The 1994 World Book

YEAR BOOK

The Annual Supplement to The World Book Encyclopedia

■■■ **A REVIEW OF THE EVENTS OF 1993** ■■■

World Book, Inc.

a Scott Fetzer company

Chicago ■ London ■ Sydney ■ Toronto

World Book, Inc.
525 W. Monroe
Chicago, IL 60661

ISBN 0-7166-0494-9
ISSN 0084-1439
Library of Congress Catalog Card Number: 62-4818

Printed in the United States of America.

Staff

Contents

▼**Page 372**

Page 182 ▶

Contributors

Contributors not listed on these pages are members of *The World Book Year Book* editorial staff.

- **ALEXIOU, ARTHUR G.,** B.S.E.E., M.S.E.E.; Assistant Secretary, Committee on Climatic Changes and Ocean. **[Ocean]**
- **ANDERSON, PORTER,** B.A., M.A., M.F.A.; Theater Critic, *Village Voice.* **[Theater]**
- **ANDREWS, PETER J.,** B.A., M.S.; free-lance writer; biochemist. **[Chemistry]**
- **APSELOFF, MARILYN FAIN,** B.A., M.A.; Associate Professor of English, Kent State University. **[Literature for children]**
- **ARNDT, RANDOLPH C.,** Media Relations Director, National League of Cities. **[City]**
- **BAKKER, ROBERT T.,** B.A., M.S., Ph.D.; Adjunct Curator, University of Colorado Museum in Boulder. **[Motion pictures Special Report: Could Dinosaurs Live in a Zoo?]**
- **BARBER, PEGGY,** B.A., M.L.S.; Associate Executive Director for Communications, American Library Association. **[Library]**
- **BARNHART, BILL,** B.A., M.S.T., M.B.A.; Financial markets columnist, *Chicago Tribune.* **[Stocks and bonds]**
- **BERGER, JIM,** B.A., M.P.A.; Editor/Publisher, Trade Reports International Group. **[International trade]**
- **BERMAN, HOWARD A.,** B.A., B.H.L., M.A.H.L.; Rabbi, Chicago Sinai Congregation. **[Judaism]**
- **BESSMAN, JIM,** contributor, *Billboard* magazine; Senior Editor, *Spin* magazine. **[Popular music]**
- **BLACKADAR, ALFRED K.,** A.B., Ph.D.; Professor Emeritus, Pennsylvania State University. **[Weather]**
- **BOWER, BRUCE,** M.A.; Behavioral Sciences Editor, *Science News* magazine. **[Psychology]**
- **BOYD, JOHN D.,** B.S.; Midwest Bureau Chief, *Journal of Commerce.* **[Economics]**
- **BRADSHER, HENRY S.,** A.B., B.J.; foreign affairs analyst. **[Asia and Asian country articles]**
- **BRETT, CARLTON E.,** B.A., M.S., Ph.D.; Professor of Geological Sciences, University of Rochester. **[Paleontology]**
- **BURKE, JUSTIN,** B.A.; Moscow Correspondent, *The Christian Science Monitor.* **[Commonwealth of Independent States and former Soviet republic articles]**

- **CAMPBELL, GEOFFREY A.,** B.J.; Staff Reporter, *The Bond Buyer.* **[Civil rights; Supreme Court of the United States]**
- **CAMPBELL, LINDA P.,** B.A., M.S.L.; National Legal Affairs Correspondent, *Chicago Tribune.* **[Civil rights; Supreme Court of the United States]**
- **CARDINALE, DIANE P.,** B.A.; Assistant Communications Director, Toy Manufacturers of America. **[Toys and games]**
- **CARMODY, DEIRDRE,** Media Reporter, *The New York Times.* **[Magazine]**
- **COLLINS, JOHN J.,** B.A., M.A., Ph.D.; Professor of Hebrew Bible at the Divinity School, University of Chicago. **[Religion Special Report: The Lure and Lore of the Dead Sea Scrolls]**
- **CORMIER, FRANK,** B.S.J., M.S.J.; former White House Correspondent, Associated Press. **[U.S. government articles]**
- **CORMIER, MARGOT,** B.A., M.S.J.; free-lance writer. **[U.S. government articles]**
- **CORNELL, VINCENT J.,** B.A., M.A., Ph.D.; Andrew W. Mellon Assistant Professor of Religion, Duke University. **[Islam]**
- **CROMIE, WILLIAM J.,** B.S., M.S.; science writer, Harvard University. **[Space exploration]**
- **DAVIDSON, ROGER H.,** B.A., M.A., Ph.D.; Loyola Professor of Government and Politics, University of Maryland. **[World Book Supplement: United States, Government of the]**
- **DeFRANK, THOMAS M.,** B.A., M.A.; White House Correspondent, *Newsweek* magazine. **[Armed forces]**
- **DeLANCEY, MARK W.,** B.A., M.A., Ph.D.; Professor of Government and International Studies, University of South Carolina. **[Africa and African country articles]**
- **DILLON, DAVID,** B.A., M.A., Ph.D.; Architect Critic, *The Dallas Morning News.* **[Architecture]**
- **DIRDA, MICHAEL,** B.A., M.A., Ph.D.; writer and editor, *The Washington Post Book World.* **[Poetry]**
- **EATON, WILLIAM J.,** B.S.J., M.S.J.; Correspondent, *Los Angeles Times.* **[U.S. government articles]**
- **ELLIS, GAVIN,** Assistant Editor, *New Zealand Herald.* **[New Zealand]**
- **FAGAN, JEFFREY,** B.S., M.A., Ph.D.; Associate Professor, Rutgers University. **[City Special Report: New Fears About Urban Gangs]**

- **FARR, DAVID M. L.,** M.A., D.Phil.; Professor Emeritus of History, Carleton University, Ottawa. **[Canada; Canadian provinces articles]**
- **FERRELL, KEITH,** Editor, *Omni* magazine. **[Computer]**
- **FISHER, ROBERT W.,** B.A., M.A.; free-lance writer; formerly a Senior Economist/Editor, U.S. Bureau of Labor Statistics. **[Labor]**
- **FITZGERALD, MARK,** B.A.; Midwest Editor, *Editor & Publisher* magazine. **[Newspaper]**
- **FORGEY, BENJAMIN,** B.S.; Architecture Critic, *The Washington Post.* **[Washington, D.C. Special Report: A Place in Which to Remember]**
- **FOX, THOMAS C.,** B.A., M.A.; Editor, *National Catholic Reporter.* **[Roman Catholic Church]**
- **FRIEDMAN, EMILY,** B.A.; Contributing Editor, *Hospitals* magazine. **[Health-care issues]**
- **GARVIE, MAUREEN,** B.A., B.Ed., M.A.; Books Editor, *The* (Kingston, Ont.) *Whig-Standard.* **[Canadian literature]**
- **GATTY, BOB,** Editor, Periodicals News Service. **[Food]**
- **GILLENWATER, SHARON K.,** B.A.; free-lance writer. **[San Diego]**
- **GOLDNER, NANCY,** B.A.; Dance Critic, *The Philadelphia Inquirer.* **[Dancing Special Report: Rudolf Nureyev: A Ballet Legend Passes; Dancing]**
- **GROSSMANN, JOHN,** B.A., M.S.J.; free-lance journalist. **[Public Health Special Report: The Dangers of Passive Smoking]**
- **HARAKAS, STANLEY SAMUEL,** B.A., B.D., Th.D.; Archbishop Iakovos Professor of Orthodox Theology, Hellenic College, Holy Cross Greek Orthodox School of Theology. **[Eastern Orthodox Churches]**
- **HAVERSTOCK, NATHAN A.,** A.B.; Affiliate Scholar, Oberlin College. **[Latin America and Latin-American country articles]**
- **HELMS, CHRISTINE,** B.A., Ph.D.; foreign affairs analyst; author. **[Middle East and Middle Eastern country articles; North Africa country articles]**
- **HENDERSON, NELL,** B.S.J., Staff Writer, *The Washington Post.* **[Washington, D.C.]**
- **HIGGINS, JAMES V.,** B.A.; Auto Industry Reporter, *The Detroit News.* **[Automobile]**
- **HILLGREN, SONJA,** B.J., M.A.; Washington Editor, *Farm Journal.* **[Farm and farming]**
- **HOWELL, LEON,** A.B., M.Div.; Editor and Publisher, *Christianity and Crisis.* **[Religion]**

- **HUEY, RAYMOND B.,** A.B., M.A., Ph.D.; Professor of Zoology, University of Washington. **[World Book Supplement: Animal]**

- **JOHANSON, DONALD C.,** B.S., M.A., Ph.D.; President, Institute of Human Origins. **[Anthropology]**

- **KING, MIKE,** Reporter, *The Montreal Gazette.* **[Montreal]**

- **KISOR, HENRY,** B.A., M.S.J.; Book Editor, *Chicago Sun-Times.* **[Literature; Literature, American]**

- **KISTE, ROBERT C.,** Ph.D.; Director and Professor, Center for Pacific Islands Studies, University of Hawaii. **[Pacific Islands]**

- **KNAPP, ELAINE S.,** B.A.; Managing Editor, Council of State Governments. **[State government]**

- **KOLGRAF, RONALD,** B.A., M.A.; Publisher, *Adweek/New England* magazine. **[Manufacturing]**

- **KORMAN, RICHARD,** Associate Editor, *Engineering News-Record.* **[Building and construction]**

- **LAWRENCE, AL,** B.A., M.A., M.Ed.; Executive Director, United States Chess Federation. **[Chess]**

- **LEWIS, DAVID C.,** M.D.; Professor of Medicine and Community Health, Brown University. **[Drug abuse]**

- **LITSKY, FRANK,** B.S.; Sportswriter, *The New York Times.* **[Sports articles]**

- **MARCH, ROBERT H.,** A.B., S.M., Ph.D.; Professor of Physics, University of Wisconsin at Madison. **[Physics]**

- **MARSCHALL, LAURENCE A.,** Ph.D.; Professor of Physics, Gettysburg College. **[Astronomy]**

- **MARTY, MARTIN E.,** Ph.D.; Fairfax M. Cone Distinguished Service Professor, University of Chicago. **[Protestantism]**

- **MATHER, IAN J.,** B.A., M.A.; Diplomatic Editor, *The European,* London. **[Ireland; Northern Ireland; United Kingdom]**

- **MAUGH, THOMAS H., II,** Ph.D.; Science Writer, *Los Angeles Times.* **[Biology]**

- **MERINA, VICTOR,** A.A., B.A., M.S.; free-lance writer. **[Los Angeles]**

- **MERLINE, JOHN W.,** B.A.; Washington Correspondent, *Investor's Business Daily.* **[Consumerism]**

- **MOORES, ELDRIDGE M.,** B.S., Ph.D.; Professor of Geology, University of California at Davis. **[Geology]**

- **MORITZ, OWEN,** B.A.; free-lance writer. **[New York City]**

- **MORRIS, BERNADINE,** B.A., M.A.; Chief Fashion Writer, *The New York Times.* **[Fashion]**

- **MUCHNIC, SUZANNE,** B.A., M.A.; Art Writer, *Los Angeles Times.* **[Art]**

- **NGUYEN, J. TUYET,** B.A.; Bureau manager, United Nations Correspondent, United Press International. **[United Nations]**

- **NOMANI, ASRA Q.,** B.A.; Reporter, *The Wall Street Journal.* **[Aviation]**

- **OPPMANN, ANDREW,** B.A., Metropolitan Editor, *The Houston Post.* **[Houston]**

- **PECK, MALCOLM C.,** A.M., M.A., Ph.D.; Former Arabian Peninsula Affairs Analyst, Bureau of Intelligence and Research, U.S. Department of State. **[World Book Supplement: West Bank]**

- **PENNISI, ELIZABETH,** B.S., M.S.; Chemistry/Materials Science Editor, *Science News* magazine. **[Zoology]**

- **PFEIFER, ELLEN,** B.S.; Music Critic, *Boston Herald.* **[Deaths Special Report: Marian Anderson: A Voice Heard Once in 100 Years]**

- **PIKE, DOUGLAS,** B.S., M.A., Ph.Bm.; Director, Indochina Studies Program, University of California at Berkeley. **[Asia Special Report: Vietnam: Emerging from a War-torn Past]**

- **PRATER, CONSTANCE C.,** B.S.J.; Reporter, *Detroit Free Press.* **[Detroit]**

- **PRIESTAF, IRIS,** B.A., M.A., Ph.D.; Geographer and Vice President, David Keith Todd Consulting Engineers, Incorporated. **[Water]**

- **RALOFF, JANET,** B.S.J., M.S.J.; Policy/Technology Editor, *Science News* magazine. **[Environmental pollution]**

- **REARDON, PATRICK T.,** B.A.; Urban Affairs Writer, *Chicago Tribune.* **[Chicago]**

- **REVZIN, PHILIP,** B.A., M.A.; Editor, *The Wall Street Journal Europe.* **[Europe and Western European country articles]**

- **ROSE, MARK J.,** M.A.; Managing Editor, *Archaeology* magazine. **[Archaeology]**

- **ROSS, ALEX,** B.A., free-lance writer. **[Classical music]**

- **SEGAL, TROY,** B.A., free-lance writer. **[Television]**

- **SHAIKEN, HARLEY,** Professor in the graduate School of Education and an Associate in the Center for Latin American Studies at the University of California at Berkeley. **[International trade Special Report: The Debate over NAFTA]**

- **SHAPIRO, HOWARD S.,** B.S.; Cultural Arts Editor, *The Philadelphia Inquirer.* **[Philadelphia]**

- **STEIN, DAVID LEWIS,** B.A., M.S.; Urban Affairs Columnist, *The Toronto Star.* **[Toronto]**

- **STILLE, ALEXANDER,** B.A., M.S., free-lance writer. **[Italy Special Report: Italy Confronts the Mafia]**

- **TANNER, JAMES C.,** B.S.J.; Senior Energy Correspondent, *The Wall Street Journal.* **[Petroleum and gas]**

- **TATUM, HENRY K.,** B.A.; Associate Editor, *Dallas Morning News.* **[Dallas]**

- **THOMAS, PAULETTE,** B.A.; Staff Writer, *The Wall Street Journal.* **[Bank]**

- **THOMPSON, WILLIAM N.,** B.A., M.A., Ph.D.; Professor of Public Administration, University of Nevada, Las Vegas. **[State government Special Report: The States Bet on Legalized Gambling]**

- **TOCH, THOMAS W.,** B.A., M.A.; Associate Editor and Education Correspondent, *U.S. News & World Report.* **[Education]**

- **TONRY, MICHAEL,** A.B., LL.B.; Sonosky Professor of Law and Public Policy, University of Minnesota Law School. **[Prison]**

- **VIZARD, FRANK,** B.A.; Electronics Editor, *Popular Mechanics.* **[Electronics]**

- **WALTER, EUGENE, J., Jr.,** B.A., free-lance writer. **[Conservation; Zoos]**

- **WIDDER, PAT,** B.A.; New York Financial Correspondent, *Chicago Tribune.* **[Telecommunications]**

- **WILLIAMS, SUSAN G.,** B.A.; free-lance journalist, Sydney, Australia. **[Australia]**

- **WILSON, W. HERBERT, Jr.,** B.S., M.S., Ph.D.; Assistant Professor, Department of Biology, Colby College. **[World Book Supplement: Animal]**

- **WOLCHIK, SHARON L.,** B.A., M.A., Ph.D.; Director, Russian and East European Studies, George Washington University. **[Eastern European country articles; World Book Supplement: Czech Republic; Slovakia]**

- **WOODS, MICHAEL,** B.S.; Science Editor, *The (Toledo, Ohio) Blade.* **[Industry articles and health articles]**

- **WUNTCH, PHILIP,** B.A.; Film Critic, *Dallas Morning News.* **[Motion pictures]**

- **ZOLA, IRVING KENNETH,** B.A., M.A., Ph.D.; Mortimer Gryzmish Professor of Human Relations, Brandeis University. **[Disabled]**

The Year's **M**ajor News Stories

From the presidential election in the United States to the fighting in former republics of Yugoslavia, 1993 was a year filled with momentous events. On these two pages are the stories that *Year Book* editors picked as the most memorable, the most exciting, or the most important of the year, along with details on where to find information about them in *The World Book Year Book.*　　*The Editors*

Russian parliament dissolved
Russian troops take over the parliament building in ▶ Moscow after extreme nationalists and hard-line Communists in October defied an order by Russian President Boris Yeltsin that dissolved parliament and called for new elections. See **Europe,** page 199; **Russia,** page 371.

Inauguration
◀ Bill Clinton, flanked by daughter, Chelsea, and wife, Hillary, takes the oath of office as the 42nd President of the United States and quickly follows through on several campaign promises. See **Clinton, Bill,** page 142; **United States, Government of the,** page 428.

Trouble in Haiti
Haiti's military rulers back out of an agreement to restore Jean-Bertrand Aristide to power. The democratically elected president was ousted in a 1991 coup. In October 1993, a wave of terror is directed at Aristide supporters. See **Haiti,** page 217; **Latin America,** page 270.

Middle East peace agreement
On Sept. 13, 1993, Israeli Prime Minister Yitzhak Rabin accepted the handshake of Yasir Arafat, chairman of the Palestine Liberation Organization, as their representatives signed a peace agreement at the White House in Washington, D.C. See **Israel,** page 245; **Middle East,** page 292.

World Trade Center bombing
A powerful car bomb left a gaping hole ▶ at the World Trade Center in New York City in February, and law enforcement officials said Muslim extremists were responsible. See **Crime,** page 158; **New York City,** page 312.

War in Bosnia-Herzegovina

The war in Bosnia-Herzegovina, a former republic of Yugoslavia, continued to rage in 1993, as several peace plans fell apart. See **Bosnia-Herzegovina,** page 99; **Europe,** page 199; **United Nations,** page 426; **Yugoslavia,** page 449.

Flooding in the Midwest

Farm buildings are surround- ▶ ed by floodwaters during record flooding in June and July in the Midwestern United States. See **Disasters,** page 180; **Water,** page 444; **Weather,** page 444.

◀ U.S. troops in Somalia

A U.S. helicopter hovers above a burning tank belonging to the forces of Somali warlord Mohamed Farah Aideed. The United States sought to capture Aideed until November, when it was decided to seek a political solution. See **Africa,** page 38; **Armed forces,** page 53; **Somalia,** page 380.

The North American Free Trade Agreement (NAFTA)

In November, the United States Congress approved the most controversial legislation it faced all year, adopting an agreement for a free-trade zone between Canada, Mexico, and the United States. See **International trade: The Debate over NAFTA,** page 230.

Siege in Waco, Tex.

The compound of a religious cult known as the ▶ Branch Davidians, located near Waco, Tex., goes up in flames in April at the end of a 51-day siege by federal law enforcement officials. See **Crime,** page 158.

ARMED FORCES ▪ ARMENIA ▪ ART

ANGLADESH ▪ BANK ▪ BASEBALL ▪

▪ BUILDING AND CONSTRUCTIO

CHICAGO ▪ CHILE ▪ CHINA

▪ COMPUTER ▪ CONSERVATIO

DEMOCRATIC PARTY ▪ DENMAR

OR ▪ EDUCATION ▪ EGYPT ▪

ARMS AND FARMING ▪ FASHIO

HEALTH-CARE ISSUES ▪ HOCKEY

ISRAEL

LATV

CTURIN

RK CITY

PTHWES ORIES

1993

THE YEAR
IN BRIEF

A pictorial review of the top news stories of 1993 is followed by a month-by-month listing of highlights of some of the year's most significant events.

▪ REPUBLICAN PAR

▪ SAUDI ARABIA ▪

VERNMENT ▪ STOC

AN ▪ TAXATION ▪

GAMES ▪ TRACK AND FIELD

NATIONS ▪ PEACE IN THE MIDDLE EAST? SEE PAGE 292 ▪ UNITED STATES, GOVERN-

ELFARE ▪ YUGOSLAVIA ▪ YUKON TERRITORY ▪ ZAIRE ▪ ZAMBIA ▪ ZOOLOGY

S	M	T	W	TH	F	S
					1	2
3	4	5	6	7	8	9
10	11	12	13	14	15	16
17	18	19	20	21	22	23
24	25	26	27	28	29	30
31						

January 1993

The oil tanker *Braer* runs aground on January 5 off Scotland's Shetland Island, home to one of Europe's largest wildlife colonies.

Dallas Cowboys quarterback Troy Aikman looks for a receiver during Dallas' 52-17 Super Bowl victory on January 31.

3 **United States President George Bush** and Russia's President Boris Yeltsin sign a sweeping arms reduction accord, called START II, in Moscow.

5 **The 103rd session of the Congress of the United States** convenes in Washington, D.C., with 110 newly elected members of the House of Representatives and 13 newly elected members of the Senate.

The oil tanker *Braer* runs aground off Scotland's Shetland Island, threatening to spill about 26 million gallons (98 million liters) of crude oil into the North Sea and the island's craggy bays, home to one of Europe's largest wildlife colonies. On January 12, after being battered by hurricane-force winds for several days, the ship broke apart, spilling its entire cargo into the sea.

Former baseball slugger Reggie Jackson is elected to the National Baseball Hall of Fame in Cooperstown, N.Y., in his first year of eligibility.

13 **United States warplanes,** joined by French and British aircraft, bomb antiaircraft missile sites and other military targets in southern Iraq in retaliation for Iraqi raids into Kuwait and other violations of the Persian Gulf War (1991) cease-fire.

The space shuttle Endeavour lifts off from Cape Canaveral, Fla., on the first of eight shuttle missions scheduled for 1993. The Endeavour's crew releases a relay satellite the same day.

17 **United States naval ships in the Persian Gulf** and Red Sea launch about 40 cruise missiles at targets near Baghdad, Iraq's capital, during President Bush's last weekend in office. The U.S. Department of Defense acknowledges on January 18 that one cruise missile crashed into the Rashid Hotel in Baghdad, where an Islamic conference was being held, killing two people.

20 **Bill Clinton takes the oath of office** as the 42nd President of the United States and in his inaugural address pledges "an end to the era of deadlock and drift" and "a new season of American renewal."

22 **Croatian forces attack** a Serb-dominated region in Croatia that was under the protection of United Nations forces, jeopardizing a cease-fire that had been in effect for almost a year.

President Clinton rescinds five executive orders handed down from previous administrations that were intended to discourage women from having abortions, including one that restricted abortion counseling at federally funded clinics and another that banned the use of fetal tissue for health research.

31 **The Dallas Cowboys win** Super Bowl XXVII in Pasadena, Calif., defeating the Buffalo Bills, 52-17, as Dallas quarterback Troy Aikman throws four touchdown passes and wins the game's Most Valuable Player award.

Bill Clinton, flanked by daughter, Chelsea, left, and wife, Hillary, takes the oath of office as the 42nd President of the United States on January 20.

S	M	T	W	TH	F	S
		1	2	3	4	5	6

February 1993

S	M	T	W	TH	F	S
		1	2	3	4	5	6
7	8	9	10	11	12	13
14	15	16	17	18	19	20
21	22	23	24	25	26	27
28						

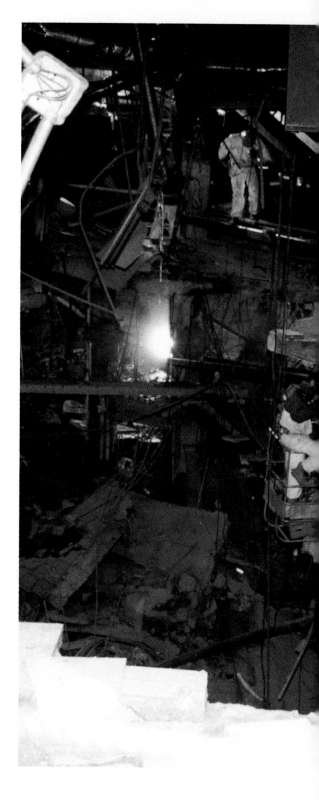

3 **Jury selection begins** in the federal trial of four white Los Angeles police officers charged with civil rights violations in the 1991 beating of black motorist Rodney King.

5 **President Bill Clinton signs into law** the Family and Medical Leave Act, which requires businesses with 50 employees or more to grant up to 12 weeks of unpaid leave for medical emergencies or to care for a new child.

11 **After weathering weeks of controversy** surrounding his original choices for attorney general, President Clinton names Janet Reno, a Florida state prosecutor in Miami, as his nominee to be the first female attorney general of the United States.

The nine hereditary rulers of Malaysia agree to a constitutional amendment that removes their immunity from criminal prosecution.

18 **South Africa's** black-led African National Congress (ANC) approves a plan for a transitional government that allows the ANC to share power for a period of five years, beginning in April 1994.

22 **The United Nations Security Council** orders the establishment of the first international war crimes tribunal since the end of World War II (1939-1945) to investigate atrocities in Bosnia-Herzegovina.

23 **Five cross-country skiers,** missing since February 21 in a snowstorm, reach safety near Aspen, Colo.

24 **Canada's Prime Minister Brian Mulroney,** battered by low popularity ratings, announces that he will resign after more than eight years in office when his Progressive Conservative Party selects a new leader.

Rioting in Mogadishu, capital of Somalia, kills 10 people and wounds 17 others, as clan violence continues.

25 **Police in New Delhi, India,** fearing a new outbreak of religious violence, prevent a scheduled rally of Hindu fundamentalists by arresting thousands of militants, including 110 members of Parliament belonging to a Hindu fundamentalist party.

26 **A powerful explosion rocks the World Trade Center** in New York City, killing six people and injuring more than 1,000 others. By August, seven people, all of whom were described as Arab militants, had been charged in connection with the bombing. On August 25, a radical Muslim cleric, Sheik Omar Abdel Rahman, and 14 others were indicted for conspiracy in the bombing of the trade center and for plotting to bomb other New York City landmarks.

28 **Four agents of the federal** Bureau of Alcohol, Tobacco, and Firearms die in a shoot-out near Waco, Tex., with members of a heavily armed religious cult. In April, law enforcement officials disclosed that six members of the cult, known as the Branch Davidians, also died in the shoot-out.

Workmen inspect a gaping hole, three stories deep, caused by a powerful car bomb that rocked the World Trade Center in New York City on February 26. The explosion killed six people and injured more than 1,000 others.

S	M	T	W	TH	F	S
March 1993		1	2	3	4	5	6
7	8	9	10	11	12	13
14	15	16	17	18	19	20
21	22	23	24	25	26	27
28	29	30	31			

1 **The United States Agriculture Department** reports that in December 1992 a record percentage of Americans received food stamps. Analysts said that the nation's economic recovery had not yet reached low-income Americans.

7 **Far right candidates in the German** state of Hesse make gains in municipal and district elections after campaigning for strong measures to stop an influx of immigrants seeking political asylum.

9, 10 **In Egypt, at least 19 people are killed** and more than 24 wounded when police launch raids against Islamic fundamentalists who have campaigned for an Islamic state by attacking foreign tourists, Coptic Christians, and intellectuals.

10 **Police in Pensacola, Fla., arrest an antiabortion** demonstrator for murdering a physician who performed abortions at several medical clinics in Florida and Alabama. It was the first slaying of its kind in the United States, according to law enforcement officials.

11 **Russia's Congress of People's Deputies,** its highest parliamentary body, votes overwhelmingly to limit the powers of President Boris N. Yeltsin and to cancel a scheduled referendum on a new Constitution. On March 20, Yeltsin declares special powers to rule by decree, but Russia's highest court on March 23 says his actions are unconstitutional.

12 **At least 11 car bombs explode in Bombay, India,** killing hundreds of people and injuring thousands of others. By March 20, authorities had arrested 13 people linked to organized crime in connection with the blasts.

13, 14 **"The worst storm of the century,"** according to the National Weather Service, strikes the East Coast from Florida to northeastern Canada, spawning 50 tornadoes in Southern states and a blizzard that paralyzed dozens of major cities, including Atlanta, Ga.; Washington, D.C.; Philadelphia; New York City; Boston; and Montreal, Canada. At least 213 people die in storm-related incidents, mostly due to heart attacks suffered while shoveling snow or to automobile accidents on icy roads.

15 **El Salvador's top military officers** and some rebel leaders are accused of human rights atrocities in a report issued by a United Nations commission, which called for the dismissal of the officers and a ban on political participation by certain military and rebel leaders.

19 **United States Supreme Court Justice Byron R. White** announces that he will retire at the end of the court's term in June, giving President Bill Clinton the opportunity to pick the first Democratic appointee to the court since 1967.

21 **France's** ruling Socialist Party suffers a crushing defeat in the first round of parliamentary elections. On March 29, French President François Mitterrand names Edouard Balladur as prime minister after another round of voting gave a center-right coalition 460 of the National Assembly's 577 seats.

Traffic is virtually halted in Boston during a blizzard, dubbed the "worst storm of the century" by the National Weather Service, that struck the East Coast on March 13 and 14.

◄ A crane is used to remove debris from the wreckage caused by a car bomb, one of a series that exploded in Bombay, India, on March 12, killing hundreds of people and injuring thousands of others.

S	M	T	W	TH	F	S
				1	2	3
4	5	6	7	8	9	10
11	12	13	14	15	16	17
18	19	20	21	22	23	24
25	26	27	28	29	30	

4 **Ending a two-day summit** with Russian President Boris N. Yeltsin in Vancouver, Canada, United States President Bill Clinton pledges his political support for Yeltsin's economic reforms with a $1.6-billion aid package.

5 **North Carolina wins college basketball's** national championship, defeating Michigan 77-71 in the final game of the men's National Collegiate Athletic Association (NCAA) tournament in New Orleans. On April 4, Texas Tech won the women's NCAA title with an 84-82 victory over Ohio State in Atlanta, Ga.

10 **South African Communist Party leader** Chris Hani is assassinated outside his home in a suburb of Johannesburg. Police charge a Polish immigrant who reportedly had close ties to a far right, white nationalist group with Hani's murder.

11 **German golfer Bernhard Langer** wins the Masters tournament in Augusta, Ga., with an 11-under-par 277, four strokes ahead of his nearest rival.

15 **The world's seven leading industrialized nations** pledge $28.4 billion in aid to Russia, much of it contingent on the Russian government's adoption of austerity measures.

A powerful car bomb explodes in a shopping mall in Bogotá, Colombia, killing 15 people and injuring more than 100 others. Government officials blame a drug trafficker for the attack.

17 **A federal jury in Los Angeles** convicts two of four police officers charged with violating the civil rights of Rodney King, the victim of a 1991 police beating. The acquittal of the four officers on state charges of excessive use of force had sparked five days of rioting in Los Angeles in 1992.

19 **The 51-day siege of the Branch Davidian-cult** compound near Waco, Tex., ends tragically as fire, deliberately set by cult members according to federal officials, engulfs the compound. An estimated 82 people, including cult leader David Koresh, died in the confrontation, but officials withheld a final death toll pending an investigation.

21 **A Republican** filibuster in the U.S. Senate succeeds in killing an economic stimulus bill proposed by President Clinton.

An 11-day prison rebellion at the Southern Ohio Correctional Facility near Lucasville ends after officials agree to improve prison conditions. Nine prisoners and a guard were killed during the cell-block take-over.

24 **A powerful bomb devastates a section of London's** financial district, killing 1 person and wounding 45 others. The Irish Republican Army claims responsibility for the attack.

25 **About 59 percent of Russian voters** give President Yeltsin a vote of confidence, and 67 percent call for early elections to Russia's parliament, the Congress of People's Deputies, which has opposed Yeltsin.

Flames engulf the compound of a religious cult known as the Branch Davidians, near Waco, Tex., on April 19, following a 51-day siege by federal authorities who sought the arrest of the cult's leader on charges of illegal possession of firearms.

May 1993

S	M	T	W	TH	F	S
						1
2	3	4	5	6	7	8
9	10	11	12	13	14	15
16	17	18	19	20	21	22
23	24	25	26	27	28	29
30	31					

1 **Sri Lanka's** President Ranasinghe Premadasa is assassinated during a May Day parade in Colombo, the capital, when a man triggered explosives fastened to his body. The explosion killed Premadasa and at least 23 other people. Officials blamed the Liberation Tigers of Tamil Eelam, a separatist guerrilla movement, for the attack.

2 **Bosnia's Serbian leader,** meeting in Athens, Greece, with other protagonists in the Balkan civil war, signs a United Nations (UN) peace plan that would divide Bosnia-Herzegovina into 10 autonomous provinces. But in a May 15-16 popular referendum, voters overwhelmingly reject the plan.

15 **French police kill a gunman** who had taken 21 children hostage on May 13 and demanded $18.5 million in ransom. The gunman had released 15 children but continued to hold 6 in their nursery school in a Paris suburb before he was killed.

16 **Detroit police arrest Jack Kevorkian,** a retired pathologist, in the suicide death of a lung cancer patient, charging Kevorkian with violating a Michigan law that prohibits assisting a suicide.

Turkey's parliament elects Prime Minister Süleyman Demirel as the country's new president.

18 **Danish voters** reverse a 1992 vote and approve the Maastricht Treaty on European unity. Two days later, the United Kingdom's House of Commons approved legislation to ratify the treaty, signaling acceptance by all 12 members of the European Community.

24 **Roman Catholic Cardinal** Juan Jesús Posadas Ocampo of Mexico is shot to death at the Guadalajara airport. Police officials say the cardinal was caught in the cross fire of a shoot-out between rival drug gangs.

25 **Guatemala's President Jorge Serrano Elías** suspends the Constitution and dissolves Guatemala's Congress and the Supreme Court of Justice. But on June 6, Congress installs the attorney general of human rights, Ramiro de León Carpio, as president after Serrano flees the country on June 2.

27 **A car bomb explodes outside the Uffizi Gallery** in Florence, Italy, killing five people, destroying 3 paintings, and badly damaging more than 30 other works of art.

28 **About 90 percent of Cambodia's** registered voters, some 4.2 million people, defy threats of violence by Khmer Rouge guerrillas and go to the polls in a UN-supervised parliamentary election that lasted six days. The largest bloc of seats went to the party led by Prince Norodom Ranariddh.

29 **Five members of a Turkish family**—two women and three young girls—die in a fire set by arsonists in Solingen, Germany, sparking riots by Turkish youths. German police later arrested four young men, members of a neo-Nazi group, on charges of murder and arson.

20

Firemen in Florence, Italy, sift through the rubble left by a powerful car-bomb explosion that damaged the west wing of the famous Uffizi Gallery on May 27, destroying 3 paintings and damaging more than 30 other works of art.

A French policeman rushes to safety one of six children held hostage by a gunman at a nursery school in a Paris suburb on May 15.
▼

S	M	T	W	TH	F	S
		1	2	3	4	5
6	7	8	9	10	11	12
13	14	15	16	17	18	19
20	21	22	23	24	25	26
27	28	29	30			

June 1993

Chicago Bulls guard Michael Jordan takes to the air during the NBA play-off finals that the Bulls went on to win on June 20. ▶

Canada's Defense Minister Kim Campbell is elected head of the Progressive Conservative Party on June 13. ▼

5 **Texas Republican Kay Bailey Hutchison** wins election to the United States Senate. Some observers saw the vote as a referendum on President Bill Clinton's tax proposals. The victory marked the first time since Reconstruction that both Senate seats from Texas were held by Republicans.

6 **Unidentified Liberian soldiers massacre** about 600 people, mostly women and children, after confiscating food from a refugee center at a former rubber plantation outside Monrovia, Liberia's capital. In September, United Nations officials blamed the slaughter on a rebel group called the Armed Forces of Liberia.

9 **Japan's Crown Prince Naruhito and Masako Owada,** daughter of a Japanese diplomat, are married in a Shinto ritual on the grounds of the Imperial Palace in Tokyo.

The Montreal Canadiens win their 24th Stanley Cup, defeating the Los Angeles Kings, 4-1, to take the series four games to one. Montreal goalie Patrick Roy was voted the Conn Smythe Trophy as the Most Valuable Player in the series.

13 **Defense Minister Kim Campbell** is elected to head Canada's Progressive Conservative Party at a convention in Ottawa, Ont. On June 25, Campbell is sworn in as the country's first female prime minister, succeeding Brian Mulroney, who resigned due to his declining popularity.

Tansu Ciller is elected head of Turkey's True Path Party, setting the stage for her appointment as Turkey's first female prime minister.

14 **President Clinton nominates federal appeals court** Judge Ruth Bader Ginsburg, noted for her legal arguments on behalf of women's rights, to the Supreme Court of the United States. The Senate confirms her nomination on August 3.

18 **Dissident members of Japan's** ruling Liberal Democratic Party join with members of the opposition to cast a no-confidence vote against the government of Prime Minister Kiichi Miyazawa.

20 **The Chicago Bulls win** the National Basketball Association (NBA) championship, defeating the Phoenix Suns 99-98 in the sixth game of the finals and becoming only the third team in NBA history to win three consecutive titles.

23 **Nigeria's military leader,** President Ibrahim Babangida, annuls the country's recent presidential elections and reneges on his promise to restore civilian leadership.

27 **Iraq's intelligence headquarters** in a suburb of Baghdad is bombed by Tomahawk cruise missiles fired from U.S. warships. The raid, which killed eight civilians after a missile failed to hit its target, was in retaliation for an alleged Iraqi plot to assassinate former President George Bush when he visited Kuwait in April. The raid was widely criticized, however, because it took place before the suspects in the plot, who were on trial in Kuwait, had been found guilty.

Japan's Crown Prince Naruhito and Masako Owada wear traditional dress for their Shinto ritual wedding on June 9. ▶

S	M	T	W	TH	F	S
July 1993				1	2	3
4	5	6	7	8	9	10
11	12	13	14	15	16	17
18	19	20	21	22	23	24
25	26	27	28	29	30	31

1 **A gunman enters the San Francisco law firm** of Pettit & Martin and begins shooting indiscriminately, killing eight people and then himself.

2 **Sheik Omar Abdel Rahman,** spiritual leader of Egypt's Islamic Group, who had been living in New Jersey, surrenders to federal authorities in New York City on immigration charges. In August, a grand jury indicts Sheik Omar on charges of masterminding the bombing of New York's World Trade Center in February and of plotting to bomb other New York landmarks.

10, 11 **The worst flooding on record** in the Midwestern United States prompts President Bill Clinton on July 10 to issue disaster declarations for the states of Illinois, Iowa, and Missouri, where more than 20,000 people were forced from their homes. On July 11, the Des Moines and Raccoon rivers spill their banks, cutting off the water supply for more than 250,000 people in Des Moines, Iowa. By August, parts of nine states are declared disaster areas, including every county in Iowa.

18 **Japan's Liberal Democratic Party** loses its majority in the Diet, Japan's parliament, for the first time since 1955. The chief opposition party, the Japan Socialist Party, also suffers a stunning defeat, losing nearly half of its seats, as three centrist parties capitalize on voters' discontent with corruption.

Pakistan's government collapses as both the president and prime minister resign, Parliament dissolves, and a caretaker regime is installed until elections can be held in October.

19 **The Joint Chiefs of Staff** express support for a new Clinton Administration policy that allows homosexuals to serve in the military only if they do not engage in homosexual conduct or openly declare their sexual preference. The new policy draws criticism from homosexual groups.

20 **A new director for the Federal Bureau of Investigation** (FBI) is nominated by President Clinton after former Director William S. Sessions, accused of misuse of government funds, is forced to resign on July 19. The nominee is Louis J. Freeh, a federal district court judge and former FBI agent.

23 **British Prime Minister John Major** survives a vote of confidence when Parliament approves the Maastricht Treaty on European unity by a vote of 339 to 299.

25 **Israeli warplanes and combat helicopters,** responding to rocket attacks on border towns, strike Palestinian guerrilla targets in Lebanon in the heaviest air attack in more than 10 years. On July 31, a cease-fire ends seven days of Israeli attacks, which officials said killed about 140 people, wounded about 500 people, and sent about 500,000 Lebanese fleeing for safety.

Miguel Indurain of Spain wins the Tour de France cycling race for the third consecutive year.

29 **Israel's** Supreme Court overturns the conviction of John Demjanjuk, accused of being a Nazi guard at Treblinka.

A family in Illinois evacuates their farm in July after floodwaters broke through a levee on the Mississippi River.

S	M	T	W	TH	F	S
August 1993						
1	2	3	4	5	6	7
8	9	10	11	12	13	14
15	16	17	18	19	20	21
22	23	24	25	26	27	28
29	30	31				

2 **A Titan 4 rocket,** launched from Vandenberg Air Force Base in California, explodes over the Pacific Ocean, destroying an $800-million spy satellite system. The accident was the second most costly disaster in the history of the United States space program.

4 **Italy's Parliament** approves a plan to alter a 45-year-old electoral system that many believed was responsible for a long history of weak governments and widespread governmental corruption.

6 **The U.S. Congress narrowly passes** President Bill Clinton's Omnibus Budget Reconciliation Act when Vice President Al Gore, Jr., casts the tie-breaking vote in the Senate. The new budget would reduce the nation's deficit by $496 billion by 1998 through a combination of spending cuts and tax hikes.

Japan's parliament, the Diet, elects a seven-party coalition candidate, Morihiro Hosokawa of the Japan New Party, as prime minister, ending 38 years of rule by Japan's Liberal Democratic Party.

8 **A mine blast in Mogadishu,** capital of Somalia, kills four U.S. soldiers, and President Clinton vows to take "appropriate action" against those responsible.

11 **United States Army General John Shalikashvili,** commander of the North Atlantic Treaty Organization (NATO), is selected as chairman of the Joint Chiefs of Staff to succeed General Colin Powell, who is retiring.

12 **A flood-relief bill** authorizing more than $6 billion in federal aid for Midwest flood victims is signed into law by President Clinton during a visit to St. Louis, Mo.

15 **Pope John Paul II leads a Mass** for more than 160,000 young Roman Catholics drawn to Denver, Colo., for the church's World Youth Day.

Palestinian deportees who were sent in December 1992 into a no man's land between Israel and southern Lebanon accept an offer from the Israeli government that will allow about half, or 200, of the deportees to return to their homes in the occupied West Bank or Gaza Strip.

19, 20 **Nicaraguan contra rebels** take 38 leftists hostage and demand the ouster of two Sandinista leaders from the government. The next day, Sandinista supporters seize Nicaragua's conservative Vice President Virgilio Godoy Reyes and 32 other people in retaliation. By August 25, both sides had released their hostages in exchange for immunity from prosecution.

23 **Two Detroit juries** find two former police officers guilty of second-degree murder in the 1992 beating death of a black man.

31 **Israel's Cabinet** approves an agreement granting Palestinians self-rule in the Gaza Strip and in Jericho in the occupied West Bank in a major breakthrough in peace negotiations.

Two former Detroit police officers hear on August 23 that they have been convicted of second-degree murder in the 1992 beating death of a black man.
▼

Nicaraguan leftists hold a press conference by telephone after seizing 33 hostages on August 20 in retaliation for a hostage-taking by Nicaraguan contra rebels. Both sides released their hostages in exchange for immunity from prosecution by August 25.

Morihiro Hosokawa, center, toasts members of his new Cabinet after he was elected prime minister of Japan on August 6 by a seven-party parliamentary coalition.

S	M	T	W	TH	F	S

September 1993

S	M	T	W	TH	F	S
			1	2	3	4
5	6	7	8	9	10	11
12	13	14	15	16	17	18
19	20	21	22	23	24	25
26	27	28	29	30		

7 **South Africa's white government** agrees to share power with a multiparty transition committee, clearing the way for blacks to have their first role in governing and thus bringing about an end to international economic sanctions against South Africa. On September 23, Parliament approved the agreement, which also called for South Africa's first free universal elections in April 1994.

8 **Canadian Prime Minister Kim Campbell** sets national elections for October 25, as polls indicate that a close race can be expected between the Liberal Party and Campbell's Progressive Conservative Party.

9 **Israel and the Palestine Liberation Organization** (PLO) reach a historic accord in Paris in which the PLO recognizes Israel's right "to exist in peace and security" and the Israeli government recognizes the PLO "as the representative of the Palestinian people."

United States troops fire on a mob in Mogadishu, capital of Somalia, killing about 100 people, including women and children, after United Nations peacekeeping forces came under attack.

13 **Israeli President Yitzhak Rabin** and PLO Chairman Yasir Arafat shake hands on the lawn of the White House during a formal ceremony in which their representatives signed a peace agreement granting limited self-rule to the Palestinians in the Gaza Strip and the West Bank city of Jericho.

19 **Poland's former Communist leaders** win the largest share of votes in parliamentary elections, signaling widespread voter dissatisfaction with free market reforms.

21 **Russian President Boris Yeltsin dissolves parliament** and declares new elections, but parliamentary leaders resist Yeltsin's decree and name Vice President Alexander Rutskoi acting head of state, setting off a constitutional crisis.

22 **United States President Bill Clinton** formally introduces his plan for universal health-care coverage in a nationally televised speech to a joint session of Congress. The plan represents the most sweeping social legislation to be proposed since Congress passed the Social Security Act in 1935.

29 **The Muslim-dominated parliament** in Bosnia-Herzegovina overwhelmingly rejects an international peace plan that would have partitioned the country into three ethnic states. The rejection makes it likely that fighting will continue throughout the remainder of the year.

30 **The most devastating earthquake to hit India** in more than 50 years flattens about 50 villages in the states of Maharashtra and Karnataka in a remote sugar-cane-growing region southeast of Bombay. The official death toll was put at 9,748. The quake was centered near the town of Killari, where an estimated 3,000 people were buried in debris. The quake measured 6.4 on the open-ended Richter scale and struck at 3:56 a.m. while people slept.

▲
Rabbi Haturi Karta, left, shakes the hand of Yasir Arafat, chairman of the Palestine Liberation Organization (PLO), prior to Arafat's departure for the United States and the signing on September 13 of a peace agreement between Israel and the PLO.

A survivor of India's ▶ worst earthquake in more than 50 years huddles among the ruins of her village after the September 30 quake killed about 10,000 people in a sugar-cane-growing region southeast of Bombay.

◄ Russian President Boris Yeltsin, in a television address on September 21, dissolves parliament, setting off a constitutional crisis.

S	M	T	W	TH	F	S
					1	2
3	4	5	6	7	8	9
10	11	12	13	14	15	16
17	18	19	20	21	22	23
24	25	26	27	28	29	30
31						

October 1993

Russian troops put down an uprising on October 4 by storming Moscow's parliament building, which burst into flames during the fighting. ▶

3, 4 **Moscow is gripped by its worst rioting** since the Bolshevik Revolution of 1917 as hard-line Communists and right wing nationalists break through police barriers surrounding the parliament, seizing the mayor's office and attacking a state-run television station. But on October 4, Army units loyal to Russian President Boris Yeltsin crushed the revolt and apprehended its principal leaders, Vice President Alexander Rutskoi and parliament Chairman Ruslan Khasbulatov.

Somali militia shoot down two United States helicopters over Mogadishu, the capital of Somalia, during a U.S. raid against the forces of warlord Mohamed Farah Aideed. Eighteen U.S. soldiers were killed in the raid, and at least 78 were wounded. The American casualties were the most in a single day since the United States joined a United Nations (UN) peacekeeping operation in Somalia in December 1992. In response to a later outcry in Congress, President Bill Clinton promises to withdraw most U.S. forces by March 1994.

Chicago Bulls superstar Michael Jordan, seated next to his wife, Juanita, announces on October 6 his retirement from professional basketball. ▼

6 **Chicago Bulls guard Michael Jordan,** considered by many to be basketball's greatest player, unexpectedly announces his retirement at age 30 from the National Basketball Association.

10 **Greece's** Pan-Hellenic Socialist Movement, led by former Prime Minister Andreas Papandreou, wins an absolute majority in parliamentary elections four years after Papandreou had been driven from office amid charges of corruption.

11 **Haiti's military blocks the arrival of U.S. troops** sent to help return to office Haiti's democratically elected President Jean-Bertrand Aristide, defying the terms of a UN-mediated agreement. On October 14, gunmen shot and killed Justice Minister Guy Malary, who had been appointed by Aristide, and two of Malary's aides in an apparent attempt to scuttle the agreement.

18 **A Los Angeles jury acquits two black defendants** of most charges in the beating of white truckdriver Reginald Denny and seven others during the Los Angeles riots of 1992.

23 **The Toronto Blue Jays** win their second consecutive World Series on a dramatic ninth inning home run by outfielder Joe Carter to defeat the Philadelphia Phillies, 8-6, and take the series, four games to two.

25 **Canadian voters** oust the Progressive Conservative government of Prime Minister Kim Campbell and give the Liberal Party, led by Jean Chrétien of Quebec, a firm majority in Parliament. The Conservatives saw their seats in Parliament drop from 152 to 2, while the separatist Bloc Québécois became the strongest opposition party.

27 **Southern California is hit by dozens of brush fires**—the worst in six years, according to state officials—that destroyed hundreds of homes and forced tens of thousands of people to evacuate.

Thugs loyal to Haiti's military rulers harass U.S. diplomats on October 11 as they arrive at a pier in Port-au-Prince to greet U.S. troops sent on a peacekeeping mission.

November 1993	S	M	T	W	TH	F	S
		1	2	3	4	5	6
	7	8	9	10	11	12	13
	14	15	16	17	18	19	20
	21	22	23	24	25	26	27
	28	29	30				

2   **The Republican Party scores** several major electoral gains, winning gubernatorial races in New Jersey and Virginia and a mayoral race in New York City. In New York, Rudolph W. Giuliani defeats incumbent Mayor David Dinkins. Virginia voters elect George Allen governor, and in New Jersey Christine Todd Whitman defeats incumbent Governor James J. Florio.

A new series of wildfires sweep along the Southern California coast and destroy more than 300 residences in the exclusive community of Malibu.

16   **The United Nations Security Council** votes to end its manhunt for Somali warlord Mohamed Farah Aideed in an effort to encourage Aideed to participate in negotiations aimed at a political settlement of the conflict in Somalia.

17   **The North American Free Trade Agreement** (NAFTA) passes the United States House of Representatives by a vote of 234 to 200, setting the stage for the creation of one of the world's largest free-trade zones. The U.S. Senate, where the outcome was not in doubt, approves the trade agreement on November 20 by a vote of 61 to 38. NAFTA will gradually remove tariffs and other trade restrictions between Canada, Mexico, and the United States when it goes into effect on Jan. 1, 1994.

New Zealand Prime Minister Jim Bolger claims victory in parliamentary elections that gave Bolger's conservative National Party a one-seat majority.

18   **President Bill Clinton arrives in Seattle** for a summit with the heads of state of 11 Asian and Pacific nations, members of a regional trade group called the Asian-Pacific Economic Cooperation forum. It was the largest gathering of Pacific Rim nations since 1966 and resulted in an agreement to seek greater trade liberalization in the region.

South Africa's main political leaders endorse a new interim Constitution that guarantees equal rights for all citizens and ends the last vestiges of the system of *apartheid* (racial segregation).

22   **Striking American Airlines flight attendants** agree to return to work after President Clinton urged both sides in the labor dispute to seek arbitration. The strike had threatened the Thanksgiving holiday plans of thousands of air travelers.

24   **The Brady bill, handgun-control legislation** that imposes a five-day waiting period so that background checks can be conducted on would-be gun purchasers, clears Congress. On November 30, President Clinton signed the legislation into law.

28   **British officials** confirm that they had made secret contacts with the outlawed Irish Republican Army in an effort to end the violence in Northern Ireland.

30   **Israeli and Palestinian leaders** meet in the Gaza Strip in an effort to end violence that threatens the peace accord.

◄ The heads of state of 11 Pacific Rim countries, hosted by U.S. President Bill Clinton, meet in Seattle from November 19 to 20 to discuss trade issues.

▲

Former press secretary Jim Brady, wounded in the 1981 assassination attempt on President Ronald Reagan, is applauded on November 30, when President Bill Clinton signed the Brady bill, requiring a five-day waiting period for handgun purchases.

◄ A mansion in the hills above Malibu, Calif., is threatened by fire on November 2. Wildfires destroyed more than 300 homes.

S	M	T	W	TH	F	S
			1	2	3	4
5	6	7	8	9	10	11
12	13	14	15	16	17	18
19	20	21	22	23	24	25
26	27	28	29	30	31	

December 1993

2 **Colombian police kill drug kingpin** Pablo Escobar Gaviria in a raid on his hideout in Medellín, the city where he based his drug trafficking operations.

5 **Italy's former Communists,** now known as the Party of the Democratic Left (PDS), claim victory in mayoral contests in Rome, Naples, Genoa, Venice, and Trieste, as Italian voters continue to reject mainstream parties tainted by a corruption scandal. The PDS fashioned coalitions in each of the contests. Only one new mayor, in Naples, was a PDS member.

7 **Astronauts on board the space shuttle Endeavour** successfully install a camera to correct an optical defect in the Hubble Space Telescope, giving astronomers hope that the telescope will begin yielding significant new discoveries. The Endeavour returned to Earth on December 13.

12 **Russian voters approve a new Constitution** that gives President Boris Yeltsin significant powers, but far right parties and hard-line Communists make a strong showing in parliamentary elections. Ultranationalist Vladimir Zhirinovsky, leader of the Liberal Democratic Party, emerges as Yeltsin's chief rival.

14 **United States and European trade representatives** set aside several major trade disputes in talks in Geneva, Switzerland, clearing the way for an agreement that will govern international trade between 117 nations.

Israel and the Vatican agree to establish full diplomatic relations. On December 24, the Vatican formally recognized Israel for the first time.

15 **French scientists** announce that they have produced the first rough map of the locations of genes on human chromosomes, an achievement that some scientists labeled a "giant step forward" in the effort to understand human heredity.

The United Kingdom and the republic of Ireland agree on a declaration of general principles that are intended to bring about peace talks with the Irish Republican Army over the future of Northern Ireland.

United States Secretary of Defense Les Aspin, Jr., announces that he is resigning for "personal reasons," after a brief tenure marked by several controversies. Aspin becomes the first member of the Cabinet to resign. On December 16, President Bill Clinton named Bobby Ray Inman, a retired admiral and former deputy director of the Central Intelligence Agency, to replace Aspin.

20 **Yugoslavia's governing Socialist Party** claims victory in parliamentary elections held on December 19. The party, which is headed by Serbian President Slobodan Milošević, retained the largest bloc of votes in the 250-seat Parliament.

22 **South Africa's Parliament** gives a strong endorsement to an interim Constitution that ends centuries of white-minority rule, adopting the Constitution by a vote of 237 to 45.

▲
Russian ultranationalist Vladimir Zhirinovsky, leader of the Liberal Democratic Party, holds a press conference after his party made significant gains in parliamentary elections on December 12.

▲
The Hubble Space Telescope, tethered to the cargo bay of the space shuttle Endeavour, appears to point toward Earth as astronauts prepare to do final repairs to the telescope on December 9. On December 7, the astronauts repaired an optical defect.

1993

WORLD BOOK
YEAR BOOK UPDATE

T he major events of 1993 are summarized in nearly 300 alphabetically arranged articles, from "Africa" to "Zoos." In
most cases, the article titles are the same as those of the articles
in *The World Book Encyclopedia* that they update. Included are
11 Special Reports that offer in-depth looks at particular subjects, ranging from urban gangs to the spread of legalized gambling. The Special Reports can be found on the following pages
under their respective Update article titles.

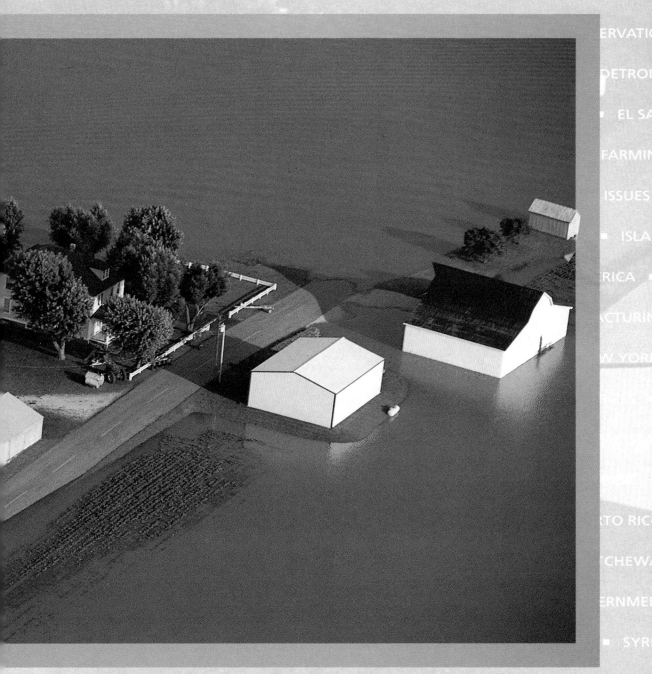

Somali warlord Mohamed Farah Aideed in November addresses supporters in Mogadishu, after the United Nations canceled a warrant for his arrest.

Africa

The movement in many African countries toward more democratic forms of government continued in 1993. There were serious setbacks in some countries, however, suggesting that further progress in achieving democratic reforms may be difficult. Adding to the continent's woes were ongoing military conflicts and ethnic strife that caused great loss of life and economic disruption in several countries.

The agony of Somalia. The United States and United Nations (UN) intervention in Somalia, widely hailed as a humanitarian relief operation when it began in December 1992, led to considerable disillu-sionment in 1993. Once the problem of widespread starvation had been brought under control, the U.S. and UN forces began pursuing one of the local warlords, General Mohamed Farah Aideed. A measure passed by the UN Security Council on March 26 shifted the burden of the operation in Somalia from the United States to a UN-commanded peacekeeping force, which included many American troops.

On October 3 and 4, U.S. soldiers fought a fierce battle with Aideed's troops in Mogadishu, the capital, in which 18 Americans died. Television footage of an American soldier's body being dragged through the streets by Aideed's supporters caused an outcry in the United States, causing President Bill Clinton to quickly revise U.S. policy in Somalia. Clin-

Addis Ababa, Ethiopia, and in April and May in Abidjan, Ivory Coast—proved fruitless. On May 19, the Clinton Administration recognized the government of Angolan President José Eduardo dos Santos, thereby putting pressure on Savimbi—a former U.S. ally—to end the civil war. The UN also exerted pressure on UNITA. In early November, Savimbi announced that he would rejoin peace talks and that he was willing to give up some of his military gains as a precondition for entering negotiations.

The conflict in Liberia remained unresolved at year's end, though the various conflicting factions and the nation's long-suffering people seemed to be growing weary of the war. UN intervention, along with the continued efforts of the Economic Community of West African States, which has had troops in Liberia since November 1990, provided some hope that peace might soon be at hand.

A peaceful and democratic solution to conflict appeared to have taken place in Burundi, where ethnic strife between the minority Tutsi and majority Hutu has killed tens of thousands of people in past years. In 1993, the Tutsi-dominated government agreed to elections, which were held under fair and free conditions on June 1. Melchior Ndadaye, the candidate of the Burundi Democracy Front, consisting mainly of Hutu, was elected president. Legislative elections were held on June 29, and the new government took power on July 10.

The appearance of successful democratic reform ended on October 21 when Tutsi soldiers rebelled, killing President Ndadaye and attempting to set up their own government. For the next few weeks, Burundi was rocked by ethnic warfare that, by some estimates, left more than 150,000 people dead. By year-end, the rebels had fled the country, and Prime Minister Sylvie Kinigi had reestablished the legitimate government.

Neighboring Rwanda was also disrupted by strife between Hutus and Tutsis during the year. Like Burundi, Rwanda has a Hutu majority and a Tutsi minority, but in Rwanda the Hutus have been in power for years. The Tutsi-dominated Rwandan Patriotic Front has been struggling for power since 1990, and severe fighting broke out in February 1993.

The two sides met for negotiations in Dar es Salaam, Tanzania, and signed a cease-fire on March 7. A military force sent by the Organization of African Unity (OAU)—an association of more than 50 African countries—arrived in Rwanda to assist in the peacemaking process, which included plans for multiparty elections in June 1995. In October 1993, a UN force was also dispatched to Rwanda.

In Mozambique, the vicious war between the government and Renamo, a rebel group, seemed to have ended in 1993 as a cease-fire signed the year before remained in effect. The country was also aided by the end of a long drought. With peace and good crops, the country began the long process of

ton promised that most American forces would be out of Somalia by March 31, 1994.

Although violence continued in the capital, peace was restored to most of the rural areas. Rainfall brought an increase in the food supply, and there was a move toward reestablishing local government. But bandit raids on UN food convoys in November 1993 were an indication of what the future holds for Somalia if UN forces were to be withdrawn.

Other conflicts. In Angola, rebel leader Jonas Savimbi and his National Union for the Total Liberation of Angola (UNITA) continued to attack government troops in 1993. Unable to accept his election defeat in September 1992, Savimbi had returned to the battlefield in late 1992 and in early 1993 won a number of victories against government troops.

Peace talks in 1993—in January and February in

returning to a normal existence. UN forces were assisting the Mozambican government in disarming Renamo troops and rebuilding roads, bridges, and other public works damaged or destroyed in the war. Elections were planned for mid- or late 1994.

Seeking an end to strife. At its 29th annual summit meeting, from June 28 to 30, 1993, in Cairo, Egypt, the OAU agreed to create permanent structures for the prevention, management, and resolution of conflicts within and between African nations. Although the organization is hampered by money shortages and other problems, observers regarded the OAU's action as a positive development in the continent's efforts to police itself.

Progress toward democracy on the continent was mixed in 1993. The most significant events occurred in South Africa. Although that nation continued to be troubled by violence, talks between the major white and black parties moved forward. Elections in which South Africa's black majority will be allowed to vote for the first time were scheduled for April 27, 1994, and an interim majority-rule Constitution was approved by the Parliament on Dec. 22, 1993.

Other hopeful developments in 1993 included successful elections on March 27 in Lesotho, where the Basotho Congress Party (BCP) defeated the incumbent Basutoland National Party, winning all 243 parliamentary seats and naming Ntsu Mokhehle as prime minister. The last elections in Lesotho had been held in 1970, when the BCP also won, but that result was canceled and the BCP outlawed. The country had been under military rule since 1986.

Malawi provided one of the most positive surprises of the year when the government allowed a referendum on June 14, 1993, to decide whether the country would continue as a one-party state or allow multiparty democracy. President H. Kamuzu Banda received a shock when citizens voted solidly against continuing one-party rule. Elections were planned for mid-1994, but there were indications that Banda and his followers were looking for ways to undermine the electoral process and stay in power.

Successful elections were also conducted in the Seychelles on July 23, 1993, with the incumbent party remaining in power. Less clear, however, were the prospects for the advancement of democracy in several other countries. Elections took place in Senegal on February 21, and the incumbent, President Abdou Diouf, won by a 2 to 1 margin. Complaints of fraud were widespread. Elections in Djibouti on May 7 returned President Hassan Gouled Aptidon to office, but that election, too, resulted in accusations of fraud. The major opposition group, the Front for the Restoration of Unity and Democracy, boycotted the event and continued its often violent opposition to the government.

Definite setbacks for democracy occurred in several countries. In Zaire, the democratization process was completely halted by the refusal of President Mobutu Sese Seko to allow an elected government to come to power. Two competing governments existed during most of the year, while the country's economy continued a disastrous downward trend. Elections in Togo on August 22 were so blatantly rigged that international observer teams, led by former U.S. President Jimmy Carter, left the country in protest before the polls opened.

The greatest disappointment of the year occurred in Nigeria, Africa's most populous country, where the planned return to civilian rule was totally disrupted. Elections were held on June 12, but the military government refused to accept the results. Although Nigeria's military ruler, President Ibrahim Babangida, bowed to pressures and stepped down on August 26, he turned the reins over to an ally, businessman Ernest Shonekan. On November 17, the military stepped in again when the defense minister, General Sani Abacha, ousted Shonekan and named himself the head of a new regime.

Nationhood for Eritrea. On May 24, Ethiopia granted independence to the province of Eritrea, which became Africa's newest country. Eritreans had fought a long and difficult war to gain their independence, helping to overthrow the military government of Ethiopian President Mengistu Haile-Mariam in 1991. Three days before independence, Eritrea's newly formed National Assembly elected former rebel leader Issaias Afeworke as the nation's first president.

Pope John Paul II made his 10th visit to Africa in February 1993, making stops in Sudan, Benin, and Uganda. In Uganda, a country severely ravaged by the AIDS epidemic, the pope stated firmly that abstinence from sexual intercourse was the only safe means of preventing the spread of AIDS. He thus made clear his opposition to the Ugandan government's U.S.-financed program to increase the use of condoms as a means of fighting AIDS.

African summit. Libreville, Gabon, was the setting for the second African/African-American Summit Conference. The purpose of the event, attended by more than 4,500 people, was to boost economic relations between Africans and black Americans. Conferees placed special emphasis on encouraging African Americans to invest in African economic development and to help influence U.S. foreign policy toward Africa. The possibility of joint U.S. and African citizenship for African Americans was also discussed. The first summit was held in 1991 in Abidjan, the capital of Ivory Coast.

Economics. The negative economic trends that have plagued most African countries in recent years showed little sign of improvement in 1993. The nations of southern Africa were benefited, however, by the ending of a long drought. The return of adequate rainfall meant that for the first time in several years good harvests were common in the region, providing an important stabilizing factor for governments struggling to institute democratic reforms or control internal unrest.

Toward the end of the year an upward surge in the world price of cocoa promised some relief for those west African countries, such as Ivory Coast and Ghana, that receive a substantial portion of their export income from the sale of that product. Most African countries depend heavily upon the export of agricultural products, such as cocoa and coffee, or of raw materials, such as ores and minerals, for their incomes. As the world prices of these commodities go up or down, so too do the economic prospects of the African countries producing them.

The African Financial Community (CFA), a group of 14 African nations that are often referred to as the Franc Zone, felt a sense of unease about their economic future in 1993. The CFA countries—all but one former colonies of France—use the same unit of currency, the CFA franc, which is guaranteed by the French treasury and tied to the value of the French franc. This arrangement has lent stability to the CFA franc, making it easier for the CFA nations to exchange their currency for the currencies of other countries and to engage in international trade.

In 1993, however, there were hints from France that it might be planning to significantly alter, or even terminate, this relationship. Rumors to that effect spread throughout Africa during the year. The CFA nations suffered a tremendous drain on their

People in the Ethiopian province of Eritrea line up in April to vote on the question of independence for Eritrea—a measure that passed overwhelmingly.

Facts in brief on African political units

Country	Population	Government	Monetary unit*	Foreign trade (million U.S.$)	
				Exports†	Imports†
Algeria	27,864,000	High State Council Chairman Ali Kafi; Prime Minister Redha Malek	dinar (19.77 = $1)	13,306	10,122
Angola	11,195,000	President José Eduardo dos Santos	new kwanza (6,500.32 = $1)	2,989	1,140
Benin	5,242,000	President Nicephore Soglo	CFA franc (293.29 = $1)	34	543
Botswana	1,467,000	President Sir Ketumile Masire	pula (2.53 = $1)	1,800	1,600
Burkina Faso	10,082,000	Popular Front President, Head of State, & Head of Government Blaise Compaoré	CFA franc (293.29 = $1)	95	322
Burundi	6,161,000	Prime Minister Sylvie Kinigi	franc (233.38 = $1)	75	230
Cameroon	13,538,000	President Paul Biya	CFA franc (293.29 = $1)	2,019	1,650
Cape Verde	423,000	President Antonio Mascarenhas Monteiro; Prime Minister Carlos Alberto Wahnon de Carvalho Veiga	escudo (74.20 = $1)	6	136
Central African Republic	3,406,000	President André-Dieudonne Kolingba	CFA franc (293.29 = $1)	74	145
Chad	6,277,000	President Idriss Deby	CFA franc (293.29 = $1)	141	419
Comoros	633,000	President Said Mohamed Djohar	CFA franc (293.29 = $1)	16	41
Congo	2,586,000	President Pascal Lissouba; Prime Minister Jacques Joachim Yhombi-Opango	CFA franc (293.29 = $1)	976	600
Djibouti	459,000	President Hassan Gouled Aptidon; Prime Minister Barkat Gourad Hamadou	franc (178.17 = $1)	17	214
Egypt	57,082,000	President Hosni Mubarak; Prime Minister Atef Sedky	pound (3.37 = $1)	3,104	8,357
Equatorial Guinea	389,000	President Teodoro Obiang Nguema Mbasogo; Prime Minister Silvestre Siale Bileka	CFA franc (293.29 = $1)	37	68
Eritrea	3,588,000	President Issaias Afeworke	Ethiopian birr	no statistics available	
Ethiopia	52,157,000	President Meles Zenawi	birr (5.00 = $1)	189	472
Gabon	1,334,000	President El Hadj Omar Bongo; Prime Minister Casimir Oye-Mba	CFA franc (293.29 = $1)	1,599	767
Gambia	957,000	President Sir Dawda Kairaba Jawara	dalasi (9.53 = $1)	43	222
Ghana	17,026,000	President Jerry John Rawlings	cedi (710.00 = $1)	1,024	1,275
Guinea	6,487,000	President Lansana Conté	franc (812.29 = $1)	788	692
Guinea-Bissau	1,049,000	President João Bernardo Vieira	peso (5,000 = $1)	14	69
Ivory Coast	13,949,000	Acting President Henri Konan Bédié	CFA franc (293.29 = $1)	2,931	2,185
Kenya	27,833,000	President Daniel T. arap Moi	shilling (68.56 = $1)	1,125	1,802
Lesotho	1,990,000	King Letsie III; Prime Minister Ntsu Mokhehle	maloti (3.36 = $1)	59	604
Liberia	2,928,000	Interim President Amos Sawyer	dollar (1 = $1)	396	272
Libya	5,240,000	Leader of the Revolution Muammar Muhammad al-Qadhafi; General People's Committee Secretary (Prime Minister) Zanati Muhammed al-Zanati	dinar (0.30 = $1)	13,877	5,599

*Exchange rates as of Oct. 29, 1993, or latest available data.
†Latest available data.
‡Defense Minister Sani Abacha ousted Ernest Shonekan on November 17 and imposed a military government.

Country	Population	Government	Monetary unit*	Foreign trade (million U.S.$)	
				Exports†	Imports†
Madagascar	13,637,000	President Albert Zafy; Prime Minister Francisque Ravony	franc (1,890.35 = $1)	306	435
Malawi	10,096,000	President H. Kamuzu Banda	kwacha (4.46 = $1)	376	699
Mali	10,443,000	President Alpha Oumar Konare; Prime Minister Abdoulaye Sekou Sow	CFA franc (293.29 = $1)	271	500
Mauritania	2,266,000	President Maaouya Ould Sid Ahmed Taya	ouguiya (113.81 = $1)	437	222
Mauritius	1,103,000	President Cassam Uteem; Prime Minister Sir Anerood Jugnauth	rupee (18.40 = $1)	1,290	1,626
Morocco	27,587,000	King Hassan II; Prime Minister Mohamed Karim Lamrani	dirham (9.34 = $1)	3,977	7,356
Mozambique	17,417,000	President Joaquím Alberto Chissano; Prime Minister Mário da Graça Machungo	metical (4,938.45 = $1)	162	899
Namibia	1,687,000	President Sam Nujoma; Prime Minister Hage Geingob	rand (3.36 = $1)	1,021	894
Niger	8,793,000	President Mahamane Ousmane; Prime Minister Mahamadou Issoufou	CFA franc (293.29 = $1)	283	389
Nigeria	102,300,000	Head of State Sani Abacha‡	naira (35.00 = $1)	11,886	8,276
Rwanda	8,292,000	President Juvénal Habyarimana	franc (145.71 = $1)	68	288
São Tomé and Príncipe	132,000	President Miguel Trovoada	dobra (240.00 = $1)	4	21
Senegal	8,180,000	President Abdou Diouf; Prime Minister Habib Thiam	CFA franc (293.29 = $1)	606	1,023
Seychelles	72,000	President France Albert René	rupee (5.23 = $1)	49	172
Sierra Leone	4,609,000	Supreme Council of State Chairman Valentine E. M. Strasser	leone (550.00 = $1)	166	131
Somalia	7,033,000	No functioning government	shilling (2,620 = $1)	104	132
South Africa	43,884,00	State President Frederik Willem de Klerk	rand (3.36 = $1)	24,000	18,800
Sudan	28,256,000	Revolutionary Command Council for National Salvation Chairman and Prime Minister Umar Hasan Ahmad al-Bashir	pound (130.00 = $1)	509	1,060
Swaziland	907,000	King Mswati III; Prime Minister Obed Mfanyana Dlamini	lilangeni (3.36 = $1)	557	632
Tanzania	31,664,000	President Ali Hassan Mwinyi; Prime Minister John Malecela	shilling (455.43 = $1)	360	1,170
Togo	4,002,000	President Gnassingbé Eyadéma	CFA franc (293.29 = $1)	253	444
Tunisia	8,882,000	President Zine El Abidine Ben Ali; Prime Minister Hamed Karoui	dinar (1.03 = $1)	4,040	6,415
Uganda	20,847,000	President Yoweri Kaguta Museveni; Prime Minister George Cosmas Adyebo	shilling (1,184.32 = $1)	201	197
Zaire	40,407,000	President Mobutu Sese Seko	zaire (4,970,000 = $1)	832	713
Zambia	9,812,000	President Frederick Chiluba; Vice President Levy Mwanawasa	kwacha (359.73 = $1)	775	801
Zimbabwe	10,974,000	President Robert Mugabe	dollar (6.72 = $1)	826	1,850

South Africa's President Frederik Willem de Klerk, right, and African National Congress President Nelson Mandela won the Nobel Peace Prize in October.

currency as citizens, fearing a devaluation of the CFA franc, rushed to transfer their francs to other currencies. On August 1, the Franc Zone countries for the first time imposed restrictions on the convertibility of their currencies in an effort to slow this drain.

The World Bank, a UN agency that has become one of the most powerful financial influences in Africa, was also moving toward policy changes in 1993. In May, World Bank President Edward Jaycox announced that African countries would in the future be required to play a greater role in their economic planning and could rely less on the bank. Jaycox said that some of the economic changes that the World Bank has required African nations to make in return for receiving the bank's assistance have caused more problems than they solved.

Public-health problems continued to be a major factor in Africa's development plans in 1993. Although AIDS has received the most publicity, tuberculosis (TB) has also become a severe problem. The World Health Organization, an agency of the UN, estimated in 1993 that TB now causes 500,000 deaths a year in Africa, a large increase from the 1980's. The increase was thought to be due to the growing prev- alence of drug-resistant strains of TB.   □ Mark DeLancey

See also various African country articles. In *World Book,* see **Africa.**

Agriculture. See **Farm and farming.**

AIDS. A major European study published on April 3, 1993, questioned the long-term benefit of administering AZT, a commonly prescribed AIDS drug, before patients develop infections or other symptoms of full-blown AIDS. The AZT study involved 1,749 patients in France, Ireland, and the United Kingdom.

Many physicians in the United States begin prescribing AZT to patients infected with the AIDS-causing human immunodeficiency virus (HIV) when the concentration of certain white cells in the patients' blood drops below 500 cells per cubic millimeter. These blood cells, known as CD-4 cells, play a key role in the body's disease-fighting immune system, and healthy adults have from 800 to 1,200 of them in every cubic millimeter of blood. HIV destroys CD-4 cells, and the concentration of these cells is used as an indicator of how far HIV infection has progressed.

The European researchers found that patients who received early treatment with AZT had a lower risk of developing AIDS symptoms during the first year of treatment, compared with HIV-infected patients who did not receive the drug. But this benefit disappeared quickly. Over three years, the patients who had been treated early with AZT became ill and died at the same rate as the patients who were not treated with the drug. The study did not question the value of AZT for patients who already have AIDS symptoms. Previous studies have shown that AZT does increase their life expectancy.

A panel of AIDS experts, brought together by the National Institute of Allergy and Infectious Diseases (NIAID), recommended on June 25 that doctors decide on an individual basis whether to administer AZT to symptomless patients with CD-4 counts in the 200 to 500 range. NIAID, a branch of the National Institutes of Health in Bethesda, Md., convened the panel after the release of the European study in order to review recommended uses of drugs in treating HIV infection.

HIV's hidden activity. HIV is active in the body much earlier than previously believed, a team of NIAID scientists reported on March 25. Anthony S. Fauci, director of NIAID and head of the research team, said the virus reproduces rapidly in lymphoid tissues during the symptomless stage of HIV infection. (Lymphoid tissues include the lymph nodes, spleen, tonsils, and other organs that make up the immune system.) Patients feel well during this stage, which may last as long as 10 years, and their blood shows little evidence of HIV infection.

Fauci said the new findings challenge the idea that HIV goes into a *latent* (resting) stage right after infection. His research group found that the virus reproduces and accumulates at high levels in lymphoid tissue. Eventually, the virus spills over into the blood, and symptoms appear as the infection progresses rapidly. The findings suggest, Fauci added, that patients might benefit if they could be identified and treated with antiviral drugs soon after HIV infection occurs.

False alarm. Researchers on February 11 concluded there is no evidence that a new AIDS virus or any other infectious agent causes a mysterious AIDS-like illness that came to public attention in 1992. People with the disorder have low white-blood-cell counts but no signs of HIV infection.

The ailment, known as idiopathic CD-4-positive T-lymphocytopenia (ICL), led to wide concern that an AIDS-causing virus, undetectable with existing blood tests, had emerged. But experts who conducted intensive studies of ICL concluded that the rare malady is neither new nor infectious and differs from HIV infection and AIDS.

AIDS in developing countries. Warning about the rapid spread of HIV infection and AIDS in developing countries, the World Health Organization (WHO) on June 7, 1993, proposed an intensive new prevention effort that would cost $2.5 billion per year. WHO is an agency of the United Nations based in Geneva, Switzerland.

Michael H. Merson, director of WHO's Global Program on AIDS, said the project would apply existing knowledge about preventing HIV infection. It would include emphasis on the use of condoms and the treatment of sexually transmitted diseases that make women in developing countries especially vulnerable to HIV infection. Merson also urged scientific research

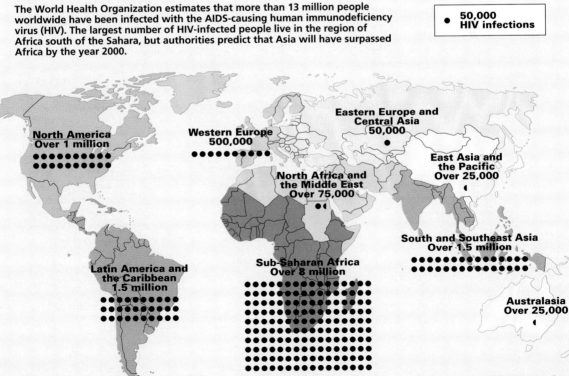

HIV infection worldwide

The World Health Organization estimates that more than 13 million people worldwide have been infected with the AIDS-causing human immunodeficiency virus (HIV). The largest number of HIV-infected people live in the region of Africa south of the Sahara, but authorities predict that Asia will have surpassed Africa by the year 2000.

● 50,000 HIV infections

North America
Over 1 million

Western Europe
500,000

Eastern Europe and
Central Asia
50,000

East Asia and
the Pacific
Over 25,000

North Africa and
the Middle East
Over 75,000

South and Southeast Asia
Over 1.5 million

Latin America and
the Caribbean
1.5 million

Sub-Saharan Africa
Over 8 million

Australasia
Over 25,000

Source: World Health Organization.

to develop an antiviral medication that women could apply to prevent infection. Women account for about 5 of every 11 new HIV infections in developing countries.

WHO reported on May 21, 1993, that the region of Africa south of the Sahara has been more severely affected by AIDS than any other region in the world. Of the more than 13 million people infected with HIV, 8 million live in sub-Saharan Africa. The region also accounts for two of every three AIDS cases that have occurred so far.

U.S. AIDS cases. The U.S. Centers for Disease Control and Prevention (CDC) in Atlanta, Ga., estimate that about 1 million Americans are infected with HIV. But the first nationwide survey of HIV infections came up with a lower estimate of 550,000. This figure, released in December, was based on a survey of 7,992 households. The National Center for Health Statistics compiled the results but added that the survey had not included people in hospitals and prisons and certain other groups at high risk. The CDC reported in October that 339,250 cases of AIDS and 204,390 deaths from AIDS had occurred in the United States from the epidemic's start in 1981 to Sept. 30, 1993. ☐ Michael Woods

See also **Drugs.** In *World Book,* see **AIDS.**

Air pollution. See Environmental pollution.

Alabama. See State government.

Alaska. See State government.

Albania. Serious differences emerged in 1993 within the Albanian government, headed by President Sali Berisha. The government failed to resolve disagreements over a proposed constitution, clouding progress toward the adoption of full-fledged democracy. Opposition leaders denounced Berisha and his ruling Democratic Party (DP) for the arrest of Fatos Nano, head of the Socialist Party (formerly the Communist Party), on corruption charges on July 30. Critics also charged that Berisha's government had become increasingly authoritarian.

By year's end, Berisha and the DP were themselves embroiled in a scandal over the alleged misuse of government funds in 1992. Meanwhile, the country's continuing economic misery, coupled with the uncertainties that accompanied the introduction of free market reforms, fueled popular support for the government's opponents.

Economic woes continued to plague Albania in 1993. Although most agricultural land had been privatized by the start of the year, few farmers could afford seeds or equipment. The country's food supply stayed at critical levels, and foreign food aid remained vital for the large portion of the population living in poverty. Privatization of industrial enterprises proceeded slowly, while foreign investors—fearful of Albania's nearness to Balkan trouble spots—steered clear of the country. As of August, about 40 percent of Albania's labor force was unemployed.

Foreign relations. The economic situation increased tension between Albania and Greece, where as many as 400,000 Albanians—a tenth of the country's population—had fled by late 1993 in search of work. Albania's efforts to normalize relations with Greece were complicated when Albania deported a Greek Orthodox priest on June 25, accusing him of trying to stir up an independence movement among ethnic Greeks in southern Albania. In response, the Greek government expelled about 25,000 Albanians, most of them illegal immigrants.

Albanian relations with Serbia, the dominant republic of Yugoslavia, and with the former Yugoslav republic of Macedonia also were tense. Albanians expressed fear for the safety of ethnic Albanians in Kosovo, a largely Albanian province of Serbia. At least 25 Albanians on both sides of the border were shot by Serbian guards in 1993. In November, Macedonia accused Albania of shipping hundreds of rifles across the border in an alleged conspiracy to arm ethnic Albanians, who make up about 25 percent of Macedonia's population. Albania denied the charge.

Albania moved closer to Turkey in 1993, receiving economic, educational, and military aid from that country. In October, Albania and the United States signed an agreement increasing military cooperation between the two nations. ☐ Sharon L. Wolchik

See also **Europe** (Facts in brief table). In *World Book,* see **Albania.**

Alberta. Powered by the popularity of Premier Ralph Klein, the Progressive Conservative Party on June 15, 1993, swept to its seventh straight electoral victory since 1971. Klein, who was chosen premier in December 1992, had distanced himself from his predecessor, Donald R. Getty, by stressing tight control of an economy handicapped by falling oil production. Klein emphasized the need for "brutal" spending cuts, a theme that played well after an impartial commission presented a picture of a skyrocketing public deficit. Klein also sponsored a law requiring a balanced budget by fiscal 1996-1997 and eliminating pensions for recent retirees of the legislature.

The Conservatives won 51 of the 83 seats in the legislature and 45 percent of the popular vote. The Liberals, who held 9 seats before the election, saw their standing grow to 32 seats. The New Democratic Party lost all 15 seats it had held before the election.

The budget, revealed on May 6, 1993, promised to reduce overall spending by 5.5 percent. The largest cuts were made in health care and social services. Income taxes were not increased, and no sales taxes were begun in the only province without any.

In September, the Klein government announced it would allow private retailers to sell liquor, but the province would remain the sole wholesaler of liquor. Alberta is the first Canadian province to allow private liquor outlets. ☐ David M. L. Farr

In *World Book,* see **Alberta.**

Albright, Madeleine K. (1937-), a professor of international affairs at Georgetown University in Washington, D.C., became United States ambassador to the United Nations on Feb. 1, 1993. A long-time Democratic foreign-policy adviser, Albright is an expert on the former Soviet Union.

Albright was born on May 15, 1937, in Prague, Czechoslovakia. She came to the United States in 1948 when her father, a diplomat, defected. She attended Wellesley College in Massachusetts, graduating with honors in 1959, and later earned master's and doctoral degrees in public law and government at Columbia University in New York City.

In 1976, Albright joined the staff of Senator Edmund S. Muskie (D., Me.) as his chief legislative assistant. Two years later, she became a member of President Jimmy Carter's National Security Council staff, responsible for foreign-policy legislation.

Albright was named a professor at Georgetown University's School of Foreign Service in 1982. During the 1980's, she also served as a foreign-policy adviser to Democratic candidates Walter F. Mondale and Michael S. Dukakis in their presidential campaigns. In 1989, while continuing at Georgetown, she became president of the Center for National Policy, a Washington, D.C.-based organization that promotes the study of national and international issues.

Albright is divorced. She has three daughters from her marriage. □ David Dreier

Algeria. Militant Islamic extremists in Algeria ambushed state security forces, assassinated public figures, and burned factories in 1993. The death total reached more than 2,000 by November in fighting that began when the military seized power in January 1992, stopping the fundamentalist Islamic Salvation Front from winning a parliamentary majority.

The ruling five-member High State Council, established by the military, responded harshly in 1993 to the militants. By mid-November, 367 militants had been sentenced to death since February 1992. In April 1993, 15,000 government troops began patrolling the capital, Algiers, to enforce order.

Assassinations. On August 21, Kasdi Merbah, former prime minister and head of military security, was assassinated. The government blamed Islamic extremists for the murder and for several other attacks on high-ranking officials. Among these were the killings of two officials in mid-March and a failed assassination attempt on February 13 against Defense Minister Khaled Nezzar, a member of the ruling council. Over 20 intellectuals and journalists who were seen as being against Islamic extremism were also murdered in 1993.

Foreigners targeted. In September and October, Islamic militants began to target foreigners, killing seven. In October, the Armed Islamic Group issued a warning that any foreigner who did not leave Algeria by November 30 could be killed. After the

deadline passed, 16 foreigners were murdered from December 1 through December 16.

Political ouster. On August 21, Foreign Minister Redha Malek was appointed by the ruling council to replace Belaid Abdesselam as prime minister. Abdesselam, who also served as economic minister, had been criticized for his failed economic programs.

Economic problems have fueled Algeria's social unrest. Interest payments on the country's $26 billion foreign debt used up about 75 percent of an estimated $11.5 billion in 1993 export revenues. One official warned that this would leave only $1 billion in foreign exchange earnings and $2 billion in gold reserves in the nation's coffers by the end of 1993. In January, the government announced an $8-billion deficit in its current $23-billion budget. Inflation remained at 30 percent.

The unemployment rate in Algeria was at least 20 percent in 1993. About 50 percent of the unemployed were adults under age 25, who make up more than 30 percent of Algeria's people. Inadequate employment, housing, and basic necessities for the population, which grew by 2.7 percent in 1993, fueled discontent. □ Christine Helms

See also **Africa** (Facts in brief table). In *World Book,* see **Algeria.**

Angola. See Africa.

Animal. See World Book Supplement section; **Conservation; Zoology; Zoos.**

Anthropology. A new analysis of finds from the Middle East may help resolve a debate over the relationship between modern human beings and Neanderthals, according to research published in May 1993. Neanderthals were a type of prehistoric people who lived in parts of Europe, Asia, and Africa from about 100,000 to 35,000 years ago. Some anthropologists believe that modern human beings evolved from Neanderthals. A competing school of thought holds that Neanderthals formed a separate evolutionary line that became extinct.

A team led by geologist Frank McDermott of University College in Dublin, Ireland, analyzed mammalian tooth fragments from three caves in northern Israel where scientists have found fossils of early *hominids* (human beings and their close prehuman ancestors). One cave, called Tabun, yielded Neanderthal remains, and the others—Qafzeh and Skhul—contained modern humans. The tooth fragments, from early cattle or oxen, were found in the same sediments that produced the hominid fossils.

The scientists measured the amount of uranium that had accumulated in the teeth since burial. They found that two teeth from Qafzeh dated to 106,000 and 89,000 years ago, and three teeth from Tabun had ages ranging from 105,000 to 98,000 years ago, suggesting that Neanderthals and modern humans coexisted in the Middle East some 100,000 years ago. McDermott's team concluded that the two groups

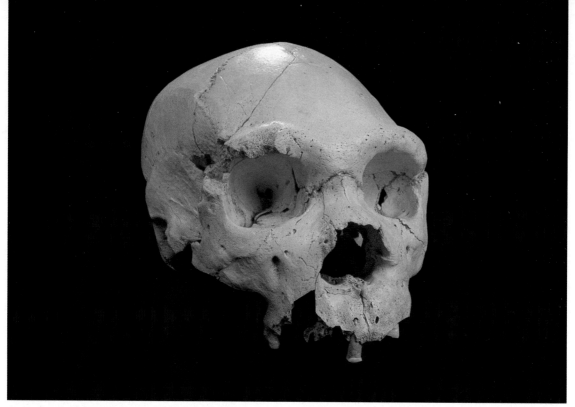

A nearly complete, 300,000-year-old skull from Spain suggests that early
Neanderthals evolved much earlier than believed, researchers said in April.

could not have an ancestor-descendant relationship.

Early Neanderthal evolution. The discovery of
three well-preserved skulls and more than 700 other
fossils has yielded new insights into the origins of
European Neanderthals, scientists reported in April.
Spanish paleontologists discovered the fossils in July
1992 in a cave called Sima de los Huesos, in the Atapuerca Mountains in northern Spain. Geological dating of a stalagmite standing just above the finds
suggests that the fossils are more than 300,000 years
old. The excavators recovered remains belonging to
at least 24 individuals, making the collection the
largest known sample of hominids from the Middle
Pleistocene Epoch (500,000 to 130,000 years ago).

The age of the Atapuerca fossils makes them at
least 200,000 years older than the earliest known
Neanderthals. However, the skulls and limb bones
exhibit several anatomical traits typical of European
Neanderthals, suggesting that Neanderthals began
to develop during the Middle Pleistocene. This, in
turn, means that if Neanderthals were not the ancestors of modern human beings, the two species had a
common ancestor even further back in time.

The new finds also may help end a debate over
the classification of other Middle Pleistocene fossils,
whose fragmentary nature and poor dating have
made them difficult to interpret. The newly found
skulls include those of two adults and one juvenile,
according to the researchers. The adult skulls vary

greatly in size, suggesting that the species was *sexually dimorphic*—that is, the males were larger than
the females. Some scientists have interpreted size
differences in other Middle Pleistocene skulls as evidence that they represented more than one species.

Earliest ancestors. The discovery of several 3.4-
million-year-old fossils belonging to *Australopithe-
cus afarensis,* widely regarded as hominids' earliest
common ancestor, was reported in November 1993.
Scientists led by anthropologist Tim D. White of the
University of California at Berkeley made the finds at
a site called Maka, in Ethiopia. The most famous *A.
afarensis* fossil is the well-preserved skeleton nicknamed "Lucy," found at Hadar, Ethiopia, in 1974.

The new finds include a partial *humerus* (upper
arm bone) and a remarkably complete lower jaw.
The jaw and humerus are both larger than Lucy's
and presumably from a male, the researchers said,
bolstering the argument that size variation in *A. afarensis* is due to sexual dimorphism. Some scientists
have thought that Hadar specimens represent more
than one species. The robust humerus exhibits deep
grooves where the muscle was attached to the arm,
indicating great strength. However, the humerus is
relatively short, unlike those of tree-climbing apes. It
thus counters the theory that *A. afarensis* spent part
of its time in trees. ☐ Donald C. Johanson

In ***World Book,*** see **Anthropology; Prehistoric
people.**

Archaeology. The discovery of an inscription bearing the first known mention outside the Bible of the House of David, the Israelite dynasty founded by the Biblical King David in about 1000 B.C., was announced by an Israeli archaeologist in August 1993. The inscription, which is in *Aramaic*—an ancient language related to Hebrew—appears on a fragment of a *stele* (monument) unearthed at the site of the Biblical city of Dan in northern Israel.

Archaeologists date the stele to the mid-800's B.C., after the Israelites split into the rival kingdoms of Israel in the north and Judah—which remained under the rule of the House of David—in the south. Scholars believe the inscription, which was published in November, commemorates a victory over Israel by Aram (present-day Syria). The part of the text surrounding the phrase House of David is incomplete, but scholars said a likely reconstruction is that the king of Aram also defeated troops belonging to the king of Judah, referred to as the king of the House of David.

Scholars noted that the stele's reference to the House of David does not prove that David himself was a historical figure. But the finding may shed light on the history of Israel and Judah during the 800's B.C., a little-understood period now known primarily from the Biblical books of I and II Kings and II Chronicles.

St. Augustine. Excavations in summer 1993 revealed what archaeologists believe is the exact site of the Spanish settlement in St. Augustine, Fla., the oldest permanent European settlement in what is now the United States. The settlement was founded in 1565 by a Spanish explorer, Pedro Menéndez de Avilés, who arrived on the Florida shore with 1,500 soldiers and colonists. Documents made by the settlers show that at first the Spaniards were guests of the Seloy tribe of the Timucuan Indians. The Spaniards converted the Seloy chief's *bujio* (long house) into a fort, digging a moat and building a palisade. The fort was burned down after seven months but then rebuilt.

The records had led scholars to believe the site of the fort might be on or near the grounds of a Roman Catholic shrine, Nuestra Señora de la Leche, near the St. Augustine waterfront. In the 1993 excavations, archaeologists uncovered part of a moat measuring 14 feet (4 meters) in width and 3 feet (1 meter) in depth, as well as traces of a row of wooden posts that could have formed part of a palisade. The dimensions of the moat are similar to those at a fort built by Menéndez on Parris Island off the South Carolina coast. The excavators also found the remains of a charred post, supporting the identification with Menéndez's original, burned-down fort.

Early writing deciphered. Two scholars have deciphered an inscription in an ancient Mexican script, making the script the earliest decipherable writing system in the Americas, the scholars reported in March. Archaeologist John S. Justeson of the State University of New York in Albany and linguist Terrence Kaufman of the University of Pittsburgh in Pennsylvania deciphered the script, called epi-Olmec, which was used from about 150 B.C. to A.D. 450 in southern Mexico.

The inscription appears in a stele found near Veracruz, Mexico, in 1986. It consists of 21 columns of *glyphs* (symbols) that tell the story of a warrior-king

A 4,600-year-old limestone statue of the high priest Kai was found in a tomb near the pyramids at Giza, Egypt, archaeologists reported in April.

named Harvest Mountain Lord. Details of the inscription suggest that the stele was carved in A.D. 159.

To decipher the text, Justeson and Kaufman assumed that the language of the inscription was an early form of the Zoquean languages used by Indians in the Veracruz region today. They also determined that the script is closely related to that of the Maya civilization, which peaked in Central America in about A.D. 250. Using their understanding of Mayan glyphs, the scholars were able to assign word meanings to the epi-Olmec symbols based on their reconstruction of the ancient Zoquean language.

Byzantine Egypt. Archaeologists have begun to explore a little-known period of Egyptian history, the A.D. 400's and 500's, when Egypt was part of the Byzantine Empire based in what is now Turkey. A University of Chicago archaeologist announced in June the discovery of a Byzantine gold-mining town at Bir Umm Fawakhir, a site in the desert some 60 miles (100 kilometers) east of the Nile River. A survey of the site located 221 structures, ranging from 1-room huts to complexes of up to 19 rooms, with walls of granite cobblestones. In nearby hills, there were traces of numerous mine shafts and outlying settlements. Archaeologists said the town's size indicates that Byzantine Egypt had a more robust economy than had been believed.

A 9,000-year-old rag. A scrap of cloth discovered in excavations at Çayönü Tepesi in southeastern Turkey has been dated to about 7000 B.C., making it the earliest known piece of fabric, American and Turkish researchers reported in July. Scientists dated the fabric, which is probably linen, by means of radiocarbon tests, which measure the relative amount of a radioactive form of carbon in an ancient material. The discovery pushes back the date for the earliest production of textiles by at least 500 years, archaeologists said.

Trojan gold found. A hoard of gold and silver vessels and jewelry from ancient Troy, missing since the end of World War II in 1945, is in Moscow, Russian officials admitted in August 1993. German archaeologist Heinrich Schliemann had excavated the treasure at the site of Troy, in northwestern Turkey, in 1873. Schliemann believed the treasure had belonged to Priam, the Trojan king mentioned in the *Iliad* of Homer, which deals with a war between Troy and Greece thought to have occurred in the 1200's B.C. Today, scholars believe the treasure dates to about 1,000 years before that era.

The Trojan treasure had been on display in Berlin, Germany, until the end of World War II. But after Germany's defeat, Russian forces secretly took the treasure to Moscow. Russia has said it would display the treasure, but it could eventually be returned to Germany or Turkey.

☐ Mark Rose

See also **Religion: The Lure and Lore of the Dead Sea Scrolls.** In *World Book,* see **Archaeology.**

A 4,300-year-old clay figurine whose discovery in northern Syria was reported in January is the oldest known sculpture of a domesticated horse.

Architecture. The year 1993 was the year of the museum. New and renovated museums not just for art, but also for history and other themes, were opened during the year. At least two dozen major institutions, and an equal number of secondary ones, opened, creating the kind of cultural bonanza that hadn't been seen since the early 1970's.

Remembering the Holocaust. The most important new museum—and the most moving—was the United States Holocaust Memorial Museum in Washington, D.C. President Bill Clinton spoke at the museum's dedication ceremony on April 22, 1993. Designed by architect James I. Freed of Pei Cobb Freed & Partners, the Holocaust Museum provides a powerful and exhaustive history of the extermination of 6 million Jews and 5 million other people during the Nazi Holocaust. Freed said that he had been so overwhelmed by the material that he nearly resigned the commission in despair, and only got his architectural bearings after visiting the Nazi death camps in Germany and Eastern Europe.

The exterior of the building evokes images of guard towers and smokestacks at Auschwitz, a concentration camp in Poland, and at the death camp at Dachau, a town in Germany. The interior is a series of skewed, unsettling spaces that create a feeling of constant surveillance. Unlike the monuments on the adjacent Washington Mall, which proclaim the power of democratic tolerance, the Holocaust Museum documents the power of evil. (See **Washington, D.C.: A Place in Which to Remember.**)

The Museum of Tolerance in Los Angeles, designed by Los Angeles' Maxwell Starkman Associates and London's James Gardner Studios, has a similar agenda but a much broader focus. Opened in February, its section on the Holocaust includes eerie animated figures representing Nazi perpetrators and conspirators. But the museum's centerpiece is the Whisper Gallery, where visitors are bombarded with racial and sexist epithets that force them to confront their own biases.

Colleges and universities also contributed to the museum bonanza in 1993. Michael Graves designed a handsomely low-keyed addition to the Michael C. Carlos Museum at Emory University in Atlanta, Ga. Its evocative forms and colors complement the museum's extensive collection of ancient art.

Spanish architect José Rafael Moneo, renowned for several major museums in Europe, made his American debut with the Davis Museum and Cultural Center at Wellesley College in Wellesley, Mass. Stark and straightforward on the outside, the building blossoms inside into a dazzling assemblage of galleries, staircases, and carefully framed views of the campus.

In November, the University of Minnesota in Minneapolis unveiled its $10.5-million museum designed by Frank Gehry. The Frederick R. Wiseman Art Museum is a silvery collection of geometrical shapes.

Upgrades. Controversy continued to shadow Louis I. Kahn's legacy. In 1989, a national protest by architects and critics scuttled plans to expand his Kimbell Art Museum in Fort Worth, Tex. In 1993, protesters rallied against expansion of the Kahn-designed Salk Institute in La Jolla, Calif. They argued that the proposed addition, to be constructed just to the east of the institute, would destroy Kahn's original plan and should be located elsewhere. Defenders, led by scientist Jonas Salk himself, countered that the institute was running out of research space and that proposed alternative sites were unacceptable. Excavation for the new building was completed in 1993, but construction had not begun at year-end, as the parties tried to work out a compromise.

The Dallas Museum of Art opened a new building in October that houses the Museum of the Americas. Containing art created in the Americas over the last 3,000 years, the Nancy and Jake L. Hamon Building covers 140,000 square feet (13,000 square meters) and cost $30 million. The museum's original architect, Edward Larrabee Barnes, also designed the addition.

Restoration of Taliesin, architect Frank Lloyd Wright's home and studio in Spring Green, Wis., began in early 1993. The Taliesin Preservation Commission, led by architect Robert Burly, is raising $24 million to restore the house, studio, and farm buildings as a portrait of America's greatest architect.

The ill-fated Central Library of Los Angeles reopened in October. The 67-year-old library, which had been damaged by three fires and an earthquake in 1986 and 1987, underwent a $214-million restoration of its buildings and an auditorium addition.

The Museum for African Art reopened in February 1993 in its new location in the SoHo district of New York City. Maya Lin, the creator of the Vietnam Veterans Memorial in Washington, D.C., designed the museum's new interior.

Awards. The American Institute of Architects' 1993 gold medal for lifetime achievement went to Kevin Roche. The Irish-American architect was a partner of Eero Saarinen's and then established a distinguished career for himself after Saarinen's death in 1961. Among his best-known projects are the Ford Foundation Headquarters in New York City and the Oakland Museum of Art in California.

The $100,000 Pritzker Architecture Prize for 1993, often described as the Nobel Prize of Architecture, was won in April by architect Fumihiko Maki of Japan. The jury praised his work for "fusing the best of both Eastern and Western cultures." Maki's best work, ranging from the Nippon Convention Center outside Tokyo to the new Yerba Buena Gardens Visual Arts Center in San Francisco, combines new technology and construction methods with a sensitivity to scale and texture that derives from the tradition of the Japanese teahouse. □ David Dillon

See also **Art.** In *World Book,* see **Architecture.**

Architect Jean Nouvel's opera house opened in Lyons,
France, in May.

Argentina. President Carlos Saúl Menem reached an agreement on Nov. 14, 1993, with the opposition Radical Civic Union that will permit Menem to seek a second term in 1995. Argentina's Constitution allows the nation's president only a single six-year term, but the opposition agreed to support Menem's plans to change the Constitution.

The agreement would shorten the presidential term to four years and shift some powers from the president to Congress. This shift would occur mainly through the creation of an office similar to that of prime minister, which Congress would control.

On Oct. 3, 1993, Menem said that he would call a national plebiscite to determine whether the Constitution should allow a second presidential term. Menem called off the plebiscite after the November 14 agreement, however.

Since taking office in 1989, Menem has been widely credited with reviving Argentina's economy. He reduced inflation from around 5,000 percent in 1989 to about 8 percent in 1993 and brought in billions of dollars through the sale of money-losing state-run enterprises. International investors signaled their confidence in Menem's economic course on December 9 with the purchase of $1 billion in Argentine government bonds.

General Motors returns. One sign that Argentina's economy had improved in 1993 was a 40 percent jump in automobile sales. This gain followed a 100 percent rise in auto sales in 1992, compared with 1991. To exploit this rapidly expanding market, General Motors Corporation (GM), the world's largest automobile manufacturer, announced in August 1993 that it would resume manufacturing autos in Argentina. GM had shut down its operations in Argentina in 1978 during a troubled period of military rule. The company said it planned to build a $100-million plant that would begin producing pickup trucks in 1994.

Privatization. By February 1993, the Argentine government had sold 33 state-run companies to private investors. The government had also allowed investors to manage 19 other companies. In return, foreign and domestic investors had paid $5.3 billion to the government and helped eliminate $7 billion of Argentina's national debt.

But there were rising complaints about some of the privatized companies. Under private ownership, Aerolineas Argentinas was seldom on time, critics said. Tickets were expensive, and some pilots questioned the thoroughness of the airline's safety procedures. Highways that the government had made into toll roads to help pay for construction and upkeep remained poorly maintained and dangerous, critics charged. Argentina's telephone bills were among the highest in the world, but many regarded the newly privatized utility's service as poor.

Despite the critics, the June public offering of half the stock of Yacimientos Petrolíferos Fiscales (YPF), the state-owned oil company, produced four times the anticipated number of buyers. The government generated more than $3 billion from the sale. It was the largest privatization on record in Latin America.

Advanced technology. On Feb. 12, 1993, the United States and Argentina signed an agreement that will permit Argentina to purchase advanced U.S. computer equipment, nuclear technology, and aeronautical guidance systems. The pact followed Argentina's agreement to surrender to the United States components of a secret ballistic missile project so that the components could be destroyed. The project, known as Condor II, was designed to produce medium-range ballistic missiles capable of delivering biological, chemical, and nuclear warheads.

Children abused. Argentine police said on September 2 that they had discovered 268 children in Buenos Aires who were allegedly subjected to sexual abuse and living "in a virtual state of servitude." The children lived in the compound of a religious group called The Family, which police said originated as the "Children of God" in Huntington Beach, Calif., in the 1960's. On Sept. 9, 1993, an Argentine federal judge ordered 18 adult members of the cult to stand trial on charges of kidnapping and corrupting children.   □ Nathan A. Haverstock

See also **Latin America** (Facts in brief table). In *World Book,* see **Argentina.**

Armed forces. As the superpower tensions of the Cold War era gave way to regional conflicts, the United States deployed its armed forces to help maintain peace in several trouble spots around the world in 1993. The U.S. military effort in Somalia, however, turned tragic on October 3 and 4, when 18 U.S. soldiers died in a fierce firefight with supporters of Somali warlord General Mohamed Farah Aideed. More than 75 U.S. soldiers were wounded in what Department of Defense officials described as the most severe combat losses for a single unit since the Vietnam War (1957-1975). Television footage of the body of a dead American soldier being dragged through the streets of the Somali capital of Mogadishu, and those of a captured U.S. helicopter pilot, galvanized public opinion against the U.S. presence in Somalia.

President Bill Clinton responded on October 7 by pledging that U.S. forces would be withdrawn from Somalia by March 31, 1994. But on the same day Clinton made that pledge, he ordered 1,700 more soldiers to Somalia, plus 13,000 soldiers to be stationed offshore. By the end of 1993, 29 U.S. soldiers had been killed in action in Somalia.

The U.S. mission to Somalia had begun as a humanitarian effort in the last weeks of 1992, when then-President George Bush ordered 28,000 troops to the impoverished African nation to help distribute food to tens of thousands of starving people.

Most of those troops returned to the United States in May 1993, but about 3,000 remained to provide security for United Nations (UN) peacekeeping forces who were distributing food and attempting to stabilize the country, which had fallen into anarchy due to clan warfare.

Clinton ordered 400 U.S. Army Rangers to Somalia in August with orders to capture Aideed after an ambush in June killed 24 Pakistani soldiers who were part of the UN peacekeeping team. Tensions escalated on September 9 when fighting between UN forces and Aideed's militia killed more than 100 civilians. On October 19, Clinton ordered the Rangers out of Somalia in an attempt to reduce tensions and reach a political settlement to the conflict.

The troubles that beset the Somali operation affected the Clinton Administration's plans for a simultaneous U.S. peacekeeping operation in Haiti. Clinton had agreed to send 600 U.S. troops to Haiti as part of a UN mission designed to assist in the return of President Jean-Bertrand Aristide, who was ousted by a military coup in 1991. On Oct. 11, 1993, armed anti-Aristide demonstrators turned away the main contingent of U.S. and Canadian peacekeepers from the docks of Port-au-Prince, Haiti's capital. Clinton then dispatched six U.S. warships to enforce U.N.-imposed trade sanctions against Haiti.

Limited U.S. military involvement in the civil war in Bosnia-Herzegovina (often called Bosnia) also created controversy. United States Air Force cargo planes began airdrops of food and medical supplies on February 28 to Muslim cities under siege by Bosnian Serbs. The humanitarian effort was widely viewed as unsuccessful, and U.S. officials began to reassess the policy of supporting European efforts to reach a negotiated settlement to the fighting.

As atrocities in the fighting mounted, the Clinton Administration disclosed on May 1 that it was prepared to launch U.S. air strikes against Bosnian Serb positions to halt the slaughter of innocent civilians. The Administration scrapped the plan, however, when European allies objected. Clinton remained committed to an offer to deploy 25,000 U.S. combat troops as peacekeepers if a negotiated settlement to the conflict could be reached.

A reinforced company of 300 U.S. Army troops from Germany arrived in the former Yugoslav republic of Macedonia in July as part of a UN peacekeeping operation along the border between Serbia and Albania. The deployment was only the second time that U.S. troops had operated under the command of the UN.

Iraqi raids. In the most serious military clash between the United States and Iraq since the end of the Persian Gulf War in February 1991, two U.S. Navy ships launched 23 Tomahawk cruise missiles on June 27, 1993, at the headquarters of the Iraqi intelligence service in a suburb of Baghdad. The United

A gay rights march in Washington, D.C., in April includes a contingent of veterans supporting the right of homosexuals to serve in the U.S. military.

States said that the raid was in retaliation for an alleged Iraqi-sponsored attempt to assassinate former President Bush when he visited Kuwait City in April. Iraq denied any involvement in the plot.

Retrenchment. With the end of the superpower confrontation between the United States and the former Soviet Union, the Clinton Administration planned substantial reductions in U.S. armed forces. For fiscal year 1994, which began on Oct. 1, 1993, the number of Army divisions would drop from 14 to 12, and the Air Force would lose 4 of its 28 fighter wings. Navy ships would be reduced from 443 to 413, including 2 of 14 aircraft carriers. The number of troops would drop by 108,000 to 1.62 million. The Pentagon also planned to cut U.S. troops in Europe from 187,000 to 100,000 by fiscal year 1996.

The reductions necessitated another round of U.S. military base closings. On Sept. 27, 1993, Congress approved the recommendations of the independent Defense Base Closure and Realignment Commission to shut down 35 major bases and reduce operations at dozens of others in 32 states.

Force review. The changing world geopolitical environment prompted the Pentagon to review its mission and force requirements in 1993. On September 1, the Pentagon adopted a new strategy of being prepared to fight two regional wars simultaneously in places such as the Middle East and South Korea. Previous strategy had envisioned fighting a

major war in Europe as well as several smaller conflicts. By 1999, military forces would fall to 1.4 million troops, active Army divisions would be cut to 10, and Air Force fighter wings would be reduced to 20.

Personnel developments. On Dec. 15, 1993, Secretary of Defense Les Aspin, Jr., became Clinton's first Cabinet member to resign. The Senate confirmed Aspin as secretary of defense on January 20. Aspin said his resignation would be effective on Jan. 20, 1994. He had come under fire from the military for his perceived inability to make decisions, his failure to reinforce U.S. forces in Somalia before the disastrous Oct. 3, 1993, attack, and continued conflict over military budget cuts and the issue of homosexuals in the military. On December 16, Clinton nominated retired Navy Admiral Bobby Ray Inman to replace Aspin.

President Clinton's attempts to overturn the ban against homosexuals serving in the armed forces provoked considerable controversy in 1993, and as a result, the existing policy was altered only slightly. On July 19, Clinton announced that recruits would no longer be asked about their sexual preference and that homosexuals would be allowed to serve in the military if they kept their sexual orientation private. Homosexuals could still be removed from the service for overtly homosexual behavior.

Clinton's "don't ask, don't tell" policy was a compromise forced by strenuous objections from the

Marine Colonel Fred Peck, far right, testifies before the U.S. Senate in May on his support for a ban on gays in the military, though his own son is homosexual.

Armed forces

Joint Chiefs of Staff and Sam Nunn, chairman of the Senate Armed Services Committee. Opponents argued that lifting the ban would have a detrimental effect on morale, discipline, and unit cohesion. On September 30, a federal judge issued a temporary injunction that blocked the new policy a day before it was to have been put into effect, but the U.S. Supreme Court lifted the injunction on October 29.

The Pentagon significantly loosened restrictions against women in combat on April 28, when Aspin ordered the military services to allow women pilots to begin flying combat aircraft. Aspin also asked that Congress repeal the prohibition against women serving aboard aircraft carriers and other warships.

Tailhook scandal. For the second consecutive year, the Navy was engulfed in controversy over a 1991 convention of naval aviators during which dozens of women were sexually assaulted. On April 23, 1993, the Pentagon inspector general issued a report alleging that sexual misconduct was far more widespread than originally believed at the Las Vegas, Nev., convention of the Tailhook Association, named for the device that brings planes to a halt after they land on aircraft carriers. The report described "a general atmosphere of debauchery" in which 83 women were assaulted during three days of drunken revels.

In addition to officers implicated in sexual misconduct, 51 others were alleged to have lied to investigators in order to conceal evidence of wrongdoing. In all, at least 175 officers were implicated in the scandal.

Efforts to bring criminal charges against many of those allegedly involved in the scandal were thwarted by conflicting testimony and a lack of evidence. The Navy dropped court-martial charges against the first of five officers scheduled to stand trial in September. A month later, charges were also dropped against the officer accused of assaulting Navy Lieutenant Paula Coughlin, who had triggered the scandal by reporting the incident to superiors.

Secret nuclear tests. The U.S. military secretly released large amounts of radiation into the atmosphere above the United States in the 1940's and early 1950's in an effort to study ways to develop a weapon that would kill enemies through nuclear fallout. That was the finding of a report released in December 1993 by the General Accounting Office, the investigative arm of the U.S. Congress. According to the report, Army scientists conducted 12 experiments in which they exploded bombs containing highly radioactive material in the atmosphere above test sites in Tennessee, Utah, and New Mexico in order to study how the radiation dispersed. The report said that the amount of radiation released in the experiments was thousands of times above current government safety limits.

Defense budget. The Clinton Administration released its first Department of Defense budget on March 27. The budget for the 1994 fiscal year requested spending authority of $263.4 billion, a decrease of $10 billion from the previous year's spending authorization. In November, Congress authorized the Defense Department to spend $261 billion in fiscal year 1994.

The budget signaled the effective end of the "Star Wars" program after 10 years of development at a cost of more than $30 billion. Begun in 1983 as a space-based shield against nuclear missiles, the Strategic Defense Initiative was for years the single largest weapons expenditure in the defense budget. Congress authorized $3 billion for the program, $745 million less than the Pentagon requested.

Command changes. The entire civilian leadership of the Pentagon changed hands in 1993 as the result of the 1992 presidential election. Togo D. West, Jr., was appointed secretary of the Army, replacing Michael P. W. Stone. John H. Dalton succeeded Sean C. O'Keefe as secretary of the Navy, and Sheila E. Widnall became the first female secretary of the Air Force, succeeding Donald B. Rice. Army General John Shalikashvili, the supreme commander of Allied forces in Europe, succeeded General Colin L. Powell, who retired on September 30 as chairman of the Joint Chiefs of Staff. (See **Shalikashvili, John.**)   □ Thomas M. DeFrank

In *World Book,* see the articles on the branches of the armed forces.

Armenia. Ongoing war over Nagorno-Karabakh, an ethnic Armenian enclave in neighboring Azerbaijan, devastated Armenia's economy in 1993. Armenia, which is mainly Christian, supported the enclave in its five-year drive for independence from the mainly Muslim Azerbaijan. But Armenia faced shortages of food and fuel, as Azerbaijan continued its blockade of Armenia and as Azerbaijani guerrillas constantly disrupted a vital gas pipeline through Georgia. In late summer, the Muslim states of Iran and Turkey temporarily blocked relief shipments into Armenia to protest Armenian actions.

The economic crisis sparked a government shakeup in February, as Armenian President Levon Ter-Petrosyan replaced his prime minister and cabinet. On February 5, at least 100,000 people rallied in the capital, Yerevan, calling for Ter-Petrosyan's ouster. The unrest eased as Karabakh Armenians launched an offensive, seizing strategic territory between Nagorno-Karabakh and Armenia in March and April. On June 15, the enclave's leaders signed a peace plan brokered by European mediators. But the accord soon broke down, and the Armenians renewed their offensive, capturing about 20 percent of Azerbaijan's territory by late summer. The warring parties signed another cease-fire in September. But in December, the fighting flared again.   □ Justin Burke

See also **Asia** (Facts in brief table); **Azerbaijan.** In *World Book,* see **Armenia.**

Art. The international art world's biggest upset of 1993 occurred at about 1 a.m. on May 27, when a car bomb exploded outside the Uffizi Gallery in Florence, Italy. After flying debris and shards of glass settled, rescuers discovered that the blast had killed five people, gutted a building adjacent to the gallery, and wreaked havoc in the Uffizi's celebrated collection of European art, which attracts about 1 million visitors a year.

Three paintings, one by Gerrit van Honthorst and two by Bartolomeo Manfredi, were destroyed. Thirty other paintings, including works by Flemish master Peter Paul Rubens, were damaged, and three sculptures were broken. The explosion hit the gallery's west wing and the Vasariano Corridor, which connects the Uffizi to the Pitti Palace across the Arno River. Fortunately, the explosion spared the east wing, where, among other famous works, the Uffizi's renowned collection of Sandro Botticelli paintings is displayed.

Offers of assistance from around the world flooded in when news of the tragedy became known. Initially, it appeared that the gallery would need to close for at least several months. But a team of conservators, custodians, and administrators poured their energy into repairing the damaged artworks and building. The east wing reopened on June 20 and welcomed 6,000 visitors in the first five hours. The west wing was not expected to reopen until the spring of 1994.

Italian government officials declared that they believed the bombing was part of a series of Mafia terrorist acts, but the perpetrators of the crime remained unknown at year's end. On May 28, 1993, more than 100,000 people in Florence marched in protest against the bombing. Many citizens in other Italian cities held similar rallies.

Collections. The fate of the famous collection of Swiss industrialist Baron Hans Heinrich von Thyssen-Bornemisza was settled with an announcement on June 18 that Spain had agreed to buy 775 works from the baron's 1,000-piece, $2-billion collection for the bargain price of $350 million. The baron is said to have the second-best private art collection in the world, eclipsed only by that of Queen Elizabeth II of the United Kingdom. Most of the artworks will be housed at the Villahermosa, a palace built in the 1800's near the Prado Museum in Madrid, Spain.

In other moves involving celebrated collections, the Metropolitan Museum of Art (MOMA) in New York City unveiled refurbished galleries on September 21 designed to hold a gift of 53 impressionist and postimpressionist works from publishing magnate Walter H. Annenberg. And the Israel Museum in Jerusalem, the capital of Israel, announced that it was the recipient of 80 pieces of art from the 1800's and 1900's, collected by the late United States film producer Sam Spiegel.

New museum buildings. Art institutions all across the United States continued to have financial difficulties in 1993 as the country struggled to recover from a recession. But several cities opened new facilities that had been funded when the economy was healthier. On October 11, San Francisco dedicated the Yerba Buena Gardens Visual Arts Center, a $45-million art and theater complex in a downtown redevelopment district. The visual art component of the new building is the first U.S. commission for the Japanese architect Fumihiko Maki, who won the Pritzker Architecture Prize in April.

The Dallas Museum of Art on September 26 opened a $30-million addition, named in honor of the building's principal donors, Nancy and Jake L. Hamon. The 140,000-square-foot (13,000-square-meter) new wing, designed by American architect Edward Larrabee Barnes, houses the institution's Museum of the Americas, which showcases 3,000 years of art from North and South America.

Two art museums in the South completed major building projects in 1993. On April 18, the New Orleans Museum in Louisiana unveiled a $23-million renovation and expansion designed by Elroy Quenroe. The refurbishing added 55,550 square feet (5,160 square meters) of space and doubled the museum's exhibition area.

The Birmingham Museum of Art in Alabama gained 50,000 square feet (4,600 square meters) of space in a $20-million renovation and expansion project. The addition, which was designed by Barnes, opened on October 2.

The renovated interior of the Brooklyn Museum's west wing opened on December 3, providing 30,000 square feet (2,800 square meters) of modern gallery space on three floors and an additional floor of office space. Designed by the architectural team of Arata Isozaki & Associates and James Stewart Polshek and Partners, the renovation completes the first phase of a $31-million project proposed in 1986 to modernize the museum's late-1800's structure.

Paris celebrated the bicentennial of the Louvre on Nov. 18, 1993, with the opening of the venerable museum's refurbished Richelieu wing. New displays feature Islamic and Oriental antiquities, a vast historical sweep of sculpture, Renaissance tapestries, and French paintings.

The National Endowment for the Arts (NEA) continued to face criticism about its grants of federal tax dollars to controversial exhibitions. The endowment suffered a blow when its budget was cut in the federal budget that President Bill Clinton signed on August 10. The budget reduced the 1993-1994 arts budget by about 5 percent of what it had been for 1992-1993, cutting it to $157.2 million from $166 million.

But Clinton's long-awaited appointment in July

The Joy of Life by Henri Matisse appeared among the outstanding but seldom-seen works from the Albert C. Barnes collection that toured in 1993.

of actress Jane Alexander as head of the NEA appeared to usher in a new period of conciliation. Alexander, whose appointment was championed by New York City art dealer Richard Feigen and a coalition of artists, was enthusiastically endorsed by both friends and foes of the endowment.

Blockbuster exhibitions are coming to an end, experts say, because even the wealthiest museums are having greater difficulty in paying the cost of insuring and shipping famous works. But a few major exhibitions of impressionist and modern art in 1993 proved to be exceptions.

The MOMA opened a major retrospective of Catalan artist Joan Miró's work on October 17. Celebrating the 100th anniversary of the artist's birth, the show examined the full range of Miró's work in a collection of some 400 paintings, drawings, prints, books, sculptures, and ceramics.

A world tour of "Great French Paintings from the Barnes Foundation" featured 80 impressionist, postimpressionist, and early modern works assembled by the late physician and art collector Albert C. Barnes. The show began May 2 at the National Gallery of Art in Washington, D.C., then traveled to the Musée d'Orsay in Paris. The tour is scheduled to continue into 1994, stopping at the National Museum of Western Art in Tokyo and the Philadelphia Museum of Art before being permanently installed at the foundation's refurbished headquarters in Merion, Pa.

Large group exhibitions of contemporary art also made news in 1993. The 45th Venice Biennale ran in Venice, Italy, from June 13 to October 10. The show, which runs every two years and dates back to 1895, provided the customary pavilions for artwork from individual nations. In 1993, curators from each country were encouraged to invite foreign artists to participate. Louise Bourgeois, a French sculptor who resides in New York City, represented the United States.

The ever-controversial "Biennial Exhibition" at the Whitney Museum of American Art in New York City opened in March and attracted a storm of negative criticism because of its sharp focus on social and political themes. Critics particularly objected to the inclusion of works that were not intended as art. For example, the videotape of the Los Angeles police beating of Rodney G. King in 1991 by onlooker George Holliday was prominently displayed. Acquittals of the police officers had sparked riots in Los Angeles in 1992.

The art market remained sluggish in 1993, with a few notable exceptions. The J. Paul Getty Museum in Malibu, Calif., made two major acquisitions. The first, purchased in January, was *Van Tromp going about to please his Masters, Ships a sea, getting a Good Wetting* (1844), a seascape done in the 1700's by British painter J. M. W. Turner. The museum paid $16 million for the painting, setting a record price for artwork by a British artist. Royal Holloway College, a small school west of London, sold the work to raise funds for an operating endowment. Objections to the purchase were raised by British art aficionados who did not want the painting to leave the country. But the British government granted an export license to the Getty in July 1993.

The second Getty purchase that made front-page news was a Michelangelo drawing, *The Holy Family With the Infant Baptist on the Rest on the Flight Into Egypt* (circa 1530). The Getty purchased the drawing on July 6 at Christie's London auction house for $6.32 million, a record price for an Old Master drawing sold at auction. The drawing had been in a private British collection for many years, but the seller was not identified.

The photography market hit a new high on October 8 at Christie's New York City auction house. Alfred Stieglitz's 1920 photograph entitled "Georgia O'Keeffe: A Portrait—Hands and Thimble," sold for $398,500, the top auction price ever paid for a photograph.

Norman Rockwell fans had cause for celebration in June 1993 when the Norman Rockwell Museum opened in Stockbridge, Mass. Located in the town where Rockwell lived and worked for 25 years, the museum became home to more than 500 Rockwell paintings and drawings and 100,000 artifacts from his life. The museum exhibits represented the largest collection of Rockwell's art in the United States. The new $4.4-million structure replaces a makeshift museum in the town that had housed a much smaller collection but, nevertheless, had attracted 150,000 visitors in 1992.

"60 Minutes," the popular news show on CBS, aroused the ire of the art world in September 1993. In the show, Morley Safer called contemporary art "worthless junk." Various gallery owners shot back that Safer is ignorant about art.

Museum people. Richard E. Oldenburg, director of MOMA since 1972, announced on Sept. 9, 1993, that he would retire in June 1994. Oldenburg said he thought it was appropriate to make way for a new leader who would guide the museum on an ambitious money-raising campaign and expansion program.

Thomas N. Armstrong III, former director of the Whitney Museum, was named director of the Andy Warhol Museum in January 1993. The museum, which was under construction in Pittsburgh, Pa., was scheduled to open in the spring of 1994 in a renovated warehouse.

Michael E. Shapiro announced his resignation as director of the Los Angeles County Museum of Art on Aug. 20, 1993, after less than a year on the job. He cited the museum's mounting financial problems and his inexperience in dealing with fiscal issues as the reasons for his leaving.

Los Angeles industrialist and art collector Norton Simon died on June 2, at age 86, following a long battle with a neurological disorder. His longtime curator, Sara Campbell, became director of the Norton Simon Museum in Pasadena, Calif. The museum planned to continue showcasing Simon's extraordinary collection of Old Masters, impressionist paintings, and Asian art.

□ Suzanne Muchnic

See also **Architecture**. In *World Book,* see **Art and the arts; Painting; Sculpture.**

Asia

Asia engaged in an arms race in 1993, though the continent was generally peaceful and its nations did not face any immediate external threats. The weapons buildup was fueled by rapid economic growth, which for the year averaged about 7 percent for East, Southeast, and South Asia, excluding Japan. In contrast, the economies of European countries, Japan, and the United States grew only about 2 percent. Asia's economic progress improved the low living standards of many of its people, but some regions remained desperately poor. Schools, health clinics, and other social programs saw little progress.

The arms race. China led the race to acquire weapons. It bought Russian arms production technology and hired Russian armaments experts. In addition, China bought advanced military technology from Israel. And on October 5, Chinese scientists exploded a nuclear device underground, despite international appeals not to break an unofficial worldwide ban on nuclear testing.

North Korea was believed to have a secret nuclear arms program. It stalled efforts by the International Atomic Energy Agency to verify that it was not acquiring nuclear weapons, as it had promised in a treaty. North Korea also tested a missile capable of carrying a nuclear warhead as far as Japan. The North Korean test prompted Japan to seek United States cooperation in the building of a missile defense system.

Japan was the only nation of the world's industrial leaders that was increasing its defense budget, despite the fact that its old enemy, the Soviet Union, had collapsed. Japan spent more on its armed forces than any nation except the United States.

Apprehension about China was the primary reason for weapons purchases by Southeast Asian nations. They were particularly concerned about China's growing ability to exert military power in the South China Sea. There, six nations made conflicting claims to the Spratly Islands because of the possibility that they are rich in oil.

Indonesia, which had bought obsolete Soviet warships in the late 1950's only to watch them rust, paid $30 million in 1993 for 39 ships of the old East German navy, which needed expensive refurbishing. Malaysia announced plans to buy 18 Russian and 8 American warplanes. Taiwan ordered American and French jet fighters. Thailand bought Chinese frigates and American jets, and it planned to buy a ship from Spain equipped to carry helicopters. Impoverished Burma took more deliveries on $1.4 billion in arms purchased from China in 1989.

Many Asian countries took advantage of sales of low-price weapons from the former Soviet bloc. But China was criticized for selling missiles and other armaments to the Middle East. And Thailand arrested

A river, swollen by monsoon rains, engulfs a village in Nepal during flooding that killed some 3,500 people and left thousands homeless in late July.

Facts in brief on Asian countries

Country	Population	Government	Monetary unit*	Foreign trade (million U.S.$) Exports†	Imports†
Afghanistan	18,405,000	President Burhanuddin Rabbani; Prime Minister Gulbuddin Hikmatyar	afghani (1,050.00 = $1)	235	937
Armenia	3,526,000	President Levon Ter-Petrosyan	C.I.S. ruble (1,184.00 = $1)	176	1,500
Australia	17,684,000	Governor General Bill Hayden; Prime Minister Paul Keating	dollar (1.50 = $1)	42,417	40,696
Azerbaijan	7,691,000	President Heydar A. Aliyev	C.I.S. ruble (1,184.00 = $1)	780	2,200
Bangladesh	128,542,000	President Abdur Rahman Biswas; Prime Minister Khaleda Ziaur Rahman	taka (39.94 = $1)	1,674	3,407
Bhutan	1,658,000	King Jigme Singye Wangchuck	ngultrum (31.38 = $1)	74	106
Brunei	294,000	Sultan Sir Hassanal Bolkiah	dollar (1.59 = $1)	2,370	1,176
Burma (Myanmar)	45,270,000	State Law and Order Restoration Council Chairman Than Shwe	kyat (6.16 = $1)	533	653
Cambodia (Kampuchea)	8,996,000	Prime Minister Norodom Ranariddh	riel (3,500 = $1)	32	147
China	1,199,460,000	Communist Party General Secretary and President Jiang Zemin; Premier Li Peng	yuan (5.79 = $1)	84,635	80,315
Georgia	5,580,000	Parliament Chairman Eduard Shevardnadze	C.I.S. ruble (1,184.00 = $1)	176	1,500
India	926,317,000	President Shankar Dayal Sharma; Prime Minister P. V. Narasimha Rao	rupee (31.38 = $1)	17,908	23,255
Indonesia	198,070,000	President Suharto; Vice President Try Sutrisno	rupiah (2,100.75 = $1)	29,142	25,869
Iran	59,132,000	Leader of the Islamic Revolution Ali Hoseini Khamenei; President Ali Akbar Hashemi Rafsanjani	rial (1,584.00 = $1)	12,587	12,537
Japan	125,551,000	Emperor Akihito; Prime Minister Morihiro Hosokawa	yen (108.28 = $1)	340,483	233,548
Kazakhstan	17,369,000	President Nursultan Nazarbayev	C.I.S. ruble (1,184.00 = $1)	1,398	469
Korea, North	23,494,000	President Kim Il-song; Premier Kang Song-San	won (2.15 = $1)	2,020	2,620
Korea, South	45,019,000	President Kim Yong-Sam; Prime Minister Lee Hoi Chang	won (808.90 = $1)	76,332	81,775
Kyrgyzstan	4,743,000	President Askar Akayev	C.I.S. ruble (1,184.00 = $1)	115	2

a business owner accused of illegally sending Thai workers to Libya to build underground facilities for producing chemical weapons.

South Asian nations trailed East Asia in economic growth and could not afford to increase arms spending. Nevertheless, India worked on missiles capable of delivering nuclear warheads, which it had the capability to make. And Pakistan's new prime minister, Benazir Bhutto, said in October that her government would "protect Pakistan's nuclear program." In July, a former Pakistani army chief said that Pakistan had simulated a nuclear test under laboratory conditions in 1987. In 1993, Pakistan bought Chinese missile technology.

Seeking security. Foreign ministers of 17 nations, including China, plus the European Community (EC, or Common Market), met in Singapore on July 25, 1993, in order to establish a forum for regular discussions of East and Southeast Asian political and security issues. A major goal was to get China involved in talks with other Asian countries, Russia, the United States, and other nations concerned with China's increased arms spending and growing ability to extend its power beyond its own borders.

Border issues. Several Asian border disputes—a major reason nations were buying weapons—moved toward settlements in 1993. China and India, which had fought over their common Himalayan border in

Country	Population	Government	Monetary unit*	Foreign trade (million U.S.$)	
				Exports†	Imports†
Laos	4,644,000	President Nouhak Phoumsavan; Prime Minister Khamtai Siphandon	kip (720.00 = $1)	81	162
Malaysia	19,564,000	Paramount Ruler Azlan Muhibbuddin Shah ibni Almarhum Sultan Yusof; Prime Minister Mahathir bin Mohamad	ringgit (2.56 = $1)	40,711	39,964
Maldives	239,000	President Maumoon Abdul Gayoom	rufiyaa (11.98 = $1)	40	189
Mongolia	2,433,000	President Punsalmaagiyn Ochirbat; Prime Minister Puntsagiyn Jasray	tughrik (400.00 = $1)	279	360
Nepal	20,999,000	King Birendra Bir Bikram Shah Dev; Prime Minister Girija Prasad Koirala	rupee (46.49 = $1)	273	790
New Zealand	3,520,000	Governor General Dame Catherine Tizard; Prime Minister James B. Bolger	dollar (1.81 = $1)	9,841	9,214
Pakistan	137,321,000	President Farooq Leghari; Prime Minister Benazir Bhutto	rupee (29.90 = $1)	7,273	9,365
Papua New Guinea	4,238,000	Governor General Sir Wiwa Korowi; Prime Minister Paias Wingti	kina (0.98 = $1)	1,812	1,522
Philippines	66,260,000	President Fidel Ramos	peso (28.70 = $1)	8,840	12,051
Russia	150,726,000	President Boris Yeltsin	ruble (1,184.00 = $1)	38,100	35,000
Singapore	2,823,000	President Ong Teng Cheong; Prime Minister Goh Chok Tong	dollar (1.59= $1)	63,516	72,216
Sri Lanka	18,101,000	President Dingiri Banda Wijetunga; Prime Minister Ranil Wickremasinghe	rupee (49.02 = $1)	2,487	3,646
Taiwan	21,299,000	President Li Teng-hui; Premier Lien Chan	dollar (26.85 = $1)	67,200	54,700
Tajikistan	5,858,000	Acting President Emomili Rakhmonov	C.I.S. ruble (1,184.00 = $1)	706	1,300
Thailand	58,771,000	King Phumiphon Adunyadet; Prime Minister Chuan Likphai	baht (25.34 = $1)	'32,156	41,039
Turkmenistan	4,024,000	President Saparmurad Niyazov	C.I.S. ruble (1,184.00 = $1)	239	970
Uzbekistan	22,677,000	President Islam Karimov	C.I.S. ruble (1,184.00 = $1)	869	929
Vietnam	71,851,000	Communist Party General Secretary Do Muoi; President Le Duc Anh; Prime Minister Vo Van Kiet	dong (10,755.00 = $1)	1,800	1,900

*Exchange rates as of Oct. 29, 1993, or latest available data.
†Latest available data.

1962, agreed on Sept. 7, 1993, "to respect and observe the line" still held by their soldiers, pending a border agreement, and to reduce the number of troops facing each other. China and Vietnam agreed in October not to threaten or use force in their dispute over land and sea boundaries as they stepped up talks to settle the dispute.

A $30-billion project to create a free-trade zone along the border of China, Russia, and North Korea moved forward in 1993. Officials of those countries plus South Korea and Mongolia met in Changchun, China, in August for talks. The zone is planned for the area where the Tumen River forms the border of North Korea and Russia. New ports where the river drains into the Sea of Japan would improve access to the sea for Mongolia and northeast China.

Refugees remained a problem along some borders. Almost half the 3 million refugees who had fled the Communist regime in Afghanistan were still in Pakistan because of continuing fighting at home, though the Communists fell in April 1992. Refugees from Burma were reluctant to leave Bangladesh due to continued fighting between government troops and rebel forces. Some 63,000 ethnic Nepali refugees from Bhutan remained in camps in Nepal. Bhutan denied that it had mistreated them.

There was a virtual end to the flow of refugees from Vietnam, who had been called "boat people" when some 675,000 fled on small boats in the late 1970's and 1980's. Tens of thousands of boat people remained in camps in Hong Kong, Malaysia, Indonesia, and other places. Most were unwilling to return home, despite cash inducements under a United Nations program, and were unable to find countries willing to take them.

Leadership changes occurred in six Asian countries, but others reelected their leaders. After Cambodia's September 1993 elections, Norodom Sihanouk became king, a position he had given up in 1955. His son Prince Norodom Ranariddh became first premier, and Hun Sen, leader of the former Communist government, became second premier.

Japan held elections in July 1993 that ended 38 years of rule by the Liberal Democratic Party. Morihiro Hosokawa became prime minister on August 6 at the head of a coalition of smaller parties that set out to reform the political system. In South Korea on February 25, Kim Yong-Sam assumed the presidency to which he had been elected in December 1992. He began attacking corruption and seeking reforms. Pakistan's Benazir Bhutto, who from 1988 to 1990 had been the Islamic world's first woman prime minister, returned to that post on Oct. 19, 1993, after her party won a narrow parliamentary election victory. Prime Minister Dingiri Banda Wijetunga was named president of Sri Lanka, after President Ranasinghe Premadasa was assassinated on May 1.

Singapore held its first direct election for president on August 28. A former deputy prime minister, Ong Teng Cheong, the candidate of the ruling People's Action Party (PAP), won 59 percent of the vote—lower than the PAP had ever won in elections for Parliament. A political unknown, Chua Kim Yeow, won 41 percent of the vote. The official Presidential Election Committee had barred two better-known opposition figures, Joshua B. Jeyaretnam and Tan Soo Phuan, from running. Prime Minister Goh Chok Tong continued to direct the government, though Ong had some supervisory powers.

The People's Consultative Assembly of Indonesia unanimously elected President Suharto to his sixth term in March. In October, Maumoon Abdul Gayoom won 93 percent of the popular vote for a fourth term as president of the Maldives republic.

Mongolia reelected Punsalmaagiyn Ochirbat as president in June, but this was an unusual political upset. He had become president in 1990, when Mongolia was emerging from control by the Soviet Union. He was then the candidate of the Mongolian People's Revolutionary Party (MPRP), the long-ruling Communist party. In 1992, the MPRP won 70 of 76 seats in parliamentary elections, but Ochirbat began opposing the party's refusal to carry out post-Communist reforms. The MPRP retaliated by denying him its nomination for the 1993 presidential elections, choosing instead a hardline Communist. Ochirbat accepted the nomination of two small opposition par-

ties and then won 60 percent of the popular vote.

Mongolia in 1993 suffered its worst economic loss in 50 years when late winter snowfalls killed 3.8 million livestock. Livestock is the backbone of the national economy. Many people endured severe cold because the government could not afford adequate amounts of imported fuel or spare parts for coal mining and power generating equipment.

Violent stalemates. Afghanistan struggled violently during 1993 to get agreement among contending factions on a successor to the Communist regime that had collapsed in 1992. Burhanuddin Rabbani, leader of one of the guerrilla groups that had vanquished the Communists, served as a weak president pending elections. He had organized a meeting of regional supporters on Dec. 30, 1992, but other groups said the meeting was invalid.

As a result, Gulbuddin Hikmatyar, a guerrilla leader who ruthlessly sought personal power, bombarded Kabul, the capital, killing thousands of residents. National unity was also threatened by ethnic and religious groups who squabbled among themselves and by warlords who continued to control some provincial areas.

Pakistan called a meeting of some guerrilla leaders. Under pressure from Pakistan, they agreed on March 6, 1993, that Rabbani would remain president for 18 months, with Hikmatyar as prime minister, until elections for president and parliament were held. However, the leaders continued to disagree over a cabinet and the division of powers. After more attacks on Kabul by Hikmatyar's forces and another Pakistani-arranged meeting, Hikmatyar was sworn in as prime minister on June 17, but he had little control of the few functioning government offices.

On September 27, a commission announced an interim constitution, which reflected the thinking of groups favored by Pakistan. But Afghanistan's Shiite Muslim minority rejected the constitution, and it was denounced by some warlords. Such ongoing disagreements dimmed prospects for holding elections that could lead to a popularly accepted government.

Nepal was also disrupted by political struggle. The secretary general and another leader of the largest faction of Communists, who form the parliamentary opposition to the ruling Nepali Congress Party, died in a car crash on May 16. A government-appointed judge investigating the accident ruled that the driver, who was not hurt, had been negligent. But many suspected that the two leaders had been murdered. Antigovernment protests erupted in the capital, Kathmandu, and the Communists called a nationwide general strike on July 4 to support demands that Prime Minister Girija Prasad Koirala resign. He refused. Rioting in Kathmandu caused 25 deaths. More died during a nationwide transport strike organized by the Communists on July 19.

South Asian floods. The Communists in Nepal called off further protests because of flooding in

Cambodians line up to cast ballots in UN-supervised elections in May, after months of intimidation by rebel and government forces fearful of losing power to moderates.

late July that killed some 3,500 people. Some reports said the flooding was the worst natural disaster in Nepal's history. Officials said that economic development of the impoverished nation was set back five years.

The floods also affected India and Bangladesh. Across the region, growing populations had cleared Himalayan forests to gain more farmland. Run-off from monsoon rains flowed down cleared mountain slopes and picked up great amounts of silt. Rivers became choked with silt and overflowed their banks downstream. The floods covered overland routes to seven states of northeast India for a week. And more than half of Bangladesh was flooded.

In China's Qinghai province, a dam burst in late August. The resulting flood killed more than 250 people and displaced more than 30,000 others.

Satellite television had an increasing impact on Asia. The region's two largest countries, China and India, plus some others, had long maintained state monopolies of television broadcasting from ground stations. But as prosperity spread, more people could afford satellite receivers, giving them access to programs outside of government control. On October 8, China announced tight controls on the purchase of satellite dishes. ☐ Henry S. Bradsher

See also the articles on the individual Asian nations. In *World Book,* see **Asia.**

65

Vietnam:

Emerging from a War-torn Past

By Douglas Pike

Twenty years after the last U.S. troops pulled out of Vietnam in 1973, this poor Southeast Asian nation is trying to awake from a long nightmare of decline.

Glossary

Boat people: Refugees from Vietnam who fled the country in small boats after 1975.

Doi moi: The policy of economic renovation adopted in 1986 that introduced free market ventures to Vietnam.

Vietminh: The informal name given to the Revolutionary League for the Independence of Vietnam, formed by Ho Chi Minh in the 1940's.

Viet Cong: Communist-trained South Vietnamese rebels.

Politburo: The top leadership of the Communist Party of Vietnam and the country's most powerful government unit.

■ **The author**

Douglas Pike is the director of the Indochina Studies Program at the University of California, Berkeley, and the author of several books on Vietnam.

Twenty years after a cease-fire agreement ended the United States combat role in Vietnam, the Vietnamese people in 1993 appeared to be emerging at last from a long nightmare of decline. Years of wasted sacrifice and dashed expectations followed the signing of the peace agreement in Paris in January 1973. The country did not become a land 10,000 times more beautiful, as its famed leader Ho Chi Minh had promised throughout the long war years. Rather, it descended into a grim time of new warfare, isolation, economic deterioration, and enormous individual suffering.

But in the 1990's, Vietnam has found itself poised on a runway of economic opportunity and about to improve relations with countries it once knew as enemies. In February 1993, French President François Mitterrand became the first Western leader to visit Vietnam since the end of the Vietnam War in 1975, touring the site of the Battle of Dien Bien Phu, where French colonial forces were defeated by Vietnamese Communists in 1954. Then, in April 1993, U.S. General John W. Vessey, Jr., traveled to Hanoi, Vietnam's capital, to discuss the search for the more than 2,200 American servicemen still missing from the war. In September, the Administration of President Bill Clinton, citing Vietnamese cooperation with that search, eased a long-standing U.S. trade embargo against Vietnam.

These and other developments appeared to signal that Vietnam's long isolation from the West was ending. In 1993, Americans were traveling to Vietnam in ever increasing numbers. Some were veterans making sentimental journeys back to wartime haunts. Some represented American businesses eager to discuss joint ventures. Some were tourists off cruise ships who had come to scuba dive or to taste the country's justly famous seafood cuisine.

What they found was a country where much had changed and much had remained the same. Economically, Vietnam had forsaken many of the features of a centrally planned socialist economy and had instead introduced free market reforms. Politically, however, it remained a rigid, one-party Communist state. And after a half century of struggle, it was once again a unified and independent nation.

Emerging from a difficult past

Vietnam has a long history of foreign occupation, going back some 2,000 years, when Chinese invaders first overtook the region now known as northern Vietnam. China was Vietnam's main ruler from about 200 B.C. to the A.D. 900's, when the Vietnamese established an independent state called *Dai Co Viet* (Great Viet State). Through the late 1800's, the Vietnamese repeatedly repelled invaders from neighboring countries. Then, in the 1860's, France forcibly took control of Vietnam and declared it a French colony.

During World War II (1939-1945), following France's defeat by Germany in June 1940, Japan, an ally of Germany, gained control of Vietnam. After Japan's defeat, France tried to reclaim its colony. But a Communist revolutionary named Ho Chi Minh had organized the Revolutionary League for the Independence of Vietnam, called the *Vi-*

etminh. In December 1946, Vietminh attacked the French in Hanoi, beginning the Indochina War. In 1954, the Vietminh defeated the French in the Battle of Dien Bien Phu. A subsequent peace settlement, reached in Geneva, Switzerland, and known as the Geneva Accords, officially ended the war and temporarily established two Vietnams, North and South.

The accords required that elections be held in 1956 to reunite the nation under one government. But Ngo Dinh Diem, the leader of capitalist South Vietnam, refused to hold elections, citing mistrust of Ho Chi Minh, the leader of Communist North Vietnam. In 1957, Vietminh in the South, who became known as the *Viet Cong,* revolted against the South Vietnamese government, headquartered in Saigon. The Viet Cong had the support of the North Vietnamese. Thus began the conflict that became known as the Vietnam War.

To aid South Vietnam and to stop the spread of Communism, the United States sent ground troops there in 1965 and began bombing the North. Five other non-Communist countries—Thailand, South Korea, the Philippines, Australia, and New Zealand—also sent troops. Some 42 other nations sent South Vietnam military supplies and economic aid. North Vietnam received military aid, but not troops, from the Communist countries of the Soviet Union, China, and Eastern Europe.

In all, about 2.7 million Americans fought in the Vietnam War, with the number of troops present there reaching a high of more than 543,000 in 1969. About 58,000 U.S. soldiers died during the war, and 365,000 were wounded, and Americans at home were bitterly divided on the U.S. role in the war. United States involvement in the war dragged on until 1973, when the United States, North and South Vietnam, and the Viet Cong signed a cease-fire agreement.

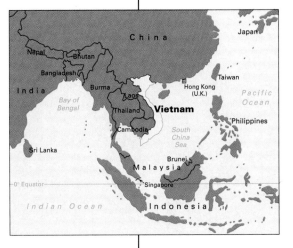

■ Vietnam lies in Southeast Asia, bordering the South China Sea on the east, China on the north, and Laos and Cambodia on the west.

■ A century of struggle in Vietnam

Foreign nations have tried to make Vietnam their own for some 2,000 years. But in the last century, struggles against foreign domination and a civil war kept Vietnam in continual turmoil and brought the nation to the brink of collapse.

■ **1883** French troops seize Hanoi, in northern Vietnam, after having taken control of the south between 1861 and 1867.

The last U.S. ground troops left the country in March 1973. Shortly thereafter, the North renewed its attacks on the South, which finally surrendered on April 30, 1975. The Communists then reunified the country in 1976 and named it the Socialist Republic of Vietnam.

The war had devastating effects on Vietnam and its people. More than 1 million South Vietnamese—about half of them soldiers—died in the war, and between 500,000 and 1 million North Vietnamese troops perished. As many as 10 million South Vietnamese became refugees as their homes and fields were destroyed or damaged and they were forced into refugee camps or crowded into cities. Bombings of North Vietnam destroyed industrial plants and large parts of the transportation system, and killed countless numbers of civilians.

Communists at the helm

After the war, the nation was united in name but was far from unified politically. To reduce the likelihood of rebellion, Communist troops were sent into the south to "break the machine." This meant ending traditional village social and political organizations.

Thousands of people of Chinese ancestry were driven from Vietnam, and millions of Vietnamese were moved from one part of the country to another. Others were sent to "reeducation" camps, where they were incarcerated—most for a few months, but many for years. Middle- and upper-class Vietnamese in the South were subjected to official acts of discrimination. They were forbidden to practice certain occupations, denied ownership of printing presses and typewriters, and refused admission to institutes of higher education.

For the most part, these drastic measures lasted only a few years. But they triggered an exodus from Vietnam of more than 1 million

■ 1945 Ho Chi Minh, the Communist leader of a revolutionary group known as the *Vietminh,* comes to power and declares Vietnam independent. In 1946, the Vietminh attack French forces and the Indochina War begins.

■ 1940 The Japanese take control of Vietnam after Germany's defeat of France during World War II. But when Japan ultimately loses the war in 1945, the French attempt to recolonize Vietnam.

■ 1954 French parachutists drop into Dien Bien Phu, a French garrison and the site of a major battle that ended the Indochina War. The subsequent peace agreement divided the country into two nations, Communist North Vietnam and non-Communist South Vietnam.

people, many of whom became known as *boat people* because they fled in small boats.

Economically, Vietnam was in near ruin in the years immediately following the war. At the same time, its population increased dramatically—from 45 million to 70 million—between 1975 and 1990. To make matters worse, the United States had imposed an economic embargo on Vietnam, and the Communists' plans for a new economic system failed to improve things.

When the Communists came to power over all of Vietnam in 1975, they tried to create a modern socialist economy based on heavy industry, similar to that in the former Soviet Union. They also tried to create giant state-owned farms, similar to those in China. But the highly centralized system needed for this approach was too complex for officials in Hanoi to manage. In addition, state ownership of factories and land removed much of the incentive for laborers and farmers. Production rapidly declined.

In 1979, a drastic shortfall of the rice crop left the population with an average food intake of 1,500 calories per day, just above the starvation level. Riots broke out that winter in the more remote villages of northern Vietnam when food ran out entirely.

Foreign developments after the war added to Vietnam's internal troubles. Relations with Cambodian leader Pol Pot, the notorious head of the Communist Khmer Rouge, grew steadily worse, as did relations with the neighboring countries of Thailand and China. In 1978, Vietnam invaded Cambodia and fought a guerrilla war there. In retaliation, China, which was allied with the Khmer Rouge, engaged in border skirmishes and occupied Vietnam's northern border for several weeks in 1979. Surrounded by hostility, Vietnam could not concentrate on recovering from the war and rebuilding its economy.

■ **1965** United States ground troops enter South Vietnam to help the nation fight the Viet Cong and the North Vietnamese.

■ **1957** The Vietnam War begins as Vietminh in South Vietnam—known as *Viet Cong*—revolt against their government with the support of North Vietnam, now ruled by Ho Chi Minh.

■ **1973** North and South Vietnam, the Viet Cong, and the United States sign a cease-fire agreement, and the last American ground troops leave the country.

■ **1975** South Vietnam, still under attack by the Communists, surrenders, ending the Vietnam War. In 1976, North and South Vietnam are united under Communist rule and called the Socialist Republic of Vietnam.

By the end of the 1970's, Vietnam's productivity had declined to the lowest in Asia. With one of the world's worst trade deficits, the nation was then forced to exist chiefly on aid—about $1 billion a year—supplied by the Soviet Union. In contrast, the economies of Vietnam's neighbors—Thailand, Indonesia, Taiwan, and even China to some extent—were booming. The need for turning the society around had become apparent to all Vietnamese, regardless of individual political or ideological differences.

Rebuilding the economy

The first signs of change began in August 1979 at a Vietnam Communist Party meeting, when new party officials were elected and economic reformers pushed through emergency economic measures. But the leaders whose wartime strategies had won them victory in battle were ineffective in constructing long-term solutions for an economy teetering on the brink of collapse.

Throughout the 1980's, however, younger political leaders who were willing to experiment with a free market economy gradually replaced the older leaders. Then, in 1986, the government adopted the policy of *doi moi* (renovation), an economic reform plan similar to that of the Soviet Union's *perestroika* (restructuring), which had introduced capitalism to a Communist society.

At the end of the 1980's, Vietnam's need to spur its economy became even more acute when the Soviet Union cut back sharply on aid, and the collapse of Communism in Eastern Europe caused Vietnam to lose its chief trading partners. Then, in 1991, the Soviet Union broke apart, and Vietnam lost its main economic benefactor.

Since then, economic change in Vietnam has come at an ever accelerating rate. By 1993, the country had what could be called a semi-

■ **1979** Vietnamese refugees transfer to a smaller boat that will take them ashore in Malaysia. The refugees became known as *boat people* and were part of an exodus of more than 1 million people who left Vietnam in the postwar years.

■ **1986** Vietnam's leaders enact the policy of *doi moi* (renovation), designed to stimulate the nation's failing economy by allowing free market ventures.

■ **1978** Vietnam invades Cambodia, overthrows the Communist Khmer Rouge government, and fights a war there until 1989.

■ **1991** The Soviet Union breaks apart, and Vietnam loses its main economic benefactor.

market economy, and the trend toward capitalism seemed to be irreversible. The main short-run economic challenge—to get the economy performing at what could be called a bare minimum level—has been accomplished. Most people now have adequate food, basic education, rudimentary health care, and sufficient, if modest, housing. Some also have a few luxuries, such as television sets.

Although the Communist Party has taken credit for the recent economic gains, successes in Vietnam today are mostly the result of a lack of government interference. For example, the average Vietnamese farmer now has a 30-year lease from the government, can grow what he wants, and sell his crop to whom he wants, at the price he wants. Not coincidentally, Vietnam has become the third-largest exporter of rice in the world (after the United States and Thailand). Crops produced for industrial use also have great potential.

With increased freedom, many Vietnamese, including many women, have started their own businesses. New stores and factories— where wages have doubled under private ownership—are prospering. The tourist industry is also beginning to flourish. Some officials have estimated that Ho Chi Minh City (formerly Saigon) will need to create 10,000 more hotel rooms by 1995 to accommodate an expected 1 million tourists annually. Pristine beaches along Vietnam's 2,000-mile (3,200-kilometer) coastline, attract travelers from throughout Asia. And Vietnamese émigrés from the United States, France, and Australia are returning in increasing numbers for short visits.

Americans, who have been allowed to travel to Vietnam since 1992, also are going over to have a look, with Vietnam War veterans making up a good portion of their ranks. Vietnamese veterans' associations market tours targeted specifically to American veterans of various di-

■ Vietnam's legislature, the National Assembly, meets in Hanoi, the capital, in December 1992. The government is now largely composed of a new generation of Communist leaders, who have embraced economic reforms but opposed political change.

■ Investing in Vietnam

Advertisements in Ho Chi Minh City (formerly Saigon), *right,* reflect Vietnam's experimentation with a free market economy in which foreign investment plays a large role. Between 1988 and 1992, foreign investors had committed a total of $4.1 billion to 562 projects in Vietnam, *below.*

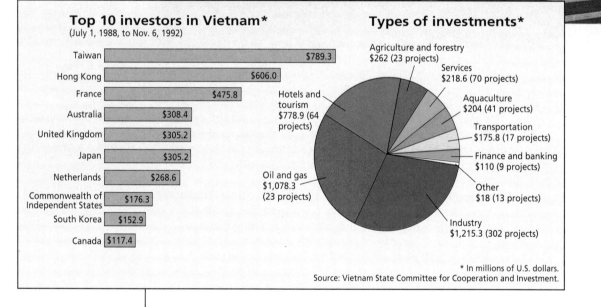

Top 10 investors in Vietnam*
(July 1, 1988, to Nov. 6, 1992)

Country	Amount
Taiwan	$789.3
Hong Kong	$606.0
France	$475.8
Australia	$308.4
United Kingdom	$305.2
Japan	$305.2
Netherlands	$268.6
Commonwealth of Independent States	$176.3
South Korea	$152.9
Canada	$117.4

Types of investments*

- Agriculture and forestry $262 (23 projects)
- Services $218.6 (70 projects)
- Aquaculture $204 (41 projects)
- Transportation $175.8 (17 projects)
- Finance and banking $110 (9 projects)
- Other $18 (13 projects)
- Industry $1,215.3 (302 projects)
- Oil and gas $1,078.3 (23 projects)
- Hotels and tourism $778.9 (64 projects)

* In millions of U.S. dollars.
Source: Vietnam State Committee for Cooperation and Investment.

visions. Such tours are typically led by a former Viet Cong soldier and wind their way through old battlegrounds.

Perhaps most important among Vietnam's economic changes is its new openness to foreign investment. In 1992, foreign investment in Vietnam totaled about $2 billion. Development contracts included such diverse ventures as the automotive industry, telecommunications, electronics, airlines, hotels, and breweries. Commodity bartering has proved particularly lucrative, especially for Thai businessmen who bring in foreign-made products, such as television sets or handheld calculators, and trade them for lumber or frozen shrimp, which they then export.

Foreign investors have also shown a continuing interest in the area off Vietnam's southern coast where vast petroleum reserves may lie.

However, no new commercially exploitable fields have yet been added to the original 1969 finds, despite 10 years of exploration by 15 oil firms.

At the end of 1992, Taiwan led investments in Vietnam with nearly $800 million. Hong Kong and France placed second and third, with Australia, the United Kingdom, and Japan following. Most of Vietnam's economic growth has been centered in Ho Chi Minh City. But many other cities and towns throughout the country are also showing a turnaround in living standards and employment opportunities. Although street vendors still predominate in the marketplace, they now hawk televisions and digital watches in addition to fruits and vegetables. In 1993, Vietnam's annual economic growth rate was about 8 percent, its currency was stable, inflation was decreasing, and, perhaps most telling, a stock exchange had been planned to open at the end of year.

Politics as usual

Despite its radical economic changes, Vietnam has experienced almost no change in its fundamental political system. The governing system in place remains officially Communist. Although Vietnam's leaders have been willing to accept recommendations from non-Communist advisers, they have been unwilling to share power in a multiparty system. To do so would mean facing the likelihood of being voted out of office in free elections.

But a changing of the guard may loosen Communism's hold on Vietnam, just as it affected the economic structure. Vietnam's Politburo is composed of about 15 men who are responsible for creating all policies set forth by the national government. Although significant changes in the Politburo membership took place in 1986, a transfer of power to a new generation was not completed until June 1991.

■ The owner of a privately held clothing factory in Ho Chi Minh City is one of Vietnam's growing number of entrepreneurs who have been allowed to test their free market skills as a result of economic reforms introduced in 1986.

How the new Politburo figures, such as Party Secretary General Do Muoi and Prime Minister Vo Van Kiet, may respond to Vietnam's changing needs in the future is still largely unknown. But so far, they have stated that they will support as much economic change in the direction of a market economy as is necessary, with no change in the political system. However, they acknowledge that eventually the moment will come when further economic progress will not be possible without political change. The intention then is to move Vietnam from a "hard" authoritarian regime to a "soft" (more democratic) authoritarian regime, such as those found in Taiwan and South Korea.

With or without Communists at the helm, economic issues are likely to dominate day-to-day thinking among the Vietnamese for the foreseeable future. And although Vietnam has come far in turning its economy around, it still faces several major challenges. Economists at the World Bank, an international lending agency, cite five goals for the nation to complete its journey toward successful modernization.

Turning the corner

First, Vietnam must recruit skilled economic leadership. Foreign economic experts have told the Politburo it must make sacrifices in other areas to serve the economy. For example, it must reallocate resources from its armed forces, which is presently the third largest in the world

■ Poverty and progress

People in Ho Chi Minh City, *opposite page,* are generally more affluent and able to purchase more consumer goods than are people farther north in Hanoi, *below.* Economic development has been uneven in Vietnam, which is among the world's poorest nations with an average annual income of $200 per person. Two-thirds of the nation's wealth is generated in the South.

with more than 650,000 full-time personnel and 1.1 million reserves. Vietnam had planned to demobilize about a third of its armed forces, but the economy currently cannot provide jobs to such a large number of people.

The leadership must also become better schooled in economics or be willing to trust policy decisions to those who are. Not one of the Politburo members who was elected to his position prior to 1991 holds even a high school diploma, and none possess any significant knowledge about the workings of a modern economic system.

World Bank economists and other experts who follow Vietnam also believe that the Vietnamese need to fashion a *social consensus*—that is, a vision of who they are as a society, what they want to become, and how they will achieve their goals. This, of course, is easier said than done. Traditional village life and geographic regionalism in Vietnam make social consensus a distant ideal. Some 80 percent of Vietnamese are villagers whose existence in many ways has not varied much over several centuries. Village life is marked by close family and community ties, shared social customs, and unchanging religious beliefs and practices. As a result, most villagers tend to identify with their own tight-knit community, rather than the nation as a whole. And although such traditionalism is dying, much of it remains.

Geographic regionalism—an attachment to and preference for a particular area and the customs and beliefs peculiar to it—can be found in almost all countries, but it is particularly strong and somewhat complex in Vietnam. In many nations, such divisions tend to be between the northern and southern areas of the country. But in Vietnam, three regions—North, Central, and South—characterize the split. The people of each area, because of their respective historical

experiences, have unique self-images and a belief in the superiority of their region. They also have a separate set of stereotypes and prejudices about the people in the other two regions. These biases make Vietnamese politics highly divisive.

Vietnam also sorely lacks an adequate *infrastructure* (the services and facilities, such as transport and sewage systems, that enable a modern economy to function). Although foreign investors are eager to set up shop in Vietnam, the nation's deficient infrastructure discourages and exasperates them. To develop its economy, Vietnam needs the type of high-tech communication networks—and corps of workers who can operate them—that other successful Asian countries have developed. Such countries, which include South Korea and Taiwan, have become known as "Asian tigers" for their economic prowess. Vietnam also needs advanced research and development facilities, good technical schools, and a strong higher education system. But currently, electrical, telephone, and transportation services are either unreliable or inadequate in most areas of Vietnam. And corrupt party and government officials make a bad situation worse.

To be able to improve its infrastructure, Vietnam must have much more money than it currently has or is able to acquire on its own. Vietnam is a poor country. The average per capita income is $200 per year, one of the lowest in the developing world. Some 70 percent of the 30-million-member labor force is engaged in agriculture or a related occupation, such as fishing—activities that do not significantly boost the economy.

Because infrastructure projects do not interest private banks, money must come from international lending agencies, such as the World Bank and the International Monetary Fund (IMF), both agencies of the United Nations. The United States—one of the major contributors to these lenders—had consistently exerted its influence to block loans to Vietnam. But then, at a World Bank and IMF meeting in April 1993, the United States lost support for its position against loans to Vietnam. In September, President Clinton announced the end of U.S. opposition to loans for Vietnam.

Mending fences

The final major requirement for Vietnam's success is development of friendly relations with its neighbors, and diplomats in Hanoi are eager to improve foreign relations. Vietnam ended its occupation of Cambodia in 1989 and now supports the United Nations peace process there. It also joined the Association of Southeast Asian Nations as an observer and is seeking full membership in the organization.

Hanoi wants stable ties with China, and their relationship has improved vastly from its low point in the 1979 border war. There remain, however, disputes over border demarcations and the territorial rights to offshore islands in the South China Sea. Both countries realize that they always will be in a struggle for power and influence in Southeast Asia. But this does not mean they cannot also have reasonably amicable relations.

Vietnam also wants and seeks diplomatic and economic relations with the United States, and particularly an end to the U.S. economic embargo. Potential American investors have had their hands tied by the continuing U.S. embargo. In the early 1990's, a number of U.S. businesses urgently petitioned the government to lift it. In 1992, former President George Bush loosened the embargo to allow American telephone companies to provide long-distance service to Vietnam. And some U.S. businesses were permitted to open offices there to prepare to do business in the event that the embargo was lifted.

Although President Clinton was expected to let the embargo end when it came up for renewal in September 1993, several organizations protested his doing so. Opponents of lifting the embargo said that Vietnam should fully account for the more than 2,200 American soldiers who were declared missing in action but whose ultimate fate is still unknown. Consequently, Clinton only loosened the embargo, allowing American businesses to bid on projects in Vietnam that would be financed by the World Bank or other international lending agencies. Given the changes that have occurred in Vietnam, combined with the end of the Cold War, many foreign policy experts believe it is in the best interest of the United States to drop the embargo completely and to establish formal diplomatic relations with Vietnam. However, many Vietnamese-Americans and many Vietnam veteran groups believe the United States should not begin normal relations until there is political freedom in Vietnam.

Although Vietnam and the United States are not yet reconciled, Vietnam has established closer ties with two of its former conquerors—Japan and France. During French President Mitterrand's visit, he promised to double the $30 million in aid France gave Vietnam in 1992, if the Vietnamese record on human rights improved. (The government continues to arrest political dissidents and to utilize "reeducation" camps.) Japan also resumed aid to Vietnam in 1992 with the offer of more than $350 million in loans.

Much work and much planning lie ahead in Vietnam's modernization effort, and important fundamental decisions have yet to be made. Only time will tell if Vietnam will successfully mix socialism with a market economy, if the one-party Communist political system will remain, or if the nation's long alienation from the West will disappear completely. Vietnam approaches the future with optimism and caution. But with a disciplined and industrious work force and an abundance of agricultural and mineral resources, the nation has faith in its ability to harness its assets and become another Asian tiger. ■ ■ ■

For further reading:

Jamieson, Neil L. *Understanding Vietnam.* University of California Press, 1993.

Trung, Thai Q., editor. *Vietnam Today: Assessing the New Trends.* Taylor & Frances, 1990.

Turley, William S. and Sheldon, Mark, editors. *Reinventing Vietnamese Socialism: Doi Moi in Comparative Perspective.* Westview, 1992.

Aspin, Les, Jr. (1938-   ), former chairman of the Armed Services Committee in the United States House of Representatives, was confirmed by the U.S. Senate as secretary of defense on Jan. 20, 1993. But he had troubles during the year and drew heavy criticism for his direction of the U.S. military role in Somalia. On December 15, he announced his resignation, effective Jan. 20, 1994. Aspin reportedly believed that President Bill Clinton and senior military leaders no longer had confidence in him.

Leslie Aspin, Jr., was born on July 21, 1938, in Milwaukee. He graduated with highest honors from Yale University in New Haven, Conn., in 1960 and earned a master's degree at Oxford University in England in 1962 and a doctorate in economics from the Massachusetts Institute of Technology in Cambridge in 1965.

Commissioned into the Army in 1966 through the Reserve Officers Training Corps, Aspin served as a Pentagon economist during the last two years of President Lyndon B. Johnson's Administration. In 1968, he returned to Milwaukee to teach economics at Marquette University.

Aspin was elected to the U.S. House of Representatives in 1970 and won reelection every two years after that. He was a member of the Armed Services Committee during his entire tenure in the House, becoming committee chairman in 1985 over six more-senior members.

☐ David Dreier

Astronomy. Several asteroids that appear to orbit at the very edges of the solar system were reported by astronomers in 1993. Asteroids are small bodies that orbit the sun, most of them between the orbits of Mars and Jupiter. They are made of leftover material from the early days of the solar system.

In March 1993, United States astronomers David Jewitt and Jane Luu, using a large telescope in Hawaii, recorded a faint dot of light which turned out to be an asteroid located just beyond the orbit of Pluto. The new body was designated 1993 FW by astronomers. Only one other asteroid was known to be so distant, 1992 QB-1, discovered by Jewitt and Luu in August 1992. These bodies are thought to be made of frozen gases and small bits of rock and dust. Ordinary asteroids are mainly rock.

By late 1993, it looked like there might be quite a number of distant icy asteroids. In September, Luu and Jewitt found two more such objects, which they called 1993 RO and 1993 RP. And a week later, astronomers in the Canary Islands detected another two, designated 1993 SB and 1993 SC.

It is possible that these small, icy objects may be the parent bodies of many comets. Astronomers have surmised that there is a large swarm of icy bodies called the Kuiper belt orbiting beyond Neptune. According to this theory, the gravitational attraction of some passing object occasionally pulls one of the members of the Kuiper belt away from its normal path and into an orbit that brings it close to the sun. A new comet is thus born.

Collision with Jupiter. One newly discovered comet, named Shoemaker-Levy 9, passed so close to Jupiter in 1992 that it was broken into about 20 fragments from the force exerted on it by the planet's gravitational field. In 1993, astronomers predicted that those pieces—which continued to orbit the sun, lined up like pearls on a string—would crash into Jupiter the next time they approach the giant planet, in mid-July 1994. The collisions were expected to take place over about six days on the side of Jupiter away from Earth.

Astronomers were not sure how much of an effect the impacts would have on Jupiter, which is made primarily of gas. But observations by the Hubble Space Telescope in 1993 showed that the fragments carried as much energy as 100 million megatons of TNT, more than 10,000 times the destructive energy of all the world's nuclear weapons.

Close view of a dying star. On March 28, 1993, Francisco García, an amateur astronomer in Spain, discovered a *supernova* (exploding star) in the galaxy M81, which lies about 11 million light-years away. (A light-year is the distance light travels in one year—about 5.9 trillion miles [9.5 trillion kilometers].) The supernova, called Supernova 1993J, was one of the closest and brightest seen in this century, and it offered astronomers a rare opportunity to study an exploding star in great detail.

Most supernova explosions, which are the final stage of stars containing more than about eight times as much matter as the sun, are seen in galaxies so far away that astronomers cannot distinguish individual stars in them. But because Supernova 1993J was relatively nearby, astronomers were able to identify the star that exploded by looking at earlier images of M81. It was a star slightly cooler than the sun and about a hundred times the sun's diameter.

Investigators also determined that before 1993J blew itself to bits, most of its matter had already boiled off into space, forming a cloud around the star. Although astronomers could not see the cloud directly, they were able to detect X rays produced when debris from the explosion collided with the cloud. Those X rays carried a great deal of information about the explosion, and astronomers think their study of the X rays will contribute to the understanding of supernovae in general.

Double nucleus in Andromeda? Astronomers discovered in July that the center of the nearest spiral galaxy, Andromeda, is a more complex place than they had imagined. Images produced by the Hubble Space Telescope revealed that Andromeda apparently has two *nuclei* (dense central clusters of stars), about 5 light-years apart, rather than a single nucleus. The nuclei appear as bright spots in the galaxy.

Double-nucleus galaxies are usually explained as two galaxies that have collided and merged, but

A *supernova* (exploding star), arrow, glowing in the outskirts of the M81 galaxy was discovered in March by an amateur astronomer in Spain.

these combined galaxies tend to have an irregular shape. Andromeda, in contrast, is a regular pinwheel of stars, similar to our own Milky Way galaxy. After the Hubble findings, some astronomers suggested that Andromeda actually has a single nucleus, which just appears double because a dark lane of dust obscures its central portion. Other researchers speculated that the bright spots are indeed separate concentrations of stars and that they surround a huge *black hole* (an object so dense not even light can escape its gravitational force).

More detailed observations will be required to determine which interpretation is correct. Repairs made to the Hubble telescope by astronauts aboard the space shuttle Endeavour in December may provide clearer pictures of Andromeda's center.

Dark matter. Astronomers in 1993 announced the discovery of faint objects that may be the first examples of *dark matter,* an undetected form of matter that most astronomers theorize makes up 90 to 98 percent of the material in the universe. The suspicion that the universe must be filled with dark matter is based in part on observations of the outermost stars in galaxies. Calculations have shown that these stars are moving too fast to be held within the galaxies by the gravitational pull of stars at the centers of the galaxies. The gravitation must come from matter that does not give off enough light to be seen from Earth.

Some astronomers have speculated that dark matter is in the form of exotic particles called WIMP's, for *w*eakly *i*nteracting *m*assive *p*articles. Other astronomers have theorized that dark matter consists of numerous large bodies of ordinary matter, including planets and dim stars. These objects have been dubbed MACHO's, for *m*assive *c*ompact *h*alo *o*bjects. They are called halo objects because they presumably form a halo around a galaxy.

If a MACHO passed between a distant bright star and the Earth, its strong gravity would act like a lens to bend the light from the star, causing the star to temporarily appear even brighter. Over the last several years, astronomers have been watching stars in a nearby galaxy, the Large Magellanic Cloud, hoping to see this gravitational lensing effect.

In September, two teams of observers announced that they had seen the phenomenon. Astronomers from the Lawrence Livermore National Laboratory in California, using a telescope in Australia, reported that a star in the Large Magellanic Cloud had brightened for 33 days before returning to normal. French observers, working in Chile, reported two similar events. Astronomers said the apparent lensing effects may indeed signal the presence of MACHO's, but further observations will be required to confirm the existence of MACHO's.   □ Laurence A. Marschall

See also **Space exploration.** In *World Book,* see **Astronomy.**

Australia. The federal Labor government was re-turned to office on March 13, 1993, marking the La-bor Party's fifth consecutive electoral victory. Prime Minister Paul J. Keating, who was facing his first election since becoming Labor Party leader in De-cember 1991, saw his party increase its majority in the lower house of Parliament, despite a weak econ-omy. Political analysts saw the election results not as an endorsement of Keating's policies but as a rejec-tion of the 15 percent goods-and-services tax pro-posed by the conservative opposition, a coalition of the Liberal Party and the National Party.

Economic growth was sluggish during 1993, held back by weak business investment and con-sumer spending, falling commodity prices, and a slide in household savings. Unemployment remained high, at about 11 percent through the year.

To reduce unemployment, the government on December 15 unveiled a five-year plan to provide a job for every person unemployed longer than 18 months. The plan also included a work-for-welfare proposal and a possible 1 percent to 5 percent tax on wages to pay for employment programs.

The budget. Treasurer John S. Dawkins on Aug. 17, 1993, handed down a controversial budget that met with strong resistance in the Senate. Conse-quently, the budget was revised and presented again on August 30. The revamped budget for fiscal 1993-1994 aimed to reduce the $16-billion federal deficit by about $10 billion or 1.2 percent of the gross domestic product by fiscal 1996-1997. (The fis-cal year runs from July 1 to June 30. All monetary figures in this article are in Australian dollars.)

Under the newly proposed budget, low-income workers—those earning less than $23,200 per year—were to receive cash rebates of $150. Smokers would pay higher taxes on cigarettes amounting to 20 per-centage points over two years. And the second half of a gasoline tax, which had been proposed and be-gun in the original budget, was scuttled.

Native title. The federal government passed legislation on Dec. 22, 1993, that clarified the condi-tions under which *Aborigines* (native peoples) could make land claims. A High Court ruling in 1992 had overthrown the doctrine of *terra nullius* (no one's land), which had been created by European colonists after they settled Australia in 1788. The doctrine held that the colonists could claim the land they found because it had no permanent residents on it (indigenous [native] peoples were nomadic) and thus belonged to no one.

The court's ruling was known as the Mabo deci-sion, named for Eddie Mabo, whose agricultural community of Torres Strait Islanders, at Australia's northeastern tip, was judged to have continuously used certain parcels of land for centuries. Although the ruling clearly recognized the entitlement of in-digenous peoples to their traditional lands, it did not lay the groundwork for how land transfers could

be achieved. The court simply specified that the rights of indigenous ownership could be recognized only when the land is government-owned rather than privately owned. However, the ruling also al-lowed the government to extinguish native land ownership under the same conditions in which any land can be claimed for the national interest.

In the year following the ruling, Aborigines filed numerous claims, causing concern among holders of mining and farming leases about the future viability of their enterprises. The new law allows that Aborig-inal hunting and fishing rights can coexist with some pastoral leases. Farmers renewing leases will not have to renegotiate terms with Aborigines, but min-ers will. In December 1993, Western Australia legis-lated to extinguish native title in that state, but Keating allowed Aborigines to have their claims de-cided at either state or federal tribunals.

State news. Queensland's worst drought on record continued for a third year, with 43.5 percent of the state, including about 16,000 farms, declared drought areas. Coming on top of the huge drop in export prices of wool and sugar—despite a record volume of sugar sales—the drought's consequences were severe, leading farmers into crippling debt that could force many off the land.

In New South Wales, Homefund, a government program to lend money to home buyers, went bust. When nearly half of the borrowers defaulted on their loans—which carried above-market interest rates—the government lost some $500 million.

Voters in the state of Western Australia went to the polls on February 6 and ousted the state's Labor Party leadership. A conservative coalition of the Lib-eral and National parties led by the Liberal Party's Richard Court won 32 seats in the 57-seat legislature. The vote was seen as a protest against the scandal known as WA Inc., in which Labor government agen-cies were accused of improper business dealings with a merchant bank.

Pay television. The federal government faced embarrassment in its efforts to establish pay TV in Australia in 1993. On April 30, the government awarded pay-TV rights to Ucom Pty. and Hi Vision Limited, the highest bidders for the contracts but relatively unknown in the television industry. Ucom had bid $177 million, and Hi Vision had bid $212 mil-lion. The companies then failed to follow through on their payment schedule. The government turned to the three next-highest bidders, but by August 20, all had withdrawn their offers. The high cost of start-up, priced at around $400 million, and license fees of $97 million and $117 million, were serious obstacles to establishing a pay TV operation.

Olympic Games. On September 23, Sydney, Aus-tralia's largest city, won the bid to host the Summer Olympic Games in the year 2000. Officials said the victory was due to the city offering a high level of technical expertise, a cooperative effort with the environmental group Greenpeace, and an emphasis on safety for the athletes. After the decision, the stock market soared and Sydney looked forward to a tourism boom.

Moving toward a republic. The movement for an Australian republic gained momentum during 1993 after Prime Minister Keating began a new push early in the year. Australia is now a constitutional monarchy and the United Kingdom's Queen Elizabeth II is Australia's head of state, though she has little power and the position is largely symbolic. In April, Keating announced the formation of the Republic Advisory Committee to install an Australian head of state by the year 2001.

International relations. Australia requested the extradition from Malaysia of Prince Kamarul Bahrin Shah to face charges for abducting his two children while on a visit to Melbourne in July 1992. The Australian Family Court in 1985 had given custody of the children—Iddin, 9, and his sister Sharina, 7—to their mother, Jacqueline Gillespie, an Australian citizen. Prince Bahrin was trying to mount his own extradition case against his former wife, alleging she abducted the children from Malaysia eight years ago. Malaysia's Prime Minister Mahathir bin Mohamad said the dispute would not affect relations between the countries.   □ Susan G. Williams

See also **Asia** (Facts in brief table). In *World Book,* see **Australia.**

Austria in 1993 formally opened talks on joining the European Community (EC or Common Market). Austrian leaders pledged to hold a popular referendum on the issue in 1994. If voters approve, Austria could become an EC member as early as Jan. 1, 1995.

However, Austria faced difficult negotiations with the EC. For one thing, the Austrian government asked for a transition period of at least four years in which it could use tariffs to help protect its farmers from EC competition while it adjusted to the EC's agricultural policies. EC negotiators had been reluctant to grant such requests in the past. Austria also sought tougher EC rules on immigration because it feared that more immigrants would settle in Austria if it had open borders with the other EC countries.

Immigration debate. Despite concerns about immigrants, especially those from the nearby wartorn countries of Croatia and Bosnia-Herzegovina, Austrians in 1993 responded coolly to moves by the right wing Freedom Party to tightly restrict the flow and activity of immigrants. An "Austria First" petition sponsored by the party called for limiting the number of immigrants allowed in Austrian schools, banning further immigration, and establishing a permanent border guard service. The petition garnered 417,000 signatures by the February 1 deadline, or about 7 percent of the electorate, well below the 1-million signatures the party had hoped for. Parliament dismissed the petition's recommendations.

The Freedom Party did relatively poorly in local elections during the year, due in part to the political extremism of party leader Jörg Haider. Nevertheless, Haider was to be the party's candidate for chancellor in parliamentary elections in 1994. The governing coalition led by the Social Democratic Party and the conservative Austrian People's Party also saw its popularity slip as the year went by.

Relationship with Israel. Austrian Chancellor Franz Vranitzky visited Israel from June 8 to 11, the first head of Austria to do so. Relations between the two countries had been sour for many decades because of Austria's ties to Nazi Germany in World War II (1939-1945). But diplomatic contacts increased in 1992 after Thomas Klestil replaced Kurt Waldheim as Austrian president. Waldheim had been accused of participating in Nazi war crimes, a charge he denied.

Airline talks. Austrian Airlines, the state-run carrier, said on April 27, 1993, that it had entered negotiations with three other airlines to merge into a single entity by the end of 1994. Under the plan, the carrier would own 10 percent of the new company, and Scandinavian Airlines System, KLM Royal Dutch Airlines, and Swissair would each own 30 percent. However, on November 21, talks between the four airlines broke down, and the project collapsed.   □ Philip Revzin

See also **Europe** (Facts in brief table). In *World Book,* see **Austria; Waldheim, Kurt.**

Automobile. Although 1993 was no boom year for automakers, it was filled with good news for the resurgent United States auto industry. After more than a decade of heavy investment in new products, better tools, and modern business methods, the Big Three automakers—Chrysler Corporation, Ford Motor Company, and General Motors Corporation (GM)—showed surprising strength against foreign competition. The trend toward a healthier U.S. car industry was helped along by Japanese and European automakers, which transferred more of their production to North American plants in 1993. And prospects for further improvement were bolstered by the ratification in November of the North American Free Trade Agreement, which gives U.S. automakers an inside track to the expanding Mexican automobile market.

Sales climb. Sales of new cars and light trucks in the United States reached an estimated 13.8 million in 1993, up a modest 7.8 percent from 1992. Most analysts said the auto industry had entered a period of slow but steady recovery from the sales slump in 1990-1992. But estimates of the pace of the rebound varied markedly. Chrysler Chairman Robert Eaton predicted that U.S. sales would reach a new record of 17 million in 1995. But the University of Michigan's prestigious Research Seminar in Quantitative Economics forecast sales of only 14.2 million in 1995.

Auto sales had surged in every post-recessionary

Chrysler in 1993 contemplated mass-producing the Prowler, a throwback
to the hot rod with an old-fashioned look but a modern-day engine.

period since the 1940's, but fundamental changes were conspiring against such a sharp upswing this time. Experts pointed to weak consumer confidence in the economy, a 4.3-cent hike in the federal gasoline tax, the increased durability of U.S.-built cars, and rising car prices as factors slowing the growth of auto sales.

New products. None of these obstacles prevented U.S. automakers in 1993 from wooing customers with new products, features, and deals. GM introduced a redesigned line of compact pickup trucks, the Chevrolet S-10 and GMC Sonoma. GM's flagship Cadillac Division also redesigned its bread-and-butter DeVille line-up of large luxury sedans, adding a 270-horsepower, high-performance version of the Concours. And the company looked forward to the 1994 unveilings of more new car and truck models, including a $35,000 Oldsmobile Aurora luxury sedan that was to serve as a vastly improved platform for all the company's future large cars.

Ford chose a nostalgia theme for its redesigned Mustang sports car, which appeared 30 years after the Mustang's fabled debut as the first American "pony" car. Numerous styling cues on the 1994 Mustang came directly from the 1964 original, and the spirit of America's muscle-car age was preserved in an optional 5.0-liter, 215-horsepower V-8 engine.

Chrysler continued its amazing recovery from near-bankruptcy in 1979 with the presentation in 1993 of its new Ram full-sized pickup truck, the first substantial redesign of that model in more than 20 years. Chrysler also previewed its Neon subcompact, an affordable small family car.

Virtually all 1994 model cars came with one or two front airbags, as did many trucks and vans. Anti-lock brakes had also become a widely offered safety feature. And leasing, not buying, was the deal of choice for a growing number of motorists, who preferred low monthly payments to actual ownership.

Japan struggles. The Honda Accord was completely redesigned for the 1994 model year, but it still showed no sign of recapturing its status as the nation's top-selling car, bowing to Ford's Taurus for the second straight year. In fact, Honda's sales fell 11 percent in 1993, a symbol of hard times for the entire Japanese auto industry. Japanese carmakers were expected to produce just 11.5 million vehicles in their home factories in 1993, down 14 percent from 1990. Overall, the Japanese auto industry in 1993 began to resemble the U.S. industry in 1981: falling profits, scattered plant closings, and shorter work hours.

One of the biggest headaches for Japanese automakers was the decline of the U.S. dollar against the Japanese yen. At the end of 1993, the yen was trading at about 108 to the dollar, down sharply from around 250 yen in the mid-1980's. Japanese carmakers thus received fewer yen for each car sold in the

United States, and they had to raise prices for profits to stay on track.

Moving to America. Some Japanese efforts to escape the strong yen helped American firms. Many Japanese automakers turned to high-quality, low-cost U.S. suppliers of parts and services in place of more expensive Japanese sources. By buying parts in the United States, the automakers avoided the exchange of dollars into yen. For a similar reason, some Japanese firms widened the production mixes at their U.S. factories. For example, Toyota said it would add production of the luxury Avalon sedan at its plant in Georgetown, Ky., and Honda was reportedly studying plans to build an Acura car alongside Accord and Civic models at its Ohio plants.

Many European automakers joined the flight to America. BMW in 1993 started construction of a car assembly plant in Spartanburg, S.C., and Mercedes-Benz in September chose Vance, Ala., as the site for its first U.S. assembly facility.

Detroit's rebirth. Buoyed by weakening competition, the Big Three automakers in 1993 experienced an enormous rise in profits. GM earned $1.3 billion in the first three quarters of the year, Ford earned $1.8 billion, and Chrysler earned $1.6 billion, not counting a $4.7-million loss to account for future retiree benefits. In most high-volume car segments, the U.S. firms had a substantial price advantage over their Japanese rivals. The Big Three also continued closing the gap in quality, according to industry observers. Perhaps the most dramatic sign of Detroit's rebirth was an agreement by Toyota to sell 20,000 GM-built cars annually in Japan.

Detroit's newfound competitiveness translated to increased market share. Through October 1993, the Big Three held 73.7 percent of the U.S. car and truck market, up from 72.2 percent for the same period in 1992. The expansion came despite continued weakness by GM, which by the end of 1993 was just completing an internal efficiency campaign expected to lead to better, less expensive products in the 1990's.

The share of the U.S. market held by Asian firms dropped from 25.2 percent in 1992 to 24.1 percent in 1993. European automakers also saw their share fall, from 2.6 percent in 1992 to 2.2 percent in 1993. However, most of that loss was due to Volkswagen of America, the one-time import leader that has plummeted to a miniscule 0.4 percent of the market.

Labor pacts. The Big Three automakers in 1993 won labor peace for three more years by reaching new contracts with the United Automobile Workers (UAW) in strike-free rounds of bargaining. The pacts gave auto workers 3 percent annual wage increases or lump-sum bonuses and improved pensions. More importantly, they preserved the job-security and income-protection features for idled workers that the UAW had won in the last round of talks in 1989. (See also **Labor.**)   □ James V. Higgins

In *World Book,* see **Automobile.**

Automobile racing. Nigel Mansell of the United Kingdom, who in 1992 won the world Formula One championship, switched to Indianapolis-type cars in 1993 and won the IndyCar World Series title. Alain Prost of France took over Mansell's car, won the world title for the fourth time, and retired at age 38. Dale Earnhardt won his sixth NASCAR series title in a year marked by aircraft accidents that killed Alan Kulwicki and Davey Allison, two of NASCAR's best drivers.

Indianapolis 500. The $7,681,300 race, the richest in the world, was run on May 30 at the Indianapolis Motor Speedway. Two weeks earlier, A. J. Foyt of Houston, who had started this race 35 consecutive years and had won four times, retired as a driver at age 58.

Mansell, driving a Lola-Ford, seemed en route to victory. But the field bunched during a caution flag on the 183rd of the 200 laps, and on the restart, Emerson Fittipaldi, a 46-year-old Brazilian, shot his Penske-Chevrolet into the lead. Fittipaldi stayed there and won by 2.862 seconds over Arie Luyendyk of the Netherlands in a Lola-Ford. Fittipaldi's average speed of 157.207 miles (253 kilometers) per hour was relatively slow because of track and car changes designed to make the race safer.

The Indianapolis 500 was the feature of the 16-race IndyCar World Series. Mansell became the first reigning world champion to switch to this series and

Alain Prost wins the French Grand Prix in Magny-Cours in July for a record sixth time.

the first rookie to win it. He earned a $5.5-million salary plus a share of prize money from his racing team, which was owned by Paul Newman and Carl Haas. Mansell won the series title with 191 points to 183 for Fittipaldi.

World drivers. This series of 16 Grand Prix races, mostly in Europe, was run in sleek, lighter versions of Indianapolis-type cars. Prost, after a one-year sabbatical, replaced Mansell on the Williams-Renault team and won seven races. Ayrton Senna of Brazil, in a McLaren-Ford, won five races, and Damon Hill, an English rookie on Prost's team, won three. Prost finished the season with 99 points, Senna 73, and Hill 69. Prost ended his career with 51 Grand Prix victories, a record.

Michael Andretti of Nazareth, Pa., became the first American Grand Prix driver in three years. He was hampered by new rules that limited his warmup laps on unfamiliar tracks, and his best finishes in 12 races were a third, a fifth, and a sixth. He decided to return in 1994 to the IndyCar series.

NASCAR. Driving a Chevrolet Lumina, the 42-year-old Earnhardt won the Winston Cup series, leaving him only one title behind the retired Richard Petty's record of seven. Earnhardt, from Kannapolis, N.C., won 6 of the Winston Cup's 31 races and led in earnings with $3,353,789. He finished with 4,526 points to 4,446 for second-place Rusty Wallace of St. Louis, Mo. Wallace, in a Pontiac Grand Prix, won 10 races, and Mark Martin of Batesville, Ark., won 5, including 4 straight in August.

In the first and most important race of the series, Dale Jarrett of Hickory, N.C., won the Daytona 500 on February 14 in Daytona Beach, Fla. His Chevrolet Lumina was owned by Joe Gibbs, who resigned a month later as coach of the Washington Redskins professional football team.

On April 1, the 38-year-old Kulwicki of Greenfield, Wis., NASCAR's defending champion, was killed when the private plane in which he was a passenger crashed near Bristol, Tenn. On July 13, the 32-year-old Allison of Hueytown, Ala., died of injuries suffered after the helicopter he was piloting crashed into the Talladega, Ala., Superspeedway track, where he was attempting to land.

Other. In the International Motor Sports Association's 11-race Camel GT series, Argentine Juan Manuel Fangio II kept his title and his Toyota teammate, P. J. Jones, finished second. This was the last year for these cars, scheduled to be replaced in 1994 by less-expensive open cars in a World Sports Car series.

In the world's most important endurance race, the 24 Hours of LeMans, held on June 19 and 20 in France, Peugeots finished first, second, and third. The winning car was driven by Geoff Brabham of Australia and Christophe Bouchut and Eric Hedlary of France. ☐ Frank Litsky

In *World Book,* see **Automobile racing.**

Aviation. For airlines in the United States, 1993 was a year of long-awaited recovery. The flow of red ink continued—experts estimated that the industry would lose at least $500 million in 1993. But signs of profitability led airline analysts to predict that the industry would break even in 1994 or even move into the black.

Industry revival. One of the earliest indicators of an economic rebound was the profit recorded by America West Airlines in the first quarter of 1993. America West was the only major airline to post a profit for that quarter besides Southwest Airlines, the industry's perennial profit generator. In the second quarter, AMR Corporation's American Airlines and UAL Corporation's United Airlines both showed profits. By the third quarter, all major domestic carriers except USAir Group Incorporated's USAir had at least meager profitability. In another strong sign, two airlines—Continental Airlines Holdings Incorporated and Trans World Airlines (TWA)—emerged during the year from court protection from creditors allowed under Chapter 11 of the U.S. Bankruptcy Code. The industry turnaround followed three years of shutdowns and losses totaling about $9 billion.

Unions take control. Labor unions gained a large role in running airlines in 1993. Several major airlines had to offer partial ownership to their employees to get the necessary financial concessions to compete with lower-cost carriers. TWA embarked on a path toward greater union participation on January 10 when Chairman Carl C. Icahn stepped down from his position, ending a stormy seven-year tenure. Icahn was replaced on July 13 by William R. Howard, former chairman of Piedmont Aviation Incorporated. On November 3, TWA finally emerged from Chapter 11 protection under a reorganization plan that gave unions a 45 percent share of the airline in return for $531 million in concessions over three years.

On December 15, United Airlines agreed to sell majority control of the carrier to a coalition of its unions in return for $5 billion in concessions. The deal still had to be approved by company directors, United shareholders, and members of the airline's unions. Also in 1993, Northwest Airlines, a unit of Wings Holdings Incorporated, reached an agreement with its pilots, machinists, and teamsters, averting a Chapter 11 filing. Under the pact, Northwest's employees provided $886 million in concessions over three years in exchange for 37.5 percent of the company's stock and three seats on the airline's board of directors.

Some analysts believed the rise of unions into positions of power would help eliminate the traditional rift between management and unions at airlines. The rockiness of that relationship was demonstrated in 1993 by a strike by flight attendants at American Airlines in November, which threatened to disrupt Thanksgiving Day travel for many people but which

A Swedish military plane burns in the forest where it crashed without causing casualties during an air show in Stockholm in August.

ended on November 22 when the two sides agreed to binding arbitration after phone calls from President Bill Clinton.

Government involvement. Revitalizing the country's airline industry was a focus of the Clinton Administration. On August 19, a panel set up to investigate the industry's problems issued a report of its findings to the President and to Congress. The commission made several important recommendations. First, it advised privatizing some functions of the Federal Aviation Administration (the branch of the U.S. Transportation Department that oversees airline safety and the U.S. air traffic control system). Second, the commission recommended lowering taxes on airline tickets and exempting airlines from any new fuel taxes for two years. Finally, it suggested raising the voting rights that a foreign carrier can possess in U.S. airlines to 49 percent from the current limit of 25 percent.

In contrast to federal policy during the 1980's, the Clinton Administration in 1993 acted to protect new airlines. For example, Transportation Secretary Federico F. Peña stepped in to stop alleged predatory pricing by Northwest Airlines against Reno Air, a small Nevada carrier. And the Justice Department, at the request of Morris Air, a small Utah airline, initiated an investigation into whether Delta Air Lines was giving travel agents above-market commissions to steer business from Morris.

Fare suit victory. On August 10, a jury decided that American Airlines had not tried to force other carriers out of business with predatory pricing during a fare war in 1992. Continental Airlines and Northwest Airlines had filed the suit, charging that American had enacted steep price cuts to try to gain monopoly control of routes. But American successfully argued that it had only been trying to compete.

Domestic consolidation. In the United States, most major airlines in 1993 reduced their capacity by dropping unprofitable routes and retiring older jets. In many cases, the airlines gave the closed routes to smaller, affiliated regional carriers. These included Atlantic Southeast Airlines, affiliated with Delta; Atlantic Coast Airlines, affiliated with United; and American Eagle, affiliated with American. As part of the retrenchment, several hubs were shut down, including American's hub in San Jose, United's hub in Washington, D.C., and USAir's hub in Baltimore.

One carrier that expanded its U.S. operations in 1993 was Southwest Airlines. For example, Southwest moved into San Jose and started service from Baltimore-Washington International Airport. The success of Southwest led to the emergence of other small carriers trying to copy its formula of low fares, short trips, and quick turnarounds. The upstarts included Kiwi International, based in Newark, N.J.; Private Jet, based in Atlanta, Ga.; and Ultrair, based in Houston. Even major players such as United Airlines and Continental Airlines established low-fare, high-use routes to better compete with Southwest.

International inroads. As airlines concentrated on their domestic operations, they slowed direct expansion abroad. Instead, many turned to creating alliances with foreign airlines. The flurry of alliance-building began on March 15 with the Transportation Department's approval of a $300-million investment in USAir by British Airways (BA). In return, BA received sizable voting and equity stakes in USAir.

Many similar deals followed. For example, Continental Airlines entered into an agreement with Air France under which the airlines will coordinate their flight schedules and share frequent-flyer programs. And Delta Airlines in 1993 finalized a patchwork of agreements with Latin-American carriers such as Varig and Aero Mexico.

Protectionist moves. The weak financial condition of airlines around the world in 1993 prompted many countries to take a more protectionist stance toward their carriers. In a typical case, Australia on June 1 said it would limit the number of passengers that Northwest Airlines could carry between Osaka, Japan, and Sydney, Australia. The move was aimed at aiding Australia's struggling Qantas Airlines. But the United States retaliated by suspending several of Qantas' Los Angeles-Sydney flights. The two sides eventually reached a settlement. □ Asra Q. Nomani

In *World Book,* see Aviation.

Azerbaijan. Disastrous defeats in a five-year war over the disputed enclave of Nagorno-Karabakh led to upheaval in Azerbaijan in 1993, as rebel forces overthrew the government. Nagorno-Karabakh lies within Azerbaijan but is populated mainly by ethnic Armenians. By late 1993, Azerbaijan had lost about 20 percent of its territory to Armenian forces and was struggling to cope with hundreds of thousands of refugees. (See **Armenia.**)

Surat Huseynov, a militia leader, launched the rebellion on June 4, after troops loyal to Azerbaijani President Ebulfez Elcibey tried to disarm Huseynov's forces. The militia then marched on Azerbaijan's capital, Baku, forcing Elcibey to flee on June 18. On June 24, parliament appointed Heydar Aliyev, formerly Azerbaijan's Communist Party chief, as acting president, and on June 30 it appointed Huseynov as prime minister. In a presidential election on October 3, Aliyev won more than 98 percent of the vote.

The new government worked to improve its ties with Russia, which it saw as the only power able to enforce a settlement in Nagorno-Karabakh. As a step in that direction, Azerbaijan on September 24 rejoined the Commonwealth of Independent States, a loose association of former Soviet republics that it had left in October 1992. □ Justin Burke

See also **Asia** (Facts in brief table); **Commonwealth of Independent States.** In *World Book,* see **Azerbaijan.**

Babbitt, Bruce (1938-), former governor of Arizona and a devoted conservationist, became United States secretary of the interior on Jan. 22, 1993. The choice of Babbitt for the Department of the Interior post was praised by environmentalists.

Born on June 27, 1938, in Los Angeles, Babbitt grew up in Flagstaff, Ariz., where his family had a ranching and trading business. He graduated with high honors from the University of Notre Dame in Indiana in 1960 and earned a master's degree in geophysics from the University of Newcastle in England in 1962. In 1965, he received a law degree from Harvard University in Cambridge, Mass.

Babbitt later returned to Arizona to join a Phoenix law firm. In 1975, he became state attorney general, and he was elected governor in 1978. As governor, Babbitt sponsored an act to protect the state's water resources. In recognition of his work, Babbitt in 1983 received a special commendation from the National Wildlife Federation.

Babbitt served as governor until 1987. The next year, he ran unsuccessfully for the Democratic presidential nomination. He returned to the private practice of law after the campaign.

Babbitt and his wife, Hattie—who is U.S. ambassador to the Organization of American States—have two children. □ David Dreier

Bahamas. See West Indies.

Bahrain. See Middle East.

Balladur, Edouard (1929-), became prime minister of France on March 29, 1993. He was named to the post by Socialist President François Mitterrand after conservative and moderate parties won 80 percent of the seats in elections for the National Assembly on March 21 and 28. Balladur was a member of the conservative Rally for the Republic (RPR) party, which won the most seats. (See also **France.**)

Edouard Balladur was born on May 2, 1929, in Turkey, but he was raised in Marseille, France. He graduated from France's Ecole Nationale d'Administration (National College of Management) in 1957. In 1963, he became an adviser to Prime Minister Georges Pompidou. When Pompidou was elected president in 1969, Balladur served as deputy chief of staff and then, beginning in 1972, as chief of staff. After Pompidou's death in 1974, Balladur moved to private industry.

In 1980, he began serving as an adviser to Prime Minister Jacques Chirac, a leader of the RPR. In 1986, Balladur became finance minister for Chirac. In that role, Balladur carried out an economic program that included privatizing government-owned firms, eliminating government controls on prices, and cutting taxes. Balladur was finance minister until 1988.

As prime minister, Balladur pledged to sell off more state-owned firms, to pursue a united Europe, and to protect the interests of French farmers in international trade talks. □ John C. Burnson

Bangladesh. Political alignments shifted during 1993 but without challenging the authority of Prime Minister Khaleda Ziaur Rahman. Her Bangladesh Nationalist Party amended its constitution on September 1 so that the party chairman would be chosen by secret ballot instead of a show of approval. The move gave party dissidents more power by enabling them to vote their choice without fear of reprisal and seemed intended to prevent the splits that occurred in two other parties in 1993.

The main opposition party, the Awami League, split on August 29. The party was led by Sheikh Hasina Wajed, a daughter of Bangladesh's independence leader and first prime minister, the late Sheikh Mujibur Rahman. Kamal Hossain, who had been a close colleague of Mujibur, opposed Hasina's focusing on political tactics and wanted more attention given to economic problems. He led some league members into a new party, the Peoples' Forum.

The Communist Party of Bangladesh, which had cooperated with the Awami League in the 1991 general elections, split on friendly terms on June 9, 1993. The smaller segment continued to advocate Marxist-Leninist principles. The larger, reformist segment called for "democracy, development, nationalism, and social justice."

Refugees leave. Throughout 1993, small groups of Muslim refugees from neighboring Burma (also called Myanmar) returned home. Since 1989, some 265,000 Muslims had fled from atrocities in Burma's Arakan province. United Nations officials supervised *repatriation* (return of the refugees) under an agreement with Burma intended to ensure good treatment for those who went home voluntarily. But by late 1993, about 200,000 refugees remained in camps in Bangladesh.

On January 11, the first Bangladeshi Muslims flew to Pakistan to live. After Bangladesh won its independence from Pakistan in 1971, Muslim residents who had supported Pakistan, known as Biharis, were put into camps. In 1992, Pakistan had agreed to accept some of the 238,000 Biharis for resettlement.

Economic gains. Although still dependent on foreign aid, Bangladesh increased its exports by 25 percent in the year ending June 30, 1993. Rice, the country's main food, was exported for the first time, but more than 90 percent of the exports were manufactured goods.

Nevertheless, in April, officials of the World Bank, an agency of the United Nations, warned that industrial investment was low. They said this was a major obstacle to faster growth and the alleviation of poverty. They urged the government to speed up the sale of its industries to the private sector.

More than 237,000 people left Bangladesh to work in foreign countries from June 1992 to June 1993. Many sent money home. ☐ Henry S. Bradsher

See also **Asia** (Facts in brief table). In *World Book,* see **Bangladesh.**

Bank. United States banks and savings and loans (S&L's), which had been rocked by failures, scandals, and steep losses during the 1980's, continued their rebound in 1993. In the first half of the year, the number of banks that closed their doors due to insolvency fell, and the industry posted record profits.

FDIC surplus. In good news for taxpayers, the Federal Deposit Insurance Corporation (FDIC), the agency that protects depositors' money in the event of a bank failure, reported a remarkable turnaround in the balance of its insurance fund. When a bank goes under, the FDIC reimburses depositors for their losses, up to $100,000 for each account. If the FDIC insurance fund is empty, the government must pay with tax dollars borrowed from the U.S. Treasury.

At the end of 1991, the FDIC was operating with a deficit of $7.03 billion, and Congress authorized the FDIC to borrow up to $70 billion from the Treasury. By June 30, 1993, the FDIC fund had come roaring back. Its balance stood at $6.8 billion, the highest level since 1990. The surplus allowed the FDIC to pay back all the money it had borrowed from the Treasury—with interest—by Aug. 6, 1993.

Banks stay afloat. The biggest reason for the FDIC's recovery was the decline in bank failures. In the first six months of 1993, only 23 banks with combined assets of $2.5 billion failed, compared with 66 banks with combined assets of about $20.1 billion during the same period in 1992. By mid-December 1993, only 42 banks had failed all year.

Most banks stayed solvent because they earned record profits. For the first six months of 1993, banks reported record earnings of $21.3 billion. Profits for S&L's for that period were also high, $3.1 billion.

The improvement in the fitness of the country's banks helped the FDIC in another way. Healthier banks and S&L's meant an increase in fees to the FDIC—28 cents per $100 of deposits in 1993, up from 23 cents per $100 of deposits in 1992. These fees make up a large part of the FDIC insurance fund.

Low interest rates. Both banks and S&L's were aided by continuing record-low interest rates. With inflation around 3 percent for 1993, banks did not have to pay high interest rates to attract depositors. For example, rates on certificates of deposits (CD's)—accounts that must be held for a certain period—sank as low as 2.56 percent. Banks thus had a comfortable spread between the money paid on their accounts and the money earned on their loans, most of which had been written at a time of higher rates.

Interest rates also fell on mortgages. In October, the rate for a 30-year, fixed-rate mortgage declined to 6.74 percent, the lowest level since 1968. Falling mortgage rates led to increased refinancing business for banks. Many people who took out a mortgage in the 1980's were paying more than 10 percent interest on the money they had borrowed. For a small fee, people could refinance their mortgages at the new, lower rates and save themselves money over

Lawyer Robert Altman walks out of a New York City courtroom with his wife, actress Lynda Carter, in August after being acquitted of bank fraud.

the long term. A record number of mortgages—some 5.3 million—were refinanced during 1993.

S&L recovery. The government continued its fitful cleanup of the S&L industry, which suffered huge losses during the 1980's. In 1993, Congress voted to add about $18 billion to the Resolution Trust Corporation, the agency created to take control of failed S&L's. The cash infusion would bring the total spent in the S&L cleanup to almost $200 billion, not counting hundreds of billions of dollars more in interest.

Wider credit. President Bill Clinton, concerned about a shortage of credit, emphasized new areas of bank lending in his Administration. On March 10, Clinton proposed lifting regulations on banks to give them greater leeway for providing credit based on a prospective borrower's character, rather than credit history or amount of collateral. The proposals were enacted by federal regulatory agencies on March 30. Then on July 15, Clinton asked Congress to establish a fund to subsidize lending by community development banks, which concentrate on making loans in poor neighborhoods. Clinton's plan earmarked $382-million for the fund through fiscal year 1998. Congress was still considering the idea at year's end.

Discrimination studied. On May 27, 1993, the Office of the Comptroller of the Currency, the agency that regulates national banks, said it would send people of various races to banks to see if minority loan applicants are discriminated against. The plan

was sparked by a 1992 report that blacks are more than twice as likely to be turned down for a loan as whites with similar incomes. On Dec. 13, 1993, the U.S. Justice Department said it had settled lending-discrimination charges against Shawmut National Corporation of Hartford, Conn. The company denied the charges but agreed to establish a fund to compensate minorities who had been denied loans.

Bank scandals. Several major court cases drew to a close in 1993. In July 1992, Clark M. Clifford, former U.S. secretary of defense for President Lyndon B. Johnson, and his law partner, Robert A. Altman, had been indicted on charges they helped the Bank of Credit and Commerce International, a corrupt Pakistani bank, hide its ownership of First American Bankshares Incorporated, a U.S. bank. On Aug. 14, 1993, a jury found Altman not guilty of fraud. Then on November 30, a judge dismissed the charges against Clifford because of his frail health.

In another global bank scandal, Christopher Drogoul on September 2 pleaded guilty to fraud in a case involving Banca Nazionale del Lavoro (BNL), an Italian bank with a branch in Atlanta, Ga. Drogoul, a former BNL manager, had been charged with issuing $5 billion in illegal loans to Iraq in the 1980's.

Law firms and accountants who were neglectful at S&L's continued to settle big cases with the U.S. government. On April 19, 1993, Jones, Day, Reavis and Pogue, a Cleveland law firm, paid the government a record $51 million to settle charges that it helped Lincoln Savings & Loan Association hide the illegal practices that eventually led to the S&L's failure in 1989. The collapse of Lincoln cost taxpayers $3.4 billion. On Aug. 3, 1993, Arthur Andersen and Company, the world's largest accounting firm, paid the federal government $79 million to settle charges of accounting lapses in connection with its work for Lincoln Savings & Loan and for Ben Franklin Savings Association, another failed institution. The demise of Ben Franklin cost taxpayers about $1 billion.

Long-term view. Although 1993 was a bright year for banks, the long-term outlook was gloomy. Newer sorts of financial institutions were grabbing larger pieces of the banking business. Since 1963, the share of financial assets held by banks in the United States had fallen from about 40 percent to less than 25 percent. People were putting an increasing portion of their money into *mutual funds* (publicly traded pools of stocks and bonds). Analysts predicted that investments in mutual funds would soon surpass the $2 trillion in deposits held in U.S. banks.

In response to this trend, Mellon Bank Corporation of Pittsburgh on Dec. 6, 1993, said it would buy Dreyfus Corporation of New York City, the country's sixth-largest mutual fund company, for about $1.8-billion. If it proceeds, the acquisition will give Mellon Bank the largest mutual-fund business of any bank in the United States. □ Paulette Thomas

In *World Book,* see **Bank.**

Baseball. The major leagues thrived in 1993, in part because of a last-to-first-place improvement by the Philadelphia Phillies and a tense battle in the National League Western Division between the Atlanta Braves and the San Francisco Giants. But in the end, the most successful team was the American League champions, the Toronto Blue Jays, who defeated Philadelphia, 4 games to 2, and won the World Series for the second consecutive year.

National League. In the Eastern Division, Philadelphia finished three games ahead of the Montreal Expos. The Phillies became only the third team in the 1900's to climb from the bottom to the top in one year.

In the Western Division, Atlanta gained its third consecutive title. It won 51 of its last 68 games and finished one game ahead of San Francisco. They were tied until the last day of the season, when Atlanta defeated the Colorado Rockies, 5-3, and the Los Angeles Dodgers routed San Francisco, 12-1. Atlanta's 104-58 record was the best in the major leagues. San Francisco became the first team since the 1954 New York Yankees to win 103 games and finish second.

Philadelphia defeated Atlanta, 4 games to 2, in the league championship series as relief pitcher Mitch Williams won two games for Philadelphia. In a memorable fourth game, Philadelphia won, 2-1, despite striking out 15 times and leaving 15 men on base.

Final standings in major league baseball

American League

Eastern Division	W.	L.	Pct.	G.B.
Toronto Blue Jays	95	67	.586	
New York Yankees	88	74	.543	7
Baltimore Orioles	85	77	.525	10
Detroit Tigers	85	77	.525	10
Boston Red Sox	80	82	.494	15
Cleveland Indians	76	86	.469	19
Milwaukee Brewers	69	93	.426	26

Western Division	W.	L.	Pct.	G.B.
Chicago White Sox	94	68	.580	
Texas Rangers	86	76	.531	8
Kansas City Royals	84	78	.519	10
Seattle Mariners	82	80	.506	12
California Angels	71	91	.438	23
Minnesota Twins	71	91	.438	23
Oakland Athletics	68	94	.420	26

American League champions—Toronto Blue Jays (defeated the White Sox, 4 games to 2)

World Series champions—Toronto Blue Jays (defeated the Phillies, 4 games to 2)

Offensive leaders

Batting average—John Olerud, Toronto	.363
Runs scored—Rafael Palmeiro, Texas	124
Home runs—Juan Gonzalez, Texas	46
Runs batted in—Albert Belle, Cleveland	129
Hits—Paul Molitor, Toronto	211
Stolen bases—Kenny Lofton, Cleveland	70
Slugging percentage—Juan Gonzalez, Texas	.632

Leading pitchers

Games won—Jack McDowell, Chicago	22
Win average (15 decisions or more)—Juan Guzman, Toronto (14-3)	.824
Earned run average (162 or more innings)—Kevin Appier, Kansas City	2.56
Strikeouts—Randy Johnson, Seattle	308
Saves—Jeff Montgomery, Kansas City; Duane Ward, Toronto (tie)	45
Shut-outs—Jack McDowell, Chicago	4

Awards*

Most Valuable Player—Frank Thomas, Chicago
Cy Young—Jack McDowell, Chicago
Rookie of the Year—Tim Salmon, California
Manager of the Year—Gene Lamont, Chicago

*Selected by the Baseball Writers Association of America.

National League

Eastern Division	W.	L.	Pct.	G.B.
Philadelphia Phillies	97	65	.599	
Montreal Expos	94	68	.580	3
St. Louis Cardinals	87	75	.537	10
Chicago Cubs	84	78	.519	13
Pittsburgh Pirates	75	87	.463	22
Florida Marlins	64	98	.395	33
New York Mets	59	103	.364	38

Western Division	W.	L.	Pct.	G.B.
Atlanta Braves	104	58	.642	
San Francisco Giants	103	59	.636	1
Houston Astros	85	77	.525	19
Los Angeles Dodgers	81	81	.500	23
Cincinnati Reds	73	89	.451	31
Colorado Rockies	67	95	.414	37
San Diego Padres	61	101	.377	43

National League champions— Philadelphia Phillies (defeated the Braves, 4 games to 2)

Offensive leaders

Batting average—Andres Galarraga, Colorado	.370
Runs scored—Lenny Dykstra, Philadelphia	143
Home runs—Barry Bonds, San Francisco	46
Runs batted in—Barry Bonds, San Francisco	123
Hits—Lenny Dykstra, Philadelphia	194
Stolen bases—Chuck Carr, Florida	58
Slugging percentage—Barry Bonds, San Francisco	.677

Leading pitchers

Games won—Tom Glavine, Atlanta; John Burkett, San Francisco (tie)	22
Win average (15 decisions or more)—Mark Portugal, Houston (18-4)	.818
Earned run average (162 or more innings)—Greg Maddux, Atlanta	2.36
Strikeouts—Jose Rijo, Cincinnati	227
Saves—Randy Myers, Chicago	53
Shut-outs—Pete Harnisch, Houston	4

Awards*

Most Valuable Player—Barry Bonds, San Francisco
Cy Young—Greg Maddux, Atlanta
Rookie of the Year—Mike Piazza, Los Angeles
Manager of the Year—Dusty Baker, San Francisco

Joe Carter jubilantly rounds the bases after his ninth-inning home run gave the Toronto Blue Jays their second consecutive World Series title on October 23.

American League. In the East, Toronto finished seven games ahead of the Yankees and won the title for the third consecutive year. The Chicago White Sox won by eight games over the Texas Rangers in the West for their first division title since 1983. After a year of recuperation following a hip replacement, outfielder Bo Jackson returned to the White Sox.

In the league championship series, Toronto and Chicago split the first four games, the visiting team winning each time. Then Toronto's pitching took over as Juan Guzman won the fifth game and Dave Stewart the sixth, and Toronto won the pennant, 4 games to 2.

World Series. After Toronto won the World Series in 1992, it dropped, traded, or did not pursue outfielders Dave Winfield and Candy Maldonado, starting pitchers Jimmy Key and David Cone, relief pitcher Tom Henke, shortstop Manuel Lee, and third baseman Kelly Gruber. It added Stewart, designated hitter Paul Molitor, outfielder Rickey Henderson, and shortstop Tony Fernandez. First baseman John Olerud (.363), Molitor (.332), and second baseman Roberto Alomar (.326) of Toronto finished 1-2-3 in American League batting.

Philadelphia was a surprise team with many cast-offs. It was led by outfielder Lenny Dykstra (143 runs and 194 hits), catcher Darren Daulton (105 runs batted in), first baseman John Kruk (.316), and third baseman Dave Hollins (93 runs batted in).

In the World Series, held from October 16 to 23, Toronto was strongly favored over Philadelphia and charged to a 3-1 lead in games. Toronto won the third game, 10-3, after Manager Cito Gaston, not allowed to use a designated hitter on a National League field, benched Olerud, the American League batting champion, and replaced him with Molitor at first base. Molitor responded with a home run, a triple, a single, and three runs batted in. The next night, Toronto won, 15-14, in the highest-scoring (29 runs) and longest (4 hours 14 minutes) Series game ever.

Toronto closed out the Series by winning the sixth game, 8-6, on Joe Carter's dramatic three-run home run off Williams in the bottom of the ninth inning. Williams, who saved 43 games during the regular season, dissipated leads in two of the last three Series games, and after the season the Phillies traded him to the Houston Astros. Molitor, with 12 hits in 24 trips and eight runs batted in, was voted the Series' Most Valuable Player.

Regular season. This was the final season for Nolan Ryan, the 46-year-old pitcher for the Rangers; Carlton Fisk, the 45-year-old catcher for the White Sox; and George Brett, the 40-year-old designated hitter for the Kansas City Royals. Ryan played in the major leagues for 27 years, Fisk for 22, and Brett for 20, and all appeared to be strong candidates for the National Baseball Hall of Fame when they become eligible in 1998. On Aug. 1, 1993, outfielder Reggie Jackson, who hit 563 home runs in 21 seasons, was inducted into the Hall of Fame.

Fisk broke the major league record for games caught (2,225) on June 22, and the White Sox released him a week later. The 41-year-old Winfield signed with the Minnesota Twins after Toronto no longer wanted him and on September 16 became the 19th player in history to get 3,000 hits in a career. On April 15, George (Sparky) Anderson of the Detroit Tigers became the seventh manager to win 2,000 games in a career. Relief pitcher Lee Smith of the St. Louis Cardinals broke the major league career record of 357 saves on April 13.

The major leagues set a regular-season attendance record of 70,257,938, helped by the National League's addition of the Colorado Rockies, based in Denver, and the Florida Marlins, based in Miami. Colorado's total (4,483,350) and average (56,751) attendance were the highest ever.

On the downside, while television viewership since 1990 rose 31 percent for basketball and 16 percent for football, it dropped 24 percent for baseball. With their four-year, $1.06-billion national television contract with CBS expiring, the major leagues created a six-year (1994-1999) joint television venture with NBC and ABC in which the networks would pay no rights fee, but would share advertising revenue with baseball. As part of the television package, the four-team play-offs were expanded to eight teams, and each major league would be realigned to three divisions from two, subject to approval by the players.

Personalities. In a determined effort to slash the club payroll, the San Diego Padres traded many high-salaried players. They included third baseman Gary Sheffield, the National League's 1992 batting champion, and first baseman Fred McGriff, its 1992 home-run champion.

A boating accident on March 22 near Clermont, Fla., killed Cleveland Indians pitchers Steve Olin and Tim Crews and badly injured Indians pitcher Bob Ojeda. Outfielder Vince Coleman of the New York Mets pleaded guilty in court to throwing a firecracker into a crowd of fans. The Mets said on August 26 that Coleman would never play for them again. The major league executive council on February 3 suspended Marge Schott, the Cincinnati Reds' owner, for most of the year for racial and ethnic slurs.

The average salary at the start of the season was $1,120,254. With a salary of $7,291,667, outfielder Barry Bonds of San Francisco was the highest-paid player. Bonds went on to hit 46 home runs, drive in 123 runs, and bat .336 and was voted the National League's Most Valuable Player for the third time in four years. The American League honor went to first baseman Frank Thomas of the White Sox, who drove in 128 runs and hit 41 home runs.   □ Frank Litsky

In *World Book,* see **Baseball.**

Basketball. In an exciting professional play-off finals that matched superstars Michael Jordan and Charles Barkley, the Chicago Bulls won the National Basketball Association (NBA) championship for the third consecutive year. Three and a half months later, Jordan retired. Duke University attempted to win the National Collegiate Athletic Association (NCAA) men's title for the third straight year, but neighboring University of North Carolina won instead. Texas Tech won its first NCAA women's championship.

NBA. Despite frequent fights during games, the NBA thrived, and television ratings rose. From November 1992 to April 1993, each team played 82 regular season games. The Phoenix Suns (62-20) and the New York Knicks (60-22) achieved the best records. The other division winners were Chicago (57-25) and the surprising Houston Rockets (55-27). At the other end, the Dallas Mavericks lost 19 consecutive games and finished with an 11-71 record.

Sixteen teams advanced to the play-offs. Chicago eliminated the Atlanta Hawks (3 games to 0), the Cleveland Cavaliers (4-0), and New York (4-2). Phoenix reached the finals with more difficulty, defeating the Los Angeles Lakers (3-2), San Antonio Spurs (4-2), and the Seattle SuperSonics (4-3).

The finals were played from June 9 to 20, and each game seemed to become a personal battle between Jordan and Barkley. In a sport in which the home team traditionally has a big advantage, the visiting team won the first three games. Chicago won the series and the title, 4 games to 2. In the final game, Chicago prevailed, 99-98, on a three-point field goal by John Paxson with 3.9 seconds remaining. Jordan averaged a record 41 points per game in the finals and was voted the Most Valuable Player (MVP) in the play-offs for the third consecutive year. Chicago became the first team to win three straight NBA titles since the Boston Celtics won their eighth in a row in 1966.

Jordan retires. Jordan announced his retirement from the NBA on Oct. 6, 1993, saying that he had "nothing more to prove in basketball." He finished his career with three regular-season MVP awards, the highest career points-per-game scoring average during the regular season, and the highest career scoring average in play-off games. (See **Jordan, Michael.**)

During the regular season, Jordan averaged 32.6 points per game and won his seventh consecutive scoring title, matching Wilt Chamberlain's NBA record. For the seventh year in a row, Jordan led all starters in voting for the all-star team.

But the season also held controversy for Jordan. He endured severe media criticism when he went to an Atlantic City, N.J., casino to gamble on the night before a play-off game in New York. Later, a book by a San Diego businessman said he won $1.25 million in golf bets from Jordan over 10 days in 1991. Jordan said he did not remember if he had won or

The 1992-1993 college basketball season

College tournament champions

NCAA	(Men)	Division I: North Carolina
		Division II: California State (Bakersfield)
		Division III: Ohio Northern
NCAA	(Women)	Division I: Texas Tech
		Division II: North Dakota State
		Division III: Central Iowa
NAIA	(Men)	Division I: Hawaii Pacific
		Division II: Willamette (Ore.)
	(Women)	Division I: Arkansas Tech
		Division II: Northern Montana
NIT	(Men)	Minnesota
Junior College	(Men)	Division I: Pensacola (Fla.)
		Division II: Owens Tech (Ohio)
		Division III: Onondaga (N.Y.)
	(Women)	Division I: Kilgore (Tex.)
		Division II: Illinois Central
		Division III: Hudson Valley (N.Y.)

Men's college champions

Conference	School
Atlantic Coast	North Carolina (reg. season)
	Georgia Tech (tournament)
Atlantic Ten	Massachusetts*
Big East	Seton Hall*
Big Eight	Kansas (reg. season)
	Missouri (tournament)
Big Sky	Idaho (reg. season)
	Boise State (tournament)
Big South	Towson State (reg. season)
	Coastal Carolina (tournament)
Big Ten	Indiana (reg. season)
Big West	New Mexico State (reg. season)
	Long Beach State (tournament)
Colonial A.A.	Old Dominion—James Madison (tie; reg. season)
	East Carolina (tournament)
Great Midwest	Cincinnati*
Ivy League	Pennsylvania (reg. season)
Metropolitan	Louisville*
Metro Atlantic	Manhattan*
Mid-American	Ball State—Miami (Ohio) (tie; reg. season)
	Ball State (tournament)
Mid-Continent	Cleveland State (reg. season)
	Wright State (tournament)
Mid-Eastern	Coppin State*
Midwestern	Xavier (Ohio)—Evansville (tie; reg. season)
	Evansville (tournament)
Missouri Valley	Illinois State (reg. season)
	Southern Illinois (tournament)
North Atlantic	Drexel—Northeastern (tie; reg. season)
	Delaware (tournament)
Northeast	Rider*
Ohio Valley	Tennessee State*
Pacific Ten	Arizona (regular season)
Patriot League	Bucknell (regular season)
	Holy Cross (tournament)
Southeastern	Kentucky (tournament)
Eastern Division	Vanderbilt (reg. season)
Western Division	Arkansas (reg. season)
Southern	Tennessee-Chattanooga*
Southland	Northeast Louisiana*
Southwest	Southern Methodist (regular season)
	Texas Tech (tournament)
Southwestern	Jackson State (reg. season)
	Southern-Baton Rouge (tournament)
Sun Belt	New Orleans (reg. season)
	Western Kentucky (tournament)
Trans America	Florida International (reg. season)
West Coast	Pepperdine (reg. season)
	Santa Clara (tournament)
Western	Utah—Brigham Young (tie; reg. season)
	New Mexico (tournament)

*Regular season and conference tournament champions.

lost, but in any event, Jordan maintained that far less money was involved.

The stars. Center Shaquille O'Neal of the Orlando Magic beat Patrick Ewing of the Knicks in voting to become the first rookie since 1985 to be named to the starting all-star team lineup. Barkley, in his first year with Phoenix after eight years with the Philadelphia 76ers, was voted MVP for the regular season. He averaged 25.6 points, 12.2 rebounds, and 5.1 assists per game. O'Neal was voted Rookie of the Year. Pat Riley of New York was named the Coach of the Year.

Tragedies. Celtics captain Reggie Lewis collapsed and died after shooting baskets on July 27, 1993, in Waltham, Mass. After collapsing in a play-off game on April 29, Lewis had sought medical advice concerning a possible heart condition. Heart specialists in Boston concluded that Lewis suffered from a life-threatening heart irregularity, but another specialist diagnosed the problem as a nerve condition.

On June 7, New Jersey Nets guard Drazen Petrovic died in an automobile accident in Germany. He was the Nets' leading scorer during the 1992-1993 season and led the Croatian national team to a silver medal in the 1992 Summer Olympics. James Jordan, father of Michael Jordan, was murdered on July 23, 1993, near Fayetteville, N.C. Authorities discovered his body on August 3 in a creek near McColl, S.C. A grand jury indicted two 18-year-olds for the murder on September 7. (See **Crime**.)

NBA to Canada. The NBA said on Nov. 4, 1993, that it would add Toronto to the league, beginning with the 1995-1996 season. The NBA's expansion committee said that it may also add another Canadian team for the 1995-1996 season.

College men. Indiana, Duke, Kentucky, and Kansas all were ranked number one nationally at some time during the regular season. In the Associated Press (AP) final regular season poll of sportswriters and broadcasters, Indiana (28-3) was ranked first, Kentucky (26-3) second, Michigan (26-4) third, and North Carolina (28-4) fourth.

Those teams were the top seeds for the NCAA's 64-team championship tournament held from March 18 through April 5. In the Midwest regional, however, California upset Duke, by a score of 82-77, in the second round, and Kansas upset Indiana, 83-77, in the regional final.

Kansas entered the Final Four in New Orleans, along with North Carolina, Michigan, and Kentucky. In the national semifinals, Michigan defeated Kentucky, 81-78, and North Carolina eliminated Kansas, 78-68. In the final, North Carolina beat Michigan, by a score of 77-71. The decisive play came with 11 seconds remaining in the game and the North Carolina team ahead by two points. Chris Webber of Michigan, trapped by two defenders, called for a time out, even though his team had no time outs remaining. North Carolina was awarded two technical-foul shots, both of which the Tar Heels' Donald Williams made to seal the victory.

Honors. On March 3, 1993, Bobby Hurley of Duke broke the NCAA career record of 1,038 assists by Chris Corchiani of North Carolina State. Calbert Cheaney of Indiana was the player of the year. The most frequent choices for All-America teams were three forwards (Jamal Mashburn of Kentucky, Cheaney, and Webber) and two guards (Anfernee Hardaway of Memphis State and Hurley). In the NBA draft, Orlando took Webber with the first choice

National Basketball Association standings

Eastern Conference

Atlantic Division	W.	L.	Pct.	G.B.
New York Knicks*	60	22	.732	
Boston Celtics*	48	34	.585	12
New Jersey Nets*	43	39	.524	17
Orlando Magic	41	41	.500	19
Miami Heat	36	46	.439	24
Philadelphia 76ers	26	56	.317	34
Washington Bullets	22	60	.268	38

Central Division				
Chicago Bulls*	57	25	.695	
Cleveland Cavaliers*	54	28	.659	3
Charlotte Hornets*	44	38	.537	13
Atlanta Hawks*	43	39	.524	14
Indiana Pacers*	41	41	.500	16
Detroit Pistons	40	42	.488	17
Milwaukee Bucks	28	54	.341	29

Western Conference

Midwest Division	W.	L.	Pct.	G.B.
Houston Rockets*	55	27	.671	
San Antonio Spurs*	49	33	.598	6
Utah Jazz*	47	35	.573	8
Denver Nuggets	36	46	.439	19
Minnesota Timberwolves	19	63	.232	36
Dallas Mavericks	11	71	.134	44

Pacific Division				
Phoenix Suns*	62	20	.756	
Seattle SuperSonics*	55	27	.671	7
Portland Trail Blazers*	51	31	.622	11
Los Angeles Clippers*	41	41	.500	21
Los Angeles Lakers*	39	43	.476	23
Golden State Warriors	34	48	.415	28
Sacramento Kings	25	57	.305	37

*Made play-off.

NBA champions—Chicago Bulls (defeated Phoenix Suns, 4 games to 2)

Individual leaders

Scoring	G.	F.G.	F.T.	Pts.	Avg.
Michael Jordan, Chicago	78	992	476	2,541	32.6
Dominique Wilkins, Atlanta	71	741	519	2,121	29.9
Karl Malone, Utah	82	797	619	2,217	27.0
Hakeem Olajuwon, Houston	82	848	444	2,140	26.1
Charles Barkley, Phoenix	76	716	445	1,944	25.6
Patrick Ewing, New York	81	779	400	1,959	24.2
Joe Dumars, Detroit	77	677	343	1,809	23.5
Shaquille O'Neal, Orlando	81	733	427	1,893	23.4
David Robinson, San Antonio	82	676	561	1,916	23.4

Rebounding	G.	Tot.	Avg.
Dennis Rodman, Detroit	62	1,132	18.3
Shaquille O'Neal, Orlando	81	1,122	13.9
Dikembe Mutombo, Denver	82	1,070	13.0
Hakeem Olajuwon, Houston	82	1,068	13.0
Kevin Willis, Atlanta	80	1,028	12.9

John Paxson releases the three-point shot on June 20 that beat the Phoenix Suns and gave the Chicago Bulls their third straight NBA championship.

overall, and the Golden State Warriors made Hardaway the third choice. Orlando then traded Webber to Golden State for Hardaway and first-round draft choices in 1996, 1998, and 2000.

College women. In the AP final regular season poll for college women, Vanderbilt (27-2) was first, Tennessee (27-2) second, Ohio State (24-3) third, Iowa (24-3) fourth, and Texas Tech (26-3) fifth. They led 48 teams into the NCAA tournament from March 17 to April 4. The star of the Final Four in Atlanta, Ga., was Sheryl Swoopes, Texas Tech's senior forward. In the semifinals, Texas Tech whipped Vanderbilt, 60-46, behind Swoopes's 31 points and 11 rebounds. Ohio State won the other semifinal against Iowa, 73-72, in overtime. In the championship game, Texas Tech defeated Ohio State, 84-82, as Swoopes scored 47 points, the most ever by a woman or man in an NCAA final. Swoopes, the player of the year, was also voted the MVP in the play-offs.

International. In May 1993, the Basketball Hall of Fame in Springfield, Mass., inducted Julius Erving, Bill Walton, Dick McGuire, Walt Bellamy, Dan Issel, Calvin Murphy, and Ann Meyers, all of the United States. Ulyana Semyonova, the 7-foot (213-centimeter) center of former-Soviet women's teams, was also inducted. □ Frank Litsky

See also **O'Neal, Shaquille.** In *World Book,* see Basketball; Jordan, Michael.

Belarus. See Europe.

Belgium in 1993 officially became a *federal* country (a country composed of states). On May 8, the Senate adopted new laws delegating most essential government powers to three regions of the country. The regions were Flanders, the area in the north whose residents speak Dutch; Wallonia, the area in the south whose residents speak French; and Brussels, Belgium's bilingual capital.

Under the new laws, each region elects its own parliament. The regional governments are responsible for matters such as education, policing, and health care. The federal government retains control of national defense and monetary policy. This structure was designed to defuse tensions between Flanders and Wallonia and to keep Belgium intact.

Monarch dies. King Baudouin I, Europe's longest reigning monarch, died on July 31 of a heart attack while at his vacation home in Motril, Spain. The king, who took the throne in 1951, is survived by Queen Fabiola. Although the Belgian monarchy has little real power, Baudouin's death revealed a deep emotional attachment to the monarchy among Belgians, as exhibited by 10 days of national mourning. Baudouin had become a symbol of Belgian unity amid the increasing discord between the country's Dutch- and French-speaking peoples.

Baudouin was succeeded by his brother, Prince Albert, who was crowned King Albert II on August. 9 in Brussels. Albert and his wife, Queen Paola, have two children, Prince Philippe and Princess Astrid. Some observers had expected Albert to pass the throne to Philippe, but Albert accepted the position. He said he would continue his brother's work of unifying Belgium under its new political structure.

European unity troubles. Belgium held the rotating presidency of the European Community's Council of Ministers during the second half of 1993. The term was marred by delays with the final ratification of the Treaty on European Union, often called the Maastricht Treaty, whose goal was the political and economic union of Europe. (See **Europe.**)

Economic woes. Belgium's economy continued to suffer in 1993 as the government kept interest rates high to support the value of the Belgian franc against other European currencies. On February 21, the regional government of Flanders and the neighboring government of the Netherlands agreed to invest $240 million in the ailing truck manufacturer DAF to help save 3,250 jobs. In November, the Belgian parliament approved an austerity plan with $3-billion in spending cuts and new taxes for 1994. Belgian workers reacted by holding the first nationwide general strike since 1936, and the government said it would reopen talks on the plan. □ Philip Revzin

See also **Europe** (Facts in brief table). In *World Book,* see Belgium.

Belize. See Latin America.

Benin. See Africa.

Bentsen, Lloyd M., Jr. (1921-   ), became United States secretary of the treasury on Jan. 20, 1993. The appointment of Bentsen, the former chairman of the Senate Finance Committee, signaled to the U.S. financial community that the Treasury Department would be in experienced hands.

Bentsen was born on Feb. 11, 1921, in Mission, Tex., and grew up in nearby McAllen. He attended the University of Texas at Austin, earning a law degree in 1942. That same year, Bentsen joined the Army air corps. He became a B-24 bomber pilot and flew missions in Europe during World War II (1939-1945), attaining the rank of major and earning the Distinguished Flying Cross. Later, he rose to the rank of colonel in the Air Force Reserve.

In 1948, Bentsen, a Democrat, was elected to the U.S. House of Representatives, becoming—at age 27—the youngest member of the House. He was reelected without opposition in 1950 and 1952. Bentsen left Congress in 1955, and, with a capital investment from his father, he founded a life insurance company in Houston.

In 1970, Bentsen was elected to the U.S. Senate, defeating Texas Congressman—later President—George Bush. He won reelection in 1976, 1982, and 1988 and was the Democratic vice-presidential candidate in the 1988 election. He became Finance Committee chairman in 1987. □ David Dreier

Bhutan. See Asia.

Biology. In 1993, researchers at the University of Colorado in Boulder attempted to lay to rest the notion that the world's largest living organisms are fungi. During the previous year, two different research teams claimed they had identified a huge fungal growth that was the largest organism. One fungus covered several acres in a Michigan forest. The other, in a Washington forest, was 40 times bigger. Each could be considered a single organism because all parts were genetically identical and appeared connected by underground tendrils.

The Colorado researchers pointed out that an aspen grove in the Wasatch Range of Utah is actually much larger than either fungus. Each of the 47,000 tree trunks in the Utah grove are part of a single *clone* (a group of organisms that are genetically identical), because the trees grow from a common root system. The grove covers 106 acres (43 hectares), and the scientists estimated that it is about 15 times heavier than the Washington fungus.

A giant among microbes. In March 1993, scientists at Indiana University in Bloomington reported the discovery of the largest known bacterium, a single-celled creature that is 0.015 inch (0.4 millimeter) long, big enough to be visible to the naked eye and 1 million times larger than the common *Escherichia coli* bacteria found in the human intestine. The bacterium was isolated from the gut of a surgeonfish caught on the Great Barrier Reef of Australia. Biolo-gists had previously believed that bacteria could not grow so large because the size would make it difficult for nutrients to reach all parts of the cell's interior.

When life began. Life may have originated on Earth earlier than scientists had previously believed, researchers at the University of California at Los Angeles reported in April. The scientists based that idea on their discovery of fossil microorganisms in rocks in western Australia. The fossils, of 11 diverse species of microbes, were 3.465 billion years old. Because millions of years must have passed before the first life form evolved into so many different species, the scientists theorized that the first living thing must have existed soon after the birth of the planet 4.5 billion years ago.

The fossil organisms looked like a type of oxygen-using bacteria that had previously been found in rocks dated to 2.1 billion years ago. If the Australian fossils are also of oxygen-using microbes, then oxygen must have existed in Earth's atmosphere 3.465 billion years ago, at least 1 billion years earlier than previously thought.

Why some corn pops. When kernels of popcorn are heated, the moisture inside the kernel is rapidly converted to steam, causing the inner starch to burst out into puffs. But kernels of normal corn of the same species barely expand when heated. Scientists at the University of Campinas in Brazil explained the

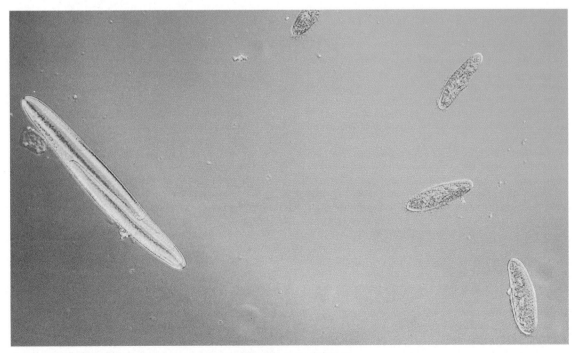

A member of the largest bacteria species ever found, left, is much larger than one-celled animals called paramecia, according to a March report.

Boating

difference in "popability" in July. Variations in the *pericarp*, the outer casing of the kernel, are the key. Molecules in the pericarp of popcorn are arranged in a much more orderly fashion than in normal corn, so that they transmit heat to the interior about twice as fast. The pericarp of popcorn is also stronger, so that higher pressure builds up before it is released in the final explosion.

Finicky cockroaches. Entomologists reported in January why some cockroach populations, particularly in Florida, avoid household roach traps. Researchers in Pleasanton, Calif., collected roaches from Florida and found that only 42 percent were attracted to the bait. The rest ignored it or were repulsed.

When the researchers started testing each bait ingredient separately, they found that the problem was the corn syrup that was used as the bait sweetener. Corn syrup is composed of two sugars, glucose and fructose. Tests showed that the bait-avoiding roaches disliked the glucose.

The research team speculated that a small fraction of roaches have a natural aversion to glucose. In a household, roaches that like the sugar are killed in the traps, and those that do not like it live to reproduce, passing on the repulsion to glucose and eventually creating a trap-avoiding population. When researchers substituted an all-fructose bait, 85 percent of the insects were attracted. □ Thomas H. Maugh II

See also **Medicine**. In *World Book*, see **Biology**.

Boating. The French sailors Alain Gautier and Bruno Peyron won around-the-world yacht races in 1993. Gautier, piloting a crewless yacht, was concerned mostly with safety. Peyron wanted to set a speed record.

On March 12, Gautier, sailing the 60-foot (18-meter) *Bagages Superior*, won the Vendée Globe Challenge, a nonstop race for skippers without crews. His time of 110 days 2 hours was only 18 hours slower than the record. One of the 14 starting skippers died at sea, and a scheduled starter was lost at sea en route to the start.

On April 20, Peyron and a four-man crew won an around-the-world race in 79 days 6 hours, the fastest ever under sail. Their craft was the 86-foot (26-meter) high-tech catamaran, *Commodore Explorer*, and they planned to sail around the world in fewer than the 80 days it took the fictional hero Phileas Fogg in Jules Verne's 1873 book *Around the World in Eighty Days*.

Other races. The first Gold Cup transatlantic race was held from July 3 to 16 from New York City to Southampton, England. The winner was the new 60-foot (18-meter) *Winston*, coskippered by Dennis Conner, the celebrated America's Cup skipper.

Economic problems in 1993 hurt the major professional sailing circuits: the Omega GP, the World Sailing Association, and the 50-Foot Circuit. All canceled races or moved them out of the United States.

America's Cup. In 1992, the last time this prestigious series was sailed, Bill Koch, the American who won, built four boats and spent $68.5 million. Italian industrialist Raul Gardini, the unsuccessful challenger, built five boats and spent $110 million. For the next cup races, in 1995, the 2 United States and 14 foreign syndicates involved agreed in May 1993 to limit each group to two new boats.

Koch wanted the six-month trials and finals condensed to two months, and he advocated the use of boats smaller than the 75-foot (23-meter) America's Cup Class sloops that were introduced in 1992. Because of the high costs, he said he did not plan to race for the cup in 1995, leaving Conner and Kevin Mahaney of Bangor, Me., to contend for the role of defender. A role for Gardini's syndicate was doubtful after Gardini was found dead on July 23, 1993, of a self-inflicted gunshot. Gardini had been accused of bribing politicians and falsifying financial records.

Powerboats. *Miss Budweiser*, driven by Chip Hanauer of Seattle, won the national series for unlimited hydroplanes for the seventh time in 11 years. He won his seventh national driving championship. There were 10 races from May to October for these powerful boats, which generate speeds up to 170 miles (274 kilometers) per hour. Hanauer won the major race, the $200,000 Gold Cup on June 6 in Detroit, for a record ninth time. □ Frank Litsky

In *World Book*, see **Boating; Sailing.**

Bolivia. Gonzalo Sánchez de Lozada began a four-year term as Bolivia's president on Aug. 6, 1993. The 63-year-old Sánchez de Lozada, a mining magnate, is a member of the Revolutionary Nationalist Movement party and was raised in the United States.

Vice President Víctor Hugo Cárdenas, Sánchez de Lozada's running mate, stole much of the limelight at the inauguration. Cárdenas, an Aymará Indian, was the first full-blooded Indian to hold such a high post in Bolivia. Cárdenas was determined to make progress on a broad Indian rights agenda. Among the most urgent tasks, he said, was rewriting school textbooks, which portray the Indians of Bolivia as outsiders in society, even though they make up the majority of Bolivia's population.

Former dictator sentenced. On April 21, the Supreme Court of Bolivia sentenced General Luis García Meza Tejada to 30 years in jail on charges of murder, looting the treasury, corruption, and abuse of constitutional power for his actions as Bolivia's military dictator in 1980 and 1981. García Meza was sentenced in absentia, as he disappeared during the course of his seven-year trial, and his whereabouts were still unknown. The court also sentenced a García Meza collaborator, former Bolivian Interior Minister Luis Arce Gómez, to 30 years in jail for the same offenses. □ Nathan A. Haverstock

Books. See **Canadian literature; Literature; Literature, American; Literature for children.**

Bosnia-Herzegovina in 1993 remained in the grip of a civil war that began soon after the former Yugoslav republic declared independence in March 1992. The fighting had pitted the government of Bosnia (as the country is often known), which sought to maintain Bosnia as a multiethnic state, against ethnic Serbs and Croats, who by December 1992 had seized about 70 percent and 20 percent, respectively, of Bosnian territory. International observers continued to express outrage at reports of atrocities by the warring forces, mainly by Serbs against members of Bosnia's Muslim ethnic group. They also denounced the Serbs and, to a lesser degree, the Croats for their policy of "ethnic cleansing"—the forced expulsion of Muslims from captured villages and towns.

Observers also deplored the Serbs' siege of Sarajevo, Bosnia's capital, and of Muslim strongholds in eastern Bosnia. In February 1993, the United States began airdrops of food and medical supplies to besieged cities after Serb forces repeatedly blocked United Nations (UN) aid convoys. International relief organizations estimated in the autumn that 2.3 million civilians in Bosnia would be dependent on aid shipments of food, medical supplies, and fuel during the coming winter. Thousands of Bosnians had already died in the nearly two years of fighting, and more than a million had become refugees.

International efforts to end the conflict made little progress in 1993. In April, the UN Security Council tightened its trade embargo on Yugoslavia, in an effort to compel Serbia—the dominant republic of what remained of Yugoslavia—to force concessions from Bosnian Serbs. In May, the Administration of U.S. President Bill Clinton failed to persuade European leaders to agree to stronger action against Serbia, including air strikes against Serbian military targets. The North Atlantic Treaty Organization (NATO) approved a list of potential targets in August but took no further action to launch air attacks.

Early in the year, it appeared that all the parties might accept a peace plan put forward in January by UN mediator Cyrus R. Vance and Lord David Owen, representing the European Community (EC or Common Market). The Vance-Owen plan would have split Bosnia into 10 semiautonomous provinces, most of them ethnically based, under a unified, multiethnic government. On March 25, Bosnian President Alija Izetbegovic joined ethnic Croat leaders in approving the plan. But by June, repeated Bosnian Serb rejections of the initiative forced all parties to admit that the Vance-Owen plan was dead.

The Bosnian government soon came under increasing pressure to accept a settlement that would entail the partition of Bosnia along ethnic lines. On June 16, President Franjo Tudjman of the former Yugoslav republic of Croatia and Serbian president Slobodan Milošević proposed a plan to partition Bosnia into a loose confederation of three ethnic republics.

A Bosnian Serb aims at Tuzla, a Muslim-held town in eastern Bosnia-Herzegovina, in July, as a fellow Serb guards the position from the rear.

Their proposal, in a slightly modified form, soon gained the backing of Lord Owen and UN mediator Thorvald Stoltenberg, who had replaced Vance.

On June 29, the UN Security Council defeated a resolution, supported by the United States, to lift a UN arms embargo against the Bosnian government. The UN had imposed the embargo against all six original Yugoslav republics in September 1991.

On July 30, 1993, Izetbegovic reluctantly agreed, in principle, to the ethnic partition of Bosnia. But on September 29, the Muslim-dominated Bosnian parliament rejected a version of the plan that would have given the Serbs 51 percent, the Croats 18 percent, and the Muslims 31 percent of Bosnia's territory. The parliament demanded that the Serbs give up more territory to the Muslims.

Lack of progress in ending the war led to divisions within Bosnia. On September 27, a provincial assembly in Bihac, a Muslim enclave in northwestern Bosnia, declared Bihac an autonomous province and named Izetbegovic's rival Fikret Abdic as its president. Bosnia's parliament then ousted Abdic from the country's 10-member collective presidency. On October 22, Abdic signed a peace accord with Serbian and Bosnian Serb leaders.   □ Sharon L. Wolchik

See also **Croatia; Europe.** (Facts in brief table); **United Nations; Yugoslavia.** In *World Book,* see **Bosnia-Herzegovina.**

Botswana. See Africa.

Bowling. The men's and women's professional tours struggled in 1993 to stay on national television. To make the sport more attractive to television, the men's Professional Bowlers Association (PBA) changed its stepladder format, adding a winner-take-all play-off between the week's winner and the previous week's play-off winner. But the American Broadcasting Companies still reduced its PBA telecasts. The Ladies Pro Bowlers Tour (LPBT), which conducted the women's tour, remained on television in the spring only after finding an 11th-hour sponsor.

Both tours worked to retain sponsors. Bridgestone-Firestone Incorporated, which had sponsored the men's showcase competition, the Tournament of Champions, for 29 years, bowed out at year's end and was replaced by General Tire Corporation.

Men. Walter Ray Williams, Jr., of Stockton, Calif., enjoyed a career year. He won seven tournaments, one short of the 1978 record held by Mark Roth. Williams reached the championship finals 15 times in 32 tournaments in 1993. His per game scoring average of 222.98 broke Roth's 1979 record of 221.66. He won $294,370 for the year, nearly breaking Mike Aulby's 1989 earnings record of $298,237.

In the three major tournaments, Williams' best performance was second place in the United States Open held from April 4 to 10, 1993, in Canandaigua, N.Y. Del Ballard, Jr., of Richardson, Tex., defeated him in the final, 237-193.

George Branham III of Indianapolis became the first black winner of a major title. In the Tournament of Champions stepladder finals held from April 20 to 24 in Fairlawn, Ohio, he eliminated Dave Husted with a 266 and Dave Ferraro with a 258. In the final, he beat Parker Bohn III of Freehold, N.J., 227-214.

Ron Palombi, Jr., of Erie, Pa., won the PBA national championship held from February 21 to 27 in Toledo, Ohio, beating Eugene McCune of Munster, Ind., 237-224, in the final.

Women. Dede Davidson of San Jose won the U.S. Open held from May 22 to 29 in Garland, Tex. She defeated Dana Miller-Mackie of Albuquerque, N. Mex., 213-194. For the year, Aleta Sill of Dearborn, Mich., led in earnings with $57,995, and Tish Johnson of Panorama, Calif., led in scoring average with 215.39. Lisa Wagner of Palmetto, Fla., passed the $500,000 career earnings mark in 1993, a first for the women's professional tour.

Seniors. The most dramatic moment on the PBA's senior tour came on July 1 in the final of a tournament in Wilkes-Barre, Pa. In the semifinal and final matches, 51-year-old Ron Winger of Tarzana, Calif., rolled 23 strikes in 24 attempts. He defeated Gary Dickinson of Edmond, Okla., 279 to 225, and then Jimmy Certain of Huntsville, Ala., 300 to 215. Dickinson led the tour with $78,250 in earnings and a 218.38 scoring average.   □ Frank Litsky

In *World Book,* see **Bowling.**

Boxing. The invincibility of 31-year-old Julio César Chávez of Mexico, generally regarded as the world's best fighter, pound for pound, was punctured in 1993. Almost everyone except two of three judges thought 29-year-old Pernell Whitaker of Norfolk, Va., had beaten Chávez on September 10 in San Antonio, but those two judges voted the fight a draw, and that became the official decision.

Because a champion keeps his title on a draw, Whitaker remained World Boxing Council (WBC) welterweight champion. This was the first fight as a welterweight for Chávez, previously the WBC super-lightweight champion. He entered the Whitaker fight a 2-to-1 favorite, had a record of 87-0 (72 knockouts), and was 25-0 in title fights in three weight divisions.

Mickey Vann, an English judge who called the fight a draw, reportedly told an English journalist that he had deducted a point from Whitaker for a low blow, a deduction the rules did not allow him to make by himself. Vann later denied the story. Another report said José Sulaiman of Mexico, the WBC president, instructed the three judges before the fight not to be entranced by boxing skills, an order that would have worked against Whitaker.

Chávez scored a fifth-round knockout in a title fight against Greg Haugen on February 20 and a sixth-round knockout in a title defense against Terrence Alli on May 8. The Haugen bout at Mexico

City's Aztec Stadium attracted 136,274 spectators, a boxing record. Whitaker had won the WBC welterweight title by outpointing James (Buddy) McGirt on March 6 in New York City.

Heavyweights. Evander Holyfield of Atlanta, Ga., recaptured the World Boxing Association (WBA) heavyweight title on November 6 in Las Vegas, Nev. Holyfield won the title back with a 12-round decision over Riddick Bowe of Brooklyn, N.Y. Bowe had beaten Holyfield a year earlier to take the title. A bizarre spectacle occurred during the seventh round, when a parachutist dropped in on the match.

Lennox Lewis of the United Kingdom maintained his WBC heavyweight title in 1993. Lewis outpointed Tony Tucker on May 8 and stopped Frank Bruno in seven rounds on October 1. George Foreman fell from the ranks of heavyweight title contenders when he was outpointed by Tommy Morrison on June 8. Foreman retired again at age 44. Michael Bentt knocked Morrison out in the first round of their October 29 fight, costing Morrison a guaranteed $7.5 million for a title fight against Lewis.

Amateur. In the 1993 world championships in Tampere, Finland, from May 7 to 16, Cuba won eight gold medals and three silver medals. Cuban superheavyweight Roberto Balado won his third consecutive title, matching the record of his celebrated countryman, Teofilo Stevenson. □ Frank Litsky

In *World Book,* see **Boxing.**

Brazil. Government ministers passed through President Itamar Franco's Cabinet in 1993 as though through a revolving door. In May, Foreign Minister Fernando Henrique Cardoso became Brazil's fourth finance minister in eight months, but he was unable to curb the country's staggering inflation rate, which was expected to reach 1,800 percent by the end of the year. As a result of the new administration's troubles, confidence in the government fell, and Brazil's parliamentary political leadership largely ignored Franco's administration. After President Fernando Collor de Mello was impeached for corruption in September 1992, Franco took power until national elections could be held in October 1994.

The country's political and economic troubles created unrest within Brazil's military. To appease the military, Franco in May 1993 replaced the country's secretary of federal administration with a retired army general. He named an admiral to run the government's shipping company, an air force general to run the telephone company, and an army general to run the national steel industry.

Another economic plan. On June 14, Cardoso announced the finalization of a sweeping economic initiative to stabilize Brazil's teetering economy. The plan, which Franco introduced in April, aimed to cut central government spending by $6 billion and raise taxes. It also called for quicker privatization of money-losing state-owned companies and a crackdown

World champion boxers

World Boxing Association

Division	Champion	Country	Date won
Heavyweight	Riddick Bowe	U.S.A.	1992
	Evander Holyfield	U.S.A.	Nov. '93
Light heavyweight	Virgil Hill	U.S.A.	1992
Middleweight	Reggie Johnson	U.S.A.	1992
	John David Jackson	U.S.A.	Oct. '93
Welterweight	Cristano Espana	Venezuela	1992
Lightweight	Tony Lopez	U.S.A.	1992
	Dingaan Thobela	South Africa	June '93
	Nazarov Olzubek	Russia	Oct. '93
Featherweight	Yong-kyun Park	South Korea	1991
Bantamweight	Jorge Julio	Colombia	1992
	Junior Jones	U.S.A.	Oct. '93
Flyweight	David Griman	Venezuela	1992

World Boxing Council

Division	Champion	Country	Date won
Heavyweight	Lennox Lewis	United Kingdom	1992
Light heavyweight	Jeff Harding	Australia	1991
Middleweight	Julian Jackson	U.S. Virgin Islands	1990
	Gerald McClellan	U.S.A.	May '93
Welterweight	James McGirt	U.S.A.	1991
	Pernell Whitaker	U.S.A.	March '93
Lightweight	Miguel Gonzalez	Mexico	1992
Featherweight	Paul Hodkinson	United Kingdom	1991
	Gregorio Vargas	Mexico	April '93
	Kevin Kelley	U.S.A.	Dec. '93
Bantamweight	Victor Rabanales	Mexico	1992
	Jung Il Byun	South Korea	March '93
Flyweight	Yuri Arbachakov	Russia	1992

Evander Holyfield, right, lunges at Riddick Bowe during the November 6 bout in Las Vegas, Nev., in which Holyfield recaptured the heavyweight title.

on tax evasion, which officials estimated was costing Brazil $40 billion to $60 billion a year. As a result of hyperinflation, the Brazilian government on August 2 lopped three zeros off the cruzeiro, Brazil's currency, and created the country's fourth new currency in seven years—the cruzeiro real.

Another scandal. On October 28, police discovered evidence that Brazilian government officials were involved in a major corruption scandal. When police searched the home of former federal Budget Director José Carlos Alves dos Santos, who was accused of murdering his wife, they found $1.7 million in bank notes, $300,000 in cash, and 212 pounds (96 kilograms) of gold.

Santos implicated 32 politicians, including the head of the budget committee of the Brazilian Congress, in a kickback scheme involving money for federal public works projects. Among those implicated was Henrique Hargreaves, President Franco's chief of staff. Hargreaves resigned on October 29. The scandal came just over a year after Collor de Mello had been impeached.

Police brutality. On July 23, three men—alleged by eyewitnesses to be military police officers—shot eight children to death who were sleeping on the sidewalks of downtown Rio de Janeiro. The killings shocked the world, as did statistics that the government later released confirming that 4,611 children under the age of 18 were killed on the streets of Brazil's cities between 1988 and 1990. The police detained three military policemen on July 27 in connection with the murders.

On August 30, squads of hooded men invaded a Rio de Janeiro slum and shot 21 people to death. Many residents of the slum claimed that military police conducted the killings. The night before, four military policemen had been shot to death in the same neighborhood by reputed drug lords, and the police had allegedly vowed vengeance.

On May 31, a report by Americas Watch, a human rights group based in New York City, detailed the extent of police violence in the state of São Paulo. The report said that São Paulo police were responsible for more than half of an estimated 2,774 murders in the state in 1992. The Brazilian government formed a police commission on Sept. 2, 1993, to investigate police death squads.

Indian massacre. Government officials said that Brazilian gold miners killed 13 Yanomami Indians near the remote town of Haximu along the Brazil-Venezuela border. The miners reportedly ambushed the Indians on July 23. About 10,000 Yanomami Indians live in Brazil on a mineral-rich reservation about the size of Portugal. They are believed to be the largest American Indian group to have preserved their way of life from outside influences.

□ Nathan A. Haverstock

See also **Latin America** (Facts in brief table). In *World Book,* see **Brazil.**

British Columbia. Premier Michael Harcourt announced on April 13, 1993, a decision to reduce but not ban commercial logging in one of Canada's last temperate rain forests located on Vancouver Island. Attempting to balance environmental and economic interests, the decision retained one-third of the area as wilderness. It also prohibited large-scale clearing of hillsides in favor of logging in small areas. Environmentalists opposed the decision, and some 700 protesters were arrested during the summer as they tried to obstruct logging operations.

The provincial government announced on June 2 the creation of a 2,367-acre (958-hectare) wilderness park in a mountainous watershed area where British Columbia, Alaska, and the Yukon Territory meet. The decision closed the gold- and copper-rich area to miners and sank a proposed multimillion-dollar mining project at Windy Craggy Mountain.

The strong provincial economy was boosted even more in 1993 by an influx of 70,000 new residents. The budget, announced on March 30, raised the sales tax from 6 percent to 7 percent, imposed a surtax on high personal incomes, and increased some government-service fees. The budget sought to reduce the deficit from $2 billion to $1.5 billion in fiscal 1993-1994 on spending of $19 billion. (Monetary figures are in Canadian dollars.) □ David M. L. Farr

In *World Book,* see **British Columbia.**

Brunei. See **Asia.**

Brown, Jesse (1944-), a former United States marine who was wounded in Vietnam and who has devoted his entire career to serving disabled veterans, was sworn in as U.S. secretary of veterans affairs on Jan. 22, 1993. Brown is just the second person, and the first black, to head the Department of Veterans Affairs since it was established as an executive department of the U.S. government in 1989.

Brown was born on March 27, 1944, in Detroit and spent his teen-age years in Chicago. He enlisted in the Marine Corps in 1963 and was later sent to Vietnam. In 1965, while on patrol near Da Nang, he was seriously wounded in the right arm by gunfire. The wounds left his arm partially paralyzed.

In 1967, after his discharge from the Marines, Brown joined the Chicago office of the Disabled American Veterans (D.A.V.), an organization that helps disabled veterans return to leading a normal life. Brown also attended Chicago City College, from which he graduated with honors in 1972 with an associate of arts degree.

Brown was transferred to the D.A.V.'s Washington, D.C., staff in 1973, and in the following years he held a series of executive posts within the organization. He became executive director in 1989, a position he held until his appointment as veterans affairs secretary.

Brown and his wife, Sylvia, have a son and a daughter. □ David Dreier

Brown, Ronald H. (1941-   ), former chairman of the Democratic National Committee, became secretary of commerce on Jan. 22, 1993. He is the first black to head the Department of Commerce.

Brown was born in Washington, D.C., on Aug. 1, 1941. He grew up in New York City and graduated in 1962 from Middlebury College in Vermont. After four years in the Army, he earned a law degree in 1970 at St. John's University in New York City.

In 1971, Brown became general counsel for the National Urban League, a New York City-based organization that works to further the interests of minority groups. He served as the league's vice president for Washington, D.C., operations from 1976 to 1979. In 1980, Brown became an attorney for the United States Senate Judiciary Committee, and in 1981 he was named its first black chief counsel.

In 1981, Brown became a partner in the Washington law firm of Patton, Boggs, and Blow. There, he served as a lobbyist for a number of foreign governments and companies. In late 1993, a federal grand jury in Miami, Fla., was investigating a charge that Brown, shortly after the election of Bill Clinton to the presidency in November 1992, accepted a bribe from the government of Vietnam to help get the U.S. trade embargo against Vietnam lifted.

Brown is married to the former Alma Arrington. They have two children.   □ David Dreier

Brunei. See Asia.

Building and construction.

Building and construction. The construction industry experienced another disappointing year in 1993. Except for specialized pockets of prosperity, there was little or no growth in most construction markets. Competition remained intense and profits low. According to the F. W. Dodge Division of DRI/McGraw-Hill, an economic consulting firm in New York City, harsh winter weather early in the year delayed work underway, and a loss of confidence in the economy delayed the start of new projects. Unemployment remained high in the construction trades, and union wage and fringe benefits increased only an average of 2.96 percent over 1992, according to an 20-city survey. Nonunion wages did not rise. But, residential construction activity overall gained a respectable 9 percent, with 1.2 billion dwelling units constructed during 1993 at a total cost of $118 billion.

Public works projects. According to figures released by the Congressional Budget Office on September 9, federal spending on *infrastructure* (such as highways and bridges) grew to $30.3 billion in 1992, up about $3 billion from 1991. Nonbuilding public works grew about 8 percent in 1993, compared with commercial, manufacturing, and institutional building construction, which grew by only 1 percent. Office building construction sank even further in 1993, as did factory construction.

What construction there was in 1993 was domi-nated by water treatment plants, incinerators, prisons, and stadiums. In Cleveland, San Antonio, and other cities, major new stadiums or arenas were erected, continuing a wave of stadium and arena construction that began in the 1980's.

Other major public works projects underway in 1993 included a $1.3-billion water treatment plant and a $5.3-billion subway system in Los Angeles, the first segment of which opened on January 30; a $331-million lock at the Bonneville Dam on the Columbia River on the Oregon-Washington border; a $70-million convention center in Columbus, Ohio; and a $95-million incinerator in Crosby, Tex., that will burn hazardous waste and then be dismantled and moved to another site. In Rotterdam, the Netherlands, $450-million floating steel floodgates that hold back tidal surges from the North Sea were under construction. In Athens, Greece, a new subway system was being constructed.

For all the attention to public works, the United States was spending less on infrastructure in the early 1990's than it had in the early 1970's, according to a Congressional Budget Office study released on Sept. 9, 1993. Congressman Norman Y. Mineta (D., Calif.), chairman of the public works and transportation committee in the U.S. House of Representatives, called for higher federal infrastructure spending as a percent of *gross domestic product* (the total value of all goods and services produced within a nation).

On February 17, President Bill Clinton unveiled a five-year economic stimulus package that would have pumped $9 billion for public works into construction in its first year. But Congress killed the stimulus measure on April 21. Then in October, Congress voted to kill construction funding for the Superconducting Super Collider, a multibillion-dollar *particle accelerator* (atom smasher) in Texas.

Japanese construction scandal. A scandal involving payoffs to politicians by construction companies reverberated through Japan in 1993. Shin Kanemaru, a key figure in Japan's Liberal Democratic Party, was indicted in March for tax evasion after failing to disclose millions of dollars in gifts from construction companies. Then, on September 20, Japanese prosecutors accused the country's most prominent construction executive of trying to buy influence over public works awards with cash gifts. They arrested 75-year-old Teruzo Yoshino, chairman of the Tokyo-based Shimizu Corporation and of the Japan Federation of Construction Contractors. Shimizu executives denied that there was any evidence to support the charges. And it was not clear whether such prosecutions could break up the old cartel system of dividing up public jobs. The system is known in Japan as *dango,* which refers to the teahouses where such arrangements often are discussed.

Rebuilding after Hurricane Andrew. Hurricane Andrew, which swept across southern Florida on Aug. 24, 1992, inflicted $16 billion in insured loss-

New home construction trends upward

New housing starts

	Total
	Single family
	Multifamily

1,400,000
1,200,000
1,000,000
800,000
600,000
400,000
200,000
0

1989 1990 1991 1992 1993* 1994*

Source: U.S. Bureau of the Census.
* Estimated, National Association of Home Builders.

New single and multifamily housing starts in 1993 continued a modest increase to an estimated 1.24 million units after dropping below 1 million in 1991.

es, according to A. M. Best Co., the insurance company rating service. The storm severely damaged or destroyed 73,000 homes in south Dade County, Fla., according to the American Red Cross, and drove tens of thousands of people from the disaster area, most of them permanently. Business activity in the general region, however, surged with the cleanup and rebuilding efforts in 1993. Just disposing of the mountains of debris that were collected cost hundreds of millions of dollars.

In south Dade County, the amount of home and roof repairs helped to keep the price of lumber surging around the country. Lumber prices climbed 28.7 percent during the first seven months of 1993, according to R. S. Means Company, a cost consultant.

Mississippi floods. The effectiveness of government construction projects in defending against natural disasters came under scrutiny after record-setting floods inundated large areas of the Midwest during the summer of 1993, especially along the Mississippi River. No one alive had seen the Mississippi so high or so wide.

Of particular interest was whether a system of levees built by the Army Corps of Engineers had contributed to the disaster by allowing river water to build up behind the levees rather than dispersing across the Mississippi's natural flood plain. Insured losses caused by the flooding reached $655 million, but many property owners were uninsured, accord-

ing to the Insurance Information Institute in New York City.

Tallest and longest structures. Foundations neared completion in 1993 for building a tower in Kuala Lumpur, Malaysia, that would be the world's tallest structure, at 1,476 feet (450 meters), beating out the Sears Tower in Chicago by 22 feet (6.7 meters). The new tower was one of the most ambitious commercial developments underway in the world during 1993.

The world's longest cable-stayed bridge span began to stretch across the Seine Estuary in Normandy, France, in 1993. The 2,808-foot- (856-meter-) long deck far exceeded the span of any existing cable-stayed bridges. In this type of bridge, the cables that support the roadway are connected directly to the supporting towers. In a suspension bridge, the cables that support the roadway are connected to other cables that are anchored to the towers. The longest completed cable-stayed bridge span is Canada's Alex Fraser Bridge near Vancouver. Its main span measures 1,526 feet (465 meters).

Tunnel opening delayed. The formal opening of the English Channel Tunnel connecting England and France was delayed from December 1993 to May 1994. The cause of the delay was a dispute with the construction company over $1 billion in extra costs.

☐ Richard Korman

In *World Book,* see **Building construction.**

Burma. Delegates selected by the ruling military junta of Burma (officially called Myanmar) convened on Jan. 9, 1993, to write a new constitution. They met sporadically under tight junta controls until September 16, when they adjourned for the remainder of the year. During the sessions, the delegates blocked junta efforts to give the armed forces constitutional authority for a leading role in national politics. On June 7, a junta representative proposed that the nation change from a parliamentary to a strong presidential system of government. Furthermore, the military wanted control over the selection of a president.

Human rights abuses. On February 25, the United Nations Human Rights Commission reported that executions and torture were widespread in Burma. Also in February, a group of Nobel Peace Prize recipients demanded the release of Burmese opposition leader Aung San Suu Kyi, who had been awarded the Nobel Peace Prize in 1991.

Kachin truce. On October 2, Khin Nyunt, chief of the secret police, announced a cease-fire with the Kachins. They are an ethnic group living along Burma's northern border with China.   □ Henry S. Bradsher

See also **Asia** (Facts in brief table). In *World Book,* see **Burma.**

Burundi. See Africa.

Bus. See Transportation.

Business. See Bank; Economics; Manufacturing.

Cabinet, U.S. President Bill Clinton in 1993 assembled one of the most diverse Cabinets in United States history. His major appointees were approved by the Senate early in the year without serious opposition, except for one: attorney general.

Clinton stumbled badly in his efforts to name the first woman attorney general. His first nominee was Zoë Baird, a senior vice president of Aetna Life and Casualty Company of Hartford, Conn. But her nomination ran into trouble when she acknowledged that she had hired an illegal-alien couple from Peru as household help in 1990, violating an immigration law barring the employment of persons who are in the United States unlawfully. In addition, Baird and her husband did not pay the required social security taxes for the couple until shortly after her nomination. Facing growing opposition, Clinton withdrew the nomination, at Baird's request, on January 22.

The President's second choice, federal Judge Kimba M. Wood, withdrew her name on February 5 when it was disclosed that she, too, had employed an illegal alien—a woman from Trinidad whom she had hired to care for her infant son. Because Wood had hired the woman months before the 1986 statute was enacted, she had not actually broken the law. But the White House felt the circumstances too closely resembled the Baird case.

Clinton finally picked a winning candidate with his nomination of veteran Miami, Fla., prosecutor

President Bill Clinton and Vice President Albert Gore, Jr., escort attorney general nominee Janet Reno to a White House news conference in February.

Janet Reno. Reno not only broke the gender barrier at the Department of Justice but also proved to be one of the most popular members of Clinton's Cabinet. She was confirmed unanimously on March 11.

Striving for diversity. Carrying out his pledge to make the heads of government departments "look more like America," Clinton included four blacks, three women, and two Hispanics in his Cabinet. The President also gave an unprecedented role to his wife, Hillary Rodham Clinton, as the unpaid head of a Task Force on National Health Care Reform. The Cabinet in 1993 had the following members: Les Aspin, Jr., secretary of defense; Bruce Babbitt, secretary of the interior; Lloyd M. Bentsen, Jr., secretary of the treasury; Jesse Brown, secretary of veterans affairs; Ronald H. Brown, secretary of commerce; Warren M. Christopher, secretary of state; Henry G. Cisneros, secretary of housing and urban development; Mike Espy, secretary of agriculture; Hazel R. O'Leary, secretary of energy; Federico F. Peña, secretary of transportation; Robert B. Reich, secretary of labor; Janet Reno, attorney general; Richard W. Riley, secretary of education; and Donna E. Shalala, secretary of health and human services.

Controversies. Several Cabinet officers found themselves in the hot seat during the year. Christopher became one of the most heavily criticized Cabinet members because of a widespread perception that he was ineffectual in carrying out U.S. foreign policy. Even Clinton openly declared his unhappiness with him.

Aspin also came under heavy fire. He was criticized particularly for refusing to send reinforcements for U.S. troops stationed in Somalia who later, in October, suffered heavy losses in combat against the forces of rebel leader Mohamed Farah Aideed.

Commerce Secretary Brown ran into a different sort of controversy. In September 1993, it was disclosed that a federal grand jury in Miami was investigating allegations that Brown had accepted at least $700,000 from the government of Vietnam. Vietnam reportedly sought his help in lifting a U.S. economic embargo against the Communist country.

Although Brown denied the charges, a spokesperson for the secretary acknowledged on September 27 that Brown met three times in late 1992 and early 1993 with Nguyen Van Hao, a Vietnamese-born U.S. businessman. Ly Thanh Binh, a former associate of Hao's, had said in August that Hao told him that arrangements were made to funnel payments to Brown through bank accounts in Singapore and Hong Kong. The Clinton Administration did slightly relax the embargo against Vietnam, but Brown said he was not directly involved with that decision. ☐ William J. Eaton

See also biographies of individual Cabinet members. In *World Book,* see **Cabinet.**
California. See **Los Angeles; San Diego; State government.**

Cambodia enthroned Norodom Sihanouk as king on Sept. 24, 1993, under a new Constitution. But Sihanouk's path to a restored constitutional monarchy had been anything but smooth.

Under a 1991 agreement to end Cambodia's 13-year civil war and establish an elected government by mid-1993, the United Nations (UN) created the UN Transitional Authority in Cambodia (UNTAC) to supervise national elections. The elections resulted in a coalition government of Sihanouk's party—the National United Front for an Independent, Neutral, Peaceful, and Cooperative Cambodia (known as FUNCINPEC), led by his son, Prince Norodom Ranariddh—and the Cambodian People's Party (CPP), the party of the Communist government that had been put in power by Vietnamese invaders in 1979. The CPP and FUNCINPEC, along with the rebel Communist Khmer Rouge (KR), had signed the 1991 agreement to end the civil war, but the KR and the CPP continued to fight for control of the country in 1993.

UNTAC woes. The KR refused to cooperate with UNTAC efforts to reduce the armed forces of all factions, a stipulation of the 1991 agreement. In January 1993, the KR launched attacks against government forces and ethnic Vietnamese living in Cambodia. The KR also killed 12 UNTAC workers from Bulgaria, Japan, the Philippines, and other nations. On April 13, the KR withdrew its officials from the capital, Phnom Penh, and boycotted the May elections, fearing a CPP victory.

Meanwhile, CPP government forces launched attacks against KR-held areas, claiming that UNTAC had failed to prevent the KR from wresting control over more territory. CPP forces attacked FUNCINPEC political workers as well. Violence intensified as the election date neared, with the CPP also fearing an election loss unless it intimidated voters.

UNTAC failed to carry out a provision of the 1991 agreement calling for it to take control of civil administration from the CPP. CPP leaders held rallies, telling crowds that ballots would not be secret and that anyone caught voting for a party other than the CPP would lose their jobs and their homes.

The election proceeded anyway. Out of more than 4.7 million voters registered by UNTAC—virtually everyone who was eligible—more than 4.2 million ballots were cast. FUNCINPEC, campaigning primarily on the Cambodian people's long-standing respect for Sihanouk, won 58 seats in the 120-seat Constituent Assembly. The CPP won 51 seats, and minor parties won 11 seats.

Results defied. The CPP was unwilling to accept its defeat. Prince Norodom Chakrapong, another son of Sihanouk's who was a deputy prime minister in the CPP government, and other CPP leaders tried to set up a secessionist regime in seven provinces along the Vietnamese border. But Vietnam refused to back them, and the secessionist moves faded. Chakrapong later received amnesty from Sihanouk.

The elected representatives convened on June 14 to begin work on a new constitution. They proclaimed the 70-year-old Sihanouk head of state. However, he said that because of poor health he would not try to run the country. On June 18, Ranariddh and the former prime minister of the CPP regime, Hun Sen, agreed to serve as copremiers in an interim government.

New government. On September 21, the Constituent Assembly ratified a new Constitution that restored monarchy to Cambodia. On September 24, Sihanouk was enthroned as king, and he immediately named Ranariddh as first premier and Hun Sen as second premier.

Sihanouk became king for the first time in 1941 at the age of 19. But after leading the country to independence from France, he abdicated in 1955 in favor of his father, Norodom Suramarit. At his father's death in 1960, Sihanouk was elected head of state, and he abolished the monarchy. He remained Cambodia's political leader until 1970, when he was ousted by a United States-supported coup.

UNTAC head Yasushi Akashi of Japan left Cambodia on Sept. 26, 1993, ending the UN's largest peacekeeping operation ever, involving 22,000 personnel. But at least 8,000 KR fighters remained a threat to national peace.   □ Henry S. Bradsher

See also **Asia** (Facts in brief table). In *World Book,* see **Cambodia.**

Cameroon. President Paul Biya found it increasingly difficult in 1993 to maintain Cameroon's reputation as an economically developing, politically stable country. Biya's regime made an outward show of moving toward democracy, but it did everything it could to hold onto power. Meanwhile, because of government mismanagement and corruption, the economy sank into depression.

Cameroon has problems common to many African countries, most importantly a weak economy based largely on a few major commodities and a multiethnic population with few common interests. The nation also suffers from having been under the control of two colonial powers, France and the United Kingdom, during much of the 1900's, which left Cameroon with a dual linguistic and cultural inheritance making it difficult to achieve political unity. Although pressures for democracy have been strong, the democracy movement has been complicated by strained relations between *Anglophones* and *Francophones*—inhabitants of areas that were once under the rule of the British or the French, respectively.

Election results protested. Biya's opponents in 1993 denounced an October 1992 presidential election that was widely perceived as fraudulent. In spite of evidence that the Social Democratic Front's candidate, John Fru Ndi, was the victor, Biya—candidate of the Cameroon People's Democratic Movement—was declared the winner.

On March 15, 1993, Fru Ndi called for a national boycott of all French products, claiming that it was France that provided the support to keep Biya, a Francophone, in power. Several people were killed in the northwest city of Bamenda on March 23 during clashes between Fru Ndi's supporters and the army as Biya took measures to stifle protest.

Drafting a new constitution. In response to Biya's actions, the United States and several other countries suspended aid to Cameroon. Biya subsequently agreed to a new constitution—but only on his terms. On May 18, his Technical Committee on the Constitution released a draft calling for a strong central government. A few days later, a prodemocracy group, the All Anglophone Conference, released its draft of a new constitution. It included provisions for a decentralized government with independent judicial and legislative branches, a system of checks and balances to prevent a concentration of power, and strong protection for human rights.

Most of Cameroon's Anglophones, along with a large part of the Francophone population, supported the Anglophone constitution. Other Francophones, out of loyalty to Biya, opposed it. But even many of those loyalists were in favor of democracy and human rights. At year-end, the debate continued, with Biya still in power.   □ Mark DeLancey

See also **Africa** (Facts in brief table). In *World Book,* see **Cameroon.**

Campbell, Kim (1947-   ), became Canada's first woman prime minister on June 25, 1993, after being elected leader of the ruling Progressive Conservative Party on June 13. But in parliamentary elections on October 25, Canadians overwhelmingly favored the Liberal Party, whose leader, Jean Chrétien, then became prime minister.

Campbell was born on March 10, 1947, in Port Alberni, British Columbia. She attended the University of British Columbia, receiving a bachelor's degree in 1969 and a law degree in 1983. She lectured in political science from 1975 to 1981.

Campbell worked as a litigator for a brief time in the mid-1980's. Her political career began in 1981, when she was elected to the Vancouver School Board. In 1985, she was named executive director for the office of British Columbia Premier Bill Bennett. She went on to win a seat in the province's legislative assembly. In 1988, she was elected to Canada's House of Commons and quickly advanced through several key posts: minister of state for Indian affairs and northern development, minister of justice and attorney general, minister of national defence, and minister of veterans affairs.

At age 12, Campbell shunned her given name of Avril Phaedra and took the nickname Kim. Twice divorced and with no children of her own, she has been characterized as exceptionally intelligent and unafraid of controversy.   □ Lori Fagan

Liberal leader Jean Chrétien runs ahead of the media on October 25, the day his party won a solid majority in Canada's parliamentary elections.

Canada

Canadians chose between two national political parties—both of which were committed to maintaining national unity—in a general election held on Oct. 25, 1993. The voters decisively rejected the Progressive Conservative Party (PC), which had governed the country for nine years, in favor of the rival Liberal Party. Liberal leader Jean Chrétien, 59, a Quebecer noted for his devotion to a unified Canada, became the country's 20th prime minister on November 4.

The PC's humiliating defeat came under a new leader, Kim Campbell, who had succeeded Brian Mulroney as head of the party and prime minister in June. Although Campbell was the first woman to become prime minister in Canada, she had to vacate the post after only 133 days, when the October election swept her government out of office.

Mulroney had announced his retirement on February 24. Although his and the PC's popularity had sunk to levels unprecedented in public opinion polls, Mulroney was confident that the party could regain its former standing under a new leader. Campbell, a 46-year-old lawyer from Vancouver, B.C., who had served as both minister of justice and of national defence in Mulroney's Cabinet, became the immediate favorite to succeed him. She was a relatively new face in national politics and was regarded as a bright woman from the West who appeared responsive to the interests of a younger generation.

Campbell's popularity within the party blossomed so rapidly that more experienced members of the Mulroney Cabinet hesitated to challenge her. Eventually, 34-year-old Quebecer Jean Charest, minister of the environment in Mulroney's Cabinet, opposed her. Although Charest made a strong bid, Campbell won the post on the second ballot at the party convention on June 13. She received the votes of 1,817 delegates to Charest's 1,630 and was sworn in as Canada's 19th prime minister on June 25.

Campbell moved quickly to transform the face of the PC government. She dropped 10 posts from the large Mulroney Cabinet of 35 members by eliminating or merging departments. She retained 18 members from her predecessor's Cabinet and brought in 7 newcomers. Her platform for the future embodied most of the policies of the Mulroney years, but she pledged a more accountable approach to the operations of government. She emphasized the seriousness of the federal deficit, running at about $35.5-billion a year (all monetary figures are in Canadian dollars), and pledged to eliminate it in five years without increasing taxes. But the PC emphasis on the role of private business in spurring the sluggish economy offered little encouragement to the voters.

PC ousted. The results of the October election proved disastrous for the PC. The 152 seats the PC had held in the 295-seat House of Commons were reduced to 2 after the election. One was retained by Jean Charest, the other by a candidate running for the first time in New Brunswick. The PC captured only 16 percent of the popular vote compared with the 43 percent they had won in the last general election, held in 1988.

The PC's overwhelming defeat—the worst for any governing party in Canada's history—was attributed not only to a platform lacking appeal but also to an inept campaign by Campbell. Her remarks that she did not have enough time to discuss serious issues during her campaign called her political judgment into question. But she also entered the campaign burdened by her party's unpopularity and difficult economic times.

The Liberals return again. The Liberal Party, which governed Canada for much of this century, saw renewed opportunity in 1993. It campaigned under an experienced leader, Chrétien, who had first entered the House of Commons in 1963 and had held several senior Cabinet posts under three Liberal prime ministers. Chrétien criticized the PC's free market approach to the country's economic problems, claiming that government intervention was necessary to stimulate economic growth. Chrétien promised to reduce the deficit, and he attacked the Mulroney government's goods-and-services tax as well as some components of the controversial free trade agreement with the United States and Mexico. Throughout his campaign, Chrétien stressed the overriding importance of creating jobs—a popular message in a country where about 1.6 million people were unemployed.

The election brought the Liberals a solid majority win, increasing their seats in the House from 79 to 177. The Liberals took 41 percent of the vote, up from 32 percent in 1988. The Liberals swept Eastern Canada, except for Quebec, and made a good showing in the West. They captured all 32 seats in the four provinces of Atlantic Canada, won 19 of Quebec's 75 seats, and took all but 1 of Ontario's 99 seats. In Manitoba, they won 12 of the province's 14 seats and about 20 percent of the seats in the three provinces west of Manitoba.

Reform Party. In 1993, the six-year-old Reform Party broadened its appeal beyond its Western origins. Under its leader from Alberta, Preston Manning, Reformers criticized the Ottawa government for its preoccupation with Quebec issues, its inability to control the deficit, and its sponsorship of the unpopular goods-and-services tax. It also spoke to concerns about immigration and crime. In the West, the Reform Party won 52 seats in the House, 46 of them from Alberta and British Columbia.

Bloc Québécois. The Bloc Québécois, founded in 1990 to promote an independent Quebec, captured 54 of Quebec's 75 seats, a gain of 46 seats. The Bloc branded both the PC's and the Liberals as architects of a system that had failed to respond to the special needs of Quebec. The Bloc, which had proclaimed that, in federal politics, its "first duty is only to Quebec," won virtually all the *ridings* (voting districts) having a French-speaking majority. The Liberal victories in Quebec were in constituencies on the island of Montreal, where the population was English-speaking or contained large groups of Italian or Portuguese minorities.

The New Democratic Party. The New Democratic Party (NDP) was almost wiped from the electoral map in the election. Its 43 members in the House were reduced to 9. Five were from Saskatchewan and the rest were scattered through the other Western provinces and the Yukon Territory. The NDP

share of the popular vote dropped to 7 percent from the 20 percent it had enjoyed in 1988. Although its leader, Audrey M. McLaughlin, won reelection, there was little doubt that much of the party's strength had slipped away to the Liberals.

A fractured House of Commons was the immediate consequence of the election, with a majority national party challenged by two powerful regional ones. The Bloc Québécois was dedicated to promoting Quebec. The Reform Party believed that the government had paid too much attention to Quebec's demands and that Quebec should not receive any special status among the 10 provinces. The new Liberal government thus faced a delicate balancing act in dealing with its opposition in Parliament. As the leader of the party with the second-largest group of members, Lucien Bouchard of the Bloc Québécois assumed the official title of leader of the opposition.

Chrétien's Cabinet reflected the new prime minister's experience and pragmatism. It consisted of only 23 members, most of them with close ties to Chrétien. He appointed Sheila Copps, his deputy during his years in the House, as deputy prime minister and minister of the environment. Paul Martin, a successful Montreal businessman, became finance minister, and Roy MacLaren of Toronto took the position of minister for international trade. Lloyd Axworthy, the most prominent Liberal elected from the West, became minister of human resources. André Ouellet, a Quebec lieutenant, became minister of the renamed department of foreign affairs.

Chrétien established eight new positions known as secretaries of state. Appointments to these posts were not full members of the Cabinet but would be responsible for such areas as multiculturalism, veterans' affairs, and Asian-Pacific relations. The secretaries of state were to report to senior ministers overseeing these areas.

The economy. During the first six months of 1993, Canada slowly emerged from the recession that had started in 1990. During the first quarter, the economy showed an annual growth rate of 3.8 percent. But the rate weakened in later months. By February, the *gross domestic product* (GDP)—the total value of all goods and services produced within a country—had climbed above the level it had reached on the eve of the recession. At the end of June, the GDP, measured on a seasonally adjusted annual basis, was estimated to be $709.2 billion.

The consumer price index in October 1993 revealed a 1.9 percent increase from October 1992. With inflation under control and the dollar stable, the Bank of Canada, which determines the commercial lending rates, dropped its prime rate to 4.79 percent in late June, the lowest level in 20 years.

By March 1993, 40 percent of the 490,000 jobs that had been lost since the beginning of the recession had been regained. But unemployment re-

Canada, provinces, and territories population estimates

	1993 estimates
Alberta	2,662,300
British Columbia	3,535,100
Manitoba	1,116,000
New Brunswick	750,900
Newfoundland	581,100
Northwest Territories	62,900
Nova Scotia	923,000
Ontario	10,746,300
Prince Edward Island	131,600
Quebec	7,208,800
Saskatchewan	1,003,100
Yukon Territory	32,000
Canada	**28,753,100**

City and metropolitan populations

	Metropolitan area 1991 census	City 1991 census
Toronto, Ont.	3,893,046	635,395
Montreal, Que.	3,127,242	1,017,666
Vancouver, B.C.	1,602,502	471,844
Ottawa-Hull	920,857	
Ottawa, Ont.		313,987
Hull, Que.		60,707
Edmonton, Alta.	839,924	616,741
Calgary, Alta.	754,033	710,677
Winnipeg, Man.	652,354	616,790
Quebec, Que.	645,550	167,517
Hamilton, Ont.	599,760	318,499
London, Ont.	381,522	303,165
St. Catharines-Niagara	364,552	
St. Catharines, Ont.		129,300
Niagara Falls, Ont.		75,399
Kitchener, Ont.	356,421	168,282
Halifax, N.S.	320,501	114,455
Victoria, B.C.	287,897	71,228
Windsor, Ont.	262,075	191,435
Oshawa, Ont.	240,104	129,344
Saskatoon, Sask.	210,023	186,058
Regina, Sask.	191,692	179,178
St. John's, Nfld.	171,859	95,770
Chicoutimi-Jonquière	160,928	
Chicoutimi, Que.		62,670
Jonquière, Que.		57,933
Sudbury, Ont.	157,613	92,884
Sherbrooke, Que.	139,194	76,429
Trois-Rivières, Que.	136,303	49,426
Saint John, N.B.	124,981	74,969
Thunder Bay, Ont.	124,427	113,946

Source: Statistics Canada.

mained alarmingly high. In November, nearly 1.6 million Canadians were unemployed, a figure representing 11 percent of the labor force.

The budget. Finance Minister Donald Mazankowski on April 26 presented a preelection, no-risk budget, which contained no new taxes and only marginal decreases in government spending. Actual spending cuts amounted to only $390 million compared with total federal spending of $159.5 billion for fiscal 1993-1994. The deficit was projected at $32.6 billion, about $3 billion lower than the deficit reached in fiscal 1992-1993. However, on Nov. 29, 1993, the new finance minister revised the deficit figure to between $44 billion and $46 billion.

The budget called for phasing out 16,500 public-sector jobs during the next five years. About 500 of these positions would be in the capital, Ottawa. The budget also cut grants to special-interest groups and axed subsidies to the Canadian Broadcasting Corporation and to VIA Rail, the passenger rail network.

Spending for defense would be allowed to grow by only 1.6 percent, or the rate of inflation, each year for the next five years. The government, however, refused to abandon its controversial plan to purchase 50 sophisticated EH-101 helicopters—aircraft that critics said were only justified by outmoded Cold War military thinking. But Campbell, under pressure during her campaign to show some commitment to reduced federal spending, cut seven heli-

Thousands of demonstrators brave the cold in Montreal in February to protest proposed changes to the Unemployment Insurance Act.

Federal spending in Canada
Estimated budget for fiscal 1993-1994*

Ministry (includes the department and all agencies for which a minister reports to Parliament):	Millions of dollars†
Agriculture	2,228
Atlantic Canada Opportunities Agency	327
Communications	
Canadian Broadcasting Corporation	1,090
Canadian Film Development Corporation	132
Other	946
Consumer and corporate affairs	204
Employment and immigration	2,125
Energy, mines, and resources	
Atomic Energy of Canada Limited	176
Other	925
Environment	1,123
External affairs	3,746
Finance	48,796
Fisheries and oceans	956
Forestry	243
Governor general	10
Indian affairs and northern development	4,586
Industry, science, and technology	
Canada Post Corporation	14
Other	2,368
Justice	750
Labour	258
Multiculturalism and citizenship	120
National defence	11,989
National health and welfare	36,739
National revenue	2,380
Parliament	299
Privy Council	172
Public works	
Canada Mortgage and Housing Corporation	2,134
Other	1,836
Secretary of state	3,412
Solicitor general	
Royal Canadian Mounted Police	1,218
Other	1,345
Supply and services	495
Transport	3,011
Treasury Board	1,206
Veterans affairs	2,118
Western economic diversification	290
Total	**139,767**

* April 1, 1993, to March 31, 1994.
† Canadian dollars; $1 = U.S. $1.3213 as of Oct. 29, 1993.

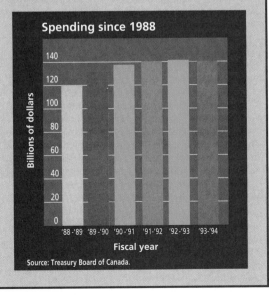

Spending since 1988

Source: Treasury Board of Canada.

Prime Minister Brian Mulroney in February announces plans to resign as Canada's leader and as head of the ruling Progressive Conservative Party.

copters from the order. Then, in November, Chrétien, fulfilling a campaign promise on his first day in office, canceled the entire $4.8-billion order.

International trade. Canadian exports to the United States were brisk in 1993, helped by a slowly recovering U.S. economy, a Canadian dollar that had slipped 12 percent against its U.S. counterpart in the 18 months preceding May, and a more competitive Canadian export sector. Lumber, natural gas, automobiles and parts, and machinery and equipment dominated the range of exports.

Canada, which had played a foremost role in recommending trade sanctions against the white regime in South Africa, lifted its own sanctions on September 24. The decision was made after the South African government approved creation of a Transitional Executive Council to run the country before its first multiracial elections, which were to be held on April 27, 1994. Canada lifted its embargo on trade and investment dealings but retained a ban on the shipment of weapons.

NAFTA. Canada's Parliament on June 23, 1993, ratified the North American Free Trade Agreement (NAFTA) between Canada, the United States, and Mexico. The approval made Canada the first of the three countries to ratify the agreement. Passage, after a stormy debate, came during the final week of Prime Minister Mulroney's term. Mulroney had actively sought the negotiation of NAFTA in 1991.

The Ministry of Canada*

Jean Chrétien—prime minister

Herbert Eser Gray—solicitor general of Canada; leader of the government in the House of Commons

André Ouellet—minister of foreign affairs

Lloyd Axworthy—minister of human resources development; minister of Western economic diversification

David Michael Collenette—minister of national defence; minister of veterans affairs

Roy MacLaren—minister for international trade

David Anderson—minister of national revenue

Ralph E. Goodale—minister of agriculture and agri-food

David Charles Dingwall—minister of public works and government services; minister for the Atlantic Canada Opportunities Agency

Ron Irwin—minister of Indian affairs and Northern development

Brian Tobin—minister of fisheries and oceans

Joyce Fairbairn—leader of the government in the Senate; minister with special responsibility for literacy

Sheila Copps—deputy prime minister; minister of the environment

Sergio Marchi—minister of citizenship and immigration

John Manley—minister of industry

Diane Marleau—minister of health

Paul Martin—minister of finance; minister responsible for the Federal Office of Regional Development-Quebec

Douglas Young—minister of transport

Michel Dupuy—minister of Canadian heritage

Arthur C. Eggleton—president of the Treasury Board; minister responsible for infrastructure

Marcel Massé—president of the Queen's Privy Council for Canada; minister of intergovernmental affairs; minister responsible for public service renewal

Anne McLellan—minister of natural resources

Allan Rock—minister of justice; attorney general of Canada

Sheila Finestone—secretary of state (multicultural) (status of women)

Fernand Robichaud—secretary of state (parliamentary affairs)

Ethel Blondin-Andrew—secretary of state (training and youth)

Lawrence MacAulay—secretary of state (veterans)

Christine Stewart—secretary of state (Latin America and Africa)

Raymond Chan—secretary of state (Asia-Pacific)

Jon Gerrard—secretary of state (science, research, and development)

Douglas Peters—secretary of state (international financial institutions)

*As of Dec. 31, 1993.

Premiers of Canadian provinces

Province	Premier
Alberta	Ralph Klein
British Columbia	Michael Harcourt
Manitoba	Gary A. Filmon
New Brunswick	Frank J. McKenna
Newfoundland	Clyde K. Wells
Nova Scotia	John Savage
Ontario	Robert K. Rae
Prince Edward Island	Catherine Callbeck
Quebec	Robert Bourassa
Saskatchewan	Roy Romanow

Government leaders of territories

Northwest Territories	Nellie Cournoyea
Yukon Territory	John Ostashek

Canadian diplomats took part in negotiating side agreements regarding the enforcement of labor and environmental standards in the agreement. The United States wished to see trade sanctions employed in the event that such standards were violated. But Canada gained endorsement for a process whereby the Federal Court of Canada could compel Canadian parties who violated the standards to pay any fines that might be levied against them. Mexico and the United States, on the other hand, agreed to follow the route of trade sanctions if the side agreements were not observed.

Canadian implementation of NAFTA depended upon the cooperation of the provinces, some of which were opposed to the trade agreement. Chrétien also voiced skepticism about NAFTA during his campaign for prime minister. And after being elected, Chrétien said he wanted changes in the pact but in December agreed to enact it on Jan. 1, 1994.

Olympia & York Developments Limited, the real estate empire created by the Reichmann family, was formally dismantled by court decision on February 5. The Reichmanns' new responsibilities were to manage for their creditors commercial properties the Reichmanns had once owned. The only part of the family empire left to them was a Toronto floor and wall tile company, which had been their first business enterprise.

Peacekeeping operations remained a major theme of Canada's foreign relations in 1993. In February, Canada transferred to Bosnia-Herzegovina 1,200 troops that had been in Croatia since March 1992. The troops were to escort food and medical supplies past Serbian lines to Muslim communities.

In January 1993, the Canadian Air Force withdrew its last jet fighters from their NATO base at Baden-Solingen in southern Germany. The force had been in Western Europe since 1953. The remaining principal Canadian military base at Lahr, Germany, was scheduled to close in 1994.

Canadian troops left Cyprus in June 1993 after 29 years of patrolling the buffer zone between the Greek and Turkish communities there. Some 515 Canadians were withdrawn, the last of about 35,000 troops who had served in Cyprus during the assignment. In May, the United Nations (UN) had appointed former Foreign Minister Joe Clark, who had retired from the Mulroney Cabinet, to mediate the long-standing hostilities in Cyprus.

Fifty-two members of the Royal Canadian Mounted Police were sent to Haiti in October to help restore to power the island's democratically elected president. But Haiti's military rulers resisted the change, and the officers had to withdraw.

In Somalia, 900 men of the Canadian Airborne Regiment helped to distribute emergency relief and attempted to restore law and order before their withdrawal in June. In April, however, the Canadian military set up an ongoing inquiry into the regi-ment's operations after four Somalis and one Canadian were killed during the mission. Beginning in May, Canada's Department of National Defence brought charges of murder, torture, or negligence against seven members of the regiment. A report in August from the ongoing inquiry revealed long-standing problems of racism and poor discipline in the Airborne Regiment. In September, the leader of the regiment, who had also been charged with negligence, was relieved of his command and reassigned to another post. The findings prompted public concern over the damage the incident brought to Canada's reputation as an experienced peacekeeper.

Superpower summit. Canada played host to the first meeting between U.S. President Bill Clinton and Russian President Boris Yeltsin in Vancouver, B.C., on April 3 and 4. Prior to the meeting, then-Prime Minister Mulroney announced a $200-million aid package to Russia. In addition to the package, new credit terms for Russia made possible the resumption of Canadian grain shipments that had been held up when Russia could not pay for them. The new aid brought Canada's total economic assistance to Russia and Eastern Europe to $2.6 billion since 1989. □ David M. L. Farr

See **International trade: The Debate over NAFTA.** See also the Canadian province and territory articles; **Campbell, Kim; Chrétien, Jean; Montreal; Toronto.** In *World Book,* see **Canada.**

Canadian literature.

Canadian literature. After Kim Campbell replaced Brian Mulroney as prime minister of Canada on June 25, 1993, a stampede of books on Canada's first woman leader hit the bookstores. The most substantial was Robert Fife's *Kim Campbell: The Making of a Politician.* The cleverest was Frank Davey's *Reading "Kim" Right.* But the most popular book regarding a political figure was *Memoirs* by former Prime Minister Pierre Elliott Trudeau. Although Trudeau has been out of office since 1984, his influence is still powerful among Canadians.

Other significant biographies included Farley Mowat's childhood memoir, *Born Naked.* The tale of family, boats, and animals identified the naturalist-humorist's inspiration. An autobiography, *Conrad Black: A Life in Progress,* offered a candid, provocative look at the outspoken newspaper czar.

A book of correspondence, *Margaret Laurence— Al Purdy: A Friendship in Letters* revealed the relationship between the late novelist (Laurence) and the poet. *Love and Duty,* newly discovered letters between novelist and poet Susanna Moodie and her husband, John, further enlivened and illuminated Canada's literary history.

The social and the political. During the year, there were a number of postmortems on the decline of the nation during the Mulroney era. Among them were Linda McQuaig's *The Wealthy Banker's Wife,* on the welfare system, and Wayne Skene's *Fade to*

113

David Adams Richards won critical acclaim for his 1993 book *For Those Who Hunt the Wounded Down,* the last in a trilogy.

Black, on the demise of public broadcasting. In *Systems of Survival,* Jane Jacobs imagined a symposium between five intellectuals on the distinct moralities of politics and commerce.

"Men's books." Works by and about men continued to claim attention in 1993. *Cracking the Armour* by sociologist Michael Kaufman, *Man Overboard* by journalist and broadcaster Ian Brown, and *From Here to Paternity* by Jay Teitel explored masculinity and the changing role of fathers.

Other nonfiction. The three-volume *Historical Atlas of Canada* was completed with the publication of Volume II (Volume III had already appeared). Subtitled *The Land Transformed, 1800-1891,* this volume made use of computer-generated rather than hand-drawn cartography.

Several books on Canadian dinosaur hunters appeared after the release of the motion picture *Jurassic Park. Dinosaur Hunters,* by David Spalding, was a "who's who" of dinosaur hunters past and present, and *The Dinosaur Project,* by Wayne Grady, discussed a joint project between paleontologists in Canada and China.

In travel writing, Ronald Wright's *Home and Away* followed its author's progress around the globe. Tim Ward's *The Great Dragon's Fleas* presented a spiritual pilgrimage through Asia that included old stories alleging that Jesus Christ had lived out his days in Kashmir.

Fiction. A big, new novel by Margaret Atwood, *The Robber Bride,* dominated the fiction scene with its sharp-tongued tale of four Toronto women. But nominations for the United Kingdom's prestigious Booker Prize gave deserved recognition to two other fine novels. Carol Shields's *The Stone Diaries* created a "biography" of the fictional Daisy Flett, from her birth on the Canadian prairies to her death in Florida. And Michael Ignatieff's *Scar Tissue* was a powerful semiautobiographical novel of a family destroyed by Alzheimer's disease.

Timothy Findley's novel *Headhunter* was a dark, monumental expedition into evil, with a setting modeled after Toronto's Clarke Institute of Psychiatry. Two sometime-Canadians, Brian Moore and Bharati Mukherjee, each published new novels. Moore's *No Other Life* placed a Quebec missionary on a Haiti-like island. Mukherjee's *The Holder of the World* was a scholarly detective thriller set in colonial Massachusetts and India.

Comebacks. Several well-respected Canadian authors broke lengthy silences in 1993. *Gentleman Death,* Graeme Gibson's novel about a writer having trouble writing, was his first publication since *Perpetual Motion* in 1982. Sarah Sheard's *The Swing Era* followed by about eight years her acclaimed first novel, *Almost Japanese.* Isabel Huggan's *You May Never Know* gave fans of her earlier *Elizabeth Stories* 12 new tales of a grown-up version of the character Elizabeth.

Other notable new fiction included the novels *Graven Images* by Audrey Thomas; *For Those Who Hunt the Wounded Down* by David Adams Richards; *The Bookseller* by Matt Cohen; and *The Wives of Bath* by Susan Swan.

Jane Urquhart was widely praised for *Away,* a lyrical, passionate novel about an Irish immigrant family on the shores of Lake Ontario. Native writer Thomas King's *Green Grass, Running Water* also garnered respect for its rich revisionist history of North America. Nino Ricci's *In a Glass House* continued the trilogy brilliantly begun with *Lives of the Saints.*

Works from new writers included Yann Martel's *The Facts Behind the Helsinki Roccamatios and Other Stories,* the title story of which had won the 1991 Journey Prize, which was established by James Michener for the year's best short story. Caroline Adderson's first book, *Bad Imaginings,* included intense depictions of children, a prospector in the 1800's, and a Victorian chambermaid.

Poetry. In Don Coles's *Forests of the Medieval World,* poems on the themes of a lost love paralleled poems on the razed forests of Europe. In Patricia Young's *More Watery Still,* poems about growing up, love, and parenthood showcased the author's increasing mastery of the genre.

Children's books. Stories for young people emphasized children living on the fringes of life. In James Houston's *Drifting Snow,* an Inuit girl taken from her parents returns home years later. Carol Matas' *Daniel's Story* followed the devastated life of a Jewish child at Auschwitz.

Awards. Winners of 1993 Governor-General's Literary Awards for books in English included Carol Shields for *The Stone Diaries* (fiction); Don Coles for *Forest of the Medieval World* (poetry); Guillermo Verdecchia for *Fronteras Americans* (drama); Karen Connelly for *Touch the Dragon* (nonfiction); Tim Wynne-Jones for *Some of the Kinder Planets* (children's literature—text); Mireille Levert for *Sleep Tight, Mrs. Ming* (children's literature—illustration); and D. G. Jones for *Categories One, Two, Three* by Normand de Bellefeuille (translation).

Winners in the French language category were Daniel Danis for *Celle-la* (drama); Nancy Huston for *Cantique des plaines* (fiction); Denise Desautels for *Le Saut de l'ange* (poetry); Francois Para for *Literatures d'exiquite* (nonfiction); Michele Marineau for *La Route de Chlifa* (children's literature—text); Stephanie Jorisch for *Le Monde selon Jean de . . .* (children's literature—illustration); and Marie José Thériault for *L'Oeuvre de Gallois* (translation), the French version of *Wales' Work* by Robert Walshe.

The 1992 Smith Books/Books in Canada First Novel Award went to John Steffler for *The Afterlife of George Cartwright.* □ Maureen Garvie

In *World Book,* see **Canadian literature.**

Cape Verde. See Africa.

Census.
In 1993, the United States Bureau of the Census projected that by the year 2050, whites will represent 52.5 percent of the U.S. population, down sharply from 75.7 percent in 1990. The figures were released by the Census Bureau on Sept. 28, 1993.

The bureau said the biggest reason for the decline in the white population will be much greater growth among Hispanics. The bureau projected that after 1996, the Hispanic population will grow by more than 870,000 people a year. Two-thirds of the increase will come from births and one-third from immigration. According to the bureau, Hispanics in 2050 will represent 22.5 percent of the U.S. population, up from 9 percent in 1990. The proportion of blacks will rise from 11.8 percent to 14.4 percent; the proportion of Asians and Pacific islanders, from 2.8 percent to 9.7 percent; and the proportion of American Indians, from 0.7 percent to 0.9 percent.

Population boom. Also in its September report, the Census Bureau said the U.S. population was increasing even faster than the agency had calculated just nine months earlier. The bureau's latest estimate for the year 2050 was 392 million people, up from a projection of 383 million people in December 1992.

Census revision. The Census Bureau on March 1, 1993, produced a revised population figure for the United States of 257 million people. After the 1990 census, the agency had announced a population of 249 million people. The bureau's new figure included an adjustment for the millions of people, particularly minorities living in the inner cities, that some studies indicated had been missed in the 1990 count.

Social changes slow. The Census Bureau on July 23, 1993, reported that the pace of many social changes that swept through America in the 1970's and 1980's was slackening. Among the findings:

▪ The explosion of the divorce rate in the 1970's has stabilized. The Census Bureau now estimates that only 4 in 10 marriages will end in divorce, down from previous projections of 5 in 10.

▪ The number of single-parent families created by births to unwed mothers is still rising but at far below the 15 percent annual rate of the 1970's. The rate of increase in 1993 was about 8 percent.

▪ Family size is no longer shrinking. The average number of children per household has remained roughly constant since 1989 after declining for about 20 years. The figure stood at 0.69 children in 1992, down from 1.09 children in 1970.

Experts attributed these changes to the aging of the population, the sluggish economy, and the life styles of recent immigrants.

□ Frank Cormier and Margot Cormier

See also **City; Population.** In *World Book,* see **Census; Population.**

Central African Republic. See Africa.
Chad. See Africa.

Chavis, Benjamin F., Jr.
(1948-), became executive director of the National Association for the Advancement of Colored People (NAACP) on April 9, 1993. He succeeded Benjamin L. Hooks, who retired after heading the organization since 1977.

Chavis was born in Oxford, N.C., on Jan. 22, 1948. In the 1960's, he was active in several civil rights organizations, including the NAACP and the Southern Christian Leadership Conference. Chavis gained national attention in 1972 as one of the "Wilmington 10," a group of civil rights activists wrongly convicted of fire-bombing a grocery store in Wilmington, N.C., during racial disturbances the year before. The group appealed the conviction up to the Supreme Court of the United States, which refused in 1976 to hear the case. Chavis spent more than four years in prison before a federal appeals court overturned the conviction in 1980, after key prosecution witnesses said they had lied under pressure from police.

Chavis received a B.A. in chemistry from the University of North Carolina at Charlotte in 1970. He earned a master of divinity degree from Duke University in Durham, N.C., in 1980 and a doctor of ministry degree from Howard University in Washington, D.C., in 1981. He was ordained a minister of the United Church of Christ in 1980. Chavis became deputy director of the church's Commission for Racial Justice in 1981 and executive director in 1986. Chavis is married and has six children. □ Meira Ben-Gad

Chemistry. Two chemists surprised the scientific world in June 1993 when they reported they had produced diamondlike carbon by baking a liquid in an oven at a relatively low temperature and at atmospheric pressure. Previously, synthetic diamond was created by subjecting graphite, the form of carbon found in coal, to pressures of 1 million pounds per square inch (70,000 kilograms per square centimeter) and to the relatively high temperature of 2500 °F (1400 °C).

Easy-bake diamonds. Chemists Patricia A. Bianconi and Glenn T. Visscher of Pennsylvania State University in University Park discovered the new diamond-making process while trying to develop better ceramics for microelectronic devices. The scientists were working with silicon and germanium compounds in the form of special *polymers* (large molecules made up of smaller molecules that are identical to each other). The smaller molecules of most polymers are linked together in a chain, but special polymers contain densely knitted links. Out of curiosity, Bianconi and Visscher tried to create a similar polymer using carbon-based compounds. To their surprise, they succeeded, ending up with a special polymer in the form of a tan powder.

The chemists dissolved this powder and heated it to between 390 and 750 °F (200 and 400 °C). The result was an extremely hard, diamondlike solid. When this solid was heated to 1000 °F (540 °C), two-thirds of it was converted to pure diamond crystals.

The unusual shape of the polymer excited chemists, and the method of creating the diamond intrigued engineers. Experts see many potential practical applications of the discovery. Everyday products, such as eyeglasses, could be endowed with diamond-hard scratch-resistant coatings, for example.

Oil from waste plastic. A promising method for turning waste plastics into a high-grade fuel oil was announced in August by fuel chemist M. Mehdi Taghiei and his colleagues at the University of Kentucky in Lexington. The ability to produce such a product could create an incentive to recycle more waste plastic, reducing the amount that is disposed of in landfills. Currently, less than 4 percent of the waste plastic produced in the United States is recycled, in part because recycled plastic tends to cost more and look worse than new plastic.

The Kentucky scientists treated plastics from soda bottles, milk jugs, and other common items by heating them, adding *catalysts* (materials that speed up chemical reactions without themselves being changed), and applying hydrogen at high pressure. The process converted more than 80 percent of the plastic compounds into a clean, high-quality oil. Adding coal to the plastic in a half-and-half mixture produced a fuel that burned even better.

The cost of the plastics-derived oil was about 50 percent higher than the cost of imported oil, but experts said that improvements in the manufacturing process could make the costs comparable in 5 to 10 years. According to estimates based on Americans' current use of plastic products, the United States is capable of producing 80 million barrels of plastics-derived oil each year.

Bone marrow bioreactor. A shortage of donors has limited the use of bone marrow transplants as a treatment for leukemia and other diseases. But a new process for growing bone marrow tissue in the laboratory holds the potential to solve that problem, according to a March report by chemical engineer J. H. David Wu of the University of Rochester in New York. Bone marrow produces the various types of blood cells that fight disease, transport oxygen, and perform other vital functions. Although other human cells can be grown in a laboratory, scientists had been unable to reproduce the mixture of cells that make up blood in a laboratory flask.

Wu and his colleagues first embedded marrow in a small plastic shell filled with *collagen* (a spongy protein found in marrow). Then they circulated fluid through the shell to provide nutrients and oxygen and remove waste products. This setup, a so-called "bioreactor," kept immature blood cells closely packed and allowed biological compounds called growth factors to build up around the growing cells. Because the bioreactor thus allowed immature cells to develop under conditions that were much closer to those found inside bone, a wide variety of cells were produced.

Cool Starlite. In July, scientists released promising results from tests of a new heat-resistant material called Starlite. According to its creator, the new material consists mostly of plastic but also contains inorganic additives, including ceramics.

Scientists at the Atomic Weapons Establishment in Foulness, England, and at the White Sands Missile Range in New Mexico each subjected Starlite to temperatures of up to 18,000 °F (10,000 °C), the equivalent of a nuclear blast. The material withstood both tests. By comparison, tungsten metal is vaporized at 6200 °F (3400 °C). In previous testing, a 0.125-inch- (0.3-centimeter) thick sample of Starlite stood up to a torch capable of cutting through a slab of aluminum 1 inch (2.5 centimeters) thick.

Starlite's creator is Maurice Ward of Hartlepool, England, a businessman with no formal training in chemistry who was trying to develop a material that could be exposed to the flames of an airline crash without producing toxic fumes. Starlite chars slowly, emitting virtually no smoke. It can slough off heat so effectively that when one side was blasted for five minutes with a blowtorch, the other side remained cool enough to touch.

Possible applications for the new material include insulation, heat shields for missiles, protective covering for fire fighters, and fire-retardant materials for airplanes, tanks, and even homes.   □ Peter J. Andrews

In *World Book,* see **Chemistry.**

Chess. Two world championship matches made 1993 a unique year in the history of chess. On January 30, Nigel Short of the United Kingdom defeated Jan Timman of the Netherlands to earn the right to challenge world champion Garry Kasparov of Russia in a match set up by the International Chess Federation (FIDE). But on February 26, Kasparov and Short announced they were breaking away from FIDE and holding their match under a new organization they had formed, the Professional Chess Association (PCA). The two were angry, alleging that FIDE had not consulted them about the location and prize money for the original match. In retaliation, FIDE removed them from its official ranking list and replaced them in its championship match with the two players who had lost to Short in the qualifying rounds, Timman and Anatoly Karpov of Russia.

The FIDE championship started on September 6 in Zwolle, the Netherlands, then moved to Jakarta, Indonesia, after the 12th game. In that match, Karpov beat Timman, 12½ games to 8½. The PCA championship opened on September 7 in London. In that match, Kasparov beat Short, 12½ games to 7½.

Challenger qualifiers. In July and August in Biel, Switzerland, Gata Kamsky of New York City and Michael Adams of the United Kingdom qualified for FIDE's candidates' cycle, the series of elimination matches to determine the challenger for the FIDE title in 1996.

Tournaments. On June 13, 1993, four players—Kamsky; Maxim Dlugy of Englewood, N.J.; Sergey Kudrin of Stamford, Conn.; and Alex Yermolinsky of Highland Park, N.J.—tied for first place at the United States National Open held in Las Vegas, Nev. On July 5, Yermolinsky won the World Open held in Philadelphia. On August 15, Alexander Shabalov of Pittsburgh, Pa., won the U.S. Open held in Philadelphia. On November 2, the United States won the gold medal, Ukraine won the silver, and Russia won the bronze at the World Team Championship held in Lucerne, Switzerland.

Women players. On February 14, Judit Polgar of Hungary defeated former world champion Boris Spassky of France in a 10-game exhibition match in Budapest, Hungary. On August 31, Elena Donaldson of Seattle and Irina Levitina of Teaneck, N.J., tied for the U.S. Women's Championship held in Bloomington, Ill. On November 17, women's world champion Xie Jun of China retained her title by beating Nana Ioseliani of Georgia by the score of 8½ games to 2½ in a match held in Monte Carlo, Monaco.

School winners. In April, Dalton School of New York City won the national elementary school championship held in Charlotte, N.C., and the national junior high school championship held in Chicago. Also in April, Edward R. Murrow High School of New York City won the national high school championship held in Dallas. □ Al Lawrence

In *World Book,* see **Chess.**

Chicago. Chicagoans were stunned on Oct. 6, 1993, when Chicago Bulls superstar Michael Jordan announced his retirement from professional basketball. In explaining his decision, the 30-year-old Jordan said, "I just don't have anything else to prove [in basketball]." He said his retirement was not related to the death of his father, James Jordan, who was murdered on July 23 while traveling in North Carolina. On June 20, Jordan had led the Bulls to their third consecutive National Basketball Association (NBA) title. (See **Basketball.**)

As in previous years, the Bulls' NBA victory was marred by violent celebrations by fans. The disturbances resulted in three shooting deaths.

Sox pennant hopes foiled. On September 27, the Chicago White Sox defeated the Seattle Mariners to clinch the American League West Division baseball championship. But the team came up short in the league play-off series against the Toronto Blue Jays, losing in 6 games. (See **Baseball.**)

Schools. The Chicago Board of Education shut down the city's entire school system on August 30 because of a $300-million gap in the system's budget. On September 13, a federal judge granted the school board a temporary reprieve from a state requirement for a balanced budget, allowing the schools to open, though a week late.

On October 9, the teachers union and the school board reached a tentative settlement in their contract talks. The federal judge gave the state legislature until November 15 to approve the settlement or come up with its own funding plan. On November 14, the legislature passed a different measure that will keep the schools open through the end of 1995.

On June 25, the Chicago Board of Education hired Argie K. Johnson, a deputy commissioner of the New York City school system, as the new superintendent of the Chicago public schools. She replaced Ted S. Kimbrough.

Riverboat casinos. On June 2, Mayor Richard M. Daley proposed the construction of an $800-million downtown entertainment complex, featuring five riverboat gambling casinos and a theme park along the Chicago River. Originally, Daley had pushed for a $2-billion land-based casino complex, but that idea ran into opposition from Illinois Governor Jim Edgar. The riverboat scheme did not get much further. Daley was unable to garner enough political support in 1993 to win state approval for the plan.

Public housing. On February 5, Vincent Lane, chairman of the Chicago Housing Authority, announced plans to transform the Cabrini-Green public housing development from an isolated enclave of poverty and crime into "a normal neighborhood." He said the effort would also include other trouble-plagued public housing developments. On October 13, United States government officials said the city would receive a $50-million federal grant for the project.

Residents of the Paxton Hotel in Chicago rest on the sidewalk on March 16 after escaping a fire that killed 19 tenants of the low-income hotel.

Crime and corruption. Statistics from the Federal Bureau of Investigation in 1993 showed that Chicago was the fourth most violent major U.S. city in 1992. Its rate of violent crime—murders, rapes, robberies, and serious assaults—was 30.3 incidents per 1,000 residents, four times the national average.

The bodies of seven employees of a fast-food restaurant in suburban Palatine were found on January 9 in two walk-in coolers at the restaurant. Each of the victims had been shot, apparently during a robbery the night before.

A two-decade-long federal effort to root out official corruption in Chicago netted its highest-ranking catch on April 5 when Walter Kozubowski, the city clerk for 14 years, pleaded guilty to mail fraud, bank fraud, and tax evasion. Kozubowski had run a "ghost" payroll operation at City Hall that cost Chicago taxpayers a total of more than $480,000 in salaries for city employees who were paid for doing nothing. In return, the employees gave part of the money to Kozubowski.

Fire tragedy. Fire swept through the Paxton Hotel, a single-room-occupancy hotel in the city's Near North Side area, on March 16, killing 19 tenants and injuring 31 other people. It was the greatest loss of life in a Chicago fire since a 1981 blaze in a similar building also killed 19. □ Patrick T. Reardon

See also **City.** In *World Book,* see **Chicago.**

Children's books. See **Literature for children.**

Chile. Senator Eduardo Frei Ruíz Tagle, son of a popular former Chilean president, was elected president of Chile on Dec. 11, 1993. Frei represented the Coalition for Democracy, Chile's five-party ruling coalition. Chileans gave Frei 58 percent of the vote, compared with 24 percent for his principal opponent Arturo Alessandri. Alessandri on August 8 had won the nomination of the right wing Union for Chilean Progress Party.

Through June 1993, Chile exported more goods to the United States than to Japan for the first time in nearly two years. Most exports of minerals, lumber, fish, and agricultural products, however, continued to go to Japan during 1993.

Japanese companies, in developing trade with Chile, have invested more than $700 million there since civilian rule was restored in 1990. For example, the Sumitomo Metal Mining Company of Japan has joined a U.S. mining company to invest $1.5 billion in a giant copper and gold mine near Copiapó.

Justice. A Chilean court sentenced two former Chilean generals—Manuel Contreras and Pedro Espinoza—on Nov. 12, 1993, to six and seven years in prison, respectively, for ordering the assassination of opposition leader Orlando Letelier. Letelier was killed by a car bomb in Washington, D.C., in 1976.

□ Nathan A. Haverstock

See also **Latin America** (Facts in brief table). In *World Book,* see **Chile.**

China in 1993 confronted world opinion that opposed the Chinese government's handling of several volatile issues, including a nuclear weapons test, human rights issues, and weapons sales to Pakistan. China's government also faced domestic opposition as it tried to solve problems stemming from an economic boom that brought prosperity to some regions and left others desperately poor.

There was political uncertainty as the health of China's aging leader Deng Xiaoping waned. At the age of 89, Deng held no official position, but he was still in control of the country. Policy statements on the 44th anniversary of the People's Republic of China, celebrated on October 1, endorsed Deng's policy of rapid economic development based on greater reliance on markets rather than on state controls.

However, conservative leaders continued to criticize the policy. And a leading conservative, 64-year-old Premier Li Peng, disappeared from public view from April 24 until June 14. He reportedly was recovering from a heart attack. During his absence, his work was handled by a deputy and political rival, Zhu Rongji, an economic liberal.

New president. On March 27, the National People's Congress (NPC), China's parliament, elected Jiang Zemin, 67 years old, to succeed Yang Shangkun, 85, as president of China. Jiang already held the posts of general secretary of the Communist Party and chairman of the Central Military Commission. With the presidency, Jiang held the country's three top jobs. Nevertheless, he was not considered to have a strong political base or the leadership skills necessary to succeed Deng. (See **Jiang Zemin.**)

The NPC reelected Li to a five-year term as premier. Although Li was widely disliked, he ran unopposed. However, in an unusual show of displeasure with Li, nearly 11 percent—210 legislators—of the 2,903 NPC delegates who voted did not approve the reelection. Another 120 delegates abstained.

Economic growing pains. The main focus of politics in 1993 was economic policy. In 1992, China's economy had grown nearly 13 percent, the fastest rate in the world. And in July 1993, China's State Statistical Bureau (SSB) reported that growth for the first half of the year had reached nearly 14 percent. Many of China's 1.2 billion people began to live better, though many others tried to immigrate illegally to the United States or Taiwan. But new economic opportunities also led to corruption. For example, three young bookkeepers and five others were executed on September 27 for embezzlement and graft.

China's many new factories created shortages in electrical power. Transportation became inadequate to move increasing amounts of goods from manufacturer to consumer.

Rapid growth also brought a rising inflation rate. Official Chinese figures put inflation at 6.4 percent for all of 1992. By mid-1993, inflation reached 14 percent, but often higher in urban areas, according

to the SSB. Therefore, on June 3, the government announced an austerity plan to reduce inflation and eliminate speculation in property and stocks. As a result, some new businesses were forced to cut production for lack of credit to purchase material. But state industries continued to absorb 70 percent of government revenues, wasting most of the money.

Conservatives and liberals in the leadership argued whether inflation or curtailing growth was the greater evil. By October, although inflation rose to more than 22 percent in many cities, the government loosened credit restraints as a wild real estate boom began to subside.

Tax revolts. Corruption and new taxes caused peasant uprisings in nearly a dozen provinces. In Sichuan province on June 3 and June 6, thousands stormed government offices in anger over official extortion linked to roadbuilding fees. Reacting to rural unrest, the government on June 21 abolished 37 taxes on farmers, including education fees. City workers complained of compulsory wage deductions to purchase government bonds, but got no relief.

Nuclear test. On October 5, China exploded a nuclear weapon underground at Lop Nor, the nation's nuclear weapons development center located in a remote western desert. American intelligence reports that a nuclear test was being prepared had been revealed in mid-September. More than 20 nations appealed for China not to break an unofficial worldwide ban on nuclear testing. China rejected the appeals, saying Western nuclear powers had conducted far more tests than China had. Chinese officials said that testing would end only when a comprehensive test-ban treaty restricted all nations.

Olympics bid. Some 12 days prior to the nuclear test, China failed in a three-year campaign to convince the International Olympic Committee (IOC) to name Beijing as the host city for the Summer Olympic Games scheduled for the year 2000. Many foreign observers thought China had delayed the test explosion while seeking the games. Foreign critics also saw China's Olympics campaign as a way of overcoming lingering condemnation for the June 1989 killing of hundreds of prodemocracy demonstrators in Tiananmen Square in Beijing. But on Sept. 23, 1993, the IOC awarded the games to Sydney, Australia, and China became less responsive to international pressure not to conduct nuclear tests.

Human rights issues. Many countries, including the United States, opposed China's hosting the Olympics because of China's poor record on human rights. They said that the games would reward a country that still jailed or exiled those who questioned its Communist system.

A U.S. official visited China in October to resume a dialogue on human rights that China had halted in 1991. But the official reported no progress in the talks. And Amnesty International, a human rights organization, said on April 16, 1993, that the torture

Representatives of Taiwan, left, and China, right, exchange copies of agreements signed in April, after talks at the highest level since 1949.

of prisoners in China had increased in the past 10 years and was "widespread and systematic."

However, during 1993, China released three men who had been leaders of China's first major public protests over the lack of democracy. Wang Xizhe was paroled in late January, Xu Wenli was released in May, and Wei Jingsheng was freed in September. Wei's release just 10 days before the IOC's vote was especially seen as intended to influence the outcome. Wei had become the foremost symbol of the human rights struggle in China.

The government also released Wang Dan, a student leader of the 1989 Tiananmen demonstrations, on Feb. 17, 1993. But another 1989 leader, Hang Dongfang, who returned to China on Aug. 13, 1993, after being treated in the United States for tuberculosis, was deported from China on August 14. On August 21, the government revoked his passport, which meant he became a man without a country.

Trade status. Analysts in the United States viewed the release of prisoners early in 1993 as China's effort to ensure continued trade opportunities with America. In 1992, China sold goods to the United States that were worth $18 billion more than what it bought from the United States.

On May 28, 1993, U.S. President Bill Clinton extended for one year China's trading status as most-favored-nation, a status that allows China to pay relatively low tariff rates on exports to the United States. But Clinton also called for greater political freedom there as a condition for continued U.S. trade concessions.

Unrest in Tibet. A delegation of diplomats from the European Community (EC, or Common Market) visited Tibet's capital, Lhasa, to investigate the extension of human rights to Tibetans under Chinese rule. China denied reports that before the delegation arrived on May 16, some 100 Tibetans were arrested to keep them from giving the diplomats documents about abuses. Tibetans said 335 independence activists were being held without trial.

The most violent demonstrations against Chinese control since 1989 erupted in Lhasa on May 24. They were touched off by an announcement of new taxes and price increases. Tibetans attacked police and Chinese-run shops. The exact number of casualties in two days of riots was unknown.

China's defense spending almost doubled from 1988 to 1993. The government bought $1.8-billion worth of weapons from Russia in 1992, and in 1993, China sought more Russian equipment to upgrade the obsolete technology of its armed forces. China also recruited hundreds of top technical experts from Russian defense industries to work in China. These major efforts to improve the quality of China's armed forces worried other countries, especially because China no longer faced a Soviet enemy or any other direct threat to its national security.

U.S. trade sanctions. On August 25, the United States issued trade sanctions restricting U.S. exports of missile-building technology to China and Pakistan for two years. On July 25, China had denied U.S. charges that it had sold such technology to Pakistan in violation of an international agreement, which China had agreed to abide by without actually signing. China claimed that the M-11 missiles it was helping Pakistan build did not exceed the payload and distance limitations cited in the agreement.

Hong Kong was the subject of tough talks between China and the United Kingdom during 1993. At issue was the reforming of the political structure of Hong Kong before June 30, 1997, when China takes control of the British colony. In 1992, Hong Kong Governor Christopher Patten had proposed political reforms, including a lowering of the legal voting age, which angered China. In March 1993, China hinted that it would set up a shadow government for Hong Kong in violation of its promise not to interfere in Hong Kong affairs before 1997. China also obstructed some development plans there.

On Oct. 6, 1993, Patten said that he would expand democratic rule in Hong Kong even without China's approval. China then warned that the colony's economy might be hurt as a result. Both sides were at an impasse. □ Henry S. Bradsher

See also **Asia** (Facts in brief table). In **World Book,** see **China.**

Chrétien, Jean (1934-   ), was elected prime minister of Canada on Oct. 25, 1993, in a landslide victory for the Liberal Party and a rout of the ruling Progressive Conservative Party. Chrétien was sworn in as prime minister on November 4.

The prime minister was born Joseph-Jacques Jean Chrétien on Jan. 11, 1934, in Shawinigan, Que. He was the 18th of 19 children in his family. Chrétien graduated in 1955 from the College of Three Rivers in Trois-Rivières, Que., with a B.A. He earned a law degree from Laval University in Quebec City in 1958.

From 1958 to 1963, Chrétien worked as an attorney. In 1963, he was elected to the House of Commons, where he served until he resigned in 1986. As a member of the Cabinets of three Liberal prime ministers, Chrétien held numerous positions, including minister of Indian affairs and northern development; minister of industry, trade, and commerce; minister of finance; minister of justice; attorney general; and deputy prime minister.

In March 1986, Chrétien returned to the legal profession and practiced until June 1990. In 1990, he was elected leader of the Liberal Party and reelected to the House of Commons.

Chrétien is a lifelong Quebecer who is more comfortable speaking French than English, but he has not supported the separatist movement in Quebec. Chrétien is married to the former Aline Chaîné and has three children. □ Lori Fagan

Christopher, Warren M. (1925-   ), a Los Angeles lawyer and former deputy United States secretary of state, became secretary of state on Jan. 20, 1993. Christopher has a reputation as a skilled negotiator who excels at bringing adversaries together.

Christopher was born on Oct. 27, 1925, in Scranton, N. Dak. He graduated with high honors from the University of Southern California in Los Angeles in 1945 and earned a law degree at Stanford University in 1949. He was a law clerk for U.S. Supreme Court Justice William O. Douglas before joining the Los Angeles law firm of O'Melveny & Myers in 1950.

In 1967, President Lyndon B. Johnson named Christopher deputy attorney general, a post he held until 1969. In 1977, he accepted the same post in the Administration of President Jimmy Carter. In 1980, he worked out an agreement that led to the freeing of the U.S. hostages in Iran in January 1981. For his service, he was awarded the Presidential Medal of Freedom, the nation's highest civilian honor.

Christopher returned to O'Melveny & Myers in 1981. In 1991, he headed a commission that called for reforms in the Los Angeles Police Department.

Christopher is married to the former Marie Wyllis. He has four children, including one by a previous marriage. □ David Dreier

Churches. See **Eastern Orthodox Churches; Judaism; Protestantism; Religion; Roman Catholic Church.**

Ciampi, Carlo Azeglio (1920-   ), became prime minister of Italy on April 29, 1993. Ciampi, who had been governor of Italy's central bank, was the first independent and the first nonparliamentarian to head Italy's government since the formation of the Republic of Italy in 1946. He succeeded Giuliano Amato, who resigned on April 22, 1993, after Italian voters approved major reforms in the country's scandal-ridden government. (See **Italy.**)

Carlo Azeglio Ciampi was born on Dec. 9, 1920, in the Italian city of Leghorn (also called Livorno). From 1941 to 1944, he served in the Italian Army. He graduated from the University of Pisa in 1946 with degrees in literature and law.

After graduation, Ciampi went to work for the Bank of Italy. He became governor of the bank in 1979. In 1981, Ciampi established the bank's independence from the Italian government. In 1992, he managed the removal of the *lira* (Italy's currency) from the European Monetary System after Germany raised its interest rates. Ciampi had a reputation for integrity and honesty, and observers noted that the Bank of Italy was one of the few institutions not implicated in Italy's scandals.

Ciampi said his top priority as prime minister was to oversee reforms in the national election process. He also pledged to cut the federal deficit, to revive the government's lagging privatization program, and to fight organized crime. □ John C. Burnson

Cisneros, Henry G. (1947-   ), the former mayor of San Antonio, was unanimously confirmed by the United States Senate on Jan. 21, 1993, as secretary of the U.S. Department of Housing and Urban Development. He was sworn in the next day.

Cisneros was born on June 11, 1947, in San Antonio. He graduated from Texas A&M University in College Station in 1970 with a master's degree in urban and regional planning. He later earned master's and doctor's degrees in public administration from Harvard University in Cambridge, Mass., and George Washington University in Washington, D.C.

In 1975, Cisneros was elected to the San Antonio City Council. After serving for six years on the council, he was elected mayor, becoming the first Hispanic to head a major U.S. city. He served in that position until 1989. During his eight years as mayor, Cisneros strengthened San Antonio's economy by increasing tourism and attracting high-technology industries and convention business to the city. He left public service in 1989 to become chairman of the newly formed Cisneros Asset Management Company, a pension-management firm.

Cisneros has won many awards and honors during his career. Among them are a 1982 citation from the United States Jaycees naming him one of the "Ten Outstanding Young Men of America."

Cisneros married Mary Alice Perez in 1969. They have three children.   □ David Dreier

City. From the bomb blast that severely damaged the World Trade Center in New York City, to the floods that engulfed large areas of the Midwest, to the choking fires that swept through southern California, events in 1993 created vivid scenes of cities affected by violence and destruction. And as always in recent years, cities had serious problems with street crime and tight budgets.

The Midwestern floods. Record floodwaters of the Mississippi River and other swollen rivers spread over parts of nine states in the Midwest in June, July, and August. Volunteers worked to assist the flood control efforts of federal and state agencies. Some cities, including St. Louis, Mo., and Kansas City, Mo., withstood the rising waters and survived with relatively little damage. Other communities, especially in Iowa and parts of Illinois, were swamped by the floodwaters.

Most of the flooded cities, including Des Moines, Iowa; St. Joseph, Mo.; Alton, Ill.; and Manhattan, Kans., quickly began to repair and rebuild as the waters receded. One did not. The 900 residents of Valmeyer, Ill., decided to abandon what remained of their town and rebuild on higher ground.

California brushfires. As the Midwest dried out, wind-driven wildfires, some believed to be the work of arsonists, swept down the dry hillsides of southern California in late October and early November, ravaging a dozen communities in the Los

The budget squeeze
Budgeted or estimated figures, in millions of dollars, from 20 large U.S. cities in fiscal 1993 show that most of the cities were keeping their spending and revenues roughly in balance. Often, however, that required drawing money from reserve funds.

	Revenue	Estimated spending
New York	31,000	31,000
Los Angeles	2,380	2,360
Chicago	1,730	1,750
Philadelphia	2,350	2,280
San Diego	481	482
Detroit	1,180	1,230
Dallas	512	512
Phoenix	479	484
San Antonio	335	337
Indianapolis	334	336
Jacksonville, Fla.	447	439
Columbus, Ohio	312	319
Milwaukee	410	410
Memphis	296	294
Washington, D.C.	4,275	4,275
Boston	1,100	1,100
Seattle	387	389
Minneapolis, Minn.	254	253
Atlanta, Ga.	353	364
Denver, Colo.	422	431

Source: National League of Cities.

Angeles area. The fires, fanned by hot, dry winds, blazed down hillsides and through canyons. In Malibu, west of Los Angeles, and Laguna Beach, to the southeast, the rampaging fires advanced all the way to the Pacific Ocean, destroying hundreds of homes and killing three people.

The World Trade Center bombing on February 26 crippled the twin 110-story structures, the tallest buildings in New York City. The blast killed 6 people and injured more than 1,000.

Seven men, all of them described as Muslim terrorists, were charged with the crime in the following months. Soon after the first arrests, an undercover informant told law-enforcement officials that the bombing was part of a plot to bomb several other major facilities in New York, including the United Nations headquarters, a federal office complex, and the tunnels that cross under the Hudson River linking New York and New Jersey.

That information led to the arrest of other suspects, including Sheik Omar Abdel Rahman, a blind Muslim cleric. Abdel Rahman was accused of being the mastermind of the World Trade Center bombing and of the thwarted bombing plot. (See also **Crime**.)

Violent crime, always a problem in recent years in United States cities, became an even more urgent issue in 1993. Crimes of violence became more vicious and deadly, with growing use of rapid-fire weapons. Statistics released by the Federal Bureau of Investigation in October showed a record 13,220 handgun murders in the United States in 1992, a 10 percent increase from 1991. Murders in 1993 were again heading toward record levels in cities around the country, and crime was far and away the top issue in public opinion polls at year-end.

Florida, where six foreign tourists were murdered in 1993 by robbers, was much in the news during the year. In one incident, on April 2 in Miami, two men robbed and beat a German woman and then ran over her with their car while the woman's mother and two children watched helplessly.

In Washington, D.C., the likelihood of another record-breaking year of homicides prompted Mayor Sharon Pratt Kelly to ask President Bill Clinton in October for authority to bring the National Guard to the city's aid. Although the President turned down her request, saying it was not in his power to grant such authority, he said he would provide additional federal support for anticrime efforts in the nation's capital.

Crime and politics. In city elections throughout the country in 1993, crime was a major campaign issue, and it contributed to victories by Republican candidates in the nation's two largest cities, Los Angeles and New York City.

In Los Angeles, where Mayor Tom Bradley decided not to run again after 20 years in office, voters on June 8 chose Richard J. Riordan, a wealthy businessman making his first run for elective office, for mayor.

50 largest cities in the world

Rank	City	Population
1.	São Paulo, Brazil	11,128,848
2.	Mexico City	10,263,275
3.	Seoul, South Korea	9,645,932
4.	Moscow	8,801,000
5.	Bombay, India	8,227,332
6.	Shanghai	8,214,436
7.	Tokyo	8,163,573
8.	Beijing	7,362,425
9.	New York City	7,322,564
10.	Jakarta, Indonesia	6,761,886
11.	Istanbul, Turkey	6,620,600
12	London	6,378,600
13.	Hong Kong	6,055,000
14.	Cairo, Egypt	6,052,836
15.	Rio de Janeiro, Brazil	6,042,411
16.	Baghdad, Iraq	5,908,000
17.	Tianjin, China	5,855,068
18.	Teheran, Iran	5,734,199
19.	Lima, Peru	5,493,900
20.	Karachi, Pakistan	5,208,170
21.	Bangkok, Thailand	5,153,902
22.	Delhi, India	4,884,234
23.	St. Petersburg, Russia	4,468,000
24.	Santiago, Chile	4,385,481
25.	Shenyang, China	4,130,000
26.	Bogotá, Colombia	3,982,941
27.	Ho Chi Minh City, Vietnam	3,934,395
28.	Sydney, Australia	3,538,970
29.	Pusan, South Korea	3,516,807
30.	Los Angeles	3,485,398
31.	Berlin, Germany	3,433,695
32.	Wuhan, China	3,340,000
33.	Calcutta, India	3,305,006
34.	Madras, India	3,276,622
35.	Yokohama, Japan	3,220,331
36.	Guangzhou, China	3,220,000
37.	Madrid, Spain	3,123,713
38.	Hanoi, Vietnam	3,058,855
39.	Melbourne, Australia	3,022,157
40.	Lahore, Pakistan	2,952,689
41.	Alexandria, Egypt	2,917,327
42.	Buenos Aires, Argentina	2,908,001
43.	Rome	2,830,569
44.	Chicago	2,783,726
45.	Chongqing, China	2,730,000
46.	Pyongyang, North Korea	2,639,448
47.	Taipei, Taiwan	2,637,100
48.	Osaka, Japan	2,623,801
49.	Kiev, Ukraine	2,616,000
50.	Harbin, China	2,590,000

Sources: 1990 census figures for U.S. cities from the U.S. Bureau of the Census; censuses or government estimates for cities of other countries.

Riordan campaigned on a promise to hire more police officers and to crack down on crime.

In New York City, Rudolph W. Giuliani defeated incumbent Mayor David Dinkins on November 2 in a rematch of their contest four years earlier. Giuliani, a former federal prosecutor with a tough anticrime reputation, became the first Republican to be elected mayor of the nation's largest city since John V. Lindsay's victory in 1965.

Financial woes. In July, the National League of Cities, a Washington, D.C.-based organization that represents the nation's cities, provided evidence of the continued strains on municipal budgets in its annual report on city finances. For the second consecutive year, the League reported that more than half of the 688 cities and towns included in the survey said their expenses would exceed revenues. Most cities maintain a cash reserve to help meet short-term budget pressures, but those reserves were in danger of running out unless conditions changed.

The pressure on city budgets provided momentum for legalizing gambling in many communities. Several Indiana cities approved riverboat casinos operating along the Lake Michigan shoreline when the issue was put on the ballot in November, and work on a huge downtown casino in New Orleans was moving ahead toward an opening by 1995. (See **State government: The States Bet on Legalized Gambling.**)

The burden of federal mandates. One of the most difficult financial problems in 1993 for local governments, and for states as well, was the growing burden of unfunded federal mandates. These are federal programs or regulations that state and local governments are required to carry out with little or no financial support from the national government. Some of the most costly mandates involved federal standards for wastewater treatment, solid waste landfills, and the removal of asbestos and lead-based paint from buildings.

Surveys issued during the year by the United States Conference of Mayors and the National Association of Counties found that 12 federal mandates were costing local governments upwards of $11.3 billion in 1993 and could cost as much as $88-billion from 1994 to 1998. Armed with that information, state and local government leaders in hundreds of communities around the United States observed the first "National Unfunded Mandates Day" on October 27. The observance was called to launch a campaign to halt the "mandates madness."

President Clinton met with leaders of organizations representing state, county, and city governments to discuss the issue. Clinton pledged his support and signed an executive order designed to reduce or eliminate unfunded federal mandates.

Meeting economic challenges. Changes in the American economy continued to challenge American cities in 1993. The work force reductions of industry giants, such as the International Business Machines Corporation and the General Motors Corporation, prompted some cities to engage in broad efforts to retrain workers for new jobs or to help make aging local businesses competitive.

In Cincinnati, Ohio, for example, the Cincinnati Technical College has developed a special cooperative curriculum with local employers seeking workers with particular skills. Workers enroll in a two-year program to obtain the required skills for the jobs being offered. College officials reported in 1993 that they had achieved a placement rate of almost 100 percent for graduates of the program.

In another Ohio city, Mansfield, local civic leaders worked with unions, financial institutions, state officials, and the Armco Steel Company during the year to save an old Armco mill. The mill was upgraded with new equipment, enabling it to once again produce steel at a competitive price.

Award-winning cities. Programs aimed at tackling a variety of problems, ranging from drug abuse to deteriorating downtown areas, were among the award-winning efforts of nine U.S. cities and one county chosen in 1993 as recipients of All-America City Awards. The awards are presented annually by the National Civic League, an organization in Denver, Colo., that seeks to improve state and local government. The 1993 winners were Cleveland; Oakland, Calif.; Fort Worth and Laredo, Tex.; Wichita, Kans.; Delray Beach, Fla.; Pulaski, Tenn.; Wray, Colo.; Washington, N.C.; and Dawson County, Nebraska.

Five other cities won 1993 Urban Enrichment Awards from the National League of Cities for outstanding collaborative projects between the public and private sectors aimed at improving city life. The cities were San Diego; Greensboro, N.C.; Macon, Ga.; Surfside Beach, S.C.; and Hoffman Estates, Ill.

Toward a new urban era. Some familiar symbols of urban life were coming full cycle in 1993. In Los Angeles, the city that defined the automobile age, the 17.3-mile (27.8-kilometer) Century Freeway—expected to be the last of the city's fabled expressways—was finally opened to traffic in October. The road cost $2.2 billion to construct, making it the most expensive highway project in history.

On Long Island, N.Y., the Northeast region's last drive-in movie theater prepared to close at year-end. Drive-ins, once a prominent part of the family and teen-age car culture, have become increasingly rare in U.S. cities.

At the same time, new features of urban life have been springing up in the form of thriving enterprises such as *microbreweries*—small breweries making premium-quality beers—and specialty coffee shops. Once considered local phenomena in just a few cities, such as Seattle and Denver, such businesses were being established in a growing number of cities in 1993. ☐ Randolph C. Arndt

In *World Book,* see **City.**

50 largest cities in the United States

Rank	City	Population*	Percent change in population since 1980	Unemployment rate†	Mayor‡
1.	New York City	7,322,564	+3.5	9.5%	Rudolph W. Giuliani (R, 1/98)
2.	Los Angeles	3,485,398	+17.4	9.5	Richard J. Riordan (NP, 6/97)
3.	Chicago	2,783,726	-7.4	6.8	Richard M. Daley (D, 4/95)
4.	Houston	1,630,553	+2.2	7.5	Bob Lanier (NP, 12/95)
5.	Philadelphia	1,585,577	-6.1	7.3	Edward G. Rendell (D, 1/96)
6.	San Diego	1,110,549	+26.8	9.2	Susan Golding (NP, 12/96)
7.	Detroit	1,027,974	-14.6	8.3	Dennis Archer (NP, 1/98)
8.	Dallas	1,006,877	+11.3	6.2	Steve Bartlett (NP, 12/95)
9.	Phoenix	983,403	+24.5	4.6	Paul Johnson (D, 1/96)
10.	San Antonio	935,933	+19.1	6.0	Nelson W. Wolff (NP, 6/95)
11.	San Jose	782,248	+24.3	7.9	Susan Hammer (NP, 12/94)
12.	Indianapolis	741,952	+4.3	3.1	Stephen Goldsmith (R, 12/95)
13.	Baltimore	736,014	-6.4	7.8	Kurt L. Schmoke (D, 12/95)
14.	San Francisco	723,959	+6.6	7.3	Frank M. Jordan (NP, 1/96)
15.	Jacksonville, Fla.	672,971	+17.9	6.4	T. Ed Austin (D, 7/95)
16.	Columbus, Ohio	632,910	+12.0	5.3	Gregory S. Lashutka (NP, 1/96)
17.	Milwaukee	628,088	-1.3	4.3	John O. Norquist (D, 4/96)
18.	Memphis	610,337	-5.5	5.0	W. W. Herenton (NP, 12/95)
19.	Washington, D.C.	606,900	-4.9	4.7	Sharon Pratt Kelly (D, 1/95)
20.	Boston	574,283	+2.0	5.8	Thomas M. Menino (NP, 1/98)
21.	Seattle	516,259	+4.5	7.1	Norman B. Rice (NP, 12/97)
22.	El Paso	515,342	+21.2	10.1	Larry Francis (NP, 5/95)
23.	Nashville	510,784	+6.9	4.1	Philip Bredesen (D, 9/95)
24.	Cleveland	505,616	-11.9	6.2	Michael R. White (D, 12/97)
25.	New Orleans	496,938	-10.9	7.1	Sidney J. Barthelemy (D, 5/94)
26.	Denver, Colo.	467,610	-5.1	5.2	Wellington E. Webb (D, 6/95)
27.	Austin, Tex.	465,622	+34.6	4.7	Bruce Todd (NP, 6/94)
28.	Fort Worth, Tex.	447,619	+16.2	6.7	Kay Granger (NP, 5/94)
29.	Oklahoma City, Okla.	444,719	+10.1	5.3	Ronald J. Norick (NP, 4/94)
30.	Portland, Ore.	437,319	+18.8	6.5	Vera Katz (NP, 12/96)
31.	Kansas City, Mo.	435,146	-2.9	5.2	Emanuel Cleaver II (NP, 4/95)
32.	Long Beach, Calif.	429,433	+18.8	9.5	Ernie Kell (NP, 6/94)
33.	Tucson, Ariz.	405,390	+22.6	3.9	George Miller (D, 12/95)
34.	St. Louis, Mo.	396,685	-12.4	6.3	Freeman R. Bosley, Jr. (D, 4/97)
35.	Charlotte, N.C.	395,934	+25.5	4.7	Richard Vinroot (R, 11/95)
36.	Atlanta, Ga.	394,017	-7.3	4.9	Bill Campbell (D, 1/98)
37.	Virginia Beach, Va.	393,069	+49.9	6.2	Meyera E. Oberndorf (NP, 6/96)
38.	Albuquerque, N. Mex.	384,736	+15.6	5.1	Martin J. Chavez (D, 11/97)
39.	Oakland, Calif.	372,242	+9.7	7.7	Elihu Mason Harris (D, 12/94)
40.	Pittsburgh, Pa.	369,879	-12.8	6.9	Thomas Murphy (D, 12/97)
41.	Sacramento, Calif.	369,365	+34.0	8.7	Joe Serna, Jr. (D, 11/96)
42.	Minneapolis, Minn.	368,383	-0.7	4.0	Sharon Sayles Belton (NP, 12/97)
43.	Tulsa, Okla.	367,302	+1.8	6.7	M. Susan Savage (D, 5/94)
44.	Honolulu, Hawaii	365,272	+0.1	3.6	Frank F. Fasi (R, 1/97)
45.	Cincinnati, Ohio	364,040	-5.5	5.4	Roxanne Qualls (D, 11/95)
46.	Miami, Fla.	358,548	+3.4	8.1	Stephen P. Clark (D, 11/97)
47.	Fresno, Calif.	354,202	+62.9	13.9	Jim Patterson (R, 3/97)
48.	Omaha, Nebr.	335,795	+7.0	3.1	P. J. Morgan (NP, 6/97)
49.	Toledo, Ohio	332,943	-6.1	7.1	Carlton Finkbeiner (D, 12/97)
50.	Buffalo, N.Y.	328,123	-8.3	7.0	Anthony Masiello (D, 12/97)

*1990 census (source: U.S. Bureau of the Census).
†July 1993 unemployment figures are for metropolitan areas (source: U.S. Bureau of Labor Statistics).
‡The letters in parentheses represent the mayor's party, with *D* meaning Democrat, *R* Republican, *I* Independent, and *NP* nonpartisan. The date is when the term of office ends (source: mayors' offices).

New Fears About Urban Gangs

By Jeffrey Fagan

Social scientists are working to understand why street gangs are a growing presence in America's urban centers.

Youths display the colors and some hand signs used by Los Angeles' Grape Street Gang. Such symbols often identify a gang. Specific colors serve as a kind of uniform and help the gang maintain its identity as a distinct group. Special hand signals help gang members communicate information about themselves and the gang.

The author

Jeffrey Fagan is an associate professor in the School of Criminal Justice at Rutgers The State University of New Jersey in Newark.

Street gangs made unusual newspaper headlines in a number of American cities in 1993. Rather than announcing new victims of gang wars, these headlines trumpeted a series of gang "summits," organized by current and former gang leaders with the declared aim of ending gang warfare. The undertaking had been initiated by about 120 gang leaders from about 24 cities at a meeting, dubbed the National Urban Peace and Justice Summit, in Kansas City, Mo., from April 30 to May 2, 1993. To some, the meeting followed logically from earlier efforts at ending gang conflict, a process that began with a truce declared in May 1992 between some factions of the Crips and the Bloods, rival gang alliances based in Los Angeles.

But skeptics—including law-enforcement officials, social scientists, and some gang members themselves—wondered whether the summit leaders would take concrete steps to make gangs less attractive to adolescents. Critics noted that the leaders failed to denounce gang membership. Others pointed out that most gangs, including a majority of Hispanic gangs, were not involved in the movement.

No observer doubted that the United States has a growing gang problem. In 1965, police departments in only 15 of the nation's 100 largest cities had reported the presence of street gangs. By 1992, police had reported gang problems in at least 92 of these cities. The toll of gang violence, too, was rising. Los Angeles, considered by many to be the nation's gang capital, had counted 39 gang-related homicides in 1973, the first year the city collected such data. In 1992, that figure was 429 homicides, up from 375 the year before. Although statistics on gangs are not wholly reliable, the U.S. Department of Justice estimated in 1993 that there were 4,881 gangs nationwide in 1991, with 249,324 members. The Justice Department said gang members in 1991 committed 1,051 homicides.

The growing presence of gangs in the streets has also coincided with a growing awareness of gangs among the general public. The portrayal of gang culture in television, motion pictures, popular music, and other media has made the public familiar with many aspects of gang life, including styles of dress and language; the adoption of particular colors, hand signs, and symbols; and the use of graffiti to mark turf and communicate with other gangs and gang members. At the same time, the participation of some gang members in illicit drug selling has created a perception that gangs have evolved into sophisticated, interstate drug-dealing organizations. These fears and perceptions have challenged social scientists to shed light on gangs so that society can fashion effective policies to combat them.

Street gangs (sometimes called urban gangs or youth gangs) are

▪ Gang graffiti

A gang uses graffiti to communicate information about the gang and its members and to help the gang in its competition for territory and status. A gang member who places a graffito within the territory of a rival gang, or who defaces a rival gang's graffito, risks retaliation and thus also gains status within the gang.

▪ Chicago gang graffiti often employ symbols that indicate the gang is allied with a larger gang *nation* (coalition of gangs). The letters SC, *left,* stand for Spanish Cobras. The pitchforks—which rise from the cobra's head, the gang's initials, and the inverted KK (lower left)—are a symbol of the Latin Disciple nation and signify that the Cobras are allied with the Disciples. The letters KK stand for King Killers, indicating the Cobras' opposition to the Disciples' rivals, the Latin Kings.

▪ Los Angeles gangs are known for their distinctive lettering styles. This graffito of the Little East Side Gang, *right,* uses a style typical of the city's Hispanic gangs, in which large block letters spell out the gang's name or initials. The Spanish inscription on the right bears the names of the gang members who drew the graffito, along with the boast "somos locos y que" ("we are crazy and so what"). Such boasts imply that the gang's members are fearless and, therefore, dangerous.

Why youths join gangs

Researchers know that gangs tend to form in low-income neighborhoods and in neighborhoods where immigrants or members of ethnic groups are concentrated. They also know that young men are more likely to join gangs than are young women. However, only a small number of male youths in communities where gang activity occurs actually join gangs. Those who do join gangs seem to be no different, in personality or social background, from youths who do not join gangs.

Investigators studied about 200 male gang members and 400 nongang male youths from gang neighborhoods in Chicago, Los Angeles, and San Diego. They found that the gang members were, overall, no different from nongang youths in their social, economic, or personal backgrounds, *right*. Gang members were, however, more likely than nonmembers to have dropped out of school.

Characteristic	Different for gang and nongang youth?	
	Yes	No
Age		X
Race		X
Makeup of family unit (for example, parents' marital status)		X
Parents' employment status		X
Parents' education level		X
In school or dropout	X	

Source: Jeffrey Fagan

Researchers do have some idea of what motivates young people to join gangs. Gang members say this is what they looked for when joining a gang, *right*.

- Respect, loyalty, and solidarity
- Intimacy and "family" feeling
- Status and power
- Security and protection
- Social life
- Economic advantage
- Maintaining ethnic tradition or culture

adolescent organizations that are usually based on ethnic solidarity and neighborhood allegiance. Although definitions of the term vary, most researchers understand street gangs at least partly in terms of their criminal or delinquent behavior. Typically, street gangs develop from so-called street-corner groups of delinquent youths—groups of friends who socialize together and engage in theft, vandalism, and other petty crimes. Social scientists distinguish between street gangs and other groups that are also sometimes called gangs, including hate groups and illegal drug distribution networks.

Evolution of America's street gangs

Street gangs have been part of America's urban landscape since at least the late 1700's. In the 1800's, as European immigration to the United States increased, gangs proliferated in neighborhoods where the immigrants settled, such as the overcrowded slums of New York City's Lower East Side. These gangs bore such names as the Plug Uglies, the Roach Guards, and the Old Slippers. Many of the gangs were born in the corner groceries that were the business and social centers of their neighborhoods. They warred regularly over territory, though they joined forces to oppose the police.

Until about 1965, street gangs were found primarily in a few large urban centers, notably Boston, Chicago, Los Angeles, New York, and Philadelphia. That situation began to change in the late 1960's, when other cities began experiencing gang problems. In the 1980's, the number of cities with gangs mushroomed, with the greatest proliferation occurring in the second half of that decade. Today, gangs can be found in both large and small cities in nearly every state.

Along with the explosion in the number of gangs came a change in their composition. For most of American history, the majority of gangs were founded by the children of immigrants from Germany, Ireland, Italy, Poland, and other European nations. By the late 1960's, however, African-American and Hispanic—chiefly Mexican-American and Puerto Rican—gangs had become predominant.

Other fundamental changes have accompanied the proliferation of street gangs. For one thing, the average age of gang members is rising. Once, members tended to end their active involvement in the gang by their early 20's, as they married, found jobs, or grew tired of fighting and the constant threat of injury or arrest. Today, members are likely to remain in the gang longer, until their late 20's or beyond.

Another change involves the scope of gang activity. In the past, gangs were likely to claim neighborhoods as their turf. Today, they may stake claims to shopping malls, schools, and other areas that extend gang territory into the larger society.

Women's roles in gangs also have evolved. Formerly, gang members were virtually all male. Women sometimes formed *auxiliaries* (branches) of male gangs, or they served as weapons carriers or decoys for male gang members. Today, there are a growing number of independent female gangs, and they fight each other just as male gangs do. There is also some evidence of sexually integrated gangs.

Street gang
emergence in
America's 100
largest cities

● Before 1965

● 1965-1974

● 1975-1984

● 1985-present

○ No gangs reported
  or no information
  available

Source: Malcolm Klein, *The American Street Gang*
(New York: Lexington Books 1994 [in press]).

■ Before 1965, street gangs were found in only 15 of the 100 largest cities in the United States. After 1965, gangs began forming in other cities, with the greatest proliferation occurring from 1985 to 1989. Many of these gangs were founded by youths who were born into economically disadvantaged neighborhoods during the 1970's. By 1993, police departments had reported the presence of gangs in 92 of the 100 largest cities.

The most dramatic and urgent change in gangs, however, has been the worsening of gang violence. Violence has always been a part of gang life—a means of commanding respect, honor, or status, whether between gangs or among members of the same gang. But in recent years, gang violence has occurred more often and more often resulted in death.

Experts do not know exactly how sharply rates of gang violence are going up. Not all law-enforcement agencies update their rosters of gang members on a regular basis, so crimes by former members may be classified as gang crimes long after the individuals have left the gang. Another problem is that agencies define gang crime in different ways. For instance, the Los Angeles Police Department defines gang-related homicide as any homicide committed by a gang member. In Chicago, only homicides committed as part of gang activity are regarded as gang-related. In 1989, researchers who applied Chicago's more restrictive definition to the Los Angeles data found that the number of gang homicides in that city dropped by about half.

Nevertheless, observers agree that gang violence is escalating at a rapid pace. In Chicago, the second leading gang city, the number of gang homicides increased more than tenfold between 1965 and 1992, rising from 11 to 116 yearly. Smaller cities show equally alarming trends. In Little Rock, Ark., the number of murders rose from less than 40 in the late 1980's to 52 in 1991 and a record 61 in 1992. Officials ascribe the increase to the appearance of gangs in the city in 1988.

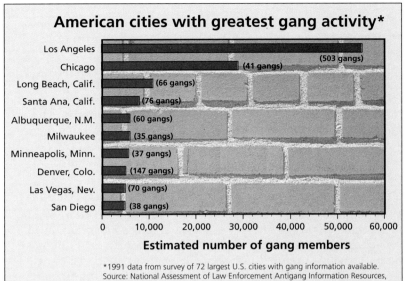

American cities with greatest gang activity*

Los Angeles **(503 gangs)**
Chicago **(41 gangs)**
Long Beach, Calif. **(66 gangs)**
Santa Ana, Calif. **(76 gangs)**
Albuquerque, N.M. **(60 gangs)**
Milwaukee **(35 gangs)**
Minneapolis, Minn. **(37 gangs)**
Denver, Colo. **(147 gangs)**
Las Vegas, Nev. **(70 gangs)**
San Diego **(38 gangs)**

0   10,000   20,000   30,000   40,000   50,000   60,000

Estimated number of gang members

*1991 data from survey of 72 largest U.S. cities with gang information available.
Source: National Assessment of Law Enforcement Antigang Information Resources,
West Virginia University.

■ **Measuring gang activity**
Among cities where offi-
cials have collected data
on gangs, Los Angeles and
nearby cities—including
Long Beach and Santa
Ana, Calif.—*left,* have the
lion's share of gang activity. There are some 55,000
gang members in Los An-
geles alone. Chicago, with
nearly 30,000 gang mem-
bers, is the second leading
gang city in the United
States.

■ Estimates of gang violence reflect, in part, agencies' differing definitions of such violence. In
Chicago, *right,* any homicide with a gang-related motive is considered a gang homicide. In Los
Angeles, officials regard any homicide committed by a gang member as a gang homicide. Nevertheless, researchers agree that gang violence
is increasing in both cities.

In part, say analysts, the rise in violence
may be due to changes in gang life since the
1970's. Studies have shown, for example, that
rates of violence tend to rise among people in
their late adolescence and early adulthood—
an age when more people now stay active in
gangs. Moreover, as the number of gangs
grows, so do the opportunities for violence.
Clashes between gangs become more likely as
new gangs emerge and compete for status
and territory. Gang members competing for
status within emerging gangs may also be
more prone to violence.

Many observers argue that the increase in
gang violence coincides with the greater violence in society at large. According to the
Centers for Disease Control and Prevention
(CDC), a federal agency based in Atlanta, Ga.,
homicide is today the second leading cause of

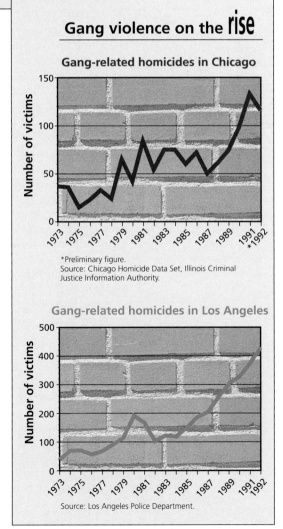

Gang violence on the rise

Gang-related homicides in Chicago

Number of victims

150

100

50

0

1973 1975 1977 1979 1981 1983 1985 1987 1989 1991 *1992

*Preliminary figure.
Source: Chicago Homicide Data Set, Illinois Criminal
Justice Information Authority.

Gang-related homicides in Los Angeles

Number of victims

500

400

300

200

100

0

1973 1975 1977 1979 1981 1983 1985 1987 1989 1991 1992

Source: Los Angeles Police Department.

death among Americans aged 15 to 24 and is the leading cause of death among blacks in that age group.

There is also broad agreement that the number and firepower of weapons in the hands of gang members have multiplied. Once, gang fights consisted of rumbles in which the weapons were knives, clubs, or fists and few people died. Today, disputes and challenges to honor often are settled with guns. Research in the 1980's found that firearms accounted for 80 to 90 percent of gang killings in Chicago and Los Angeles, compared with 60 to 65 percent of all murders nationwide.

Gangs and drugs: A complex connection

Some people link the rise in gang violence to two other relatively new phenomena among gangs. One is a shift, among some gangs, away from the goal of neighborhood defense and toward a focus on making money, usually through drug selling. Some researchers call these gangs *entrepreneurial gangs* to distinguish them from more traditional turf-based gangs, sometimes called *fighting gangs.* The other is the creation of large gang alliances, known as supergangs or nations, that have arisen in Chicago and Los Angeles. These alliances are Los Angeles' Bloods and Crips and the People and Folks of Chicago (which are themselves made up of the gangs in the Vice Lord, Latin King, Gangster Disciple, and Latin Disciple nations). These developments have fostered concern that gangs have evolved into sophisticated criminal organizations reaping great profits from drug distribution.

The evidence suggests, however, that most gangs have not become major distributors of illicit drugs. Rather, analysts believe, people perceive gangs as controlling the drug trade simply because gangs proliferated at the same time as this trade reached crisis proportions. In the 1980's, Malcolm Klein, a sociologist at the University of Southern California in Los Angeles, showed that the advent of *crack cocaine*—an inexpensive and highly addictive form of cocaine—during that decade created opportunities for both gang members and other youths to earn ready cash through drug sales. Images of gang leaders sporting expensive clothes, jewelry, and other luxury items grew common in certain neighborhoods—and in the media and popular culture. At the same time, the appearance of gangs using well-known names such as Crips and Bloods in cities across the country created concern that gangs were migrating to expand their drug-selling territories.

There is no question that some gang members are heavily involved in drug selling. A 1992 report prepared for the Los Angeles County district attorney, for example, found that gang members sold drugs at roughly seven times the rate of nonmembers. According to the report, however, this activity does not reflect a transformation of street gangs into organized drug distribution networks. Instead, many gang members operate as small-time dealers earning only modest incomes. The report also suggests that many gang members move into full-time dealing as they reach the age when they would traditionally have left the gang. These individuals are often unable to find conventional jobs or are unwilling to accept the lower-rung work available to them.

Researchers have documented isolated instances of gangs establishing business locations in other cities. Detroit gangs, for example, have set up drug-selling operations in Cleveland and in cities that lie along Interstate 75 between Detroit and Cincinnati, Ohio. A similar pattern is found in California, where Bloods and Crips operate along Interstate 5 between Los Angeles and the state's Central Valley.

According to experts, however, what appears to be the movement of a gang into another city is often just the activity of an individual gang member. In other cases, members whose families move or send them away from home may bring their gang traditions with them. In the mid-1980's, for instance, Chicago gang graffiti began to appear in Mississippi as parents sent their sons there to live with relatives, chiefly to escape gang violence. Even more often, youths mimic the gang culture of established gang cities, adopting their names, graffiti, and other symbols.

Basis of the gang crisis

The first major researcher to explore the question of gang formation was the sociologist Frederic M. Thrasher, who studied more than 1,300 gangs in Chicago in the 1920's. Thrasher viewed these gangs as symptoms of the deteriorating neighborhoods and shifting populations that accompanied the city's industrialization. Beginning in the late 1800's, hundreds of thousands of immigrants thronged to work in Chicago's steel mills and meat-packing plants, crowding into hastily erected housing that rapidly became slums. Under these conditions, Thrasher believed, institutions such as families, schools, churches, and businesses were no longer effective in controlling the behavior of young males, thus enabling street-corner groups to evolve into gangs.

Researchers have developed many other theories about gang formation. But Thrasher's views remain the foundation for much thinking about gangs today. Like Thrasher, many researchers look toward changing social and economic conditions to explain today's gang crisis and, in particular, the proliferation of gangs during the 1980's.

Today's gangs were formed by youths born between the late 1960's and the mid-1970's, who belonged to the first generation to grow up as members of what some social theorists call the *underclass*. The term *underclass* refers to people who live in acute, long-term poverty, typically in racially segregated urban communities. They tend to be chronically unemployed and to have low educational levels and job skills, and they often come from single-parent families.

The trends that helped create the underclass began in the early 1900's. But they gained momentum following World War II (1939-1945), when several factors combined to propel the center of econom-

■ Gang leaders from across the country meet in Kansas City, Mo., in April and May 1993 for a four-day summit designed to promote gang peace and address the problems of the nation's inner cities. But skeptics question whether this summit, and others that followed it, would lead to a resolution of the gang crisis.

ic life out of the central cities. Intensive highway construction and government-subsidized home loans, for example, enabled growing numbers of middle-class workers to move to suburban communities. The departure of these taxpayers led to mounting tax rates at the same time as crime increased and municipal services declined. Partly as a result, factories and businesses began to join the exodus from the cities. Meanwhile, the growing burden on schools, hospitals, and other institutions harshly affected many of the residents left behind.

As the middle class left the cities, the urban poor became increasingly black and Hispanic. Millions of Southern blacks had migrated north after World War I (1914-1918) and again during World War II, seeking the jobs they hoped would raise their standard of living. At the same time, Mexican immigrants poured into the cities of California and the Southwest. And in the 1940's, Puerto Ricans began moving to the mainland, settling primarily in New York City.

As the cities changed, blacks and Hispanics found themselves in a bind. These groups were most likely to work in the occupations hardest hit by the loss of manufacturing firms and other industries. The cities did continue to serve as a reservoir of well-paying jobs—but these were mainly in service industries, such as banking and insurance, and required either higher education or specialized skills. The remaining jobs were unskilled and poorly paid.

Some analysts argue that failed social policies added to the plight of urban minorities. In the 1950's and 1960's, for instance, many cities sought to aid people in poor communities by offering them low-cost homes in public housing projects. Over time, however, many of these projects became ridden with crime, drugs, and other social problems. In addition, some observers say, government welfare programs reduced people's incentives for seeking employment. And as the number of female-headed households rose, multiple generations of families became dependent on welfare.

Many experts believe that the trends that created the urban underclass laid the groundwork for today's gang crisis. First, as men's role as wage earners declined, they became increasingly marginal at home as well, and so lost the ability to supervise delinquent youths. But the ability of mothers to supervise adolescents also suffered as women entered the workplace as primary wage earners. A growing number of children compared to adults also limited the ability of communities to control youths. In addition, the increasing unemployment disrupted the family networks that formerly had linked youths with potential jobs, and it reduced the incentives of young people to succeed in school. Meanwhile, intensifying racial and class segregation fueled resentment at the growing disparity in income between the urban poor and the suburban middle class.

Working to resolve the gang crisis

Looming beyond the effort to understand gangs is the job of designing policies to weaken the attraction of gangs to young people. Over the decades, public and private agencies have tried many approaches to controlling gangs. Some programs, for instance, target actual or potential gang members. They try to offer youths an alternative to gang involvement through counseling, structured recreation, instruction in basic skills, and vocational training. Other programs work to mobilize community residents against gangs, teaching them to patrol their neighborhoods, provide tutoring and other programs, or mediate gang conflicts. Many of these programs have not been fully evaluated, and others have produced, at best, mixed results.

In recent years, state and local governments have emphasized law-enforcement responses to gangs. Among these responses are strategies to break up gangs by eliminating their leadership—for example, through sentencing laws that ensure harsh punishments for gang leaders convicted of crimes. Other strategies are designed to harass gang members through such tactics as street sweeps to round up suspected gang members for arrest or questioning. In Los Angeles, officials have claimed some success with tactics that use laws designed to prohibit acts constituting a public nuisance. Under these laws, police officers can arrest an individual for loitering, wearing gang clothing, or other acts that suggest the individual is engaged in gang activity.

Critics of rigid law-enforcement responses to gangs suggest that these strategies are more likely to increase gang activity than to reduce it. They point out that gangs may become more cohesive and organized in response to conflict with the police. Moreover, they argue, imprisoning gang leaders often simply carries gang rivalries into the prisons. Some of these researchers point to what they regard as more promising law-enforcement approaches to gang control, such as programs in which police work with schools and community organizations to teach students how to avoid getting involved in gangs. In other programs, currently being tried in Los Angeles and Chicago, plainclothes police work with gang members in their communities as well as make arrests when necessary. They mediate gang fights, counsel gang members and their families, and even help youths find jobs.

Many observers suggest, however, that the United States cannot solve its gang crisis until it resolves broader social problems. First, they say, the country must reverse its growing culture of violence, through means that include regulations to limit access to firearms. Even more important is whether America can resolve its urban ills. This query has, as yet, no sure reply. But experts say more and more Americans are asking the question. That, they say, is at least a hopeful first step. ■ ■ ■

For further reading:

Gangs. Ed. by Scott Cummings and Daniel Monti. State University of New York Press, 1993.

Gangs in America. Ed. by C. Ronald Huff. Sage Publications, 1990.

Hagedorn, John M. *People and Folks: Gangs, Crime and the Underclass in a Rustbelt City.* Lake View Press, 1988.

Vigil, James Diego. *Barrio Gangs.* University of Texas Press, 1988.

Civil rights. For most of 1993, the top civil rights post in the United States remained vacant under the Administration of President Bill Clinton. On June 3, President Clinton abandoned his efforts to appoint Lani Guinier, a law professor at the University of Pennsylvania in Philadelphia, as head of the U.S. Justice Department's Civil Rights Division.

Clinton nominated Guinier, a respected civil rights lawyer and former Justice Department official, on April 29. However, Guinier's nomination became controversial as critics claimed that she held radical views about voting rights and opposed the principle of one person-one vote. Supporters of Guinier said that she had proposed controversial ideas about voting in order to explore ways to help minorities gain political power. When Republican senators and some Democrats said that they would not confirm Guinier, President Clinton withdrew her name, angering many civil rights groups that strongly favored her. In October, the Administration said it planned to nominate District of Columbia Corporation Counsel John Payton, but Payton later withdrew his name.

Restaurant settlements. Shoney's, Inc., which owns more than 900 restaurants in 38 states, in January agreed to a record $105-million settlement with about 40,000 current and former employees. According to a 1989 lawsuit, Shoney's denied promotions to black workers, fired blacks without cause, and tried to limit the number of blacks employed. The settlement required Shoney's to adopt equal opportunity policies.

A group of 32 black customers claiming discrimination by Denny's restaurants in California sued the restaurant chain on March 24, 1993. Two days later, the U.S. Justice Department also sued Denny's for a pattern of discrimination in California. The company resolved that suit by signing a court-ordered settlement on April 1, agreeing not to discriminate against minorities in the future. However, six black Secret Service agents filed a new suit against Denny's on May 24 claiming they were denied service at a Denny's in Annapolis, Md. On July 1, the agents' complaint was expanded to include nationwide claims—outside of California—against the company.

On July 1, Flagstar Companies, parent of Denny's, worked to repair its public relations by signing an agreement with the National Association for the Advancement of Colored People (NAACP). The agreement required Denny's to start a minority recruiting and training program, offer minorities more chances to open restaurants, and use more goods and services from minority-owned firms. NAACP leaders said the plan would generate about $1 billion in wages and revenues for minorities by the year 2000.

Homosexual rights. President Bill Clinton announced on July 19 a new policy allowing homosexuals to serve in the armed forces as long as they do not discuss their sexual orientation or engage in homosexual acts. Referred to as the "don't ask, don't

tell" policy, it was meant to relax the military's long-standing rule barring homosexuals from the armed services. However, homosexual-rights activists protested that the new policy continues to discriminate against homosexuals and restricts their freedom of speech. (See also **Armed forces.**)

On April 25, hundreds of thousands of gay-rights activists and sympathizers marched in Washington, D.C.. They called for equal rights and freedom from discrimination for homosexuals.

Police brutality. On August 4, a federal judge sentenced white Los Angeles police officers Stacey C. Koon and Laurence M. Powell to 30 months in prison each for their role in the 1991 beating of black motorist Rodney G. King. A federal jury on April 17, 1993, had convicted the officers of violating King's civil rights in a beating that was videotaped by a bystander and broadcast worldwide. Two other officers were acquitted.

The case was prosecuted in federal court after a state court jury on April 29, 1992, had found Koon, Powell, and the two other officers not guilty of assaulting King. That verdict touched off rioting in Los Angeles that lasted five days, claimed more than 50 lives, and caused more than $1 billion in damages.

In a case stemming from an incident in the Los Angeles riots, two black men were tried in the beating of white truck driver Reginald Denny. In late October 1993, a racially mixed jury acquitted Damian Williams and Henry Watson of attempted murder. They were convicted only on lesser charges. Many people viewed the lenient verdicts as an effort to prevent another riot in Los Angeles. Many blacks had viewed the attempted murder charges as too harsh. On December 7, a judge sentenced Williams to 10 years in prison. Watson was put on probation. (See also **Los Angeles.**)

In Michigan, state court juries on August 23 convicted two former Detroit police officers of second-degree murder in the 1992 beating death of a black man. A third former officer, who faced an assault charge, was found not guilty. The prosecution contended that officers Larry Nevers and Walter Budzyn used their metal flashlights to beat to death Malice W. Green, after stopping him outside a suspected drug house. The three officers, who were white, were fired shortly after the incident. On Oct. 12, 1993, a Detroit judge sentenced Nevers to a 12-to-25-year prison term and Budzyn to an 8-to-18-year prison term. (See also **Detroit.**)

Sex discrimination. A District of Columbia jury on June 24 awarded $2.4 million to Sandra Tyler, a women's basketball coach at Howard University in Washington, D.C. The jury found that the school had violated local and federal laws by paying her less and giving her worse facilities than the men's coach. The judge in the case reduced the award to $1.1 million on June 28, but the university still appealed the case. The award was the first given by a jury in a

Church members in Los Angeles rejoice at hearing the jury verdict in April convicting two policemen of violating motorist Rodney King's civil rights.

school sex discrimination case since the Supreme Court of the United States ruled in 1992 that victims can collect monetary damages for violations of Title IX of the Education Amendment Act of 1972, barring sex discrimination at schools receiving federal aid.

Racial violence. On Sept. 7, 1993, a jury in West Palm Beach, Fla., convicted two white men of kidnapping, robbery, and attempted murder for dousing a black tourist with gasoline and setting him on fire on New Year's Day. The tourist, Christopher Wilson, 32, testified that Mark Kohut, 27, and Charles Rourk, 33, abducted him at gunpoint from a shopping mall and forced him to drive to a field where they attacked him. On October 22, the two defendants were sentenced to life in prison.

The U.S. Supreme Court on June 11 said that states can punish crimes motivated by racial, religious, or other forms of bias more harshly than similar crimes that are not motivated by bias. Voting 9 to 0 in a Wisconsin case, the court said laws that enhance penalties for hate crimes do not violate free speech protections in the Constitution.

In a separate 5 to 4 ruling, the court on June 28 said states may be violating the equal protection rights of white voters by drawing bizarrely shaped voting districts to favor minority candidates. The ruling reinstated a lawsuit challenging the constitutionality of two voting districts in North Carolina and called into question similar districts in other states.

Marshall dies. Legendary civil rights lawyer and retired Supreme Court Justice Thurgood Marshall died on January 24 at age 84. As head of the NAACP Legal Defense and Educational Fund, Marshall won the 1954 *Brown v. Board of Education of Topeka* case in which the Supreme Court declared racially separate public schools unconstitutional. In 1967, President Lyndon B. Johnson named him as the first black Supreme Court justice. Marshall retired from the court in 1991 because of poor health.

A march remembered. An estimated 75,000 people marched in Washington, D.C., on Aug. 28, 1993, to celebrate the 30th anniversary of the historic March on Washington when Martin Luther King, Jr., gave his "I Have a Dream" speech. Labor union members, NAACP members, religious groups, and others joined in demanding more jobs and a renewed commitment to civil rights.

Amnesty International, in its 1993 report, accused governments around the world of using a double standard in protecting human rights. The London-based human rights organization highlighted human rights abuses in 161 countries. Its report said some countries were silent on human rights violations of allies while publicly condemning violations by declared enemies.

☐ Linda P. Campbell and Geoffrey A. Campbell
See also **Deaths: Marian Anderson: A Voice Heard Once in 100 Years.** In *World Book,* see **Civil rights.**

Classical music. Dozens of young pianists went to Fort Worth, Tex., in May 1993 for the Ninth Van Cliburn International Piano Competition. Promoters of this most famous of piano competitions sought to counteract its reputation as a battlefield for showy virtuosos by broadening the repertory and encouraging experimentation. However, most critics found the gold-medal winner, Simone Pedroni of Italy, to be a flashy performer in the Van Cliburn tradition, storming his way through Russian composer Sergei Rachmaninoff's Third Piano Concerto (1909). The second-prize winner was Valery Kuleshov of Russia, and the third prize went to Christopher Taylor of the United States, who explored offbeat repertory.

Luciano Pavarotti made a confident return to the concert platform in 1993 after an unfavorable turn in his career. The Italian tenor had received a run of bad press in 1992 for an alleged lip-synching episode, a disastrous opening night at La Scala in Milan, Italy, and his severe weight problem. Some people expected him to announce his retirement. But following a period of recuperation during which he lost about 30 pounds (14 kilograms), Pavarotti made a triumphant reappearance before an audience of 500,000 in New York's Central Park on June 26, 1993. He then sang alongside Spanish tenor Placido Domingo at the opening night of the Metropolitan Opera in New York City on September 27. Both tenors debuted at the Met in 1968, so the event also celebrated their 25th anniversaries.

Monteverdi anniversary. Numerous revivals of the works of Italian Renaissance composer Claudio Monteverdi were performed in 1993, the 350th anniversary of his death. The Salzburg Festival of Austria presented Monteverdi's *The Coronation of Poppea* (1642) and *Orfeo* (1607). The Boston Early Music Festival staged *Orfeo* in June. And also in June, the Netherlands Opera brought *The Return of Ulysses* (1641) to the Brooklyn Academy of Music in New York City. *The New Yorker* magazine called it ". . . the most wholly fine, the most candid and expressive piece of operatic staging seen in the city during the entire season."

Opera in Europe. The Bayreuth Festival, held each summer in Bayreuth, Germany, home of the composer Richard Wagner, opened with a new production of Wagner's opera *Tristan and Isolde* (1865). Directed by German playwright Heiner Muller, the production featured severely abstract sets by artist Erich Wonder and austere Japanese costumes by designer Yohji Yamamoto. Although some Wagnerian traditionalists dissented, the *Frankfurter Rundschau* newspaper called the production "among the most gripping, most perfect" ever seen in Bayreuth.

Two major world premieres took place at the Vienna (Austria) Festival in May 1993. The highly eclectic Russian composer, Alfred Schnittke, unveiled his second opera, *Homage to Zhivago,* a freewheeling adaptation of Russian novelist Boris Pasternak's *Dr.*

Zhivago (1957). Prepared in collaboration with Yuri Lyubimov and his Taganka Theater of Moscow, the opera blended theater, dance, classical music, and fragments of pop styles.

American composer Steve Reich discarded tradition altogether in what he called a "documentary music video theater work." *The Cave* told the Biblical story of Abraham from the viewpoint of modern-day Israelis, Palestinians, and Americans. Reich's music along with his artist wife Beryl Korot's computer-enhanced designs surrounded an array of "talking head" interview subjects. *The Cave* went to New York City in October, headlining the Next Wave Festival at the Brooklyn Academy of Music.

American operatic premieres included Daron Aric Hagen's *Shining Brow*, about the life of American architect Frank Lloyd Wright, at the Madison (Wis.) Opera in April; Philip Glass's *Orpheus*, based on French writer Jean Cocteau's 1950 motion picture of the same name, at the American Repertory Theater in Cambridge, Mass., in May; and *The Midnight Angel*, David Carlson's portrait of Edwardian high society, at the Opera Theater of St. Louis in June. The New York City Opera celebrated its 50th anniversary with three operatic premieres in October. The three operas were Ezra Laderman's *Marilyn*, based on the life of actress Marilyn Monroe; Lukas Foss' *Griffelkin*, a children's opera; and Hugo Weisgall's *Esther*, a Biblical story that won acclaim from New York critics for its high seriousness.

Opera companies became increasingly adventurous in 1993, reviving neglected repertory or importing contemporary works from overseas. In late May and early June, the Spoleto Festival USA in Charleston, S.C., featured Italian composer Gioacchino Rossini's *Le Comte Ory* (1828) and Alexander von Zemlinsky's *Birthday of the Infanta* (1922). The San Francisco Opera performed four operas of German composer Richard Strauss in June, including the seldom performed *Daphne* (1938). A rare Kurt Weill double bill played at the Santa Fe (N.M.) Opera in September with *The Tsar Has His Photograph Taken* (1928) and *The Protagonist* (1926). Michael Tippett's *The Midsummer Marriage* (1955) played at the New York City Opera in September.

Contemporary orchestral music. A compact disc recording of Henryk Górecki's Symphony No. 3, subtitled the *Symphony of Sorrowful Songs* (1976), became a phenomenal success in 1993. It topped the U.S. classical music charts for many months and even reached sixth place on the pop charts in the United Kingdom. It features a soprano voice and orchestra in the *minimalist* style, which uses repeated short patterns of music and complex rhythmic variations.

John Tavener's cello concerto, *Protecting Veil*, also scored a great success in Britain. The increasingly symphonic scores of Philip Glass continued to draw large U.S. audiences.

Orchestral premieres in the United States in

The Metropolitan Opera in New York City performs a new staging of Richard Strauss's *Ariadne auf Naxos* (1916) in March.

1993 included Witold Lutosławski's Symphony No. 4 by the Los Angeles Philharmonic in January; Ellen Taaffe Zwilich's Symphony No. 3 by the New York Philharmonic in February; Charles Wuorinen's *Microsymphony* by the Philadelphia Orchestra in March; and John Adams' *Chamber Symphony* by the San Francisco Orchestra in the spring. Other premieres included Nicholas Maw's Violin Concerto by the St. Luke's Orchestra in New York City in October and Bernard Rands's *. . . where the murmurs die. . .,* which was performed by the New York Philharmonic in December.

American orchestras in 1993 looked for ways to stop a decline in attendance. Several orchestras initiated programs with themes on various topics.

The American Symphony Orchestra League issued an alarming report in 1993 on the financial crisis of American orchestras. The report, called "Americanizing the American Orchestra," stirred controversy by calling for drastic changes. The report claimed that American orchestras were "exclusive, arrogant, possibly racist institutions." It also argued that orchestras should transform themselves in order to "reflect more closely the cultural mix, needs, and interests of their communities." The suggested changes included an increase in repertory aimed at minority groups as well as a flashier approach involving choreography, lighting, and graphic design. Critics of the report saw it as hostile to artistic values and condescending to minorities.

Grammy Award winners in 1993

Classical Album, Gustav Mahler, Symphony No. 9, Berlin Philharmonic Orchestra, Leonard Bernstein, conductor.

Orchestral Performance, Gustav Mahler, Symphony No. 9, Berlin Philharmonic Orchestra, Leonard Bernstein, conductor.

Opera Recording, Richard Strauss, *Die Frau Ohne Schatten,* Vienna Philharmonic, Sir Georg Solti, conductor.

Choral Performance, Carl Orff, *Carmina Burana,* San Francisco Girls/Boys Chorus, Symphony Chorus, and Symphony Orchestra, Herbert Blomstedt, conductor.

Classical Performance, Instrumental Solo with Orchestra, Sergei Prokofiev, *Sinfonia Concertante;* Peter Ilich Tchaikovsky, *Variations on a Rococo Theme;* Yo-Yo Ma, cello, with Pittsburgh (Pa.) Symphony Orchestra, Lorin Maazel, conductor.

Classical Performance, Instrumental Solo Without Orchestra, *Horowitz-Discovered Treasures (Chopin, Clementi, Liszt, Scarlatti, Scriabin),* Vladimir Horowitz, piano.

Chamber Music Performance, Johannes Brahms, Sonatas for Cello and Piano, Yo-Yo Ma, cello, and Emanuel Ax, piano.

Classical Vocal Performance, *Kathleen Battle at Carnegie Hall,* Kathleen Battle, soprano.

Contemporary Composition, *The Lovers,* Samuel Barber, composer.

Dvořák tributes. The Czech composer Antonín Dvořák composed his best-known symphony, *From the New World,* in 1893 while living in the United States. The symphony's 100th anniversary gave rise to several commemorations of Dvořák's work in 1993. The town of Spillville, Iowa, where Dvořák spent the summer of 1893, honored him with a folk festival and performances of his music. Bard College in Annandale-on-Hudson, N.Y., selected Dvořák as the subject for its annual summer festival of performances, symposia, and lectures. In addition, the Metropolitan Opera offered its first production of Dvořák's opera *Rusalka* (1900) in November 1993.

Deaths. The classical music world lost several great singers in 1993. The incomparable American contralto Marian Anderson died on April 8 (See **Deaths: Marian Anderson: A Voice Heard Once in 100 Years**).

The no less incomparable Bulgarian bass Boris Christoff died on June 28, the great soprano Arleen Auger died on June 10, and the gifted mezzo-soprano Tatiana Troyanos died on August 21. Opera soprano Lucia Popp died on November 16.

At age 100, pianist Mieczyslaw Horszowski died on May 22. Others who passed away were conductors Erich Leinsdorf on September 11 and Maurice Abravanel on September 22. Violinist Alexander Schneider died on February 2. □ Alex Ross

In *World Book,* see **Classical music; Opera.**

Clinton, Bill. United States President Bill Clinton was sworn into office on Jan. 20, 1993. Clinton began his term with boundless optimism, but his first year in office turned out to be fairly rocky. He managed, however, to get his economic plan through Congress—though barely—and to advance many of his new Democratic priorities despite strong Republican opposition on many fronts. Even so, he was criticized for showing a lack of strong leadership in foreign policy, and he suffered several embarrassing setbacks on his domestic agenda as well.

Searching for an attorney general. Trouble began early as Clinton on January 22 withdrew the name of Zoë Baird, an insurance company executive, as his nominee for attorney general. Baird admitted that she had unlawfully hired an illegal-alien couple from Peru as household servants in 1990. A second nominee, federal judge Kimba M. Wood, withdrew for similar reasons on February 5. Clinton finally got through this difficult period when he tapped Janet Reno, a Miami, Fla., prosecutor, for the attorney general's post. The Senate confirmed Reno unanimously on March 11. (See **Reno, Janet.**)

A new course on abortion. Dramatizing his differences with previous, Republican administrations, Clinton on January 22 reversed federal abortion policy. Acting by executive order, he lifted a controversial "gag rule" that barred abortion counseling by clinics receiving federal aid and ended a ban on the use of fetal tissue from abortions in federally funded research. The President also abolished a prohibition against performing abortions at U.S. military hospitals overseas.

Homosexuals in the military. In trying to lift a ban against gays and lesbians in the armed forces, the President retreated before a fire storm of criticism in Congress. In July, he agreed to a more limited change in rules that was dubbed the "don't ask, don't tell" policy. That plan eliminated questions about sexual preference from enlistment forms but still barred avowed homosexuals from the armed forces. Congress approved the policy but amended it to make it even more restrictive.

The issue took a new turn on September 3, as a U.S. district court judge in Los Angeles decreed that the military could not discharge homosexuals because of their sexual orientation. The ruling came in the case of a Navy petty officer who was fighting his dismissal for being a homosexual. On October 29, the Supreme Court of the United States granted a request from the Clinton Administration that the ruling be delayed while it was being appealed.

Family leave bill. The first bill passed by Congress in 1993, the Family and Medical Leave Act, represented another change in political direction. Similar measures had been vetoed twice by President George Bush. The 1993 legislation required companies with 50 or more employees to grant workers up to 12 weeks of unpaid leave in any 12-month period to care for a new baby or a seriously ill family member. Clinton signed the bill into law on February 5.

Economic package. The biggest domestic test for Clinton in 1993 came on the economic plan that he presented to Congress on February 17. The proposal, which called for big tax increases on upper-income Americans and corporations, was designed to reduce federal budget deficits by almost $500 billion over five years. Also included in the plan was a provision to stimulate the economy by spending $30 billion (later reduced to $16.3 billion) through 1997 by creating short-term and summer jobs.

The plan came under immediate attack from Republicans for its tax hikes and spending. And some key Democrats objected to a proposed tax on all forms of nonrenewable energy. Because of the opposition to the energy tax, Clinton dropped the idea and agreed instead to a 4.3-cents-a-gallon increase in the federal gasoline tax.

On April 21, Senate Republicans killed the stimulus package—by that time reduced to $15.4 billion—by waging a filibuster that prevented the measure from coming to a vote. Clinton charged "political gridlock," but his critics said the package would not have helped the economy, in any case.

After many changes, the final version of the economic plan squeaked through Congress by the narrowest of margins in early August. The House passed the plan 218 to 216 on August 5, and the Senate approved it the next day by a 51 to 50 vote.

White House woes. After several months in office, Clinton had little to cheer about. National polls in late May showed that only 36 percent of Americans approved of his performance—an all-time low for a new President so early in his administration.

Compounding its sinking image, the White House on May 19 dismissed seven staff members of its travel office, which makes travel arrangements for the White House press corps, citing evidence that the employees had been guilty of financial mismanagement. But five of the staffers were rehired less than a week later. An initial inquiry suggested that they had been fired at the behest of friends and relatives of Clinton's who wanted a share of the White House travel business.

In July, after an internal investigation of the matter, four White House aides were reprimanded for their role in the firings. They included Catherine Cornelius, 25, a distant cousin of Clinton's, who had been named to head the travel office in the wake of the staff dismissals. She was removed from that post after the report was issued.

Such internal disarray, along with strained relations with the news media, added to the President's woes. On May 29, seeking help in improving his image, Clinton brought in David R. Gergen, a former adviser to Republican Presidents, as a press counselor. At the same time, Clinton announced that his communications director, George Stephanopoulos,

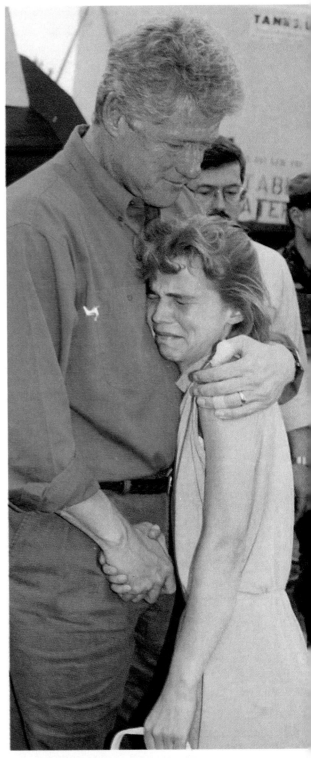

President Clinton comforts flood victim Christina Hein at a water distribution area in Des Moines, Iowa, in July as the Midwest is hit by record floods.

would be assuming a new position as a policy adviser to the President. On June 7, Clinton named his deputy chief of staff, Mark D. Gearan, as the new communications director.

Triumph on NAFTA. Despite opposition from many Democrats, Clinton became a strong advocate of the North American Free Trade Agreement (NAFTA), which called for the creation of a huge free trade zone encompassing Canada, Mexico, and the United States. NAFTA's chances were looking dim in November, but Clinton's tireless efforts in its behalf brought success. Congress approved the pact on November 17 and 20. Partly as a result of that victory, Clinton's approval ratings were rising late in the year.

Foreign policy. Clinton's foreign policy successes were few in 1993. Early in the year, he tried and failed to get European support for intervening militarily in the former Yugoslavia to halt Serbian aggression against Muslims in Bosnia-Herzegovina. (See **Europe; Bosnia-Herzegovina.**)

Responding to events in Somalia, Clinton set a March 31, 1994, withdrawal deadline for U.S. forces there. Clinton made the move after U.S. Army troops suffered heavy casualties on Oct. 3 and 4, 1993, in a battle in Mogadishu with forces of rebel leader Mohamed Farah Aideed. (See **Armed forces; Somalia.**)

Haiti was another sore point. Despite a campaign promise to the contrary, Clinton continued the policy—begun during the Bush Administration—of returning Haitian refugees to Haiti without allowing them to seek political asylum. Haiti's military leaders signed an accord in July calling for ousted Haitian President Jean-Bertrand Aristide to be reinstated at the head of a democratic government by October 30, but they refused to abide by it. Clinton ordered a naval blockade of Haiti to shut off imports and bring pressure on Haiti's leaders to allow Aristide's return. The stand-off continued at year-end. (See **Haiti.**)

But Clinton enjoyed a clear diplomatic triumph at a September 13 White House ceremony bringing together two once-bitter enemies, Israeli Prime Minister Yitzhak Rabin and Yasir Arafat, chairman of the Palestine Liberation Organization. The two signed an agreement calling for Palestinian self-rule in Jericho and the Gaza Strip. (See **Israel; Middle East.**)

Health care. Clinton launched his much-delayed plan for health-care reform with a speech to Congress on September 22, triggering a national debate. Members of Congress offered several competing plans. First Lady Hillary Rodham Clinton, who directed a White House task force on health care, testified extensively about the proposal before congressional committees. Although no action was taken in 1993, health-care reform was expected to be high on the legislative agenda in 1994. □ William J. Eaton

See also **Clinton, Hillary Rodham; Congress of the United States; United States, Government of the.** In *World Book,* see **Clinton, Bill.**

Clinton, Hillary Rodham (1947-   ), wife of President Bill Clinton, moved in 1993 to become one of the most activist first ladies in United States history. The President named her to head his Task Force on National Health Care Reform.

Hillary Clinton was born Hillary Diane Rodham in Chicago on Oct. 26, 1947. She grew up in the Chicago suburb of Park Ridge and attended Wellesley College in Massachusetts, graduating with honors in 1969. She then attended Yale University Law School in New Haven, Conn., where she met Bill Clinton.

In 1973, after obtaining her law degree, Hillary Rodham became a staff attorney for the Children's Defense Fund, an organization based in Washington, D.C., that develops programs for child welfare and family services. The following year, she was recruited to work for the U.S. House of Representatives Judiciary Committee in its impeachment proceedings against President Richard M. Nixon.

In 1975, Hillary Rodham married Bill Clinton. Their daughter, Chelsea, was born in 1980, two years after Bill Clinton was elected to his first term as Arkansas governor.

As first lady of Arkansas, Hillary Clinton resumed her work on behalf of children. She also became a prominent private lawyer with a Little Rock firm. For her achievements, she was named Arkansas Woman of the Year in 1983. □ David Dreier

Clothing. See **Fashion.**

Coal. On Dec. 7, 1993, negotiators reached an agreement to settle a series of strikes by the United Mine Workers of America (UMW) union that began May 10. The strikes, aimed at winning a new contract, had targeted several coal companies belonging to the Bituminous Coal Operators Association (BCOA), which represents the 12 largest coal-mining companies in the United States. The first strike involved about 2,000 miners in Indiana and Illinois. On May 18, miners struck in West Virginia and on June 16, the strike spread to Kentucky. By late October, the strike included 17,700 miners in several states.

The contract between BCOA and the UMW, which covers about 60,000 coal miners, is important in setting a pattern for collective bargaining agreements with hundreds of smaller mining companies. In the 1993 negotiations, the UMW wanted new job-security provisions from BCOA. The union also wanted assurance that new mines would employ union workers and that unionized coal companies would stop setting up nonunion subsidiaries.

U.S. coal production during the first half of 1993 dropped 4 percent below the amount produced in the first half of 1992, the U.S. Department of Energy reported on August 26. The National Coal Association (NCA), an industry group based in Washington, D.C., attributed the decline to poor worldwide economic conditions. In January 1993, the NCA reported that U.S. coal exports in 1992 declined by about 6 percent from 1991. The NCA predicted that exports would decline by about 3 percent in 1993.

Britain's coal industry. On January 12, a special committee of the United Kingdom's House of Commons recommended a government subsidy to keep 10 to 20 of Britain's 50 coal mines open. The committee warned that Britain's coal industry would not survive unless the government invested in technology that reduces the air pollution caused by burning coal. Otherwise, air pollution regulations would severely restrict the use of coal in the future, the panel said. British Coal, the state-owned coal company, agreed in March to subsidies that would keep 12 mines open. But by August, as the mines grew more unprofitable, British Coal announced that mine closings would be necessary.

Making oil. On August 23, members of the Consortium for Fossil Fuel Liquefaction Science (CFFLS), a group of university researchers, released a report on their progress in converting mixtures of plastic waste and coal into a fuel oil suitable for refining into gasoline. Newly discovered chemical agents have increased the efficiency of the liquefaction process, they reported. The director of CFFLS said the process, which could be ready for large-scale use within a few years, could help the United States make use of its large coal reserves and reduce waste plastics that are now disposed of in landfills. ☐ Michael Woods

See also **Chemistry**. In *World Book,* see **Coal**.

Colombia. Pablo Escobar Gaviría, 44, one of the world's most notorious criminals, died in a shoot-out with police and soldiers in Medellín, Colombia, on Dec. 2, 1993. Escobar was the multibillionaire head of the Medellín cocaine cartel and was wanted in the United States on murder and drug-trafficking charges. The Colombian government had increased the bounty on Escobar from $4 million to $7 million early in the year. The United States had agreed to pay $2.5 million of the total.

Police found Escobar by tracing phone calls he made from his hideout. As police stormed the house, Escobar tried to escape over the roof. He was killed by members of a 3,000-member security force that had searched for him since he escaped from a federal prison in 1992.

Pipeline bombings. Given their importance to Colombia's economy, oil installations increasingly became a target for antigovernment terrorist attacks in 1993. In July, rebel bomb attacks on a 500-mile (800-kilometer) oil pipeline that runs from the interior of the country to the Caribbean coast forced the government to halt oil exports for three days. In April, guerrillas blew up a bridge about 185 miles (300 kilometers) north of Bogotá that carried eight oil pipelines.

To counter the threat, the Colombian government offered bounties of up to $1.4 million each for the capture of top guerrilla leaders. The government

said that it would also institute sanctions against banks found handling rebel accounts.

Beginning in January 1993, Colombia began setting aside 20 percent of its oil revenues in a national defense fund. The central government said it would use the money to train and deploy 44 military intelligence units and to station 18,000 additional police and soldiers around oil installations. The government also moved to purchase thousands of acres of land surrounding the oil fields to create military security zones.

Bombings by drug traffickers. Drug traffickers continued to terrorize Colombians with bombings in 1993. In a typical incident on January 30, a vehicle packed with dynamite exploded in Bogotá and killed 20 people, including 5 children.

The government blamed Escobar for much of Colombia's terrorism in 1993, including the killing of more than 100 Medellín police officers. In January, an anti-Escobar vigilante group formed. It was called "People Persecuted by Pablo Escobar," or PEPES from its Spanish acronym. Many PEPES members were former Escobar associates. In its first month, PEPES reportedly killed 20 Escobar loyalists. ☐ Nathan A. Haverstock

See also **Latin America** (Facts in brief table). In *World Book,* see **Colombia**.

Colorado. See State government.

Common Market. See Europe.

Commonwealth of Independent States.

Led by Russia, the former Soviet republics that made up the Commonwealth of Independent States (C.I.S.) took steps in 1993 to transform the confederation into a viable political and economic alliance. After its formation following the breakup of the Soviet Union in December 1991, the commonwealth had lacked effective means to forge closer ties among its member states. But by the end of 1993, tensions within the C.I.S. remained, in part over Russia's efforts to dominate the confederation.

The effort to revitalize the C.I.S. began on January 22, when seven members—Armenia, Belarus, Kazakhstan, Kyrgyzstan, Russia, Tajikistan, and Uzbekistan—signed a charter that called for increased political and economic integration. Three states— Moldova, Turkmenistan, and Ukraine—did not sign the charter but remained members of the C.I.S.

On February 28, Russian President Boris Yeltsin angered fellow C.I.S. leaders when he suggested that international organizations grant Russia special powers to stop conflicts in the former Soviet Union. Russia viewed ethnic conflicts in several states, notably Tajikistan, as potentially destabilizing for the entire region. Some C.I.S. leaders saw Yeltsin's statement as an expression of Russian imperialist designs.

A deepening economic crisis in the spring and summer sparked efforts to increase economic cooperation. The Soviet Union's breakup had severed trade links and other ties that had made the former republics economically interdependent. Some states, including Ukraine, feared that restoring these ties would lead to Russian domination. Nevertheless, C.I.S. leaders at meetings in April and May promoted the idea of economic integration. On July 10, the mostly Slavic states of Russia, Ukraine, and Belarus agreed to form a customs union and single market.

Russia on July 24 moved to withdraw all pre-1993 ruble notes from circulation, greatly disrupting the economies of many former republics that used the ruble as their currency. But by September, Russia had eased conditions of the reform.

Another blow came in October, when a "ruble zone" formed in September by Russia and five other C.I.S. members fell apart. The republics had agreed to coordinate economic and monetary policies. However, the C.I.S. continued to work toward eventual economic union. C.I.S. members had agreed to form such a union in a treaty signed on September 24.

New members. On September 24, Azerbaijan, which had withdrawn from the C.I.S. in October 1992, rejoined the commonwealth. The former Soviet republic of Georgia became the confederation's 12th member on Oct. 23, 1993. □ Justin Burke

See also **Armenia; Azerbaijan; Georgia; Russia; Tajikistan; Ukraine.** In *World Book*, see **Commonwealth of Independent States.**
Comoros. See **Africa.**

Computer. Increasingly powerful personal computers, the introduction of "personal digital assistants," and the convergence of computing, telecommunications, and television were among the leading developments in the computer industry during 1993. But these stories were overshadowed by disastrous financial setbacks and resulting personnel changes at two of the industry's largest and most important companies—International Business Machines Corporation (IBM) of Armonk, N.Y., and Apple Computer Incorporated of Cupertino, Calif.

IBM, having lost billions of dollars and seen its stock value decline by almost 75 percent over five years, replaced long-time chairman John F. Akers in spring 1993. The company's new head, Louis V. Gerstner, Jr., took quick action to restructure the corporation to make it more consumer-oriented.

Apple Computer likewise suffered severe business losses that resulted in replacement at the top. John Sculley, head of Apple since 1985 and one of the computer industry's best-known executives, resigned as chief executive officer in June 1993. He was replaced by Apple executive Michael Spindler. Sculley remained chairman of Apple until October, when he resigned that position as well. Observers said the resignation was prompted by severe declines in Apple's stock value, as well as a perception that the company was ill-equipped to compete against less-expensive personal computers flooding the market.

A decline in computer prices, in fact, lay at the heart of the business woes of both Apple and IBM. IBM, which had built much of its success on the sale and service of huge mainframe computers used in business, saw those computers increasingly replaced by much smaller, far-less-expensive machines.

By late 1993, industry analysts detected signs that IBM was beginning to turn itself around, though its stock prices remained in the doldrums. Experts remained concerned about Apple's long-term future.

Personal digital assistants. Apple and other manufacturers pinned some of their hopes for the future on a new consumer item dubbed the personal digital assistant (PDA). PDA's are computers barely larger than a paperback book. They are designed to keep records, recognize handwriting, fax or modem documents, and accomplish other tasks that previously required larger desktop machines.

Apple's Newton MessagePad was one of the first PDA's. Priced at between $700 and $1,000, Newton captured a great deal of attention during its August introduction. Some of that attention turned to ridicule when it became clear that the Newton had flaws, particularly in its handwriting-recognition feature. Nevertheless, Apple sold more than 10,000 Newtons during its first few weeks on the market.

The Pentium microprocessor, the latest version of the most successful computer chips ever made, was introduced in March by Intel Corporation

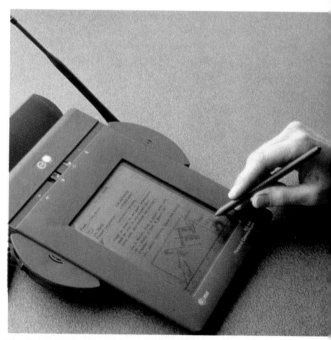

The Personal Communicator 440 was one of several small computers dubbed "personal digital assistants" that hit the market in 1993.

of Santa Clara, Calif. A microprocessor is the "brains" of the personal computer, a tiny electronic device that makes possible all the computer's functions. The Pentium is the fastest and most sophisticated Intel microprocessor yet produced.

The first Pentium-based personal computers had been expected to cost around $5,000, with prices holding steady throughout 1993. Pentium machines were available for under $4,000 by autumn, however, in another indication of the fierce price wars raging throughout the personal computer industry.

Meanwhile, IBM and Apple prepared for the 1994 release of personal computers containing another new microprocessor, the PowerPC chip. Apple and IBM had developed that chip in partnership with Motorola Incorporated of Schaumburg, Ill., in an attempt to challenge Intel's dominance as a chip maker.

Multimedia computing. The increase in power and decline in price for information-processing technology also accelerated the spread of sophisticated computer technology to the home. New computers for home use are capable of handling programs that allow a user to interact with data in the form of audio, animation, video, and graphics.

Multimedia technology is at the heart of interactive television, in which a viewer uses a special keypad to control what appears on the television screen—for example, by summoning an instant replay during a televised sporting event. Industry experts believe the business potential for interactive television is enormous, and mid-1993 saw an explosion of interest in this new field. Telephone companies, publishers, TV and motion-picture companies, computer manufacturers, and software developers all began forming alliances and partnerships aimed at dominating sections of the emerging industry. (See **Telecommunications.**)

In November, Compton's NewMedia of San Diego announced that it had secured a fundamental patent on the software used to store and retrieve video, graphics, and other items in multimedia programs. The patent, which had been granted on August 31, affected software for interactive television as well as for many new products in the CD-ROM (compact disc read-only memory) format.

Information superhighway. Multimedia computing and interactive TV are two key aspects of the National Information Infrastructure envisioned by the Administration of United States President Bill Clinton. The infrastructure, also called the *information superhighway*, would provide high-speed data transmission among business and personal computers across the United States and eventually around the world. In September, the Clinton Administration issued a report detailing principles for developing the network. Observers predicted that building the highway would become a major focus of industry, university, and government activity.   □ Keith Ferrell

See also **Electronics.** In *World Book,* see **Computer.**

Congress of the United States. The first session of the 103rd Congress gave President Bill Clinton a narrow victory on his budget package and enacted much of his domestic agenda in 1993. Despite sharp criticism of some of the new Administration's foreign policy actions, Congress approved the controversial North American Free Trade Agreement (NAFTA) with Mexico and Canada by decisive majorities in both the House of Representatives and the Senate. Action on the President's comprehensive plan for universal health care was put off until 1994.

Although it was the first time in 12 years that a Democratic-controlled Congress was able to work with a Democrat in the White House, the relationship was far from trouble-free. Clinton had to make countless concessions to members of his own party to win their votes for his $1.5-trillion budget package and other major legislation. Even so, Congress approved 88 percent of Clinton's proposed legislation, an achievement unmatched by any President since Lyndon B. Johnson in 1965. Moreover, Clinton did not once use his veto power, in sharp contrast to former President George Bush, who used his veto power 34 times in four years. As the congressional session drew to a close on November 24, the President and his allies declared that gridlock between the White House and Capitol Hill had at last been broken.

Controversial nominee. The year began on a sour note when the Senate Judiciary Committee balked at Clinton's nominee for U.S. attorney general, corporate attorney Zoë Baird, after disclosures that Baird had violated aspects of a 1986 immigration law. On Jan. 14, 1993, five days before the start of Baird's confirmation hearings, media reports revealed that she and her husband had unlawfully employed two illegal aliens from Peru beginning in 1990 and had not paid social security taxes for the couple until soon after her nomination. On Jan. 22, 1993, Clinton accepted Baird's request that her nomination be withdrawn. After another false start, Clinton chose Janet Reno, the former state attorney for Dade County, Florida, to head the Department of Justice. Reno was confirmed easily on March 11.

Rejected measures. Over Clinton's objections, Congress finally killed the Superconducting Super Collider (SSC), a mammoth *particle accelerator* (atom smasher) under construction near Dallas. The House had cut off funding for the $11-billion project in 1992, but the SSC had then been saved by the Senate. In 1993, Congress's anti-SSC mood was bolstered by a large number of freshmen anxious to fulfill campaign promises to help cut the federal budget deficit. By year's end, freshmen made up 14 percent of the Senate and nearly 25 percent of the House, the largest class of newcomers since 1947.

Clinton's chief loss was his $16.3-billion short-term economic stimulus package, which included funding for highway construction projects and loans

Members of the United States House of Representatives

The House of Representatives of the second session of the 103rd Congress consisted of 258 Democrats, 176 Republicans, and 1 independent (not including representatives from American Samoa, the District of Columbia, Guam, Puerto Rico and the Virgin Islands), when it convened on Jan. 25, 1994. There were also 258 Democrats, 176 Republicans, and 1 independent when the first session of the 103rd Congress convened. This table shows congressional district, legislator, and party affiliation. Asterisk (*) denotes those who served in the 102nd Congress; dagger (†) denotes "at large."

Alabama
1. Sonny Callahan, R.*
2. Terry Everett, R.
3. Glen Browder, D.*
4. Tom Bevill, D.*
5. Bud Cramer, D.*
6. Spencer Bachus, R.
7. Earl Hilliard, D.

Alaska
† Donald E. Young, R.*

Arizona
1. Sam Coppersmith, D.
2. Ed Pastor, D.*
3. Bob Stump, R.*
4. Jon L. Kyl, R.*
5. Jim Kolbe, R*
6. Karan English, D.

Arkansas
1. Blanche Lambert, D.
2. Ray Thornton, D.*
3. Tim Hutchinson, R.
4. Jay Dickey, R.

California
1. Dan Hamburg, D.
2. Wally Herger, R.*
3. Vic Fazio, D.*
4. John Doolittle, R.*
5. Robert T. Matsui, D.*
6. Lynn Woolsey, D.
7. George E. Miller, D.*
8. Nancy Pelosi, D.*
9. Ronald V. Dellums, D.*
10. Bill Baker, R.
11. Richard Pombo, R.
12. Tom Lantos, D.*
13. Fortney H. (Peter) Stark, D.*
14. Anna Eshoo, D.
15. Norman Mineta, D.*
16. Don Edwards, D.*
17. Sam Farr, D.
18. Gary Condit, D.*
19. Richard H. Lehman, D.*
20. Calvin Dooley, D.*
21. William M. Thomas, R.*
22. Michael Huffington, R.
23. Elton Gallegly, R.*
24. Anthony Beilenson, D.*
25. Howard McKeon, R.
26. Howard L. Berman, D.*
27. Carlos J. Moorhead, R.*
28. David Dreier, R.*
29. Henry A. Waxman, D.*
30. Xavier Becerra, D.
31. Matthew Martinez, D.*
32. Julian C. Dixon, D.*
33. Lucille Roybal-Allard, D.
34. Esteban E. Torres, D.*
35. Maxine Waters, D.*
36. Jane Harman, D.
37. Walter Tucker, D.
38. Steve Horn, R.
39. Edward Royce, R.
40. Jerry Lewis, R.*
41. Jay Kim, R.
42. George E. Brown, Jr., D.*
43. Kenneth Calvert, R.
44. Al McCandless, R.*
45. Dana Rohrabacher, R.*
46. Robert K. Dornan, R.*
47. C. Christopher Cox, R.*
48. Ronald C. Packard, R.*
49. Lynn Schenk, D.
40. Bob Filner, D.
41. Randy (Duke) Cunningham, R.*
42. Duncan L. Hunter, R.*

Colorado
1. Patricia Schroeder, D.*
2. David E. Skaggs, D.*
3. Scott McInnis, R.
4. Wayne Allard, R.*
5. Joel Hefley, R.*
6. Daniel Schaefer, R.*

Connecticut
1. Barbara B. Kennelly, D.*
2. Sam Gejdenson, D.*
3. Rosa DeLauro, D.*
4. Christopher Shays, R.*
5. Gary Franks, R.*
6. Nancy L. Johnson, R.*

Delaware
†Michael Castle, R.

Florida
1. Earl Hutto, D.*
2. Pete Peterson, D.*
3. Corrine Brown, D.
4. Tillie Fowler, R.
5. Karen Thurman, D.
6. Clifford B. Stearns, R.*
7. John Mica, R.
8. Bill McCollum, R.*
9. Michael Bilirakis, R.*
10. C. W. Bill Young, R.*
11. Sam M. Gibbons, D.*
12. Charles Canady, R.
13. Dan Miller, R.
14. Porter J. Goss, R.*
15. Jim Bacchus, D.*
16. Tom Lewis, R.*
17. Carrie Meek, D.
18. Ileana Ros-Lehtinen, R.*
19. Harry A. Johnston II, D.*
20. Peter Deutsch, D.
21. Lincoln Diaz-Balart, R.
22. E. Clay Shaw, Jr., R.*
23. Alcee Hastings, D.

Georgia
1. Jack Kingston, R.
2. Sanford Bishop, D.
3. Mac Collins, R.
4. John Linder, R.
5. John Lewis, D.*
6. Newt Gingrich, R.*
7. George Darden, D.*
8. J. Roy Rowland, D.*
9. Nathan Deal, D.
10. Don Johnson, D.
11. Cynthia McKinney, D.

Hawaii
1. Neil Abercrombie, D.*
2. Patsy T. Mink, D.*

Idaho
1. Larry LaRocco, D.*
2. Michael Crapo, R.

Illinois
1. Bobby Rush, D.
2. Mel Reynolds, D.
3. William O. Lipinski, D.*
4. Luis Gutierrez, D.
5. Dan Rostenkowski, D.*
6. Henry J. Hyde, R.*
7. Cardiss Collins, D.*
8. Philip M. Crane, R.*
9. Sidney R. Yates, D.*
10. John Edward Porter, R.*
11. George Sangmeister, D.*
12. Jerry F. Costello, D.*
13. Harris W. Fawell, R.*
14. J. Dennis Hastert, R.*
15. Thomas W. Ewing, R.*
16. Donald Manzullo, R.
17. Lane A. Evans, D.*
18. Robert H. Michel, R.*
19. Glenn Poshard, D.*
20. Richard J. Durbin, D.*

Indiana
1. Peter J. Visclosky, D.*
2. Philip R. Sharp, D*
3. Tim Roemer, D.*
4. Jill Long, D.*
5. Steve Buyer, R.
6. Danny L. Burton, R.*
7. John T. Myers, R.*
8. Frank McCloskey, D.*
9. Lee H. Hamilton, D.*
10. Andrew Jacobs, Jr., D.*

Iowa
1. Jim Leach, R.*
2. Jim Nussle, R.*
3. Jim Ross Lightfoot, R.*
4. Neal Smith, D.*
5. Fred Grandy, R.*

Kansas
1. Pat Roberts, R.*
2. James C. Slattery, D.*
3. Jan Meyers, R.*
4. Dan Glickman, D.*

Kentucky
1. Tom Barlow, D.
2. William H. Natcher, D.*
3. Romano L. Mazzoli, D.*
4. Jim Bunning, R.*
5. Harold (Hal) Rogers, R.*
6. Scotty Baesler, D.

Louisiana
1. Robert L. Livingston, Jr., R.*
2. William J. Jefferson, D.*
3. W. J. (Billy) Tauzin, D.*
4. Cleo Fields, D.
5. Jim McCrery, R.*
6. Richard Hugh Baker, R.*
7. James A. (Jimmy) Hayes, D.*

Maine
1. Thomas H. Andrews, D.*
2. Olympia J. Snowe, R.*

Maryland
1. Wayne T. Gilchrest, R.*
2. Helen Delich Bentley, R.*
3. Benjamin L. Cardin, D.*
4. Albert Wynn, D.
5. Steny H. Hoyer, D.*
6. Roscoe Bartlett, R.
7. Kweisi Mfume, D.*
8. Constance A. Morella, R.*

Massachusetts
1. John W. Olver, D.*
2. Richard E. Neal, D.*
3. Peter Blute, R.
4. Barney Frank, D.*
5. Martin Meehan, D.
6. Peter Torkildsen, R.
7. Edward J. Markey, D.*
8. Joseph P. Kennedy II, D.*
9. John Joseph Moakley, D.*
10. Gerry E. Studds, D.*

Michigan
1. Bart Stupak, D.
2. Peter Hoekstra, R.
3. Vernon Ehlers, R.
4. Dave Camp, R.*
5. James Barcia, D.
6. Frederick S. Upton, R.*
7. Nick Smith, R.
8. Bob Carr, D.*
9. Dale E. Kildee, D.*
10. David E. Bonior, D.*
11. Joseph Knollenberg, R.
12. Sander M. Levin, D.*
13. William D. Ford, D.*
14. John Conyers, Jr., D.*
15. Barbara-Rose Collins, D.*
16. John D. Dingell, D.*

Minnesota
1. Timothy J. Penny, D.*
2. David Minge, D.
3. Jim Ramstad, R.*
4. Bruce F. Vento, D.*
5. Martin O. Sabo, D.*
6. Rod Grams, R.
7. Collin C. Peterson, D.*
8. James L. Oberstar, D.*

Mississippi
1. Jamie L. Whitten, D.*
2. Bennie Thompson, D.
3. G. V. (Sonny) Montgomery, D.*
4. Mike Parker, D.*
5. Gene Taylor, D.*

Missouri
1. William L. (Bill) Clay, D.*
2. James Talent, R.
3. Richard A. Gephardt, D.*
4. Ike Skelton, D.*
5. Alan D. Wheat, D.*
6. Pat Danner, D.
7. Mel Hancock, R.*
8. Bill Emerson, R*
9. Harold L. Volkmer, D.*

Montana
† Pat Williams, D.*

Nebraska
1. Doug Bereuter, R.*
2. Peter Hoagland, D.*
3. Bill Barrett, R.*

Nevada
1. James H. Bilbray, D.*
2. Barbara F. Vucanovich, R.*

New Hampshire
1. Bill Zeliff, R.*
2. Dick Swett, D.*

New Jersey
1. Robert E. Andrews, D.*
2. William J. Hughes, D.*
3. H. James Saxton, R.*
4. Christopher H. Smith, R.*
5. Marge Roukema, R.*
6. Frank Pallone, Jr., D.*
7. Bob Franks, R.
8. Herbert Klein, D.
9. Robert G. Torricelli, D.*
10. Donald M. Payne, D.*
11. Dean A. Gallo, R.*
12. Richard A. Zimmer, R.*
13. Robert Menendez, D.

New Mexico
1. Steven H. Schiff, R.*
2. Joe Skeen, R.*
3. William B. Richardson, D.*

New York
1. George J. Hochbrueckner, D.*
2. Rick Lazio, R.
3. Peter King, R.
4. David Levy, R.
5. Gary L. Ackerman, D.*
6. Floyd H. Flake, D.*
7. Thomas J. Manton, D.*
8. Jerrold Nadler, D.*
9. Charles E. Schumer, D.*
10. Edolphus Towns, D.*
11. Major R. Owens, D.*
12. Nydia Velazquez, D.
13. Susan Molinari, R.*
14. Carolyn Maloney, D.
15. Charles B. Rangel, D.*
16. Jose E. Serrano, D.*
17. Eliot L. Engel, D.*
18. Nita M. Lowey, D.*
19. Hamilton Fish, Jr., R.*
20. Benjamin A. Gilman, R.*
21. Michael R. McNulty, D.*
22. Gerald B. Solomon, R.*
23. Sherwood L. Boehlert, R.*
24. John McHugh, R.
25. James Walsh, R.*
26. Maurice Hinchey, D.
27. William Paxon, R.*
28. Louise M. Slaughter, D.*
29. John J. LaFalce, D.*
30. Jack Quinn, R.
31. Amory Houghton, Jr., R.*

North Carolina
1. Eva Clayton, D.
2. Tim Valentine, D.*
3. H. Martin Lancaster, D.*
4. David E. Price, D.*
5. Stephen L. Neal, D.*
6. Howard Coble, R.*
7. Charles Rose III, D.*
8. W. G. (Bill) Hefner, D.*
9. J. Alex McMillan III, R.*
10. Cass Ballenger, R.*
11. Charles H. Taylor, R.*
12. Melvin Watt, D.

North Dakota
† Earl Pomeroy, D.

Ohio
1. David Mann, D.
2. Rob Portman, R.
3. Tony P. Hall, D.*
4. Michael G. Oxley, R.*
5. Paul E. Gillmor, R.*
6. Ted Strickland, D.
7. David L. Hobson, R.*
8. John A. Boehner, R.*
9. Marcy Kaptur, D.*
10. Martin Hoke, R.
11. Louis Stokes, D.*
12. John R. Kasich, R.*
13. Sherrod Brown, D.
14. Thomas C. Sawyer, D.*
15. Deborah Pryce, R.
16. Ralph Regula, R.*
17. James A. Traficant, Jr., D.*
18. Douglas Applegate, D.*
19. Eric Fingerhut, D.

Oklahoma
1. James M. Inhofe, R.*
2. Mike Synar, D.*
3. Bill Brewster, D.*
4. Dave McCurdy, D.*
5. Ernest Jim Istook, R.
6. Glenn English, D.*

Oregon
1. Elizabeth Furse, D.
2. Robert F. Smith, R.*
3. Ron Wyden, D.*
4. Peter A. DeFazio, D.*
5. Mike Kopetski, D.*

Pennsylvania
1. Thomas M. Foglietta, D.*
2. Lucien Blackwell, D.*
3. Robert A. Borski, Jr., D.*
4. Ron Klink, D.
5. William F. Clinger, Jr., R.*
6. Tim Holden, D.
7. W. Curtis Weldon, R.*
8. Jim Greenwood, R.
9. E. G. (Bud) Shuster, R.*
10. Joseph M. McDade, R.*
11. Paul E. Kanjorski, D.*
12. John P. Murtha, D.*
13. Marjorie Margolias-Mezvinsky, D.
14. William J. Coyne, D.*
15. Paul McHale, D.
16. Robert S. Walker, R.*
17. George W. Gekas, R.*
18. Rick Santorum, R.*
19. William F. Goodling, R.*
20. Austin J. Murphy, D.*
21. Thomas J. Ridge, R.*

Rhode Island
1. Ronald K. Machtley, R.*
2. John F. Reed, D.*

South Carolina
1. Arthur Ravenel, Jr., R.*
2. Floyd Spence, R.*
3. Butler Derrick, Jr., D.*
4. Bob Inglis, R.
5. John M. Spratt, Jr., D.*
6. James Clyburn, D.

South Dakota
† Tim Johnson, D.*

Tennessee
1. James H. Quillen, R.*
2. John J. Duncan, Jr., R.*
3. Marilyn Lloyd, D.*
4. James H. Cooper, D.*
5. Bob Clement, D.*
6. Bart Gordon, D.*
7. Donald K. Sundquist, R.*
8. John S. Tanner, D.*
9. Harold E. Ford, D*

Texas
1. Jim Chapman, D.*
2. Charles Wilson, D.*
3. Sam Johnson, R.*
4. Ralph M. Hall, D.*
5. John W. Bryant, D.*
6. Joe Barton, R.*
7. Bill Archer, R.*
8. Jack Fields, Jr., R.*
9. Jack Brooks, D.*
10. J. J. (Jake) Pickle, D.*
11. Chet Edwards, D.*
12. Preston P. (Pete) Geren, D.*
13. Bill Sarpalius, D.*
14. Greg Laughlin, D.*
15. Eligio (Kika) de la Garza, D.*
16. Ronald D. Coleman, D.*
17. Charles W. Stenholm, D.*
18. Craig A. Washington, D.*
19. Larry Combest, R.*

20. Henry B. Gonzalez, D.*
21. Lamar S. Smith, R.*
22. Tom DeLay, R.*
23. Henry Bonilla, R.
24. Martin Frost, D.*
25. Michael A. Andrews, D.*
26. Richard K. Armey, R.*
27. Solomon P. Ortiz, D.*
28. Frank Tejeda, D.
29. Gene Green, D.
30. Eddie Bernice Johnson, D.

Utah
1. James V. Hansen, R.*
2. Karen Shepherd, D.
3. William Orton, D.*

Vermont
† Bernard Sanders, Ind.*

Virginia
1. Herbert H. Bateman, R.*
2. Owen B. Pickett, D.*
3. Robert Scott, D.
4. Norman Sisisky, D.*
5. Lewis F. Payne, Jr., D.*
6. Robert Goodlatte, R.
7. Thomas J. (Tom) Bliley, Jr., R.*
8. James P. Moran, Jr., D.*
9. Frederick C. Boucher, D.*
10. Frank R. Wolf, R.*
11. Leslie Byrne, D.

Washington
1. Maria Cantwell, D.
2. Al Swift, D.*
3. Jolene Unsoeld, D.*
4. Jay Inslee, D.
5. Thomas S. Foley, D.*
6. Norman D. Dicks, D.*
7. Jim McDermott, D.*
8. Jennifer Dunn, R.
9. Mike Kreidler, D.

West Virginia
1. Alan B. Mollohan, D.*
2. Robert E. Wise, Jr., D.*
3. Nick J. Rahall II, D.*

Wisconsin
1. Peter W. Barca, D.
2. Scott Klug, R.*
3. Steven Gunderson, R.*
4. Gerald D. Kleczka, D.*
5. Thomas Barrett, D.
6. Thomas E. Petri, R.*
7. David R. Obey, D.*
8. Toby Roth, R.*
9. F. James Sensenbrenner, Jr., R.*

Wyoming
† Craig Thomas, R.*

Nonvoting representatives
American Samoa
Eni F. H. Faleomavaega, D.*

District of Columbia
Eleanor Holmes Norton, D.*

Guam
Robert Underwood, D.

Puerto Rico
Carlos Romero-Barceló, D.

Virgin Islands
Ron de Lugo, D.*

to small businesses. The House passed the package in March. But Senate Republicans, sticking together in an unbreakable filibuster, scuttled the program—by then reduced to $15.4 billion—on April 21. However, the Senate approved by voice vote a portion of the bill authorizing $4 billion to give the long-term jobless up to 20 extra weeks of unemployment compensation. The House passed that measure the next day.

A second chance for vetoed bills. Democratic leaders in the House and Senate spearheaded moves during the year to pass again a number of bills that President Bush had vetoed. In February, both houses approved the Family and Medical Leave Act, twice vetoed by Bush. The bill requires large companies to offer workers up to 12 weeks of unpaid leave per year for family or medical emergencies, including the birth or adoption of a child or a family member's serious illness.

In May, Congress passed the so-called motor voter bill, requiring states to permit citizens to register to vote when they apply for driver's licenses. The bill, due to take effect in 1995, also permits registration at military recruitment stations and welfare offices. Congress also approved legislation during the year lifting some restrictions on political activity by most federal and Postal Service employees.

Economic program. Clinton faced his most difficult task in obtaining congressional approval for his proposed fiscal 1994 budget, which set targets for a long-term plan to bring down record-high budget deficits through a combination of tax increases and spending cuts. Clinton contended that the proposed tax increases would affect primarily upper-income Americans. Opponents, including all congressional Republicans, attacked the program as a job-killing measure that would harm the middle class.

In early spring 1993, the President presented Congress with the broad outlines of his economic plan, which the President said would reduce the deficit by $473 billion over five years. But Republicans and conservative Democrats demanded deeper spending cuts, especially after the Congressional Budget Office announced that the White House had overestimated the deficit reduction by about $70 billion. In late March and early April, the House and Senate approved a resolution calling for a reduction of $496-billion over five years.

On April 8, Clinton sent Congress his proposed $1.5-trillion 1994 budget, which projected a deficit reduction of only about $450 billion through 1998. The move sparked weeks of intense lobbying by the President and Democratic leaders in preparation for the House vote on May 27, culminating in a last-minute agreement on a mechanism to help curb the growth of Medicare, social security, and other so-called entitlement programs. The budget, with the $496-billion deficit reduction goal restored, cleared the House by a vote of 219 to 213. On June 25, the Senate's version squeezed through that chamber

with the aid of Vice President Albert Gore, Jr., who broke a 49-to-49 tie. No Republican voted for the budget in either chamber.

The drama drew toward its close as House and Senate negotiators worked on a final version of the legislation. In a key compromise, the conferees submitted to a demand by lawmakers from energy-producing states and eliminated the President's proposed broad-based energy tax, replacing it with an increase in the federal tax on gasoline. In the end, the bill passed by the narrowest of margins, again without the support of even one Republican. In the House, it was approved on August 5 by 218 to 216—effectively a margin of one vote, since a tie would have counted as defeat. The next day, Gore again had to break a tie to save the program in the Senate by 51 votes to 50.

Gays in the military. Congress in September enacted a bill permitting homosexuals to serve in the armed forces as long as they neither engage in homosexual activity nor openly proclaim their sexual orientation. The move enshrined into law a policy announced by Clinton in July, after he gave up his earlier efforts to lift unconditionally the military's ban on homosexuals. The congressional version of the "don't ask, don't tell" compromise, unlike the White House version, left open the possibility that the military could in the future reintroduce its practice of asking recruits about their sexual orientation. (See also **United States, Government of the.**)

NAFTA. Another drama unfolded in the fall, as Clinton pushed hard for NAFTA. The accord, hotly opposed by organized labor, eliminates trade barriers between the United States, Canada, and Mexico. After an all-out campaign marked by last-minute concessions to citrus growers and other groups, the House passed NAFTA on November 17 by a vote of 234 to 200. The issue split the Democrats, with 156 voting against the pact and only 102 in favor, forcing Clinton to rely on 132 Republican votes to win. The Senate approved NAFTA on November 20, voting 61 to 38. (See **International trade: The Debate over NAFTA.**)

Crime and gun control. The House and Senate passed competing crime-fighting bills in late 1993. On November 19, the Senate approved a broad, $23-billion package that would put 100,000 more police officers on the streets, erect high-security prisons for violent offenders, and ban certain *assault weapons* (guns that fire large numbers of bullets very rapidly). Earlier in the month, the House had passed a less sweeping package that added only 50,000 more police, along with expanded drug treatment programs in prisons and a variety of measures aimed at youth gang members. A Senate-House conference was expected to reconcile the bills in 1994.

Also in November, Congress passed the long-debated Brady gun control bill over the opposition of the highly influential gun lobby, led by the National

The Senate passes the President's budget program on August 6 by a single vote, a day after the bill was saved by one vote from defeat in the House.

Rifle Association (NRA). The bill, first introduced in 1986, imposes a waiting period of five business days for handgun purchases so officials can check that the buyer is not a convicted felon, drug addict, minor, or other person prohibited from buying such guns. It is due to expire in five years, by which time a computerized system permitting instant background checks is due to be in place. The bill was named for James S. Brady, former White House press secretary, who was wounded in an assassination attempt on President Ronald Reagan in 1981. It was the first major gun control measure passed since Congress banned the mail-order sale of rifles and shotguns in 1968.

Foreign policy issues. On Oct. 15, 1993, the Senate voted to support President Clinton's timetable for the withdrawal of U.S. troops from Somalia by March 31, 1994. Congress had become highly critical of the Administration's actions in the African nation, where an original U.S. mission to ensure the distribution of relief supplies had been expanded into what some lawmakers feared would be a longterm peacemaking mission. After 18 American soldiers were killed in a firefight on Oct. 3 to 4, 1993,

many congressional leaders had demanded the immediate pullout of U.S. troops. (See **Armed forces.**)

On September 30, Clinton signed into law a $13-billion foreign aid package, including $2.5 billion in economic and technical aid to Russia and other former Soviet states. Congress had acted quickly on the bill as a gesture of support to Russian President Boris Yeltsin in his struggle against Russian nationalists and hard-line Communists who opposed his political and economic reforms.

Other achievements:
- Congress passed a national service initiative designed to create a corps of young volunteers who would receive federal education grants in return for community service. Congress authorized $1.5 billion over three years for the program, under which students could receive up to $4,725 a year for two years to help pay their tuition for college or technical training. The bill, a scaled-back version of one originally proposed by President Clinton, received bipartisan backing.
- The House and the Senate approved bills to reform campaign financing through voluntary limits on

Members of the United States Senate

The Senate of the second session of the 103rd Congress consisted of 56 Democrats and 44 Republicans when it convened on Jan. 25, 1994. Kay Bailey Hutchison of Texas was elected June 5, 1993, to fill the Senate seat left vacant after Lloyd M. Bentsen, Jr., became secretary of the treasury. The first date in each listing shows when the senator's term began. The second date in each listing shows when the senator's term expires.

State	Term	State	Term	State	Term
Alabama		**Louisiana**		**Ohio**	
Howell T. Heflin, D.	1979-1997	J. Bennett Johnston, Jr., D.	1972-1997	John H. Glenn, Jr., D.	1974-1999
Richard C. Shelby, D.	1987-1999	John B. Breaux, D.	1987-1999	Howard M. Metzenbaum, D.	1976-1995
Alaska		**Maine**		**Oklahoma**	
Theodore F. Stevens, R.	1968-1997	William S. Cohen, R.	1979-1997	David L. Boren, D.	1979-1997
Frank H. Murkowski, R.	1981-1999	George J. Mitchell, D.	1980-1995	Don Nickles, R.	1981-1999
Arizona		**Maryland**		**Oregon**	
Dennis DeConcini, D.	1977-1995	Paul S. Sarbanes, D.	1977-1995	Mark O. Hatfield, R.	1967-1997
John McCain III, R.	1987-1999	Barbara A. Mikulski, D.	1987-1999	Bob Packwood, R.	1969-1999
Arkansas		**Massachusetts**		**Pennsylvania**	
Dale Bumpers, D.	1975-1999	Edward M. Kennedy, D.	1962-1995	Arlen Specter, R.	1981-1999
David H. Pryor, D.	1979-1997	John F. Kerry, D.	1985-1997	Harris L. Wofford, D.	1991-1995
California		**Michigan**		**Rhode Island**	
Barbara Boxer, D.	1993-1999	Donald W. Riegle, Jr., D.	1976-1995	Claiborne Pell, D.	1961-1997
Dianne Feinstein, D.	1993-1995	Carl Levin, D.	1979-1997	John H. Chafee, R.	1976-1995
Colorado		**Minnesota**		**South Carolina**	
Hank Brown, R.	1991-1997	David F. Durenberger, R.	1978-1995	Strom Thurmond, R.	1955-1997
Ben N. Campbell, D.	1993-1999	Paul D. Wellstone, D.	1991-1997	Ernest F. Hollings, D.	1967-1999
Connecticut		**Mississippi**		**South Dakota**	
Christopher J. Dodd, D.	1981-1999	Thad Cochran, R.	1978-1997	Larry Pressler, R.	1979-1997
Joseph I. Lieberman, D.	1989-1995	Trent Lott, R.	1989-1995	Thomas A. Daschle, D.	1987-1999
Delaware		**Missouri**		**Tennessee**	
William V. Roth, Jr., R.	1971-1995	John C. Danforth, R.	1976-1995	James Sasser, D.	1977-1995
Joseph R. Biden, Jr., D.	1973-1997	Christopher S. (Kit) Bond, R.	1987-1999	Harlan Mathews, D.	1993-1995
Florida		**Montana**		**Texas**	
Bob Graham, D.	1987-1999	Max Baucus, D.	1978-1997	Phil Gramm, R.	1985-1997
Connie Mack III, R.	1989-1995	Conrad Burns, R.	1989-1995	Kay Bailey Hutchison, R.	1993-1995
Georgia		**Nebraska**		**Utah**	
Sam Nunn, D.	1972-1997	J. James Exon, D.	1979-1997	Orrin G. Hatch, R.	1977-1995
Paul Coverdell, R.	1993-1999	Robert Kerrey, D.	1989-1995	Robert F. Bennett, R.	1993-1999
Hawaii		**Nevada**		**Vermont**	
Daniel K. Inouye, D.	1963-1999	Harry M. Reid, D.	1987-1999	Patrick J. Leahy, D.	1975-1999
Daniel K. Akaka, D.	1990-1995	Richard H. Bryan, D.	1989-1995	James M. Jeffords, R.	1989-1995
Idaho		**New Hampshire**		**Virginia**	
Larry E. Craig, R.	1991-1997	Robert C. Smith, R.	1991-1997	John W. Warner, R.	1979-1997
Dirk Kempthorne, R.	1993-1999	Judd Gregg, R.	1993-1999	Charles S. Robb, D.	1989-1995
Illinois		**New Jersey**		**Washington**	
Paul Simon, D.	1985-1997	Bill Bradley, D.	1979-1997	Slade Gorton, R.	1989-1995
Carol Moseley-Braun, D.	1993-1999	Frank R. Lautenberg, D.	1982-1995	Patty Murray, D.	1993-1999
Indiana		**New Mexico**		**West Virginia**	
Richard G. Lugar, R.	1977-1995	Pete V. Domenici, R.	1973-1997	Robert C. Byrd, D.	1959-1995
Dan R. Coats, R.	1989-1999	Jeff Bingaman, D.	1983-1995	John D. Rockefeller IV, D.	1985-1997
Iowa		**New York**		**Wisconsin**	
Charles E. Grassley, R.	1981-1999	Daniel P. Moynihan, D.	1977-1995	Herbert Kohl, D.	1989-1995
Tom Harkin, D.	1985-1997	Alfonse M. D'Amato, R.	1981-1999	Russell D. Feingold, D.	1993-1999
Kansas		**North Carolina**		**Wyoming**	
Robert J. Dole, R.	1969-1999	Jesse A. Helms, R.	1973-1997	Malcolm Wallop, R.	1977-1995
Nancy Landon Kassebaum, R.	1979-1997	Lauch Faircloth, R.	1993-1999	Alan K. Simpson, R.	1979-1997
Kentucky		**North Dakota**			
Wendell H. Ford, D.	1974-1999	Kent Conrad, D.	1987-1995		
Mitch McConnell, R.	1985-1997	Byron Dorgan, D.	1993-1999		

152

spending. But the chambers differed on whether the legislation should establish public financing of campaigns, as sought by the House, or eliminate political action committee (PAC) contributions, as was called for by the Senate. (A PAC collects contributions from special-interest groups and gives them to candidates the group favors.) A Senate-House conference was due to tackle the issue in 1994.

■ Both chambers passed measures making it a federal crime to bomb, burn, or block access to abortion clinics or to threaten doctors or nurses who perform abortions. A final version of the legislation was expected to be sent to Clinton in 1994.

■ Breaking an 18-month stalemate, Congress in November approved the release of $18.3 billion to finish the federal bailout of insolvent savings and loan institutions. The money would allow the last of the failed thrifts to be taken over, and their depositors paid, by March 1995. (See also **Bank.**)

Scandal continued to tarnish Congress in 1993. Robert V. Rota, who had resigned as House postmaster in 1992, pleaded guilty on July 19, 1993, to charges that he had illegally converted stamps into cash for two lawmakers. Rota admitted that he or his subordinates had bought back large quantities of stamps that the lawmakers had purchased with campaign funds or expense account vouchers. His statements appeared to implicate Representative Dan Rostenkowski of Illinois, chairman of the House

Ways and Means Committee, as one of the lawmakers. Rostenkowski, who had been under investigation by a federal grand jury since May 1992, denied any wrongdoing.

Oregon Senator Bob Packwood remained the focus of a widening investigation on sexual misconduct and other charges in 1993. On December 16, a federal judge took custody of Packwood's personal diaries after hearing evidence that Packwood had altered the diaries soon before they were subpoenaed by the Senate Ethics Committee in October. The ethics panel sought the diaries as part of its investigation into charges by 26 women that Packwood had made unwanted sexual advances toward them over a period of two decades. On November 2, the Senate voted 94 to 6 to back the subpoena. During the debate before the vote, Ethics Committee members revealed that the panel was also investigating charges that Packwood had improperly asked lobbyists to offer jobs to his estranged wife several years earlier.

The Department of Justice, which was pursuing a separate criminal inquiry into the pressuring of lobbyists, had also subpoenaed the diaries on November 19. Packwood denied any criminal activity. □ William J. Eaton

See also **Elections; United States, Government of the.** In *World Book,* see **Congress of the United States.**

Connecticut. See State government.

"...SO WE'RE LOCKED IN A STRUGGLE TO DEFINE WHO ULTIMATELY HAS THE MOST POWER— CONGRESS OR THE PRESIDENT!"

TELL ME ABOUT IT!

BORIS

Conservation. Two of United States President Bill Clinton's Cabinet appointments won praise from conservationists in 1993: Bruce Babbitt as secretary of the interior and Carol M. Browner as head of the Environmental Protection Agency. The U.S. Senate confirmed both candidates in January.

When Babbitt was governor of Arizona from 1978 to 1987, he was known for his sensitivity to the environment and his ability to work successfully with people on many sides of environmental conflicts. As secretary of the Florida Department of Environmental Regulation, Browner played a leading role in the early 1990's in the attempt to settle a major federal lawsuit over the pollution of the Everglades National Park by sugar and vegetable growers. But a tentative agreement to help protect the Everglades, reached in July 1993, was at an impasse in mid-December when the federal government refused to guarantee agricultural interests that future Everglades accords would not harm their businesses.

Public land management. In February, Clinton directed Babbitt to eliminate subsidies to various groups that use public lands for profit-making activities. On these lands—which are the property of all U.S. citizens and are managed by the federal government—the new policy would increase fees to ranchers who graze livestock at below-market rates. The policy would also, for the first time, charge royalties to miners, require farmers to pay extra for using

The California gnatcatcher, a threatened species, is the subject of an agreement in March to protect its habitat but allow some development on it.

large amounts of water for irrigation, and end the sale of timber at below-cost prices.

The new policy would radically reverse management practices in existence for more than a century on nearly 500 million acres (200 million hectares) of land in Western states. Conservationists have long advocated such changes, arguing that existing policies not only cost taxpayers millions of dollars every year, but that they also severely damage the environment. Ranchers, miners, and others affected by the new policy claimed it would drive small operators out of business.

In March, a group of Democratic senators from Western states warned Clinton that they would likely oppose his economic program if he instituted the plan. Knowing their support was essential, Clinton withdrew the revised management policies from his budget proposal on March 30.

The battle over land issues resumed after Congress passed Clinton's deficit-reduction package in August. On August 9, Babbitt announced that grazing fees on federal land would increase from $1.86 a month for each *animal unit* (a cow and calf or five sheep) to $4.28 a month in three years. Rates for grazing on private land range from $5 to $15 per month.

In late October, Western senators blocked action on the Interior Department's entire $12-million budget by leading a filibuster against the increased fees. On November 9, the Senate dropped its attempt to increase the grazing fees.

Timber issues. Another long-standing environmental dispute centered on the forests of the Pacific Northwest. Many trees in these forests are hundreds of years old, and some are more than 1,000 years old. Only about 10 percent of the original forests remain, and they have been closed to logging in order to protect the spotted owl and other endangered species whose survival depends on this habitat. Residents of the region fear a loss of thousands of jobs if the logging prohibition continues.

As a first step toward resolving the conflict, President Clinton held a forestry conference in Portland, Ore., on April 2. Loggers, labor leaders, and other timber representatives told Clinton that the logging prohibition would cause continued unemployment in communities where timber is the dominant industry. Representatives of conservation organizations pleaded for a large preserve that would leave the forests intact.

On June 30, Clinton announced a compromise that would allow reduced logging and establish reserves for the spotted owl. The plan would restrict logging in federal forests in the Northwest to 1.2 billion board feet (2.8 million cubic meters) a year—down from a high of more than 5 billion board feet (11.8 million cubic meters) in the 1980's—and would protect spotted owl habitats. The plan would also provide about $1.2 billion over five years for job training for displaced loggers and for economic development in communities hardest hit by reduced logging.

Environmental treaties move forward. On June 4, the United States signed an international treaty designed to protect Earth's *biodiversity* (variety of plant and animal species). The treaty requires biotechnology companies that create marketable products from biological resources to share profits with countries where those resources originated.

The signing was a reversal of U.S. policy. Former U.S. President George Bush declined to sign the treaty when it was drafted at the United Nations Earth Summit in Rio de Janeiro, Brazil, in June 1992. Bush claimed that the treaty would be too expensive to enforce and could be too costly to American businesses. Conservationists around the world criticized Bush harshly for not signing the treaty.

President Clinton announced in April that he planned to seek limits on U.S. emissions of so-called "greenhouse gases" as part of another treaty that stemmed from the Earth Summit. This treaty aims at cutting emissions of gases produced largely by burning *fossil fuels* (gasoline, coal, and oil). Burning fossil fuels produces certain gases, chiefly carbon dioxide, that trap heat in Earth's atmosphere, much in the way that glass in a greenhouse traps heat. Some scientists fear that if too many greenhouse gases build up, the heat they trap could cause *global warming* (a significant warming of Earth's atmosphere). Global warming could threaten crops over wide areas, melt polar icecaps, and flood coastal areas.

Although Bush signed the global warming treaty, he refused to commit the United States to a specific reduction in greenhouse gas emissions. Clinton said on April 21, 1993, that he planned to reduce U.S. emissions of greenhouse gases to 1990 levels by the year 2000. On Oct. 19, 1993, the Clinton Administration announced a plan to spend about $200 million a year to encourage greenhouse gas emission cuts. The plan relied mainly on voluntary measures by businesses and industries to cut emissions.

A new strategy for saving species. In February, Babbitt proposed a major revision in the method for saving endangered species. Babbitt's plan would focus on preserving whole ecosystems before the species that inhabit them become endangered. The existing Endangered Species Act attempts to save plants and animals on a species-by-species basis only after their numbers dwindle so low that their existence is endangered. Usually, emergency measures are required, placing every square inch of land inhabited by endangered species off-limits to further development. The new approach also opens the way for conservationists and business interests to collaborate on plans to allow for some development while leaving most of the ecosystems intact.

As a first step toward implementing the new plan, Babbitt proposed conducting a scientific assessment of all U.S. ecosystems and the biological diversity within them. In March, he appointed conservation biologist Thomas E. Lovejoy of the Smithsonian Institution in Washington, D.C., and botanist Peter H. Raven of the Missouri Botanical Garden in St. Louis, Mo., to conduct this assessment.

An early test of the proposed method began in four coastal counties of southern California in late March. A small blue-gray songbird, the California gnatcatcher, lives exclusively in some 250,000 acres (100,000 hectares) of coastal sage scrub, a locale that is also extremely valuable for real estate development. About 90 percent of the scrub has been destroyed, and the U.S. Fish and Wildlife Service estimates only 2,562 gnatcatcher pairs remain.

On March 25, the U.S. Fish and Wildlife Service declared the California gnatcatcher a threatened species. Babbitt brokered a deal in which conservationists and developers will collaborate with federal and state agencies to save most of the bird's habitat and still allow development on some of it. The state plans to create 12 gnatcatcher preserves in California. Developers will be allowed to build on them as long as they help preserve enough of the critical habitat to ensure the gnatcatcher's survival. □ Eugene J. Walter, Jr.

See also **Environmental pollution.** In the World Book Supplement section, see **Animal.** In *World Book,* see **Conservation.**

Consumerism. The United States economy performed more poorly than expected in 1993. Early in the year, reports forecast economic growth of 3.1 percent. In September, the Administration of President Bill Clinton was estimating a 2 percent growth rate. Interest rates fell dramatically. By August, interest rates on 30-year fixed mortgages had dropped to below 7 percent, the lowest in nearly 30 years. The low rates prompted many homeowners to refinance their mortgages, and many other Americans bought their first homes.

Inflation, as measured by the Consumer Price Index, remained at low levels in 1993. Prices rose only 2.8 percent over a 12-month period ending in October. Consumer confidence continued to linger at relatively low levels as measured by the Consumer Confidence Index, a monthly survey that asks consumers about the confidence they have in their financial status for the next six months. By November, the Index stood at 71, slightly above its November 1992 mark. An index of 100 represents the level of consumer confidence in 1985, when the U.S. economy was growing steadily.

Taxes. Federally imposed taxes on gasoline increased by 4.3 cents to 18.4 cents per gallon on Oct. 1, 1993, as part of President Clinton's five-year deficit reduction plan. Other taxes were increased under the plan, including income taxes and taxes on businesses. In addition, 85 percent of social security benefits for elderly people with incomes above $34,000 were taxed. Previously, only 50 percent of benefits could be taxed. (See also **Taxation.**)

Health care. On September 22, President Clinton unveiled the outline of a sweeping health-care reform bill, the American Health Security Act, to a joint session of Congress. The controversial plan, which took eight months to complete, would guarantee every American a health insurance policy with a basic minimum standard of benefits. It would also expand benefits for people already receiving health care through the government's Medicare and Medicaid programs. The plan would require every employer to pay for at least 80 percent of the insurance costs of their employees. Policies would be bought through newly created Regional Health Alliances, which would offer consumers a choice of three or more types of health-care plans that conform to federal guidelines. The government would subsidize insurance costs for small businesses, the unemployed, retired and elderly Americans, and children of low-income families. The plan would also place cost controls on the health-care industry. (See also **Health-care issues.**)

Cable TV. In 1993, a law allowing the Federal Communications Commission (FCC) to regulate the prices cable television companies could charge consumers received criticism. The law, passed by the U.S. Congress on Oct. 5, 1992, was designed to lower the consumers' cable TV rates. On April 1, 1993, the FCC approved regulations designed to make deep rate cuts. The regulations went into effect on September 1. However, on September 24, 130 members of Congress complained to the FCC that the regulations caused rate increases for some cable consumers. In September, Congress began hearings to determine why rates went up under the bill, and the FCC began a consumer survey to determine why the increase occurred. (See also **Television.**)

Trade. The Clinton Administration in 1993 encouraged Congress to pass the North American Free Trade Agreement (NAFTA), signed by President George Bush in 1992. NAFTA would create a free-trade zone between Mexico, the United States, and Canada. On Nov. 17, 1993, the House of Representatives voted to pass the agreement. The Senate approved it on November 20. Supporters of NAFTA had argued that it would lower U.S. prices on imported goods from Canada and Mexico and create jobs among U.S. companies that export goods to those countries. Opponents had said it would cause American jobs to be lost because many companies would move to Mexico where wages are lower. They also feared that NAFTA could cause harm to the environment because Mexico reportedly has lax enforcement of its pollution-control laws.   ☐ John Merline

See **International Trade: The Debate over NAFTA.** In *World Book,* see **Consumerism; Economics.**

Costa Rica. See **Latin America.**

Courts. An Iowa couple won their fight to regain custody of their two-year-old daughter, known as Baby Jessica, in August 1993. On July 30, the Supreme Court of the United Sates refused to block an order requiring Jan and Roberta DeBoer of Ann Arbor, Mich., to return the girl to her biological parents, Cara and Daniel Schmidt of Blairstown, Iowa. The DeBoers had taken Jessica home three days after her birth in February 1991, after Cara Schmidt, then unmarried, named the wrong man as the father and had him consent to the adoption. A few days later, Cara revealed that Daniel Schmidt was the true father, and the two began trying to get the child back.

The DeBoers appealed the case through the Iowa Supreme Court, which in autumn 1992 ruled that Cara's false declaration of the father made their consent to the adoption nonbinding. On July 2, 1993, Michigan's Supreme Court deferred to the Iowa ruling and ordered Jessica returned by August 2.

Parental rights denied. A 14-year-old girl who was switched after birth with another baby cannot be forced to have contact with her biological family, a Sarasota, Fla., judge ruled on August 18. The girl, Kimberly Mays, had been sent home from a Florida hospital with Robert and Barbara Mays, whose child was given to Ernest and Regina Twigg. The mistake came to light soon before the Twiggs' daughter, Arlena, died of a heart ailment in 1988. Medical tests revealed that she was not the Twiggs' biological child. In 1989, genetic tests showed that Arlena had been switched with Kimberly.

In 1989, the Twiggs accepted a settlement giving them visitation rights but leaving custody of Kimberly with Robert Mays. (Barbara Mays had died in 1981.) Mays halted the visits in October 1990, saying they were upsetting Kimberly. The Twiggs then launched a bitter custody battle. Kimberly sued to sever her ties with the Twiggs in May 1993, after hearing of a successful 1992 suit by Gregory Kingsley (now Shawn Russ) of Leesburg, Fla., to terminate his mother's parental rights.

Free speech rights. A federal jury in New York City ruled on May 11, 1993, that officials of the City University of New York (CUNY) violated the First Amendment when they removed Leonard Jeffries, Jr., as chairman of the black studies department at CUNY's City College in 1992. Witnesses supported Jeffries' charge that he was removed because of a 1991 speech, widely criticized as racist, in which he said that Jews and Italians had conspired to denigrate blacks in motion pictures. CUNY officials said they had acted because Jeffries was a lax administrator and a poor scholar. On May 18, 1993, the jury awarded Jeffries $400,000 in damages. On August 4, a judge ordered Jeffries reinstated as chairman.

Student's killer cleared. On May 23, a Baton Rouge, La., jury found Rodney Peairs not guilty of manslaughter in his October 1992 shooting of a 16-year-old Japanese exchange student. The case, which centered on a homeowner's right to use lethal force against perceived threats, came at a time of heightened debate about the desirability of gun control laws in American society.

The student, Yoshihiro Hattori, and a friend had come to the Peairs home while looking for a Halloween party. Peairs testified that Hattori rushed toward him in a threatening way, waving what turned out to be a camera. Hattori's companion said Hattori apparently did not see the gun in Peairs's hands and did not understand the man's command to freeze.

Several racially charged cases were concluded in 1993. On May 28, an Orlando, Fla., court acquitted former Miami police officer William Lozano, a Hispanic, of manslaughter charges in the 1989 deaths of two black motorcyclists. Lozano had shot the motorcycle driver, and the other man had died of injuries from the ensuing crash. The racially mixed jury accepted Lozano's claim that the driver had been veering wildly and that he had fired in self-defense. A Miami court had convicted Lozano in 1989, but in June 1991 an appeals court said the conviction may have been influenced by fears of racial violence and ordered that Lozano be retried outside Miami.

Also in 1993, courts issued judgments in cases involving alleged racially motivated violence in Los Angeles, Detroit, and Florida. (See **Civil rights.**)

Repressed memory. The archbishop of Chicago, Joseph Cardinal Bernardin, was charged with sexual abuse in November 1993, in a civil lawsuit involving the supposed recovery of a forgotten memory. The charges were filed by a 34-year-old Philadelphia man who said he had been molested by Bernardin as a teen-ager and had repressed the memory until October 1993. Bernardin denied the charges. According to analysts, hundreds of cases involving repressed memories were in American courts by the end of 1993.

Repressed memory is a poorly understood phenomenon in which the memory of a traumatic experience is stored outside the reach of consciousness. Psychologists believe that such memories can be retrieved through therapy or triggered by a related situation, even decades after the event. But many experts charge that it is often difficult to distinguish between such retrieved memories and false memories suggested, perhaps inadvertently, by a therapist or other source.

A loss for atheists. A federal appeals court in Chicago ruled on May 17 that the Boy Scouts of America is a private organization that can bar individuals who refuse to take an oath in which Scouts promise to do their "duty to God." The court rejected an argument that the Scouts were subject to federal civil rights laws because they hold meetings in public places, such as schools. In December, the U.S. Supreme Court refused to hear the case.

Obesity bias. On November 22, a federal appeals court in Boston found that the state of Rhode

"Baby Jessica" is carried in August from the home of Jan and Roberta DeBoer after they lost a two-year custody fight with the girl's biological parents.

Island had violated the rights of a 320-pound (145-kilogram) woman by refusing to hire her because of her weight. The state had argued that the obesity did not qualify as a disability protected under a 1973 federal law. The court said the state's action was discriminatory whether obesity is a disability or not.

Term limits. Thomas S. Foley, the Speaker of the House of Representatives, on June 7 joined with the League of Women Voters in a suit challenging a Washington state law that imposes limits on terms for elected federal officials. Fifteen states had enacted such laws by late 1993. Critics of the laws say the Constitution prohibits states from imposing any restrictions on congressional candidates. Proponents, however, noted that the U.S. Supreme Court has upheld state laws that regulate who may appear on a ballot for federal office.

Gay rights. Several federal court rulings in 1993 cast doubt on the constitutionality of a new policy regarding the right of gays to serve in the military. The policy prevents the military from asking about a recruit's sexual orientation but prohibits members of the military from engaging in homosexual acts or openly declaring their homosexuality. In September, a federal judge issued an injunction that effectively barred the policy, but the U.S. Supreme Court lifted the injunction. (See **Armed forces.**)   □ Meira Ben-Gad

See also **Crime; Supreme Court of the United States.** In *World Book,* see **Court.**

Crime. Most forms of crime fell to 20-year lows in the United States during 1993, but the number of violent crimes increased slightly. Religious fanaticism appeared to be the common element in the year's two most staggering incidents of violence.

Tragedy in Waco. About 82 members of a religious cult, including many children, died in an inferno on April 19 near Waco, Tex., when federal law-enforcement agents assaulted the cult's headquarters. By year-end, officials were still trying to identify all of the victims and were unable to provide a final death count. The incident ended a 51-day stand-off that began on February 28, when agents of the federal Bureau of Alcohol, Tobacco, and Firearms (ATF) raided the compound of the Branch Davidians, as the cult members called themselves. The raid was an attempt to search for illegal weapons and arrest the Branch Davidian leader, 33-year-old David Koresh. But the raid ended in a gun battle in which four ATF agents and as many as six cult members died.

Koresh, whose name at birth was Vernon Howell, was a high school dropout who at times claimed to be Jesus Christ. Early in the stand-off, Koresh told authorities that he would surrender. He did not, and some cult members who left the compound during the stand-off said that Koresh believed the cult was fated to engage in a fiery confrontation with law-enforcement officials that would signal the end of the world.

The Federal Bureau of Investigation (FBI) assumed control of the siege after the shoot-out and seemed prepared to wait out the crisis. But after weeks of fruitless negotiations, federal authorities assaulted the compound early on April 19. Armored vehicles punched large holes in the side of the compound and sprayed tear gas off and on for several hours. Just after noon, flames suddenly broke out in several areas of the compound. The expansive wooden structure burned to the ground in 30 minutes with nearly all of the remaining cult members still inside, including Koresh.

The FBI claimed that cult members set the fires on Koresh's orders. Some surviving cult members said that Koresh had no plans for mass suicide and that the fires must have been caused by government action. A government investigation of the incident released in October supported the FBI's claim that cult members started the fire, but a separate government report on September 30 sharply criticized the ATF for mishandling the February raid.

World Trade Center bombed. Terror struck New York City on February 26 when a huge bomb exploded in a parking garage beneath the World Trade Center. The blast killed 6 people and injured more than 1,000 others. The explosion ripped a hole 3 stories deep below the 110-story towers, knocking out the buildings' telephone lines and power systems, collapsing the ceiling of a nearby subway line, and paralyzing much of lower Manhattan. The blast caused an estimated $591 million in damages and lost business to trade center tenants, according to the Port Authority of New York and New Jersey, which operates the trade center complex.

On February 28, law-enforcement authorities determined that a car bomb had caused the explosion. Police arrested Mohammed A. Salameh on March 4 in Jersey City, N.J., in connection with the bombing. Authorities described Salameh as a Muslim fundamentalist. By August, seven suspects had been charged in the bombing, all of whom investigators described as Arab militants. The trial for four of the suspects began in New York City on October 4.

On March 27, officials said that one of the defendants had sent a letter to *The New York Times* four days after the blast. The letter said the bombing was in retaliation for U.S. support of Israel and other U.S. policies in the Middle East. But the defendant's lawyer denied that his client had anything to do with the letter.

In June, the FBI said it had uncovered a plot to bomb other landmarks in New York City, including the United Nations (UN) building. According to the FBI, the plot also involved the assassination of public officials, including UN Secretary-General Boutros Boutros-Ghali and Egyptian President Hosni Mubarak.

On August 25, a federal grand jury indicted Sheik Omar Abdel Rahman, a radical Muslim cleric, on charges that he orchestrated both the plot to bomb the New York landmarks and the World Trade Center bombing, as well as the 1990 killing of militant Rabbi Meir Kahane in New York City. The jury also indicted 14 other co-conspirators. All 15 defendants pleaded not guilty.

Abdel Rahman had been in U.S. custody since July 2, 1993, on charges that he had violated U.S. immigration laws. He had lived in the United States since 1990. Abdel Rahman had been charged with plotting to assassinate Egyptian President Anwar el-Sadat in 1981 but was acquitted.

Michael Jordan's father killed. James Jordan, father of basketball superstar Michael Jordan, was murdered in a roadside robbery near Fayetteville, N.C., on July 23, 1993. Authorities discovered his body on August 3 in a creek near McColl, S.C. Medical examiners identified the body on August 13 using dental records.

Police said that the elder Jordan was killed as he slept in his car. The case came to light when a car that was found stripped in a wooded area near Fayetteville on August 5 was identified as belonging to James Jordan. A grand jury on September 7 indicted two 18-year-olds—Larry Martin Demery of Rowland, N.C., and Daniel Andre Green of Lumberton, N.C.—for the murder. (See **Basketball; Jordan, Michael.**)

Foreign tourists slain in Florida. Six foreign tourists were slain in Florida in 1993, continuing a pattern of violence against foreign visitors to the state that began in late 1992. Nine foreign tourists were killed in Florida from October 1992 through September 1993, raising concerns for Florida's $31-billion tourism industry.

The killings occurred during robbery attempts. Several victims were attacked as they drove rental cars, prompting rental agencies to issue safety warnings and to remove company logos and special license plates that identified cars as rental vehicles. These measures did not save the life of a 33-year-old German man in September, however. Uwe-Wilhelm Rakebrand was gunned down as he drove a rental car with his wife along a Miami expressway on September 8. Six days later, a 34-year-old English tourist died after he was shot in a rental car in a rest area near Monticello, Fla. On October 6, police charged four teen-agers—the youngest 13 years old—with murdering the Englishman.

Mass murder in Long Island. When police stopped 34-year-old Joel Rifkin of East Meadow, N.Y., on June 28 for driving without license plates, they noticed a foul smell coming from his pickup truck. Police officers discovered the decaying body of a woman in the back of the truck. Under questioning, Rifkin admitted to killing 17 women in the New York City metropolitan area dating back at least to 1991. In July, police found personal items from an 18th victim in Rifkin's home. By the end of the year, police had recovered 14 of the bodies and charged Rifkin with seven of the murders.

Terror in San Francisco. A man began firing semiautomic weapons in the offices of a San Francisco law firm on July 1, 1993, killing eight people and wounding six others before killing himself. Police said the 55-year-old gunman—Gian Luigi Ferri (also spelled Gianluigi Ferri)—had a list of 30 employees of the law firm on him when he died, but no one on the list was injured. Ferri had been involved in a lawsuit with a party represented by the law firm, Pettit and Martin.

Shooting on a New York train. A man shot 23 people and killed 6 on a Long Island Railroad commuter train in New York on December 7. The suspect was 35-year-old Colin Ferguson, a native of Jamaica. He allegedly fired a semiautomatic pistol at passengers as the train was approaching Garden City in Long Island.

Massacre in an Illinois restaurant. Unknown assailants shot seven people to death in a fast-food restaurant in Palatine, Ill., a suburb of Chicago. The victims, all of whom worked at the restaurant, were found on Jan. 9, 1993, in the restaurant coolers. Police said that the slayings probably occurred during a robbery. No suspects had been charged in the slayings by the end of the year.   □ Mark Dunbar

See also **City: New Fears About Urban Gangs.** In *World Book,* see **Crime.**

An agent of the Bureau of Alcohol, Tobacco, and Firearms comes under fire during a failed assault on the Branch Davidian cult compound near Waco, Tex., on February 28.

Croatia. In January 1993, Croatia renewed its fight to regain territory seized by ethnic Serbs and the Serb-dominated federal Yugoslav army during a seven-month war that followed Croatia's declaration of independence from Yugoslavia in June 1991. Croatian forces also took action in 1993 against ethnic Muslims in the former Yugoslav republic of Bosnia-Herzegovina (often called Bosnia).

Croatian troops on January 22 broke a year-old United Nations (UN)-sponsored cease-fire and attacked the Krajina region, part of a self-proclaimed Serbian republic comprising about a third of Croatian territory. The Croatians said the Serbs had failed to honor the terms of the cease-fire, which required that the Serbs place their heavy weapons under UN control and negotiate terms of autonomy with Croatia. In the offensive, the Croatians recaptured a destroyed bridge in the town of Maslenica, on Croatia's Adriatic coast, in order to establish a land link between northern Croatia and ports to the south. Maslenica lay in an area that was to have been turned over to the UN under the cease-fire terms.

The Croatian government agreed on July 16 to withdraw its forces from captured areas and to place the rebuilt Maslenica bridge under UN control. However, Croatian officials then refused to pull back their troops until the Serbs handed over their heavy weapons to the UN. In response, Serb forces on August 1 attacked Maslenica but did not capture the bridge. At year's end, the two sides continued to engage in sporadic fighting.

Bosnian role. Croatia drew international condemnation in 1993 as reports spread of atrocities committed by Croat troops in Bosnia, including massacres of Muslim civilians and mass expulsions of Muslims from their homes. At various times during the year, European countries and the United Nations threatened Croatia with economic sanctions unless it halted the attacks on its southeastern neighbor.

On June 16, Croatian President Franjo Tudjman announced a plan, endorsed by Serbian leaders, to partition Bosnia into three ethnic republics. But the plan fell through in September after the Bosnian parliament demanded greater territorial concessions from the Serbs. (See **Bosnia-Herzegovina.**)

Internal developments. In elections on February 7, Tudjman's Croatian Democratic Union won nearly 54 percent of the seats in the Chamber of Districts (upper house of parliament).

The war and disruption caused by Yugoslavia's breakup began to shatter Croatia's economy in 1993. Croatians faced high rates of unemployment and shortages of food and other goods. In September, inflation reached a monthly rate of 30 percent. The economic problems were compounded by the estimated 600,000 refugees who had entered the country by the end of March. ☐ Sharon L. Wolchik

See also **Europe** (Facts in brief table); **Yugoslavia.** In *World Book,* see **Croatia.**

Cuba. Those favoring a peaceful conclusion to the 34-year political stand-off between Cuba and the United States spoke out boldly in 1993. Their numbers included moderate Cuban exiles in the United States, who suggested various formulas for coping with what many see as the inevitable end to the rule of Cuba's Communist dictator Fidel Castro.

U.S. economic embargo. Looking ahead, many observers argued that the 31-year-old U.S. trade embargo against Cuba was a major obstacle to easing U.S.-Cuban tensions. The embargo, along with lingering effects from the 1991 loss of foreign aid from the former Soviet Union, caused severe hardship in Cuba during 1993. According to a July 29 report by the U.S. Central Intelligence Agency (CIA), Cuba's economic output during the first half of 1993 was half the level of the same period in 1989. Half of the island's workers were without steady jobs, and the public transportation system had all but collapsed. Cuba had no hard currency to buy imports of basic consumer goods, resulting in food shortages, malnutrition, and disease.

Twenty-one Latin-American nations, along with Spain and Portugal, called for an end to the embargo on July 16 at a conference in Salvador, Brazil. Castro suggested in a February 25 interview with U.S. television reporter Diane Sawyer—broadcast in the United States on March 4—that lifting the embargo could possibly sway him to give up power peacefully.

U.S.-Cuban diplomatic agreements. Cuba and the United States reached agreements on immigration and narcotics matters in 1993. On September 28, the U.S. Justice Department announced that Cuba would take back up to 1,500 Cuban prisoners who had been in U.S. jails on felony charges since 1984. The prisoners had come to the United States in 1980 during a mass departure from Cuba.

On Sept. 19, 1993, Cuban authorities returned two suspected cocaine smugglers to the United States for prosecution. The suspects, who were Cuban residents of Miami, Fla., allegedly used a speedboat to pick up bales of cocaine that had been dropped from a plane off the Florida coast. When U.S. drug enforcement agents chased the suspects, they fled to Cuba, where they were captured.

A baffling disease. A mysterious disease that impairs vision and damages nerves spread rapidly through Cuba in 1993, affecting about 51,000 people. The epidemic first appeared in western Cuba in January 1992, according to Cuban officials. Medical investigators said they were unsure what caused the disease, but they speculated that a vitamin deficiency combined with a toxin, such as a pesticide, may have caused the epidemic. The disease appeared to peak in September 1993, the investigators said. ☐ Nathan A. Haverstock

See also **Latin America** (Facts in brief table). In *World Book,* see Cuba.

Cyprus. See **Middle East.**

Czech Republic. On Jan. 1, 1993, the Czech Republic became an independent state, as a 1992 agreement dividing Czechoslovakia into two separate nations went into effect. The transition to independence for the Czech Republic and neighboring Slovakia was peaceful and orderly, in contrast to the upheaval that had accompanied the breakup of two other formerly Communist multinational states—the Soviet Union and Yugoslavia—during the preceding years.

Czechoslovakia's parliament had approved the separation of the republics in November 1992, despite evidence from public opinion polls that most Czechs and Slovaks opposed splitting the federation. The separation issue had dominated Czechoslovakia's political stage since the end of Communist rule in 1989.

Václav Klaus, who became the Czech Republic's prime minister in June 1992, continued to head the government of the newly independent state. On Jan. 26, 1993, the Czech parliament elected Václav Havel as the country's president. Havel, a playwright who had helped spearhead the movement that toppled Communism, had opposed the federation's division in his role as federal president in 1992.

Czech and Slovak leaders pledged in 1992 and 1993 to minimize disruption from the breakup to both sides. However, a number of disputes came to the fore early in 1993. On February 8, the two countries switched to separate currencies, both called the koruna, after disagreements over monetary policy forced them to abandon plans to maintain a common currency for six months. On March 17, the Czech government froze the distribution of stock in Czech companies in which Slovak investors had bought shares under a 1992 privatization program. The Czechs restarted the distribution on May 12, 1993, after the two sides resolved most of their disputes over the division of federal assets.

Economic reform. The Czech government continued to pursue its rapid restoration of a market economy in 1993. The policy enjoyed high support in the Czech Republic, where unemployment levels remained below 3 percent for much of the year. Unemployment rates were expected to rise over time, however, as larger numbers of unprofitable enterprises were allowed to fail.

The Czech economy failed to recover as much as expected during the year, in part because of the disruption of economic links with Slovakia. In addition, foreign investment, which had declined toward the end of 1992, continued to fall slightly in 1993. However, Czech firms saw a sizable increase in exports, especially to Western Europe. By November, officials said, about 80 percent of Czech export income came from markets in the West. ☐ Sharon L. Wolchik

See also **Europe** (Facts in brief table); **Slovakia.** In the World Book Supplement section, see **Czech Republic; Slovakia.**

Dallas. The entire downtown area was declared a public improvement district in January 1993 as Dallas strove to upgrade its image. Construction crews worked during the year to transform downtown Dallas into a showcase area that, city leaders hope, will spur economic development and attract tourists.

The city spent $30 million to convert a nine-block stretch of Main Street into a landscaped and brightly lit boulevard for new retail shops and restaurants. Another $100 million was spent to enlarge the Dallas Convention Center.

The popular Farmer's Market on the southeast side of downtown Dallas underwent a $15-million face-lift, and the Dallas Museum of Art opened a new $30-million wing. Special assessments of businesses within the public improvement district have been used to pay for additional police officers and to finance extended cleanup programs.

Also during the year, Dallas Area Rapid Transit began construction of a light-rail system. The trains will provide passenger service between suburban communities and the downtown area.

Dallas Plan. In October, the Dallas City Council authorized a long-range project known as The Dallas Plan, which lays out a course of development for the city through the year 2025. Included in the $30-billion plan are an expanded downtown area, a new sports and entertainment center in west Dallas, and a new commercial airport southeast of the city.

City government. Dallas Police Chief William Rathburn resigned in January 1993 to accept a position as chief of security for the 1996 Summer Olympic Games in Atlanta, Ga. During Rathburn's two years as head of the Dallas Police Department, the city's homicide rate dropped by more than 20 percent. Ben Click, a deputy chief with the Phoenix police force, was named to succeed Rathburn.

Dallas public schools Superintendent Marvin Edwards resigned in April to become head of the Elgin, Ill., public school district. Edwards' first assistant, Chad Woolery, was appointed acting superintendent. In November, Dallas City Manager Jan Hart resigned after clashing with Mayor Steve Bartlett over policy matters. The City Council chose Assistant City Manager John Ware as Hart's successor.

New senator elected, indicted. Texas State Treasurer Kay Bailey Hutchison, a Dallas resident, won a landslide victory in June to fill the seat in the United States Senate vacated by former Senator Lloyd M. Bentsen, Jr., who had become U.S. secretary of the treasury. Hutchison was the first woman ever elected to the Senate from Texas.

Less than a week after her election, the district attorney in Austin, the state capital, began a probe into allegations that Hutchison had misused her treasury post to support her Senate campaign. She was indicted on five felony counts on September 27. Hutchison denied the allegations. Later, the indictments were dropped after it was discovered that a

Aspiring dance stars perform in March at the 15th anniversary celebration of the tuition-free New Ballet School in New York City.

grand jury member was not qualified. But Hutchison was reindicted on December 8.

Superfund site. In May, the U.S. Environmental Protection Agency declared west Dallas a Superfund site—an area requiring cleanup of toxic wastes under a special Superfund program—after finding serious lead contamination in neighborhoods around an abandoned smelting plant. A planned federal renovation project at a housing development across the street from the smelter was then postponed.

Sports. On January 31, the Dallas Cowboys football team won a 52 to 17 Super Bowl victory over the Buffalo Bills at the Rose Bowl in Pasadena, Calif. A parade in downtown Dallas celebrating the Cowboys' win attracted more than 300,000 people but was marred by fighting among unruly teen-agers.

In March, Dallas became the sixth city in the United States to have franchises in all four major professional sports—baseball, basketball, football, and hockey—when the Minnesota North Stars hockey team announced it would relocate to Dallas. The team was renamed the Dallas Stars.

Dallas, chosen to be one of the U.S. host cities for the 1994 World Cup soccer matches, began making preparations in 1993. The Cotton Bowl stadium, where the matches will be played, underwent a major renovation, including the replacement of its artificial turf with natural grass. ☐ Henry K. Tatum

See also **City.** In **World Book,** see **Dallas.**

Dancing. Two of the major dance companies in the United States, the American Ballet Theater (ABT) and the Joffrey Ballet, began 1993 in serious debt. ABT's debt of $5.7 million was so staggering it almost forced the troupe to declare bankruptcy. However, under the new leadership of Kevin McKenzie as artistic director and Gary Dunning as executive director, ABT took drastic measures to ensure survival. They cut the ABT budget by $3 million, to $13.5 million. Dancers agreed to a wage freeze for 1993, and they had their employment cut from 36 to 26 weeks. The roster, which had close to 100 dancers in the late 1980's, was reduced to 68.

ABT canceled tours to cities, such as Chicago and San Francisco, where the troupe had traditionally presented itself without the help of a sponsor. ABT's annual run at the Metropolitan Opera House in New York City, which began May 3, was cut from nine to six weeks. ABT also formed a special fund-raising task force to raise $8 million. On June 1, management announced that $3 million had already been raised and that one-third of it would go toward a new production of The Nutcracker (1892). With choreography by McKenzie and a *libretto* (story) by playwright Wendy Wasserstein, the modernized holiday classic opened December 3 at the Orange County Performing Arts Center in Costa Mesa, Calif.

Given ABT's dire financial situation, McKenzie selected a modest repertory for the six weeks the company did perform. Their major production, which began May 28, was the lavish, three-act *Manon* (1974), originally choreographed for the United Kingdom's Royal Ballet by the late Kenneth MacMillan. McKenzie revived such once-familiar ballets as Harald Lander's *Études* (1948) and works by Agnes De Mille, who died on October 7.

The Joffrey Ballet found itself more than $2-million in the red at the beginning of 1993 but was able to get through the year on the coattails of a successful premiere, *Billboards.* The dance was conceived by artistic director Gerald Arpino, who used the music of rock star Prince. Arpino invited such diverse choreographers as Laura Dean, Charles Moulton, Peter Pucci, and Margo Sappington each to create a section of the ballet. Originally, Prince was supposed to compose new music. That did not happen, but Prince's name was enough to bring new, young audiences to the Joffrey. In June 1993, Prince changed his name to a symbol that did not correspond to any known word.

Billboards premiered on January 27 at the University of Iowa's Hancher Auditorium, followed by performances in Chicago in March and Washington, D.C., in June. The dance was also performed at the prestigious Next Wave Festival in November at the Brooklyn Academy of Music.

The New York City Ballet sparked controversy with an event that was acclaimed for its heroism. The troupe honored the 10th anniversary of the death of George Balanchine, founder of the City Ballet and widely regarded as the greatest choreographer ever, by mounting a chronological retrospective of his work. Under artistic director Peter Martins, it began with *Apollo* (1928) and ended with ballets from 1981. The Balanchine Celebration ran at the New York State Theater at Lincoln Center from May 4 to June 27 and consisted of 73 works.

To perform so many ballets was a monumental undertaking and to see Balanchine's work in such concentrated form was revealing, critics agreed. But the occasion also gave rise to consideration of the quality of the dancing, and by extension, of Martins' performance as artistic director. Many professional observers felt that the troupe was becoming increasingly mechanical in its dancing. The discussion came to a crisis when people from within the City Ballet broke ranks and criticized Martins in a May article published in *The New Yorker* magazine. Among the "defectors" was Suzanne Farrell, Balanchine's favorite ballerina. She had retired from dancing in 1989 but was still employed by the company. On July 30, Martins caused a scandal when he fired Farrell.

Twyla Tharp. Without a permanent company, choreographer Twyla Tharp nevertheless had a busy year. In February, she and a temporary ensemble including Mikhail Baryshnikov began a 25-city American tour in a program billed *Cutting Up,* the highlight of which was a section of solos and duets for the two stars. In September, Tharp and her group played at City Center for two weeks, during which Tharp taught her dancers a new phrase of choreography at every performance. She also invited amateurs from the audience to come up on stage and join in the dancing. Tharp's year culminated in a premiere of her *Demeter and Persephone* for the Martha Graham Dance Company on October 6 at New York's City Center. It was the first time a choreographer outside of the Graham fold created a work for the company.

Merce Cunningham, the grand old man of modern dance, was more creative than ever in 1993. Four of the choreographer's dances were seen in the United States for the first time. He also premiered two dances, *Doubletoss,* which began February 26 at Northrup Auditorium in Minneapolis, Minn., and *CRWDSPCR,* on July 15 at the American Dance Festival (ADF) in Durham, N.C. The odd title is a computer variant of the words "crowd spacer" and "crowds pacer." Cunningham used an animation computer program in making the dance. *CRWDSPCR* was commissioned by the ADF in honor of its 60th anniversary. The festival also commissioned choreographer Paul Taylor's 100th dance, *Spindrift,* which refers to sea foam cast upon the shore. Taylor's second new dance of 1993 debuted on October 27 during his troupe's two-week season at the City Center. Set to songs written by singer Harry Nilsson in the 1960's and 1970's, *A Field of Grass* was about "flower children," or hippies, from that era.

Dance festival. The most ambitious dance event from abroad in 1993 was presented by the Kennedy Center for the Performing Arts in Washington, D.C., in late March. Called France Danse, this festival of six groups included the Paris Opera Ballet and the Ballet du Rhin from Strasbourg. The Ballet du Rhin offered a reconstruction of *La Fille Mal Gardée* (1789), which is considered the first modern ballet because it is about common people rather than nobles and gods. The Paris Opera Ballet presented Serge Lifar's *Icare* (1935) and *Suite en Blanc* (1943), and Roland Petit's *Les Rendezvous* (1945). Both choreographers were once the backbone of French ballet but were cast aside as tastes changed in the 1960's. The potent atmosphere of Petit's work, about the seamy side of Parisian life, especially impressed critics.

John Neumeier, a Milwaukee-born choreographer whose work is fairly rare in North America, premiered his *Now and Then* with the National Ballet of Canada in Toronto on February 24. Neumeier, director of the Hamburg (Germany) Ballet, received great acclaim for the premiere.

Metropolitan Ballet Theater, launched on October 7, became Detroit's first professional ballet group. This group had 22 dancers. Karl Condon, formerly a dancer with the Boston Ballet, was artistic director. □ Nancy Goldner

In *World Book,* see **Ballet; Dancing.**

Rudolf Nureyev:
A Ballet

By Nancy Goldner

Dancer and choreographer Rudolf Nureyev brought a special grace, power, and charisma to the world of ballet.

Rudolf Nureyev, who died on Jan. 6, 1993, at the age of 54, was one of the greatest ballet dancers of the 1900's. But the Russian-born Nureyev *(nu RAY yuhf)* was more than a great ballet dancer. When he defected from the Soviet Union in 1961, Nureyev became an international symbol of courage and defiance.

The appeal of Nureyev's artistry lay in its contradictions. His language was classical ballet, yet he was able to break through its rigid technical boundaries with his own athletic charisma. Audiences swooned over the romantic passion that seemed to enable him to leap into the air higher than other dancers.

At the peak of his career, Nureyev's virtuosity was unbeatable. Although most ballet dancers try to create the illusion of effortlessness, with Nureyev one could always sense the physical effort and care that went into his leaps and turns. This feature made his dancing more intense. And yet, his dancing at its best was textbook perfect.

Nureyev's drive for perfection was matched by his drive to stay on the stage. This tenacity remained with him despite the illness that plagued his final years. At the time of his death in Paris, Nureyev held the title of first *choreographer* (creator of dances) for the Paris Opera Ballet, the troupe he had directed from 1983 to 1989. According to his closest friends,

Legend Passes

■ Rudolf Nureyev and Dame Margot Fonteyn dance in *Raymonda* (1898) with the Australian Ballet in 1965. The two became one of ballet's most famous duos.

■ **The author:**

Nancy Goldner is dance critic for *The Philadelphia Inquirer.*

on days when he was strong enough to talk, he was full of plans for the future. When Nureyev died of complications due to AIDS, it seemed hard to believe that his restless energy would no longer enliven the era we live in.

Rudolf Hametovich Nureyev was born on March 17, 1938, on a train that was just passing Irkutsk as his mother traveled to Vladivostok to join his father, who was stationed there as a soldier. Rudolf grew up in the city of Ufa, near the Ural Mountains. The family, which included three sisters, was poor. His father despised his son's interest in dancing, which he was exposed to in school. Nureyev later told of his father dragging him on hunting and fishing trips to make a "man" of him. He said his father even beat him up, but he went on dancing anyway.

When he was 17 years old, Nureyev scraped together train fare for the journey to Leningrad (now St. Petersburg), home of the esteemed Kirov Ballet and the school associated with it. Although for a ballet dancer he was old to begin serious training, teachers at the school recognized his talent and admitted him. Nureyev worked hard and when he completed training, he was quickly promoted to soloist in the Kirov Ballet. However, he displayed defiance by such acts as refusing to join the Communist Youth League. Communist officials came to regard Nureyev as a troublemaker.

In June 1961, the Kirov performed in Paris, and critics singled out Nureyev for his blazing virtuosity. However, as the company waited to board an airplane for London, the next stop on the tour, Nureyev learned that he was to return to the Soviet Union instead. Suspecting that this was punishment for his insubordination, Nureyev slipped away from the troupe and threw himself at two nearby French policemen, crying "Protect me!" His "leap to freedom," as the press dubbed his defection, brought him international fame.

Within months, renowned ballerina Dame Margot Fonteyn of the United Kingdom's Royal Ballet invited Nureyev to be her partner. His debut with her in 1962 in *Giselle* (1841) created a sensation. Nineteen years younger than Fonteyn, Nureyev inspired new life in one of the world's most beloved ballerinas. Their partnership helped spur the new interest in ballet that developed in the 1960's and the 1970's. Nureyev's good looks, his flair for fashion, and his taste for the high life made him an idol for young people.

While Nureyev was bringing a flashy touch to ballet, he was also introducing to the West the purest examples of Russian classical ballet. In 1963, the Royal Ballet performed Nureyev's first staging of a Russian classic, the Shades scene from *La Bayadère* (1877), a ballet written by French choreographer Marius Petipa. Petipa had directed the

Kirov from 1862 to 1903 (when it was known as the Imperial Theater) and had helped make St. Petersburg the world center of ballet. Nureyev went on to restage nearly every available Petipa ballet for scores of companies around the world. Nureyev often inserted his own choreography into these productions and reinterpreted them from a point of view based on the psychoanalytic theories of Austrian physician Sigmund Freud. Critics said that Nureyev's original choreography was fussy and that his psychological orientation was a distortion of Petipa's intentions. The critics may not have approved, but fans bought tickets, especially since he usually danced in his own productions.

By the mid-1970's, Nureyev's physical powers began to decline, so he turned to the less rigorous demands of modern dance. In 1975, he performed as a guest artist with the troupe of Martha Graham, an American dancer and choreographer who was a pioneer of modern dance. Graham created the title role in *Lucifer* (1975) for Nureyev. Also in 1975, Nureyev formed a group called Nureyev and Friends in which other dancers would mainly perform classical material while he mainly performed modern dances. Nureyev and Friends was a staple of the international dance circuit until as late as 1991.

Nureyev also ventured into completely new areas by working in motion pictures, theater, and music. He starred in two movies, *Valentino* (1977) and *Exposed* (1983). In 1989, he performed the role of the king in an American touring production of the musical *The King and I* (1951). He conducted classical music performances in Eastern Europe in 1991 and Russia in 1992.

Only after his death did the world learn that Nureyev had been ill for about 10 years. Knowing that, one can say that the heroic passion Nureyev brought to the stage was more than an aspect of his public image, that his discipline was more than an aspect of his technique. These attributes were the essence of his character. ■ ■ ■

Deaths

Deaths in 1993 included those listed below, who were Americans unless otherwise indicated.

Abe, Kobo (1924-January 22), Japanese novelist, short-story writer, and playwright, best known in both Japan and the United States for his 1962 novel *The Woman in the Dunes,* which was made into an award-winning motion picture in 1964.

Adams, Diana (1926?-January 10), former leading ballerina with the New York City Ballet and American Ballet Theater.

Alexandra, Queen (1921-January 30), Greek-born daughter of Alexander, king of the Hellenes, who married King Peter II of Yugoslavia.

Allison, Davey (1961-July 13), automobile racer who was a star on the National Association for Stock Car Racing circuit with 19 victories.

Ameche, Don (1908-December 6), motion-picture actor whose versatile career culminated in an Academy Award for best supporting actor in *Cocoon* (1985).

Anderson, Marian (1897-April 8), singer whose contralto voice was described by conductor Arturo Toscanini as a "voice . . . heard once in a hundred years"; known mostly for her performances on the recital stage due to racial prejudice that barred her from American opera for most of her career. See **Deaths: Marian Anderson: A Voice Heard Once in 100 Years.**

Antall, Jozsef (1932-December 12), Hungary's prime minister from 1990 until his death in office.

Ardolino, Emile (1943?-November 20), motion-picture and documentary-film director known for films that focused on dancing, such as *Dirty Dancing* (1988) and *Nutcracker* (1993).

Ashe, Arthur (1943-February 6), tennis star and civil rights activist; first black to win the U.S. Open men's singles championship and the first black to win the Wimbledon singles title in England.

Auger, Arleen (1939-June 10), singer known especially for her roles in operas by the Austrian composer Wolfgang Amadeus Mozart.

Baudouin I (Baudouin Albert Charles Leopold Axel Marie Gustave) (1930-July 31), king of Belgium.

Bauza, Mario (1911?-July 11), Cuban-born bandleader who helped pioneer the synthesis of Afro-Cuban music and jazz.

Bazelon, David L. (1909-February 19), federal appeals court judge who wrote several landmark rulings that expanded the rights of criminal defendants and individual civil liberties.

Berberova, Nina (1901-September 26), Russian-born poet, novelist, playwright, and critic.

Bérégovoy, Pierre (1925-May 1), former prime minister of France and leader of France's Socialist Party.

Bixby, Bill (1934-November 21), motion-picture and television actor, perhaps best known for his role in "The Incredible Hulk," a TV series that ran from 1978 to 1982.

Bridges, James (1936?-June 6), motion-picture director and screenwriter who wrote and directed *The Paper Chase* (1973) and *The China Syndrome* (1979).

Buell, Marjorie (1904-May 30), cartoonist who created the cartoon character Little Lulu.

Burdett, Winston (1913-May 19), broadcast reporter for CBS News from 1940 to 1978, known for his coverage of the Vatican as CBS's correspondent in Rome.

Burgess, Anthony (1917-November 25), English novelist, composer, and critic, best known for his novel *A Clockwork Orange* (1962).

Burkitt, Denis P. (1911-March 23), British surgeon whose study of cancer among African children led to a finding that high-fiber diets protect against colon cancer, changing the eating habits of millions of people around the world.

Burr, Raymond (William Stacy) (1917-September 12), Canadian-born television and motion-picture actor best known for his leading role in the "Perry Mason" TV series.

Butts, Alfred M. (1899-April 4), inventor of the Scrabble board game.

Cahn, Sammy (Samuel Cohen) (1913-January 15), lyricist who won four Academy Awards for his words to songs that were popularized by Frank Sinatra, with whom he was long associated. Among his hits were "All the Way," "Three Coins in the Fountain," "High Hopes," and "My Kind of Town."

Caldwell, Toy Talmadge, Jr. (1947?-February 24), rock guitarist and songwriter who was a founding member of the Marshall Tucker Band.

Campanella, Roy (1921-June 26), catcher for the Brooklyn Dodgers who was voted the National League's Most Valuable Player in 1951, 1953, and 1955; the sec-

Thurgood Marshall, Supreme Court justice.

Cesar Chavez, labor union organizer.

Lillian Gish, motion-picture actress.

Raymond Burr, television actor.

ond black player to be voted into the National Baseball Hall of Fame.

Cantinflas (Mario Moreno Reyes) (1911-April 20), Mexico's most famous comic actor and most revered celebrity, often called the "Latin-American Charlie Chaplin"; best known in the United States for his role in the motion picture *Around the World in 80 Days* (1956).

Chavez, Cesar (1927-April 23), labor union organizer and civil rights activist who founded the first successful union of farmworkers in the United States.

Collins, Albert (1932-November 24), blues guitarist who was regarded as the leading heir of the legendary Texas blues tradition.

Conn, Billy (1918-May 29), boxer who won the light-heavyweight title in 1939 and who nearly defeated heavyweight champion Joe Louis in 1941.

Connally, John B., Jr. (1917-June 15), former governor of Texas who was wounded when President John F. Kennedy was assassinated in Dallas in 1963; later became secretary of the treasury under President Richard M. Nixon.

Cooley, Austin G. (1900?-August 31), telecommunications pioneer who helped develop the fax machine.

Crichton, Robert (1925-March 23), author known for two best-sellers, *The Great Imposter* (1959) and *The Secret of Santa Vittoria* (1966), both of which were made into motion pictures.

De Mille, Agnes (1909-October 7), choreographer known for creating ballets based on American themes, such as *Rodeo* (1942), and for choreographing dances for musicals, such as *Oklahoma!* (1943).

DeRita, Joe (Curly) (1909-July 3), comedian who was the last surviving member of the Three Stooges comedy team, which he joined in the late 1950's.

Dickey, Bill (1907-November 12), catcher for the New York Yankees for 17 seasons from the late 1920's to the mid-1940's and later a coach and manager for the Yankees; considered one of the greatest catchers of all time with a .313 career batting average; inducted into the National Baseball Hall of Fame in 1954.

Diebenkorn, Richard (1922-March 30), painter noted especially for his abstract expressionist work.

Donald, James (1917-August 3), British actor who often played military officers; best known for his role in *The Bridge on the River Kwai* (1957).

Donner, Frank J. (1911?-June 10), civil liberties attorney who authored several books on government surveillance and the use of informers against dissidents.

Doolittle, James H. (Jimmy) (1896-September 27), famous American flier who led the first U.S. air raid on Japan during World War II (1939-1945) and later rose to the rank of lieutenant general in the Air Force.

Dopsie, Rockin' (Alton Rubin, Sr.) (1932-August 26), musician and a prominent figure in zydeco music, a fusion of Cajun folk music and rhythm and blues.

Drysdale, Don (1936-July 3), star baseball pitcher for the Brooklyn and Los Angeles Dodgers from 1956 to 1969; voted into the National Baseball Hall of Fame in 1984.

Duke, Doris (1912-October 28), tobacco heiress and

River Phoenix, motion-picture actor.

John Connally, former governor of Texas.

Don Drysdale, Hall of Fame baseball pitcher.

Dizzy Gillespie, jazz composer and trumpeter.

philanthropist once widely regarded as the wealthiest woman in the world.

Eckstine, Billy (1914-March 8), popular ballad singer and jazz band leader who had several hits in the 1940's and 1950's and who assembled a legendary jazz orchestra that included such bebop innovators as Art Blakey, Dizzy Gillespie, Charlie Parker, and Sarah Vaughn.

Farr, Heather (1965?-November 20), professional golfer who became one of the youngest players on the Ladies Professional Golf Association's Tour in 1985.

Feld, Bernard T. (1919-February 19), physicist who helped develop the first atomic bomb and later became a leading advocate of nuclear disarmament.

Fellini, Federico (1920-October 31), Italian motion-picture director whose career spanned five decades and earned him numerous awards, including four Oscars and a lifetime achievement prize at the Academy Awards in March 1993; best known for *La Dolce Vita* (1960), *8 ½* (1962), and *Juliet of the Spirits* (1965).

Fine, Reuben (1914-March 26), chess genius and author of several books on chess.

Gallo, Julio (1910-May 2), vintner who as president of the E.&J. Gallo Winery helped increase wine consumption in America and turned a family business into one of the world's largest wineries.

Gehringer, Charlie (1903-January 21), major league baseball player who was voted into the National Base-

Davey Allison, race car driver.

Helen Hayes, theater and motion-picture actress.

Fred Gwynne, noted television actor.

Donald K. Slayton, Mercury astronaut.

Granger, Stewart (James Lablanche Stewart) (1913-August 16), British-born actor known for his roles as the handsome adventurer in such motion pictures as *King Solomon's Mines* (1950) and *Bhowani Junction* (1956).

Gwynne, Fred (1926-July 2), stage, motion-picture, and television actor known best as Herman Munster on the TV series "The Munsters."

Haber, Joyce (1932-July 29), author and Hollywood gossip columnist for *The Los Angeles Times.*

Haldeman, H. R. (1926-November 12), chief of staff in the Nixon Administration; convicted of conspiring to obstruct justice and of lying to a federal grand jury in the investigation of the 1972 Watergate break-in.

Hamlin, Vincent T. (1900?-June 14), cartoonist who created the "Alley Oop" comic strip.

Hani, Chris (1942-April 10), leader of South Africa's Communist Party.

Harken, Dwight (1910?-August 27), pioneering heart surgeon who developed and implanted the first internal pacemaker.

Hayes, Helen (Helen Hayes Brown) (1900-March 17), stage and motion-picture actress often called the first lady of American theater. Although she won two Academy Awards for best actress in 1931-1932 and best supporting actress in 1970 for her role in *Airport,* she was best known for her stage role as Queen Victoria in *Victoria Regina* (1935).

Hearst, William Randolph, Jr. (1908-May 14), publisher and Pulitzer Prize-winning journalist who headed a media empire founded by his father, William Randolph Hearst.

Hepburn, Audrey (Edda van Heemstra Hepburn-Ruston) (1929-January 20), Belgian-born actress and motion-picture star who won an Academy Award for best actress in her first major film role, as a princess in *Roman Holiday* (1953). She received five Oscar nominations during her film career, which included such motion pictures as *Sabrina* (1954), *Breakfast at Tiffany's* (1961), *Charade* (1963), and *Two for the Road* (1967).

Herlihy, James Leo (1927?-October 21), novelist and playwright best known for his novels *All Fall Down* (1960) and *Midnight Cowboy* (1965), the latter of which was made into a motion picture.

Hersey, John (1914-March 24), novelist and journalist best known for his work on World War II, including the novel *A Bell for Adano,* which won the Pulitzer Prize for fiction in 1945, and *Hiroshima* (1946), a non-fiction account of six people who survived the atomic bombing of that Japanese city.

Hibbert, Eleanor (1906?-January 18), British novelist who wrote about 200 historical and Gothic novels under many pen names, including Jean Plaidy, Victoria Holt, and Philippa Carr.

Hodes, Art (1904-March 4), jazz pianist who played in the traditional style.

Holley, Robert W. (1922-February 11), biologist who shared the Nobel Prize for physiology or medicine in 1968 for his discovery of the genetic code of ribonucleic acid, or RNA.

ball Hall of Fame in 1949 after a 19-year career as a second baseman for the Detroit Tigers.

Gentry, Alwyn (1945-August 3), botanist and senior curator at the Missouri Botanical Garden who was considered among the world's leading authorities on the flora of Latin America.

Gesell, Gerhard A. (1910-February 19), federal district court judge who presided over several historic cases, including the Watergate investigations, the release of the Pentagon Papers, and the Iran-contra affair.

Gillespie, Dizzy (John Birks Gillespie) (1917-January 6), jazz trumpeter and composer who was a co-creator of the be-bop style. With his distinctive turned-up trumpet and bullfrog cheeks, Gillespie became a landmark in the jazz landscape during an almost 60-year career. He was known especially for his composition "A Night in Tunisia."

Gilliatt, Penelope (1932-May 9), British motion-picture critic, screenwriter, and novelist, whose reviews as *The New Yorker* film critic from 1967 to 1979 made her one of America's best-known critics.

Gish, Lillian (1893-February 27), motion-picture and stage actress whose career spanned nearly a century, including starring roles in the silent films *The Birth of a Nation* (1915) and *Intolerance* (1916) and later work in *Sweet Liberty* (1986) and *The Whales of August* (1987).

Golding, Sir William (1911-June 19), English writer who won the Nobel Prize for literature in 1983. A novelist, playwright, short-story writer, essayist, and poet, Golding was best known for his 1954 novel *Lord of the Flies.*

Houphouët-Boigny, Félix (1905?-December 7), president of the Ivory Coast since 1960 and Africa's oldest and longest-serving head of state.

Hourani, Albert (1915-January 17), noted scholar and authority on Middle Eastern history.

Howe, Irving (1920-May 5), literary and social critic and founding editor of *Dissent* magazine.

Hunt, James (1947-June 15), British racing car driver who won the Formula One championship in 1976.

Iba, Henry (1904-January 15), basketball coach who won two national championships, in 1945 and 1946, at Oklahoma State University during a 41-year coaching career; member of the Basketball Hall of Fame.

Janeway, Eliot (1913-February 8), political economist and author.

Juan Carlos, Count of Barcelona (1913-April 1), Spanish aristocrat known throughout Spain as Don Juan; the father of King Juan Carlos, he renounced his claim to the throne in 1977.

Kadoorie, Lord (Lawrence) (1899?-August 25), British businessman and billionaire credited with helping spark an economic boom in the British colony of Hong Kong.

Kauffman, Ewing M. (1916-August 1), founder of the drug firm Marion Laboratories Incorporated and owner of the Kansas City Royals baseball team.

Keeler, Ruby (1910-February 28), Canadian-born dancer who starred in such motion-picture musicals of the 1930's as *42nd Street* (1933).

Knebel, Fletcher (1911-February 26), novelist and former newspaper columnist known for his best-selling Cold War novel *Seven Days in May* (1962).

Knowles, Warren P. (1909?-May 1), former Republican governor of Wisconsin who gained notoriety in 1969 when he summoned National Guard troops to the University of Wisconsin campus at Madison to quell student protests.

Kulwicki, Alan (1955?-April 1), automobile racer and winner of the 1992 Winston Cup championship.

Kusch, Polykarp (1911-March 20), physicist who shared the Nobel Prize in physics in 1955 for determining the magnetic moment of the electron.

Lamborghini, Ferruccio (1916-February 20), Italian industrialist who produced the Lamborghini sports car.

Lee, Brandon (1965?-March 31), motion-picture actor.

Lee, Pinky (Pincus Leff) (1908?-April 3), comedian who hosted a popular children's television show in the 1950's and 1960's.

Leinsdorf, Erich (1912-September 11), Austrian-born music conductor who directed the Boston Symphony from 1962 to 1969 and then became a guest conductor for several major orchestras.

Lewis, Reggie (1965-July 27), star basketball player for the Boston Celtics.

Loy, Myrna (Myrna Williams) (1905-December 14), motion-picture actress who played Nora Charles in the popular comedy-mystery series that began with the 1934 film *The Thin Man*.

MacDougall, Roger (1911-May 27), British playwright and screenwriter known for cowriting *The Man in the White Suit* (1951) and *The Mouse That Roared* (1959).

Mankiewicz, Joseph (1909-February 5), motion-picture director and screenwriter who won Academy Awards for writing and directing *A Letter to Three Wives* in 1949 and who won the same two awards for *All About Eve* in 1950.

Marshall, Thurgood (1908-January 24), first black justice of the Supreme Court of the United States and a pioneering civil rights attorney who won the landmark 1954 Supreme Court ruling that found segregated public school systems unconstitutional.

Mayer, Jean (1920-January 1), French-born nutritionist who pioneered research into problems of poverty, malnutrition, aging, and obesity; chancellor and former president of Tufts University in Boston.

Maynard, Robert C. (1937-August 17), publisher of *The Oakland* (Calif.) *Tribune* and the first black to own a large metropolitan daily newspaper.

McCollum, Leonard F. (1902?-June 13), oilman who transformed the Continental Oil Company into a major energy giant known as Conoco and who later became a philanthropist, helping fund medical projects such as HOPE hospital and Project Orbis.

McFarland, George (Spanky) (1928-June 30), child actor who gained fame as the character Spanky in the motion-picture comedy series "Our Gang."

Mickelson, George S. (1941-April 19), Republican governor of South Dakota from 1986 until his death.

Mize, Johnny (1913-June 2), baseball player and mem-

Reggie Lewis, star basketball player.

Pat Nixon, former first lady.

Federico Fellini, motion-picture director.

Conway Twitty, country music singer.

Deaths

ber of the National Baseball Hall of Fame who played 15 seasons with the St. Louis Cardinals and New York Giants and retired with a .312 career batting average, 359 home runs, and an eighth-best .562 slugging average.

Montoya, Carlos (1903-March 3), guitarist and composer who helped create an international audience for the flamenco music of Spain.

Moore, Garry (Thomas Garrison Morfit) (1915-November 28), pioneer of early television who hosted a variety show, "The Garry Moore Show," and two quiz programs, "I've Got a Secret" and "To Tell the Truth."

Mosconi, Willie (1913-September 16), pocket billiards champion.

Mosley, Zack (1906?-December 21), cartoonist.

Most, Johnny (1923?-January 3), radio broadcaster for the Boston Celtics basketball team for almost 40 years.

Negulesco, Jean (1900-July 18), Romanian-born motion-picture director known for directing such films as *How to Marry a Millionaire* (1953) and *Three Coins in the Fountain* (1954).

Nikolais, Alwin (1910-May 8), modern-dance choreographer known for his experiments with lighting and fabric.

Nixon, Pat (Thelma Catharine Ryan) (1912-June 22), former First Lady who many regarded as the perfect political wife.

Nureyev, Rudolf (1938-January 6), ballet star who was considered one of the most charismatic and athletic male dancers of the 1900's. See **Dancing: Rudolf Nureyev: A Ballet Legend Passes.**

Ochoa, Severo (1905-November 1), Spanish-born molecular biologist who shared the Nobel Prize in physiology or medicine in 1959 for his discovery of an enzyme that can synthesize ribonucleic acid (RNA), a nucleic acid that plays an important role in the formation of proteins.

O'Connell, Helen (1920-September 9), singer known for her hit recording "Green Eyes" and as a leading female vocalist during the big band era of the 1940's.

Özal, Turgut (1927-April 17), president of Turkey from 1989 until his death and Turkey's prime minister from 1983 to 1989; known for the measures he took to revive Turkey's economy.

Parish, Mitchell (1900-March 31), lyricist who wrote the words to "Star Dust," "Sophisticated Lady," "Sweet Lorraine," and "Ruby," among others.

Parker, Theodore A., III (1953-August 3), renowned ornithologist.

Paul, Wolfgang (1913-December 6), German physicist who shared the Nobel Prize in physics in 1989 for his work in isolating electrons and ions.

Peale, Norman Vincent (1898-December 24), one of America's most influential clergymen, known for his 1952 bestseller *The Power of Positive Thinking.*

Pennel, John (1940?-September 26), pole vaulter who set eight world records during the 1960's.

Petrovic, Drazen (1964-June 7), Yugoslav-born basketball player who starred for the New Jersey Nets and for Croatia's basketball team in the 1992 Summer Olympics.

Philbrick, Herbert A. (1915-August 16), informer for the Federal Bureau of Investigation who described his infiltration of the Communist Party of the United States in an autobiography, *I Led Three Lives* (1950), that inspired a popular television show of the 1950's.

Phoenix, River (1970-October 31), motion-picture actor known for his youthful, coming-of-age roles in such films as *Stand by Me* (1986), *Running on Empty* (1988), and *My Own Private Idaho* (1991).

Price, Vincent (1911-October 25), motion-picture, television, and stage actor who became best known as the suave villain of seemingly countless horror movies.

Pulitzer, Joseph, Jr. (1913-May 26), media magnate and noted art collector.

Reid, Kate (1930-March 27), British-born stage and motion-picture actress known for a career that spanned more than 40 years in Canada, the United Kingdom, and the United States.

Ridgway, Matthew B. (1895-July 26), World War II and Korean War (1950-1953) general; he led the 82nd Airborne Division in the World War II invasions of Sicily, Italy, and Normandy and later became the first U.S. Army officer to hold supreme commands in both the Pacific and Atlantic areas; Army chief of staff from 1953 to 1955.

Sabin, Albert (1906-March 3), Polish-born medical researcher who developed an oral vaccine for polio that helped

Roy Campanella, baseball player.

Audrey Hepburn, motion-picture actress.

Hervé Villechaize, television actor.

Matthew B. Ridgway, World War II general.

provide immunization for millions of people.

Salant, Richard S. (1914-February 16), television news executive who headed CBS News for most of the 1960's and 1970's.

Salisbury, Harrison (1908-July 5), reporter, editor, and author who won the Pulitzer Prize in 1955 for his coverage of the Soviet Union as a correspondent for *The New York Times.*

Sauvé, Jeanne (1922-January 26), first woman Speaker of the House of Commons in Canada and Canada's first woman governor general.

Schneider, Alexander (1908-February 2), violin virtuoso, conductor, and music teacher.

Sharkey, Ray (1952-June 11), television and motion-picture actor noted for playing tough guys, especially in the TV series "Wiseguy."

Shirer, William (1904-December 28), author and journalist who wrote the highly regarded *The Rise and Fall of the Third Reich* (1960).

Slayton, Donald K. (Deke) (1924-June 13), astronaut who was one of the original seven Mercury astronauts and who later became chief of flight operations at the Johnson Space Center near Houston.

Smith, Alexis (1921-June 9), actress who appeared in motion pictures in the 1940's and 1950's and then emerged in 1971 as a Tony Award-winning star in the Broadway musical *Follies.*

Stark, Dame Freya (1893-May 9), British travel writer known for her explorations of the Middle East.

Stegner, Wallace (1909-April 13), novelist and short-story writer known for his depictions of the Western United States in such novels as *The Big Rock Candy Mountain* (1943) and *The Spectator Bird* (1976).

Sulzberger, C. L. (1912-September 20), foreign correspondent and foreign affairs columnist for *The New York Times* for almost 40 years.

Sun Ra (Herman Blount) (1914?-May 30), jazz band leader known for his theatrical and avant-garde performances.

Tambo, Oliver R. (1917-April 24), South African opponent of apartheid who led the African National Congress from 1967 to 1991.

Tanaka, Kakuei (1918-December 16), former prime minister of Japan known as the kingpin behind Japan's Liberal Democratic Party.

Thomas, James (Son) (1926-June 26), blues guitarist and singer known for his renditions of traditional Mississippi Delta blues.

Thomas, Lewis (1913-December 3), physician and author who won the National Book Award for *The Lives of the Cell: Notes of a Biology Watcher* (1974), regarded as a classic of popular science writing.

Thompson, E. P. (1924-August 28), British historian and social and peace activist best known for his book *The Making of the English Working Class* (1963).

Troyanos, Tatiana (1938-August 21), opera singer known for her wide range of roles.

Twitty, Conway (Harold L. Jenkins) (1933-June 5), coun-

Sir William Golding, British author.

Billy Eckstine, jazz singer and bandleader.

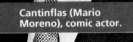

Cantinflas (Mario Moreno), comic actor.

Vincent Price, motion-picture actor.

try and western singer who, during his career, had more than 50 number-one songs on the country charts.

Valvano, Jim (1946-April 28), basketball coach who helped lead North Carolina State to the college basketball championship in 1983.

Villechaize, Hervé (1943-September 4), French-born actor best known for his role as Tattoo on the television series "Fantasy Island."

Webb, Richard (1915-June 10), actor who portrayed Captain Midnight on the 1950's television series of that name.

Williams, Archie (1915?-June 24), black Olympian who won a gold medal in the 400-meter race at the 1936 Olympic Games in Berlin, Germany, helping blunt Adolf Hitler's efforts to use the games as a forum for racist propaganda.

Wise, Gloria E. (1937?-June 7), civil rights activist and one of the five sit-in protesters who tried to integrate a lunch counter at a Woolworth's store in Greensboro, N.C., in 1960.

Zappa, Frank (1940-December 4), rock music composer, guitarist, and bandleader known for his range of musical inventions.

Zuckerman, Lord (Solly Zuckerman) (1904-April 1), British scientist and adviser to British prime ministers, beginning with Winston Churchill; known for his expertise on military matters and his opposition to stockpiling nuclear weapons.   □ Rod Such

Marian Anderson:

A Voice Heard Once in 100 Years

By Ellen Pfeifer

A singer known for her great range and for her unique part in a landmark civil rights protest dies at the age of 96.

174

Marian Anderson, one of the world's greatest concert singers and a trailblazer for black performers, died on April 8, 1993, at age 96. She was known and loved for her fervent performances of classical vocal music and spirituals, for a voice of enormous range and color, and for a personal demeanor of great simplicity and dignity. "Yours is a voice such as one hears once in a hundred years," the Italian conductor Arturo Toscanini once told her. But Anderson was more than a great singer. She broke through many racial barriers, making possible the careers of subsequent generations of black American musicians.

Anderson was born in Philadelphia on Feb. 27, 1897. As her career progressed, she used Feb. 27, 1902, as her birthdate on the advice of her manager, and many standard reference works cite this date. When she was 10 years old, her father died from an accidental injury received at work, leaving her mother to support Marian and her two younger sisters. The family moved in with Marian's grandparents, and Marian's mother took in laundry and worked as a cleaning woman.

Anderson joined the junior choir of her family church, the Union Baptist, at the age of 6. Quite soon, church members recognized the unique beauty of her contralto voice and her unusually wide range, which extended three octaves. Anderson joined the senior church choir at age 13 and could also sing baritone, tenor, or soprano parts. While still in her teens, Anderson was much sought after in Philadelphia as a performer. She sang in churches, schools, and choral festivals, often accompanying herself on the piano. These engagements allowed her to begin contributing to the family income.

Anderson struggled to obtain music lessons, as her family had little money. Once the great tenor Roland Hayes appeared at Union Baptist and was so impressed by Anderson that he arranged for her to study with his teacher in Boston. However, Marian could not go because her grandmother opposed the idea of her living away from home. Nevertheless, Hayes had inspired Anderson deeply. In 1917, she tried to enroll in a small Philadelphia music school with money donated by her church. To her shock, the school denied her an application because of her race.

In spite of these setbacks, Marian's great talent attracted the help she needed. A locally known black soprano, Mary Patterson, gave Anderson free voice lessons. Anderson later auditioned to study with a prominent vocal coach, Giuseppe Boghetti, who eventually taught her without pay and remained her primary teacher until his death. With Boghetti, Anderson learned many of the *arias* (operatic solos) and *art songs* (classical vocal solos) for which she became known.

After completing high school, Anderson began performing more and also began touring. A major step in her career came when she competed against 300 singers and won first prize—an appearance with the New York Philharmonic on April 26, 1925. She was soon signed on by Arthur Judson, head of a highly prominent concert-management agency.

Judson secured higher fees for Anderson, but—partly be-

■ **European debut**

Marian Anderson confers with her German voice coach, Michael Raucheisen, during a European tour in the early 1930's.

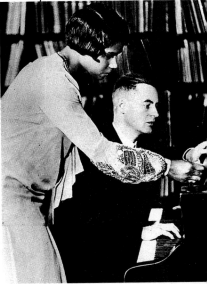

▪ Lincoln Memorial

Anderson performs for more than 75,000 people at the Lincoln Memorial in Washington, D.C., on April 9, 1939, in a landmark civil rights protest. The Daughters of the American Revolution had denied Anderson use of Constitution Hall in the nation's capital.

cause of the higher fees—she began to have fewer concert dates. So in the early 1930's, she went to Europe where her career took off. She sought coaching in foreign languages and made her European debut in Berlin, Germany, in 1930. From 1930 to 1934, she gave nearly 200 concerts in Denmark, Finland, Norway, and Sweden. Anderson sang at the home of Finland's famous composer Jean Sibelius, whose enthusiastic response to her singing was, "My roof is too low for you."

In 1934 and 1935, Anderson toured the Soviet Union, Poland, and the Baltic countries. In Moscow, the famous theater director Konstantin Stanislavski offered to coach her in the lead role of the opera *Carmen* (1875), but she declined because of her busy tour. Stanislavski died not long after, and Anderson later regretted the missed opportunity. Recitals followed in Paris; London; Vienna, Austria; Budapest, Hungary; and The Hague in the Netherlands. While in Europe, Anderson caught the attention of successful concert manager Sol Hurok. He offered to manage Anderson and did so for the rest of her career. She returned to America in the late 1930's and began a grueling schedule of performances in the United States and South America.

During this tour, a furor broke out that became a defining point in Anderson's life and a historical moment in America's struggle for racial equality. In February 1939, Hurok was unable to book Anderson into Washington, D.C.'s Constitution Hall, then the city's largest auditorium. The hall, owned by the Daughters of the American Revolution (DAR), was not available for black performers. When Hurok made this news public, protests began to pour in from many people. Most notably, First Lady Eleanor Roosevelt announced in her syndicated newspaper column that she had resigned her DAR membership in protest.

The U.S. Secretary of the Interior, Harold Ickes, responded to the incident by inviting Anderson to sing at the Lincoln Memorial. Such a public show of defiance was contrary to Anderson's modest nature. She later recounted her dilemma: "In principle the idea was sound, but it could not be comfortable to me as an individual. As I thought further, I could see that my significance as an individual was small in this affair. I had become, whether I liked it or not, a symbol, representing my people. I had to appear." The free Easter Sunday concert on April 9, 1939, drew an audience of more than 75,000 people.

Although the DAR received great criticism for the Constitution Hall scandal, racial discrimination in the United States was common—including at other performance halls in Washington, D.C., and elsewhere. Anderson had faced constant, daily humiliations as a black person. While touring, she traveled in segregated railroad cars. In the South, she had to worry about offending audiences when she took her white piano accompanist's hand to bow at the end of a concert. When she became famous, some white-only hotels would allow her to stay but only as an exception to their usual policy of segregation.

Perhaps the most unfortunate discrimination Anderson faced during her career was the unspoken bias displayed by opera companies, which, with minor exceptions, ignored the great contralto. As a result, Anderson sang only one operatic role in her life—that of the old sorceress Ulrica in Giuseppe Verdi's *A Masked Ball* (1859). With this 1955 debut, she became the first black soloist to perform with the Metropolitan Opera in New York City. By then, Anderson was 58 years old and her voice had declined with age. Thus the occasion was more a milestone in race relations than an important artistic achievement.

In 1943, Anderson married her long-time beau Orpheus Fisher, a New York City architect whom she had met while still in her teens. The couple settled on an estate in Connecticut. They never had children. In 1956, Anderson's autobiography, *My Lord, What a Morning*, was published.

In her later years, Anderson was honored at the highest levels of American government. The State Department asked her to represent the United States as a goodwill ambassador in concerts throughout Asia in 1957. In 1958, President Dwight D. Eisenhower named her an official delegate to the United Nations (UN). At his request, she sang "The Star-Spangled Banner" for Eisenhower's second inauguration, as she also did for the inauguration of President John F. Kennedy in 1961. On a sadder occasion, she also sang at a New York memorial service for Kennedy after his assassination in November 1963. Kennedy had nominated Anderson for the Presidential Medal of Freedom and, that December, President Lyndon B. Johnson awarded her the medal. In 1977, she won the UN peace prize, and the U.S. Congress voted to strike a gold medal in honor of her 80th birthday.

Anderson retired from the concert stage in 1965. Unpretentious and modest, she stated that she was looking forward to becoming a "homemaker" and helping children. ■ ■ ■

■ **Presidential honor**
Anderson accepts the Presidential Medal of Freedom from President Lyndon B. Johnson in 1963. President John F. Kennedy had nominated her for the award before his death.

Democratic Party

Democratic Party. Buoyed by its first presidential election victory in 16 years, the Democratic Party began 1993 with boundless optimism. But the gala inaugural of President Bill Clinton on January 20 proved to be a high point, with troubles mounting for Democrats after that. They spent much of the year wondering how to regain momentum and stem a Republican revival spurred by Clinton's woes. Their doubts were compounded in the November elections, when Republican candidates won governorships of New Jersey and Virginia and the mayoralty of New York City. In June, Los Angeles also got a Republican mayor, for the first time in 32 years.

Clinton selects his team. As is customary, Clinton picked his own team to run the party machinery through the Democratic National Committee (DNC). For chairman, Clinton tapped David C. Wilhelm, 36, a liberal Illinois politician who had been his 1992 campaign manager. Clinton picked Craig Smith, a longtime adviser of his, to be DNC political director.

The DNC membership ratified Clinton's choices on January 20. Upon taking office, Wilhelm emphasized that winning the presidency was only the first step toward regaining majority party status. He said he aimed "to build a new Democratic majority for the 21st century" by appealing to disenchanted Republicans and supporters of billionaire Ross Perot, an independent candidate for President in 1992. Clinton had won only 43 percent of the popular vote.

Wilhelm succeeded Ronald H. Brown, a lawyer and lobbyist who was Clinton's choice for secretary of commerce. During his tenure as DNC chairman, Brown transformed a sleepy organization into a major political force. Brown's chairmanship ended on an embarrassing note, however. He canceled plans for a January 17 corporate-financed gala at the Kennedy Center for the Performing Arts when the event came under fire. Critics suggested that future conflicts of interest might arise because the companies paying for the affair might be affected by Brown's actions as commerce secretary.

The new chairman takes flak. For all the optimism displayed when Wilhelm took office, he ran into trouble within months. With Clinton pressing for a budget plan aimed at curbing enormous federal deficits, the new DNC chairman strove to counter Republican attacks on the proposed measure.

But many Democrats in Congress were less than impressed with Wilhelm's efforts. House members reportedly received hundreds of telephone calls opposing the Clinton program but almost none supporting it, and Republicans in Congress formed a solid bloc in opposition to the budget proposal. When the bill received final congressional approval on August 5 and 6, it received a 50 to 50 vote in the Senate, requiring Vice President Albert Gore, Jr., to cast the tie-breaking vote in favor of the plan.

During the lengthy budget battle, Congressman Richard A. Gephardt of Missouri, Democratic leader of the House of Representatives, was quoted as calling the DNC effort in behalf of the Clinton budget plan "a disaster." Another, unnamed Democrat was quoted as saying that the DNC had conducted "the most inept political operation I've ever seen."

Wilhelm acknowledged that he had been criticized but insisted he had established a good working relationship with Democrats in Congress. Reports that Wilhelm might be replaced were denied.

Clinton slides in polls. Discontent in Democratic ranks reflected more than dissatisfaction with DNC operations. Clinton himself was seen as being partly responsible, as a series of early political missteps and policy shifts triggered a historic slide in the polls. Between late March and late May, Clinton's approval rating in national opinion polls fell from 57 percent to 36 percent—the lowest level ever recorded for a President so early in his administration.

Democratic election setbacks during the year reflected, to some extent, the President's problems. The party's most important loss came on June 5 when Texas Republican Kay Bailey Hutchison won a special election to take the Senate seat of Lloyd M. Bentsen, Jr., who had become Clinton's secretary of the treasury. Her election marked the first time since the Reconstruction era (1865-1877) that Texas had two Republican senators. Republicans also scored a string of victories in special elections for seats in state legislatures.

A split over NAFTA. The Democrats in Congress were deeply divided over the proposed North American Free Trade Agreement (NAFTA), a pact that would create a tariff-free trading zone encompassing Canada, Mexico, and the United States. Opponents of NAFTA said it would lead to a loss of American jobs as more U.S. companies moved to Mexico to take advantage of that nation's low-wage labor force. Clinton argued that NAFTA would ultimately strengthen the economies of both Mexico and the United States and would show the world that the United States remained committed to free trade.

Clinton finally convinced a sizable minority of Democrats in the House of Representatives to support the measure. On November 17, 102 House Democrats joined with 132 Republicans to pass NAFTA, 234 to 200. The Senate approved NAFTA, 61 to 38, on November 20. The victory enhanced Clinton's stature and helped raise his standing in the polls.

Wilhelm makes waves. In September, Wilhelm was invited to address a Washington, D.C., meeting of the conservative, Republican-leaning Christian Coalition, an organization founded in 1989 by evangelist Pat Robertson. The DNC chairman attracted wide media coverage when he assailed the coalition for sponsoring "mean-spirited, misleading commercials" and criticized its opposition to abortion and homosexuality. ☐ Frank Cormier and Margot Cormier

See also **Clinton, Bill; Republican Party.** In *World Book,* see **Democratic Party.**

Denmark in 1993 reversed a 1992 vote against the Treaty on European Union, also known as the Maastricht Treaty. The treaty, set forth by the 12-nation European Community (EC or Common Market), calls for much closer political, economic, and defense cooperation among the member countries.

Maastricht ratified. In a national referendum on May 18, 1993, Danes voted 57 percent to 43 percent to approve the treaty. The outcome was a sharp turnaround from the vote one year earlier, when treaty opponents outnumbered supporters by 51 percent to 49 percent. The change in public opinion resulted largely from agreements with the EC obtained in late 1992 that allow Denmark to opt out of some joint activities, such as a single EC currency and a common EC defense policy. Opinion polls taken after the 1992 vote showed that many Danes feared the Maastricht Treaty would undermine national sovereignty and damage the Danish economy.

The Danish "yes" vote removed a major obstacle to the enactment of the Maastricht Treaty, which had to be approved by all EC members to take effect. The vote also provided political momentum that helped the treaty pass the United Kingdom's House of Commons on May 20, 1993.

New prime minister. Danish Prime Minister Poul Schlüter resigned on January 14 after a government report determined that he had deliberately misled the Folketing (parliament) to try to cover up his government's role in a 1987 scandal. The incident involved a minister in Schlüter's Cabinet who ordered the delay of entry visas for refugees from Sri Lanka who sought to join relatives in Denmark. Danish courts later ruled that the minister's order violated Denmark's liberal asylum laws.

Schlüter, a conservative who had led Denmark since 1982, was succeeded by Poul Nyrup Rasmussen, leader of the Social Democratic Party. On Jan. 25, 1993, Rasmussen formed a new center-left coalition government with members from the Social Democratic Party, the Center Democratic Party, the Radical Liberal Party, and the Christian People's Party. Rasmussen's government had the support of 90 members of the 179-seat Folketing, a majority of just one.

Budget proposed. In May, Rasmussen unveiled a budget for 1994 that lowers taxes and increases spending to stimulate the sluggish Danish economy. Rasmussen's plan would inject about $2 billion into the economy and create a budget deficit of $8.44-billion, similar to the government's 1993 shortfall.

Unemployment in 1993 topped 12 percent, the highest level since the 1930's. Inflation was among the lowest in Europe at about 1.4 percent, but economists said the figure could rise to more than 3 percent in 1994. Many economists predicted that the government would have to boost already high interest rates to keep price rises in check. □ Philip Revzin

See also **Europe** (Facts in brief table). In *World Book,* see **Denmark.**

Detroit. Democrat Dennis Archer, a former justice on the Michigan Supreme Court, was elected mayor of Detroit on Nov. 2, 1993. Archer succeeded five-term Democratic Mayor Coleman A. Young, 75, who had announced in June that he would retire after 20 years. Archer—who, like Young, is black—defeated Democratic contender Sharon M. McPhail, a division chief in the Wayne County Prosecutor's Office. Archer received 147,838 votes (57 percent of the total) to McPhail's 114,758 votes (43 percent). McPhail, also black, had been endorsed by Mayor Young. Archer and McPhail were the two top vote-getters in a September 14 nonpartisan primary election.

The mayoral race split many of the city's traditional political organizations for the first time in 20 years. Archer received heavy support from city labor unions, the clergy, and the media. McPhail was backed by women's groups and the two local Democratic organizations. Archer appealed to voters with promises to improve city services.

Police on trial. On Aug. 23, 1993, separate juries convicted two former Detroit police officers, Larry Nevers and Walter Budzyn, of second-degree murder in the 1992 beating death of Detroit motorist Malice W. Green. A third patrolman, Robert Lessnau—who had been present at the scene of the beating but did not take part in it—was acquitted of lesser assault charges in a separate trial on August 16. On October 12, Nevers was sentenced to 12 to 25 years in prison, and Budzyn received a sentence of 8 to 18 years.

On Nov. 5, 1992, Nevers and Budzyn confronted Green in a car outside a suspected *crack house* (a house where crack cocaine is sold). When Green refused the officers' demands to open his clenched hand, which they suspected concealed a packet of crack, they pulled him out of the car. According to the testimony of witnesses, Nevers and Budzyn then struck Green repeatedly in the head with their police flashlights. Medical examiners testified that Green died from at least a dozen blows to the head.

The trial raised tensions in Detroit because of its racial aspects. Green was black, and the three officers are white. The summerlong trials, broadcast live daily on cable television, were followed closely by members of the city's black community. After the convictions, some white suburbanites and a few city residents signed petitions asking Michigan Governor John Engler to pardon the officers, but he refused to interfere with the court's decision.

After the trial, Green's family won a $5.25-million civil-court settlement against the city. Meanwhile, the convicted police officers filed appeals to their sentences.

Southwest takes flight. Southwest Airlines, the only major passenger airline flying out of Detroit's newly renovated City Airport, on September 14 announced that it was ceasing operations there. Southwest continued to fly out of Detroit Metropolitan Airport in suburban Romulus.

Detroit had spent more than $25 million expanding City Airport and had planned to spend another $175 million to extend a runway. Southwest, which began service from City Airport in July 1988, said it needed a longer runway to fly larger planes in and out of the airport. But city officials were stymied by opposition from nearby residents and business owners who objected to the noise and possible dangers associated with expanded air service. Many of them also opposed having their property condemned by the city to make room for the longer runway.

Lots of laughs. A taste of Chicago came to the Motor City on September 16 with the opening of the Second City comedy club. The club originated in Chicago, which has long been nicknamed the Second City. The $6.5-million club was the latest addition to Detroit's theater district, which is developing around the renovated Fox Theater.

New schools chief. Detroit schools Superintendent Deborah McGriff announced her resignation on October 14, after just 27 months on the job. McGriff, 44, left amid tensions with members of the school board and uncertainty over school funding reforms being considered in the state legislature. The board named David Snead, a former school administrator and principal, to be interim superintendent of the 177,000-student district. □ Constance C. Prater

See also **City.** In *World Book,* see **Detroit.**

Dinosaur. See Paleontology.

Disabled. The impact of the Americans with Disabilities Act (ADA), a federal civil rights law whose major provisions took effect in July 1992, was difficult to assess in 1993. The difficulty stemmed in part from legal challenges to some ADA provisions that had yet to work their way through United States courts. By July, 11,500 complaints had been filed with the Equal Employment Opportunity Commission (EEOC) under ADA's employment provisions. Only a few were under investigation, however, because the EEOC did not have an expanded staff to deal with the surprisingly high number of cases. Most of the charges were made by disabled employees against their employers for failing to provide appropriate accommodations to the workplace.

In response to another ADA provision, many public facilities and commercial enterprises contracted for "accessibility surveys" in 1993. The surveys identified the minimum number of changes a business would have to make in order to comply with the ADA provision calling for the removal of structures that might be barriers to people with disabilities.

Federal appointments. By September, the disabled had won appointments to nearly 30 top-level positions, including assistant secretary in the Office of Special Education and Rehabilitation Services of the Department of Education and commissioner of aging in the Administration on Aging, an agency of the Department of Health and Human Services. Oth-

er positions filled by people with disabilities were in the departments of Justice and Agriculture, the White House, and the office of the Vice President.

A voice in health-care reform. President-elect Bill Clinton appointed a transition team in late 1992 to work on a plan to reform the nation's health-care system. Disability rights advocates served on a subgroup of the team that dealt with long-term care. The subgroup recommended that any national health-care plan include such basic reforms as the elimination of clauses in health insurance that exclude coverage for preexisting conditions or that delay coverage for certain conditions. The subgroup also recommended that a national plan cover services that would enable a disabled person to live at home. For example, the plan should cover the cost of having someone assist a disabled person who needed help dressing and the cost of widening doorways to accommodate a wheelchair.

The disabled then brought these concepts to First Lady Hillary Rodham Clinton after the President named her to head the Task Force on National Health Care Reform in January 1993. Disabled people served on other task force subgroups and met with the President and White House staff to ensure that people with disabilities would be represented in key decision-making health-care agencies. □ Irving Kenneth Zola

In *World Book,* see **Disabled.**

Disasters. The worst natural disaster of 1993 was an earthquake that struck a sugar-growing region of India, southeast of Bombay, in September. The official government death toll was 9,748 people. The quake, which measured 6.4 on the Richter scale, was the most destructive to hit India since 1935. It leveled almost 50 villages in the states of Maharashtra and Karnataka.

Disasters that resulted in 25 or more deaths in 1993 included the following:

Aircraft crashes

February 8—Teheran, Iran. An Iranian airliner collided with an Iranian air force jet on take-off from Teheran's main airport. All 132 people on board the airliner were killed, but the two-man crew of the air force jet ejected safely before the collision.

March 5—Skopje, Macedonia. A twin-engine passenger airplane crashed in a snowstorm shortly after take-off from Skopje's Petrovac airport, killing 81 people among the 97 people on board.

April 27—Aurangabad, India. The undercarriage of an Indian Airlines jet struck a truck that was on a road abutting the runway. The plane crashed, killing 70 of the 118 passengers and crew.

April 27—Libreville, Gabon. A military airplane transporting most of Zambia's national soccer team crashed into the Atlantic Ocean shortly after take-off, killing all 30 people on board.

April 27—Tashqurgan, Afghanistan. A military transport plane crashed in northern Afghanistan, killing all 76 people on board, including General Mohammad es'Haq and 15 members of an army wrestling team.

May 19—Near Medellín, Colombia. A Colombian jetliner crashed into a mountain as it prepared to land at Medel-

Rescuers sift through the rubble left by a powerful earthquake that killed almost 10,000 people in a region southeast of Bombay, India, in September.

lin's airport. All 132 passengers and crew members on board were killed.

July 1—Sorong, Indonesia. An Indonesian airliner on a regular flight from Jakarta to Surabaya crashed as it tried to land at the airport in Sorong, killing 40 of the 43 people on board.

July 23—Yinchuan, China. A China Northwest Airlines jetliner, en route to the capital, Beijing, crashed on take-off from Yinchuan, killing at least 59 people.

July 26—Near Haenam, South Korea. A South Korean airliner crashed into a mountain near Haenam after bad weather prevented it from landing at its destination, Mokpo, South Korea. Airline officials said 66 of the 110 people on board were killed in the crash.

August 28—Khorog, Tajikistan. A Tajik passenger jet crashed on take-off from Khorog, killing 76 people. Officials said the jet was carrying more than twice the number of passengers it could safely transport.

November 20—Near Ohrid, Macedonia. A Macedonian airliner crashed into a hill and exploded near the resort of

Ohrid, killing 115 of the 116 people on board. The sole survivor was thrown from the airplane by the impact.

Earthquakes

July 12—Northern Japan. An earthquake measuring 7.8 on the Richter scale struck northern Japan, triggering tidal waves and killing about 200 people. The quake, the strongest in that region since 1968, was centered about 50 miles (80 kilometers) from the island of Hokkaido. The tiny island of Okujiri, with a population of about 4,600, was the worst hit, suffering more than half of the casualties. There, tidal waves washed away a number of homes and automobiles, and fires caused by the quake destroyed about half of the 680 homes in the island village of Aonae.

September 30—Maharashtra and Karnataka states, India. The most destructive earthquake to strike India in more than 50 years leveled almost 50 villages in the states of Maharashtra and Karnataka in a remote sugar-cane-growing region southeast of Bombay. The official death toll was 9,748. The quake, which measured 6.4 on the Richter scale, was centered near the village of Killari, where an estimated 3,000 people were buried in the debris of their homes.

October 13 and 16—Eastern Papua New Guinea. An earthquake measuring 7.2 on the Richter scale struck the eastern region of Papua New Guinea on October 13, causing avalanches that killed at least 60 people. On October 16, an aftershock from the quake, measuring 6.8 on the Richter scale, killed at least 3 other people.

Explosions and fires

January 7—Chongju, South Korea. South Korea's worst fire tragedy in more than 20 years killed at least 29 people when a fire that started in the basement of an apartment building ignited liquefied natural gas tanks.

February 14—Tangshan, China. A fire ripped through a three-story department store in Tangshan during a peak shopping hour, killing 79 people.

March 24—Dakar, Senegal. At least 60 people were killed and 250 were injured when a truck carrying liquid ammonia exploded at a peanut-processing factory in Dakar.

May 10—Near Bangkok, Thailand. What may have been the worst factory fire in history claimed the lives of at least 188 people when a doll factory in an outlying area of Bangkok burst into flames. At least 80 people were listed as missing after a weeklong search of the fire debris ended. About 800 workers were in the factory when the fire broke out.

August 5—Shenzhen, China. An explosion caused by a leak of nitric acid at a warehouse led to a blaze that ignited a nearby natural gas plant, which in turn led to several other explosions. Chinese officials said that as many as 70 people were killed.

September 28—Near Caracas, Venezuela. A natural gas pipeline alongside a highway ruptured and exploded near Caracas, the capital of Venezuela. The explosion occurred during rush hour. Flames engulfed a commuter bus and several automobiles, killing at least 51 people. A state telephone company crew laying fiber-optic cables reportedly ruptured the pipeline and triggered the explosion.

November 19—Near Shenzhen, China. A toy factory in the Shenzhen Economic Zone went up in flames, killing 81 workers. Officials said most of the doors and windows in the factory were locked to keep people inside during working hours.

Landslides and avalanches

January 18—Ozengeli, Turkey. An avalanche of snow buried most of the village of Ozengeli in northeastern Turkey, killing at least 53 people.

March 29—Near Cuenca, Ecuador. A landslide caused by heavy rains killed about 300 people in a mining town.

May 10—Near Zamora, Ecuador. A mud slide swept through a gold mining camp, killing at least 200 people. Officials said the landslide occurred on a mountain slope denuded of trees and vegetation by mining and logging activities. Heavy rains further loosened the soil.

August 8—Caracas, Venezuela. About 150 people living in shantytowns around Caracas were buried in mud slides triggered by the heavy rains of Tropical Storm Bret. More than 4,000 people were left homeless by the storm, which lashed Venezuela's Caribbean coast.

December 11—Kuala Lumpur, Malaysia. Heavy rains caused a landslide that demolished a luxury 12-story apartment building. Police said at least 51 people were killed.

December 14—Cairo, Egypt. A landslide sent huge limestone boulders rolling down a mountain into a residential section of Cairo, the capital, killing at least 34 people.

December 17, 18—Dabeiba, Colombia. Heavy rainfall triggered a landslide that crushed homes and killed at least 30 people in this farming community.

Mine disasters

May 13—Near Johannesburg, South Africa. A methane-gas explosion ripped through a coal mine located near Johannesburg, the capital, killing at least 49 miners. Four other miners were reported missing and were feared dead. Union officials accused mine owners of ignoring safety measures by increasing production with fewer workers.

Shipwrecks

January 14—Baltic Sea off Germany. A Polish ferry en route to the Swedish port of Ystad capsized in the Baltic Sea during a storm that lashed the boat with hurricane-force winds. Authorities said 54 people drowned.

February 17—Off the coast of Haiti. An overcrowded ferry en route from the town of Jérémie, Haiti, to the capital, Port-au-Prince, sank in a storm in one of the worst maritime disasters in history. The official death toll was 275 people. About 300 people survived. The ferry reportedly carried no lifeboats or life jackets and was licensed to transport a maximum of 260 passengers and crew.

March 15—Off Nova Scotia. A freighter sank in a storm that created waves 60 feet (18 meters) high, and 32 crew members were missing.

July 2—Near Manila, Philippines. A pagoda being carried by three boats that were lashed together in a religious procession toppled onto the boats and sank them in the Bocaue River. More than 230 people drowned.

October 10—Off Puan, South Korea. A ferry sank in a storm off Puan, South Korea, killing at least 261 people. Officials could not determine how many people were on board because no passenger list could be found.

December 19—Off Desaru, Malaysia. Two fishing trawlers collided in high waves off the town of Desaru on Malaysia's southeastern coast. Police said that 49 people were missing.

Storms and floods

January 17—Tijuana, Mexico, and southern California. Heavy rains that began on January 7 and continued for almost two weeks caused extensive flooding, claiming the lives of at least 32 people in Tijuana. The same storm system also caused flooding in San Diego and Riverside counties in southern California, killing 17 people there.

April 26—Andes, Colombia. A flash flood along the Taparto River in a mountainous region of northwest Colombia destroyed homes and triggered landslides near the town of Andes, killing at least 67 people.

June 17—Dhaka, Bangladesh. Floods and storms killed more than 100 people, including 40 fishermen who drowned after their trawlers sank in the Bay of Bengal.

July 6, 7—Off Mexico's Pacific Coast. Hurricane Calvin swept along Mexico's Pacific Coast, striking the resort cities of Acapulco and Manzanillo and killing at least 28 people in accidents caused by high winds. About 14,000 people were left homeless.

June, July—North-central United States. At least 48 people died as a result of record flooding along the Mississippi, Missouri, and other rivers in the Midwestern United States, according to the Climate Analysis Center of the National Oceanic and Atmospheric Administration. The federal government declared parts of the states of Illinois, Kansas, Minnesota, Missouri, Nebraska, North and South Dakota, and Wisconsin as disaster areas. Every county in Iowa was declared a disaster area.

July—South Asia. Four weeks of flooding caused by monsoon rains killed more than 4,500 people in several South Asian countries. Authorities said that more than 3,500 people died in Nepal, about 700 were killed in India, and about 300 people died in Bangladesh. By July 24, nearly half of Bangladesh was flooded.

July—Hunan and Sichuan provinces, China. Heavy summer rains caused floods that killed at least 78 people in Hunan province and at least 41 people in Sichuan province.

August 7—Southwestern Japan. Typhoon Robyn caused at least 40 deaths as it swept along the southwestern part of Japan. Hardest hit was Kagoshima City on Kyushu Island.

August 27—Near Xining, China. A dam burst near the city of Xining, capital of Qinghai province, and the resulting floodwaters killed more than 250 people, according to government officials.

September 4, 5—Southern and western Japan. Typhoon Yancy left at least 37 people dead after storming across southern and western Japan. The storm triggered more than 200 landslides and badly damaged more than 1,200 residences.

October 31 to November 2—Yoro and Colón departments, Honduras. Three days of heavy rains in the Atlantic Coast *departments* (provinces) of Colón and Yoro caused flooding and mud slides that killed at least 110 people. Authorities said that 263 people were missing.

November 23—South-central Vietnam. Typhoon Kyle struck four coastal provinces of Vietnam, killing at least 45 people and injuring at least 244 others. The storm also destroyed or damaged tens of thousands of residences.

December 4—Southern India. A cyclone roared through coastal districts of southern India, killing at least 47 people in the state of Tamil Nadu and the district of Pondicherry.

Train wrecks

January 30—Near Darajani, Kenya. Five railway cars, part of a train carrying about 600 passengers, plunged off a bridge into a flooded river. At least 140 people were killed, and more than 250 people were reported missing. The bridge had been battered by floodwaters.

March 28—Pusan, South Korea. A crowded passenger train veered off the tracks and into a hole created when rain-soaked ground collapsed into a tunnel below the tracks. At least 78 people were killed and 120 people were injured in South Korea's worst train accident.

September 22—Near Mobile, Ala. An Amtrak train plunged into a bayou near Mobile, Ala., when a section of a bridge gave way, killing 47 passengers and crew members in the worst wreck since Amtrak was founded in 1970. Federal officials determined that the bridge had been struck earlier by a barge. More than 150 passengers and crew members survived the wreck.

November 2—Jakarta, Indonesia. At least 69 people were killed and more than 75 people were injured when two commuter trains collided during the morning rush hour on the outskirts of Jakarta, the capital of Indonesia.

Other disasters

January 4—Near Cancún, Mexico. A bus carrying tourists to the Mayan ruins at Chichén Itza swerved on a rain-slickened road and crashed into a high-tension power pole, killing 25 people.

January 9—Santo Tomé, Argentina. Three tour buses collided on a narrow highway, bursting into flames and killing at least 55 people.

January 31—Liaoning province, China. A bus tried to speed across a railway crossing and was struck by a train. Sixty-six people were killed.

February 2—Near Legazpi, Philippines. The eruption of the Mount Mayon volcano on the island of Luzon killed at least 75 people and forced the evacuation of about 45,000 people.

March 2—Brazzaville, Congo. A ferryboat captain reportedly pulled away from a dock while hundreds of passengers were still standing on a gangway. Estimates of the death toll ranged from at least 147 to as many as 219 people. Most drowned when they fell into the deep waters and fast-moving currents of the Congo River, but others were crushed to death when the captain maneuvered the ferry back to the dock.

August 13—Nakhon Ratchasima, Thailand. At least 123 people were killed when the Royal Palace Hotel in this provincial capital collapsed. More than 200 people were injured. Police arrested six people on charges of criminal negligence following news reports that three stories had been added to the hotel's original three-story structure without adequate safeguards. □ Rod Such

Djibouti. See Africa.

Dole, Robert J. (1923-), United States senator from Kansas and Senate minority leader, became a leading spokesman for the Republican Party in 1993. In his role as party spokesman, Dole especially attacked President Bill Clinton's economic plans. (See **Republican Party**.)

Dole was born on July 22, 1923, in Russell, Kans. His father worked in agribusiness and his mother sold sewing machines. In World War II (1939-1945), Dole served as a platoon leader in the U.S. Army. After he was struck by a shell in Italy, he spent three years in hospitals and lost the use of his right arm. In 1952, Dole completed law school at what is now Washburn University of Topeka, in Topeka, Kans. Dole was elected to the Kansas House of Representatives in 1950. In 1952, he began a four-term stint as the prosecuting attorney of Russell County.

Starting in 1960, Dole served four terms in the U.S. House of Representatives. In 1968, he was elected to the Senate and has remained there ever since. Dole unsuccessfully ran for his party's presidential nomination in 1980 and 1988.

In 1975, Dole married Elizabeth Hanford, who later became secretary of transportation in the Administration of President Ronald Reagan. Dole has a daughter, Robin, from a previous marriage. □ Mary Carvlin

Dominican Republic. See Latin America.
Drought. See Water; Weather.

Drug abuse. Discussions about health-care reform in the United States in 1993 helped to focus attention on the economic toll of drug abuse. Experts estimated that substance abuse costs the nation $238 billion annually. The largest expense, $99 billion, came from alcohol-related problems. Cigarette smoking was estimated to cost $72 billion, and abuse of other drugs costs about $67 billion. These estimates include direct expenses, such as medical care, and indirect costs, such as lost work time.

Government spending on treatment. Research showing the costliness of untreated substance abuse encouraged health-care policymakers to include this treatment in shaping an affordable national health-care plan. According to results of a nationwide study published in September 1993, alcohol problems accounted for 38 percent of hospital costs paid by Medicare, the government medical insurance program for people over 65 and for people with disabilities. The study, performed by physicians at the Medical College of Wisconsin in Milwaukee, showed greater alcohol problems among the elderly than previously recognized.

Another study, released in September 1993 by the Center for Addiction and Substance Abuse in New York City, found that 18 percent of Medicaid hospital costs were related to substance abuse. Medicaid is a government program that pays medical expenses for people who qualify for public assistance.

Drugs

Drug use surveys. In June 1993, the U.S. National Institute on Drug Abuse (NIDA) released the results of the 1992 National Household Survey. It showed downward trends in alcohol, tobacco, and other drug use. The number of people using any illicit drug in any given month in 1992 was just over 11 million, down from 23 million in 1985. Cocaine users declined from about 6 million in 1985 to 1.3 million in 1992.

However, the annual NIDA survey of college students, conducted by the University of Michigan Institute for Social Research in Ann Arbor, showed that marijuana use in 1993 was up slightly. Use of hallucinogenic drugs, notably LSD, was also up. Cocaine use among this group, however, continued to drop.

Drug use among high school seniors continued to decline, according to the survey, which questioned 15,800 seniors. Students who reported using illicit drugs in 1992 dropped to 27 percent from 29 percent in 1991. Marijuana use in 1992 decreased to 22 percent from its peak of 51 percent in 1979. Cocaine use declined to 3.1 percent from a peak of 13 percent in 1985. The survey also showed that in 1992, those using alcohol within the month prior to the survey dropped to 51 percent from 54 percent in 1991. About 30 percent of the seniors reported smoking cigarettes, about the same percentage that has been reported since 1980.   □ David C. Lewis

In *World Book,* see **Drug abuse.**

Drugs. The first drug capable of treating the abnormalities that underlie multiple sclerosis (MS) was approved by the United States Food and Drug Administration (FDA) on July 23, 1993. Berlex Laboratories of Richmond, Calif., will sell the genetically engineered drug, interferon beta-1b, under the brand name Betaseron.

MS is a chronic, often disabling disease of the nervous system that affects about 300,000 Americans. The disease destroys patches of *myelin,* a material made of fat and protein that coats and insulates nerve fibers. This loss, or demyelination, causes difficulties with movement, vision, and other body functions. Drugs currently given to MS patients only relieve symptoms.

In clinical tests, interferon beta-1b helped patients with a form of MS characterized by episodes of symptoms followed by *remissions* (periods with few or no symptoms). About 30 percent of MS patients have this form. In the studies, patients on interferon beta-1b experienced fewer flare-ups, had milder symptoms, and required less hospital treatment than did patients given a *placebo* (substance with no active ingredients). In addition, computerized brain scans showed that the patients also experienced less demyelination. Experts do not know exactly how the drug works, however.

Physicians on an FDA medical advisory panel emphasized that Betaseron does not cure MS but said it could help many people with early, mild MS. Researchers have begun testing Betaseron on patients with a more severe, progressive form of MS.

Betaseron was the first drug approved under a new FDA program to make certain drugs available to patients faster than previously possible. The FDA approved Betaseron in 12 months, compared with an average of 28 months for other drugs. But a short supply of the drug limited its availability.

Alzheimer's drug. Tacrine, the first drug shown to have any effect on symptoms of Alzheimer's disease, was approved by the FDA on September 9. Warner-Lambert Company of Morris Plains, N.J., manufactures tacrine, which will be sold under the brand name Cognex. FDA Commissioner David A. Kessler emphasized that tacrine is not a cure but may improve memory in some patients with mild or moderate forms of Alzheimer's disease.

Alzheimer's is a disease of the brain that slowly destroys memory and reasoning ability. It affects about 4 million Americans, most of whom are elderly. Members of an FDA advisory committee, which recommended approval of tacrine, said that the drug produced only slight improvement in symptoms and might help only about 12 percent of patients.

Epilepsy drug. The FDA on August 2 approved felbamate, the first new drug for treating epilepsy in 15 years. About 2.5 million Americans have epilepsy, a brain disorder that causes seizures. Clinical trials showed that felbamate reduces the number of seizures and causes fewer side effects, such as drowsiness, than existing drugs do. Felbamate was developed by Wallace Laboratories of Cranbury, N.J., and is sold under the brand name Felbatol.

Felbamate also proved effective in treating children who have Lennox-Gastaut syndrome. This disorder is an extremely serious and difficult to treat form of epilepsy in which the head suddenly drops or the child falls to the ground without warning. Many children with the rare condition have to wear protective headgear to prevent head injuries.

Cystic fibrosis drug. An FDA advisory committee on August 9 recommended approval of the drug DNase I for the treatment of cystic fibrosis (CF). CF affects about 30,000 Americans and is the most common serious inherited disease among Caucasians.

The drug, developed through genetic engineering, breaks up the thick mucus that accumulates in the lungs of CF patients and thereby reduces the frequency of respiratory tract infections. Clinical trials showed that DNase I allows CF patients to breathe more easily and lead more active lives. The drug, manufactured by Genentech Incorporated of South San Francisco, Calif., would be sold under the brand name Pulmozyme.

Regulating vitamins. Expressing concern about exaggerated health claims made for vitamins, minerals, herbs, and other dietary supplements, the FDA on June 14 proposed new labeling rules for these popular products. The FDA said labels on dietary supplements would be permitted to make health claims only when there is "significant agreement" among scientists that the claim is valid.

Agreement exists, for example, on folic acid's ability to prevent a group of birth defects termed neural tube defects, and so the FDA said it planned to authorize that claim. In addition, the FDA was considering authorizing the claim that antioxidant vitamins, such as C and E, may help prevent cancer.

The FDA rules also would require labels to carry the nutritional information that appears on food packages. Manufacturers of dietary supplements reacted angrily to the action, claiming that it was an attempt by the FDA to restrict consumer access to vitamin and mineral supplements.

AIDS collaboration. In a pioneering effort to speed the search for new AIDS drugs, 15 pharmaceutical companies in the United States and Europe on April 19 announced an agreement to cooperate in testing AIDS drugs on human subjects. The companies said they would share data on early test results, share supplies of potential new drugs, and collaborate on other aspects of drug development. Participants in the collaboration noted that such cooperation was unusual because pharmaceutical companies traditionally are secretive about products that are under development. □ Michael Woods

See also **Medicine.** In *World Book,* see **Drug.**

Eastern Orthodox Churches. Ecumenical Patriarch Bartholomew I of Constantinople (Istanbul, Turkey) visited Serbia, the dominant republic of Yugoslavia, on Aug. 5 to 12, 1993. He called for respect for human rights and an end to fighting in Bosnia-Herzegovina, a former republic of Yugoslavia that declared its independence in 1992.

Bartholomew I called an assembly in Istanbul in July 1993 to discuss tensions involving Patriarch Diodoros of Jerusalem. Diodoros had purchased properties and set up dioceses in Australia that were in competition with established Orthodox churches. As a result of the meeting, the Jerusalem church announced it would withdraw from the disputed area.

In Russia, the parliament passed a law on July 31 requiring foreign missionaries to register with a special government board. The purpose was to limit missionary activity other than that of the Eastern Orthodox Church. Russian President Boris N. Yeltsin returned the measure to parliament unsigned because he believed it contradicted international human rights agreements. The parliament revised the legislation, but Yeltsin again returned it unsigned just before he dissolved parliament on September 21.

On October 2, Alexei II, patriarch of Moscow and All Russia, served as a mediator at talks at the Danilov Monastery between Yeltsin backers and those supporting Vice President Aleksandr V. Rutskoi, who had demanded Yeltsin's resignation. The patriarch

sought to disarm rebel deputies, who were under siege in the parliament building, and the government forces that surrounded them. (See **Russia.**)

Other developments. The Orthodox Church in Albania continued in 1993 its struggle to reestablish itself following near extinction under Communist rule. Archbishop Anastasios Yannoulatos presided over the building of new churches and the establishment of a seminary.

The Inter-Orthodox Preparatory Commission for the Great and Holy Council of the Orthodox Church met in Chambesy, Switzerland, from November 7 to 13 to decide on the way a national or local Orthodox church could become *autocephalous* (self-governing). A procedure was adopted in which the church would get approval from its mother church, the Ecumenical Patriarchate of Constantinople, and, finally, the other autocephalous Orthodox churches.

The Jan. 1, 1993, division of Czechoslovakia into the Czech Republic and Slovakia brought about a unique change in the Orthodox Church of Czechoslovakia. The Orthodox Church had been organized on an ethnic basis, but the divided populations were too small to warrant two separate churches. Thus, the chief hierarch, Metropolitan Dorotheos, was to be known as the metropolitan of Czech Lands and Slovakia and to minister to two ethnically different populations. □ Stanley Samuel Harakas

In *World Book,* see **Eastern Orthodox Churches.**

Economics. The United States economy in 1993 continued on a course of moderate growth with low inflation and low interest rates. By the end of the year, the pace of growth appeared to be strengthening, and many analysts predicted the economy might be poised for accelerated growth in 1994. However, the two-year-old expansion remained slower than typical recoveries following past recessions.

GDP growth. The year opened on a sharply positive note, as statistics showed that the *gross domestic product (GDP)*—the total value of all goods and services produced within a country—grew at a robust 5.7 percent annual rate in the final quarter of 1992. But the picture of renewed economic health painted by that figure turned out to be faulty. In the first three months of 1993, GDP growth braked to a very slow 0.8 percent annual rate. GDP growth improved to an annual rate of 1.9 percent in the second quarter and 2.7 percent in the third quarter. For all of 1993, economists predicted a GDP growth rate of 2.8 percent.

Unemployment remained stubbornly high at almost 7 percent of the work force for most of 1993, and many companies continued to lay off workers. However, in October, factories added jobs for the first time since February even though the overall jobless rate edged up.

Inflation in check. The slow economic growth helped keep inflation under control. Inflation at the

Economics

consumer level rose at a yearly rate of almost 3 percent, and increases at the wholesale and producer levels were even smaller. Slow growth countered upward price pressures that included a 4.3-cent boost in the federal gasoline tax, the growing use of more expensive low-sulfur diesel fuel in commercial trucking, and massive flooding in Midwest farm regions in June and July, which led to fears of higher food prices.

The absence of a serious inflation threat prompted financial lenders to lower interest rates on loans. Some types of interest rates hit their lowest levels since the 1960's. Low rates helped homeowners save money by refinancing old mortgages at the newer levels, allowed businesses to lighten debt loads they had accumulated when interest rates were higher, and reduced the federal deficit by lowering the yield to investors that the government offered on new U.S. Treasury debt notes.

Weak trading partners. Weighing on the U.S. economy in 1993 was economic weakness among many other industrial nations. Slowdowns and, in some cases, outright recessions in foreign countries reduced their demand for imports and so helped deflate the U.S. export sector, which had been a major source of new jobs in the past.

Reacting to a stubborn recession in Japan, Japanese voters on July 18 deprived Prime Minister Kiichi Miyazawa's Liberal Democratic Party of a majority in the lower house of parliament for the first time since 1955. Shortly thereafter, Miyazawa resigned, and a seven-party coalition government headed by Morihiro Hosokawa of the Japan New Party took over on August 6. To help revive Japan's economy, Hosokawa on September 16 unveiled a $58-billion economic stimulus package and dozens of deregulation proposals for business.

Economic weakness—reflected by an unemployment rate of about 11 percent—also helped create political change in Canada, the single-largest trading partner of the United States. Declining popularity for the ruling Progressive Conservative Party forced Prime Minister Brian Mulroney to announce his resignation. Then in elections on October 25, the Liberal Party swept into office, and leader Jean Chrétien became prime minister. He pledged to reduce Canada's budget deficit and shift public funds away from defense and business programs and toward social programs such as day care and education.

Recession plagued much of the European continent during 1993. The slowdown helped trigger a currency market crisis that weakened the Exchange Rate Mechanism (ERM), the framework that links the values of the currencies of many countries in Western Europe. Germany, trying to fight off inflation after the reunification of West and East Germany in 1990, kept its interest rates high. Countries trying to promote growth wanted to lower their rates, but

The heads of the world's leading industrialized nations meet to discuss global trade at their annual summit, which was held in Tokyo in July.

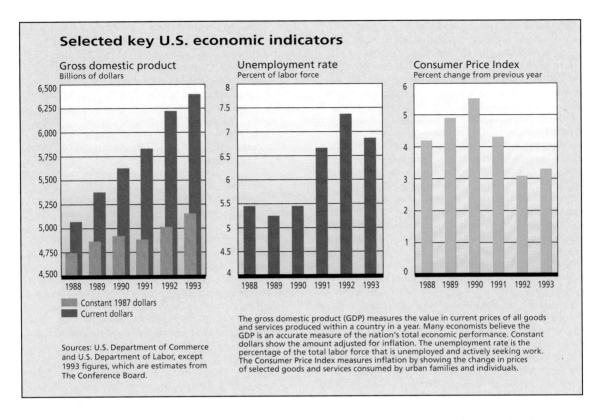

Selected key U.S. economic indicators

Gross domestic product
Billions of dollars

6,500
6,250
6,000
5,750
5,500
5,250
5,000
4,750
4,500

1988 1989 1990 1991 1992 1993

■ Constant 1987 dollars
■ Current dollars

Sources: U.S. Department of Commerce and U.S. Department of Labor, except 1993 figures, which are estimates from The Conference Board.

Unemployment rate
Percent of labor force

8
7.5
7
6.5
6
5.5
5
4.5
4

1988 1989 1990 1991 1992 1993

Consumer Price Index
Percent change from previous year

6
5
4
3
2
1
0

1988 1989 1990 1991 1992 1993

The gross domestic product (GDP) measures the value in current prices of all goods and services produced within a country in a year. Many economists believe the GDP is an accurate measure of the nation's total economic performance. Constant dollars show the amount adjusted for inflation. The unemployment rate is the percentage of the total labor force that is unemployed and actively seeking work. The Consumer Price Index measures inflation by showing the change in prices of selected goods and services consumed by urban families and individuals.

they were constrained by the high German rates. Currency speculators used the opportunity to bid down the values of linked currencies, such as the French franc. On Aug. 2, 1993, EC ministers were finally forced to loosen the ERM and allow the member currencies to move more freely.

Trade pacts. Worries about the slow pace of job creation in the United States threatened approval of the North American Free Trade Agreement (NAFTA). The pact, which eliminates most trade barriers between Canada, Mexico, and the United States, met considerable opposition from many Democrats and labor groups. Many people feared NAFTA would encourage U.S. businesses to relocate to Mexico, where wages are lower and environmental oversight is reportedly less stringent. But President Bill Clinton argued that the future of American prosperity rested on free trade. After intense lobbying by the Clinton Administration, the House of Representatives passed NAFTA on November 17. Senate approval followed. Passage of NAFTA helped spur completion of global trade negotiations under the General Agreement on Tariffs and Trade, which ended on December 15. (See **International trade: The Debate over NAFTA.**)

Economic policies. Shortly after taking office, Clinton on February 17 unveiled two economic packages, a short-term job creation bill and a long-term deficit reduction budget. The $16.2-billion job creation bill included spending for highway construc-

tion, small business loans, and community development grants, as well as funds for extending unemployment benefits for the long-term unemployed. Congressional approval was blocked by Senate Republicans, who claimed the bill would expand the federal deficit because spending increases in the bill were not matched by spending cuts elsewhere.

The Republican victory helped slow Clinton's momentum and made it more difficult for him to sell his broader budget plan, the Omnibus Budget Reconciliation Act. In that bill, Clinton proposed shrinking the deficit through spending cuts and higher taxes on corporations and upper-income individuals, plus a new energy tax on nonrenewable fuels. Clinton contended that the burden of higher taxes on the economy would be more than offset by lower interest rates that would result from reducing the deficit and thus curbing inflation fears. But businesses attacked the energy tax, claiming it would cost large numbers of jobs and push up inflation, and Clinton eventually settled for a tax only on transport fuel. On August 5 and 6, the House and then the Senate narrowly passed the bill. The final version aimed to reduce the deficit by a total of $496 billion over five years. □ John Boyd

See also **Consumerism; Health-care issues; Labor; Manufacturing; Stocks and bonds.** In *World Book,* see **Economics.**

Ecuador. See Latin America.

Education. The United States Congress on Jan. 21, 1993, confirmed Richard W. Riley as the sixth secretary of education. As governor of South Carolina from 1979 to 1986, Riley convinced the state's legislature to pass sweeping school reforms and to raise taxes to pay for them. Upon becoming President Bill Clinton's top education adviser, Riley announced five major goals for the nation's schools: a national system of standards and testing in core subjects; a national service program that would help students pay for their college education in return for volunteer work; an apprenticeship system for students going directly into the work force after high school; an overhaul of the federal program that provides tuition loans to college students; and improvements in a $6-billion Department of Education program that supplies educational help to students from poor families.

The national service plan proposed by the Clinton Administration received Senate approval in September, one month after the House of Representatives had voted for it. The plan calls for the creation of a Corporation for National and Community Service that will operate a program overseeing up to 100,000 volunteers. The volunteers will receive up to $9,450—or $4,725 per year for two years—in college grants in return for two years of public service. The first volunteers are scheduled to go to work in September 1994.

A new student-loan plan also received congressional approval in August. Under the initiative, by 1998, at least 60 percent of college students eligible for federal student loans will be able to borrow directly from the government—via college financial aid offices—rather than receiving student loans through banks and other lending agencies. Riley argued that the move would reduce paperwork, lower students' interest rates, and save the government more than $1 billion annually.

Under the current arrangement, the government pays fees and accumulated interest to lending agencies that handle the government-backed student loans. A chorus of critics has charged that this system has been not only expensive, but also plagued by waste and fraud in recent years.

Adult illiteracy. In September, the Department of Education reported that nearly half of all adult Americans lack the English literacy skills needed to fully exercise "the rights and responsibilities of citizenship." The four-year study, which tested 26,000 people over the age of 15, was called the most comprehensive literacy study in 20 years. These Americans, the department reports, are unable to perform such day-to-day functions as writing a letter about an error on a credit card bill or comprehending information contained in a paycheck stub. The report said inadequate education and a large population of people whose native language is not English were possible reasons for the illiteracy problem.

Students' knowledge. The American Association for the Advancement of Science (AAAS), the country's leading organization of professional scientists, endorsed the idea of establishing national standards and tests in core subjects. In October, the AAAS published a detailed list of facts and theories that every 2nd-, 5th-, 8th-, and 12th-grader should know. According to the AAAS, by the end of the 2nd grade, students should know that the look of the moon changes daily, and 12th-graders should know that most scientists believe the universe was created by a gigantic explosion, known as the big bang, that occurred about 10 billion to 20 billion years ago.

A sobering report card was released in September on the performance of the nation's elementary and secondary school students. The annual federally funded study of student achievement reported that many of the nation's students read very poorly. The "Reading Report Card for the Nation and the States" reported that 41 percent of 4th-graders, 31 percent of 8th-graders, and 25 percent of 12th-graders are inadequate readers. The study tested 140,000 students in 41 states during 1992.

Paying for education. Many states responded to the bad news on student achievement by attempting to improve the funding of schools in impoverished communities. From January to July 1993, courts in four states—Alabama, Tennessee, Missouri, and Massachusetts—declared the states' school funding formulas unconstitutional on the grounds that they deny students in poor communities an opportunity to receive a solid education. In requiring the states to rewrite their formulas for funding public education, the courts dealt a blow to the widespread practice of using local property taxes as a major source of public school funding.

In August, Michigan Governor John Engler took the attack on the local school tax further. He signed a bill to scrap the state's local property taxes altogether, eliminating $6.5 billion in funding for the state's public schools. The move set off a furious debate within Michigan over how best to fund the state's schools. In October, Engler proposed issuing grants to allow students to attend the public school of their choice. He also suggested increasing Michigan's sales and business taxes to fund schools. The plan was working its way through the state's legislature at year's end.

College critics continued to attack higher education in 1993. High tuition, shorter classroom calendars at many campuses, and the tendency of many senior professors to concentrate on research rather than teaching were among the criticisms leveled at colleges and universities. The College Board, an organization of colleges and schools, supported the arguments of campus critics when it reported in September that tuition at the nation's colleges and universities rose 6 percent to 10 percent, outpacing inflation for the 10th consecutive year.

Politically correct campus. Higher education also struggled with the often-conflicting issues of tolerance and free speech. An incident at the University of Pennsylvania in Philadelphia in January touched off a national debate over the question of whether a student should be disciplined for making degrading remarks to other students. The university brought charges of "racial harassment" against a white male freshman who called a group of black female students "water buffalo."

The student said he yelled at the women because their noise was interfering with his ability to study, and that his remark was not racially motivated. But the university said he violated its speech code, which prohibits "abusive language or conduct" designed to cause "direct injury to an identifiable individual, on the basis of his or her race, ethnicity, or national origin."

In May, the female students dropped the case on the grounds that the extensive publicity it was receiving made it impossible for the university to rule fairly. In November, the university abandoned its controversial speech code, which had been criticized as an example of "political correctness." The university's interim president, Claire Fagin, said the code limited free expression while failing to sufficiently protect minorities from harassment.

The largest private gift to education in history came from retired publisher Walter H. Annenberg,

one of the nation's richest people. Annenberg announced in June that he would give a total of $365-million in cash to several private schools by the end of 1993. The University of Southern California in Los Angeles and the University of Pennsylvania were each to receive $120 million. Harvard University in Cambridge, Mass., would get $25 million, and the preparatory school Annenberg attended in Hightstown, N. J., the Peddie School, would get $100 million. On December 16, Annenberg announced that he intended to give as much as $500 million of his personal fortune to several education groups involved in public school reform.

Privatization. Christopher Whittle, chairman of Whittle Communications, reported in August that he was scaling back his plan to build a national system of private, low-cost, for-profit schools. Whittle had announced in 1992 that he planned to open 200 schools by 1996 and 1,000 schools educating 2 million students by 2010. But Whittle was unable to attract the corporate investors he needed to help fund his ambitious Edison Project. Rather than open new schools, he said, he would invest in managing existing schools.

In November, California voters rejected a proposal to give parents a publicly funded voucher of $2,600 annually to spend at any public or private school in the state. Seventy percent of the voters turned down the plan. The vouchers represented

High school dropouts stand at attention in August as they participate in a new National Guard program aimed at helping them earn a high school equivalency degree.

about one-half of what the state spends per child in the public school system.

Despite Whittle's announcement and the California vote, the privatization movement gained some ground. In September, the Puerto Rican legislature passed a bill establishing the nation's first school voucher experiment. The law permits over half of Puerto Rico's families to receive a government voucher of $1,500 per child to spend at the public or private school of their choice. About 1,700 students signed up for the first round of vouchers in the fall of 1993.

Meanwhile, the school board in Minneapolis, Minn., in an unprecedented step, in November hired a for-profit consulting company to operate the city's 79 schools. The president of the firm, Peter Hutchinson, was slated to become the superintendent of the schools.

Preschool benefits. A study released in April suggested that high-quality preschool programs can impart long-term benefits to both the students in the program and to society. The study, begun nearly 30 years ago by the High/Scope Educational Research Foundation in Ypsilanti, Mich., found that low-income students who attended a good preschool as 3- and 4-year-olds were leading much more productive lives at the age of 27 than similar individuals who did not attend the preschool program. The Perry Preschool Study concluded that each dollar spent on the program netted society $7.16 from increased taxes on earnings as well as reduced welfare, special education, and criminal justice costs.

Students with disabilities won a victory in November when the U.S. Supreme Court upheld the right of parents of disabled students to sue public schools for the cost of educating their children in private schools when public schools fail to offer them needed educational assistance. Advocates of the disabled hailed the ruling, but many leaders in public education said the ruling gives parents a blank check drawn on school districts.

Enrollment and costs. The Department of Education estimated that preschool and kindergarten enrollments would increase in the 1993-1994 school year by 200,000 to 6.6 million. Elementary and secondary school enrollment was expected to reach 48.9 million, up 1.3 million. And the number of college students enrolled in public and private institutions was predicted to reach a new high of 15 million, an increase of 700,000.

The Department of Education estimated that the nation's education bill would be $493 billion for the 1993-1994 school year, representing a 3 percent increase after adjusting for inflation. Spending on public elementary, secondary, and higher education was predicted to be $397 billion, and spending on private schools and colleges was expected to be $96-billion.   □ Thomas Toch

In *World Book,* see **Education.**

Egypt. Egypt's severe economic problems were overshadowed in 1993 by violent attacks from Islamic fundamentalists. In their efforts to topple the government of President Hosni Mubarak, the militants struck public officials, tourists, Coptic Christians, and other targets. The fundamentalists, who seek an Islamic government, were also the targets of government reprisals. More than 220 civilians, militants, and government officials were killed from the spring of 1992 to November 1993.

On August 18, a bombing by Muslim extremists failed to kill Interior Minister Hassan Mohammed Alfi, but four people died in the blast. On July 18, a general escaped an ambush that resulted in four deaths. On November 25, a car bomb killed one girl and injured 20 people in an assassination attempt on Prime Minister Atef Sedki near his home in Cairo.

Attacks on Western tourists decimated Egypt's largest foreign revenue source. Tourism, which netted about $3.5 billion in 1992, dropped by more than 60 percent in early 1993. Six tourists were killed, and about 20 were wounded from October 1992 to November 1993. Militants ambushed cruise boats and buses and bombed cafes and ancient sites.

Coptic Christians suffered increasingly brutal attacks in 1993. The Copts are the largest religious minority in Egypt, which is about 90 percent Muslim. The Copts complained that the government did not act to protect them against the militants until foreign tourists also became targets.

Government crackdowns on Islamic militants were harsh in 1993, and some critics blamed the crackdowns for turning popular sentiment toward the pro-Islamic groups. By mid-December, 23 pro-Islamic militants had been hanged, the largest number of political executions in a year in Egypt in the 1900's. Sweeps for alleged Islamic radicals in 1993 were said to have netted thousands of people who were held under emergency law. Egypt's prisons were severely overcrowded due to mass arrests and long prison terms aimed at quelling the unrest. Two prison riots in late August and early September left three dead and 175 injured. Officials admitted that the militants were influential within the prisons.

Government reprisals against Islamic fundamentalists provoked criticism when authorities stormed 500 worshipers in a mosque in the city of Aswan on March 9. Nine people died, 41 were injured, and 87 were arrested. At various times in 1993, the Egyptian Organization for Human Rights, Amnesty International, and others criticized Egyptian authorities for human rights abuses.

Although many believed Egypt's extremism was a home-grown problem, Mubarak blamed other nations for fomenting the unrest in his country. He accused Pakistan and Afghanistan of offering militants a safe haven. In March and April, Mubarak stated that Iran had directed and trained Egyptian militants and that terrorist training camps existed in Sudan.

United States and Egypt. Relations between the two allies became strained in 1993. Egypt complained that U.S. Embassy officials in Cairo, the capital, had sought contacts with militants from 1991 until February 1993. Embassy officials claimed that some contacts had been made for the purpose of understanding militant grievances. The United States rebuffed Mubarak's repeated advice in 1993 to pressure Israel to take back 400 Palestinians expelled to Lebanon. Mubarak's attempts to resolve United Nations sanctions against Libya were also rebuffed. He viewed both activities as adding to anti-American, pro-Islamic fundamentalist sentiment in the region.

Sheik Omar Abdel Rahman, an Egyptian Islamic spiritual leader, was jailed in the United States after his followers allegedly bombed the World Trade Center in New York City on February 26. A federal grand jury indicted the sheik on August 25 on charges of overseeing the bombing and plotting other bombings and assassinations. (See also **Crime.**)

Referendum. On July 21, Mubarak was nominated by a vote of 439 to 7 in the People's Assembly to serve a third six-year term as president. His National Democratic Party controlled the assembly after opposition groups boycotted the 1990 election. On Oct. 5, 1993, Mubarak, the only candidate, won a referendum to remain president. □ Christine Helms

See also **Crime; Islam; Middle East** (Facts in brief table). In *World Book,* see **Egypt.**

Elections. Bouncing back from the loss of the White House, the Republican Party (GOP) scored big election victories in 1993 at state and local levels. GOP candidates won governor's races in New Jersey and Virginia and, against the odds, captured mayor's seats in Los Angeles and New York City. In addition, a Republican woman captured a United States Senate seat in Texas that had been held by a Democrat.

Although individual personalities and local conditions played a role in these outcomes, political analysts said the results also reflected voter anxieties and a continuing anti-incumbent mood.

Governors' races. Republican Christine Todd Whitman narrowly defeated New Jersey Democratic Governor Jim Florio on November 2. Florio had been handicapped in the race by a big tax increase enacted during his first year in office and by the state's high unemployment rate. Whitman, the first woman ever elected governor of New Jersey, promised to reduce income taxes by 30 percent.

The outcome of the New Jersey race was called into question on November 9, when Edward J. Rollins, a GOP strategist who had managed Whitman's campaign, told reporters that Republicans in the state had distributed money in an effort to suppress the black, largely Democratic vote. Rollins retracted his statement the next day. Florio, who briefly considered contesting the election, accepted his defeat.

In Virginia, former Republican U.S. Representa-

Surrounded by well-wishers in Dallas on June 5, Republican Kay Bailey Hutchison savors her victory in a special election for a U.S. Senate seat.

tive George F. Allen easily defeated Democrat Mary Sue Terry, a former state attorney general, on November 2. Allen appealed to voters with a pledge to get tougher on criminals.

Mayoral contests. In the New York City election on November 2, former U.S. prosecutor Rudolph W. Giuliani narrowly defeated Mayor David N. Dinkins, who squeaked to victory over Giuliani in 1989. The electorate was sharply polarized, with black and Hispanic voters favoring Dinkins and the white middle class backing Giuliani. Giuliani was the first Republican to be elected mayor in the city since 1965.

In Los Angeles, where riots in April 1992 were a vivid memory, millionaire businessman Richard J. Riordan defeated Democratic City Council member Michael Woo on June 8 to become that city's first GOP mayor in 32 years. Riordan promised to work to make Los Angeles a "safe and friendly" place.

There were some unexpected breakthroughs in other mayors' races on November 2. In Boston, voters elected Democratic Acting Mayor Thomas M. Menino, an Italian-American, ending a 64-year tradition of electing Irish-American mayors. In Minneapolis, City Council President Sharon Sayles Belton became that city's first woman and first black mayor.

Races for Congress. Republicans scored a major triumph in Texas on June 5, when GOP challenger Kay Bailey Hutchison defeated Democrat Bob Krueger for a seat in the U.S. Senate. Krueger had been appointed to the Senate seat vacated when Lloyd M. Bentsen, Jr., became secretary of the treasury.

In special elections for the U.S. House of Representatives, however, there was a stand-off, between Republicans and Democrats. In California, Democrat Sam Farr on June 8 won the seat held by Democratic Congressman Leon Panetta before he resigned to become director of the Office of Management and Budget. In Wisconsin, Democrat Peter Barca was elected on May 4 to succeed Democratic Representative Les Aspin, Jr., who had become secretary of defense. In Mississippi, Democrat Bennie Thompson was elected on April 13 to the seat vacated by Democratic Congressman Mike Espy, who had left the House to become secretary of agriculture.

On May 4, Republican Rob Portman won the seat that had been held by GOP Congressman Willis D. Gradison, Jr., of Ohio before he resigned to become a lobbyist. On December 7, Republican Vernon Ehlers won the seat held by GOP Representative Paul B. Henry of Michigan, who died of cancer on July 31.

Crime referendum. In Washington state, voters on November 2 favored by a 3 to 1 margin a plan for stiffer sentencing of violent criminals. A third conviction for a violent felony will now bring an automatic life prison term without parole. □ William J. Eaton

See also **Congress of the United States; Democratic Party; Republican Party; State government.** In *World Book,* see **Election; Election campaign.**

Electric power. See Energy supply.

Electronics. In 1993, people could see and buy a number of new products that were expected to point electronics in a new direction. Among those products, long awaited in the United States, was a wide-screen television, introduced by RCA Corporation. This TV had a screen ratio of 16 inches (41 centimeters) of width per 9 inches (23 centimeters) of height, one-third wider than traditional models, which have a 4:3 ratio. The 16:9 TV provides a cinematic viewing experience. Other TV manufacturers soon followed RCA, generally with large projection-TV models. The new wide-screen TV's are the first step in the expected conversion to a high-definition TV system, which produces supersharp images and high-quality sound.

Panasonic Video Systems introduced its Flat Vision TV in 1993, which was less than 4 inches (10 centimeters) deep. Unlike standard TV's built around a single, large cathode ray tube (CRT), the Flat Vision TV used nearly 10,000 miniature CRT's to form a picture on the screen. Although the initial model had a 14-inch (36-centimeter) screen, manufacturers hoped to use the new technology for larger screens.

LCD camcorder. Sharp Corporation introduced ViewCam in 1993, a camcorder video camera with a 4-inch liquid-crystal-display color monitor mounted on it. The operator uses the monitor as a viewfinder as the action being filmed is displayed on the monitor screen. Sony Corporation soon followed with a similar camcorder.

Multimedia player. Panasonic began marketing a multimedia player, called a Video CD, developed by 3DO Corporation. The 3DO player is a component that connects to a TV and uses software in a compact disc (CD) form. Motion-picture CD's are available for the multimedia player, providing a superior quality picture and more durable material than that of videotapes. Using a remote control device, the Video CD operator can play high-quality games on the TV screen. The Video CD provides graphics superior to previous devices.

Personal digital assistants. By November 1993, Apple Computer Incorporated, Sharp Corporation, Tandy Corporation, and Casio Incorporated had all introduced a version of a personal digital assistant (PDA). About the size of a hard-cover book, PDA's perform many computer functions but are designed to organize information better than previous hand-held models. Their data entry system is a pen that the operator uses to write electronically on a small screen. PDA's can also be used to fax or modem documents.

This new category of electronic device was expected to grow considerably as more companies debut models. In addition, PDA's that are capable of working with wireless or regular telephones were being developed. □ Frank Vizard

See also **Computer.** In *World Book,* see **Computer; Electronics; Television.**

El Salvador. A March 15, 1993, report by a United Nations (UN) commission blamed the Salvadoran army for most of the human rights abuses that occurred during the Salvadoran civil war from 1981 to February 1992. The commission said the army was responsible for 85 percent of the human rights abuses, in which at least 75,000 people died. Antigovernment rebels committed about 5 percent of the atrocities, the report said.

The commission was formed as part of the UN-sponsored peace plan that officially ended the civil war. The commission called for a purge of top military officers who had been involved in abuses and for the resignation of all judges of the Salvadoran Supreme Court for failure to protect human rights.

El Salvador's Legislative Assembly, controlled by the right wing National Republican Alliance of President Alfredo Cristiani Burkard, voted on March 20, 1993, to give amnesty to all those named in the UN report. The measure led to the release in April of two army officers who were convicted of the November 1989 murder of six Jesuits, their housekeeper, and her daughter.

Under international pressure, Cristiani replaced the top leadership in El Salvador's armed forces on July 1, 1993.   □ Nathan A. Haverstock

See also **Latin America** (Facts in brief table). In *World Book,* see **El Salvador.**

Electric power. See **Energy supply.**

A Salvadoran investigator in San Salvador uncovers the skull of an antigovernment rebel in March. The rebel died in 1989 in El Salvador's civil war.

Energy supply. The three biggest automobile manufacturers in the United States said on Sept. 29, 1993, they would join forces with the federal government to develop a new generation of cars with three times the fuel efficiency of existing vehicles. Officials of General Motors Corporation (GM), the Ford Motor Company, and the Chrysler Corporation said their scientists and engineers would work with those at U.S. Department of Energy (DOE) and U.S. Department of Defense laboratories in the effort.

The goal was to develop cars with high fuel efficiency, improved safety, and low exhaust emissions. The cars, which would go on sale early in the 2000's, may be capable of traveling 80 miles (130 kilometers) on 1 gallon (3.8 liters) of gasoline and would be built from advanced materials that are light but strong and could run on propulsion systems other than conventional internal combustion engines.

The same auto companies on April 13 said they were considering a joint effort to build an electric car that would meet requirements of antipollution laws passed by California and several other states. The laws require that by 1998 at least 2 percent of all cars sold within these states emit virtually no pollution, a goal that electric vehicles could meet. Both Chrysler and Ford have developed prototype electric vans, and GM has developed a two-seat electric car. The joint program would seek to reduce the costs of the vehicles and increase their driving range, which was generally less than 100 miles (160 kilometers) between battery charges.

Energy production, consumption. The United States produced 38.51 quadrillion British thermal units (Btu's) of energy during the first seven months of 1993, the DOE reported in November. That figure was slightly less than the 38.96 quadrillion Btu's produced during the same period in 1992. (A Btu is the amount of heat needed to raise the temperature of one pound [0.45 kilogram] of water by 1 Fahrenheit degree [0.56 Celsius degree].)

Coal was the number-one source of energy, followed by natural gas, crude oil, nuclear power, and hydroelectric power. The United States consumed 49.02 quadrillion Btu's during the first seven months of 1993, compared with 48 quadrillion Btu's during the same period in 1992. Imports totaled 9.50 quadrillion Btu's during the seven months of 1993, compared with 8.19 quadrillion Btu's in the 1992 period.

Nuclear power plants in the United States performed more reliably from 1990 through 1992 than during any other three-year period, the American Nuclear Society (ANS) said in a May 10, 1993, report. The ANS, based in La Grange Park, Ill., is an organization of 17,000 engineers and scientists.

The study compared *capacity factors* of U.S. nuclear power plants from 1990 through 1992 with those during earlier three-year periods. Capacity factor is the amount of electricity that a plant could have produced if there were no shut-downs due to mechanical and other problems. The ANS considers reactors with a 70 percent capacity factor to be good performers, and those with 50 percent or less to be poor performers. The ANS found that for the first time since nuclear power plants began widespread operation in 1974, more than half of the reactors received a good rating.

Chernobyl to remain open. The Ukrainian parliament on Oct. 21, 1993, voted to keep the remaining two reactors at the Chernobyl power plant in operation, reversing a previous decision to shut the plant by the end of 1993. Chernobyl was the site of a 1986 explosion that destroyed one of the plant's four reactors. Authorities shut down a second reactor in 1991 after a fire. The Ukrainian parliament also voted to end a 1990 moratorium on construction of nuclear power plants to alleviate serious energy shortages in the former Soviet republic.

Fuel cell plant. Final plans to construct the first full-scale electric generating station that uses fuel cells rather than conventional turbines were announced on Sept. 22, 1993, by the Electric Power Research Institute (EPRI) in Palo Alto, Calif., the DOE, and a group of electric utilities. The molten carbonate fuel cell plant will be built as part of a $46-million test project in Santa Clara, Calif. The plant was expected to begin operation in early 1995 and will have a capacity of 2 megawatts, or 2 million watts, enough to supply about 1,000 average homes.

Most conventional generating stations use heat from burning *fossil fuels* (coal, oil, or natural gas) or from nuclear reactions in uranium fuel pellets to produce steam. The steam turns a turbine, which runs a generator that produces electricity. But *fuel cells*, most familiar as the electricity source on the U.S. space shuttle, convert fuel directly into electricity without combustion. In a manner similar to electricity production in batteries, fuel cells transform either natural gas or hydrogen into electricity through electrochemical reactions. The Santa Clara plant, which will be about the size of a tennis court, will use natural gas. The type of fuel cell depends on the material that is used as an *electrolyte* (conductive material) to carry electrons between the cell's electrodes. The Santa Clara plant uses an electrolyte of molten carbonate, a form of carbonic acid.

Fuel cells have advantages that could lead to their widespread use. They convert 60 to 65 percent of the energy in their fuel to electricity, compared with only about 30 to 35 percent for conventional power plants. Because fuel cells do not actually burn fuel, they produce no sulfur air pollutants, up to 250 times less nitrogen oxide pollution, and less carbon dioxide than existing generators.

Wind energy is on the verge of a major expansion in the United States, the American Wind Energy Association (AWEA) predicted in a report issued on May 6. AWEA, an industry group headquartered in Washington, D.C., predicted that wind energy could produce about 22 billion kilowatt hours of electricity by the year 2000. That would be 8 times more electricity than wind turbines currently produce and enough to supply the residential electricity needs for about 5.4 million people. The expansion was possible because of several rapid advances in wind energy technology, including decreased cost and improved reliability of wind turbines, which use wind to generate electric current. AWEA noted that the costs of producing electricity with wind have decreased from about 50 cents per kilowatt hour in 1980 to 6 to 9 cents today. As the next generation of wind turbines goes into operation in the mid-1990's, costs may drop below 5 cents per kilowatt hour. The average cost to produce a kilowatt hour through conventional methods was about 8 cents.

A "revolutionary" compressor. The U.S. Environmental Protection Agency (EPA) on June 3, 1993, announced a "revolutionary development" in refrigerator technology that could reduce the consumption of energy in home refrigerators and air conditioners by 15 percent. The compressors in refrigerators and air conditioners are the biggest consumers of electricity in most homes. The EPA financed research on the new technology, which was developed by Sunpower, Incorporated, of Athens, Ohio.

Conventional compressors use a cylinder and piston similar to those in an auto engine. An electric motor turns a crankshaft attached to the piston via a connecting rod. The piston's back-and-forth motion compresses the refrigerant gas, and it eventually becomes a fluid that collects heat inside a refrigerator or the rooms in a building. The new compressor eliminates the crankshaft and connecting rods, reducing friction and other energy loss. Its piston attaches to a spring and a ring of magnets encased by a wire coil. When electricity from the motor passes through the coil, it creates a magnetic field, causing the magnets and piston to move back and forth. The new compressor also saves energy by using an electronic control system that allows the compressor to run continuously, adjusting its speed according to the cooling demand. This avoids the use of the extra electricity needed to restart an idle compressor.

The Whirlpool Corporation of Benton Harbor, Mich., on June 29 won a $30-million prize for the best design of a refrigerator that both saves energy and helps prevent depletion of Earth's protective layer of atmospheric ozone. Twenty-four U.S. electric utility companies provided the prize money. Whirlpool claimed that the new design would save consumers $100 to $125 a year in energy costs because of a more efficient defrost system, compressor, and better insulation. It uses a new refrigerant that does not contain *chlorofluorocarbons* (ozone-depleting substances). ☐ Michael Woods

In *World Book*, see Energy supply.
Engineering. See Building and construction.
England. See United Kingdom.

The oil tanker *Braer* lies underwater after running aground off the Shetland Islands in January, spilling about 26 million gallons (98 million liters) of oil.

Environmental pollution. The amount of ozone in Earth's *stratosphere* (upper atmosphere) fell to record low levels in 1993. Ozone, a molecule made up of three oxygen atoms, protects life by absorbing the sun's biologically damaging ultraviolet radiation. Scientists fear that increased exposure to ultraviolet radiation could cause increased instances of skin cancer.

Since 1987, scientists have detected signs of a seasonal thinning in stratospheric ozone everywhere except over the tropics. Atmospheric scientists have linked the thinning to the release of *chlorofluorocarbons* (CFC's)—chlorine-containing gases that are often used as coolants in refrigerators and air conditioning systems. Many scientists also believe that sulfur particles emitted from the massive June 1991 eruption of Mount Pinatubo in the Philippines also helped further ozone destruction by traveling into the stratosphere and promoting chemical reactions that enhance the destructive effects of CFC's on ozone molecules.

In mid-March 1993, atmospheric scientists at the United Nations (UN) World Meteorological Organization in Geneva, Switzerland, reported record low levels of stratospheric ozone above the Northern Hemisphere's middle and high latitudes. Using readings from ground instruments and measurements from satellites, the UN scientists reported that ozone levels thinned between 9 and 20 percent between December 1992 and February 1993, depending on the region. This drop was twice the normal year-to-year variation, the scientists said. In September, scientists reported all-time lows in summertime levels of stratospheric ozone over Canada. Although the thinning averaged about 7 percent, losses in some areas were much higher. Average July ozone levels over Toronto, Ont., for instance, were about 12 percent lower than levels typical before 1980.

Between late August and October 1993, the annual thinning of the ozone layer above Antarctica reached 70 percent—the highest loss ever recorded anywhere, according to scientists with the National Oceanic and Atmospheric Administration in Suitland, Md. The thinning affected 9 million square miles (23 million square kilometers)—an area about the size of North America.

Oil spills. On January 5, the U.S.-owned tanker *Braer* ran aground in a fierce storm off Scotland's Shetland Islands in the North Sea. Seven days later, the ship broke apart, releasing about 26 million gallons (98 million liters) of Norwegian crude oil. Waves dispersed most of the oil before it could wash ashore and damage marine life.

By contrast, much of the oil from the March 1989 *Exxon Valdez* spill in Alaska's Prince William Sound, which involved less than half the oil in the *Braer* spill, remained on Alaskan beaches in 1993. In February, a panel of biologists and ecologists reported in Anchorage, Alaska, on the effects of the *Valdez* spill. Although Exxon, the state of Alaska, and the U.S. government employed more than 10,000 people in a massive $2.5-billion, three-year cleanup effort, about 324,000 gallons (1.2 million liters) of *Valdez* oil, mostly in the form of tarry deposits, still remained on beaches, the scientists said. The meeting offered government-funded scientists their first opportunity to report on the effects of the *Valdez* oil.

The *Valdez* spill killed an estimated 500,000 birds, more than 10 times as many as any other U.S. spill, according to the panel. Many surviving birds later failed to breed, according to marine biologist D. Michael Fry of the University of California at Davis. Other scientists linked the spill to large losses of harbor seals, killer whales, and sea otters, and to lingering reproductive problems in some fish.

But in an April 26 statement, Exxon concluded that Alaska "has almost fully recovered" from the *Valdez* spill. The oil company based its conclusion on 25 papers delivered during an April technical meeting in Atlanta, Ga., by scientists it had funded.

Exxon scientists acknowledged that crude oil still taints Prince William Sound, but they revealed new data indicating that much of the oil still littering the area's seabed comes from coastal oil deposits that seep petroleum. Such data, the Exxon scientists said, suggest that aquatic species in the area have coexisted with crude oil for more than a century and can recover from occasional heavy spills.

Pesticides and children's health. Pesticide residues on most foods in the United States tend to be small and well within legal limits. However, two major studies released on June 28 claim that pesticide residues could pose some long-term risks—especially to children.

Richard Wiles, director of the agricultural pollution prevention program at the Environmental Working Group in Washington, D.C., an environmental research organization, studied the amount of pesticide residue on some 20,000 samples of fruits and vegetables. Wiles used information about the toxicity of those pesticides and data on the types and amounts of food that youngsters eat to determine whether the amount of pesticides that the average American child consumes before his or her first birthday increases the risk of developing cancer. He determined that pesticides can increase a child's risk of cancer to more than 1 in 1 million—a risk that exceeds the federal government's acceptable threshold. The National Academy of Sciences issued a related report which concluded that pesticide regulations must be strengthened in order to protect children from potential harm.

On September 21, the Environmental Protection Agency, the Food and Drug Administration, and the Agriculture Department announced plans to adopt many recommendations contained in the reports. The changes would revise how the United States regulates pesticides and speed the phase-out of the most dangerous ones.

DDT and cancer. On April 21, epidemiologist Mary S. Wolff and her colleagues at the Mount Sinai School of Medicine in New York City linked the pesticide dichloro-diphenyl-trichloroethane (DDT) with breast cancer. Their study of 14,290 women found that chances of developing breast cancer rose with the levels of DDE (a breakdown product of DDT) in a woman's blood.

Although the United States banned almost all uses of DDT in 1972, many Americans retain traces of the chemical. Once absorbed by the body, DDT can persist for years. And traces of the chemical continue to be found in food products.

Cancer agents in water? Two studies reported in 1993 suggest that a by-product of chlorine used to kill microorganisms in drinking water may increase the risk of developing cancer. In May, researchers at the National Institute of Environmental Health Sciences in Research Triangle Park, N.C., reported that trihalomethanes—chemicals that form in public drinking water as a by-product of chlorination—cause cancer in the kidneys and colorectal tract of rats. A study in the May/June 1993 issue of *Archives of Environmental Health* found that drinking large quantities of chlorinated water, or beverages made with it, increases one's risk of developing bladder cancer.

Reduction of greenhouse gases. The Administration of U.S. President Bill Clinton announced a plan on October 19 to reduce U.S. emissions of so-called greenhouse gases. Such gases result largely from the burning of *fossil fuels* (gasoline, coal, and oil) in industry and transportation. Burning fossil fuels produces certain gases, chiefly carbon dioxide, that trap heat in Earth's atmosphere, much in the way that glass in a greenhouse traps heat. Some scientists fear that if too many greenhouse gases build up, the heat they trap could cause *global warming* (a rapid warming of Earth's atmosphere). Global warming could threaten crops over wide areas, melt polar icecaps, and flood coastal areas.

Most initiatives in the plan were voluntary, such as a program whereby manufacturers would collaborate to develop more efficient electric motors. But some programs were mandatory, such as new limits on how much methane, a significant greenhouse gas, can escape from landfills.

The Administration estimated that these efforts could lower U.S. emissions of greenhouse gases to 1990 levels by the year 2000. The initiative was intended to comply with the Convention on Climate Change, an international agreement that the United States signed in June 1992 at the Earth Summit in Rio de Janeiro, Brazil.   □ Janet Raloff

See also **Consumerism; Food; Safety.** In *World Book,* see **Environmental pollution.**

Equatorial Guinea. See Africa.

Eritrea. More than 99 percent of the people casting ballots in a referendum from April 23 to 25 in the Ethiopian province of Eritrea voted to separate from Ethiopia. On May 21, the newly formed National Assembly elected Issaias Afeworke, secretary general of the Eritrean People's Liberation Front (EPLF)—a rebel group that helped overthrow Ethiopia's President Mengistu Haile-Mariam in 1991—as the country's first president. Eritrea declared itself an independent nation on May 24, 1993.

The new nation contained the seeds for possible internal conflict. The 3.6 million Eritrean people belong to nine ethnic groups, and the population is split roughly half and half between Christian and Muslim. Moreover, besides the EPLF, which is now in control of the government, there is a rival political group, the Eritrean Liberation Front, which actually began the independence war in 1961. But balancing those potentially divisive factors is a strong national identity forged by the long war.

The war left Eritrea severely damaged, with the economy in shambles. In 1993, agricultural production, although rising with the aid of good rains, was still inadequate, and three-fourths of the nation's people needed food aid. But Eritrea has untapped resources of copper, gold, oil, and natural gas, so the future could be bright. □ Mark DeLancey

See also **Africa** (Facts in brief table). In *World Book,* see **Eritrea.**

Espy, Mike (1953-), became United States secretary of agriculture on Jan. 22, 1993. Espy, who had been serving on the Agriculture Committee of the U.S. House of Representatives until being appointed secretary, is the first black to head the Department of Agriculture.

Espy was born on Nov. 30, 1953, in Yazoo City, Miss. He earned a bachelor's degree at Howard University in Washington, D.C., in 1975 and a law degree at Santa Clara University in California in 1978.

In 1978, Espy returned to Mississippi and entered public service. After two years in Yazoo City as managing attorney for Central Mississippi Legal Services, he became assistant secretary of state in charge of public lands and later, in 1984, assistant state attorney general for consumer protection.

Espy was elected to the U.S. House of Representatives in 1986, representing the rural Second District. He was the first black member of Congress from Mississippi since the Reconstruction era after the Civil War (1861-1865). In the House, he served on the Budget Committee as well as the Agriculture Committee and also held the leadership position of majority whip at large. While on the Agriculture Committee, Espy made numerous proposals to reform U.S. agriculture, such as cutting bureaucratic "red tape," and to help farmers.

Espy is married to the former Sheila Bell. They have two children. □ David Dreier

Estonia. Estonia's economy in 1993 was the most prosperous of all 15 former republics of the Soviet Union. Inflation was about 25 percent, down from 1,000 percent in 1992. But despite economic improvement, voters devastated Estonia's governing Fatherland Party in local elections on Oct. 17, 1993. The party's defeat resulted in part from ethnic Russians' support for political parties that advocated minority rights. Ethnic Russians, who comprise about 40 percent of Estonia's population of 1.6 million, are angry at what they perceive as Estonian discrimination against them.

Relations between Russia and Estonia suffered when the Estonian parliament passed a strict residency law on June 21. Russia denounced the law as discriminatory against ethnic Russians and threatened economic sanctions. On June 25, Russia cut off natural gas supplies to Estonia, citing unpaid debts. Estonian President Lennart Meri defused the crisis by refusing to sign the residency law. Estonia paid its debt, and gas supplies were resumed. But in July, Meri signed an amended version of the law.

Tensions flared again on July 17, when the ethnic Russians who make up most of the city of Narva, in eastern Estonia, voted in a referendum to establish an autonomous region. Estonian authorities ruled the referendum illegal. □ Justin Burke

See also **Europe** (Facts in brief table). In *World Book,* see **Estonia.**

Ethiopia in 1993 continued its slow recovery from the civil war that ended in 1991 with the overthrow of President Mengistu Haile-Mariam. But political problems still threatened the nation.

From April 23 to 25, people in the province of Eritrea who helped depose Mengistu voted overwhelmingly to become free of Ethiopia. On May 24, the province declared its independence. The loss of Eritrea, which borders the Red Sea, made Ethiopia a landlocked nation. Ethiopia's President Meles Zenawi and Eritrea's President Issaias Afeworke promised to cooperate. But Eritrea's secession angered many Ethiopians, prompting fears that hostilities would erupt between the two nations in the future.

The threat of ethnic conflict within Ethiopia remained a serious problem in 1993. The Transitional Government of Ethiopia (TGE) has followed a controversial policy of allowing the nation's various ethnic groups to have more control over their own affairs. Some Ethiopians worried that this policy will lead to the political disintegration of the country.

Another concern in 1993 was the TGE's move toward authoritarian rule. The TGE had agreed to hold democratic elections by the end of February 1994, but throughout 1993 there were signs that the military rulers were laying plans to rig the election and retain power. □ Mark DeLancey

See also **Africa** (Facts in brief table); **Eritrea.** In *World Book,* see **Ethiopia.**

Fireworks light up revelers in the new European nation of Slovakia, which
was created when Czechoslovakia split into two countries on January 1.

Europe

The year 1993 was supposed to have ushered in an era of increased harmony for Europe, but it turned out instead to be filled with problems that will not be easy to resolve. Many of the difficulties centered on the implementation of the Treaty on European Union, or Maastricht Treaty, which calls for tighter economic and political integration of the European Community (EC or Common Market). In 1993, the Maastricht Treaty was finally ratified by all 12 EC members—Belgium, Denmark, France, Germany, Greece, Ireland, Italy, Luxembourg, the Netherlands, Portugal, Spain, and the United Kingdom. But plans to further unify the continent by creating a single currency and adopting common defense policies suffered setbacks.

Maastricht adopted. After many months of debate, the Maastricht Treaty was ratified by all EC countries by October 1993. Ratification, which had to be unanimous for the treaty to take effect, had been delayed by the defeat of the treaty in a referendum in Denmark in June 1992. But Danes reversed their vote and approved the treaty on May 18, 1993, after being assured that Denmark could choose not to participate in a future single currency or common defense policy. The Parliament of the United Kingdom then approved the treaty on July 23, and Germany's highest court removed the final hurdle to the treaty's approval on October 12 by ruling that the treaty would not infringe upon German sovereignty. The EC Council of Ministers said Maastricht would enter into force as scheduled on Jan. 1, 1994.

The Maastricht Treaty is actually two agreements. One agreement allows the EC Council of Ministers to take over certain functions now fulfilled by the national governments of the EC members, including the formulation of foreign and defense policies. The other agreement calls for the creation of a European Central Bank, which will assume responsibility for a common EC monetary policy and oversee the creation of a single currency.

Political issues. The continuation in 1993 of the brutal civil war in the former Yugoslav republic of Bosnia-Herzegovina despite the efforts of EC negotiators to bring about a peaceful settlement was viewed by many observers as a failure of European leadership. Exacerbating the problem were the hundreds of thousands of refugees who fled to Western Europe. The influx of asylum seekers touched off a political backlash and aided the fortunes of nationalist, anti-immigrant political parties.

Much of Western Europe remained mired in a severe recession in 1993. The inability of leaders to reverse the slide led to significant political change across the continent. For example, the governing Socialist Party in France suffered a massive election defeat in March, and Andreas Papandreou and his Pan-

hellenic Socialist Party came back into power in Greece in October after having been ousted in 1989.

The Northern League, an Italian political party that calls for more power for Italy's regions, did well in elections in 1993 as Italians rejected traditional parties whose members were implicated in government corruption scandals. More than 2,600 Italian politicians and businessmen were charged with offenses, including bribery and extortion, in an investigation that spread into most aspects of Italian life. In November, Italy's former Communists formed alliances that won mayoral contests in five major cities. (See **Italy: Italy Confronts the Mafia.**)

Currency problems. The EC took the first step toward the creation of a European Central Bank by choosing Frankfurt, Germany, as the site of the new European Monetary Institute. EC ministers also restated their commitment to have their countries meet the strict economic guidelines set out in the Maastricht Treaty. If a country does not meet the specified targets for inflation rate and federal budget deficit by 1996, it will not be allowed to participate in the planned EC currency. Because of the recession in Europe, economists predicted that most EC countries would be unable to meet the targets by 1996, so the start of a single currency could be put off until 1999 or later.

Hopes for a single European currency were also hurt in the summer when the Exchange Rate Mechanism (ERM) nearly fell apart under pressure from currency speculators. The ERM links the values of many EC currencies in order to stabilize them. During 1993, many European countries sought to revive their sagging economies by lowering interest rates. But Germany, still struggling with the reunification of East and West Germany, had to maintain high interest rates to keep inflation at bay. Therefore, all the countries linked to Germany in the ERM also had to keep their rates high.

By late July, the strain on the system from currency speculators had become too great, so EC officials on August 2 decided to temporarily widen the range within which the values of the currencies could fluctuate. This action relieved the speculation pressure, but it also underscored the various monetary needs of the EC members and made prospects for a single European currency more remote. By the end of 1993, EC officials still had not returned to the original range within which currency values could fluctuate.

Recession lingers. Economic slowness and high unemployment continued to plague Europe in 1993. Experts estimated that some 22 million people—more than 10 percent of the total work force—went jobless in Western Europe. With most major economies showing either zero or negative growth in 1993, prospects for improvement were dim.

The poor economic conditions around Europe fed nationalist revivals in some countries, especially Germany. Nationalist groups accused immigrants

Country	Population	Government	Monetary unit*	Foreign trade (million U.S.$) Exports†	Imports†
Albania	3,462,000	President Sali Berisha; Prime Minister Aleksander Gabriel Meksi	lek (110.00 = $1)	80	147
Andorra	57,000	The bishop of Urgel, Spain, and the president of France	French franc & Spanish peseta	1	531
Austria	7,598,000	President Thomas Klestil; Chancellor Franz Vranitzky	schilling (11.77 = $1)	44,430	54,116
Belarus	10,583,000	Supreme Soviet Stanislav Shushkevich	C.I.S. ruble (1,184.00 = $)	751	1,061
Belgium	9,979,000	King Albert II; Prime Minister Jean-Luc Dehaene	franc (36.31 = $1)	123,066	125,058 (includes Luxembourg)
Bosnia-Herzegovina	4,408,000	President Alija Izetbegovic	not available	2,054	1,891
Bulgaria	9,032,000	President Zhelyu Zhelev; Prime Minister Lyuben Berov	lev (29.51 = $1)	4,071	4,239
Croatia	4,840,00	President Franjo Tudjman	not available	2,900	4,400
Czech Republic	10,473,000	President Václav Havel; Premier Václav Klaus	koruna (29.42 = $1)	no statistics available	
Denmark	5,155,000	Queen Margrethe II; Prime Minister Nyrup Rasmussen	krone (6.75 = $1)	39,577	33,613
Estonia	1,653,000	President Lennart Meri	kroon (13.44 = $1)	186	1,200
Finland	5,019,000	President Mauno Koivisto; Prime Minister Esko Aho	markka (5.76 = $1)	23,530	20,756
France	57,352,000	President François Mitterrand; Prime Minister Edouard Balladur	franc (5.87 = $1)	231,948	238,911
Germany	81,193,000	President Richard von Weizsäcker; Chancellor Helmut Kohl	mark (1.67 = $1)	430,272	408,305
Greece	10,315,000	President Constantinos Karamanlis; Prime Minister Andreas Papandreou	drachma (239.50 = $1)	9,511	23,222
Hungary	10,342,000	President Arpad Goncz; Acting Prime Minister Peter Boross	forint (99.03 = $1)	10,680	11,122
Iceland	262,000	President Vigdis Finnbogadóttir; Prime Minister David Oddsson	krona (71.15 = $1)	1,515	1,692
Ireland	3,863,000	President Mary Robinson; Prime Minister Albert Reynolds	pound (punt) (0.71 = $1)	28,333	22,478
Italy	57,107,000	President Oscar Scalfaro; Prime Minister Carlo Azeglio Ciampi	lira (1,629.00 = $1)	178,471	188,712 (includes San Marino)
Latvia	2,762,000	President Guntis Ulmanis; Prime Minister Valdis Birkavs	lat (0.61 = $1)	239	9,000
Liechtenstein	29,000	Prince Hans Adam II; Prime Minister Markus Buechel	Swiss franc	no statistics available	

from Eastern Europe and the war-torn former Yugo-slavia of stealing jobs and diverting welfare benefits. Anti-immigrant parties in Germany and France performed well in some elections, as did a small nationalist party in the United Kingdom.

Trade zone widened. The EC in May invited the seven nations of the European Free Trade Association (EFTA) into its own free-trade zone, the European Economic Area (EEA). EFTA members Austria, Finland, Iceland, Liechtenstein, Norway, and Sweden accepted the offer, but Switzerland could not because a referendum on the issue did not win enough support. Swiss backers of EEA membership said they would try again for approval in 1994, and the other six EFTA countries agreed in the meantime to pay

the share of EEA membership that would have been owed by Switzerland. The EEA was to enter into force on Jan. 1, 1994.

Because membership in the EEA does not give countries a full say in EC affairs, four EFTA nations—Austria, Finland, Norway, and Sweden—also applied to join the EC. The EC pledged to speed negotiations with the countries with the aim of making them full EC members as early as Jan. 1, 1995.

The EC in 1993 also strengthened its association agreements with Central and Eastern European nations such as Bulgaria, the Czech Republic, Hungary, Poland, and Romania. However, none of the countries were expected to become EC members until at least the year 2000.

Country	Population	Government	Monetary unit*	Foreign trade (million U.S.$) Exports†	Imports†
Lithuania	3,849,000	President Algirdas Brazauskas	litas (3.97 = $1)	700	2,200
Luxembourg	376,000	Grand Duke Jean; Prime Minister Jacques Santer	franc (36.31 = $1)	123,066	125,058 (includes Belgium)
Macedonia	2,096,000	President Kiro Gligorov	not available	578	1,112
Malta	359,000	President Vincent Tabone; Prime Minister Eddie Fenech Adami	lira (0.39 = $1)	1,238	2,114
Moldova	4,521,000	President Mircea Ivanovich Snegur; Prime Minister Andrei Sangheli	C.I.S. ruble (1,184.00 = $1)	400	1,900
Monaco	29,000	Prince Rainier III	French franc	no statistics available	
Netherlands	15,313,000	Queen Beatrix; Prime Minister Ruud Lubbers	guilder (1.88 = $1)	139,944	134,475
Norway	4,259,000	King Harald V; Prime Minister Gro Harlem Brundtland	krone (7.31 = $1)	35,150	26,076
Poland	39,006,000	President Lech Walesa; Prime Minister Waldemar Pawlak	zloty (20,497.00 = $1)	13,187	15,913
Portugal	10,401,000	President Mário Alberto Soares; Prime Minister Aníbal Cavaço Silva	escudo (172.50 = $1)	17,905	29,726
Romania	23,703,000	President Ion Iliescu; Prime Minister Nicolae Vacaroíu	leu (1,036 = $1)	4,031	5,394
Russia	150,726,000	President Boris Yeltsin	ruble (1,184.00 = $1)	33,100	35,000
San Marino	24,000	2 captains regent appointed by Grand Council every 6 months	Italian lira	178,471	188,712 (includes Italy)
Slovakia	5,366,000	President Michal Kovac; Prime Minister Vladimir Mečiar	koruna (31.88 = $1)	no statistics available	
Slovenia	1,979,000	President Milan Kucan; Prime Minister Janez Drnovsek	tolar (125.23 = $1)	4,120	4,679
Spain	39,770,000	King Juan Carlos I; Prime Minister Felipe González Márquez	peseta (134.25 = $1)	64,329	99,766
Sweden	8,495,000	King Carl XVI Gustaf; Prime Minister Carl Bildt	krona (8.12 = $1)	56,021	49,835
Switzerland	6,667,000	President Adolf Ogi	franc (1.48 = $1)	65,783	65,924
Turkey	60,355,000	President Süleyman Demirel; Prime Minister Tansu Ciller	lira (13,195.65 = $1)	14,883	22,507
Ukraine	52,226,000	President Leonid Kravchuk	karbovanet (31,000.00 = $1)	13,500	16,700
United Kingdom	57,875,000	Queen Elizabeth II; Prime Minister John Major	pound (0.67 = $1)	190,052	222,655
Yugoslavia	10,100,000	President Zoran Lilic; Prime Minister Radoje Kontic	new dinar (105.00 = $1)	4,400	6,400

*Exchange rates as of Oct. 29, 1993, or latest available data.
†Latest available data.

Trade and investment increased between Western Europe and the emerging democracies in Eastern Europe in 1993. But relations with the nations of the former Soviet Union proved more difficult because of concerns about Russia's political stability.

Open borders. The EC's single market program, which reduces many barriers to the movement of people, goods, services, and money throughout the EC, came into effect in 1993. In one of the most visible aspects of the program, the so-called Schengen Group—a nine-member organization that includes all the EC countries except Denmark, Ireland, and the United Kingdom—agreed to open their borders to each other completely as of December 1, permitting travelers to cross without passports. This agree-ment was supposed to have entered into effect on January 1, but France had objected to some of the provisions on immigration and the control of illegal drug traffic. In addition to free movement for EC nationals, the Schengen countries also adopted a common visa that allows visitors from more than 100 countries to cross borders freely within the group's boundaries.

Military debate. The North Atlantic Treaty Organization (NATO), which for decades had provided for the common defense of Western Europe against a military threat from the Communist Soviet Union, continued to seek a new role as a peacekeeper in the wake of the Soviet Union's collapse in 1991. But in the most pressing military problem of 1993—the civil war in the former country of Yugoslavia, where Croats, Muslims, and Serbs fought each other for territory—the organization was unable to find either a military or political solution. Plans for NATO to enforce a no-fly zone over parts of Bosnia-Herzegovina or to station thousands of troops for enforcing a peace settlement did not come to fruition.

NATO members also could not reach a consensus on extending membership in NATO to Central and Eastern European countries that had belonged to the Warsaw Pact, the Soviet-led military alliance. Some NATO members favored admitting the countries, arguing that such a move would signal Western acceptance of their progress toward democracy. But other members, including the United States, opposed the idea on the grounds that moving the NATO umbrella eastward could antagonize Russia.

NATO closely followed events in Russia in 1993, especially the violent confrontation in October between forces led by reform-minded President Boris Yeltsin and those led by hard-liners in the parliament. Much Western aid was delayed because of the uncertain political situation.

In another military matter, Belgium and Spain in November agreed to join the Eurocorps, an army unit run jointly by France and Germany. Although the current role of the Eurocorps was limited, EC officials hoped the unit would provide the basis for an EC army of the future.

Trade disputes. Trade continued to be a difficult issue between Europe and its trading partners. Many of the problems revolved around a planned global trade pact, the so-called Uruguay Round of negotiations being held under the auspices of the General Agreement on Tariffs and Trade (GATT). The negotiations, which included representatives from 112 countries, were to set the rules for global trade in manufactured goods, farm products, and services through the year 2000. France voiced the loudest objections to GATT, saying proposals that reduced the amount of subsidies that could be paid to farmers were unfair. But France finally agreed to a last-minute compromise that enabled the agreement to be completed successfully on Dec. 15, 1993.

Culture was also a hot trade issue in Europe in 1993 as countries sought to shield their citizens from foreign—particularly American—influences. Many French objected to the Euro Disney amusement park, located near Paris, labeling it "cultural imperialism" by the United States. The park, created by the U.S.-based Walt Disney Company, lost several hundred million dollars in 1993. The EC also moved to enforce quotas on the number of non-European television shows that could be broadcast in Europe. For example, France decreed that 60 percent of its television time must be devoted to programs made in Europe, and EC ministers ruled that 50 percent of programs beamed across national borders should be European.

Mourners attend the funeral of former French Prime Minister Pierre Bérégovoy, who committed suicide on May 1 after losing power in March.

The first victim of these rules was the TNT channel, owned by Turner Broadcasting System of the United States, which was banned from showing its mix of American-made cartoons and old movies on cable television systems in France and Belgium.

Macedonia recognition. Macedonia, which became an independent nation in 1991 after the breakup of Yugoslavia, finally won international recognition in 1993. The country joined the United Nations on April 8 as the Former Yugoslav Republic of Macedonia, and it was formally recognized in December by Denmark, Germany, Italy, and the United Kingdom. Greece had objected to recognition of the country as Macedonia because that is also the name of a Greek province and Greece feared that formal recognition might tempt the country to make territorial claims on the province. Macedonia had maintained it was contemplating no such claims.

Chunnel completed. The English Channel Tunnel, or Chunnel, was finally completed in 1993. The tunnel runs under the English Channel and links the port cities of Dover in England and Calais in France. It will officially open to freight traffic in March 1994 and to passenger traffic in May 1994. The Chunnel cost more than $14 billion and took more than five years to build. □ Philip Revzin

See also the various European country articles. In *World Book,* see Europe and the country articles.

Explosion. See Disasters.

Farm and farming. Floods, drought, and frost devastated crops in the United States in 1993. Water from the rain-swollen Mississippi and Missouri rivers covered thousands of farms in the Midwest. Heat and summer drought destroyed crops in states along the Atlantic Coast from Virginia to Florida and west to Tennessee and Alabama. From mid-September to early October, frost struck parts of the Midwest before late-planted crops had matured.

Floods. Spring rainfall left fields so soggy that many Midwestern farmers were unable to plant crops. The rains continued throughout the summer, raising the Mississippi and Missouri rivers and their tributaries to flood level as early as June. Sandbags stacked along riverbanks and on levees failed to keep the rivers from overflowing their banks. Farmers moved livestock to high ground or sold them at sale prices. Barges loaded with grain could not move down the Mississippi to ports in the Gulf of Mexico. On September 13, for the first time in 80 days, the Mississippi fell below flood stage at St. Louis, Mo.

Flood damage. Receding rivers left behind pools of standing water and fallen trees. Silt and sand accumulated from a few inches in depth to more than 8 feet (2.4 meters). Floodwater carved out large holes in the ground, some exceeding 50 feet (15 meters) in depth and covering more than 50 acres (20 hectares). Crops not destroyed by floods were damaged by high-moisture diseases.

The U.S. Department of Agriculture (USDA) estimated that 12.8 million acres (5.2 million hectares) of land were inundated in the Midwest. Storms affected 40 million acres (16.2 million hectares) of cropland, creating severe erosion in areas far from any river. Many terraces constructed to control soil erosion and grass waterways designed to eliminate gullies were covered with sediment. The USDA predicted that some cropland would not be planted until 1995 or 1996. An estimated 500,000 acres (202,000 hectares) were rendered useless. Economists predicted some financially devastated farmers would need as long as a decade to recover.

Disaster aid. United States President Bill Clinton declared parts of Illinois, Kansas, Minnesota, Missouri, Nebraska, North and South Dakota, and Wisconsin as disaster areas. Every county in Iowa was declared a disaster area. On August 12, Clinton signed an aid bill that included $2.35 billion to compensate farmers who had enrolled in the federal farm program and had purchased federally subsidized crop insurance for 65 percent of crop losses. Farmers without crop insurance were paid 60 percent of their losses. A special program aided farmers who were unable to plant, whose fields were flooded or burned up by drought, or who destroyed poor-quality crops.

Most production drops. Damaged by too much or too little water, the U.S. corn crop fell to 6.5 billion bushels, 31 percent below the record 1992 harvest. Soybean production was 1.83 billion bushels, down 16 percent. Wheat production fell only 2 percent to 2.42 billion bushels. The winter wheat harvest was up 10 percent to 1.77 billion bushels. Spring-planted durum wheat was down 25 percent to 73.2 million bushels, and other spring-planted wheat was down 23 percent to 579 million bushels.

The cotton crop was up less than 1 percent and peanut production declined by 24 percent. Oats declined by 29 percent for the smallest crop since estimates were first made in 1866. Rice declined by 10 percent. Beef production rose less than 1 percent and poultry rose 4 percent. Pork fell 2 percent.

World production. In 1993, world wheat production declined by less than 1 percent; rice, 2 percent; corn, 14 percent; and soybeans, 5 percent. Cotton was unchanged. World beef production fell less than 1 percent. World pork rose 1.5 percent and poultry, nearly 4 percent.

Depressed Russian market. U.S. crop prices rose less than farmers had hoped, in part because economically depressed Russia could no longer afford to buy massive quantities of U.S. grains. On May 3, Clinton announced a $700-million food aid package to keep at least some U.S. commodities flowing to Russia.

Farm subsidies. In an economic plan unveiled on Feb. 17, 1993, Clinton proposed to increase the planted acreage on a farm that would be ineligible

The rain-swollen Mississippi River flows over its banks, submerging acres of Iowa farmland during record Midwestern floods in July.

for crop subsidies from the current 15 percent to 25 percent. Members of Congress from farm states managed to block the cuts. Economists estimated Clinton's package would have reduced farm income by $5.2 billion from 1995 to 1998.

Farm-state lawmakers also joined a congressional coalition from oil-producing states that blocked Clinton's energy tax proposal. On August 10, Clinton signed into law an economic package with a scaled-back 4.3-cent increase in gasoline taxes from which on-farm fuel use was exempt. But Congress on October 15 approved a fiscal 1994 spending bill that effectively eliminated federal subsidies for honey, wool, and mohair producers.

New agriculture secretary. On Jan. 22, 1993, Mike Espy, a six-year Mississippi congressman, was sworn in as U.S. secretary of agriculture. He was the first black to hold the job. (See **Espy, Mike.**)

On January 24, Espy went to Washington state to respond to an outbreak of illness traced to a microorganism found in undercooked hamburgers at Jack-in-the-Box restaurants. Illness in more than 500 people and 4 deaths in the Pacific Northwest were linked to the tainted hamburgers.

The outbreak prompted Espy to order reform of meat inspection in processing plants. The new system would use scientific technology to test meat and poultry for bacteria, rather than have inspectors rely on sight and touch. Espy attempted to require cook-

ing and handling labels be put on all raw meat and poultry. But a U.S. district court in Texas blocked mandatory labeling on October 14, the day before new rules were to go into effect.

On September 7, Espy unveiled a proposal to reorganize the USDA. Subject to congressional approval, it would reduce the number of USDA agencies from 43 to 30, most notably merging agencies that deal directly with farm finances into a Farm Service Agency. Espy also proposed to close or consolidate 1,215 county offices out of a total of 3,700.

Canada-Mexico trade agreement. After a bruising political fight, the U.S. Congress approved the North American Free Trade Agreement (NAFTA) with Canada and Mexico in November. The agreement gradually eliminates trade barriers between the three nations.

President Clinton had made last-minute deals with lawmakers representing regions with fruit, vegetable, sugar, and wheat farmers to get a winning margin of votes. Produce and sugar growers were promised protection against imports. Wheat growers won a pledge that Espy would press U.S. objections to Canadian wheat subsidies.

Under NAFTA, U.S. exports of corn, grain, sorghum, soybeans, wheat, beef, pork, dairy, and poultry were expected to increase over the next 15 years. According to a pro-NAFTA agricultural coalition, the biggest gains would be nearly a fourfold increase in beef and corn exports. (See **International trade: The Debate over NAFTA.**)

World trade agreement. The NAFTA victory set the stage for completion of worldwide trade reform talks on December 15 among 117 member nations of the General Agreement on Tariffs and Trade (GATT). The agreement, signed on the deadline day, was scheduled to become effective on July 1, 1995, if approved by the governments of participating nations. The pact reduces industrial tariffs by an average of 33 percent and establishes rules for the first time to govern trade in services, investments, and intellectual property. International trade disputes are to be resolved by a successor agency to GATT, to be called the World Trade Organization.

Agricultural disputes between the United States and the European Community (EC, or Common Market) had caused GATT talks to drag on for seven years. During that time, many nations sought modifications to agreements made in earlier sessions, virtually up to the deadline day. For example, France forced a modification on Nov. 20, 1993, to an agreement worked out in 1992. The modification in effect allows the EC to subsidize over six years about 8.8 million more short tons (8 million metric tons) of exported wheat than it could have done under the 1992 version. Similarly, the United States could subsidize 8.21 million more short tons (7.45 metric tons) of wheat than it could have under the 1992 version. In other trade agreements, Japan and South Korea agreed to lift bans on rice imports. (See also **International trade.**)

New regulations. On August 24, Clinton gave the Soil Conservation Service, a USDA agency, authority to determine the wetlands that cannot be farmed. The Administration exempted from regulation 53 million acres (21 million hectares) of wetlands that had been drained and planted in crops before Dec. 23, 1985.

On Sept. 21, 1993, the Clinton Administration proposed a compromise, subject to congressional approval, that would allow pesticide residues on both raw and processed foods, if there were a "reasonable certainty of no harm." The current law allows tiny amounts of residue from cancer-causing pesticides to remain on raw foods but not in processed foods. Without congressional approval, the U.S. Environmental Protection Agency would have to take as many as 60 pesticides off the market as a result of a 1992 U.S. Court of Appeals decision requiring strict application of the residue ban in processed foods.

Bovine somatotropin (BST), a genetically engineered version of a naturally occurring growth hormone in cows, was approved by the U.S. Food and Drug Administration on Nov. 5, 1993. In clinical trials, dairy cows injected with BST increased milk production by 10 to 15 percent. □ Sonja Hillgren

See also **Weather.** In *World Book,* see **Agriculture; Farm and farming.**

Fashion. There was a brief flurry of interest in 1993 in bell-bottom pants and platform shoes. But many fashions presented by the world's leading designers never affected styles in the ready-to-wear market, as expected. The designs simply fizzled.

For example, top-ranking designers had reintroduced the long skirt with great enthusiasm in 1991, and others had followed suit in 1992. But in 1993, a significant segment of the fashion-conscious public rejected the long skirt. Stores reported that calf- to ankle-length skirts sold well and in reasonable quantities early in the year, but many women seemed to be leaving them in the closet. The styles with a slit at the front, side, or back to provide a glimpse of leg were awkward to wear, and there was too much fabric to deal with easily. So women frequently went back to their short skirts or chose pants.

What went wrong? Many fashion experts believed that designers had lost touch with what women like to wear. Some experts said designers were putting too much effort into the fashion shows that introduced their collections. The extravagance and polish of the shows in such fashion capitals as Paris, Milan, and New York City approached that of the best Broadway productions. Furthermore, to add excitement to their shows, designers introduced styles inspired by such diverse sources as ancient Greece and Victorian England. But these clothes were unsuited to the electronic age.

Designers also hired the best models, including Linda Evangelista, Claudia Schiffer, Kate Moss, and Christy Turlington, who have acquired movie star status and movie star salaries. Observers noted that the top models look great in almost anything they wear, but other women wearing the same style find it difficult to achieve the same effect.

A surprising success during autumn 1993 was the long, fitted winter coat. For some years, many women had wrapped themselves in shawls, bulky down coats, and sweaters under raincoats during cold weather. But in 1993, even before cold weather set in, they began ordering long, fitted coats, most frequently in black. The long coat could cover skirts of any length, or pants, and was appropriate for day or evening wear. Plus, it provided warmth.

First Lady fashions. First Lady Hillary Rodham Clinton, wife of United States President Bill Clinton, chose a violet lace bouffant dress by Sarah Phillips, a virtual unknown, to wear to inaugural balls on January 20. For her daily activities in Washington, D.C., she preferred casual suits by Randy Kemper and other moderate-priced designers. Her predecessor in the White House, Barbara Bush, wore made-to-order clothes by Arnold Scaasi, and Nancy Reagan chose styles by top-priced American designers, including James Galanos, Bill Blass, and Adolfo.

Paris reigns. Designers worldwide held seasonal shows in Paris, strengthening the city's position as the world's fashion capital. Oscar de la Renta, the

The Anne Klein collection for fall 1993 features a black chenille bolero with gold seams. Black was the most prevalent color in Klein's new collection.

American who had introduced his own ready-to-wear designs in Paris for a few seasons, took over as designer for Pierre Balmain's custom-made collection. De la Renta introduced his first ready-to-wear line for Balmain in Paris in March.

Italian-based designers, such as Valentino and Gianni Versace, and Japanese designers, including Rei Kawakubo of Comme des Garçons, Yohji Yamamoto, and Issey Miyake, had introduced their collections in Paris for several years. In 1993, Vivienne Westwood, John Galliano, and Rifat Ozbek, all of London, moved their shows to Paris, because, they said, of the greater exposure to retailers and the press.

Belgian designers attracted attention from the fashion world in 1993, the best known being Martin Margiela, Ann Demeulemeester, and Dries van Noten. They had studied clothing design at the Royal Academy in Antwerp, Belgium, in the early 1980's. In 1993, they were the leaders in a style known as deconstruction, in which fabrics are rough-textured, the seams are visible, as if the clothes were turned inside out, and edges are unfinished. Their styles began to influence the work of more polished designers.

A new high-tech center under the Louvre museum in Paris was scheduled to hold its first fashion show in January 1994. Shows had been held in tents in the museum courtyard. ☐ Bernadine Morris

In *World Book,* see **Clothing; Fashion.**

Finland. The 1991 collapse of the Soviet Union, formerly a ready market for Finnish goods, and a recession in Western Europe caused Finland's economic output to drop by about 10 percent from 1990 to 1993. During 1993, unemployment hovered around 20 percent, one of the highest rates in Europe.

Stimulus measures. In late 1992, Finland lowered the value of its currency, the markka. The move boosted exports by making Finnish products less expensive in foreign markets. By mid-1993, Finland was running an annual trade surplus of $2 billion. But Finnish companies were still reluctant to hire more workers, so the exports surge had little effect on unemployment.

The Finnish government also began a program to reduce its growing foreign debt. In late 1993, it approved a budget for 1994 that called for almost $2 billion in cuts in government spending and higher taxes for most Finns. Despite the austerity measures, most economists did not expect a significant economic upturn in Finland before at least 1995.

Unity talks. On Feb. 1, 1993, Finland formally opened talks on joining the European Community (EC or Common Market). The ministers of the EC countries set a target date for entry of Jan. 1, 1995. Finland's negotiations with the EC centered on the EC's agricultural framework, which provides subsidies for much farm production and sets rules to curb the production of some surplus goods, such as milk and sugar. The EC said Finland may have to cut its generous subsidies to farmers to bring them in line with lower EC payments. Finnish farmers may also have to accept lower prices for their produce. Poorer EC members, such as Spain and Portugal, also complained about contributing money to the EC to help subsidize Finland's relatively rich farmers.

In a significant development, Finland indicated that it no longer ruled out participating in EC defense. Previously, Finland's political neutrality would have kept it out of any EC political or defense union. But the fall of the Soviet Union, with which Finland had signed a neutrality pact, gave Finland more leeway to take part in military operations in Europe.

Bank victory. Finland's banks on March 8, 1993, won an increase in funding from the Government Guarantee Fund, which had already spent more than $4 billion to bail out ill financial institutions. Many of the banks lent money to firms that went out of business and were unable to repay the loans.

Finland's President Mauno Koívisto said he would not run for reelection in January 1994. Koívisto's Center Party chose Foreign Minister Paavo Vayrynen as its candidate.　□ Philip Revzin

See also **Europe** (Facts in brief table). In *World Book,* see **Finland.**

Fire. See **Disasters.**

Flood. See **Disasters.**

Florida. See **State government.**

Food. The United States Department of Agriculture (USDA) announced on Aug. 11, 1993, that labels on packages of all raw and partially cooked meat and poultry products must carry instructions for safe handling. The new requirements were designed to reduce the risk of contamination from bacteria, which the U.S. Centers for Disease Control and Prevention (CDC) in Atlanta, Ga., described as the most serious public health threat to the food supply. Illnesses attributable to meat and poultry contamination cost the nation between $3.9 billion and $4.3-billion each year, according to USDA estimates.

The labeling rules apply to meat and poultry sold in supermarkets and to restaurants and institutions. The handling instructions advise consumers to keep meats separate from other foods and to thoroughly wash hands, cutting boards, and other equipment before and after they come into contact with raw meat. The USDA further advises consumers to thaw frozen meats in either a refrigerator or a microwave, to cook all meat thoroughly, and to refrigerate unused cooked portions within two hours.

The labeling requirements were to become effective on October 15 but were blocked by a federal judge who ruled that the changes were not immediately necessary. The USDA then changed the effective date to April 15, 1994.

The new procedures were prompted by an outbreak of food poisonings early in 1993 in the Pacific Northwest. The poisonings occurred after people ate hamburgers contaminated with bacteria and then not thoroughly cooked. Four people died from the tainted meat, and hundreds became ill.

Meat inspection. On March 16, U.S. Secretary of Agriculture Mike Espy announced that the USDA would develop new procedures for its meat inspection system. The new system would largely replace visual inspections of meat with scientific techniques that detect the presence of harmful microbes in meat. The new plan also called for federal inspectors to be periodically stationed at agricultural sites to evaluate the safety of meat-producing operations.

Pesticides in food. In August 1993, the Administration of U.S. President Bill Clinton proposed a uniform standard for pesticides in both fresh and processed foods. The new "negligible risk" standard would replace the Delaney Clause, a principle in federal law that prohibits any amount of a *carcinogenic* (cancer-causing) pesticide in processed foods. The new rule would allow processed foods to have trace amounts of a carcinogen as long as the rate of cancer that could be caused by the pesticide would be no more than 1 per 1 million people.

Proponents of the negligible risk standard, including the National Academy of Sciences, an organization that advises the U.S. government, and many food manufacturers, said the 1958 Delaney Clause is outdated. But supporters of the Delaney Clause argued there is no way to determine a "safe" level of a cancer-causing substance. Several congressional committees were formed to study the proposal.

The proposal also sought to have the U.S. Environmental Protection Agency (EPA) review all pesticides and to expand the EPA's power to remove harmful pesticides from the market. The proposal promoted the use of safer pesticides and nonchemical methods of pest control. It also banned exports of pesticides that are illegal in the United States.

Preventing birth defects. On Oct. 8, 1993, the U.S. Food and Drug Administration (FDA) issued proposed regulations requiring manufacturers of grain products to add folic acid, one of the B vitamins, to their enriched grain products. Studies have shown that pregnant women taking folic acid can reduce the risk of having a baby with a *neural tube defect*—a serious malformation of the brain or spinal cord, such as spina bifida. Because a fetus's brain and spinal cord form during the first few weeks of pregnancy—before a woman may even realize she is pregnant—the CDC in 1992 advised women of childbearing age to consume 0.4 milligrams of folic acid daily. A number of grain products, including bread, rolls, buns, pasta, and rice, may be enriched with vitamins and minerals. The FDA proposal would also allow manufacturers of folic acid enriched products to advertise the beneficial effects of the nutrient.

School lunches. On Sept. 8, 1993, the USDA initiated the "Fresh Start" program to double the amount of fresh fruits and vegetables it provides through the National School Lunch Program. The USDA also said it would introduce reduced-fat cheddar and mozzarella cheeses on a test basis and develop a low-fat turkey sausage for school lunches. According to the USDA, approximately 25 million children in 95 percent of the nation's schools receive food through the school lunch program.

Food relief overseas. In September, the U.S. Department of Defense began using a vegetarian meal in its humanitarian food relief programs. The new product, called humanitarian daily ration (HDR), is an alternative to the meal ready-to-eat (MRE) field ration designed for U.S. soldiers. The vegetarian meal, designed specifically for humanitarian crises, reflects the military's growing relief efforts in starvation areas such as Somalia and Bosnia-Herzegovina.

The 3,600-calorie-per-day MRE diet that is suitable for an American soldier is unsuitable, and may even be harmful, to those suffering from malnutrition, the agency determined. Thus, the HDR consists of two meatless entrees, such as lentil stew, vegetable pilaf, or beans, and five other products, such as bread, granola, or fruit. The meal provides about 2,000 calories per day. Because the HDR contains no animal products, it is also more culturally acceptable to some groups. The HDR costs $3.95 per day compared with $13.80 for an MRE. □ Bob Gatty

In *World Book*, see Food; Food supply.

Football.

Football. The Dallas Cowboys, professional football's best team in 1992, were strong again in 1993, but not as dominant, sharing the honor of most regular season wins with the Buffalo Bills and the Houston Oilers. Four college teams entered the postseason bowl games with a chance of earning the national championship. But despite a regular-season loss to the University of Notre Dame, the eventual second-place team, Florida State University emerged as the champion, giving coach Bobby Bowden his first national title.

Professional. Free agency and more equal competition came to the National Football League (NFL) in 1993. As a result, few teams ran away with division honors and, more often than usual, good teams lost games they were expected to win.

In the National Conference, the division winners were Dallas (12-4), the San Francisco 49ers (10-6), and the Detroit Lions (10-6). They qualified for the play-offs in January 1994 along with three wild-card teams —the New York Giants (11-5), the Minnesota Vikings (9-7), and the Green Bay Packers (9-7).

The division champions in the American Conference were the Oilers (12-4), the Bills (12-4), and the Kansas City Chiefs (11-5). The wild-card teams were the Pittsburgh Steelers (9-7), the Los Angeles Raiders (10-6), and the Denver Broncos (9-7)

Regular season. There were many significant moments. On Nov.14, 1993, Don Shula, the head

coach of the Miami Dolphins, in his 31st year as an NFL head coach, broke the record of 324 victories by George Halas of the Chicago Bears. Joe Montana, perhaps the greatest quarterback ever, was traded on April 20 at his request from San Francisco to Kansas City. When healthy, Montana was as dominant a player as he had been with the 49ers. The Pro Football Hall of Fame in Canton, Ohio, inducted running back Walter Payton, quarterback Dan Fouts, offensive guard Larry Little, and coaches Bill Walsh and Chuck Noll on July 31.

But there were negatives, too. Quarterback Bernie Kosar of the Cleveland Browns lost his job over disagreements with coach Bill Belichick and was waived. Two days later, Kosar signed with Dallas as a backup. Coach Joe Gibbs unexpectedly left the Washington Redskins on March 5, and the team won only four games during the season. Quarterback Randall Cunningham missed most of the season with a broken leg, and his Philadelphia Eagles struggled. Dan Marino of Miami and Cunningham were among the starting quarterbacks lost to injury.

For the first and perhaps only time, each team played its 16 games over an 18-week schedule. To speed up games, the 45-second maximum between plays was reduced to 40 seconds, leading to frequent confusion by offenses lacking time to make adjustments at the line of scrimmage.

To deal with injuries in a more orderly way, the 47-man rosters were expanded to 53, though teams could still dress only 45 for games. Tied to that, any player placed on injured reserve could not return during the year.

Free agency. On January 6, after five years without a collective-bargaining agreement, the league and the NFL Players Association agreed on the outlines of a seven-year pact. On May 6, they concluded negotiations.

The players achieved their main goal, unrestricted free agency, and the owners agreed to pay them $195 million in damages and $850 million in benefits over seven years. The owners achieved a main goal, a salary cap that would begin in 1994.

Unrestricted free agency was available to almost all players who had been in the league at least five years and whose contracts had expired. From April 1 to July 15, they could sign with any team without their original team receiving compensation. Restricted free agency was available to almost all four-year players, but clubs that signed them had to compensate their previous clubs.

Of the 298 unrestricted and 140 restricted free agents, 129 moved. Defensive end Reggie White of Philadelphia received the highest free-agent contract, $17 million over four years from Green Bay. Quarterback Steve Young stayed with San Francisco for $26.75 million over five years, giving him the highest average salary in NFL history. Dallas made sure Emmitt Smith would not leave when he became

National Football League final standings

American Conference

Eastern Division

	W.	L.	T.	Pct.
Buffalo Bills*	12	4	0	.750
Miami Dolphins	9	7	0	.563
New York Jets	8	8	0	.500
New England Patriots	5	11	0	.313
Indianapolis Colts	4	12	0	.250

Central Division

	W.	L.	T.	Pct.
Houston Oilers*	12	4	0	.750
Pittsburgh Steelers*	9	7	0	.563
Cleveland Browns	7	9	0	.438
Cincinnati Bengals	3	13	0	.188

Western Division

	W.	L.	T.	Pct.
Kansas City Chiefs*	11	5	0	.688
Los Angeles Raiders*	10	6	0	.625
Denver Broncos*	9	7	0	.563
San Diego Chargers	8	8	0	.500
Seattle Seahawks	6	10	0	.375

*Made play-off.

National Conference

Eastern Division

	W.	L.	T.	Pct.
Dallas Cowboys*	12	4	0	.750
New York Giants*	11	5	0	.688
Philadelphia Eagles	8	8	0	.500
Phoenix Cardinals	7	9	0	.438
Washington Redskins	4	12	0	.250

Central Division

	W.	L.	T.	Pct.
Detroit Lions*	10	6	0	.625
Minnesota Vikings*	9	7	0	.563
Green Bay Packers*	9	7	0	.563
Chicago Bears	7	9	0	.438
Tampa Bay Buccaneers	5	11	0	.313

Western Division

	W.	L.	T.	Pct.
San Francisco 49ers*	10	6	0	.625
New Orleans Saints	8	8	0	.500
Atlanta Falcons	6	10	0	.375
Los Angeles Rams	5	11	0	.313

Individual statistics

Leading scorers, touchdowns

	TD's	Rush	Rec.	Ret.	Pts.
Marcus Allen, Kansas City	15	12	3	0	90
Barry Foster, Pittsburgh	9	8	1	0	54
Shannon Sharpe, Denver	9	0	9	0	54
Gary Brown, Houston	8	6	2	0	48
Tim Brown, L.A. Raiders	8	0	7	1	48
Ben Coates, New England	8	0	8	0	48
Robert Delpino, Denver	8	8	0	0	48
Michael Jackson, Cleveland	8	0	8	0	48
Natrone Means, San Diego	8	8	0	0	48

Leading scorers, kicking

	PAT	FG	Longest	Pts.
Jeff Jaeger, L.A. Raiders	27/29	35/44	53	132
Al Del Greco, Houston	39/40	29/34	52	126
John Carney, San Diego	31/33	31/40	51	124
Jason Elam, Denver	41/42	26/35	54	119
Gary Anderson, Pittsburgh	32/32	28/30	46	116

Leading quarterbacks

	Att.	Comp.	Yds.	TD's	Int.
John Elway, Denver	551	348	4,030	25	10
Joe Montana, Kansas City	298	181	2,144	13	7
Vinny Testaverde, Cleveland	230	130	1,797	14	9
Boomer Esiason, N.Y. Jets	473	288	3,421	16	11
Scott Mitchell, Miami	233	133	1,773	12	8
Jeff Hostetler, L.A. Raiders	419	236	3,242	14	10
Jim Kelly, Buffalo	470	288	3,382	18	18
Neil O'Donnell, Pittsburgh	486	270	3,208	14	7
Jeff George, Indianapolis	407	234	2,526	8	6

Leading receivers

	Number caught	Total yards	Avg. gain	TD's
Reggie Langhorne, Indianapolis	85	1,038	12.2	3
Anthony Miller, San Diego	84	1,162	13.8	7
Shannon Sharpe, Denver	81	995	12.3	9
Tim Brown, L.A. Raiders	80	1,180	14.8	7
Brian Blades, Seattle	80	945	11.8	3
Webster Slaughter, Houston	77	904	11.7	5
Terry Kirby, Miami	75	874	11.7	3
Ronnie Harmon, San Diego	73	671	9.2	2
Ernest Givins, Houston	68	887	13.0	4
Pete Metzelaars, Buffalo	68	609	9.0	4

Leading rushers

	No.	Yards	Avg.	TD's
Thurman Thomas, Buffalo	355	1,315	3.7	6
Leonard Russell, New England	300	1,088	3.6	7
Chris Warren, Seattle	273	1,072	3.9	7
Gary Brown, Houston	195	1,002	5.1	6
Johnny Johnson, N.Y. Jets	198	821	4.1	3
Rod Bernstine, Denver	223	816	3.7	4
Marcus Allen, Kansas City	206	764	3.7	12
Leroy Thompson, Pittsburgh	205	763	3.7	3
Marion Butts, San Diego	185	746	4.0	4
Barry Foster, Pittsburgh	177	711	4.0	8
Roosevelt Potts, Indianapolis	179	711	4.0	0

Leading punters

	No.	Yards	Avg.	Longest
Greg Montgomery, Houston	54	2,462	45.6	77
Tom Rouen, Denver	67	3,017	45.0	62
Rick Tuten, Seattle	90	4,007	44.5	64
Brian Hansen, Cleveland	82	3,632	44.3	72

Individual statistics

Leading scorers, touchdowns

	TD's	Rush	Rec.	Ret.	Pts.
Jerry Rice, San Francisco	16	1	15	0	96
Andre Rison, Atlanta	15	0	15	0	90
Sterling Sharpe, Green Bay	11	0	11	0	66
Ricky Watters, San Francisco	11	10	1	0	66
Edgar Bennett, Green Bay	10	9	1	0	60
Emmitt Smith, Dallas	10	9	1	0	60
Calvin Williams, Philadelphia	10	0	10	0	60
Cris Carter, Minnesota	9	0	9	0	54
Ron Moore, Phoenix	9	9	0	0	54

Leading scorers, kicking

	PAT	FG	Longest	Pts.
Jason Hanson, Detroit	28/28	34/43	53	130
Chris Jacke, Green Bay	35/35	31/37	54	128
Eddie Murray, Dallas	38/38	28/33	52	122
Morten Andersen, New Orleans	33/33	28/35	56	117
Norm Johnson, Atlanta	34/34	26/27	54	112

Leading quarterbacks

	Att.	Comp.	Yds.	TD's	Int.
Steve Young, San Francisco	462	314	4,023	29	16
Troy Aikman, Dallas	392	271	3,100	15	6
Phil Simms, N.Y. Giants	400	247	3,038	15	9
Bubby Brister, Philadelphia	309	181	1,905	14	5
Bobby Hebert, Atlanta	430	263	2,978	24	17
Steve Beuerlein, Phoenix	418	258	3,164	18	17
Jim McMahon, Minnesota	331	200	1,967	9	8
Brett Favre, Green Bay	522	318	3,303	19	24
Jim Harbaugh, Chicago	325	200	2,002	7	11

Leading receivers

	Number caught	Total yards	Avg. gain	TD's
Sterling Sharpe, Green Bay	112	1,274	11.4	11
Jerry Rice, San Francisco	98	1,503	15.3	15
Michael Irvin, Dallas	88	1,330	15.1	7
Andre Rison, Atlanta	86	1,242	14.4	15
Cris Carter, Minnesota	86	1,071	12.5	9
Herschel Walker, Philadelphia	75	610	8.1	3
Mike Pritchard, Atlanta	74	736	9.9	7
Michael Haynes, Atlanta	72	778	10.8	4
Brent Jones, San Francisco	68	735	10.8	3
Eric Martin, New Orleans	66	950	14.4	3
Larry Centers, Phoenix	66	603	9.1	3

Leading rushers

	No.	Yards	Avg.	TD's
Emmitt Smith, Dallas	283	1,486	5.3	9
Jerome Bettis, L.A. Rams	294	1,429	4.9	7
Erric Pegram, Atlanta	292	1,185	4.1	3
Barry Sanders, Detroit	243	1,115	4.6	3
Rodney Hampton, N.Y. Giants	292	1,077	3.7	5
Reggie Brooks, Washington	223	1,063	4.8	3
Ron Moore, Phoenix	263	1,018	3.9	9
Ricky Watters, San Francisco	208	950	4.6	10
Herschel Walker, Philadelphia	174	746	4.3	1
Derek Brown, New Orleans	180	705	3.9	2

Leading punters

	No.	Yards	Avg.	Longest
Jim Arnold, Detroit	72	3,207	44.5	68
Reggie Roby, Washington	78	3,447	44.2	60
Rich Camarillo, Phoenix	73	3,189	43.7	61
Tommy Barnhardt, New Orleans	77	3,356	43.6	58

The 1993 college football season

College conference champions

Conference	School
Atlantic Coast	Florida State
Big East	West Virginia
Big Eight	Nebraska
Big Sky	Montana
Big Ten	Wisconsin—Ohio State (tie)
Big West	Southwestern Louisiana—Utah State (tie)
Gateway	Northern Iowa
Ivy League	Pennsylvania
Mid-American	Ball State
Mid-Eastern	Howard
Ohio Valley	Eastern Kentucky
Pacific Ten	UCLA—Arizona—Southern California (tie)
Patriot	Lehigh
Southeastern	Florida
Southern	Georgia Southern
Southland	McNeese State
Southwest	Texas A&M
Southwestern	Southern
Western Athletic	Brigham Young—Fresno State—Wyoming (tie)
Yankee	Boston University

Major bowl games

Bowl	Winner	Loser
Alamo	California 37	Iowa 3
Aloha	Colorado 41	Fresno State 30
Amos Alonzo Stagg (Div. III)	Mount Union 34	Rowan 24
Blue-Gray	Gray 17	Blue 10
Carquest	Boston College 31	Virginia 13
Copper	Kansas State 52	Wyoming 17
Cotton	Notre Dame 24	Texas A&M 21
Fiesta	Arizona 29	Miami (Fla.) 0
Florida Citrus	Penn State 31	Tennessee 13
Freedom	Southern California 28	Utah 21
Gator	Alabama 24	North Carolina 10
Hall of Fame	Michigan 42	North Carolina State 7
Heritage	Southern 11	South Carolina State 0
Holiday	Ohio State 28	Brigham Young 21
Independence	Virginia Tech 45	Indiana 20
John Hancock	Oklahoma 41	Texas Tech 10
Las Vegas	Utah State 42	Ball State 33
Liberty	Louisville 18	Michigan State 7
Orange	Florida State 18	Nebraska 16
Peach	Clemson 14	Kentucky 13
Rose	Wisconsin 21	UCLA 16
Sugar	Florida 41	West Virginia 7
NCAA Div. I-AA	Youngstown State 17	Marshall 5
NCAA Div. II	North Alabama 41	Indiana (Pa.) 34
NAIA Div. I	East Central (Okla.) 49	Glenville State (W. Va.) 35
NAIA Div. II	Pacific Lutheran 50	Westminster (Pa.) 20

All-America team (as picked by AP)

Offense
Quarterback—Charlie Ward, Florida State
Running backs—LeShon Johnson, Northern Illinois; Marshall Faulk, San Diego State
Wide receivers—J. J. Stokes, UCLA; Johnnie Morton, Southern California; Ryan Yarborough, Wyoming
Center—Jim Pyne, Virginia Tech
Guards—Mark Dixon, Virginia; Stacy Seegars, Clemson
Tackles—Aaron Taylor, Notre Dame; Wayne Gandy, Auburn
All-purpose—David Palmer, Alabama
Place-kicker—Bjorn Merten, UCLA

Defense
Linemen—Rob Waldrop, Arizona; Dan Wilkinson, Ohio State; Sam Adams, Texas A&M; Kevin Patrick, Miami (Fla.)
Linebackers—Trev Alberts, Nebraska; Derrick Brooks, Florida State; Dana Howard, Illinois
Backs—Antonio Langham, Alabama; Aaron Glenn, Texas A&M; Jeff Burris, Notre Dame; Jaime Mendez, Kansas State
Punter—Terry Daniel, Auburn

Player awards
Heisman Trophy (best player)—Charlie Ward, Florida State
Lombardi Award (best lineman)—Aaron Taylor, Notre Dame
Outland Trophy (best interior lineman)—Rob Waldrop, Arizona

Quarterback Charlie Ward of Florida State University, who won the 1993 Heisman Trophy in December, unloads a pass against Notre Dame.

eligible in a year, signing him for $13.6 million over four years, a record for a running back.

Other. On October 26, the NFL granted an expansion franchise to Charlotte, N.C., for 1995 for $140 million. On November 30, the NFL awarded a franchise to Jacksonville, Fla., for the same amount. The Charlotte team announced its name as the Carolina Panthers, and Jacksonville said it would call itself the Jaguars. In December, the Fox network outbid CBS Inc. for the rights to televise NFL games. Fox bid $1.58 billion for the four-year deal, about $100-million more per year than the CBS bid. Fox will begin televising NFL games in 1994.

Canadian. In January 1993, the Canadian Football League (CFL) for the first time moved into the United States, establishing a team in Sacramento, Calif. The team, the Gold Miners, finished with a 6-12 record. The CFL also announced that a Las Vegas, Nev., franchise would begin play in 1994. A San Antonio team was also to begin play in 1993, but the team's organizers said they needed more time to organize. In the Grey Cup championship game on November 28 in Calgary, the Edmonton Eskimos defeated the Winnipeg Blue Bombers, 33-23.

College. There was strong disagreement over which team was the best in the nation. Because major-college football was the only college sport without a national championship, unofficial champions were determined by The Associated Press (AP) poll of sportswriters and broadcasters and the *USA Today*/CNN poll of coaches.

Notre Dame seemed headed for the national title after it upset top-ranked Florida State, 31-24, on November 13 in South Bend, Ind. But on November 20, also in South Bend, Boston College, then ranked 17th, upset Notre Dame, 41-39. When the regular season ended, the best records belonged to Nebraska (11-0), West Virginia (11-0), Auburn (11-0), Florida State (11-1), Notre Dame (10-1), Texas A&M (10-1), Wisconsin (9-1-1), Ohio State (9-1-1), and Tennessee (9-1-1).

At that point, the AP poll ranked Florida State number one, and the *USA Today*/CNN poll ranked Nebraska number one. The poll of the bowl coalition, which combined the results of the other two, ranked Nebraska first, Florida State second, and West Virginia third. The National Collegiate Athletic Association had placed Auburn on probation for recruiting violations. As a result, Auburn was ineligible for postseason play and lost some consideration in the polls.

The rules of the coalition required the first two teams to be matched, if possible, and Nebraska and Florida State were paired in the Orange Bowl on Jan. 1, 1994, in Miami, Fla. Although Florida State was a 17-point favorite, the Seminoles trailed Nebraska, 16-15, late in the game. Aided by two Nebraska penalties, Florida State drove to the Cornhusker 5-yard-line and kicked a 22-yard field goal with 21 seconds remaining. Nebraska rallied for a 45-yard field goal attempt with 1 second remaining, but the kick missed, and Florida State won, 18-16.

On the same night, West Virginia, disappointed it could not play Nebraska or Florida State, opposed Florida in the Sugar Bowl in New Orleans. Florida won, 41-7, ending the Mountaineers' hopes of a national title. The next day, the *USA Today*/CNN poll and the AP poll declared Florida State the national champion.

Honors. Charlie Ward, the Florida State quarterback, won the Heisman Trophy as the nation's outstanding player with 740 of 790 first-place votes, the most ever. He received 2,310 points to 688 for Heath Shuler, the Tennessee quarterback; 292 for David Palmer, the Alabama wide receiver and quarterback; and 250 for Marshall Faulk, the San Diego State running back.

Nose guard Rob Waldrop of Arizona won the Outland Trophy as the nation's best interior linemen; offensive tackle Aaron Taylor of Notre Dame won the Lombardi Trophy for linemen; Trev Alberts of Nebraska won the Butkus Award for linebackers; and Byron Morris of Texas Tech won the Doak Walker Award for running backs. Terry Bowden of Auburn, the son of Florida State coach Bobby Bowden, was voted the Bear Bryant Trophy as Coach of the Year. ☐ Frank Litsky

In *World Book,* see **Football.**

France. Conservative political parties won a stunning victory in parliamentary elections on March 21 and 28, 1993. The conservative Rally for the Republic Party (RPR) won 247 seats in the 577-seat National Assembly, one of the two houses of Parliament. Center-right parties, including the moderate Union for French Democracy (UDF), controlled 460 seats in the body.

The Socialist Party, which had been in power since 1988, suffered a humiliating defeat. The party won only 54 seats, down from 260 seats. The Socialists had been weakened by controversies on party funding, a scandal involving transfusions of blood tainted with the AIDS virus, and a poor economy.

New prime minister. As a result of the conservative victory, Edouard Balladur, a member of the RPR, was named prime minister on March 29 by Socialist President François Mitterrand. The move forced Mitterrand and Balladur into an uneasy political *cohabitation*—an arrangement where the government is shared by a president of one political party and a prime minister of an opposing party. (See **Balladur, Edouard.**)

Suicide stuns. France was shaken when Pierre Bérégovoy, the Socialist politician who was prime minister from April 1992 until the 1993 election defeat, shot himself to death on May 1. Bérégovoy was said to have been depressed by the Socialists' political setback and by rumors of financial impropriety.

Bérégovoy's suicide underlined the turmoil in the demoralized Socialist Party. After the March election defeat, Michel Rocard, who was prime minister from 1988 until 1991, wrested leadership of the Socialists from Laurent Fabius. Rocard hoped to become the Socialists' presidential candidate in 1995.

Privatization underway. Banque Nationale de Paris, one of France's largest banks, on Oct. 18, 1993, became the first company privatized under an ambitious plan to sell off 21 large state-owned firms. The plan, released on May 26, could raise more than $50-billion for the French treasury. The government targeted three other companies for early sale: Elf Aquitaine, an oil company; Rhône-Poulenc SA, a chemical and drug maker; and Banque Hervet, a small bank.

Trade disputes. French farmers in 1993 tried to block a world trade accord under the auspices of the General Agreement on Tariffs and Trade. The farmers claimed that agreements between the European Community (EC or Common Market) and the United States to eliminate many subsidies would jeopardize their livelihoods. The French government threatened to veto any EC agreement on a farm deal.

In a minor but symbolic trade action, France on September 17 refused to allow a television channel owned by U.S. businessman Ted Turner to be broadcast in France. The government said the largely U.S.-produced cartoon fare violated quotas designed to protect European television producers.

Trade also caused friction with Germany, which

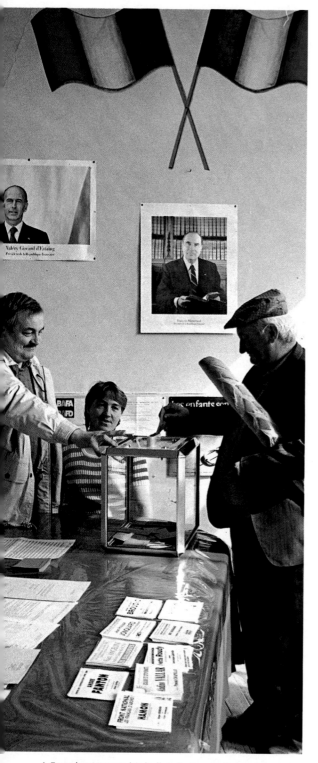

A Frenchman casts his ballot during parliamentary elections in March in which conservative parties triumphed over the governing Socialists.

declined to support France in some European trade disputes. The friction was worsened by high German interest rates, which forced the French to maintain similarly high rates to avoid a devaluation of the French franc against the German mark. Pressure on the franc eased on August 2 when rules were loosened in the Exchange Rate Mechanism, which links the values of European currencies. But high interest rates continued to contribute to a sluggish economy and unemployment of more than 11 percent.

Political murder. René Bousquet, who had been chief of police during the Vichy government—the French government during World War II (1939-1945) that had cooperated with Nazi occupation forces— was murdered by a lone gunman on June 8, 1993. French courts had been in the process of deciding whether to bring Bousquet to trial for war crimes.

Soccer scandal. France's 1993 champion soccer team, Olympique Marseilles, won the European Cup title on May 26 but then was banned on September 6 from defending its title in next year's tournament and was stripped of its French title on September 22. The actions followed allegations that a player and a manager of the team had bribed members of an opposing team not to play hard in a league match so that Olympique Marseilles could rest up for the cup final. (See also **Soccer.**) □ Philip Revzin

See also **Europe** (Facts in brief table). In **World Book,** see **France.**

Freeh, Louis J. (1950-   ), a former agent of the Federal Bureau of Investigation (FBI) and more recently a United States district court judge in New York City, became director of the FBI on Sept. 1, 1993. Freeh took over an agency shaken by the firing of its previous director, William S. Sessions.

Freeh was born on Jan. 6, 1950, in Jersey City, N.J. He graduated from Rutgers University in New Brunswick, N.J., in 1971 and earned a law degree at Rutgers in 1974. He became an FBI agent the following year and spent the next six years involved in several investigations. One probe, of New York City waterfront rackets, resulted in the conviction of 125 mobsters, labor leaders, and shipping executives.

In 1981, Freeh moved to the U.S. Attorney's office in New York City. He was an investigator and the chief prosecutor in a probe that destroyed an international heroin-smuggling ring—the so-called Pizza Connection—run by the Sicilian Mafia. He was appointed chief of the organized-crime unit in 1987.

In 1990, Freeh headed an investigation of mail bombings in Georgia that killed a federal judge and a civil rights lawyer in 1989. The bomber was found and convicted in 1991. That same year, President George Bush appointed Freeh to the federal bench.

Freeh and his wife, Marilyn, have four young sons. □ David Dreier

Gabon. See Africa.
Gambia. See Africa.

Gates, Bill (1955-   ), cofounder, chairman, and chief executive officer of Microsoft Corporation in Redmond, Wash., one of the world's largest computer software companies, was involved in 1993 in a dispute with the federal government over alleged antitrust violations. (See **Computers.**)

William H. Gates III was born on Oct. 28, 1955, in Seattle. In high school, he worked as a consultant in computer programming on mainframe and mini-computers. In 1974, while attending Harvard University in Cambridge, Mass., he teamed up with another consultant, Paul Allen, to create a version of the BASIC programming language for the first widely available line of personal computers (PC's). After that project, Gates and Allen in 1975 formed Microsoft to develop more computer software for the growing PC market.

In 1980, Microsoft signed a contract with International Business Machines Corporation (IBM) to furnish all of IBM's new PC's with Microsoft's MS-DOS, a piece of software that tells a computer's electronic circuits how to act like a computer. In 1993, more than 80 percent of the world's PC's used MS-DOS.

In fiscal year 1992, Gates's company employed more than 10,000 people worldwide and had sales of $3.2 billion. Gates's own worth was estimated in 1993 at about $6.1 billion. On March 24, 1993, Gates announced his engagement to Melinda French, a manager at Microsoft.   □ John C. Burnson

Geology. Earth's strongest earthquake since 1990 struck the Sea of Japan west of the northern Japanese island of Hokkaido on July 12, 1993. The quake, which measured 7.8 on the Richter scale, occurred in an active fault zone where geologists believe the Eurasian tectonic plate is grinding beneath the North American plate. (Tectonic plates are huge, rigid segments of Earth's outer shell that carry the oceans and continents.)

The earthquake triggered a series of *tsunamis*, large tidal waves that can travel for thousands of miles and cause damage at great distance from their source. The tsunamis reached heights of up to 98 feet (30 meters) near the quake's epicenter, some 50 miles (80 kilometers) west of the small island of Okujiri off southwestern Hokkaido. The earthquake and tsunamis caused the deaths of about 200 people. They destroyed or damaged at least 600 homes and 270 fishing boats in Okujiri and caused damage in other coastal areas.

Formation of the Himalaya. Researchers reported in October on new evidence for the presence of Indian continental crust beneath Tibet. Geologists have long known that the Tibetan Plateau and the neighboring Himalaya mountain chain, which divides Tibet from India, constitute Earth's largest region of high elevation. They also know that this region has unusually thick continental crust. Geologists believe the region formed about 40 million years

ago, when the Indian land mass, which lies on the Indian-Australian tectonic plate, collided with what is now the continent of Asia, on the Eurasian plate. But just how this collision caused the rise of the mountains and plateau remained a mystery.

In the research reported in October, a team of geoscientists led by Wenjin Zhao of the Chinese Academy of Geological Sciences in Beijing and K. D. Nelson of Syracuse University in New York used *seismic tomography* to profile the continental crust beneath southern Tibet. In this technique, researchers set off explosions that generate *seismic waves* (vibrations in the earth), which travel downward and reflect off geological features. A computer measures the time the waves take to return to the surface and uses that data to construct a three-dimensional image of the features.

Zhao and Nelson confirmed a previously unproven theory that as the Indian-Australian plate collided with the Eurasian plate, the Indian continental crust was thrust beneath the southern edge of the Asian crust, forming a crust of double thickness. The underthrusting caused layers of the Asian crust to crumple and fold, pushing up the Himalaya. The researchers planned to study how the underthrusting might have formed the Tibetan Plateau.

Deep mantle recycling. According to the theory of plate tectonics, tectonic plates are built as *magma* (liquefied rock) and hot solid rock rise from the *asthenosphere,* a region near the top of the *mantle* (the part of Earth underneath the crust). As the magma rises, it hardens, creating new crust on the edges of plates and pushing them away from each other. Plates return to Earth's interior at *subduction zones*, where one plate slides beneath another. Geologists have long wondered where the material from such plates ends up. Earthquakes at subduction zones have occurred at depths of 435 miles (700 kilometers), but seismic measurements have hinted at the presence of plate material at far greater depths.

In April, geologists led by J. D. Woodhead of Australia National University in Canberra published a study that seems to confirm one theory: that the material from subducted plates is recycled through volcanic activity. Woodhead and his team analyzed *isotopes* (forms) of oxygen molecules from volcanic rocks in the South Pacific Ocean near Pitcairn Island and the Society Islands of French Polynesia. These islands were formed by *mantle plumes,* upwellings of hot molten rock that rise from deep in the Earth's mantle, as much as 1,800 miles (2,900 kilometers) below the ocean floor.

The analysis of the oxygen isotopes suggests that as much as 9 percent of the material at the source of the plumes was sedimentary rock from close to Earth's surface. The sedimentary material could only have come from a tectonic plate that descended deep within the mantle.   □ Eldridge M. Moores

In *World Book,* see **Geology; Plate tectonics.**

Georgia

Georgia endured civil war in 1993. The government of Parliament Chairman Eduard A. Shevardnadze faced separatists who were fighting to establish an independent homeland in the western region of Abkhazia. Shevardnadze accused Russia of backing the Abkhazians, but Russian officials denied it.

On July 27, 1993, Russia brokered a cease-fire in which Georgian forces withdrew tanks and artillery from the conflict zone. But separatists mounted a surprise attack on September 16, and, with no armor to stop them, they rapidly advanced on Sukhumi, the regional capital. Shevardnadze held emergency talks with Russian leaders, but talks halted when he refused a Russian military peacekeeping force. He then went to Sukhumi to lead its defense. But the capital fell to the Abkhazians on September 27, and Georgian forces were driven from the area.

Meanwhile, former President Zviad K. Gamsakhurdia, exiled in 1992, returned. Guerrillas loyal to him attacked the shattered government forces in western Georgia. But their offensive stalled on Oct. 23, 1993, before Georgia's second largest city, Kutaisi. The national chaos forced Shevardnadze to seek support from the Russian-dominated Commonwealth of Independent States, which Georgia formally joined on October 23. ☐ Justin Burke

See also **Asia** (Facts in brief table). In *World Book,* see **Georgia.**

Georgia. See State government.

Germany in 1993 struggled through economic, social, and political problems arising from the reunification of Communist East Germany and democratic West Germany in October 1990. The country also worked to find a military role in world affairs that it—and its neighbors—could accept.

Economic slowdown. The high cost of rebuilding industries in the former East Germany and providing welfare payments to its 17 million residents forced Germany to increase taxes and keep interest rates high in 1993. But those actions slowed economic growth. Germany's *gross domestic product*—the total value of goods and services produced in the country—declined by about 2 percent in 1993.

To fight price increases, the Bundesbank, Germany's central bank, lowered interest rates during the year, but only gradually. This cautious approach created friction with other Western European countries, which wanted to cut their interest rates faster but were unable to do so because the values of their currencies were linked to that of the German mark through the Exchange Rate Mechanism (ERM) of the European Community (EC). By August, though, the pressure on the other countries to lower rates had become too great, so the EC on August 2 effectively freed the currencies from their ties to the mark.

Foreigners attacked. Violence against immigrants flared throughout 1993. The hostile atmosphere was fueled by extreme right wing, neo-Nazi

Turks pray in front of a house in the German town of Solingen where a bomb killed five Turks in May. Police arrested four neo-Nazis in the attack.

214

groups. In one of the worst attacks, five Turks died when their home in the city of Solingen was fire-bombed on May 29, 1993. Police arrested four neo-Nazis in the attack. On October 29, a white member of the United States luge federation was attacked by neo-Nazis in the German town of Oberhof when he tried to protect a black teammate.

On December 8, two neo-Nazis who killed three Turks in the town of Mölln in November 1992 were given stiff sentences, one of life imprisonment and the other of 10 years in prison. The two men had firebombed the house where the Turks lived.

Although horrified by the violence, a growing number of Germans in 1993 supported new political restrictions against immigrants. In response to this mood, the German parliament on March 26 and 28 approved changes to the Constitution limiting the rights provided by Germany's political asylum laws.

Communists in court. Trials continued in 1993 for officials of the former East Germany who had been charged for their actions while serving under that nation's Communist regime. On May 27, Hans Modrow, a former East German prime minister, was convicted of altering the results of a 1989 election to favor Communist candidates. On December 6, former East German intelligence chief Markus Wolf received six years in prison for bribery and treason.

Erich Honecker, the head of East Germany from 1971 until 1989, was released from a jail in the German capital of Berlin on Jan. 13, 1993. A court ruled that Honecker, who was 80 years old at the time and suffering from liver cancer, was too ill to continue standing trial. Honecker had been charged with ordering border guards to shoot East Germans trying to flee to West Germany. After his release, Honecker flew to Chile to live in exile.

Party shakeups. German Chancellor Helmut Kohl remained the head of the Christian Democratic Union (CDU) in 1993, but Germany's other two main political parties changed their leadership in preparation for elections in 1994. On June 11, 1993, Foreign Minister Klaus Kinkel was chosen leader of the Free Democratic Party, succeeding Otto Lambsdorff. Then on June 25, Rudolf Scharping, the prime minister of the state of Rhineland-Palatinate, became the new leader of the Social Democratic Party.

Kohl sparked a controversy within the CDU when he nominated Steffen Heitmann, the justice minister of the state of Saxony, to be the CDU's candidate for president in 1994. Kohl said having Heitmann, an Easterner, as president would help ease the reunification process. But Heitmann came under fire for his remarks that women should spend more time in the home and that Germany should someday be forgiven for its Nazi past. On November 25, Heitmann withdrew from the race.

Maastricht ruling. The Federal Constitutional Court, Germany's highest judicial body, on Oct. 12, 1993, said the Treaty on European Union, also called the Maastricht Treaty, does not infringe on German sovereignty. The ruling paved the way for the enactment of the treaty across the EC on November 1.

AIDS scandal. In November, state health investigators revealed that a German medical firm called UB Plasma may have failed to properly screen thousands of units of blood for the virus responsible for AIDS. Doctors said a small number of people had contracted AIDS through transfusions of UB Plasma blood. The scandal undermined trust in Germany's health-care system, one of the oldest in the world.

Military moves. Germany in 1993 continued to ease its way into a larger role in world military affairs. On April 8, the Federal Constitutional Court ruled it was legal for German troops to help allies enforce a "no-fly" zone over the war-torn nation of Bosnia-Herzegovina. Then on April 20, Germany said it would send a contingent of 1,600 troops to join the United Nations-led forces trying to restore order in the African nation of Somalia. The German Constitution, drawn up under the supervision of the victorious Allied forces at the end of World War II (1939-1945), forbids the deployment of German soldiers outside Germany. But supporters of a German military role successfully argued that peacekeeping missions do not fall under that ban. □ Philip Revzin

See also **Europe** (Facts in brief table). In *World Book,* see **Germany.**

Ghana. See Africa.

Ginsburg, Ruth Bader (1933-   ), was sworn in as an associate justice of the Supreme Court of the United States on Aug. 10, 1993, succeeding retiring Justice Byron R. White. Ginsburg became the second woman ever to sit on the high court.

Ginsburg was born Joan Ruth Bader on March 15, 1933, in the New York City borough of Brooklyn. She attended Cornell University in Ithaca, N.Y., where she met her future husband, Martin D. Ginsburg, a fellow prelaw student who became one of the nation's top tax lawyers. They were married in 1954.

Ruth Ginsburg attended Harvard University Law School in Cambridge, Mass., but transferred to the Columbia University School of Law in New York City for her final year. She graduated in 1959 at the top of her class and then clerked for two years for a U.S. district court judge in New York City.

Ginsburg joined the faculty of the Rutgers University Law School in New Jersey in 1963, where she taught until 1972. From 1972 to 1980, she was a law professor at Columbia. As head of the Women's Rights Project of the American Civil Liberties Union from 1973 to 1976, Ginsburg won five important Supreme Court decisions for women's rights.

In 1980, President Jimmy Carter appointed Ginsburg to the U.S. Court of Appeals in Washington, D.C. There, she gained a reputation as a moderate.

Ruth and Martin Ginsburg have a son, James, and a daughter, Jane. □ David Dreier

Golf

Golf. Nick Price of Zimbabwe and Betsy King and Dave Stockton of the United States won major honors on the 1993 professional golf tours. Prize money rose to $46 million for the Professional Golfers Association (PGA) men's tour, $26 million for the PGA senior tour, and $21 million for the Ladies Professional Golf Association (LPGA) tour.

PGA. Price won four tournaments on tour: the Players Championship by five strokes, the Greater Hartford Open by one stroke, the Western Open by five, and the St. Jude Classic by three strokes. He also won the $1 million first prize in the season-ending Million Dollar Challenge in Sun City, South Africa. Paul Azinger won three times on the tour. Price led the tour in earnings ($1,478,557) and won the Vardon Trophy for low scoring average with 69.11.

The grand slam tournaments began with the Masters from April 8 to 11 in Augusta, Ga. Bernhard Langer of Germany became the fifth foreign Masters winner in six years. He shot rounds of 68, 70, 69, and 70 for a 72-hole score of 277 and beat Chip Beck by four strokes.

In the United States Open from June 17 to 20 in Springfield, N.J., Lee Janzen surprisingly won, his 272 beating Payne Stewart by two strokes. The turning point of the tournament came on the 16th hole of the last round when Janzen sank a 30-foot (9-meter) chip shot from the rough.

In the British Open from July 15 to 18 in Sandwich, England, Greg Norman of Australia won with a record 267, beating Nick Faldo by two strokes and Langer by three.

Norman, who had wasted many opportunities for victory in major tournaments, missed another in the PGA championship held from August 12 to 15 in Toledo, Ohio. He and Azinger tied at 272, a stroke ahead of Faldo. Norman narrowly missed a winning putt on the last hole, and when he missed a similar putt on the second play-off hole, Azinger won.

On December 8, Azinger announced that he had a type of cancer called lymphoma in his right shoulder. He was expected to return to golf in about six months after treatment.

Ryder Cup. In 1991, on Kiawah Island, S.C., the United States regained this biennial international trophy. From Sept. 24 to 26, 1993, in Sutton Coldfield, England, the United States won again, defeating the European team, 15 to 13. The Americans rallied to win 7½ of the 12 points in the final day's singles matches. Their big victory that day was Jim Gallagher's upset of Seve Ballesteros of Spain, and other points came from Stewart, Azinger, Chip Beck, Tom Kite, Davis Love 3rd, and Raymond Floyd.

LPGA. Betsy King's only tour victory came when she sank a 20-foot (6-meter) birdie putt on the last hole of the last tournament. She earned the most money ($595,992) during the year and also had the lowest scoring average (70.85). She was also named

Bernhard Langer of Germany blasts out of a sand trap on the way to winning the Masters in April.

Player of the Year. Helen Alfredsson of Sweden won one major championship, and Patty Sheehan won a major on the way to earning a place in the LPGA Hall of Fame.

In the first women's major, the Nabisco Dinah Shore from March 25 to 28 in Rancho Mirage, Calif., Alfredsson's score of 284 won by two strokes. In the United States Open held from July 22 to 25 in Carmel, Ind., Alfredsson seemed headed for victory, but Lauri Merten made up five shots with a final-round 68 for a 280 total and beat Alfredsson and Donna Andrews by a stroke.

When Sheehan won the Standard Register Ping tournament on March 21 in Phoenix, it was her 30th career victory, automatically putting her in the Hall of Fame. From June 10 to 13 in Bethesda, Md., her 275 gave her a third LPGA championship.

Heather Farr of Phoenix, one of the top players on the LPGA tour, died on November 20 of breast cancer. She was 28 years old.

Seniors. Tom Wargo of Centralia, Ill., a club professional for 17 years, won the PGA Seniors championship on April 18 in Palm Beach Gardens, Fla. Jack Nicklaus, at age 53, overtook Tom Weiskopf to win the United States Senior Open by a stroke on July 11 in Englewood, Colo. Stockton led the tour in victories (five) and in earnings ($1,175,944).   □ Frank Litsky

In **World Book,** see **Golf.**

Gore, Al (1948-   ), 45th Vice President of the United States, became the most visible U.S. Vice President in modern times after taking the oath of office on Jan. 20, 1993. At scores of public ceremonies and announcements during the year, Gore shared the spotlight with President Bill Clinton.

On September 7, Gore and Clinton introduced a plan, developed by the Vice President, to "reinvent government." The plan, which is subject to approval by Congress, would save the federal government an estimated $108 billion over five years through workforce reductions and the streamlining of inefficient procedures.

Clinton met with Gore for lunch once a week during the year, and he consulted the Vice President frequently, particularly on environmental and technological issues. Clinton also entrusted Gore with such typical vice presidential chores as campaigning for Democratic candidates, raising money for the party, and lobbying for White House initiatives.

In April, Gore went to Poland for the 50th anniversary commemoration of the uprising of the Warsaw Jewish ghetto against the Nazis during World War II (1939-1945). In December, he traveled to Moscow to confer with Russian President Boris Yeltsin and make arrangements for a Moscow summit meeting between Yeltsin and Clinton in January 1994.   □ Frank Cormier and Margot Cormier

In *World Book,* see **Gore, Al.**

Greece. Andreas Papandreou, who was prime minister of Greece from 1981 to 1989, returned to the post in 1993 after his Panhellenic Socialist Movement (PASOK) won the most seats in parliamentary elections held on October 10. The victory capped a remarkable comeback by Papandreou, who had left office in ill health, enmeshed in a much-publicized extramarital affair, and facing a long trial on corruption charges, of which he was acquitted in 1992.

Election results. The elections were called on Sept. 9, 1993, by then Prime Minister Constantinos Mitsotakis after he lost his majority in the 300-seat parliament. In July 1993, former Foreign Minister Antonis Samaras had defected from Mitsotakis' New Democracy Party (NDP) and founded the center-right Political Spring party. Samaras then encouraged NDP deputies opposed to Mitsotakis to withdraw their support.

In the elections, the liberal PASOK won 47 percent of the votes and 170 seats, giving it an outright parliamentary majority. The conservative NDP won only 39 percent of the votes and 111 seats. Political Spring won 10 seats. After the election, Mitsotakis quit as the leader of the NDP.

Papandreou's task. Papandreou faced major problems with the Greek economy. Although inflation had fallen to below 13 percent, the rate was still higher than elsewhere in the European Community (EC or Common Market). Also, the govern-

ment's budget deficit continued to grow. To reduce the government's burden, Mitsotakis had encouraged foreign investment in Greece, and more than $1 billion had poured into the country. However, Papandreou said he would cancel all of Mitsotakis' plans to sell off state-owned industries, including the national airline and telephone company.

Papandreou's new government also had to prepare quickly for the rotating presidency of the EC's Council of Ministers, which it was scheduled to hold for six months starting on Jan. 1, 1994. In that role, Greece was to guide the enactment of the Treaty on European Union, also known as the Maastricht Treaty.

Macedonia settlement. Greece in 1993 softened its previously fierce objections to the international recognition of Macedonia, a country on its northern border. Under a compromise agreement, Macedonia was able to join the United Nations on April 8 under the temporary name of the Former Yugoslav Republic of Macedonia. Greece had objected to recognition of the country as Macedonia, saying the name implied that the country wanted to annex the northern Greek region of Macedonia. The new name was to be used until a permanent one could be worked out.   □ Philip Revzin

See also **Europe** (Facts in brief table). In *World Book,* see **Greece.**

Grenada. See Latin America.

Haiti. Efforts to restore democracy to Haiti failed miserably in 1993. A United Nations (UN) plan to return exiled President Jean-Bertrand Aristide to power fell apart on October 11 when armed opponents of Aristide prevented UN peacekeepers from landing in the capital, Port-au-Prince, to initiate the plan. The Haitian military, led by Lieutenant General Raoul Cédras, overthrew Aristide, Haiti's first democratically elected president, in September 1991.

United Nations mediation. In spring and early summer 1993, UN negotiators worked out an agreement that would allow Aristide to return to power by October 30. In exchange, Cédras and other military leaders would receive amnesty for their parts in the September 1991 coup. On July 3, 1993, Cédras and Aristide signed the agreement in New York City.

The agreement allowed Aristide to choose a prime minister. If the Haitian parliament approved Aristide's choice, the UN said, it would lift an international oil and arms embargo that had gone into effect against Haiti in June. Aristide named Robert Malval, a prominent Haitian known for his independence and support for human rights, as prime minister. The Haitian parliament approved Malval on August 25, and the UN lifted the oil and arms embargo two days later. Malval was sworn in at the Haitian Embassy in Washington, D.C., on August 30.

Terror reigns. Malval returned to take office in Haiti on September 2, but Aristide's opponents, aid-

United States President Bill Clinton confers with exiled Haitian President Jean-Bertrand Aristide in Washington, D.C., in March.

ed by the military and the police, initiated a wave of killing. On September 11, gunmen dragged a prominent Aristide supporter, Antoine Izmery, from a church service and shot him to death. According to UN officials, more than 100 such killings occurred during August and September in Port-au-Prince.

UN officials attributed the Izmery killing to *attaches,* a shadowy paramilitary force created by Colonel Joseph Michel François, head of Haiti's military police force. On September 21, Aristide called Cédras and François "killers" and called for their immediate removal.

Turbulence and violence continued into October. The day after 31 UN soldiers arrived in Haiti as part of the peace plan, Aristide opponents staged a general strike on October 7 that shut down Port-au-Prince. As a larger UN force prepared to land on October 11, armed civilian supporters of the government, assisted by police, shut down the port and refused to allow the troops to land.

On October 13, the UN reinstated the oil and arms embargo against Haiti. The next day, Haitian Justice Minister Guy Malary, a key Aristide ally, was assassinated in Port-au-Prince. Malval resigned on December 15, criticizing Aristide for withdrawing support for compromises aimed at returning him to power.   □ Nathan A. Haverstock

See also **Latin America** (Facts in brief table). In *World Book,* see **Haiti.**

Health-care issues. Health-care news in the United States was dominated in 1993 by the promise of newly elected President Bill Clinton to reconfigure the nation's health-care system. Clinton wasted little time in trying to make good on his vow. He appointed his wife, attorney Hillary Rodham Clinton, to head a task force charged with developing a proposal by May 3, 1993. Ira C. Magaziner, a corporate consultant and family friend, was named the Administration's senior adviser for policy development and given responsibility for directing the reform effort.

Health-care reform. The road to reform proved rockier than the President had anticipated, however. The task force, which comprised some 500 consultants, academicians, congressional staff members, state officials, and others, failed to meet the May deadline, as well as several subsequent target dates.

A draft of the plan was widely distributed in early September, and on September 22, Clinton presented the outline of his American Health Security Act before a joint session of Congress. It included:

- The phasing in of mandatory universal coverage for basic health services.
- The establishment of so-called health alliances, regional groups to which most Americans would be assigned. Leaders of the alliances would then negotiate contracts with health plans, such as health maintenance organizations and networks of hospitals and physicians, which would provide health services to alliance members.
- Reliance on competition among health plans to control costs, backed up by limits on total health-care spending for each state.
- The reform of private insurance practices that exclude many sick or high-risk applicants from coverage or that terminate coverage of people with a history of poor health.

Under the plan, every employer was to be required to provide insurance for its employees, with the federal government subsidizing coverage of workers employed by small businesses; the unemployed; retired and elderly Americans; children from low-income families; and others. Clinton planned to finance the subsidies through increased taxes on cigarettes and cuts in spending on the government health payment programs Medicare and Medicaid.

Reactions to the proposal split largely along party lines. Republicans quickly offered their own plans. And some members of Congress advocated a single-payer system, under which a single public or private entity pays for all health care. Clinton formally presented the legislation to Congress on October 27.

Health-care reform progressed at the state level as well. Oregon received permission in March to ration the number of procedures covered by Medicaid and thereby spread Medicaid benefits to more people. The Administration of former President George Bush had rejected Oregon's original application in 1992 on the grounds that it discriminated against people with disabilities. The state made several revisions before resubmitting the rationing plan.

Florida and Washington passed comprehensive health-care reform legislation in 1993. Minnesota, Montana, and Vermont continued work on programs passed in 1991 or 1992.

Physician-assisted suicide. Michigan in February 1993 passed a law making it a felony to assist in a suicide. The law was intended to prevent further suicides aided by Jack Kevorkian, a retired pathologist and advocate of assisting the suicides of very ill patients. A circuit court judge in May struck down the law on a technicality, but an appellate court reinstated the law in June.

While the Michigan law was under review, Kevorkian assisted in another suicide. He was charged with a felony and freed on bail on September 9. Undeterred, Kevorkian was present at another suicide—the 18th in his presence—the same day. Two more suicides took place in October and November in an apartment he rented, and Kevorkian was jailed on November 30 on charges stemming from the October suicide. Kevorkian was released from jail on December 17, after a judge reduced his bail from $50,000 to $100. In return, Kevorkian pledged not to assist in any more suicides until a final ruling was reached on the disputed law. ☐ Emily Friedman

See also **Medicine.** In *World Book,* see **Health.**

Hobbies. See **Toys and games.**

Hillary Rodham Clinton in June tells physicians that the medical community and the government must work together to keep health-care costs down.

Hockey. The Pittsburgh Penguins, who had won the Stanley Cup championship two consecutive seasons, rolled into the play-offs in April 1993 with an 18-game undefeated streak and the best regular-season record, only to lose in the second round. The Montreal Canadiens, who had finished only third in their division, roared through the play-offs and won the Stanley Cup for the 24th time, a record number of championships for any North American team sport. The New York Rangers, who posted the best record in the National Hockey League (NHL) the year before, finished last in their division during the 1992-1993 season and did not make the play-offs.

NHL season. The league changed its look for the 1992-1993 season. It had its first commissioner in Gary Bettman and a longer schedule (84 games per team rather than 80). It sought more national television coverage. New teams started play in Tampa, Fla., and Ottawa, Canada. Franchises were awarded to Anaheim, Calif., and Miami, Fla., for the 1993-1994 season.

The four division champions—Pittsburgh, the Boston Bruins, the Chicago Blackhawks, and the Vancouver Canucks—were eliminated before the conference finals. Montreal and the Los Angeles Kings reached the Stanley Cup finals held from June 1 to 9, 1993. Montreal won, 4 games to 1.

Heroes and goats. Mario Lemieux, the Pittsburgh center, signed the richest contract in NHL history, for $42 million over seven years. Although he missed 20 games while undergoing treatment for Hodgkin's disease, a cancer that mainly affects lymph nodes, he won the Ross Trophy as the league scoring champion and the Hart Trophy as the Most Valuable Player.

The Winnipeg Jets' right wing Teemu Selanne broke NHL single-season records for goals (76) and points (132) by a rookie. Selanne was the unanimous choice for the Calder Trophy, which honors the NHL's most outstanding rookie.

In an April 28 play-off game in Uniondale, N.Y., a frustrated Dale Hunter of the Washington Capitals smashed Pierre Turgeon of the New York Islanders into the boards. Turgeon suffered a separated right shoulder. Bettman suspended Hunter for the first quarter of the 1993-1994 season, the longest suspension for on-ice behavior in NHL history.

World. The world championships were held from April 18 to May 2 in Munich and Dortmund, Germany. The United States and Canada used mostly NHL players whose teams had already been eliminated from the Stanley Cup play-offs. In the final round of eight, Sweden eliminated the United States, 5-2. Russia won the gold medal over Sweden, which took the silver medal. The Czech Republic turned back Canada, 5-1, for the bronze medal. ☐ Frank Litsky

See also **Lemieux, Mario.** In *World Book,* see **Hockey.**

Honduras. See **Latin America.**

National Hockey League standings

Clarence Campbell Conference

James Norris Division

	W.	L.	T.	Pts.
Chicago Blackhawks*	47	25	12	106
Detroit Red Wings*	47	28	9	103
Toronto Maple Leafs*	44	29	11	99
St. Louis Blues*	37	36	11	85
Minnesota North Stars	36	38	10	82
Tampa Bay Lightning	23	54	7	53

Conn Smythe Division

Vancouver Canucks*	46	29	9	101
Calgary Flames*	43	30	11	97
Los Angeles Kings*	39	35	10	88
Winnipeg Jets*	40	37	7	87
Edmonton Oilers	26	50	8	60
San Jose Sharks	11	71	2	24

Prince of Wales Conference

Charles F. Adams Division

Boston Bruins*	51	26	7	109
Quebec Nordiques*	47	27	10	104
Montreal Canadiens*	48	30	6	102
Buffalo Sabres*	38	36	10	86
Hartford Whalers	26	52	6	58
Ottawa Senators	10	70	4	24

Lester Patrick Division

Pittsburgh Penguins *	56	21	7	119
Washington Capitals*	43	34	7	93
New York Islanders*	40	37	7	87
New Jersey Devils*	40	37	7	87
Philadelphia Flyers	36	37	11	83
New York Rangers	34	39	11	79

*Made play-off.

Stanley Cup winner—
Montreal Canadiens (defeated
Los Angeles Kings, 4 games to 1)

Scoring leaders

	Games	Goals	Assists	Pts.
Mario Lemieux, Pittsburgh	60	69	91	160
Pat LaFontaine, Buffalo	84	53	95	148
Adam Oates, Boston	84	45	97	142
Steve Yzerman, Detroit	84	58	79	137
Teemu Selanne, Winnipeg	84	76	56	132
Pierre Turgeon, N.Y. Islanders	83	58	74	132
Alexander Mogilny, Buffalo	77	76	51	127
Doug Gilmour, Toronto	83	32	95	127
Luc Robitaille, Los Angeles	84	63	62	125
Mark Recchi, Philadelphia	84	53	70	123
Mats Sundin, Quebec	80	47	67	114
Kevin Stevens, Pittsburgh	72	55	56	111

Leading goalies

(27 or more games)	Games	Goals against	Avg.
Felix Potvin, Toronto	48	116	2.50
Ed Belfour, Chicago	71	177	2.59
Tom Barrasso, Pittsburgh	63	186	3.01
Curtis Joseph, St. Louis	68	196	3.02
Kay Whitmore, Vancouver	31	94	3.10

Awards
Calder Trophy (best rookie)—Teemu Selanne, Winnipeg
Hart Trophy (most valuable player)—Mario Lemieux, Pittsburgh
Lady Byng Trophy (sportsmanship)—Pierre Turgeon, New York
 Islanders
Masterton Trophy (perseverance, dedication to hockey)—
 Mario Lemieux, Pittsburgh
Norris Trophy (best defenseman)—Chris Chelios, Chicago
Ross Trophy (leading scorer)—Mario Lemieux, Pittsburgh
Selke Trophy (best defensive forward)—Doug Gilmour, Toronto
Smythe Trophy (most valuable player in Stanley Cup)—
 Patrick Roy, Montreal
Vezina Trophy (most valuable goalie)—Ed Belfour, Chicago

Los Angeles Kings defenders (in white) battle Brian Bellows of the Montreal Canadiens in the Stanley Cup finals in June. Montreal won, 4 games to 1.

Horse racing. The tragedies that struck thoroughbred racing in recent years returned during the 1993 Triple Crown series for 3-year-olds. Prairie Bayou, a gelding who was favored in the first Triple Crown race and won the second, died in the third.

Triple Crown. In the $985,900 Kentucky Derby on May 1 at Churchill Downs in Louisville, Ky., Sea Hero defeated Prairie Bayou by 2½ lengths. Sea Hero was owned by 85-year-old Paul Mellon and trained by 71-year-old MacKenzie Miller.

In the $725,900 Preakness on May 15 in Baltimore, Prairie Bayou beat Cherokee Run by a half-length, with Sea Hero fifth. Union City suffered a compound fracture of his right front ankle and was destroyed.

In the $750,900 Belmont Stakes on June 5 in Elmont, N.Y., Colonial Affair won by 2¼ lengths and made Julie Krone the first female jockey to win a Triple Crown race. But Prairie Bayou suffered a compound fracture of the left front foot, and he, too, was destroyed. Sea Hero won the $1-million bonus for the best overall Triple Crown finishes, and Mellon donated the money to equine research.

Breeders' Cup. When the Breeders' Cup series was run on November 6 at Santa Anita in Arcadia, Calif., the richest of the seven races, the $3-million Classic, produced the greatest upset in the 10-year history of these season-ending races. Arcangues, a 5-

year-old from France, won at odds of 133 to 1 and paid $269.20 for a $2 win bet. Jerry Bailey, the jockey, never saw the horse until he climbed on him just before the race, could not understand the instructions from the French trainer, and could not even pronounce the horse's name.

The strongest favorite of the day was the 2-year-old Dehere. But in the $1-million Juvenile, Dehere ran his worst race ever and finished eighth. The winner was Brocco, owned by Albert Broccoli, who produced James Bond films. Losses by Bertrando and Best Pal in the Classic and Dehere in the Juvenile made Kotashaan, who won the $2-million Turf, the strongest candidate for Horse of the Year.

Harness. Staying Together, a 4-year-old pacer, won 21 of his 26 races, including the Breeders Crown for older pacers on October 8 in Campbellville, Canada. Cambest paced the fastest harness mile ever in 1 minute 46⅕ seconds at a time trial on August 16 in Springfield, Ill. Silver Almahurst set a world record for a half-mile track in 1 minute 50⅗ seconds April 24 in Yonkers, N.Y.

Among 3-year-old pacers, Life Sign won the Little Brown Jug and the Breeders Crown, and Riyadh took the Cane and the Messenger Stakes. Among 3-year-old trotters, Pine Chip won the Kentucky Futurity and the Breeders Crown and American Winner the Yonkers Trot and the Hambletonian. □ Frank Litsky

In *World Book,* see **Harness racing; Horse racing.**

Hosokawa, Morihiro (1938-   ), leader of the Japan New Party (JNP), was elected prime minister of Japan on Aug. 6, 1993. Hosokawa presided over a seven-party coalition of Socialists and conservatives that won 262 out of 511 votes in the lower house of the Diet, Japan's parliament. (See **Japan.**)

Hosokawa was born on Jan. 14, 1938, in Tokyo to one of Japan's most famous warlord families. His maternal grandfather, Fumimaro Konoe, was prime minister of Japan from 1937 to 1939 and from 1940 to 1941. Hosokawa graduated from Sophia University in Tokyo in 1963. Upon graduating, he began working as a reporter for Japan's most liberal newspaper, the *Asahi Shimbun.*

Hosokawa entered politics in 1971, when he was elected a councilor to the upper house of the Diet as a candidate of the conservative Liberal Democratic Party (LDP). By 1983, he had held various posts, including vice minister in the Ministry of Finance. In 1983, he left the Diet to serve as governor of Kumamoto prefecture (a division similar to a state in the United States). In 1992, Hosokawa became increasingly frustrated with the LDP and decided to form his own party, the JNP. The party's goals included bringing more women into politics.

Hosokawa is married, and he and Kayoko, his wife, have three children. □ Carol L. Hanson

Hospital. See Health-care issues.
Housing. See Building and construction.

Sea Hero (with jockey Jerry Bailey standing) wins the 119th Kentucky Derby in Louisville, Ky., on May 1.

Major horse races of 1993

Race	Winner	Value to winner
Arlington Million	Star of Cozzene	$600,000
Belmont Stakes	Colonial Affair	$444,540
Breeders' Cup Classic	Arcangues	$1,560,000
Breeders' Cup Distaff	Hollywood Wildcat	$520,000
Breeders' Cup Juvenile	Brocco	$520,000
Breeders' Cup Juvenile Fillies	Phone Chatter	$520,000
Breeders' Cup Mile	Lure	$520,000
Breeders' Cup Sprint	Cardmania	$520,000
Breeders' Cup Turf	Kotashaan	$1,040,000
Derby Stakes (England)	Commander in Chief	$671,146
Hollywood Gold Cup Handicap	Best Pal	$412,500
Irish Derby (Ireland)	Commander in Chief	$550,226
Japan Cup (Japan)	Legacy World	$1,378,612
Jockey Club Gold Cup	Miner's Mark	$510,000
Kentucky Derby	Sea Hero	$735,900
King George VI and Queen Elizabeth Diamond Stakes (England)	Opera House	$405,253
Molson Export Million	Peteski	$600,000
Pacific Classic	Bertrando	$550,000
Pimlico Special Handicap	Devil His Due	$510,000
Preakness Stakes	Prairie Bayou	$471,835
Prix de l'Arc de Triomphe (France)	Urban Sea	$893,650
Rothmans International (Canada)	Husband	$623,100
Santa Anita Handicap	Sir Beaufort	$550,000
Super Derby	Wallenda	$450,000
Travers Stakes	Sea Hero	$600,000
Woodward Stakes	Bertrando	$525,000

Major U.S. harness races of 1993

Race	Winner	Value to winner
Cane Pace	Riyadh	$216,400
Hambletonian	American Winner	$550,000
Little Brown Jug	Life Sign	$197,371
Meadowlands Pace	Presidential Ball	$500,000
Messenger Stakes	Riyadh	$164,152
Woodrow Wilson	Magical Mike	$373,850

Sources: *The Blood-Horse* magazine and U.S. Trotting Association.

Houston. Mayor Bob Lanier easily won election to a second term on Nov. 2, 1993. The millionaire developer, who was first elected in 1992 on a platform of improving neighborhoods and beefing up law enforcement, had high approval ratings and faced no serious opponents in the election. During the campaign, Lanier promised to continue his efforts to rebuild the city's *infrastructure* (roads, bridges, and other public works), which he said had been allowed to deteriorate in the 1980's.

Houston voters rejected the city's first zoning ordinance in the November balloting. The regulations, approved by the City Council in September, would have divided the city into zones for commercial, residential, and industrial development. But many members of Houston's business community were against the proposed ordinance, arguing that it would hamper the city's future growth. Houston is the only major city in the United States with no zoning laws.

Crime. During Lanier's first term, studies by local and federal law-enforcement agencies showed a significant drop in Houston's crime rate. A report issued by the Federal Bureau of Investigation in 1993 said Houston led the nation's top 50 cities in crime reduction in 1992. The study also showed that Houston—the largest city in Texas and the fourth-largest in the United States—had the lowest crime rate of any of the state's major metropolitan areas.

Houstonians were increasingly concerned, however, about rising violence by youth gangs in 1993. In one case that attracted national attention, six youths were charged with raping and brutally murdering two Houston girls, 14-year-old Jennifer Lee Ertman and 16-year-old Elizabeth Peña. Police investigators said the girls had been walking along a deserted railroad track on the night of June 24 when they accidentally encountered a gang initiation ritual. The gang members then attacked the girls.

NASA facility. In August, the National Aeronautics and Space Administration (NASA) named the Johnson Space Center as the new headquarters of the U.S. space station project. NASA said it would open a 300-person office to run the program. Houston officials predicted the move would bring 600 new high-paying jobs to the Houston area.

Education. Academic accountability became one of the watchwords of the Houston Independent School District in 1993. In one of his boldest moves, Superintendent Frank Petruzielo overhauled Rusk Elementary School in June, citing serious faculty infighting and poor student performance. Petruzielo removed the principal from her post and ordered the teachers and support staff of the school to reapply for their jobs. A new administration and faculty greeted students when the school's doors reopened in the autumn.

Joann Horton, a community college administrator from Iowa, was selected in August to be the first woman president of Texas Southern University, a largely black institution in Houston. Horton succeeded William H. Harris, who resigned.

In June, Rice University officials announced that S. Malcolm Gillis, dean of the arts and sciences faculty at Duke University in Durham, N.C., would become Rice's sixth president. Gillis succeeded George E. Rupp, who resigned to become president of Columbia University in New York City.

Shakeup for the Astros. In October, the new owner of the Houston Astros baseball team, Drayton McLane, fired manager Art Howe and general manager Bill Wood, saying a change in leadership was needed to make the team more competitive. The Astros finished third in the National League Western Division in 1993.

McLane named Robert Watson, the team's former assistant general manager, as the new general manager. Watson became the second black general manager in the major leagues. In November, Terry Collins, a former bullpen coach for the Pittsburgh Pirates and before that a minor-league manager for 11 years, was hired as the Astros' new manager.

The Bushes come home. In October, former U.S. President George Bush and his wife, Barbara, moved into a new home in Houston's Tanglewood neighborhood. The Bushes planned to divide their time in their retirement years between Houston and their seaside home in Maine. □ Andrew Oppmann

See also **City.** In *World Book,* see **Houston.**

Hungary. Hungary's internal political divisions became more confused in 1993 when Prime Minister Jozsef Antall, leader of the Hungarian Democratic Forum (HDF), died in office on December 12. President Arpad Goncz appointed Interior Minister Peter Boross as acting prime minister.

Antall became prime minister in May 1990 after his non-Communist HDF won Hungary's first free elections in 43 years. It was unclear how Antall's death would affect parliamentary elections set for 1994. On June 22, 1993, Antall and his allies had ousted Istvan Csurka, leader of a nationalist right wing in the HDF. Although the ouster calmed fears that the HDF might move to the right, it did not stop an erosion of voter support for the HDF. The Alliance of Young Democrats, which modified its rules to admit members over 35 years old, was reportedly gaining in popular support, as was the Hungarian Socialist Party.

Media control. A conflict over control of television and radio continued in 1993. In January, the two chiefs of the state-run television and radio networks quit in protest following the parliament's failure to approve a law to overhaul the media in December 1992. Antall had favored tight monitoring of programs, staff, and budgets, but Goncz had wanted the media to be independently run.

Hungary's economy continued to benefit in 1993 from foreign investment. Analysts predicted that the economy would show modest growth. However, unemployment averaged 15 percent for the first half of 1993, and the living standards of many people continued to drop. Private business ventures with 50 or more employees accounted for only 16 percent of the labor force and 42 percent of the *gross domestic product* (the total value of goods and services produced within a country). Small, newly established businesses accounted for much of the private sector economy. In early 1993, the government had introduced a plan to hasten the privatization of state firms and agricultural cooperatives. The program, which was to begin in 1994, will extend zero-interest credits to those who wish to purchase shares in state-owned enterprises.

Regional relations improved in 1993. On May 11, the Hungarian parliament ratified a treaty with Ukraine to confirm their mutual border. On April 7, 1993, Hungary and Slovakia agreed to turn to the World Court, a United Nations body, to resolve an ongoing dispute related to a hydroelectric dam Slovakia had constructed on the Danube River. The dam had diverted the Danube and caused water shortages in Hungary. In July, representatives from Hungary and Romania met to discuss how to meet the needs of the large number of Hungarians in the Transylvanian region of Romania. □ Sharon L. Wolchik

See also **Europe** (Facts in brief table). In *World Book,* see **Hungary.**

Fifteen-year-old Oksana Baiul of Ukraine celebrates her gold-medal performance at the world figure skating champhionship in Prague in March.

Ice skating. In 1992, Oksana Baiul of Ukraine could not pass junior qualification tests in figure skating. But in March 1993, at age 15, Baiul won the world figure-skating championship for women in Prague, capital of the Czech Republic. In the 1993 European championships held from January 10 to 16 in Helsinki, Finland, Baiul surprisingly finished second to Surya Bonaly of France. Still, Baiul was an outsider in the world championships from March 7 to 14. But the favored Nancy Kerrigan of Stoneham, Mass., the American champion, faltered badly in her free-skating program, and Baiul became the youngest world champion since Sonja Henie of Norway, a 14-year-old, in 1927. Bonaly placed second and a crushed Kerrigan was fifth.

Mark Mitchell of Hamden, Conn., also stumbled in the world championships. Mitchell was second to Kurt Browning of Canada in the men's technical program, but Mitchell faltered in the free skating and finished fourth. Browning won his fourth world title in five years.

Lloyd Eisler and Isabelle Brasseur of Canada won the pairs title, and Aleksandr Zhulin and Maya Usova of Russia won the ice dancing championship. Russia finished with 5 of the 12 medals, and Canada finished with 3 medals. The United States had no medals for the first time since 1964. However, hopes of U.S. skaters for the 1994 Winter Olympics in Lillehammer, Norway, may improve since Brian Boitano, who won the 1988 Olympic gold medal, was reinstated as an amateur in June 1993. His amateur status made him eligible for the Olympic team.

At age 21, Falko Zandstra of the Netherlands became the world's best male speed skater. On January 22 and 23 in his hometown of Heerenveen, he won the European championship with a world record of 156.882 points. On February 13 and 14 in Hamar, Norway, he won the world championship.

Gunda Niemann-Kleemann of Germany maintained her supremacy among women. She retained the world championship from February 6 to 7 in Berlin, Germany, and she won the titles at 1,500, and 3,000 meters in the World Cup season series.

In the world sprint championships on February 27 and 28 in Ikaho, Japan, Ye Qiaobo of China won her second consecutive women's title, and Igor Zhelezovski of Belarus won his third consecutive men's title. Bonnie Blair of Champaign, Ill., took the World Cup women's title at 1,000 meters. Dan Jansen of Greenfield, Wis., won his third World Cup title at 500 meters and became the first speed-skater to break 36 seconds for 500 meters when he covered the distance in 35.92 seconds in a World Cup meet in Hamar, Norway, on December 4. □ Frank Litsky

In *World Book,* see **Ice skating.**

Iceland. See Europe.

Idaho. See State government.

Illinois. See State government.

Immigration

Immigration emerged as a hot political issue in the United States in 1993. Opinion polls during the year found a majority of Americans favored curbs on immigration. In 1992, some 1.1 million immigrants entered the United States, the most since 1907.

Haitian policy kept. President Bill Clinton made immigration news even before he took office on Jan. 20, 1993. On January 14, he said he would continue indefinitely the policy of forcibly returning any refugees from Haiti who were intercepted at sea while trying to reach the United States. During his 1992 campaign, Clinton had said he was "appalled" by the policy, which had been formulated by his predecessor, President George Bush.

On June 21, 1993, the Supreme Court of the United States upheld the Bush-Clinton policy. The court said refugees were entitled to hearings on claims for political asylum only if they reached U.S. territory.

Ban on AIDS carriers. On February 18, the Senate voted 76 to 23 to keep a ban on immigration by foreigners infected with the virus that causes AIDS. On March 11, the House adopted the same position by a vote of 356 to 58. During his campaign, Clinton had vowed to repeal the ban, but he accepted Congress's decision and signed the bill on June 10.

Battling illegal immigration. On July 27, Clinton asked Congress for more money, more personnel, and tougher laws to fight illegal immigration. The most controversial aspect of Clinton's plan was a proposal to speed the interviews of immigrants seeking political asylum.

Under the current system, asylum seekers can stay in the United States while their claims are being investigated, a process that takes an average of 18 months. Clinton proposed instead that expedited hearings be given to asylum seekers within days of the initial asylum claim. The preliminary hearings would allow officials to quickly identify and deport people with doubtful claims. But critics contended the expedited hearings could infringe on the rights of immigrants.

Clinton also sought $172.5 million in added outlays for the Immigration and Naturalization Service (INS), a 600-person increase in the Border Patrol, and stiffer criminal penalties for smugglers of illegal immigrants. Although most illegal immigrants come from Mexico, experts said crime syndicates smuggle thousands of Asians into the country each year.

New INS head. Clinton on June 18 nominated Doris M. Meissner to be commissioner of the INS. She had served as acting INS commissioner for President Ronald Reagan and had directed immigration studies at the Carnegie Endowment for International Peace in Washington, D.C., since 1986. Meissner was confirmed on October 14.

☐ Frank Cormier and Margot Cormier

In *World Book,* see **Immigration.**

Income tax. See **Taxation.**

Illegal Chinese immigrants are escorted off a New York City beach in June after the ship that was carrying them ran aground off the coast.

Police secure the area around an apartment building destroyed by a car bomb, one of a series of bombings in March that killed more than 300 people in Bombay.

India. South Asia's deadliest earthquake since 1935 struck a rural area southeast of Bombay in the predawn hours of Sept. 30, 1993. About 10,000 people were killed. Entire villages were virtually wiped out as brick and stone buildings collapsed.

The earthquake followed unusually heavy monsoon rains across northern India that caused severe flooding and damaged farmlands in July. About 700 people died. The floods temporarily cut road and rail ties to the northeastern state of Assam.

Religious tensions remained high between India's Hindus and Muslims after fundamentalist Hindus destroyed a 430-year-old Islamic mosque at Ayodhya in December 1992. In January 1993, riots in Bombay killed more than 1,700 people, most of them Muslims, who are a minority in India. A judicial report found that a radical Hindu nationalist group, Shiv Sena, was directly responsible, but the report also criticized the government for its reluctance to prosecute the group's leader, Bal Thackeray, an admirer of Adolf Hitler.

The religious strife had political ramifications for the two major political parties—the ruling Congress Party of Prime Minister P. V. Narasimha Rao and the Bharatiya Janata Party (BJP), the largest opposition party in Parliament. The BJP, based on Hindu revivalism, gained support and called a massive rally in the capital, New Delhi, for February 25 to demand Rao's resignation. The BJP wanted new elections in the four states that the BJP controlled, including Uttar Pradesh, where the mosque had been destroyed. Rao had dismissed the four state governments, claiming that the BJP had failed to provide protection for the mosque. Rao's government prevented the rally from taking place by arresting some 25,000 people in New Delhi and 75,000 people elsewhere in India.

The BJP believed that state elections in November would restore it to power in those four states. But the BJP lost all four states. Significantly, voters in Uttar Pradesh dealt the BJP its most severe blow. Rao's Congress Party also lost support.

Rao's handling of the Ayodhya case and of Hindu-Muslim relations in general was widely criticized. Education Minister Arjun Singh challenged his leadership of the Congress Party in March, but other party leaders rallied around Rao. He defeated a no-confidence vote in Parliament on July 28 by only 14 votes, and then only after frantic lobbying to split a small opposition group.

In June, Rao was accused of accepting $317,000 from a stockbroker just prior to Rao's election as prime minister in 1991. The broker was facing criminal charges for a $2-billion scandal involving Bombay's stock market. The scandal had surfaced in April 1992. Rao denied taking the money, but the accusations hurt him in the eyes of the public, who believed political corruption was rampant in India.

Bombing toll. On March 12, 1993, a series of bombs exploded in Bombay, killing 317 people and injuring hundreds. One bomb wrecked India's primary stock exchange. Police blamed a network of Muslim criminals. Police also accused Pakistan of helping the bombers, who were said to be seeking revenge for Muslim deaths in the January riots in Bombay.

On March 17 in Calcutta, 68 people were killed and 125 injured in an explosion that occurred while local criminals were assembling bombs. The Madras office of a Hindu group accused of leading the Ayodhya mosque destruction was destroyed by a bomb on August 8, killing 10 people. A bomb killed 8 people in New Delhi on September 11 but missed the head of the Congress Party's youth organization, who apparently was its target.

Separatist battles. A brutal war continued in the state of Jammu and Kashmir between 400,000 Indian security forces and Muslim guerrillas seeking independence. The guerrillas attacked police and army troops, who often retaliated against civilians. Western human rights groups accused Indian authorities of a "campaign of terror against civilians." The government denied the accusations.

Separatists in the Nagaland and Manipur hills of eastern India, bordering Burma, ambushed government forces several times. The biggest attack killed 32 soldiers in an army convoy on June 29.

In Punjab state, a campaign for independence by militants from the Sikh religious community finally waned. After militants began killing families of policemen, authorities intensified efforts to kill terrorist leaders.

Economic growth. Finance Minister Manmohan Singh extended on February 27 a program begun in 1991 to remove economic controls. For the first time, India's currency, the rupee, became convertible to foreign currency, and also for the first time, the government allowed the export of many farm products.

The Reserve Bank of India estimated the growth rate late in 1993 at more than 5 percent. Although industrial production dropped slightly, foreign investment proposals to modernize some industries amounted to $3.5 billion.

Foreign relations. Russian President Boris N. Yeltsin visited New Delhi on January 27 to 29 to reaffirm ties between the two nations that were in effect before the Soviet Union collapsed in 1991. Nevertheless, under pressure from the United States, Russia agreed in July 1993 not to carry out a 1988 agreement in which India was to receive Russian technology to make certain rocket engines. India said it wanted to launch commercial satellites, but the United States argued that the deal would violate an international agreement against the transfer of military missile technology. India said it would try to develop the engines on its own.   □ Henry S. Bradsher

See also **Asia** (Facts in brief table). In *World Book,* see **India.**

Indian, American. Concern was aroused in the Southwestern United States in 1993 when people on and near the Navajo reservation on the Arizona-New Mexico border began dying of a mysterious viral infection. The disease first surfaced in the spring in the Four Corners area, the juncture of Arizona, Colorado, New Mexico, and Utah. Later cases surfaced in several other states, and by mid-November, 45 cases of infection and 27 deaths from the virus had been reported.

The disease starts with flulike symptoms and quickly becomes fatal when the victims' lungs fill with fluid. On June 11, the United States Centers for Disease Control and Prevention (CDC) in Atlanta, Ga., reported that a virus called a hantavirus was the likely cause. On June 25, the CDC said that victims probably contracted the virus by inhaling airborne particles of the dried urine and feces of deer mice. Even before the hantavirus was suspected, Navajo tribal elders had told state health officials that the disease coincided with an unusual amount of rain in the area. The rain had created ideal conditions for mice to flourish by helping spur an abundant crop of seeds from piñon trees, called piñon nuts, which deer mice like to eat.

Tension developed between some Navajo people, health officials, and news media. Some Navajo believed that the disease resulted from the corruption of their traditional way of life. Suspicion of the U.S. government and Western medicine fueled distrust. In addition, Navajo traditions regarding death, including a custom of not talking about the dead soon after burial and discomfort with autopsies, hindered epidemiological investigations. In early June, Peterson Zah, president of the Navajo Nation, called upon tribe members to work with medical investigators in solving the puzzle of the disease. In late 1993, researchers isolated the virus and began steps to create a vaccine. (See also **Public health.**)

Gambling. In mid-July 1993, the Oneida Indians of central New York opened a casino that they expected to generate over $100 million annually. They became one of about 70 U.S. tribes to offer gambling since the Indian Gaming Regulatory Act was signed in 1988 to permit some types of gambling on Indian reservations. By 1993, gambling had become a major revenue source, allowing some previously impoverished tribes to build schools, hospitals, and homes and to virtually eliminate unemployment.

In September, the Mashantucket Pequot tribe opened the second largest casino in the world near Ledyard, Conn. The tribe expected to be one of the state's largest employers and to add $113 million to state coffers by the end of 1993. However, some area residents worried about the Pequot buying up land to expand operations.

As gambling on reservations became an estimated $6-billion-a-year business, governments struggled to interpret the gaming act. On April 2, real estate tycoon Donald Trump sued the federal government, claiming that Indians were given preference in casino licenses and that parts of the gaming act were illegal. Trump saw Indian casinos as a threat to the gambling industry of Atlantic City, N.J., where he owns three casinos. (See also **State government: The States Bet on Legalized Gambling.**)

The first woman assistant secretary for Indian affairs in the U.S. Department of the Interior, Ada Deer, was nominated on May 11 by U.S. President Bill Clinton and confirmed by the U.S. Senate on July 16. Deer, a Native American rights activist, is a Menominee from Wisconsin.

Two custody battles. A British Columbia court in Canada ruled in late August that two-year-old David James Tearoe remain with his adoptive parents. His biological mother, Cecilia Sawan, a Cree Indian, had tried to regain custody of her son with the help of her tribe, who thought the boy should be raised as a Native American.

At the end of 1993, an Idaho district court had yet to resolve a case of Oglala Sioux Indians seeking custody of 4-year-old Casey Swenson, who had been adopted by non-Indians. The child's biological father was a Sioux, and the tribe wanted the boy to be raised by a relative on the Pine Ridge Indian Reservation in South Dakota.   □ Mary Carvlin

In *World Book,* see **Indian, American.**
Indiana. See **State government.**

Indonesia. On March 10, 1993, the People's Consultative Assembly unanimously elected 71-year-old President Suharto to his sixth consecutive five-year term. The next day, the assembly approved Suharto's choice as vice president, Try Sutrisno. Speculation arose whether Sutrisno, who was Suharto's sixth vice president, had enough political skill and support to eventually succeed Suharto to the presidency.

Sutrisno was a former presidential aide and, until his retirement in February, the commander of the armed forces. However, diplomats speculated that there was a growing rift between the armed forces and Suharto over the presidential succession. On October 25, Suharto's ruling political organization, Golkar, named its first civilian chairman, Harmoko, in a move possibly intended to reduce the influence of the military.

New cabinet. Suharto named a new cabinet on March 17. He dropped several Western-educated ministers, who had promoted deregulating the economy and had encouraged low-wage export industries. Their policies were credited with Indonesia's solid economic growth. Nevertheless, Suharto replaced those ministers with economic nationalists—men who favored large state investments in key industries. Suharto gave the military fewer and less important posts than in his previous cabinet.

Liberal signals. After decades of authoritarian rule, Suharto's government appeared to be liberaliz-

Native Americans in February commemorate the 20th anniversary of a 1973 clash between Indians and U.S. authorities at Wounded Knee, S. Dak.

ing in 1993. For example, Suharto met twice with General A. H. Nasution, a hero of Indonesia's independence struggle against the Netherlands and former armed forces commander. Nasution had been isolated by the regime since the 1970's, when he criticized its dictatorial tendencies. Other former leaders, shunned for similar reasons, also began to get official attention. The media were allowed to be a bit more critical than in the past, such as suggesting that official rulings favored the rich. However, criticizing Suharto or his family was still off-limits.

The standard of living rose in 1993, despite low wages—$2.40 or less a day for factory workers. The government tried to keep wages low, and thus help keep the price of goods low, so that Indonesia's export industries could compete with less-developed countries with low-wage labor.

Trial in East Timor. On May 21, a court sentenced Xanana Gusmao to life in prison for plotting against the state and illegally possessing firearms. Until his capture in November 1992, Gusmao had been the leader of the Revolutionary Front for an Independent East Timor, a resistance movement that continued its fight during 1993. On August 13, Suharto reduced Gusmao's sentence to 20 years in prison as foreign criticism of Indonesia's human rights record in East Timor continued.   □ Henry S. Bradsher

See also **Asia** (Facts in brief table). In *World Book,* see **Indonesia**.

International trade. The Administration of United States President Bill Clinton scored two big victories for freer international trade in 1993. One triumph led to a free-trade zone in North America, and the other reduced tariffs around the world.

NAFTA win. The first test of Clinton's commitment to free trade came with the North American Free Trade Agreement (NAFTA), which would create a barrier-free trade zone between the United States, Canada, and Mexico. Clinton argued that NAFTA was essential to boosting U.S. trade with a developing Mexico. But opponents said it would depress working conditions for Mexican laborers, threaten the job security of thousands of Americans, and lead to ecological destruction along the border between the United States and Mexico.

Officials from the three nations spent the early part of 1993 negotiating supplemental agreements to NAFTA, which were a condition of Clinton's support. The side agreements addressed the resolution of environmental problems along the U.S.-Mexican border, the raising of labor standards in Mexico, and the enactment of emergency U.S. tariffs in the event of surging imports from Mexico. The entire NAFTA package was then sent to Congress in the early fall.

Passage was fought by a well-organized coalition of citizens groups, environmental groups, and labor unions. Billionaire businessman H. Ross Perot also led attacks. But Clinton lobbied fiercely for the pact,

and on November 17, the House of Representatives cleared it by a vote of 234 to 200. The Senate then approved the bill on November 20. The provisions of NAFTA, which will be phased in over several years, were to start taking effect on Jan. 1, 1994.

Asian summit. On Nov. 18, 1993, Clinton flew to Seattle to host the annual meeting of the Asian-Pacific Economic Cooperation (APEC) forum, an organization of 15 countries in Southeast Asia. At the meeting, Clinton discussed the opening of trade barriers in the area, but no agreements were reached.

GATT conclusion. Trade concerns between the United States and the European Community (EC) in 1993 almost thwarted completion of the so-called Uruguay Round of talks under the auspices of the General Agreement on Tariffs and Trade (GATT). GATT is an organization that has overseen international trade since 1947. The U.S. Congress had set a deadline of Dec. 15, 1993, for the completion of the current round of talks, which began in 1986.

The largest obstacle involved agriculture. In November 1992, the United States and the EC reached an understanding on reducing agricultural subsidies. But in 1993, France found new problems with the arrangement, and negotiators had to rework the settlement in last-minute talks in early December. Another sticking point involved proposed limits on the entry of U.S.-made motion pictures and television shows in European markets. But that matter was set aside for future resolution.

The talks were finally completed on December 15, five hours before Congress's deadline. Under the new agreement, the 117 member nations of GATT were to cut their tariffs by an average of one-third. The agreement also provides for global patent protection and calls for the creation of an official body, the World Trade Organization (WTO), to replace GATT. The WTO was to have greater powers than GATT for governing trade and resolving disputes.

The provisions of the GATT agreement were to go into effect on July 1, 1995. Congress still had to vote on the pact, but approval was expected.

Trade with Japan. Gaining access to the huge Japanese market has been a recurring headache for U.S. administrations in recent years. Japan is the nation that possesses the largest trading surplus with the United States. In 1993, the surplus was expected to reach more than $60 billion, a record high.

Early in the year, Clinton decided to take a hard-line approach. His model was a successful agreement on computer chips negotiated with Japan in 1991 that had set a target for foreign manufacturers of 20 percent of the Japanese market by the end of 1992. But Japan objected to a replay of that format, saying it forced the Japanese government to manage trade.

In Tokyo on July 10, 1993, Clinton and Japanese Prime Minister Kiichi Miyazawa finally arrived at a framework for trade talks. Japan said it would work to reduce its trade surplus with the United States, in

Police in the French town of Perpignan survey boxes of Spanish tomatoes, smashed by farmers to protest the lowering of trade barriers in 1993.

particular by increasing its imports of manufactured goods by one-third by 1999. However, Japan refused to set any specific import targets as it had done in the computer chip agreement.

Trade with China. China was the country with the second largest trade imbalance with the United States in 1993. For the year, China was expected to enjoy a $20-billion trade surplus in the relationship.

On May 28, the Clinton Administration extended for one year China's most-favored-nation trading status. Such a designation allows countries to pay the lowest allowable tariffs in trade with the United States. However, Clinton said he would not renew the status in 1994 unless China had made significant progress toward reducing its import barriers, improving its human rights conditions, and abiding by multilateral rules on the transfer of missile technology to developing countries.

Trade with Russia. The United States in 1993 tried to encourage trade with the ailing countries of the former Soviet Union. The U.S. Export-Import Bank (Eximbank) and the Overseas Private Investment Corporation both worked on arrangements with Russia and the other former Soviet republics to spur U.S. investment. By mid-December, the Eximbank had established an innovative framework with Russia that was intended to help U.S. banks finance modernization of the country's decaying energy production sector.

Trade with Vietnam. The normalization of U.S. diplomatic relations with Vietnam, which had proceeded steadily during the Administration of President George Bush, slowed under Clinton. The White House in 1993 awaited more information from Vietnam on the fates of U.S. soldiers missing during the Vietnam War (1957-1975). But on July 2, the Clinton Administration withdrew its objection to loans to Vietnam by international lending institutions. And on September 13, the Administration said it would allow U.S. firms to bid on projects financed by such loans. However, direct trade with Vietnam by U.S. firms was still prohibited. (See also **Asia: Vietnam: Emerging from a War-torn Past.**)

Trade with South Africa. The United States had eliminated most of its trade restrictions with South Africa in 1992 after the repeal of the laws that had permitted apartheid. But plans announced in 1993 to establish a multiracial government in South Africa in 1994 prompted Clinton to push for more investment in the country. On Nov. 23, 1993, Clinton removed the last existing U.S. trade restrictions. Then on November 26, Commerce Secretary Ronald H. Brown headed the first U.S. trade promotion mission to South Africa since 1973. During the trip, officials from both countries signed an agreement that insures U.S. firms investing in South Africa against losses due to civil disruption.   □ Jim Berger

In *World Book*, see **International trade.**

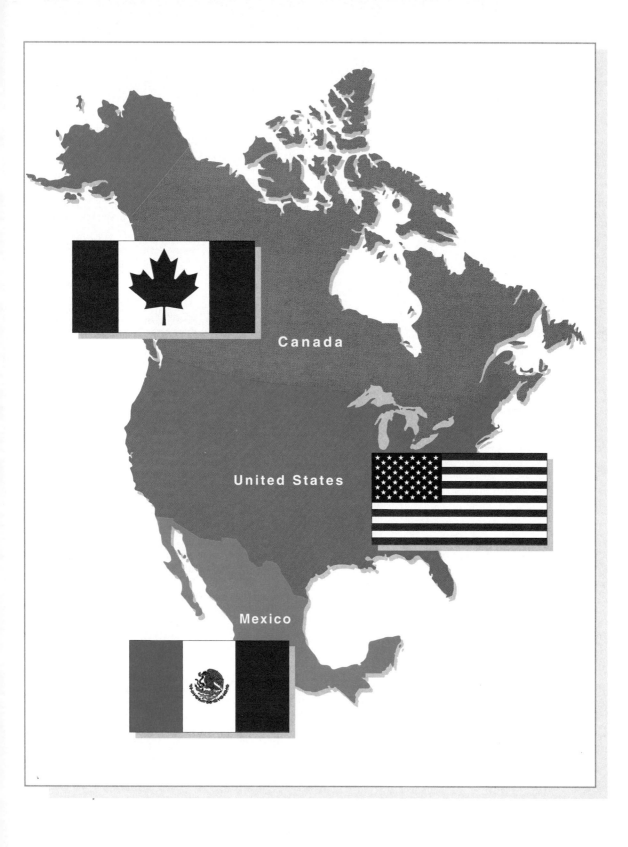

Canada

United States

Mexico

The Debate over NAFTA

By Harley Shaiken

Supporters say the North American Free Trade Agreement will spur an economic boom, but critics say it will cost jobs and create more pollution.

In the dry, scrub-covered hills and valleys of Tijuana, Mexico, near the United States border south of San Diego, gleaming new factories rise next to ramshackle wooden houses with dirt floors and no running water or electricity. Modern office buildings underscore the city's economic growth, yet the cost of industrial development is also apparent in streams and rivers polluted with hazardous chemicals.

Tijuana and Mexican cities like it along the U.S. border in 1993 became symbols of controversy in an impassioned debate over the adoption of the North American Free Trade Agreement (NAFTA). The agreement will create one of the world's largest free-trade zones, encompassing the economies of Canada, Mexico, and the United States. Despite much opposition, the U.S. Congress approved NAFTA in November 1993, and the Mexican Senate followed, assuring that the agreement will take effect on Jan. 1, 1994. The two houses of the Canadian legislature passed NAFTA earlier in 1993.

But the prospect of such an agreement raised many questions. Will the expanded economic integration between Mexico and the United States that NAFTA promised help pull these Tijuana residents out of poverty, as its proponents hoped? Will it create jobs in the United States to service the growing Mexican market in the process? Or, will

Glossary

Free trade: Trade between countries that is free from barriers, such as tariffs.

Free-trade zone: An area where countries conduct free trade.

North American Free Trade Agreement: An agreement between the United States, Mexico, and Canada that will eliminate tariffs and quotas on trade between the countries.

Protectionism: Trade practices designed to bolster a country's industries by discouraging foreign products from entering that country.

Trade quota: A form of protectionism that limits the quantity of a foreign good allowed into a country.

Tariff: A form of protectionism that taxes foreign goods.

■ **The author:**

Harley Shaiken is a professor in the graduate School of Education and an Associate in the Center for Latin American Studies at the University of California at Berkeley.

lowering trade barriers reduce wages in the United States as American companies try to counter low-wage competition from across the border, as critics charged? Will NAFTA prod the cleanup of the environment, or will it result in even more dangerous levels of pollution?

The move toward free trade in North America mirrors evolving trade practices around the world. The 12-nation European Community (EC) moved closer to eliminating all barriers to trade among its members in 1993, though with far greater attention to social issues such as income disparities. Seven other nations in the region also signed an agreement with the EC that was to begin in 1993. Thailand, Malaysia, the Philippines, Indonesia, Brunei, and Singapore have said that they will begin a free-trade pact in January 1994, and many nations in Latin America announced plans for free-trade alliances in the early 1990's. It is uncertain how long these trade blocs will last, but they will probably be a major influence in international trade well beyond the year 2000. And a successful NAFTA could become the basis on which the United States develops closer economic ties with other nations through additional trade pacts, especially in Latin America.

NAFTA will create a vast new market of 370 million people, stretching from the Arctic Circle to the Guatemalan border. In U.S. dollars, the total value of goods and services produced in these three economies was more than $6.5 trillion a year in 1992, rivaling the EC as the largest single market in the world. The EC comprises 345 million people and produces $6.8 trillion in goods.

Considerable trade already exists between these three North American neighbors. Canada is the largest trading partner of the United States, and Mexico is third behind Japan. The United States is Mexico's most important trading partner by a wide margin, accounting for 70 percent of Mexico's imports and exports. Because a free-trade agreement between the United States and Canada went into effect in 1989, most of the economic integration that will result from NAFTA will take place between the United States and Mexico. Trade between Canada and Mexico is small. Canadian trade with Mexico in 1991 represented only 3.6 percent of U.S.-Mexican trade, according to the International Trade Commission in Washington, D.C.

How NAFTA will work

NAFTA will expand trade by knocking down barriers to trade between the three countries. Such trade barriers take many forms, but collectively they are called *protectionism*. Protectionism is a trade policy that tries to bolster a country's industries by making products from other countries more expensive than similar goods produced at home or by limiting the number of foreign goods allowed into the country. The most common form of protectionism is *tariffs*. Tariffs raise prices on foreign goods by placing taxes on them. NAFTA proposes to do away with most tariffs between the three participants within 5 years and to eliminate 99 percent of tariffs within 10 years. Lowering tariffs continues a decadelong trend. Tariffs on Mexican goods coming into the United States in 1993 averaged less than 4 percent of the man-

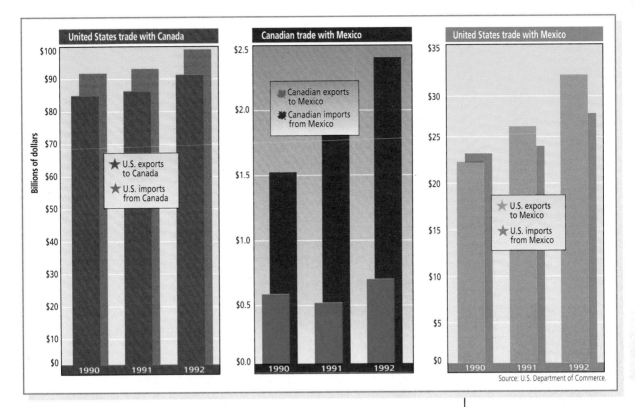

United States trade with Canada

Billions of dollars

★ U.S. exports to Canada
★ U.S. imports from Canada

1990 · 1991 · 1992

Canadian trade with Mexico

Canadian exports to Mexico
Canadian imports from Mexico

1990 · 1991 · 1992

United States trade with Mexico

★ U.S. exports to Mexico
★ U.S. imports from Mexico

1990 · 1991 · 1992

Source: U.S. Department of Commerce.

ufactured value of the goods, while the levies on U.S. goods entering Mexico were about 10 percent of the goods' manufactured value.

NAFTA was also designed to sharply reduce other trade barriers. These barriers include quotas limiting the amount and kind of imports, "local content" laws requiring that products contain a minimum percentage of parts or material made in the home country, or regulations requiring governments to buy products made at home. The treaty will eliminate almost all import quotas, such as U.S. restrictions on Mexican textiles or Mexican limits on U.S. and Canadian cars and trucks. Regulations in the auto industry now demanding that a company balance the value of its imports and exports will expire over a 10-year period. Moreover, U.S. and Canadian businesses will be able to sell their products to Mexican government agencies as well as the other way around.

The agreement will be more than just a trade treaty: It will spell out important guarantees for investors. The underlying idea is that a company should have the same rights to operate in any of the three countries as it does in its home country. Foreign ownership of and investment in Mexican companies have been restricted in many areas, but NAFTA will allow U.S. and Canadian firms to own most Mexican companies or invest in them. Industries such as insurance or telecommunications that previously barred foreign companies will be open. The exception will be the Mexican energy industry. Oil, natural gas, and electricity production are state-run enterprises in Mexico, and under

■ Trade each year between the United States, Canada, and Mexico totals more than $6.5 trillion worth of goods, placing the trade bloc among the largest in the world. NAFTA proponents claim that the treaty will increase this trade even more. The elimination of trade barriers between the United States and Mexico, in particular, will help trade between the two countries continue to increase, supporters claim.

NAFTA, the Mexican government will retain ownership of these industries, with only limited opportunities for foreign investment.

NAFTA is really a managed rather than a free-trade agreement, as the colossal length of the written agreement indicates. It would probably take only several paragraphs to do away with all trade barriers in North America. But the actual agreement contains 22 chapters and almost 2,000 pages of dense legal language. These pages detail how and when tariffs and quotas will be phased out.

The history of NAFTA

The idea of a free-trade agreement was proposed to United States President George Bush in spring 1990 by Mexican President Carlos Salinas de Gortari. The proposal reversed the long-standing policy of Mexican leaders, who historically have tried to distance themselves from the

| 1982 | 1987 | 1992 |
| $59 | $107 | $99 |

Billions of dollars

Source: Office of Trade of
Mexico's U.S. Embassy.

■ Why Mexico wants NAFTA

Mexico's foreign debt nearly doubled from 1982 to 1992, *left*, primarily as a result of the declining price of oil, Mexico's chief export. The increasing debt burdened the Mexican economy and worsened poverty for many workers, such as those living in the slums surrounding an oil refinery in Minatitlán, Mexico, *below*.

Goliath to the north. This departure from traditional Mexican policy stems from Mexico's painful economic experience during the 1980's.

Mexico went through one of the worst economic traumas in its history then. It was a period so dismal that it is often called the "lost decade." Oil was and still is Mexico's chief export, but after global oil prices collapsed in the early 1980's, Mexico's economy went into a tailspin.

In response to the crisis, President Miguel de la Madrid Hurtado, who governed from 1982 to 1988, embarked on a major restructuring of the economy. President Salinas continued these initiatives when he took office in 1988. The new direction emphasized selling government-owned enterprises to help pay the country's huge debt. Such sales involved many major companies, including banks, airlines, telephone companies, and steel manufacturers.

A free-trade agreement with the United States was seen as another step to aid the Mexican economy. But it will not come without potential problems. A 1988 free-trade agreement between the United States and Canada, which eliminates all tariffs between the two countries by 1999, provided an important precedent. NAFTA built on this earlier agreement but went further in many areas, such as protecting patents and allowing for easier transportation between the three countries. Although proponents of the U.S.-Canada agreement projected large job gains, Canada actually lost almost 25 percent of its manufacturing jobs during the treaty's first three years. Defenders of the agreement say that a Canadian recession and a fall in value of the Canadian dollar caused the job losses, but critics insist that the treaty is at fault as well.

Presidents Salinas and Bush both endorsed the idea of a free-trade agreement between Mexico and the United States in early June 1990, and formal negotiations began several months later. Prime Minister Brian Mulroney of Canada joined the negotiations in February 1991, and negotiators reached agreement on the text of the new treaty on Aug. 12, 1992.

The debate over NAFTA in the United States centered around four issues. These issues were whether the United States would gain or lose jobs if NAFTA passed; whether U.S. wages would slide toward Mexican levels; whether the treaty would have an adverse environmental impact; and whether rejecting NAFTA would have serious economic and political consequences.

Arguments for NAFTA

Proponents of NAFTA claimed that free trade is beneficial because it spurs economic growth, allowing each country's most important industries to expand through increased efficiency. Increasing the size of the pie means everyone can have a larger slice, they maintained.

As a result of the partial opening of the Mexican economy, supporters of the agreement pointed out, U.S. trade with Mexico ballooned to $76 billion in 1992, almost double 1988 levels. Moreover, the United States exported $5 billion more than it imported from Mexico in 1992, creating jobs in the United States. (According to the

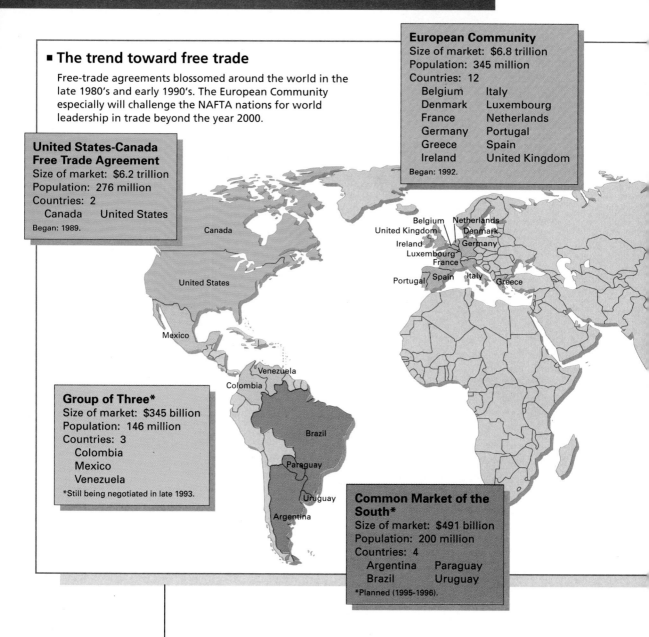

■ **The trend toward free trade**

Free-trade agreements blossomed around the world in the late 1980's and early 1990's. The European Community especially will challenge the NAFTA nations for world leadership in trade beyond the year 2000.

European Community
Size of market: $6.8 trillion
Population: 345 million
Countries: 12
Belgium Italy
Denmark Luxembourg
France Netherlands
Germany Portugal
Greece Spain
Ireland United Kingdom
Began: 1992.

United States-Canada Free Trade Agreement
Size of market: $6.2 trillion
Population: 276 million
Countries: 2
Canada United States
Began: 1989.

Group of Three*
Size of market: $345 billion
Population: 146 million
Countries: 3
Colombia
Mexico
Venezuela
*Still being negotiated in late 1993.

Common Market of the South*
Size of market: $491 billion
Population: 200 million
Countries: 4
Argentina Paraguay
Brazil Uruguay
*Planned (1995-1996).

International Trade Commission, for each $1 billion of exports, 17,000 jobs are created.) The removal of Mexican tariffs, which averaged more than twice U.S. tariffs, will give firms in the United States access to a rapidly growing market of more than 90 million people.

An expanding domestic market in Mexico combined with free trade with the United States will create jobs in both countries, NAFTA proponents said. They supported this argument with results from complex computer models that analyze trade and investment patterns. A widely cited outcome from such modeling released in January 1993 by economists at the Institute for International Economics in Washington, D.C., pointed to a gain of 170,000 U.S. jobs from 1990 to

Association of Southeast Asian Nations (ASEAN) Free Trade Area*

Size of market: $300 billion
Population: 341 million
Countries: 6

Brunei	Philippines
Indonesia	Singapore
Malaysia	Thailand

*Planned (1994).

Thailand
Philippines
Brunei
Malaysia
Singapore
Indonesia

1995 as a result of NAFTA and internal Mexican reforms. Economists were uncertain which industries these gains will favor, however. Conceding that some jobs might be lost despite the overall gain, supporters argued that displaced workers will primarily be in low-paying, unskilled occupations that would likely leave the United States for less developed countries anyway. Moreover, they said, the small size of the Mexican economy—its annual production is about 5 percent of U.S. levels—limited the number of jobs that could relocate from the United States. The potential increase of jobs in Mexico will also reduce undocumented immigration to the United States, lessening the pressure on workers in the United States, at least in the long run, supporters say.

Will low Mexican wages—currently about 15 percent of U.S. levels in manufacturing—drag down U.S. wages? Not really, said NAFTA supporters, because United States and Mexican workers do not usually compete. The United States has an advantage in highly skilled, automated production, while Mexico's edge is in less skilled, labor-intensive jobs. Mexican labor is low wage because Mexican workers, on average, produce considerably less than do U.S. workers, and the different wage levels in each country should therefore not significantly affect one another. Low wages alone are overrated as an attraction for automated production, proponents of NAFTA argued, because for such production to be successful, productivity must also be high. As former U.S. Trade Representative Carla A. Hills put it, in a frequently cited remark, "If wages were the only factor, many developing countries would be economic superpowers."

NAFTA supporters also claimed that the treaty will benefit the environment. NAFTA is "the greenest trade treaty ever," according to former U.S. Environmental Protection Agency (EPA) Director William Reilly. The treaty allows each country to maintain its existing environmental standards and even toughen them. Concern centered on Mexico's lax enforcement of its environmental laws. Many kinds of hazardous wastes have accumulated to dangerous levels in the soil and water in Mexico along the U.S. border, where many factories operate.

Such wastes include acidic chemicals, sometimes at levels thousands of times beyond EPA limits, pesticides that are illegal in the United States due to their harmful effects on human health, and sewage. But NAFTA supporters argued that Mexico has strong environmental protection laws and is devoting more resources to enforce those laws. For example, Mexico increased the number of environmental inspectors from about 100 in 1991 to more than 300 in 1992 and promised to spend more than the United States—almost $500-million through 1995—on border cleanup.

Finally, NAFTA advocates contended that Mexican political and economic stability could be seriously undermined if the U.S. Congress turned down the treaty. Due to President Salinas' strong support of NAFTA, its failure in the U.S. Congress could have badly damaged the governing party in Mexico—the Institutional Revolutionary Party (PRI)—possibly creating political instability in Mexico as the 1994 presidential elections approached. Moreover, much of the foreign investment that has been attracted to Mexico in recent years by the prospect of NAFTA could very well leave the country, leading to economic turmoil. Overall, supporters warned, U.S.-Mexican relations would be dealt a severe blow.

Arguments against NAFTA

Although the business community in the United States was generally enthusiastic about the treaty, most labor, environmental, and consumer groups were not. These critics did not oppose further economic integration with Mexico but questioned how NAFTA will accomplish this. NAFTA critics pointed out that before economies as different as those of Mexico and the United States could be brought closer together, significant social issues, such as wage differences, labor rights, and how judicial systems settle disputes, had to be addressed. Opponents contended that NAFTA provided strong guarantees for investors but ignored protection for workers and the environment.

NAFTA critics feared that the treaty will threaten jobs in the United States. Many computerized economic models that showed job gains in the United States as a result of NAFTA relied on false assumptions, opponents maintained, such as the assumption that investment in U.S. business will not suffer from increased investment in Mexico. Instead of the pie becoming larger, the bakery will move to Mexico, critics contended. Moreover, continued low wages will prevent Mexican workers from benefiting dramatically from any increased investment.

The explosive growth of export-oriented assembly plants known as *maquiladoras* during the late 1980's fueled many of the critics' fears. Maquiladoras import parts from manufacturers in the United States, paying no duty, and then ship assembled products back to the United States, paying tax only on the value of the work done in Mexico. There are maquiladoras that assemble automobile parts and others that assemble electronic products or other manufacturing components. The numbers of such maquiladoras grew from 620 employing 120,000 workers in 1980 to over 2,000 employing 550,000 workers in 1993. Proponents boast that these plants have become the second largest earner of foreign exchange for Mexico. Critics charge that maquiladora workers barely earn enough to survive.

Well-paying manufacturing jobs that require sophisticated skills could prove as vulnerable to export as low-paying assembly jobs, the treaty's adversaries maintained. Far from being unsophisticated and undeveloped, many Mexican companies have developed powerful technological capabilities. The productivity of the most advanced Mexican manufacturing plants and the quality of goods they produce compare well to U.S. or Japanese plants.

But Mexican salaries are a fraction of those in the United States. As U.S. manufacturers in industries ranging from electronics to automobiles consider this combination of high efficiency and low wages, they could decide to move plants to Mexico. Mexico is already one of the world's largest exporters of automobile engines, a highly complex product. More realistic computer models, according to critics, showed about 500,000 jobs—many of them core middle-class occupations—being lost from the United States by the year 2000 as a result of NAFTA.

Not only will the United States lose jobs to Mexico as a result of NAFTA, critics charged, but the treaty will also lower wages in the United States. Although the productivity and skills of Mexican workers have risen considerably since 1980, their wages have fallen by about 40 percent. Many factors, including government-controlled unions, employer federations, government policies to attract investment, and a large surplus labor force, pushed wages down, NAFTA opponents contended. If automobile manufacturers could assemble cars paying workers little more than $2 an hour in Mexico, opponents pointed out, this will put tremendous pressure on workers earning $18 an hour for the same work in the United States. If a U.S. firm moved even a single plant to Mexico, this would exert a chilling effect on wages in the plants that remained in the United States. Wage levels, like water, in this view, flow downhill.

Environmental concerns

NAFTA foes claimed that less rigorous environmental standards in Mexico could lower environmental standards in the United States and Canada. Environmentalists conceded that the laws designed to protect the environment in Mexico were comparable to those in the United States and Canada, but these critics expressed concern about the haphazard enforcement of Mexican regulations. Many environmentalists charged that Mexican officials often endorse environmental protection regulations without actually enforcing them. Environmentalists applauded some of Mexico's recent cleanup campaigns but were skeptical that stricter enforcement will continue after

■ Pros and cons of NAFTA

The debate over the benefits and drawbacks of NAFTA is complex, involving possible effects on each country's standard of living, and changes in the quality of the natural environment.

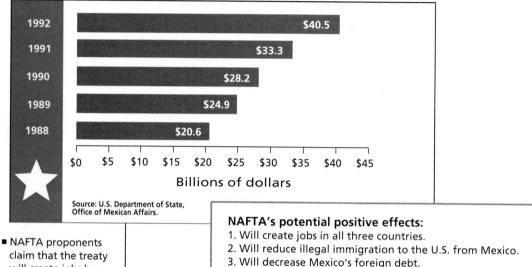

Year	Billions of dollars
1992	$40.5
1991	$33.3
1990	$28.2
1989	$24.9
1988	$20.6

Source: U.S. Department of State, Office of Mexican Affairs.

NAFTA's potential positive effects:
1. Will create jobs in all three countries.
2. Will reduce illegal immigration to the U.S. from Mexico.
3. Will decrease Mexico's foreign debt.
4. Will ensure markets for all three countries' goods in face of increasing competition from other free-trade blocs.

■ NAFTA proponents claim that the treaty will create jobs by helping continue the trend toward free trade with Mexico. Since Mexico began lowering tariffs on U.S. goods on its own in the late 1980's, U.S. exports to Mexico have soared, *above*. NAFTA supporters claim that each $1 billion of U.S. exports to Mexico creates about 17,000 jobs.

NAFTA was approved. Moreover, they said the language in the treaty itself was inadequate in a number of areas, such as specifying standards for how a product is made. The maquiladoras were a preview of the future, the critics contended. Although these factories expanded rapidly after 1980, wages did not rise, and the environment continued to worsen.

Critics acknowledged that the treaty's defeat in the U.S. Congress could disrupt Mexican politics, but they believed that the impact was overstated. A defeat might encourage greater democracy by strengthening the opposition in the next election and loosening the PRI's iron grip on government, NAFTA critics claimed. A NAFTA defeat would allow an opportunity to negotiate a new agreement emphasizing improved social and environmental standards throughout North America as the basis for economic integration.

Side agreements strengthen treaty

In August 1993, the three countries worked out side agreements on labor and environmental issues. These agreements set up provisions to ensure that each country upholds its existing laws in limited labor and environmental areas. The agreements also set up methods for re-

■ Pollution fouls the New River just across the U.S.-Mexican border at Calexico, Calif., *left.* The river is one of the most polluted in the United States. Much of the pollution comes from poisonous chemicals released by *maquiladoras*—U.S.-owned assembly plants just across the border in Mexico. NAFTA critics claim that Mexico's environmental standards are too lax and that increased manufacturing along the U.S.-Mexican border as a result of NAFTA will result in increased pollution.

NAFTA's potential negative effects:
1. Will damage the environment along the U.S.-Mexican border and possibly lead to a weakening of U.S. environmental laws.
2. Will cost U.S. jobs.
3. Will allow unfair labor practices by Mexico.
4. Will lower U.S. wages.

■ A worker assembles an automobile at a Ford Motor Company plant in Cuautitulán, Mexico, *above.* NAFTA critics claim that Mexico's low wages and skilled workers will attract high-paying manufacturing jobs away from the United States.

solving differences regarding these issues, including fines and trade sanctions against any government that violates these agreements.

The debate over NAFTA turned into one of the most passionate debates over trade issues in many years. Until several weeks before the vote in the U.S. House of Representatives on November 17, it seemed that opponents would garner enough votes to defeat the treaty. But President Clinton waged a fevered campaign that resulted in the passage of the treaty by a vote of 234 to 200. The U.S. Senate passed the treaty three days later. An open debate gave the U.S. public a broader understanding of how trade issues affect their lives. Future U.S. trade negotiations may thus become more politically charged as the public demands a similar debate.

For further reading:

Ebrahim, Margaret, and Lewis, Charles. "Can Mexico and Big Business USA Buy NAFTA?" *The Nation,* June 14, 1993, p. 826.

Prestowitz, Clyde. "Making the Free-Trade Agreement Work." *Technology Review,* April 28, 1993, p. 22.

Richman, L. S. "How NAFTA Will Help America." *Fortune,* April 19, 1993, p. 95.

"The Mexican Worker." *Business Week,* April 19, 1993, p. 84.

Iran. In March 1993, officials of the Administration of United States President Bill Clinton declared that Iran was the world's most dangerous sponsor of terrorism and stated U.S. intentions to curb Iran's armament program and regional influence. Iranian officials denied the U.S. claims, accusing the United States of having anti-Islamic policies.

In the spring of 1993, the United States began to pressure other nations not to sell military equipment or technology to Iran. Iran reportedly sought to buy biological, chemical, and nuclear weapon technology. Observers also believed that Iran bought antiship missiles, mines, and long-range ballistic missiles from North Korea and China. In August, Iran accepted delivery of the second of three nuclear submarines from Russia. The first submarine was delivered in 1992. These arms purchases and Iran's alleged attempts to export Islamic fundamentalism dashed hopes in 1993 by some Western officials that Iranian-U.S. relations would improve.

Terrorism. Mohammed Hussein Nagdi, a former Iranian diplomat who defected from Iran in 1982, was slain in Rome on March 16, 1993. His murder was reportedly the work of Iran's Islamic fundamentalist regime, which is thought to be responsible for the deaths of more then 30 Iranian dissidents since coming to power in 1979. On Feb. 4, 1993, Turkish officials accused pro-Iranian extremists of murdering two Turkish writers and an Iranian dissident living in Turkey for speaking against militant Islam. These murders occurred in late 1992 and early 1993.

On January 31, Iran's President Ali Akbar Hashemi Rafsanjani stated that he would not cancel a 1989 call for Muslims to kill British author Salman Rushdie. Iran considers Rushdie's novel, *The Satanic Verses* (1988), blasphemous to Islam.

Economic ills. Iran's national debt, $6.5 billion in 1989, rose to $40 billion in 1993. Unemployment topped 30 percent and inflation rose to 40 percent during the year. Floods and earthquakes of 1991 and 1992 and the nearly 4 million Afghan and Kurdish refugees in Iran also burdened the country. Oil, accounting for about 80 to 90 percent of Iran's export revenues, earned just $17 billion in 1993.

In March, the World Bank, an international lending agency of the United Nations, approved three loans totaling nearly $460 million for Iran, against U.S. wishes. The United States pressured the World Bank to suspend consideration of another $475 million in loans to Iran later in the year.

Regional relations. In 1993, Egypt and Algeria openly accused Iran of supporting Islamic extremists within their countries. The extremists were intent upon toppling the governments of Egypt and Algeria and sought an Islamic state similar to Iran's. On March 27, Algeria broke off relations with Iran.

On May 25, Iran sent two military planes into Iraq to attack guerrilla bases there. Iran said that the attacks were in retaliation for guerrilla raids into Iran

by the People's Mujaheddin, a group of exiled Iranians opposed to the current regime.

Iranian pilgrims came close to conflict during the annual Islamic *hajj* (pilgrimage) to Mecca, Saudi Arabia. On May 27, Saudi soldiers kept 100,000 Iranian pilgrims from conducting a protest against the United States and Israel. In 1987, 402 people died in a violent clash between Iranians and Saudi security forces in Mecca during the hajj.

On Sept. 14, 1993, Iranian President Rafsanjani condemned the peace accord that granted limited self-rule to Palestinians in the Israeli-occupied Gaza Strip and the West Bank town of Jericho. The accord between Israel and the Palestine Liberation Organization was signed on September 13 in Washington, D.C. Pro-Iranian groups in parts of the Arab world, particularly the Hezbollah in Lebanon, staged protests against the agreement that resulted in several deaths. (See also **Lebanon.**)

Elections. On June 11, President Rafsanjani won reelection in a four-way race for the Iranian presidency. Only 56 percent of eligible Iranian voters cast ballots, and Rafsanjani won only 63 percent of the votes. By contrast, in 1989 Rafsanjani won almost 95 percent of the votes with a 70 percent voter turnout. The low turnout in 1993 was interpreted as a sign of frustration with the regime. □ Christine Helms

See also **Islam; Middle East** (Facts in brief table). In *World Book,* see **Iran.**

Iraq. Iraq's President Saddam Hussein clung to power in 1993 in spite of harsh United Nations (UN) sanctions. The United States hoped that the economic sanctions, imposed after Iraq invaded Kuwait in 1990, would help topple Hussein. However, Hussein was untouched, and Iraqis complained that the sanctions only hurt average citizens.

In July 1993, Rolf Ekeus, head of the UN team dismantling Iraq's weapons, said their work was mainly finished. Under the terms of the cease-fire that ended the Persian Gulf War (1991), Iraq had agreed to allow UN inspectors to destroy its facilities for producing biological, chemical, and nuclear weapons.

During September 1993 meetings at UN headquarters in New York City, Iraq indicated it would accept weapons monitoring but wanted assurances that the UN sanctions would be eased. On November 26, Iraq formally agreed to long-term monitoring of its weapons programs. This appeared to remove the last remaining obstacle, many UN officials believed, to lifting or easing the sanctions that prohibited Iraqi oil sales. Nonetheless, officials said on November 29 that this could not happen until Iraq had shown willing compliance for a period of six months.

The United States, however, insisted that other resolutions against Iraq had to be met before the embargo could be lifted. These resolutions included monitoring human rights in Iraq and Iraqi acceptance of a redefined Iraq-Kuwait border.

Iraqis survey damage to housing facilities in a Baghdad suburb after a U.S. missile attack that also destroyed Iraqi intelligence headquarters there in June.

Allied bombings. In mid-January, American-led allied forces conducted several bombings of Iraqi military sites. These took place after Iraq was told to remove antiaircraft missiles from southern Iraq and stop impeding UN arms inspectors.

On January 17, the United States launched about 40 cruise missiles against an industrial complex near the Iraqi capital, Baghdad. One of the missiles hit the Al Rashid Hotel in Baghdad, killing two Iraqi civilians and wounding several Iraqis and foreigners. On January 20, France became the first allied coalition member to criticize the United States for the attack, which France said went beyond UN resolutions.

Alleged plot. On June 27, a U.S. cruise-missile attack destroyed Iraq's intelligence headquarters in Baghdad and killed eight civilians. President Bill Clinton said the attack was in retaliation for an alleged Iraqi plot to assassinate former U.S. President George Bush during a mid-April visit to Kuwait. The U.S. attack was widely criticized because it took place before the suspects, including 11 Iraqis, were found guilty. On October 30, a Kuwaiti judge postponed a verdict in the suspects' trial.

UN sanctions created severe hardships in Iraq in 1993. Although one Iraqi dinar was officially valued at $3.20, one U.S. dollar could buy 150 dinars on Iraq's black market in November. Food and spare parts were scarce and costly. Consequently, general health conditions deteriorated, and protein deficiencies became common. The percentage of Iraqi babies born under 5.5 pounds (2.5 kilograms), a risk factor in newborn deaths, rose from 4.5 percent in 1990 to more than 17 percent in 1993. Diseases such as cholera and polio reemerged. Amebic dysentery was widespread due to a lack of chemicals for purifying water.

Kurds. The troubled economy also hurt northern Iraq, which is populated mainly by Kurds. Hussein maintained an economic blockade of the region in order to squelch Kurdish rebel activity. The rebels, who receive foreign aid, set up their own government in defiance of Baghdad. However, insufficient foreign aid in 1993 fueled disputes in the north between rival Kurdish groups, between Kurds and non-Kurds, and between Muslims and Christians. Turkey, Iran, and Syria also expressed concern in 1993 that spreading Kurdish unrest could destabilize their shared border area.

Currency change. On May 5, Iraq sealed its borders and set a six-day deadline for Iraqis to exchange older 25-dinar notes for a new bill, claiming the measure was necessary because hoarding of Iraqi money by speculators had contributed to inflation. Kurds condemned the action as political pressure. In April, agents reportedly sold more than $3 million in Iraqi-owned gold in Jordan.　　　□ Christine Helms

See also **Middle East** (Facts in brief table). In *World Book,* see **Iraq; Persian Gulf War.**

Ireland. After an inconclusive general election on Nov. 25, 1992, plunged Ireland into political turmoil, a new coalition government was finally sworn in on Jan. 12, 1993. Prime Minister Albert Reynolds retained office and forged a coalition between his conservative Fianna Fáil (Soldiers of Destiny) party and the left wing Labour Party headed by Dick Spring. It was the first time in the republic's history that Fianna Fáil shared power with Labour. The coalition held 101 seats in the 166-seat parliament—a record 36-seat majority. Reynolds gave 6 of the 15 Cabinet seats to Labour. Spring became deputy prime minister as well as minister for foreign affairs.

Five-year plan. Reynolds and Spring worked out a coalition agreement that called for a five-year blueprint for change. The two parties pledged support for a program that would cost 270 million Irish pounds (U.S. $432 million) to create 30,000 jobs. Nearly 20 percent of the people were unemployed during 1993. The program would be financed largely through funds provided by the European Community (EC, or Common Market), of which Ireland is a member. Other aspects of the plan included an ambitious program to improve roads and railways.

Pummeling the pound. The new government faced an ongoing economic recession and crippling interest rates. But the first challenge it faced directly was defending the value of the Irish pound. Foreign currency speculators bought the pound with loans, anticipating that the Irish government would be forced to devalue the currency and then they would make a profit by repaying the loans with cheaper pounds. The Irish pound is in the EC's Exchange Rate Mechanism, which calls for members to maintain the value of their currency at prescribed levels.

On January 27, speculator demand forced the Irish Central Bank to raise overnight interest rates from 14 percent to 100 percent. Reynolds insisted that devaluation was not an option. But the wave of selling continued unabated across Europe, and on January 30, Ireland reluctantly devalued the pound by 10 percent. Irish leaders expressed bitter disappointment with the failure of other EC banks to support the Irish pound. The experience raised questions about the capacity and the willingness of the EC to defend any currency against speculators.

Social issues. On June 24, the government legalized homosexual activities for people age 17 and above. It also announced plans to hold a referendum on divorce in 1994. Conservatives and the Roman Catholic hierarchy opposed both moves. On July 20, 1993, the Irish Supreme Court by a vote of 4 to 1 refused to overturn a ban on a Dublin clinic's distribution of information about overseas abortion facilities. The court delivered its ruling in spite of a 1992 referendum that supported guaranteed access to abortion information. □ Ian J. Mather

See also **Northern Ireland.** In *World Book,* see **Ireland.**

Islam. Ethnic, religious, and political conflicts continued to shape the public image of Islam in 1993. Among the main concerns were strife between Hindus and Muslims in India and atrocities against Muslims in Bosnia-Herzegovina. Terrorist attacks by Islamic militants continued in Egypt, Israel, and elsewhere. But there were also acts of reconciliation, such as a peace accord signed in September granting limited self-rule to Palestinians, who are mostly Muslims, in the Israeli-occupied Gaza Strip and Jericho.

A radical Muslim cleric and his followers became the focus of United States legal proceedings after they were implicated in the February 26 bombing of the World Trade Center in New York City and in plots, reported in June, to bomb other New York locations and assassinate political figures. Sheik Omar Abdel Rahman—a native Egyptian who presided over a small mosque in Jersey City, N.J.—was indicted on August 25, along with 14 associates, on charges of conspiring to engage in a war of terror against the United States. The indictments prompted fears of reprisals against American Muslims.

Sheik Omar, who was blind from childhood, had been a militant activist since the 1970's, when he became religious adviser to al-Jama'at al-Islamiya (the Islamic Group), an organization that opposed the Egyptian regime. In 1982, he was acquitted in Egypt on charges of advocating the assassination of Egyptian President Anwar Sadat in 1981. (See **Crime.**)

Muslim cleric Sheik Omar Abdel Rahman, a suspect in terrorist plots in New York City, prepares to surrender to U.S. immigration officials in July.

Islam in America. A poll reported by the Gallup organization in 1993 found that 1 percent of adult Americans identify themselves as Muslims, meaning that American Muslims numbered about 3.5 million people. Most American Muslims are immigrants from the Middle East and South Asia, but an estimated 500,000 to 1.5 million are native-born. The Islamic Resource Institute, a research organizaion based in Tustin, Calif., reported in June that there were more than 1,500 mosques and Islamic centers in the United States.

British author Salman Rushdie remained in hiding in 1993, four years after Iran's Ayatollah Ruhollah Khomeini condemned him to death for his treatment of Islam in his novel *The Satanic Verses* (1988). Arab and Muslim intellectuals offered their most significant defense of Rushdie to date with the autumn publication in France of *Pour Rushdie (For Rushdie),* an anthology of writings in defense of the right to publish works of religious controversy. Included was an opinion by a Shiite Muslim jurist declaring Khomeini's decree invalid on the basis of Islamic law.

Women's gains. Two Muslim women—Benazir Bhutto of Pakistan and Tansu Ciller of Turkey—were elected their nations' prime ministers in 1993. The two overcame the opposition of Islamic and secular opponents to win office. □ Vincent J. Cornell

In *World Book,* see **Muslims; Islam.**

Israel. On Sept. 13, 1993, representatives of Israel and the Palestine Liberation Organization (PLO) signed a "Declaration of Principles" in Washington, D.C., setting forth details for Palestinian self-rule in the Israeli-occupied Arab territories of the Gaza Strip and the town of Jericho in the West Bank. With a historic handshake, Israeli Prime Minister Yitzhak Rabin and PLO leader Yasir Arafat pledged to seek a peaceful end to more than 45 years of bloody Arab-Israeli conflict. The signing ceremony, attended by world leaders and presided over by United States President Bill Clinton, was broadcast worldwide.

News that Israel and the PLO had been secretly negotiating peace under Norwegian sponsorship since January 1993 stunned the world when it was revealed in August. The final obstacle to the accord was overcome several days prior to the signing when Rabin and Arafat exchanged letters in which Israel recognized the PLO as the sole representative of the Palestinian people and the PLO acknowledged Israel's right to exist as a nation.

Despite hopes raised by the ceremony, Jewish and Arab extremists vowed to derail the agreement. Many Israeli Jews, who have long thought of Arafat as a terrorist, doubted his sincerity. And many Arabs felt that Arafat had accepted too little on their behalf. Nonetheless, the Israeli parliament approved the agreement on September 23 in a 61 to 50 vote.

Due to an outbreak of violence in reaction to the peace agreement, a December 13 deadline for the withdrawal of Israeli troops from the Gaza Strip and Jericho was postponed. By December 15, at least 44 Arabs and 18 Israelis had died in the clashes.

Violent prelude to peace. By March, more than 75 Palestinians and 17 Israelis had been killed in strife that began on Dec. 17, 1992, when Rabin deported 415 Palestinian men to a remote area of southern Lebanon. Most of the men were accused of being members of the Islamic militant group Hamas.

In March 1993, 15 Israelis and more than 25 Palestinians were killed, making it the bloodiest month since the Palestinian *intifada* (uprising) began in 1987. On March 30, Rabin sealed off the West Bank and Gaza Strip, and violence abated. But the ban allowed only 50,000 of 120,000 Arabs to commute to daily jobs in Israel. The resulting loss of income fueled Arab extremism as the economic plight of Palestinians worsened. The incomes of Arab laborers working in Israel in 1992 reportedly accounted for 50 percent of earnings in the Gaza Strip and 30 percent in the West Bank. Israeli agriculture and construction, much of it dependent on Arab labor, lost millions of dollars as a result of the ban.

In a peace gesture on Sept. 9, 1993, Israel readmitted 189 of the 415 Arab deportees, and the remainder returned by the year's end. Israel had received criticism for its failure to abide by UN resolution 799, passed Dec. 18, 1992, which demanded the immediate return of all the deportees.

Assault on Lebanon. In late July 1993, Israel bombarded targets north of a security zone maintained by Israel in southern Lebanon. The bombardment was in response to rocket attacks on Israel by the pro-Iranian Hezbollah (Party of God). Rabin hoped the offensive, the largest since Israel invaded Lebanon in 1982, would force the Lebanese government to restrain the Hezbollah. Following what Rabin termed a cease-fire "understanding" on July 31, 1993, Israeli officials said Syria and Lebanon had agreed to help halt Hezbollah attacks on Israel. The offensive killed about 130 Lebanese, wounded 600, and displaced about 300,000 from 70 villages.

Economic news. The Israeli economy was projected to grow by 4 percent in 1993. Inflation fell to just under 10 percent, the lowest figure in more than a decade. Statistics showed that, in 1992, Israeli exports had risen by 14 percent and there were a record 1.8 million tourists.

Unemployment remained at 11 percent in 1993, mainly because of the influx of about 6,000 immigrants a month. Servicing Israel's $23-billion debt ate up almost 30 percent of the 1993 budget, defense took 18 percent, and social services used 25 percent. Many Israelis disliked the nation's dependency upon an annual $3 billion in U.S. aid. Some also faulted Rabin for his failure to move more quickly to privatize state-owned banks and companies, which allegedly discouraged foreign investment.

Israeli soldiers shield their ears as they fire heavy artillery aimed at targets in southern Lebanon in July.

Foreign relations. Responding to U.S. pressure, Israel announced on August 16 that it was suspending trade talks with North Korea which began in October 1992. Israel had hoped that it could induce North Korea not to sell its Rodong-1 missiles to Syria and Iran. The missiles have a range of 700 miles (1,100 kilometers), which puts them within striking distance of Israel if fired from Syria or Iran. The United States hoped that economic isolation would prompt North Korea to allow international inspections of its nuclear-energy sites.

In mid-December 1993, Israel and the Vatican agreed to establish full diplomatic ties. Although the Roman Catholic Church had recognized Israel as a nation, it had long refused a diplomatic exchange. An agreement to formalize relations was to be signed December 30.

John Demjanjuk. On July 29, 1993, the Israeli Supreme Court overturned a 1988 death sentence against John Demjanjuk. Citing new evidence, the court said it was not certain Demjanjuk was guilty of being Ivan the Terrible, a Nazi concentration camp guard during World War II (1939-1945). Appeals that he be tried for other war crimes were rejected on Sept. 19, 1993, by a Supreme Court justice, and Demjanjuk was deported to the United States three days later.   □ Christine Helms

See also **Middle East** (Facts in brief table). In *World Book,* see **Israel.**

Italy endured political, social, and economic turmoil in 1993 as a corruption scandal spread to nearly every aspect of Italian life. Public outrage helped usher in a new government and voting system.

Scandal widens. A local investigation in 1992 into the Socialist Party in Milan mushroomed in 1993 into a national probe in which more than 2,600 people, including some 150 politicians, were investigated or jailed, most on charges involving bribes for political or business favors. The probe snared members of politics, business, the judiciary, and the Mafia.

The scandal shook up several political parties. On February 11, Bettino Craxi, a former prime minister, was forced to resign as head of the Socialist Party because of corruption charges. Craxi's successor, Giorgio Benvenuto, then quit on May 20 in frustration at his party's effort to block reform proposals. Leaders of the Republican and Liberal parties also resigned in 1993 in the face of corruption allegations.

Another fallen leader was Giulio Andreotti, who had been prime minister seven times and who was one of Italy's most respected politicians. On March 27, Andreotti revealed that he was being investigated for ties to the Mafia. Then on May 13, the upper house of Parliament, the Senate, lifted Andreotti's parliamentary immunity to criminal prosecution, clearing the way for a wider probe into his conduct.

Electoral changes. Disgusted with the scandal, voters on April 18 and 19 approved eight referendums on government reform. In the most significant result, Italians voted to change the electoral system for three-quarters of the Senate seats from one of *proportional representation,* in which political parties are awarded seats based on the percentage of votes won, to one of electoral districts, in which candidates vie for individual seats. The proportional representation system had allowed numerous political parties to gain parliamentary seats, leading to the weak coalition governments that were at the root of Italy's corruption problems.

The success of the referendums prompted the lower house of Parliament, the Chamber of Deputies, to adopt similar reforms on June 30. On August 4, Parliament wrote the electoral reforms for both houses into law. The first elections under the new system were expected sometime in early 1994.

New prime minister. The approval of the reforms led Prime Minister Giuliano Amato to resign on April 22, 1993. Amato was succeeded by Carlo Azeglio Ciampi, the governor of Italy's central bank. Ciampi was not a member of any of Italy's political parties, and he responded to the public mood of disgust at official corruption by appointing a government mainly of independent experts. Ciampi took office on April 29. (See also **Ciampi, Carlo Azeglio.**)

Communist victories. On December 5, candidates backed by Italy's former Communist Party defeated right wing opponents in mayoral elections in

five major cities—Rome, Naples, Genoa, Venice, and Trieste. Among the losers was Alessandra Mussolini, granddaughter of Fascist dictator Benito Mussolini.

Suicides shock. On July 20, Gabriele Cagliari, former chairman of the state-run energy company ENI, committed suicide in his prison cell in Milan. Cagliari was under investigation for allegedly paying kickbacks to political parties during ENI's purchase in 1990 of a chemical company from the Italian conglomerate Montedison SpA. Then on July 23, 1993, Raul Gardini, who had been chairman of Montedison's parent company, Ferruzzi, during the ENI transaction, shot himself to death at his home in Milan. Police speculated that Cagliari and Gardini feared the testimony of another former Montedison executive who had been arrested on July 13.

Bomb attacks. On May 27, a car bomb exploded near the Uffizi Gallery in Florence, killing five people and destroying numerous artworks. Car bombs also went off in Rome and Milan. Investigators believed the bombs were planted by the Mafia in retaliation for the arrest of several top Mafia leaders.

In other crime news, Italian police on November 12 announced that they had issued arrest warrants for 18 people suspected in the May 1992 murder of Italy's top Mafia prosecutor, Giovanni Falcone. □ Philip Revzin

See also **Europe** (Facts in brief table). In *World Book,* see **Italy.**

Italians march in Rome in July to show their outrage at three car bombings that killed five people in Rome and Milan.

How did a secret criminal organization that originated in Sicily in the 1860's infiltrate the top levels of the Italian government?

Italy Confronts the Mafia

By Alexander Stille

O n Jan. 15, 1993, Italian police arrested the alleged "boss of bosses" of the Italian Mafia, Salvatore Riina, on a street in Palermo, Sicily. Riina had eluded arrest for 23 years. On May 18, the police raided a Sicilian farmhouse and captured Riina's ally and heir-apparent to head the Mafia, Benedetto Santapaola. He had evaded capture for 11 years. During the year, 501 "men of honor," the traditional name for Mafia members, were cooperating with Italian prosecutors, revealing the secrets of the mob and the names of its political protectors. The once impregnable wall of *omertà* (silence) that surrounded the Mafia in Italy appeared to be shattering in 1993.

Observers have long considered the Mafia's alliance with Italy's politicians to be the secret source of its extraordinary power. But proving that the link existed had been beyond the grasp of Italian prosecutors. In 1993, however, the government used information from Mafia informants to indict 11 members of the Italian Parliament, including Italy's most powerful politician and seven times its prime minister, Giulio Andreotti. Prosecutors accused the politicians of being in league with the Mafia, doling out public works projects to

Mafia-controlled companies in return for illegal payments and using their influence to get Mafia convictions overturned.

Italian authorities do not claim to have defeated the Mafia. Indeed, many think that the Mafia engineered several terrorist bombings that rocked Italian cities in the spring and summer of 1993. But undoubtedly, the year marked a major turning point in Italy's war against organized crime.

Organization and origins

The Mafia in Italy is made up of three main criminal organizations based in the south, Italy's most underdeveloped region. The Camorra group is active in the Naples area. The N'Drangheta group is based in the Calabria region. And the Cosa Nostra operates throughout the island of Sicily, the birthplace of Mafia traditions. Nevertheless, in Italy, the Mafia has come to mean any one of these groups, or all of them.

Unlike other kinds of modern, organized crime groups, the Mafia is a secret association with strict rules of internal discipline that have helped make it resistant to outside penetration. In the case of Cosa Nostra (*Our Thing*), members are required to be Sicilian and cannot have relatives in law enforcement. They take an initiation oath never to betray the organization and to maintain silence about the group's activities. Each "man of honor" is a member of a "family" that controls a specific territory.

Unlike bandits or common thieves who usually live outside respectable society, most *mafiosi* (Mafia members) work at normal jobs and appear to be law-abiding citizens. But when the need arises, they use force or the intimidating power of the organization to extort advantage from others. Although mafiosi have often cultivated the image of being modern-day "Robin Hoods" who rob the rich to give to the poor, they have always been dedicated to self-enrichment, never hesitating to use violent force to get what they want. The Mafia draws on a centuries-old code of behavior that requires its members to refuse to cooperate with police authorities and to carry out their own form of private justice, which includes torture and murder.

Many historians view the Mafia as a product of Sicily's tumultuous history. For example, the Mafia's code of behavior can be traced back to centuries of corrupt and brutal government by foreign conquerors of Sicily, which taught most Sicilians to regard government with suspicion and hostility. To some extent, the Mafia is rooted in Sicilian feudal society that lasted until the 1800's, when most of Sicily's land belonged to a few people. Peasants cultivated the fields for the benefit of the landowners, and the landlords hired armed guards to maintain order, with force if necessary. These armed guards, the precursors of the mafiosi, became intermediaries between the peasants and the landowner, on the one hand keeping the peasants in line and on the other guaranteeing the landlord that the harvest would be gathered and the animals tended.

Gradually, the landlords moved off their estates to cities, especially to Palermo. The early mafiosi then began to use their control of the

■ *Preceding pages:*
Salvatore Riina, the alleged "boss of bosses" of the Sicilian Mafia, awaits trial for multiple murders in a Rome prison in 1993. Hundreds of convicted mobsters are imprisoned on the island of Pianosa (background).

■ **The author**
Alexander Stille is a free-lance writer who is currently at work on a book about the war on the Mafia in Sicily.

▪ What is the Mafia?

The Mafia is a secret criminal society based in three main groups that operate out of southern Italy, *right*. The Camorra group operates in the Naples area; the N'Drangheta in the Calabria region; and the Cosa Nostra in Sicily. Beginning in the 1940's, according to the authorities, the Mafia forged an unofficial link with the Christian Democratic government, guaranteeing votes in return for relative freedom to continue its criminal activities in Italy. In the 1970's, the Mafia began amassing huge sums from international drug trafficking and took over legitimate businesses in order to "launder" its illegal drug profits, according to police. In the 1990's, Mafia crime reportedly included a wide variety of activity, *below*.

Europe

Adriatic Sea

Italy

Sardinia

Mediterranean Sea

Africa

Sicily

★ Rome

Italy

● Naples

Tyrrhenian Sea

Calabria

Ionian Sea

Trapani ●

● **Palermo**

● Reggio di Calabria

● Corleone

Sicily ● **Catania**

Agrigento ●

Alleged Mafia activities

- ❏ Arms and drug trafficking
- ❏ Bribery
- ❏ Construction rackets
- ❏ Control of wholesale markets
- ❏ Electoral fraud
- ❏ Extortion
- ❏ Gambling
- ❏ Infiltration of all levels of government
- ❏ Insurance fraud
- ❏ Kidnapping
- ❏ Money laundering
- ❏ Murder
- ❏ Political assassination
- ❏ Smuggling
- ❏ Infiltration of real estate and other legitimate businesses

▪ Corleone, Sicily, *above*, is the symbolic center of the world of Mafia power. It is home to Salvatore Riina, the reputed "boss of bosses" of the main Cosa Nostra group. With about 600 members, the Corleone clan under Riina was linked to the deaths of nearly 1,000 people during its climb to the top of the mob in the 1980's.

■ **Mafia trials and retaliation**
Judges confer during the 1987 trial of more than 450 mobsters in the largest Mafia trial in Italian history, *above*. For security reasons, the defendants were kept in cages at the back of the courtroom. A car bomb attack in Palermo, *left,* killed former trial prosecutor Paolo Borsellino, who had become the chief anti-Mafia prosecutor in Sicily, on July 19, 1992.

land to extract concessions from the now absentee landlord. For example, they charged the landlord for guaranteeing his safety in traveling to his estate. And the early mafiosi had a free hand in dealing with the peasants, punishing those who disobeyed, settling disputes, and even allocating plots of land and other resources. In effect, the functions of government became the domain of these early mafiosi.

Sicily's long history as a conquered possession also meant that the island was out of the mainstream of Italian cultural development. The island remained in the grip of feudal traditions long after feudalism ended in Italy and elsewhere. The contrast between Sicily and the Italian mainland was perhaps most apparent during the 1860's and 1870's. That was when Italy completed its drive to unite the many separate states

of the mainland with the Kingdom of Sardinia, which consisted of the island of Sardinia and the northern region of Piedmont on the mainland, to form a modern nation. Northern Italian troops under the command of Giuseppe Garibaldi, Italy's most popular national hero, invaded Sicily in 1860, when the island was part of the Kingdom of the Two Sicilies under the rule of Spain. Garibaldi's mission was to help Sicilians fight the Spanish forces for Sicily's freedom. Then Sicily could join a united Italy ruled by an elected Parliament and King Victor Emmanuel II.

However, when the new government took control of Sicily, it encountered rampant crime. After unification, which occurred in 1861,

253

The Mafia-government connection

Christian Democrats have been the main party in power in Italy since Fascism fell at the end of World War II (1939-1945). After the war, coalition governments controlled by the Christian Democrats set out to develop southern Italy's traditionally weak economy through public works projects. Early on, the Mafia reportedly recognized an opportunity to enrich its coffers by infiltrating the south's construction industry. The mob traded votes for public contracts and judicial protection, and the Christian Democrats built a power base in southern Italy. According to investigators, a typical case of corruption might work in this way:

The national government in Rome plans to build a subway in Naples.

⇩

The subway contract goes to a legitimate construction company.

⇩

The Mafia forces the legitimate company to subcontract to smaller companies that the Mafia controls.

⇩

The project drags on for years, keeping workers employed and inflating the project's cost through overruns.

⇩

The Mafia rewards politicians responsible for appropriating money for the project.

⇩

At election time, the Mafia brings out the vote for candidates favored by the mob.

⇩

The favored parties remain in power, providing more public works and protecting Mafia interests.

■ Seven times prime minister of Italy, Christian Democrat Giulio Andreotti, *above* (center), faced an investigation in 1993 for alleged links to the Mafia. He denied the allegations. Andreotti's close associate, Salvatore Lima, *above* (right), was shot dead on March 12, 1992, reportedly for not getting Mafia convictions overturned.

the northern Italians were struck by the Sicilians' refusal to cooperate with the new government. Unification expanded trade and opened up possibilities for the lower classes to participate in the chaotic grab for land and wealth that ensued. But with no tradition of law or public administration to fall·back on, violence or the threat of violence became the easiest way to gain a leg up on the competition.

The word "Mafia" entered the Italian vocabulary at this time to describe organized crime in Sicily. Bandits terrorized the countryside, murdering government troops. The new government broke up the great feudal estates and auctioned off the land to the peasants. But criminal bands manipulated the sales for their own advantage, acquiring more parcels than the rules allowed and stationing "guards"at the sales. Criminals extorted money from new businesses, demanding payment for "protection."

Mafia members were generally of the lower and middle classes, but they influenced all social strata because people came to them for help rather than to government authorities whom Sicilians regarded with their traditional distrust. The Mafia intruded in all aspects of daily life, and Mafia power grew. Crime in Sicily reached such epidemic proportions that it became the subject of an enormous national debate in the Italian Parliament in 1874. The conservative national government proposed emergency police measures to regain control of the island. But the Sicilian police were implicated in Mafia crime, and Sicilian politicians, rather than calling for investigations, covered up criminal activity.

Ultimately, the crime issue brought down the

national government in 1876. Public order in Sicily was finally restored through a compromise between the Mafia and the national government that set a pattern for the future. The Mafia helped track down and arrest bandits, who were the most visible threat to public security, and in exchange, the government allowed the Mafia to continue its criminal activities with little or no punishment.

Politics: a new source of power

The Mafia also began to corrupt political life in the early days of unified Italy. Sicilian politicians sought Mafia help in getting votes in local and national elections. At the time, only the wealthy could vote. In 1913, voting privileges were extended to all adult males, and the Mafia lost no time in recognizing new opportunities to acquire political influence among these new voters.

The first effective attempt to control the Mafia came from Italian dictator Benito Mussolini. In October 1922, Italy's King Victor Emmanuel III named Mussolini prime minister. Mussolini not only abolished elections in 1925, taking away a source of the Mafia's power, but in 1926, he began a bloody attempt to suppress the Mafia in Sicily. Mussolini could not tolerate an authority parallel to his own. The campaign of suppression mainly hit the less important Mafia bosses, leaving the top leaders untouched. Nevertheless, Mussolini's era was a difficult one for Sicily's crime bosses, and they were quick to throw it off at the earliest possible moment.

The moment came in 1943, when Sicily was liberated by Allied troops during World War II (1939-1945). Military leaders of the occupying forces from the United Kingdom and the United States were anxious to exclude both Communists and Fascists from power. Allied military occupation lasted only six months, but during that time, Allied authorities installed several prominent mafiosi as town mayors. Also during this time, many mafiosi backed a new movement of Sicilian separatism. The movement's goal was to free Sicily from Italy. The Mafia helped organize a small guerrilla army to fight national forces on the island, but the cause of separatism faded once it became clear that the Allies did not support separatism.

Determined to avoid the persecution it had suffered under Fascism, the Mafia strove for political protection in the postwar order. New parties had emerged, and the Italian Communist Party seemed to be on the brink of winning national power at the polls. Mafia bosses sensed that their fortunes lay with the new anti-Communist parties, such as the Christian Democratic Party, which accepted Mafia support as a bulwark against Communism.

The Mafia's opposition to the Communists and other parties of the left could be brutal. For example, from 1945 to 1948, the Mafia and Sicilian bandits had dozens of union organizers and Communists murdered in Sicily, often around election time. Perhaps the most infamous incident occurred on May 1, 1947. Ten days earlier, on April 20, the united left (Communists and Socialists) had won an impressive 30 percent of the vote against 21 percent garnered by the Christian

Democratic Party in regional elections. Communist farmers from the area around the town of Portella della Ginestra gathered to celebrate May Day and the electoral victory. With the protection and support of the Mafia, a Sicilian bandit named Salvatore Giuliano and his gang opened fire on the crowd, killing 11 people.

Once Sicilian bandits like Giuliano had exhausted their usefulness and had become a public menace and embarrassment, the Mafia captured or killed them, handing them over dead or alive to the Italian police. Italian judges of the period openly praised the Mafia's role as intermediary. In 1955, a member of Italy's highest court, Giuseppe Guido Lo Schiavo wrote an outright defense of the Mafia: "People say the Mafia does not respect the police and the judiciary. It's untrue. The Mafia has always respected the judiciary and justice, has bowed before its sentences, and has not interfered with the judge's work. In the persecution of bandits and outlaws . . . it has actually joined together with the police."

This benign view of the Mafia made it easier for some politicians to accept the Mafia's backing and to overlook its corrosive effects on Italian life. For example, since the 1950's, the Christian Democrats have depended heavily on southern Italy as a reservoir of votes. With Mafia help, the party consistently won between 40 and 50 percent of the vote in most parts of Sicily, but struggled to win more than 30 percent in many northern cities, where Mafia influence was minimal.

The Mafia and drugs

During the 1950's and 1960's, attempts to combat organized crime were at best sporadic and were generally only in response to public outrage over a particularly grisly killing. More often, the Mafia avoided killing public officials, seeking compromise and not conflict. The picture changed in the late 1970's, however, when illegal drugs became an important part of the Mafia's business. Police and judges in Palermo became more vigilant as they discovered that Sicily had replaced France as the principal gateway for heroin destined for the United States. A new generation of law enforcement officials tried to break up this traffic, and the Mafia reacted by murdering them.

During the 1980's, the Mafia killed chief prosecutors, police officials, and major politicians, shocking many Italians into realizing how mistaken they had been to tolerate the growth of Mafia power. Investigations showed that not only had the Mafia polluted life through the drug trade, but also it had taken advantage of Italy's public works projects, threatening the country's ability to control its national debt.

By the 1990's, public spending had grown to represent 52 percent of Italy's *gross domestic product* (the total value of goods and services produced within a nation). Much of this spending went into public works projects, and investigations showed that as a result of collusion between the Mafia and the government, the Mafia was systematically awarded public works contracts. Furthermore, politicians added in an amount that went directly to the Mafia—at times as much as 10 percent of a contract worth millions of dollars.

■ A member of Parliament in April 1993 urges citizens to *vota si* (vote yes) on a referendum to change Italy's electoral system, *left.* A campaign for electoral change began in 1990. In June 1991, voters approved a referendum to simplify their proportional voting system, which had led to a stream of coalition governments and invited widespread fraud. But the reform proved to be inadequate. The April 1993 referendum discarded the old system altogether.

This was especially true in the south, where public money accounted for 70 percent of the economy in 1992. Because the Mafia dominates southern Italy's construction industry, many well-intentioned efforts to industrialize southern Italy ended up financing and expanding the Mafia's power. For example, the government spent billions of dollars during the 1980's trying to build a huge electric plant in Gioia Tauro in Calabria only to abandon it, after the Camorra crime group had taken control of all the contracts to build the plant. The Mafia was reaping a fortune, but work had come to a virtual halt. Furthermore, the Mafia model was being imitated by other criminal groups in areas of southern Italy once considered free of organized crime.

Italians were also stunned by scandal in the north that began surfacing in February 1992. The business community there, which had once been content to pay bribes for a share of government contracts, rebelled against the system. Companies realized that they could never compete internationally if they continued to be drained by larger and larger kickbacks to politicians. The cooperation of business leaders with prosecutors in Milan, who were conducting a bribery investigation known as "Operation Clean Hands," led to thousands of arrests. Since the investigation began in February 1992, nearly one-third of the Italian Parliament has been indicted on corruption charges.

In the early 1990's, the public attitude toward the Mafia also began to change because of new political alignments following the end of the Cold War. In the past, many Italian voters were prepared to overlook widespread corruption rather than accept a Communist-led government. "Hold your nose and vote Christian Democrat," conservative editor Indro Montanelli advised his readers in the mid-1970's, when the Communists were on the verge of overtaking the Christian Democrats as Italy's largest party. But with the end of the Cold War and the demise of the Communist Party, which had renounced Leninist doctrine and renamed itself the Democratic Party of the Left, the stench of Mafia murder and corruption became unbearable.

Assassinations jolt the public

Under public pressure, the government began an aggressive campaign to capture and convict Mafia members. The Mafia reacted with escalating violence. On March 12, 1992, Mafia killers allegedly murdered Salvatore Lima, a former mayor of Palermo, a member of the European Parliament, and a close adviser and friend of then Prime Minister Giulio Andreotti. Lima had long been rumored to be the Mafia's "ambassador" in Rome, using his influence to intervene on its behalf. Lima had failed to get Mafia convictions from the 1980's overturned, previously a routine occurrence. Many observers interpreted Lima's murder as punishment for his lapse.

Then, on May 23, 1992, the Mafia reportedly killed Giovanni Falcone, Italy's most prominent anti-Mafia prosecutor, his wife, and three bodyguards. On July 19, anti-Mafia prosecutor Paolo Borsellino and five of his bodyguards were killed in a car-bomb explosion. But rather than stop the war against the Mafia, these killings jolted the government into intensifying its anti-Mafia efforts, including an investigation of the Christian Democrats' ties to the Mafia in the south.

The twin scandals of Mafia infiltration of the government and corruption among politicians have had the effect of radically altering Italy's political landscape. In April 1993, Italians, fed up with corrupt politicians and the Mafia's political influence and violence, resoundingly approved a referendum proposal to change the way senators are elected. Previously, Italians voted for a list of candidates that each political party drew up. The number of parliamentary seats each party received was in proportion to the percentage of votes the party received in national elections. This system was designed to prevent a recurrence of the one-party rule that Italy experienced under Fascism. But the system created a proliferation of political parties and enabled the Christian Democratic Party and the Socialist Party to dominate a succession of coalition governments since the end of World War II.

In August, acting on the referendum, the Italian Parliament passed legislation affecting both chambers of the Italian Parliament, making politicians more directly responsible to the people. The new laws meant that most members of Parliament would be elected directly: The candidate receiving the most votes in a district wins the seat.

The Christian Democratic Party, Italy's largest political party, has been seriously weakened by the charges of corruption and collusion with the Mafia. The party has been forced to cleanse its ranks of those touched by scandal and was even proposing to change its name to The Popular Party. The Socialist Party also has been affected. For example, evidence of the Mafia's efforts on behalf of the Socialists surfaced when police raided a Mafia hideout in Calabria. They found thousands of electoral leaflets supporting local Socialist candidates. Furthermore, in February 1993, Bettino Craxi , Socialist Party leader for 17 years and a former prime minister, was forced to resign. He was under six separate government investigations into political corruption involving millions of dollars in bribes given to the Socialist Party since 1985. He allegedly solicited some bribes personally.

Is Mafia dominance ending?

The emerging new political force in Italy's changed climate is the Northern League, a movement that wants regional autonomy for Italy. The League insists that Italy's industrial north is being drained by a corrupt government in Rome to finance projects of the Mafia-dominated economy of southern Italy. Some League leaders have even proposed dividing Italy into three separate republics.

Paradoxically, the Mafia may be rooting for the Northern League. Some observers have interpreted Mafia terrorist campaigns of 1992 and 1993 in this light. These observers believe that the Mafia hopes to stir public anger against the government through terrorist attacks, such as bombing the Uffizi Palace in Florence. Disaffection with the government might strengthen the League's hand. In a new, divided Italy, the Northern League would govern the north and wash its hands of the south, perhaps giving the Mafia freedom to retain its power in the lower third of the country. On the other hand, in the coming years, if the government keeps pressure on the Mafia, 1993 may go down in history as the beginning of the end of Mafia dominance in Italian life. ■ ■ ■

For further reading:

Catanzaro, Raimondo. *Men of Respect: A Social History of the Sicilian Mafia.* Free Press, 1991.
Duggan, Christopher. *Fascism and the Mafia.* Yale University Press, 1989.
Gambetta, Diego. *The Sicilian Mafia: The Business of Private Protection.* Harvard University Press, 1993.

Japan

Japan experienced a political revolution in 1993. The Liberal Democratic Party (LDP) that had governed since 1955 split and lost power to a coalition of seven parties. Prime Minister Kiichi Miyazawa resigned on July 22, 1993, and on August 6, the Diet (Japan's parliament) elected Morihiro Hosokawa as prime minister. (See **Hosokawa, Morihiro.**)

Public anger over corruption in politics had been rising with the number of scandals that had surfaced since the late 1980's. For years, the LDP had won elections with money from big businesses to whom it granted political favors. But the system began to unravel in 1992 when the LDP's most powerful leader, Shin Kanemaru, admitted that he had improperly accepted $4 million from a parcel delivery firm. He was arrested on March 6, 1993, but after negotiating and paying a small fine, he was released. Pressured by public outrage at such light punishment, the government later indicted him on charges of tax evasion after a search of his office uncovered hidden assets, including gold bars worth $50 million.

The recent movement to clean up Japan's political system had begun as early as May 1992, when Hosokawa, a former LDP member who had been calling for reform, established the Japan New Party (JNP). In December, an LDP faction formed a group called Reform Forum 21 to urge Prime Minister Miyazawa to seek political reforms. The group was led by Tsutomu Hata, a former finance minister, and

Ichiro Ozawa, a former protégé of Kanemaru and LDP secretary-general.

But reform seemed to be a lost cause by June 11, 1993, when Miyazawa and LDP leaders abandoned efforts to work out a compromise reform bill that would pass the Diet before it adjourned on June 20. The key reform was the abolition of multiseat constituencies for the Diet. In these districts, members of the same political party competed against each other, though they usually supported party positions on campaign issues. The candidate who had the most money to give to voters usually won, an arrangement that led to corrupt fund-raising schemes.

Miyazawa's decision to drop the reform bill led to a brawl on the floor of the Diet. And on June 18, opposition parties introduced a motion of no-confidence over the issue of election reform. Members of Reform Forum 21 defected from the LDP and voted with the opposition. Miyazawa's government fell, and new elections for the lower house of the Diet were called for July 18.

New parties campaign. Before the elections, however, on June 21, the LDP split as 10 members formed the New Party Harbinger. On June 23, the LDP split again, when Hata and Ozawa, with 42 other LDP members, formed the Japan Renewal Party.

The new parties campaigned on the need for political reform. Another election theme promoted the idea that new professional politicians, such as Hata

Debris litters the town of Aonae on the Japanese island of Okujiri in the aftermath of an earthquake that struck in July, the strongest there in 25 years.

and Ozawa, who had taken over seats in the Diet from their fathers, should oust entrenched bureaucrats, such as Miyazawa, who had entered LDP politics as a retired bureaucrat.

A third theme stressed consumer interests. Bureaucratic government had allocated resources into capital growth rather than consumer products. This policy, in combination with an overrepresentation of farmers in the Diet who opposed cheap food imports, caused the Japanese to pay high prices for food and other goods despite Japan's prosperity.

Election results. Only 67 percent of voters cast ballots on July 18. The LDP won 223 seats, down from its previously held 275, and though it became the largest party in the new house, it did not win the required majority of seats to form a new government. Instead, seven diverse parties agreed to some common policies on July 29, enabling them to form a government. The coalition intended to implement political reforms, maintain stable foreign and economic policies, and decentralize government.

Hosokawa elected. Coalition leaders selected Hosokawa as prime minister because he was untainted by scandal. The new Diet elected Hosokawa as prime minister on August 6. In a 262 to 224 vote, he defeated Yohei Kono, who had succeeded Miyazawa as LDP president. Also on August 6, the Diet elected Takako Doi as its first woman speaker. She was a former leader of the Social Democratic Party.

Hosokawa's new Cabinet, announced on August 9, included Hata as deputy prime minister and minister of foreign affairs. Although Ozawa did not get a Cabinet post, he was widely regarded as the main power behind the scenes. Other former LDP members became ministers of finance, defense, agriculture, and trade and industry. The Social Democrats got six Cabinet posts, including the politically sensitive ministry of construction and a new Cabinet post responsible for overseeing political reform. Hosokawa's appointments brought the total number of ministers to 21.

However, Hosokawa quickly ran into disagreements within his coalition and with critics among the LDP in the Diet. The Renewal Party complained about Hosokawa's attention to economic and foreign policy, arguing that the Cabinet's only mandate was to implement political reforms. Ozawa indicated that he regarded the coalition as only transitional until a two-party system could develop.

But Hosokawa claimed victory on November 18, when the lower house of the Diet passed landmark electoral reform legislation. One of the four bills passed altered the electoral formula, reducing the lower house to 500 seats from 511. Another bill transformed multiseat districts to single-seat districts. A third measure took some seats away from rural constituencies and gave them to cities. The fourth bill stipulated that corporations may contribute campaign funds only to political parties, not

Morihiro Hosokawa, leader of a reformist coalition, became Japan's new prime minister in August, ousting a party that had been in power since 1955.

to individuals, and it provided for subsidies to the parties. The bills had to pass the upper house, where Hosokawa's coalition held the majority of seats.

War apology criticized. Some coalition colleagues as well as LDP members criticized Hosokawa for giving the most direct apology for Japan's actions in World War II (1939-1945) ever made by a Japanese official. Japan had long tried to avoid or deny any blame for its wartime actions. On Aug. 10, 1993, Hosokawa said Japan had fought "a war of aggression and it was wrong." He extended official sympathies to all war victims and their surviving families in Asia as well as all the world.

Economic troubles. Japan's Economic Planning Agency, which had long expected a recovery from economic decline, said on September 7 that the economy was "stagnating." The agency blamed low consumer spending, falling capital investment, and rising imports for the economy's poor performance.

On September 16, Hosokawa announced the third economic stimulus package in a year. It included public works spending and tax incentives for business. But neither the $57-billion package nor a lowering of business-loan interest rates sparked a recovery. For the first time since World War II, a car factory closed. Many Japanese companies were building factories in less developed parts of Asia to escape Japan's high labor costs.

Bad weather reduced Japan's rice crop, forcing

the importation of 200,000 short tons (181,500 metric tons) of the grain. Officials said the move did not mean the import ban on rice had been lifted.

Royal wedding. Crown Prince Naruhito married Masako Owada on June 9. The bride, a daughter of Japan's most senior career official in the foreign ministry, had turned Naruhito down twice in six years before agreeing to a traditional wedding and restricted life within Emperor Akihito's palace.

Foreign relations. On July 6, Japan announced that it would seek a permanent seat on the United Nations Security Council. Japan worried about a new missile that North Korea tested in the summer. The missile could carry nuclear, chemical, or biological warheads and was capable of hitting the Japanese islands. The United States proposed on September 22 to help Japan build a missile defense system in return for access to advanced commercial technologies of value to U.S. industries. But negotiations were slow in getting underway.

Russian President Boris Yeltsin visited Tokyo, the capital of Japan, in October. Yeltsin's visit failed to resolve a deadlock over Japan's desire to recover four of the Kuril Islands that Russia had acquired after the Soviet Union collapsed. The islands had belonged to Japan until the end of World War II, when the Soviets seized them. ☐ Henry S. Bradsher

See also **Asia** (Facts in brief table); **Owada, Masako.** In *World Book,* see **J**apan.

Jiang Zemin (1926-   ) was elected president of the People's Republic of China on March 27, 1993, by the National People's Congress, China's parliament. He has been general secretary of the Chinese Communist Party since June 1989 and chairman of the Chinese government's Central Military Commission since March 1990. Jiang's election to the presidency meant that, for the first time since the 1970's, one man held the top positions in the party, the military, and the government, though the presidency is largely a ceremonial office. (See **China.**)

Jiang was born in August 1926 in Yangzhou in Jiangsu province. He joined the Chinese Communist Party in 1946, and the following year, he graduated from Jiao Tong University in Shanghai with an engineering degree. He spent a year in Moscow in the mid-1950's as a trainee in an automobile factory and upon returning to China held technical positions in several cities.

In the early 1980's, Jiang served on government trade commissions. In 1982, he was first elected to the Central Committee of the Communist Party, and in 1985, he was appointed mayor of Shanghai.

In addition to his political accomplishments, Jiang speaks fluent English, as well as French, Russian, and Romanian. He also plays the flute, among other musical instruments.

Jiang and his wife, Wang Yeping, have two sons. ☐ Carol L. Hanson

Jordan. Representatives of Jordan and Israel on Sept. 14, 1993, initialed an agenda in Washington, D.C., establishing a process by which the two countries hope to normalize relations. Jordan's King Hussein I, though initially angered by the revelation in August of an impending agreement between Israel and the Palestine Liberation Organization (PLO), became one of the first Arab leaders to offer support. Hussein's anger stemmed from the fact that Israel and the PLO reached their accord through secret talks, even though Jordan and the PLO had formed a joint negotiating team for the Arab-Israeli peace talks that began in 1991.

Peace issues. The Jordanian-Israeli agenda, signed one day after the PLO-Israeli agreement, paved the way for communication links and sharing water from the Yarmuk and Jordan rivers. The two countries also hoped to settle a dispute over two parcels of land Israel took from Jordan during the 1967 Arab-Israeli war. One is an acre (0.4 hectare) near the main Yarmuk tributaries in the north and the other is a 125-square-mile (324-square-kilometer) area extending from the Dead Sea to Aqaba. Jordan sought Israeli cooperation on the development of Dead Sea mineral resources and permission to fly aircraft over Israeli airspace.

The PLO-Israeli agreement, which granted eventual self-rule for Palestinians in the Israeli-occupied West Bank and Gaza Strip, created uncertainty about the status of 1.5 million Palestinians in Jordan. These are people and their descendants who sought refuge in Jordan after the 1948 and 1967 Arab-Israeli conflicts or who were deported there later. In addition to the financial burden they incur, Jordanian politics have been influenced by this growing group who make up a sizable part of Jordan's 3.8 million people. Jordan also feared that a PLO failure to provide stability in the Gaza Strip and the West Bank could result in another refugee influx.

Economy. Jordan rescheduled part of its $7-billion debt in 1993 but was less successful in attracting badly needed foreign investment. Although Jordan's economy grew by 11 percent in 1992 and an estimated 7 percent in 1993, growth was mainly due to the return of about 350,000 Palestinians and Jordanians from some Persian Gulf nations around the time of the Persian Gulf War (1991). The war cost Jordan about $500 million in aid from oil-rich Arab nations, which spurned Jordan's overtures to improve relations after Jordanians expressed sympathy with Iraq in the war.

Jordan-United States relations improved in 1993 following a trip by Hussein to meet U.S. President Bill Clinton on June 18 and the September Jordanian-Israeli agreement. On September 16, Clinton released $30 million in aid for economic, military, and multilateral regional projects. A U.S. team also went to Jordan in September to explore how United Nations sanctions against Iraq could be amended to ease the negative impact they have had on the Jordanian economy. One result of the sanctions has been the loss of fees for transporting goods to Iraq through the Jordanian port of Aqaba.

Elections. Voter turnout was heavy on November 8 for Jordan's first multiparty parliamentary elections since 1956. Candidates from 20 parties ran for the 80 seats in the lower half of Parliament. Hussein appoints the 40 members of the upper half.

Islamic fundamentalists lost 6 of their 22 seats but remained the largest voting bloc in Parliament. A new voting system allowed each voter only one vote. Previously, voters could vote for as many candidates as there were seats in their district. The new system drew fewer votes for the fundamentalists, who had great support in populous districts. Toujan al-Faisal, a women's rights activist, won a seat. She became the first woman ever elected to Parliament.

Assassination plot. Ten suspects were indicted in September in a plot to assassinate Hussein. The plot was foiled before it was to take place during a military graduation in June at Mutah University near Kerak, 55 miles (88 kilometers) south of Amman, the capital. The accused were members of al-Tahrir, Islamic Liberation Party, whose larger aim was to overthrow national governments in the region and establish a unified Islamic state. ☐ Christine Helms

See also **Middle East** (Facts in brief table). In *World Book,* see **Jordan.**

Jordan, Michael (1963-), widely considered history's greatest basketball player, announced his retirement from professional basketball on Oct. 6, 1993. After leading the Chicago Bulls to their third straight National Basketball Association (NBA) championship in June 1993, Jordan declared that he had nothing more to prove in basketball.

Jordan was born on Feb. 17, 1963, in Brooklyn, a borough of New York City. His family moved to North Carolina when Jordan was less than 1 year old. Jordan went on to star in basketball at the University of North Carolina (UNC) at Chapel Hill. He left UNC after his junior year to enter the NBA draft, and the Bulls chose him third overall in 1984.

Jordan won seven straight NBA scoring titles beginning with the 1986-1987 season, tying him with Wilt Chamberlain for the most consecutive scoring titles and the most total scoring titles. Jordan won the NBA regular season Most Valuable Player award three times—in 1988, 1991, and 1992—and his career 32.3-points-per-game scoring average for the regular season was an NBA record. He won three consecutive NBA play-off finals MVP awards, and his 41- points-per-game finals average also established an NBA record.

Jordan's father, James, was murdered during a roadside robbery on July 23, 1993, near Fayetteville, N.C. Jordan and his wife, Juanita, live in Highland Park, Ill. They have three children. ☐ Mark Dunbar

Judaism. The commemoration of milestone anniversaries of events associated with the Holocaust, and the opening of two major new museums preserving the memory of the Holocaust, were the highlights of developments in the Jewish community in 1993. During 1993, several events reinforced the importance of keeping alive the memory and the lessons of the Holocaust, in which 6 million European Jews were exterminated during World War II (1939-1945). These events included the violent spread of racism and anti-Semitism in Germany and the continuing tragedy of "ethnic cleansing" in Bosnia-Herzegovina.

Historic anniversaries. The year 1993 marked the 50th anniversaries of two important events in the history of the Holocaust, both symbolic of the courage and resistance to tyranny that brightened this tragic period. On April 19, a solemn commemoration was held in Poland to mark the anniversary of the famous Warsaw ghetto uprising. On April 19, 1943, after most of the ghetto's inhabitants had died of starvation or illness or had been sent to concentration camps, about 60,000 surviving Jews—led by a small underground that had arisen in the walled ghetto—revolted against their oppressors. They fought the German army with few weapons and no outside support for more than three weeks, until the Nazis killed most of the resistance fighters. On May 16, the last survivors committed suicide rather than be taken prisoner.

The Warsaw ghetto uprising has become a symbol of the bravery and faith that led many to stand up against the evil of the Nazis. At the anniversary ceremonies, Poland's President Lech Walesa, United States Vice President Albert Gore, Jr., and Israeli Prime Minister Yitzhak Rabin led thousands of Poles and Jews in recalling this heroic chapter.

Another example of courage and resistance was recalled in the autumn of 1993—the 50th anniversary of the rescue of the Jews of Denmark. During the Jewish High Holy Days of 1943, the invading Germans had planned to arrest and deport Danish Jews to the death camp at Auschwitz in Poland. But the Danish government, Christian church leaders, and common citizens protected their Jewish neighbors by secretly ferrying them at night across the Baltic Sea to neutral Sweden. More than 7,000 Jews were saved. Many events were scheduled in Denmark, the United States, and Israel in autumn 1993 to commemorate these events and to express the gratitude of the Jewish community to the Danish people.

U.S. Holocaust Museum. On April 22, the new United States Holocaust Memorial Museum was dedicated in Washington, D.C., by President Bill Clinton. Housed in a beautiful and impressive building rich in symbolic design, on the famous Mall in the nation's capital, the museum tells the story of the Holocaust in various ways. Exhibits of artifacts, photographs, and documents, as well as specially designed spaces

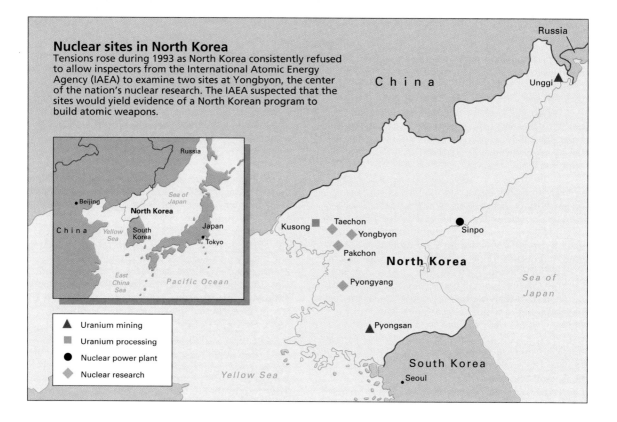

Nuclear sites in North Korea
Tensions rose during 1993 as North Korea consistently refused to allow inspectors from the International Atomic Energy Agency (IAEA) to examine two sites at Yongbyon, the center of the nation's nuclear research. The IAEA suspected that the sites would yield evidence of a North Korean program to build atomic weapons.

▲ Uranium mining
■ Uranium processing
● Nuclear power plant
◆ Nuclear research

for contemplation, are combined to help people understand the Holocaust and the moral challenge it poses. The museum also pays tribute to others who suffered from Nazi oppression—the Romany people (as Gypsies prefer to be called) and homosexuals.

In his dedication address, President Clinton said, "I believe that this museum will touch the life of everyone who sees it, and that no one who sees it will emerge without being changed." The museum has already become one of the most sought-after destinations in Washington, with attendance breaking all anticipated figures. (See also **Washington, D.C.: A Place in Which to Remember.**)

Peace accord. The historic signing of the peace agreement between Israel and the Palestine Liberation Organization (PLO), in Washington, D.C., on September 13, 1993, was the other major development of 1993 affecting the Jewish community. While most Jews around the world hailed the breakthrough and supported the dramatic peace effort, some Orthodox Jews and right wing Israelis opposed the agreement as a dangerous threat to Israel's security.   □ Howard A. Berman

See also **Religion: The Lure and Lore of the Dead Sea Scrolls.** In *World Book,* see **Jews; Judaism.**
Kampuchea. See **Cambodia.**
Kansas. See **State government.**
Kazakhstan. See **Asia.**
Kentucky. See **State government.**

Korea, North. Throughout 1993, North Korea stalled international efforts to determine whether it was making nuclear weapons in violation of the nuclear Non-Proliferation Treaty (NPT), which North Korea had signed in 1985. While stalling, the government successfully tested a missile, the Rodong 1, which was powerful enough to deliver a nuclear weapon or other kinds of warheads as far as Japan.

Under NPT terms, North Korea was obligated to permit inspections of its nuclear facilities by the International Atomic Energy Agency (IAEA), an agency affiliated with the United Nations (UN). During January 1993, IAEA inspectors examined nuclear facilities in North Korea, but the government refused to allow them to see two questionable sites at Yongbyon, the center of North Korea's nuclear development. On February 9, the IAEA demanded "special inspection" rights. It also was expected to ask the UN Security Council to impose economic sanctions against North Korea if inspections were not allowed.

However, on March 12, North Korea announced that it would withdraw from the NPT on June 12. Four rounds of talks with the United States culminated in North Korea's stating on June 11 that it would suspend its withdrawal. A fifth round of talks with the United States produced an agreement by North Korea to resume inspection talks with the IAEA. However, further IAEA efforts were frustrated. In late December, the U.S. intelligence community concluded that North Korea probably had developed one or two nuclear weapons.

Missile test. The military fired Rodong 1 missiles into the Sea of Japan on May 29 and 30, according to Japanese reports. Japan feared that the missiles could reach Japanese targets. North Korea sold Scud missiles to Iran, Libya, and Syria, so the United States worried that the Rodong might also be sold in the Middle East, heightening tensions in that region.

Domestic problems. Neither President Kim Il-song nor his son and designated heir, Kim Chong-il, appeared at Army Day celebrations on April 25. Both men's later appearances reduced foreign speculation that dissension had arisen between father and son.

The government said on December 9 that the economic situation was grave. Diplomats reported widespread hunger, perhaps starvation, during 1993. Industrial production had dropped by an estimated 15 to 30 percent from 1990 to 1993, and a Russian institute said North Korean industry was running at 50 percent of capacity because of power shortages.

Agreement signed. North Korean and United States generals signed an agreement on August 24 to cooperate in efforts to trace American military personnel still unaccounted for from the Korean War (1950-1953). The whereabouts of 8,140 servicemen were still unknown. ☐ Henry S. Bradsher

See also **Asia** (Facts in brief table). In *World Book,* see **Korea.**

Korea, South.
Kim Yong-Sam was inaugurated on Feb. 25, 1993, as South Korea's first civilian president after more than three decades of military rule. An opponent of the military, Kim had been kept under house arrest for years. On Dec. 18, 1992, running as a candidate of the ruling Democratic Liberal Party (DLP), he had captured 42 percent of the vote in a three-way presidential race. When he joined the DLP in 1990, he was criticized for selling out his reformist principles, but Kim's presidential inaugural address attacked the generals for having led the country into corruption and moral drift, indicating that his views had not changed. In the following months, he instituted sweeping political and economic reforms.

Cabinet problems. Kim named former General Hwang In-song as prime minister on Feb. 22, 1993, but overall, the old ruling elite got few places in the new Cabinet, named on February 26. On March 8, however, Kim fired three Cabinet members. Korean newspapers reported that the three had indulged in unethical, activities. On December 11, Kim replaced Hwang with Lee Hoi Chang, a former Supreme Court justice who had fought corrupt military leaders.

Military purge. Also on March 8, Kim fired the army chief of staff and another senior general, and on April 2, he fired two more top generals. The dismissals were viewed as the reassertion of civilian authority over the military. On May 24, Kim further reshuffled the military command, firing four senior

generals for their leading roles in a December 1979 coup that led to the consolidation of army rule.

On July 17, 1993, two generals who were former defense ministers were arrested on charges of having taken bribes from military suppliers in return for defense contracts. Some 30 other top officers and industrialists were ensnared in a widespread investigation of corruption in weapons purchases.

Civil corruption. Several of Kim's conservative political critics faced bribery or tax evasion charges or were forced to retire. A bank president was accused of taking bribes to grant loans and then using the bribe money to pay off politicians for access to government-controlled credit.

A new ethics law enacted in June forced 6,000 top politicians and civil servants to reveal the value of their assets. The average net worth of 1,500 senior civil servants was $1.8 million. The chief justice of the supreme court, the prosecutor-general, and the head of the national police were among top officials who resigned in September because of the controversial source of their wealth.

On August 12, Kim issued a ban on the use of false names in financial transactions, such as in the opening of bank accounts. As much as $14.85 billion was estimated to be in accounts under false names in order to evade taxes, conceal sources of income, or avoid regulators.

Political opposition fades. Kim's reforms upset his opponents in the DLP. However, a vote-buying scandal in a by-election for parliament discredited these same opponents. And Kim's old rival as the country's leading dissident, Kim Dae Jung, resigned the leadership of the opposition Democratic Party and was succeeded by Lee Ki Taek in a party election on March 11. These moves left the president with little effective opposition in the National Assembly.

Economic slowdown. South Korea's economy grew in 1993 at a rate faster than most countries' but slow according to its own standards. Annual growth had fallen from about 8.5 percent in 1991 to about 4.8 percent in 1992. On March 19, 1993, Kim unveiled a 100-day economic stimulus package intended to get the growth rate up to 6 percent. However, in September, the government said that it expected only a 4.7 percent growth for all of 1993.

The anticorruption drive was blamed for a 15 percent fall in capital investment by domestic investors, as they sought to conceal undeclared wealth from tax collectors. Foreign investment also fell, as poorer Asian countries with fewer governmental regulations and lower wages attracted funds away from South Korea.

Accidents. The nation's worst rail accident occurred near Pusan on March 28, when a rail bed collapsed under a train, killing 78 people. Blasting for a tunnel nearby was blamed. ☐ Henry S. Bradsher

See also **Asia** (Facts in brief table). In *World Book,* see **Korea.**

Suspects charged with plotting to assassinate former U.S. President George Bush are seated in a cage at their trial, which began in June in Kuwait.

Kuwait. Financial troubles plagued Kuwait in 1993. The ruling Sabah family faced a newly elected opposition majority in angry parliamentary debates over how to deal with the growing national debt, estimated at between $20 billion and $30 billion.

The country's financial problems stemmed in part from Iraq's 1990 invasion, which resulted in the Persian Gulf War (1991). Kuwait was forced to spend about 60 percent of its estimated $90 billion in financial reserves on war-related costs. A budget deficit of nearly $3.4 billion was projected for the fiscal year beginning July 1, 1993. The previous fiscal year's deficit was more than $6 billion.

The opposition in parliament criticized government proposals that Kuwait slash civil service salaries —which account for about one quarter of state spending—and decrease government subsidies on services. They called for a reduction in special building projects and military spending instead.

Financial scandal. On April 15, Kuwaiti officials filed a civil suit in London against former officials of the Kuwaiti Investment Office (KIO) to recoup $500-million allegedly embezzled through Kuwaiti investments in Spain. KIO, the government investment department, was accused of losing $5 billion through theft and mismanagement from 1986 through 1992. Two members of the ruling Sabah family were among the officials accused in the case. Many opposition legislators, elected in October 1992, had called

for close scrutiny of alleged corruption and abuse of public funds by the ruling family.

Bush assassination plot. On Oct. 30, 1993, a Kuwaiti judge postponed a verdict in the trial of 12 suspects accused of plotting to assassinate former United States President George Bush during Bush's visit to Kuwait in mid-April. The prosecution sought the death penalty for 1 Kuwaiti and 11 Iraqi suspects. In retaliation for the alleged plot, the United States on June 26 launched a missile attack on the Iraqi capital, Baghdad. In October 1993, an article in *The New Yorker* magazine by investigative journalist Seymour Hersh claimed there was insufficient evidence of a plot.

Regional relations. Throughout 1993, Kuwait rebuffed diplomatic overtures to mend relations from Jordan, Sudan, Tunisia, Morocco, Mauritania, Yemen, and the Palestine Liberation Organization, because they had not renounced their sympathy with Iraq's invasion of Kuwait. Kuwait demanded that they uphold United Nations sanctions against Iraq and also seek the return of some 600 Kuwaitis allegedly still being held in Iraq. In June, the Kuwaiti military began digging a fortified trench 10 feet (3 meters) deep and 16 feet (5 meters) wide along its border with Iraq.   □ Christine Helms

See also **Middle East** (Facts in brief table). In *World Book,* see Kuwait.

Kyrgyzstan. See Asia.

Labor. In 1993, the United States economy continued its unsteady recovery from the 1990-1991 recession, and the labor market struggled along with it. Unemployment fell from 7.1 percent in January 1993 to 6.4 percent in November, but 8.3 million people remained jobless. Plans to lay off thousands of workers were announced by some of the country's largest multinational firms, including high-tech leaders such as Apple Computer Corporation, International Business Machines Corporation, and Wang Laboratories. More than 1.7 million jobs were created in 1993, but this level of job growth was still well below the average in previous recoveries, and many workers were uneasy about the prospects for keeping their jobs.

Pay and benefits continued rising at historically modest rates in 1993. Together, they were up only 3.6 percent through September. Pay alone rose a mere 3.0 percent. Inflation remained low—about 3 percent for the year—so employers felt little pressure to give larger wage hikes.

Given the uncertain economic outlook, companies in 1993 tried to gain more control over wages and benefits. In many collective bargaining sessions, employers sought longer-term agreements to help them forecast labor costs. They also tried to shift more of the costs of health insurance onto workers and to award profitability-based bonuses instead of wage increases. Unions, on the other hand, sought standard-length contracts, earlier adjustments to changing circumstances, steady health costs, and both wage increases and bonuses. Many unions also sought job and income guarantees.

Steel industry. On July 21, members of the United Steelworkers of America (USW) ratified a six-year contract with Inland Steel Industries Incorporated that analysts said would serve as a model for future steel industry settlements. The agreement provides for pay bonuses rather than direct wage increases and gives workers control of one seat on Inland's board of directors. In return, Inland can reduce its payroll through attrition and can implement plans to reduce health-care costs.

The Inland deal set the tone for other negotiations. On August 30, USW members approved a similar contract with Bethlehem Steel Corporation. The Bethlehem agreement provides for bonuses in 1994 and 1995, a 50-cent-an-hour wage increase in 1995, and then more bonuses in 1996 if the company has become profitable.

Coal mining. On Jan. 31, 1993, the contract expired between the United Mine Workers (UMW) and the Bituminous Coal Operators Association (BCOA), a group of the largest coal producers in the United States. The two sides agreed to extend the contract while the union pressed for new provisions on job security. However, by early May, no resolution was in sight, so the UMW on May 10 began a selective strike against the BCOA. First, they walked away from mines in Illinois and Indiana. When the BCOA did not budge, the UMW expanded the strike to include mines in West Virginia on May 18 and in Kentucky on June 16. On December 7, negotiators finally reached an agreement to settle the strike.

Aluminum industry. On May 25, the Aluminum, Brick, and Glass Workers Union and the USW authorized strikes against Reynolds Metals Company and the Aluminum Company of America (Alcoa), the two largest U.S. producers of aluminum. But on June 1, the two sides reached agreement on three-year pacts that provide for 25-cent-an-hour wage increases in 1993 and 1995 and immediate lump-sum bonuses. Members of the unions approved the pacts shortly thereafter.

Airline industry. In March, Trans World Airlines Incorporated (TWA) reached agreement with the Air Line Pilots Association (ALPA), the International Association of Machinists and Aerospace Workers (IAMAW), and the Independent Federation of Flight Attendants on proposed changes in work rules and cuts in wages and benefits. The moves were needed to help the airline emerge from federal bankruptcy protection. As part of the deal, TWA Chairman Carl C. Icahn relinquished control of the airline.

After drawn-out negotiations that had started in 1992, United Airlines on Dec. 15, 1993, finally agreed to sell majority control of the airline to 60,000 of its employees for $5 billion in wage concessions and changes in work rules. If the deal was approved by company directors, United shareholders, and members of the airline's unions, United would become the largest employee-owned business in the country.

Northwest Airlines in 1993 sought $886 million in labor concessions over three years so the airline could remain solvent. On June 2, the airline and the unions reached tentative agreement on a package of concessions. However, members of the IAMAW rejected the pact in mid-June, and the International Brotherhood of Teamsters (IBT) stopped considering it. Northwest then threatened to seek relief on labor costs in federal bankruptcy court. But on July 6, the ALPA finally agreed to the concessions. The IAMAW and the IBT followed suit later in the month.

The Association of Professional Flight Attendants went on strike against American Airlines on November 18—one week before Thanksgiving Day—to apply pressure for changes in work schedules and pay. The attendants had planned to return to work after the holiday, before replacements could be trained and certified. But the strike ended after only four days when both sides responded to an appeal by President Bill Clinton and agreed to binding arbitration in the event of a continuing impasse.

Aerospace industry. Aerospace companies in 1993 were buffeted by cuts in defense spending and reduced orders from private carriers. To remain competitive, many firms turned to layoffs. Cuts for 1993 and 1994 included 2,000 jobs at Martin Marietta Corporation; 4,000 jobs at Douglas Aircraft Company;

10,000 jobs at United Technologies Corporation; and 28,000 jobs at Boeing Company.

Automobile industry. The three-year contracts between auto workers and the leading U.S. automakers expired in 1993, but they were renegotiated without strikes. In a prelude to these settlements, the United Automobile Workers (UAW) and Navistar International Corporation, a maker of truck parts, on January 25 reached agreement on a two-year pact that provides for lump-sum payments to workers and a larger worker voice in decisions on plant closings, health-care plans, and purchasing services from outside the company.

Some of those ideas were carried over to the bargaining sessions during the summer with the Big Three automakers: Chrysler Corporation, Ford Motor Company, and General Motors Corporation (GM). The UAW followed its usual script for contract talks. First, it selected a *strike target*—the company to which the union would apply the most pressure for acceptance of its demands. The union chose Ford. Ford was considered the healthiest of the three automakers and the one with the most to lose from a strike, so the UAW believed it would be the most eager to reach a deal. After a settlement with Ford, the union would negotiate with the other two companies to accept the same contract.

On September 15, Ford and the UAW reached agreement on a new three-year contract. The pact provides for 3 percent annual raises on top of cost-of-living adjustments, and it boosts pension benefits for workers with at least 30 years of experience by 17 percent. Also, Ford was to continue paying all health-care costs. In return, new workers were to earn only 70 percent of full wages, rather than the current 85 percent, and they must work for three years to reach the full-wage level, rather than the current 18 months.

The UAW quickly made similar agreements with Chrysler and GM. Chrysler agreed to the new pact on October 1, and GM signed off on October 24. However, GM was able to wrest a few more concessions from the union because the company was still recovering from billions of dollars in losses in recent years.

Transit industry. On May 7, bus drivers who were members of the Amalgamated Transit Union ended their bitter three-year strike against Greyhound Lines, Incorporated. The two sides agreed to a lengthy six-year pact that provides for wage increases of 20 percent over the life of the contract, $22 million in back pay to striking workers, the rehiring of 550 union drivers, and amnesty and reinstatement for 250 union drivers who had been fired for alleged misconduct during the strike. Also, the 2,100 replacement drivers that Greyhound had hired could keep their jobs.

Other strikes and settlements. On January 12, some 200,000 New York City employees settled with

Pallbearers in Delano, Calif., carry the body of Cesar Chavez, the pioneering head of the United Farm Workers of America, who died in April.

the city on a wage-and-benefit package totaling 8.25 percent over 39 months. Also in January, the Oil, Chemical, and Atomic Workers Union reached agreement with the American Oil Company on a 3-year contract that provides for a 3.5 percent pay increase in the first and second years and a 3.7 percent hike in the third year. On December 1, the National Hockey League Officials Association ended a 16-day strike against the National Hockey League.

Union membership. Statistics showed that the slide in the proportion of U.S. workers in unions has slowed but not bottomed out. In 1992, less than 17 percent of workers belonged to unions, down from almost one-third in the 1950's. The American Federation of Labor and Congress of Industrial Organizations (AFL-CIO), a group of about 100 labor unions, reported in September 1993 that union membership has fallen by a total of 633,000 workers since 1991, partly as a result of layoffs caused by the recession. However, unions won almost 50 percent of employee votes for union representation in 1992, up from about 47 percent in 1991.

Government policy. With the election of President Bill Clinton, organized labor faced a friendlier Administration than it had since 1980. Clinton and Secretary of Labor Robert B. Reich voiced support for many union positions during 1993, such as increasing the federal minimum wage, extending unemployment compensation for people who have exhausted their benefits, and instituting a payroll tax to help fund retraining programs for laid-off workers.

Labor leaders applauded many of Clinton's decisions. On Feb. 5, 1993, Clinton signed the Family and Medical Leave Act. The law allows workers in companies with 50 or more employees to take up to 12 weeks of unpaid leave for the care of newborn or adopted children or sick relatives. Clinton's predecessor, President George Bush, had twice vetoed similar legislation. On August 12, Clinton approved the rehiring of air traffic controllers who had been fired by President Ronald Reagan in 1981 after they started a nationwide strike. However, Clinton's act was largely symbolic, because the Federal Aviation Administration was in the midst of a hiring freeze.

But the Administration's strong support of the North American Free Trade Agreement (NAFTA) dismayed union officials, who believed the pact would encourage American businesses to relocate to Mexico, where labor costs were lower. Unions lobbied hard to defeat NAFTA, which will create a free-trade zone between the United States, Canada, and Mexico, but their efforts failed. Clinton signed the agreement in December. In retaliation for the defeat, the AFL-CIO said it would withhold support for all Democratic candidates nationwide for three months. The AFL-CIO was reportedly the single largest contributor to Democratic campaigns. □ Robert W. Fisher

See also **Economics; Manufacturing.** In *World Book,* see **Labor force; Labor movement.**

Changes in the United States labor force

	1992	1993
Civilian labor force	126,982,000	127,856,700
Total employment	117,598,000	119,039,100
Unemployment	9,384,000	8,815,900
Unemployment rate	7.4%	6.9%
Changes in real weekly earnings of production and nonsupervisory workers (private nonfarm sector)*	−1.1%	0.4%
Change in output per employee hour (private nonfarm sector)†	3.1%	1.6%

*Constant (1982) dollars. 1992 change from December 1991 to December 1992; 1993 change from October 1992 to October 1993 (preliminary data).

†Annual rate for 1992; for 1993, change is from third quarter 1992 to third quarter 1993 (preliminary data).

Source: U.S. Bureau of Labor Statistics.

Laos. The restructuring of the Laotian leadership was completed in February 1993, following the death on Nov. 21, 1992, of the president and leader of the Laos Communist Party, Kaysone Phomvihane. A new Supreme National Assembly confirmed Nouhak Phoumsavan as president on Feb. 22, 1993. He had first been elected in November 1992 by the previous assembly. The new assembly also reelected Prime Minister Khamtai Siphandon, who had succeeded Kaysone as chairman of the Communist Party. Saman Vignaket replaced Nouhak as assembly chairman, the third-ranked position.

On March 19, 1993, Khamtai blamed difficulties in completing economic development plans during 1993 on "increasingly rampant corruption" by Communist Party officials, who had stolen property, taken bribes, and evaded taxes, among other crimes. But the economy grew by 6 percent, aided by an agricultural recovery after the 1992 drought ended.

Relations with Thailand, which borders Laos on the west, improved in 1993. Thai Prime Minister Chuan Likphai visited the Laotian capital of Vientiane on June 4 to 6. Thailand agreed to buy one of Laos' few potential exports, power from new hydroelectric projects. The first bridge across the Mekong River between the two countries was being built at Vientiane. □ Henry S. Bradsher

See also **Asia** (Facts in brief table). In *World Book,* see **Laos.**

Latin America

Six present or former Latin-American leaders faced trial in 1993 on charges of corruption or abuse of human rights while in office. Charges ranged from looting the public treasury to murder.

In Venezuela, one of the region's most durable democracies, President Carlos Andrés Pérez was suspended on May 21 when the Venezuelan Senate authorized the Supreme Court to try Pérez on charges that he embezzled government funds. Pérez, 70, once one of Latin America's most respected leaders, yielded office to be tried along with two of his former ministers on charges of embezzling $17 million during his second term in office. He had narrowly been cleared of similar charges following his first presidential term.

On April 29, the Brazilian Supreme Court indicted the nation's former president, Fernando Collor de Mello, on corruption charges. Collor de Mello was impeached on corruption charges in September 1992. If convicted, Collor de Mello, Brazil's first popularly elected chief executive since 1960, could spend up to eight years in jail.

Trials of former leaders. Former chief executives faced similar charges of theft in office in four other Latin-American nations in 1993. In Costa Rica, former President Luís Alberto Mongé, who ruled from 1982 to 1986, appeared in court on May 17. Together with his vice president and 17 other officials of his administration, Mongé was charged with stealing $6 million earmarked for disaster relief.

In Panama, Manuel Solís Palma, who was president in 1988 and 1989, faced trial in absentia on charges that he directed paramilitary mobs to beat up political opponents after dictator Manuel Noriega dismissed the results of the 1989 national election. Palma was living in exile in Venezuela. Noriega controlled Panama from 1983 to 1989.

In Peru, officials sought in vain to extradite former President Alan García Pérez (1985-1990) from Colombia, where he was living in exile. On February 11, the Colombian government refused Peru's request to send García Pérez back to Peru to stand trial on charges that he embezzled $400,000 from the national treasury and stole $50 million from the Peruvian central bank. In 1992, the Peruvian Congress withdrew the immunity from prosecution that former heads of state customarily enjoy so that García Pérez could stand trial.

On April 21, the Supreme Court of Bolivia sentenced former dictator Luís García Meza Tejada, who ruled in 1980 and 1981, to 30 years in jail without parole. The court found him guilty of murder, looting the treasury, corruption, and abuse of constitutional power. The court tried García Meza in absentia. The former dictator is still in hiding. Fourteen of his closest associates, including his interior minister,

who was serving 30 years in jail in the United States for drug trafficking, also received stiff sentences.

Atrocity report. Presidents, dictators, and drug traffickers were not the only ones called to account for their crimes in 1993. The United Nations (UN) issued a report on March 15 that implicated the Salvadoran army in most of the human rights violations that occurred during that nation's civil war from 1981 through February 1992. At least 75,000 people died in the war. Antigovernment rebels committed about 5 percent of the atrocities, the report said. (See also **El Salvador.**)

The report also blamed high-ranking U.S. officials for the killing. The report named former Secretary of State Alexander Haig, Jr., and his subordinates for covering up atrocities by El Salvador's military in an effort to persuade the U.S. Congress to continue

Guatemalan demonstrators gather in Guatemala City on June 1 after President Jorge Serrano Elías resigned following his failed coup attempt.

supplying billions of dollars in assistance to the Salvadoran government. The report blamed an elite Salvadoran military unit that had been trained by U.S. forces for the 1981 massacre of about 1,000 civilians in the vicinity of the town of El Mozote.

Guatemalan leadership change. Guatemala's President, Jorge Serrano Elías, dissolved Congress and the Supreme Court on May 25, 1993, claiming that the institutions had contributed to uncontrollable corruption in Guatemala. Under pressure from the military and widespread domestic and international opposition to his power grab, however, Serrano fled the country on June 2. Opponents in the Guatemalan Congress disallowed Vice President Gustavo Espina Salguero's claim to the presidency, and

on June 5, the Congress elected Ramiro De León Carpio, the nation's chief human rights advocate, as president.

Haitian troubles. Political turmoil reigned in Haiti throughout 1993. A UN-sponsored plan to return exiled Haitian President Jean-Bertrand Aristide to power by October 30 collapsed when an armed mob closed the port in the capital, Port-au-Prince, and refused to allow UN peacekeepers to land on October 11. The peacekeepers were to begin retraining the Haitian military, as well as the police force, for civilian rule.

A military coup, led by Lieutenant General Raoul Cédras, overthrew Aristide in September 1991. Aristide had been Haiti's first democratically elected president. On July 3, 1993, Cédras had signed a UN-mediated agreement in New York City to return Aristide to power in exchange for a guarantee of amnesty for Cédras and other military leaders involved in the 1991 coup. (See **Haiti.**)

New Honduran president. Hondurans elected 67-year-old Carlos Roberto Reina of the Liberal Party as the nation's new president on Nov. 28, 1993. A lawyer, Reina won with 53 percent of the vote over Oswaldo Ramos Soto of the conservative incumbent National Party. Reina said he would challenge the military's influence in government and fight to end corruption.

Toward greater free trade. Latin America continued its trend toward increased free trade in 1993. On November 17, the U.S. House of Representatives passed the North American Free Trade Agreement (NAFTA), assuring that the agreement would take effect on its scheduled start-up date of Jan. 1, 1994. NAFTA will eliminate trade barriers between the United States, Mexico, and Canada over 15 years.

Most Mexicans regarded NAFTA as an opportunity to attract more foreign investment, reduce the nation's foreign debt, and increase its standard of living. The treaty's fate in the United States was uncertain until nearly a day before the congressional vote, however. Proponents claimed that as trade barriers with Mexico fall, prices for U.S. goods will fall accordingly, increasing demand for those goods and jobs for the people who make them. U.S. opposition to NAFTA centered on the possibility that U.S. companies would move to Mexico to take advantage of cheaper labor. Many people in the United States also feared that Mexico's less-stringent enforcement of environmental laws would lead to increased pollution along the U.S.-Mexican border, where many U.S. companies set up factories. (See also **International trade: The Debate over NAFTA.**)

Beyond NAFTA's immediate focus, the debate over the treaty's merits sparked interest among Latin Americans everywhere in continental free trade. In February 1993, El Salvador, Guatemala, Honduras, and Nicaragua reached a free trade agreement that will allow goods from these four nations free access to Venezuela and Colombia by 1999. Under the agreement, tariffs on goods from Venezuela and Colombia to the four Central American nations will be eliminated by 2003. This agreement follows several other similar accords in the region in recent years, including one between Argentina, Brazil, Uruguay, and Paraguay in 1990, and another between Colombia and Venezuela in 1992.

Increased investments. The free trade debate of 1993, plus the acceptance of market-oriented policies in almost all Latin-American nations, triggered a heightened flow of new investment into the region. Indicative of the potential that many U.S. business leaders see in Latin America, Pepsico Incorporated of Purchase, N.Y., the giant U.S. soft drink

maker and fast food conglomerate, said on March 4 that it would invest $750 million over five years to expand its operations in Mexico. Pepsico said it would open more Pizza Hut, Taco Bell, and Kentucky Fried Chicken franchises throughout Latin America.

Latin America's automotive market attracted great interest from foreign investors in 1993. Sales of new cars and trucks in the first six months of the year were up 32 percent compared with 1992, and automobile manufacturers predicted that 1993 sales would easily break the 1980 record of 2.4 million vehicles. On the same day in August 1993 that the General Motors Corporation of Detroit announced that it would begin manufacturing pickup trucks again in Argentina, Mazda executives signed a contract to establish a $35-million assembly plant there.

Computer-related investments also bloomed in Latin America in 1993. Digital Equipment Corporation of Maynard, Mass., teamed up with Chile's largest software producer to sell its equipment throughout Latin America. Business possibilities prompted Memotech, a California computer disk-drive maker, to move all of its manufacturing operations to Chile.

In most major U.S. cities, companies prepared to meet the expansion opportunities that NAFTA will provide in Mexico. Typically, Forest City Enterprises of Cleveland, a real estate development company, entered into a venture with Grupo Protexa of Monterrey, Mexico, to build shopping malls in Mexico. Diebold Incorporated of Canton, Ohio, reached an agreement with Hidromex to buy an 80 percent interest in the Mexican company's automated teller machine and security equipment business.

Oil boom. The oil industry had a strong year in Latin America in 1993. Huge oil strikes in 1992 and 1993 in Latin America and the Caribbean pushed the region's known oil reserves above 123 billion barrels—five times the known level of those in the United States. Moreover, the region led the world in new discoveries from 1982 to 1991, according to a 1993 report by Petroconsultants S.A., a research firm in Geneva, Switzerland.

In Peru from 1990 through mid-1993, 14 foreign oil companies signed oil exploration or production contracts. To further encourage foreign oil companies, the Peruvian congress moved toward approval of a new oil investment law in 1993 that would permit international arbitration of disputes and a stable tax regime.

In Venezuela, the most recent Latin-American nation to nationalize its oil industry, the government welcomed foreigners back in 1993, inviting in August some 80 companies from overseas to bid on reactivating old oil fields with reserves totaling an estimated 1.7 billion barrels. Venezuela sought to obtain $22 billion of the $40 billion it had pledged to invest in its oil industry by the year 2000 from joint ventures with foreign companies. The government was working in 1993 on large projects to de-

Facts in brief on Latin-American political units

Country	Population	Government	Monetary unit*	Foreign trade (million U.S.$) Exports†	Imports†
Antigua and Barbuda	77,000	Governor General James B. Carlisle; Prime Minister Vere C. Bird, Sr.	dollar (2.70 = $1)	22	225
Argentina	33,767,000	President Carlos Saúl Menem	peso (1.00 = $1)	11,978	8,275
Bahamas	272,000	Governor General Clifford Darling; Prime Minister Hubert Ingraham	dollar (1.00 = $1)	2,678	2,920
Barbados	260,000	Governor General Dame Nita Barrow; Prime Minister Lloyd Erskine Sandiford	dollar (2.01 = $1)	202	695
Belize	204,000	Governor General Dame Minita E. Gordon; Prime Minister Manuel Esquivel	dollar (2.00 = $1)	141	273
Bolivia	8,171,000	President Gonzalo Sanchez de Lozada Busta-mente	boliviano (4.39 = $1)	858	942
Brazil	163,949,000	President Itamar Franco	cruzeiro real (168.00 = $1)	36,148	20,501
Chile	14,009,000	President Patricio Aylwin Azócar	peso (444.30 = $1)	9,986	10,129
Colombia	35,487,000	President César Gaviria Trujillo	peso (818.98 = $1)	7,269	4,967
Costa Rica	3,296,000	President Rafael Angel Calderón Fournier	colón (147.51 = $1)	1,741	2,445
Cuba	10,991,000	President Fidel Castro	peso (1.32 = $1)	3,585	3,690
Dominica	90,000	President Clarence Augustus Seignoret; Prime Minister Eugenia Charles	dollar (2.7 = $1)	55	118
Dominican Republic	7,755,000	President Joaquín Balaguer Ricardo	peso (13.00 = $1)	545	2,262
Ecuador	10,608,000	President Sixto Durán Ballén Cordovez	sucre (1,815.00 = $1)	3,008	2,491
El Salvador	5,790,000	President Alfredo Cristiani Burkard	colón (8.71 = $1)	412	902
Grenada	84,000	Governor General Reginald Palmer; Prime Minister Nicholas Brathwaite	dollar (2.7 = $1)	32	89
Guatemala	10,303,000	President Ramiro De León Carpio	quetzal (5.83 = $1)	1,058	2,463
Guyana	822,000	President Cheddi Jagan	dollar (126.00 = $1)	264	307
Haiti	6,731,000	President Jean-Bertrand Aristide‡	gourde (12.00 = $1)	103	374
Honduras	5,783,000	President Rafael Leonardo Callejas	lempira (6.96 = $1)	782	880
Jamaica	2,552,000	Governor General Howard Cooke; Prime Minister P. J. Patterson	dollar (27.50 = $1)	1,142	1,615
Mexico	95,939,000	President Carlos Salinas de Gortari	new peso (3.12 = $1)	27,531	48,138
Nicaragua	4,389,000	President Violeta Barrios de Chamorro	gold córdoba (6.24 = $1)	300	923
Panama	2,607,000	President Guillermo Endara	balboa (1 = $1)	510	2,019
Paraguay	4,756,000	President Juan Carlos Wasmosy	guaraní (1,720.00 = $1)	1,163	695
Peru	23,354,000	President Alberto Fujimori	new sol (2.16 = $1)	3,379	2,955
Puerto Rico	3,522,000	Governor Pedro Rossello	U.S. dollar	no statistics available	
St. Christopher and Nevis	44,000	Governor General Clement Atholston Arrindell; Prime Minister Kennedy Alphonse Simmonds	dollar (2.70 = $1)	25	103
St. Lucia	161,000	Governor General Sir Stanislaus James; Prime Minister John Compton	dollar (2.70 = $1)	123	313
St. Vincent and the Grenadines	121,000	Governor General David Jack; Prime Minister James F. Mitchell	dollar (2.70 = $1)	75	130
Suriname	453,000	President Ronald R. Venetiaan	guilder (1.79 = $1)	473	472
Trinidad and Tobago	1,355,000	President Noor Hassanali; Prime Minister Patrick Manning	dollar (5.52 = $1)	1,869	1,431
Uruguay	3,166,000	President Luis Alberto Lacalle	peso (4.23 = $1)	1,701	2,024
Venezuela	19,876,000	Interim President Ramon José Velasquez	bolívar (100.41 = $1)	13,173	12,946

*Exchange rates as of Oct. 29, 1993, or latest available data.
†Latest available data.
‡Democratically elected President Jean-Bertrand Aristide remained in exile following a military coup.

velop natural gas fields and liquefied natural gas plants with such giants as Exxon, Mitsubishi, Royal Dutch/Shell, Total S.A. of France, and Conoco Incorporated, a subsidiary of E. I. du Pont de Nemours.

Colombia, which had previously opened the door to foreign companies, confirmed in 1993 that with their help it has discovered the largest find in the Americas since the 1968 strike in Alaska's Prudhoe Bay. A May 20, 1993, analysis of the amount of oil in two large oil fields confirmed that they hold up to 5 billion barrels. The fields are about 100 miles (160 kilometers) northeast of Bogotá in the Cuisiana region. Workers began pumping oil from one of the oil fields, estimated to have 2 billion barrels of low-sulfur oil, on June 29. Half the oil will go to Colombia's state oil company. The balance will go to three foreign partners: British Petroleum, Total S.A. of France, and the Triton Energy Corporation of Dallas.

Although Mexico retained control of its oil industry, it also remained open to the possibility of foreign investment in 1993. Petróleos Mexicanos (PEMEX), the Mexican state oil company, announced plans to sell some 60 petrochemical plants to private investors. In another departure, PEMEX invited foreign companies to help finance a $1.4-billion refinery and to drill dozens of offshore wells.

Indian massacre. On July 23, gold miners working illegally within tribal reserve lands in Brazil's northernmost state near Venezuela allegedly slaughtered 13 Yanomami Indians near the remote town of Hoximú. The 10,000 Yanomami Indians in Brazil live on mineral-rich land that miners have heavily exploited since the mid-1980's. The Yanomami are believed to be the largest American Indian group to have preserved their way of life from outside influences. Brazilian President Itamar Franco called upon military forces to help track down the killers.

Scientists killed. On August 3, two U.S. biologists, who ranked among the world's leading scientists in their fields, died when an airplane they were in crashed while making a tree-top survey of the rain forest along Ecuador's coast near the town of Guayaquil. Theodore A. Parker III, 40, an ornithologist and senior scientist with Conservation International of Washington, D.C., an ecological conservation organization, and Alwyn Gentry, 48, a botanist and senior curator at the Missouri Botanical Garden in St. Louis, Mo., died in the crash. Eduardo Aspiazú, an Ecuadoran ecologist, also died in the crash.

Six scientists who were studying the Galeras volcano near Pasto, Colombia, died on January 14 when the volcano erupted. The catastrophe struck as 90 scientists from 15 nations met in Pasto as part of a UN effort to reduce the death toll from such natural disasters. ☐ Nathan A. Haverstock

See also articles on the individual nations. In **World Book**, see **Latin America** and articles on the individual nations.

Homeless children sleep on the street in Rio de Janeiro, Brazil, in April. Police allegedly shot eight homeless children to death in Rio de Janeiro in July.

Latvia in 1993 held its first elections since gaining independence from the former Soviet Union in 1991. But the country failed to achieve economic or political stability or to mend relations with Russia, which accused Latvia of violating human rights over its treatment of ethnic Russians there. In 1992, Latvia had passed a law that had the effect of denying citizenship to about 48 percent of Latvia's people who are not ethnic Latvians.

In elections on June 5 and 6, the Latvian Way—an alliance dominated by former Communist Party officials—emerged with 36 of 100 seats in parliament. The party formed a coalition with the Farmers' Association Party. On July 7, after two votes ended in bitter deadlock, the parliament elected banker Guntis Ulmanis of the Farmers' Association as Latvia's first post-Soviet president. The Latvian Way's Anatolijs Gorbunovs, who had served as the country's acting president, was reelected chairman of parliament.

Tension with Russia reached a peak in late August, as Russia again suspended its withdrawal of between 15,000 and 20,000 Soviet troops remaining in Latvia. (Russia had resumed the withdrawal in January after suspending it in late 1992.) In late October 1993, Latvia and Russia held talks on the withdrawal but reached no agreement.   □ Justin Burke

See also **Europe** (Facts in brief table). In *World Book,* see **Latvia.**

Law. See **Courts; Supreme Court of the U.S.**

Lebanon. Hopes of prosperity and peace, buoyed by Prime Minister Rafik Hariri's $10-billion plan to rebuild Lebanon by the year 2000, faltered when Israel bombed southern Lebanon for a week in late July 1993. The Israelis said they were retaliating for rocket attacks against northern Israel by the pro-Iranian Hezbollah (Party of God). The Israeli bombardment hit 70 villages north of a security zone maintained by Israel in southern Lebanon. About 130 Lebanese died and 600 were injured. Lebanese officials estimated that about 10,000 homes were destroyed and 20,000 were heavily damaged. The country was already struggling to rehouse the 20 percent of its people who were displaced during Lebanon's civil war from 1975 to 1991.

Eight Hezbollah activists were killed on September 13 by Lebanese troops in Beirut, the capital, during violent demonstrations protesting the peace agreement signed that day between Israel and the Palestine Liberation Organization. Hezbollah also resumed attacks against Israeli troops in the security zone during the rest of 1993.

In June, the parliament approved $2 billion for national reconstruction, including roads, electrical networks, telecommunications, and sewage and water systems. Lebanon also secured a $175-million loan from the World Bank.   □ Christine Helms

See also **Middle East** (Facts in brief table). In *World Book,* see **Lebanon.**

A city in Lebanon, An Nabatiyah, suffers damage during a seven-day Israeli bombardment in July that affected 70 villages in southern Lebanon.

275

Lemieux, Mario (1965-   ), overcame cancer to win the Hart Trophy in June 1993 as the National Hockey League's (NHL) Most Valuable Player for the 1992-1993 season. He also won the award in 1988.

Lemieux was born on Oct. 5, 1965, in Montreal, Canada. One of three children, he left high school during 10th grade to play Canadian junior hockey. The Pittsburgh Penguins drafted Lemieux first overall in the 1984 NHL draft.

Lemieux established himself quickly, winning the Calder Memorial Trophy (Rookie of the Year) in 1985 and becoming only the third player in NHL history to score more than 100 points in his first season. He has won four NHL scoring titles. On March 22, 1992, he scored his 1,000th point. Only Wayne Gretzky scored 1,000 points sooner in his career. Lemieux also led the Penguins to Stanley Cup championships in 1991 and 1992.

In January 1993, the Penguins announced that Lemieux had developed Hodgkin's disease, a cancer of the *lymph nodes* (structures that filter out harmful microbes). After treatment, he returned to hockey on March 2. He finished the season with a 2.67-points-per-game average, the third highest average in NHL history.

Lemieux married the former Nathalie Asselin of Montreal in summer 1993. They have a daughter, and the family lives in Pittsburgh, Pa.   □ Mark Dunbar

Lesotho. See Africa.

Liberia. The civil war in Liberia continued into 1993. By year-end, however, Liberians had renewed hopes for peace.

The first months of the year were marked by heavy fighting as an offensive launched in October 1992 by rebel commander Charles Taylor against the capital, Monrovia, raged on. Taylor and the troops of his National Patriotic Front of Liberia (NPFL) were one of two major rebel groups that overthrew President Samuel K. Doe in 1990. Taylor in 1992 refused to abide by a 1991 peace agreement that established an Interim Government of National Unity, headed by Interim President Amos Sawyer. The NPFL attack on Monrovia resulted in severe retaliation by forces of the Economic Community of West African States (ECOWAS). That multinational coalition had been trying since 1990 to bring an end to the war.

Massacre. On June 6, unidentified soldiers massacred as many as 600 people, most of them women and children, at a refugee camp near the town of Harbel, about 35 miles (56 kilometers) east of Monrovia. Survivers blamed the NPFL for the atrocity, but Taylor insisted that his forces had not been involved. United Nations (UN) investigators said on September 10 that another group, the Armed Forces of Liberia (AFL)—the remnants of the original Liberian Army—had conducted the slaughter.

The massacre was just one of many atrocities that have taken place during the Liberian conflict. By

mid-1993, more than 150,000 people had died in the war, and hundreds of thousands were homeless.

New peace agreement. The years of fighting, and particularly the heightened violence of the first half of 1993, seemed to have exhausted the combatants. Also, an anti-Taylor alliance of ECOWAS, the AFL, and a rebel group known as ULIMO, together with the blockading of ports and supply routes used by Taylor, put further pressure on the NPFL.

These factors led the warring parties to the negotiating table, and UN-supervised talks opened in Geneva, Switzerland, on July 10. On July 17, an agreement was announced that called for a cease-fire, disarmament, the introduction of a UN force, and elections in February 1994. The accord, signed on July 25, 1993, also provided for the broadening of the ECOWAS force to include troops from other African countries. That change diminished the prominent role played by Nigeria, which Taylor believed was not neutral and was opposed to the NPFL.

On July 31, the cease-fire went into effect. A UN Observer Mission in Liberia was established on September 22 to oversee the peace process. By November, a few members of the UN mission were in Liberia, but the disarmament process was proceeding slowly, and there were reports of renewed fighting in several areas.   □ Mark DeLancey

See also **Africa** (Facts in brief table). In *World Book,* see **Liberia.**

Library. Not even libraries were immune in 1993 to the epidemic of violence in the United States. On April 18, a gunman went on a shooting spree in a public library in Sacramento, Calif., killing two reference librarians. The murders occurred right before the 5 p.m. closing of the new Central Library, which had just concluded a celebration for the restoration of Sunday hours. The gunman was shot to death by Sacramento police officers. On September 1, a librarian on duty alone was fatally stabbed at the Seminole County Library in Donalsonville, Ga. Twelve hours later, a 16-year-old youth was arrested and charged with armed robbery and murder.

Funding problems. Faced with a $2-million budget shortfall in 1993, the Baltimore County Library in Maryland made an unpopular decision to permanently close nine libraries and lay off 24 librarians rather than cut hours and materials across the system. Library director Charles Robinson said, "I'd rather run a smaller, excellent library than a larger, lousy one." The New Orleans Public Library handled a budget shortfall by closing all of its 15 libraries on Fridays. In Multnomah County, Oregon, county commissioners wanted the library to charge for the 250,000 calls for reference information it receives each year, but librarians succeeded in maintaining free information services.

These crises were small compared with those of California's county library districts, which serve 250 communities, or 43 percent of the state's population. The state budget for 1993-1994 threatened to cut as much as 50 percent of the county library service. The Los Angeles County Public Library stood to lose $29.4 million—half of its budget—which could force the closing of 43 of its 87 branches and the cutting of hours by half in the remaining libraries. Ventura County planned to close 12 of its 15 libraries, and Orange County foresaw cutting hours by 44 percent. The state had already suffered the closing of more than half of its school libraries and eight of its public library systems.

The Los Angeles Public Library, a city system, rededicated its Central Public Library on Oct. 3, 1993. The landmark library had been severely damaged by an arson fire in 1986. The gala reopening, following a $214-million renovation, was one of the largest free public parties in Los Angeles history. Celebrities, politicians, business leaders, and thousands of citizens toured the facility, which is now twice its former size.

Midwestern floods seriously damaged three libraries in Missouri and three more in Kansas in 1993, but many were spared in otherwise ravaged areas. Nine Illinois libraries were affected but only one remained closed. Almost every library in the flooded areas saw increased use after the flooding. Library officials believed that flood victims came for refuge and information.

Information technology. On September 15, Ronald H. Brown, U.S. secretary of commerce and chairman of a task force on information technology, issued a position paper on behalf of the Administration of President Bill Clinton concerning the National Information Infrastructure (NII), also called the information superhighway. In September, 15 library and information associations met to consider policies for the NII. (See also **Telecommunications.**)

In 1993, the Cleveland Public Library became the first U.S. library to offer public access to Internet. Many other libraries linked up to Internet, a collection of computer networks that spans the globe. These connections provide electronic mail, access to computers in many parts of the world, and access to numerous databases. Internet users can search the catalogs of libraries around the world.

School library media centers received a boost in 1993. The DeWitt Wallace-Reader's Digest Fund, a philanthropic foundation, expanded a $45-million initiative to make media centers an educational focal point in elementary and middle schools. The project is administered by the American Association of School Librarians, a division of the American Library Association. The project gives grants to match state or local funds for refurbishing school library media centers. Nine grants were announced in the spring of 1993, and the fund is to be extended to up to 25 communities by 1996. ☐ Peggy Barber

In *World Book*, see **Library.**

Libya failed to meet an Oct. 1, 1993, deadline to hand over two terrorist suspects, so the United Nations (UN) Security Council voted on November 11 to toughen economic sanctions against Libya. Previous UN sanctions, including bans on air traffic and sales of military equipment to Libya, went into effect on April 15, 1992, when Libyan leader Muammar Muhammad al-Qadhafi failed to meet an earlier deadline.

The suspects are wanted for the bombing of a Pan American World Airways jetliner over Lockerbie, Scotland, in 1988, which killed 270 people. France also wants to question Libyan suspects about the downing of a French plane in 1989 that killed 171 people. The 1993 UN resolution went into effect December 1, freezing Libya's overseas assets and banning some sales of oil equipment to Libya. Libya claims the suspects will not receive a fair trial.

Nearly 200 Libyan Muslims went to Israel to tour holy sites in May 1993. Observers discounted the event as an attempt by Qadhafi to improve his image during the ongoing UN sanctions dilemma.

On February 16, German officials confirmed that three German firms had supplied Libya with materials that were used to construct a chemical-weapons factory southeast of Tripoli. ☐ Christine Helms

See also **Middle East** (Facts in brief table). In *World Book*, see **Libya.**

Liechtenstein. See **Europe.**

Literature. As a group, Irish writers produced the finest fiction in English in 1993. They were led by Roddy Doyle, whose *Paddy Clarke Ha Ha Ha* was a beautifully realized story of childhood in Dublin, Ireland, in the 1960's. On Oct. 27, 1993, the novel won the Booker Prize, the United Kingdom's most prestigious literary award. Other important books with Irish roots were Michael Collins' *The Man Who Dreamt of Lobsters;* Patrick McCabe's *The Butcher Boy;* and Colm Toibin's *The Heather Blazing.*

England also produced many fine novels, including A. S. Byatt's *Angels and Insects;* Michael Frayn's *Now You Know;* John Le Carré's *The Night Manager;* Penelope Lively's *Cleopatra's Sister;* John Mortimer's *Dunster;* and Rose Tremain's *Sacred Country.*

One of the year's most striking debuts in English was the Indian Vikram Seth's *A Suitable Boy.*

Major biographies were Victoria Glendinning's *Anthony Trollope;* Andrew Motion's *Philip Larkin;* and William Shawcross' *Murdoch.* In *The Downing Street Years,* Margaret Thatcher recalled her career as the United Kingdom's first female prime minister.

Translations. Japanese author Banana Yoshimoto's *Kitchen* portrayed the lives of young Japanese. Dutch author Peter Hoeg's *Smilla's Sense of Snow* was a suspense novel with a complex heroine. ☐ Henry Kisor

See also **Canadian literature; Literature, American; Literature for children.**

Literature, American. The year 1993 produced no new trend in any genre in American literature. First-rate books were published in many areas, by both veteran writers and newcomers.

James Dickey's *To the White Sea,* a novel of survival during World War II (1939-1945), demonstrated that the distinguished poet still possessed a powerful narrative skill. Stanley Elkin's *Van Gogh's Room at Arles* was a brilliant collection of three novellas that showed astonishing range and depth. Mary Gordon's own collection of three novellas, *The Rest of Life,* also showed amazing breadth and insight.

Barbara Kingsolver's *Pigs in Heaven* was a fierce and stylish novel centered on a self-professed Kentucky hillbilly's adoption of a Native-American child. Bobbie Ann Mason's *Feather Crowns* was a richly layered novel of quintuplets and miracles in Kentucky in the early 1900's. *Operation Shylock,* by the always inventive Philip Roth, was a farcical yet reflective tale about a novelist named Philip Roth who learns that an impostor bearing his name is operating in Israel and may be a secret agent.

T. Coraghessan Boyle drove home his claim as one of America's best younger novelists with *The Road to Wellville,* a satirical tale set in the breakfast-cereal capital of the world, Battle Creek, Mich. Bob Shacochis, who had made his name as a short-story writer, wrote *Swimming in the Volcano,* an epic portrait of a fictional Caribbean island.

Other notable novels were Alice Adams' *Almost Perfect;* Richard Bausch's *Rebel Powers;* Charles Baxter's *Shadow Play;* Louis Begley's *The Man Who Was Late;* Madison Smartt Bell's *Save Me, Joe Louis;* Robert Boswell's *Mystery Ride;* Mark Childress' *Crazy in Alabama;* Steve Erickson's *Arc D'X;* Abby Frucht's *Are You Mine?;* Kaye Gibbons' *Charms for the Easy Life;* William Gibson's *Virtual Light;* Sue Miller's *For Love;* Brian Moore's *No Other Life;* Mary Morris' *A Mother's Love;* T. R. Pearson's *Cry Me a River;* E. Annie Proulx's *The Shipping News;* Richard Russo's *Nobody's Fool;* and Charlie Smith's *Chimney Rock.* In November 1993, *The Shipping News* won the National Book Award for fiction.

Multicultural voices. The most vivid entry in multicultural fiction in 1993 was the Cuban-American Oscar Hijuelos' *The Fourteen Sisters of Emilio Montez O'Brien,* an exuberant celebration of life in a Cuban-Irish family in a small Pennsylvania town. The Indian-American Bharati Mukherjee's *The Holder of the World* was an engaging novel that spanned from the early 1600's to the present and from Salem, Mass., to the coast of India. The Mexican-American writer Ana Castillo explored magic at work in New Mexico in *So Far from God.*

First novels. Among the year's best debuts were Robert O'Connor's *Buffalo Soldiers,* a tale of absurdity in the military during the armed peace after the Cold War; Alan Lightman's *Einstein's Dreams,* a fable about the physics of time; Fae Myenne Ng's *Bone,*

a novel about cultural assimilation and the younger generation in San Francisco's Chinatown area; and Mark Richard's *Fishboy,* a hybrid of Gothic horror novel and sea story.

Short stories. Notable collections of short stories included Alison Baker's *How I Came West, and Why I Stayed;* Maxine Chernoff's *Signs of Devotion;* Mavis Gallant's *Across the Bridge;* Thom Jones's *The Pugilist at Rest;* Reynolds Price's *The Collected Stories;* Francine Prose's *Stories;* William Styron's *A Tidewater Morning;* and Peter Taylor's *The Oracle at Stoneleigh Court.*

Literary biographies. In *The Man Who Wasn't Maigret,* author Patrick Marnham portrayed Georges Simenon as being as energetic in his womanizing as he was in his mystery writing. *The Passion of Michel Foucault* by James Miller was a highly critical biography of the French philosopher whose arcane ideas on the nature of literature have become popular in American universities. In *Genet: A Biography,* Edmund White explored how the great French writer turned the violent experience of his life into art.

Other biographies. Several biographies of black Americans reached bookstores in 1993. Two books about Thurgood Marshall, the first black to become a Supreme Court justice, were published right after his death in January. The books were Carl T. Rowan's *Dream Makers, Dream Breakers* and Michael D. Davis and Hunter R. Clark's *Thurgood Marshall.* David Levering Lewis' *W. E. B. Du Bois: Biography of a Race: Volume I, 1868-1919* covered the first half of the complex life of the black scholar-activist. Two illuminating autobiographies of black civil rights activists of the 1970's were Elaine Brown's *A Taste of Power* and David Hilliard's *This Side of Glory.*

Other important biographies were Daniel Mark Epstein's *Sister Aimee,* about Aimee Semple McPherson, the colorful American evangelist; William Innes Homer's *Thomas Eakins: His Life and Art,* a study of the great American painter; William Lanouette and Bela Silard's *Genius in the Shadows,* a biography of physicist Leo Szilard; Richard Reeves' *President Kennedy,* a cool portrait of John F. Kennedy; and *Marlene Dietrich,* a riveting demystification of the motion-picture star by her daughter, Maria Riva.

Memoirs. *Days of Grace* was the late Arthur Ashe's memoir of life as a black tennis star in a sport dominated by whites. *My Life as Author and Editor* was the long-awaited autobiography by the late H. L. Mencken. The work, which the writer had asked not to be published until at least 35 years after his death, was by turns fascinating, disappointing, and repulsive. In *New York Days,* Willie Morris told of his editorship of *Harper's* magazine during the 1960's, a time of upheaval in journalism. In *Turmoil and Triumph,* George P. Shultz discussed his tenure as President Ronald Reagan's secretary of state.

Terry Anderson's *Den of Lions* related the author's ordeal as a hostage of Shiite Muslims in the

Author Toni Morrison, who in October became the first black American to win the Nobel Prize for literature, reads from her book *Beloved* (1987).

Middle Eastern country of Lebanon in the 1980's. *Picasso and Dora* was James Lord's memoirs of his relationship in the 1950's and 1960's with painter Pablo Picasso and one of his mistresses, Dora Maar. In *Remembering Denny,* Calvin Trillin recalled and traced the life of a Yale classmate who committed suicide in middle age after building a promising future in college.

Letters. Among important collections of correspondence published in 1993 were *The Gonne-Yeats Letters 1893-1938,* edited by Anna McBride White and A. Norman Jeffares, which told of the love story between Irish poet William Butler Yeats and aristocratic countrywoman Maud Gonne, and *Delmore Schwartz and James Laughlin: Selected Letters,* edited by Robert Phillips, an enlightening exchange of letters between Schwartz, a troubled American poet, and Laughlin, a far-sighted publisher of experimental literature.

Criticism. In *Culture of Complaint,* the perceptive and curmudgeonly art critic Robert Hughes dissected the struggle over "political correctness" in American intellectual life. More scholarly was Edward W. Said's *Culture and Imperialism,* in which the Palestinian-born American critic brilliantly discussed the importance of imperial conquest in themes of Western culture. *The Sixties: The Last Journal, 1960-1972* was the fifth and final volume of the late critic Edmund Wilson's magisterial journals.

Essays. *United States: Essays 1952-1992* brought together the elegant and witty essays that the distinguished novelist Gore Vidal had written over 40 years. In November 1993, *United States* won the National Book Award for nonfiction.

History. Several significant history books covered events related to World War II. *The Warburgs* was Ron Chernow's engrossing study of a remarkable German-Jewish family important in finance and the arts in both Europe and the United States, and the betrayal of the family during the Holocaust, the mass murder of Jews by the Nazis. In *Denying the Holocaust,* Deborah E. Lipstadt brilliantly examined the perverse rationales of the people who declare that the Nazis did not exterminate 6 million Jews. Thomas Powers' controversial *Heisenberg's War* contended that the Nobel Prize-winning physicist Werner Heisenberg, who remained in Germany during World War II, deliberately tried to hinder Nazi progress toward atomic weapons.

David Halberstam's popular history *The Fifties* demonstrated that a period of American history often thought stodgy—the 1950's—was actually a lively and consequential time.

Contemporary nonfiction. Two interesting books on religion in American life were Ronald L. Numbers' *The Creationists,* which looked at the roots of the conflict between believers in a literal interpretation of the Biblical book of Genesis and believers

279

in evolutionary science, and Stephen L. Carter's *The Culture of Disbelief,* which charged that contemporary political and legal decisions unwisely exclude all consideration of religion in American life.

Paul Kennedy's *Preparing for the Twenty-First Century* was a gloomy prognosis for the world after the millennium. David Remnick's *Lenin's Tomb* expertly and invitingly relived the collapse of the former Soviet Union from the point of view of ordinary Russians whose lives were thrown into turmoil.

Two books on aging in America were Betty Friedan's *The Fountain of Age* and Tracy Kidder's *Old Friends.* The first book was notable for its optimism, the second for its pessimism. In *Conduct Unbecoming,* Randy Shilts produced a powerful and disturbing study of the contributions that gay and lesbian soldiers have made to the U.S. military and argued that the military has treated them unjustly.

Several writers made names for themselves with controversial books. David Brock's *The Real Anita Hill* attacked the woman who brought charges of sexual harassment against Supreme Court Justice Clarence Thomas during his nomination hearings in 1991. In *Case Closed,* Gerald Posner claimed to establish an irrefutable case that Lee Harvey Oswald acted alone in the assassination of President John F. Kennedy in 1963. Katie Roiphe's *The Morning After* charged that an overemphasis on date rape on college campuses places women in the role of helpless victims, hindering the larger cause of feminism.

Science. Several excellent books on science and natural history for nonscientists appeared in 1993. *Eight Little Piggies* was the sixth collection of essays from the distinguished paleontologist Stephen Jay Gould. *Assembling California* was the fourth and final volume in John McPhee's "Annals of the Former World," his account of the rise of the theory of plate tectonics in geology.

Three books took widely differing views of the Neanderthals. They were Christopher Stringer and Clive Gamble's *In Search of the Neanderthals,* Jeffrey H. Schwartz's *What the Bones Tell Us,* and Erik Trinkhaus and Pat Shipman's *The Neandertals.*

George B. Schaller's *The Last Panda* was an affecting group portrait of the threatened species. *The Hidden Life of Dogs,* by the anthropologist-novelist Elizabeth Marshall Thomas, was a speculative look inside canine minds.

Best-selling romances. *The Bridges of Madison County,* a sentimental story by Robert James Waller about an affair between a photographer and an Iowa farmer's wife, appeared in 1992 and sold more than 4 million copies before it was toppled from the number-one spot on the best-seller lists late in 1993 by a second, similar Waller novel, *Slow Waltz in Cedar Bend.*   □ Henry Kisor

See also **Canadian literature; Literature; Literature for children; Poetry.** In **World Book,** see **American literature.**

Literature for children. Children's books published in 1993 were noteworthy for the number of books that emphasized multiculturalism and the environment. Many picture books were of folk tales, and books for middle and upper grades addressed getting along with others. Informational books on a wide variety of subjects continued to be published, and more fantasy appeared. Outstanding books of 1993 included the following:

Picture books. *Too Many Cooks: And Other Proverbs* illustrated by Maggie Kneen (Green Tiger Pr.). Twenty-three familiar sayings are illustrated. An explanation of the proverbs is in the back. All ages.

The Sweetest Fig by Chris Van Allsburg (Houghton Mifflin). A fussy, self-centered dentist is given magic figs and gets what he deserves. All ages.

Lester's Dog by Karen Hesse, illustrated by Nancy Carpenter (Crown). A boy follows a deaf friend past a mean dog, then must return alone. Ages 4 to 8.

A Small Tall Tale from the Far Far North by Peter Sis (Knopf). This Arctic saga combines humor with action. All ages.

Fox Song by Joseph Bruchac, illustrated by Paul Morin (Philomel). When Jamie remembers what her grandmother told and showed her, she knows Grama is near. Ages 4 and up.

We Are All in the Dumps with Jack and Guy illustrated by Maurice Sendak (HarperCollins). Illustrations of two nursery rhymes show homeless children finding love amid hard times. All ages.

The Bee Tree by Patricia Polacco (Philomel). When Grandpa and Mary Ellen go after a bee tree, they are joined by many others. Ages 4 to 8.

Magic Spring by Nami Rhee (Putnam). In a Korean tale, an old couple finds a special spring and a greedy neighbor gets what he deserves. Ages 4 to 8.

Waiting for the Whales by Sheryl McFarlane, illustrated by Ron Lightburn (Philomel). In a Canadian award winner, an old man watches for killer whales to return each summer, sharing his joy and knowledge with his granddaughter. All ages.

Square Beak by Chyng Feng Sun, illustrated by Chihsien Chen (Houghton Mifflin). A chick born with a square beak has other talents. Ages 4 to 8.

Author's Day by Daniel Pinkwater (Macmillan). This wildly funny book should delight all children's book authors as well as children. Ages 5 to 8.

Chin Yu Min and the Ginger Cat by Jennifer Armstrong, illustrated by Mary Grandpre (Crown). Chin Yu Min scorns others until she learns appreciation and contentment from a cat. Ages 5 to 8.

The Dragon's Pearl by Julie Lawson, illustrated by Paul Morin (Clarion). Xiao Sheng finds a magic pearl that brings food and money until robbers come and Xiao swallows the pearl. Ages 5 to 9.

Julius by Angela Johnson, illustrated by Dav Pilkey (Orchard Bks.). Grandaddy brings Maya an unusual present that creates problems for her parents, but Maya is delighted. Ages 3 to 6.

The Boy Who Lived with the Seals by Rafe Martin, illustrated by David Shannon (Putnam). A Chinook Native American legend of a lost boy. Ages 4 to 8.

Monster Mama by Liz Rosenberg, illustrated by Stephen Gammell (Philomel). Patrick Edward's mama is a monster, but that is just fine. Ages 4 and up.

Zoom at Sea by Tim Wynne-Jones, illustrated by Eric Beddows (Laura Geringer/HarperCollins). Zoom has seafaring cats' blood in his veins, and it leads to a magical trip. Canadian award winner. Ages 4 to 8.

The Singing Snake by Stefan Czernecki and Timothy Rhodes, illustrated by Stefan Czernecki (Hyperion Bks.). Australian tale shows why snakes hiss and how the didgeridoo was made. Ages 4 to 8.

Kinda Blue by Ann Grifalconi (Little, Brown). Sissy feels sad and lonely until her uncle shows her something special about plants and herself. Ages 4 to 7.

Rude Giants by Audrey Wood (Harcourt Brace Jovanovich). Tale of a young girl's witty reformation of two rude giants. Comical illustrations. Ages 3 to 7.

Babysitting for Benjamin by Valiska Gregory, illustrated by Lynn Munsinger (Little, Brown). When Frances and Ralph, two mice, baby-sit with Benjamin the rabbit, he gets into everything. Ages 4 to 8.

Raven by Gerald McDermott (Harcourt Brace Jovanovich). In this Native American trickster tale, Raven brings daylight to the people. Ages 4 to 8.

Fish Story by Katharine Andres, illustrated by DeLoss McGraw (Simon & Schuster). Craig meets a wish-granting fish and takes him home. Ages 4 to 7.

The Man Who Tricked a Ghost by Laurence Yep, illustrated by Isadore Seltzer (BridgeWater Bks.). Sung goes and meets a ghost at night. Ages 5 to 9.

Strega Nona Meets Her Match by Tomie De Paola (Putnam). This girl has a competitor. Ages 4 to 8.

The Story of a Boy Named Will, Who Went Sledding Down the Hill by Daniil Kharms, translated by Jamey Gambrell, illustrated by Vladimir Radunsky (North-South Bks.). Ages 1 to 5.

Bamboo Hats and a Rice Cake adapted by Ann Tompert, illustrated by Demi (Crown). Japanese characters act like pictures. Ages 4 to 8.

Fiction. *Bull Run* by Paul Fleischman (HarperCollins). Individuals tell of their experiences in this Civil War novel. Ages 12 and up.

Timothy of the Cay by Theodore Taylor (Harcourt Brace). Readers of *The Cay* learn more about Timothy and blind Phillip. Ages 10 to 14.

Lydia, Queen of Palestine by Uri Orlev, translated by Hillel Halkin (Houghton Mifflin). Lydia travels to a new country and confronts problems. Ages 8 to 11.

Haveli by Suzanne Fisher Staples (Knopf). A sequel to *Shabanu*. Ages 12 and up.

For the Life of Laetitia by Merle Hodge (Farrar, Straus & Giroux). Laetitia can go to school but must live with her father and his wife. Ages 12 and up.

Annie Is Still Here by Ida Voss, translated by Terese Edelstein and Inez Smith (Houghton Mifflin). Annie adapts after hiding from Nazis. Ages 8 to 12.

Molly Donnelly by Jean Thesman (Houghton Mifflin). World War II erupts and Molly's Seattle world becomes irreversibly changed. Ages 10 and up.

Make Lemonade by Virginia Euwer Wolff (Henry Holt). Verna answers a baby-sitting ad and becomes enmeshed in the lives of a family. Ages 12 and up.

Echoes of the White Giraffe by Sook Nyul Choi (Houghton Mifflin). In a sequel to *Year of Impossible Goodbyes*, Sookan, a refugee in Pusan, South Korea, faces love and restlessness. Ages 12 and up.

Leaving Eldorado by Joann Mazzio (Houghton Mifflin). Maude, 14, left on her own in a mining town, is determined to be an artist. Ages 10 to 14.

Alice in April by Phyllis Reynolds Naylor (Atheneum). Another delightful saga about Alice and the trials she faces as she is about to become 13. Ages 9 to 13.

Shizuko's Daughter by Kyoko Mori (Henry Holt). After her mother commits suicide, Yuki's life changes when she goes to live with her father and her new stepmother. Set in Japan. Ages 12 and up.

Harper & Moon by Ramon Royal Ross (Atheneum). Trust and friendship between Harper and Moon are threatened by a mysterious death. Ages 10 and up.

For the Love of Pete by Jan Marino (Little, Brown). Gram goes into a nursing home and her granddaughter, Phoebe, goes to the father she's never met. Ages 10 and up.

Poetry. *Rich Lizard and Other Poems* by Deborah Chandra, illustrated by Leslie Bowman (Farrar, Straus & Giroux). Familiar objects and sights take on a new radiance in these original poems. Ages 8 to 10.

The Dragons Are Singing Tonight by Jack Prelutsky, illustrated by Peter Sis (Greenwillow). Poems about dragons. Ages 4 to 8.

Brown Angels by Walter Dean Myers (HarperCollins). A variety of poems is illustrated with turn-of-the-century photos of African-American children. All ages.

It's Hard to Read a Map with a Beagle on Your Lap by Marilyn Singer, illustrated by Clement Oubrerie (Henry Holt). Laughable lyrics and comical illustrations about dogs. All ages.

Zoomrimes: Poems about Things that Go by Sylvia Cassedy, illustrated by Michelle Chessare (HarperCollins). Imaginative rhymes. Ages 8 to 12.

Extra Innings: Baseball Poems selected by Lee Bennett Hopkins, illustrated by Scott Medlock (Harcourt Brace Jovanovich). Paintings catch the spirit of the game revealed in the poems. Ages 8 to 12.

A. Nonny Mouse Writes Again! selected by Jack Prelutsky, illustrated by Marjorie Priceman (Knopf). Children will have fun guessing which rhymes are by Prelutsky while enjoying lots of nonsense. All ages.

Animals, people, places, and things. *Powwow* by George Ancona (Harcourt Brace Jovanovich). Native American culture and dances at the summer Crow Fair powwows. Ages 6 to 12.

Mirette on the High Wire, the story of a young girl and a high-wire artist, earned a Caldecott Medal in January for author and illustrator Emily Arnold McCully.

Eleanor Roosevelt: A Life of Discovery by Russell Freedman (Clarion). One of the most important women of the 1900's is portrayed in prose and 200 photos. Bibliography, index. Ages 10 and up.

Wolves by Seymour Simon (HarperCollins). Bad myths surrounding this species are dispelled. Fine color photos. Ages 6 and up.

Dear World: How Children Around the World Feel About Our Environment edited by Lannis Temple (Random House). Children's hopes and observations about the world. Ages 6 and up.

Many Thousand Gone: African Americans from Slavery to Freedom by Virginia Hamilton, illustrated by Leo and Diane Dillon (Knopf). Profiles of familiar and unfamiliar people. Ages 10 and up.

Whaling Days by Carol Carrick, illustrated by David Frampton (Clarion Bks.). Text and woodcuts give history and description of whaling. Ages 6 to 9.

Animals Observed: A Look at Animals in Art by Dorcas McClintock (Scribner's). Information and artwork of animals are presented. All ages.

Amish Home by Raymond Bial (Houghton Mifflin). In color photos and an engaging text, readers learn about Amish lives and beliefs. Ages 8 and up.

Tentacles: The Amazing World of Octopus, Squid, and Their Relatives by James Martin (Crown). Information and color photos. Ages 10 and up.

The Sierra Club Book of Small Mammals by Linsay Knight (Sierra Club). Ages 10 and up.

I Was a Teenage Professional Wrestler by Ted

Lewin (Orchard Bks.). A well-known illustrator talks about an earlier career. Ages 11 and up.

A Short Walk Around the Pyramids & Through the World of Art by Philip M. Isaacson (Knopf). Explains sculpture, color, and more. Ages 8 and up.

Lincoln in His Own Words edited by Milton Meltzer, illustrated by Stephen Alcorn (Harcourt Brace Jovanovich). Abraham Lincoln's thoughts on a variety of subjects. Ages 10 and up.

Fantasy. *The Boggart* by Susan Cooper (McElderry Bks.). When the Volniks inherit a Scottish castle, they get more than they bargained for. Ages 9 to 12.

More Rootabagas by Carl Sandburg, illustrated by Paul O. Zelinsky (Knopf). Ten previously unpublished zany stories have unusual characters and events and rollicking language, with fine illustrations. All ages.

The Flying Emu and Other Australian Stories by Sally Morgan (Knopf). Humorous tales, many about creation and animal characteristics. Ages 8 and up.

The Wainscot Weasel by Tor Selden, illustrated by Fred Marcellino (Michael di Capua/HarperCollins). Bagley cannot forget his famous father and how he disappeared. Ages 8 to 12.

Flight of the Dragon Kyn by Susan Fletcher (Atheneum). Kara must call down dragons, but that leads to trouble and adventure. Ages 10 and up.

The Giver by Lois Lowry (Houghton Mifflin). When Jonas becomes a Receiver in the time of Sameness, he learns about the wonders and terrors of earlier generations. Ages 12 and up.

Matthew and the Sea Singer by Jill Paton Walsh (Farrar, Straus & Giroux). Birdy buys Matthew, but the sea queen kidnaps him. Ages 7 to 10.

Strange Objects by Gary Crew (Simon & Schuster). An iron pot and its contents, found by a boy, trigger visions into the past of a shipwreck. Australian award winner. Ages 12 and up.

Switching Well by Peni R. Griffin (McElderry Bks.). Ada and Amber, a century apart, wish to change centuries, so they switch places. Ages 10 to 14.

The Crystal Drop by Monica Hughes (Simon & Schuster). Megan and Ian set out across the drought-stricken West in 2011. Ages 12 and up.

Dragon Sword and Wind Child by Noriko Ogiwara (Farrar, Straus & Giroux). In this Japanese myth, Saya, torn between the warring forces of Light and Darkness, is in constant danger. Ages 12 and up.

Awards. Cynthia Rylant won the 1993 Newbery Medal for her novel *Missing May*. The medal is given by the American Library Association (ALA) for outstanding children's literature published the previous year.

The ALA's Caldecott Medal for "the most distinguished American picture book for children" went to Emily Arnold McCully, the illustrator and author, for *Mirette on the High Wire*.

□ Marilyn Fain Apseloff

In *World Book*, see **Caldecott Medal; Newbery Medal; Literature for children.**

Lithuania. Lithuanians on Feb. 14, 1993, elected Algirdas Brazauskas, head of the governing Democratic Labor Party (formerly the Communist Party), as president in Lithuania's first presidential election since it regained independence in 1991. Brazauskas won 60 percent of the vote, defeating Stasys Lozoraitis, who had been endorsed by the nationalist movement Sajudis. The results indicated that Lithuanians favored a gradual transition from the centrally planned Communist system to a market economy.

On March 10, 1993, Brazauskas appointed Adolfas Slezevicius as prime minister to oversee the cautious reforms. The year's chief reform came on June 25, when Lithuania began circulating a national currency, the litas, a step designed to solidify economic independence from Russia.

Relations with Russia took center stage beginning August 22, when Russia announced that it was suspending its withdrawal of 2,500 remaining former Soviet troops from Lithuania. Observers said the Russian action was meant to protest Lithuanian demands that Russia compensate Lithuania for economic damage allegedly caused by the 50-year Soviet occupation of the Baltic nation. But Brazauskas persuaded Russian President Boris Yeltsin to put the compensation issue aside, and the last Russian soldier left Lithuania on August 31. □ Justin Burke

See also **Europe** (Facts in brief table). In *World Book,* see **Lithuania.**

Los Angeles. On April 17, 1993, a federal jury returned guilty verdicts against two Los Angeles police officers for violating the civil rights of motorist Rodney G. King in March 1991. The officers, Sergeant Stacey C. Koon and patrolman Laurence M. Powell, were convicted for their roles in the arrest and beating of King, an incident that was videotaped by an onlooker and widely broadcast. Two other officers, Theodore J. Briseno and Timothy E. Wind, were acquitted.

The trial heightened racial tensions in Los Angeles because all the officers are white, and King is black. In April 1992, a state jury had acquitted the same officers of assaulting King, touching off rioting that left more than 50 people dead. Los Angeles residents feared a new outbreak of violence if the officers were also acquitted on the federal charges. On Aug. 4, 1993, a federal judge sentenced Koon and Powell to 2½ years in prison. Prosecutors in the case had requested longer sentences for the two men.

Denny trial. Another case that stemmed from the 1992 riots ended in October 1993. Two Los Angeles men—Damian M. Williams and Henry K. Watson—were acquitted of most of the felony charges against them resulting from attacks on truckdriver Reginald O. Denny and other people on April 29, 1992. Williams and Watson are both black, and the victims were white, Hispanic, or Asian-American.

On Oct. 18, 1993, Williams was convicted on a single felony charge of committing mayhem and on four misdemeanor assault charges. Two days later, he was acquitted on the most serious charge, attempted murder. The jury deadlocked on a felony assault charge against Watson, whose only conviction was for one count of misdemeanor assault.

On November 1, Watson pleaded guilty to the felony assault charge. As part of the plea agreement, he was spared a prison term. On December 7, Williams was given the maximum sentence of 10 years in prison.

New mayor. Richard J. Riordan, a 63-year-old multimillionaire businessman, was inaugurated on July 1 as the 39th mayor of Los Angeles. Riordan became the city's first Republican mayor in 32 years. He succeeded Democrat Tom Bradley, mayor since 1973.

In winning his first bid for elective office, Riordan defeated City Council member Michael Woo in the June 8, 1993, election. Riordan promised to work toward making Los Angeles "safe and friendly." His first budget won the unanimous approval of the City Council on October 6. The budget provided funding for the police department to continue hiring until it reaches its authorized level of 7,900 officers.

Rampaging fires. Devastating brushfires, spread by strong winds, swept through southern California in late October and early November, destroying hundreds of homes in Los Angeles County. Three people were reported killed. The first blaze began in a canyon northeast of Los Angeles, reportedly when a campfire that a transient had started to keep warm spread to dry underbrush. Fire officials said at least two acts of arson touched off new fires in other areas around the city.

By November 2, the fires seemed to be under control. But then a new fire, perhaps caused by arson, began to rage in a canyon just west of Los Angeles. The flames moved toward the coast, where they burned about 300 homes in the Malibu area. That last fire was finally subdued on November 4.

Smoking ban. On June 23, despite heavy lobbying by restaurateurs, smokers, and the tobacco industry, the City Council approved a smoking ban in all the city's restaurants. The move made Los Angeles the largest city in the nation to adopt such a law. Restaurant owners who resist the ban will face a misdemeanor charge, punishable by up to six months in jail or a $1,000 fine. Smokers who light up despite warnings are subject to a $50 fine. (See also **Public health: The Dangers of Passive Smoking.**)

Subway opens. The first segment of Los Angeles' new subway, the Metro Red Line, opened on January 30 amid much fanfare. The segment stretches for 4.4 miles (7 kilometers) from downtown Union Station to MacArthur Park.   □ Victor Merina

See also **City.** In *World Book*, see **Los Angeles.**

Louisiana. See **State government.**

Luxembourg. See **Europe.**

Madagascar. See **Africa.**

Businessman Richard J. Riordan exults on June 8 after winning election as the first Republican mayor of Los Angeles since 1961.

Magazine. *The New Yorker* continued to dominate magazine news in 1993 as it had in 1992 after appointing Tina Brown editor. Long-time readers of the magazine held their breath waiting to see how the former editor in chief of the flamboyant *Vanity Fair* would jazz up the venerable *New Yorker.*

In early 1993, Richard Avedon became the magazine's first staff photographer. Avedon's striking fashion photographs have appeared in magazines for half a century. *The New Yorker* carried dramatic full-page photos by Avedon in almost every issue.

Some long-time readers continued to criticize *The New Yorker* for abandoning its traditionally discreet tone. But with Brown at the helm, the magazine's newsstand sales doubled, and subscription renewals and advertising sales were very strong.

Libel trial. *The New Yorker* was also in the spotlight in 1993 because of a celebrated trial in which psychoanalyst Jeffrey M. Masson accused the magazine and writer Janet Malcolm of defaming him in a 1983 article. On June 2, a federal jury in San Francisco decided that Malcolm had defamed Masson by fabricating five quotations. The jury also found that two of the quotations were libelous, meaning that the author had fabricated or substantially altered them; that she knew they would harm Masson's reputation; that she acted with "reckless disregard" for their accuracy; and that Masson had been damaged by them.

The jury, however, found *The New Yorker* not guilty of libel. It determined that Malcolm was an independent contractor rather than a magazine employee, and that the magazine was unaware that the quotes were fabricated. When the jury could not decide on a monetary award that might be due Masson, the judge ruled in September that a new trial must take place. But he severed *The New Yorker* from the case, making Malcolm the only defendant.

New acquisitions. In April 1993, Condé Nast Publications Incorporated announced it was ceasing publication of *HG,* a leading decorating magazine since its founding as *House & Garden* in 1901. In May, Condé Nast had agreed to acquire Knapp Communications' *Architectural Digest,* which was *HG*'s main rival. The company said that it could not sustain both magazines and that its own publication was not as profitable as the one it was buying.

As part of the agreement with Knapp, Condé Nast also acquired another competitor, *Bon Appétit,* a food magazine. Condé Nast already owns *Gourmet* but decided there would continue to be a market for both magazines. *Gourmet* is an upscale publication for people who are interested in travel, sophisticated food, and deluxe restaurants, but *Bon Appétit* caters more to mainstream appetites.

Newcomers. A major new magazine arrived on the scene in September when Jann S. Wenner launched *Family Life.* Wenner said he was targeting the same readers he had courted 25 years ago, when he started *Rolling Stone.* In those days, his audience was a young counterculture group interested in rock music and drugs. Because most of those people are in their 40's and raising children, Wenner is betting on their having radically different interests.

Hachette Filipacchi Magazines Incorporated, publisher of *Elle,* launched a magazine called *Tell* for teen-age girls in October. *Tell* entered the already crowded teen-age field, which includes *Seventeen, YM, Sassy,* and *'Teen.*

Many of the other start-ups in 1993 were either one-time-only or biannual magazines spun off by traditional publications to test whether readers wanted them on a regular basis. In the spring, *Esquire* launched *Esquire Gentleman,* a fashion magazine for men. *Esquire* was so pleased with the reception of the magazine that, in addition to publishing *Gentleman* as a stand-alone magazine twice a year, it decided to introduce a 20-to-30-page fashion section titled "Gentleman" in every issue of *Esquire.*

Life magazine announced in February that it would continue publication as a monthly. The decision capped more than two years of intense self-examination about the future of one of Time Warner Incorporated's most famous titles, which has been going through troubled times. □ Deirdre Carmody

In *World Book,* see **Magazine.**
Maine. See **State government.**
Malawi. See **Africa.**

Malaysia. A contest for the future leadership of the governing party, United Malays National Organization (UMNO), dominated Malaysian politics during 1993. The UMNO president, and Malaysia's prime minister since 1981, was 69-year-old Mahathir bin Mohamad. The UMNO's dominance of Malaysia's government was such that winners in party election for top offices become government leaders. Thus, when Anwar Ibrahim, Malaysia's finance minister, won the UMNO election for deputy president of the party on Nov. 4, 1993, he also became deputy prime minister of Malaysia. Anwar, widely believed to be Mahathir's favorite, replaced incumbent Ghafar Baba. Under the party's constitution, Anwar would succeed Mahathir as prime minister should he decide to step down, which he showed no signs of doing.

The election results reflected the changing demographics of Malaysia. At age 68, Ghafar represented the old rural base of the UMNO, a party of the country's dominant Malay ethnic group. At age 45, Anwar came from a younger generation that had moved away from the villages to build Malaysia's economy under Mahathir's plan to fully industrialize by the year 2020.

Anwar had been a student leader and was imprisoned for 22 months for demonstrating against the government in 1974. He ran the Muslim Youth Organization until Mahathir persuaded him to enter politics in 1982. He had held three other Cabinet posts before becoming finance minister in 1991.

Critics accused Anwar of using his political connections to raise money to influence delegates voting at the UMNO conference. He denied the accusations. Critics also raised questions about UMNO's growing business interests and how they were used to further the party leadership's political aims.

Sultans restricted. Mahathir pursued efforts begun in 1992 to limit the influence of hereditary sultans, who head 9 of Malaysia's 13 state governments. On Jan. 20, 1993, Parliament passed constitutional amendments that eliminated the sultans' legal immunity from prosecution. However, the sultans, who by law had the power to block any changes to their status, rejected the amendments. Mahathir then halted all privileges traditionally, not legally, given to the sultans. Parliament then passed modified amendments on March 9, and the sultans accepted them on March 23. These amendments called for the attorney general's approval before any legal action could be brought against the sultans.

The economy grew steadily in 1993, as the nation recorded its sixth consecutive year of growth at 8 percent or more. Exports pushed foreign trade toward a surplus. □ Henry S. Bradsher

See also **Asia** (Facts in brief table). In *World Book,* see **Malaysia.**
Maldives. See **Asia.**
Mali. See **Africa.**
Malta. See **Europe.**

Manitoba. Yvon Dumont, 41, a leader of the *métis* (people of mixed Indian and white ancestry), was selected as lieutenant-governor of Manitoba on Jan. 22, 1993, by then Prime Minister Brian Mulroney. The largely ceremonial post corresponds in each province to that of governor general of Canada. Dumont in 1983 had helped organize a lawsuit laying claim to lands in Manitoba's Red River Valley allegedly promised to the métis in the 1870's.

On March 4, 1993, the Supreme Court of Canada instructed the provincial government to give French-speaking citizens exclusive control over French-language education "without delay." The court ruled that Manitoba's Public Schools Act violated minority language rights guaranteed by the 1982 Charter of Rights and Freedoms.

Finance Minister Clayton Manness brought in a budget on April 6, 1993, stressing deficit reduction. The budget was expected to cost Manitobans at least $400 each in disposable income for fiscal 1993-1994. Total spending was projected to be $5.35 billion, with a deficit of $367 million. (Monetary figures are in Canadian dollars.)

After by-elections on Sept. 21, 1993, the governing Progressive Conservatives held 29 seats in the legislature, a one-seat majority. The New Democratic Party held 21 seats, and the Liberals had 7.

□ David M. L. Farr

In *World Book,* see **Manitoba.**

Manufacturing. Coming off a strong last quarter of 1992, and having spent years cutting costs, enhancing productivity, and boosting exports, manufacturers in the United States in 1993 had appeared poised to roar ahead. But cuts in defense spending, recessions across Europe, an economic downturn in Japan, and restrained consumer spending caused manufacturers to limp through the first half of 1993 before finally rebounding later in the year.

While the United States was emerging from a recession in 1993, most of the other industrialized nations of the world were entering one. The economic weakness abroad prompted reduced demands for U.S. manufactured goods. At home, continuing layoff announcements shook consumer confidence. Consumers' reluctance to spend led retailers to draw down existing inventories rather than purchase new goods. These circumstances gave manufacturers little reason to increase their payrolls. Manufacturing in 1993 accounted for less than 17 percent of nonfarm employment and less than 19 percent of the *gross domestic product* (the total value of all goods and services produced within a country).

In the second half of the year, low interest rates and low inflation finally sparked increased consumer spending. Manufacturing sectors that were especially boosted by renewed spending were automobile, housing, and related industries such as glass, rubber, home appliances, and building equipment.

Industrial output. Industrial production grew erratically during the first six months of 1993. The first solid sign of growth came in July, with a 0.4 percent rise in production that would have been higher if not for a 6.5 percent drop in auto production. Another encouraging sign appeared in August when industrial output rose 0.1 percent despite sagging exports and continuing defense cutbacks. The improving health of the economy, as indicated by these figures, was confirmed when industrial output rose 0.4 percent in September, and then jumped 0.8 percent in October, the largest monthly increase in manufacturing production since November 1992.

Factory orders. Factory orders were weak in the first part of 1993. Orders dropped 1.6 percent in March, 0.3 percent in April, and 1.4 percent in May for the first three-month decline since the recession. However, in June, orders jumped 2.6 percent, fueled by growth in the transportation equipment sector. Orders slid again in July, but then rose in August, September, and October.

Despite the increases in orders, factories ran at relatively low capacity. The capacity at the end of the last recession in March 1992 was 76.6 percent. By September 1993, the rate was not much higher— only 81.9 percent.

Durable goods orders. *Durable goods* are items expected to last three or more years. Orders for durable goods fell 2.3 percent in January, rose 2.2 percent in February, and then fell 3.7 percent in March. Despite the unevenness, first-quarter orders were still 3.5 percent above the level in the fourth quarter of 1992 and 11.6 percent above the level in the first quarter of 1992.

Durable goods orders continued to seesaw in the spring and early summer, and in July 1993, they fell to $127.5 billion, their lowest level since 1988. But orders finally picked up for good late in 1993 as carmakers increased production and new homeowners went on a buying spree for household goods. Orders for durable goods rose 2.5 percent in August and 1.1 percent in September, the first back-to-back increases in a year. A 2.6-percent rise in October—to a record $135.8 billion—marked the third straight gain.

Exports. One of the biggest growth areas for U.S. manufacturers in recent years has been the export market, which now accounts for almost 20 percent of all the goods manufactured in the United States. Exports continued to grow in 1993 but at a much slower rate than in recent years. Japan and Europe, which together take in almost one-third of U.S. exports, were both mired in recessions. Through April, U.S. exports grew only 3.2 percent over the same four-month period in 1992. In the third quarter of 1993, exports actually fell 1.1 percent.

One of the bright spots in the export market was China. Exports to China rose 19 percent through September. The industrializing countries of Latin America and Southeast Asia were also growing markets.

Exports grew 5.4 percent in the second quarter of 1993, compared with the same period in 1992. Exports to Europe were down 3.6 percent for the year, but exports to parts of Asia were up 8 percent and exports to Latin America were up 4.7 percent.

Productivity among all U.S. workers had risen 2.6 percent in 1992, the largest gain since 1972. But in the first half of 1993, productivity fell for the first time since the first quarter of 1991. Productivity got back on track in the third quarter of 1993 with an annual rate of increase of 4.3 percent.

Overall productivity was down in 1993, but productivity in manufacturing soared. Manufacturing productivity rose at an annual rate of 4.9 percent in the first quarter, 5.2 percent in the second quarter, and 3.1 percent in the third quarter. These gains, which came at a time when wages and benefits rose at only a 3.8 percent annual rate, reduced production costs and enabled manufacturers to squeeze out profits in an economic climate where raising prices was difficult.

Machine tools are used in many manufacturing processes to cut and form metal for use in other machines. Machine tools are considered a barometer of future economic activity because they are usually ordered 9 to 18 months before they can be shipped and so reflect manufacturers' investment plans.

For the first quarter of 1993, orders for machine tools totaled $785.3 million, up 16.1 percent over the same period in 1992. Orders rose 4.8 percent in April 1993 to $348.2 million, their highest level since 1988 and an increase of 58.6 percent over April 1992. Much of the rise was due to increased demand from automakers. Through October 1993, orders were up 29.5 percent over the same period in 1992.

Capital spending. Manufacturers stepped up investments in more efficient products in 1993. Analysts estimated that capital spending on new plants and high-tech equipment would rise about 9 percent in 1993, after a 7.5 percent increase in 1992. In total, U.S. companies were expected to invest more than $580 billion in plants and equipment in 1993.

Manufacturing survey. The National Association of Purchasing Management (NAPM) surveys 300 industrial companies monthly on orders, exports, and employment and confidence levels. The resulting index is a closely watched indicator of manufacturers' health. Index readings above 50 percent indicate that the manufacturing sector is expanding.

In January, the NAPM index stood at 58 percent, the highest level since July 1988. But in April 1993, the index dropped to 49.7 percent, the first time it had fallen below 50 percent in seven months. After rising to 51.1 percent in May, the index slipped to 48.3 percent in June, the lowest level since November 1991. The index remained at just over 49 percent until it surged to 53.8 percent in October 1993.

However, the NAPM's employment index in October was only 45.5 percent. A reading below 48 per-

Waiting for the recovery

After a strong fourth quarter of 1992, manufacturers were ready to enjoy a rebound in 1993. But they saw little to celebrate for most of the year, as factory orders stalled, retail inventories soared, and the trade deficit climbed. The main culprits for the weakness were recessions in Europe and Japan, which reduced the demand for U.S. goods abroad, and low consumer confidence, triggered by regular news of layoffs. The recovery eventually solidified late in the year, led by growth in the automobile and housing sectors.

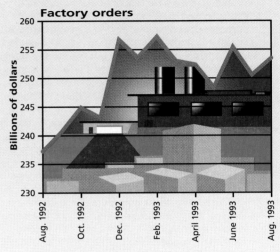

Factory orders

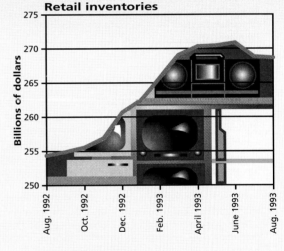

Retail inventories

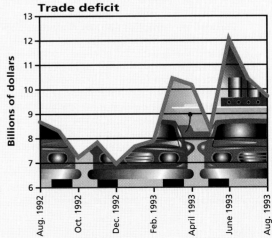

Trade deficit

Source: Commerce Department.

cent indicates that manufacturing employment is shrinking. So manufacturers were increasing their output, but productivity gains were allowing them to reduce employment at the same time. Manufacturers increased overall output by 4.9 percent from September 1992 to September 1993 but cut their work force by more than 250,000 jobs.

Employment. Responding to a strong surge in demand in the last quarter of 1992, factories added 34,000 workers in January 1993, the largest monthly job increase among manufacturers since 1990. In February 1993, manufacturers added 10,000 more jobs. However, they then began cutting jobs. By September, a total of 219,000 jobs had been lost. Late in the year, the trend reversed, and some 42,000 jobs were created in October and November.

Manufacturing employment in 1993 stood at the lowest level since 1965. Since 1989, when industry employment reached its peak, manufacturers have shed more than 1.8 million jobs, or 9 percent of their work force. Manufacturers coped in part by asking more from their current workers. The average factory workweek rose to 41.7 hours in 1993, the longest workweek since the 1940's.   □ Ronald Kolgraf

In *World Book,* see **Manufacturing.**

Maryland. See State government.

Massachusetts. See State government.

Mauritania. See Africa.

Mauritius. See Africa.

Medicine. French researchers on Dec. 15, 1993, announced a major advance in an international effort to identify all the genes in the human body—a 15-year undertaking known as the Human Genome Project. The French breakthrough amounted to a rough map of the 23 pairs of *chromosomes*—structures that carry genes—in every human cell. Each cell has about 100,000 genes that together define all human functions and traits.

Genetic researchers emphasized that much more work was needed to identify individual genes but said that the map would speed that process. Scientists hope eventually to use genetic information to treat—or even prevent—such diseases as AIDS, Alzheimer's disease, cancer, and diabetes.

Controlling complications of diabetes. People with diabetes can delay or prevent many serious complications of the disease by closely monitoring the level of sugar in their blood and by taking multiple insulin injections to keep their blood sugar at a fairly constant level, researchers reported on June 13. Researchers at 29 medical centers in the United States and Canada cooperated in the 10-year Diabetes Control and Complications Trial (DCCT), which was described as the largest and most important study ever conducted on diabetes.

The study compared two methods of treatment in 1,441 patients with Type I diabetes, also known as insulin-dependent diabetes. This form of diabetes most often occurs in people under the age of 30 whose immune systems destroy insulin-producing cells of the pancreas. Insulin is a hormone that enables the body to utilize sugar in producing energy. Without insulin, sugar levels in the blood rise, and patients eventually can develop such complications as eye disease, kidney disease, and nerve damage. Type I diabetes, which affects about 1.5 million Americans, is treated with insulin injections.

In the study, one group of patients received the customary treatment for Type I diabetes, which included one or two insulin injections a day, daily blood sugar tests, and a standard diet and exercise program. The other group received more intensive treatment aimed at keeping blood sugar levels as close to normal as possible. Patients in this group followed a special diet and tailored their daily insulin dose according to food intake, exercise patterns, and the results of four or more daily tests for blood sugar. Compared with patients receiving the standard treatment, patients in the second group had a 76 percent lower risk of diabetic eye disease; a 56 percent lower risk of serious kidney disease; and a 60 percent lower risk of serious nerve damage.

Aspirin and cancer prevention. People who take aspirin regularly may reduce their risk of developing cancers of the colon, esophagus, stomach, and rectum, according to an American Cancer Society study published on March 15. By examining data on 635,031 adults, researchers found that death rates for all four digestive tract cancers were about 40 percent lower among men and women who took aspirin at least 16 times a month.

The researchers were not sure why aspirin seems to protect against cancers of the digestive tract. They speculated that aspirin may bolster immune defenses, inhibit the growth of cancer cells, and suppress the spread of cancer from its original site to other organs. Experts cautioned people to consult a physician before taking aspirin regularly, because the drug can cause bleeding in the digestive tract.

Screening babies' hearing. A panel of medical experts recommended in March that all infants be screened for signs of hearing impairment during the first three months of life. The panel, assembled by the National Institutes of Health in Bethesda, Md., said that about 1 of every 1,000 babies born in the United States is deaf or has a serious hearing disorder. Yet only about half of the children are diagnosed before the disorder impairs their speech and language development.

The panel recommended that all newborns receive a hearing test before leaving the hospital. The test uses a tiny microphone probe to measure inner ear function. Infants who fail the test should receive a second test, which measures nerve signals produced in response to various sounds.

Ultrasound overuse? A study of 15,530 pregnant women, reported on September 15, questioned the benefits of routine ultrasound examinations for healthy women. An ultrasound examination, or sonogram, can help determine the age and health of a fetus by using high-frequency sound waves to produce an image of the unborn child. Many physicians routinely order sonograms for women who have no specific risks for problems during pregnancy.

The study, conducted at 109 sites in six states, found that sonograms do not improve the outcome of low-risk pregnancies. In the study, the researchers compared a group of women who had an average of 2.2 sonograms with a control group that averaged 0.6 tests. They found no difference in the percentage of unhealthy babies born to mothers in the sonogram group. In both groups, about 5 percent of babies were born prematurely or had a low birth weight or other problems. The researchers emphasized that the recommendation applies only to low-risk pregnancies and that sonograms can be beneficial for women who are at high risk for problems during pregnancy because of high blood pressure, diabetes, or other ailments.

Newly identified genes. Researchers during 1993 identified defects in genes associated with a number of different diseases. These discoveries marked an important first step toward developing blood tests to screen people for the diseases as well as developing new methods of treatment.

The discovery of the genetic basis for about 1 in 7 cases of colon cancer was announced on May 5 by an international team of scientists from the University of Helsinki in Finland and Johns Hopkins University in Baltimore. The gene itself was identified in December. Colon cancer is second to lung cancer as the leading cause of cancer deaths in the United States, killing about 57,000 Americans annually.

Geneticists believe that about 1 person in 200 carries the flawed gene responsible for the form of colon cancer known as familial or inherited colon cancer. This would make familial colon cancer the most common inherited disease ever identified in human beings. The researchers advised people who had close relatives with colon cancer to see their physicians for screening tests and advice. The risk is

One of two girls who pioneered a gene therapy treatment in 1990, Cynthia Cutshall, left, underwent a new experiment in May to cure a faulty immune system.

especially high if a family member developed colon cancer before age 50.

Although only sophisticated laboratories at present can conduct tests to identify the genetic defect linked with familial colon cancer, researchers predicted that a simpler lab test might soon be available. People who tested positive for the gene could then have frequent screening tests to detect the disease at an early and highly curable stage.

The discovery of the gene that causes Huntington's disease was announced on March 23, 1993, after a 10-year search, by scientists at the Massachusetts General Hospital (MGH) in Boston. This disorder of the nervous system destroys brain cells and eventually causes death.

Many victims of Huntington's disease first develop symptoms around age 35, when they may already have passed the faulty gene to another generation. An estimated 30,000 Americans have Huntington's disease, and as many as 150,000 may have inherited the gene from an affected parent.

The discovery of a flawed gene that causes a hereditary form of amyotrophic lateral sclerosis (ALS) was announced on March 3 by scientists at MGH and the Massachusetts Institute of Technology in Cambridge. A team of 32 scientists from 13 institutions worked on the project.

ALS is a fatal disease of the nervous system that causes a slowly progressing paralysis. It is often called Lou Gehrig's disease after the baseball star who died of it in 1941. ALS affects about 30,000 Americans, and 5 percent to 10 percent of these cases are believed to result from the faulty gene. The remaining cases develop from unknown causes. The gene linked with ALS normally helps the body destroy certain potentially toxic substances. The discovery suggests that drugs might someday help in treating ALS by breaking down these substances.

An experimental gene therapy was first used to treat cystic fibrosis (CF), a common genetic disorder, starting in April 1993 at the National Heart, Lung, and Blood Institute (NHLBI) in Bethesda. As the result of an abnormal gene, thick mucus builds up in the lungs of CF patients, leading to frequent respiratory infections. CF occurs in about 1 of every 2,500 births and is the most common hereditary disease among Caucasians in the United States.

In the therapy, the NHLBI researchers inserted a copy of a normal CF gene into a common cold virus and administered the modified virus into the respiratory passages of a 23-year-old CF patient. The virus was intended to infect cells in the lungs, just as an ordinary cold virus would, and to transfer the normal gene to lung cells in the process. The NHLBI researchers planned to try the experimental therapy on 10 CF patients to determine whether larger studies would be justified. □ Michael Woods

See also **AIDS; Health-care issues.** In *World Book,* see **Medicine.**

Mental health. A major gap exists in the United States between the number of adults who have mental or addictive disorders and the number who seek treatment for those disorders, according to a comprehensive study reported in February 1993. The study was sponsored by the National Institute of Mental Health (NIMH) in Rockville, Md.

The study included 20,291 adults who were interviewed on several occasions to identify those with mental health problems. From the results, researchers estimated that 1 out of 4 adults—nearly 45 million people—suffered from a mental or addictive disorder during the course of a year. But only 28.5 percent of them received any professional help.

Phobias, the most common disorder, afflicted 10.9 percent of the adults surveyed. They were followed by alcohol abuse (7.4 percent); mild depression (5.4 percent); severe depression (5.0 percent); drug abuse (3.1 percent); and obsessive-compulsive disorder (2.1 percent). Another 8 percent suffered from other disorders. Researchers said that the findings spotlight the need to develop new health insurance benefits and other means of encouraging people to obtain needed mental health care.

Seeking help. In a related NIMH study, researchers found that mental health or drug abuse problems caused 22.8 million Americans to make 326 million visits in a year to physicians, psychiatrists, psychologists, or other caregivers. Each person made an average of 14.3 visits. About 50 percent of those who sought care saw a family physician, internist, or other primary-care physician or a doctor in a hospital emergency department, rather than a psychiatrist or psychologist. The study confirmed previous research showing that primary-care physicians and other nonspecialists play an important role in diagnosing and treating mental illness and drug addiction.

An agency of the U.S. Public Health Service in April urged primary-care physicians to take a more active role in diagnosing and treating clinical depression. The agency said that most people with depression turn to their family doctors when symptoms first appear. But it noted that primary-care doctors fail to properly diagnose and treat two-thirds of patients with depression. The agency emphasized the importance of early diagnosis, because depression, when left untreated, is a major cause of suicide. It added that most cases of depression can be treated with medication or some form of psychotherapy.

Hostility between husbands and wives can weaken the immune system and make both partners physically ill, researchers at Ohio State University in Columbus reported in August. Psychiatrist Janice Kiecolt-Glasser, who led the study, looked at marital strife and immune system function in 90 couples.

The researchers found that couples who behaved negatively toward each other had reduced levels of key immune system cells, compared with couples who behaved in a more positive manner. Negative behavior included the use of put-downs, sarcasm, dismissiveness, and nastiness in discussions of problems. Kiecolt-Glasser said the findings provide further evidence of a link between stress and a weakening of the immune system that can lead to illness.

Violent behavior. A panel of experts organized by the American Psychological Association (APA) concluded in August that steps can be taken to reduce violent behavior among young people. The APA noted that a dramatic rise in youth violence has created an impression that violence is unavoidable.

On the basis of a two-year study, the panel concluded that violent behavior is not an unavoidable result of extreme anger, impulsiveness, poverty, or other situations. Instead, they claimed, violence is a learned behavior, a result of various cultural and social factors that teach young people to resolve conflicts through aggression and violence.

To control the epidemic of youth violence, the APA recommended a number of steps, which included reducing the amount of violence on television and establishing early intervention programs for children at high risk for violent behavior. Such children, the APA said, include those who have used violence in the past; those whose parents have a criminal record; and those whose parents discipline them through physical abuse. □ Michael Woods

See also **Psychology.** In *World Book,* see **Mental illness.**

Mexico. Debate over the North American Free Trade Agreement (NAFTA) dominated the news in Mexico during 1993. The treaty will eliminate tariffs on goods traded between Mexico, the United States, and Canada over 15 years, beginning on Jan. 1, 1994. The presidents of the three nations signed NAFTA on Dec. 17, 1992. The national legislatures of each nation had to pass the treaty before it could take effect. Canada's Parliament voted for the treaty in mid-1993. The U.S. Congress approved it in November, and Mexico's legislature soon followed.

The administration of Mexican President Carlos Salinas de Gortari and that of U.S. President Bill Clinton supported NAFTA. Many large corporations on both sides of the Mexican-U.S. border also supported the trade pact. But U.S. trade unions, fearful of losing jobs to low-wage Mexican workers, and environmentalists, critical of what many regard as Mexico's lax enforcement of antipollution laws, spoke out against the treaty.

Many Mexican and U.S. companies positioned themselves for a boom in operations once NAFTA went into effect. Pepsico Incorporated of Purchase, N.Y., the giant U.S. soft drink maker and fast food conglomerate, announced plans on March 4 to invest $750 million over a five-year period to expand its operations in Mexico. As part of its expansion plans, Pepsico acquired an interest in Mexican soft drink bottling plants in Guadalajara, Monterrey, and Mexico City. On March 22, Anheuser-Busch Incorporated of St. Louis, Mo., the largest U.S. brewer, announced that it would pay $477 million for an 18 percent stake in Mexico's largest brewer, Grupo Modelo S.A. de C.V., which makes Corona beer.

Salinas, who has pegged his Institutional Revolutionary Party's (PRI) future to NAFTA, seemed disposed to do whatever was necessary to ensure that the U.S. Congress passed the treaty. On August 13, the United States, Mexico, and Canada, at the insistence of the Clinton Administration, reached agreement on additions to NAFTA designed to settle any disputes that may arise over labor practices and pollution. In a further effort to win support from U.S. workers, Salinas announced a complex plan on October 3 to boost wages in Mexico. Under the plan, the Mexican government will spend an anticipated $6-billion to increase the country's minimum wage and cut corporate and individual taxes. (See also **International trade: The Debate over NAFTA.**)

1994 elections. On Feb. 5, 1993, Cuauhtémoc Cárdenas, 58, became the first publicly declared candidate for the presidency in elections scheduled for August 1994. The son of Lázaro Cárdenas, Mexico's president from 1934 to 1940, the younger Cárdenas provided the PRI its stiffest challenge in 60 years when he ran for president as the head of a coalition called the National Democratic Front in the 1988 national election, winning 3 of every 4 votes in Mexico City. Salinas beat Cárdenas with just 50.4 percent of the vote. Salinas was ineligible by law from running in the 1994 election. On Nov. 28, 1993, the PRI announced that Social Development Minister Luís Donaldo Colosio would be its candidate for president. Colosio won the nomination over Finance Minister Pedro Aspe Armella and Mexico City Mayor Manuel Camacho Solís.

Fund-raising scandal. About 30 of Mexico's most powerful businessmen attended a private dinner on February 23, hosted by Salinas, who reportedly asked each guest to contribute $25 million to PRI's campaign chest. After news of the request leaked out, Salinas' administration claimed he had merely intended to shift the source of party funding from government sources to private citizens. On March 9, Salinas endorsed limits on political contributions.

Cardinal killed. On May 24, Roman Catholic Cardinal Juan Jesús Posadas Ocampo was killed at Guadalajara's international airport. Police claimed that the cardinal and six other people, including his driver, died in cross fire during a shoot-out between rival drug traffickers. Many observers wondered whether the police helped the suspected killers escape, because eight suspects fled on a commercial airline flight that officials made no effort to stop. □ Nathan A. Haverstock

See also **Latin America** (Facts in brief table). In *World Book,* see **Mexico.**

Michigan. See **Detroit; State government.**

Israeli Prime Minister Yitzhak Rabin, left, in September takes the hand of PLO leader Yasir Arafat in a historic gesture of peace as U.S. President Bill Clinton looks on.

Middle East

The Middle East was once again the site of startling developments in 1993 when the Palestine Liberation Organization (PLO) and Israel revealed in August that they had been conducting secret peace negotiations in Norway since January and were close to reaching agreement. So secret were these talks that Jordan and Syria, which were also conducting peace talks with Israel, were dumbfounded. Within Israel, only a small circle of people who reported directly to Israeli Prime Minister Yitzhak Rabin and Foreign Minister Shimon Peres were informed. Indeed, only on January 19 had the Israeli parliament voted to drop a law against contacts with the PLO. Even the

United States, which since January had been trying to revive the stalled Arab-Israeli peace talks that began in 1991, was stunned by the breakthrough.

On Sept. 9, 1993, PLO leader Yasir Arafat and Rabin exchanged letters. In the letters, Arafat recognized Israel's right to exist as a nation, and Rabin acknowledged the PLO as the representative of the Palestinian people.

Prospects for peace. On September 13, after more than 45 years of Arab-Israeli violence, a "Declaration of Principles" between Israel and the PLO was officially signed in a historic ceremony hosted by U.S. President Bill Clinton in Washington, D.C. The defining moment of the day came when Arafat, who had been reviled by Israel and the United States as a

nation, the declaration is not a peace treaty. However, the document sets forth a five-year timetable for Palestinian self-rule in the Gaza Strip and the West Bank town of Jericho. After that, if stability has been maintained, a permanent accord will be signed that could lead to the creation of a Palestinian nation.

Although many details remained to be negotiated, the timetable for when the details were to be concluded was specific. Both parties decided to begin the withdrawal of Israeli troops from areas populated by Palestinians in Gaza and Jericho on December 13, and to provide for the protection of Israeli settlements within those areas. That process, which could be extended to other West Bank areas, was due to be completed by January 1994.

By June 1994, Palestinians are to hold elections for a municipal council to regulate such functions as education, taxation, economic development, and health care. These affairs have been controlled by the Israeli army. Also in June, a Palestinian police force, which was being trained in 1993, is slated to assume security duties that were being overseen by Israeli authorities.

In addition, both parties were expected to negotiate before September 1996 the status of Jerusalem, Israel's capital, as well as that of Israeli settlements and security forces in the occupied Arab territories. Talks were also expected to decide the future borders of Palestinian territories and the return of Palestinian refugees exiled during the Arab-Israeli conflict. Only then could limited Palestinian autonomy be extended and a permanent accord ratified.

Regional reaction. Official reactions to the September 1993 declaration were mixed in the Middle East. King Hassan II of Morocco welcomed Rabin and Peres for a rare meeting in his country on the day after the signing of the PLO-Israeli declaration, though he decided not to establish full diplomatic relations with Israel. In December, Hassan said that he would broaden economic cooperation with Israel.

After initial anger at not being included in the secret talks, Jordanian officials moved swiftly to initial preliminary accords with Israel that could include long-term agreements on issues such as energy, the environment, banking, refugees, and economic development. On October 1, Crown Prince Hassan of Jordan, brother of King Hussein I, joined Peres in a meeting sponsored by U.S. President Clinton.

Syria's response was muted. It had hoped that peace talks with Israel would lead to the return of the Golan Heights, which Israel had captured in 1967. However, most experts believed that Israeli leaders would be reluctant to cede more territory any time soon because they must first accustom the Israeli people to granting limited Palestinian autonomy. Syria harbored at least 10 radical groups that opposed an Arab-Israeli peace accord. Some of these radicals vowed after the signing of the declaration to kill Arafat.

terrorist, reached forward and offered his hand to Rabin. As Rabin accepted his hand, the attending world leaders, former U.S. Presidents, and those who had worked over the decades for Middle East peace erupted in applause.

Ratification of peace. The Israeli parliament voted to approve the declaration by only 61 to 50 on September 23. On October 11, the Palestinian legislature, known as the Palestine National Council, ratified the accord with a vote of 63 to 8 with 9 abstentions. Arafat, however, was said to have purged earlier in October many PLO leaders who had criticized him throughout 1993 for his monopoly of power, alleged misuse of PLO finances, and ceding of too many Palestinian rights to Israel.

Terms of peace. Since the 1.7 million Palestinians living under Israeli control do not constitute a

On Sept. 14, 1993, Iranian President Ali Akbar Hashemi Rafsanjani openly condemned the peace accord. Pro-Iranian groups in parts of the Arab world staged protests against the agreement.

Violent reactions to the peace agreement occurred in various parts of the Middle East. In Beirut, capital of Lebanon, troops killed eight Hezbollah (Party of God) activists on September 13 as they demonstrated against the accord. By mid-November, five moderate PLO leaders had been assassinated by Arab radicals. An Israeli settler was killed on October 29 by supporters of Al Fatah, the largest and most moderate group of the PLO. Further, right wing Israelis opposed to the accord also attacked Arabs.

In an effort to quell the violence, on November 24, Israeli troops killed the leader of the radical Islamic group Hamas, which was blamed for much of the unrest. A second Hamas leader was killed on November 26. As the December 13 deadline approached for the withdrawal of Israeli troops from the Gaza Strip and Jericho, violence increased in the Gaza Strip. As a result, the deadline passed without a troop withdrawal, though talks were underway in hopes of resolving the issue before 1994. By December 15, at least 44 Arabs and 18 Israelis had been killed. In late December, the Israeli army was ordered to take strong action against anti-Arab violence by Jewish settlers in the occupied territories.

Refugees. One of the most sensitive issues remaining to be resolved between the PLO and Israel was the status of Palestinian refugees. The United Nations (UN) Relief and Works Agency for Palestine Refugees in the Middle East, which has aided the refugees since 1949, estimates that there are 2.8 million in the region, including descendants. Of these, about 700,000 were exiled by the 1948 creation of Israel, and another 200,000 fled the West Bank and Gaza in the 1967 Arab-Israeli war, called the Six-Day War. The PLO wants to see the 1967 refugees allowed to return and those of 1948 either allowed to return or be compensated with money. There are a total of about 5.5 million Palestinians worldwide, many of whom have relocated in other countries.

Deportees and prisoners. As a concession to peace, Israel agreed on Sept. 9, 1993, to readmit about half of the 415 Palestinians it had deported to southern Lebanon in late 1992 for their alleged radical Islamic affiliation. The rest were readmitted by the end of 1993. In October, Israel released about 600 Palestinian prisoners.

West Bank and Gaza Strip needs. Many experts believed that peace would be impossible unless conditions in the West Bank and Gaza improved quickly. The World Bank, an agency of the UN, reported in September that the Gaza Strip and the West Bank needed at least $2.4 billion just to establish basic services such as electricity, sewage, water, schools, and clinics over the next five years. On October 1, at a conference in Washington, D.C., 43 nations pledged a total of $2 billion for development projects in the occupied territories.

Conditions in the territories had deteriorated after oil-rich Arab nations cut financial aid to the PLO because of its support of Iraq during the 1991 Persian Gulf War. The situation worsened when Israeli authorities closed off the territories in March 1993 to halt conflicts between Arabs and Israelis. Before that, more than 30 percent of West Bank residents and 38 percent of Gazans were commuting to work in Israel.

Boycott. The United States continued to pressure Arab states during 1993 to renounce their economic boycott of Israel in support of peace. The boycott, which was begun by Arab nations in 1946, bans direct trade with Israel as well as with foreign companies that trade with Israel. Only Egypt, which signed a peace treaty with Israel in 1979, allows commercial relations with Israel, though such trade remains small.

In late September 1993, however, moderate Arab states, which had openly greeted the tentative steps to peace, announced that their people would not be ready for such a move until peace became more certain. Unofficially, however, Kuwait and Saudi Arabia were reported by mid-1993 to be ignoring the boycott in recognition of Western support for them against Iraq during the Persian Gulf War.

Middle East-U.S. relations. Despite peace prospects, Middle East leaders feared that U.S. policies during 1993 would accelerate the growth of anti-Western, pro-Islamic fervor within their own countries. One central concern was the diffuse, but growing, anger among the region's Muslims toward the United States and other Western nations for failing to protect Bosnian Muslims, who were brutally treated by Christian Serbs and Croats in the civil war in Bosnia-Herzegovina, a former republic of Yugoslavia. In a policy of "ethnic cleansing," Muslims were being murdered and forced out of captured villages and towns.

On August 13, a group of Islamic officials, including representatives from Turkey and Pakistan, unsuccessfully requested that the United States intervene militarily in the Bosnian conflict. Throughout 1993, a number of Arab and Muslim countries took in Bosnian war casualties for medical treatment. Saudi Arabia alone had raised nearly $130 million in private and official contributions by late August to help war-ravaged Bosnia. (See **Bosnia-Herzegovina.**)

Another cause of rising Arab concern about U.S. policies were two U.S. cruise missile attacks on Iraq, on January 17 and June 27, in which civilians were killed. Officials of nearly all Middle Eastern governments, though not Kuwait or Israel, criticized the raids as excessive and counterproductive to regional stability. Both raids renewed widespread accusations that the United States was guilty of a double standard and anti-Islamic bias. Critics contended that

Country	Population	Government	Monetary unit*	Foreign trade (million U.S.$)	
				Exports†	Imports†
Bahrain	583,000	Amir Isa bin Salman Al-Khalifa; Prime Minister Khalifa bin Salman Al-Khalifa	dinar (0.38 = $1)	3,404	4,066
Cyprus	727,000	President Glafcos Clerides (Turkish Republic of Northern Cyprus: Acting President Rauf R. Denktas)	pound (0.51 = $1)	1,002	3,289
Egypt	57,082,000	President Hosni Mubarak; Prime Minister Atef Sedky	pound (3.37 = $1)	3,104	8,357
Iran	59,132,000	Leader of the Islamic Revolution Ali Hoseini Khamenei; President Ali Akbar Hashemi Rafsanjani	rial (1,584.00 = $1)	12,587	12,537
Iraq	21,619,000	President Saddam Hussein	dinar (0.31 = $1)	10,530	11,344
Israel	4,882,000	President Ezer Weizman; Prime Minister Yitzhak Rabin	new shekel (2.93 = $1)	11,889	16,906
Jordan	3,855,000	King Hussein I; Prime Minister Abd al-Salam al-Majali	dinar (0.70 = $1)	1,194	3,257
Kuwait	2,279,000	Amir Jabir al-Ahmad al-Jabir al-Sabah; Prime Minister & Crown Prince Sad al-Abdallah al-Salim al-Sabah	dinar (0.30 = $1)	6,690	7,505
Lebanon	2,947,000	Prime Minister Rafik Hariri; President Ilyas Harawi	pound (1,719.00 = $1)	700	1,800
Oman	1,740,000	Sultan Qaboos bin Said Al-Said	rial (0.39 = $1)	5,428	3,769
Qatar	421,000	Amir and Prime Minister Khalifa bin Hamad Al-Thani	riyal (3.64 = $1)	3,107	1,720
Saudi Arabia	16,509,000	King & Prime Minister Fahd bin Abd al-Aziz Al-Saud	riyal (3.75 = $1)	44,417	24,069
Sudan	28,256,000	Revolutionary Command Council for National Salvation Chairman and Prime Minister Umar Hasan Ahmad al-Bashir	pound (130.00 = $1)	509	1,060
Syria	14,434,000	President Hafiz al-Assad; Prime Minister Mahmud Zubi	pound (21.50 = $1)	3,143	3,151
Turkey	60,355,000	President Süleyman Demirel; Prime Minister Tansu Ciller	lira (13,195.65 = $1)	14,883	22,507
United Arab Emirates	1,736,000	President Zayid bin Sultan Al-Nuhayyan; Prime Minister Maktum bin Rashid Al-Maktum	dirham (3.67 = $1)	15,837	6,422
Yemen	12,847,000	President Ali Abdallah Salih; Prime Minister Haydar Abu Bakr al-Attas	rial (18.00 = $1)	101	1,378

*Exchange rates as of Oct. 29,1993, or latest available data.
†Latest available data.

though the United States continued its military pressure on Iraq, it had been unwilling to use force or even permit arms to be sent for Bosnia's defense.

Democracy. During 1993, two notable elections took place in the Middle East. On November 8, Jordan held its first multiparty parliamentary elections since 1956, and voters elected a woman to Parliament for the first time ever. On April 27, Yemen held its first multiparty parliamentary elections since North Yemen and South Yemen united as the Republic of Yemen in 1990. It was also the first time that women, some of whom were also candidates, were allowed to vote in Yemen.

Salman Rushdie. More violence occurred in 1993 over the controversial novel *The Satanic Verses* (1988), as its British author Salman Rushdie entered his fourth year in hiding. Police believed that outraged Muslims, who view Rushdie's book as blasphemous to Islam, shot William Nygaard, the Norwegian publisher of Rushdie's novel, outside his home near Oslo on October 11.

On July 2, angry Muslims set fire to a hotel in Turkey where Rushdie's Turkish publisher was attending a conference. Although the publisher escaped, 37 people died.

Iranian President Rafsanjani rebuffed numerous

pleas during 1993 by Western governments to lift the death sentence against Rushdie. In early February, Rafsanjani stated that the 1989 Rushdie death sentence could never be revoked because it had been decreed by Ayatollah Ruhollah Khomeini, Iran's deceased but revered spiritual leader.

In late November 1993, President Clinton met briefly with Rushdie, which angered many Muslims. Ayatollah Mohammed Yazdi, the head of Iran's justice system, called Clinton "the most hated man before all the Muslims of the world." Clinton was surprised when even moderate Arabs disapproved of his meeting with Rushdie.

Gulf war cost tallied. The chairman of the Arab Monetary Fund, based in Abu Dhabi, United Arab Emirates, said in April that his organization calculated that the Persian Gulf War against Iraq had cost the Arab nations $676 billion. The cost estimate was based on a fall in economic growth after the war, spending on war-related expenses, transfer of money out of Arab nations, and damage to the region's infrastructure. Of this figure, Kuwait and Iraq each suffered losses of more than $230 billion. □ Christine Helms

See also articles on the various Middle Eastern countries. In *World Book,* see **Middle East** and individual Middle Eastern country articles; **Palestine; Palestine Liberation Organization (PLO); Persian Gulf War.**

Mining. The United States mining industry was poised for a period of more rapid growth after years of effort to modernize facilities and reduce operating costs, the U.S. Bureau of Mines (BOM) reported in February 1993. If the U.S. economy shows sustained, moderate growth, the production and sale of nonfuel minerals could increase by 25 percent, to $40 billion annually, by 1997, according to the BOM report. Nonfuel minerals include metal ores; fertilizer materials, such as phosphate rock; and construction materials, such as crushed stone and sand. It does not include coal or other materials used as fuel. The BOM said that improved economic conditions would stimulate demand for mined products in road and commercial building construction, automobile manufacturing, and other industries.

However, the U.S. mining industry experienced relatively little growth during 1992, the BOM reported. Mines produced about $32 billion worth of nonfuel minerals, 3 percent more than they did in 1991. The United States exported metal ores worth about $900 million in 1992, a decline of about 12 percent. Exports of other types of nonfuel minerals increased by about 1 percent to $1.1 billion. Imports of metal ores decreased by about 5 percent to $1.2 billion.

Mine safety. The U.S. Department of Labor on Jan. 13, 1993, said it would advise coal companies about a potentially hazardous coal mining practice that had been used prior to four recent cave-ins that

Marchers in Beirut, Lebanon, protest the peace agreement between Israel and the Palestine Liberation Organization in September.

had killed 12 miners and injured 7 others. The procedure involves removing pillars or columns of coal that usually are left intact to support the mine's ceiling. The Labor Department said it had not determined that removing the pillars was a factor in causing the accidents, but that coal mining firms should be aware of a possible connection. The department's action came after concerns were expressed by the United Mine Workers of America union.

Clearing water. The BOM announced in August that it would begin the first field tests in September of a new technology designed to clean metal contaminants from mine waste water and to recover metals from low-grade ores. The process involves creating a special *emulsion* (a mixture of liquids) that, like oil and water, would not normally mix. The emulsion contains a chemical that attracts metals in mine waste water or *leaching solutions* (chemical liquids used to dissolve metals from large piles of low-grade ore). The metals are recovered and the emulsion can be recycled. □ Michael Woods

See also **Coal; Petroleum and gas.** In *World Book,* see **Mining.**

Minnesota. See State government.
Mississippi. See State government.
Missouri. See State government.
Moldova. See Europe.
Mongolia. See Asia.
Montana. See State government.

Montreal added to its reputation as a successful sports town on June 9, 1993, when the Montreal Canadiens won their 24th National Hockey League championship at Montreal's Forum stadium. But the Stanley Cup victory was tarnished by a downtown riot that erupted moments after the Canadiens defeated the Los Angeles Kings 4-1 in the fifth game of the best-of-seven series. While players and fans celebrated inside the Forum, thousands of people outside the arena went on a rampage, overturning vehicles, smashing store windows, and looting shops. Theft losses and property damages totaled $2.3 million. There were 168 injuries reported and police made 115 arrests.

The Quebec Public Security Minister Claude Ryan appointed retired Quebec Court of Appeal Judge Albert Malouf to head an inquiry into the Montreal Urban Community (MUC) police's handling of the riot. Malouf's report, released October 12, concluded that police at the riot were disorganized and lacked adequate communication and leadership.

Sylvi Fréchette. It took 16 months, but synchronized swimmer Sylvi Fréchette finally received the gold medal she had been denied due to a judging error at the 1992 Summer Olympics. The 26-year-old Montreal woman received her medal at a ceremony in the Forum on Dec. 15, 1993. Fréchette said that she still felt cheated because she had lost the opportunity to receive the medal at the Olympics.

Police. On September 9, the Supreme Court of Canada, in a unanimous decision, ordered a new trial for former MUC police officer Allan Gosset. An all-white jury in 1988 had acquitted Gosset in the 1987 death of an unarmed black teen-ager, Anthony Griffin, whom Gosset had shot in the head as he tried to escape custody in a police station parking lot.

A Quebec police ethics committee in May 1993 began an investigation of 20 MUC police officers. The officers had been involved in a bungled operation that resulted in the shooting death of a 24-year-old black man in July 1991.

Money matters. Montreal imposed a two-year wage freeze on its 12,300 unionized employees. The move sought to cut $40 million from the payroll in an effort to balance the 1994 budget of nearly $1.9-billion. Mayor Jean Doré promised no new tax hikes and, instead, opted to reduce municipal spending. (All monetary figures are in Canadian dollars.)

City budget plans suffered a major blow, however, when the Quebec Superior Court declared on Sept. 29, 1993, that the province's two-year-old surtax on nonresidential property was unconstitutional. Montreal had collected $553.5 million from the surtax, which Doré said was already spent.

New entertainment. The world's first International Museum of Humor opened its doors in Montreal on April 1. Four years in the planning, the museum drew frowns from opponents who balked at its $21-million cost, of which $13.5 million came from public monies. The not-so-funny admission price of up to $17.75 for adults was later reduced to $11, but the $8 fee for children, students, and senior citizens was retained.

On October 9, Montreal became home to the largest casino in Canada and the 20th largest in the world. The casino is located in the middle of the St. Lawrence River in the former Palais de la Civilisation, which was France's pavilion at Expo 67. The $95-million facility, capable of holding 5,300 people, attracted more than 36,000 people during its opening over the three-day Canadian Thanksgiving weekend. Gross earnings of $114 million were expected for the first year, with a net profit of $50 million going into Quebec government coffers.

Montreal-based Nationair, the country's largest charter operation and third-largest air carrier, was permanently grounded May 12. Robert Obadia, president and chief shareholder of the company he founded in 1984, had officially declared bankruptcy, leaving $75 million in unpaid bills, more than 1,350 creditors up in the air, and 1,300 employees out of work. Nationair's insurance had expired April 1, leading to a considerable loss of business. Two weeks later, Saudi Arabia and Indonesia canceled large contracts with Nationair to carry pilgrims to Mecca. □ Mike King

See also **Canada; Quebec.** In *World Book,* see **Montreal.**

Morocco. One day after the Sept. 13, 1993, signing of the Israeli-Palestinian peace accord in Washington, D.C., Morocco's King Hassan II hosted Israeli Prime Minister Yitzhak Rabin and Foreign Minister Shimon Peres at his palace near Rabat, the capital. It was the first official visit of an Israeli prime minister to an Arab country other than Egypt. Hassan, a veteran peacemaker in Middle Eastern disputes, praised the Israeli-Arab peace talks. Rabin placed a wreath on the tomb of Hassan's father, Muhammad V, who protected Moroccan Jews during World War II (1939-1945). About 8,000 Jews still live in Morocco.

Moroccan officials negotiated with European nations during 1993 to improve Morocco's economic and political status. As a result of Morocco's fragile economy, many Moroccans had fled to Europe, seeking jobs and raising immigration concerns among European nations. Hassan's government tried to stem this emigration by seeking to improve access to the European Community market for Moroccan products, thereby creating new domestic jobs.

High unemployment and inflation hit the young hard in Morocco, where about 65 percent of the population is under the age of 25. In 1993, the country still relied heavily on the $2 billion that comes in annually from Moroccans working in Europe. □ Christine Helms

See also **Africa** (Facts in brief table); **Middle East.** In *World Book,* see **Morocco.**

Motion pictures. With director Steven Spielberg's dinosaur thriller *Jurassic Park* breaking attendance records, the entire 1993 year also seemed destined as a recordbreaker. Box-office revenues in the United States were expected to climb to $5.3 billion by the end of 1993, compared with 1989's previous record of $5.1 billion. The 1993 summer box-office tally alone reached $2 billion.

Jurassic Park, which buoyed Spielberg's critical reputation following the disappointments of *Always* (1989) and *Hook* (1991), became a worldwide money-making machine. By November, it had earned more than $800 million at box offices across the globe, compared with the previous worldwide record of $701 million, earned by Spielberg's *E.T.: The Extra-Terrestrial* (1982). Tom Pollack, chairman of Universal Pictures' parent corporation, MCA Incorporated, predicted his company's film would eventually gross nearly $900 million.

The picture, which tells of a dinosaur theme park in which genetically reproduced dinosaurs run amok, was noted for the advanced technology of its special effects. As might be expected, it proved to be a merchandising bonanza. A conservative estimate reported that, in a period of four months, 1,000 *Jurassic Park*-inspired products earned $300 million in worldwide retail revenues.

Spielberg's reputation also was enhanced by the year-end release of a serious three-hour film shot in black and white. *Schindler's List* was a drama about a German businessman in Poland who saves Jews from Nazi concentration camps. The release of the two films reflected the director's practice of alternating dramatic films with high-tech adventure extravaganzas. *Schindler's List* emerged as the most universally acclaimed American film of many years. Without the use of newsreel footage, Spielberg recreated the terror of the Holocaust with harrowing authenticity. With *Jurassic Park* and *Schindler's List,* 1993 was definitely Spielberg's year.

Other box-office hits. *Jurassic Park* was not the only smash of the 1993 record-breaking year. *The Fugitive,* a lean and exciting version of the classic 1960's television series, became Harrison Ford's most popular film, with the exception of his *Indiana Jones* trilogy. The action-drama about a doctor's efforts to clear his name in the murder of his wife brought Andrew Davis to the forefront of American directors. His handling of the movie's spectacular train crash was universally admired.

Novelist John Grisham proved to be as popular at the box office as he has been in bookstores. Despite mixed reviews, *The Firm,* in which audience charmer Tom Cruise was aided by a superb supporting cast, was a big hit in the United States, Europe, and Asia. Another Grisham thriller, *The Pelican Brief,* premiered in December and signaled the return of actress Julia Roberts to the screen after a two-year absence.

Sleepless in Seattle starred Tom Hanks and Meg Ryan as would-be sweethearts who don't meet until the final scene. The movie rekindled the romantic comedies of Hollywood's past and was a worldwide favorite.

Clint Eastwood continued his success by starring in the profitable *In the Line of Fire,* about a still-active Secret Service man who had been on duty when President John F. Kennedy was assassinated. Eastwood also directed and starred in *A Perfect World,* in which Kevin Costner played an escaped convict who develops a bond with the 8-year-old boy he has kidnapped.

The critically slammed *Indecent Proposal* ignited the ire of some feminists with its theme of a billionaire, played by Robert Redford, who pays $1 million for one night with another man's wife, played by Demi Moore. Nevertheless, the film was a magnet for moviegoers across the world.

Highly praised movies sprang from renowned writers and directors in 1993. Robert Altman's direction of *Short Cuts,* based on a selection of nine short stories by Raymond Carver, solidified his resurgence following the success of 1992's *The Player.*

Director James Ivory and producer Ismail Merchant again teamed up with last year's *Howards End* actors Anthony Hopkins and Academy Award-winner Emma Thompson in *The Remains of the Day.* Departing from their trend of making movies based on

The Piano, starring Holly Hunter as a mute woman, was a co-winner of a Palme d'Or, the top prize at the 1993 Cannes International Film Festival.

Academy Award winners in 1993

Best Picture, *Unforgiven.*

Best Actor, Al Pacino, *Scent of a Woman.*

Best Actress, Emma Thompson, *Howards End.*

Best Supporting Actor, Gene Hackman, *Unforgiven.*

Best Supporting Actress, Marisa Tomei, *My Cousin Vinny.*

Best Director, Clint Eastwood, *Unforgiven.*

Best Original Screenplay, Neil Jordan, *The Crying Game.*

Best Screenplay Adaptation, Ruth Prawer Jhabvala, *Howards End.*

Best Cinematography, Philippe Rousselot, *A River Runs Through It.*

Best Film Editing, Joel Cox, *Unforgiven.*

Best Original Score, Alan Menken, *Aladdin.*

Best Original Song, Tim Rice and Alan Menken, "Whole New World" from *Aladdin.*

Best Foreign-Language Film, *Indochine* (France).

Best Art Direction, Luciana Arrighi and Ian Whittaker, *Howards End.*

Best Costume Design, Eiko Ishioka, *Bram Stoker's Dracula.*

Best Sound, Chris Jenkins, Doug Hemphill, Mark Smith, and Simon Kaye, *The Last of the Mohicans.*

Best Sound Effects Editing, Tom C. McCarthy and David E. Stone, *Bram Stoker's Dracula.*

Best Makeup, Greg Cannom, Michele Burke, and Matthew W. Mungle, *Bram Stoker's Dracula.*

Best Animated Short Film, *Mona Lisa Descending a Staircase.*

Best Live-Action Short Film, *Omnibus.*

Best Feature Documentary, *The Panama Deception.*

Best Short Subject Documentary, *Educating Peter.*

Clint Eastwood stars in *Unforgiven,* which he also directed and which won four Academy Awards in 1993, including best picture and best director.

E. M. Forster novels, the Merchant-Ivory team brought Kazuo Ishiguro's 1989 novel to the screen. The film depicts the unspoken love between a British butler and a housekeeper.

Kenneth Branagh directed a sunny, witty adaptation of *Much Ado About Nothing,* his second Shakespearean screen success, following *Henry V* in 1989. The varied, star-studded cast included Branagh, his wife Emma Thompson, Denzel Washington, and Keanu Reeves.

Director Martin Scorsese, noted for such angry pictures as *Taxi Driver* (1976) and *Raging Bull* (1980), enjoyed a change of pace by adapting Edith Wharton's *The Age of Innocence* for the screen. Daniel Day-Lewis and Michelle Pfeiffer starred as thwarted lovers.

Jane Campion's critically praised *The Piano* featured a superb performance by Holly Hunter as a mute woman in the early 1900's who becomes awakened to her sensuality. The picture brought fresh attention to New Zealand filmmaking and shared the top prize at the 1993 Cannes International Film Festival with Chinese director Chen Kaige's *Farewell My Concubine*. Kaige's film told the story of two boys who enter the Peking (now Beijing) Opera and pursue a 50-year friendship against the backdrop of social and political changes. The Chinese government briefly allowed a censored version of the film to be shown in China, then banned it altogether.

Other notables. Ivan Reitman, the director of the popular *Ghostbusters* (1984), charmed audiences again with *Dave*. Kevin Kline played the title character who is cast as a stand-in look-alike for a philandering U.S. President, also played by Kline.

In *Fearless,* Jeff Bridges plays an architect who survives a disastrous plane crash. The movie won acclaim for its no-easy-answers probing of questions regarding immortality.

In *Menace II Society,* twin brothers Allen and Albert Hughes directed actors alongside gang members in a violent story of the bleak life of black inner-city males. The movie was the first feature-length film by the 20-year-old directors.

Brains and brawn fall equally hard. The year of one of Hollywood's greatest hits, *Jurassic Park*, also brought one of its most high-profile flops. *Last Action Hero* marked the end of Arnold Schwarzenegger's string of hits. The movie cost more than $100 million to produce and market but earned only $50 million in the United States and was headed for a similar total in Europe and Asia.

Among other disappointments was David Cronenberg's film version of the stage success *M. Butterfly*. The film told the story of a French diplomat who had a 17-year romantic relationship with a man he was duped into thinking was a woman.

Year-end films that were among the most eagerly awaited were *Philadelphia, In the Name of the Father,* and *Mrs. Doubtfire. Philadelphia,* director Jonathan Demme's first film since his 1991 Oscar-winning *The Silence of the Lambs,* was Hollywood's first major feature about the AIDS epidemic. It starred Tom Hanks as an AIDS-afflicted attorney fired from his law firm and Denzel Washington as a homophobic lawyer. *In the Name of the Father* also had a lawyer-client theme, with Emma Thompson as a counselor defending activist Daniel Day-Lewis against terrorist charges. *Mrs. Doubtfire* featured Robin Williams as a divorced man who poses as a British nanny so that he can see his children. Tim Burton advanced the art of animation with *The Nightmare Before Christmas*.

Foreign flicks. The Spanish-language film *Like Water for Chocolate,* a mystical romance of doomed love in Mexico, seemed destined to become the highest-grossing foreign-language film in U.S. history. Ironically, it had been only a moderate success in its native Mexico, where its running time included 38 minutes that had been cut for the U.S. release. During the summer, 179 prints of the film were running in the United States, a record for a foreign-language film.

Claude Berri's $30-million version of Émile Zola's classic 19th-century novel *Germinal* (1885) became the most expensive French-speaking film ever made. Starring Gerard Depardieu, the movie's story of conflict within an impoverished mining community would seem to present a commercial challenge, yet it became an immediate box-office gold mine in France.

In Europe, filmmaking continued to be on the rebound. Among the celebrated Italian directors with 1993 features were Ermanno Olmi with *Secret of the Old Wood;* Giuseppe Ferrara, whose *Giovanni Falcone* told of the assassination of an anti-Mafia investigator; and Giuseppe Tornatore, whose *A Simple Formality,* featured Depardieu and Roman Polanski in a story about an amnesiac who is suspected of murder. Spanish cinema, which had blossomed in recent years with the works of director Pedro Almodovar, continued to flourish with Vicente Aranda's *Amantes* and Bigas Luna's *Jamon*.

In general, Hollywood hits translated to equal success overseas. *Sommersby,* starring Richard Gere and Jodie Foster in a remake of the 1982 French hit *The Return of Martin Guerre,* and *Falling Down,* with Michael Douglas as an angry urban dweller, were more successful in Europe and Asia than in the United States.

Filmgoing in the United Kingdom during 1993 increased 11 percent over the previous year. Taiwan became the latest country to duplicate the American practice of constructing multiplex theaters. And Japan experienced a growing trend in the construction of drive-in theaters.

Many deaths were universally mourned. The death of Italian film master Federico Fellini brought worldwide mourning for the creator of such classics as *La Dolce Vita* (1960) and *La Strada* (1954). Actress Lillian Gish's death severed the last living link to the days of American silent films. Ruby Keeler's demise erased one of our final connections with the Busby Berkeley musicals of the Great Depression era. Vincent Price's death also signaled the end of an era—in this case of elegant horror films based in part on the works of Edgar Allan Poe.

The death of Audrey Hepburn was mourned not only for the sophisticated actress's contributions to film but also because of her efforts on behalf of children in underdeveloped nations. And with the demise of Helen Hayes, the world lost one of Hollywood's most long-standing leading ladies. Twenty-three-year-old actor River Phoenix, who earned critical respect in *Stand By Me* (1986), *Running on Empty* (1988), and *My Own Private Idaho* (1991), died outside a Hollywood nightclub after ingesting multiple drugs. Phoenix' death caused much media discussion about young actors' lifestyles. ☐ Philip Wuntch

See also **Pacino, Al; Thompson, Emma.** In *World Book,* see **Motion pictures.**

Mozambique. See Africa.

Mulroney, Brian. See Canada.

Music. See Classical music; Popular music.

Myanmar. See Burma.

Namibia. See Africa.

Nebraska. See State government.

Nepal. See Asia.

Could Dinosaurs Live in a Zoo?

By Robert Bakker

Taking a cue from the 1993 motion picture *Jurassic Park,* a prominent paleontologist explores the idea of running a real dinosaur zoo—and reaches some surprising conclusions.

Jurassic Park—the novel by Michael Crichton that was turned into a motion picture in 1993—makes scientists like me think, and that's good. Sure, the central assumption of the story is wrong—genetic engineers can't take a bit of fossil dinosaur blood, extract the DNA (deoxyribonucleic acid, the basic unit of heredity), and create an entire, living *Tyrannosaurus rex,* and they'll probably never be able to. Paleontologist Jack Horner and his colleagues in 1993 announced that they had obtained small fragments of DNA from fossil *T. rex* bones, but not nearly enough to give scientists a complete genetic blueprint of *Tyrannosaurus rex.* DNA simply can't survive tens or hundreds of millions of years in any reasonable shape—it's too vulnerable to chemical attack by water and oxygen molecules. And even if scientists could get a full set of DNA from dinosaur fossils, would we be able to stick it into an ostrich egg and grow a baby dinosaur, as hypothesized in the novel and movie? Again, probably not.

Nevertheless, *Jurassic Park* makes a wonderful launching pad for the imagination, coaxing us paleontologists to push our basic understanding of dinosaurs far beyond the usual limits. In that spirit, I accepted the premise of the story and decided to explore how a real-life dinosaur park would work. I wanted to know how zookeepers would respond if the zoo director suddenly announced, "We're going to get live *T. rex, Velociraptor,* and *Triceratops* in a few months!" Those are three of the dinosaurs most popular among children, and any dinosaur park worth its salt would have to have them. *Tyrannosaurus rex* was a monstrous *carnivore* (meat-eater) that stood about 10 feet (3 meters) tall at the hips, walked on two legs, and lived about 66 million years ago. *Velociraptor* was another meat-eater that resembled *T. rex,* but it was smaller and more agile. Raptors lived 120 million to 70 million years ago. *Triceratops* was a *herbivore* (plant-eater) that walked on four legs, had three horns on its face, and lived about the same time as *T. rex.*

A trip to the zoo

In pursuit of answers, I traveled to the San Diego Wild Animal Park—reputedly the best zoo in the world when it comes to handling large animals—and discussed dinosaurs with the keepers of the rhinoceroses, elephants, giraffes, and tigers. "You folks couldn't handle a 4-ton (3.6-metric-ton) *Triceratops* or *Tyrannosaurus,* could you?" I asked.

"Sure, we could!" they answered. "We take care of bull Indian rhinos. They weigh 4 tons, just as much as a *T. rex.* And they can gallop at 32 miles per hour (52 kilometers per hour), just as fast as a *T. rex* probably could."

The keepers had no worries about handling a *Velociraptor,* either, even though that dinosaur could probably jump about 12 feet (3.6 meters). "Our Sumatran tigers can jump the same distance, and we have no problem keeping them in the park," they said. Like other zoos, the San Diego Wild Animal Park keeps animals from escaping their exhibits with simple yet effective architecture, such as a deep moat encircling the animal's exhibit and an overhanging fence.

■ **The author**

Robert Bakker is a paleontologist at the University of Colorado in Boulder and author of *The Dinosaur Heresies* (1986).

A piece of amber containing a weevil that lived in the time of the dinosaurs.

■Step 1:
Find dinosaur DNA.

In *Jurassic Park*, fictional scientists extract dinosaur DNA (deoxyribonucleic acid, the basic unit of heredity) by obtaining dinosaur blood from the stomach of a prehistoric mosquito that fed on a dinosaur before it was embedded in *amber* (fossilized tree resin).

- In the real world, finding prehistoric DNA is extremely difficult, though it has been done. However, DNA is very unstable, breaking up in even the best laboratory conditions after only a few hours. It cannot survive tens of millions of years in a completely intact state, so only segments of DNA can be found.

- Once scientists obtained prehistoric DNA, they would have a hard time proving it came from a dinosaur because there are no living dinosaurs to compare it with. At best, they could try to make a case by comparing the DNA with that from modern dinosaur relatives, such as birds.

- Scientists would also have trouble ruling out contamination of the dinosaur DNA by DNA from other organisms. Scientists might mistakenly *clone* (make identical copies of) other DNA that happened to become mixed with the dinosaur DNA. They would then not be certain which DNA came from dinosaurs and which did not.

- Dinosaur DNA would not be protected inside a prehistoric mosquito because the mosquito would digest the DNA. Even if the mosquito had been trapped in amber and killed right after a meal of dinosaur blood, its stomach acids would remain active and continue chewing up the DNA.

- Scientists have found insects in amber dating from the time of the dinosaurs, but such amber is very rare. Most amber was formed more recently than 65 million years ago, after the dinosaurs died out. Also, amber tends to trap insects that live amidst trees, such as ants and termites, rather than insects that feast on blood, such as mosquitoes and ticks.

- **Step Z:**
  Fill in the gaps.

  In *Jurassic Park,* fictional scientists use DNA from frogs to complete missing segments in the dinosaur DNA.

- In the real world, scientists would not use frog DNA, because frogs are amphibians and dinosaurs are reptiles. For a better match, scientists would instead choose DNA from closer relatives, such as an alligator or other reptile or birds.

- The gaps in the dinosaur DNA would be too numerous and large for scientists to reconstruct a dinosaur. Scientists estimate that a full set of dinosaur DNA would include 1 billion to 10 billion *base pairs* (the units of DNA). But none of the pieces of prehistoric DNA yet found is longer than about 250 base pairs. So the number of DNA gaps would likely be far greater than the number of actual DNA fragments.

- Even if scientists obtained most of a dinosaur's DNA, they would still probably be missing some critical *genes* (the segments of DNA that dictate cell functioning). The DNA of human beings and chimpanzees is 98 percent identical, so a relatively small number of genes is responsible for the great differences between the two species. The odds are high that a few key dinosaur genes would fall in the gaps and be lost to scientists.

- Also, scientists would have to organize all the DNA pieces into the right order along *chromosomes* (the structures in cells that carry genes). The order of genes on chromosomes is very important for their proper working. But scientists have little idea about the correct order of genes on human chromosomes, let alone dinosaur chromosomes.

The main comment the keepers had about *Jurassic Park* was that a real zoo never relies on computers and electrified fences to keep animals under wraps. In the story, a computer malfunction knocks out the electrified fences, and the dinosaurs escape. But at San Diego, none of the gates require electricity or computers. Every important gate is operated manually and is checked four times daily by an experienced keeper. In addition, there are emergency generators for the lights that kick in automatically if the main power fails, so keepers never have to fumble around in the dark. A real dinosaur park would be run the same way.

Getting the upper hand

The San Diego keepers also said they knew how they would manipulate the behavior of a big plant-eater such as *Triceratops.* "We'd find out what food to use as *Triceratops* yummies," they said. "Big bull

■ Step 3:
Make a baby dinosaur.

In *Jurassic Park,* fictional scientists replace the DNA in an ostrich egg with reconstructed dinosaur chromosomes and then grow the embryo into a baby dinosaur, *below.*

■ In the real world, scientists cannot yet substitute DNA in an embryo and grow a baby animal, even using DNA from living animals.

■ Only DNA from an embryo can lead to a complete animal with all the different types of cells that enable it to function. As an embryo develops, the DNA in different cells becomes physically altered so that each cell assumes a specialized role, such as a bone cell or nerve cell. Scientists do not yet know how to return the altered DNA to its original state. Therefore, to clone a dinosaur, they would have to find dinosaur DNA from an embryo—an unlikely happening.

■ Also, chromosomes do not float randomly inside a cell but are anchored and oriented in a specific way for the genes to control the cell correctly. However, the proper orientation of dinosaur chromosomes would probably not be preserved in fossils of dinosaur DNA.

■ Finally, the DNA of an organism alone does not provide all the information needed to create a new individual. The development of an embryo also depends on chemicals provided by the mother in her womb. But the chemicals manufactured by mother dinosaurs probably cannot be recovered.

rhinos are potentially very dangerous, but we found out that they love apples and will do anything for apple slices. So we use apples as rhino yummies—special treats to lure the rhino where we want him to go. We'd do the same thing with dinosaurs. We'd try out all sorts of food with *Triceratops* to find out what special treats we could use to lead it around."

The keepers would also gain control over the dinosaurs by watching their social behavior. For example, bull rhinos are fiercely competitive and will fight each other if they have a chance. So at San Diego, the keepers allow only one bull rhino in the main pen with the cow rhino. Any other bull rhinos are kept apart in their own compounds. This arrangement eliminates most aggression by the bull rhinos. "We'd work with dinosaurs the same way," the keepers said. "We'd watch a group of *Triceratops* to figure out the social system, and then manipulate the composition of the herd to keep the animals under control."

A meal fit for a dinosaur

What about feeding the dinosaurs? Well, finding the proper food for meat-eating dinosaurs would be easy, because the chemical composition of meat probably hasn't changed very much since the first land animal evolved 300 million years ago. Meat from most present-day reptiles—even a primitive one like the tuatara, a lizardlike reptile found on New Zealand—tastes like chicken and can be digested by any living carnivore. Herbivorous dinosaurs, the natural prey for meat-eating dinosaurs, probably tasted like chicken, too, since all dinosaurs are close kin of birds. So *Velociraptor* and *T. rex* would probably dive right in to a huge slab of chicken meat.

Feeding herbivorous dinosaurs would be much tougher. Every plant-eating species tends to have special adaptations for eating the type of plant found in its native habitat. For example, the different rhino species kept at San Diego all have distinct features for chewing and digesting plants of a specific shape and texture. White rhinos have square lips, huge teeth, and large intestines for picking and grinding the tough grass that they favor, whereas black rhinos have pointed lips, smaller teeth, and shorter intestines for eating the softer leaves and branches of shrubs that they

▪ Step 4:
Give the dinosaur a nice home.

In *Jurassic Park,* the dinosaurs live contentedly in the modern world, *above.*

- ▪ In the real world, scientists would have difficulty finding edible food for *herbivorous* (plant-eating) dinosaurs. The digestive system of each herbivorous dinosaur evolved to consume the specific types of plants that existed in the dinosaur's native habitat. But most plants from the era of the dinosaurs have gone extinct.

- ▪ For a cloned dinosaur to digest food, scientists would also need to clone the prehistoric bacteria that lived inside the dinosaur's stomach and assisted in digestion. But DNA from these bacteria would probably be impossible to find.

- ▪ Also, over the millions of years since dinosaurs went extinct, plants have developed new poisons to deter animals from eating them. Dinosaurs would not be prepared to handle these modern poisons.

- ▪ Finally, the dinosaurs would fall prey to the countless new diseases that have arisen since prehistoric times. Their immune systems simply would not be able to recognize or defeat the new disease agents.

309

prefer. The rhinos have trouble eating plants they aren't designed for, so the keepers must make sure that each rhino gets the right food.

Now consider the case of a revived *Brachiosaurus*, a gigantic plant-eating dinosaur that stood about 40 feet (12 meters) tall and lived about 144 million years ago. In the time of *Brachiosaurus*, there were no grasses or broadleaf trees or shrubs. Instead, the forests were composed of *conifers* (needle-bearing trees). So a *Brachiosaurus* would have a digestive system suited for prehistoric conifers.

Could we keep a cloned *Brachiosaurus* from starving in our world? The closest we could find to food of the right texture would be primitive existing conifers such as the Norfolk Island pine or the podocarp, which can be found on islands in the tropical South Pacific Ocean. We would just have to hope that the trees would be to the *Brachiosaurus'* liking. A somewhat easier task would be getting plants of the right size and texture for a later dinosaur such as *Triceratops*, since it evolved only about 65 million years ago, when primitive broadleaf trees such as the magnolia and the sycamore were present.

Digestion difficulties

However, finding the proper plant food would be only part of the problem in keeping herbivorous dinosaurs happy, because a modern-day counterpart to some prehistoric plant could still pose a danger. Over time, many plant species evolve poisons in their leaves and fruits to deter herbivores from eating them. To ensure a steady diet, plant-eating species must constantly coevolve with the plants, developing ways of detoxifying the latest plant defenses. For example, many deer and antelope species have extra stomach chambers where microbes break down plant poisons, rendering them harmless. But the gut of the *Brachiosaurus* stopped evolving when the species went extinct about 144 million years ago, whereas the plant world has continued to evolve better deterrents right up to the present day. A *Brachiosaurus* just wouldn't be able to cope with modern plant chemical defenses. That dinner of podocarp could turn out to be lethal.

For a cloned *Brachiosaurus* to be able to digest any food at all, we would also have to bring back its gut microbes. But where are we going to find 144-million-year-old *Brachiosaurus* gut microbes? Gut microbes aren't passed on from parent to child like genes but must be obtained by an animal after it is born. Today, for example, young antelope get their gut microbes by eating grass that has been smeared with feces from adult antelope. But *Brachiosaurus* gut microbes probably went extinct many millions of years ago without leaving any of their DNA in an intact state. Microbial DNA just wouldn't have the protection from the environment that bones or *amber* (fossilized tree resin) may provide to fragments of dinosaur DNA.

The invisible threat

Still, the most serious danger to cloned dinosaurs in a modern zoo wouldn't be improper diets, plant poisons, or even escaped *Velociraptors*. Instead, the deadliest threat would come from the microscopic bacteria, viruses, tapeworms, and parasitic protozoans that inhabit the modern world. All through evolutionary history, disease-causing microbes have evolved new strategies to outwit their intended targets' defenses. In turn, the animal species must keep evolving *immune* (disease-fighting) systems that can combat the disease agents. But the dinosaurs' immune systems stopped evolving when they went extinct, whereas the disease agents have continued to evolve. Thus, a dinosaur in the present world would be hopelessly underprotected, like a medieval knight in armor dropped into battle against modern-day tanks and attack helicopters.

Zookeepers have to deal with the problem of unfamiliar diseases even with modern animals. When the San Diego staff brings in a species from out of the United States—say, a koala from Australia—they have to be very careful that the foreign animal doesn't catch a disease from an animal native to America, because the new animal would have no evolved immunity against the disease. A *Brachiosaurus* would be even more at risk, because its immune system would be vulnerable to modern diseases from anywhere in the world.

What's the bottom line? Well, the San Diego Wild Animal Park and other zoos probably could safely contain dinosaurs and manipulate their behavior and could even supply a healthy diet to the meat-eating ones. But the modern ecosystem, with its new and deadly plant poisons, would be very hard on the plant-eaters. And modern diseases would probably overwhelm the immunological defenses of any dinosaur.

Hopeless? No, not quite. There have been spectacular advances in recent years in the field of immunology. Scientists are gradually learning how to strengthen an animal's immune system by giving it disease-fighting genes from other species. If genetic engineers ever could bring back the dinosaurs, immunologists might be ready to insert modern antimicrobial defenses into the dinosaurs' DNA. Thereby protected from disease, the dinosaurs might at last return to enjoy life on Earth after being away for 65 million years.   ■ ■ ■

For further reading:

Bakker, Robert T. *The Dinosaur Heresies.* Morrow, 1986.

Begley, Sharon. "Here Come the DNAsaurs." *Newsweek,* June 14, 1993, pp. 56-61.

Crichton, Michael. *Jurassic Park.* Knopf, 1990.

Morell, Virginia. "Dino DNA: The Hunt and the Hype." *Science,* July 9, 1993, pp. 160-162.

Rensberger, Boyce. "Bringing Back the Dinosaurs Is Possible Only in Hollywood." *Washington Post,* June 28, 1993, p. A3.

Netherlands. The Netherlands in 1993 stayed committed to a more united European Community (EC or Common Market). The Dutch currency, the guilder, was one of the strongest in the European Monetary System (ERM), which links the values of the EC members' currencies. The Netherlands during the year kept the value of the guilder tied closely to that of the strongest currency, the German mark, whereas the other ERM countries loosened their ties.

Unemployment rises. The Netherlands withstood most of the worst effects of Europe's recession in 1993. However, the strong guilder led to relatively high prices for exports and low prices for imports. As a result, Dutch businesses faced increasing competition from foreign companies. Some Dutch firms responded by cutting their payrolls, causing unemployment to grow to almost 9 percent by September. To fight this trend, the Dutch government on September 21 announced a series of job creation measures for 1994, including increased spending on infrastructure; tax benefits for firms that hire workers; and more flexible working hours for employees.

Also in 1993, to help cut its swelling budget deficit, the Dutch government unveiled plans to trim some social programs, reduce defense spending, and tighten rules on political asylum, which were among the most liberal in Europe. More than 800 asylum seekers a week entered the Netherlands in 1993.

Euthanasia approved. The Netherlands on February 9 enacted guidelines governing euthanasia, also called assisted killing or mercy killing. Under the new law, euthanasia was still a crime, but doctors who followed the guidelines would not be prosecuted. The Netherlands has long been one of the countries in the world most tolerant of euthanasia.

Business developments. The Dutch government was involved in several major business transactions in 1993. On February 21, it worked out an agreement with the regional government of Flanders in neighboring Belgium to save 3,250 jobs in their countries by investing more than $240 million in near-bankrupt truck manufacturer DAF. On March 17, the Dutch government finally agreed on terms to sell 51 percent of Fokker NV, a partly state-owned aircraft maker, to a private German firm, Deutsche Aerospace AG. The government had held up the deal for months until it received assurances from Deutsche Aerospace that Fokker factories located in the Netherlands would remain in operation.

On March 22, the government confirmed plans to sell a majority share of the state-run postal and telecommunications monopoly Koninklijke Nederlandse PTT NV in 1994. On April 27, state-run KLM Royal Dutch Airlines said it was trying to merge with three other European airlines to form a giant carrier. But talks fell apart on November 21.   □ Philip Revzin

See also **Europe** (Facts in brief table). In *World Book,* see **Netherlands.**

Nevada. See **State government.**

New Brunswick. Deriving 40 percent of its revenue from the federal government, the New Brunswick Liberal government under Premier Frank J. McKenna sought to raise more funds within the province. The 1993-1994 budget, introduced on March 31, 1993, raised the provincial income tax rate by 2 percent, to 62 percent of the federal rate, the second highest level in Canada. The 11 percent sales tax, also the second highest in Canada, was extended to certain nonessential consumer products. Government spending increases were restricted to 1.7 percent, one of the lowest among the provinces.

On May 6, the provincial legislature passed a bill requiring the provincial administration to balance its operating budget by the last year of its four-year term. On September 28, McKenna announced a plan to transfer the administration of New Brunswick's medicare (health-care) system to a group of private companies, which would save the province $60 million a year.

Angry that Quebec prohibits New Brunswickers from competing for provincial contracts, New Brunswick took the same step against Quebec on April 21. The move will shut Quebecers out of a planned expansion of the Trans-Canada Highway in New Brunswick.   □ David M. L. Farr

New Hampshire. See **State government.**
New Jersey. See **State government.**
New Mexico. See **State government.**

New York City. Republican Rudolph W. Giuliani, a former prosecutor, was elected mayor of New York City on Nov. 2, 1993. He narrowly defeated Democratic incumbent David N. Dinkins, the city's first black mayor.

Although the city was in the grip of a prolonged recession, Dinkins had sought to govern on a theme of racial peace rather than on economics. But his single term in office was marked by controversies over his handling of racial disturbances in the boroughs of Manhattan and Brooklyn. Dinkins also fell victim to an anti-incumbent mood that swept most high-profile officials in the Northeast out of office.

Giuliani, who lost to Dinkins in 1989, made his mark as a crusading federal prosecutor in the 1980's. He became the first Republican to win the mayor's office since 1965 and is just the second Republican mayor since 1945. In one of his first actions, aimed at making good on a promise to fight crime, Giuliani named William J. Bratton, Boston police commissioner, to be the new commissioner of the New York City Police Department.

Other election results. A referendum on term limits for elected city officials carried overwhelmingly. All local officeholders, from the mayor to borough presidents to members of the City Council, will now be limited to two consecutive four-year terms.

Meanwhile, residents of the borough of Staten Island, which lost political power under a recent charter revision, voted to secede from New York City. Staten Island, with a population of about 380,000, would become the state's second most populous city if New York's governor and legislature concur.

Trade Center bombing. The twin-tower 110-story World Trade Center in lower Manhattan was rocked by an underground explosion on Feb. 26, 1993, that left 6 people dead and more than 1,000 injured. In the following months, seven men described as Muslim terrorists were charged with taking part in the bombing.

On July 2, law enforcement authorities detained Sheik Omar Abdel Rahman, a blind Egyptian Muslim cleric who serves as a spiritual leader of Muslim fundamentalists, on immigration charges. Abdel Rahman was soon accused of masterminding the World Trade Center bombing and other terrorist activities. In August, he and 14 of his followers were charged with planning to blow up a number of New York City structures—including the United Nations headquarters and two Hudson River tunnels—and to assassinate U.S. officials and Egyptian President Hosni Mubarak.

The first trial, of four defendants charged in the World Trade Center bombing, began on October 4. Two of the other bombing suspects were believed to be in Iraq, and the seventh defendant was waiting to be tried separately. Abdel Rahman and the other alleged conspirators were also awaiting trial at year-end. (See also **Courts; Crime.**)

Police corruption. Tales of illicit activities by many New York City police officers were disclosed to a blue-ribbon mayoral commission investigating corruption in the police department during two weeks of hearings that began on September 27. The panel heard details of illegal drug activities, the acceptance of payoffs, the use of excessive force, and a "blue wall of silence" that protected rogue officers.

The star witness, former detective Michael Dowd, told of collecting $8,000 a week in payoffs from cocaine dealers. Other witnesses said police department administrators followed an unwritten policy of discouraging internal investigations in order to avoid scandals. The revelations were the worst since 1971, when the Knapp Commission uncovered widespread corruption in the police department.

New schools chancellor. The Board of Education voted on February 10 to remove public schools Chancellor Joseph A. Fernandez, who had clashed with parents and the school board over school policies. A program to distribute condoms in city schools and a multicultural curriculum for grade schoolers that discussed alternate life styles and homosexuality were particularly controversial.

On August 30, just days before the scheduled opening of classes, the board hired Ramon C. Cortines, the former superintendent of San Francisco schools, as Fernandez' successor.   □ Owen Moritz

See also **City.** In *World Book,* see **New York City.**

New York City Mayor-elect Rudolph W. Giuliani delivers his acceptance speech on November 3 after defeating incumbent Mayor David N. Dinkins.

New Zealand. Political fortunes hung in the balance for 11 days after the Nov. 6, 1993, elections for Parliament. Early tallies on election night gave the ruling National Party of Prime Minister James B. Bolger only 49 seats in the 99-seat House of Representatives. The major party in opposition, the Labour Party, held 46 seats. Two smaller parties, the Alliance and New Zealand First, each claimed 2 seats.

The initial results seemed to indicate that Bolger would have to share power in a coalition government formed with the minor parties. This possibility had an immediate effect on financial markets. Prices of stocks fell, and the value of the New Zealand dollar dipped sharply.

However, nine of the parliamentary seats were held by the most slender of margins. And officials had yet to count the votes of an additional 200,000 citizens who had been unable to reach a polling booth in their districts on election day. After officials counted these special votes, the National Party won a seat previously thought to have been won by Labour. With a single-seat majority, Bolger announced on November 17 that he would form a government without having to rely on the voting power of the minor parties. Financial markets quickly rebounded.

New electoral system. Also on November 6, voters approved a referendum to change the way most members of Parliament (MP's) are elected. Under the old system, all candidates won a parliamentary seat by winning a simple majority of votes in a district. In the referendum, 53.9 percent of the voters approved a proposal that provided for the election of most MP's under a new system of proportional representation. With this system, 56 seats will be filled from lists of names that each party will draw up. The number of candidates each party may seat in Parliament will depend on the percentage of votes the party wins in national elections. However, 64 MP's will continue to be elected under the old system of simple majority.

The referendum called for an expanded Parliament. The new Parliament will increase from 99 seats to 120.

Economic reforms, restructuring, and deregulation that had begun in the mid-1980's helped produce sustainable growth, low inflation, and an increased number of jobs during 1993. By the end of September, unemployment had fallen to a three-year low of 9.1 percent of the work force. The *gross domestic product* (GDP)—the total value of all goods and services produced within a nation—rose by 2.6 percent during the first half of 1993. The GDP reflected an annual growth rate of 5.3 percent. From September 1992 to September 1993, overall inflation was 1.5 percent, slightly higher than the previous 12 months, and exports rose 6.5 percent. □ Gavin Ellis

See also **Asia** (Facts in brief table). In *World Book,* see **New Zealand.**

Newfoundland. The province reeled from an ongoing crisis in its fishing industry, the mainstay of its economy for 400 years. A two-year closing of the northern cod fishery in 1992 was followed in 1993 by fishing quotas and bans. Overfishing both within and without Canada's 200-nautical-mile (370-kilometer) fishing zone had prompted the bans. Thousands of Newfoundland fishermen and plant workers were put out of work, joining the 20,000 whose livelihood had been cut off the year before. The federal government offered a compensation package and retraining for those affected by the closings.

Canada unsuccessfully fought for enforceable international fishing agreements at a United Nations conference on high-seas fishing in September. It claimed that foreign vessels caught many times the quota of fish allotted to them by the Northwest Atlantic Fisheries Organization.

Premier Clyde K. Wells and his Liberal government won a second victory in elections held on May 3. Making no campaign promises and emphasizing restraint in facing acute economic problems, Wells and his party captured 35 seats in the 52-seat legislature. The Progressive Conservatives won 16 seats, and the New Democratic Party 1 seat. The Wells government had previously vowed to reduce the province's deficit for 1993-1994 by cutting $70 million from public-servants' salaries. □ David M. L. Farr

In *World Book,* see **Newfoundland.**

Newsmakers of 1993 included the following people and events:

Fermat's last theorem—proved at last? In 1637, the French mathematician Pierre de Fermat jotted down a simple mathematical proposition in the margin of a book, adding that he had found "a rather marvelous proof" for it that the margin was too small to hold. Fermat never wrote down his supposed proof, and after his death in 1665, "Fermat's last theorem" remained to torment generations of mathematicians. The theorem states that the equation $x^n + y^n = z^n$ has no whole-number solutions if n is greater than 2. That is, no whole number raised to the third or fourth power—or the 100th power or any other—can be expressed as the sum of two other whole numbers raised to the same power.

In 1993, mathematician Andrew Wiles of Princeton University in New Jersey apparently succeeded where others had failed. Speaking at a gathering of mathematicians at Cambridge University in England on June 23, he offered a 200-page proof of Fermat's theorem that one ecstatic colleague described as "beautiful." In late 1993, mathematical reviewers going through Wiles's proof step by step found a small error, but it was thought to be correctable.

One-in-a-million shot nets $1 million. As Don Calhoun entered Chicago Stadium on the evening of April 14, the woman from the Chicago Bulls public relations department spotted his yellow suede hik-

American mathematician Andrew Wiles reported in 1993 that he had found an apparent proof for a long-standing problem called Fermat's last theorem.

ing boots. The boots decided it for her. Calhoun was the guy she wanted for a promotional stunt during that night's basketball game with the Miami Heat. So when a time out was called in the second half, the 23-year-old office-supplies clerk from Bloomington, Ill., was handed a basketball and given one throw to sink a basket from a distance of 79 feet (24 meters). If he made the shot, he would win $1 million—$50,000 a year for 20 years. Calhoun reared back and flung the ball—right through the center of the hoop.

Calhoun's prize seemed to be in jeopardy a few days later when the insurance company underwriting the promotion balked at paying. But the sponsors—a local restaurant chain and the Coca-Cola Company—said he would receive the money.

Three tales of survival. What personal quality is it that enables some individuals to survive in life-threatening situations that would spell death for most people? It was a cool head that saved 13-year-old Gary Mahr from drowning on July 23 when he and six other people were caught by a flash flood in a cave near St. Louis, Mo. Mahr and his companions—four fellow residents of a Catholic home for boys and two adult counselors—were exploring the cave when it suddenly began filling with rushing water from heavy rains. Swept away by the current, Mahr held his breath underwater until he surfaced in an air pocket, where he found a ledge of rock he could cling to. Eighteen hours later, a rescue party found him. His friends had all panicked when the flood hit, and all had drowned.

A few days earlier, on July 20, Pennsylvania logger Donald Wyman escaped almost certain death by summoning the courage to take a grim but necessary action after an oak tree fell on his leg. Alone in the woods, pinned to the ground, and bleeding heavily, Wyman tied off his upper leg with a makeshift tourniquet and sawed off his lower leg with a pocket knife. He then drove to a farm for help and was taken to a hospital.

In a remarkable replay of Wyman's experience, William Jeracki of Conifer, Colo., amputated his lower leg on October 5 after a boulder fell on him. Jeracki lay for three hours, his leg broken beneath the rock, before deciding to free himself by cutting off the leg with a fishing knife.

Jean Harris goes free. On January 20, a New York state parole board granted freedom to Jean Harris, convicted in 1981 of murdering her lover, physician Herman Tarnower. The board acted after New York Governor Mario M. Cuomo commuted Harris' sentence for health reasons. Harris was suffering from severe heart disease and had undergone coronary bypass surgery in December 1992.

Tarnower, originator of the so-called Scarsdale diet, was shot to death in 1980. At her trial, Harris, the former headmistress of an exclusive girls' school, testified that the shooting had been an accident.

She said she had gone to Tarnower's Purchase, N.Y., estate with the intention of seeing the doctor one last time before committing suicide. She said that when she tried to shoot herself in Tarnower's bedroom, he struggled with her for the gun, which discharged twice, wounding him fatally.

Biospherians return to Earth. Looking tired and thin but otherwise healthy, the four men and four women of Biosphere II, a 3.15-acre (1.27-hectare) glass and steel habitat in the Arizona desert, ended their confinement on September 26. The artificial world was designed to duplicate the conditions of "Biosphere I"—the Earth—on a small scale as an experiment in sustaining life in a sealed environment. But things went wrong from the start. Crop failures in the biosphere's tiny farm led to food shortages and caused the crew to experience weight losses averaging 13.5 percent. Even more troublesome was a mysterious decline in oxygen levels that made it necessary for project officials to replenish the habitat's atmosphere. In summer 1993, scientists determined that the oxygen loss was caused by the proliferation of oxygen-consuming bacteria in the biosphere's overly enriched soils.

Despite the setbacks, Biosphere II administrators said a new crew would enter the structure in February 1994 for a one-year stay. They said they hoped to have the oxygen problem under control by then, perhaps by replacing some of the soil.

Subway commando. Keron Thomas was in love with New York City's subway system. Since immigrating to New York with his family from the West Indian nation of Trinidad in 1990, the 16-year-old boy had ridden the trains for hours at a time, pored over subway operations manuals, and talked endlessly of becoming a motorman.

On May 8, Thomas could wait no longer to get his hands on the controls of a train. Impersonating a motorman, he fooled a subway dispatcher and was assigned to pilot a train between the boroughs of Manhattan and Brooklyn. All went well until the youth accidentally tripped an emergency brake. The train sat motionless until the brake was released by an inspector. Thomas was summoned for drug and alcohol testing, but he fled home, where transit detectives tracked him down and arrested him two days later. In July, prosecutors allowed Thomas to plead guilty to three misdemeanors, and he was placed on probation. Thomas' final word on the episode: "I'm going to become a train operator."

Death atop a volcano. A tragic incident took the lives of six *volcanologists* (volcano researchers) on January 14 high in the Andes Mountains of Colombia. As an international group of volcanologists ranged over the Galeras volcano collecting data, the volcano suddenly exploded, throwing lava, ash, and glowing-hot boulders into the air. Of seven scientists in or near the crater, only Stanley N. Williams of Arizona State University in Tempe escaped being killed,

At Chicago Stadium in April, Bulls fan Don Calhoun accepts the basketball he threw to sink a shot from 79 feet (24 meters) for $1 million.

though he suffered a fractured skull and two broken legs as he scrambled down the slope to safer ground. Williams and his colleagues had been studying Galeras as part of a United Nations effort aimed at reducing the death toll from volcanoes by learning how to predict their eruptions.

A ticket to Easy Street. Leslie C. Robins of Fond du Lac, Wis., on July 8 joined the ranks of the super-rich when he became the sole winner of a $111-million pot in a lottery drawing encompassing 14 states and Washington, D.C. Robins, an English teacher and assistant track coach at a Fond du Lac junior high school, had bought the ticket in the Powerball lottery as a gift for his fiancée, nurse Colleen De Vries. At last word, the two were sharing the incredible windfall equally. The prize was the largest sum ever won with a single lottery ticket.

Woody loses custody battle. A New York City judge ruled in June that motion picture actor-director Woody Allen was an unfit parent and not entitled to custody of his three children. The judge gave custody of the children—Satchel, 5; Dylan, 7; and Moses, 15—to their mother, actress Mia Farrow. In one of the few bright spots in the ruling for Allen, the judge said there was probably insufficient evidence to prosecute Allen for alleged sexual abuse of Dylan. In 1992, Farrow had accused Allen of molesting the girl at Farrow's summer home in Connecticut. Allen contended that Farrow cooked up that ac-

cusation out of spite because he had become romantically involved with another of Farrow's daughters, 21-year-old Soon-Yi Farrow Previn. Allen filed his custody suit in August 1992, a week after Farrow made the sex-abuse allegation.

A 60's-era fugitive surrenders. No longer able to cope with the stress of hiding from her past, Katherine Ann Power, a fugitive from justice for 23 years, turned herself in to Massachusetts law-enforcement authorities on Sept. 15, 1993. Power had been on the run since September 1970, when, as a student radical at Brandeis University in Waltham, Mass., she took part in a bank robbery that resulted in the shooting death of a police officer.

After the crime, she went into hiding and broke off all contact with her family. In the late 1970's, she settled in Oregon, where she established herself as a gourmet cook and was known to everyone as Alice Metzinger. Along the way she got married and had a son, who was age 14 at the time of her surrender. On Oct. 6, 1993, having pleaded guilty to armed robbery and manslaughter, Power was sentenced in a Boston state court to 8 to 12 years in prison.

Johnny Carson honored. Television star Johnny Carson was one of five Americans saluted at the 1993 Kennedy Center Honors celebration on December 5 at the Kennedy Center for the Performing Arts in Washington, D.C. Carson was described as a "national icon" for his 30-year career as host of "The

Tonight Show." The other award recipients were ballet dancer and director Arthur Mitchell; Sir Georg Solti, former conductor of the Chicago Symphony Orchestra; Broadway composer and lyricist Stephen Sondheim; and gospel singer Marion Williams.

Epic balloon flight ends a bit short of goal. Some days it doesn't pay to get out of bed. January 12 was just such a day for Larry Newman, commander of a huge $5-million balloon named Earthwinds. Newman, who in 1978 became the first person to cross the Atlantic Ocean in a balloon, had hopes in 1993 of succeeding at an even grander feat that no balloonist had ever accomplished—a nonstop flight around the world. A large crowd was on hand at an airfield near Reno, Nev., as Newman and his two fellow crewmen lifted off on a frigid morning. But within minutes, after struggling for altitude, Earthwinds plowed into a nearby mountain. Newman repaired the badly damaged balloon and planned a new attempt for November 6, but that trip had to be aborted. He said he would try again in early 1994.

Fragments of "True Cross"? At a Paris auction in May, an unidentified woman paid 100,000 francs (about $18,500) for two tiny slivers of wood that supposedly came from the cross on which Jesus was crucified. The wood fragments, laid one across the other in the shape of a cross and encased in a tiny oval bronze box, were accompanied by two alleged certificates of authenticity from the mid-1800's. One of those documents was said to have been issued by the Vatican in Rome, but Vatican officials said they had no way of determining whether the document was genuine. Moreover, Roman Catholic authorities have often remarked that if all the pieces of wood reputed to be from Jesus' cross were put together, they would make a truly massive object.

U.S.-born sumo grand champ. Many people in Japan believe that only native Japanese sumo wrestlers possess the right qualities to be named a *yokozuna,* or grand champion. So there was some discomfort in Japan when Akebono—formerly Chad Rowen, a hulking 23-year-old from Hawaii—became the first foreign-born sumo wrestler granted that exalted title. Sumo officials named Akebono a *yokozuna* in January after he chalked up victories in two consecutive sumo tournaments. Only 63 other wrestlers in the history of the ancient sport have risen to the rank of grand champion, and Akebono is the only *yokozuna* among currently active wrestlers. In 1992, another former Hawaiian, Salevaa Atisanoe, who wrestles in Japan under the name Konishiki, was denied *yokozuna* status.

Oldest bungee jumper. "If I die, I die," said 100-year-old S. L. Potter on October 13 as he prepared to bungee jump from a 210-foot (64-meter) tower in Alpine, Calif. Potter, a resident of La Mesa, Calif., was seeking to become the oldest person in the world to make a bungee jump. After being cinched into an upper-body harness, with the bungee cord attached at the back, Potter leaped into space. At the end of his jump, he dangled motionless for several seconds, causing many in the onlooking crowd to think that the dive had indeed been too much for the old man's heart. But then he kicked his feet and gave a wave, as if to say he had only been joking. It seems fairly certain that Potter did set an age record for a bungee jump, but that could not be confirmed. *The Guinness Book of Records* has no listing for feats of bungee jumping.

Las Vegas sleuths nab elusive bank robber! Well, not exactly. It didn't exactly require Sherlock Holmes to track down the most likely suspect in the robbery of a Bank of America branch in Las Vegas, Nev., on July 23. He was handing out $100 bills to people on the street and urging them to "have a nice day." The Las Vegas police said the alleged robber, Ronald M. Chrontak, 46, was still cheerfully acting the part of Robin Hood when officers found him and placed him under arrest.

Romanov bones. British scientists reported in July that some of the bones found in a mass grave in 1991 were, as suspected, the remains of Russia's last czar, Nicholas II, and several other members of the Romanov family. Czar Nicholas, his wife, and their five children were executed in 1918 by Bolshevik revolutionaries, who disposed of the bodies in secret. The researchers analyzed genetic material from the bones to make the confirmation.   □ David Dreier

Newspaper. American newspaper publishers in 1993 continued their forays into the electronic market. Bell South Advertising & Publishing Company Incorporated and Cox Enterprises Incorporated, the publisher of *The Atlanta* (Ga.) *Journal and Constitution* and the *Palm Beach* (Fla.) *Post,* agreed on Oct. 25, 1993, to jointly offer electronic advertising. *The San Jose Mercury News* began offering electronic news access in May 1993, and the *Los Angeles Times* planned to start electronic publishing through Prodigy Services Company in early 1994.

Knight-Ridder Incorporated, the second-largest newspaper chain in the United States, was experimenting with an electronic newspaper that would eliminate paper entirely. Its research lab in Boulder, Colo., is developing a flat computer tablet, about the size of a thick magazine, that would let readers receive news articles and photographs from satellite transmissions.

Changing hands. New York City newspaper competition remained vigorous in 1993 as two feisty but financially hurting tabloids, the *New York Post* and the *New York Daily News*, were bought by wealthy investors. The soap-operalike story of the *Post*'s rescue saw three potential buyers commit to purchasing the paper only to be undermined by either financial troubles or striking employees. On October 1, billionaire media mogul Rupert Murdoch officially purchased the paper.

Daily News editorial employees bitterly protested the $36.3-million sale of their paper on January 7 to real estate investor Mortimer B. Zuckerman, who owns *U.S. News & World Report* magazine. Zuckerman dismissed about 170 news and editorial employees but spent generous sums to attract popular columnists and editors from other publications.

The New York Times Company on June 10 agreed to buy New England's largest newspaper, the *Boston Globe.* The $1.1-billion merger represented the highest price ever paid for an American newspaper.

Pittsburgh, Pa., welcomed the return of the *Pittsburgh Post-Gazette* on January 18 after an eight-month delivery drivers' strike. However, the city's other daily newspaper, *The Pittsburgh Press,* which the *Post-Gazette* had purchased in December 1992, did not survive the strike.

Staying afloat. Newspaper readership and advertising revenues increased slightly in 1993 after three years of a serious industry recession. Every day, 115 million people read a daily newspaper, a figure that jumped to 125 million on Sundays, according to the Newspaper Association of America. Newspaper advertising grew slowly—at about 3 percent—but newspapers still attracted the largest share of advertising dollars, 23.5 percent. By comparison, advertisers spent 22 percent of their ad budgets on television commercials. ☐ Mark Fitzgerald

In *World Book,* see **Newspaper.**

Nicaragua. President Violeta Barrios de Chamorro tried to mend relations in 1993 with former supporters who had become some of her harshest critics. She also faced the possibility of armed conflict between right and left wing militants. General Humberto Ortega Saavedra, the leftist army commander and former Sandinista, announced on February 22 that the government would form a national reconciliation commission to address conflicts remaining from the country's civil war from 1981 to 1990. Satisfied that the commission would broaden investigations into alleged human rights abuses, the United States announced on April 2, 1993, that it would release $50 million in aid to Nicaragua.

On Aug. 19, 1993, about 400 right wing, former contra rebels took 38 members of a government delegation hostage near the town of Quilali and demanded that Ortega and other high-ranking former Sandinistas be fired. In retaliation, Sandinista rebels seized the country's vice president and about 32 other officials in Managua, the capital. On August 25, both sides released their hostages unharmed. On September 2, Chamorro said that she would replace Ortega in 1994—a move that angered her remaining Sandinista supporters and appeared to end hopes for national reconciliation. ☐ Nathan A. Haverstock

See also **Latin America** (Facts in brief table). In *World Book,* see **Nicaragua.**

Niger. See Africa.

Nigeria. The military regime of President Ibrahim Babangida had set 1993 as the year that the nation would return to democratic, civilian government, and on June 12 Nigerians went to the polls to elect a new president. On June 23, however, the Babangida administration annulled the results of the election. Later in the year, Babangida stepped down, but a new military government soon took control.

Two parties compete. In March, the two government-sponsored parties—the National Republican Convention (NRC) and the Social Democratic Party (SDP)—had selected well-known Muslim business leaders as their presidential candidates. The moderately conservative NRC chose Alhaji Bashir Tofa, and the left-of-center SDP nominated Chief Moshood Abiola. Both men are friends and allies of Babangida, so the public had little reason to expect that a civilian government would embark on a radically new political or economic course. Many Nigerians were dubious that elections would even take place.

In late April, an organization called the Association for a Better Nigeria went to the nation's highest court and argued that the presidential election should be postponed because of alleged rampant fraud by the two parties. On June 10, the court ordered a postponement, but the government ignored it, and the election was held on June 12.

Observers described the election as the most honest in Nigerian history. But on June 15, when it began to appear that Abiola had won, the government set aside the results, claiming widespread fraud. A week later, the election was officially annulled. This was the fourth time Babangida had postponed the transition to civilian rule.

More military rule. On June 26, Babangida announced that a new election would be held, and a civilian government would be sworn in on August 27. But despite his announcement, at least 30 high-ranking military officers who favored democratic rule announced plans to resign in protest against the annulment of the election. On July 26, violence broke out in Lagos, the country's largest city. A general strike followed.

On August 26, with protests and strikes increasing, Babangida resigned, turning power over to an interim government of 13 of his military and civilian friends. He appointed an ally, businessman Ernest Shonekan, to head the interim government. But the situation changed yet again on November 17, when Defense Minister Sani Abacha ousted Shonekan and declared himself the leader of a new military government.

Nigeria's economy continued to falter in 1993 due to government mismanagement and the political uncertainties facing the country. During the year, the government devalued the currency, and the inflation rate exceeded 50 percent. ☐ Mark DeLancey

See also **Africa** (Facts in brief table). In *World Book,* see **Nigeria.**

Nobel Prizes in literature, peace, economics, and the sciences were awarded in October 1993 by the Norwegian Storting (parliament) in Oslo and by the Royal Swedish Academy of Sciences, the Karolinska Institute, and the Swedish Academy of Literature in Stockholm, Sweden. The value of each prize was $825,000 in United States currency.

The literature prize was awarded to Toni Morrison, an African-American novelist whose books explore the experience of blacks, and particularly black women, in the United States. The 62-year-old novelist was the first black American and the eighth woman to win the prize. In her writing, Morrison draws on the language and traditions of black American culture as well as the literary heritage exemplified by the Southern writer William Faulkner. The Nobel committee said her work was "characterized by visionary force and poetic import [that] gives life to an essential aspect of American reality."

Morrison has been a professor of humanities at Princeton University in New Jersey since 1987. Her best-known books include *Song of Solomon* (1977), *Beloved* (1987), and *Jazz* (1992).

The peace prize was shared by African National Congress (ANC) President Nelson Mandela and South African President Frederik Willem de Klerk for their efforts to dismantle South Africa's system of rigid racial segregation, called *apartheid,* and to transform the country into a nonracial democracy. The committee cited the 75-year-old Mandela and 57-year-old de Klerk for their "personal integrity and great political courage" in working peacefully for change in South Africa.

Mandela had been imprisoned from 1962 to 1990, when the government of de Klerk—who became president in 1989—released him. After his release, Mandela suspended the ANC's armed struggle against the government. In 1990 and 1991, de Klerk led the government in repealing the laws that had formed the legal basis for apartheid. In December 1991, negotiations began between the ANC and the government on a new constitution—adopted in November 1993—that would establish full political equality for all of South Africa's racial groups.

The economics prize went to two American economic historians, Robert W. Fogel of the University of Chicago and Douglass C. North of Washington University in St. Louis, Mo. The two were cited for founding a new branch of economic history, called *cliometrics,* that applies economic theory and modern statistical techniques to past economies.

Fogel's award was the fourth in a row to go to a University of Chicago economist. The 67-year-old economist is best known for his controversial work on American slavery, *Time on the Cross* (1974), cowritten with Stanley Engerman. The book argued that, contrary to the then-accepted view, slavery was economically efficient and came to an end for moral and political reasons, not economic ones. The book aroused the anger of critics who accused Fogel of defending slavery, a charge that Fogel said rested on a misunderstanding of his work.

The 72-year-old North was honored for exploring the economic effects of legal and social institutions, such as labor unions and legal systems. His work included studies on the relation between the legal protection of private property rights and the success of some Western European economies.

The chemistry prize was shared by American biochemist Kary B. Mullis, who works from his home in California, and Michael Smith, a British-born biochemist at the University of British Columbia in Vancouver, Canada. The two scientists were cited for their separate work in genetic research. The 48-year-old Mullis was the inventor in 1985 of the *polymerase chain reaction* (PCR), a technique that allows scientists to make millions of copies of a tiny fragment of DNA, the molecule of which genes are made. PCR has numerous applications, including testing for infections and linking specific individuals to DNA from blood or hair found at crime scenes.

The 61-year-old Smith was honored for his invention of *site-directed mutagenesis*, a method used to modify the proteins produced by an organism by splicing foreign genetic material into the organism's genes. The technique, developed in the 1970's, enables scientists to create specific *mutations* (changes) in a gene in order to determine the function of the genes and the proteins they code for.

The physics prize was given to two American astronomers, Joseph Taylor and Russell Hulse, both of Princeton University. The pair won the prize for their discovery in the 1970's of the first *binary pulsar.* A pulsar is a small, dense star that emits pulses of radio waves. In a binary system, two pulsars orbit around a common axis, pulling each other into a closer, faster orbit. Taylor and Hulse did their work when the two were at the University of Massachusetts in Amherst. At the time, Hulse was a postgraduate student working with Taylor.

The physiology or medicine prize was shared by two molecular biologists, Phillip Sharp of the Massachusetts Institute of Technology (MIT) in Cambridge and the British-born Richard Roberts of New England Biolabs in Beverly, Mass. The two scientists were honored for their independent work in the 1970's on how DNA is organized in genes. Before 1977, biologists believed that genes were continuous strands of DNA. Sharp and Roberts found that active segments of DNA in genes are interrupted by inactive segments that do not contain genetic instructions. The discovery of these so-called split genes has led to new theories on the evolution of genes as well as advances in the study of cancer and other diseases. □ Meira Ben-Gad

In *World Book,* see **Nobel Prizes.**
North Carolina. See State government.
North Dakota. See State government.

Northern Ireland. Peace efforts appeared to take a fresh turn in September 1993, when John Hume, the leader of the moderate Social Democratic and Labour Party (SDLP), met with Gerry Adams, the leader of Sinn Fein, the political wing of the outlawed Irish Republican Army (IRA). They agreed on a set of principles for peace, which they gave to the Irish government in Dublin on October 7.

But on October 23, the IRA set off a bomb in a fish market on Shankill Road, which is the center of Protestant businesses in Belfast, the capital of Northern Ireland. The blast killed 10 people, including one of the bombers. During the following five days, Protestant terrorists retaliated in a campaign of violence that left four Catholics dead.

Analysts feared that the IRA attack also killed the Hume-Adams peace plan. The plan set up a mechanism through which the IRA would abandon its terrorist tactics and Sinn Fein would be included in future peace talks. Sinn Fein was excluded from the talks by the British and Irish governments because it would not renounce IRA terrorism.

Reactions to the Hume-Adams initiative were mixed. Ian Paisley, Protestant leader of the Ulster Unionist Party, said it had on it "the bloody thumbprint of the IRA." Britain's Secretary of State for Northern Ireland, Sir Patrick Mayhew, said there could be no change in the province's status without the support of its 1.6 million people, around two-thirds of whom are Protestant. However, Albert Reynolds, the prime minister of Ireland, gave an initial favorable response.

Secret meetings. In late November, a British newspaper reported that the government had been meeting in secret with the IRA. On November 27, British Prime Minister John Major admitted that such meetings to promote peace had been occurring since February. Protestants in Northern Ireland immediately accused the government of breaking its vow not to deal with the terrorist group and called for Major's resignation.

Major and Reynolds announced on December 15 a historic declaration of principles designed to bring about peace talks that would include Sinn Fein if the IRA agreed to renounce violence. Britain went further than ever in adopting a neutral position on the possible unification of Ireland and Northern Ireland, providing all parties consent. Dublin prepared to drop its constitutional claim to Northern Ireland.

IRA attacks in England. On March 20, the IRA planted two bombs in trash cans in the main shopping street of Warrington in northern England, killing two boys, ages 3 and 12, and injuring more than 50 others. The young ages of the two victims sparked a wave of revulsion against the violence in Ireland and included the largest demonstration ever in Dublin on March 28. □ Ian J. Mather

See also **Ireland.** In *World Book,* see **Northern Ireland.**

Rescuers search the rubble for survivors of a terrorist bombing that killed 10 people and injured 57 others in a crowded shopping area of Belfast in October.

Northwest Territories. The Northwest Territories moved closer to division in 1993 as proceedings continued for the creation of Nunavut, a future home for Canada's *Inuit* (Eskimo) people. On May 25, 1993, then Prime Minister Brian Mulroney signed the final land-claims agreement that will eventually give the Inuit a land mass amounting to about one-fifth the size of Canada. On June 10, the Canadian Parliament ratified the agreement.

A smaller but also important land-claims agreement was signed on September 6 between the federal government and the 2,000 members of the Sahtu tribe, which includes Dene Indians and *métis* (people of Indian and European ancestry). The accord grants the Sahtu ownership of 16,000 square miles (41,000 square kilometers) of land, as well as subsurface mineral rights to a 700-square-mile (1,800-square-kilometer) area between Great Bear Lake and the Mackenzie River.

The Territories' budget, presented on February 19, emphasized the elimination of the deficit. Revenues and expenditures were to be almost balanced at $1.2 billion (in Canadian dollars). Expenditure increases were to be kept below inflation, and revenues were estimated to grow 4.4 percent. A special 1 percent payroll tax was levied on people who work in the Territories but pay income tax in another province. □ David M. L. Farr

In *World Book,* see **Northwest Territories.**

Norway. Norwegian Prime Minister Gro Harlem Brundtland on Sept. 13, 1993, won reelection as the head of the minority Labor Party government. But the most striking feature of the national elections was the strong showing of the Center Party, which had based its campaign on opposition to Norway's joining the European Community (EC or Common Market). Brundtland, who applied for EC membership for Norway in 1992, faced a difficult campaign to win approval for her plan in a national referendum to be held in 1994. Opinion polls taken at the time of the 1993 elections showed that a substantial majority of Norwegians opposed joining the EC.

Legislative elections. In parliamentary elections, Brundtland's Labor Party won 37 percent of the vote and 67 seats in the Storting (parliament), up from 63 seats. The Center Party, whose leader was Anne Enger Lahnstein, won almost 18.5 percent of the vote, more than twice its total in the previous elections in 1989. The party captured 32 seats in the Storting, up from 11 seats. The big losers were right-of-center parties. For example, the Conservative Party fell from 37 seats to 28 seats and the Progress Party dropped from 22 seats to 11 seats.

Commitment to EC. After her victory, Brundtland pledged to continue the drive for EC membership, saying Norway would find itself politically and economically isolated if it rejected the EC. Nearby Denmark joined the EC in 1973, and Norway's neighbors Sweden and Finland were negotiating membership in 1993. But opponents of EC membership maintained that Norway would give up too much control over economic, defense, and domestic issues if it joined. If Norwegians approve membership in 1994, the country could join the EC as early as Jan. 1, 1995.

Whaling controversy. Norway in 1993 defied a moratorium by the International Whaling Commission (IWC) on the hunting and killing of certain species of whales for commercial use. On May 18, four days after the IWC voted to retain its strict ban, the Norwegian government announced that whalers would be allowed to kill 296 minke whales in 1993, with 136 allotted for scientific study. The government used IWC data to argue that the minke population would not be in danger from limited whaling. Norway's decision was severely criticized by environmental groups as well as by the EC's executive commission, which said the stance could make Norway's EC membership negotiations more difficult. All 12 EC countries have agreed to the whaling ban.

Role in peace talks. Norway won international praise for its role in secret talks between Israel and the Palestine Liberation Organization, which culminated in a historic peace agreement between the two parties signed on September 13. Foreign Minister Johan Jorgen Holst kept months of intricate talks alive. (See **Middle East.**) ☐ Philip Revzin

See also **Europe** (Facts in brief table). In **World Book,** see **Norway.**

Nova Scotia. In provincial legislative elections on May 25, 1993, the Liberal Party toppled the Progressive Conservative government, which had been in office for 15 years. The Conservatives had held 25 seats in the 52-seat legislature, compared with the Liberals' 20 seats. After the election, the Conservatives were left with 9 seats. The Liberals, under John Savage, a 60-year-old physician and former mayor of Dartmouth, N.S., acquired 40 seats. The New Democratic Party won 3. After the defeat, Premier Donald Cameron resigned as leader of the Conservatives and left active politics.

The federal government announced on August 31 that five Atlantic cod-fishery areas would be closed indefinitely. The closings threw some 12,000 fishery workers—of whom half were Nova Scotians—out of work. The layoffs brought the total number of unemployed workers to almost 40,000.

The budget, announced on September 30, raised taxes to bring in $78 million in revenue. Government expenditures were reduced by 2 percent and civil servants earning more than $22,000 a year were required to take five days off without pay. Even so, the province's operating deficit was projected to reach $396 million during the 1993-1994 fiscal year. ☐ David M. L. Farr

In **World Book,** see Nova Scotia.

Nuclear energy. See Energy supply.
Nutrition. See Food.

Ocean. The TOPEX-Poseidon satellite, a joint project of the United States and France, was a spectacular success in 1993. The satellite was launched in August 1992 to map the *topography* (shape) of the ocean surface. During the first six months of its operation, the satellite recorded the most accurate measurements to date of global sea level changes. The satellite detected a 1-foot (30-centimeter) winter sea level drop in the Northern Hemisphere due to lower sea temperatures and a corresponding rise in summer sea level in the Southern Hemisphere. Seawater expands when it warms and contracts when it cools.

Scientists could use such accurate measurements of sea level changes to determine whether *global warming* is occurring. Global warming is a rise in Earth's average temperature that could occur due to the accumulation of heat-trapping gases in the atmosphere. Chief among these gases is carbon dioxide, which is released through burning *fossil fuels* (coal, oil, and natural gas). Scientists fear that global warming could disrupt agriculture in many areas and melt polar icecaps, causing widespread flooding of coastal areas.

Unexpectedly, the satellite detected a large *Kelvin wave* in the western Pacific Ocean. A Kelvin wave is a large surge of warm water that moves eastward along the equator in the Pacific. A Kelvin wave can contribute to *El Niño* conditions. El Niño is a periodic warming in the eastern tropical Pacific

Ocean that alters weather conditions in the tropics and elsewhere in the world. The satellite's detection of the Kelvin wave in December 1992 allowed scientists to predict the wave's arrival in March 1993 along the western coast of South America.

El Niño hangs on. The duration of El Niño well into 1993 provided an extraordinary surprise. The most current El Niño began in late 1991. After weakening in late 1992, the El Niño reappeared in early 1993. It is not unprecedented to have two successive years of El Niño conditions, as occurred in 1991 and 1992, but 1993 marked only the second time since weather records have been kept that an El Niño has spanned three years. Some scientists suggested that this extended warming in the eastern tropical Pacific caused the long period of rainfall that resulted in the record-breaking summer floods in the Midwestern United States during 1993. El Niño appeared to strengthen in fall 1993, raising the possibility that it would continue into 1994.

A sunken nuclear submarine. In late July 1993, Russian, American, Norwegian, and Dutch scientists examined a nuclear-powered Russian submarine that sank in 1989 in waters 1 mile (1.6 kilometers) deep 300 miles (500 kilometers) off the coast of Norway. Prior to the scientists' expedition, experts worried about a plutonium leak from nuclear-tipped torpedoes. They feared that plutonium from the corroding weapons could be swept into North Atlantic fishing areas by strong currents. Such pollution could threaten human health if people ate contaminated fish. However, the scientists found currents in the area to be weak. They also found that sediment, about 1 inch (2.5 centimeters) annually, was accumulating on the ocean floor around the submarine. Scientists determined that the sediment would bind to any leaking radioactive particles and bury them on the bottom. But the Russian government in September 1993 said that it would seal the submarine in 1994, regardless of the cost, to eliminate even the slightest chance of plutonium pollution.

Vast undersea volcanoes. Scientists mapping the sea floor 600 miles (960 kilometers) northwest of Easter Island in the South Pacific Ocean said they found the greatest concentration of active volcanoes on Earth in February 1993. The scientists found more than 1,100 volcanoes on the sea floor. Many of them rise more than 1 mile above the ocean floor with their peaks 2,500 to 5,000 feet (760 to 1,500 meters) below the sea's surface. The undersea volcanoes occur in an area that covers about 55,000 square miles (140,000 square kilometers). One potential benefit of the discovery is that the volcanic eruptions are generating large new mineral deposits, including copper, iron, sulfur, and gold. □ Arthur G. Alexiou

In *World Book,* see **Ocean.**

Ohio. See **State government.**

Oklahoma. See **State government.**

Old age. See **Social security.**

O'Leary, Hazel R. (1937-   ), a lawyer and power company executive from Minneapolis, Minn., became secretary of energy on Jan. 22, 1993. She is the first woman and the first black to head the United States Department of Energy.

O'Leary was born Hazel Reid on May 17, 1937, in Newport News, Va. She graduated with honors from Fisk University in Nashville in 1959 and earned a law degree at Rutgers University in Newark, N.J., in 1966.

After obtaining her law degree, O'Leary worked as an assistant prosecutor in Essex County, N.J., and later became an assistant attorney general for the state of New Jersey. In the 1970's, she served as an energy official in the administrations of Presidents Gerald R. Ford and Jimmy Carter.

From 1981 to 1989, O'Leary was vice president and general counsel for O'Leary Associates, a Washington, D.C., consulting firm that she founded with her late husband, John F. O'Leary. The company helped with the development of power plants and lobbied state and federal legislatures on energy issues. John O'Leary died in 1987.

In 1990, Hazel O'Leary was named executive vice president of the Northern States Power Company, a Minneapolis-based power utility. She was named president of the company's natural-gas operations just before being confirmed as energy secretary.

O'Leary has a son, Carl G. Rollins, from a previous marriage. □ David Dreier

Olympic Games. In a controversial decision, the International Olympic Committee (IOC) voted on Sept. 23, 1993, to award the Summer Olympics in the year 2000 to Sydney, Australia, over Beijing. The United States Congress adopted a resolution on July 26, 1993, saying Beijing should be rejected due to China's poor human rights record. The European Parliament later adopted a similar resolution.

The IOC regarded the resolutions as political interference, and Beijing became the voting favorite. But the committee selected Sydney in the fourth round of voting in Monte Carlo, Monaco. The IOC eliminated Istanbul, Turkey; Berlin, Germany; and Manchester, England, in earlier rounds.

On July 27, the IOC awarded U.S. television rights for the 1996 Summer Olympics in Atlanta, Ga., to the National Broadcasting Company for $456 million, a record for an Olympics. The American Broadcasting Companies bid $450 million, and CBS Inc. bid $415 million.

Major competitions in 1993 included the two World University Games. In the Winter Games in February in Zakopane, Poland, Japan won 18 medals, followed by the United States and Russia with 15 each. In the Summer Games in July in Buffalo, N.Y., U.S. athletes led with 75 medals compared with 40 medals for second-place Canada. □ Frank Litsky

In *World Book,* see **Olympic Games.**

Oman. See **Middle East.**

O'Neal, Shaquille (1972-   ), was named the National Basketball Association's (NBA) Rookie of the Year on May 6, 1993. He was the youngest player ever to win the award. The 7-foot 1-inch (216-centimeter) center for the Orlando Magic received 96 of 98 possible votes from a nationwide panel of basketball writers and broadcasters to claim the honor.

O'Neal was born on March 6, 1972, in Newark, N.J. One of six children, O'Neal moved with his family to Germany, where his father served in the United States military. The family moved to San Antonio when O'Neal was 16 years old. There he attended Cole High School and excelled in basketball. O'Neal, nicknamed "Shaq," attended Louisiana State University (LSU) in Baton Rouge, where he was a two-time first-team All-American. He left LSU after his junior year to become the first pick in the 1992 NBA draft.

O'Neal is known for his rebounding skills, shot blocking, and his backboard-smashing slam dunks. He led all NBA rookies in four offensive categories during the 1992-1993 season: rebounding (13.9 rebounds per game); shots blocked (3.53 per game); shooting percentage (.562); and scoring (23.4 points per game). He was second in the league in rebounding and shots blocked per game, fourth in shooting percentage, and eighth in scoring.

In his spare time, O'Neal enjoys acting, watching karate movies, and listening to rap music. He is single and lives in Orlando, Fla.   □ Mark Dunbar

Ontario. The New Democratic Party (NDP) government of Premier Robert K. Rae undertook decisive steps in 1993 to reduce a ballooning public deficit. Ontario had secured lower-than-anticipated revenues because of a recession. At the same time, a loss of manufacturing jobs meant that 1 in every 9 residents, including children, was forced to rely on some form of social welfare assistance.

On April 23, Finance Minister Floyd Laughren described a three-pronged approach to cut back government spending. First, the fiscal 1993-1994 budget was to be cut by $4 billion. (Monetary figures are in Canadian dollars.) To that end, up to 11,000 public service jobs would be eliminated—3,800 from government departments and 7,200 from such sectors as schools and health care. Second, revenues from taxes and fees were to be boosted by $2 billion. And third, payroll expenses for workers in the public sector would be reduced by $2 billion through a voluntary austerity package called a social contract. By these means and others, the government expected to cut from $7 billion to $9 billion from the projected fiscal 1993-1994 deficit of $17 billion.

The budget, announced on May 19, 1993, boosted income taxes by three percentage points, to 58 percent of the federal tax rate. Taxpayers earning over $51,000 were also hit with an increase in the income surtax. Revenues for 1993-1994 were expected to total $43.9 billion, leaving a deficit of $9.2 billion.

The government negotiated the austerity plan with the public sector unions through the summer. The three-year plan sought to secure voluntary agreements to cut payroll spending through wage freezes, early retirement options, and unpaid leaves. The scheme, which involved overriding 8,000 union contracts covering 900,000 public employees, met stiff resistance from the unions. But by August 2, agreements had been negotiated with the representatives of unions and employers in eight major sectors, including schools, universities, and municipalities. In sectors such as health care, agreements could not be reached and the finance minister imposed settlements. New local agreements were then hammered out, leading to a savings of $1.9 billion a year in payroll costs. A reduction in government pension contributions also helped save $470 million.

Casino approved. In July, the Ontario government announced that the province's first gambling casino would be located in Windsor, just across the border from Detroit. The casino's temporary home would be the downtown Art Gallery of Windsor.

NDP candidates in two Toronto by-elections on April 1 fared poorly, each receiving less than 1,500 votes, but the NDP retained a comfortable majority of 73 seats in the legislature. The Liberals had 36 seats and the Progressive Conservatives had 21.   □ David M. L. Farr

In *World Book,* see Ontario.

Owada, Masako (1963-   ), gave up a promising career in foreign relations to marry Japan's Crown Prince Naruhito on June 9, 1993. She is the first career woman to become crown princess and the third commoner to marry into the royal family.

Owada was born in Tokyo on Dec. 9, 1963. As the daughter of a Japanese diplomat, she had lived in Moscow and New York City. When her father took a position as a lecturer in international relations at Harvard University in Cambridge, Mass., the family moved to Belmont, Mass., where Masako completed her high school education. She then enrolled at Harvard, graduating magna cum laude in 1985 with a bachelor's degree in economics. In 1986, she attended law school at Tokyo University and, in 1987, entered Japan's Ministry of Foreign Affairs. The ministry sent Owada to Oxford University in England, where she studied international relations from 1988 to 1990.

Back in Japan in June 1990, Owada began working for the ministry's North American Affairs Bureau. There she was involved in negotiations between Japan and the United States, which included the thorny issues of semiconductor trade and Tokyo's restrictions on the activities of foreign lawyers. Life in the royal palace has been traditionally controlled and near-cloistered. But observers speculated that Owada's intellect, skills, and ambitions might crack some of the rigid customs.   □ Lori Fagan

Country	Population	Government	Monetary unit*	Foreign trade (million U.S.$)	
				Exports†	Imports†
Australia	17,684,000	Governor General Bill Hayden; Prime Minister Paul Keating	dollar (1.50 = $1)	42,417	40,696
Fiji	811,000	Prime Minister Sitiveni Rabuka	dollar (1.54 = $1)	435	624
Kiribati	75,000	President Teatao Teannaki	Australian dollar	6	27
Nauru	10,000	President Bernard Dowiyogo	Australian dollar	93	73
New Zealand	3,520,000	Governor General Dame Catherine Tizard; Prime Minister James B. Bolger	dollar (1.81 = $1)	9,841	9,214
Papua New Guinea	4,238,000	Governor General Sir Wiwa Korowi; Prime Minister Paias Wingti	kina (0.98 = $1)	1,812	1,522
Solomon Islands	386,000	Governor General Sir George Lepping; Prime Minister Francis Billy Hilly	dollar (3.18 = $1)	70	92
Tonga	94,000	King Taufa'ahau Tupou IV; Prime Minister Baron Vaea	pa'anga (1.50 = $1)	13	63
Tuvalu	10,000	Governor General Sir Toaripi Lauti; Prime Minister Bikenibeu Paeniu	Australian dollar	1	3
Vanuatu	164,000	President Fred Timakata; Prime Minister Maxime Carlot Korman	vatu (122.76 = $1)	20	83
Western Samoa	170,000	Head of State Malietoa Tanumafili II; Prime Minister Tofilau Eti Alesana	tala (2.60 = $1)	9	75

*Exchange rates as of Oct. 29, 1993, or latest available data.
†Latest available data.

Pacific Islands. The year 1993 was marked by natural disasters in the Pacific Islands. On January 2 and 3, Typhoon Kina struck Fiji and Tonga, causing at least 20 deaths and leaving thousands of people homeless. Also on January 2 and 3, Typhoon Nina hit the Solomon Islands, killing at least three people. On October 13, an earthquake left about 60 people dead in eastern Papua New Guinea.

Fiji. In spite of predictions that his fragile political coalition would be short-lived, Prime Minister Sitiveni Rabuka celebrated his first year in office on June 2. Rabuka, a major general who twice overthrew Fiji's democratically elected government in military coups in 1987, formed a governing coalition after no party won enough votes in the May 1992 parliamentary election to choose a prime minister. Rabuka declared his commitment to national unity. By year's end, he had entered into a conciliatory dialogue with some leaders of Fiji-Indians, descendants of indentured laborers brought from India around 1900 who now control much of Fiji's economy.

Papua New Guinea. Two major events marked Papua New Guinea's political scene in 1993. In September, Parliament proposed a fundamental overhaul of the way the nation is governed, including the abolition of its 19 provincial governments. With 4.2 million people divided among a variety of cultures who speak more than 800 languages, national unity has always been an elusive goal for Papua New Guinea. The provincial system was designed to accommodate such diversity and ward off secession sentiments on the mineral rich island of Bougainville. But many Papua New Guineans have criticized the provincial governments as inefficient and corrupt. In sporadic attempts at reform, the central government has suspended 10 provincial governments since 1975. Provincial premiers rejected Parliament's September 1993 move, and six provinces threatened to secede.

Prime Minister Paias Wingti attempted a clever maneuver to hold onto power in September, after being elected in July 1992 by the slim margin of 55-54. First, Wingti resigned. In a matter of minutes, however, he was reelected as the sole nominee for the post. Wingti's gambit was designed to avoid a no-confidence motion in Parliament. Under Papua New Guinea's Constitution, such a motion is not allowed until a new prime minister has served at least 18 months. Wingti's 18 months would have expired in December 1993, so his resignation and reelection reset the clock on any possible parliamentary ouster. The opposition stormed out of Parliament and challenged the maneuver in court.

The armed rebellion on Bougainville continued throughout 1993. Ignited by disputes over the sharing of revenues from Bougainville's lucrative Panguna copper mine and other grievances, the revolt erupted in 1988 when the island demanded independence. During 1993, the Papua New Guinea defense force appeared to regain control over much of Bougainville, and rebel forces appeared to lose some of their support among local people. Tension also continued in 1993 between Papua New Guinea and the Solomon Islands over the island of Bougainville. Culturally and linguistically, the people of Bougainville are linked to the Solomon Islands to the east.

Tonga. King Taufa'ahau Tupou IV of Tonga, Polynesia's only surviving monarch, celebrated his 25th year on the throne in July. The nation's 1875 Constitution guarantees the king and 33 noble families control of 21 seats of a 30-member parliament.

But political change seemed inevitable. In November 1992, reformists held a conference on democracy in Tonga, a previously unthinkable event. Representatives of the Pro-Democratic Movement won six of the nine seats held by commoners in elections on Feb. 4, 1993. Although this was only a gain of one seat, support appeared likely from the other three newly elected commoners.

Solomon Islands. A climate of dissatisfaction existed for the May 1993 parliamentary election. A deteriorating economy, problems with the nation's education and health systems, charges of corruption, and strained relations with Papua New Guinea over Bougainville contributed to the electorate's mood.

The elections failed to produce a ruling majority, so six parties formed the National Coalition Partnership (NCP). Francis Billy Hilly, a former premier of the Solomons' Western Province, was elected prime minister when Parliament met in June.

Nauru. On August 9, Nauru and Australia concluded a long-standing dispute over mineral rights on the island. The dispute grew out of the Nauru government's demands that Australia pay more for phosphate deposits that it had mined on Nauru since the early 1900's. Australia agreed to provide compensation of more than $70 million and assist with the restoration of the island.

Using the position it gained after World War I (1914-1918) as administrator of Nauru, Australia mined the island's rich layer of phosphate rock. Nauruans received little benefit from this, however, and when the island became independent in 1968, much of the deposit was depleted. The Nauruans sued for compensation in the International Court of Justice, the highest judicial agency of the United Nations, headquartered at The Hague in the Netherlands.

Milestones. Frank Liu became premier of Niue in June 1993. He succeeded Robert Rex, who died at age 83 in December 1992. Rex had served as premier since Niue became self-governing in free association with New Zealand in 1974. He was the longest-serving head of government in the region. A strong personality whose influence was greater than the small size of his country, Rex was a leader of the movement to decolonize the Pacific. ☐ Robert C. Kiste

In *World Book,* see **Pacific Islands.**

Pacino, Al (1940-   ), won the Academy Award for best actor in March 1993 for his role as a blind, retired military officer in *Scent of a Woman* (1992). It was Pacino's first Oscar after several nominations.

The actor was born Alfredo James Pacino on April 25, 1940, in New York City. He attended the High School for the Performing Arts in Manhattan but dropped out. He went on to study acting at the Herbert Berghof Studio and then at the Actors' Studio, both in New York City.

In 1968, he won an Obie Award for best actor for his off-Broadway debut in *The Indian Wants the Bronx.* The next year he made his Broadway debut in *Does a Tiger Wear a Necktie?,* for which he won a Tony Award. Another Tony came his way for his role in *The Basic Training of Pavlo Hummel* (1972).

Pacino's first motion picture was *Me, Natalie* (1969). His performances in subsequent movies—*The Godfather* (1972); *Serpico* (1973), for which he won a Golden Globe Award; *Scarecrow* (1973), for which he won the best actor award at the Cannes Film Festival; *The Godfather, Part II* (1974); and *Dog Day Afternoon* (1975)—established him as a star. His next films won little acclaim, however, until 1989 and 1990, when he starred in three well-received releases: *Sea of Love, Dick Tracy,* and *The Godfather, Part III.* Three more films secured his renewed success— *Frankie and Johnny* (1991); *Glengarry Glen Ross* (1992); and *Scent of a Woman.* ☐ Lori Fagan

Pakistan had a politically tumultuous 1993 that was punctuated in midyear by the resignations of President Ghulam Ishaq Khan and Prime Minister Nawaz Sharif. An interim prime minister ushered in a three-month period of reform to prepare for elections in the fall. On October 6, the Pakistan People's Party (PPP), led by former Prime Minister Benazir Bhutto, won the most seats in parliament, and she formed a government. The Pakistan Moslem League (PML) under Sharif became the party in opposition.

Sharif's troubles. Beginning in January 1993, Sharif and Ishaq Khan were involved in a dispute over the power of the presidency. Sharif sought to repeal the constitutional amendment that gave the presidency the power to dissolve parliament. Also in January, Ishaq Khan selected General Abdul Waheed Kakar as army chief of staff, but Sharif had recommended another general. In Pakistan, the army chief of staff, the president, and the prime minister effectively run Pakistan together. The previous chief of staff, General Asif Nawaz, had died on January 9.

Then, Sharif threatened to work with Bhutto to limit the president's powers. In retaliation, Ishaq Khan dismissed Sharif's government on April 18 on charges of corruption similar to those he had used to dismiss Bhutto's government in 1990. The president scheduled new elections for July 1993, but the Supreme Court of Pakistan voted on May 26, 1993, that Sharif's ouster was unlawful. He resumed office.

Pakistan

Army intercedes. On July 11, Bhutto threatened a massive march on Islamabad, the capital, unless elections were called. Fearing a violent uprising by Bhutto's supporters, Waheed forced the resignations of Ishaq Khan and Sharif on July 18. Wasim Sajjad, chairman of the Senate, became acting president. Moeen A. Qureshi, a retired senior vice president of the World Bank, an international lending agency, who had lived outside his native Pakistan for 40 years, was named acting prime minister.

Qureshi's reforms. Qureshi found the country near financial collapse with many public services not operating. On August 19, he introduced an economic reform program that reduced government subsidies on electricity, transportation, and wheat and imposed new taxes on wealthy landowners who had used their political power to evade taxation. Qureshi also barred prominent people from seeking election until they paid off previously defaulted state loans.

The parliamentary elections on October 6 pitted Sharif against Bhutto in what was widely viewed as one of the nation's few fair elections. Bhutto's PPP won 86 of parliament's 211 contested seats to 72 for Sharif's PML. On November 13, Bhutto's candidate, Farooq Leghari, easily won the presidential election against Sharif's candidate. Leghari supported reducing presidential power. □ Henry S. Bradsher

See also **Asia** (Facts in brief table). In *World Book,* see **Pakistan.**

Paleontology. A fossilized insect dating to the early Cretaceous Period (135 million to 120 million years ago) has yielded the first genetic material recovered from the age of the dinosaurs, researchers reported in June 1993. The researchers extracted DNA—the molecule of which genes are made—from a weevil preserved in *amber* (fossilized tree resin) found near Jazzin, Lebanon. The DNA is about 80 million years older than any previously recovered.

Cambrian explosion. The *Cambrian explosion*—the rapid appearance of nearly all the major body plans known in animals—may have taken far less time than previously believed, according to research published in September. Scientists had long placed the start of the Cambrian Period at about 570 million years ago. However, geologists have now determined the age of volcanic rocks—which can be dated more reliably than other rocks—that were laid down in Siberia, in Russia, slightly before the oldest Cambrian fossils. The scientists dated the rocks at 544 million years, making the start of the Cambrian almost 30 million years later than had been thought. This in turn suggested that the Cambrian explosion took place within only 5 million to 10 million years, an extraordinarily brief span in paleontological terms. The finding has challenged scientists anew to determine what caused the evolutionary explosion.

A "living fossil"? A British amateur zoologist reported in March that he had discovered what may

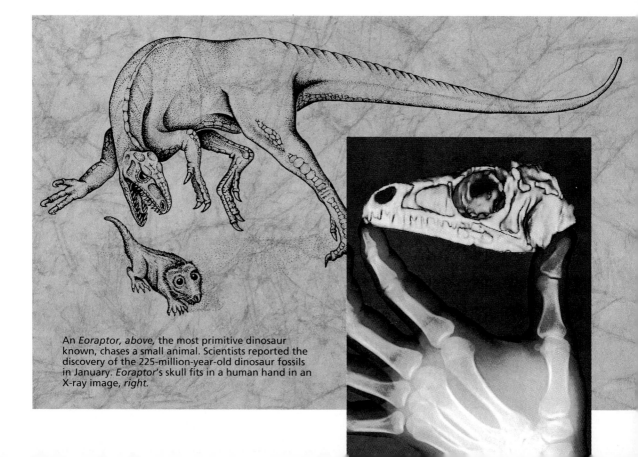

An *Eoraptor, above,* the most primitive dinosaur known, chases a small animal. Scientists reported the discovery of the 225-million-year-old dinosaur fossils in January. *Eoraptor*'s skull fits in a human hand in an X-ray image, *right.*

be living *graptolites*—small, colony-forming marine invertebrates—in samples of marine life dredged from the deep Pacific Ocean floor near New Caledonia. Graptolites are among the most important fossils of the Ordovician and Silurian Periods (500 million to 410 million years ago). They are thought to have become extinct some 320 million years ago.

The new animal, dubbed *Cephalodiscus graptolitoides,* is a previously unknown member of the *pterobranchs,* a class of wormlike marine organisms. The tiny tentacle-bearing animals live in tubes arranged in colonies. The tubes, and spinelike structures that extend from them, resemble those of fossil graptolites. Whether or not the organism is a graptolite, the finding may help scientists resolve a debate over the relation between graptolites and pterobranchs.

Angiosperms (flowering plants) may have become the predominant form of plant life less rapidly than had been believed, according to a May report on plant fossils from central Wyoming. The earliest angiosperm fossils date to about 100 million years ago. Because angiosperms reproduce quickly, scientists had thought that in many environments, they displaced lower plants such as ferns soon after they evolved. But in the Wyoming fossils, which date to 72 million years ago, angiosperms remain overshadowed by the lower plants. □ Carlton E. Brett

See **Motion pictures: Could Dinosaurs Live in a Zoo?** In *World Book,* see **Paleontology.**

Panama. Panamanians were reconsidering the wisdom in 1993 of the impending withdrawal of United States armed forces from the Panama Canal Zone, according to a poll conducted in May by *La Prensa,* a Panamanian daily newspaper. Nearly 71 percent of those polled said Panama would be better off if U.S. military bases remained in the country after the end of 1999. This is the deadline for removal of the bases in accord with a 1977 treaty that calls for the return to Panama of the Canal Zone and the military bases in it.

The departure of U.S. troops and their estimated 20,000 dependents would deprive Panama of about $500 million annually in U.S. spending. This figure is about one-tenth of Panama's *gross domestic product* (the value of all goods and services produced in a country).

Illegal weapons seized. The Panamanian government confirmed on Aug. 16, 1993, that it had seized $21 million worth of weapons and ammunition earlier in the year that were destined for war-torn Bosnia-Herzegovina in violation of a United Nations embargo. Arms traffickers had used false papers, citing Panama as the ultimate destination of the weapons, which originated in Austria and the former Czechoslovakia. □ Nathan A. Haverstock

See also **Latin America** (Facts in brief table). In *World Book,* see **Panama.**

Papua New Guinea. See Asia; Pacific Islands.

Paraguay. On May 9, 1993, Juan Carlos Wasmosy of the ruling Colorado Party won the first democratic, multiparty presidential elections in Paraguay's 182-year history. He was sworn in for a five-year term on August 15.

Wasmosy, a wealthy civil engineer, had headed a consortium that won lucrative contracts in the 1970's for the construction of the huge Itaipú hydroelectric dam in southeastern Paraguay along the country's border with Brazil. Wasmosy had never before held elected office.

Opponents charged that Wasmosy's election was marred by fraud, sabotage, and overt politicking by military officers who supported the Colorado Party. But a 300-member international team of election observers, headed by former U.S. President Jimmy Carter and federal Senator Al Graham of Canada, concluded that disruptions were not sufficient to have influenced the outcome of the election.

A conservative, Wasmosy pledged to liberalize Paraguay's often oppressive government, which the Colorado Party has dominated since 1948. He also supported Latin-American economic integration and the construction of a 1,584-mile (2,550-kilometer) international waterway that would link ports on the South Atlantic Ocean with the South American interior via rivers in Paraguay. □ Nathan A. Haverstock

See also **Latin America** (Facts in brief table). In *World Book,* see **Paraguay.**

Peña, Federico F. (1947-), the former mayor of Denver, Colo., was sworn in as United States secretary of transportation on Jan. 21, 1993, becoming the first Hispanic to hold that Cabinet post. Peña has spent much of his political career working on transportation issues, and he was a driving force behind the construction of a new international airport—the world's largest—for the Denver area.

Peña was born on March 15, 1947, in Laredo, Tex. He received a bachelor's degree from the University of Texas at Austin in 1968 and earned a law degree there in 1972. He later moved to Colorado.

In 1983, Peña became the first Hispanic mayor of Denver. Prior to his election, he served for four years in the Colorado House of Representatives and became minority leader. While in that position, he began working on the state's transportation needs.

As mayor, Peña worked to improve transportation throughout the Denver metropolitan area. In addition to pushing for a new airport, he oversaw the development of a ground-transportation plan calling for improved highways and mass transit, including the construction of a light-rail system.

Peña was reelected in 1987 and served until 1991. During his administration, the city engaged in a massive public works program.

Peña is married to attorney Ellen Hart. They have two children. □ David Dreier

Pennsylvania. See State government.

327

Peru. Peruvians voted to approve a new Constitution on Oct. 31, 1993. The new Constitution dissolved Peru's two houses of Congress in favor of a smaller, one-house legislature. It also allowed the president to run for a second term and to promote military officers. The new law also approved the death penalty for convicted terrorists. Many saw the vote as a sanction of President Alberto Fujimori's actions of April 5, 1992, when he dissolved Congress and suspended the previous Constitution in an attempt to quell what he said was a government crisis due to "terrorism, drug trafficking, and corruption."

War on terror. Speaking before the United Nations (UN) General Assembly on Oct. 1, 1993, Fujimori said that he was confident of victory in the continuing war against the Shining Path leftist guerrillas, a conflict that has killed about 25,000 people since 1980. Fujimori displayed a letter from jailed Shining Path leader Abimael Guzmán Reynoso as proof that the guerrilla group was near defeat. In the letter, Guzmán reportedly offered to negotiate a peace agreement with the government. Fujimori rejected the offer, saying that he would not negotiate with "genocidal terrorists." Since Guzmán had called for an all-out war against the government after his capture, Fujimori said the peace offer proved that the Shining Path had "accepted total defeat."

Peruvian police had captured Guzmán on Sept. 12, 1992. A military tribunal then convicted him of treason and sentenced him to life in prison. On April 3, 1993, the government transferred Guzmán to an underground cell in Callao.

Liberalization of the economy. Fujimori continued his efforts to introduce free market principles to the Peruvian economy in 1993. One of his major strategies was to sell money-losing government industries. In June, the Peruvian government began soliciting bids for ownership of up to 100 percent of Centromin Peru, the country's largest state-owned mining company. Centromin accounts for about 70 percent of Peru's mineral exports.

Military uneasiness. Peru's military refused attempts in 1993 to investigate its role in atrocities committed during the 1980's and early 1990's. On April 20, 1993, Army General Nicolás de Bari Hermoza Ríos refused to answer questions from a member of Peru's Congress regarding the role of paramilitary death squads in the killings of nine students and a professor at a university outside Lima in 1992.

On April 21 and 22, 1993, army tanks appeared on Lima streets in a show of support for Hermoza Ríos. A day later, Bernard Aronson, United States assistant secretary of state for Latin American affairs, phoned Fujimori to warn that the action jeopardized Peru's democratic process, as well as its eligibility for international aid. ☐ Nathan A. Haverstock

See also **Latin America** (Facts in brief table). In *World Book,* see **Peru.**

The Peruvian military transfers guerrilla leader Abimael Guzmán Reynoso from an island prison in the Pacific Ocean to one on the mainland in April.

Petroleum and gas. An oversupply of oil in 1993 caused a decline in prices for much of the year, which benefited petroleum consumers. However, producers of crude oil suffered financially as a result of lowered fuel prices. By autumn, values of some crude oil had dropped by as much as $4 a barrel from prices a year earlier. Consequently, Saudi Arabia, the wealthy Persian Gulf kingdom that is the world's largest oil producer, had a budget deficit for the year. Saudi Arabia and the 11 other members of the Organization of Petroleum Exporting Countries (OPEC) felt considerable economic pressure to stop the declining prices as the reference price for their crudes dropped below $14 a barrel, $7 below a target price they had set.

The main reason that the oversupply of oil developed was that the OPEC nations as well as the major oil-consuming nations had overestimated world petroleum demand for 1993. At the beginning of the year, it was generally assumed that worldwide oil consumption would climb. Indeed, in January 1993, the International Energy Agency, an organization of 21 countries that are major importers of oil, had predicted that 1993 petroleum use would rise by some 600,000 barrels a day.

But sluggish economies in the bigger oil-consuming nations failed to recover as fast as expected, and this held down demand for oil, the economic lifeblood of most industrial nations. As a result, total 1993 consumption of petroleum worldwide averaged slightly under the 1992 level of 67 million barrels a day.

Meanwhile, most of the world's oil-producing countries, in desperate need of revenues, continued to produce close to their capacity. The exception to this was the former Soviet Union. In Russia and the other former Soviet republics, output plunged because of economic and political turmoil. However, the chaos also caused petroleum consumption to drop in these nations, so their oil exports remained relatively high, adding to the world oversupply.

OPEC action. Among OPEC members, which are the main oil-exporting nations, petroleum output remained near 25 million barrels a day during 1993. That was close to the highest rate in a decade even though one major producer, Iraq, remained banned from the world oil market for the year. Economic sanctions that were imposed by the United Nations (UN) against Iraq in August 1990 after its invasion of Kuwait remained in effect for 1993 despite periodic efforts by Iraq to have the bans lifted.

In late September, the OPEC members finally took a major step to curb their runaway production, or at least to keep it from rising further over the winter months, the peak period for oil use. At a meeting that began on September 25 in Geneva, Switzerland, representatives of the OPEC nations set a new production ceiling of 24.5 million barrels a day for six months. That was 200,000 barrels a day less than the nations had been producing. It also was well below the 25 million barrels a day expected to be required from OPEC for world oil needs to be met over the winter.

Although oil analysts doubted that all the OPEC exporters would adhere to their new production quotas, the action helped to put a floor under falling oil prices for a few weeks. Then oil prices resumed their plunge, falling by December to the lowest level in five years.

Throughout 1993, the average price of West Texas Intermediate, the main type of United States crude, was down about $2 a barrel from $20.58 a barrel in 1992. Oil economist Paul Mlotok estimated that West Texas Intermediate, usually $2 a barrel higher than the OPEC crudes, would average around $18.50 a barrel in 1994 if Iraq remained excluded from the market, as was likely.

Prices at the pumps. Because of the cheaper costs of crude oil for refiners, fuel prices remained relatively low in 1993. In the United States, however, prices of gasoline at the pumps rose after a federal 4.3-cent gas tax went into effect on October 1 and some state gas taxes rose. Prices also rose because of higher manufacturing costs resulting from some federal clean-air laws and regulations that took effect in late 1993.

Natural gas, which had dropped to a near-record low of $1 per 1,000 cubic feet in early 1992, remained above $2 per 1,000 cubic feet for 1993. And U.S. gas consumption, which had reached 19.8 trillion cubic feet (560 billion cubic meters) for all of 1992, continued to rise in 1993.

Although deliveries of natural gas to industrial consumers were down 2 percent during the first six months of 1993, deliveries to residential consumers were up 8 percent, according to the U.S. Department of Energy. Total output of the nation's gas producers during July 1993 was an estimated 1.5 trillion cubic feet (42.5 billion cubic meters), 4 percent more than the volume during July 1992.

For the first eight months of 1993, domestic production of gas rose. It reached 12 trillion cubic feet (340 billion cubic meters), up from 11.8 trillion cubic feet (334.1 billion cubic meters) during the same period in 1992.

U.S. oil production. The optimistic outlook for gas contributed to increased drilling for oil, as companies that drill for both oil and gas together could devote the increased gas revenues to drilling. The number of drilling rigs active in the United States had dropped from a high of 4,500 in late 1981 to 610 units a decade later, the lowest level ever recorded. But rig activity rebounded in 1993, approaching 900 units late in the year.

Still, the drilling gains failed to stop the decline in U.S. crude oil production. Domestic output was down to 6.7 million barrels a day by late 1993 from 7 million a day a year earlier. Although U.S. petroleum

Petroleum and gas

demand was up only slightly, to some 17.2 million barrels a day, oil imports increased.

Indeed, 20 years after an Arab oil embargo introduced American motorists to gasoline lines in late 1973, the nation depended more on foreign oil than ever. Saudi Arabia and Venezuela were jockeying for position as the top source of U.S. oil imports. In 1993, imports of petroleum products and crude oil were averaging a total of more than 8 million barrels a day.

Taking note of the 20th anniversary of the Arab oil embargo, the October 1993 issue of *Petroleum Outlook,* a publication that monitors and analyzes the petroleum industry worldwide, cited some of the results: "While the embargo stimulated renewed interest in oil exploration in the United States through the mid-1980's, oil exploration and production spending in this country has been falling steadily since 1986 as oil companies continue to seek cheaper reserves abroad. And the United States' dependence on oil imports, after a brief lull, continues to grow sharply."

In 1993, the article said, the United States imported about 42 percent of its total supply of petroleum, with OPEC countries responsible for 25 percent of the total. "Imports are expected to climb to 55 percent of the total (10.1 million barrels a day) by the end of the decade," *Petroleum Outlook* reported. "By 1995," it added, "OPEC will again be in a powerful position not seen since 1979 when the cartel supplied 30 percent of all the U.S.'s supply of petroleum products."

Although the OPEC nations had problems of their own, recovering economies in the industrial nations and a very cold winter in 1993-1994 could increase oil demand enough to bail the OPEC nations out of their slump. This would force worldwide oil prices sharply higher.

Kuwait and Iraq. The Kuwaiti oil industry, although still recovering from the Persian Gulf War (1991), restored its ability to produce as much as 2.5 million barrels a day. However, Kuwait agreed in September 1993 to a six-month output quota of 2 million barrels a day.

Iraq made no such agreement, and, even though it was kept out of the world oil market by UN sanctions, it was eager to sell crude again. Before the war, Iraq was producing 3.2 million barrels a day. It will be months, or perhaps years, before Iraq's damaged oil industry can reach that level again. But Iraq's oil reserves were second only to those of Saudi Arabia, and the country was under severe economic stress. Once the UN lifts the bans, the Iraqis are expected to market their oil aggressively, discounting prices to regain their former customers.

☐ James Tanner

See also **Middle East.** In *World Book,* see **Gas; Gasoline; Organization of Petroleum Exporting Countries (OPEC); Petroleum.**

Philadelphia. Democratic Mayor Edward G. Rendell, who was elected in 1991 on a pledge to restore the financial health of the nearly bankrupt city, was delivering on that promise in 1993. In fiscal 1993, which ended on June 30, the city balanced its budget for the first time in seven years, and city officials said the fiscal 1994 budget would also be balanced. The Rendell administration achieved the fiscal turnaround through a higher sales tax and wage concessions from city employees.

New convention center. The city opened its $522-million Pennsylvania Convention Center on June 26, 1993. United States Vice President Albert A. Gore, Jr., officially dedicated the center. Located downtown in the shadow of City Hall, the convention center is the most expensive public works project in Philadelphia history. The huge facility could hold seven football fields in its main hall.

From the time it was first proposed in the 1980's, the center had stirred controversy over how much money the state should provide to pay for it, who would oversee its construction, and whether such a massive project should even be built. But the debate ended once the building was completed—on time and on budget. Most public officials heralded the center, predicting that it would attract great numbers of people to Philadelphia and inject a flow of much-needed money into the city's economy.

Avenue of the Arts. While one massive public works project was being completed, another—a street devoted to the arts—was begun just blocks away. The idea, developed in the early 1960's, was adopted by Mayor Rendell and has been promoted as a key part of his economic revitalization plan for the city. Under the plan, a stretch of South Broad Street, one of the city's major boulevards, will become the Avenue of the Arts. The avenue will be lined with theaters, a center dedicated to jazz, and other facilities, including a public high school that will train students for careers in the arts.

Considerable money has been earmarked for the avenue. At the end of 1992, the Pennsylvania legislature authorized $60.6 million for the project, and in 1993 billionaire philanthropist Walter H. Annenberg contributed $20 million. In addition, Sidney Kimmel, founder of a large clothing company, announced that he would donate $12 million toward the construction of a new concert hall for the Philadelphia Orchestra if the orchestra could raise twice as much from other sources within the next two years. The orchestra had already raised $25 million in donations and pledges for a new hall, and orchestra officials said they believed they could attract the additional $24 million to match Kimmel's donation.

Mob violence. Different factions of Philadelphia's organized-crime families warred through 1993 in what the police called a power struggle for control of the underworld in the city and in suburban southern New Jersey. Eight shootings—some in public during daylight hours—occurred during the year. On August 31, Joseph Stanfa, son of alleged mob leader John Stanfa, was wounded in daylight as he was riding in a car with his father on one of the city's major expressways. And on September 17, a reputed associate of another mob leader was shot to death in the parking lot of the Melrose Diner, one of the city's landmark diner restaurants.

Phillies fever. The Philadelphia Phillies baseball team won the National League Eastern Division title in 1993 for the first time in 10 years. After defeating the Atlanta Braves to capture the pennant, the Phillies faced the Toronto Blue Jays in the World Series. The Phillies lost the series, four games to two. The turning point of the series might have been game four, when the Phillies blew a five-run lead in the eighth inning and went on to lose 15 to 14. That game set a series record for number of runs scored and length—4 hours 14 minutes. (See **Baseball.**)

De Klerk and Mandela honored. On July 4, South Africa's State President Frederik Willem de Klerk and Nelson Mandela, president of the African National Congress, received the Philadelphia Liberty Medal, an annual award presented by a private civic group. United States President Bill Clinton spoke at the ceremony, lauding the two men's efforts to end *apartheid* (racial separation) in South Africa. ☐ Howard S. Shapiro

See also **City.** In *World Book,* see **Philadelphia.**

Philippines. President Fidel V. Ramos struggled with economic problems during 1993 in an effort to combat his nation's widespread poverty. On April 5, he signed a bill that granted him emergency powers for one year to deal with the chronic shortage of electrical power. But on June 30, he said that the economy was still sluggish, mainly because of the power shortage.

Factories in metropolitan Manila, the capital, received reduced, or no, electricity from 11 a.m. to 7 p.m. each workday. The power shortage forced businesses to lay off about 71,000 workers and to reduce hours for another 2 million workers. Ramos set a goal of ending electricity shortages by the end of 1993, but late in the year, officials said the goal could not be met. Although businesses increased their imports of small generators early in 1993, contracting for more efficient, large generators met with financial, bureaucratic, and other problems.

Reform efforts. The government also tried to break up the monopolies and cartels that dominated Filipino business activity, despite the fact big business had supported Ramos in the 1992 presidential election. Ramos wanted to reduce the concentration of wealth in the hands of a few and to weaken businessmen who had benefited from political favoritism under the late President Ferdinand E. Marcos.

Nevertheless, the economy barely kept up with the growth in population, which was increasing 2.3

percent annually, one of the highest rates in Asia. The total population was 66 million in 1993. Ramos told Congress on July 26 that the population growth rate was straining resources for jobs, education, housing, health clinics, and other services. It also contributed to food shortages and migration of people abroad to seek jobs. Thus, on August 2, Ramos announced a birth control program with a goal of cutting the growth rate to below 2 percent by 1998.

Communism wanes. After 24 years of trying to overthrow the government, the Philippine Communist Party appeared to be weakening in 1993. One factor was an internal disagreement on strategy. The founder of the Philippine party, Jose Maria Sison, argued from exile in the Netherlands that a peasant insurrection was still needed against the cities. But the party's regional committees in Manila and two other areas, backed by more than half of the estimated 24,000 party members, broke with the Sison-led central committee. The rebel groups argued that new tactics were needed, including participation in congressional contests and agrarian reforms.

The Philippine armed forces had focused on Communist insurgency for years. But with the guerrilla war waning, Ramos ordered the armed forces to turn over counterinsurgency responsibilities to the National Police by 1995 and to refocus on external defense.

Police shakeup. On April 24, Ramos fired 62 top-ranking National Police officials in the largest shakeup of the law enforcement department in Philippine history. An investigation had uncovered widespread corruption and abuse of power. Ramos also authorized the forced retirement of 23 police generals and the shifting of some 175 other officers to positions of less importance.

Marcos entombed, Imelda convicted. The body of former President Ferdinand Marcos was returned to Batac, his home in the northern province of Ilocos Norte, on September 7. Loyal followers held demonstrations, but they were smaller and less disruptive than the government had feared. Marcos was ousted from office in 1986 and died in exile in Hawaii in 1989.

Imelda Marcos, widow of the late president, was convicted on Sept. 24, 1993, on two charges of corruption. They were the first of 94 criminal and civil cases filed against her. She appealed the two convictions, which had combined prison sentences of 18 to 24 years. Meanwhile, the government sought to recover from her billions of dollars they said Marcos had looted while he was in office.

The Moro National Liberation Front, a Muslim separatist group in the southern Philippines, signed a cease-fire agreement with the Philippine government in Indonesia on November 7. Peace talks were planned for 1994. ☐ Henry S. Bradsher

See also **Asia** (Facts in brief table). In *World Book,* see **Philippines.**

Physics. In October 1993, the United States Congress halted construction of the world's largest experimental physics instrument, the Superconducting Super Collider (SSC) particle accelerator near Waxahachie, Tex. A particle accelerator is a device that produces violent collisions of subatomic particles such as protons or electrons to generate a variety of other particles that scientists believe existed in the early moments of the universe. Although continued funding for the SSC had been approved by the Senate, a majority in the House of Representatives opposed it, and their view prevailed. Legislators said they voted against the project because it was too costly, given the need to reduce the federal budget deficit. About $1.8 billion of the projected $11-billion budget for the SSC had already been spent.

With the SSC's demise, physicists turned their attention to the European Organization for Nuclear Research (CERN), which was in the final stages of approving plans for a similar machine, the Large Hadron Collider (LHC). A significant number of U.S. physicists were already working at CERN and other European laboratories, and the end of the SSC meant that many more Americans were likely to join them.

The Large Hadron Collider will share an existing 17-mile (27-kilometer) oval tunnel with an older accelerator at CERN's labs near Geneva, Switzerland. That will make it considerably cheaper to build than the SSC, which required digging a 54-mile (87-kilometer) tunnel. But because the LHC's tunnel is much shorter than the one planned for the SSC, the LHC device will be only about one-third as powerful.

The LHC will generate two beams of protons circulating in opposite directions. Where the beams cross and protons collide violently, particle detectors will track the particles created as the energy of the collision is converted into mass. Each proton in the LHC's two beams will carry up to 7.7 trillion electronvolts (TeV) of energy. (An electronvolt is equivalent to the energy gained by an electron passing through an electric potential of 1 volt.) The SSC would have produced beams with 20 TeV of energy.

One goal of particle research is to determine whether the most fundamental particles ever discovered—objects called *quarks* and *leptons*—are composed of still-smaller particles. Data from the LHC will enable physicists to construct pictures of quarks and leptons with about nine times finer detail than is now obtainable.

The primary goal set for the SSC was to probe the origins of mass itself by testing the idea that mass is conferred by a theoretical particle called the Higgs boson. Physicists are not sure whether the LHC will produce enough energy to prove or disprove that particle's existence.

New heavy isotopes. In September 1993, a joint team of Russian and American scientists announced the discovery of two new and surprisingly stable *isotopes* (forms) of the unnamed element 106.

Team leaders Ron W. Lougheed of the Lawrence Livermore Laboratory in Livermore, Calif., and Yuri A. Lazarev of the Joint Institute for Nuclear Research in Dubna, Russia, found the isotopes during experiments performed at Dubna, using particle detectors built at Livermore.

Isotopes of an element differ only in the number of neutrons contained in the atomic nucleus. One of the new isotopes has 149 neutrons, and the other has 150. The nuclei of both isotopes also contain the 106 protons that give the element its designating number. The discovery was exciting because the two new isotopes are extraordinary long-lived for nuclei this massive. Both existed for more than a minute—an impressive length of time given that the only other known isotope of element 106, with 147 neutrons in its nucleus, lasts less than a second.

The September finding indicates that heavy isotopes with more neutrons are stabler than those with fewer. The notion that additional neutrons can stabilize a heavy nucleus revived interest in a prediction that an "island of stability" exists for nuclei that contain about 114 protons and 174 neutrons. Such nuclei might have lifetimes of years—possibly even millions of years. They would be extremely hard to produce, however, because the lighter nuclei that must be joined to form them have too few neutrons to go with the protons. □ Robert H. March

In *World Book*, see **Particle accelerator; Physics.**

Poetry. The year 1993 opened for American poetry with a flourish, as Maya Angelou was invited to compose a poem for the inauguration of Bill Clinton as United States President on January 20. Angelou's "On the Pulse of Morning" celebrated the nation's diversity and reaffirmed, in rolling Biblical cadences, America's need to ensure equality for all its people.

New volumes. John Updike, perhaps the greatest living master of light verse, brought out his *Collected Poems, 1953-1993* during the year. In the collection are reflections on golfers, celery, and a wrist watch, along with an ode to rot and a paean to food: "It's always there/Man's *real* best friend./It never bites back; it is already dead. . . . /It simply begs, *Take me;*/it cries out, *I'm yours.*"

More soberly, John Haines's *The Owl in the Mask of the Dreamer* contains acute observations on being, nature, and the search for stillness. "Meditation on a Skull Carved in Crystal" opens: "To think that the world/lies wholly in this mind; that this frozen water/this clarity of quartz,/this ice, is all."

In addition to Updike, many poets brought out retrospective volumes in 1993. May Sarton's *Collected Poems: 1930-1993* showed again why this sturdy survivor is still a model to young readers. John Hollander issued a new *Selected Poetry*, as well as a volume of fresh work, *Tesserae*. Hollander, a formally inventive writer, has sometimes been dismissed as merely a cool virtuoso, a skilled hand with compli-

Rita Dove, named the seventh poet laureate of the United States in May, was the first black poet and, at 40, the youngest poet ever to hold the title.

Another autobiographical work was James Merrill's *A Different Person,* in which Merrill artfully chronicles his early years in Europe and their effect on his writing. New paperback editions of Merrill's *Selected Poems, 1946-1985* and his epic *The Changing Light at Sandover* confirmed his standing as one of the nation's finest and most refined poets.

Other collections. Rita Dove, named the nation's newest poet laureate in May, issued her *Selected Poems* in 1993. Richard Kenney's *The Invention of the Zero* densely intertwines modern science and history. In Margaret Gibson's *The Vigil,* four women review their lives. Critic Bruce Bawer produced a book of poetry, *Coast to Coast.* Roseanna Warren's *Stained Glass Elegies* contains a sequence of elegies for her father, the novelist, poet, and critic Robert Penn Warren. *The Book of Light,* by Lucille Clifton, delivers poems of praise and protest.

Anthologies. *American Poetry: The Nineteenth Century,* a groundbreaking anthology edited by John Hollander, includes poems by long-neglected giants such as Henry Wadsworth Longfellow and Sidney Lanier, as well as African-American spirituals and American Indian poetry. For an expression of the year's sheer variety, no better survey exists than *The Best American Poetry 1993,* the latest in an annual series, edited by Louise Gluck with series editor David Lehman. ☐ Michael Dirda

In *World Book,* see **Poetry.**

cated verse patterns. In fact, few can match Hollander's wit, as in "The Art of Fiction" from *Tesserae:* "The poet who pretends to read/John Austin's essay on 'Pretending'/Need never grasp its condescending/Point that pretending can't succeed." But the books are also replete with achingly beautiful word-music.

Hollander is matched in economy of phrase by the gnomic William Bronk, who offered *The Mild Day* in 1993. Most of Bronk's poems are as tight as epigrams and as brief as haiku. In contrast, Albert Goldbarth's *Across the Layers: Poems Old and New* is pure excess. Whether writing about James Joyce or Miss Aluminum Siding, Goldbarth is like a torrent spouting lines of such gusto they become poetry by their sheer verbal energy.

A. R. Ammons treated the topic of excess in 1993 by taking up the subject of civilization's detritus in *Garbage.* This book-length poem—which received the National Book Award for poetry in 1993—examines, in unrhymed two-line stanzas, both America's production of waste and the waste our lives can seem to become as we grow older.

Poetry and prose. Donald Hall's collection *The Museum of Clear Ideas* included meditations on issues from baseball to living with sickness and the approach of death. Hall, one of America's most highly esteemed writers, also brought out his contemplative memoir *Life Work* in 1993. In the book, the poet candidly discusses his fight against cancer.

Poland. Foreign investment and steady economic growth in 1993 gave Poland the strongest economy in the former Communist Eastern Europe. However, the economic situation of many Poles remained difficult. By September, officials estimated that about 15 percent of workers were unemployed. For most jobholders, wage increases lagged substantially behind the steadily rising cost of living.

Discontent with its tight budget policies brought down Poland's 10-month-old government on May 28, as the coalition led by Prime Minister Hanna Suchocka lost a no-confidence motion by a single vote. On May 29, President Lech Walesa dissolved parliament and called new elections for September 19. Poland got its third government in three years on October 13, when the Democratic Left Alliance (SLD) and Polish Peasant Party (PSL) formed a coalition. The next day, Walesa named the PSL's Waldemar Pawlak as prime minister.

New parliament. The SLD—the successor to Poland's Communist Party—had won about 20 percent of the vote in the election, picking up 171 of the 460 seats in the Sejm (lower house of parliament). The PSL, another party with roots under Communism, won 132 seats. Suchocka's Democratic Union retained only 74 seats. In all, only 7 parties were represented in the new Sejm, down from 29 before the election. On May 28, in an effort to end the factionalism that had hampered previous governments,

333

parliament had passed a law requiring that parties win at least 5 percent of the popular vote to receive seats in the Sejm. Walesa's Nonparty Bloc to Support Reform barely cleared that hurdle, gaining 16 seats. Solidarity, the labor union once headed by Walesa, did not pass the 5-percent threshhold.

The election results demonstrated discontent with the impact of the move to a free market economy, as well as with the increasing role of the Roman Catholic Church in Poland's political life. In January, parliament had passed a bill sharply restricting the right to abortion, a move opposed by many voters. Many Poles also objected to compulsory religious instruction in public schools.

Privatization. Suchocka's government increased the pace of privatization early in the year. On April 30, the Sejm reversed a March vote and passed a plan to privatize about 600 large state-owned enterprises. Under the plan, every adult citizen was offered a share in one of 20 funds responsible for selling off some of the firms. There was also a rise in the number of new businesses. In September, officials estimated that approximately 1.7 million new businesses had been formed since 1989. By October, the private sector employed an estimated 60 percent of the work force. □ Sharon L. Wolchik

See also **Europe** (Facts in brief table). In *World Book,* see **Poland.**

Pollution. See **Environmental pollution.**

Popular music. Many music retailers reacted against high compact disc (CD) prices in 1993 by selling used CD's. This move created conflict with the major record labels and their distribution companies, who saw the practice as damaging to the sale of new CD's and threatened early in 1993 to withhold advertising dollars from any dealers who sold used CD's. In the face of lawsuits from music store owners who cited unreasonable restraint of trade and commerce, however, most distributors restored their advertising support to music retailers by mid-1993—provided that the money would not be used to promote used CD's.

Controversy over lyrics and graphics continued to create headlines in 1993. Still smarting over the 1992 stir caused by his song "Cop Killer," hardcore rapper Ice-T started his own label after leaving Warner Brothers in January 1993 over differences regarding violent artwork accompanying his new album *Home Invasion.*

The back cover for Nirvana's album *In Utero* depicted human fetuses, and the K-mart and Wal-Mart retail chains refused to carry it. *In Utero* nonetheless debuted at number one in September. Also, in September, the Black Entertainment Television cable network in Washington, D.C., imposed a month-long ban on videos with gun images to protest violence in the African-American community.

The rap group Cypress Hill, whose album *Black*

Sunday debuted at number one in July, drew attention for a promarijuana stance. Their position was echoed by such varied acts as Black Crowes, Lemonheads, and Sacred Reich. After losing a March 3 television booking on "The Tonight Show," Jamaican reggae rapper Shabba Ranks apologized for remarks he made in December 1992 supporting fellow reggae artist Buju Banton, whose song "Boom Bye Bye" advocated killing homosexual men.

Michael Jackson's 1993 overseas tour attracted even greater than usual publicity in late August after a 13-year-old boy accused Jackson of sexually abusing him. Police were investigating the charges as the year ended. Jackson canceled the remaining stops on his tour in November, claiming that he was addicted to pain medication. Jackson also performed a 30-minute Super Bowl half-time show on January 31 before an estimated 133 million people—the largest viewing audience in U.S. history.

Tours and comebacks. A backlash against Madonna seemed to subside as her year-end "Girlie Show" tour sold out quickly. Tina Turner toured on the heels of her autobiographical motion picture *What's Love Got to Do with It?* (1993). Prince in April announced his retirement from studio recording and changed his name in June to a symbol, for which there was no known word, representing male and female unity. The Velvet Underground, an influential New York City group in the late 1960's that included Lou Reed, reunited and issued a new album in October 1993. The hugely successful 1970's acts Meat Loaf and Steely Dan staged strong comebacks in 1993. Fleetwood Mac reunited during the U.S. presidential inaugural festivities in January to sing their 1977 hit "Don't Stop," which had served as President Bill Clinton's campaign theme.

Benefit concerts. John Mellencamp held two concerts in July to help victims of the devastating summer floods in the U.S. Midwest. Jon Bon Jovi and Clint Black also held concerts to aid the flood victims. Former Eagles star Don Henley organized a Labor Day concert and raised $1.25 million to benefit the Walden Woods Project to help preserve Walden pond, which was immortalized in Henry David Thoreau's 1854 book *Walden.* The benefit concert also starred Elton John, Sting, and Aerosmith.

Rock. Alternative rock bands, whose designation derives from their lack of mainstream appeal, became more mainstream in 1993. The shift occurred as album rock radio shifted from the long dominant 1960's and 1970's rock mainstays and embraced younger, harder guitar-based bands. Bands such as Stone Temple Pilots, Blind Melon, Soul Asylum, and Alice in Chains led the way along with top groups Nirvana and Pearl Jam, whose album *Vs.* debuted at number one on November 6, having sold a record 950,000 copies in the first week after its release.

Meanwhile, stalwarts such as U2, Billy Joel, and Janet Jackson celebrated major album releases, all of

John Mellencamp performs in a benefit for flood victims in the Midwestern United States during a concert in Tinley Park, Ill., in July.

which debuted at number one. Pete Townshend returned with a solo album in June 1993, but it was overshadowed by the soundtrack to the Grammy-winning Broadway production of *Tommy*, the smash hit album by Townshend's old band, The Who. Elvis Costello, one of the key figures in modern rock, issued an album in January of classical string quartet music with England's Brodsky Quartet and also oversaw the reissue of his landmark early recordings.

Country music. The success of the 10-day Country Takes Manhattan country music festival in May in New York City underscored country music's increased popularity. Festival performers included Clint Black, Tricia Yearwood, Travis Tritt, Willie Nelson, and Mary-Chapin Carpenter. Garth Brooks re-

tained his dominant position when his album *In Pieces* debuted in August at the top of the pop album charts. Foremost among country music artists whose albums sold more than 1 million copies in 1993 were established artists Billy Ray Cyrus, Alan Jackson, Brooks & Dunn, Vince Gill, and Wynonna, and newcomers John Michael Montgomery and Aaron Tippin. Country music legends Dolly Parton, Tammy Wynette, and Loretta Lynn united to put out the album *Honkey Tonk Angels* in November.

Adult-oriented pop music received a boost in 1993 from the popularity of the softer-sounding Music Television's (MTV) "MTV Unplugged" style, which Eric Clapton successfully set forth in 1992 and Rod Stewart followed in 1993. In the unplugged style, musicians perform concerts using only acoustic instruments. Mariah Carey followed a 1992 album in the unplugged style with a hit studio album in 1993, and Barbra Streisand released an album of show tunes entitled *Back to Broadway*. The soundtrack to *Sleepless in Seattle* (1993) revived interest in standards by singers Jimmy Durante (1893-1980) and Nat "King" Cole (1917-1965), as well as trumpet player and singer Louis Armstrong (1901?-1971).

Rhythm and blues. En Vogue's runaway success in 1992 spawned their September 1993 release *Runaway,* an album of two new songs and four remixes. Whitney Houston's single "I Will Always Love You" from the soundtrack of her movie *The Bodyguard* (1992) became the longest-running number-one single of the rock era, topping the pop charts for 14 straight weeks and selling 4 million copies. The duet Peabo Bryson and Regina Belle toppled Houston's song on Feb. 26, 1993, with their "A Whole New World (Aladdin's Theme)" from the *Aladdin* (1992) motion-picture soundtrack.

Rap and reggae. Led by Dr. Dre, Eazy-E, Onyx, Naughty By Nature, and Cypress Hill, the hardcore rap style enjoyed unprecedented airplay on Top 40 and rhythm-and-blues radio stations in 1993. Female rappers, including Boss, MC Lyte, Yo-Yo, and Patra, also gained popularity. The pioneer rap group Run-D.M.C. returned strong with a May album, *Down with the King.*

Rap musicians earned notoriety for their arrests on felony charges in 1993. On October 31, police in Atlanta, Ga., arrested Tupac Shakur and charged him with shooting two off-duty police officers. On November 18, police in New York City arrested Shakur and charged him with sexually assaulting a woman in a Manhattan hotel. On November 1, Flavor Flav of the group Public Enemy was arrested and charged with attempted murder after allegedly shooting a neighbor during an argument. In September, rapper Snoop Doggy Dog was charged with murder in the August 25 shooting of a Los Angeles man.

Canadian dancehall rapper Snow helped lift reggae to its greatest popularity ever in the United States. But the more song-oriented form of reggae was also very popular, as British group UB40 had a chart-topping single with their version of Elvis Presley's hit "Can't Help Falling in Love."

Jazz continued to merge with outside influences in 1993. A new group, Digable Planets, blended rap and cool jazz in the hit "Rebirth of Slick (Cool Like Dat)." Saxophonist Greg Osby's May album release *3-D Lifestyles* explored what he called "street jazz" and featured Philadelphia rappers 100X. On June 18, trumpeter Wynton Marsalis and singer Rosemary Clooney were among the artists who joined President Bill Clinton for a jazz celebration at the White House.   □ Jim Bessman

In *World Book*, see **Country music; Jazz; Popular music**.

Grammy Award winners in 1993

Record of the Year, "Tears in Heaven," Eric Clapton.

Album of the Year, *Unplugged,* Eric Clapton.

Song of the Year, "Tears in Heaven," Eric Clapton and Will Jennings, songwriters.

New Artist, Arrested Development.

Pop Vocal Performance, Female, "Constant Craving," k. d. lang.

Pop Vocal Performance, Male, "Tears in Heaven," Eric Clapton.

Pop Performance by a Duo or Group with Vocal, "Beauty and the Beast," Celine Dion and Peabo Bryson.

Traditional Pop Vocal Performance, *Perfectly Frank,* Tony Bennett.

Pop Instrumental Performance, "Beauty and the Beast," from *Symphonic Hollywood,* Richard Kaufman, conductor, and the Nuremberg Symphony Orchestra.

Rock Vocal Performance, Female, "Ain't It Heavy," Melissa Etheridge.

Rock Vocal Performance, Male, *Unplugged,* Eric Clapton.

Rock Performance by a Duo or Group with Vocal, *Achtung Baby,* U2.

Hard Rock Performance, "Give It Away," Red Hot Chili Peppers.

Metal Performance, "Wish," Nine Inch Nails.

Rock Instrumental Performance, "Little Wing," Stevie Ray Vaughan and Double Trouble.

Rock Song, "Layla," Eric Clapton and Jim Gordon, songwriters.

Alternative Music Album, *Bone Machine,* Tom Waits.

Rhythm-and-Blues Vocal Performance, Female, *The Woman I Am,* Chaka Khan.

Rhythm-and-Blues Vocal Performance, Male, *Heaven and Earth,* Al Jarreau.

Rhythm-and-Blues Performance by a Duo or Group with Vocal, "End of the Road," Boyz II Men.

Rhythm-and-Blues Song, "End of the Road," L. A. Reid, Babyface, and Daryl Simmons, songwriters.

Rap Solo Performance, "Baby Got Back," Sir Mix-a-Lot.

Rap Performance by a Duo or Group, "Tennessee," Arrested Development.

New-Age Album, *Shepherd Moons,* Enya.

Contemporary Jazz Performance, *Secret Story,* Pat Metheny.

Jazz Vocal Performance, "'Round Midnight," Bobby McFerrin.

Jazz Instrumental Solo, "Lush Life," Joe Henderson.

Jazz Instrumental Performance, Individual or Group, *I Heard You Twice the First Time,* Branford Marsalis.

Large Jazz Ensemble Performance, *The Turning Point,* McCoy Tyner Big Band.

Country Vocal Performance, Female, "I Feel Lucky," Mary-Chapin Carpenter.

Country Vocal Performance, Male, *I Still Believe in You,* Vince Gill.

Country Performance by a Duo or Group with Vocal, *Emmylou Harris and the Nash Ramblers at the Ryman,* Emmylou Harris and the Nash Ramblers.

Country Vocal Collaboration, "The Whiskey Ain't Workin'," Travis Tritt and Marty Stuart.

Country Instrumental Performance, *Sneakin' Around,* Chet Atkins and Jerry Reed.

Bluegrass Album, *Every Time You Say Goodbye,* Alison Krauss and Union Station.

Country Song, "I Still Believe in You," Vince Gill and John Barlow Jarvis, songwriters.

Rock/Contemporary Gospel Album, *Unseen Power,* Petra.

Population. United States President Bill Clinton in January 1993 reversed the so-called Mexico City policy that had been instituted by former President Ronald Reagan in 1984. The policy denied U.S. funding to organizations that included abortion counseling in their services. Clinton's decision restored funds to the United Nations Fund for Population Activities, the International Planned Parenthood Federation, and the World Health Organization Human Reproductive Program—the major providers of family-planning services for Third World countries.

According to the U.S. Agency for International Development, which administers the funds, family-planning programs are vital because "the world's rapidly increasing population presents a tremendous hindrance to sustainable development, strains natural resources, and threatens the environmental future of the planet." However, the U.S. funding was renewed with the stipulation that U.S. monies be segregated and tracked to ensure that they are not used in China—the most populous nation on Earth—because of charges that women there have been forced to have abortions and sterilizations.

Ranking aid contributors. Among developed nations, only Norway has met internationally agreed upon goals for providing aid to worldwide family-planning programs, according to a June 1993 report from Population Action International (PAI), a nonprofit group based in Washington, D.C. Among the 20 industrialized nations the PAI ranked, only Norway received a grade of "A." Five countries received a "B" grade, including the United States and the United Kingdom; and three, including Germany, garnered "C's." Japan was one of four nations receiving a "D," and France, Italy, Ireland, and four other countries merited an "F."

Norway contributes 4 percent of its foreign aid to family planning, amounting to more than $12 for every Norwegian citizen. By comparison, the United States targets about 2 percent of aid to such programs. Japan devotes less than 1 percent, and France and Italy give less than one-tenth of 1 percent.

Another PAI report, released in March, commended Indonesia, Bangladesh, Iran, Peru, and Zimbabwe for progress in improving access to their own nations' family-planning services. It also cited Russia, Pakistan, Poland, Iraq, and Ireland for their lack of progress in this area.

Looking ahead. According to projections made by the UN Fund for Population Activities in March 1993, the world's population has become so large (5.5 billion people) that it will grow to at least 8 billion by the year 2025 even if the worldwide birth rate fell to 2.1 children per woman. Population experts note that such growth will lead to heightened pressure on developed countries to accept immigrants from poor nations. ☐ Lori Fagan

See also **Census; Immigration.** In **World Book,** see **Population.**

Portugal in 1993 continued to try to modernize its economy within the European Community (EC or Common Market). However, the country suffered an economic recession along with the rest of Western Europe. Economic growth remained very slow, with Portugal's economic output rising only about 1 percent in 1993. Also, inflation fell to about 6 percent.

Portugal's gloomy economic picture could prevent the country from meeting the economic standards required under the EC's Treaty on European Union, also called the Maastricht Treaty. If Portugal does not meet these standards by 1996, it may not be eligible to join the single European currency, set to take effect in 1999.

Currency devalued. On May 13, 1993, Portugal was forced to devalue its currency, the escudo. The escudo's value dropped yet again on August 2 after the effective suspension of the Exchange Rate Mechanism, which links the values of EC currencies.

Privatization proceeds. Prime Minister Aníbal Cavaço Silva in 1993 continued his program to privatize Portuguese industry. For example, several state-run banks were sold off in 1993. The moves were helped along by a new government report issued on August 22 that said state-owned companies lost more than $700 million in 1992 and most continued to lose money in 1993. ☐ Philip Revzin

See also **Europe** (Facts in brief table). In **World Book,** see **Portugal.**

Postal Service, United States. The Postal Service recorded an operating deficit of $500 million in the fiscal year ending Sept. 17, 1993. Postmaster General Marvin T. Runyon, Jr., had aimed for break-even operations in 1993, mostly by eliminating more than 47,000 postal jobs in 1992 through early retirement and restructuring. But personnel costs were larger than expected, notably for overtime work.

Despite the deficit, Runyon on Aug. 3, 1993, said he hoped the 29-cent letter rate adopted in 1991 would remain until at least 1995. But other developments threatened this goal. In the federal budget passed in August 1993, the Postal Service was forced to pay $1 billion for health benefits for postal workers who had taken early retirement. The agency also had to make up a $360-million reduction in Congress's subsidy for mailings by nonprofit groups.

Congressional criticism. On March 17, Senator Theodore F. Stevens (R., Alaska) complained that veterans were not being given preference for new positions created in Runyon's restructuring. Runyon countered that the restructuring was not a reduction in force (RIF) and therefore was not subject to federal RIF provisions. But on July 21, the Merit Systems Protection Board, a federal agency that oversees the personnel practices of the U.S. government, ruled that the reorganization was indeed a RIF and that thousands of displaced postal workers were entitled to a broad range of benefits.

An "AIDS Awareness" postage stamp was issued in December by the United States Postal Service to coincide with World AIDS Day.

On April 27, Representative William L. Clay (D., Mo.) complained that the percentage of blacks and women working at Postal Service headquarters had dropped as a result of the reorganization. Runyon said there had been a 20 percent drop in the number of black workers at headquarters but that agencywide percentages for minorities had not changed.

Union victory. On May 28, President Moe Biller of the American Postal Workers Union announced an arbitrator's ruling that the Postal Service must offer mail-sorting jobs to postal workers instead of hiring lower-cost private contractors. The agency in 1992 had begun using outsiders to handle mail that could not be processed by post office machines.

Post office violence. Two postal workers were killed and four were injured in two separate shootings on May 6, 1993, at Postal Service facilities in Dana Point, Calif., and Dearborn, Mich. The gunmen in the two cases were, respectively, a fired postal worker and a disgruntled one. Since 1983, a total of 29 postal workers have been killed by coworkers.   □ Frank Cormier and Margot Cormier

In *World Book,* see **Post office; Postal Service, United States.**

President of the United States. See
Clinton, Bill; United States, Government of the.

Prince Edward Island voters on March 29, 1993, affirmed Catherine Callbeck as leader of their province. She became the first woman ever elected to head a Canadian province. British Columbia's Rita Johnston had been appointed interim premier in 1991, but she did not win a subsequent election.

The island's Liberal Party chose Callbeck as its leader on Jan. 23, 1993. The 53-year-old former business administration teacher, provincial minister, and member of the federal Parliament was sworn in as premier on January 25. She then called for the general election, in which her party won the largest electoral victory in the history of the province. The Liberals captured 31 of the provincial legislature's 32 seats, with 1 seat going to the leader of the Progressive Conservative Party, Patricia Mella.

On April 15, Callbeck reduced the number of government departments from 13 to 8 by combining ministers' duties. The budget, announced on June 17, aimed to reduce the annual deficit to $25.4 million in fiscal 1993-1994, contrasted with the $83.4-million deficit on the books in fiscal 1992-1993. (Monetary figures are in Canadian dollars.)

On June 23, the federal government assented to a plan to build an 8-mile (13-kilometer) bridge between Prince Edward Island and New Brunswick to replace the ferry crossing that has been used since 1873.   □ David M. L. Farr

In *World Book,* see **Prince Edward Island.**

Prison. At the end of 1992, state and federal prisons held 883,593 prisoners, according to the United States Department of Justice's Bureau of Justice Statistics (BJS). The number reflects a 7.2 percent increase in the prison population over 12 months. Although the Justice Department noted that prisons should operate at 95 percent of capacity or less, federal prisons in 1992 operated at 37 percent above capacity, and state prisons exceeded capacity by 18 percent to 31 percent.

Jails, which typically house people serving short sentences or awaiting hearings and trials, also became more crowded, operating at 99 percent capacity from July 1, 1991, to June 30, 1992. Jails held 444,584 inmates as of mid-1992, an increase of 4 percent from the previous year.

Drug-related offenses. The increasing number of arrests related to illegal drugs accounted for much of the population growth in jails and prisons. In 1981, for example, 8 percent of admissions to state prisons were convictions for drug crimes; 36 percent, for violent crimes; and 44 percent, for property crimes. In 1990 (the latest year for which figures were available), 32 percent of admissions to prisons were convictions for drug crimes; 32 percent, for property crimes; and 27 percent, for violent crimes.

Demographics. The proportion of women in prisons and jails was small compared with that of men. Women accounted for 9 percent of all jail inmates in 1992 and 5.7 percent of prisoners, according to the BJS. But from December 1980 to June 1990, the rate of incarceration for women was almost twice as great as that for men. The trend was reversed, however, in 1991 and 1992. In 1992, the rate of growth in the number of women prisoners was 5.9 percent, compared with 7.3 percent for men. In jails, the average daily population of men increased by 4.7 percent from 1991, and the rate for women increased by 2.8 percent.

White inmates made up 40 percent of the jail population as of mid-1992, and blacks and Hispanics comprised 59 percent. The incarceration rate for whites was 109 inmates per 100,000 U.S. residents. Blacks' incarceration rate was 619 per 100,000. As of mid-1992, jails held 233,000 white inmates and 195,200 black inmates.

AIDS in prisons. The BJS reported in September 1993 that 2.2 percent of state and federal prisoners in 1991 were infected with the human immunodeficiency virus (HIV), which causes AIDS. It further noted that 28 percent of all inmate deaths were caused by AIDS. HIV infection was most common in prisons in the Northeast, affecting more than 5 percent of Connecticut and Massachusetts prisoners and a staggering 13.8 percent of New York prisoners.   □ Michael Tonry

See also **Crime.** In *World Book*, see **Prison.**

Prizes. See **Nobel Prizes; Pulitzer Prizes.**

Protestantism. During his first year in office in 1993, United States President Bill Clinton drew criticism from various Christian right movements, notably the Christian Coalition of evangelist Pat Robertson. The Christian Coalition opposed many of Clinton's liberal positions. Among them were his pledge to lift the ban on gays serving in the military and his removal on January 22 of five restrictions on abortion established during the administrations of former Presidents Ronald Reagan and George Bush.

The Southern Baptist Convention (SBC) also rebuked Clinton and Vice President Albert A. Gore, Jr., at the denomination's annual convention in Houston in June for their stands on gay and abortion rights. Both Clinton and Gore belong to churches affiliated with the SBC.

However, Clinton worked for a close association with mainstream Protestant leaders during 1993. He invited the leaders of Protestant as well as other religious groups to a nondenominational prayer breakfast on February 4. Evangelist Billy Graham moderated the breakfast. Some 2,000 people attended the affair. On March 24, the President invited leaders of the largely Protestant National Council of Churches (NCC) to the White House. During their administrations, Reagan and Bush had distanced themselves from the NCC, which is known for its liberal positions. And in August, Clinton again hosted a prayer breakfast.

National Guardsmen in April surround the Southern Ohio Correctional Facility in Lucasville during an 11-day take-over of a cell block by inmates.

Protestantism

Cult under siege. David Koresh, the leader of a cult called the Branch Davidians, died along with 81 of his followers when a siege by federal law enforcement officials ended in a fire on April 19 at the cult compound near Waco, Tex. There were 9 survivors.

The Branch Davidians are an offshoot of the Davidians, which split from the Seventh-day Adventists in the 1930's. Branch Davidians believe that this world belongs to Satan and that it will soon end. Koresh, born Vernon Howells, joined the cult in the late 1970's or early 1980's and assumed its leadership in 1987. He sometimes claimed to be the messiah.

Agents of the Bureau of Alcohol, Tobacco, and Firearms (ATF) moved against the group on Feb. 28, 1993, to arrest Koresh for illegal possession of fully automatic firearms and explosive devices. During the assault on the compound, four ATF agents were killed, and the officers failed to gain entry. Federal agents then surrounded the cult compound and demanded that Koresh and his followers surrender. For 51 days thereafter, Koresh made extravagant and not always coherent prophecies, frequently from the book of Revelation. The siege ended when armored vehicles punched holes through the walls and fired tear gas into the compound. About six hours later, fire broke out, and within 30 minutes, the compound burned to the ground. (See also **Crime.**)

Sexual-orientation issues. The question of whether to allow gays and lesbians to serve as Protestant ministers was included on most Protestant agendas in 1993. For example, delegates at the annual meeting of the Presbyterian Church (U.S.A.) in Orlando, Fla., in June voted to keep the ban on the ordination of sexually active homosexuals as pastors. The delegates also called for congregations to discuss the issue of homosexuality as it relates to the church and report on their discussions in 1996.

The Southern Baptist Convention amended its constitution to give the convention authority to expel congregations that condone homosexuality. Church officials called the action unprecedented in the denomination's history. Other convention matters included discussions on the ordination of women and controversies over seminary appointments. Officials also announced a downturn in financial support from its member congregations. Fundamentalist Albert Mohler was named to replace moderate Roy L. Honeycutt as president of the Southern Baptist Theological Seminary in Louisville, Ky.

A Baptist Cooperative Fellowship, made up of dissidents who nevertheless remained in the Convention, met in May in Birmingham, Ala., where its delegates adopted a constitution. The fellowship had attracted former U.S. President Jimmy Carter and former First Lady Rosalyn Carter as members. The group founded their own seminaries and supported their own missionaries. □ Martin E. Marty

See also **Religion: The Lure and Lore of the Dead Sea Scrolls.** In *World Book,* see **Protestantism.**

Psychology. From adolescence to young adulthood, boys and girls differ in the development of self-esteem, according to a study reported in June 1993 by psychologists Jack Block and Richard W. Robins of the University of California at Berkeley. The researchers studied 47 girls and 44 boys. About two-thirds of the subjects were white and the rest were black or Asian. At ages 14, 18, and 23, participants arranged two lists of adjectives, one describing themselves and one the person they would ideally like to be. The researchers viewed close agreement between these two lists to show high self-esteem.

A major difference found between boys and girls was that feelings of self-worth from age 14 to age 23 tended to increase for boys but decrease for girls. The researchers attributed this to socialization processes that broaden the range of experience for boys growing up, but narrow the girls' range.

Psychologists rating the youngsters' personalities also found that in early adolescence, girls with high self-esteem had much different personalities than boys with high self-esteem. The girls reporting high self-esteem were well adjusted at all ages. The psychologists rated them as cheerful, assertive, emotionally open and warm, spontaneous, and unwilling to give up when frustrated. In contrast, 14-year-old boys citing high self-esteem were rated as stern, humorless, unemotional, and lacking in social skills. At later ages, however, this difference decreased and high-self-esteem boys showed more of the traits typical of the high-self-esteem girls.

Females with close friends and other social relationships proved most likely to report high self-esteem in the study. In contrast, high self-esteem in males was tied to ability to manage their anxiety in social situations and to control their emotions when dealing with others.

Early memories. Even though most adults cannot remember experiences from before about 3½ years old, memory of some significant experiences may extend back to age 2, according to research published in June 1993 by JoNell Adair Usher and Ulric Neisser, psychologists at Emory University in Atlanta, Ga. They studied 222 college students, each of whom experienced one of four events at age 1, 2, 3, 4, or 5. The events were the birth of a sibling, being hospitalized, the death of a family member, or a family move. Information recalled by the students was largely accurate, Usher and Neisser asserted; the mothers of 53 volunteers reviewed their children's testimony and considered it on the mark.

Most of those who were 2 years old at the time of a hospitalization or a sibling's birth recalled key aspects of those events. Few of the students who were 1 year old at the time of such occurrences recalled much.

In contrast, only a small minority of students who were 2 years old at the time of a move or a death in the family remembered circumstances surrounding those events. Memory for these experiences improved substantially if they happened by age 4.

Memory. A report in June 1993 indicated that though people often cite vivid "flashbulb memories" of what they thought and did just before, during, and after very startling events, those memories are often inaccurate. Yet people place great confidence in those memories, said psychologist Charles A. Weaver III of Baylor University in Waco, Tex.

Weaver instructed a group of college students to remember all the details surrounding their next meeting with a friend or roommate and immediately write them down. The day that Weaver gave these instructions was Jan. 16, 1991, the day the Persian Gulf War began. Two days later, the same students were instructed to write down their memories of the day the war began.

In subsequent checks, Weaver found that students' memories of both events decreased similarly over the next three months. That level of recall held steady one year after the events occurred. Yet they expressed far more confidence in their memories of the first day of the war than in their memories of the meeting. Weaver contended that people may feel great confidence in memories of individual experiences that connect their personal histories to a public event. But those memories are as prone to error as any others, he argued.   ☐ Bruce Bower

In *World Book,* see **Psychology.**

Public health. In May 1993, the United States Centers for Disease Control and Prevention (CDC) began investigating a mysterious flulike illness in the Four Corners area, where Arizona, Colorado, New Mexico, and Utah meet. On June 11, the CDC reported that the disease was caused by a hantavirus, a microbe never before known to cause disease in the United States. Other strains of the virus have led to serious illnesses elsewhere in the world, however.

On June 25, the CDC reported that victims probably contracted the virus by inhaling airborne particles of the dried urine and feces of deer mice. The CDC warned people in the Southwest to avoid contact with rodent excrement and dust from rodent nests. By mid-November, 45 cases of infection and 27 deaths from hantavirus had been reported. Many of the cases occurred among residents of a Navajo Indian reservation in the Four Corners area.

Smoking hazards. A long-awaited report from the U.S. Environmental Protection Agency (EPA) on January 7 classified environmental tobacco smoke as a *carcinogen* (cancer-causing substance) and concluded that it poses a serious public health threat to nonsmokers. The EPA found that inhaling the smoke from another person's cigarette causes 3,000 cases of lung cancer in nonsmokers each year and as many as 300,000 cases of respiratory ailments in children of smokers. See **Public health: The Dangers of Passive Smoking.**

The Canadian government on July 22 announced that tobacco products will be required to carry what it termed the world's most explicit warning labels. The labels, which must be in use by August 1994, will cover one-fourth of tobacco packaging, both front and back, and display such warnings as "Cigarettes are addictive" or "Smoking can kill you."

Less cholesterol. Almost half of all Americans have healthy blood cholesterol levels, a government study reported on June 15, 1993. The study, from the National Center for Health Statistics (NCHS), found that average cholesterol levels are continuing a long-term decline. The decline began in the 1960's but has accelerated since the late 1970's, paralleling a decline in America's death rate from heart disease.

Since 1978, the percentage of Americans with a "desirable" level of blood cholesterol has increased from 44 percent to 49 percent, the NCHS reported. A blood cholesterol reading of 200 milligrams per deciliter or less is defined as desirable. Average blood cholesterol readings have fallen from 213 to 204, a decline of 4 percent.

Sexually transmitted diseases. On June 15, 1993, the FDA approved a faster, simpler laboratory test for chlamydia, a sexually transmitted disease (STD) that affects about 4 million Americans each year. Many chlamydia infections occur in sexually active teen-agers and young adults. Left untreated, chlamydia can cause infertility and other problems.

Men are the primary carriers of the disease, but detecting chlamydia in men has been difficult. Previous tests were either painful or unreliable. The new test uses genetic engineering techniques to identify the genetic material of chlamydia. The FDA said this test is more accurate than existing tests and can be completed in about four hours, compared with three to seven days for conventional tests.

The FDA on May 10 approved the sale of the first female condom, which was developed to protect women from STD's as well as from unwanted pregnancy. The device, called Reality, is a flexible pouch made of polyurethane, a thin plastic, that fits into the vagina. The manufacturer said Reality would be sold for about $2.50 at pharmacies and other outlets. The FDA emphasized that the male latex condom better protects women against STD's and unwanted pregnancy. But experts said Reality was the first device that women could use themselves to prevent exposure to STD's.

Vaccines for kids. President Bill Clinton on August 10 signed a budget bill that included $500-million to provide free vaccines for children in low-income families. The new program resulted from concern that preschoolers are not adequately immunized against measles, mumps, and other childhood diseases. Clinton originally wanted to spend $1.1 billion on a more ambitious program, but members of Congress objected to the cost.   ☐ Michael Woods

See also **AIDS.** In *World Book,* see **Public health.**

The Dangers of Passive Smoking

**The health risks of cigarette smoking are not
confined to smokers but extend to illnesses
such as lung cancer and asthma
in nonsmokers, said the United
States Environmental Protection
Agency in 1993.**

By John Grossmann

All over the United States in 1993, smokers found fewer and
fewer places where they were free to light up. In January, for
example, newly elected President Bill Clinton invoked a ban
on smoking at White House dinners and throughout the residential
and nonoffice sections of the White House. In April, the Vermont legislature approved a bill that outlaws smoking in all the state's public
buildings as well as in many private buildings open to the public, such
as grocery stores, libraries, and airport waiting areas. And in June, Los
Angeles Mayor Tom Bradley signed legislation prohibiting smoking in
all of Los Angeles' 7,000 restaurants.

Steps such as these to limit smoking in public places reflect growing concerns about the health hazards of *passive smoking*—breathing

in the smoke from someone else's cigarette. Passive smoking is the other shoe dropped by smoking—in this case, on nonsmokers.

The dangers of cigarette smoking have been well documented. Lung cancer, *emphysema* (a disease of inadequate lung function), heart disease, and other ailments kill a smoker in the United States almost every minute of every day. More than one in six deaths nationwide—an estimated 419,000 each year—can be attributed to tobacco use, according to the federal government's Centers for Disease Control and Prevention (CDC) in Atlanta, Ga. But people have generally considered smoking a self-inflicted harm, at worst an irritant to those within puffing range.

A new view

That perception was dealt a severe blow in 1993 by the U.S. Environmental Protection Agency (EPA). After reviewing scores of studies about the effects of secondhand smoke—formally known as environmental tobacco smoke (ETS)—the EPA in January announced that passive smoking was a "serious and substantial" threat to public health. The EPA concluded from its review that passive smoking is responsible for about 3,000 lung cancer deaths annually among nonsmokers. In light of this finding, the agency labeled ETS a "Group A"— or proven—*carcinogen* (cancer-causing compound), comparable to asbestos. The EPA also reported that secondhand smoke is especially harmful to children, causing up to 300,000 cases of respiratory infection in children each year and leading to increased risks for other ailments such as *asthma* (a disease involving breathlessness) and ear infections.

Many physicians are hailing the EPA's report as a milestone in the effort to improve public health in the United States, as significant as the surgeon general's 1964 report that first warned of the dangers of smoking. "I think [the EPA's report] makes smoking socially unacceptable," says Alfred Munzer, president of the American Lung Association (ALA) and director of pulmonary medicine at Washington Adventist Hospital in Takoma Park, Md. "Smoking is no longer just a private habit but rather a public health problem."

Signs of trouble

Since the surgeon general's 1964 report, the percentage of Americans age 18 or over who smoke has slowly but steadily declined. In 1965, about 40 percent of American adults smoked cigarettes. By 1991, the percentage had fallen to 25.7 percent, according to the CDC. Despite the decline, other numbers reveal some discouraging information. For example, the highest smoking rate for women exists for those from age 25 to 34, the prime childbearing and child-rearing years. This high incidence of smoking raises concerns among doctors for the health of the women, of developing fetuses, and of young children exposed to secondhand smoke.

Moreover, although smoking rates are down, the number of Americans who smoke is still enormous. The CDC puts the number at more

■ **The author**

John Grossmann is a free-lance journalist.

than 45 million people. Figuring an average of 1½ packs of cigarettes per smoker per day, the total number of cigarettes puffed daily in the United States easily surpasses 1 billion. So plenty of smoke still swirls.

One of the first indications that all this smoke spells danger to nonsmokers appeared in 1981. In a 14-year study of some 265,000 individuals, Japanese researcher Takeshi Hirayama found higher levels of lung cancer in nonsmoking wives of men who smoked heavily than in nonsmoking wives of men who smoked moderately or not at all. In fact, Hirayama found that the risk of lung cancer for a nonsmoking wife increased proportionally with the number of cigarettes that her husband smoked.

"Since then [1981], the scientific evidence against passive smoking has been accumulating at an increasing pace," says Stanton Glantz, a cardiologist at the University of California at San Francisco. In 1986, the surgeon general and the National Research Council, a nonprofit organization in Washington, D.C., that does much of the work of the National Academy of Sciences, warned the American public of the health risks of secondhand smoke. Every year thereafter, researchers have uncovered additional reasons for concern. The EPA's 1993 report was only the latest warning about passive smoking, though it was by far the loudest.

Debating the merits

The tobacco industry, however, called the EPA's conclusions unfounded. In June 1993, industry giants R. J. Reynolds Tobacco Company and Philip Morris Companies Incorporated, both based in New

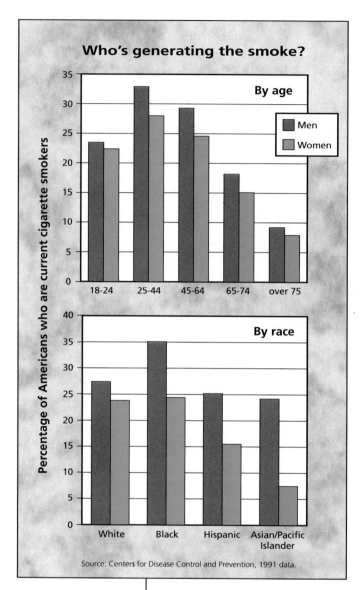

Who's generating the smoke?

By age

Men
Women

Percentage of Americans who are current cigarette smokers

18-24 25-44 45-64 65-74 over 75

By race

White Black Hispanic Asian/Pacific Islander

Source: Centers for Disease Control and Prevention, 1991 data.

■ In 1991, about 26 percent of adults in the United States smoked cigarettes. The smoking rate for men was well above that for women, and the rate for black men was highest of all.

York City, along with groups representing tobacco growers, distributors, and marketers, filed suit against the EPA to overturn its classification of secondhand smoke as a carcinogen. Industry spokespeople complained that the EPA had reviewed only studies that supported its conclusions, had deviated from normal statistical methods in order to obtain a predetermined result, and had ignored the role in health played by other factors, such as diet and exercise. The Tobacco Institute, a trade group representing cigarette manufacturers located in Washington, D.C., termed the EPA's assessment of secondhand smoke "another step in a long process characterized by a preference for political correctness over sound science."

Such rebuttals, say Glantz and others who have locked horns with the tobacco industry for years, ring increasingly hollow. They maintain that the dangers of passive smoke are many, varied, and serious. Much of the harm is due to the particular nature of secondhand smoke. Secondhand smoke is a combination of two types of smoke: *mainstream smoke* (smoke that is exhaled by smokers) and *sidestream smoke* (smoke that escapes from the end of a burning cigarette). Of the two, the sidestream smoke is more dangerous.

The nature of secondhand smoke

Not only does sidestream smoke contain the same array of more than 40 carcinogens that mainstream smoke contains, but also the particles in sidestream smoke tend to be smaller, so they can travel deeper into the nonsmoker's lungs and thus have a smaller chance of becoming dislodged by breathing. Furthermore, mainstream smoke usually travels through a filter. Sidestream smoke, on the other hand, enters the air directly from a cigarette. Partly for this reason, research indicates that sidestream smoke may contain twice as much nicotine and up to three times as much carbon monoxide as mainstream smoke. Nicotine, a chemical substance, and carbon monoxide, a gas, are both poisonous to human beings in large amounts.

Harm before birth

In covering the EPA's report, the media have focused much attention on the dangers of passive smoking to adults, but many public health officials are more alarmed by the EPA's conclusions about the impact of passive smoking on children. "Even I was surprised by the magnitude of the harm done to kids," says John Banzhaft, executive director and chief counsel of Action on Smoking and Health (ASH), an anti-smoking organization located in Washington, D.C.

Scientists have known for many years that smoking by pregnant women poses dangers to fetuses. In 1979, the surgeon general warned that smoking by mothers hampers fetal development, doubles the chance of having a low-birth-weight baby, and increases the risk of stillbirth. In 1986, the National Academy of Sciences reiterated those warnings, noting that research had found that smoking during pregnancy is associated with an average reduction in a baby's birth weight of about 5 to 9 ounces (140 to 260 grams) and a drop in the average duration of the pregnancy of one or two days. These numbers may seem small, but their impact on the health of a newborn can be large.

Researchers are still investigating how cigarettes alter fetal development. Scientists know that nicotine causes arteries to become constricted. This effect may hinder the passage of nutrients across the placenta to the fetus. Scientists also speculate that normal fetal growth is inhibited because carbon monoxide in the cigarette smoke takes the place of some oxygen in the mother's—and thereby the fetus's—blood.

Infants in danger

Passive smoking poses different—and potentially more serious—health risks for newborns. Some recent research has found a link between maternal smoking and the mysterious disease known as sudden infant death syndrome (SIDS), or crib death. According to the American Academy of Pediatrics, SIDS is the leading cause of death in children 1 month to 1 year old, claiming the lives of about 6,000 infants in the United States each year. Scientists have not yet pinned down the cause of SIDS, but some researchers have discovered that the risk of the disease is associated with maternal smoking both before and after a child's birth.

For example, a 1990 study by Swedish researchers of more than 279,000 infants found a correlation between the risk of SIDS and the number of cigarettes smoked by the infant's mother during pregnancy. Infants of mothers who smoked one to nine cigarettes a day were almost twice as likely to die of SIDS as were children of nonsmoking

■ How passive smoking harms nonsmokers

Secondhand smoke has different adverse effects depending on a nonsmoker's age. Fetuses and young children are especially vulnerable to the health risks.

Passive smoking increases a nonsmoker's risk of lung cancer. Research suggests that living with a person who smokes a pack of cigarettes a day increases one's chance of getting lung cancer by about 30 percent.

Cigarette smoke may help cholesterol build up along artery walls. It may also promote the formation of blood clots, increasing the risk of a heart attack.

Secondhand smoke may increase a child's chance of suffering chronic ear infections and a build-up of fluid in the middle ear.

The chemicals in cigarette smoke can hamper the flow of nutrients in the blood to a fetus and lead to a low-birth-weight or premature baby.

By inflaming a child's lungs, cigarette smoke can lead to respiratory problems and even, after repeated exposures, asthma.

The toll from passive smoking

Ailment	Estimated impact
Lung cancer	3,000 deaths per year
Heart disease	37,000 deaths per year
Respiratory problems	150,000 to 300,000 cases per year in children
Asthma	8,000 to 26,000 new cases per year in children

mothers. When the mother smoked more than nine cigarettes a day, the relative risk of dying by SIDS rose to almost three times. And a 1992 study by the National Center for Health Statistics in Hyattsville, Md., found a connection between SIDS and smoking by mothers after the birth of their children. The researchers discovered that babies born to mothers who began smoking only after their birth were twice as likely to die from SIDS as were infants born to nonsmoking mothers.

Researchers are not sure whether maternal smoking is a contributing factor for SIDS or only an innocent associate of the actual cause. But if passive smoking is responsible, almost one-seventh of all SIDS cases may be due to maternal smoking, estimates the surgeon general.

Risks for children

By far the most common adverse consequences of passive smoking for young children are respiratory problems. In its report, the EPA concluded that secondhand smoke is responsible for the following illnesses:

- From 150,000 to 300,000 cases each year of lower respiratory tract infections, such as bronchitis and pneumonia, in children up to 18 months old;
- From 7,500 to 15,000 infants hospitalized each year due to respiratory ailments; and
- From 8,000 to 26,000 new cases of childhood asthma, and worsened symptoms in 200,000 to 1 million children who already have asthma.

Research indicates that respiratory problems can arise in children as a result of passive smoking during or after pregnancy. For example, a 1992 study by doctors at Brigham and Women's Hospital in Boston reported that children born to mothers who smoked during pregnancy have as little as 50 percent of the lung function of children born to nonsmokers. The decreased lung function may make the children prone to respiratory problems. The researchers said that a fetus's lungs are especially vulnerable to the chemicals in cigarette smoke because they develop early in the pregnancy, when environmental factors can have a greater impact.

Another 1992 study, this one by researchers at Mount Sinai Medical Center in New York City, indicated that children who are exposed to high levels of tobacco smoke after birth are twice as likely to develop asthma as children who are not exposed. Tobacco smoke can inflame the lungs and, over time, cause them to constrict too readily in response to particles in the air. A rapid constriction of the lungs is a hallmark of asthma.

As children get older, other effects of secondhand smoke may emerge. Several studies have suggested that chronic ear infections and a build-up of fluid in the middle ear are more common among children whose parents smoke cigarettes. For example, a 1989 study by British researchers compared the home lives of 112 children aged

■ **Restrictions on smokers**
Cigarette smokers congregate outside an office building. In the wake of studies revealing the dangers of passive smoking, many businesses have instituted smoke-free workplaces to protect their employees and customers, thereby forcing smokers to venture outdoors for a cigarette.

1 to 12 who had been admitted to a hospital for treatment for ear infections with the home lives of children with no ear problems. The researchers found that the children with recurrent ear infections were twice as likely to have parents who smoked cigarettes than were the children without ear problems.

Other research has raised the possibility that cigarette smoking by parents may dull their children's reasoning and learning skills. Researchers at the University of North Carolina in Chapel Hill in 1991 discovered that children of cigarette smokers scored lower on tests of reasoning ability and vocabulary than did children of nonsmokers. The scientists speculated that exposure to secondhand smoke reduces the amount of oxygen available for the brain in the blood and thus hampers thinking ability. Another idea was that ear infections arising as a result of environmental tobacco smoke make it more difficult for children to concentrate. The researchers said they considered their findings suggestive rather than definitive and planned further study.

Some research has even hinted of a link between passive smoking and behavioral problems in young children. A 1992 study of more than 2,000 children aged 4 to 11 by researchers at the University of Rochester School of Medicine and Dentistry in Rochester, N.Y., found that the more cigarettes a mother smoked, the more likely her children were to exhibit behavioral problems such as anxiety, depression, and hyperactivity. Children whose mothers smoked a pack of cigarettes or more a day after pregnancy were twice as likely to have behavioral problems as were children of nonsmoking mothers. However, the researchers could not conclusively determine whether the children's behavioral problems stemmed from the exposure to secondhand smoke or from other factors, and they called for more investigation.

A message for parents

Scientists point out that many studies of the effects of passive smoking on children focus on maternal smoking because mothers commonly spend more time with their children than fathers do. But smoking by fathers has ramifications on their children's health similar to those of smoking by mothers, say experts. The lesson for all parents, say many researchers, is not to smoke. Some doctors even see a silver lining in the magnitude of the EPA's findings concerning children. "I think [the EPA's report] will really hit home in terms of finally getting parents interested in quitting smoking," says ALA President Munzer.

Attacking the lungs and heart

Because the bodies of adults are larger and more fully developed than those of children, adults are not as vulnerable to relatively brief exposure to passive smoking. But adults can be harmed by longer-term exposure to secondhand smoke generated year after year by smoking family members or friends. The most well-known illness associated with smoking is lung cancer, and recent studies have tied passive smoking to that disease in nonsmokers as well. For example, a 1991 study of 1,500 women by researchers at Louisiana State University Medical Center in New Orleans found that living with a husband who smokes about one pack of cigarettes a day increases a nonsmoking wife's risk of lung cancer by 30 percent. The risk jumps to 70 percent higher when the husband smokes about two packs a day. And a study reported in 1993 by researchers at the University of California at Berkeley found that restaurant workers and bartenders have a 50 percent greater risk of lung cancer due to their regular exposure to secondhand smoke in the workplace.

Direct evidence of passive smoking's effects on a nonsmoker's lungs came to light in 1992 in a study using autopsy samples. Scientists at the Harvard University School of Public Health in Boston examined lung samples taken during autopsies of men and women who died of causes other than respiratory illness or cancer. Tissue analysis revealed a significantly higher level of potentially precancerous changes in the lungs of nonsmoking women married to smoking husbands than in the lungs of nonsmoking women married to nonsmoking husbands.

Lung cancer was the only ailment in adults that the EPA decided was definitely connected to passive smoking. However, many scientists believe that an even deadlier link exists between passive smoking and heart disease, or *atherosclerosis* (the build-up of fat and cholesterol on artery walls). After reviewing 10 recent studies on that link, Glantz and his colleague William Parmley at the University of California at San Francisco concluded that as many as 37,000 Americans—or more than 10 times the EPA's estimated annual lung cancer toll from passive smoking—die each year from heart disease attributable to passive smoking.

Wanting to know why, the doctors placed rabbits in smoke-filled enclosures in a laboratory. The enclosures had a level of environmental tobacco smoke comparable to that found in the air of a smoking section of a restaurant. The doctors also fed the rabbits a high-fat diet, which promotes heart disease. The rabbits spent 6 hours a day in the smoke-filled enclosures for 10 weeks.

At the end of the experiment, the researchers found 10 percent more fatty deposits along the blood vessels of rabbits exposed to environmental tobacco smoke, compared with the vessels of rabbits that had been given the high-fat diet but had not spent time in the smoke-filled enclosures. The doctors believe that particles in cigarette smoke bind to cholesterol and help facilitate its build-up in arteries. The researchers also discovered that exposure to environmental tobacco smoke activated blood *platelets* in the rabbits. Platelets are disklike structures in blood essential in clotting at the sites of cuts. However, if they are activated unnecessarily, they can form clots in blood vessels that can block blood flow and cause a stroke or a heart attack.

Fortunately, the researchers discovered that the artery-impairing effects of passive smoking drop off sharply when exposure ends. "Most of the effects [on the blood vessels] are due to the short-term poisoning," says Glantz, "and if you stop the exposure, the effects are resolved fairly quickly."

Making public air safer

Reducing bystander exposure to smoking—for the sake of both the comfort and the health of nonsmokers—has been the aim of smoking restrictions and bans since the 1970's. The airline industry provides a good example of the course of antismoking activity. In 1972, separate smoking and nonsmoking sections were introduced on airplanes. In 1988, a ban on smoking on flights of two hours or less went into effect. In 1990, the ban was expanded to include all domestic flights, except those scheduled to last six hours or more. And in 1993, a ban loomed for smoking on overseas flights, as the Clinton Administration began trying to negotiate agreements with other governments to ban smoking on all international flights by 1996.

Many groups in the public and private sectors had acted to limit smoking even before the EPA's report. Forty-six states, the District of Columbia, and more than 300 cities had curbed smoking in public places in some manner. Restrictions ranged from laws limiting smoking in schools and on public transportation, as in West Virginia, to a ban on smoking in virtually all public places, as in Minnesota. Nonsmoking corporate offices were also common, often identifiable by a clutch of smokers huddled outside the buildings' front doors, even in winter.

Nevertheless, the EPA's explicit warnings about the dangers of passive smoking fueled new antismoking moves. In February 1993, for example, McDonald's Corporation of Hinsdale, Ill., became the first fast-food company to announce that it would test smoke-free restaurants. Companies were implementing antismoking regulations not only to limit the costs of medical coverage for their employees but also to avoid lawsuits from nonsmoking workers and customers who say they became ill as a result of exposure to tobacco smoke at the company's workplace.

Antismoking laws were even extended to relatively open arenas. In February, the Philadelphia Phillies announced that smoking would no longer be permitted in the stands at Veterans Stadium. They thus became the 11th major league baseball team to restrict smoking at the ball park.

But antismoking advocates clamored for more active measures than merely designating some areas "smoke-free." They pointed to California, where an aggressive antismoking advertising program, financed by a hefty 25-cents-a-pack cigarette tax, has helped decrease smoking prevalence among adults by 23.5 percent since 1989. Possibly as a result of the campaign, only 20 percent of Californians over the age of 18 were smokers in 1992, well under the national average of 25.7 percent.

In the wake of the EPA's report, many health-care experts believed that the public—especially the nonsmoking segment—would take the health threat from cigarettes seriously and support stricter antismoking measures. Even longtime tobacco fighter John Banzhaft of the ASH was optimistic about the elimination of passive smoking: "I work in a smoke-free building in Washington. When I fly, I fly out of Washington National, a smoke-free airport. On my last trip, I changed planes in Denver at another smoke-free airport, flew coast-to-coast in smoke-free planes, and checked into a smoke-free room in my hotel." If the trend continues, Banzhaft says, "a smoke-free society by the year 2000 may be possible." ■ ■ ■

For further reading:

Altman, Lawrence K. "The Evidence Mounts on Passive Smoking." *New York Times*, May 29, 1990, p. B5.

Boyle, Peter. "The Hazards of Passive—and Active—Smoking." *The New England Journal of Medicine*, June 10, 1993, pp. 1708-1709.

Respiratory Health Effects of Passive Smoking: Lung Cancer and Other Disorders. CERI, United States Environmental Protection Agency, 26 W. Martin Luther King Drive, Cincinnati, Ohio, 45268. (Publication number EPA/600/6-90/006F.)

Stone, Richard. "Bad News on Second-Hand Smoke." *Science,* July 31, 1992, p. 607.

Puerto Rico. Puerto Ricans voted on Nov. 14, 1993, to keep Puerto Rico a commonwealth of the United States. As residents of a commonwealth, Puerto Ricans have some, but not all, rights of U.S. citizens. Although the vote was nonbinding, voters were asked whether they favored Puerto Rico becoming the 51st state, remaining a commonwealth, or pursuing independence. Puerto Rico's Governor Pedro J. Rosselló campaigned hard to persuade Puerto Ricans to vote for statehood.

NAFTA concern. With the island's unemployment at 18 percent, Puerto Ricans in 1993 were fearful that the North American Free Trade Agreement (NAFTA) could be harmful to their already beleaguered economy. Beginning on Jan. 1, 1994, NAFTA will gradually eliminate trade barriers over the next 15 years between the United States, Mexico, and Canada. (See also **International trade: The Debate over NAFTA.**)

Puerto Ricans feared that, as a result of NAFTA, many jobs would leave the island as U.S. companies sought lower-wage workers in Mexico. Puerto Rico has attracted many U.S. manufacturing firms because of the tax breaks it can offer them. But the same manufacturers may now find the low wage scale in Mexico more attractive than Puerto Rico's tax breaks. □ Nathan A. Haverstock

See also **Latin America** (Facts in brief table). In *World Book,* see **Puerto Rico.**

Pulitzer Prizes in letters, drama, music, and journalism were awarded for the 77th year in April 1993 by Columbia University in New York City, on the recommendation of the Pulitzer Prize Board.

Letters and the arts. Robert Olen Butler won the Pulitzer Prize for fiction for *A Good Scent from a Strange Mountain,* a collection of stories told from the viewpoint of Vietnamese immigrants in Louisiana. The drama prize went to Tony Kushner for *Angels in America: Millennium Approaches,* the first half of a two-part play about homosexuality and AIDS. The prize for poetry went to Louise Gluck for her collection *The Wild Iris.* David McCullough won the biography prize for *Truman.* Garry Wills won the general nonfiction prize for *Lincoln at Gettysburg.* The history prize went to Gordon S. Wood for *The Radicalism of the American Revolution.* Christopher Rouse won the music prize for Trombone Concerto.

Journalism. The public service award went to the *Miami* (Fla.) *Herald* for its coverage of Hurricane Andrew, which struck the Florida coast in August 1992. The *Herald* also won the prize for commentary for reports by Liz Balmaseda on conditions in Haiti and on Cuban-Americans in Miami.

The Washington Post won three Pulitzers in 1993. The *Post* received the national reporting prize for a series by David Maraniss on the life and character of then-presidential candidate Bill Clinton. The feature writing prize went to *Post* reporter George Lardner,

An image of Democratic presidential candidate Bill Clinton addressing a rally in Boston helped the Associated Press win a 1993 Pulitzer Prize.

QUEBECOIS

Lucien Bouchard, a vocal Quebec separatist, meets with the press after Canada's October parliamentary elections made him the opposition leader.

Jr., for his investigation of his daughter's murder by a former boyfriend. Michael Dirda earned the *Post* the criticism prize for his essays and book reviews.

Other journalism awards: Spot news reporting, the *Los Angeles Times* for its coverage of riots in that city in April 1992, following the acquittal of four white police officers in the beating of black motorist Rodney King. Investigative reporting, Jeff Brazil and Steve Berry of the *Orlando* (Fla.) *Sentinel* for their reports exposing corruption in a sheriff's drug squad. International reporting, John F. Burns of *The New York Times* for coverage of war-torn Bosnia-Herzegovina and Roy Gutman of *Newsday* for disclosures of atrocities in Bosnia-Herzegovina and Croatia. Beat reporting, *The Wall Street Journal*'s Paul Ingrassia and Joseph B. White for coverage of management turmoil at General Motors Corporation. Explanatory journalism, Mike Toner of the *Atlanta* (Ga.) *Journal-Constitution* for a series on the diminishing effectiveness of antibiotics and pesticides.

Feature photography, the staff of the Associated Press news service for its documentation of the Clinton campaign. Spot news photography, the *Dallas Morning News* for images by William Snyder and Ken Geiger of the 1992 Summer Olympics in Barcelona, Spain. Editorial cartooning, Stephen R. Benson of *The Arizona Republic* of Phoenix. No prize was awarded in editorial writing.   □ Meira Ben-Gad

In *World Book,* see **Pulitzer Prizes.**

Quebec and Canada were stunned on Sept. 14, 1993, when Quebec Premier Robert Bourassa, leader of the provincial Liberal Party, announced he would retire from active politics as soon as a successor could be named. Daniel Johnson, a Bourassa Cabinet member, was chosen on December 14 to become leader of the party and be sworn in as premier in January 1994. Bourassa, who had battled skin cancer since 1990, said he was retiring for personal and family reasons. He had served 14 years as premier.

Bourassa's retirement will remove from Quebec politics a leader committed to a unified Canada. In so doing, the change has given hope to individuals promoting Quebec's independence. Bourassa delivered a parting shot to the separatists as he prepared to leave office. "Quebec independence is geopolitical nonsense," he said.

English returns. Bourassa moved Quebec closer to a lasting peace over the sensitive language issue when he won approval in the legislature on June 17, 1993, to modify the province's controversial language law. The law banned English on outdoor commercial signs. Many of Quebec's 5.5 million French-speaking residents had seen the law as an aid to the preservation of their language and, therefore, to their unique culture.

In 1988, the Supreme Court of Canada ruled Quebec's original language ban unconstitutional. But the Bourassa government had used its powers to override the charter of rights and reimpose a unilingual sign law. However, recent polls showed that two-thirds of Quebecers had come to accept bilingual signs. Then, in April 1993, a United Nations human rights committee declared that the ban on bilingual signs violated individual rights in Quebec.

Thus, the government decided to allow bilingual signs in stores, museums, and tourist establishments. Public opposition to the change was much less than the nationalists had predicted. For the first time in 15 years, people entering Quebec now see English-language welcome signs at border crossings.

Language in the schools. The Supreme Court of Canada on June 17 approved a provincial plan to reorganize Quebec's denominational school system along linguistic rather than religious lines. The plan limited enrollment in Roman Catholic and Protestant schools and established new secular language-based school boards. The transition, to be completed by July 1996, marked the end of the Roman Catholic Church's historic authority in Quebec's educational system.

The Bloc Québécois, a political party founded in 1990 to promote an independent Quebec, made great gains in Canada's Oct. 25, 1993, national election. The Bloc captured 54 of Quebec's 75 seats in the House of Commons, a gain of 46 seats. The Bloc won virtually all the province's *ridings* (voting districts) having a French-speaking majority.

Lucien Bouchard, as the leader of the Bloc Québécois, became the leader of the official opposition in Parliament. He vowed to make Quebec's interests his first priority.

The budget. Finance Minister Gérard-D. Levesque presented his ninth budget on May 20. It included no new stimulants for a sluggish economy nor major cuts in government services. But the budget did extract $1.1 billion (all monetary figures are in Canadian dollars) from individual taxpayers. Workers also lost an employment deduction, worth an average of $150 a year. Wage earners who pay from $5,000 to $10,000 per year in income taxes would be obliged to pay an additional 5 percent surtax. The surtax was doubled for those paying taxes of more than $10,000. Public-sector employee salaries would be frozen for a second year. The budget also cut health-care coverage for optometrist services, except for people under age 18 and over age 65.

Through the revenue increases for fiscal 1993-1994, the government hoped to cut its deficit from $4.9 billion to $4.1 billion. Levesque projected expenditures to be $40.8 billion, of which 65 percent would be devoted to education, health, and social services. The tough new budget was not enough to stave off a downgrading of the province's credit rating on June 3 from a double-A to an A-1, which still is an above-average rating. ☐ David M. L. Farr

See also **Canada.** In *World Book,* see **Quebec.**

Railroad. See **Transportation.**

Reich, Robert B. (1946-   ), became secretary of the United States Department of Labor on Jan. 21, 1993. He promised to develop Labor Department policies that would help American workers upgrade their skills, better enabling them to compete for jobs in the new global economic marketplace.

Reich (pronounced *Ryshe*) was born on June 24, 1946, in Scranton, Pa., and grew up in South Salem, N.Y. He attended Dartmouth College in Hanover, N.H., graduating with highest honors in 1968. He then studied for two years as a Rhodes scholar at Oxford University in England, where he was a classmate and friend of future President Bill Clinton.

In 1970, Reich returned to the United States to study law at Yale University in New Haven, Conn. After receiving his degree in 1973, he served as a law clerk at the U.S. Court of Appeals in Boston.

Reich held several positions in the federal government during the administrations of Presidents Gerald R. Ford and Jimmy Carter. In 1981, he left government to become a lecturer on political economics at Harvard University in Cambridge, Mass. In the following years, Reich became a widely known economic theorist. He argued that the United States must repair its *infrastructure* (roads and other public works) and improve its educational system if it is to compete successfully with other nations.

Reich is married to the former Clare Dalton. They have two sons, Adam and Samuel. ☐ David Dreier

Religion. Church attendance has been dramatically lower than was previously estimated, according to survey results presented to the American Sociological Association in August 1993. The survey reported that 28 percent of Roman Catholics and 20 percent of Protestants attend church in any given week. Over many decades, Gallup polls have estimated church attendance to be more than 40 percent of those claiming church membership. The media in recent years have reported declining attendance.

Six black denominations have shown steady growth and are now among the 15 largest denominations in the United States, according to the 1993 edition of *Yearbook of American and Canadian Churches.* Furthermore, several African-American Pentecostal denominations were among the fastest growing of any religious group in America. For example, Church of God in Christ, with headquarters in Memphis, has gained nearly 200,000 members and 600 congregations each year since 1982, and in 1992, the membership reached 5.5 million. Pentecostal churches in general were expanding rapidly across the United States, Latin America, and Africa.

Religious commitment was strongly linked to involvement in human service programs, according to Independent Sector, a large nonprofit coalition. The group reported that 258,000 congregations in the United States gave some $6.6 billion to relief organizations, advocacy groups, and needy individuals in 1991, the latest available data. More than 90 percent of those congregations reported supporting one or more programs, such as food kitchens.

Islam grew in the United States in 1993 to an estimated 5 million members, according to the American Muslim Council. The council also reported that since 1978, the number of incorporated Islamic mosques has doubled to about 1,000. Most Muslims in America were immigrants or their descendants from the Middle East, South Asia, Southeast Asia, and Africa. But about 42 percent of the American Muslim population were black Americans, according to the council.

Trade Center bombing. A Muslim cleric was charged with conspiracy in August 1993 in the bombing of the World Trade Center in New York City on February 26. Many Muslims deeply resented media coverage that they felt distorted Islam and Islamic fundamentalism. (See **Crime.**)

A Parliament of the World's Religions convened in Chicago on August 28. More than 7,000 people, twice as many as expected, attended the eight-day conference. The first parliament had been held in 1893, also in Chicago. The purpose of both meetings was to debate the critical religious issues of the day and ultimately to agree on a united response to those issues, which proved to be a difficult task. At the conclusion, representatives of more than 125 of the world's religions signed "The Declaration of a Global Ethic." The document restated some of the Biblical commandments in general terms without referring to God. Some religions represented at the parliament do not recognize a single creator.

The Christian Coalition, a politically active, religious-right group led by television evangelist Pat Robertson, took a lower profile in 1993 than it had at the 1992 Republican National Convention. The coalition campaigned quietly to elect its candidates in local and state contests. The Roman Catholic Archdiocese of New York endorsed the coalition's voters' guide in the May New York City school board elections, but with little apparent impact on the outcome. The coalition claimed several victories in city and state elections in November, but its long-term impact remained to be seen.

The Religious Freedom Restoration Act was signed into law on Nov. 16, 1993. The act, supported by diverse religions, was framed in response to a 1990 Supreme Court decision that upheld a state law denying the use of *peyote* (a hallucinogen derived from peyote cactus) in religious ceremonies of certain American Indian tribes. The new law will make it more difficult for the government to interfere with, or bar, religious practices by requiring more stringent standards under which the government can intervene in those practices. □ Leon Howell

See also **Eastern Orthodox Churches; Islam; Judaism; Protestantism; Roman Catholic Church.** In *World Book,* see **Religion.**

Religious groups with 150,000 or more members in the United States*

African Methodist Episcopal Church	3,500,000
African Methodist Episcopal Zion Church	1,200,000
American Baptist Association	250,000
American Baptist Churches in the U.S.A.	1,527,840
Antiochian Orthodox Christian Archdiocese of North America	350,000
Armenian Apostolic Church of America	150,000
Armenian Church of America, Diocese of the	275,000
Assemblies of God	2,234,708
Baptist Bible Fellowship International	1,430,000
Baptist Missionary Association of America	230,127
Christian and Missionary Alliance	267,853
Christian Church (Disciples of Christ)	1,022,926
Christian Churches and Churches of Christ	1,070,616
Christian Methodist Episcopal Church	718,922
Christian Reformed Church in North America	224,921
Church of God (Anderson, Ind.)	214,743
Church of God (Cleveland, Tenn.)	620,393
Church of God in Christ	5,499,875
Church of God in Christ, International	200,000
Church of Jesus Christ of Latter-day Saints	4,336,000
Church of the Nazarene	573,834
Churches of Christ	1,690,000
Conservative Baptist Association of America	210,000
Coptic Orthodox Church	260,000
Episcopal Church	2,471,880
Evangelical Free Church of America	187,775
Evangelical Lutheran Church in America	5,245,177
Free Will Baptists	209,223
General Association of Regular Baptist Churches	160,123
Greek Orthodox Archdiocese of North and South America	1,500,000
International Church of the Foursquare Gospel	208,150
International Council of Community Churches	250,000
Jehovah's Witnesses	914,079
Judaism	5,981,000
Liberty Baptist Fellowship	180,000
Lutheran Church—Missouri Synod	2,607,309
National Baptist Convention of America	3,500,000
National Baptist Convention, U.S.A., Inc.	8,000,000
National Missionary Baptist Convention of America	2,500,000
National Primitive Baptist Convention, Inc.	500,000
Orthodox Church in America	1,030,000
Pentecostal Assemblies of the World	500,000
Presbyterian Church in America	233,770
Presbyterian Church (U.S.A.)	3,778,358
Progressive National Baptist Convention, Inc.	2,500,000
Reformed Church in America	340,991
Reorganized Church of Jesus Christ of Latter Day Saints	150,143
Roman Catholic Church	58,267,424
Salvation Army	446,403
Seventh-day Adventist Church	733,026
Southern Baptist Convention	15,232,347
United Church of Christ	1,583,830
United Methodist Church	8,785,135
United Pentecostal Church International	550,000
Wisconsin Evangelical Lutheran Synod	420,039

*A majority of the figures are for the years 1991 and 1992. Includes only groups with at least 150,000 members within the United States itself.
Sources: Representatives of individual organizations; National Council of the Churches of Christ in the U.S.A.; *Yearbook of American and Canadian Churches* for 1993.

The Lure and Lore

of the
Dead Sea Scrolls

By John J. Collins

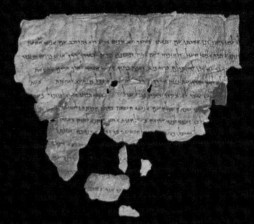

After almost 50 years under the control of a small group of editors, fragments of ancient religious scrolls are at last available to all scholars eager to discover their significance for the history of Judaism and Christianity.

On April 29, 1993, the doors of the United States Library of Congress in Washington, D.C., opened on an exhibition of the Dead Sea Scrolls. These fragments of parchment brought from Israel contain words in ancient Hebrew that reflect Jewish religious thought of 2,000 years ago, when Jesus lived and Christianity was in its infancy. An inkwell, pottery bowls and cups, ancient coins, and frayed linen cloth enhanced the display of the scrolls. The artifacts came from Qumran, a ruin near the caves where Bedouin shepherds found the first scrolls in 1947. The people who once ate from the bowls probably read the scrolls and placed them in the caves.

Or did they? Therein lies one of the controversies surrounding the Dead Sea Scrolls. There are many others, including why did it take so long for all of the scrolls to be published and was their publication deliberately suppressed? And what exactly have the scrolls revealed about the relationship between Judaism and early Christianity?

Scholars called the Dead Sea Scrolls the archaeological find of the century when the first cache was discovered in a cave near the northwestern shore of the Dead Sea in what is now the West Bank. The scrolls consist of all the books of the Old Testament except Esther and are the oldest known manuscripts of any books of the Bible. They also consist of original writings of a Jewish religious sect that apparently lived in the cave area from 150 B.C. to A.D. 68.

The attention still being paid to these manuscripts in 1993, some 46 years after their discovery, testifies to their importance for the religions of Judaism and Christianity. Before the scrolls' discovery, scholars had few documents on Judaism written in Hebrew and dated from the period about 200 B.C. to A.D. 135. The study of Judaic history of this period had relied on translations of religious texts that were preserved by Christians. When the scrolls came to light, scholars at last had documents that they were quite sure accurately reflected the original Jewish texts.

Christian scholars, as well, were excited by the discovery of the ancient scrolls. Some were written during the time of Jesus, the founder of Christianity. Jesus and his followers were Jews who shared many of the ideas of other Jews of the time. Thus, Christian scholars were intrigued by the possibility that the views of the Jewish sect expressed in the scrolls might have found their way into early Christian beliefs.

But the current fascination with the scrolls also is due in no small part to a controversy that came to a head in recent years. Scholars, eager to see all of the thousands of fragments that constitute the Dead Sea Scrolls, accused the editors who were piecing together and translating the texts of monopolizing the ancient works. Publication of all the texts had been delayed for years, but the editors justified the delay by noting the difficulty of putting together bits of parchment, some no larger than a dime, and then carefully translating the text into English and French.

Discovery of the scrolls had taken place over several years. The first ancient documents were found in a cave near Qumran Valley, about 8 miles (13 kilometers) south of the city of Jericho. The initial find consisted of seven antique leather rolls, including a well-worn copy of the

■ **The author**

John J. Collins is professor of Hebrew Bible at the Divinity School of the University of Chicago.

■ A barren desert yields priceless treasure

The Dead Sea Scrolls derive their name from the region where Bedouin shepherds found the first cache in 1947 on the northwestern shore of the Dead Sea in what is now called the West Bank, *below* (inset). By 1956, archaeologists and shepherds had discovered thousands of fragments in 11 caves and had also excavated the nearby ruins of Qumran, *below.*

■ The entrances to some of the caves, *above,* were difficult to gain access to, leading scholars to speculate that the scrolls were placed there for safekeeping.

Lebanon
Syria
Golan
Heights
Mediterranean
Sea
Israel
West
Bank
Jericho
Jerusalem
Qumran site
Gaza Strip
En Gedi
Dead Sea
Jordan
Egypt
Gulf of
Suez
Gulf of
Aqaba
Saudi
Arabia

Cave 3
Cave 11
Escarpment
Wadi Jaweat Zabin
Cave 1
Cave 2
Wadi Dababit
Qumran
Cave 7
Cave 5
Cave 8
Cave 6
Cave 9
Cave 4
Cave 10
Dead Sea Plain
Wadi Qumran
Dead
Sea

0   1/2 Mile
0   1/2 Kilometer

361

complete book of Isaiah, carefully preserved in jars. The Isaiah scroll is the largest, measuring about 1 foot by 24 feet (30 centimeters by 7 meters). Six scrolls were written in ancient Hebrew, and one, a paraphrase of Genesis, was in *Aramaic,* the language spoken in Palestine at the time of Jesus. This discovery set off a search both by trained archaeologists and by local Bedouin shepherds. By 1956, they had recovered thousands of fragments from hundreds of manuscripts in 11 caves in the region. The most spectacular discovery occurred in 1952, when shepherds found about 15,000 scroll fragments in a cave that archaeologists designated as cave 4.

At first, the process of publishing the scrolls went along smoothly. The American School of Oriental Research and the Hebrew University, both in Jerusalem, each acquired a part of the initial seven scrolls. They were in good condition, so that publishing photographs of them proceeded promptly but without any accompanying commentary.

Publication slows

On the other hand, publication of the scrolls discovered in cave 4, many of which were in an advanced state of decay, took many years. The process was complicated by political turmoil in the region resulting from the creation of the Jewish state of Israel. In 1947, the United Nations agreed to divide Palestine into an Arab state and a Jewish state and to place Jerusalem under international control with East Jerusalem in Jordanian hands. War quickly broke out between Arab and Jewish forces. In the midst of the turmoil, the Jordanian government purchased the scroll fragments that had been found in cave 4 and deposited them at the Palestine Archaeological Museum in East Jerusalem. The government then appointed an international team of eight scholars to edit them at the museum.

The official team worked in Jerusalem for a few years, but then, in 1960, funding ran out. This forced the scholars to leave the city in search of other livelihood. No team ever again assembled in Jerusalem. Instead, the scholars worked on the scrolls mainly by using photocopies that they took to the institutions where they were employed.

The scholars had found that identifying which fragments belonged together was an excruciatingly slow process. They analyzed handwriting, the parchment or papyrus the texts were written on, and the texts themselves to bring together the appropriate bits. By 1960, much of the work of identifying the fragments was finished. But actual publication of a complete edition of the scrolls proceeded slowly, complicated once again by political turmoil: the Six-Day War of 1967. Israeli forces occupied the West Bank and took over East Jerusalem.

During the Six-Day War, the Israelis acquired from an Arab dealer one of the most important scroll documents, the Temple Scroll, which had been recovered from cave 11 in 1956. Its 66 columns of text are a rewriting of Biblical laws from Leviticus and Deuteronomy, presented as the laws God gave to Moses.

By the mid-1980's, a chorus of complaint was rising over the delay in publication of the remaining scrolls. Several respected scholars,

Sacred songs, hidden treasure

The Psalms Scroll, *above,* found in cave 11 in 1956, dates from between A.D. 30 and 50, according to an analysis of the carefully drawn script. The scroll contains parts of 41 Biblical psalms, as well as previously unknown hymns and a passage about the psalms composed by King David.

■ The copper scroll, *above,* lists treasures and their hiding places. It had split in two before it was found in cave 3 in 1952. A British researcher carefully separated the fragile metal into readable sections. Scholars now argue whether such treasures, never located, could have belonged to the religious sect that apparently lived at Qumran.

such as Géza Vermès of Oxford University in England and Norman Golb of the University of Chicago, complained that they were excluded from the editorial process. Hershel Shanks, a Washington, D.C., publisher, launched a campaign for the release of the unpublished scrolls. Then, in September 1991, the Huntington Library in San Marino, Calif., made available to any qualified researcher a set of scroll photographs that it had obtained several years earlier. Soon, Shanks published a set of scroll photographs. And about the same time, the official group of editors was enlarged to more than 50 members, including some long-time critics.

Scholars were eager to examine all of the scrolls primarily because they sought to resolve the question of their authorship. Among the most intriguing of the Dead Sea Scrolls are the original writings relating to a religious sect, its liturgy, hymns, and rituals. One such original work was a Community Rule book remarkably like the rule books that were written for later Christian monasteries. Because the Qumran ruins were near the caves where the scrolls were found, scholars inferred that the community described in the rule book had lived at Qumran. In addition, the scholars believed all of the scrolls to be the

■ The Qumran question

Were the inhabitants of Qumran, now a ruin, *above,* responsible for the Dead Sea Scrolls? Most scholars concluded that they were, after pottery from cave 1 proved to be identical to pottery found in Qumran. An inkwell found in the ruins, *inset,* led to the early assertion that scribes at Qumran created the scrolls. Later analysis showed that too much variation existed in the handwriting for all the scrolls to have been written at Qumran.

library of the community. Pottery found in the caves matched pottery found in the ruins, confirming this hypothesis for many scholars.

Archaeological evidence indicated that Qumran had been occupied from about 150 B.C. to A.D. 68. Other evidence, such as a great quantity of Roman arrowheads, charred timbers, and ash, indicated that Qumran was destroyed by a Roman army putting down a Jewish revolt that had erupted in A.D. 66. The Jews were attempting to throw off their Roman rulers, but without success. The revolt ended with the destruction of the Jerusalem temple in A.D. 70.

The question remained as to who exactly were the inhabitants of Qumran before it was destroyed. Scholars looked to the accounts of ancient writers for clues. Pliny the Elder, a Roman writer, reported that there was a settlement near the western shore of the Dead Sea, south of Jericho and above the town of Engedi, that was occupied by a group called Essenes. He might have taken his account of the site from an older source, but most scholars are convinced that Qumran was the site Pliny was describing.

Then, scholars looked at the work of two writers whose descriptions of the way of life of the Essenes aligned with the life style laid out in the Community Rule scroll from Qumran. Philo, a Jewish philosopher who wrote until about A.D. 40, provided the earliest account of the Essenes. He described their way of life as communal and dedicated to the service of God. Flavius Josephus, a Jewish historian who wrote an account between A.D. 70 and 75 called *The Jewish War*, related that the Essenes were a third sect of Jews in addition to the Pharisees and the Sadducees, who are frequently mentioned in the New Testament and in writings by ancient Jewish rabbis. Josephus wrote that the Essenes had a complicated process of admission, by which candidates were tested for several years. The Community Rule from Qumran describes a similar process. Other similarities between Josephus' description and the Community Rule range from communal ownership of possessions to a prohibition against spitting.

Perplexing inconsistencies

Some differences exist, however, between the Essenes described by ancient writers and the community described in the scrolls. For example, Josephus and Pliny noted that the Essenes were celibate, though Josephus also described one order of the Essenes who married. None of the Qumran scrolls prohibit marriage. In fact, some of the documents clearly assume that marriage is normal and accepted. However, the Community Rule is silent on the subject of marriage, and some scholars argue that this omission implies that the members were celibate. Some female skeletons have been found at the cemetery at Qumran, but only a fraction of the graves have been excavated.

For some scholars, the evidence proving or disproving the Qumran community's marital arrangements, if any, remains inconclusive. Other scholars refer to another ancient document discovered in the early 1900's called the Damascus Document. This text is a rulebook with many features in common with the Qumran Community Rule, but it envisages various "camps" where some members may take wives and have children. Most scholars have concluded that the Damascus Document refers to the "marrying Essenes," but that the Community Rule was written for celibate Essenes at Qumran.

Another difference between Josephus' account of the Essenes and what is found in the Dead Sea Scrolls concerns some specific beliefs of the Qumran community. The Community Rule states that the world is divided between the spirits of Light and the spirits of Darkness. The rule further states that the conduct of people is determined by how much of each spirit they inherited. Josephus' account of the Essenes does not mention such beliefs. The rule also mentions messiahs "of Aaron and Israel"—that is, a messiah priest and a messiah king, who were expected to appear in the future. Another Qumran document, called the War Scroll, describes a great war between "the sons of Light" and "the sons of Darkness," which would end with the intervention of God on behalf of the sons of Light. No such events are mentioned in Josephus' account of the Essenes.

Scholars, then, have two options with regard to the identification of the community that inhabited Qumran. If it was an Essene settlement, then the account in Josephus is incomplete and somewhat misleading. If it was not an Essene settlement, the community nonetheless resembles the Essenes more closely than any other known group.

Other issues complicate the identification of the Dead Sea Scrolls with the Essenes. Most scholars have assumed that the community described in the Community Rule lived at Qumran, because the caves where the scrolls were found are very close to the ruins. Roland de Vaux, director of the École Biblique in East Jerusalem, who excavated the site in the early 1950's, theorized that the ruins resembled a monastery. Although most of de Vaux's theory is still accepted, a few scholars deny any connection between the ruins and the scrolls. Two Belgian archaeologists, Robert and Pauline Donceel, who have examined the site, have proposed that the building was a luxurious villa with an area for making pottery and for mining minerals. They claim that the scrolls came from somewhere else. Historian Norman Golb at the University of Chicago has argued for many years that the building was a military fort. In his view, the scrolls were brought from Jerusalem during the Jewish revolt to save them from destruction by the Roman army.

Underlying Golb's theory, however, is another point of more far-reaching importance: Do the scrolls represent the beliefs of an isolated religious sect or are they part of the mainstream beliefs of most Jews living at that time? Fragments of more than 700 documents have now been recovered from the caves. From the handwriting, it appears that they were copied by hundreds of scribes, because only rarely is more than one document in the same hand. It seems unlikely that all these writings were copied at Qumran. Golb supposes that they came from a major center and that they represent a cross section of Jewish thought at the time.

Other scholars argue that the scrolls do not represent such a cross section. There is no trace of the Books of the Maccabees, which were widely known at the time. The books relate how the Maccabees rebelled against the Seleucid rulers of the Jews about 165 B.C. The scrolls also do not reflect the views of the Pharisees, which were important politically and philosophically when Qumran was inhabited.

Many scholars believe that the scrolls can still be explained as the library of a religious sect. Many of the scrolls share a distinctive view of the world that may be called *apocalyptic* (giving a revelation of violent upheaval), such as the War Scroll's description of the forces of Light and Darkness clashing in a great battle at the end of history. There is the expectation of two messiahs, a priest and a king, who would come in the final days of the world. The sect thought that it was living on the verge of the last days and that its own history was foretold in the prophetic books of the Bible. The sect was guided by the Teacher of Righteousness, who was regarded as the definitive interpreter of the Scriptures.

Much of the controversy that has surrounded the Dead Sea Scrolls has concerned the relationship between this view of the world and early Christianity. In the 1950's, Edmund Wilson, a literary critic, claimed that similarities between the scrolls and the New Testament were being suppressed to protect the uniqueness of Christianity. Many journalists have repeated the charge, most recently in *The Dead Sea Scrolls Deception* (1992) by Michael Baigent and Richard Leigh. But most scholars agree that there is no substance to those charges.

Some parallels between certain Dead Sea Scrolls and the New Testament do exist. One scroll refers to the messiah as "Son of God." A claim that one fragment spoke of a dying messiah received wide publicity in the newspapers in the autumn of 1991, but subsequently was shown to be mistaken. Perhaps the most extreme theory is that of Robert Eisenman of California State University at Long Beach, who holds that the members of the Dead Sea sect were early Christians, and that the Teacher of Righteousness was James, the brother of Jesus. Virtually no other scholar supports this interpretation of the texts.

Now that the scrolls are available to all scholars, some controversies will probably be resolved. But the intriguing fragments often lack the context necessary for a correct interpretation, making them a fertile breeding ground for conflicting theories. Nevertheless, the scrolls have greatly enriched our knowledge of ancient Judaism and of the setting in which Christianity arose. ■ ■ ■

For further reading:

Baigent, Michael, and Leigh, Richard. *The Dead Sea Scrolls Deception.* Summit Books, 1992.

Ringgaren, Helmer. *Faith of Qumran: Theology of the Dead Sea Scrolls.* Crossroad Publishing, 1993.

Understanding the Dead Sea Scrolls: A Reader. Ed. by Hershel Shanks. Random House, 1993.

Vermès, Géza. *The Dead Sea Scrolls: Qumran in Perspective.* Augsburg Fortress, 1981.

Yadin, Yigael. *The Message of the Scrolls.* Crossroad Publishing, 1991.

Reno, Janet (1938-   ), the former state attorney for Dade County, Florida, became United States attorney general on March 12, 1993. She is the first woman ever to head the U.S. Department of Justice.

Reno was born in Miami, Fla., on July 21, 1938. She received a bachelor's degree, with a major in chemistry, at Cornell University in Ithaca, N.Y., in 1960 and graduated from Harvard University Law School in Cambridge, Mass., in 1963.

Reno returned to Florida in 1963 to enter the private practice of law. She switched to the public arena in 1971, serving until 1973 as a lawyer for the state legislature and until 1976 as an assistant state attorney in Miami. In 1976, she returned briefly to private practice.

In 1978, Reno was appointed Dade County state attorney. She made enemies in Miami's black community in 1980 when she failed to win convictions against four white Miami police officers charged with fatally beating a black man. She later mended fences with the city's minority population by hiring many blacks and Hispanics for her department and becoming perhaps the most accessible public official in the state.

She continued to have critics, however. Police groups, for instance, contended that she had been too lenient with criminals.

Reno has never been married. She is an outdoor enthusiast and enjoys camping.   □ David Dreier

Republican Party. Disheartened and nearly demoralized after the 1992 defeat of incumbent President George Bush, the Republican Party (GOP, for Grand Old Party) rebounded smartly in 1993. In June, Los Angeles got a Republican mayor for the first time since 1961. And in the November elections, the GOP captured the governorships of New Jersey and Virginia and the mayor's office of New York City. Democrats claimed that the election results reflected anti-incumbent sentiment and not a pro-Republican trend, but the GOP looked ahead with optimism to the 1994 elections. (See **Elections**.)

United against taxes. Republicans found unity in opposing the economic programs of Democratic President Bill Clinton. After Clinton in February proposed a combination of tax increases and spending cuts to pare about $500 billion from federal deficits over five years, Republicans found their voice. Emphasizing tax hikes in labeling Clinton a "tax-and-spend Democrat," they convinced many voters that enactment of his program would hurt them in their pocketbooks. Although Clinton countered that his income tax proposals would affect only the wealthiest 1.2 percent of Americans, polls showed a solid Republican victory in the battle for public opinion.

When voting time came on the budget bill on August 5 and 6, Republicans in both the Senate and House of Representatives showed unity of a sort almost never seen on major legislation. They not only

voted "no" unanimously, but they also picked up enough Democratic support to come within one vote of winning in the Senate and within one vote in the House. Moreover, they succeeded in killing a companion proposal to stimulate the sluggish economy through new spending programs.

The GOP got an inadvertent boost from Clinton himself, many observers believed. As a consequence of missteps and a seeming eagerness to please everyone, Clinton wound up satisfying a shrinking minority of Americans. By late May, polls gave him an approval rating of just 36 percent, the lowest ever recorded for a new President so early in his term.

Through all of these developments, the most visible spokesman for the Republican Party was Senate Republican leader Robert J. Dole of Kansas. Dole acknowledged in August that he was thinking about seeking the 1996 Republican presidential nomination. (See **Dole, Robert J.**)

New Republican Committee chairman. Haley Barbour, a lawyer and lobbyist from Mississippi, was elected chairman of the Republican National Committee (RNC) on January 29 at a national party meeting in St. Louis, Mo. He bested four rivals to succeed Richard N. Bond in the top GOP post. Barbour also had to fend off an effort by Senator Dole to install an ally, Senator Mitch McConnell of Kentucky, as the party's "general chairman."

After his election, Barbour said that the key to a Republican comeback would be to stress GOP economic policies. He said the party should soften its opposition to abortion rights, though he stopped short of committing himself to removing the antiabortion plank in the GOP platform.

New GOP organizations. The party's unanimity against Clinton's economic plans was underscored by the formation of organizations within the party aimed at appealing to various factions of the electorate. On January 12, key conservative GOP leaders formed Empower America, a tax-exempt think tank and advocacy group. One goal of Empower America was to bridge the gap between GOP moderates and evangelical Christians. Vin Weber, a former congressman from Minnesota, became president of Empower America. Founding directors included Jack F. Kemp, the former United States secretary of housing and urban development, and William J. Bennett, the former U.S. secretary of education.

In December 1992, Republican moderates had formed the Republican Majority Coalition. Its aim was to counter the Christian right's influence on the party and strip the antiabortion plank from the 1996 GOP platform. In June 1993, the RNC formed a National Policy Forum. Party leaders hoped this group, by emphasizing grass-roots concerns, would help draw Democrats and supporters of independent presidential candidate Ross Perot to the GOP.

New GOP senator runs into trouble. The party scored its first big election victory of the year on

In April, Senate Republican leader Robert J. Dole and other GOP senators present their report card of President Bill Clinton's first 100 days in office.

June 5, when Texas Treasurer Kay Bailey Hutchison easily defeated Democrat Bob Krueger to fill the unexpired term of former Senator Lloyd M. Bentsen, Jr. Krueger had been appointed to the seat when Bentsen joined the Clinton Cabinet as secretary of the treasury.

Hutchison became an instant GOP celebrity. In September, however, the new senator was indicted in a Texas court on charges that she had misused her state treasury post to support her campaign for the U.S. Senate, allegations that she denied. The indictments cast a cloud of doubt over Hutchison's prospects of winning reelection in 1994.

In October, the situation seemed to brighten as Hutchison learned that the indictments against her would be withdrawn. Texas officials discovered that a member of the grand jury that drafted the indictments was ineligible to serve on the jury. But on December 8, Hutchison was reindicted.

Bush declines GOP stipend. On June 21, former President Bush notified the RNC that he had decided not to accept a $150,000-a-year GOP stipend. Former President Ronald Reagan had been receiving that amount since 1989. The money was described as reimbursement for their GOP political activities. ☐ Frank Cormier and Margot Cormier

See also **Democratic Party.** In *World Book,* see **Republican Party.**

Rhode Island. See State government.

Riley, Richard W. (1933-   ), former governor of South Carolina, became United States secretary of education on Jan. 22, 1993. On April 21, Riley and Labor Secretary Robert B. Reich introduced a plan for developing national standards for academic proficiency and providing occupational training for students who have not attended college.

Riley was born near Greenville, S.C., on Jan. 2, 1933. He graduated with honors from Furman University in Greenville in 1954 and then enlisted in the Navy, serving for two years as an officer on a minesweeper. In 1959, he earned a law degree at the University of South Carolina in Columbia. From 1960 to 1963, he worked at his family's law firm in Greenville and Simpsonville, S.C.

Riley entered politics in 1963, getting elected to the state House of Representatives. He served for 4 years in the House and then for 10 years in the South Carolina Senate.

In 1978, Riley was elected South Carolina governor. A new amendment in the state Constitution allowed him to become the first governor in modern times to run for a second term, and he was reelected in 1982. As governor, Riley worked to improve the state's public school system, attracting national attention as an educational reformer. After leaving office, he resumed the private practice of law.

Riley is married to the former Ann Yarborough. They have four children. ☐ David Dreier

Roman Catholic Church.

Pope John Paul II, in his 15th year as pope, continued his worldwide travels in 1993. No other pope has traveled outside Italy as much as he has. From 1978 to 1993, the pope made more than 60 trips.

On August 12, he visited the United States for the third time since his election to the papacy in 1978. He participated in celebrations in Denver, Colo., for World Youth Day, a festival sponsored by the Vatican. The 73-year-old pope spent his four-day visit encouraging some 160,000 young Catholics from 70 countries to be strong in their faith. Upon arrival at Denver's Stapleton International Airport, the pope was greeted by President Bill Clinton. It was the first meeting of the two men since Clinton took office as U.S. President in January 1993. Clinton praised the pontiff for his moral leadership.

On September 4, the pope made his first papal visit to the newly independent Baltic nations of Estonia, Latvia, and Lithuania. In the 1980's, when these nations were republics within the Soviet Union, the pope had sought greater religious freedom for them and other Communist-dominated nations of Eastern Europe. Observers viewed the visit as an ideological and emotional triumph for the pope.

The pope's conservative voice. Many Catholics viewed Pope John Paul II as a strong upholder of traditional church teachings. Throughout his papacy, he has criticized Catholics who have advocated liberal church reforms, such as allowing priests to marry or ordaining women into the priesthood. The pontiff stirred controversy on Oct. 5, 1993, when he issued a strongly worded *encyclical* (papal message), considered to be one of his most important statements. The October encyclical, *Veritatis Splendor* (*The Splendor of Truth*), stated that morals are based on objective truths, which can be known by human reason. *Veritatis Splendor* condemned what it called the loosening of Catholic moral theology, especially on sexual matters. It encouraged bishops to discipline offending theologians. The encyclical also encouraged Catholic theologians to speak out strongly against sin, particularly sexual sins.

The birth-control issue. Catholics observed the 25th anniversary of Pope Paul VI's encyclical *Humanae Vitae* (*Of Human Life*) on July 29. The encyclical restated the Catholic Church's 1968 ban on the use of artificial contraception. Catholics have been divided on the issue of birth control ever since. Supporters of the encyclical say it is wrong for couples to control the births of their children by means other than sexual abstinence. Critics say couples ought to be able in good conscience to limit the size of their family by artificial means. Surveys of U.S. Catholics, including a *USA Today*/Cable News Network Gallup poll reported on July 10, found that 8 out of 10 U.S. Catholics disagree with the church's teaching on birth control.

Pope John Paul II greets some of the 160,000 Roman Catholics who came to Denver, Colo., in August for World Youth Day, a Vatican-sponsored festival.

Misconduct charges. Reports continued to arise in 1993 that a small percentage of Roman Catholic priests had sexually abused children. The Vatican announced in June the formation of a committee of Vatican and U.S. bishops to study church law for ways to more quickly expel proven sex offenders.

The archbishop of Santa Fe, N. Mex., Robert F. Sanchez, announced on March 19 that he had submitted his resignation to the pope. Earlier published reports indicated that Sanchez had engaged in sexual relationships with several young women during the 1970's and early 1980's. In November 1993, a Philadelphia man brought charges of sexual abuse against the archbishop of Chicago, Joseph Cardinal Bernardin. The man said that Bernardin had sexually assaulted him during the mid-1970's, while, at age 17, he was studying at a preseminary in Cincinnati, Ohio, where Bernardin was then archbishop. The man said he recalled the incident in October 1993. He claimed that he had experienced repressed memory, a controversial and little understood reaction that psychologists say sometimes follows trauma. Bernardin denied the charges.

The pope underwent tests on July 2, almost one year after colon surgery. A Vatican spokesman declared him to be in good health. □ Thomas C. Fox

See also **Religion: The Lure and Lore of the Dead Sea Scrolls.** In *World Book,* see **Roman Catholic Church.**

Romania. The Romanian government continued to face serious economic problems in 1993. Industrial production was still in decline, and unemployment neared 11 percent by the end of 1993. Wages continued to fall, and inflation ran about 200 percent in late November. The World Bank, an international lending agency, estimated that Romanians spent about 80 percent of their income on food.

Since the Communist government was toppled in 1989, Romania has continued to privatize industry. In 1992, the private sector accounted for about 25 percent of the *gross domestic product* (the total of all goods and services produced within a country). However, about 65 percent of all those employed were in the state or cooperative sector.

Foreign investment in Romania increased modestly but remained lower than in other post-Communist countries. Government officials tried to attract foreign investors by promoting their country as a politically stable, untapped market with a trained work force. The International Monetary Fund, a UN agency, refused to lend money to Romania in 1993, partly because the government had done poorly in reorganizing industry. Divisions among the ruling party's leaders, some of whom came out of the Communist leadership, were seen as blocking economic reform.

Party politics. President Ion Iliescu's party, the Democratic National Salvation Front, changed its name to the Democratic Party at its July conference. The party also merged with several independent small parties. Changes in Iliescu's Cabinet in August reflected divisions within the party and appeared to reduce the influence of reformists. Right wing nationalist forces, including the Greater Romanian party, which held its first national congress in March, continued to be active in Romania in 1993.

Labor strikes. On August 2, 45,000 coal miners in the Jiu Valley went on strike to increase their wages. Prime Minister Nicolae Vacaroiu refused to meet with the workers, and they returned to work on August 11 without winning major demands.

Just as coal miners returned to work, the nation's railway workers struck for higher wages. Romania's rail system and international rail service were disrupted. After they were threatened with replacement, the workers returned to work on August 18. Numerous other labor strikes took place in 1993.

Human rights. In 1993, the government established a Council of National Minorities and promised to improve its treatment of ethnic minorities. About 8 percent of Romania's people are Hungarian. In July, Romanian and Hungarian representatives signed an accord to improve educational and language conditions for Hungarian Romanians.

□ Sharon L. Wolchik

See also **Europe** (Facts in brief table). In *World Book,* see **Romania.**

Rowing. See Sports.

Russia. On Dec. 12, 1993, Russian voters went to the polls to remake the country's governing institutions for the first time since Russia gained independence following the Soviet Union's collapse in December 1991. The voters approved a new Constitution to replace the Soviet-era basic law. They also elected representatives to a new parliament, called the Federal Assembly.

The new Constitution gave sweeping powers to Russian President Boris Yeltsin, who favored Western-style reform. But conservative forces made significant gains in parliament, both in the 176-seat upper house, the Federation Council (reserved for representatives of Russia's administrative regions), and the 450-seat lower house, the State Duma, half of whose members were elected according to party lists and half in individual balloting. The Liberal Democratic Party, led by Vladimir Zhirinovsky—an extreme nationalist whose goals included restoring the Russian empire—was expected to control 64 seats in the Duma. The Communist Party won about 48 seats, and the allied Agrarian Party 33 seats. Russia's Choice, headed by radical reformer Yegor T. Gaidar, was the strongest of the reform-minded parties. It was expected to hold 58 seats in the Duma.

The elections became possible after troops loyal to Yeltsin stormed the Russian parliament building in Moscow on Oct. 4, 1993, crushing an uprising by hard-line lawmakers. The conclusion of the 12-day stand-off ended a bitter struggle between the president and legislature that had paralyzed economic and political reform.

The stage for these events was set in December 1992, when Yeltsin lost a showdown with the Congress of People's Deputies, then Russia's highest legislative body, which favored a cautious transition to a market economy. The congress forced Yeltsin to replace Gaidar as prime minister. In return, the congress accepted Yeltsin's demand for a nationwide referendum on whether the president or legislature should control the pace of reform.

Political wrangling continued through spring, as parliament Speaker Ruslan Khasbulatov sought to pressure Yeltsin into giving up the referendum. On March 10, 1993, the Congress of People's Deputies, meeting in a special four-day session, voted overwhelmingly to cancel the referendum and to limit Yeltsin's powers. Yeltsin said he would hold a referendum on April 25 in defiance of the congress.

On March 20, Yeltsin signed a degree establishing presidential rule. Khasbulatov, backed by Vice President Alexander Rutskoi, denounced the move and called for Yeltsin's impeachment. Meanwhile, Russia's Constitutional Court, the country's top judicial body, on March 23 declared Yeltsin's action unconstitutional. Negotiations failed to resolve the crisis, and on March 28, the congress voted on an impeachment motion. The motion fell only 72 votes

Russian President Boris Yeltsin, right, walks with U.S. President Bill Clinton at the two leaders' first summit, in Vancouver, Canada, in April.

short of the 689 deputies necessary to approve it.

Referendum. On March 29, the congress approved the April 25 referendum, but it insisted that the questions should require a majority of all registered voters to pass, rather than a majority of those voting. Yeltsin appealed to the Constitutional Court, which ruled that two questions—votes of confidence in Yeltsin and his economic policies—would require only a simple majority. The other two questions, asking whether there should be early presidential and early parliamentary elections, would require the approval of a majority of registered voters.

About 65 percent of registered voters took part in the referendum. Of these voters, some 59 percent said they had confidence in Yeltsin, and 53 percent said they approved of his economic policies. About 67 percent, representing 43 percent of all voters, supported early elections for parliament, and 50 percent, or 32 percent of all voters, favored an early presidential election. Yeltsin and his supporters hailed the results as a clear popular endorsement.

Constitutional assembly. On April 29, Yeltsin asked representatives of Russia's nearly 90 administrative regions, including about 20 *autonomous republics* (partially self-governing ethnic homelands), to form an assembly that would complete work on a draft constitution. (The Chechen Republic, which had split from Chechen-Ingush, had declared independence and did not take part in the assembly.) The assembly convened on June 5 and approved a draft of the constitution on July 12. The document replaced the congress and its standing legislature, the Supreme Soviet, with the two-chamber Federal Assembly. It also expanded the president's powers and abolished the posts of vice president and parliament speaker.

Work on the constitution almost bogged down in June, as regional leaders opposed proposals to give the autonomous republics disproportionate power in the upper house. Eventually, the draft allotted two seats to each of the republics and other regions. The draft also increased the autonomy of both the republics and the other regions, which resisted what they saw as efforts by Moscow to restore centralized rule. But the autonomy provisions were removed from the final draft of the constitution, signed by Yeltsin in November.

Economic reform slowed. As conservative factions in parliament became increasingly powerful, the government fought a losing battle to curb inflation, which by summer hovered at about 20 percent monthly. Russia's central bank, which was nominally controlled by parliament, continued through spring to issue credits to struggling industries, arguing that the policy was necessary to prevent massive unemployment. In May, the bank agreed to phase out the issuing of credits. But the agreement had little effect, and inflation reached 25 percent by October. Meanwhile, the value of the ruble plummeted from

Hard-line Communists and nationalists clash with police during an antigovernment demonstration in Moscow on May Day.

415 per United States dollar on January 1 to 1,247 per dollar in December.

On July 24, the bank sparked panic when, in a surprise move, it announced that all pre-1993 ruble notes were being withdrawn from circulation. The withdrawal, designed to curb inflation, led to a further rift with the Yeltsin government. Yeltsin issued a decree softening the conditions of the withdrawal.

On September 1, Yeltsin suspended Rutskoy from his post pending results of a corruption investigation. The Supreme Soviet then voted to lift the suspension. On September 19, prosecutors said there were insufficient grounds to bring charges against the vice president.

Parliamentary revolt. On September 21, Yeltsin dissolved parliament and called elections for the Federal Assembly. He justified the move, widely recognized as unconstitutional, on the grounds of his success in the April referendum. The Supreme Soviet, followed by the Congress of People's Deputies—which met in an emergency session on September 23—immediately impeached Yeltsin and replaced him with Rutskoi. Rutskoi, meanwhile, sought to seize control of the vital Defense, Security, and Interior ministries, replacing their pro-Yeltsin ministers with his own appointees. However, the ministries remained loyal to Yeltsin.

As the stand-off heated up, Yeltsin cut telephone and electricity links to the White House, the Russian parliament building. Seeking to ease resistance, he also said on September 23 that he would call early presidential elections for June 12, 1994. Parliament, in turn, called for simultaneous elections for parliament and president, a demand Yeltsin rejected.

On Sept. 28, 1993, Yeltsin ordered some 2,000 Interior Ministry troops to seal off the White House, where about 230 parliamentarians and several hundred aides and parliamentary guards were holed up with a supply of light arms. Over the next few days, minor clashes between pro-parliament demonstrators and security forces stiffened the resistance of parliamentary leaders. Mediation efforts by the Russian Orthodox Church made little progress.

On October 3, about 5,000 protesters smashed through cordons of underprepared security forces, lifting the siege of the White House. Within hours, rioters also seized the Moscow mayor's office as pro-Yeltsin police fled in panic. The rioters failed, however, to capture the Ostenkino television complex, Moscow's main broadcasting station.

End of the uprising. On the evening of October 3, Yeltsin imposed a state of emergency in Moscow as he and his supporters overcame initial confusion and rallied wavering security forces to their side. Pro-parliament forces retreated to the White House.

The next morning, armored units advanced on the White House and launched an assault. For eight hours, troops battled the building's occupants, even-

Riot police prevent demonstrators from joining lawmakers holed up in the Russian parliament building during a parliamentary uprising in September.

tually shelling the building's upper floors. By late afternoon, the uprising's ringleaders—including Rutskoi and Khasbulatov—were in custody. According to official estimates, approximately 190 people were killed and 430 injured in the revolt, which came to be called the October Uprising. Critics claimed the number of casualties was far higher.

In the wake of the revolt, Yeltsin dissolved some regional councils—many of which had opposed his dissolution of parliament—and banned extremist publications and organizations, including the Communist Party. The ban on the party was later lifted. Yeltsin also suspended the Constitutional Court pending adoption of a new constitution. On October 18, Yeltsin lifted the state of emergency imposed on

October 3. Yeltsin sought to restart the process of economic reform on October 27, issuing a decree lifting Communist-era restrictions on the purchase and sale of land. However, vague wording left parts of the decree open to interpretation.

As the campaign for the December 12 balloting began, Yeltsin drew increasing criticism for what some called authoritarian tendencies. Yeltsin threatened to deprive parties that campaigned against the constitution of free broadcast time, and his government sought to have such parties banned from the election. On December 2, the election commission ruled that all parties were free to criticize the draft.

Foreign policy. On January 3, Yeltsin and outgoing U.S. President George Bush signed the START

II (Strategic Arms Reduction Treaty II) arms control pact, designed to drastically cut the number of warheads in both nation's nuclear arsenals. But progress in arms control was threatened by Ukraine, which was hedging on commitments to make Russia the sole nuclear power in the former Soviet Union. The issue was one of several disputes between Russia and Ukraine in 1993. (See **Ukraine.**)

In July, Russia canceled a planned sale of rocket engines to India under strong American pressure. The United States said the sale would violate international agreements on the proliferation of missile technology. Many Russians charged that the United States was trying to shut Russia out from lucrative international arms trade markets. In November, Russia signed an agreement with China that was expected to help China obtain Russian military technology.

Also in November, Russia announced a new military doctrine that renounced a 1982 Soviet pledge not to initiate the use of nuclear weapons. The doctrine stressed the security threat posed by small regional conflicts. Earlier, Russia had troubled Western nations and angered its former Soviet neighbors by claiming a sphere of influence in the former Soviet Union. (See **Commonwealth of Independent States; Georgia; Tajikistan.**) □ Justin Burke

See also **Europe** (Facts in brief table). In *World Book,* see **Russia.**

Rwanda. See Africa.

Safety. Nationwide concern over the safety of Diet Pepsi cola arose in June 1993 after people in more than 20 states reported finding hypodermic syringes or other objects in Pepsi cans. But an investigation by the United States Food and Drug Administration (FDA) and PepsiCo Incorporated concluded on June 17 that the reports were hoaxes, and that the complainants themselves had placed objects inside Pepsi cans.

FDA Commissioner David A. Kessler warned that such false reports could result in prison sentences of up to five years and fines of up to $250,000. At least five people were arrested for making false reports about finding objects in Pepsi cans. In one instance, a surveillance camera in a Colorado store taped a woman who appeared to be placing a syringe in a Pepsi can.

Iron supplement tablets have become the most common cause of fatal poisonings in children, according to a February report issued by the U.S. Centers for Disease Control and Prevention (CDC) in Atlanta, Ga. Iron supplements caused 5,144 reported poisonings and 11 deaths among children in 1991, the last year for which complete data were available. Children may mistake iron tablets with a red or green coating for candy. Just five or six high-potency tablets can kill a young child, the report said, so parents should store iron pills in a place out of children's reach.

Automobile deaths. The U.S. Department of Transportation reported in January 1993 that the number of traffic fatalities recorded for 1992 was the lowest since 1962. Total deaths in motor vehicle accidents declined to 39,000, or 5 percent less than in 1991. Experts noted a number of possible factors responsible for the decline, including more widespread use of safety belts, improvements in car design, and fewer drunk drivers.

Water wrongs. Many states are not conducting proper inspection programs for monitoring the safety of public drinking-water supplies, according to a study reported on April 15, 1993. The study, conducted by the U.S. General Accounting Office (GAO), an independent agency that advises the U.S. Congress, found that states often fail to verify whether water-treatment plants have corrected problems identified during inspections. It also found that inadequate inspections occur at about 50 percent of the 59,000 large U.S. public water-supply systems, and at 20 percent of the 139,000 smaller systems. States failed to inspect frequently enough, and many inspectors were inadequately trained, the GAO found.

Cellular phone scare. In January, a Florida man triggered concern over the safety of portable cellular telephones by claiming on a television talk show that a cellular phone caused his wife's brain cancer. Several other people later made similar claims. Scientists from the FDA, the National Cancer Institute, the Environmental Protection Agency, and the Federal Communications Commission on February 2 said there was no evidence that cellular phones cause or promote cancer, but that further studies were needed to rule out any danger from the devices.

New warning labels. In an effort to ensure that consumers use over-the-counter drugs safely, the FDA announced on August 26 that several groups of nonprescription drugs must carry new warning labels within six months to one year. The labels will be required on antacids, laxatives, and antidiarrhea drugs. The labels will give consumers more information about proper use of nonprescription drugs, their possible interactions with other drugs, and potentially adverse effects in people with certain medical conditions.

On May 12, the FDA announced a proposal to require new safety labels on sunscreen and suntan products. Such products would carry a statement such as: "Sun Alert: the sun causes skin damage. Regular use of sunscreens over the years may reduce the chance of skin damage, some types of skin cancer and other harmful effects due to the sun." The FDA said the highest permissible sun protection factor (SPF) that could be carried on sunscreen labels would be 30. Products with SPF's higher than 30 do not significantly reduce damage to the skin, the FDA noted. □ Michael Woods

In *World Book,* see **Safety.**

Sailing. See Boating.

San Diego. Drenching rains in January 1993 ended San Diego's six-year drought. The rainfall, coupled with melting snow in the nearby mountains, kept municipal reservoirs 90 percent full through the summer. The month was the wettest January, and the second-wettest month of any in the calendar, in San Diego history. A string of storms dumped a total of 9.1 inches (23.1 centimeters) of rain on the city, nearly as much as typically falls in an entire year.

On the downside, the winter storms were blamed for the deaths of 12 San Diego County residents and $193 million in property damage. Just across the border in Tijuana, Mexico, the toll was even worse, with flooding, mud slides, and exposure to the cold killing more than 30 people. San Diegans participated in a massive effort to aid their Mexican neighbors, donating blankets and food items.

President's town hall meeting. United States President Bill Clinton was in San Diego on May 17 for one of his televised "town hall meetings." Clinton visited the studios of KGTV, Channel 10, for an hour-long question-and-answer session with an audience of 65 San Diegans. Most of the questions focused on Clinton's new economic plan and, particularly, concerns about the fate of San Diego's defense industry. Clinton said his plan would encourage defense companies to develop nonmilitary products and would fund programs to retrain workers.

Narcotics tunnel discovered. On May 31, Mexican authorities discovered an unfinished 1,450-foot (442-meter) tunnel that was being secretly constructed from just inside the Mexican border to San Diego. According to U.S. and Mexican officials, the tunnel was being built by Mexican drug traffickers to smuggle narcotics into the United States.

The existence of the tunnel was discovered when Mexican law-enforcement agents were trying to track down drug kingpin Joaquín Guzman Loera. Guzman (who was finally apprehended on June 9) was being sought in connection with the May 24 shooting deaths of Roman Catholic Cardinal Juan Jesús Posadas Ocampo and six others in Guadalajara, Mexico. While searching a house in Tijuana used for drug operations, Mexican officials found documents describing the tunnel and showing that it began under a warehouse owned by Guzman.

College tuition controversy. In January, many older students at community colleges in San Diego and elsewhere in California were sent reeling by a more than eightfold increase in tuition. Fees for most students were raised from $6 to $10 per unit of credit, but for students already holding degrees the cost per unit jumped to $50. Thus, degreed students had to pay $150 to $200 for most classes.

The "differential fee," instituted to ease a strain on community college admissions and on the cash-strapped state budget, was aimed at discouraging students from enrolling in classes purely for enjoyment. But state officials underestimated the effect of the increase on people seeking training for new careers. Complaints about the fee hikes poured in to community colleges throughout San Diego. Meanwhile, the number of degree-holders enrolled at San Diego's community colleges declined by more than 50 percent during the year.

Naval training center slated to close. The San Diego Naval Training Center was one of 35 major U.S. military facilities recommended for closure on June 27 by the federal Defense Base Closure and Realignment Commission. Although Congress had not formally approved the commission's recommendations by year-end, it was expected that the training center would shut down by 1999.

***Tommy* gets Tonys.** *The Who's Tommy,* a new version of the rock opera *Tommy* that premiered at the La Jolla Playhouse in suburban San Diego in summer 1992, won five major Tony Awards on June 6, 1993. Des McAnuff, artistic director of the La Jolla Playhouse, captured the prize for best direction of a musical, and rock musician Peter Townshend, composer of the opera in the late 1960's for the British rock group The Who, shared a Tony for best original score. The musical also collected awards for choreography, lighting design, and scenic design. But the playhouse's proudest moment came when it received a special Tony for excellence by a regional theater.   □ Sharon K. Gillenwater

See also **City.** In *World Book,* see **San Diego.**

Saskatchewan. The difficulty of managing public finances during a recession became apparent on Jan. 8, 1993, when Saskatchewan's deputy premier and minister of finance, Edward Tchorzewski, resigned his position because of stress. Associate Finance Minister Janice MacKinnon took over his post in the New Democratic Party administration led by Premier Roy Romanow. MacKinnon was the first woman to become a minister of finance in Canada.

The new minister delivered a tough budget on March 1 but noted that it continued to show concern for those less fortunate. Although government operating expenses of $4.9 billion (all monetary figures are in Canadian dollars) were cut by 3.4 percent, MacKinnon maintained assistance for families of the working poor, single mothers, low-income seniors, and Indian and *métis* (people of mixed Indian and white ancestry) children. With a cumulative public debt of $14.9 billion and a population in which less than one-third of 1 million people pay income tax, prospects for revenue growth were dim.

Saskatchewan, which introduced the first medicare (public health care) system in North America in 1962, began a second stage of health-care reform in 1993. It set up 30 autonomous boards to administer its medicare system and planned to reduce its number of hospital beds from 7,284 to 4,300.   □ David M. L. Farr

In *World Book,* see **Saskatchewan.**

Saudi Arabia. King Fahd and other members of Saudi Arabia's ruling Saud family came under increasing criticism from the Saudi people in 1993. They were accused of autocratic rule, corruption, and financial mismanagement.

Economic woes. Western press reports in late August said that reckless spending had caused Saudi financial reserves to fall from $121 billion in 1984 to less than $51 billion in 1993. Of the $51 billion, only $7 billion was said to be *liquid reserves* (money easily accessed).

The reports, which Fahd condemned as a smear campaign, also claimed that the Saudi banking system was unstable. Government debt to Saudi banks was said to be $20 billion, 40 percent of all deposits. Further, Saudi royals were accused of not repaying billions in loans to the National Commercial Bank, the kingdom's largest bank. Observers noted that the government has the ability to generate considerable income. Saudi Arabia has the world's largest oil reserves and pumped about 8 million barrels of oil per day in 1993.

Dissenters. With few avenues to voice dissent, Islamic reformists and technocrats aired their criticisms by disseminating faxes and tape cassettes. Trying to quell criticism, Fahd appointed 60 citizens to a Consultative Council in August. But critics noted that the council had no legislative or veto power.

Human rights. International human rights activists increased their criticism of Saudi Arabia's human rights record in 1993. On May 12, Saudi authorities banned a Saudi human rights group, the Committee for the Defense of Legitimate Rights, that had announced its formation on May 3. Several of its members, some of whom were professors and lawyers, were stripped of their jobs, and some were arrested. At least nine academics alleged to be Islamic activists at King Saud University in Riyadh, the capital, were reportedly arrested in a similar crackdown in early September.

The highest number of recorded executions since 1987 were carried out in 1993. By August, about 60 people of different nationalities had been beheaded. Nearly half of those executed had been convicted of drug dealing. Human rights groups charged that the accused had inadequate guarantees for fair arrests and trials.

Regional tensions. Saudi-Iranian antagonisms flared on May 27 when Saudi authorities stopped an anti-American, anti-Saudi demonstration by Iranian pilgrims during the annual Islamic *hajj* (pilgrimage) to Mecca. In mid-August, Saudi Arabia warned foreign oil companies, as it had in 1992, to cease activities in a disputed, oil-rich area on the Yemen-Saudi border. □ Christine Helms

See also **Middle East** (Facts in brief table). In *World Book,* see **Saudi Arabia.**

School. See Education.

Senegal. See Africa.

Shalala, Donna E. (1941-   ), former chancellor of the University of Wisconsin at Madison, became United States secretary of health and human services on Jan. 22, 1993. She was expected to play a major role in one of President Bill Clinton's promised reforms, overhauling the nation's welfare system.

Shalala (pronounced *shuh-LAY-luh*) was born on Feb. 14, 1941, in Cleveland. After graduating in 1962 from Western College for Women in Oxford, Ohio, she joined the Peace Corps, serving as a teacher in Iran until 1964. Later, she studied political science at Syracuse University in Syracuse, N.Y., earning a master's degree in 1968 and a doctorate in 1970.

That same year, Shalala accepted a teaching position at the City University of New York (CUNY). From 1972 to 1979, she taught politics and education at Columbia University, also in New York City.

In 1977, Shalala was named an assistant secretary in the Department of Housing and Urban Development in the Administration of President Jimmy Carter. She left in 1980 to become president of Hunter College, part of CUNY. She was named chancellor of the University of Wisconsin in 1988.

At Wisconsin, Shalala sparked controversy. Conservatives criticized her emphasis on multiculturalism. On the other hand, several student groups said she was not truly committed to progressive ideas.

Shalala is single. She enjoys golf, mountain climbing, and tennis. □ David Dreier

Shalikashvili, John M. (1936-   ), the former commander of North Atlantic Treaty Organization (NATO) forces in Europe, became head of the United States Joint Chiefs of Staff on Oct. 25, 1993. Shalikashvili, the first foreign-born head of the Joint Chiefs, is a strong supporter of using military force to exercise American leadership in the world.

Shalikashvili (pronounced *shah lee kosh VEE lee*) was born on June 27, 1936, in Warsaw, Poland. His father was a senior officer in the Polish military who served with the German Army during World War II (1939-1945). The family immigrated to the United States in 1952, settling in Peoria, Ill.

Shalikashvili graduated from Bradley University in Peoria in 1958 and then joined the Army. He attended Officer Candidate School at Fort Sill, Okla., and was commissioned a second lieutenant in 1959.

After rising to the rank of major, Shalikashvili was sent to Vietnam in 1968, where he served as an adviser to South Vietnamese forces. In 1970, he received a master's degree in international affairs at George Washington University in Washington, D.C.

Shalikashvili held a number of command posts in the 1970's and 1980's and took command of NATO forces in June 1992. He and his wife, Joan, have a son, Brandt. □ David Dreier

Sierra Leone. See Africa.

Singapore. See Asia.

Skating. See Hockey; Ice skating; Sports.

Lasse Kjus of Norway celebrates on the way to winning the combined competition at the world alpine skiing championships in Shizukuishi, Japan, in January.

Skiing. Kjetil-Andre Aamodt, age 21, of Norway established himself as the sport's newest superstar at the Alpine events of the 1993 World Ski Championships. Marc Girardelli of Luxembourg and Anita Wachter of Austria won two world medals each en route to World Cup overall titles.

World championships. In competition from February 3 to 14 in Japan, Aamodt won the men's slalom and giant slalom and finished second in the combined (a special downhill and a special slalom). The super giant slalom, which Aamodt won in the 1992 Winter Olympics, was snowed out on the final day. Lasse Kjus of Norway won the combined, and Urs Lehmann of Switzerland won the downhill.

In women's competition, Kate Pace of Canada won the downhill. She skied with a cast protecting her left wrist, which she broke less than three weeks before the competition. The other winners were Katja Seizinger of Germany in the super giant slalom, Carole Merle of France in the giant slalom, Karin Buder of Austria in slalom, and Miriam Vogt of Germany in the combined.

Of the 27 medals, Austria won 8; Norway, 7; and the United States and Germany, 3 each. American Julie Parisien of Sugarloaf Mountain, Me., won a silver medal in the women's slalom; Picabo Street of Sun Valley, Ida., won a silver medal in the women's combined; and A. J. Kitt of Rochester, N.Y., won a bronze medal in the men's downhill.

World Cup. In races held from November 1992 through March 1993 in Canada, Europe, and the United States, Girardelli won a record fifth overall title. (Gustavo Thoeni of Italy and Pirmin Zurbriggen of Switzerland had won four each.) The 29-year-old Girardelli, a native Austrian, finished with 1,379 points to 1,347 for Aamodt, the runner-up. The leading American was Tommy Moe of Palmer, Alaska, who finished 31st with 240 points. Wachter won the women's title with 1,286 points to 1,266 for the second-place Seizinger. Kerrin Lee-Gartner of Canada finished 9th with 565 points, and Parisien was 27th with 292 points. A month after the season began, Petra Kronberger of Austria, overall champion the three previous years, unexpectedly retired at age 23.

Other. In the Nordic events of the World Ski Championships, held from February 18 to 28 in Falun, Sweden, Bjorn Dahlie of Norway won three gold medals in cross-country. Dahlie was the men's World Cup champion, and Lyubov Yegorova of Russia was the women's champion.

In freestyle skiing, four skiers won both the world championship and World Cup titles in their respective specialties. They were Ellen Breen of Los Angeles (for women's ballet), Jean-Luc Brassard of Canada (for men's moguls), Stine Lise Hattestad of Norway (for women's moguls), and Lina Tcheryazova of Uzbekistan (for women's aerials). □ Frank Litsky

In *World Book*, see **Skiing.**

Slovakia became an independent state on Jan. 1, 1993, when the Czechoslovak federation broke apart into its two republics. The separation of Slovakia and the Czech Republic, approved by Czechoslovakia's parliament in November 1992, created problems for both new countries.

Economic woes. Slovakia, poorer and less industrialized than its Czech neighbor, had suffered most from efforts to reintroduce a market economy after the fall of Communism in 1989. Slovaks' standard of living fell more sharply in 1993, as industrial output shrank and exports plummeted. At the end of July, more than 13 percent of Slovak workers were unemployed, and inflation, fueled by a growing foreign debt, stood at more than 14 percent.

Plans for the Czech Republic and Slovakia to use one currency for six months gave way on February 8 to the creation of separate currencies. On July 10, the Slovak government devalued the Slovak koruna by 10.4 percent as a condition for receiving an $89-million loan from the International Monetary Fund, an international agency associated with the United Nations (UN). Meanwhile, Slovakia's trade with the Czech Republic dropped about 30 percent in the first half of 1993.

Support for the government of Prime Minister Vladimir Mečiar, who had led Slovakia's drive for independence, plummeted after January 1993. Mečiar also faced opposition from within his Movement for a Democratic Slovakia (HZDS), especially from Foreign Affairs Minister Milan Knazko. On March 19, Slovak President Michal Kovac, who had been elected by parliament on February 15, dismissed Knazko under pressure from Mečiar. Knazko and seven other HZDS deputies left the party, leaving the HZDS controlling only 66 of 150 seats in parliament. On November 10, after several months of negotiation, the HZDS formed a new coalition with the Slovak National Party, which had left the government in March.

Early fears that Mečiar would move dramatically to restrict political liberties proved unfounded. However, opposition critics denounced government efforts to control Slovak newspapers and other media.

Relations with Hungary. Critics also pointed to the government's treatment of Slovakia's 600,000 ethnic Hungarians as evidence of its insensitivity to minority concerns. In January, the government began removing Hungarian street signs in predominantly Hungarian districts. The issue complicated Slovakia's relations with Hungary, already on edge because of Slovakia's 1992 construction of a controversial dam on the Danube River between the two countries. (See **Hungary.**)   □ Sharon L. Wolchik

See also **Czech Republic; Europe** (Facts in brief table). In the World Book Supplement section, see **Slovakia.**

Slovenia. See Europe.

Soccer.
The most significant moments of 1993 soccer involved France's Olympique Marseilles team, first on the playing field, then before police interrogators and in court. On May 26, in the European Cup final in Munich, Germany, Olympique Marseilles defeated AC Milan of Italy, 1-0, to become the first French team to win a major European championship.

Within weeks, Olympique Marseilles was involved in a bribery scandal. One player, Jean-Jacques Eydelie, and the general manager, Jean-Pierre Bernes, were accused of trying to bribe two players on the Valenciennes team to play at less than their best in a league match against Olympique Marseilles on May 2. The plan was for Olympique Marseilles to save energy for the European Cup final six days later.

Eydelie admitted his role in July. Bernes said he was innocent and resigned on July 25. In September, the Union of European Football Associations (UEFA) banned Olympique Marseilles from defending its European Cup title, and the French federation banned Bernes and the players involved.

Parma of Italy won the European Cup Winners Cup on May 19, and Juventus of Italy won the UEFA Cup, also on May 19. In April, Arsenal won the English League Cup and the English Football Association Cup in May to become the first team to win both titles in the same year. São Paulo of Brazil won the Libertadores Cup that crowns the South American club champion.

The U.S. National Team, preparing for the 1994 World Cup tournament in the United States, experienced highs and lows. It upset England, played respectably in a 4-3 loss to Germany, struggled against lesser teams, such as Panama and Honduras, and was badly beaten by Mexico. Before the U.S. Cup, which was held from June 6 to 19 against England, Germany, and Brazil in four U.S. cities, the Americans had won only 1 of 14 international matches during 1993. But on June 9, the U.S. team shocked England, 2-0.

Next came the Gold Cup held from July 10 to 25 in Mexico City for national teams from North America and the Caribbean. The United States won four consecutive matches, then lost to Mexico, 4-0, in the final.

World Cup. Qualifying continued for the 1994 World Cup competition in the United States. The 24 qualifiers were the United States as host, Germany as defending champion, Mexico, Argentina, Brazil, Colombia, Bolivia, Italy, Spain, the Netherlands, Belgium, Ireland, Switzerland, Romania, Bulgaria, Norway, Sweden, Greece, Russia, Morocco, Saudi Arabia, Nigeria, Cameroon, and South Korea.

Zambia's 18-man team was killed April 28 in a plane crash en route to a qualifying match. A new Zambian team formed, but it failed to get beyond the qualifying competition.   □ Frank Litsky

In *World Book,* see Soccer.

Social security.
A Cabinet nominee's woes in 1993 provoked a months-long debate over a law requiring social security taxes to be paid on household help. A violation of the law helped lead to the withdrawal on January 22 of Zoë Baird as President Bill Clinton's nominee for attorney general.

Baird, who was senior vice president at Aetna Life and Casualty Company of Hartford, Conn., had been nominated on Dec. 24, 1992. But during Senate confirmation hearings in January 1993, Baird admitted that she and her husband had not paid social security taxes on a couple from Peru who worked in the Bairds' household. Under federal law, if a household worker earns at least $50 in a quarter, the employer must pay social security and Medicare taxes on the worker's wages.

Change debated. The Internal Revenue Service in 1993 estimated that about 1.5 million American families failed to pay social security taxes for household help. For many violators, the trouble with the law stemmed from the low threshold wage for triggering tax payments. When the law was enacted in 1950, a worker had to earn $50 a quarter to warrant social security taxes and to become eligible for social security benefits later in life. Since that year, the threshold wage for receiving benefits has gradually increased. It equaled $590 a quarter in 1993. But the threshold wage for paying taxes has remained at $50.

A U.S. helicopter hovers over burning tanks commanded by Somali warlord Mohamed Farah Aideed in June after an air strike against the rebel leader.

During the debate on Clinton's budget bill in the summer of 1993, the House voted to raise the quarterly threshold for paying taxes to $450. However, the amendment was not included in the Senate-House compromise bill that was signed into law on August 10.

New commissioner. On August 3, Clinton said he would nominate Shirley S. Chater, president of Texas Woman's University in Denton, for commissioner of the Social Security Administration. White House officials also revealed that Chater from 1969 to 1975 had failed to pay social security taxes on part-time baby sitters but that she had since settled her tax bill. Chater was confirmed on Oct. 7, 1993.

Benefits rise. Monthly social security benefits were set to rise by 2.6 percent beginning on Jan. 3, 1994, under the annual cost-of-living adjustment program. The increase, the second smallest in almost 20 years, would boost the average monthly check by $17, from $657 to $674. On the same date, the maximum wage subject to the social security payroll tax was to rise from $57,600 to $60,600.

As part of the federal budget package passed in August 1993, the percentage of social security benefits subject to income tax rose from 50 percent to 85 percent for individuals earning more than $34,000 and couples earning more than $44,000.

☐ Frank Cormier and Margot Cormier

In *World Book,* see **Social security.**

Somalia. United States and United Nations (UN) forces managed in 1993 to end the terrible famine that killed more than 300,000 Somalis in 1992. They were unable, however, to resolve the civil war that, along with drought, had led to the mass starvation.

United States-led forces, which arrived in Somalia in December 1992, moved swiftly to distribute food to the populace and to end the fighting between rival warlords. On January 15, the warlords signed a cease-fire in Addis Ababa, Ethiopia.

But strife continued. On February 23, the troops of one of the principal warlords, General Mohamed Farah Aideed, were attacked by soldiers of a rival rebel leader. The next day, after Aideed blamed the attack on the foreign intervention forces, Aideed's supporters rioted in Mogadishu, the capital.

Shifting the burden. On March 26, the UN Security Council voted to replace U.S.-led forces with a UN-commanded peacekeeping force that was to remain until a Somali government formed.

On March 27, rival Somali leaders meeting in Addis Ababa agreed to establish a transitional government. On May 4, the UN force took over from the U.S. forces. Some U.S. military units were placed under UN command, but most of the American troops were transported back to the United States.

The UN forces lacked a clear policy on how to deal with the Somali warlords. General Aideed insisted on retaining his weapons and continuing his dominance in Mogadishu, and violence rocked the capital almost daily. Only in the countryside was there some success in restoring peace.

On June 5, Somali rebels attacked UN forces in Mogadishu, killing 24 Pakistani troops. Aideed was blamed for the violence, and the UN put out a reward for his capture. United States forces joined the search but failed to capture Aideed.

Americans question mission. In the United States, there was growing public concern about the U.S. role in Somalia. Concern became outrage after a battle in Mogadishu with Aideed's forces on October 3 and 4 in which 18 U.S. soldiers were killed. Americans were shocked by a photograph of Somalis dragging an American soldier's body through the streets.

On October 7, President Bill Clinton announced that he was sending reinforcements to Somalia, and he promised that most U.S. forces would leave there by March 31, 1994. Clinton also sent diplomat Robert B. Oakley to Somalia to seek peace terms.

Another peace attempt. In November, it appeared that Somalia might return to chaos, as battles between warlords increased. On December 1, Somali leaders meeting again in Addis Ababa agreed to work toward peace. Aideed participated in the conference but was unable to agree on terms for a settlement. ☐ Mark DeLancey

See also **Africa** (Facts in brief table). In *World Book,* see **Somalia.**

South Africa. Negotiations aimed at establishing a multiracial democracy in which South Africa's black majority will finally be granted political power made great progress in 1993. But that progress—which included the adoption of an interim Constitution in November—was marred by many outbreaks of violence.

On January 29, State President Frederik Willem de Klerk instructed Parliament to draft laws to end white rule. On February 2, the government proposed a bill of rights that would protect the white minority after it loses power. But the African National Congress (ANC), the major black group in the long fight against *apartheid* (racial separation), rejected the document, saying it would preserve white privileges.

On February 18, the government and the ANC agreed on a plan by which whites and other sizable minority groups would participate in a transitional government for five years after the end of white rule. White rule would end with elections to be held by April 1994, in which blacks would vote for the first time. Voters would elect a 400-member Parliament charged with drafting a new constitution.

Several white and black groups voiced strong opposition to the transitional-government plan. The principal opponents on the black side were the right wing Inkatha Freedom Party—an organization based on the Zulu ethnic group and led by Chief Mangosuthu Gatsha Buthelezi—and the left wing Pan Afri-

Residents of a township near Johannesburg, South Africa, demonstrate in April to protest the murder of black leader Chris Hani by white extremists.

can Congress (PAC). Among whites, a number of right wing proapartheid groups came together to form the Afrikaner People's Front, which demanded the formation of a state for *Afrikaners* (South Africans of largely Dutch descent).

Discussions in Johannesburg. Talks aimed at hammering out the details of the transitional government began in April in Johannesburg. The assembly included 26 political parties and interest groups. On June 3, the conferees set April 27, 1994, as the date for elections. Inkatha and right wing white groups opposed the decision. ANC President Nelson Mandela tried to win Buthelezi over but without success. On July 18, Inkatha withdrew from the talks.

On September 7, the conferees agreed to form a multiparty committee known as the Transitional Executive Council to oversee the police, army, budget, and civil service from October 1993 until the April elections. The transitional council held its first meeting on December 7, which was hailed as the beginning of a new democratic era.

Murder and violence. On April 10, Chris Hani, head of the South African Communist Party and a leader of the ANC, was shot to death outside his Boksburg home by white extremists. Hani's murder led to rioting in several black townships. On October 14, two white men affiliated with the South African right wing were convicted of killing Hani. The next day, they were sentenced to death.

Violence by both blacks and whites provided an ugly counterpoint to the negotiations in Johannesburg. The white community was particularly horrified by a crime that occurred at a Cape Town church on July 25. While a service was in progress, black gunmen burst through the door and attacked the white worshipers with automatic rifles and hand grenades, killing 11 and wounding more than 50.

A dramatic incident of white violence occurred on June 25, when hundreds of members of the right wing Afrikaner Resistance Movement stormed the constitutional talks in Johannesburg. The shock of the event was thought to increase support for the constitutional proceedings among white moderates.

South Africa's economy showed little signs of improvement during the year. Unemployment remained high and foreign investment low. Both Mandela and de Klerk visited the United States in late June and early July to meet with President Bill Clinton and other U.S. leaders, mainly to seek funds for the renewal of the South African economy.

Peace Prize. For their efforts to bring racial harmony and democracy to South Africa, Mandela and de Klerk were jointly awarded the 1993 Nobel Peace Prize in October. ☐ Mark DeLancey

See also **Africa** (Facts in brief table); **Nobel Prizes**. In *World Book*, see **South Africa**.

South America. See Latin America.

South Carolina. See State government.

South Dakota. See State government.

Space exploration. Mission failures and delays troubled the National Aeronautics and Space Administration (NASA) in 1993. An unmanned mission to Mars disappeared in space. Three spy satellites blew up, and communications were lost with a weather satellite and a science satellite. Congress almost eliminated the space station program, and the project was scaled back to cut its rapidly rising costs. Several space shuttle missions were delayed repeatedly, one of them five times. On the positive side, the Jupiter-bound Galileo spacecraft took rare close-up photographs of an asteroid. Also, NASA flew seven successful shuttle missions during the year, including one to fix the Hubble Space Telescope.

A spacewalk and child's play. The space shuttle Endeavour lifted off from the Kennedy Space Center (KSC) in Florida on January 13. Six hours later, the crew of five launched a Tracking and Data Relay Satellite into an orbit 22,300 miles (35,900 kilometers) above the equator. The satellite is part of a space-based network that provides communications with shuttles and other spacecraft in Earth orbit.

On January 17, two astronauts took a 4½-hour spacewalk to practice tasks that will be required for building the proposed space station. During the six-day mission, the crew also measured X rays coming from regions of space between stars; conducted experiments aimed at obtaining a better understanding of how near-weightless conditions affect plant reproduction; and did a live television show in which they used toys to demonstrate principles of physics.

Discovery and Columbia flights. After two delays because of technical problems, the shuttle Discovery blasted into orbit on April 8 in a spectacular night launch from KSC. The five-person crew operated instruments to measure Earth's protective ozone layer and determine how it is affected by energy from the sun and the chemical makeup of the atmosphere. The astronauts also released, and later retrieved, a small satellite to obtain measurements of the solar wind, an outflow of charged particles from the sun. After a one-day delay caused by stormy weather, Discovery landed in Florida on April 17.

Nine days later, the shuttle Columbia blasted off on a mission delayed since February. While in orbit, the crew of five Americans and two Germans conducted 88 experiments in materials science, biology, robotics, astronomy, and Earth observation. The experiments were carried out in the so-called German Spacelab, designed and built by Germany and carried in the shuttle's cargo bay. Columbia ended the mission with a landing at Edwards Air Force Base in California on May 6.

Satellite retrieval. Endeavour soared into orbit again on June 21. During the mission, the crew of six used a robot arm to snag a European Space Agency satellite, named EURECA, in orbit since August 1992. Two astronauts took a spacewalk to help bring the satellite into the cargo bay.

The DC-X, a light, single-stage experimental rocket being developed by the Department of Defense, lifts off from a test site in New Mexico in August.

Endeavour also carried a commercial facility known as Spacehab in its cargo bay. NASA, private companies, and universities leased space in this laboratory for space-based experiments. Endeavour landed in Florida on July 1.

Testing tools. After a total of five delays, Discovery carried five astronauts into orbit on September 12. They launched an Advanced Communications Technology Satellite, designed to rapidly relay large amounts of information to various ground locations. The mission also included a spacewalk to test tools for repairing the Hubble Space Telescope. On September 22, Discovery returned to Earth, touching down for the first nighttime landing of a shuttle at KSC at about 4 a.m.

Longest shuttle flight. Columbia went into orbit again on October 18, following two launch delays. The seven-person crew included two physicians and the first veterinarian to fly in space. The astronauts conducted medical experiments on the effects of weightlessness on themselves and four dozen rats in a specially equipped Spacelab module. The shuttle landed in California on November 1 after a mission lasting 14 days 13 minutes, nearly five hours longer than any previous shuttle flight.

Fixing the Hubble. Endeavour flew in space from December 2 to 13 to carry out repairs to the flawed Hubble Space Telescope. The telescope was brought into the shuttle's cargo bay on December 4. In the following days, the astronauts installed new optics and a new camera on the Hubble and also re-placed gyroscopes and solar panels. The shuttle landed at KSC shortly after midnight on December 13.

Mars goes unobserved. The worst setback for the U.S. space program in 1993 came in August when the Mars Observer spacecraft, a $980-million project, was lost in space. Launched on Sept. 25, 1992, the unmanned spacecraft made a 450-million-mile (725-million-kilometer) trip to the vicinity of Mars in 11 months. The Mars Observer, the first U.S. mission to the red planet since 1975, was to have studied surface features and weather on Mars for one Martian year (687 Earth days). On August 21, three days before the space probe was scheduled to fire its braking rockets and go into a polar orbit around Mars, NASA lost radio contact with the craft. Experts speculated that the Mars Observer may have exploded as the braking rockets attempted to fire. Another possibility is that the automatic control systems failed, and the spacecraft kept going in space.

Other losses. On August 2, a Titan 4 rocket carrying three spy satellites exploded shortly after its launch from Vandenberg Air Force Base in California. On August 21, contact was lost with a weather satellite launched on August 9. Another failure occurred on October 8 when ground controllers lost contact with the $228-million Landsat 6 satellite, launched three days earlier for the purpose of collecting environmental data about Earth.

Space station. Congress, by a narrow vote on June 23, approved funding for a scaled-back version of the proposed U.S. space station, Freedom. The name of the space station was due to be changed to reflect the altered design. Freedom would have cost at least $31 billion, by estimates in early 1993. The smaller version of the space station was expected to be placed in orbit in 10 years for $19.4 billion. Part of the savings may be achieved by bringing Russia into the venture.

Russian moonlight. On February 4, an unmanned Russian cargo spaceship, which had delivered supplies to the Russian Mir space station, deployed a large plastic reflector 66 feet (20 meters) in diameter. The reflector automatically unfurled from the spaceship like an opened parachute and went into orbit around the Earth. The aluminum and plastic "mirror" cast a diffuse beam of reflected sunlight 2.5 miles (4 kilometers) wide onto the nightside of the Earth. The experiment tested the idea that such space mirrors might someday enable society to save on electricity by using sunlight to illuminate selected areas of the Earth at night.

Asteroid watch. On Aug. 28, 1993, the Galileo spacecraft, launched in 1989, took photographs of an asteroid called Ida from a distance of about 1,500 miles (2,400 kilometers). Ida is about 32 miles (52 kilometers) long. □ William J. Cromie

See also **Astronomy.** In *World Book,* see **Space travel.**

Spain. Prime Minister Felipe González Márquez lost his parliamentary majority in national elections on June 6, 1993, but he and his Socialist Workers' Party (PSOE) were able to stay in power with the support of two smaller nationalist parties. It was González' fourth consecutive term as prime minister. González later named a moderate Cabinet to run the government until 1997.

Legislative elections. Opinion polls before the elections for the 350-seat Chamber of Deputies, the lower house in the Cortes (parliament), had suggested the PSOE would finish second to the conservative Popular Party (PP). The PSOE had been hit by financial scandals in 1993, and it had overseen Spain's recent economic downturn. But the party made a surprisingly strong showing, winning 39 percent of the vote and 159 seats, down from 40 percent and 176 seats in the previous election in 1989. The PP did surpass its 1989 tally, winning 35 percent of the vote and 141 seats, up from 26 percent and 106 seats.

The United Left, a coalition of left wing groups led by the Communist Party, won 10 percent of the vote and 18 seats, up slightly from 9 percent and 17 seats. Of the sizable nationalist parties, the Catalán Convergence and Union Party (CIU) won 5 percent of the vote and 17 seats, one fewer than in 1989, and the Basque Nationalist Party (PNV) won 1 percent of the vote and 5 seats, the same as in 1989.

Minority rule. González sought a coalition government with the CIU and PNV, whose 22 seats, combined with the PSOE's 159 seats, would have given González a 181-seat majority. But the two parties wanted more power for the governments in their regions than González was willing to give, so González rejected that idea. Instead, for lesser concessions, the two parties agreed simply to not topple González' government in confidence votes in the Chamber of Deputies, thus giving Spain its first minority government since democracy was restored in 1975.

On July 13, 1993, González named a moderate Cabinet with eight new ministers. None came from the CIU or the PNV, but the parties were expected to get Cabinet representation later in González' term.

Economic crisis. Spain in 1993 suffered through a deep recession that sent unemployment above 20 percent, one of the highest rates in the European Community (EC). On August 4, González unveiled a special budget that drastically reduced government spending and raised taxes. The government's budget deficit rose sharply in 1993, partly due to higher-than-expected unemployment payments.

For most of 1993, Spain kept interest rates above 10 percent to fight inflation and keep the value of Spain's currency, the peseta, linked to the values of other European currencies in the EC's Exchange Rate Mechanism (ERM). Rates stayed high even after the ERM eased its rules on August 2. □ Philip Revzin

See also **Europe** (Facts in brief table). In *World Book,* see **Spain.**

Sports. Some of the fun in sports suffered from fan violence, continued sanctions against college athletic programs for breaking recruiting rules, and escalating franchise fees and salaries in 1993.

Violence. On February 9, during the victory parade after the Dallas Cowboys won professional football's Super Bowl, violence by onlookers sent 26 people to the hospital and resulted in 25 arrests. On June 9, the night the Canadiens won the National Hockey League's (NHL) Stanley Cup championship, looting and vandalism marred Montreal's downtown celebration, resulting in 115 arrests, 168 injuries, and millions of dollars of property damage. On June 20, the night the Bulls won the National Basketball Association (NBA) championship, Chicago placed 5,000 police officers on duty downtown. Even so, violent celebrations resulted in three deaths and 682 arrests.

NCAA. A major function of the National Collegiate Athletic Association (NCAA), the major governing body for college sports, is to ensure that athletes receive no more financial help than the rules allow. In 1993, one case proved especially embarrassing.

The University of Virginia was accused of illegally providing no-interest loans to athletes from 1987 to 1991. Dick Schultz, the NCAA's executive director, had been Virginia's athletic director from 1981 to 1987. NCAA investigators found Virginia guilty and on May 6, 1993, placed the university on probation for two years.

Schultz said he had no knowledge of the loans, but James Park, Jr., a lawyer hired by the NCAA to determine the facts, said Schultz did know about some of the loans. On May 11, Schultz resigned as the NCAA executive director, and on November 5, the NCAA hired Cedric Dempsey, the athletic director at the University of Arizona, as his replacement.

Among the major colleges that the NCAA penalized for illegal payments to athletes were Auburn and the University of Nevada, Las Vegas (UNLV). On August 18, Auburn's football program received a two-year probation, a two-year ban on postseason play, and a one-year ban on television appearances. The UNLV basketball program admitted to 26 violations and was placed on a three-year probation and given several minor penalties.

Big dollars. Costs continued to climb for expansion franchises in major sports. The National Football League awarded 1995 franchises to Charlotte, N.C., on Oct. 26, 1993, and Jacksonville, Fla., on November 30 for $140 million each. On November 4, the NBA awarded a 1995-1996 franchise to Toronto for $125-million. The Colorado Rockies and the Florida Marlins joined major league baseball in April 1993 after paying franchise fees of $95 million each. The Anaheim, Calif., Mighty Ducks and the Florida Panthers started playing in the NHL in October for franchise fees of $50 million each.

Salaries climbed in the four major team sports, especially in basketball. Larry Johnson signed a contract extension with the Charlotte Hornets that raised his salary to $84 million over 12 years. Chris Webber, a rookie, signed with the Golden State Warriors for $74.4 million over 15 years. Anfernee Hardaway, another rookie, signed with the Orlando Magic for $68 million over 12 years. Derrick Coleman of the New Jersey Nets turned down an offer of $69-million over 8 years that would have given him the highest annual salary in team sports.

The money was not all for the athletes. Mike Krzyzewski, the Duke University basketball coach, switched his team from Adidas to Nike shoes and agreed to do occasional endorsements. In return, Nike agreed to pay him $375,000 per year for 15 years plus a $1-million signing bonus.

Little League World Series. Long Beach, Calif., won its second consecutive Little League World Series championship on September 4 with a 3-2 win over Panama. Long Beach was the first U.S. team to repeat as champion in the 47-year history of the series.

Among the winners in 1993 were:

Cycling. Miguel Indurain of Spain, over a nine-week span from May to July, won the Tour de France for the third consecutive year and the Tour of Italy for the second consecutive year. But in the world championships on August 29 in Oslo, Norway, he finished second to 21-year-old Lance Armstrong of Austin, Tex. On June 6 in Philadelphia, Armstrong won a $1-million bonus by sweeping an American three-race series.

Diving. China won all six gold medals in the World Cup competition in May and June in Beijing. Its winners included 14-year-old Chi Bin on the women's platform. The United States, normally a diving power, won only two fourth places. Germany swept the four springboard titles, and Russia won the platform titles in the European championships in Sheffield, England.

Fencing. Germany won three of the 10 titles and Russia, Hungary, and Italy two each in the world championships in July in Essen, Germany. The best individual placing by an American was 25th in women's foil by Ann Marsh of Royal Oak, Mich. In the United States championships, Michael Marx of South Bend, Ind., won the men's foils for the eighth time, and his wife, Leslie, won the women's epee.

Gymnastics. Sixteen-year-old Shannon Miller of Edmond, Okla., won the gold medals in the women's all-around, uneven bars, and floor exercise in the world championships held from April 13 to 18 in Birmingham, England. Vitali Scherbo of Belarus won the men's all-around, parallel bars, and vault. Miller also won the all-around in the United States championships held from August 25 to 28 in Salt Lake City, Utah, and the United States Olympic Festival in San Antonio in July.

Rowing. The German men and Romanian women won the eight-oared titles in the world championships, which ended on September 5 in Roudnice, Czech Republic. Germany's eight, competing as Hansa Dortmund, also won the Grand Challenge Cup in England's Henley Royal Regatta. Brown University's men and Princeton's women won the United States collegiate and Eastern sprint titles.

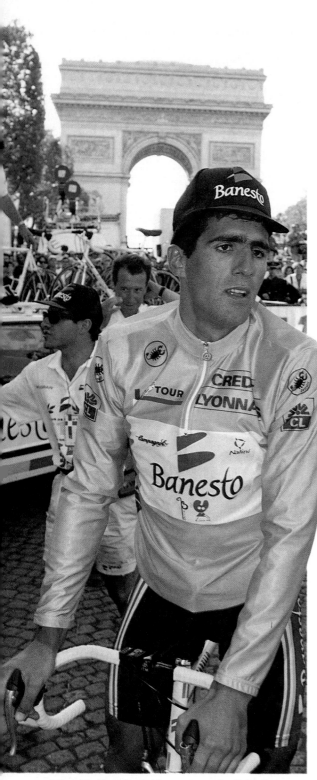

Miguel Indurain of Spain rests near the finish line in Paris after winning his third consecutive Tour de France in July.

Wrestling. The United States won its first-ever team title in the world freestyle championships held from August 25 to 28 in Toronto, Canada. The U.S. team produced three individual champions in Terry Brands of Iowa City, Iowa, at 57 kilograms (125.7 pounds); Tom Brands, his twin, at 62 kilograms (136.7 pounds); and Bruce Baumgartner of Cambridge Springs, Pa., super heavyweight. Russia won the world Greco-Roman team title.

Other champions

Archery, world target champions: men, Kyung Mo Park, South Korea; women, Hyo Jung Kim, South Korea.

Badminton, world champions: men, Joko Suprianto, Indonesia; women, Susi Susanti, Indonesia.

Biathlon, world champions: men's 10-kilometer, Mark Kirchner, Germany; men's 20-kilometer, Andreas Zingerle, Italy; women's 7.5-kilometer, Myriam Bedard, Canada; women's 15-kilometer, Petra Schaff, Germany.

Bobsledding, world champions: two-man sled, Christoph Langen, Germany; four-man sled, Gustav Weder, Switzerland.

Canoeing, world champions: men's 500-meter canoe, Nikolai Buhalov, Bulgaria; men's 500-meter kayak, Mikko Kolehmainen, Finland; women's 500-meter kayak, Birgit Schmidt, Germany.

Cross-country, world champions: men, William Sigei, Kenya; women, Albertina Dias, Portugal.

Equestrian, World Cup champions: jumping, Ludger Beerbaum, Germany; dressage, Monica Theodorescu, Germany.

Handball, U.S. four-wall champions: men, David Chapman, Long Beach, Calif.; women, Anna Engele, St. Paul, Minn.

Judo, world open champions: men, Rafael Kubacki, Poland; women, Beata Maksymow, Poland.

Lacrosse, World Cup women's champion: United States.

Luge, world champions: men, Wendel Suckow, Marquette, Mich.; women, Gerda Weissensteiner, Italy.

Modern pentathlon, world champions: men, Richard Phelps, England; women, Eva Fjellerup, Denmark.

Motorcycle racing, world 500-cc champion: Kevin Schwantz, Paige, Tex.

Racquetball, U.S. pro series champions: men, Cliff Swain, Boston; women, Michelle Gould, Boise, Ida.

Shooting, world skeet champions: men, Dean Clark, Hendersonville, Tenn.; women, Svetlana Diomina, Russia.

Softball, U.S. fast-pitch champions: men, National Health Care, Sioux City, Iowa; women, Redding (Calif.) Rebels.

Table tennis, world champions: men, Jean-Philippe Gatien, France; women, Hwa Hyunjung, China.

Synchronized swimming, World Cup solo champion: Becky Dyroen-Lancer, Campbell, Calif.

Triathlon, world champions: men, Spencer Smith, Australia; women, Michellie Jones, Australia.

Volleyball, World Grand Champions Cup winners: men, Italy; women, Cuba.

Water polo, FINA Cup champions: men, Italy; women, the Netherlands.

Water skiing, world overall champions: men, Patrice Martin, France; women, Natalia Rumiantseva, Russia.

☐ Frank Litsky

See also articles on the various sports. In *World Book,* see articles on the sports.

Sri Lanka suffered in 1993 more of the violence that has killed some 50,000 people in the last 10 years. On May 1, 1993, President Ranasinghe Premadasa and 23 others were killed in Colombo, the capital, when a youth on a bicycle rode into a May Day parade and detonated a bomb strapped to his body. Police believed the assassinations were organized by the Liberation Tigers of Tamil Eelam. The Tigers have been fighting since 1983 to gain independence for the Tamil ethnic minority in the northeast section of Sri Lanka.

Eight days earlier, on April 23, a gunman shot Lalith Athulathmudali, a leading political opponent of Premadasa and long a leader in the fight against Tamil separatists. Athulathmudali's supporters blamed the president for their leader's death.

Tamil Tigers denied murdering either of the political leaders. But on May 9, police said that they identified the assassins of both leaders as Tamils.

New president. Prime Minister Dingiri Banda Wijetunga was sworn in as acting president several hours after Premadasa's death. On May 7, Parliament held a special presidential election in which Wijetunga ran and won unopposed. He will serve out Premadasa's term, which ends in December 1994. Even without a strong political base, the 71-year-old Wijetunga assumed broad powers under Sri Lanka's form of government. He immediately appointed Ranil Wickremasinghe as prime minister.

Election setback. In what many observers considered a referendum on Premadasa's rule, the United National Party (UNP) on May 17, 1993, suffered its first electoral setback since 1977. A coalition of leftist parties that was led by the Sri Lanka Freedom Party won control of the Western Provincial Council, which governs Colombo and the surrounding area. The UNP won majorities in four other provincial councils and pluralities in two councils. Elections were not held in the northern and northeastern provinces, where Tamils predominate, because of the guerrilla war.

Army offensive. On Sept. 28, 1993, the army launched its largest offensive against the Tamils in two years. Troops supported by planes and tanks tried to destroy Tiger supply facilities in the Jaffna area near Sri Lanka's northern tip. More than 200 guerrillas and 119 soldiers were killed by the time the offensive ended on October 4. The Tigers said that the bombardments killed 100 civilians.

Tamils strike back. The Tigers retaliated against the government on November 11 by attacking the main Sri Lankan army and navy base at Pooneryn in the Jaffna area. In the largest battle of the civil war, more than 1,000 people on both sides were killed. The Tigers captured large amounts of ammunition and artillery. The four-day battle was a major setback for the government. □ Henry S. Bradsher

See also **Asia** (Facts in brief table). In *World Book,* see **Sri Lanka.**

State government. Fewer states found themselves running out of money as they approached the end of their fiscal year on June 30, 1993. Less than half the states made midyear cuts to their fiscal 1993 budgets, contrasted with 35 states that had belatedly slashed their 1992 budgets. An April 1993 report by the National Association of State Budget Officers attributed the improvement to more conservative revenue estimates.

Taxes. Most states also adopted their budgets on time—before June 30—and without major tax hikes. State taxes increased by only 1.2 percent nationwide, the smallest increase in dollar amounts since 1989. But California, Illinois, Maine, New York, and Vermont continued tax hikes that had been scheduled to expire in 1993. California, for example, took from local governments $2.6 billion in property taxes to finance schools, but cushioned the blow to those governments by extending a half-cent sales tax until December.

The lack of state tax activity could be partly attributed to a tax revolt among the public. Citizens voted down tax proposals in Michigan, Montana, and Texas. In Washington state, Governor Mike Lowry faced protest rallies against his proposal to tax services. In response, the legislature increased business and income taxes and taxed only a few consumer services.

Most states experienced significant budget increases in the areas of Medicaid (the federal and state health program for the poor) and correctional facilities. Medicaid spending increased 7.5 percent overall. Corrections spending nationwide increased 11 percent in fiscal 1994, compared with a 7 percent increase in 1993. Most of the increase was for new prison construction.

Education. In Michigan, the legislature voted in July to eliminate property taxes to fund schools. The law wiped out $6.5 billion that schools had been counting on for the next academic year. Governor John Engler signed the measure in August and asked the legislature in October to raise sales taxes and give parents the revenues to pay for their children's education at the school of their choice. The legislature faced a deadline of December 31 to approve the plan or to come up with a new one.

Texas school districts in June sued the state over a new plan to equalize funding among wealthy and poor school districts. The plan would allow less wealthy school districts to impose and collect property taxes on more affluent areas.

Tennessee received a go-ahead from a lower court in September to begin a five-year plan to increase school funding by $664 million. Alabama schools and state officials on October 1 submitted to a court a joint proposal for equalizing school aid. Governor Jim Folsom, Jr., prepared to call a special legislative session to adopt the plan.

Wisconsin Governor Tommy G. Thompson ap-

Selected statistics on state governments

State	Resident population*	Governor†	House (D)	House (R)	Senate (D)	Senate (R)	State tax revenue‡	Tax revenue per capita‡	Public school expenditures per pupil§
Alabama	4,062,608	Jim Folsom, Jr. (D)	82	23	26	9	$ 3,943,000,000	$ 960	$3,780
Alaska	551,947	Walter J. Hickel (I)	20	18#	9	10**	1,806,000,000	3,170	9,550
Arizona	3,677,985	J. Fife Symington (R)	25	35	12	18	4,711,000,000	1,260	5,160
Arkansas	2,362,239	Jim Guy Tucker (D)	88	11**	30	5	2,366,000,000	1,000	3,930
California	29,839,250	Pete Wilson (R)	47	33	21	16††	44,874,000,000	1,480	4,620
Colorado	3,307,912	Roy Romer (D)	31	34	16	19	3,214,000,000	950	5,180
Connecticut	3,295,699	Lowell P. Weicker, Jr. (I)	87	64	19	17	4,983,000,000	1,510	8,840
Delaware	688,696	Tom Carper (D)	17	24	15	6	1,165,000,000	1,710	6,270
Florida	13,003,362	Lawton M. Chiles, Jr. (D)	71	49	20	20	13,764,000,000	1,040	5,280
Georgia	6,508.419	Zell Miller (D)	128	52	39	17	7,154,000,000	1,080	5,000
Hawaii	1,115,274	John Waihee (D)	47	4	22	3	2,639,000,000	2,330	5,750
Idaho	1,011,986	Cecil D. Andrus (D)	20	50	12	23	1,205,000,000	1,160	3,850
Illinois	11,466,682	Jim Edgar (R)	65	53	27	32	13,292,000,000	1,150	5,320
Indiana	5,564,228	Evan Bayh (D)	55	45	22	28	6,182,000,000	1,100	5,790
Iowa	2,787,424	Terry E. Branstad (R)	49	51	27	23	3,447,000,000	1,230	5,240
Kansas	2,485,600	Joan Finney (D)	59	66	14	26	2,796,000,000	1,020	5,430
Kentucky	3,698,969	Brereton C. Jones (D)	71	29	25	13	5,043,000,000	1,360	5,130
Louisiana	4,238,216	Edwin W. Edwards (D)	88	16**	33	6	4,309,000,000	1,010	4,740
Maine	1,233,223	John R. McKernan, Jr. (R)	93	58	20	15	1,558,000,000	1,260	6,090
Maryland	4,798,622	William D. Schaefer (D)	116	25	38	9	6,401,000,000	1,320	6,440
Massachusetts	6,029,051	William F. Weld (R)	122	34‡‡	31	9	9,684,000,000	1,620	6,540
Michigan	9,328,784	John Engler (R)	55	55	16	22	11,103,000,000	1,190	6,240
Minnesota	4,387,029	Arne H. Carlson (R)	85	49	45	22	7,051,000,000	1,590	5,310
Mississippi	2,586,443	Kirk Fordice (R)	91	29#	37	15	2,461,000,000	950	3,520
Missouri	5,137,804	Mel Carnahan (D)	97	66	20	14	4,996,000,000	970	4,450
Montana	803,655	Marc Racicot (R)	47	53	30	20	818,000,000	1,010	5,180
Nebraska	1,584,617	E. Benjamin Nelson (D)	unicameral (49 nonpartisan)				1,767,000,000	1,100	5,000
Nevada	1,206,152	Bob Miller (D)	29	13	10	11	1,683,000,000	1,310	4,990
New Hampshire	1,113,915	Steve Merrill (R)	135	258§§	11	13	625,000,000	570	5,650
New Jersey	7,748,634	Christine Todd Whitman (R)	22	58	13	27	11,645,000,000	1,500	10,560
New Mexico	1,521,779	Bruce King (D)	53	17	27	15	2,086,000,000	1,350	4,720
New York	18,044,505	Mario M. Cuomo (D)	100	50	25	35##	28,300,000,000	1,570	8,740
North Carolina	6,657,630	James B. Hunt, Jr. (D)	78	42	39	11	7,850,000,000	1,170	5,130
North Dakota	641,364	Edward T. Shafer (R)	33	65	25	24	755,000,000	1,090	4,420
Ohio	10,887,325	George V. Voinovich (R)	53	46	13	20	11,556,000,000	1,060	6,250
Oklahoma	3,157,604	David Walters (D)	70	31	37	11	3,862,000,000	1,220	4,020
Oregon	2,853,733	Barbara Roberts (D)	28	32	16	14	3,030,000,000	1,040	6,210
Pennsylvania	11,924,710	Robert P. Casey (D)	104	99	25	25	13,021,000,000	1,090	6,450
Rhode Island	1,005,984	Bruce Sundlun (D)	85	15	39	11	1,257,000,000	1,250	6,880
South Carolina	3,505,707	Carroll A. Campbell, Jr. (R)	71	52**	30	16	3,933,000,000	1,100	4,620
South Dakota	699,999	Walter Dale Miller (R)	28	42	20	15	528,000,000	750	4,520
Tennessee	4,896,641	Ned Ray McWherter (D)	63	36	19	14	4,311,000,000	870	4,010
Texas	17,059,805	Ann W. Richards (D)	91	58‡‡	18	13	16,017,000,000	920	4,830
Utah	1,727,784	Michael O. Leavitt (R)	31	44	10	19	1,861,000,000	1,050	3,130
Vermont	564,964	Howard Dean (D)	87	57***	14	16	685,000,000	1,210	7,670
Virginia	6,216,568	George Allen (R)	52	47**	22	18	6,852,000,000	1,090	5,240
Washington	4,887,941	Mike Lowry (D)	65	33	28	21	7,990,000,000	1,590	5,580
West Virginia	1,801,625	Gaston Caperton (D)	79	21	32	2	2,328,000,000	1,290	5,690
Wisconsin	4,906,745	Tommy G. Thompson (R)	52	46##	16	17	7,017,000,000	1,420	6,730
Wyoming	455,975	Mike Sullivan (D)	19	41	10	20	637,000,000	1,390	5,940

*1990 Census (source: U.S. Bureau of the Census).
†As of January 1994 (source: state government officials).
‡1991 figures (source: U.S. Bureau of the Census).
§1992-1993 figures for elementary and secondary students in average daily attendance (source: National Education Association).
#Two independents.

**One independent.
††Two independents, one vacancy at time of publication.
‡‡One independent, one vacancy at time of publication.
§§One independent; four libertarians; two vacancies at time of publication.
##One vacancy at time of publication.
***Four independents, two progressives.

proved a charter schools experiment on August 10 in which 10 school boards can open schools for which they may hire teachers and administrators either from other public schools or from private schools. Californians in November voted down an initiative to provide $2,600-a-year vouchers for students to use at the schools of their choice.

Welfare. A trend among state governments to require welfare recipients to work and to attend educational programs continued in 1993. At least 15 states by 1993 had received federal approval to change their welfare systems. Vermont, for example, gained approval for an experimental program to cut welfare benefits to people who refuse work after 30 months on welfare. Virginia approved a pilot program to place 600 welfare recipients in jobs that pay more than welfare. Georgia joined the states that deny increased welfare benefits to women who have additional children while receiving state aid.

Health care. State legislators marched ahead with their own health-care plans as the nation awaited a federal proposal from President Bill Clinton. Some of the state proposals, especially those for managed health-care systems, contained many of the same elements as the federal plan, which was released in October. A managed health-care plan approved by the Washington state legislature was hailed as a model for federal action. The bill, signed in May, called for extending medical benefits to all state residents and for employers to pay at least half of the cost of health insurance premiums for their employees. In November, the public approved the plan by voting for tax hikes that were to pay for the program. The tax hikes were to be imposed on cigarettes, beer, hospitals, and businesses.

A managed health plan to cover all of a state's residents passed in April in Florida and in May in Minnesota. A similar 1993 Iowa law sought to test the concept.

Tennessee moved to extend health coverage to all its poor and uninsured citizens by adopting a state health insurance plan to replace the Medicaid system starting in 1994. The state received federal approval in November. Oregon on March 19, 1993, obtained federal approval for its plan to extend coverage to 120,000 poor and uninsured residents by restricting health procedures for which the state will pay.

Measures designed to prevent antiabortion groups from limiting a woman's access to health clinics took effect in Connecticut in October and in Oregon in September. Colorado passed a measure that establishes a safety zone around abortion clinics to stop harassment by protesters.

Gay rights. On December 14, a state district court judge in Denver, Colo., ruled that a state ban on gay rights laws violates the United States Constitution's guarantee of equal protection. As a result of the ruling, organizations that had been calling for a boycott of Colorado said they were suspending the boycott, which was estimated to have cost Colorado about $38 million in lost convention business.

Crime. Colorado in 1993 passed new laws to clamp down on juvenile crime. Youths were banned from possessing handguns, and teen-agers charged with certain violent crimes were to be tried in court as adults. In addition, funds for new prisons for violent young criminals were approved. Utah in October passed a bill to outlaw handguns for youths under age 18. North Carolina and Oregon passed laws cracking down on youths who take guns to school.

Virginia also forbade juveniles from possessing handguns in a new law passed in February that reportedly sought to end the state's reputation as a gunrunner's haven. The law limited handgun purchases to one per month and required more record keeping on gun sales. Then-Governor L. Douglas Wilder of Virginia signed pacts with the governors of Delaware, Maryland, New Jersey, and New York to work together to stem the illegal flow of firearms across state lines.

Connecticut on October 1 became the third state in the nation to ban the sale and possession of military-style semiautomatic assault rifles. California and New Jersey also have such laws.

Gambling. States continued to expand gambling opportunities. Nebraska became the latest state to approve a state lottery, which was scheduled to start by 1995. Georgia launched its new lottery on June 29, 1993, and Indiana cleared the way for riverboat casinos in June.

States where Indian reservations have established casino gambling continued to sign agreements with tribes. New York Governor Mario M. Cuomo in April signed an agreement allowing the Oneida Indians to open a high-stakes casino. Connecticut agreed to grant the Pequots exclusive casino rights in return for a minimum $100-million annual fee.

Political offices. Two lieutenant governors moved up to governor in 1993. Lieutenant Governor Jim Folsom, Jr., a Democrat, replaced Guy Hunt, a Republican, as governor of Alabama on April 22. Hunt was removed from office after being convicted of violating a state ethics law. In South Dakota, Lieutenant Governor Walter Dale Miller replaced fellow Republican George S. Mickelson, who died in a plane crash on April 19.

In Arkansas, Republican Mike Huckabee on July 27 was elected lieutenant governor to fill the vacancy created by Jim Guy Tucker, who had become governor on Dec. 12, 1992. Tucker replaced Bill Clinton after Clinton was elected U.S. President.

In September 1993, Democratic Governor Joan Finney of Kansas and independent Governor Lowell P. Weicker, Jr., announced they would not seek re-election in 1994. □ Elaine Stuart Knapp

See also **Elections.** In *World Book,* see **State government** and the articles on the individual states.

The States Bet on Legalized Gambling

By William N. Thompson

Seeking new sources of revenue, state governments are turning increasingly to lotteries, casino gaming, and other forms of legalized gambling, but critics warn that the social costs can be high.

With the force of a locomotive, legalized gambling is spreading across the land. The gambling train got rolling in the 1970's as states began to establish government-run lotteries. It gathered steam in the 1980's with the spread of betting and bingo parlors. And now, in the 1990's, that train looks unstoppable. It is highballing on a downhill run as many states legalize casino games and other forms of gambling.

But why has gambling, once widely denounced as a sinful pastime that should be outlawed, now become so popular among government leaders? The answer is simple: money. Gambling generates huge amounts of cash, and part of the take goes to state and city treasuries.

Today, gambling in America is a very big business, with well over $300 billion wagered each year. Perhaps another $30 billion annually is bet illegally, most of it on sporting events. Only Nevada and Oregon allow betting on sports. In 1992, legal gambling generated revenues—the money remaining after all winnings had been paid out—of $29.9-billion. State lotteries collected the largest share of the pot—$11.5 billion, or 38.5 percent. Coming in a close second were casinos, with $10.1 billion, or 33.8 percent. The $29.9 billion raked in by legal gambling operations in 1992 was more than double the amount spent on motion-picture tickets and recorded music. If those gambling revenues had been spent on the products of a single company, that company would have ranked among the 15 largest in the nation.

For state and city governments, which are experiencing their biggest budget deficits ever, this money fountain is irresistible. Political leaders hope that lottery revenues and taxes on private gambling enterprises will enable them to balance their budgets without having to resort to large hikes in income or property taxes—increases that can be politically dangerous. The taxes on gambling are largely hidden, so the public has received lotteries and other forms of gambling with enthusiasm, or at least tolerance.

Still, not everyone has been receptive to the growth of gambling. In some states, there has been strong opposition from groups and business interests that already run legal gambling operations and are fearful of competition. For instance, charitable organizations that rely on bingo or other gambling activities to raise funds have taken a dim view of expanding wagering opportunities.

Other opposition is based on moral and crime issues. The public's moral opposition to gambling has greatly diminished in recent years, due in part to the spread of bingo and other games of chance, many sponsored by churches, that are conducted for charity. Still, many people continue to oppose gambling on the grounds that it is an immoral activity. Their main argument is that gambling leads individuals susceptible to compulsive gambling to squander their money. The specter of crime is an even bigger concern, particularly with regard to casinos. Many people fear that casinos will lead to both increased street crime and the take-over of casino operations by mobsters.

Politicians, as well as business people seeking to open new gambling establishments, have tried to overcome such objections. They acknowledge that gambling has its dark side, but they say that crime and compulsive gambling can and will be controlled. To clinch the sale, they argue that gambling can be a great social good, revitalizing run-down cities, providing needed jobs, and generating money for education and other social programs.

New support for an age-old pursuit

Gambling is certainly nothing new. It has been a part of human society throughout history. Archaeologists have found dice in the tombs of Egyptian pharaohs, and surviving artworks and historical accounts reveal that the ancient Greeks and Romans loved to wager. The Bible is brimming with references to lotteries and other forms of gambling.

In the United States, gambling halls were common, and legal, until the late 1800's. But then, as a rising tide of social reform swept the nation, gambling came into disrepute, and it was soon prohibited across most of the nation. By the mid-1900's, casino-style gambling was legal only in Nevada (which reauthorized gambling in 1931 after having banned it in the early 1900's). In a handful of other states, gamblers could bet on horse and dog races and on jai alai (*HY ly*), a game resembling handball.

But by the 1970's, the public's opposition to gambling had begun

■ **The author**
William N. Thompson is a professor of public administration at the University of Nevada at Las Vegas.

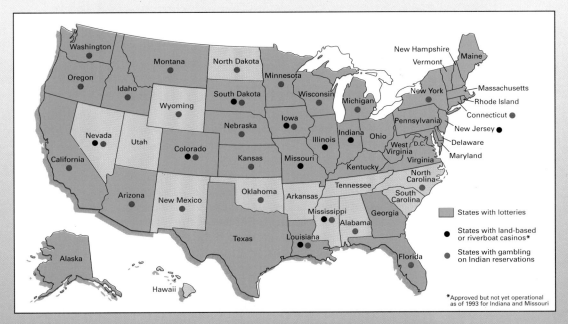

States with lotteries

● States with land-based or riverboat casinos*

● States with gambling on Indian reservations

*Approved but not yet operational as of 1993 for Indiana and Missouri

	1992 total wagering [in billions]	Percent increase 1982-1992	1992 revenues (income after payoffs to bettors) [in billions]	Percent increase 1982-1992
Casinos	$252.9	149.4%	$10.1	140.5%
Lotteries	$24.4	495.9%	$11.5	428.0%
Pari-mutuel betting (horse and dog racing, jai alai)	$17.8	22.8%	$3.7	32.0%
Commercial bingo	$4.3	43.5%	$1.1	39.7%
Charitable games	$4.8	297.9%	$1.3	228.0%
Gambling on Indian reservations	$15.2	N/A*	$1.5	N/A
Other legal gambling activities†	$10.5	585.0%	$.758	897.4%
Totals	$329.9	162.3%	$29.9	177.9%

*Not applicable.   †Bookmaking, card rooms.

Source: *Gaming and Wagering Business.*

▪ Gambling fever

Lotteries and other forms of gambling are spreading across much of the nation, *above*. In 1992, a total of $329.9 billion was wagered in the United States, and gambling operations had revenues of $29.9 billion, figures that were more than 150 percent higher than in 1982, *left*.

to soften, and in later years gambling in one form or another became an increasingly common part of the American scene. As of 1993, 48 states permitted some kind of legalized gambling. Only Hawaii and Utah continued to prohibit all gambling activity.

Lotteries get the train rolling

The year things began to change was 1963, when New Hampshire established the first legal lottery in the United States since the 1890's. Other states, seeing the popularity and profitability of the New Hampshire lottery, soon followed suit. By 1993, 37 states and the District of Columbia had authorized lotteries. A state typically keeps 50 percent of the money it raises from lottery sales—that is, it imposes a 50 percent tax on lottery tickets—and returns the other 50 percent as prizes to the holders of winning numbers. About 80 percent of a state's share of lottery revenue is used to fund public programs, with the remainder going to cover the cost of administering the lottery.

State lotteries started out as low-key affairs, with tickets sold just twice a year. But soon, monthly drawings became the norm. Then came weekly and daily games, including games enabling players to select a three- or four-digit number of their own choosing. In 1974, Massachusetts started an instant-winner game, in which players simply rub a ticket to reveal a hidden number and then compare it with a list of winning numbers. Almost at once, nearly every other state with a lottery imitated the idea.

Another major event in lottery development came when New York instituted the lotto format in 1978. In lotto, a player selects a series of numbers—usually 5 or 6—from 1 to about 50, and is given a ticket with those numbers. Tickets can also be purchased with a series of numbers randomly generated by a lottery-operated computer. After the close of ticket sales, lottery officials draw the winning numbers for that round of lotto. Drawings are usually held once or twice a week. With each drawing, if no ticket has the exact series of winning numbers, the prize money is "rolled over" into a pool for the next drawing.

Lotto pots can be huge. In July 1993, a Wisconsin man and his fiancée were the sole winners of a prize of $111 million in a lotto drawing encompassing 14 states and the District of Columbia. It was the most money ever won with a single lottery ticket.

As the lottery craze picked up speed, other forms of gambling also began to proliferate. Many states legalized horse and dog racing with a track-run system called *pari-mutuel betting*. Under this arrangement, the track, the state, and the owner of the horse or dog each get a part of the money from each bet, though most of the money is divided among the winning bettors. As of 1993, 35 states had legalized wagering on horse races, and 18 allowed betting on dog races.

Casino gambling has been making a slow comeback since New Jersey decided in 1978 to allow casinos in Atlantic City, making it the first city outside of Nevada to have Las Vegas-style gambling. At that time, there were predictions that as many as 20 other states would soon permit casinos. But those forecasts proved to be premature. In one state after another, voters and legislators, fearful of the crime and social problems traditionally associated with big-time gambling, said no to the idea of legalizing casinos.

Then, in the late 1980's, two states—South Dakota and Iowa—decided to loosen up on gambling. In 1988, the voters of South Dakota agreed to allow casinos in the historic town of Deadwood, where frontiersman Wild Bill Hickok met his end in 1876—shot dead while playing poker in a saloon. But the state balked at restoring the unlimited-stakes gambling that existed in Wild Bill's day. Under the new rules, money fed into slot machines or wagered at poker and blackjack tables would be limited to $5 per play. A $5 betting limit was also imposed in Iowa, which in 1989 approved casino gambling for riverboats on the Mississippi River.

Another impetus to the spread of casinos has been the growing phenomenon of gambling on Indian reservations, which was authorized by Congress in 1988. As of 1993, there were at least 185 Indian gaming operations in 26 states. Most of the Indian gaming halls were high-stakes bingo parlors with prizes up to $1 million, but many reservations offered casino gambling. In September 1993, the Mashantucket Pequot tribe in Connecticut showed that Indian reservation gambling had become a very big business indeed when it opened the second-largest casino in the world, surpassed in size only by one in Malaysia. By 1993, gambling on Indian reservations was pulling in an estimated $6 billion a year.

With casinos sprouting on Indian lands, the remaining opposition to casino gambling in many states has begun to melt away. After all, some lawmakers have reasoned, if Native Americans can have casinos, why shouldn't other people be able to as well?

Besides wanting to tap into a new source of tax revenue, these states have been anxious to prevent neighboring states from establishing a commercial advantage over them. In 1990, the voters of Colorado approved limited-stakes ($5 per play) casino games in three historic mountain towns—Black Hawk, Central City, and Cripple Creek. That same year, Illinois approved riverboat gambling, and soon Indiana, Louisiana, Mississippi, and Missouri also authorized gambling boats. The boats in Indiana and Missouri were not due to begin operating until 1994. These states did not impose limits on the size of bets permitted.

Big growth for big-time casinos

In 1992, Louisiana authorized an immense land-based high-rise casino for downtown New Orleans. That casino, which is expected to open in 1995, will be larger than any other casino now operating in the world. And as 1993 unfolded, it appeared that casino gambling could expand to several other cities and states. There were proposals for casinos in Hartford, Conn.; Detroit; Chicago; and Kansas City, Mo.

Like any expanding industry, the gambling business is trying to attract new customers. Some of the major players, eager to change the unsavory image that many people have of casinos, are striving to

■ **New gambling experiences**

Gamblers have a lot to choose from in the 1990's, from riverboat casinos on the Mississippi River to fantasy-oriented casino hotels in Las Vegas, Nev., that cater to the whole family.

■ The *President* riverboat casino, *right,* plies the Mississippi River at Davenport, Iowa.

■ Video poker machines, *right,* and other kinds of electronic gambling devices are an appealing option for those who prefer to gamble solo.

■ The Luxor, *left,* one of the most spectacular new casino hotels in Las Vegas, opened in October 1993. Many new casinos are located on Indian reservations, such as the Grand Casino, *below,* in Hinckley, Minn., on the Mille Lacs reservation.

make gambling establishments more family oriented. Some casinos are becoming more like theme parks than traditional gambling halls. A leader in this trend has been Circus Circus Enterprises of Las Vegas. In October 1993, Circus Circus opened its most dramatic Las Vegas casino hotel yet, the pyramid-shaped Luxor. The Luxor offers an entertainment floor with a video arcade and three "participatory adventures" that take visitors on simulated trips through time.

Gambling's economic benefits

It takes a lot of people to run an extravaganza like the Luxor. The largest casino hotels in Las Vegas employ an average of 3,300 people each, and a few of the hotels there and in Atlantic City have staffs of up to 7,000. The entire U.S. gambling industry employed about 160,000 people in 1993, a number that was bound to grow. The hope of providing jobs has been a major factor in the scramble to legalize casino gambling around the nation.

But studies have shown that gambling operations create a net increase in jobs in an area only when most of their customers are from outside that area. Those customers enrich the local and state economy with the dollars they spend in the hotels and lose at the gaming tables, and that results in an expansion of employment. Gambling has produced many thousands of jobs in Nevada and Atlantic City because the great majority of the people frequenting their casinos are from other states—more than 80 percent in the case of Nevada.

The employment increases resulting from most gambling operations are illusory. The purchasers of lottery tickets and the patrons of race tracks are almost exclusively local residents. The money they wager comes from the local economy, and each dollar they spend on a lottery ticket or lose on a horse is a dollar they can no longer spend at a store or restaurant. This situation benefits the gambling operations but works to the detriment of other kinds of business.

Moreover, revenues from gambling do not appreciably fatten most municipal or state budgets. Although Nevada derives more than 40 percent of its revenues from gambling taxes, it is the exception. In New Jersey, the money raised from casino taxes amounts to about 3 percent of the state budget. Nowhere else do they amount to even 2 percent. Lotteries, too, though they unquestionably raise significant amounts of money for public treasuries, are not exactly gold mines. No lottery produces much more than 4 percent of a state's budget, and the average is about 2 percent.

With the continued proliferation of gambling, these numbers are likely to drop even further as the pool of gamblers gets spread ever thinner. For example, analysts have predicted that if Chicago gets casino gambling, Illinois river towns will lose business on the casino riverboats that they had been counting on for an economic boost.

Not that gambling has lived up to its promises as an engine for revitalizing cities, or even for providing extra revenues for education or social programs. Opponents of gambling contend that the glowing promises have in fact gone largely unfulfilled. Lotteries are a case in

■ Legalized gambling: A roll of the dice

Advocates of gambling say that lotteries, casinos, and other gambling enterprises can give an economic boost to cities and states. At the Mille Lacs Indian reservation in Minnesota, for example, gambling revenues paid for a new school, *above left*. But opponents argue that gambling's benefits are often overstated and its negative aspects downplayed. They point to Atlantic City, N.J., where substandard housing still stands within shouting distance of gleaming new casinos, *above right*. The following are the main arguments usually presented for and against legalized gambling.

■ Advocates of gambling say:

- Gambling can be an important source of revenue for cash-starved states.
- Income from state lotteries provides needed money for education and other social programs.
- Gamblers pump large amounts of money into the local economy.
- Casinos and other large gambling enterprises provide jobs that ordinarily would not exist.
- Large casinos can serve as a stimulus for the revitalization of the urban areas in which they are located.
- With proper regulation, organized crime can be prevented from gaining control of casinos.
- Surveillance at casinos and increased street patrols by police can protect gamblers from robbers and muggers.
- Casinos can identify compulsive gamblers and stop them before they lose all their money.

■ Opponents of gambling say:

- Gambling revenues are unlikely to fatten state budgets by more than a few percent.
- Lotteries rarely provide extra money for social programs. Legislators typically reduce allotments for social services from the general fund by about the same amount they raise from the lottery.
- Unless gambling enterprises draw customers from outside the immediate area, they do not enrich the local economy—they simply absorb money that would have gone to other local businesses.
- Just as most gambling enterprises do not boost the local economy, neither do they create a net increase in jobs.
- Despite their glitter, casinos do little or nothing to uplift the urban areas around them.
- Even if mobsters are effectively barred from casinos, they may still take control of unions and businesses that provide services to the casinos.
- Street crime around casinos and other gambling operations is almost impossible to control.
- Casinos do very little to prevent compulsive gambling by patrons.

point. In 13 states, lotteries were instituted with the stipulation that all the proceeds would be used to fund public schools. The public assumed that the schools would thus benefit by having more money to spend. In most of those states, however, legislators have reduced education allotments from the general fund by about the same amount raised by the lottery, so there has been no extra money for schools.

With regard to casinos and their supposed influence in revitalizing shabby urban areas, critics say, one need look no farther than Atlantic City. Gambling advocates claimed that casinos would bring a rebirth to this aging resort community. The casinos did generate tens of thousands of jobs and billions of dollars in construction contracts, and millions of gamblers flocked to the casino-lined Boardwalk. In addition, the state has used some $400 million in gambling revenues to make improvements in the city, half of it in upgrading housing.

Nonetheless, the critics say, Atlantic City has not been revived. Most of the city's housing is still substandard. Landlords, anxious to sell their property to casino developers, reportedly have often raised rents and refused to make needed repairs in an effort to force tenants out. And store owners have not only failed to attract new customers, they have lost many of their old customers to shops at the casinos.

Compulsive gambling and crime

Opponents of gambling are quick to point out the mixed verdict on Atlantic City. They also warn that compulsive gambling and crime are problems that must be faced in any debate about legalized gambling.

Studies have found that a small percentage of people—about 2 to 5 percent of the population—are susceptible to becoming compulsive gamblers. Those people share certain personality traits, including a tendency to be anxious, restless, and impulsive and a need for immediate gratification. But those who fit that personality profile often are not gamblers. If they have no opportunity to gamble, they may never realize that they carry the seeds of an addiction within them. It is the experience of gambling, with all its excitement and tension, that can turn susceptible individuals into compulsive gamblers who bring financial ruin on themselves.

Some casino operators are becoming sensitive to the problem of compulsive gambling. They recognize that although only a small minority of their customers are compulsive gamblers, the devastation that those few cause to themselves and their families hurts the image of the industry. A growing number of casinos now train their employees to recognize compulsive gamblers and to intervene when it appears that the individuals are spinning out of control.

Crime, particularly the infiltration of casinos by mobsters, is an even bigger issue. The worry that gangsters will muscle their way into casino operations is based on the experience of Las Vegas. As far back as the 1950's, it was widely assumed, though not proved, that some of the major Las Vegas casinos were controlled by organized crime.

The mob's hold on several Las Vegas casinos was confirmed beginning in 1979, when Nevada gaming authorities closed down the Aladdin Casino after an investigation showed that its management had ties with Detroit gangsters. Then in 1983, the Stardust, Fremont, and Sundance casinos were placed in receivership after a Federal Bureau of Investigation probe of their operations revealed mob involvement. The U.S. Justice Department indicted 15 organized-crime figures, charging them with stealing more than $2 million from the casinos.

Major casinos in Nevada and elsewhere are now under strictly controlled corporate managements, greatly reducing the chances of their being taken over by mobsters. Moreover, both the U.S. Securities and Exchange Commission and state regulators have the power to close down any casino in which they find evidence of criminal activities.

Still, anywhere money is flowing like water, it is difficult to keep organized crime completely out of the picture. Following the legalization of gambling in Atlantic City, New Jersey authorities instituted strict control over casino operations to ensure that they stayed in honest hands. Barred effectively from the casinos, the mob turned instead to some of the labor unions that furnished services to the casinos. According to law-enforcement investigators and confessions from organized-crime figures, several unions were firmly in mob control by the 1980's. The mobsters then extorted money from casino owners, threatening to call strikes if payoffs weren't made. Not until the 1990's were state and federal law-enforcement authorities able to clean up the unions and stop, or at least limit, the illegal activities.

The most prevalent kind of crime associated with gambling is street crime. Casinos, race tracks, and other large gambling operations attract great numbers of people with pockets full of cash, and they in turn attract robbers, muggers, pickpockets, and prostitutes. Advocates of gambling argue that vigilant surveillance at gambling facilities and increased street patrols by the police can minimize this form of crime. But critics contend that little can be done to protect gamblers from those who are intent on taking their money.

Possible future trends

Despite the problems associated with gambling, a large portion of the American public seems to favor gambling as a way to spend its entertainment dollar and perhaps to make a fast buck. The spread of gambling in the United States is thus likely to continue well into the next century, with new forms of wagering making it even easier to bet. Some experts, for example, foresee the day when television viewers will be able to bet on sporting events through interactive TV hookups.

But opposition to gambling may also increase as many people come to realize that gambling, though it does offer some benefits to states and communities, has its downside and is often not the horn of plenty it is touted to be. Citizens' groups may demand that some kinds of gambling, such as casinos, be limited to certain parts of the country and that the federal government strictly regulate gambling activities. Such steps may indeed be needed if we are to minimize the social costs that are an unavoidable side effect of gambling. The gambling train is a potent force, and it must be kept on the track. ■ ■ ■

Stocks and bonds

Stocks and bonds. Lower interest rates were the engine that drove financial markets in 1993 in the United States and abroad. Falling interest rates led many people to move their money out of low-paying accounts with banks and savings and loan associations and into riskier but potentially more profitable stocks and bonds. As a result, stock and bond markets boomed for most of the year, fueled by a spectacular flow of money into *mutual funds* (publicly sold pools of stocks and bonds). Many companies responded to the hungry investment climate by selling stocks and bonds to help pay off any high-interest debt.

New highs. The Dow Jones Industrial Average (the Dow), a composite of the stock prices for 30 major U.S. companies, reached a record closing high of 3,794.33 on December 29. On December 31, the Dow stood at 3,754.09, up 13.7 percent for 1993.

The Standard & Poor's 500-Stock Index, a broader measure of the U.S. market, reached a record closing high of 469.50 on October 15. On December 31, the index stood at 466.45, a 7 percent gain for the year.

Prices also soared on the National Association of Securities Dealers Automated Quotation (NASDAQ) system, which tracks smaller, more speculative companies than do the other U.S. stock exchanges. The NASDAQ composite index reached a record closing high of 787.42 on October 15. On December 31, the NASDAQ index closed at 776.82, up 14.8 percent for the year.

Winners and losers. Stocks that scored well in 1993 included those of older manufacturing firms, which gained from lower interest rates and from years of corporate cost-cutting, and those of newer, communications-based firms, which gained from advances in technology and from an increasing consumer appetite for computers and the like. Examples of the first category were Caterpillar Incorporated, General Electric Company, and General Motors Corporation. Examples of the second category were Bell Atlantic Corporation, US West Incorporated, and other of the so-called Baby Bells, the regional telephone companies that span the United States.

On the other hand, stocks of many well-known consumer-products companies faltered in 1993. The uncertain U.S. economy increasingly led consumers to make purchases on the basis of price, not brand. That change in behavior meant greater competition and lower profits for firms with long-established brands. Some consumer-products companies whose stock struggled in 1993 were Coca-Cola Company, Philip Morris Companies, and Sara Lee Corporation.

International stock markets. In Europe, central banks cautiously nudged interest rates lower in an effort to spark economic growth without rekindling inflation. Although a significant recovery never developed, lower interest rates and the prospects of better times ahead spurred heavy investing. In the United Kingdom, the London Financial Times-Stock

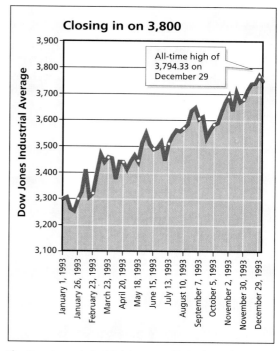

Closing in on 3,800

All-time high of 3,794.33 on December 29

The Dow Jones Industrial Average climbed steadily in 1993, rising more than 450 points to end within reach of the 3,800 mark.

Exchange Index of 100 stocks (FT-SE 100) closed on December 31 at 3,418.40, up 20 percent for 1993. Stock exchanges in France and Germany also did well.

In Canada, the Toronto Stock Exchange's 300-Stock Index began the year at 3,350.44. It closed on December 31 at 4,321.40, up 29 percent.

In Japan, political scandals, continued slow economic growth, and the lingering effects of a collapse in real estate prices worried investors throughout 1993. Stock prices, which began a steep slide in 1990, reversed course in the spring of 1993 but then resumed their plunge in the autumn. The Nikkei Index of 225 large Japanese companies stood at 17,417.24 on December 31, up just 3 percent for the year.

Slow growth in most industrialized countries of the world turned the attention of many investors to the more rapidly growing economies of countries in Southeast Asia and Latin America. Stock exchanges in those areas that performed particularly well were those of Malaysia, Mexico, and Hong Kong.

The U.S. bond market. The yield on 30-year U.S. Treasury bonds dropped to a record-low 5.78 percent on October 15 from 7.39 percent at the start of the year. But then interest rates began to creep up in reaction to signs of economic growth. By December 31, the yield on 30-year Treasury bonds had risen to 6.34 percent. ☐ Bill Barnhart

In *World Book,* see **Bond; Investment; Stock.**

Sudan. Efforts by Sudan's Prime Minister, General Umar Hasan Ahmad al-Bashir, to moderate Sudan's radical image abroad failed in 1993. On August 18, the Administration of United States President Bill Clinton added Sudan to a list of six other nations considered supportive of terrorism. Administration officials accused Sudan of providing safe haven, passage, and training to Middle Eastern terrorist groups. Egyptian President Hosni Mubarak, who increased security along Egypt's Sudanese border, in March accused Sudan of aiding radical Islamic Egyptian rebels. Among the terrorist groups Sudan reportedly hosted were the Lebanese-based Islamic Party of God, also known as Hezbollah, and the Palestine Islamic Holy War.

Speculation also arose in 1993 that Sudan was involved in providing weapons to the anti-American Somali warlord, General Mohamed Farah Aideed, whose supporters clashed several times in 1993 with United Nations (UN) peacekeeping forces in Somalia.

Experts believe Sudan's support for terrorism is championed by Hasan al-Turabi, leader of Sudan's National Islamic Front party and the reputed power behind Bashir. Turabi has supported the Sudanese government's attempt to impose Islamic law in southern Sudan where most people practice Christianity and local religions. The conflict has caused Sudan's 11-year civil war.

The civil war, which has claimed more than 500,000 lives since it began, raged on in 1993. Peace talks started in April stalled over the rebels' demands that the government decentralize control and stop forced Islamization. Other complications arose because the opposition group, the Sudan People's Liberation Army, split into hostile factions.

Human rights. International relief agencies, many of which were barred from providing aid in 1993, said that more than 1 million people were at risk of starving in southern Sudan alone. The UN heard brutal allegations in March. The bombing of towns and deliberate destruction of homes in southern Sudan during 1993 reportedly added tens of thousands of people to Sudan's 3 million displaced people and refugees. A U.S. State Department report claimed in May that Sudanese troops were massacring civilians and kidnapping children for forced labor in Libyan farms and military camps. On November 22, an agent of the UN Commission on Human Rights presented a report charging the Sudanese government with torture, murder, and extra-judicial executions.

Papal visit. Hoping to dispel charges of religious persecution against his government, Bashir allowed Pope John Paul II to conduct an open-air mass on February 10 in the capital, Khartoum. About 200,000 people heard the pope call for religious freedom, civil peace, and human rights.   □ Christine Helms

See also **Middle East** (Facts in brief table). In *World Book*, see **Sudan.**

Supreme Court of the United States.

In its 1992-1993 term, which ended on June 28, 1993, the Supreme Court of the United States lowered the constitutional wall between church and state and made it easier to challenge government actions designed to protect minority voting rights.

New justice. The court welcomed a new member after the end of the term, when Associate Justice Ruth Bader Ginsburg was sworn in on Aug. 10, 1993. Ginsburg, the 107th justice, was the second woman ever to sit on the high court. (Justice Sandra Day O'Connor, appointed by President Ronald Reagan in 1981, was the first.) President Bill Clinton nominated Ginsburg, 60, on June 14 to replace Justice Byron R. White, who had announced his retirement after 31 years on the court. Ginsburg was instrumental in the 1970's in winning legal protections for women in a series of cases she argued before the Supreme Court. As a judge on the U.S. Court of Appeals for the District of Columbia in the 1980's, Ginsburg developed a reputation for moderation and a conviction that legislators, not judges, should lead society in new directions. (See **Ginsburg, Ruth Bader.**)

Voting rights. In one of the year's most controversial rulings, the court on June 28 said bizarrely shaped electoral districts that favor minority candidates could violate the rights of white voters. The 5 to 4 decision returned to a lower court a lawsuit challenging two North Carolina congressional districts, one of which—the 12th District—was a 160-mile (257-kilometer) ribbon no wider in places than one lane of the interstate highway it follows. The state had created the two black-majority districts in 1991 to comply with an amendment to the 1965 Voting Rights Act that was designed to increase minority political representation. The two districts had enabled North Carolina voters in 1992 to elect the state's first black members of Congress since 1901. The ruling made it likely that oddly shaped districts in other states would be challenged.

Job discrimination. The justices on June 25 increased the burden on workers charging employers with discrimination on the basis of race or other personal characteristics. The 5 to 4 majority held that a worker could not win a discrimination suit simply by showing that an employer lied in court about the reasons for a dismissal or other action. Instead, the worker must prove that the employer was motivated by bias. Lower courts had frequently interpreted an employer's failure to offer an honest explanation for an action as evidence of an intent to discriminate.

On November 9, during its 1993-1994 term, the court made it easier for workers to show that they had been subjected to sexual harassment on the job. Ruling unanimously, the court reinstated a lawsuit brought by a female employee of a Nashville truck-leasing firm, who charged that the company's president had repeatedly subjected her to sexual innuendos and demeaning remarks. The high court rejected

Supreme Court of the United States

a standard adopted by some lower courts under which an employee had to show that harassment had caused severe psychological harm. Instead, the court ruled that plaintiffs need only show that the offensive conduct made the workplace environment hostile or abusive.

Religion. On June 18, the court ruled that public school districts do not violate the constitutional separation of church and state by paying for sign-language interpreters for deaf students attending parochial schools. A Tucson, Ariz., student had argued that he was entitled to the interpreter under a federal law requiring schools to provide appropriate services for students with disabilities. Ruling 5 to 4, the court held that sign-language interpreters differ from forms of assistance that public schools may not give to parochial schools, such as teachers and audio-visual equipment, because the interpreter would aid the student, not the school.

On June 11, the court ruled 9 to 0 that the Constitution's guarantee of religious freedom prevents governments from banning animal sacrifice performed in religious rites. The decision struck down four Hialeah, Fla., ordinances that the court said were aimed at suppressing observance of the Santería religion. Santería combines African tribal and Roman Catholic rituals and involves animal sacrifice.

In another unanimous ruling, the court on June 7 said public schools that allow community organizations to meet in school buildings after hours also must let religious groups use the facilities. Ruling in a case from Center Moriches, N.Y., the justices said that denying access solely to groups promoting a religious viewpoint amounted to a violation of the First Amendment's guarantee of freedom of speech.

Hate crimes. The court on June 11 ruled that cities and states can set harsher punishments for crimes that are motivated by bias than for other crimes. Voting 9 to 0, the justices upheld a Wisconsin law that allows judges to give longer sentences to defendants who choose their victims on the basis of race, religion, ethnicity, sexual orientation, or disability. The justices said such penalty-enhancement laws differ from laws prohibiting speech motivated by bias. In 1992, the court had said the Constitution prohibits laws directed at hate speech because they violate the First Amendment.

Abortion protests. The justices on January 13 said a federal civil rights law enacted to protect blacks from conspiracies to deprive them of their rights does not permit judges to bar abortion protesters from blocking access to medical clinics. Voting 6 to 3 in a case from Alexandria, Va., the court said antiabortion groups were not conspiring to discriminate against women, a necessary condition if the law were to apply. Congress passed the law, known as the Ku Klux Klan Act, in 1871 to protect newly freed slaves from attacks by the Ku Klux Klan, a white supremacist group.

Federal Appeals Court Judge Ruth Bader Ginsburg accepts her nomination to the U.S. Supreme Court in June as U.S. President Bill Clinton listens.

Immigration. On June 21, the court upheld, 8 to 1, a U.S. government policy of stopping boats carrying Haitian refugees bound for the United States and returning the refugees to Haiti without asylum hearings. The practice, begun by the Administration of President George Bush and continued under President Clinton, was widely criticized by human rights groups. Government officials said the policy was designed to prevent Haitians from risking their lives by sailing on flimsy, overcrowded boats. The government also said that many of the Haitians would not qualify for asylum because they were fleeing poverty instead of political persecution.

In its decision, the high court noted that it was not ruling on whether or not the government should send the refugees back to Haiti. The ruling held only that neither U.S. law nor international treaties prevented the United States from requiring that refugees apply for asylum before leaving their country.

Scientific evidence. In a 7 to 2 decision, the justices on June 28 made federal judges responsible for determining whether scientific evidence offered as testimony in the courtroom is relevant and reliable. Formerly, judges had relied on a standard, dating to 1923, under which expert evidence had to conform to "generally accepted" scientific methods—for example, experiments that had been reported in a prestigious scientific journal.

Criminal law. On June 7, the court held 9 to 0 that police do not need a search warrant to confiscate illicit drugs they find while frisking criminal suspects for weapons, as long as the officers can plainly feel that an object must be an illegal drug. Ruling on a case from Minneapolis, Minn., the court extended an earlier doctrine known as "plain view," under which seizing illicit drugs that are clearly visible to police does not violate the Fourth Amendment's ban on unreasonable searches and seizures.

Marshall papers controversy. A furor erupted in May when newspaper stories revealed that the Library of Congress in Washington, D.C., had opened to researchers and scholars the personal papers of former Justice Thurgood Marshall, who died in January. Chief Justice William H. Rehnquist and other justices strongly protested the release of the papers, which included early drafts of court opinions and memos exchanged by the justices, some involving recent cases. The justices argued that maintaining the secrecy of court proceedings is necessary to ensure the integrity of the court. The library said that it had acted according to Marshall's instructions.

☐ Geoffrey A. Campbell and Linda P. Campbell

See also **Courts.** In *World Book,* see **Supreme Court of the United States.**

Surgery. See Medicine.
Suriname. See Latin America.
Swaziland. See Africa.

Sweden in 1993 continued in its deepest recession since World War II (1939-1945). The country's economic output declined almost 2 percent in 1993. And Sweden's currency, the krona, plummeted almost 25 percent after the Swedish government in late 1992 allowed it to trade freely on foreign exchange markets. Previously, Sweden's central bank had kept interest rates high to tie the krona's value to the values of other Western European currencies.

Government overhaul. Prime Minister Carl Bildt on April 22, 1993, announced a five-year plan to drastically reduce Sweden's massive government budget. Bildt's plan, which signaled a major retreat from Sweden's generous social welfare system, included proposals to freeze government spending at the 1993 level for the rest of the 1990's and slash government pensions, unemployment benefits, and other payouts. The plan was passed by the Riksdag (parliament) on June 10 and went into effect on July 1. But the austerity measures were opposed by the Social Democratic Party, which was expected to provide stiff opposition for Bildt and his Moderate Party in the next elections, scheduled for June 1994.

Automaker merger fails. On Sept. 6, 1993, Volvo AB, the Swedish car and truck maker, agreed to merge most of its operations with carmaker Renault SA of France. The new company was to become the world's sixth-largest vehicle maker. However, many of Volvo's shareholders and executives began voicing concerns about the intentions of the French government, which owns Renault. Faced with growing opposition, Volvo on December 2 backed out of the deal. The collapse of the merger prompted the resignation of Volvo Chairman Pehr Gyllenhammar, who had headed the company since 1971.

Privatization continues. The Swedish government's plan to privatize 35 state-owned companies, which could raise more than $38 billion by the end of the 1990's, continued hesitantly in 1993. On April 28, the government announced plans to privatize arms maker Celsius Industries Corporation by reducing its stake in the company from 89 percent to 25 percent. On June 3, the long-running battle over the privatization of food and pharmaceutical conglomerate Procordia AB was settled when Volvo and the Swedish government, which each owned about 43 percent of the voting shares, agreed to split up the company. Under the plan, Volvo gained control of Procordia's consumer products operations, whereas the government gained control of its drug and biotechnology operations. The government planned to sell shares in its part of Procordia to the public.

EC talks. Sweden on February 1 formally opened talks on joining the European Community (EC or Common Market). Sweden could become a member of the EC as early as Jan. 1, 1995. ☐ Philip Revzin

See also **Europe** (Facts in brief table). In *World Book,* see **Sweden.**

Swimming. After five years of disappointments, Janet Evans of Placentia, Calif., regained most of the sharpness that made her the world's best swimmer at the age of 16. Even so, she had to share attention in 1993 with 15-year-old Franziska van Almsick of Germany, who won six women's gold medals and one silver medal in the European championships.

Evans. At the Pan Pacific Games held from August 12 to 15 in Japan, United States swimmers won 23 of the 34 gold medals. Evans won the women's 400-meter and 800-meter freestyles, raising her record to 20-1 in major meets over seven years in the 400 meters and 18-0 over six years in the 800 meters.

Evans swept the 400-meter, 800-meter, and 1,500-meter freestyles in the United States spring nationals from March 31 to April 4 in Nashville and the summer nationals held from July 26 to 30 in Austin, Tex. Those victories gave her 36 national titles, tying Johnny Weissmuller for second place on the all-time list behind Tracy Caulkins, who won 48. In the summer championships, Evans' time of 15 minutes 59.44 seconds was the third fastest ever; her 4 minutes 5.85 seconds for 400 meters was the fifth fastest ever; and her 8 minutes 23.61 seconds for 800 meters was faster than her gold-medal time in the 1992 Summer Olympics in Barcelona, Spain.

Evans won the 400-meter and 800-meter titles in the first world short-course championships from Dec. 2 to 5, 1993, in Palma de Majorca, Spain. China won

10 gold medals, and the United States, with many stars absent, won 7.

European. In the European championships from August 2 to 8 in Sheffield, England, German swimmers won 10 of the 16 women's events, and Russians took 7 of the 16 men's events. Van Almsick won gold medals in the three shortest freestyle races (50, 100, and 200 meters) and all three relays. She took the silver medal in the 100-meter butterfly. In these championships, Krisztina Egerszegi of Hungary won four individual gold medals for women, and Alexander Popov of Russia won two individual and two relay gold medals for men.

Karoly Guttler of Hungary set a world record of 1 minute 0.95 second in his heat before the men's 100-meter breaststroke, then won the final in 1 minute 1.04 seconds. That was the only world record set by a man or woman during 1993. In 1992, there were seven world records for men and six for women.

Other. Among the women, Jenny Thompson of Dover, N.H., won three gold medals in the U.S. spring nationals and a record of six medals (three in relays) in the Pan Pacific Games. Among the men, Jon Olsen of Jonesboro, Ark., won four gold medals (two in relays) in the Pan Pacific Games. Kieren Perkins of Australia took the three longest freestyle finals in Australia's national championships and the same three in the Pan Pacifics. □ Frank Litsky

In *World Book,* see **Swimming.**

Switzerland in 1993 continued to negotiate for membership in the European Community (EC or Common Market) even though Swiss voters in late 1992 rejected participation in another multinational group, a free trade zone that links many Western European countries. Public opinion among the Swiss ran well against EC membership in 1993, especially after a currency crisis hit the EC in August.

Election controversy. The coalition of parties that have shared power in Switzerland since 1959— the Social Democratic Party, the Radical Democratic Party, the Christian Democratic Party, and the People's Party—was disturbed in 1993 when the Swiss legislature on March 3 refused to elect the Social Democratic Party's chosen candidate, lawyer Christiane Brunner, to the governing Federal Council. Brunner, who would have been the only woman on the seven-person council and only the second woman ever to serve in the Swiss government, created unease in the legislature with her support of abortion rights and her criticism of the military.

In response to the rejection, the Social Democratic Party threatened to pull out of the power-sharing arrangement. But calm returned on March 10 when the legislature elected a less controversial female candidate, trade union leader Ruth Dreifuss, to the council with Brunner's support. □ Philip Revzin

See also **Europe** (Facts in brief table). In *World Book,* see **Switzerland.**

Syria. A peace agreement between the Palestine Liberation Organization (PLO) and Israel signed on Sept. 13, 1993, drew criticism from Syrian President Hafiz al-Assad. The agreement allowed limited Palestinian self-rule in the Israeli-occupied Gaza Strip and the West Bank town of Jericho. This undercut Syria's leading position in the Arab-Israeli peace talks, which began in 1991. Assad criticized the PLO and Israel for working out their own deal in secret talks.

After the agreement, experts believed that a Syrian-Israeli peace accord would be stalled. As its price for peace, Syria had been demanding the return of the Golan Heights, which Israel captured in 1967 and annexed in 1981. But experts predicted the Israeli government would find it difficult to sell another land-for-peace swap to a nervous Israeli public.

As recently as August 1993, experts had predicted that a five-day Israeli raid in July against positions held by the pro-Iranian guerrillas of Hezbollah in southern Lebanon had created an opportunity for a Syrian-Israeli breakthrough in the Arab-Israeli peace talks. This was due to the fact that Syria, which still had 35,000 troops stationed in Lebanon and held sway over Lebanese politics, had helped broker a cease-fire between Israel and Lebanon. Following the September accord, however, U.S. officials and experts worried that Syria could attempt to subvert support for PLO leader Yasir Arafat's bid for peace. Syria harbors 10 radical, non-PLO Palestinian groups and maintains links with anti-American Iran.

Syrian-American relations. Syria continued to receive criticism from the United States in 1993. In a May 20 letter to U.S. President Bill Clinton, nearly 75 percent of the U.S. Senate condemned Syria for allegedly backing down on its agreement to allow exit visas for its remaining 1,400 Jewish citizens. Western officials also criticized Syria for supporting various terrorist groups active in the Middle East and for its failure to withdraw Syrian troops from Lebanon by September 1992 in accord with a 1989 agreement.

Adding to U.S.-Syrian tensions in 1993 were lingering suspicions based on a 1992 report by the U.S. House Subcommittee on Crime and Criminal Justice. The report claimed that about 90 percent of the land in Lebanon's Bekaa Valley, where Syrian troops are located, was being used to grow poppies, the source of heroin destined for the United States.

Internal events. Salah Jedid, a leader of Syria's Baath Party who effectively ran Syria from 1966 until 1970, died of a heart attack Aug. 19, 1993. Jedid was ousted by Assad in 1970 and jailed for 23 years.

The state-run Syrian press stated that 57 inmates died and another 50 were injured during a fire at Hasaka prison, 400 miles (640 kilometers) north of Damascus, on March 24, 1993. The fire was blamed on five inmates who were then executed in May. □ Christine Helms

See also **Middle East** (Facts in brief table). In *World Book,* see **Syria.**

Taiwan. In late April 1993 in Singapore, Taiwan and China held their highest-level talks since 1949, when Nationalist Chinese retreated to Taiwan after the Communist victory in China. Because Taiwan forbids any direct contact with China, semiofficial organizations had been set up in each state to deal with practical matters concerning the other.

The leaders of these organizations signed four historic agreements on April 29, 1993. Two agreements called for the delivery of registered letters and the verification of official documents within each state. A third agreement called for meetings "as needed" between the semiofficial leaders and more frequent meetings between their lower-level deputies. The fourth agreement outlined areas of future cooperation, including repatriation from Taiwan of illegal Chinese immigrants and joint efforts to halt crime, particularly smuggling.

Trade with China was the fastest growing element in Taiwan's economy, despite Taiwan's forbidding direct contact with China. In 1993, the two states traded some $10 billion in goods through Hong Kong, and Taiwan had an estimated $20 billion invested in mainland enterprises.

Political strife. The power of the Kuomintang (KMT) party that has ruled Taiwan since 1945 continued to wane in 1993. The first signs of decline had occurred in December 1992, when elections for the Legislative Yuan, Taiwan's lawmaking body, gave the KMT only 53 percent of the popular vote. Fighting among KMT liberal and conservative factions increased during 1993. On February 3, conservative KMT Premier Hao Po-ts'un resigned, due in part to pressure from the party's mainstream liberals. He was accused of blocking the democratic reforms of President Li Teng-hui, who has the liberals' support.

On February 23, the Legislative Yuan approved Li's nomination of Lien Chan as premier. Lien had been Taiwan's foreign minister, deputy premier, and governor. On June 8, the KMT suffered its first major legislative defeat. Despite government objections, KMT party rebels and members of the opposition Democratic Progressive Party (DPP) joined forces to pass legislation that required some 23,000 elected and appointed officials to disclose their wealth.

The political strife finally caused the KMT to split for the first time on August 10. Six KMT members of the Yuan, protesting KMT corruption and favoring closer ties with China, formed a new political party, the Chinese New Party (CNP). On August 18, running unopposed, Li was reelected as party chairman. But about 17 percent of the delegates cast spoiled ballots, indicating their opposition to him. Nevertheless, Li's supporters won control of the KMT's policymaking bodies. Despite strong opposition from the DPP in elections for 23 county and city offices on November 27, the KMT won 15 contests.   □ Henry S. Bradsher

See also **Asia** (Facts in brief table). In *World Book,* see **Taiwan.**

Tajikistan in 1993 was the scene of violent conflict, as an alliance of prodemocracy and Islamic forces continued their rebellion against the former Soviet republic's Communist government. The fighting calmed somewhat in January but flared up again in June, as rebels operating out of bases in neighboring Afghanistan staged raids against Tajik government forces and Russian troops patrolling the Tajik-Afghan border. Russia had allied itself with the Tajik government in late 1992 in an effort to keep radical Islamic influences from penetrating into other areas of the former Soviet Central Asia.

On July 13, 1993, Tajik rebels killed 25 soldiers at a Russian border post. Skirmishes continued during the summer, as Russia attacked Tajik positions in Afghanistan. On August 24, Russia, Tajikistan, Kazakhstan, Kyrgyzstan, and Uzbekistan agreed to set up a peacekeeping force on the border.

At year's end, opposition guerrillas remained active, chiefly in eastern Tajikistan. Officials said that tens of thousands of people had died and hundreds of thousands had lost their homes in two years of fighting. Human rights groups accused the Tajik government of torturing and killing political opponents. Tajik officials denied the charges.   □ Justin Burke

See also **Asia** (Facts in brief table); **Commonwealth of Independent States.** In *World Book,* see **Tajikistan.**

Tanzania. See Africa.

Taxation. President Bill Clinton and congressional Democrats enacted new tax legislation in 1993 that Republicans labeled the biggest tax increase in the history of the world. Democrats countered that the measure, designed to raise about $241 billion through fiscal year 1998, was topped by President Ronald Reagan's 1981 tax increases, when adjusted for inflation. The tax provisions were part of a budget bill that was passed by Congress on Aug. 5 and 6, 1993. The bill aimed at paring $496 billion from annual federal deficits during the five years. An object of intense partisan controversy, the package barely squeaked through the Senate and House of Representatives. No Republican voted for what was the centerpiece of Clinton's economic program.

Income tax hikes. Retroactive to Jan. 1, 1993, the top income tax rate of 31 percent was raised to 36 percent and affects single filers with taxable incomes above $115,000 and couples making above $140,000. Also, a 10 percent surtax was imposed on those with taxable incomes of more than $250,000. The surtax created a top tax rate of 39.6 percent.

Talk of a monster income tax hike led many of the nation's 110 million taxpayers to fear that they would be adversely affected. The Clinton Administration argued that the income tax changes affected only the top 1.2 percent of taxpayers.

Congress boosted the highest corporate income tax rate, also making it retroactive to January 1. The rate, which was increased to 35 percent from 34 percent, applies to taxable incomes over $10 million.

Additional taxes. Effective October 1, the federal gasoline tax was boosted by 4.3 cents a gallon (3.8 liters) to 18.4 cents. The tax on diesel fuel was increased by 4.3 cents to 24.4 cents a gallon.

Starting in 1994, the 2.9 percent Medicare tax will apply to all wages and self-employment income. Previously, the Medicare tax had applied only to the first $135,000 of income. Also beginning in 1994, some social security recipients will pay taxes on up to 85 percent of their benefits. This change will affect retirees whose total income, including social security benefits and tax-free interest, exceeds $34,000 for singles and $44,000 for couples.

Also to go into effect in 1994 were new curbs on business deductions for meals and entertainment. The deductible portion of such spending will drop to 50 percent from 80 percent. Outlays for lobbying and club dues will no longer be deductible.

Low-income taxpayers. The revenue package included tax cuts and cash benefits for the poorest taxpayers, starting in 1994. The Earned Income Tax Credit was extended to cover families earning up to $27,000 a year. And for the first time, the credit will be offered to childless people between ages 25 to 64.

☐ Frank Cormier and Margot Cormier

See also **Clinton, Bill; Congress.** In *World Book,* see **Taxation.**

Telecommunications. Companies from once separate industries such as telephone, cable television, and motion pictures rushed to form alliances in 1993. They were preparing for a new telecommunications era in which video, voice, and data will be carried over the same networks and controlled by the same firms. Key players in many of the deals were the long-distance telephone carrier American Telephone and Telegraph Company (AT&T) and the seven regional carriers, the so-called Baby Bells, which were created in 1984 when AT&T was forced to sell its local telephone operations.

Strategic partnerships. On May 17, 1993, US West Incorporated, the Baby Bell that serves most of the western United States, bought a $2.5-billion stake in the entertainment division of Time Warner Incorporated, one of the world's largest information and entertainment conglomerates. The move gave US West a vast storehouse of programming to support any ventures into the television market.

On August 16, AT&T said it would buy McCaw Cellular Communications Incorporated, the nation's largest cellular telephone company, for $12.6 billion. The acquisition will allow AT&T to assemble a telecommunications network that completely bypasses the Baby Bells.

On October 12, Bell Atlantic Corporation, the Baby Bell that serves the Pennsylvania-Virginia area, said it was purchasing Tele-Communications Incor-

© Jeff Danziger, *The Christian Science Monitor,* Los Angeles Times Syndicate.

porated (TCI), the nation's largest provider of cable television. If approved by regulators, the merger would be the biggest in U.S. history at more than $31 billion.

Paramount battle. The fiercest fight in telecommunications in 1993 took place over motion-picture and television studio Paramount Communications Incorporated. On September 12, Viacom Incorporated, the owner of cable channels MTV and Nickelodeon, said it was purchasing Paramount in a friendly deal for about $8.2 billion. But the news sparked a bidding war for Paramount. On September 20, QVC Network Incorporated, a home-shopping cable channel, made a hostile counterbid of about $9.5 billion.

Nynex Corporation, the Baby Bell that serves the upper Northeast, along with Blockbuster Entertainment Corporation, the biggest video store chain in the United States, then invested $1.8 billion in Viacom to help it match QVC's offer. On November 12, QVC countered by raising its offer to $10.6 billion after securing a $1.5-billion investment from Bell South, the Baby Bell that serves the Southeast.

Paramount's directors decided to ignore QVC's higher bid and go with Viacom. But on December 9, the Delaware Supreme Court ruled that Paramount must consider both bids on an equal basis. On December 22, Paramount's directors accepted a QVC offer of $10.2 billion.

Regulatory easing. On August 24, a federal judge overturned a law that prohibits telephone companies from providing television programming over their phone lines to subscribers in their own service areas. The judge ruled that the plaintiff in the case, Bell Atlantic, could compete with cable television carriers to provide television services to its customers. If upheld on appeal, the ruling would open the door to full competition between telephone and cable television companies.

Wireless services. On September 23, the Federal Communications Commission (FCC), the agency that regulates interstate communication, voted to reserve part of the airwaves for so-called wireless networks, also known as personal communications services (PCS). Wireless networks are similar to cellular networks, but they can carry more information and require less expensive receivers. The FCC's decision paved the way for new types of cordless telephones, computers, and fax machines.

Superhighway construction. Planning began in 1993 on the *information superhighway*—a telecommunications network that will link a person with a computer to information databases. Officials in the Administration of President Bill Clinton said they would try to spur private investment in the network by setting communication standards, making government data available on the network, and proposing laws that foster competition.   □ Pat Widder

See also **Computer; Electronics.** In *World Book,* see **Cable; Telecommunication.**

Television. The television industry's fondness for sensational subjects reached new heights in 1993. During the first week of January, three networks—CBS Inc., the American Broadcasting Companies (ABC), and the National Broadcasting Company (NBC)—televised docudramas about Amy Fisher, a teen-ager who shot the wife of her lover. The movies drew huge audiences, and inspired other TV dramas from headline stories. One program, "In the Line of Duty: Ambush in Waco," about Branch Davidian cult leader David Koresh, was being filmed even as the Federal Bureau of Investigation laid siege to Koresh's compound in Texas on April 19. The program aired on May 23.

The made-for-TV movie *The Positively True Adventures of the Alleged Texas Cheerleader-Murdering Mom* satirized the media's penchant for lurid docudramas. It aired on the Home Box Office network in April.

Targeting TV violence. The United States Congress in 1993 held hearings on television violence and threatened to pass legislation requiring a rating system for TV programs. In response, the four national networks—ABC, CBS, NBC, and Fox Broadcasting Corporation—volunteered to preface some prime-time shows with a warning label reading: "Due to some violent content, parental discretion advised." The warnings began in September, with the networks themselves deciding which programs would receive them.

"Educational" programming. The Federal Communications Commission (FCC) on March 2 announced that television stations could no longer consider cartoons such as "G.I. Joe" and "The Flintstones" as educational fare. The FCC also delayed the renewal of broadcast licenses for seven local television stations, calling their record in providing educational programs inadequate. Under the Children's Television Act of 1990, local broadcasters are required to show a commitment to educational shows for children.

Tinkering with the truth. Two scandals hit the NBC news division in 1993. In February, anchors on "Dateline NBC" issued an on-air apology to viewers for a report that the show had aired the previous November. The report addressed the safety of a type of truck manufactured by the General Motors Corporation (GM) and showed a pickup truck catching fire in a test crash. However, the report did not reveal that the testers had rigged the truck with explosives. GM filed a defamation suit.

Also in February 1993, Tom Brokaw, the anchor of "NBC Nightly News," admitted that "dead" fish displayed in a story on industrial pollution had not been killed by pollution but had just been stunned for a scientific experiment. These two incidents led to the resignation of NBC's news division President Michael Gartner on March 2. Andrew Lack, a producer of news-magazine shows at CBS, replaced him.

A scene from the last episode of "Cheers" airs on May 20. The popular show had been televised for 11 years.

Top-rated U.S. television series

The following were the most-watched television series for the 31-week regular season—Sept. 21, 1992, through April 18, 1993—as determined by Nielsen Media Research.

1. "60 Minutes" (CBS)
2. "Roseanne" (ABC)
3. "Home Improvement" (ABC)
4. "Murphy Brown" (CBS)
5. "Murder, She Wrote" (CBS)
6. "Coach" (ABC)
7. "NFL Monday Night Football" (ABC)
8. (tie) "CBS Sunday Movie" (CBS)
   "Cheers" (NBC)
10. "Full House" (ABC)
11. "Northern Exposure" (CBS)
12. "Rescue 911" (CBS)
13. "20/20" (ABC)
14. (tie) "CBS Tuesday Movie" (CBS)
    "Love and War" (CBS)
16. (tie) "The Fresh Prince of Bel Air" (NBC)
    "Hangin' With Mr. Cooper" (ABC)
    "The Jackie Thomas Show" (ABC)
19. "Evening Shade" (CBS)
20. (tie) "Hearts Afire" (CBS)
    "Unsolved Mysteries" (NBC)
22. "Primetime Live" (ABC)
23. "NBC Monday Night at the Movies" (NBC)
24. "Dr. Quinn, Medicine Woman" (CBS)
25. (tie) "48 Hours" (CBS)
    "Seinfeld" (NBC)

Night talkers. David Letterman announced on January 14 that his talk show would move from NBC to CBS and air at 11:30 p.m. Eastern Standard Time (EST)—directly opposite NBC's "The Tonight Show" with Jay Leno. CBS agreed to pay Letterman an annual salary of $14 million for the "Late Show." It premiered on August 30. Letterman's ratings got off to a fast start and by late October had surpassed Leno's. Meanwhile, NBC chose 30-year-old Conan O'Brien as Letterman's replacement. O'Brien was a virtually unknown writer and producer of television comedies.

The Fox network launched its own talk show hosted by Chevy Chase, a comic actor who became famous portraying inept TV anchors on "Saturday Night Live" in the 1970's. Chase's show debuted on Sept. 7, 1993, and fizzled fast. Fox canceled his program in October.

The new and the blue. Veteran producer Steven Bochco brought out a new series, "NYPD Blue," that became the most controversial new show of the fall season. Similar in theme to "Hill Street Blues," Bochco's influential police series of the 1980's, "NYPD Blue" contained raw language and nudity that was more frank than that seen on other network shows, but still mild compared with cable programs and motion pictures. Alarmed by the program's content, 57 of the 225 ABC affiliate stations across the country refused to air the premiere on

September 21. Nevertheless, the show had the greatest number of viewers in its time period. Several of the reluctant affiliates began carrying the series after it looked as if it could become one of the season's hits.

Most of the programs debuting in autumn were comedies, concerned with single-parent families or high school counselors and coaches. Influenced by the success of "Seinfeld," a racy sitcom starring comedian Jerry Seinfeld, many new programs starred stand-up comics. Harry Anderson played the humor columnist Dave Barry in "Dave's World"; Richard Lewis and Don Rickles played a father and son in "Daddy Dearest"; and Brett Butler portrayed a divorced mom in "Grace Under Fire."

Two competing science-fiction shows airing opposite each other on Sunday nights had mixed success. Motion-picture director Steven Spielberg produced "seaQuest DSV," an expensive underwater adventure series full of computer-generated graphics and special effects. Despite a highly watched debut on September 12, ratings began to sink in subsequent weeks. In contrast, "Lois and Clark: The New Adventures of Superman" initially seemed like a failure but began emerging as a sleeper hit.

Filling famous chairs. On June 1, Connie Chung became co-anchor of the "CBS Evening News" with Dan Rather. The change was seen as an effort to boost the CBS show into the number-one slot among nightly news reports.

Alistair Cooke, the articulate host of the Public Broadcasting Service's (PBS) "Masterpiece Theatre," retired after almost 22 years on the program. *New York Times* columnist Russell Baker replaced him in the emcee's chair beginning in October.

So long, farewell. After 11 years, the situation comedy "Cheers" ended its run with a 90-minute finale on May 20. The occasion was heavily promoted, with specials preceding and following the final episode. "I'll Fly Away," a drama about a Southern white family and its black housekeeper during the civil rights movement of the early 1960's, also folded. The show had won critical acclaim and Emmy nominations but never achieved high ratings.

Cable concerns. Responding to consumer complaints that cable TV subscription rates had nearly doubled in the past six years, the FCC on April 1 set down regulations for charges for basic cable packages. The FCC's determination of "reasonable" rates for cable services resulted in many cable companies having to cut prices by about 10 percent. However, some consumers were expected to receive higher bills. The FCC also ordered cable operators to retract any price increases they had imposed since passage of the Cable Television Consumer Protection and Competition Act of 1992. Originally intended to take effect in 120 days, the rate reductions were later delayed until early 1994, and prices remained frozen at their April 1993 levels.

The networks and other broadcasters in 1993 sought to take advantage of provisions in the 1992 cable act that allowed them to charge cable companies for their broadcast signals. But the cable systems refused to pay, and, on Oct. 6, 1993, subscribers in several cities awoke to find that they were no longer receiving network programs. However, most broadcasters agreed to an arrangement that allowed them to form new cable channels instead of receiving cash fees from cable systems. The first channel to arrive was ESPN2, a sports channel developed by ABC.

Information highway. In October, Bell Atlantic Corporation and Tele-Communications Incorporated (TCI) announced a merger that would bring the *information superhighway* closer to reality. The superhighway is a plan to combine video, telephone, cable, and computer technologies so that television can provide viewers with a vast number of channels, databanks, and interactive services. Bell Atlantic is one of the country's largest telephone companies, and TCI is the nation's largest cable operator, with the technology to provide TV's with 500 channels. The $31-billion deal, the largest in American business history, reflected a wave of mergers and acquisitions among cable, telephone, and entertainment companies during the year.   □ Troy Segal

See also **Telecommunications.** In *World Book,* see **Television.**

Tennessee. See State government.

Emmy Award winners in 1993

Comedy
Best Series: "Seinfeld"
Lead Actress: Roseanne Arnold, "Roseanne"
Lead Actor: Ted Danson, "Cheers"
Supporting Actress: Laurie Metcalf, "Roseanne"
Supporting Actor: Michael Richards, "Seinfeld"

Drama
Best Series: "Picket Fences"
Lead Actress: Kathy Baker, "Picket Fences"
Lead Actor: Tom Skerritt, "Picket Fences"
Supporting Actress: Mary Alice, "I'll Fly Away"
Supporting Actor: Chad Lowe, "Life Goes On"

Other awards
Drama or Comedy Miniseries or Special: *Mystery!: Prime Suspect 2*
Variety, Music, or Comedy Series: "Saturday Night Live"
Made for Television Movie: *Barbarians at the Gate* and *Stalin*
Lead Actress in a Miniseries or Special: Holly Hunter, *The Positively True Adventures of the Alleged Texas Cheerleader-Murdering Mom*
Lead Actor in a Miniseries or Special: Robert Morse, *Tru*
Supporting Actress in a Miniseries or Special: Mary Tyler Moore, *Stolen Babies*
Supporting Actor in a Miniseries or Special: Beau Bridges, *The Positively True Adventures of the Alleged Texas Cheerleader-Murdering Mom*

Tennis

Tennis. Steffi Graf of Germany and Pete Sampras of the United States won the major honors in 1993, but greater attention went to an attack on Monica Seles and the death of Arthur Ashe. Ashe, the only black male winner of the Wimbledon and United States Open championships and a celebrity beyond sports, died at age 49 of pneumonia, a complication of AIDS. Ashe's doctors said he probably contracted HIV, the virus that causes AIDS, from an unscreened blood transfusion in 1983, when he underwent open-heart surgery. He died on Feb. 6, 1993.

Seles. The 19-year-old Seles, the world's top-ranked woman, was stabbed by a psychologically disturbed spectator and did not play the rest of the year. Seles, an ethnic Hungarian, was born in Yugoslavia and had lived in Florida since 1986. She had won three of the four grand slam titles in 1991 and again in 1992, displacing Graf as the best female player.

Seles was sitting with her back to the stands at courtside during a match in Hamburg, Germany, on April 30, 1993, when a man walked up behind her and stabbed her between her left shoulder blade and spine with a serrated knife. Although the knife narrowly missed her spinal column and did not damage vital organs, the wound, an inch (2.5 centimeters) wide and a half-inch (1.3 centimeters) deep, cut at least two muscles.

The attacker was Gunther Parche, a 38-year-old

Monica Seles collapses after a spectator stabbed her in the back during a match on April 30 in Hamburg, Germany.

German who said he did not want to hurt Seles but did want to help Graf regain the number-one ranking. On October 13, a Hamburg District Court let Parche off with a two-year suspended sentence, citing a psychiatrist's testimony that Parche's "highly abnormal personality" could have diminished his ability to reason.

Seles said she was "shocked and horrified" by the light sentence, and tennis officials said the same. They tightened security at all tournaments. At the French Open, even paté knives were confiscated.

Women. In the Australian Open, the first grand slam tournament, Graf was the runner-up. But with Seles sidelined later in the year, the 24-year-old Graf won the last three grand slams—the French Open, Wimbledon, and the United States Open.

In the final of the Australian Open on January 30 in Melbourne, Seles defeated Graf, 4-6, 6-3, 6-2, for her third consecutive title there. Seles had won three consecutive French Opens, but this time, she was recovering from the stabbing. On June 5 in Paris, Graf defeated Mary Joe Fernandez in the final, 4-6, 6-2, 6-4.

In the Wimbledon championships held from June 21 to July 4 in England, Graf trailed Jana Novotna of the Czech Republic, 4-1, in the final set before winning, 7-6, 1-6, 6-4. In the final of the $9-million United States Open, held from August 30 to September 12 in Flushing Meadow, N.Y., Graf defeated Helena Sukova of the Czech Republic, 6-3, 6-3.

Men. Sampras and Jim Courier, also a U.S. player, exchanged the number-one ranking during the year, with Sampras holding it at year's end. Courier fell to number three at year's end behind Germany's Michael Stich. Sampras led men and women in earnings with $3,648,075. Courier's major victory came when he won his second consecutive Australian Open, defeating Stefan Edberg of Sweden in the final on January 31, 6-2, 6-1, 2-6, 7-5.

In the French Open, which Courier won in 1991 and 1992, Sergi Brugera of Spain upset him in the June 6, 1993, final, 6-4, 2-6, 6-2, 3-6, 6-3. On July 4 at Wimbledon, in the first all-U.S. final since John McEnroe beat Jimmy Connors in 1984, Sampras defeated Courier, 7-6, 7-6, 3-6, 6-3.

In the fourth round of the United States Open, 15th-seeded Cédric Pioline of France upset Courier, 7-5, 6-7, 6-4, 6-4. In the final on Sept. 12, 1993, the 22-year-old Sampras whipped Pioline, 6-4, 6-4, 6-3.

In Davis Cup play in 1993, the best U.S. players—Sampras, Courier, McEnroe, Andre Agassi, and Michael Chang—were unavailable for the team's first match, against Australia in March. With Brad Gilbert and David Wheaton playing singles for the United States, Australia won, 4-1. Germany, led by Stich, beat Australia, 4-1, in the finals on December 5 in Dusseldorf, Germany. ☐ Frank Litsky

In *World Book,* see **Tennis.**

Texas. See **Houston; State government.**

Thailand. Two major accidents in 1993 focused attention on the unregulated nature of Thailand's rapid economic growth. On May 10, a fire swept through a toy factory outside Bangkok, the capital, killing 188 workers. Investigators reported that most doors in the four-story building were locked, and there were no fire alarms or fire escapes. Building inspectors reportedly had been bribed to approve faulty construction and overlook safety violations.

On August 13, a hotel in a provincial capital 150 miles (240 kilometers) northeast of Bangkok collapsed, killing more than 120 people. Three floors had been added in 1990 to the original three-story hotel, causing cracks to appear in the foundation. The cracks had widened under the weight of water tanks recently erected on the roof. The accident followed a number of other building collapses, as construction companies ignored building codes and safety regulations and bribed inspectors.

The economy continued to grow at an estimated 6 to 7 percent a year. Foreign-owned factories began to shift from making simple labor-intensive products to high-technology products such as computer parts that required skilled labor to operate sophisticated equipment. However, manufacturers found it difficult to find highly skilled workers because of Thailand's poor educational system.

Thailand's armed forces, which usually had dominated the government in recent decades, became less politically visible during 1993. The military lost control of the government in 1992, after its attack on demonstrators in May led to the election of a civilian government under Chuan Likphai, who became prime minister on Sept. 23, 1992.

The army commander, General Wimol Wongwanich, asserted that the army no longer maintained special links to certain political parties in order to exert influence on governmental affairs. The annual round of military promotions on Oct. 1, 1993, emphasized professionalism, and officers associated with the May 1992 attacks on demonstrators were given unimportant posts. Wimol also reassigned many army commanders stationed along the border with Cambodia. The Thai army had long been accused of aiding the Khmer Rouge (KR), a Cambodian Communist movement blamed for numerous atrocities, in the illegal trade of timber and gems.

Guerrilla attacks. In July and August 1993, two small guerrilla organizations wanting independence for Thailand's four southern provinces burned 35 schools and ambushed government troops and a train in the south. The Thai army accused a Muslim separatist faction of setting the fires. The people of the provinces are mostly Muslims in a nation that is predominantly Buddhist. Muslims had complained that Buddhists had too much influence on Thailand's educational system. □ Henry S. Bradsher

See also **Asia** (Facts in brief table). In *World Book,* see **Thailand.**

Theater. On Sept. 29, 1993, noted actress Jane Alexander was confirmed as the new director of the National Endowment for the Arts, the federal agency that awards grants to artistic groups. Alexander's appointment led some observers to hope for a new attention to theater in the United States. But others were unsure whether even the presence of such a powerful friend could help stabilize the country's financially shaken nonprofit theater community.

Regional theater. Long considered the risk-taking heartland of American new-play development, the regional theater community in 1993 found itself forced into a drastic retreat from that role. American audiences, hotly wooed by television and motion pictures, proved warier than ever of unfamiliar plays. To avoid losing desperately needed ticket sales at the box office, regional theater directors often felt compelled to stage previously produced works.

The extent of the pullback was revealed in April when the Theater Communications Group (TCG), the national organization of regional theaters, reported that script workshops, staged readings, and other new-drama programs had been cut back more than 60 percent since 1989 in the TCG's surveyed theaters. The TCG also reported that corporate donations to nonprofit theaters dropped in 1993 for the first time since 1974, when TCG began its annual surveys.

Despite these discouraging figures, regional theater did show some signs of life in 1993. Important new productions were Mame Hunt's *Unquestioned Integrity: The Hill-Thomas Hearings* at San Francisco's Magic Theatre; *The Times,* a musical by Joe Keenan and Brad Ross at the Long Wharf Theatre in New Haven, Conn.; and Anna Deavere Smith's *Twilight: Los Angeles, 1992* at Los Angeles' Mark Taper Forum.

Broadway. The country's commercial-theater industry, based in New York City, watched a real-life melodrama unfold in 1993 as the economy's halting recovery from recession led to the quick closures of many productions. Among the casualties were Brian Friel's *Wonderful Tennessee,* Jonathan Tolins' *Twilight of the Golds,* Lanford Wilson's *Redwood Curtain,* and Tug Yourgrau's *The Song of Jacob Zulu.* The low turnout for these plays was especially disappointing because 1993 was the 50th anniversary of the landmark Broadway musical *Oklahoma!* and the year chosen by the League of American Theaters and Producers to represent Broadway's centennial.

Even the usually reliable musical struggled. For example, Neil Simon's *The Goodbye Girl,* an expensive new musical treatment of his 1977 motion picture with a score by Marvin Hamlisch and a cast featuring Bernadette Peters and Martin Short, played only 188 performances. Yet producers remained optimistic about the drawing power of musicals. Late Broadway openings included a Dutch-born musical version of *Cyrano de Bergerac* and a stage-musical treatment of the 1948 ballet film *The Red Shoes.*

An angel visits a character in *Angels in America: Millennium Approaches,* a drama by Tony Kushner that won the Tony Award for best play in June.

Acclaimed works. Both the 1993 Pulitzer Prize for drama and the 1993 Tony Award for best play went to *Millennium Approaches,* the first half of Tony Kushner's two-part *Angels in America,* which explores issues of political power and human relationships in the era of AIDS. The second half of the work, *Perestroika,* joined *Millennium Approaches* in rotating repertory on Broadway in November. A second significant Broadway opening in November was Robert Schenkkan's six-hour, nine-play *The Kentucky Cycle,* the 1992 Pulitzer Prize winner for drama.

However, many financiers considered these innovative works too risky to bankroll, and most backed only shows with the widest appeal. The leader in this category was *The Who's Tommy,* an eye-popping adaptation of Pete Townshend's 1968 rock opera about an autistic boy who rises to cult-level popularity through his wizardry with a pinball machine. Featuring stagewide projections, flying actors, computer-controlled set changes, and blinding lighting effects, *Tommy* brought live theater to a new level of technological spectacle.

Other theater backers clung to the safest of stage havens, revivals. Standards appearing on Broadway in 1993 included *Guys and Dolls* (1950), *She Loves Me* (1963), and *Joseph and the Amazing Technicolor Dreamcoat* (1967).

Financial troubles. Ever-mounting production costs helped fuel a desperate atmosphere among Broadway producers. For example, *My Fair Lady* is estimated to have cost only $350,000 to stage when it opened in 1956 and to have recouped that investment in 12 weeks. By comparison, *The Will Rogers Follies* closed in 1993 without recovering its initial $7.2-million investment, despite running for more than two years. Rising labor costs, combined with the costly fad of increasingly sophisticated visual effects, steadily widened the gap that producers faced between revenue and cost.

The money crunch resulted in a new phenomenon: a glut of shows opening in the weeks before May 5, the eligibility deadline for the Tony Awards. A Tony victory can add weeks and even months to a show's run, so the closer a show opens to the cutoff date, the less time the show has to stay open before the announcement of a win. In 1993, no fewer than 14 new shows hit Broadway from March 4 to May 5. However, few survived. Of the 14 late-season openers, only 5 were still running six months later. These included the musicals *Kiss of the Spider Woman* and *Blood Brothers,* and *Fool Moon,* a comedy by mime artists Bill Irwin and David Shiner.

Off-Broadway. The off-Broadway theater scene emerged in 1993 as the country's most vital outlet for new dramatic work. Directors such as Lynne Meadow at Manhattan Theatre Club and Tanya Berezin at Circle Repertory chose promising playwrights and stuck with them regardless of the critical welcome. For example, Meadow staged Terrence McNally's *A Perfect Ganesh* and John Patrick Shanley's *Four Dogs and a Bone* despite the uneven reception that both writers' works had received in the past. And Berezin responded to a severe panning of Paula Vogel's *And Baby Makes Seven* by promising to stage Vogel's new *Desdemona*. Most encouraging, the subscriber bases of both the Manhattan Theatre Club and the Circle Repertory grew in 1993, suggesting that audiences were willing to join theaters in a long-term commitment to young, talented dramatists.

Other key events off-Broadway in 1993 included the Signature Company's inauguration of a full season of works by American playwright Edward Albee; the Vineyard Theatre's production of Nicky Silver's *Pterodactyls*; and Second Stage's premiere of Tina Howe's *One Shoe Off*. Winners of the 1993 *Village Voice* Obie Awards for best off-Broadway playwriting were Harry Kondoleon's *The Houseguests,* Larry Kramer's *The Destiny of Me,* Jose Rivera's *Marisol,* and Paul Rudnick's *Jeffrey.*

Director dismissed. On March 11, JoAnne Akalaitis was abruptly dismissed as artistic director of the Joseph Papp Public Theater and the New York Shakespeare Festival. Akalaitis had been chosen for the job by Papp, the theater's legendary founder, before his death in October 1991. But the theater's board of trustees did not approve of Akalaitis' preference for dark, unpopular works, such as her own much-praised but rigorously expressionistic staging

of Georg Büchner's play *Woyzeck* (1836) in 1992.

Akalaitis was replaced by George C. Wolfe, the playwright-director who scored big on Broadway in 1992 with the musical *Jelly's Last Jam* and went on to direct Kushner's *Angels in America* in 1993. The board of trustees chose Wolfe both for his knack for commercial success and for his record for serious accomplishments, such as the television presentation in 1993 of Anna Deavere Smith's *Fires in the Mirror.*

Women in charge. Female artistic directors continued to grow as a nurturing force for new theater nationwide in 1993. The efforts of women directors were especially felt in California, where women led four highly acclaimed theaters: Mame Hunt at San Francisco's Magic Theater, Timothy Near at the San Jose Repertory Theater, Sharon Ott at the Berkeley Repertory Theater, and Carey Perloff at San Francisco's American Conservatory Theater.

Revolving critics. After 13 years in the most influential theater critic's post in the country, Frank Rich on Dec. 1, 1993, stepped down from the job of chief theater critic at *The New York Times*. David Richards, the *Times'* Sunday theater critic, succeeded Rich, and Vincent Canby, former chief film critic at the *Times,* moved into Richards' old seat. Also, Ben Brantley, a former film critic with *Elle* magazine, in August took over Mel Gussow's post as the *Times'* principal off-Broadway critic. ☐ Porter Anderson

In *World Book,* see **Theater.**

Tony Award winners in 1993

Best Play, *Angels in America,* Tony Kushner.
Best Musical, *Kiss of the Spider Woman.*
Best Revival, *Anna Christie.*
Leading Actor in a Play, Ron Leibman, *Angels in America.*
Leading Actress in a Play, Madeline Kahn, *The Sisters Rosensweig.*
Leading Actor in a Musical, Brent Carver, *Kiss of the Spider Woman.*
Leading Actress in a Musical, Chita Rivera, *Kiss of the Spider Woman.*
Featured Actor in a Play, Stephen Spinella, *Angels in America.*
Featured Actress in a Play, Debra Monk, *Redwood Curtain.*
Featured Actor in a Musical, Anthony Crivello, *Kiss of the Spider Woman.*
Featured Actress in a Musical, Andrea Martin, *My Favorite Year.*
Direction of a Play, George C. Wolfe, *Angels in America.*
Direction of a Musical, Des McAnuff, *Tommy.*
Book of a Musical, Terrence McNally, *Kiss of the Spider Woman.*
Original Musical Score, (tie) John Kander and Fred Ebb, *Kiss of the Spider Woman,* and Pete Townshend, *Tommy.*
Scenic Design, John Arnone, *Tommy.*
Costume Design, Florence Klotz, *Kiss of the Spider Woman.*
Lighting, Chris Parry, *Tommy.*
Choreography, Wayne Cilento, *Tommy.*
Regional Theater, La Jolla Playhouse, California.

Thompson, Emma (1959-   ), won the Academy Award for best actress in March 1993 for her portrayal of a liberated Englishwoman living in the early 1900's in the motion picture *Howards End* (1992).

Thompson was born in London on April 15, 1959, to parents who were actors. Thompson herself did not become involved in the performing arts until she entered Cambridge University, near London. While at Cambridge, she joined the comedy troupe Footlights and quickly proved herself a superior actor.

After graduating from Cambridge, Thompson worked in the theater, motion pictures, and television (for which she wrote as well as acted). Thompson won the British Academy of Film and Television Arts award for best actress for her 1987 roles in two television miniseries, *Tutti Frutti* and *Fortunes of War*. In 1988, she wrote and starred in a miniseries mixing political and social issues with comedy.

Thompson acted in her first film, *The Tall Guy*, in 1988. She subsequently starred in *Henry V* (1989), *Impromptu* (1990), *Dead Again* (1991), and *Peter's Friends* (1992). Many of her roles have been opposite her husband, actor and director Kenneth Branagh, whom she married in 1989.

In 1993, Thompson had leading roles in the films *Much Ado About Nothing* and *The Remains of the Day*.   □ Lori Fagan

Togo. See Africa.

Toronto. The Toronto Blue Jays won their second World Series in a row on Oct. 23, 1993, setting off a huge, spontaneous celebration in the city's streets. The Blue Jays beat the Philadelphia Phillies 8-6 in the sixth game of the series with a dramatic ninth-inning home run by outfielder Joe Carter at Toronto's SkyDome. People immediately began to pour into the center of the city for a nightlong celebration that police estimated drew nearly 1 million people. But the party was remarkable for its general good humor and lack of violence.

Fallen Leafs rise. For many years, Toronto was considered a "hockey town," but the rise of the Blue Jays and a decade of lackluster seasons by the Toronto Maple Leafs made it appear that baseball had eclipsed hockey. In 1993, however, the Leafs advanced to the Campbell Conference finals by eliminating the St. Louis Blues and the Detroit Red Wings in dramatic play-off competition. The Toronto team entered the conference finals for the first time since 1978 but lost in seven games to the Los Angeles Kings. Nevertheless, Toronto was so pleased with its rejuvenated hockey players that a parade and reception was held for them at City Hall in June 1993.

Professional basketball was soon to be a part of Toronto's sports scene. In November 1993, the National Basketball Association granted a franchise to restauranteur John Bitove and a group of Toronto business people. The team owners planned to build a $100-million arena two blocks north of Toronto City Hall and begin their first season in 1996. (Monetary figures in this article are in Canadian dollars.)

New theaters. In June, businessman Ed Mirvish opened the 2,000-seat, $22-million Princess of Wales Theatre. The new theater opened with a production of *Miss Saigon* (1989), which brought in $30 million in advance ticket sales—a record for the city.

The suburban city of North York opened the Performing Arts Centre in October. The new $48-million complex includes a 1,750-seat theater, a 1,032-seat concert hall, a 250-seat studio theater, and an art gallery. The theater staged its first production in October with *Show Boat* (1927), which local black leaders protested as promoting racial stereotypes. Producer Garth Drabinsky argued that the script in his production had been modernized to eliminate any suggestions of racism. Nevertheless, there were an estimated 100 demonstrators outside the theater on opening night. Despite the controversy, *Show Boat* opened with healthy advance sales of $6 million and good reviews. The concert hall began its musical season in November with a performance by the opera star Dame Kiri Te Kanawa. The first season boasted scheduled performances by such well-known stars as violinist Pinchas Zukerman, cellist Yo-Yo Ma, and soprano Kathleen Battle.

The addition of the Princess of Wales Theatre and the North York Performing Arts Centre helped reinforce Toronto's position as the third largest city in the English-speaking world—after New York and London—for gross theater revenues.

The unemployment rate in 1993 dropped slightly from the previous year but still remained high at about 10.6 percent most of the year. Analysts estimated that 500,000 of the Municipality of Metropolitan Toronto's 2.2 million people received unemployment insurance or welfare during the year. Daily Bread, the supplier to local food banks, delivered more than 32 million pounds (15 million kilograms) of food for distribution to needy people.

Getting around. In February, provincial Premier Robert K. Rae announced his government would support "Let's Move," a program to spend $2.5 billion on new subways and transit lines. Four of the lines were to be built in the Municipality of Metropolitan Toronto. Another was slated for Mississauga, which is immediately to the west of Toronto.

The provincial government was to pay 75 percent of the cost of "Let's Move," and local municipalities were to pay 25 percent. But over the summer, the provincial government decided to try reducing its deficit by cutting grants to municipalities. These losses forced municipalities to cut their payrolls by 5 percent. This was accomplished by requiring municipal employees to take up to 12 days of unpaid leave. Declining revenues, however, cast doubt on the future of the transit program.   □ David Lewis Stein

See also **Ontario.** In *World Book,* see **Toronto.**

Dinosaur-related toys and games, many of them inspired by the motion picture *Jurassic Park,* were among the most popular product lines in 1993.

Toys and games. Retail toy sales in the United States leveled out in 1993 to gain just under 4 percent over 1992 levels, down from a 5 percent gain the year before. Continued sluggishness in the U.S. economy, along with apprehension about possible tax increases, prompted most consumers to spend cautiously, industry analysts said. Discount stores and chain stores offering competitive pricing and a wide selection of merchandise fared best during the year.

It's a small world. The Littlest Pet Shop, premiered by Kenner Products of Cincinnati, Ohio, is a line of tiny plastic animals, including dogs, cats, rabbits, hamsters, and turtles, that come with their own palm-sized "homes." The "homes" range from simple pet carriers to playhouses equipped with miniature scratching posts, dog baskets, and other items. Each pet chews on a bone, chases its tail, or performs some other appropriate action.

Toy Biz Incorporated of New York City introduced Mini Caboodles in 1993. The toy consists of a tiny carrying case that opens to reveal a thematic playset and miniature doll. The Workout Gym Playset, one of the 12 playsets available, includes an exercise bike, balance beam, high bar, hand weights, and pool and hot tub that can be filled with water.

Mighty Max, from Mattel Toys of El Segundo, Calif., is a miniature adventurer who travels to scary microworlds. The toy is packaged in plastic cases that come in a variety of shapes, including snakes and skulls. The cases open to reveal the tiny Max figure in such places as a mad scientist's dungeon.

Toys that talk to the TV. Two toys that respond to signals broadcast from television programs or videotapes were unveiled in 1993. Both toys, Toby Terrier, from Tiger Electronics Incorporated of Vernon Hills, Ill., and TV Teddy, from YES! Entertainment Corporation of Pleasanton, Calif., are geared to the younger children's market and come with their own videocassettes.

Toby Terrier's videotapes portray Toby's animated adventures with his Video Pals, a group of puppets. Signals encoded in the videos and emitted from the TV screen are picked up by a sensor on Toby's collar, which transmits them to a computer chip in the toy. The chip prompts Toby to bark, wag his tail, sing, and say such things as "I love you."

In TV Teddy's system, a transmitter attached to the TV set transmits radio signals to a speaker inside the animal. Teddy moves his eyes and mouth as he comments on the action in his videos or encourages children to recite the alphabet or join him in a song. Unlike Toby, Teddy can also respond to television shows that carry signals like those on the videotapes. A number of children's programs designed to work with Teddy are scheduled to be broadcast in 1994.

Snuggly, scary, and sublime. Barney the purple dinosaur, host of the "Barney & Friends" children's series on public television, continued to rule the television screen in 1993, and his success was

417

mirrored in the toy industry. Even a backlash from adults tired of what they regard as the plush reptile's syrupy sentimentalism failed to diminish sales of Barney products. Hasbro Inc. of Pawtucket, R.I., added to the numerous Barney dolls already on the market with its Talking Barney in 1993. The talking dinosaur repeats hundreds of phrases heard on the TV show and Barney videos. Barney also starred in a new video game—"Barney the Dinosaur's Hide & Seek Adventure"—from Sega of America, Incorporated, of Redwood City, Calif.

Two motion pictures—*Jurassic Park* (1993) and the animated *Aladdin* (1992)—inspired new toys in 1993. The fantastic dinosaurs of *Jurassic Park* translated into big sellers for more than 100 manufacturers licensed to sell *Jurassic Park*-related products. These included a video game from Sega and a line of action figures from Kenner Products. Sega also produced an *Aladdin* video game, with animation by the same Disney Studios artists who drew the animation for the movie. Dolls based on Aladdin and Jasmine, the heroine of the movie, were big hits for Mattel.

Watch those babies go! The first radio-controlled doll was on a roll in 1993. Mattel's Baby Walk 'N Roll comes in her own walker, which is guided by a remote-control device shaped like a baby's rattle. The doll giggles when moved forward and squeals when moved backward, while her head bounces and her legs and arms move. Also on offer was Baby Giggles 'N Go, manufactured by Tyco Toys of Mount Laurel, N.J. The soft-bodied, cuddly doll giggles when her tummy is tickled. When placed in her two-speed walker, she runs and bumps into things, giggling and turning around whenever she does so.

Although not on the run, fashion queen Barbie still left tracks in 1993. Mattel's Western Stampin' Barbie comes with stamps on rollers attached to her Western-style boots. An enclosed inkpad allows the doll to stamp a trail of "B's" in turquoise ink that can be sprinkled with accompanying glitter. Barbie's horse Stomper can stamp a trail of hoof marks and stars in a similar fashion. And don't forget Barbie's boyfriend—Western Stampin' Ken's bootmarks leave a trail of "K's" encircled in a horseshoe design.

Video ratings. The manufacture of increasingly realistic video games that incorporate actual film footage and enhanced graphics led to concern in 1993 about whether such games were too violent for young children. In May, Sega announced its introduction of a rating system for its games, much like that adopted by the motion-picture industry. Sega's ratings include GA (general audiences), MA-13 (mature audiences aged 13 and up), and MA-17 (aged 17 and up). Sega also established a toll-free hot line to let parents learn about the contents of a Sega game before buying it.   □ Diane P. Cardinale

In *World Book,* see **Doll; Game; Toy.**

Track and field. Chinese women stunned everyone in 1993 when they won the gold medals in three of the middle-distance and long-distance races in the world outdoor championships and weeks later shattered the world records in all three events. Many runners and coaches from other nations said the Chinese had to be using illegal body-building drugs, but the Chinese denied it.

China. Hardly anyone expected the kind of performances that the Chinese women registered in the

Michael Johnson sets off on the last leg of the 1,600-meter relay as the United States broke the world record at Stuttgart, Germany, in August.

world outdoor championships held from August 14 to 22 in Stuttgart, Germany. Liu Dong won the 1,500 meters in 4 minutes 0.50 second; Qu Yunxia won the 3,000 meters in 8 minutes 28.71 seconds; and Wang Junxia won the 10,000 meters in 30 minutes 49.30 seconds.

The Chinese then returned home for their national games in Beijing, the capital, where from September 8 to 13 they shattered world records four times in three events. The 20-year-old Wang ran 10,000 meters in 29 minutes 31.78 seconds, breaking the record by 42 seconds. In the 1,500, Qu Yunxia lowered the record by more than 2 seconds to 3 minutes 50.46 seconds. Although she finished second in the 1,500, Wang also broke the world record, with a time of 3 minutes 51.92 seconds. Then Wang lowered the 3,000-meter record to 8 minutes 12.19 seconds in a qualifying round and to 8 minutes 6.11 seconds in the next day's final, breaking the old record of 8 minutes 22.62 seconds by more than 16 seconds.

The Chinese attributed their success to hard work and a hunger to excel. Ma Junren, who coached the record-breaking women, said their energy came from a potion made from caterpillar fungus that Chinese have been drinking for hundreds of years. He said his runners had been tested regularly for drugs and had never tested positive.

World championships. No Chinese women ran in the world indoor championships, held from March 12 to 14 in Toronto, Canada. The United States and Russia led with 14 medals each, and the gold-medal leaders were Russia with 7 and the United States with 5. Harry (Butch) Reynolds of Columbus, Ohio, in his return to major international competition, won the men's 400 meters in 45.26 seconds.

Reynolds had served a two-year suspension from the sport's governing body, the International Amateur Athletic Federation (IAAF), which said he had tested positive in 1990 for banned performance-enhancing drugs. Reynolds blamed faulty testing procedures and won a $27.3-million judgment against the IAAF in December 1992 in a U.S. federal court. He had not collected any money from the judgment as 1993 ended, however.

Reynolds helped the United States dominate the outdoor world championships with 26 medals (13 gold, 7 silver, 6 bronze) to Russia's 16 (3 gold, 8 silver, 5 bronze). He ran on the U.S. 1,600-meter relay team that set a world record of 2 minutes 54.29 seconds. The U.S. men who won were Michael Johnson in the 400 meters (43.65 seconds, with Reynolds second); Kevin Young in the 400-meter hurdles (47.18 seconds); Mark Plaatjes in the marathon (2 hours 13 minutes 57 seconds); Mike Powell in the long jump (28 feet 2 inches [8.59 meters]); Mike Conley in the triple jump (58 feet 7¼ inches [17.86 meters]); Dan O'Brien in the decathlon (8,817 points); and the 400-meter and 1,600-meter relay teams.

World outdoor track and field records established in 1993

Men

Event	Holder	Country	Where set	Date	Record
4 x 100 meters	Jon Drummond Leroy Burrell Dennis Mitchell Andre Cason	U.S.A.	Stuttgart, Germany	Aug. 21	0:37.40†
4 x 400 meters	Andrew Valmon Quincy Watts Michael Johnson Butch Reynolds	U.S.A.	Stuttgart, Germany	Aug. 22	2:54.29
Mile	Noureddine Morceli	Algeria	Rieti, Italy	Sept. 5	3:44.39
10,000 meters	Yobes Ondieki	Kenya	Oslo, Norway	July 10	26:58.38
110-meter hurdles	Colin Jackson	United Kingdom	Stuttgart, Germany	Aug. 20	0:12.91
High jump	Javier Sotomayor	Cuba	Salamanca, Spain	July 27	8 ft. ½ inch (2.45 meters)
Javelin throw	Jan Zelezny	Czech Republic	Sheffield, England	Aug. 29	313 ft. 10 inches (95.66 meters)

Women

Event	Holder	Country	Where set	Date	Record
400-meter hurdles	Sally Gunnell	United Kingdom	Stuttgart, Germany	Aug. 19	0:52.74
Triple jump	Ana Biryukova	Russia	Stuttgart, Germany	Aug. 21	49 ft. 6 ¼ inches (15.09 meters)
1,500 meters	Qu Yunxia	China	Beijing	Sept. 11	3:50.46
3,000 meters	Wang Junxia	China	Beijing	Sept. 13	8:06.11
10,000 meters	Wang Junxia	China	Beijing	Sept. 8	29:31.78
20,000 meters	Izumi Maki	Japan	Amagasaki, Japan	Sept. 19	1:06.48.8

†Tied record.

The U.S. women's winners included Gail Devers in the 100-meter dash (10.82 seconds) and the 100-meter hurdles (12.46 seconds, an American record); Jearl Miles in the 400 meters (49.82 seconds); Jackie Joyner-Kersee in the heptathlon (6,837 points); and the 1,600-meter relay team anchored by Miles. Merlene Ottey of Jamaica won the 200-meter dash in 21.98 seconds.

Sergei Bubka of Ukraine won the pole vault at 19 feet 8¼ inches (6.00 meters) and became the first track and field athlete to capture the same event in four consecutive world championships. Linford Christie of the United Kingdom won the 100 meters in 9.87 seconds.

Two runners from the United Kingdom broke world records. Sally Gunnell set a world record in the 400-meter hurdles with a time of 52.74 seconds, and Colin Jackson bettered the world mark in the men's 110-meter hurdles with a time of 12.91 seconds.

Noureddine Morceli of Algeria won the men's 1,500 meters in 3 minutes 34.24 seconds. On September 5, he set a world record of 3 minutes 44.39 seconds for the mile. Between winning world championships indoors (7 feet 10¾ inches [2.41 meters]) and outdoors (7 feet 10½ inches [2.40 meters]), Cuban high jumper Javier Sotomayor improved his world record outdoors to 8 feet ½ inch (2.45 meters) on July 27. □ Frank Litsky

In *World Book,* see **Track and field.**

Transportation. In October 1993, Rodney E. Slater, administrator of the United States Federal Highway Administration, proposed that private companies be allowed to operate the nation's highways. The proposal sought to head off projected costs to the government of some $200 billion in necessary road construction and repairs and another $90 billion in bridge work. The federal government cannot afford the road repairs the nation needs, Slater said, but private industry, which could make a profit from such an undertaking, can.

If the proposal, which had the support of the U.S. Department of Transportation, was approved by Congress and the states, private enterprises would be allowed to charge new tolls and raise existing ones. Supporters of the proposal said that public pressure would prevent road operators from raising tolls extravagantly, and that increased toll costs are inevitable no matter who is in charge of roads.

Fuel tax. United States President Bill Clinton on February 17 introduced his economic plan, which included an extension of a gasoline tax and new taxes on nonrenewable fuels based on their energy content. The proposal met stiff resistance from lawmakers from oil-producing states. The energy tax was abandoned in June after Senator John B. Breaux (D., La.) suggested taxing only transportation fuels at a rate of 7.3 cents per gallon. Railroad, airline, and trucking industries cried "unfair," and the new Sec-

retary of Transportation Federico F. Peña supported them. After extensive debate in Congress, the tax was reduced to 4.3 cents per gallon, and the economic plan was signed into law in August.

Los Angeles opened its first subway on January 30. The underground railway, called the Red Line, runs 4.4 miles (7 kilometers) from downtown Los Angeles to MacArthur Park and makes stops at five stations. The line is one leg of the city's planned Metro system, which calls for the use of subways, buses, aboveground railways, car pooling, bikeways, and other forms of transit to help relieve congestion on the city's roadways.

In August, the safety of the subway's wall construction became a matter of public concern. A report from a consulting firm showed that the thickness of the walls at some locations did not meet the specifications called for in the design contract. Both the federal government and local authorities began investigations into the problem.

Channel tunnel delayed. A dispute over who would pay for cost overruns on the English Channel Tunnel railway scuttled the tunnel's planned opening in December, the tunnel's operator announced in April. Eurotunnel, the British-French company that will operate the underwater railway, and the tunnel's contractors agreed on July 27 on a system for determining who will be responsible for some $1.5-billion in unplanned costs. The tunnel's opening date was then rescheduled for May 6, 1994. The tunnel will connect Folkestone, England, and Calais, France.

Railroads. Major flooding in the Midwestern United States in the summer of 1993 disrupted the nation's railroad industry. The Association of American Railroads reported in August that the cost of damaged rails, lost service, and delays due to rerouting would cost the railroad industry about $200 million. About 25 percent of freight or passenger trains in the United States begin, end, or pass through the areas devastated by the floods. The financial loss was not, however, expected to seriously damage the growing $27.5-billion railroad industry.

Amtrak's worst accident since it was founded in 1970 occurred on Sept. 22, 1993, near Mobile, Ala. Forty-seven passengers and crew died when a train plummeted from a bridge in the middle of the night. Three of the train's locomotives and the first four cars—of which two were passenger cars—fell into a bayou below the bridge. Federal investigators reported on September 26 that a barge traveling down the bayou had hit and damaged the bridge shortly before the train's arrival. But various subsequent reports gave conflicting information on the details of the accident, and further investigations were underway. □ Lori Fagan

See also **Automobile; Aviation.** In *World Book,* see **Bus; Electric railroad; Subway; Transportation.**
Trinidad and Tobago. See **Latin America.**

Turkey. A political era ended in Turkey when President Turgut Özal, leader of the Motherland Party (ANAP), died unexpectedly on April 17, 1993. Although popular in the West for his support of a free market economy and of the coalition against Iraq during the Persian Gulf War (1991), Özal's legacy in Turkey was controversial. The war, which hit the Turkish economy hard, fueled radical nationalism among Kurds, Turkey's largest minority. In addition, Özal's plans to extend Turkish influence and trade to the former central Asian republics of the Soviet Union, had produced no tangible results. Özal was Turkey's prime minister from 1983 until 1989 when, fearing an ANAP electoral defeat, Özal forced his election as president while ANAP still held a parliamentary majority.

Succession. Süleyman Demirel, head of the True Path Party and Turkey's prime minister since 1991, was elected president by the National Assembly on May 16, 1993. Tansu Ciller, a United States-educated economist, became Turkey's first female prime minister after she won a formal parliamentary vote on July 5.

Economic ills. Despite a yearly economic growth rate of about 5 percent in recent years, Turkey's 60 million people earned only an average per capita income of $2,000 in 1993. Inflation was over 60 percent. Moreover, Turkey posted a budget deficit of $3.2 billion in the first quarter of 1993.

Foreign policy. After meeting with Russian President Boris Yeltsin, Ciller announced on September 9 that Russia would aid Turkey in seeking to lift the United Nations (UN) trade sanctions against Iraq. On August 24, Ciller's foreign policy adviser announced that abiding by the sanctions was costing Turkey an estimated yearly loss of $3 billion in trade with Iraq and in revenues generated from transporting Iraqi crude oil to the Mediterranean Sea. The UN sanctions against Iraq have been in place since 1990.

On October 18, Ciller met with U.S. President Bill Clinton in Washington, D.C., to persuade him to help lift the UN sanctions. Clinton did not agree to do so.

Kurdish-Turkish fighting. On March 17, Marxist Kurdish Workers' Party (PKK) leader, Abdullah Ocalan, declared a cease-fire. The PKK had fought Turkey since 1984 to establish an independent Kurdish state. Analysts believed that Ocalan called the cease-fire in response to pressure from Syria and Iran, his former benefactors, who wish to maintain stability in the region. On May 24, 1993, PKK guerrillas broke the cease-fire and set off a new wave of violence when they ambushed and killed 34 Turkish army recruits. The government's swift retaliation led to the deaths of hundreds of civilians, rebels, and Turkish troops in battles, air strikes, and ambushes.

About 10,300 people have died since the fighting began. Half of those deaths have occurred since 1990 as the violence escalated.

Tansu Ciller, an economist, celebrates in June after she was named to head a new government and become Turkey's first female prime minister.

Kurdish violence in Europe. On June 24, Kurds and their supporters launched simultaneous attacks against Turkish businesses and diplomatic missions in Denmark, England, France, Germany, Sweden, and Switzerland. In France and Germany, the militants briefly took hostages. One Kurdish protester died in Switzerland. Similar attacks occurred on November 4, killing one person and wounding 23.

Water rights. On January 21, Syria and Turkey announced that they would begin renegotiations on a 1987 accord over water-sharing rights to the Euphrates River. Friction between Turkey, Syria, and Iraq began in 1990 when Turkey started building dams on the river in a $365-million plan to irrigate 4.2 million acres (1.7 million hectares) of its impoverished southeast.

Salman Rushdie. Thirty-seven people died on July 2 when Muslim extremists set fire to a hotel in Sivas where Turkish newspaper publisher Aziz Nesan was attending a conference. Nesan, who survived the fire, had published excerpts from British author Salman Rushdie's novel *The Satanic Verses* (1988) in May. Iran's Ayatollah Ruhollah Khomeini condemned the book in 1989 and called for Rushdie's death. □ Christine Helms

See also **Middle East** (Facts in brief table). In *World Book,* see Turkey.

Turkmenistan. See Asia.
Uganda. See Africa.

Ukraine. Internal struggles over the pace of economic reform brought Ukraine to the point of economic collapse in 1993. Reform-minded Prime Minister Leonid Kuchma resigned in September, leaving most power in the hands of President Leonid Kravchuk. At the time of Kuchma's resignation, inflation stood at 70 percent a month, and Ukraine's temporary currency, the karbovanet, had fallen to more than 8,000 per United States dollar, from 2,000 to the dollar in March. The economy had shrunk by about a third since the end of 1991, and the government estimated that about 80 percent of Ukraine's people were living in poverty.

Ukraine's foreign relations also were tense in 1993. Ukraine and Russia failed to resolve several disputes that arose after the countries gained independence following the Soviet Union's breakup in December 1991. Ukraine also drew the anger of Russia and Western nations over its reluctance to give up its share of the former Soviet nuclear arsenal.

Struggle over reform. Kuchma, who had taken office in October 1992, worked early in 1993 to place the country on a path of market-oriented reform. Kuchma said his plans to cut subsidies to failing industries, to loosen price controls, and to cap wages and welfare benefits were necessary if Ukraine was to reduce its budget deficit and reverse its economic decline.

It quickly became apparent, however, that parliament was bitterly divided on a strategy for reform. And Kuchma was unable to control the Ukrainian central bank. On March 30, the karbovanet lost almost half its value against the U.S. dollar after the bank issued credits worth more than a million karbovanets to failing state-owned enterprises.

On May 18, Kuchma asked parliament to extend his power, granted six months earlier, to make economic policy by decree. Two days later, Kravchuk called for a constitutional amendment that would make the president, not the prime minister, the head of government. In response, Kuchma resigned. Parliament rejected Kuchma's resignation, but it refused to extend his economic powers.

Following a wave of price rises in early June, coal miners in the Donetsk region of eastern Ukraine went on strike. Kravchuk offered state credits to pay off mounting debts at inefficient coal mines. The move, however, sparked further inflation, which soon was running close to 50 percent a month.

In late August, parliament sought to increase Ukrainians' buying power by fixing the exchange rate for the karbovanet. As a result, the karbovanet lost a third of its value against the dollar, setting off another government crisis. On September 9, Kuchma again resigned, after parliament failed to act on an emergency reform plan that he had presented on August 31. Parliament accepted his resignation on September 21. On September 27, Kravchuk took control of the government. He said he favored a slow transition to a market economy.

On September 24, parliament voted to hold early legislative elections in March 1994 and a presidential election in June of that year. Local elections were set for January 1994.

Relations with Russia. The Soviet Union's collapse had left in dispute two issues of symbolic importance to both Ukraine and Russia: the Black Sea naval fleet and the Crimean Peninsula. The Crimea had belonged to Russia until 1954, when the Soviet Union placed it under the jurisdiction of Ukraine. The Black Sea Fleet had been a central part of Russia's navy before the formation of the Soviet Union. The fleet, comprising about 300 aging vessels, was based in the Crimean port city of Sevastopol, and Ukrainians regarded it as an important symbol of their independence.

Under an August 1992 treaty, Ukraine and Russia were to jointly control the Black Sea Fleet until 1995. However, tensions rose in May 1993, when about 200 vessels raised the Russian naval ensign in violation of that accord. On June 17, Kravchuk and Russian President Boris Yeltsin agreed to divide the fleet beginning in September. They also agreed that Sevastopol's port facilities would be leased by Russia.

On September 3, Kravchuk enraged Ukrainian nationalists by agreeing to transfer Ukraine's part of the fleet to Russia to settle a debt for billions of dollars' worth of fuel supplies. Kravchuk also promised to send to Russia all remaining nuclear warheads in Ukraine for dismantling, in return for the nuclear fuel they contained. But the deal came into doubt after Russia accused Ukraine in late September of amending it to exclude some nuclear weapons.

Arms control. In May 1992, Ukraine had promised to destroy or transfer to Russia all long-range nuclear weapons on its territory and to become a nuclear-free state. But since then, the country had hedged on these commitments. Ukrainian officials cited the danger posed to Ukraine's security by nationalist forces in Russia. They also demanded compensation for the cost of destroying the weapons.

On July 2, 1993, parliament passed a resolution claiming ownership of all the nuclear weapons on Ukrainian soil, including the long-range weapons covered by the first Strategic Arms Reduction Treaty (START I), an accord reached by the United States and the Soviet Union in 1991 and signed by Kravchuk in May 1992. On Nov. 18, 1993, parliament ratified START I but said Ukraine would comply with the treaty only if it received security guarantees and as much as $5 billion in aid. It also rescinded Ukraine's pledge to become a nuclear-free state. Kravchuk criticized the action and said he would resubmit the issue to parliament in 1994.   □ Justin Burke

See also **Commonwealth of Independent States.** In *World Book,* see **Ukraine.**

Unemployment. See Economics; Labor.

United Kingdom. British Prime Minister John Major saw a dramatic slump in his Conservative Party's fortunes and in his own popularity during 1993. His premiership was marked by economic difficulties, party divisions, policy reversals, and a public perception that he cast a gray image. Yet Major hung on, and at year-end, no potential successor had emerged to challenge him.

Voters delivered a stunning rebuff to ruling Conservative governments in local and national elections held on May 6. In elections for 47 county councils in England and Wales, the Conservatives lost 15 out of the 16 councils they had previously controlled.

In parliamentary by-elections on the same day, Conservatives lost Newbury, a seat in west Berkshire that they had held since 1924. The Liberal Democratic Party won 65 percent of the votes to the Conservatives' 27 percent, cutting the government's already slim majority in the House of Commons to 19.

Cabinet changes. In the wake of the Newbury disaster, Major made sweeping Cabinet changes, including the removal of Norman S. Lamont as chancellor of the exchequer on May 27. Lamont had been implicitly branded as the scapegoat for the calamity that began on Sept. 16, 1992, known as "Black Wednesday." That day speculators began selling pounds on foreign exchange markets. This ultimately led to the withdrawal of the pound from the Exchange Rate Mechanism of the European Communi-

The Blue Drawing Room in London's Buckingham Palace is one of 18 areas in the palace that opened for the first time to paying visitors in August.

Glass and bricks litter London's financial district in April, after Irish terrorists exploded a bomb on a Saturday morning that killed 1 man and injured more than 40 other people.

ty (EC, or Common Market). In 1993, Lamont's policies were blamed for the country's economic problems, including an unemployment rate that reached 10 percent of the labor force—more than 3 million workers. Major replaced Lamont with Kenneth Clarke, who had been secretary of the home office.

On June 24, Michael J. Mates, the minister for Northern Ireland in charge of security, resigned from the Cabinet as the result of revelations about his personal ties to Asil Nadir, a businessman who had jumped bail set at 3.5 million pounds (U.S. $5.25 million) and fled to Turkish Cyprus in May. Nadir was to have been tried in September on 13 counts of fraud and false accounting involving millions of dollars, stemming from the collapse in 1990 of his Polly Peck conglomerate. Political opponents called for Mates's resignation after the disclosure that he had accepted the loan of a car from one of Nadir's associates and had given Nadir a watch with an inscription referring to the activities of government lawyers who were preparing the case against Nadir.

The uproar over Nadir had also embarrassed the government on June 15, 1993, when the Conservative Party acknowledged that the fugitive businessman had donated at least 440,000 pounds (U.S.

$650,000) to the party. The opposition Labour Party demanded that the Conservatives release all the names of donors to party funds.

Maastricht showdown. A lengthy parliamentary process for ratifying the Maastricht Treaty on European unity turned into a nightmare for the government. The treaty called for closer political and monetary ties among EC nations. But during treaty negotiations in 1991, Major had argued that a section of the treaty called the "Social Protocol" was too costly for British industry. The protocol would have given British workers the same rights as those in the other EC countries, including a maximum 48-hour work week and paid maternity leave. Major was able to get the treaty negotiators to exempt the United Kingdom from the protocol.

However, about 20 to 25 Conservative members of Parliament (MP's), popularly called "Euroskeptics," were opposed to the Maastricht Treaty altogether. They united with Labour MP's, who wanted Major to sign the Social Protocol. On July 22, 1993, Parliament voted twice on the Maastricht Treaty. In the first round of balloting, on a motion to force Major to adhere to the Social Protocol, 23 Euroskeptics voted with Labour, producing a tie. Speaker Bet-

and interest rates were below the European average. On April 26, 1993, Lamont announced that the recession was officially over. But the recovery proved to be elusive, and the ballooning national deficit preoccupied the government.

The government embarked on a major review of spending. The Cabinet was divided between those who wanted to keep taxes low and cut public spending and those, including Major, who believed there was no choice but to raise taxes. The rising cost of programs, such as welfare, pensions for government employees, and the National Health Service, all came under review, and the government announced one of the toughest budgets on record on November 30.

Privatizing the railroad. On January 22, Transport Secretary John R. MacGregor introduced to the House of Commons a bill establishing a new entity called Railtrack, which would own track and other railroad facilities. British Rail would continue to own the trains. Franchises to provide freight and passenger service would be sold to private companies.

The Labour Party said that privatization would be a bureaucratic nightmare, and many Conservative MP's with commuters in their constituencies were also wary of the plan. The government insisted that privatization would benefit passengers. But on May 25, bowing to MP demands that cheap tickets for retirees and young people should continue, the government said it would regulate those ticket prices.

Labour's labors. The Labour Party continued its efforts to attract voters by moving away from its socialist roots. On September 29, at the party's annual conference, leader John Smith staked his political fortune on a proposal that would curb the power of trade unions, which had founded and funded the party. Previously, unions affiliated with the Labour Party had control over 40 percent of the local voting to select parliamentary candidates. However, Smith proposed a one-member, one-vote system, which meant that individual party members would select nominees for Parliament.

Student testing. Secretary of State for Education John H. Patten faced a widespread teachers' boycott in April over government plans to introduce testing for 7- and 14-year-olds as a way of gauging the progress of school reform. The three biggest unions said that the tests were poorly designed and difficult to administer. The teachers objected to publishing test results, in effect ranking the schools. Patten argued that the results had to be published to justify the spending of substantial amounts of taxpayers' money on school reform. But in August, due to widespread teacher hostility, the government announced it was scrapping plans to publish test results. It also decided to limit the tests to core subjects of English, mathematics, and science.

Royal wrangles. Prince Charles and Princess Diana separated in December 1992. But the royal family was plunged into a fresh scandal on Jan. 12, 1993,

ty Boothroyd broke the tie, casting her vote against Labour's motion. In the second round of balloting, a vote on the treaty as negotiated, at least 20 Euroskeptics joined the opposition, and the government lost by a vote of 324 to 316. The treaty appeared to be in limbo. Acting quickly, Major called for a vote of confidence on his handling of the treaty issue for the next day, July 23. The motion was worded so as to endorse the treaty. Faced with the certainty of a general election if Major lost the vote of confidence, which would likely have cost many Conservative MP's their seats, the Euroskeptics capitulated, and the treaty was approved 339 to 299.

Conservative plunge. The results of a poll taken on July 6 indicated that Major was the most unpopular prime minister ever. Only 14 percent of those polled said he was doing a good job. The government faced added humiliation on July 29, when Conservatives lost the parliamentary seat of Christchurch to the Liberal Democrats in a by-election. Conservatives had held the seat for 83 years. A major election issue was a Conservative plan to collect a 17.5 percent tax on domestic fuel consumption to begin in the spring of 1994.

The economy. Inflation dropped to 1.2 percent in June, the lowest rate since 1964. The pound remained competitive with other foreign currencies,

when an Australian magazine published details of a sexually explicit conversation that reportedly took place in 1989 between Prince Charles and his long-time friend, Camilla Parker Bowles. Buckingham Palace refused to comment on the story. The same day, a British newspaper leaked the contents of a letter that accused Princess Diana of using the media to publicize her personal account of the marriage breakup.

On June 28, Queen Elizabeth's second son, Prince Andrew, and his wife, the Duchess of York, known informally as "Fergie," announced their legal separation. Thus, the way was cleared for a divorce.

Royal finances. Major announced details on February 11 of an agreement under which Queen Elizabeth and Prince Charles had agreed to pay taxes on their income. However, the monarchy could "opt out" of the agreement after April 1994. Major did not disclose details regarding the sources of Queen Elizabeth's income, a closely guarded secret.

The queen also agreed to pay most of the bill to repair Windsor Castle, which had been badly damaged by a fire in 1992. The money would come in part from admission fees to sections of Buckingham Palace, which would be open to visitors in August and September, the months when the queen stays in Scotland. □ Ian J. Mather

See also **Ireland; Northern Ireland.** In *World Book,* see **United Kingdom.**

United Nations (UN) peace efforts ran into serious difficulties in 1993, particularly in Somalia, Bosnia-Herzegovina, and Haiti. On March 27, leaders of 15 Somali factions signed a UN-brokered agreement to end the nation's bloody two-year civil war and reestablish a legitimate government. The agreement called for disarmament, reconstruction, and setting up a two-year transitional national council composed of 74 representatives from throughout Somalia. Subsequent to the agreement, the UN took control of the United States-led relief mission in Somalia on May 4.

The UN Operation in Somalia (UNOSOM) had begun in 1992 and sought to provide humanitarian relief and to disarm the Somali factions so that food distribution could be carried out unimpeded. But the UNOSOM efforts had continually encountered fierce opposition, particularly from the supporters of General Mohamed Farah Aideed, the warlord who controlled the southern part of Mogadishu, the capital of Somalia. After the March agreement, Aideed continued to block UN relief efforts and escalated his attacks on UN peacekeepers.

On June 5, 1993, 24 Pakistani peacekeepers were ambushed and killed after inspecting weapons facilities operated by Aideed. As many as 35 Somalis also died as UN forces returned fire. UN officials accused Aideed of planning the attack.

In retaliation for the attack against the Paki-

stanis, UN forces from June 12 to 16 bombed munitions depots and captured hundreds of Aideed's militia. On June 16, U.S. forces bombed the headquarters of Aideed as UN ground troops attacked the area. At least 60 Somalis and 5 UN troops were killed.

The mission was tainted when Pakistani troops reportedly opened fire on Somalis demonstrating in support of Aideed. About 20 men, women, and children were killed and about 50 injured. UN officials said the demonstrators had fired on the Pakistanis first, but some witnesses claimed otherwise.

UN military strength in Somalia during July stood at nearly 20,000 troops from 28 countries. It included 3,935 Americans and 4,718 Pakistanis, the two largest contingents. In August, U.S. President Bill Clinton decided to send 400 Army Rangers to help capture Aideed.

On October 3 and 4, Aideed's forces shot down three U.S. helicopters during a U.S. attack. Eighteen Americans were killed during the attack. After Somalis had dragged the naked body of one of the dead U.S. soldiers through the streets of Mogadishu, American outrage prompted Congress to call for a complete withdrawal of U.S. forces from Somalia.

Clinton, however, decided to send an additional 1,700 U.S. troops to Somalia and ordered an offshore stand-by of 13,000 more troops. On October 7, he announced that U.S. troops were back under U.S., rather than UN, command, and that the United States would withdraw almost all of its troops from Somalia by March 31, 1994. Several other nations also laid plans for the return of their forces.

The deterioration of the UN operation in Somalia prompted the UN to focus on a political rather than a military solution. On November 9, UN Secretary-General Boutros Boutros-Ghali reported that 26,000 UN troops from 32 countries were in Somalia, and that at least 85 peacekeepers had been killed. The operation suffered the highest casualty toll among the 17 peace missions underway in 1993. The UN said UNOSOM's humanitarian efforts had helped revive the economy in many parts of the country, where schools were reopened and security reestablished. But at year's end, no overall political solution was in sight.

Progress in Bosnia-Herzegovina, which had declared independence from Yugoslavia in March 1992, continued to be thwarted by fierce ethnic rivalries between Croats, Muslims, and Serbs. By February 1993, the Serbs had captured more than 70 percent of the territory in Bosnia-Herzegovina (often called Bosnia). On March 11, UN Commissioner for Refugees Sadako Ogata said that Serbs continued to expel Muslims from Bosnian villages under a policy of "ethnic cleansing."

Mediators Lord David Owen, representing the European Community, and Cyrus R. Vance, representing the UN, continued negotiations to work out a political settlement among the factions. On March 25, the Muslims and Croats signed a peace plan that called for a permanent cease-fire, a new constitutional framework, the creation of an interim government, and a division of Bosnia into 10 semiautonomous provinces. The division would allow each of the three factions to control three areas, with Sarajevo, the capital, as an open city. The Serbs agreed to all the provisions except for the land division and continued their siege of Bosnian towns.

On March 31, the UN Security Council voted 14 to 0, with China abstaining, to allow the UN protection force in Bosnia to shoot down unauthorized military aircraft entering a no-fly zone over the country. But Bosnian Serb forces were undeterred by the order and continued to violate the ban.

On April 17, the Security Council expanded its economic sanctions against Serbia and Montenegro, the two remaining Yugoslav republics. The Council banned shipments of most goods across borders, blocked ships carrying goods to Serbia, and froze assets abroad belonging to the Serbian government.

On May 6, in a futile effort to protect Muslims, the Council declared six Bosnian towns as "safe areas," meaning that Serbian forces were not to attack them. Those towns were Tuzla, Zepa, Gorazde, Bihac, Srebrenica, and the capital. The Council in June authorized air strikes and the dispatch of protective UN troops to these towns, but the measures were never fully implemented, and the Serbs overtook all the towns but Sarajevo.

Peace talks resumed in July, and by the end of the summer, a new plan called for Bosnia to be transformed into a federation of three separate ethnic states, with Serbs receiving 52 percent of the republic, Muslims obtaining 30 percent, and Croats 18 percent. On August 31, all parties met to sign the plan, but the next day the Serbs demanded alterations that sank the agreement.

Haiti. On February 14, Haiti's military leader Lieutenant General Raoul Cédras agreed to allow UN human rights observers to begin implementing a UN plan to restore democracy to the country. About 250 UN and Organization of American States (OAS) workers then began arriving in Haiti.

Cédras had ousted democratically elected President Jean-Bertrand Aristide in September 1991. In retaliation, the United States and the OAS imposed a trade embargo on Haiti.

From March to June, UN-OAS envoy Dante Caputo negotiated with Cédras and Aristide, who was living in exile in Washington, D.C. The United States and the UN Security Council pressured Cédras to accept a plan for the return of Aristide. But Cédras and his government refused, and on June 16, the Council unanimously voted to impose on Haiti a weapons, oil, and economic embargo. Cédras then agreed to settle the crisis through diplomacy.

On July 3, on Governors Island in New York Harbor, Cédras and Aristide signed a peace agreement. The agreement called for a political truce, technical assistance to modernize Haiti's army and police, a conditional end to the embargo, and Aristide's reinstatement as Haiti's legitimate leader by October 30. Cédras reneged on the agreement, and on October 19, the Security Council reimposed its embargo.

Fearing for the safety for its personnel, the UN ordered most of its observers to leave Haiti. About 30 stayed with Caputo to continue efforts aimed at convincing the military government to step down and restore democracy.

Libya. On November 11, the Security Council decided to impose additional sanctions against Libya for refusing to hand over Libyan suspects sought in the bombings of two aircraft. One bombing in 1988 killed 270 people aboard a Pan American World Airways flight. The second bombing in 1989 killed 171 people aboard a French UTA airliner. The Council favored the new sanctions by a vote of 11 to 0. China, Djibouti, Morocco, and Pakistan abstained. The new sanctions were aimed at crippling Libya's oil and gas production by banning exports of equipment related to that industry. The sanctions also froze Libya's overseas investments and prohibited its import of construction materials and aircraft parts.

Cambodia. The UN Transitional Authority in Cambodia (UNTAC) successfully organized and supervised elections in Cambodia from May 23 to May 28 without any major incidents. Prior to the elections, UNTAC registered more than 4.7 million voters, or more than 90 percent of those eligible to vote. UNTAC also helped repatriate about 350,000 Cambodian refugees. After the elections, UNTAC began withdrawing from Cambodia. On November 4, the Security Council declared that UNTAC would complete its withdrawal by December 31, formally ending one of the UN's largest peacekeeping operations, with more than 22,000 military and civilian personnel and a cost of nearly $2 billion.

Human rights. The first World Conference on Human Rights in 25 years was held in Vienna, Austria, from June 14 to 25. On December 20, the UN General Assembly established the post of UN High Commissioner for Human Rights.

The General Assembly began its 48th session on September 21 with President Clinton making his first UN address since being elected. Clinton said the UN must make changes to become more effective and, specifically, "to know when to say no."

The 184-member Assembly included five new enrollees for 1993. They were the Czech Republic, Slovakia, Eritrea, Monaco, and Andorra. On October 29, the Assembly elected Argentina, the Czech Republic, Oman, Nigeria, and Rwanda as the five new, nonpermanent members of the Security Council for the 1994-1995 term. □ J. Tuyet Nguyen

See also **Bosnia-Herzegovina; Cambodia; Haiti; Somalia.** In *World Book,* see **United Nations.**

United States, Government of the.

President Bill Clinton took office on Jan. 20, 1993, promising to be an agent of change, something voters seemed to favor in electing him over incumbent George Bush in November 1992. Change was at the top of Clinton's agenda, with legislative proposals to restrain record federal deficits and, for the first time, guarantee health insurance for all Americans. He also embraced a blueprint for "reinventing government" that faced an uncertain future in Congress.

Clinton was able to implement some changes on his own. On Aug. 12, 1993, he had the Federal Aviation Administration (FAA) announce that 11,400 air traffic controllers fired by President Ronald Reagan after a 1981 strike could apply for rehiring. Administration officials conceded, however, that because of limited openings in the agency, only a handful of the controllers were likely to get their old jobs back.

Clinton announced on Feb. 9, 1993, that he intended to set an example for frugal government by reducing the White House staff by 25 percent and paying senior aides 6 to 10 percent less than their Bush-appointed predecessors. On October 1, he claimed to have achieved the staff cuts, but critics said some of the purported reductions were more imaginative bookkeeping than real cuts. Clinton also vowed to reduce the federal work force by 100,000 employees, to 2 million, by 1996.

Radiation experiments revealed. The U.S. Department of Energy disclosed in December 1993 that from 1945 through the mid 1970's, researchers at a number of government laboratories and private institutions exposed more than 1,000 people to high doses of radiation. The medical experiments—in which many individuals apparently were not asked for their consent or were not fully informed about the possible dangers involved—were aimed at determining the effects of radioactivity on the human body. Some people in the studies were exposed to intense beams of radiation, and others were injected with radioactive substances. Secretary of Energy Hazel R. O'Leary pledged a full investigation of the experiments, and on December 27 she called for the government to provide compensation for individuals, or their surviving families, who were harmed by the experiments.

Fixing the federal government. Far more ambitious than the proposed work force reductions was the "reinventing government" plan announced on Sept. 7, 1993, by Clinton and Vice President Albert Gore, Jr. The plan emerged from a study of government waste headed by Gore. By cutting, consolidating, and reorganizing government, Clinton said, the plan would save $108 billion over five years. However, Congress would have to take such measures as voting to close hundreds of Department of Agriculture field offices.

Clinton seeks diversity. Clinton's appointees to Cabinet posts and other top government positions reflected his promise to make his Administration a model of diversity. His Cabinet included four blacks, three women, and two Hispanics. (See biographies of individual Cabinet members.)

On March 19, Justice Byron R. White announced plans to retire after 31 years on the Supreme Court of the United States. Clinton nominated Ruth Bader Ginsburg, a federal appeals court judge, to succeed him. Sworn in as the 107th Supreme Court justice on August 10, she became the second woman ever to sit on the high court, joining Sandra Day O'Connor.

Conservatives in Congress vowed to block the appointment of other Clinton nominees. One of their targets was M. Joycelyn Elders, the President's choice for U.S. surgeon general. Elders, who had been director of the Arkansas Health Department when Clinton was governor of Arkansas, is an outspoken advocate of sex education programs in schools. But the confirmation battle that many had feared never materialized. She was confirmed by the Senate on September 7 by the comfortable margin of 65 to 34.

Likewise, conservative senators failed to prevent the appointment of Roberta Achtenberg as assistant secretary for fair housing and equal opportunity at the Department of Housing and Urban Development (HUD). Achtenberg, a lesbian who was a former municipal supervisor in San Francisco, became the first openly homosexual nominee to be confirmed by the Senate to a high office in the U.S. government.

Conservatives scored a victory on June 3 when the President withdrew his nomination of Lani Guinier, a black law professor at the University of Pennsylvania in Philadelphia, as head of the civil rights division of the Department of Justice. Guinier had been attacked because in some of her writings in law journals she discussed unorthodox ways of increasing the political power of minorities.

Gays in uniform. In seeking to honor a campaign promise to end the ban on homosexuals in the military, Clinton faced the united opposition of the Joint Chiefs of Staff and some influential senators, including fellow Democrat Sam Nunn of Georgia, chairman of the Senate Armed Services Committee. Seeking a compromise, Clinton gave Secretary of Defense Les Aspin, Jr., six months to come up with a new policy, meanwhile halting efforts to root out homosexuals already in uniform.

On July 19, Clinton announced a so-called "don't ask, don't tell" compromise plan. Starting October 1, military recruits would no longer be asked to reveal their sexual orientation, and the armed services could not discriminate against homosexuals in any way. An exception to that rule would be cases where individuals announced their homosexuality or were found to have engaged in homosexual acts. In September, Congress approved the policy but amended it to make it somewhat more restrictive.

Closing military bases. On September 20, the Senate joined Clinton in approving the closure of

Executive Office of the President
President, Bill Clinton
Vice President, Albert Gore, Jr.
White House Chief of Staff, Thomas F. McLarty III
Presidential Press Secretary, Dee Dee Myers
Assistant to the President for National Security Affairs, W. Anthony Lake
Assistant to the President for Science and Technology, John H. Gibbons
Council of Economic Advisers—Laura D'Andrea Tyson, Chairman
Counselor to the President for Domestic Policy—Carol H. Rasco
Office of Management and Budget—Leon E. Panetta, Director
Office of National Drug Control Policy—Lee P. Brown, Director
U.S. Trade Representative, Mickey Kantor

Department of Agriculture
Secretary of Agriculture, Mike Espy

Department of Commerce
Secretary of Commerce, Ronald H. Brown
Bureau of Economic Analysis—Carol S. Carson, Director
Bureau of the Census—Harry A. Scarr, Acting Director

Department of Defense
Secretary of Defense, Les Aspin, Jr.
Secretary of the Air Force, Sheila E. Widnall
Secretary of the Army, Togo D. West, Jr.
Secretary of the Navy, John H. Dalton
Joint Chiefs of Staff—
General John Shalikashvili, Chairman
General Merrill A. McPeak, Chief of Staff, Air Force
General Gordon R. Sullivan, Chief of Staff, Army
Admiral Frank B. Kelso II, Chief of Naval Operations
General Carl E. Mundy, Jr., Commandant, Marine Corps

Department of Education
Secretary of Education, Richard W. Riley

Department of Energy
Secretary of Energy, Hazel R. O'Leary

Department of Health and Human Services
Secretary of Health and Human Services, Donna E. Shalala
Public Health Service—Philip R. Lee, Assistant Secretary
Centers for Disease Control and Prevention—David Satcher, Director
Food and Drug Administration—David A. Kessler, Commissioner
National Institutes of Health—Harold Varmus, Director
Surgeon General of the United States, M. Joycelyn Elders
Social Security Administration—Shirley S. Chater, Commissioner

Department of Housing and Urban Development
Secretary of Housing and Urban Development, Henry G. Cisneros

Department of the Interior
Secretary of the Interior, Bruce Babbitt

Department of Justice
Attorney General, Janet Reno
Bureau of Prisons—Kathleen M. Hawk, Director
Drug Enforcement Administration—Stephen H. Greene, Acting Administrator
Federal Bureau of Investigation—Louis J. Freeh, Director
Immigration and Naturalization Service—Doris M. Meissner, Commissioner
Solicitor General, Drew S. Days III

Department of Labor
Secretary of Labor, Robert B. Reich

Department of State
Secretary of State, Warren Christopher
U.S. Ambassador to the United Nations, Madeleine K. Albright

Department of Transportation
Secretary of Transportation, Federico F. Peña
Federal Aviation Administration—David R. Hinson, Administrator
U.S. Coast Guard—J. William Kime, Commandant

Department of the Treasury
Secretary of the Treasury, Lloyd M. Bentsen, Jr.
Internal Revenue Service—Margaret Milner Richardson, Commissioner
Treasurer of the United States, vacant
U.S. Secret Service—Eljay Bowron, Director
Office of Thrift Supervision—Jonathan L. Fiechter, Acting Director

Department of Veterans Affairs
Secretary of Veterans Affairs, Jesse Brown

Supreme Court of the United States
Chief Justice of the United States, William H. Rehnquist
Associate Justices—
Harry A. Blackmun
John Paul Stevens
Sandra Day O'Connor
Antonin Scalia
Anthony M. Kennedy
David H. Souter
Clarence Thomas
Ruth Bader Ginsburg

Congressional officials
President of the Senate pro tempore, Robert C. Byrd
Senate Majority Leader, George J. Mitchell
Senate Minority Leader, Robert J. Dole
Speaker of the House, Thomas S. Foley
House Majority Leader, Richard A. Gephardt
House Minority Leader, Robert H. Michel
Congressional Budget Office—Robert D. Reischauer, Director
General Accounting Office—Charles A. Bowsher, Comptroller General of the United States
Library of Congress—James H. Billington, Librarian of Congress
Office of Technology Assessment—Roger C. Herdman, Director

Independent agencies
Agency for International Development—J. Brian Atwood, Administrator
Central Intelligence Agency—R. James Woolsey, Jr., Director
Commission on Civil Rights—Mary Frances Berry, Chairperson
Commission of Fine Arts—J. Carter Brown, Chairman
Consumer Product Safety Commission—Ann Winkelman Brown, Chairman
Corporation for National and Community Service—Eli J. Segal, Chief Executive Officer
Environmental Protection Agency—Carol M. Browner, Administrator
Equal Employment Opportunity Commission—Tony E. Gallegos, Chairman
Federal Communications Commission—James H. Quello, Chairman
Federal Deposit Insurance Corporation—Andrew C. Hove, Jr., Acting Chairman
Federal Election Commission—Scott E. Thomas, Chairman
Federal Emergency Management Agency—James Lee Witt, Director
Federal Reserve System Board of Governors—Alan Greenspan, Chairman
Federal Trade Commission—Janet D. Steiger, Chairman
General Services Administration—Roger W. Johnson, Administrator
Interstate Commerce Commission—Gail C. McDonald, Chairman
National Aeronautics and Space Administration—Daniel S. Goldin, Administrator
National Endowment for the Arts—Jane Alexander, Chairman
National Endowment for the Humanities—Sheldon Hackney, Chairman
National Labor Relations Board—James M. Stephens, Chairman
National Railroad Passenger Corporation (Amtrak)—W. Graham Claytor, Jr., Chairman
National Science Foundation—Neal F. Lane, Director
National Transportation Safety Board—Carl W. Vogt, Chairman
Nuclear Regulatory Commission—Ivan Selin, Chairman
Peace Corps—Carol Bellamy, Director
Securities and Exchange Commission—Arthur Levitt, Jr., Chairman
Selective Service System—Robert Gambino, Director
Small Business Administration—Erskine Bowles, Administrator
Smithsonian Institution—Robert McC. Adams, Secretary
U.S. Arms Control and Disarmament Agency—John D. Holum, Director
U.S. Information Agency—Joseph D. Duffey, Director
U.S. Postal Service—Marvin T. Runyon, Jr., Postmaster General

*As of Dec. 31, 1993.

130 bases and scaling back 45 others. The independent Defense Base Closure and Realignment Commission estimated these moves would save about $4-billion through fiscal 1999.

Marine directive reversed. On Aug. 5, 1993, the Marine Corps commandant, General Carl E. Mundy, Jr., ordered a halt to the enlistment of married individuals after Sept. 30, 1995. Mundy took the action because of high levels of marital stress among many young marines, caused by long separations. On Aug. 11, 1993, Aspin reversed the directive.

Star Wars ended. On May 13, Aspin announced that the Strategic Defense Initiative (SDI)—the space-based antiballistic-missile system known popularly as Star Wars—was being canceled. Antimissile research efforts, he said, would be redirected into ground-based defenses under a new name. Aspin said it would focus on devising shields against missile attacks on forces in the field and against limited attacks on the nation's cities. In September, Aspin said the Reagan Administration had a secret plan to deceive the Soviet Union by rigging SDI space tests so they would appear successful even if they failed. But he said the plan was never actually carried out.

In other moves reflecting the winds of change, Aspin announced on April 28, 1993, that he had lifted a ban on women in combat aviation slots and said he would seek repeal of a law barring women from the Navy's combat ships. And on September 8,

he agreed to joint training exercises for American and Russian heavy combat divisions.

A rough year for Aspin. In February, Aspin was stricken with shortness of breath caused by thickening of the heart muscle. On March 18, a pacemaker was implanted in his chest to relieve the condition.

Aspin was widely criticized for his handling of U.S. military activities in Somalia and for his overall performance as defense secretary. On December 15, he resigned, effective Jan. 20, 1994. The next day, Clinton nominated Bobby Ray Inman, a retired admiral and former deputy director of the Central Intelligence Agency (CIA), as Aspin's successor.

Supercollider, space station. Funding for the Superconducting Super Collider (SSC)—a huge *particle accelerator* (atom smasher) under construction in Texas—was ended in late October. Hopes that the SSC would be in the budget were extinguished after the House of Representatives voted 282 to 143 on October 19 to end the $11-billion project.

Congress, decided, however, to continue funding for the proposed U.S. space station. Clinton on June 17 backed a simpler version of the space station that would cost much less than the design being planned in early 1993, which was estimated at $31 billion. In October, Congress authorized $2.1 billion for the space station in the budget for fiscal year 1994.

NAFTA passes. After months of wrangling between Democrats and Republicans in Congress, the

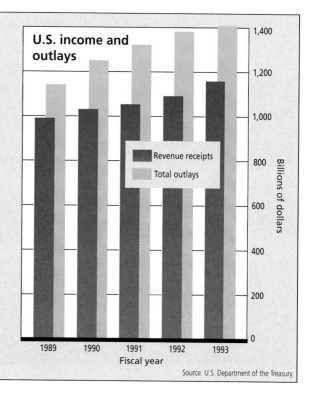

Federal spending
United States budget for fiscal 1993*

	Billions of dollars
National defense	290.6
International affairs	17.2
General science, space, technology	17.1
Energy	4.4
Natural resources and environment	20.1
Agriculture	20.3
Commerce and housing credit	–23.5
Transportation	35.2
Community and regional development	10.4
Education, training, employment, and social services	48.9
Health	99.2
Social security	304.6
Medicare	130.6
Income security	207.9
Veterans' benefits and services	35.7
Administration of justice	15.0
General government	13.0
Interest	198.9
Undistributed offsetting receipts	–37.4
Total budget outlays	**1,407.9**

*Oct. 1, 1992, to Sept. 30, 1993.
Source: U.S. Department of the Treasury.

U.S. income and outlays

Revenue receipts
Total outlays

Fiscal year

Billions of dollars

Source: U.S. Department of the Treasury.

A helicopter replaces the repaired statue of Freedom atop the Capitol dome in Washington, D.C., in October during celebrations of the Capitol's 200th anniversary.

North American Free Trade Agreement (NAFTA) won the approval of the House, 234 to 200, on November 17. The Senate passed the bill 61 to 38 on November 20. NAFTA, which had President Clinton's strong backing despite much fierce opposition from U.S. labor organizations, brings Canada, Mexico, and the United States together into one huge free-trade zone. (See also **International trade: The Debate over NAFTA.**)

Waco and its aftermath. A February 28 raid by agents of the Bureau of Alcohol, Tobacco, and Firearms (ATF) on a building near Waco, Tex., housing followers of a religious cult ended in an ambush of the raiders, four of whom were killed. A lengthy siege followed. The stand-off ended on April 19, when the building caught fire during a raid by Federal Bureau of Investigation (FBI) agents. An estimated 82 cult members perished in the ensuing blaze. (See **Crime.**)

The ATF raid led to a major shakeup in that agency. A September 30 report released by the Department of the Treasury, of which the ATF is part, was highly critical of the agency's handling of the raid. The report charged that supervising agents on the scene ordered the attack to proceed even though they learned that the cultists had been tipped off about the raid. It also accused some ATF officials of trying to cover up their mistakes.

Treasury Secretary Lloyd M. Bentsen, Jr., replaced ATF Director Stephen E. Higgins and suspended five officials who had directed the raid. Two of the suspended officials resigned, and Higgins announced that he would retire.

A second report, focusing on the April 19 attack, was issued on October 8 by the Department of Justice, parent department of the FBI. That evaluation concluded that the cultists—not FBI agents, as some people had contended—had set the fatal fire at the compound. Still, the report was criticized by some observers as a whitewash because it excused Attorney General Janet Reno of any wrongdoing in the raid. Reno had given the go-ahead for the disastrous attack.

The Central Intelligence Agency on November 19 admitted that a CIA-supported antidrug program in Venezuela shipped about 2,000 pounds (900 kilograms) of nearly pure cocaine to the United States in 1990. The shipments, which originated in Colombia, were arranged by CIA agents to win the confidence of Colombian drug traffickers and thereby infiltrate their operation. Although no agents are thought to have profited from the shipments, much of the cocaine wound up being sold on U.S. streets. At year-end, a federal grand jury in Miami, Fla., was investigating the incident.

New FBI director. On January 15, before Clinton took office, a Justice Department investigation concluded that FBI Director William S. Sessions had repeatedly violated FBI regulations and made unethical personal use of bureau resources. Sessions was accused of using government funds for private travel, making his FBI bodyguards do chores and run errands, and several other transgressions. Sessions later rejected repeated requests by the Clinton Administration that he resign.

On July 19, the President fired Sessions and then named U.S. District Judge Louis J. Freeh, a former FBI agent and federal prosecutor, to succeed him. (See **Freeh, Louis J.**)

HUD scandal. A continuing inquiry into the activities of the Department of Housing and Urban Development (HUD) during the Reagan Administration brought more convictions in 1993. The probe had focused on appointees of Samuel R. Pierce, Jr., who was secretary of HUD during the Reagan years. The most prominent of those convicted in 1993 was Deborah Gore Dean, Pierce's executive assistant, who was found guilty on October 26 of funneling millions of dollars in housing grants to private developers and consultants who had close ties to the Republican Party. □ Frank Cormier and Margot Cormier

See also **Clinton, Bill; Congress of the United States.** In the World Book Supplement section, see **United States, Government of the.**

Uruguay. See Latin America.

Utah. See State government.

Uzbekistan. See Asia.

Vanuatu. See Pacific Islands.

Venezuela. Venezuelans returned former President Rafael Caldera to the presidency on Dec. 5, 1993. Caldera served as president of Venezuela in the early 1970's. He will take office again for a five-year term on Feb. 2, 1994.

The elections capped a tumultuous year. On May 21, 1993, President Carlos Andrés Pérez was suspended from office to face charges, along with two former ministers of his administration, of embezzling $17 million in government funds. It was the first time that a Venezuelan president had faced an impeachment trial.

The National Congress elected Senator Ramón José Velásquez, 76, as acting president on June 5. Although widely respected, Velásquez could not push the Congress ahead on urgent legislation to offset an anticipated deficit of from $3 billion to $5 billion.

Under Pérez, Venezuela had welcomed foreign investment in the oil industry for the first time since it was entirely nationalized in 1976. On March 25, 1993, Petróleos de Venezuela, the government oil monopoly, signed an agreement for a $3-billion natural gas project, which will include participation by three foreign companies. □ Nathan A. Haverstock

See also **Latin America** (Facts in brief table). In *World Book,* see **Venezuela.**

Vermont. See State government.

Vice President of the U.S. See Gore, Albert, Jr.

Vietnam. The secretary general of the ruling Communist Party of Vietnam (CPV), Do Muoi, visited a Buddhist pagoda and a Roman Catholic cathedral in early 1993. Buddhism and Roman Catholicism are the country's two main religions, but both have suffered years of government oppression. Muoi's visit was viewed as the Communist leadership's recognition of the two religions' influence among the people and as an attempt to win popular support. But the government still tried to control Vatican appointments to Catholic church positions.

Buddhists opposed the CPV's atheistic regime throughout 1993. On May 21 in Hue, a man burned himself to death at Thien Mu pagoda, long a center of resistance to the government. Antigovernment demonstrations followed.

Other unrest was suppressed. On March 30, a court in Ho Chi Minh City (formerly Saigon) sentenced eight intellectuals to prison for their activities in an antigovernment organization called Freedom Forum.

Economic aid. Decades of war and a wasteful Communist bureaucratic system left the country's infrastructure in an advanced state of disrepair. But on July 2, 1993, U.S. President Bill Clinton ended official opposition to the granting of international loans to Vietnam. The U.S. move opened the way for France, Japan, and Australia to grant a loan to pay off Vietnam's $140-million debt to the International Mone-

Vietnam's foreign minister, left, greets U.S. Secretary of State Warren Christopher in July, before discussions on American servicemen missing since 1975.

tary Fund (IMF). IMF rules stipulate that no new loans can be made until outstanding debt is paid off. The IMF and the World Bank, both agencies of the United Nations, and the Asian Development Bank then granted new loans to Vietnam.

On September 13, the Clinton Administration announced that it would permit U.S. companies to bid on development projects financed with those loans. But an embargo on most U.S. commercial dealings with Vietnam, imposed after the Vietnam War ended in 1975, remained in place.

United States diplomats were stationed in Vietnam beginning on Aug. 18, 1993, for the first time since the Vietnam War ended. Their main task was to investigate the whereabouts of American servicemen missing in action (MIA). During 1993, Vietnam continued to turn over remains of MIA's, but some 2,200 were still unaccounted for. In January, a document relating to MIA's was reportedly found in Soviet intelligence archives in Moscow. The document was a Russian translation of a 1972 report to the Vietnamese Politburo indicating that North Vietnam was holding 1,205 American prisoners, not 368 as it had claimed to have. Vietnam denounced the document as fraudulent.   □ Henry S. Bradsher

See also **Asia: Vietnam: Emerging from a War-torn Past.** In *World Book,* see **Vietnam.**

Virginia. See State government.
Vital statistics. See Census; Population.

Washington, D.C. John A. Wilson, chairman of
the Washington, D.C., City Council, committed suicide on May 19, 1993. Wilson's death left open the second most powerful job in the District government at a time when the city was facing continuing fiscal problems and increasing criminal violence.

Wilson, 49, a former civil rights activist, hanged himself in the basement of his home at the end of a lifelong struggle with mental depression. Elected to the chairman's job in 1990, he had been the longest-serving elected official in the District government, having joined the first elected City Council in 1974.

Council Chairman Pro Tempore John Ray served as acting chairman through the summer until the election of a new chairman. On Sept. 14, 1993, District voters returned former Chairman David A. Clarke to the job, which he had held for two terms, from 1983 through 1990. Clarke had left the seat in 1990 to run unsuccessfully for mayor.

The chairman's race was the first election in the District since voters imposed some of the strictest campaign contribution limits in the country. Candidates could receive no more than $100 from individual donors. As predicted, the restriction enhanced the role of independent political action committees, which are not subject to the limits.

District legislation. During the year, the City Council responded to complaints about aggressive panhandling by passing legislation placing limits on how and where individuals may solicit money on city streets. And yielding to criticism that it was too easy for minors to buy liquor in the city, the council enacted a measure making it illegal for anyone under age 21 to purchase alcohol in the District.

Crime. The number of murders in the District started to climb again in 1993, after dipping the year before for the first time in five years. By December 10, a total of 442 homicides had been reported, up from 420 at that time in 1992. The pace of killings was just short of the record rate logged in 1991.

Several apparently random acts of gun violence generated wide public concern in 1993. During an eight-week period from late February to late April, a man who came to be known as "the shotgun stalker" terrorized two northwest-side neighborhoods with a series of drive-by shootings. The stalker killed four people and wounded five. On April 19, the day of the fourth slaying, the police arrested a suspect in the shootings, James E. Swann, Jr., age 29, a former security guard. Swann was charged with committing 14 shooting attacks and four murders.

In June, a gunman fired a semiautomatic handgun at a crowded public pool, wounding six children. Also in June, a 72-year-old British tourist was shot and killed after he got off at the wrong subway stop. In September, a gunman killed a 4-year-old girl and a 26-year-old man when he sprayed gunfire at an elementary school playground. And during the year, Asian-American shopkeepers in the District demanded increased police protection after a series of slayings.

On October 22, Mayor Sharon Pratt Kelly asked President Bill Clinton to give her the authority to call out the national guard to help control crime in the District. Clinton responded that he could not delegate that power directly but would support legislation in Congress to do so. Clinton said he would also direct federal law-enforcement agencies to give the city more help in fighting crime.

City jobs. Public school teachers in the District, who are forbidden by law to strike, staged a two-day "sick-out" in January. The teachers were protesting nine unpaid "furlough days" imposed on all city government employees in 1993 to help balance the District's $3.4-billion budget. By March, the continuing deterioration of the city's finances prompted Mayor Kelly and the City Council to agree to cut at least 3,000 positions from the District's work force of 46,000. By June, the mayor and council agreed to eliminate another 853 positions, and Kelly promised to cut at least another 355 on her own authority.

Statehood. Mayor Kelly was among 38 protesters arrested on August 26 for blocking an intersection during a nonviolent demonstration. The demonstrators were calling on Congress to make the District the nation's 51st state.   □ Nell Henderson

See also **City; Crime.** In *World Book,* see **Washington, D.C.**

A Place in Which to Remember

By Benjamin Forgey

By the end of World War II, Nazi Germany had murdered two-thirds of the Jews of Europe in a campaign of genocide known as the Holocaust. A new museum in Washington, D.C., stands as a national memorial to these Jews and other victims of the Nazi horror.

In the late winter and spring of 1945, during the last months of World War II in Europe, soldiers in advancing Allied armies began to encounter the network of concentration camps that Nazi Germany had established to eradicate Europe's Jews. As the American, British, and Soviet troops reached the camps, many partially destroyed by hastily fleeing guards, terrible scenes met their eyes. At the camp near Dachau, Germany, liberated by American forces in April 1945, hundreds of emaciated bodies lay stacked in rows. At Belsen, another German camp liberated in April, British soldiers found 10,000 decaying corpses. The living lay amid the dead, their skeletal forms clothed in rags and covered with lice and filth. In the weeks following liberation, thousands of these individuals would succumb to starvation, exhaustion, and disease.

Forty-eight years later, on April 22, 1993, United States President

■ Visitors enter the United States Holocaust Memorial Museum on the east, *above left,* through arches set in a curved limestone facade. At the west side of the building, *above right,* stands a six-sided memorial hall, the Hall of Remembrance.

Bill Clinton, the leaders of a dozen other countries, and a crowd that included survivors and their liberators gathered in the cold to dedicate the United States Holocaust Memorial Museum in Washington, D.C. The ceremony marked the opening of a unique institution. The new museum is a national memorial to the approximately 11 million victims of the Holocaust, the Nazis' program of mass murder that claimed the lives of 6 million Jews and 5 million others, among them Gypsies, Poles, Soviet prisoners of war, homosexuals, Jehovah's Witnesses, the mentally ill, and political opponents of the Nazi regime. The museum also, in the words of director Jeshajahu Weinberg, is an educational institution designed "to tell America and the world the factual story of this most terrible event in modern history, and to illuminate the crucial moral lessons it entails."

A museum to tell the unspeakable

The story the museum tells took place between 1933 and 1945, when Adolf Hitler and his National Socialist German Workers' Party held power in Germany. (The word *Nazi* comes from the first two syllables of the party's German name.) At the core of Nazi ideology was the doctrine that Germans represented a superior form of humanity, and that Jews—and, to a lesser degree, members of other ethnic and social groups—were a corrupting influence on German culture and racial purity.

■ **The author**

Benjamin Forgey is architecture critic at *The Washington Post.*

After Germany invaded Poland in 1939, starting World War II, the Nazis undertook to wipe out Europe's Jewish population. At first, Jews were crowded into walled areas called ghettos, where many fell prey to hunger, cold, and disease. Later, the killing began in earnest. Millions of Jews were shot in mass executions by mobile killing squads. Millions more were imprisoned in concentration camps, where those not killed on arrival were used as slave labor until they could no longer work. In some camps, inmates perished at the hands of Nazi doctors, who used them as subjects for medical experiments. And in

■ Visitors begin their tour in the Hall of Witness, the museum's central space. The
hall's brick walls, exposed steel, and twisted skylight are designed to disorient
and upset the viewer.

■ A freight car thought to have been used to transport Jews to concentration camps stands in the museum's permanent exhibition. As many as 100 people were often packed into these cars for several days, with little water and no food. Many died on the journey.

certain notorious "death camps," the Nazis established special gas chambers that killed hundreds of victims at once with factorylike efficiency, by means of poison gas piped into rooms disguised as shower facilities. After the gassings, the bodies were shoveled into pits or, later, furnaces and burned, the smoke wafting over nearby villages.

The Holocaust Memorial Museum was conceived in 1978, when President Jimmy Carter established a commission to explore ideas for a national memorial to victims of the Nazis. Two years later, the U.S. Congress passed legislation authorizing the transfer of federal land for the institution. Today, the museum stands just off the National Mall, a long, parklike area that stretches westward from the Capitol, linking some of the nation's most important buildings and monuments.

Constructed and equipped with nearly $170 million in privately raised donations, the building contains both a memorial hall and extensive exhibition space, including two temporary exhibition galleries and a 36,000-square-foot (3,345-square-meter) permanent exhibition occupying nearly three floors. In addition, the museum houses two auditoriums; classrooms; a library and archive for scholarly research; and a computer-based learning center that provides access to texts, maps, and videotapes not displayed in the permanent exhibition.

The work of collecting material for the exhibits began well before the start of construction in September 1988. By its opening day on April 26, 1993, the museum housed about 5,000 objects, making it the world's largest collection of Holocaust-related artifacts.

Its very size and scope makes the institution different from most other memorials to Holocaust victims. There are thousands of such memorials in Europe, Israel, and the United States, most ranging from simple displays on synagogue walls to large sculptures in public places. The only institution comparable to the Memorial Museum is Yad Vashem in Israel, founded in 1953 and gradually expanded to include archives, outdoor monuments, and exhibition halls. And, of course, there remain the sites of the concentration camps themselves, where in many cases the gas chambers and wooden barracks stand as the Allied soldiers found them.

Designing the Memorial Museum

The architect of the Memorial Museum was James Ingo Freed of the prominent New York City firm of Pei Cobb Freed & Partners. Freed, himself a Jew, was born in Essen, Germany, in 1930. He escaped the

■ Shoes collected from Jews and others murdered at the Auschwitz and Majdanek death camps in Poland, *above,* fill a room at the museum. A purple triangle affixed to a camp uniform, *right,* identifies its wearer as a Jehovah's Witness. Similar badges identified members of each group imprisoned in the camps.

Nazi terror in 1939, when he emigrated to the United States with his older sister. (His parents followed in 1941.) After he was commissioned to design the museum in 1986, Freed studied the Holocaust obsessively, immersing himself in books and documentary motion pictures. A museum for such an unprecedented human catastrophe, he thought, must be "a sort of unimaginable building." After a trip to his birthplace and to the sites of concentration camps in Germany and Eastern Europe, he was able to imagine it.

Freed faced three major challenges. The building had to accommodate the diverse needs of an institution designed to serve scholars, Holocaust survivors, and the public at large. It had to fit comfortably into the setting of monumental Washington. And it had somehow to represent the Holocaust.

Freed responded to these challenges with a design of striking and unique architectural character. On the outside, his structure consists of geometric forms—pyramids, cubes, and other shapes—that stand out from the museum's surroundings without overpowering them. At the same time, nearly every architectural element, both outside and inside the building, alludes in some way to the Holocaust. The structure, like its contents, is designed to be upsetting. However, the prominent Hall of Remembrance, which protrudes from the building's western side, is meant to calm the emotions rather than disrupt them. The Hall of Remembrance is a *hexagonal* (six-sided) limestone memorial hall, its shape symbolizing both the six-pointed Star of David, the universal symbol of Judaism, and the 6 million Jewish victims of the Holocaust. From the hall and the plaza on which it stands, visitors can glimpse two of the nation's great monuments: the towering Washington Monument, commemorating the first U.S. President, and the memorial to Thomas Jefferson, author of the Declaration of Independence with its ringing affirmation of human rights.

The main portion of the five-story Memorial Museum building is divided into two parts: a row of four brick towers on the north and, on the south, a larger space capped with four pyramid-shaped roofs. Between these two areas is a three-story central hall, the Hall of Witness, roofed by a skylight that angles upward from the second floor. On the fifth floor, reserved for the library, four steel-and-glass bridges link the northern and southern sections. A similar, two-story bridge on the third and fourth floors links the sections on the building's western side. The bridges and towers are subtly prisonlike in character.

Freed designed the exterior of the building in materials that match those of its immediate neighbors. On three sides—east, south, and west—the museum is sheathed in limestone, the most familiar building material in official Washington and that of the building that houses the Bureau of Engraving and Printing, which stands next to the museum on the south. The northern facade is of red brick, matching the ensemble of brick buildings that flanks the museum on that side.

However, the materials also serve the more important, evocative function of the design. At the museum's main entrance on the east, visitors pass first through arches set in a curved limestone facade. From outside, the arches appear to be the entrance to the building, but in fact they lead to an open space that visitors must cross to reach the real entrance into the brick structure behind it. Symbolically, this facade recalls the way the Nazis concealed their program of extermination—for example, by telling Jews destined for death that they were being sent to labor camps. The open space behind the facade also serves to emotionally distance visitors from the bustling atmosphere of the Mall, preparing them for the sober experience ahead.

Once inside the museum, visitors proceed into the Hall of Witness, the building's three-story central space. Here, the deliberately upsetting aspects of Freed's design become even more powerful. The brick walls of the hall are reinforced with steel beams, as were the death-camp ovens in which thousands of bodies were cremated. At the end of the hall, a stairway of gray-painted steel narrows as it ascends toward a brick arch, recalling the railroad tracks that led into the camps. The hall's massive skylight is warped and twisted. Throughout the

■ Displays in the museum chronicle the story of the Holocaust beginning with the Nazis' rise to power in Germany in 1933, *below.*

room, the concrete, brick, and steel structural elements are exposed, down to the bolts that hold the steel in place. Everything acts to disorient and unsettle the visitor, creating a deepening sense of oppression.

Objects that bear witness

In contrast to the indirect means by which the architecture evokes the Holocaust, the comprehensive permanent exhibition is straightforward. The exhibits circle around the Hall of Witness, proceeding downward chronologically from the rise of Nazism and the prelude to the war (fourth floor) to the mass murders of 1940 to 1944 (third floor) and, finally, the aftermath of the Holocaust and the world's moral response to it (second floor). At the end of the fourth- and third-floor circuits, visitors can rest in areas designed to encourage quiet reflection before continuing with the exhibition.

To reach the exhibits, visitors ascend in claustrophobic, gray steel elevators to the fourth floor. Upon exiting, the first images they see are those seen by American soldiers when they stumbled upon the camps: the human corpses organized in stacks; the skeletal survivors. Then, the chronology shifts to the beginning. First, the exhibition traces Hitler's rise to power, with his illegal manipulation of democratic means to impose a totalitarian regime in 1933. It happened very fast. Hitler was named chancellor of a coalition government at the end of January. By late March, despite the fact that the Nazi Party had never won a majority vote in a free election, Hitler had become Germany's dictator. Civil liberties, including freedom

■ **A vanished world**
Several exhibits memorialize Jewish life in Europe before the Holocaust. The three-story Tower of Faces, *top*, displays photographs of Jews from Ejsyszki, Poland, virtually all of whom were massacred on a single day. The names of obliterated Jewish communities are etched on the glass wall of a bridge, *above*.

of the press, speech, assembly, and religion, were suspended. Legal safeguards and property rights were abandoned. And on April 1 began the official persecution of Jews, as the Nazis organized a nationwide boycott of Jewish businesses and stores.

Methodically, the exhibits document the mounting state-organized terror. Photographs, films, drawings, maps, interactive videos, and numerous artifacts (or, in rare cases, carefully made replicas) reinforce one another to give viewers a sense of what it would have been like to live in Germany (and, later, almost all of Europe) during the Hitler years. Visitors learn from real identity cards, for example, that initially the concentration camps were used to imprison or kill political opponents of the Nazis. A cart used by Gypsies evokes the nomadic life of this persecuted people. A synagogue entrance defaced on Kristallnacht (Night of the Broken Glass)—the Nazi-led attack on Jewish institutions and business on Nov. 9, 1938—tells unforgettably of the increasing intensity of hate and violence. And a hospital bed, a blanket, and restraint straps speak of the mentally ill and disabled men, women, and children who were systematically killed in so-called *euthanasia* (mercy-killing) centers. In its thoroughness, its technology, and its justification by bogus theories of racial purity, the euthanasia program prefigured the campaigns of murder to follow.

As the German armies spread across Europe in triumph, the number of Jews under Nazi control expanded immensely. In 1942, the Nazi leadership made the decision to kill them all. They nearly succeeded: Two out of three Jews in the nations under Hitler's control did not survive the Holocaust. The Final Solution, as the extermination plan was known, was served by an organization and technology capable of handling vast numbers. Thousands of people at a time were transported by rail to the camps, crammed for days in freight cars with little water and no food or toilets. One of the museum exhibits is a boxcar thought to have been used in the transports and donated to the museum by the Polish government. Visitors also see canisters of Zyklon B, the powerful gas that the Nazis used in the gas chambers. Nearby is a heat-twisted metal frame, originally part of the frame of a truck, that was used to support bodies during cremation. Its users called it a "roast."

Helping visitors comprehend

The photographs and film images exhibited at the museum, some of them taken by the Nazis themselves, include the most explicit—and sickening—Holocaust images ever displayed or published. The worst images are screened off from the view of children by low walls.

Children were a special concern of the exhibition planners. At all times, one of the museum's two temporary exhibition spaces is to hold an exhibit targeted especially to young people. The opening exhibition, on view indefinitely, is entitled "Remember the Children: Daniel's Story." Here, visitors walk through a series of environments that trace the story of a fictional German Jewish child called Daniel, who is deported with his family to the Lodz ghetto in Poland and then to the Auschwitz concentration camp. The exhibition encourages children to touch the objects and furnishings in these environments, imagining themselves in Daniel's place as they lift the lid of his suitcase or walk across the rough boards that form the floor of his ghetto room. Interested children can also trace Daniel's story in his diary, which was composed by exhibition curators, based on actual experiences, and copied out by a New York fifth-grader.

"Daniel's Story" helps children understand the Holocaust by reducing it to a single story about a single child and his family. For adults, too, the very enormity of the Holocaust makes it difficult to comprehend. As a counterpoint to the almost numbing series of anonymous images in the permanent exhibition, the museum also presents the Holocaust as the tragedies of identifiable people. As visitors enter the museum, each one is offered a computer-generated identity card bearing the name, picture, and brief history of an actual person who experienced the Holocaust. Eventually, the museum hopes, visitors will receive cards that display only the person's name, picture, and origin. Then, at various points in the exhibition, visitors will insert the cards into computer terminals that will print out paragraphs tracing the individual's history and ultimate fate, whether to death or to refuge.

Elsewhere, too, the museum seeks to help visitors comprehend the Holocaust as the sum of countless individual tragedies. On the third and fourth floors, visitors circling through the exhibition cross bridges that carry them from the southern to the northern exhibition spaces. The fourth-floor bridge, overlooking the skylight, is walled by glass panes etched with the names of some 5,000 communities whose Jewish population was obliterated by the Nazis. On the third-floor bridge, the glass is etched with the first names of thousands of Holocaust victims. And the northeast tower in the exhibition houses the Tower of Faces, a three-story memorial to Jewish life in Eastern Europe before the war. The walls of the tower are covered with more than 1,000 photographs of Jews from Ejsyszki, Poland, virtually all of whose 4,000 Jewish inhabitants were massacred on a single day in 1941.

The exhibition ends at the entrance to the Hall of Remembrance, a quiet, light-filled space designed for contemplation and ceremonies. Through a skylight and narrow windows, the sun casts a soft glow on the limestone walls and the eternal flame that burns in memory of the dead. For those who wish, there are candles to be lit. Much that seems horrifically unreal has passed before the visitor's eyes during the preceding hours. But the truth is inescapable: It happened. There is much to think about. ■■■

■ The Hall of Remembrance is a light-filled space designed for quiet contemplation.

Water. Rain returned to southern and eastern Africa in 1993, ending what many had regarded as the worst drought of the 1900's. The drought affected an estimated 120 million people, with Zimbabwe, Mozambique, Tanzania, Kenya, and Somalia hardest hit. Rains nearly ceased in late 1991, killing 90 percent of crops in some areas and causing famine.

California drought ends. California Governor Pete Wilson declared the state's six-year drought over on Feb. 24, 1993. Because the state's reservoirs would require at least another year to refill, however, cities and farms did not receive full water deliveries in 1993.

Midwest floods. Heavy rains began in April and continued through most of the summer in a nine-state region of the Midwest, causing severe flooding along the Mississippi River and its tributaries. On July 11, 1993, flooding along the Des Moines and Raccoon rivers overwhelmed the water treatment plant in Des Moines, Iowa, leaving 250,000 people without drinking water. Water surged over protective levees, submerging the plant's pumping system beneath 10 feet (3 meters) of water and contaminating its water purification system. Residents had no running water to drink, bathe, wash clothes, or flush toilets. In suburban areas where running water was still available, officials warned residents not to drink from their taps. The Iowa National Guard trucked drinking water into the city during the emergency.

The water system was unable to supply drinking water for more than a week. Workers drained the water treatment plant, pulled the equipment out, dried and reconstructed it. At the same time, workers flushed the city's 800 miles (1,300 kilometers) of pipeline of the floodwater and tested for disease-causing organisms. On July 19, workers refilled part of Des Moines's water system. City officials warned people not to drink tap water for another month, until all pipelines had been flushed clean, but some businesses and residents began abusing the warning. The city punished people who used water prematurely by shutting off their water supply.

On July 25, flooding closed the water treatment plant at St. Joseph, Mo., leaving nearly 80,000 residents without drinking water. On August 1, flooding along the Mississippi also shut down the water treatment plant in Alton, Ill., leaving more than 60,000 people without drinking water. (See also **Weather**.)

Lead in drinking water. A U.S. government survey released on May 11, 1993, claimed that drinking water in 819 city water supply systems serving 30 million people in the United States contained lead levels above federal safety limits. The U.S. Environmental Protection Agency (EPA) survey did not represent the average lead levels in the cited cities' water systems, however. It reflected lead levels only in residences that the EPA defined as high-risk—those served by lead service lines or containing lead interior piping. The EPA deemed city water systems to be

in violation of lead safety limits if more than 10 percent of high-risk residences had drinking water lead levels of more than 15 parts per billion (ppb). One ppb is equivalent to a grain of salt in about 78 gallons (300 liters) of water.

Excessive lead in drinking water can retard children's physical and mental growth. High lead levels have also been linked with damage to the brain, kidneys, and nervous system in adults. To reduce lead levels, the EPA recommended running tap water for 15 to 30 seconds before drinking it.

Milwaukee waterborne disease. In March and early April 1993, contaminated drinking water caused an intestinal illness in up to 281,000 residents of Milwaukee, sending hundreds to the hospital and killing up to six people. Health officials determined that a parasite called *cryptosporidium*, which usually lives in the intestines of livestock, caused the illnesses. Water runoff from farms and dairies probably washed animal feces containing the organism into the Milwaukee River and then into Lake Michigan, from which the city draws its water, officials said. One of the city's water treatment plants may have contributed to the problem by switching to a less effective chemical purification system, officials said. The city ordered 800,000 people to boil their drinking water or to buy bottled water until the mayor lifted the warning on April 14. ☐ Iris Priestaf

In *World Book,* see **Water.**

Weather. Persistent heavy rainfall created havoc in many parts of the world during 1993. The central United States experienced the costliest flooding in its history, estimated at between $10 billion and $20 billion in damages, during the summer. Excessive rainfall also ravaged several South Asian countries and Japan.

Droughts adversely affected other portions of the world. Large areas of the eastern and southern United States experienced long periods of high temperature and reduced rainfall during the summer of 1993. South Carolina recorded its lowest summer total rainfall since meteorologists began keeping such records in 1895. Florida, North Carolina, and Virginia experienced their second driest summers on record. Many portions of eastern Africa south of the Sahara, particularly Ethiopia, also experienced drier-than-normal conditions.

Winter storms. The year opened with a series of fierce winter storms that battered the California coast with torrential rains. Heavy snows up to 11 feet (3.4 meters) deep buried portions of the Sierra Nevada. Later in January, stormy weather brought up to 12 inches (30 centimeters) of rain to northern California and wind gusts of more than 100 miles (160 kilometers) per hour.

The same series of storms also battered northern Mexico, southern California, Nevada, Utah, and Arizona. In Tijuana, Mexico, the storms claimed 32 lives,

An agricultural inspector surveys drought damage to a grain field near Anderson, S.C., in August. Drought hit the Southern United States hard in 1993.

left 2,800 people homeless, and caused $27 million in damages. By January 9, the seasonal total snowfall at Salt Lake City, Utah, reached a record 59 inches (150 centimeters). During the first half of January, extensive flooding along the Gila River in southwest Arizona damaged or destroyed more than 800 homes and caused up to $25 million in damages.

By the end of April, most of northern California had registered a five-month total exceeding 23.6 inches (60 centimeters) of melted precipitation, and amounts up to 92.8 inches (235.7 centimeters) were registered in the Sierra Nevada. Water content in the Sierra snowpack was 150 percent of normal. On February 24, California Governor Pete Wilson declared the state's six-year drought was at an end.

The blizzard of 1993. One of the most severe storms of the 1900's hit the East Coast of the United States on March 13 and 14. Beginning in the Gulf of Mexico, the storm intensified rapidly as it moved through eastern Georgia on March 13. The storm created a 10-foot (3-meter) surge of seawater along the Florida coast and a large outbreak of tornadoes that killed 26 people in the interior of the state, according to the National Weather Service in Silver Spring, Md. As it moved through the Carolinas, the storm intensified, setting numerous low-pressure records. The lowest pressure, 960 millibars (28.35 inches) of mercury, which scientists observed over eastern Maryland and Delaware, was the lowest of any winter storm in the 1900's. After dumping up to

445

A turbulent summer

Heavy rains in the Midwest throughout most of the summer of 1993 produced the worst flooding in the history of the United States. Floodwaters surround a farm near West Alton, Mo., in July, *below*.

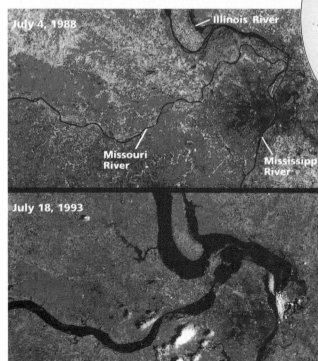

July 4, 1988

Illinois River

Missouri River

Mississippi River

July 18, 1993

A combination of meteorological conditions produced the heavy rains in the Midwest in 1993. The *jet stream* (a high-altitude, high-speed current of air) remained farther north than usual for many weeks, *above*. This allowed warm, moist air from the Gulf of Mexico to rush north into the central United States, producing rain. At the same time, a mass of hot air remained stationary over the East, creating months of excessive heat and drought. The Missouri, Illinois, and Mississippi rivers converge in a 1988 photograph taken from a satellite, *left* (top). In a satellite photograph of the same location taken on July 18, 1993, *left* (bottom), the rain-swollen rivers are far beyond their banks.

The Mississippi River bursts through a levee south of Quincy, Ill., on July 25, *left.* Floodwaters broke through more than 1,200 levees in nine states, flooding more than 8 million acres (3.2 million hectares) during June and July.

Missouri River floodwaters, *below,* force goats onto their only remaining high ground in Lupus, Mo., in July.

50 inches (127 centimeters) of snow over a broad path from Georgia through New England, the storm center left land near Portsmouth, N.H., and continued up the coast into Canada. The storm knocked out electricity in about 3 million homes. At least 213 people died in storm-related incidents, mostly from heart attacks suffered while shoveling snow or automobile accidents caused by icy roads. Insured damages were estimated at about $1.6 billion, and snow removal was estimated to cost another $150 million. The storm was followed by an outbreak of bitterly cold Arctic air that set 68 low-temperature records from the Great Plains to the Atlantic Coast on March 14, and another 70 records the following day.

Costliest flood in U.S. history. Excessive rainfall over the north-central United States during June and July resulted in the worst flooding ever experienced in the United States. Excessive rainfall had begun in the summer of 1992, leaving the ground over a wide area saturated. Excess rainfall resumed in early April 1993 in Iowa and neighboring states, severely hampering the planting of crops. The summer rainfall total exceeded 37 inches (94 centimeters) in central Iowa, and most of this fell in June and July.

The rains affected northern portions of the Mississippi River Valley first. Reservoirs overflowed, and numerous levees began breaking at the end of June. Some portions of the Mississippi River were more than 7 miles (11 kilometers) wide. On June 28, the river was closed to barge traffic from St. Paul, Minn., to St. Louis, Mo. All-time high water levels occurred in Keithsburg, Ill., and Burlington, Iowa. All but two bridges over the 230-mile (370-kilometer) stretch of river between Fort Madison, Iowa, and Alton, Ill., were closed. The Missouri River was also closed to barge traffic from Jefferson City, Mo., to St. Louis to prevent possible damage to levees.

Excessive rainfall continued over the northern plains throughout July, and rivers rose to all-time levels almost daily. The lengthy submersion gradually weakened earthen levees, and levee failures occurred frequently. On July 16, officials closed the last bridge across a 275-mile (440-kilometer) stretch of the Mississippi River north of St. Louis. Only Interstate 70 remained open across the Missouri River between St. Louis and Kansas City, Mo. According to the National Weather Service, the Mississippi River crested on August 1 at a record 49.4 feet (15.1 meters) at St. Louis, nearly 19.5 feet (5.9 meters) above flood stage. The highest previous crests were 43.3 feet (13.2 meters) in April 1973 and 41 feet (12.5 meters) in 1844.

During August 1993, there was relatively light rainfall, river levels slowly receded, and barge traffic resumed at the end of August. On September 13, the river fell below flood stage at St. Louis for the first time in 80 days.

The federal government declared nine states disaster areas as a result of the flooding. They were Iowa, Illinois, Minnesota, Missouri, Wisconsin, South Dakota, Nebraska, Kansas, and North Dakota. Every county in Iowa was declared a disaster area.

According to data compiled by the Climate Analysis Center at the National Oceanic and Atmospheric Administration in Suitland, Md., at least 48 people died as a result of the floods, and damage totaled between $10 billion and $20 billion. Flood waters forced more than 54,000 people from their homes and damaged or destroyed more than 50,000 residences. Seventy-seven towns were completely flooded, nearly 500,000 people were deprived of drinkable water, and 1,272 levees either broke or were damaged. High waters closed about 1,000 miles (1,600 kilometers) of rivers to navigation, and the flooding prevented farmers from planting nearly 8 million acres (3.2 million hectares)—more than twice the area of Connecticut—according to the U.S. Department of Agriculture. (See also **Farm and farming; Water.**)

Monsoons in South Asia. The Indian monsoon rainy season began in May and produced heavy rains through July. Rains caused severe flooding that resulted in the deaths of at least 700 people in northern India. More than 1,400 people died in floods in neighboring Nepal and Bangladesh. In some regions, rainfall was 370 percent more than normal. In late July, the Sutlej River overflowed its banks and flooded large sections of the state of Punjab in India. In Nepal, floods caused more than $20 million in damages and made Kathmandu, the capital, inaccessible by roads for more than three weeks. In Bangladesh, more than 17,000 cattle perished and 1,550 miles (2,500 kilometers) of roads were damaged. In early August, a landslide killed 50 people and destroyed 100 dwellings near Calcutta, India.

In mid-September, there was renewed flooding in the northern region of the state of Uttar Pradesh and southwest Nepal. Late in September, 12.2 inches (30.9 centimeters) of rain fell in one night in Bombay, India, claiming a dozen lives.

Tropical storms. The 1993 Atlantic hurricane season was relatively quiet. On August 31, the eye of Hurricane Emily passed within 25 miles (40 kilometers) of Cape Hatteras, N.C. Tropical storm Gert reached hurricane strength briefly on September 20 before entering Mexico at the Bay of Campeche. Gert crossed Central America into the Pacific Ocean.

Six weeks of heavy rainfall over the Japanese island of Kyushu preceded the passage of Typhoon Nathan on July 24 and 25. Typhoon Robyn hit the Japanese island of Kyushu and South Korea on August 9 and 10. On August 27 to 28, Typhoon Vernon moved up the east coast of Honshu with maximum winds of 100 mph (160 kph), causing more than 67 landslides, flooding 7,800 homes, and damaging downtown Tokyo. ☐ Alfred K. Blackadar

See also **Disasters.** In *World Book*, see **Weather.**

Weightlifting. See **Sports.**

Welfare. The number of Americans in poverty increased for the third straight year in 1992, but the rise was statistically insignificant, the United States Bureau of the Census reported in October 1993. The agency said the number of impoverished Americans totaled 36.9 million in 1992, up from 35.7 million in 1991. The poor accounted for 14.5 percent of the population in 1992, up slightly from 14.2 percent in the previous year. The percentage of poor Americans was the highest since 1983.

A single individual was defined as poor in 1992 if he or she had an annual income of less than $7,143. For a family of four, the poverty line was $14,335. The median income for all Americans—the point at which half the households had a higher income and half a lower income—was $30,786 in 1992.

Among ethnic groups, blacks had the highest poverty rate—33 percent. The rate for Hispanics was 29.3 percent; for Asians and Pacific islanders, 12.5 percent; and for whites, 11.6 percent. The figures were virtually unchanged from 1991.

The Census Bureau report noted that many poor Americans worked in 1992. Of the impoverished, 40.3 percent worked at some time during the year, and 9.2 percent of those worked full-time.

Federal assistance. A sluggish economy in 1993 contributed to a record number of Americans—more than 27 million—receiving federal food stamps. The feeding program cost the Department of Agriculture $24 billion.

The federal Health Care Financing Administration reported that a record number of Americans in 1992 took part in Medicaid, the federal program that provides health care for the poor. Medicaid rolls rose from 28.3 million in 1991 to 31.6 million in 1992.

Welfare reform. President Bill Clinton during his 1992 campaign vowed "to end welfare as we know it" by shifting the emphasis in the welfare system from increasing federal aid to encouraging personal initiative. On Aug. 10, 1993, Clinton signed a budget that increased tax rebates to the working poor by $20.8 billion through 1998. The hike in the earned-income tax credit was expected to provide a work incentive by cutting the taxes of more than 10 million working families earning up to $27,000 annually. The budget also included $3.5 billion for the creation of so-called *empowerment zones* and *enterprise communities*—low-income areas where the government uses tax incentives to help attract businesses.

On Nov. 1, 1993, the Clinton Administration allowed Wisconsin to cut off cash benefits to welfare recipients in two counties after two years. The experiment was to take effect in 1995.

□ Frank Cormier and Margot Cormier

In *World Book,* see **Welfare.**

West Indies. See **Latin America.**
West Virginia. See **State government.**
Wisconsin. See **State government.**
Wyoming. See **State government.**

Woolsey, R. James, Jr. (1941-   ), became director of the United States Central Intelligence Agency (CIA) on Feb. 5, 1993. Woolsey was expected to oversee significant cuts in the CIA budget to help control government expenditures.

Woolsey was born on Sept. 21, 1941, in Tulsa, Okla. He graduated with high honors from Stanford University in California in 1963 and was awarded a Rhodes scholarship to Oxford University in England. After earning a master's degree at Oxford in 1965, he attended Yale University Law School in New Haven, Conn., receiving his law degree in 1968.

From 1968 to 1970, Woolsey served as a captain in the U.S. Army, during which time he was an adviser to the American delegation to the Strategic Arms Limitation Talks with the Soviet Union. For the next two years, Woolsey was general counsel to the U.S. Senate Committee on Armed Services.

Woolsey joined a Washington, D.C., law firm in 1973. He served as undersecretary of the Navy from 1977 to 1979 and then returned to private practice. He once again entered public life in 1989 when he was sent to Vienna, Austria, for two years as ambassador and U.S. representative to the Negotiation on Conventional Armed Forces in Europe.

Woolsey is married to the former Suzanne Haley. They have three children.   □ David Dreier

Wyoming. See **State government.**
Yemen. See **Middle East.**

Yugoslavia remained a focus of the world's attention in 1993, as the violence that had accompanied the country's breakup in 1991 and 1992 continued to flare. Political and economic life in Serbia and Montenegro—the only two of the six original Yugoslav republics that remained in the federation—continued to revolve around the war in the former republic of Bosnia-Herzegovina (often called Bosnia). International observers widely denounced Serbian President Slobodan Milošević, Yugoslavia's most powerful leader, for failing to take steps to end Serb aggression in Bosnia or to halt atrocities by Bosnian Serbs against Muslim civilians there. Milošević denied that he had influence over the Bosnian Serbs.

As 1993 progressed, Yugoslavia's economy drew close to collapse under the weight of soaring inflation and international sanctions designed to force Serbia to rein in the Bosnian Serbs. Meanwhile, Milošević came under increasing attack from opponents on both sides of the political spectrum. By the end of the year, however, Milošević had consolidated his hold on power as his Socialist Party of Serbia (SPS) gained seats in elections for the Serbian parliament on December 19.

Economic breakdown. The United Nations (UN) Security Council on April 27 tightened its trade embargo on Yugoslavia, first imposed in May 1992, after the self-declared Bosnian Serb parliament rejected a UN-backed peace plan for Bosnia. The new sanctions froze Yugoslav assets abroad and closed a loophole that had enabled goods nominally bound for other countries to be unloaded in Yugoslavia. The UN called on member states to seize any commercial vessel found in Yugoslav waters. On Oct. 4, 1993, the Council expanded its conditions for lifting the sanctions by linking them to an end to hostilities in the former Yugoslav republic of Croatia. Ethnic Serbs in Croatia had declared an independent state.

Some goods, including luxury items from Western Europe, continued to trickle into the country despite the embargo. But few people could afford these goods. Inflation, fueled partly by government subsidies of Serb operations in Bosnia and Croatia, stood at a staggering 20,190 percent monthly rate in November. Government-imposed rationing and price controls were withdrawn when they escalated the shortage of basic goods. Meanwhile, industrial output plummeted. As winter approached, UN officials estimated that more than 3 million of Yugoslavia's 10 million inhabitants were living in poverty.

Milošević was at a political crossroads as 1993 drew to a close. The worsening economic crisis—along with threats of Western air strikes against Yugoslavia, announced by the North Atlantic Treaty Organization (NATO) in August—had led to growing calls for an end to the war in Bosnia. Opposition leaders attacked Milošević for his totalitarian rule, including his control over Serbia's state-run radio and television stations. But Milošević also came under fire from the extreme nationalist Serbian Radical Party, an ally of Milošević's SPS. The Radical Party was the second largest party in both the Serbian and Yugoslav parliaments, after the SPS.

Hopes for a settlement of the Bosnian conflict rose in the spring, as Milošević called on the Bosnian Serbs to accept the UN-backed peace plan. The Bosnian government and ethnic Croat forces, the two other warring parties, agreed to the plan by March. After the Bosnian Serbs repeatedly rejected the plan, Milošević on May 6 said that Yugoslavia would impose an embargo on all supplies except food and medicine to the Bosnian Serbs. He also agreed to allow UN observers to monitor Yugoslavia's border with Bosnia. But on May 25, Yugoslav leaders said they would not permit observers on the border.

On May 31, the SPS supported the Radical Party in ousting Yugoslav President Dobrica Cosic, a former hard-liner who had favored the peace plan. Cosic was replaced on June 25 by Zoran Lilic of the SPS, with the backing of the Radical Party.

The conflict between Milošević and his radical opponents in the Serbian parliament came to a head in October, as the Radical Party threatened to oust Milošević in a no-confidence vote. On October 20, Milošević dissolved the parliament and called the December 19 elections. ☐ Sharon L. Wolchik

See also **Bosnia-Herzegovina; Croatia; Europe** (Facts in brief table). In *World Book*, see **Yugoslavia.**

Yukon Territory. The Yukon's largest employer, Curragh Incorporated, owner of a lead and zinc mine at Faro, went into receivership in September 1993. Beset by high costs and falling metal prices, the mine had not operated through the year, leaving almost 1,000 employees out of work and striking a serious blow to a region with a 14 percent unemployment rate. Attempting to avoid bankruptcy, receivers had looked unsuccessfully for possible buyers.

The new government formed by the Yukon Party in 1992 released its first budget on March 25. John Ostashek, government leader and minister of finance, predicted a balanced budget of $483 million for operations and capital projects. (Monetary figures are in Canadian dollars.) The budget called for increased taxes on personal incomes, corporate incomes, diesel and aviation fuel, gasoline, and tobacco. Financial analysts predicted that the average family would pay $500 more per year in income tax alone. The budget held overall spending at 1992 levels and called for a streamlined government.

A wolf hunt in southwestern Yukon to reduce the territory's estimated 4,500 wolves preying on migratory caribou herds and moose took place in early 1993. Biologists originally thought that 150 wolves should be shot, but only one-fourth of that number had to be destroyed to restore ecological balance in the area. ☐ David M. L. Farr

In *World Book,* see **Yukon Territory.**

Zaire. A political crisis that began in 1990 continued throughout 1993 as President Mobutu Sese Seko stubbornly hung onto power. During the year, the country seethed with unrest. In late January in Kinshasa, the capital, violence erupted after soldiers who had gone for weeks without pay were paid with new bank notes that merchants refused to accept. By February 2, the death toll from looting and rioting was at least 1,000 people.

Underlying the political crisis was an ongoing economic depression. In May, as hardships deepened, there were reports of widespread starvation. And throughout the year, inflation raged at an estimated annual rate of 5,000 percent.

Mobutu's control of the treasury and of the best units in Zaire's military forces allowed him to maintain a semblance of control and to hold his prodemocracy opponents at bay. Since 1992, two governments have been vying for power—Mobutu's and one that was led by interim Prime Minister Etienne Tshisekedi.

In May 1993, United States Secretary of State Warren Christopher urged Mobutu to give up power. But neither foreign pressures nor the demands of Zairians could end Mobutu's rule. ☐ Mark DeLancey

See also **Africa** (Facts in brief table). In *World Book,* see **Zaire.**

Zambia. See Africa.

Zimbabwe. See Africa.

Zoology. Elaborate ornamentation on male birds, such as fancy feathers, attract female birds of the same species, enabling the fancy males to acquire mates more easily than less conspicuous males. But in crested auklets, a sea bird, both males and females have long crests of feathers. Furthermore, both sexes are involved in the selection of a mate, according to findings reported in March 1993 by zoologists at the University of Cambridge in England. The researchers found that both males and females preferred individuals of the opposite sex that had the longest, most elaborate crests. The study refuted the hypothesis that female ornamentation in auklets has no function.

The scientists made models of male and female auklets and placed the models on Buldir Island, Alaska, where auklets gather to court mates. During the breeding season, auklets have on average 12 feathers in a crest that protrudes and curves forward from the forehead. In their models, the zoologists created longer and shorter crests, but always within the range found in the wild. Both male and female auklets were more attracted to models with the longer crests. Also, there was a correlation between crest size and dominance, with the larger crests indicating the more dominant individual in both sexes.

Brothers influence sisters. The position of a female gerbil embryo inside the mother gerbil affects the sex of babies that the developing female embryo will produce in the future, according to an August report by biologists at McMaster University in Ontario, Canada. When a female embryo is positioned between two males, it is exposed to a chemical substance called testosterone that is produced and released by the brothers. Female embryos that developed between male embryos produced more male offspring as adults than did female embryos that developed between other females. The biologists said that testosterone in effect transmits reproductive characteristics to the female embryo. Also, the female exposed to testosterone matures later and has a reproductive life half as long as those developed between two female embryos.

Swimming muscle. Most biologists believed that fish swim by tightening powerful muscles along the sides of their bodies and that most of the power originates in muscles toward the head. But biologist Lawrence C. Rome at the University of Pennsylvania in Philadelphia reported in July that fish get their power from bundles of red muscle that extend in a narrow band along the length of a fish.

Rome monitored the activity of red muscles in a fish called a scup. Most of the power for swimming was generated by the red muscles near the tail. Red muscle is only 4 percent of a fish's mass, but it powered all the steady swimming.   □ Elizabeth Pennisi

In the World Book Supplement section, see **Animal.** In *World Book,* see **Zoology.**

A reconstruction shows how a newly discovered mammal resembles a goat and an antelope. In June, scientists confirmed that the mammal, found in Vietnam, was a new species.

Zoos and aquariums in the United States opened a broad spectrum of naturalistic exhibits in 1993, virtually all of them emphasizing endangered species. Tropical rain forests and American waterways were the most frequently represented habitats.

Jungle journey. The Cincinnati Zoo brought realistic simulations of Asian and African rain forests to Ohio with the opening on July 9 of Jungle Trails, an exhibit focusing on primates. The exhibit features lavish tropical vegetation, machine-generated mist, recorded sound effects, and other techniques that create an illusion of being part of the animals' environment. In the Asian portion of the exhibit, visitors cross a swinging rope bridge past a tree-covered island where gibbons hoot and swing from branch to branch. A mist-shrouded trail leads to encounters with other primates, as well as reptiles and birds.

The exhibit's African rain forest features two primates not usually found in zoos. One is the bonobo, also called the pygmy chimpanzee, a rare species that lives in the wild only in Zaire. The other is the aye-aye, a type of lemur native to Madagascar that has never before been exhibited in a North American zoo. The aye-aye is considered the most endangered primate on Earth. This part of the exhibit allows visitors to experience the African rain forest at night, when aye-ayes are most active.

The Denver Zoo on November 15 unveiled Tropical Discovery, a global array of habitats stressing the diversity of tropical life. The exhibit, topped by a glass pyramid 45 feet (14 meters) tall, holds nearly 200 plant species and more than 1,000 animals representing 243 species. Among them are *capybaras*, semiaquatic mammals that are the world's largest living rodent species. Visitors can observe the capybaras swimming in a simulated South American river. Other habitats include a shadowy mountain cave, home to a clan of bats; and a jungle complete with the "ruins" of an ancient temple populated by cobras, boa constrictors, and vipers.

A safari in Chicago. On May 1, Chicago's Brookfield Zoo launched its 5-acre (2-hectare) Habitat Africa, an exhibit devoted to tropical grasslands. The exhibit's mythical Makundi National Park features a replica of a *kopje* (pronounced *KAHP ee*)—a small hill formed by rocks that thrust through the surface of the African *savanna* (plain), providing a habitat for many wildlife species. At Brookfield, small, sure-footed antelope called *klipspringers* scamper over the boulders that they share with *rock hyraxes* (small gopherlike mammals). A pack of African wild dogs—highly endangered predators—prowl the savanna around the kopje. Across a nearby waterhole, visitors can spot other savanna residents, including giraffes, Grant's zebras, and ostriches.

Tropical waters. On May 29, the Columbus Zoo in Ohio premiered Discovery Reef, a 100,000-gallon (378,500-liter) saltwater aquarium housing more than 100 species of animals that live near coral reefs. Besides brightly colored fishes, the residents include sharks, sting-rays, and a sea turtle. Their native environment is simulated by some 1,400 pieces of artificial coral, water maintained at 76 °F (24 °C), and the surging of artificial waves.

The St. Augustine Alligator Farm in St. Augustine, Fla., celebrated its 100th anniversary with the opening on May 20 of Land of Crocodiles, the only exhibit in the world to display all 22 species of *crocodilians* (crocodiles, alligators, and their relatives). Visitors walk through sections representing Africa, Asia, and the Americas, observing such rare species as Chinese alligators, Philippine crocodiles, and gavials (also spelled gharials).

Aquatic mammals were featured in two exhibits introduced in late May. Manatees: The Last Generation?, which opened on May 28 at Sea World of Florida in Orlando, stars one of America's most endangered species, the huge but docile *manatee* (sea cow). Despite their bulk—the largest one weighs 2,200 pounds (998 kilograms)—the manatees seem graceful as they meander through a 300,000-gallon (1.1-million-liter) reproduction of a Florida river. Other habitats in the complex feature alligators and birds that are the manatee's neighbors in the wild.

Bottle-nosed dolphins take center stage at Rocky Point Preserve, a new exhibit that opened on May 29 at Sea World of California in San Diego. A craggy Western coastline frames a 700,000-gallon (2.6-million-liter) simulated bay that is home to a lively group of these friendly creatures. In an interactive area, visitors can pet and feed the dolphins. An adjacent pool serves as a habitat for a group of Alaskan sea otters.

The dry side. On September 23, the North Carolina Zoological Park in Asheboro opened Sonora Desert, a glass-domed structure that duplicates areas in the American Southwest. In the "Sonoran Flats" section, road-runners scurry around slow-moving desert tortoises. On the cactus-dominated "Saguaro Uplands," visitors encounter *ocelots* (small spotted cats), elf owls, and a variety of lizards. "The Desert at Night" reveals a different aspect of this hot, dry land, as rattlesnakes, kangaroo rats, and *cacomistles* (small relatives of raccoons) emerge into the darkness. Sonora Desert is the first of seven habitats that will make up the zoo's 200-acre (81-hectare) American section, expected to be completed in 1994.

Missing amphibians. The Indianapolis Zoo directed public attention to the mysterious worldwide decline of amphibian populations with its Toads, Frogs, and Pollywogs exhibit, introduced in midsummer. The exhibit features more than 30 species of frogs and toads in realistic reproductions of five types of amphibian habitat: aquatic, tropical rain forest, grassland, Amazonian, and desert.

□ Eugene J. Walter, Jr.

In the World Book Supplement section, see **Animal.** In *World Book,* see **Zoo.**

shadow economy, the production and distribution of goods and services outside the normal channels of business activity, and conducted without government regulation.

elec|tron|ic|mailbox, a system for receiving and storing electronic mail

seismic analysis of the rhythms of the heart, especially the left ventr

seis|mo|car|di|og|ra|phy

to detect abnormalities and indicate the presence of heart disease.

play | list

fog-forest (fog´ fôr´ ist), a forest that is sustained by water droplets contained in fog.

1993

DICTIONARY SUPPLEMENT

A list of new words added to the 1994 edition of **The World Book Dictionary** because they have been used enough to become a permanent part of our ever-changing language.

mag|no|cel|lu|lar, a visual pathway of specialized ce that processes impulses of motior

tech|no

kick-start (kik´ stärt´), *v.t.* **1.** to start an engine or machine by a downward kick or pressure on a pedal **2.** *Figurative.* to start an enterprise or process by additional effort or

A a

action doll or **action figure**, a doll with jointed arms and legs that can be moved into different positions, usually portraying a fictional superhero. *As Rambo packed theatres with audiences who howled with pleasure, . . . the nation was flooded with Rambo "action dolls"* (Atlantic).

Af|ro|cen|trism (af rō sen′triz′əm), *n.* the doctrine that African cultures are a principal source of European and American ideas and customs: *Afrocentrism, a cult within the multicultural movement, displays some distressing signs of authoritarianism* (Time). —**Af′ro|cen′trist**, *n.*

alternative medicine, medicine that uses remedies and methods of treatment developed outside modern Western medicine: *The article on alternative medicine seemed to dwell on the schism between holistic therapies and mainstream medicine* (Compuserve).

ar|chae|om|e|try (är′kē om′ə trē), *n.* the science of dating archaeological specimens, as by carbon dating or archaeomagnetism. Also, **archeometry**. [< *archaeo-* + *-metry*] —**ar′chae|om′e|trist**, *n.*

B b

blended family, a family in which one or both of the parents have children from a previous marriage living with them: *Remarriage and blended families are becoming mainstream phenomena* (Wall Street Journal).

body double, a person who stands in for a motion-picture actor in photographic shots that focus on a part of the body: *body doubles . . . women whose body parts are being passed off as movie-star flesh* (New York Newsday).

brown dwarf, a hypothetical object in outer space similar to a star but too small to burn hydrogen steadily: *A new class of objects, brown dwarfs . . . are believed to be too small to get their nuclear fires ignited and become true stars* (New York Times).

C c

car|jack (kär′jak′), *v., n.* —*v.t.* to steal an automobile with a driver in it by force: *Sunday, Bush signed a bill that makes carjacking a federal crime* (USA Today). —*n.* the act or crime of stealing an automobile by force.

com|mu|ni|tar|i|an|ism (kə myü′nə tãr′ē ən iz əm), *n.* political principles that stress both a citizen's individual rights and an obligation to the community and its institutions: *Where environmentalism focuses on the degradation of nature, communitarianism concentrates on the social environment* (New York Times).

D d

Dis|ney|land (diz′nē land), *n.* an ideal place of fantasy and diversion: *Tibetan Buddhism has tremendous entertainment value. As a lama in Kathmandu put it, it is the Disneyland of religions*

(Vanity Fair). [American English, name of a theme park centered around the characters and stories of Walt Disney cartoons]

domino practice, the donation of a functioning organ by a transplant patient who is to receive a group of organs: *To make way for the new heart, they [patients] gave up the old one [for a heart-lung transplant]; doctors call it the "domino practice"* (Time).

E e

e|co|tour (ē′kō tür′), *n.* a trip to a natural area that preserves its environment: *Many ecotour operators support limiting the number of visitors allowed in natural parks* (New York Times).

e|co|tour|ism (ē′kō tür′iz əm), *n.* travel to a natural area that preserves or enhances its environment: *To some companies, ecotourism is . . . a trackless type of travel to natural habitats . . . others say that ecotourism also means improving sites visited* (New York Times).

electronic mailbox, a system for receiving and storing electronic mail: *A computer-user in Finland . . . posted a copy in an electronic "mailbox," where it was retrieved by a Michigan engineering student* (Wall Street Journal).

electronic warfare, warfare conducted by using computer-controlled weapons: *A squadron of Marine Corps electronic-warfare planes . . . would try to destroy Iraqi missile sites* (Wall Street Journal).

ethnic cleansing, the use of intimidation and violence to force an ethnic group out of a geographic area: *The overwhelming, all-pervasive terror . . . has a clear objective: uprooting the Muslim and Croat population in what has been called ethnic cleansing* (Time).

F f

fog-for|est (fog′fôr′ist, -for′-, fôg′-), *n.* a forest that is sustained by water droplets contained in fog: *Fog-forests . . . have been found sitting in the middle of arid deserts, obviously sustained for millennia by the water that is collected by leaves from fog* (New York Times).

G g

gen|dered (jen′dərd), *adj.* divided according to sex: *Women don't want to exchange places with men. We wanted better places, in a kinder, gentler, less rigidly gendered world* (Time).

green|tail|ing (grēn′tā′ling), *n.* retailing that sets aside a percentage of its profits for environmental causes: *The Nature Co. is a prime example of "greentailing," or riding the wake of the environmental movement* (Time).

green tax, a tax on goods, services, or activities which reflects their impact on the environment: *The institute . . . [advanced] "green taxes" as the cure to ailments ranging from global warming to traffic congestion to the scarcity of places to dump garbage* (New York Times).

H h

habitat island, a small area with a uniform habitat: *The same relation holds for "habitat islands," such as patches of forest surrounded by a sea of grassland* (Edward O. Wilson).

hard drive, **1** a mechanism in a computer for reading from and storing information on a hard disk. **2** = hard disk.

hate speech, derogatory speech directed at an individual or group and motivated by prejudice: *The Michigan rule was voided because it prohibited hate speech directed not only at a specific person but also at broad groups of people* (New York Times).

I i

initial public offering, a first-time sale to public investors of company securities on a stock exchange: *An initial public offering . . . will provide you with cash . . . in exchange for pieces of paper* (Spy Magazine). *Abbr:* IPO (no periods).

insider crime, a crime committed by members or trusted associates of an organization or group: *the growing problem of insider crime [where] recent thefts . . . have turned out to be the work of trusted staff members or scholars* (New York Times).

installation art, art that consists of ordinary objects assembled into a composition or installation: *her installations, the first of which she conceived decades before installation art came into its own* (New York Times).

intellectual property, a creative work such as a book, movie, recording, or computer program in which a person has rights protected by patents, trademarks, or copyrights: *With intellectual property now accounting for more than 25% of U.S. exports . . . protection against international piracy ranks high* (Time).

Iron John, a man who is both strong and sensitive: *[Schwarzkopf] even sports the fashionable "Iron John" image of a tough guy who can cry* (Newsweek).

in-your-face (in yür fās′, -yər-), *adj.* in a hostile and aggressive manner: *Hers is a far cry from the in-your-face style that has been the hallmark of mostly male police forces for years* (Time).

J j

ju|ku (jü′kü′), *n.* a Japanese tutorial school that provides extra courses to prepare students for their competitive national examination: *Juku . . . are as much a part of the lives of young Japanese as baseball and skinned knees* (New York Times).

junk call, a telephone call by a telemarketer: *The 550 members . . . answer junk calls cordially and lease out all the information they can* (Wall Street Journal).

Pronunciation Key: hat, āge, cãre, fär; let, ēqual, tėrm; it, īce; hot, ōpen, ôrder; oil, out; cup, pút, rüle; child; long; thin; ᵺen; zh, measure; ə represents **a** in about, **e** in taken, **i** in pencil, **o** in lemon, **u** in circus.

junk caller, a person who engages in telemarketing: *Robert Bulmash has spent years thinking up ways to outfox junk callers* (Wall Street Journal).

K k

kar|a|oke (kar′ē ō′kē), *n.* an entertainment in which patrons of a club or bar sing alone or in groups accompanied by recorded music: *Karaoke . . . lets pop fans act out the way they feel about a song . . . or becomes a show-off's springboard* (New York Times). [< Japanese *karaoke* empty orchestra]

kick-start (kik′stärt′), *v.t.* **1** to start an engine or machine by a downward kick or pressure on a pedal. **2** *Figurative.* to start an enterprise or process by additional effort or action: *Tories called for a realignment of currencies . . . to provide scope for cuts in interest rates to kick-start the economy* (Manchester Guardian Weekly).

L l

Lazarus drug, a drug or medication capable of curing a disease diagnosed as incurable: *Such stories have given ta-crine a reputation as a Lazarus drug, the one medication that could recall to life loved ones who are losing control of their minds and bodies* (Time).

living donor, a person who, while still alive, donates all or part of an organ for transplantation: *Most organs come from cadavers, but the number of living donors is rising* (Time).

low-im|pact (lō′im′pakt), *adj.* causing little or no damage; not harmful or aggressive: *She gradually regained her strength through three months of hydrotherapy, followed by low-impact aerobic sessions* (New York Times).

M m

mag|no|cel|lu|lar system (mag′nō-sel′yə lər), a visual pathway of specialized cells in the brain of humans and other primates that processes impulses of motion, low-contrast light, and depth perception: *The magnocellular system is composed of large cells that carry out fast processes* (New York Times).

ma|qui|la|dor|a (mə kē′lə dôr′ə), *n.* an industrial plant located in Mexico and owned by a U.S. corporation. It assembles finished products from component parts shipped into Mexico, duty-free, from other countries. *Mexican peasants drawn to the maquiladoras are paid as little as fifty-five cents an hour* (Rolling Stone).

mass extinction, the destruction of a whole species by forces of nature: *Scientific skeptics hold that natural causes, like volcanoes or slow climate change, are mainly responsible for the five mass extinctions revealed in the geologic record* (New York Times).

O o

old-growth forest (ōld′grōth′), a forest that has reached its final or stable stage of growth; climax forest: *If finalized, the designation [of the spotted owl as an endangered species] will protect 1.5 million acres . . . of old-growth forest* (Eugene J. Walter).

o|ver|draft|ing (ō′vər draf′ting, -dräf′-), *n.* the extraction of ground water in amounts that are greater than the amount of water normally replaced through rainfall or snowmelt: *Overdrafting ground water . . . is a third option, but the region could pay dearly for that choice . . . unless it finds enough water somewhere to recharge the basins* (New York Times Magazine).

P p

par|vo cel|lu|lar system (pär′vō sel′-yə lər), a visual pathway of specialized cells in the brain of humans and other primates that processes impulses of color, detailing form and contrast and stationary objects: *The parvocellular system is composed of smaller cells that carry out slower processes* (New York Times).

pay-per-view (pā′pər vyü′), *n., adj.* —*n.* a cable television program service in which the subscriber pays a fee for each program viewed: *It would suit the owners—men who seem bent on making baseball a pursuit to follow on TV—if you can get cable and pay-per-view* (Time). —*adj.* of or having to do with pay-per-view: *In the U.S., the concert is being presented via pay-per-view cable TV* (Rolling Stone). *Abbr:* PPV (no periods).

play|list (plā′list), *n.* a catalog of recordings in the library of a radio station: *The Los Angeles heavy-metal radio station . . . features a turbo-charged playlist* (Deanne Stillman).

R r

razor wire, wire fencing with slivers of sharp metal attached to it every few inches: *All you can see . . . is acres of low, mean-looking buildings, girded by fences topped with miles of razor wire glittering in the sun* (Leslie Bennetts).

S s

seis|mo|car|di|og|ra|phy (sīz′mə kär′-dē og′rə fē), *n.* seismic analysis of the rhythms of the heart, especially the left ventricle, to detect abnormalities indicating the presence of heart disease.

shadow economy, the production and distribution of goods and services outside the normal channels of business activity, and conducted without government regulation: *Stanislav Shatalin . . . estimates that by 1989 annual turnover in the "shadow economy" was one-fifth of the entire Soviet GDP* (New Republic).

SLAPP suit (slap), a lawsuit to force an individual to end public criticism, protest, or demonstration against land development projects, dangerous products, controversial actions of public officials, and the like: *A SLAPP suit is an attempt to shift debate out of a public arena and into a more private, judicial forum and to dead-end opposition* (Thomas Clavin). [< S(trategic) L(awsuit) A(gainst) P(ublic) P(articipation)]

surgical strike, **1** an attack, especially by aircraft, against a specific target to eliminate it without causing much damage to the surrounding area: *And quick, it was understood, would mean clean—*

a fact conveyed in the constant bandying-about of "clean sweep," "precision bombing," and "surgical strikes" (Washington Monthly). **2** an advertisement, press release, speech, or public statement that is directed against a specific person, problem, or point of view, as in a political campaign: *Victory requires blowing the current campaign dynamic across the board; surgical strikes won't do* (Michael Kramer).

T t

tech|no (tek′nō), *n.* dance music with a fast beat, produced by an array of highly amplified electronic instruments and equipment: *At the pounding heart of every rave is the galvanizing metronomic beat of techno . . . an intensely synthetic, hyperkinetic form of dance music* (Time).

V v

vid|e|o|scope (vid′ē ō skōp′), *n.* a thin fiber-optic tube with a telescopic lens attached to a miniaturized video camera: *Videoscopes . . . project images of the patient's internal organs and . . . the snippers, staplers and graspers that the surgeons manipulate* (Time).

vid|e|o|sur|ger|y (vid′ē ō sėr′jər ē), *n.* surgery performed with a videoscope: *[Misjudging] the distance to a blood vessel or organ . . . is a major hazard of videosurgery* (J.M. Nash). —**vid′e|o-sur′geon,** *n.*

voice-rec|og|ni|tion technology (vois′rek′əg nish′ən), a system that permits the operation of an appliance or a machine by using the human voice to activate it: *A microphone picks up the sound of your voice, and within seconds your route is plotted on the video display. This same voice-recognition technology is used to control the car stereo* (Rolling Stone).

W w

watch list, a list of individuals, groups, or organizations whose activities are monitored by a governmental agency: *The Florida department of insurance seized two insolvent insurers . . . and placed about a dozen others on its "watch list"* (Time).

white-shoe (hwīt′shü′), *adj. Especially U.S. Informal.* of or associated with individuals thought of as having special rank and privilege; elitist: *A white-shoe Princetonian and onetime political operative for Nelson Rockefeller, Gillies had gone on to head up the John Hay Whitney Foundation* (Christopher Byron).

Z z

zero lot, a small building lot on which a building is placed along one edge with zero or no setback from the property line to maximize the use of available land: *The . . . new house . . . sits on . . . a zero lot, one of several oddly named layouts that builders are using to make the most of indoor and outdoor space* (New York Times).

1993

WORLD BOOK SUPPLEMENT

To help World Book owners keep their encyclopedias up to date, the following articles are reprinted from the 1994 edition of the encyclopedia.

AEOLOGY ▪ ARCHITECTURE ▪ ARGENTINA ▪ ARMED FORCES ▪ ARMENIA ▪ ART

ACING ▪ AVIATION ▪ BAHRAIN ▪ BANGLADESH ▪ BASEBALL ▪ BASKETBALL

CONSTRUCTIO

ER

RATIC PARTY

EDUCATION

S AND FARMIN

▪ HEALTH-CA

AQ ▪ IRELAN

LATIN AMERI

▪ MANITOBA

THERLANDS ▪

RIO

PHILIPPIN

ROTESTANTISM

H ▪ ROMAN

▪ SPACE EXP

NDS ▪ SUDAN ▪ SUPREME COURT OF THE U.S. ▪ ANIMAL, SEE PAGE 458 ▪ SWEDEN

TIONS ▪ TELEVISION ▪ TENNIS ▪ THAILAND ▪ THEATER ▪ TORONTO ▪ TOY

RAINE ▪ UNITED KINGDOM ▪ UNITED NATIONS ▪ UNITED STATES, GOVERNMENT

▪ YUGOSLAVIA ▪ YUKON TERRITORY ▪ ZAIRE ▪ ZAMBIA ▪ ZOOLOGY ▪ ZO

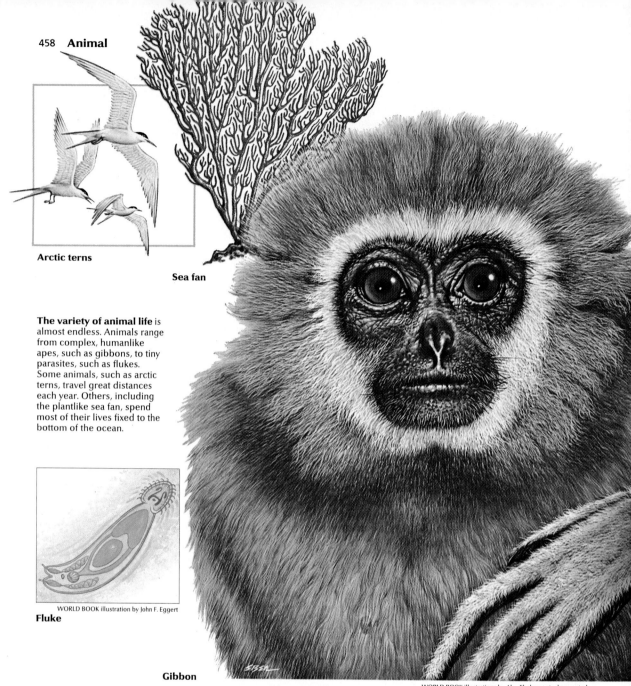

Arctic terns

Sea fan

The variety of animal life is almost endless. Animals range from complex, humanlike apes, such as gibbons, to tiny parasites, such as flukes. Some animals, such as arctic terns, travel great distances each year. Others, including the plantlike sea fan, spend most of their lives fixed to the bottom of the ocean.

WORLD BOOK illustration by John F. Eggert

Fluke

Gibbon

WORLD BOOK illustrations by Alex Ebel except where noted

Animal

Animal. Animals come in many shapes and sizes. They live throughout the world. Animals walk or crawl on land and dig through the soil. They swim in the water and fly through the air. They even live inside the bodies of other animals. Bats, dogs, horses, kangaroos, and

The contributors of this article are Raymond B. Huey, Professor of Zoology at the University of Washington, and W. Herbert Wilson, Jr., Assistant Professor of Biology at Colby College.

moles are all animals. So are butterflies, frogs, jellyfish, pigeons, sharks, snakes, and worms.

Most kinds of animals are less than 1 inch (2.5 centimeters) long. Many are so tiny that they can be seen only with a microscope. The largest animal is the blue whale. It is about as long as five elephants in a row.

Animals are not the only kind of living things. Scientists divide living things into five main *kingdoms* (groups)—animals, plants, fungi, protists, and monerans. *Fungi* include molds, mushrooms, and yeasts. *Protists,* such as amebas, cannot be seen without a microscope. *Monerans,* which include bacteria and certain algae, are some of the smallest, simplest forms of life.

Interesting facts about animals

Kinds of animals. No one knows exactly how many kinds of animals there are. New kinds are found every year. So far, scientists have identified more than $1\frac{1}{2}$ million types of animals. About 1 million of these are insects. There are about 21,000 kinds of fish, 9,700 kinds of birds, 6,500 kinds of reptiles, 4,000 kinds of amphibians, and 4,500 kinds of mammals.

Largest ears and eyes. The largest ears of all animals are those of the African elephant. Elephant ears grow as large as 4 feet (1.2 meters) across. The largest eyes of all land animals are those of the horse and the ostrich. They measure about $1\frac{1}{2}$ times the size of human eyes.

Elephant

Blue whale

Giraffe

The flying dragon is another name for the draco lizard. This lizard can spread out folds of skin to form "wings" that it uses to glide through the air from tree to tree. It lives in Asia and the East Indies.

The huge blue whale is far bigger than the elephant, the biggest land animal, or the giraffe, tallest of all the animals.

Mayfly

The hummingbird, *right,* can fly straight up like a helicopter. It can hover in front of a flower to suck the nectar. The *bee hummingbird,* which grows to only 2 inches (5 centimeters) long, is the smallest of all birds.

The chameleon's tongue is as long as its body. This lizard swiftly shoots out its tongue to capture insects for food. Certain chameleons can quickly change color and even develop spots and streaks that make them seem to be part of their background.

A tree-climbing crab, *left,* lives on many tropical islands. It is called the *coconut crab* because it cracks coconuts with its powerful claws and eats the sweet meat.

Giant tortoise

Lives of animals range from several hours to many years. An adult mayfly survives only a few hours or days. Some giant tortoises have lived more than 100 years.

The world's only known poisonous bird is the hooded pitohui, which lives on the island of New Guinea. This brilliantly colored orange-and-black bird has poison on its feathers and skin. This poison serves as a defense against hawks, snakes, and other enemies. It is the same type of poison as that carried by the deadly poison-dart frog of South America.

The platypus, a mammal, has a bill like a duck and lays eggs as birds do, *right.* But it nurses its young with milk as do other mammals. It lives only on mainland Australia and the island of Tasmania.

WORLD BOOK illustrations by Alex Ebel and Robert Kuhn

Animals are different from other living things in many ways. For example, the bodies of animals are made up of many cells. But the bodies of monerans and most protists have only one cell. Like animals, plants and fungi also are made up of many cells. However, animals can move around. Most plants and fungi are held to one place in the soil by roots or rootlike structures. For a more complete discussion of the differences between the members of the five kingdoms, see the article on **Kingdom** in *World Book Encyclopedia*.

No one knows exactly how many *species* (kinds) of animals there are. So far, scientists have *classified* (grouped) and named more than $1\frac{1}{2}$ million kinds of animals. Over half of these are types of insects. Many new species are discovered each year. Scientists believe there may be from 2 million to as many as 50 million kinds of animals alive today. Many other kinds of animals used to live on the earth but have died out. They include dinosaurs and dodos.

This article provides general information on animals other than human beings. It includes a classification table and pictures of many animals. Separate *World Book Encyclopedia* articles give details about hundreds of animals.

Importance of animals

Animals and the web of life. Living things depend on one another. They are connected in what is sometimes called the *web of life*. Plants capture the energy from sunlight and use it to make roots, stems, leaves, flowers, and fruits. Animals eat the plants, or they eat other animals that feed on the plants. When animals die, their bodies decay and release materials that help fertilize the soil for plants.

Animals and plants are also connected in other ways. When animals breathe, they take in oxygen from the air and give off carbon dioxide. Green plants take in carbon dioxide and give off oxygen in a food-making process called *photosynthesis*. Many plants with flowers need insects or birds to carry their pollen from plant to plant. Without this transfer of pollen, these plants are not able to *reproduce* (create new individuals of their own kind). Some seeds are prickly and cling to the fur or feathers of animals. When the animals move from place to place, they take the seeds with them. In this way, the seeds get dropped in new areas where they can grow into plants.

The web of life relies on balance among its parts. A change in one part may mean disaster for the others. For

WORLD BOOK illustration by John F. Eggert

Animals and plants are linked in a pattern of nature often called the *web of life*. This pattern can be seen in a garden or backyard. There, many kinds of animals keep themselves alive by eating some of the plants. Likewise, much of the food that plants need comes from the body wastes of animals. In most cases, natural forces keep the total number of living things in balance.

example, if all the trees in an area are cut down, then many animals that depend on them will die. For more information on how living things are linked, see **Ecology** in *World Book Encyclopedia.*

Animals and people. Animals have provided people with food and clothing since prehistoric times. Without animals, people would not have such things as meat, honey, eggs, wool, leather, or silk.

At least 10,000 years ago, people began *domesticating* (taming) animals. Some of these animals provide food and clothing. For example, cattle supply meat, milk, and leather. Chickens lay eggs. Sheep provide wool.

Some domesticated animals help people work. Water buffaloes pull plows in Asian rice fields. Horses and camels carry people from one place to another. At first, people kept cats in their houses to catch rats and mice. They raised dogs to help them hunt and to warn them when danger approached. Today, cats and dogs are kept largely as pets.

Certain insects are useful to people. Bees make honey, which people harvest for food. Bees also pollinate many food crops, including fruits and vegetables. Silk comes from fiber made by silkworms.

Some animals harm people. On rare occasions, croc-

Melissa Grimes-Guy, Photo Researchers

Some animals make wonderful pets. Cats and dogs are favorite pets around the world. They are affectionate and loyal, and they provide companionship to people of all ages.

Larry Stessin, Photo Researchers

Some animals can be dangerous to people. A great white shark, *above,* usually feeds on tuna and other large sea animals. But sharks sometimes kill and eat people.

Anna E. Zuckerman, Tom Stack & Assoc.

Some animals help people work. Through the centuries, cattle and horses have pulled plows, carts, and wagons and carried products and riders on their backs. The water buffaloes shown at the left are helping a farmer plow a rice field in Southeast Asia.

odiles, lions, and tigers attack and kill people. So do grizzly bears and polar bears. Sharks sometimes kill and eat human beings. Bites from such poisonous snakes as rattlesnakes and cobras can cause death. The black widow spider has a poison that makes people extremely sick.

Some animals pass diseases along from person to person. Certain mosquitoes transmit malaria and yellow fever. Some ticks carry the bacteria that cause Lyme disease and Rocky Mountain spotted fever. Some animals cause disease themselves. Worms called *flukes,* which live in human organs, can cause *schistosomiasis.* This disease infects millions of people in many African, Asian, and Latin-American countries.

Kinds of animals

People often divide animals into various groups based on certain similarities the animals share. For example, some animals can be kept as pets, but others are wild. Arranging animals according to their similarities is a handy way of remembering and understanding them.

Some common ways of grouping animals. Animals can be grouped in many ways. They can be arranged according to whether they live on land or in water. Animals that live on land are known as *terrestrial animals.* They include cats, dogs, lizards, mice, and worms. Animals that live in water are called *aquatic animals.* They include eels, fish, lobsters, octopuses, and whales.

Animals can be arranged by the number of legs they have. Dogs, frogs, and lizards have four legs. Bats and birds have two legs. Insects have six legs, and spiders have eight. Snakes and worms have no legs.

Another way to group animals is according to how they move. Bats, most birds, and many insects fly. Whales, fish, and squid swim. Snakes and worms crawl. Antelope and cheetahs run. Frogs, kangaroos, and rabbits hop.

Some animals are *cold-blooded,* and others are *warm-blooded.* The bodies of cold-blooded animals are warm when their surroundings are warm and cool when their surroundings are cool. Warm-blooded animals, on the other hand, almost always have the same body temperature, regardless of the warmth of their surroundings. Birds, *mammals* (animals whose babies drink the mother's milk), and a few species of fish and insects are warm-blooded. All other kinds of animals are cold-blooded.

Animals are also commonly divided into groups according to whether they have backbones. *Invertebrates* do not have backbones, but *vertebrates* do. The vast majority of animals are invertebrates. They include clams, insects, jellyfish, sea urchins, snails, spiders, sponges, and worms. Birds, fish, mammals, and reptiles are vertebrates. So are *amphibians*—frogs, salamanders, and other animals that spend part of their lives in water and part on land.

The scientific classification of animals involves grouping animals according to the biological relationships among them. This orderly arrangement of animals depends in part on the features the animals share. In general, the more features they share, the more closely they are related. However, the scientific classification of animals is based mainly on the belief that certain animals share a common ancestor. Animals with a more recent common ancestor are more closely related than those who share an ancestor further back in time. In a somewhat similar way, brothers and sisters are more closely related than are cousins. Brothers and sisters share parents. First cousins share grandparents.

In classifying animals, *zoologists* (scientists who study animals) divide them into ever-smaller groups that have more and more features in common. The largest group is the kingdom Animalia itself, which includes all animals. Next, each animal is placed in a group called a *phylum.* Each phylum is divided into groups called

The cat and its relatives

The cat family includes many kinds of wild animals with similar body characteristics. Most members of the cat family have many of the same habits. They are clever hunters and stalk their prey on padded feet. They use their sharp claws and teeth to tear their food. Some also use their claws to climb trees to seek food or escape enemies.

Domestic cat

Lion

Tiger

Snow leopard

Leopard

Ocelot

Lynx

Jaguar

Cheetah

Mountain lion

Length of life of animals

Figures in this list are average life spans in years for animals in the wild, unless otherwise noted.

Mammals				Birds			
Buffalo, American	20	Horse	20-30*	Blue jay	6-9	Owl (snowy)	10
Cat	14*	Lion	13	Canada goose	12-23	Penguin (emperor)	20
Chimpanzee	50-60	Monkey (rhesus)	27-28	Canary	6-8	Pigeon	6
Deer (fallow)	20	Mouse (field)	1	Cardinal	13	Raven	5
Dog	12-20*	Sheep	10-20	Chickadee	6-8	Robin, American	17
Elephant	50-70	Squirrel	7	Condor	35-40	Skylark	9
Goat, Mountain	14-18	Tiger	20	Heron	10-20	Sparrow	2½-7
Grizzly bear	25	Wolf (gray)	12-16	Macaw	64	Starling	9-16
Hippopotamus	41	Zebra	22	Ostrich (African)	40		

Fish				Reptiles and amphibians			
Dogfish (lesser spotted)	8	Perch	3-10	Bullfrog	5	Rattlesnake (diamondback)	14-15
Goldfish	10	Pike	60-70	Chameleon	4-5		
Halibut	25	Salmon (Pacific)	4-5	Cottonmouth	18-20	Salamander (spotted)	20
Lamprey	7	Seahorse	4½	Crocodile (Nile)	25-50	Turtle (box)	80
Lungfish (African)	18	Sturgeon	50	Garter snake	3-4	Water snake	11
		Trout (rainbow)	11	King snake	3		
				Puff adder	14		

*Domesticated animal; life span in captivity.

---

classes. The classes are broken down into *orders,* and the orders into *families.* The families are split into *genera,* and the genera into *species.* The singular form of *genera* is *genus,* but the word *species* may be either singular or plural.

Among the animals that scientists have classified are about 13,000 species of flatworms; 50,000 species of clams, oysters, and other *mollusks* (soft-bodied animals, most of which have a hard shell); 1,000,000 species of insects; 30,000 species of spiders; 21,000 species of fish; 4,000 species of amphibians; 6,500 species of reptiles; 9,700 species of birds; and 4,500 species of mammals. Each species belongs to one phylum, one class, one order, one family, and one genus. For example, tigers belong to the kingdom Animalia, the phylum Chordata, the class Mammalia, the order Carnivora, the family Felidae, and the genus *Panthera.* They are members of the species *Panthera tigris.* Lions are related to tigers. They belong to the same kingdom (Animalia), phylum (Chordata), class (Mammalia), order (Carnivora), family (Felidae), and genus (*Panthera*) as tigers. But lions are classified in a different species—*Panthera leo,* also written simply as *P. leo.*

A *table* of animal classification, showing some of the major groups of animals, appears at the conclusion of this article.

Where animals live

Animals live in many kinds of places. The place where an animal lives is called its *habitat.* Each type of habitat presents a special challenge to animals. For example, animals that live in polar regions must withstand bitter cold. Those that inhabit the tropics face extreme heat. In spite of these challenges, animals can be found everywhere on the earth. They live on the highest mountains and in the deepest oceans. They roam the driest deserts and the wettest rain forests. They swim in fresh water and salt water.

Each habitat supports many kinds of animals. In most cases, the animals are the same kinds that have lived in those surroundings for thousands of years. As a result, the animals have developed bodies and ways of life that suit them to that particular habitat. No single species of animal can survive everywhere. For example, tropical fish from the Amazon River thrive in warm water but cannot withstand the cold streams of the Andes Mountains. On the other hand, many kinds of fish that live in the Arctic Ocean would die if they were exposed to the warm waters of the Caribbean Sea. However, some animals may travel between habitats from time to time. For example, African elephants eat both grass and tree parts and so move between grassland and forest. But these animals would not be able to withstand the freezing temperatures of the polar regions.

Some habitats, including many forests and grasslands, are being destroyed by human beings. The destruction of these habitats usually causes the death of many animals. When people convert grassland to farmland, for example, they destroy the homes and source of food of many species. Without these necessities, some animals will die immediately. Others may try moving to another grassland. But the new area may not have enough food and shelter to support the additional wildlife. As a result, many more animals will die.

This section tells about some of the major animals, grouped according to seven types of habitats: (1) mountains, (2) grasslands, (3) temperate forests, (4) tropical forests, (5) deserts, (6) polar regions, and (7) oceans. For descriptions and pictures of animals grouped according to the continent on which they live, see the articles on **Africa; Antarctica; Asia; Australia; Europe; North America; South America** in *World Book Encyclopedia.*

Animals of the mountains

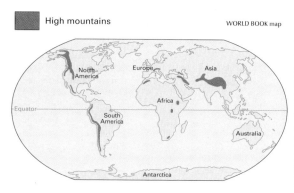

█ High mountains

WORLD BOOK map

Leonard Lee Rue III

Vicuña   South America

Jane Burton, Bruce Coleman Ltd.

Chinchilla   South America

Mountains support a variety of animal life. The numbers and kinds of animals found on mountains vary with altitude. More animals and more kinds of animals live at lower altitudes than at higher ones, largely because of the differences in climate between elevations. Generally, mountain climates become colder, wetter, and windier with increasing altitude. The air also gets thinner and has less oxygen. In addition, fewer plants are found at higher elevations, and therefore less food is available for animals.

Bears, deer, elk, and mink make their homes on the forested lower slopes and in the wooded or grassy valleys of mountains. Rainbow trout and graylings swim in mountain streams. Many mountains have meadows of grasses and herbs. These meadows are home to chinchillas, ibexes, llamas, vicuñas, and yaks. Butterflies, grasshoppers, and spiders also live there.

Above the *timber line*—that is, the line beyond which trees will not grow because of the cold—stand rocky cliffs and peaks dotted with shrubs, mosses, and other plants. Small meadows are also found there. Sure-footed bighorn sheep and mountain goats dwell among the windswept rocks, as do furry marmots and pikas. High on the snow-capped peaks, only a few insects, spiders, and ice worms can survive. Golden eagles and some other birds fly above the mountains. A large African vulture, Rüppell's griffon, has been known to soar as high as 36,600 feet (11,150 meters).

Bighorn sheep   North America

Rocky Mountain pika
North America

Rocky Mountain goat
North America

Nepalese swift
Asia

Yak
Asia

Wolf spider
North America

Lynn M. Stone, Animals Animals

Himalayan ibex
Asia

Russ Kinne, Photo Researchers

Giant panda Asia

Marco Polo sheep
Asia

Snow leopard
Asia

WORLD BOOK illustrations by Margaret L. Estey

Animals of the grasslands

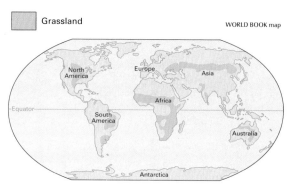

☐ Grassland

WORLD BOOK map

Grasslands include the prairies of North America, the pampas of South America, the plains of Europe, and the steppes of Asia. The savannas of east Africa have more grassland animals than any other area.

Rainfall in grasslands is seasonal, and animals sometimes travel great distances to find green grass. Gazelles, gnus, and zebras migrate by the thousands through the African savannas. Smaller groups of ele-phants and rhinoceroses also feed on the grasses there. Such meat-eating mammals as cheetahs, hyenas, and lions roam the savannas in search of prey. The savannas are also home to giraffes, jackals, ostriches, secretary birds, and termites. In addition, hippopotamuses live in and near bodies of water in African grasslands. Animals of other grasslands include the kangaroos and wombats of Australia, the cavies and rheas of South America, and the coyotes and prairie dogs of North America.

Many animals of the grasslands have become endangered due to loss of their habitat and to overhunting. The rich soils of grasslands are ideal for farming, and people have converted many such areas to farmland. Many of the large grassland animals are favorite big game for hunters. For example, the once-plentiful pampas deer of South America have become extremely rare. As the pampas are converted to farmland, the tall grass that grows there disappears. Without this grass, the pampas deer have no shelter and become easy prey. Bison once grazed in huge herds in the Great Plains of North America. But so many of these animals were killed by hunters or died as their grassland habitat was converted to farmland that they were nearly wiped out.

Giraffe

Zebra

Ostrich

Aardvark

Termite mound

Gnu

Africa

Pronghorn
North America

Blackbuck
Asia

Eland
Africa

Ylla, Rapho Guillumette

Indian rhinoceros Asia

Guggisberg, Photo Researchers

Secretary bird Africa

Conzett & Huber

Hippopotamus Africa

Peterson, Photo Researchers

African vulture

African elephant

Simon Trevor

African lion

Kangaroo
Australia

Prairie dog
North America

WORLD BOOK illustrations by John F. Eggert and René Martin

Animals of the temperate forests

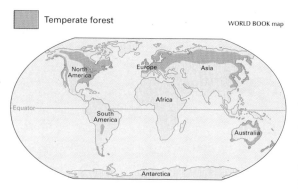

Temperate forest

WORLD BOOK map

Temperate forests consist largely of *deciduous trees* and *evergreen trees*. Deciduous trees shed their leaves in the fall and grow new ones in the spring. Evergreen trees have leaves that live two or more years. Some evergreens have needle-shaped leaves. Most temperate forests are in Asia, Europe, and North America. Australia also has some temperate forests.

Many forest animals have small bodies that allow them to move easily through the underbrush. Forest mammals include chipmunks, mice, opossums, porcupines, raccoons, skunks, and squirrels. Bears, deer, and wild boars also live in temperate forests. Bobcats and wolves were once common in woodland areas. However, so many of these predators have been hunted and trapped through the years that they have become rare.

Salamanders are often plentiful in temperate forests. They hide in the leaf litter or under rocks, where they feed on insects and other small organisms. In wet forests, slugs and other snails are common. Beavers, fish, frogs, muskrats, otters, salamanders, and turtles live in or near woodland streams, ponds, and lakes. Great numbers of birds nest in the trees and shrubs.

Many temperate forests have been cleared for farms and cities, and many others have been cut down for fuel and lumber. This *deforestation* (destruction of forests) places woodland animals in danger. Extensive logging in the Pacific Northwest of the United States, for example, has destroyed much of the habitat of the spotted owl, threatening the existence of that species.

Redstart
North America

Gray squirrel
North America

Russ Kinne, Photo Researchers

FPG

European brown bear

Moose   North America

Otter   North America

Spotted owl
North America

Red-backed salamander
North America

Wood frog
North America

Beaver
North America

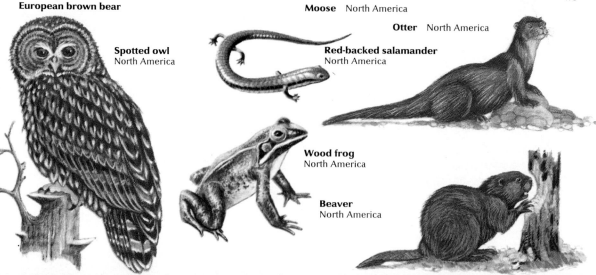

Downy woodpecker

Ovenbird

White-tailed deer

Chipmunk

Raccoon

Muskrat

Woodchuck

Porcupine

Opossum

Skunk

Snapping turtle

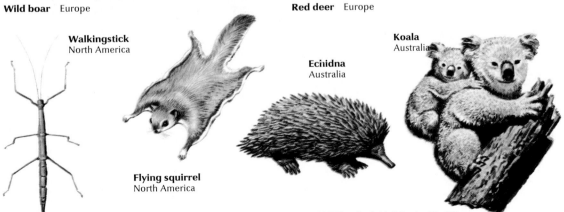

Wild boar Europe

Okapia, Publix

Red deer Europe

Geoffroy Kinns, Photo Researchers

Walkingstick
North America

Flying squirrel
North America

Echidna
Australia

Koala
Australia

WORLD BOOK illustrations by John F. Eggert and Stan Galli

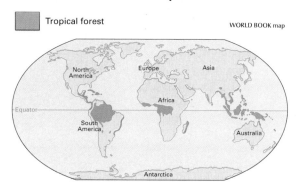

Tropical forest

WORLD BOOK map

Tropical forests stay warm all year and receive plentiful rainfall. These forests are found in Africa, Asia, Australia, Central and South America, and the Pacific Islands. More kinds of animals live in tropical forests than in any other habitat. Scientists estimate that perhaps as many as 30 million species of tropical animals have not even been discovered yet.

Insects make up the largest single group of animals that live in tropical forests. They include brightly colored butterflies, huge colonies of ants, mosquitoes, and camouflaged stick insects. Spiders are also plentiful. Many tropical birds, such as quetzals and parrots, are spectacularly colored.

The broad leaves of trees in tropical forests form a thick overhead covering called a *canopy* that blocks nearly all sunlight from reaching the forest floor. Many kinds of animals live in the canopies of tropical forests. They include harpy eagles and toucans; tree frogs; flying dragons; spider monkeys and howlers; gibbons and orangutans; sloths; slow lorises; tree boa constrictors; bats; and wasps, beetles, and leaf-cutting ants.

Jaguars, tapirs, and bushmaster snakes live on the ground in tropical forests. Chimpanzees and lowland gorillas alternate between the ground and the trees. Crocodiles, fish, and turtles inhabit rivers and ponds.

People are rapidly destroying tropical forests for wood and for farming. The continuing destruction of this habitat means that many animals will disappear forever. Scientists believe countless species have already been wiped out.

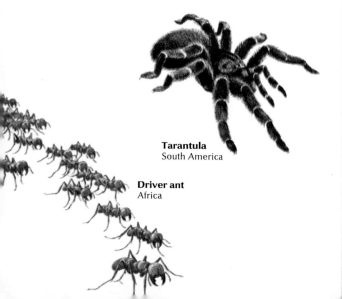

Tarantula
South America

Driver ant
Africa

Black howler monkey

Common marmoset

Macaw

Spider monkey

Coati

Iguana

Two-toed sloth

Parasol ant

Ocelot

Tree frog

Tree boa constrictor

South American rain forest

Axis deer Asia

South American tapir

Malayan tapir Asia

Chevrotain Asia

Des Bartlett, Photo Researchers

Bongo Africa

Nancy Adams, Tom Stack & Assoc.

Gorilla Africa

Orangutan Asia

James Simon, Photo Researchers

Woolly monkey South America

James Simon, Photo Researchers

Giant anteater South America

Tiger Asia

Ylla, Rapho Guillumette

Leopard Africa, Asia

Jaguar Central and South America, Mexico

WORLD BOOK illustrations by John F. Eggert and Robert Kuhn

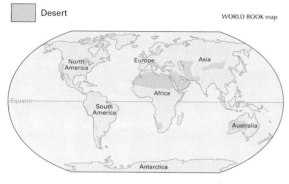

☐ Desert

Southwestern United States

Most deserts lie near the edges of the tropics. Food and water are often scarce in deserts, and temperatures in the summer can be scorching. Despite these conditions, many kinds of animals live there. They include geckos, iguanas, and skinks; bees, butterflies, and moths; spiders; elf owls and roadrunners; sidewinders; dorcas gazelles and mule deer; and bobcats, coyotes, and dingoes.

Animals of the deserts have developed special bodies and ways of life that enable them to survive the extreme heat. Centipedes, kangaroo rats, rattlesnakes, and scorpions spend the day in burrows. They come out to search for food only when temperatures drop at night. Many insects, lizards, and tortoises can tolerate high desert temperatures and are active in the daytime. But even they must retreat underground or find the shade of a tree during the hottest part of the day. Some snails, insects, frogs, lizards, mice, and ground squirrels *estivate* (sleep through the summer).

Many desert dwellers have light-colored skin, which helps keep them cool by reflecting sunlight. Desert foxes and hares have long ears. When overheated, these animals move to a cool cave or burrow where they can get rid of excess body heat through their ears. The Cape ground squirrel makes its own shade by using its fluffy tail like a parasol. Fairy shrimp and spadefoot toads may spend months or years underground waiting for rain to create ponds. Then they quickly feed and reproduce before the ponds dry again.

Dingo   Australia

Roadrunner   North America

Scorpion   North America

Pallid bat

Coyote

Bobcat

Mule deer

Antelope
jack rabbit

Cactus wren

Kit fox

Gila monster

Shovel-nosed snake   North America

Saiga   Asia

Elf owl   North America

Addax   Africa

Animals of the polar regions

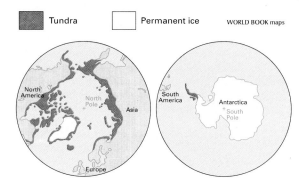

Tundra   Permanent ice   WORLD BOOK maps

Animals that live in polar regions must withstand extremely cold temperatures. No land animals except ice worms and a few species of insects live in polar regions that have ice and snow the year around. But the seas of the Arctic and Antarctic have large numbers of wildlife, including fish, giant sponges, whales, and tiny shrimp-like creatures called *krill.* In addition, polar bears, sea lions, and walruses spend much of their time on floating sheets of ice in the Arctic. Penguins and seals live on the Antarctic coast.

Many animals inhabit the vast arctic *tundras* (cold treeless plains) of northern Asia, North America, and Europe. They include caribou, ermine, musk oxen, reindeer, lemmings, snowy owls, and wolves. Shallow ponds in the region provide a place for mosquitoes and many other insects to lay their eggs. These insects serve as food for the birds that migrate to the tundra each summer to nest.

Animals that live in polar regions have developed bodies and ways of life that enable them to deal with the frigid winter weather. Caribou, musk oxen, and polar bears have thick fur, which helps them stay warm. The arctic fox and arctic hare have short ears and tails that keep them from losing much body heat. Arctic ground squirrels *hibernate* (sleep through the winter). They curl up in a burrow, and their body temperature drops, saving energy during the long winter. They also do not eat in the winter. They live off fat stored in their bodies.

Snowy owl

Musk ox

Arctic hare

Rock ptarmigan

Ermine

Arctic winter

Polar bear   Arctic

Cy LaTour

Arctic bumble bee

Emperor penguin   Antarctica

Emil Schulthess, Black Star

Kodiak bear North America

St. Meyers/Okapia, Photo Researchers

Sandhill crane

Arctic loon

Golden plover

Caribou

Arctic fox

WORLD BOOK illustrations by John F. Eggert and Guy Tudor

Arctic summer

Krill
Polar seas

Collared lemming
Arctic

Walrus Arctic

Steve McCutcheon

Animals of the oceans

Animals of many kinds are found everywhere in the vast oceans. Some of the smallest animals live in the sea, as does the world's largest, the blue whale. Cod, halibut, seals, and whales swim the frigid waters of the polar regions. Lobsters, sea urchins, and many types of brightly colored fish inhabit coral reefs in warm tropical seas. Some ocean animals live near the shore—in shallow water, in tide pools, and on rocks. They include anemones, barnacles, mussels, octopuses, and starfish. Other marine animals—mostly such tiny shrimplike creatures as krill and copepods—are found in the open sea. Krill and some species of copepods form part of the group of organisms called *plankton.* Many fish and some whales feed on plankton.

The great depths of the ocean are completely dark, and the water there is bitterly cold. Even so, anglerfish, clams, and certain other creatures live there. On the other hand, flyingfish, manta rays, marlins, and porpoises generally swim near the ocean surface. Albatrosses, gulls, and petrels fly above the sea.

Oceans provide people with such foods as crab, fish, lobster, and shrimp. However, the demand for seafood has led to the overfishing of halibut, herring, and some other marine animals. Millions of dolphins, which are mammals, have drowned in fishing nets that were intended to catch cod, tuna, and other fish. In addition, spills of toxic materials and other forms of pollution have reduced the numbers of some ocean species.

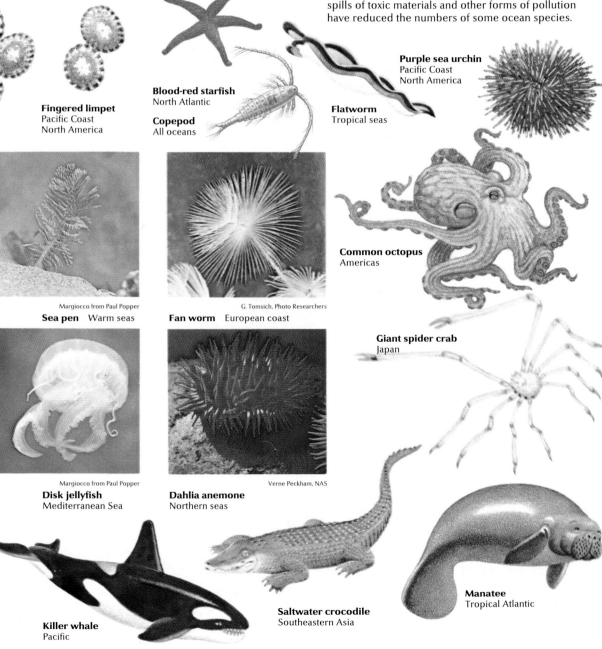

Fingered limpet
Pacific Coast
North America

Blood-red starfish
North Atlantic

Copepod
All oceans

Flatworm
Tropical seas

Purple sea urchin
Pacific Coast
North America

Margiocco from Paul Popper
Sea pen   Warm seas

G. Tomsich, Photo Researchers
Fan worm   European coast

Common octopus
Americas

Giant spider crab
Japan

Margiocco from Paul Popper
Disk jellyfish
Mediterranean Sea

Verne Peckham, NAS
Dahlia anemone
Northern seas

Manatee
Tropical Atlantic

Killer whale
Pacific

Saltwater crocodile
Southeastern Asia

Mike Bacon, Tom Stack & Assoc.

Raccoon butterflyfish and coral Red Sea

Flyingfish Warm seas

Deep-sea angler Atlantic and Pacific

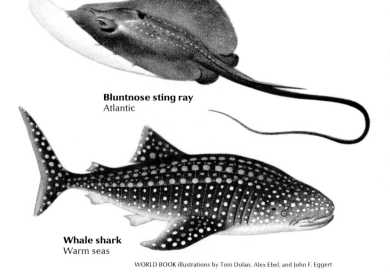

Bluntnose sting ray
Atlantic

Whale shark
Warm seas

WORLD BOOK illustrations by Tom Dolan, Alex Ebel, and John F. Eggert

The bodies of animals

Animals have special body features that enable them to survive in their environment. These special features, called *adaptations,* result from the ability animal species have to *adapt* (adjust) over time to changes in their surroundings. Adaptations for survival enable animals to move about, to eat, to breathe, and to sense their environment. Legs, wings, and fins help animals move. Teeth and jaws help them eat. Lungs and gills help them obtain oxygen. Eyes and ears help them find food and detect predators.

Animals live in many kinds of environments. The body features of an animal that work well in one type of environment may not work in others. For example, the adaptations that enable fish to breathe in water do not let them breathe on land. Even in the same environment, animals may have different adaptations for survival. Shrimp, fish, and sea turtles can all swim in the ocean, but they have different body features for doing so.

Invertebrates and vertebrates

The animal kingdom is often divided into two main groups—animals without backbones, called *invertebrates,* and animals with backbones, called *vertebrates.* Invertebrates include sponges, worms, centipedes, starfish, mollusks, and insects. Vertebrates include fish, amphibians, reptiles, birds, and mammals. Invertebrates are commonly known as the *lower animals.* Vertebrates are known as the *higher animals.* The backbone of a vertebrate helps protect the *spinal* (main nerve) *cord.* The main nerve cord of invertebrates is unprotected. A small sea animal, the amphioxus, has a *notochord,* which is a rod of cartilage that serves as a backbone and partly protects the animal's main nerve. The amphioxus is considered to be a link between the lower animals and the higher animals.

WORLD BOOK illustrations by Patricia Wynne

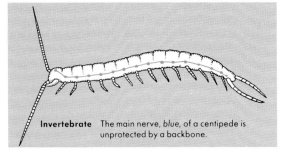

Invertebrate The main nerve, *blue,* of a centipede is unprotected by a backbone.

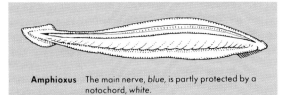

Amphioxus The main nerve, *blue,* is partly protected by a notochord, *white.*

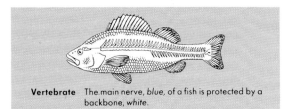

Vertebrate The main nerve, *blue,* of a fish is protected by a backbone, *white.*

Shrimp have tiny swimming legs, fish have fins and muscular tails, and turtles have flippers. Because animals adapt to their surroundings in many ways, there is a wide diversity of animals in any environment.

This section describes some of the ways animal bodies are adapted for moving, eating, breathing, and sensing the environment. For more information on adaptation, see **Adaptation** in the *World Book Encyclopedia.*

Adaptations for moving about

Legs and feet. Mammals, birds, insects, and many reptiles and amphibians have legs with feet that enable them to walk or run on land. Most amphibians, mammals, and reptiles walk on four legs. Birds and people walk on two. Insects have six legs, and spiders have eight. Millipedes may have up to 200 legs.

Animals can crawl without legs and feet. Such tiny creatures as planarians and other flatworms slide by moving many small hairlike structures, called *cilia,* back and forth like miniature oars. Snails move by coating the ground with a sticky fluid from their bodies. They then crawl through the fluid using a muscular organ called a *foot.* Most snakes slide along the ground by bending their bodies from side to side. An earthworm crawls through the soil by alternately lengthening and shortening parts of its body.

Many walking and crawling organisms live in water. Crabs and lobsters have legs that enable them to walk across the bottom of a body of water.

Wings. Three groups of animals have the ability to fly under their own power: (1) insects, (2) bats, and (3) birds. Most insects have two pairs of wings. Muscles inside the *thorax* (middle section of an insect's body) move the wings up and down.

Bats are the only mammals with wings. Batwings are

Jacana

Long, powerful legs and a stride of 15 feet (4.6 meters) make the ostrich one of the fastest land animals. Ostriches can reach speeds as high as 40 miles (64 kilometers) per hour.

Comparative speeds of animals The speeds of animals vary greatly. Birds are the fastest of all animals, with flying speeds of more than 200 miles (320 kilometers) per hour. The speediest land animals outstrip the fastest water animals. Many of the figures given in the table below are estimates because scientists have difficulty measuring the speeds of wild animals. In addition, the maximum speed of an animal may differ widely from its usual speed. A rabbit runs faster than a greyhound for a short time. But the greyhound can keep up its speed for longer distances.

WORLD BOOK illustrations by Linda Kinnaman and Robert Klunder

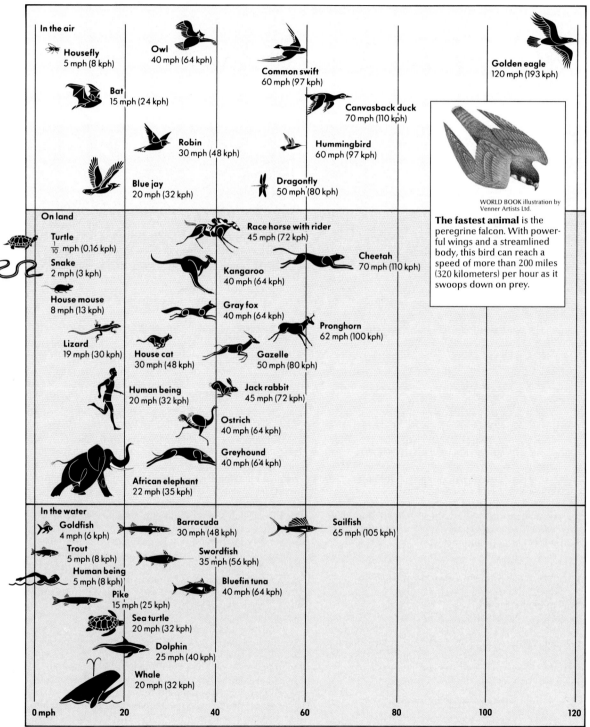

In the air

Housefly 5 mph (8 kph)

Owl 40 mph (64 kph)

Common swift 60 mph (97 kph)

Golden eagle 120 mph (193 kph)

Bat 15 mph (24 kph)

Canvasback duck 70 mph (110 kph)

Robin 30 mph (48 kph)

Hummingbird 60 mph (97 kph)

Blue jay 20 mph (32 kph)

Dragonfly 50 mph (80 kph)

WORLD BOOK illustration by Venner Artists Ltd.

The fastest animal is the peregrine falcon. With powerful wings and a streamlined body, this bird can reach a speed of more than 200 miles (320 kilometers) per hour as it swoops down on prey.

On land

Turtle 1/10 mph (0.16 kph)

Race horse with rider 45 mph (72 kph)

Cheetah 70 mph (110 kph)

Snake 2 mph (3 kph)

Kangaroo 40 mph (64 kph)

House mouse 8 mph (13 kph)

Gray fox 40 mph (64 kph)

Pronghorn 62 mph (100 kph)

Lizard 19 mph (30 kph)

House cat 30 mph (48 kph)

Gazelle 50 mph (80 kph)

Human being 20 mph (32 kph)

Jack rabbit 45 mph (72 kph)

Ostrich 40 mph (64 kph)

Greyhound 40 mph (64 kph)

African elephant 22 mph (35 kph)

In the water

Goldfish 4 mph (6 kph)

Barracuda 30 mph (48 kph)

Sailfish 65 mph (105 kph)

Trout 5 mph (8 kph)

Swordfish 35 mph (56 kph)

Human being 5 mph (8 kph)

Bluefin tuna 40 mph (64 kph)

Pike 15 mph (25 kph)

Sea turtle 20 mph (32 kph)

Dolphin 25 mph (40 kph)

Whale 20 mph (32 kph)

0 mph 20 40 60 80 100 120

G. I. Bernard, Oxford Scientific Films from Animals Animals

Long, slender front wings and small hind wings enable the fast-flying hawk moth to hover like a hummingbird.

E. R. Degginger

The measuring worm crawls by pulling the back part of its body toward the front, then pushing the front part forward.

E. R. Degginger

A tail and fins serve most fish in swimming. The tail of a male fancy guppy, *above,* may grow longer than its body.

Stephen Dalton, Animals Animals

Powerful hind legs make the frog a champion jumper on land, *above,* and an expert swimmer when in the water.

made up mostly of skin stretched over long finger bones. Muscles in the wings raise and lower them.

Birds have powerful muscles attached to their wings and breastbone. Bird wings are covered with feathers, which also aid in flight.

Some animals, including flying squirrels and flying lemurs, can glide but not fly. Such animals jump from trees or mountains. They have big feet or folds of skin that spread out to serve as "wings" for gliding.

Fins, tails, and flippers. Many types of animals swim in fresh or salt water. Fish have well-developed tails and fins. Most fish swim by bending their powerful, muscular tail from side to side. Fins on the top, bottom, and sides of fish are used to maintain balance and to maneuver in tight areas. Dolphins, porpoises, and whales swim by moving their massive tails up and down rather than side to side. Turtles swim by paddling with their webbed feet or their flippers.

Jellyfish and squids swim by jet propulsion. When a jellyfish pushes water out from under its body, it is thrust in the opposite direction. A squid takes water into its body cavity and then squirts the water out through a small opening called a *funnel.* This action repeated many times pushes the squid forward.

A number of species of birds can swim. Some ducks and gulls paddle on the surface of the water using their webbed feet as oars. Torrent ducks and loons dive underwater, where they swim by kicking their feet. Penguins use their feet and their wings to swim.

Adaptations for eating

All animals need food to survive. Animals eat plants, other animals, or both plants and other animals. Animals

that eat plants are called *herbivores.* Zebras, cows, and moose are herbivores. Animals that eat other animals are called *carnivores* or *meat-eaters.* Dogs, lions, and sharks are carnivores. Animals that eat both plants and animals are known as *omnivores.* Bears are omnivores.

Biologists describe the relationships between animals in a habitat and the foods they eat as a *food chain.* Technically, a food chain involves the flow of energy from the sun to green plants to animal consumers. For example, a simple food chain in a meadow links the grasses, the deer that eat the grasses, and the wolves that eat the deer. Sometimes, many kinds of animals and plants are involved in complex networks of food chains. Such networks are called *food webs.*

Most animals eat a variety of foods. For example, pigeons eat fruits, grains, and nuts, and they sometimes feed on insects, snails, and worms.

Some animals eat only a few foods. A snail called a cone shell preys only on a single species of marine worm. Several kinds of snakes eat only slugs or other snails. Hummingbirds and honey possums live on the nectar of flowers. A sapsucker drills holes in trees and eats the sap that flows from the holes. The koala of Australia dines only on the leaves of eucalyptus trees.

Filtering mechanisms. Huge numbers of tiny organisms called plankton float or swim slowly near the surface of oceans, lakes, and other bodies of water. Plankton make up a part of an important food chain in the ocean. Plankton are too small to be captured individually by animals that feed on them. Some animals, such as barnacles, sweep water past themselves while straining out the tiny plankton, which are thereby captured. This process is called *filter feeding.*

A **gray whale** filters food from water by squeezing the water out of its mouth through thin plates called *baleen*.

A **snake** swallows food whole. It has loose jaws that enable it to swallow eggs or animals much larger than its own head.

A **lion** has long, razor-sharp *canine* (pointed) teeth for killing and tearing such prey as antelope and zebras. It does not have teeth for chewing, however. It swallows its food in chunks.

Baleen whales are probably the best-known filter feeders. These animals, which do not have teeth, feed by gulping huge mouthfuls of water containing plankton, small fish, and other marine organisms. They then force the water out of their mouths through a series of strainers called *baleen*. The food is captured on the baleen and then swallowed. A baleen whale can consume as much as 4 short tons (3.6 metric tons) of food a day.

Teeth and jaws. Many animals eat food that they need to tear into pieces small enough to be swallowed and digested easily. Teeth and jaws are adaptations for tearing food. Teeth may also be used to kill prey.

Teeth are adapted for the particular type of food an animal eats. Deer, giraffes, and other herbivores have teeth with broad surfaces for grinding grasses and plants into small bits. The powerful front teeth of beavers enable these animals to cut down trees for food and shelter. Lions have razor-sharp *canine* (pointed) teeth for killing and then tearing prey.

Birds have bills that are adapted for certain types of feeding. A hawk has a sharp, hooked beak for tearing prey. A woodpecker uses its long, pointed bill to drill into the bark of trees to find insects.

Insects have jaws and movable mouthparts that act like teeth. The jaws of grasshoppers are adapted for cutting and chewing plants. Mosquitoes have needle-shaped mouthparts for piercing skin and sucking blood.

Adaptations for breathing

Most animals need a continuous supply of oxygen to survive. The entire process of obtaining and using oxygen is called *respiration.* That part of the process that involves how an animal takes oxygen from its environment and gives off carbon dioxide is known as *breathing.* This section focuses on breathing. For a complete description of how oxygen flows to various cells of an animal's body and how it is used by those cells, see **Respiration** in *World Book Encyclopedia.*

The way that animals breathe depends on where they live. Land animals get oxygen from the air. Aquatic animals obtain oxygen from water.

Many land animals have lungs for breathing. As blood flows through the lungs, it picks up oxygen from the air

A **water spider breathes underwater** by means of large air bubbles held close to its body. Small bubbles of air trapped by the spider's body hair help supply extra air.

and releases carbon dioxide. The blood then carries oxygen to the rest of the body.

Many aquatic organisms, such as fish and tadpoles, use gills to obtain oxygen that is dissolved in water. Some animals pump water across their gills to increase the efficiency of breathing. Sharks do this by swimming continuously.

Tiny tubes called *tracheae* allow insects to breathe in air. Tracheae branch throughout an insect's body. They open to the outside air through holes called *spiracles.* When air enters the tracheae, oxygen is carried to every cell in the body.

Some animals that live in damp environments have unusual ways of breathing. For example, some small salamanders have no lungs or gills. They breathe through their moist skin.

Adaptations for sensing the environment

Most kinds of animals have special body parts that respond to changes in the animal's environment. Such a

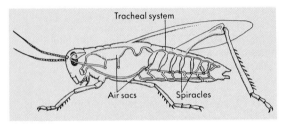

Spiracles are openings on the outside of an insect's body. Air enters the body through these openings and flows into air sacs. A *tracheal* (air tube) system distributes the air.

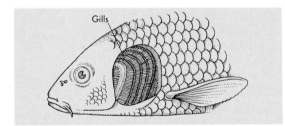

Gills are the breathing organs of most fish. The thin tissues of the gills absorb oxygen from the water. A fish gulps in water, and then forces it out through the gill openings.

WORLD BOOK illustrations by Patricia Wynne

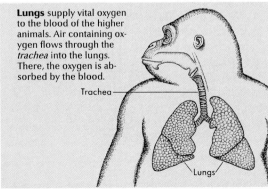

Lungs supply vital oxygen to the blood of the higher animals. Air containing oxygen flows through the *trachea* into the lungs. There, the oxygen is absorbed by the blood.

Trachea

Lungs

Touch. Woodcocks and many other birds can use the tips of their beaks to locate worms underground.

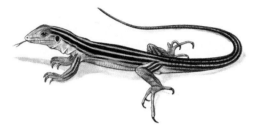

Smell. The forked tongues of snakes and some lizards are used to smell as well as to touch.

Taste. Catfish and certain other fish have cells called *taste buds* in the skin that covers their bodies.

Hearing. Bats navigate by the echoes that result from their high-pitched sounds striking objects.

Sight. A dragonfly's large compound eyes enable it to detect moving objects at great distances.

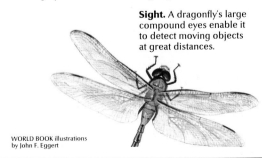

WORLD BOOK illustrations by John F. Eggert

A table of animal intelligence

Many animals can learn to do some tricks if they are carefully trained. But the ability to do tricks is not a sign of intelligence. Even fleas can be trained as circus performers.

Scientists measure the intelligence of animals by giving them problems to solve and by studying their behavior. In the past, most animals were studied in isolation from other animals. They were tested for how they performed tasks when given food as a reward.

Today, however, many studies of animal intelligence focus on animals in group settings. Such research concentrates on the intelligence animals use in their dealing with others of their kind and in solving group problems. Scientists believe this *social intelligence* may be closely related to the development of language skills. The ability to use language represents a high degree of intelligence.

The following table provides information on the intelligence of a number of types of animals, based on various scientific studies.

Apes and monkeys have the most humanlike intelligence. Chimpanzees seem to be the most advanced. They can make tools, plan complicated searches for food, and even count. They can also communicate by means of symbols. For example, they may use certain gestures to symbolize particular objects, actions, or states of being.

Large aquatic mammals, such as dolphins, whales, and sea lions, have brains much like those of human beings. They are capable of learning symbolic communication that may have properties like those of language. For example, dolphins seem to recognize differences in meaning based on the order in which the symbols are presented.

Carnivorous mammals in the cat and dog families show learning ability as good as, or better than, all animals except apes, some monkeys, and large aquatic mammals. Lions, tigers, and wolves probably can learn more rapidly than domesticated cats or dogs can.

Hoofed animals. Elephants and pigs are the best problem solvers among the hoofed animals.

Rodents are generally good at solving problems that involve finding their way through complicated pathways.

Birds, such as the raven and the pigeon, can solve simple counting problems. Parrots can learn to say human words and use them meaningfully in naming and counting objects.

Amphibians and reptiles are difficult to test, but alligators, crocodiles, turtles, and large monitor lizards may rival mammals and birds in locating sources of food and in some other forms of nonsocial learning.

Fish. Salmon and some other kinds of fish can remember odors for as long as several years. Sharks have brains as large as those of some birds and mammals. They have keen senses, and they are surprisingly clever at finding food and avoiding danger.

Animals without backbones often seem to learn very little. But some have remarkable and specialized abilities involving communication, food, and place learning. Many scientists consider octopuses to have the most complex brains of all the invertebrates. Octopuses learn rapidly and have distinct personalities.

stimulus (change) might come from an odor, a sight, a sound, a taste, or a touch. The simplest kinds of animals, such as sponges, have no special body parts and react to stimuli with their body cells. Animals with more complex physical structures, especially vertebrates, have highly developed organs for reacting to stimuli. These organs are described in the articles on **Brain** and **Nervous system** in *World Book Encyclopedia*.

Some simple animals, such as hydras, react to stimuli with special cells. These sensory cells are scattered among the outermost cells of the body. The reactions of most other kinds of animals depend largely on one or more of the major senses. These senses are sight, hearing, smell, taste, and touch.

Some senses are more important to one kind of animal than to another. Most birds cannot find food if they cannot see it. Hearing is vital to bats. If the ears of a bat are covered, the animal will crash into objects when it tries to fly. A keen sense of smell enables dogs and wolves to find food, follow trails, and recognize danger. Taste is highly important to many insects. The butterfly finds its food by sensing the sweetness of flowers with its feet. A cat's long whiskers serve as touch organs. They enable the cat to feel its way through underbrush and avoid bumping into objects.

A number of animals have special senses. A rattlesnake has *pit organs* on the side of its face that sense heat. These organs enable the snake to tell if a mouse or some other warm-blooded prey is nearby, even in total darkness. Many scientists believe that some birds and insects can detect the direction of the earth's magnetic field. This ability may help these animals navigate.

How animals protect themselves

The world of an animal is filled with danger from enemies. This section describes some of the many ways animals protect themselves from such danger.

Hiding in a safe place. The best protection against a predator is to avoid being seen by it. Many animals rest or sleep in a safe hiding place. Some desert toads crawl down a crack in the mud. A cricket hides under a large rock or under the loose bark of a tree. Worms and moles dig underground tunnels.

Many species, such as rabbits, leave their nests mainly or only at night, when they are harder for enemies to spot. Other species become active for only short periods so they are not exposed to predators for long.

Camouflage. Many animals are difficult for enemies to see because they resemble their surroundings. The various ways animals blend with their surroundings are called *camouflage*. For camouflage to be effective, the animals must remain motionless or nearly so.

Protective coloration is coloring that helps animals to hide. A dark moth lying against the brown or black bark of a tree is hard to see. However, that same moth would be clearly visible if it sat on a green leaf.

A number of animals can change their colors and thus remain camouflaged even when moving among backgrounds that have different colors. The chameleon, a type of lizard, is green when surrounded by leaves but

Animals defend themselves from enemies by a variety of means. Some use such weapons as sharp teeth and claws. Others simply run away from attackers. In some cases, the weapons an animal uses for defense are the same ones it uses to capture prey.

Leonard Lee Rue III

The armadillo's armor protects the animal from harm. The bony plates of the armor fit together so well that the armadillo can roll up tightly into a ball when an enemy comes near.

E. R. Degginger

Speed is the impala's main defense. An impala can run as fast as 50 miles (80 kilometers) per hour in bounding leaps.

E. R. Degginger

Sharp quills help protect a porcupine from attack. When touched, the barbed quills come off the porcupine and hook into the attacker's flesh, where they can cause painful wounds.

Zig Leszczynski, Animals Animals

A lobster's claws are powerful weapons. The animal uses its claws to seize crabs, fish, snails, and other prey. The strong, toothed claws then crush the prey and tear it into pieces.

Ted Levin, Animals Animals

Sharp claws called *talons* are used by owls to defend their nests from intruders and to capture prey. A saw-whet owl spreads its talons to catch a mouse, *above*.

A. J. Deane, Bruce Coleman Ltd.

Large, heavy horns protect the slow-moving Cape buffalo of southern Africa from enemies. A fierce and powerful fighter, this animal can kill even an attacking lion.

Alan Blank, Bruce Coleman Inc.

Rattlesnake fangs inject deadly poison. The needlelike fangs fold back against the roof of the mouth when not in use. They move forward when the snake opens its mouth to strike.

© Stouffer Productions, Ltd. from Animals Animals

Eric A. Soder, Tom Stack & Assoc.

David G. Allen

Alexander B. Klots

Pierre Labout, Jacana

Protective coloration helps many animals hide from their enemies. In winter, ptarmigan feathers match the snow, *top left*. The spotted fawn of the roe deer is hard to see because its colors resemble those of its woodland home. The gray bark crypsis is typical of many moths whose coloring makes them seem to disappear when they rest on certain trees. The pheasant's colors make it seem part of its surroundings.

Denise Tackett, Tom Stack & Assoc.

E. R. Degginger

Breck Kent, Animals Animals

Mimicry helps many animals avoid predators. Some animals *mimic* (resemble) other objects in their environment or other animals. The wings of a dead-leaf mantis, *above,* resemble leaves. Some robber flies look so much like a bumble bee that enemies often avoid them. The razor fish has a long, slender body that resembles the thin leaves of a sea plant. A treehopper on the stem of a rosebush looks so much like a thorn that birds often overlook the insect.

turns brown when moving slowly on bark or on the ground. The ptarmigan, an arctic bird, is brown in summer but becomes white in winter, when snow covers the ground.

Mimicry helps many animals avoid predators. Some animals *mimic* (resemble) other objects in their environment. For example, many green insects are shaped like leaves. Some caterpillars look like lizards or bird droppings. Walkingstick insects are shaped and colored like twigs. Anglerfish resemble rocks on the ocean floor.

Batesian mimicry is a form of mimicry in which an otherwise harmless animal strongly mimics an offensive animal. This type of mimicry was named after the English naturalist Henry W. Bates, who studied it in the 1800's. Bates observed that some harmless species have coloring and behavior that make them look like a dangerous or bad-tasting animal. A predator spotting such a species may mistake it for the undesirable animal and leave it alone. For example, viceroy butterflies are believed to be tasty to birds. But birds rarely attack them because they look like foul-tasting monarch butterflies.

Escaping by flight. Many animals run away from an attacker. Antelope sprint away at high speed when charged by a lion or a cheetah. Many animals stay near safe places, such as burrows, and run to them if attacked. The octopus squirts a black inky fluid to conceal itself and then quickly swims for safety.

Armor. Some species have a hard shell or covering that is used as armor against predators. Clams pull back into their shells when a predator approaches. Many turtles can pull in their head, legs, and tail when attacked.

Armadillos and pangolins are covered by hard, bony plates. When frightened, these animals roll into a tight ball that is difficult for enemies to penetrate.

Playing dead. A few species sometimes fool predators by lying motionless and appearing to be dead. If the predator does not deliver a killing blow or bite, then the animal may have a chance to escape. A threatened opossum goes limp. The hognose snake flips onto its back when a predator approaches.

Giving up a body part. Many animals break off a nonessential part of their body when attacked. The glass lizard breaks off its tail, which flops about and attracts the attention of the predator. While the attacker struggles with the tail, the lizard escapes. In most cases, the lost body part grows back quickly.

Fighting. Many animals have special weapons for fighting predators. The sharp hooves of a moose or the claws of an ostrich can rip open an enemy. Porcupines have long, sharp quills on their back, sides, and tail. These animals strike attackers with their quilled tails. The quills come out easily and stick in the attackers. Bees and wasps sting animals that appear to threaten them by approaching their nests.

Chemical defenses. A number of animals use special chemicals for defense. Hagfish and one kind of starfish give off huge quantities of slime when disturbed. The bombardier beetle squirts irritating chemicals at an enemy. Some cobras spit blinding venom at the eyes of attackers. Skunks spray foul-smelling chemicals. Birds from New Guinea called hooded pitohuis have poisonous feathers and skin.

How animals reproduce

All types of animals reproduce. Many animals have special organs that are used in reproduction. These organs are called *gonads*. Some simple animals do not have gonads, but they are still able to reproduce. The various methods used by living things to reproduce are described in detail in the **Reproduction** article in *World Book Encyclopedia*.

There are two general forms of animal reproduction: (1) *asexual reproduction* and (2) *sexual reproduction*. In asexual reproduction, only one parent produces the offspring. In sexual reproduction, two parents of opposite sexes are needed to produce the offspring. Many of the simplest animals, including sponges, sea anemones, and some flatworms, reproduce asexually most of the time. Sometimes, they reproduce sexually as well. Most other kinds of animals reproduce only sexually.

Asexual reproduction. Planarians and some other flatworms can reproduce by *fragmentation,* the division of the body into two or more pieces. When a planarian reproduces asexually, it typically divides into two sections, one with the head and the other with the tail. Each section then grows the parts that are missing and becomes a complete new individual.

Hydras and some sea anemones reproduce by *budding.* The animal produces small projections, called *buds,* from its side. These buds develop into miniature copies of the parent. The buds eventually detach from the parent, and the individuals produced by budding grow to be as large as their parents.

Sexual reproduction. Most animals that reproduce only sexually do so with special sex cells known as *gametes*. Female sex cells are called *eggs* and are produced in the female gonads, the *ovaries*. The male sex cells are known as *sperm* and are made in the male gonads, the *testes*. Sperm are much smaller than eggs and have a tail that enables them to swim toward eggs. When a sperm cell unites with an egg cell, a new animal starts to form. The process in which the sperm unites with the egg is called *fertilization*.

External fertilization occurs outside an animal's body. Many aquatic animals reproduce sexually without ever meeting. Female sea urchins release millions of egg cells directly into the water. About the same time, the males release their sperm. The sperm swim through the water, and some unite with eggs, leading to fertilization. The fertilized eggs develop into swimming offspring, which are called *larvae*. The larvae grow and eventually sink to the bottom of the sea, where they become small sea urchins with bodies similar to those of their parents.

Internal fertilization occurs within an animal's body. If gametes are released on land, they dry up and die. Consequently, land-dwelling animals that reproduce sexually have developed ways for fertilization to take place inside their bodies.

Animals mate in many ways. Males of such species as snakes, lizards, birds, and mammals mate by releasing sperm directly into an opening in the female's body. Fertilization occurs in the female's reproductive organs.

Male salamanders do not release sperm directly into the female's body. Instead, they deposit a packet of sperm at the bottom of a stream or pond. When the female passes over the sperm, she draws them into an opening in her body that leads to her reproductive organs. Several other animals, including mites and scorpions, mate in a manner similar to that of salamanders. Males deposit packets of sperm on the ground, which are then picked up by females.

In almost all mammals and some reptiles, the *embryo* (undeveloped animal) grows inside the female's body after fertilization. However, in birds and some reptiles, the embryo develops outside the body. The female lays an egg in which the embryo develops.

Courtship behavior consists of actions that help animals find and choose suitable mates. This behavior tends to follow a specific pattern according to species. As a result, courtship behavior helps ensure that animals mate with members of their own species. If two different species mate, they may not produce young, or their offspring may be unhealthy or unable to reproduce. Such courtship behaviors as singing and displaying colors help animals recognize their own species.

Animal mates find each other in a number of ways. Female birds are attracted to the beautiful songs and bright feathers of males. Female grasshoppers, cicadas, bullfrogs, and toads also are attracted to the calls made by males of their species. Female silkworm moths release into the air a perfumelike chemical called a *pheromone* to attract males from as far away as several miles or kilometers. At certain times of the year, female dogs give off a pheromone that attracts male dogs. Female fireflies watch for male fireflies that flash their lights in a certain rhythmic pattern. Male fence lizards bob their heads rhythmically when a female approaches. Siamese fightingfish perform a complicated courtship dance, followed by the release of eggs and sperm into the water.

Some animals choose particular mates. The female anole lizard typically prefers to mate with the largest

Animal reproduction

Animal	Approximate gestation period	Typical number of newborn
Alligator (American)	9 weeks*	50-60†
Bat (common vampire)	210 days	1
Cat	65 days	4
Dog	9 weeks	1-10
Elephant	21-22 months	1
Frog (bullfrog)	5-20 days*	20,000†
Gerbil	19-21 days	4-7
Guinea pig	68 days	1-5
Hamster (golden)	16 days	6-9
Horse	332-342 days	1
Lion	100-119 days	3-4
Monkey (spider)	226-232 days	1
Mouse (field)	21-23 days	5-6
Rabbit (cottontail)	25-40 days	3-6
Robin, American	12-14 days*	4†
Sheep	150-180 days	1-2
Squirrel (red)	33-35 days	4-6
Tiger	104-106 days	2-3

*Approximate incubation period.
†Approximate number of eggs a female lays. Not all of them hatch into newborns.

male. The peacock spreads his fantastic tail feathers, hoping to coax a peahen into becoming his mate. Peahens choose males with many spots on their tail feathers. Male birds of paradise gather in a tree. When a female appears, the brilliantly colored males strut and dance to show off their bright feathers. If a female chooses to watch this display, she will usually mate with the male that has the brightest colors.

Male bowerbirds build chambers or runways, called *bowers,* made of sticks or other material. They decorate these structures with brightly colored stones, bones, or other objects. The male dances and bows in front of his bower, hoping that a passing female will accept him as a mate. If one does, she enters the bower with him, and they mate there.

Some male animals give food to possible mates. A male tern catches a fish and places it into the mouth of

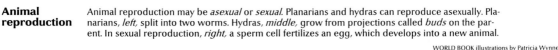

Animal reproduction   Animal reproduction may be *asexual* or *sexual.* Planarians and hydras can reproduce asexually. Planarians, *left,* split into two worms. Hydras, *middle,* grow from projections called *buds* on the parent. In sexual reproduction, *right,* a sperm cell fertilizes an egg, which develops into a new animal.

WORLD BOOK illustrations by Patricia Wynne

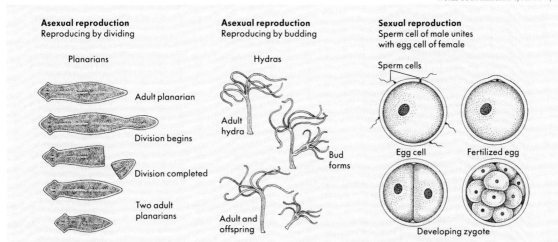

Asexual reproduction
Reproducing by dividing

Planarians

Adult planarian

Division begins

Division completed

Two adult
planarians

Asexual reproduction
Reproducing by budding

Hydras

Adult
hydra

Bud
forms

Adult and
offspring

Sexual reproduction
Sperm cell of male unites
with egg cell of female

Sperm cells

Egg cell

Fertilized egg

Developing zygote

The courtship ritual of the albatross involves an elaborate dance between a male and female, *left*, before they mate. Through courtship rituals, animals can identify members of their own species for mating. In some cases, such rituals help them choose specific mates.

the female he wants for his mate. A male dance fly brings a dead insect to a female. She eats the insect while mating with the male. A male that does not bring a dead insect risks being eaten by the female.

Mating is dangerous for some male spiders and insects. Male black widow spiders are sometimes eaten by females after mating. A female praying mantis may pounce unexpectedly on a male in her vicinity. Sometimes, she mates with a male and then eats him.

Regeneration. Some kinds of animals, mostly simple animals, can replace lost body parts by *regeneration*. If a sponge is broken into small pieces, some of the fragments will grow into new sponges. Earthworms and their marine relatives can regenerate their heads or tails if those parts are broken off. Crabs and lobsters can grow new claws. Sea cucumbers sometimes throw out their intestines and other internal body parts to distract attackers. New parts grow back quickly.

Even some vertebrates can regenerate parts of their bodies. A salamander that loses a leg will grow a new one. Many salamanders can break off their tails to escape the grip of an enemy. These animals soon grow new tails. Mammals can regenerate hair, nails, and some other body tissues.

How animals raise their young

The newborn young of many species need no care from their parents. Even from birth, they can move about and find food on their own. The young of other species need parental care for some time after birth. One or both parents provide them with food and protection until they are old enough to manage for themselves.

Most kinds of animals never see their parents. For example, clams and many other invertebrates release their eggs and sperm into the water, where fertilization takes place. Carried around by ocean currents, the young of these animals may travel far from where their parents live. The female leatherback turtle swims thousands of miles or kilometers in the ocean to tropical beaches. She then digs a hole on the beach and lays her eggs. The eggs hatch in the warm sand after the female has returned to the sea.

Providing food is one of the main ways animals care for their young. Even females who never see their offspring provide them with food. The female's eggs contain yolk and other nourishing substances that serve as food for the developing embryos. Female sea urchins and herring produce vast numbers of small eggs, each of which has little yolk. Offspring from these eggs are extremely tiny when they hatch and must find their own food to grow. Their chance for survival is relatively small. Female birds, on the other hand, lay only a few eggs, each with large amounts of yolk. Offspring from these eggs are relatively large and have a higher chance of survival.

Some animals that do not see their offspring provide their young with food in addition to that in the egg. Many flies lay their eggs on rotting fruits, which supply the young flies with food. The female digger wasp lays her egg on a grasshopper that she has stung, paralyzed, and buried. After hatching, her offspring feeds on the grasshopper. The female dung beetle finds fresh *dung* (manure), rolls a piece into a ball, and then buries it. She lays her egg on the dung ball. After hatching, the young beetle feeds on the dung.

Mammals *nurse* their babies—that is, they feed them on the mother's milk. The nursing period lasts only a few weeks in mice, hares, and many other species. But among some larger mammals, such as elephants and rhinoceroses, the young may nurse several years before they are *weaned*—that is, taken off the mother's milk.

Incubation. In many species, the mother and sometimes the father remain with their eggs and young. Birds incubate their eggs by sitting on them in a nest. Incubation keeps the eggs warm and helps the embryo inside to develop quickly into a young bird. After the eggs hatch, the parents may make many hunting trips each

B. Amadeus Rubel, Shostal

Monkeys take good care of their babies. These crab-eating macaques show great affection for their young and train them carefully. Most monkeys fight fiercely to protect their babies.

David Fleay

A baby wallaby stays in its mother's pouch until it can care for itself. Wallabies belong to a group of animals called *marsupials,* which give birth to extremely undeveloped young.

Joyce Photographics from Photo Researchers

A male Adélie penguin incubates an egg by holding it between his feet to protect it from the Antarctic chill. The male does not eat while incubating—a period of 33 to 38 days.

day, trying to catch enough insects to feed the hungry *nestlings* (young birds). When the young are old enough to hunt, they leave the nest and fly away.

Among many species of birds, including pigeons and starlings, the parents take turns incubating the eggs. Among ducks, geese, and some other birds, the females are the only incubators. In most species of hornbills, the

Names of animals and their young

Animal	Male	Female	Young
Ant		queen	antling
Antelope	bull	doe	kid
Bear	boar	sow	cub
Cat*	tom	tabby	kitten
Cattle*	bull	cow	calf
Chicken	cock, rooster	hen	chick
Deer	buck, stag	doe	fawn
Dog	dog	bitch, dam	puppy, whelp
Dolphin	bull	cow	calf
Duck	drake	duck	duckling
Elephant	bull	cow	calf
Fox	renard, dog	vixen, bitch	kit, cub
Goat	billy, buck	nanny, doe	kid
Hog	boar	sow	piglet, shoat
Kangaroo	buck, boomer	doe, flier	joey
Lion	lion	lioness	cub
Sheep	buck, ram	dam, ewe	lamb, lambkin
Swan	cob	pen	cygnet
Tiger	tiger	tigress	cub
Turkey	cock, tom	hen	poult

*There are numerous alternate names for this animal and its young.

Fur seals start life in a group with many other pups and their mothers. Mother seals divide their time between eating at sea and nursing their pups on land. Each mother seal nurses and tends only her own young.

Karl W. Kenyon, NAS

female even imprisons herself inside a walled-up nest chamber to incubate eggs. The male passes food to the female through a tiny slit in the wall. In a few species of birds, the male does all the incubating. For example, a female emperor penguin lays a single egg, which the male then incubates on top of his toes. He tucks his toes and the egg under the fluffy feathers of his belly. When the egg hatches, the little penguin stays warm and grows in this cozy "nest."

Female pythons also incubate their eggs. They produce the heat to warm their eggs by twitching their muscles, much as people do when shivering. After the baby pythons hatch, they must find food and shelter on their own.

Providing shelter. Some species provide shelter for their young. A female lizard may lay her eggs in an underground nest, where they are hidden from predators. The huge nests of sociable weavers, a type of African bird, protect the baby birds from bad weather and enemies. Some frogs and fish build nests for their eggs and young. A few tropical frogs carry their tadpoles around on their backs until they find a safe pool of water for the young frogs.

Parents sometimes provide shelter for their offspring within their own bodies. The male seahorse carries the female's eggs in a pouch. When the young seahorses hatch, the male releases them from the pouch. Female kangaroos, koalas, opossums, wallabies, and other *marsupials* give birth to tiny, poorly developed offspring. The babies mature in a pouch on the mother's abdomen. There, they nurse and are protected by the mother. One kind of Australian frog swallows her eggs into her stomach, where they develop. After the eggs hatch, the female opens her mouth, and tadpoles and small froglets come out.

Providing protection. Parents often protect their young from enemies. A male stickleback fish will attack any predatory fish or insect that approaches its young. A female scorpion carries her babies on her back and defends them with the poisonous sting on the tip of her long tail. Female crocodiles guard their nests and will fight any predator that comes near. As young crocodiles begin to hatch, they cry out, and the female helps them dig out of the nest. She then gently picks them up in her jaws and carries them to a nearby pond. A female bear

Names of groups of animals

Animal	Group	Animal	Group
Bear	sloth	**Lion**	pride
Cat	clowder		troop
Dog	kennel	**Monkey**	troop
Donkey	pace	**Quail**	covey
Fox	skulk	**Seal**	herd
Frog	army		trip
Goose (in flight)	skein	**Toad**	knot
(on land or		**Whale**	herd
in water)	gaggle		pod
Kangaroo	herd	**Wolf**	pack
	mob		

will sometimes attack hikers who venture too close to her cubs. A female pet dog may attack even her owner if she fears that her puppies are threatened.

Group care. Some animals live together in groups of several families. As many as a hundred pairs of sociable weavers raise their chicks together in a large nest. Several female lions may care for their young cubs together. Naked mole rats live in underground colonies. One female produces offspring. Most of the other females help tend the young. Many monkeys and baboons live in small groups. All the adults in a group will work together to defend their young from an attacking leopard. When attacked by a wolf, a herd of musk oxen will protect their calves by placing them between adults.

Learning and play. Young animals may learn many things about the world from their parents. By watching what foods its parents eat and reject, a young animal can learn to recognize the kinds of foods that are safe. If young animals see their mother show fear of another type of animal or of certain locations, they learn to avoid those animals and places. Thus, they learn which types of animals, foods, and environments are safe and which are dangerous.

Many animals play while they are young. Lion cubs may try to pounce on the twitching tail of an adult lion. They also play with one another as though they were fighting. Such games help young animals develop coordination and strength. Play also helps them learn how to defend themselves and to fight effectively. In addition, it enables some animals to learn how to stalk and capture prey.

Animals' homes provide shelter from harsh weather or protection against enemies. Some animals have shelters that they use only once. Others make homes where they live for many years. However, a number of animals, such as fish that live in the ocean, spend their whole lives moving about. They never have homes.

A number of animals use caves, cracks in the ground, logs, plants, or rocks as temporary shelter. Garter snakes and many insects spend the night under rocks but leave this shelter the next day to hunt for food.

Some animals build their homes. Field mice collect dried grass and then construct a small nest under a protective log. Many birds and squirrels collect grass and twigs to build nests in the trees or on the ground. Gophers and moles dig burrows in the soil.

Home ranges. Most animals live within certain areas that form their *home range*. An animal's home range includes all the resources an animal needs to survive. By living within a specific area, an animal can learn where best to find food or shelter there.

The size of an animal's home range depends typically on the animal's size. Crickets and sea urchins have small home ranges. But elephants and lions may have home ranges that cover vast distances. Big animals require extensive home ranges to obtain the large amounts of food they need to survive.

Some animals defend their home ranges from other animals. A defended home range is called a *territory*. The song of a warbler, the hoot of an owl, or the roar of a lion warns other animals of their kind to stay away. Some animals use chemical warnings rather than sounds to ward off invaders from their own species. Intruders can easily smell the urine of wolves and the scent marks of cats and hyenas and know that a territory is already occupied. Often the intruder leaves without a

Dennis Green, Bruce Coleman Ltd.

A raven's nest is usually built on a cliff in late winter. The bird makes its nest out of sticks and lines it with bark, moss, cattle hair, wool, seaweed, grasses, or rabbit fur.

E. R. Degginger

A mountain lion's den is usually in a hidden, protected place. The animal may use a cave, a thicket, or a group of rocks.

Anthony Bannister, Animals Animals

A male antelope marks his territory by rubbing his face on plants within its borders. His facial glands release a fluid with a scent that warns other males to stay away.

WORLD BOOK illustration by James Teason

A hermit crab's home is an empty sea snail shell. When the crab grows too large for the shell, it hunts for a larger one.

Meerkats live in colonies of up to 30 individuals. These burrowing animals of southern Africa leave their underground homes only during the day. Meerkats stand upright to watch for large birds that may attack them, *left.*

fight. Sometimes, however, fights break out over territory, resulting in injury or death.

Group living. Many animals live in groups. Some groups, such as herds of elephants, remain together for many years. Others are small families that come together only during the breeding season. A mother and father bird may cooperate in raising their nestlings but may separate when the young leave the nest.

Wolf packs and some other animal groups have a social order called a *dominance hierarchy.* In such groups, every member has a certain rank in the hierarchy. High-ranking members are called *dominant individuals,* and low-ranking ones are known as *subordinate individuals.*

The dominant individuals have first choice of such resources as food and water. They also have their pick of mates.

Some groups are large and complex. Ants, bees, and termites live in huge colonies that consist of many thousands or even millions of individuals. The individuals in these colonies often have specific tasks. With honey bees, the *queen bee* is responsible for producing eggs. *Workers* search for pollen, make honey, and feed and care for the queen and her offspring. *Drones* do little but fertilize the queen's eggs.

Fish may form large schools in the open ocean. Herring schools may consist of hundreds of millions of fish.

Animal migration

Why animals migrate. The environment of some animals becomes extremely harsh at certain times of the year. In winter, for example, high mountains become bitterly cold. Snow and ice cover the peaks, and food becomes hard for animals to find. Some animals survive by hibernating. Others travel to places where the weather is milder and more food is available. The next spring, these animals return home. This type of regular round-trip journey is called a *migration.* Many animals that migrate live in the mountains or far from the equator. Migrating animals usually travel in large groups.

Animals migrate for other reasons than to escape cold weather. Some travel to favorite feeding areas or to special places to produce their young.

Animal travelers. Many birds make seasonal migrations. Some simply move short distances from the mountains to the valleys below. Others make remarkable long-distance journeys. In the fall, huge flocks of ducks and geese fly south for the winter. European white storks spend the spring and summer in northern Europe, where they breed and raise their young. They fly as far south as southern Africa for the winter.

The arctic tern is the champion long-distance traveler. Terns breed on islands in the Arctic Ocean. In late summer, they begin a long journey and fly all the way to Antarctica. They feed on the fish that are plentiful there before flying north to the Arctic to breed the following summer. A tern making this round trip may fly as many as 22,000 miles (35,400 kilometers).

Humpback whales and blue whales also make long

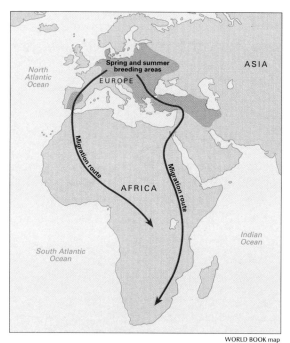

Repeated round-trip migrations are made by the European white stork. This bird lives in northern Europe in spring and summer. Every fall it flies to Africa over one of the routes on the map. The white stork returns to Europe by the same route.

migrations. They spend the summer in polar oceans, which have plentiful food. In the autumn, they swim toward the equator until they reach the warm tropical seas. There, the females that are pregnant give birth. Others mate and then give birth the next year. The warm waters provide a comfortable environment for the babies. The whales spend the winter in the tropics before returning to the polar feeding area in the spring.

Monarch butterflies and many other insects also migrate. When winter approaches, swarms of monarch butterflies travel from Canada and the northern United States to California and Florida. Some even fly as far south as southern Mexico. The butterflies begin the return trip in the spring, but few of the adults that flew south live long enough to complete it. Female monarchs lay eggs along the way back. The offspring, after maturing, continue the northward journey.

Some animals travel long distances to find a breeding site. The green sea turtle feeds along the east coast of South America. It then swims 1,200 miles (1,900 kilome-ters) of open ocean to breed on Ascension Island, a small island in the middle of the Atlantic Ocean. When the baby turtles hatch, they swim to South America, where they may remain for many years. When they are mature, they swim back to Ascension Island and breed.

Most salmon live for years in ocean waters. When the time comes for them to *spawn* (lay their eggs), they travel thousands of miles or kilometers. The salmon swim to inland waters, where they produce their young. The adult salmon die before the young hatch.

Dangers of migration. Migrating animals may face a number of dangers, including new predators, during their long journeys. Some dangers come from human beings. For example, the fences that farmers use to corral their livestock prevent antelope from making their seasonal migrations. Farmers often shoot migrating animals that stop to feed on their crops. The draining of wetlands makes it harder for ducks and geese to find a safe place to rest and feed during migration. Some winter feeding areas are also being destroyed.

The origin and development of animals

Most scientists believe that all plant and animal species probably developed from a single form of life that arose about $3\frac{1}{2}$ billion years ago. The basic life form gradually changed so that through the centuries, millions of kinds of animals have come into being. Some kinds are still alive. Others are *extinct* (no longer living). All animals, whether living or extinct, are related to one another.

This set of ideas about how species change over time is called the theory of evolution. The theory is supported by a vast amount of evidence from many fields, and most scientists consider the occurrence of evolution to be a scientific fact. However, many people reject the concept of evolution because it conflicts with their religious beliefs. The Biblical account of the Creation, for example, says that God took only a few days to create all living things essentially as they exist today.

This section uses evolutionary theory as the basis of a discussion of when some animals originated and how species change. For a discussion of religion and evolution and for more information on evolution, see **Evolution**. For more information on creationism, see **Creationism**. Both articles are in *World Book Encyclopedia*.

When animals appeared on the earth. Most scientists believe that the earth formed as a planet at least $4\frac{1}{2}$ billion years ago. The first life forms were simple, single-celled organisms that appeared about 1 billion years later. More complex animals and plants gradually evolved from these simple organisms. Many groups of invertebrates arose about 650 million years ago. The first vertebrates—fish—developed about 500 million years ago, and the first mammals appeared more than 200 million years ago.

Another way of looking at these times is to imagine the history of life on the earth in terms of a single year. Start with the formation of the earth on New Year's Day, January 1. Bacteria, the first types of living things, would not appear until March 22. Many invertebrates would not show up until November 9. Fish would evolve from their invertebrate ancestors about November 20. Mam-mals would appear on December 16. Monkeys and apes would not be found until December 28. Human beings would appear only a few minutes before the end of the year, on December 31.

For more information on when various types of animals appeared on the earth, see **Earth** (History of the earth) in *World Book Encyclopedia*.

How new species are formed. Scientists consider groups of animals to represent distinct species when they become so different that they cannot produce fertile offspring together. Imagine a group of birds that lived only on one island. Then imagine that a few individuals got lost in a storm and landed on a different island. The two groups, now separated from each other, may gradually develop different traits as they adapt to different environments. If they become dissimilar enough, they cannot produce fertile offspring if they mate. They are then two separate species. This process can repeat itself many times over many millions of years, resulting in great numbers of species.

How species change. The individuals of any given species are not the same. Some individuals are larger, some are darker, some tolerate heat better, and some are stronger. Some individuals have traits that make them better able than others of their species to survive and reproduce in their environment. Over long periods, those animals will produce more young that survive than will individuals with less desirable traits. The offspring of the better-suited species will probably share some of the desirable traits of their parents. For example, dark moths will be well hidden in a shady forest. More of their offspring will probably survive than will those of lighter moths, which may be easily seen and eaten by hungry predators. In the next generation, more moths in the forest will be dark. This process, which causes the traits of animal groups in nature to change through time, is called *natural selection*. See **Natural selection** in *World Book Encyclopedia*.

Why species become extinct. Scientists estimate that, left to natural processes, most species of animals live 1 million to 10 million years before becoming extinct. Natural causes that lead to the extinction of animals include drastic changes in climate and failure of a species to compete with other animals for food. For example, the dinosaurs died out rather suddenly about 65 million years ago. Many scientists believe that these huge reptiles became extinct because of a rapid change in climate and the dinosaurs' inability to survive those climate changes.

Some human activities also cause animals to become extinct. Such activities are discussed in the next section of this article.

The future of animals

Some scientists believe that we are living in a period of mass extinction. In the United States alone, about 40 species of birds, 35 species of mammals, and 25 other species of animals have become extinct during the last 200 years. Many of these species became extinct as a result of human activities. Hundreds of other species in the United States have become *endangered* (in danger of going extinct). Today, however, more and more people are working to preserve the variety of animal life for future generations.

How human beings endanger animals

Destruction of habitat. When people build cities or cut down forests to obtain wood or to clear land for farming, they destroy the habitats that animals need to survive. For example, grizzly bears and mountain lions once roamed freely where the city of San Francisco now stands. But a wild grizzly bear or mountain lion could not survive in San Francisco today.

The habitats of animals in tropical forests are particularly threatened today. People are rapidly cutting down these forests to obtain such valuable hardwoods as mahogany and teak. They are also clearing the land to plant crops. However, soils in such areas are not especially fertile, and farms there produce crops for only a few years. To continue farming in such areas, people have to keep cutting down more of the forests to create new farmland. By the early 1990's, about two-fifths of the world's tropical forests had already been destroyed.

Many scientists and other people are especially concerned about the destruction of tropical forests. They point out that these forests have more *biodiversity*—that is, a greater variety of plant and animal species—than any other place. One square mile (2.6 square kilometers) of forest in South America may have more species of birds and insects than many countries do. In fact, biologists discovered a single tree in a tropical forest in Peru that supported 43 species of ants. That is as many species of ants as live in the entire United Kingdom.

Even though many types of plant and animal life can be found in one place in the tropics, the total range of many tropical species is extremely small. As a result, when a large area of forest is cleared, all the members of some species are killed.

Pollution. Various types of pollution can also destroy animals and their habitats. Agricultural chemicals and industrial wastes sometimes drain into ponds and streams and kill the plants and animals there. Air pollution produced by factories that burn such fossil fuels as coal and oil has seriously damaged forests and wildlife. *Acid rain* —rainfall with a high concentration of sulfuric and nitric acids due to air pollution—kills fish and other animals.

An increase in carbon dioxide in the atmosphere presents a long-term threat to animals and habitats. Many factories—as well as automobiles and power plants—release carbon dioxide into the air. Forest trees and plants help absorb this gas, but as more of them are cut down, carbon dioxide levels rise. Many scientists believe that higher amounts of carbon dioxide in the atmosphere speed up global warming caused by the phenomenon known as the *greenhouse effect.* A major global warmup could produce significant changes in the earth's climate. Such changes could destroy many kinds of plants and animals.

W. K. Fletcher, Photo Researchers

Destroying a forest results in the loss of habitat for many animal species. Animals that live in tropical forests are especially threatened today. People cut down these forests to obtain wood and fuel and to clear land for farms and cities. This photograph shows a logging operation in a tropical rain forest in Malaysia.

Introduction of new species into an area can sometimes have unexpected consequences. In the mid-1800's, for example, people introduced rabbits into the wild in Australia for sport. However, the rabbits had no natural enemies there, and their population grew quickly. Partly as a result of the rapid increase and spread of rabbits, rabbit-eared bandicoots, which are native to Australia, disappeared from some areas of the continent. The bandicoots had to compete with the rabbits for burrow space. The traps and poisons people set out for rabbits also killed bandicoots.

People may unintentionally cause new species to enter an area. Zebra mussels are shellfish that are native to the area around the Caspian Sea, which lies between Europe and Asia. They were first found in North America in 1988. Their larvae had been unintentionally released into the Great Lakes in *ballast water,* the water kept in the hold of a ship to keep the vessel stable. Today, the mussels are a major pest in North America. The explosive growth of zebra mussel populations may threaten the food supply of many species of fish and shellfish that are native to the Great Lakes. See **Zebra mussel** in *World Book Encyclopedia.*

Hunting. Through the centuries, people have overhunted certain animals and caused them to become extinct. For example, prehistoric hunters probably helped make woolly mammoths and mastodons extinct.

Overhunting in the past 200 years has been especially destructive of animal life. It contributed to the extinction of such animals as the great auk, the passenger pigeon, and the Steller's sea cow.

Human population growth. The human population is growing rapidly. In the early 1990's, the world had about $5\frac{1}{2}$ billion people—nearly five times as many as it had in 1850. Some experts predict that by 2150 the population will have about doubled from what it is now—to more than $11\frac{1}{2}$ billion people. Such a huge increase in the number of people on the planet would place additional pressure on natural habitats. People would need more land for food and housing. In addition, human industrial activities would probably increase to process the food and manufacture the goods the growing population would need. Many such activities cause pollution, which also can damage or destroy habitats.

For more information on why animals become endangered, see the **Endangered species** article in *World Book Encyclopedia.*

How human beings protect animals

Since the late 1800's, people have become increasingly concerned about the world's vanishing wildlife. Such concerns have resulted in part from a growing awareness of the interconnectedness of species—the web of life. Greater numbers of people now recognize that the disappearance of large numbers of species threatens the survival of other living things, including human beings. People who help protect habitats and animals are called *conservationists.*

Protected areas. The United States and many other countries have created national parks, game reserves, and wildlife refuges. In these areas, habitats are protected from development and hunting is banned. Many conservationists believe that these areas may represent the last hope for saving some threatened species in the

Stephen J. Krasemann, Nature Conservancy from Photo Researchers

People protect some animals by raising them in captivity. A peregrine falcon chick receives a meal, *above.* Peregrine falcons are rare or absent in many of their former habitats.

wild. Yellowstone National Park is one of the largest wildlife preserves in the United States. Grizzly bears and bison roam the park freely, and bald eagles and trumpeter swans nest there. All these species are rare. The African elephant and black rhinoceros are protected in parks and reserves in the African savannas.

Laws. State and federal laws also protect wildlife in the United States. For example, under the Endangered Species Act of 1973, officials in the Department of the Interior keep an up-to-date list of species that are in danger of extinction. The act prohibits federal projects that would destroy the habitat of an endangered species. In 1982, the act was amended to require anyone who wants to develop or change a habitat occupied by an endangered species to show that the planned changes will not harm that species.

Federal and state agencies in the United States also determine the number of certain game animals that can be hunted and fished each season. If an animal starts to become rare, the agencies can reduce the number of that species that can be taken legally. The population of that species then has an opportunity to recover.

Breeding in captivity. Some species have become so rare that scientists believe the only hope of saving them is to breed them in captivity. For example, nearly all the California condors that are still alive are in zoos in the United States. A condor chick raised in captivity has a better chance of survival than one in nature does. As the number of condors grows, biologists are beginning to reintroduce a few birds back into the wild. Other endangered species being bred in captivity include the Arabian oryx and the whooping crane.

In spite of conservation efforts, the future of wildlife remains uncertain. The human population continues to grow. Forests and grasslands are still being destroyed. People continue to hunt African elephants, snow leopards, and other vanishing species. Air pollution, acid rain, and water pollution also still threaten the survival of wild species. Raymond B. Huey and W. Herbert Wilson, Jr.

A classification of the animal kingdom

Scientists classify animals chiefly according to the animals' ancestry. Those with a common ancestor nearer in time are more closely related than those who share an ancestor further back in time. Closely related animals share certain unique features. Scientists today arrange animals into 33 major groups called *phyla* (singular *phylum*). The classification below lists some of the phyla and some of the features of their members. It is arranged, roughly, from the smallest animals to the largest. However, sizes of animals within a phylum can vary greatly.

Phylum	Characteristics	Example
Rotifera (Rotifers or "wheel animals")	Rotifers live in lakes, rivers, streams, and the oceans. They have cylinder- or vase-shaped bodies. On their heads are circles of hairlike projections known as *cilia*. The largest rotifers are about $\frac{1}{10}$ inch (3 millimeters) long. About 2,000 species have been identified.	*Brachionus calyciflorus*
Bryozoa (Bryozoans)	Bryozoans live in water, and most form colonies. Some colonies are jellylike masses. Others form branchlike networks on water plants. Bryozoans have a boxlike or tube-shaped body that holds fluid. *Tentacles* (feelers) cluster on the head. About 5,000 species have been identified.	**Bowing ectoproct**
Cnidaria (Cnidarians or coelenterates)	Cnidarians may be shaped like a cylinder, a bell, or an umbrella. Their bodies contain a jellylike material between two layers of cells. This phylum includes jellyfish, sea fans, sea anemones, and corals. About 9,000 species have been identified.	**Sea anemone**
Brachiopoda (Lamp shells)	Lamp shells have two hard shells that cover a soft body. They live in the oceans. Some attach themselves to rocks and other hard surfaces. Others burrow or lie loose in sand or mud. About 335 living species have been identified, and about 30,000 extinct species have been described.	**Lamp shell**
Acanthocephala (Spiny-headed worms)	These parasites live in many animals. They have a spiny tubelike structure called a *proboscis* on their head that attaches them to the wall of their hosts' intestines. Most measure about $\frac{3}{4}$ inch (2 centimeters) or less in length. About 600 species have been identified.	*Leptorynchoides thecatus*
Porifera (Sponges)	Sponges attach themselves to rocks and other objects at the bottom of oceans, lakes, or rivers. Many take the shape of such objects. Sponges have cells called *choanocytes* or *collar cells* that trap food particles within chambers in their bodies. About 5,000 species of sponges have been identified.	**Vase sponge**
Ctenophora (Comb jellies or sea walnuts)	These transparent animals live in oceans. They have eight bands of comblike organs on the side of their bodies. Most are pea-sized to thimble-sized. Comb jellies of a group called *Venus' girdle* can be over 3 feet (90 centimeters) long. About 90 species have been identified.	**Venus' girdle**
Nematoda (Roundworms or nematodes)	Many roundworms live in soil, water, or dead tissue. Some are parasites that are found in living plants and animals. Roundworms range from microscopic to about 3 feet (90 centimeters) long. The phylum includes filariae, hookworms, pinworms, and trichinae. About 12,000 species have been identified.	**Hookworm**
Platyhelminthes (Flatworms)	Many flatworms live as parasites in other animals. Flatworms have soft, thin, flattened bodies with three layers of cells. Most are less than 1 inch (2.5 centimeters) long. The largest flatworms, called *tapeworms,* are as long as 100 feet (30 meters). About 13,000 species have been identified.	**Planarian**
Nemertea or **Rhynchocoela** (Ribbon worms or proboscis worms)	Most ribbon worms live in the oceans. They have a slender, often flattened, body. They shoot out a proboscis from their head to capture prey. These worms range from less than 1 inch (2.5 centimeters) to about 100 feet (30 meters) in length. About 900 species of ribbon worms have been identified.	**Bootlace worm**

Annelida (Segmented worms)	The bodies of these worms consist of segments. Many of these worms have tentacles on their heads and a pair of leglike projections called *parapodia* on each body segment. Earthworms and leeches belong to this phylum. About 8,800 species have been identified.

Earthworm

Chaetognatha (Arrow worms)	These worms have an arrow shape. They range from about $\frac{1}{4}$ to 6 inches (0.5 to 15 centimeters) long. They have movable hooks on their heads that they use to catch prey. They live in open seas, particularly in warm waters. About 100 species have been identified.

Arrow worm

Arthropoda (Arthropods)	Arthropods have jointed legs, segmented bodies, and an outside shell called an *exoskeleton*. This phylum includes insects, such as ants, bees, beetles, and butterflies; crustaceans, such as crabs, lobsters, and shrimps; arachnids, such as mites, ticks, and spiders; centipedes; and millipedes. More than 1 million species have been identified.

Beetle

Echinodermata (Echinoderms)	Echinoderms are spiny-skinned animals that have an internal bony skeleton. They are the only animals that have tiny tubelike structures called *tube feet*. This phylum includes brittle stars, sand dollars, sea urchins, sea cucumbers, and starfish. About 6,000 species have been identified.

Starfish

Mollusca (Mollusks)	Mollusks make up the largest group of water animals, though some species live on land. Most mollusks have a hard shell that protects a soft body. The phylum includes clams, mussels, octopuses, oysters, snails, and squids. About 50,000 living species have been identified, and fossils of 100,000 extinct species have been found.

Snail

Chordata (Chordates)	At some point in their life cycle, all chordates have a *notochord* (a rodlike, flexible cord that runs down the back of the body). A hollow nerve tube runs above the notochord. This phylum is the one to which human beings and many familiar animals belong. It includes amphibians, birds, mammals, and reptiles, as well as hagfishes, lampreys, and bony fishes. About 45,000 species have been identified.

WORLD BOOK illustrations by John D. Dawson; Alex Ebel; John F. Eggert; Alan Male, Linden Artists Ltd.; Donald Moss; Peter Snowball; James Teason

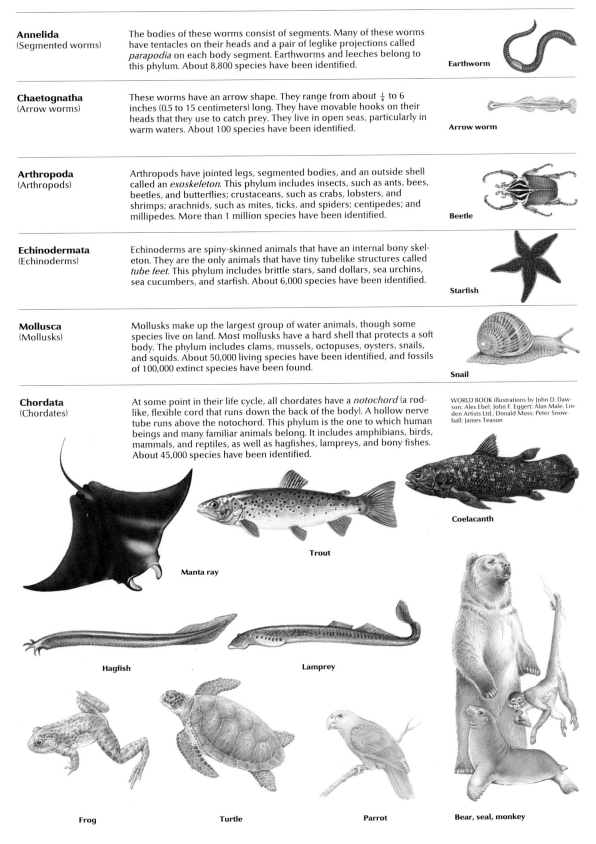

Coelacanth

Trout

Manta ray

Hagfish

Lamprey

Frog

Turtle

Parrot

Bear, seal, monkey

Study aids

The study of animals

Biology	Embryology	Marine biology
Classification,	Entomology	Ornithology
Scientific	Ethology	Paleontology
Comparative	Gnotobiotics	Sociobiology
psychology	Herpetology	Zoology
Ecology	Ichthyology	

Groups of animals

Amphibian	Fish	Reptile
Arachnid	Herbivore	Rotifer
Arthropod	Insect	Ruminant
Bird	Invertebrate	Sponge
Carnivore	Mammal	Vertebrate
Cnidarian	Mollusk	Viviparous animal
Cold-blooded	Omnivore	Warm-blooded
animal	Oviparous animal	animal
Crustacean	Parasite	Worm
Echinoderm	Primate	

Individual animals

World Book has hundreds of separate articles on specific animals. Many are listed below.

Cnidarians

Coral	Jellyfish	Sea anemone
Hydra	Portuguese man-of-	Sea fan
	war	

Worms

Earthworm	Horsehair worm	Ribbon worm
Eelworm	Leech	Roundworm
Filaria	Lugworm	Tapeworm
Flatworm	Nematode	Trichina
Fluke	Pinworm	Vinegar eel
Hookworm	Planarian	

Echinoderms

Brittle star	Sea cucumber	Sea urchin
Sand dollar	Sea lily	Starfish

Mollusks

Abalone	Cowrie	Nautilus	Shipworm
Argonaut	Cuttlefish	Octopus	Slug
Chiton	Geoduck	Oyster	Snail
Clam	Limpet	Periwinkle	Squid
Cockle	Mussel	Scallop	Whelk
Conch			

Crustaceans

Barnacle	Crayfish	Krill	Water flea
Blue crab	Fiddler crab	Lobster	Wood louse
Crab	Hermit crab	Shrimp	

Arachnids

Black widow	Mite	Tarantula
Brown recluse	Scorpion	Tick
Chigger	Spider	Trap-door spider
Daddy longlegs		

Insects

For a list of separate articles on insects, see the *Related articles* at the end of the **Insect** article.

Fish

For a list of separate articles on fishes, see the *Related articles* at the end of the **Fish** article.

Amphibians

Bullfrog	Newt	Toad
Frog	Salamander	Tree frog
Midwife toad	Surinam toad	
Mudpuppy	Tadpole	

Reptiles

See **Lizard** and **Snake**, with their lists of *Related articles*. See also the following articles:

Alligator	Gavial	Tortoise
Crocodile	Terrapin	Turtle

Birds

For a list of separate articles on birds, see the *Related articles* at the end of the **Bird** article.

Mammals

See the following general articles and the lists of *Related articles* at the ends of these articles:

Antelope	Dog	Ox
Ape	Edentate	Rabbit
Bat	Goat	Raccoon
Bear	Hog	Rodent
Camel	Horse	Sheep
Cat	Human being	Sirenia
Cattle	Insectivore	Ungulate
Cetacean	Marsupial	Weasel
Deer	Monkey	Whale

Extinct and prehistoric animals

Allosaurus	Elephant bird	Prehistoric animal
Ankylosaurus	Extinct animal	Pterosaur
Apatosaurus	Ground sloth	Saber-toothed cat
Archaeopteryx	Hesperornis	Stegosaurus
Brachiosaurus	Mammoth	Tarpan
Dinosaur	Mastodon	Triceratops
Diplodocus	Moa	Trilobite
Dodo	Passenger pigeon	Tyrannosaurus

The history of animal life

Adaptation	Endangered species	Heredity
Earth (History	Evolution	Life
of the earth)	Fossil	Natural selection

Animal habitats

For a general discussion of animal habitats, see the articles on **Biome, Habitat,** and **Environment.** See also:

Desert	Prairie	Tropical rain
Forest	Savanna	forest
Mountain	Seashore	Tundra
Ocean	Steppe	Wetland

Animal traits and behavior

Biological clock	Metamorphosis	Sleep (Sleep
Dominance	Migration	among animals)
Estivation	Mimicry	Sound (Animal
Growth	Pheromone	sounds)
Hibernation	Protective coloration	Territoriality
Instinct	Reproduction	

Animal body parts

Antennae	Hand (Animal hands)
Blubber	Hoof
Brain (The brain in animals;	Horn
illustration)	Scale
Coelom	Shell
Compound eye	Skin (Animal skin)
Ear (The ears of animals)	Tail
Eye (Eyes of animals)	Teeth (Teeth of animals)
Feather	Tentacle
Gill	Tongue
Gizzard	

Animal diseases

Anthrax	Glanders
Brucellosis	Heaves
Canine parvovirus	Mange
Distemper	Psittacosis
Foot-and-mouth	Rabies
disease	Spavin
Fungal disease	Tularemia

Organizations

Audubon Society, National
Fish and Wildlife Service
Greenpeace
Izaak Walton League of America
National Wildlife Federation
Nature Conservancy
Sierra Club
Society for the Prevention of Cruelty to Animals

Other related articles

Animal experimentation	Game
Animal rights movement	Livestock
Animal worship	Magnetism (Magnetism
Aquarium	in living things)
Biogenesis	Nature study
Breeding	Pet
Circus	Safari
Conservation	Taxidermy
Farm and farming	Veterinary medicine
Fauna	Wildlife conservation
Fishing industry	Zoo

Outline

I. Importance of animals
 A. Animals and the web of life
 B. Animals and people
II. Kinds of animals
 A. Some common ways of grouping animals
 B. The scientific classification of animals
III. Where animals live
 A. Animals of the mountains
 B. Animals of the grasslands
 C. Animals of the temperate forests
 D. Animals of the tropical forests
 E. Animals of the deserts
 F. Animals of the polar regions
 G. Animals of the oceans
IV. The bodies of animals
 A. Adaptations for moving about
 B. Adaptations for eating
 C. Adaptations for breathing
 D. Adaptations for sensing the environment
V. How animals protect themselves
 A. Hiding in a safe place E. Playing dead
 B. Camouflage F. Giving up a body part
 C. Escaping by flight G. Fighting
 D. Armor H. Chemical defenses
VI. How animals reproduce
 A. Asexual reproduction C. Courtship behavior
 B. Sexual reproduction D. Regeneration
VII. How animals raise their young
 A. Providing food D. Providing protection
 B. Incubation E. Group care
 C. Providing shelter F. Learning and play
VIII. Animal homes and communities
 A. Home ranges
 B. Group living
IX. Animal migration
 A. Why animals migrate
 B. Animal travelers
 C. Dangers of migration
X. The origin and development of animals
 A. When animals appeared on the earth
 B. How new species are formed
 C. How species change
 D. Why species become extinct
XI. The future of animals
 A. How human beings endanger animals
 B. How human beings protect animals
XII. A classification of the animal kingdom

Questions

What is the largest animal of all?
What groups of animals are warm-blooded?

What are some ways in which animals and plants are connected?
How do the long ears of desert foxes and hares help them survive desert heat?
What is the difference between *protective coloration* and *mimicry*? What is *Batesian mimicry*?
What are the two general forms of animal reproduction?
Why do animals engage in courtship behavior?
What is *filter feeding*?
What animal is the champion migrator? How far does it usually travel each year?
What is the difference between a *home range* and a *territory*?

Additional resources

Level I

Batten, Mary. *Nature's Tricksters: Animals and Plants That Aren't What They Seem.* Sierra Club, 1992.
Brooks, Bruce. *Nature by Design.* Farrar, 1991. *Predator!* 1991.
Facklam, Margery. *Do Not Disturb: The Mysteries of Animal Hibernation and Sleep.* Sierra Club, 1989. *Partners for Life: The Mysteries of Animal Symbiosis.* 1989. *Bees Dance and Whales Sing: The Mysteries of Animal Communication.* 1992.
Few, Roger. *Macmillan Animal Encyclopedia for Children.* Macmillan, 1991.
Fichter, George S. *Poisonous Animals.* Watts, 1991.
Flegg, Jim, and others. *Animal Builders.* Newington Pr., 1991. *Animal Helpers.* 1991. *Animal Hunters.* 1991. *Animal Travelers.* 1991.
Gutfreund, Geraldine M. *Animals Have Cousins Too: Five Surprising Relatives of Animals You Know.* Watts, 1990.
Johnson, Rebecca L. *The Secret Language: Pheromones in the Animal World.* Lerner, 1989.
Lambert, David. *The Children's Animal Atlas: How Animals Have Evolved, Where They Live Today, Why So Many Are in Danger.* Millbrook, 1992.
McGrath, Susan. *The Amazing Things Animals Do.* National Geographic Soc., 1989.
Nielsen, Nancy J. *Animal Migration.* Watts, 1991.
Pollock, Steve. *Animal Life.* Gareth Stevens, 1989.
Seddon, Tony. *Animal Parenting.* Facts on File, 1989.
Staple, Michele, and Gamlin, Linda. *The Random House Book of 1001 Questions and Answers About Animals.* Random Hse., 1990.
Taylor, Barbara. *The Animal Atlas.* Knopf, 1992.

Level II

Alcock, John. *Animal Behavior: An Evolutionary Approach.* 5th ed. Sinauer, 1993.
Behavioural Ecology: An Evolutionary Approach. 3rd ed. Ed. by J. R. Krebs and N. B. Davies. Blackwell Scientific, 1991.
Beyond Captive Breeding: Re-Introducing Endangered Mammals to the Wild. Ed. by J. H. W. Gipps. Oxford, 1991.
Current Mammalogy. Ed. by Hugh H. Genoways. 2 vols. Plenum Pr., 1987, 1990.
Dorit, Robert L. *Zoology.* Saunders Coll. Pub., 1991.
Drickamer, Lee C., and Vessey, S. H. *Animal Behavior: Mechanisms, Ecology, and Evolution.* 3rd ed. Wm. C. Brown Pubs., 1991.
Forsyth, Adrian. *The Architecture of Animals.* Camden Hse. (Camden East, Ont.), 1989.
Griffin, Donald R. *Animal Minds.* Univ. of Chicago Pr., 1992.
Grzimek's Encyclopedia of Mammals. Ed. by Bernhard Grzimek. 5 vols. McGraw, 1990.
The Illustrated Encyclopedia of Wildlife. 15 vols. Grey Castle Pr., 1991. Individual volumes cover mammals, birds, reptiles and amphibians, fish, and invertebrates.
Manning, Aubrey, and Dawkins, Marian S. *An Introduction to Animal Behaviour.* 4th ed. Cambridge, 1992.
Nowak, Ronald M. *Walker's Mammals of the World.* 2 vols. 5th ed. Johns Hopkins, 1991.
Patent, Dorothy H. *How Smart Are Animals?* Harcourt, 1990.
Predators and Predation: The Struggle for Life in the Animal World. Ed. by Pierre Pfeffer. Facts on File, 1989.
Rezendes, Paul. *Tracking and the Art of Seeing: How to Read Animal Tracks and Signs.* Camden Hse. (Camden East, Ont.), 1992.
Waterman, Talbot H. *Animal Navigation.* Scientific Am. Lib., 1989.

Travelpix from FPG

Prague, the capital and largest city of the Czech Republic, is one of the most beautiful cities in central Europe. The Charles Bridge, *above,* is a major tourist attraction.

Czech Republic

Czech Republic is a country in central Europe that became independent on Jan. 1, 1993. It is bordered by Poland to the north, Slovakia to the east, Austria to the south, and Germany to the west. Prague is the capital and largest city. From 1918 until Dec. 31, 1992, the area that is now the Czech Republic was united with Slovakia in a larger nation called Czechoslovakia.

Most of the people in the Czech Republic belong to a Slavic group called *Czechs.* Two regions—Bohemia in the west and Moravia in the east—make up most of the republic. The country also includes a small part of a region called Silesia.

The area that is now the Czech Republic has been an industrial center since the 1800's. From 1948 until 1989, when Communists ruled Czechoslovakia, the people in the region had one of the highest standards of living in Communist central and eastern Europe. However, their prosperity declined in the 1980's, and dissatisfaction with the Communist government grew. In 1989, following mass protests, the country's top Communist leaders resigned. Non-Communists took over the government.

Soon after the Communists left office, tensions began to build between Czechoslovakia's two main ethnic groups, the Czechs and the Slovaks. In mid-1992, Czech

Sharon L. Wolchik, the contributor of this article, is Director of Russian and East European Studies at George Washington University and author of Czechoslovakia in Transition.

and Slovak leaders decided to split Czechoslovakia into two nations, one for Czechs and one for Slovaks. On Jan. 1, 1993, the Czech Republic and Slovakia were formed to replace Czechoslovakia.

This article deals with the area that is now the Czech Republic from its early history to the present. For more information on Czechoslovakia, see **Czechoslovakia** in *World Book Encyclopedia.*

Government

National government. The Czech Republic is a parliamentary democracy. A two-house Parliament makes the country's laws. The 81 members of the smaller house, called the Senate, serve six-year terms. Voters

Facts in brief

Capital: Prague.
Official language: Czech.
Official name: Česká Republika (Czech Republic)
Area: 30,450 sq. mi. (78,864 km²). *Greatest distances*—east-west, 305 mi. (491 km); north-south, 175 mi. (282 km).
Elevation: *Highest*—Sněžka, 5,256 ft. (1,602 m) above sea level. *Lowest*—377 ft. (115 m) along the Elbe River near the German border.
Population: *Estimated 1994 population*—10,470,000; density, 344 persons per sq. mi. (133 per km²). *1980 census*—10,291,927. *Estimated 1999 population*—10,661,000.
Chief products: *Agriculture*—barley, cattle, corn, hogs, hops, oats, potatoes, poultry, rapeseed, rye, sheep, sugar beets, wheat. *Manufacturing*—footwear, glass, iron and steel, textiles. *Mining*—coal.
National anthem: "Kde domov můj?" ("Where Is My Home?")
Money: *Basic unit*—koruna. See **Money** (table: Exchange rates).

elect one-third of the senators every two years. The 200 members of the larger house, called the Chamber of Deputies, are elected to four-year terms. The Parliament elects a president, who serves as head of state. The president appoints a prime minister, who heads the government and oversees its day-to-day operations. The prime minister names a cabinet to help carry out the executive functions of government.

Local government. The Czech Republic is divided into seven regions, excluding Prague, which is a separate administrative unit. Each region is governed by an elected council. Cities, towns, and villages also have their own local governments.

Politics. The Czech Republic has many political parties. The Civic Democratic Party and the Christian Democratic Union, two moderate non-Communist parties, form a coalition in the government. Together, they are the strongest parties. The Left Bloc, a group that includes former Communists, is the next most important party. Several smaller parties also hold seats in the Chamber of Deputies. All Czech citizens 18 years of age and older may vote.

Courts. The Supreme Court is the Czech Republic's highest court. The Czech Republic also has a constitutional court and high, regional, and district courts.

Armed forces. Men are required to serve for one year in the armed forces of the Czech Republic after reaching the age of 18. Women serve in the military on a voluntary basis.

People

Population. The Czech Republic has a population of about $10\frac{1}{2}$ million. About 80 percent of the people are Czechs and about 15 percent are Moravians. Slovaks make up the largest minority group. Small numbers of Germans, Gypsies, Hungarians, and Poles also live in the Czech Republic.

Before World War II (1939-1945), Czechoslovakia had a large Jewish population. But almost all the Jews were killed by Nazis during the war. Today, between 15,000 and 18,000 Jews live in the Czech Republic. Most of the Jews make their homes in Prague, which has a well-preserved Jewish synagogue and cemetery.

Ancestry. The Czechs are descendants of Slavic tribes who settled in the region by about A.D. 500. Bohemia gets its name from the Boii, a Celtic tribe that probably lived in the region in about the 400's B.C. There have been large German settlements in what is now the Czech Republic for much of the region's history.

Language. The official language of the Czech Republic is Czech. Moravians speak a form of Czech that is slightly different from that spoken in Bohemia. Slovaks speak Slovak, a language closely related to Czech. Gypsies speak Romany, which belongs to the Indo-Iranian group of languages. Other minority groups speak their own languages at home but generally also speak Czech.

Way of life

City life. Most of the people in the Czech Republic live in towns and cities. Prague, with a population of more than 1 million, is the largest city. Other cities with more than 150,000 people are Brno, Ostrava, and Plzeň.

The Czech Republic has a severe housing shortage. Most people in urban areas live in apartment buildings, many of which are poor quality high-rises built during the Communist era.

Air pollution is a health threat in the Czech Republic, especially in the cities. Alcoholism, crime, and drug abuse are also serious problems.

The Czech government is working to move the country from a Communist state-controlled economy to one based on private enterprise. Despite disruptions caused by the shift, the people of the Czech Republic still have one of the highest standards of living in post-Communist central and eastern Europe. Most households have automobiles, refrigerators, televisions, and washing machines. Many city families have country cottages.

Rural life. People in rural areas usually work in agriculture or travel to cities or nearby factories to work. Rural families often live in single-family homes.

Food and drink. The Czech diet is close to that of Germany. Pork is a popular dish, as are sliced, boiled dumplings and pickled cabbage. Carp with potato salad is a traditional Christmas menu. Apple strudel is a favorite dessert. World-famous Czech beer is the main alcoholic beverage consumed in the Czech Republic. Several fine wines are made in Moravia.

Recreation. Favorite forms of recreation in the Czech Republic include attending and playing in soccer matches and other sporting events, and watching motion pictures and television. Many people gather in pubs

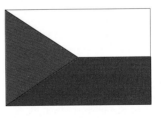

Symbols of the Czech Republic include a flag adopted in 1993. It is the same flag that Czechoslovakia used. The coat of arms features a white lion with a double tail on a red field. The Holy Roman emperor granted it to Bohemia in the 1100's.

WORLD BOOK map

The Czech Republic is in central Europe. It borders four countries including Slovakia, its former partner in Czechoslovakia.

to chat, play games, and drink. Outdoor activities, including gardening, hiking, and such winter sports as skiing and skating, are also popular.

Religion. The Communist rulers of Czechoslovakia tried to keep people from practicing religion. But Czechoslovakia's new government granted the people full religious freedom in 1990. About 40 percent of the people are Roman Catholics. Other active churches include the Orthodox Church and Protestant denominations such as the Czech Brethren and the Czechoslovak Church. The country's Jewish population is working to revive Jewish culture and customs.

Education. Czech law requires children to attend nine years of elementary school. A student may then attend a vocational or technical secondary school, a teacher training institute, or a general education school.

Charles University in Prague is one of the oldest universities in Europe. It was founded in 1348. Other universities are in Brno, Olomouc, and Opava. Most schools and all universities are state-owned.

The arts. The composers Antonín Dvořák and Bedřich Smetana, who wrote their major works in the late 1800's, are considered the founders of the Czech national school of music. Composer Leoš Janáček created operas in the early 1900's that show his interest in Moravian folk music. Today, popular music, including country, jazz, and rock, is also popular in the Czech Republic.

The first major works of literature in Czech were written in the 1300's. Czech literature flowered during an awakening of national identity that began in the late 1700's and continued into the early 1900's. Outstanding authors from the later period include Karel Čapek; Jaroslav Hašek; and Franz Kafka, who wrote in German.

Czechoslovakia's Communist government attempted to limit artistic expression. However, many Czech artists, filmmakers, and writers resisted political control. Miloš Forman, Jiří Menzel, and other Czech *New Wave* filmmakers achieved worldwide acclaim during the 1960's for motion pictures that criticized social and political conditions. A large number of Czech writers became known outside of Czechoslovakia for their works. These writers include the novelist Milan Kundera; the playwright Václav Havel, who later became president of Czechoslovakia and of the Czech Republic; and the poet Jaroslav Seifert, who won the Nobel Prize for literature in 1984. The non-Communist government removed restrictions on art in 1990.

Land and climate

The Czech Republic consists of five main geographic regions: (1) the Bohemian Mountains; (2) the Sudeten Mountains; (3) the Bohemian Basin; (4) the Bohemian-Moravian Highlands; and (5) the Moravian Lowlands.

The Bohemian Mountains are a series of mountain ranges in the western part of the Czech Republic. These ranges include the Ore Mountains in the northwest and the Bohemian Forest in the west and southwest. This region, which rises more than 2,500 feet (762 meters) above sea level, is known for its ski slopes and *spas* (health resorts). Many people visit the spas at Karlovy Vary (also called Karlsbad) and Mariánské Lázně (also called Marienbad) to drink waters from the mineral springs there or bathe in them. Coal mining in the Ore Mountains and industrial pollution have damaged the

region's environment. The Bohemian Forest is an important source of lumber and wood products.

The Sudeten Mountains form much of the Czech Republic's northern border. The *Krkonoše* (Giant) Mountains of the Sudeten system have one of the country's largest nature preserves. But acid rain and other kinds of pollution threaten the animal and plant life there.

The Bohemian Basin lies in north-central Bohemia. This region of low plains and rolling hills has much fertile farmland. Prague and Hradec Králové are among the region's industrial centers. Several major rivers, including the Elbe, Ohře, and Vltava, flow through the basin.

The Bohemian-Moravian Highlands cover much of the central part of the Czech Republic. High plains, plateaus, and low hills make up this largely agricultural region. Plzeň, the largest city in the area, is a major manufacturing center noted for automaking and beer brewing. The city's breweries produce a famous pale beer called Pilsner. The Sázava, the Vltava, and several smaller rivers drain the highlands.

The Moravian Lowlands occupy the southeastern part of the country. Farmers grow a variety of crops in the fertile valley of the Morava River. Many farmers also raise cattle there. The city of Ostrava is an industrial and mining center. Important coal fields lie nearby. The Morava and Oder are the chief rivers of the lowlands.

Climate. The Czech Republic has warm summers and cold winters. Temperatures vary greatly by elevation. They range from an average of 23 °F (−5 °C) in winter to 68 °F (20 °C) in summer. Annual *precipitation* (rain, melted snow, and other forms of moisture) ranges from 18 to 41 inches (45 to 103 centimeters).

Economy

After the Communists came to power in Czechoslovakia in 1948, they began managing all aspects of the economy. They put all factories and almost all farms under state control. They changed the economy's focus from light industry, such as glass and textiles, to heavy industry, such as machinery and steel. The economy thrived until the 1960's, when poor planning, labor shortages, and other problems caused it to decline. After the Communist government resigned in 1989,

STR from Bavaria

The Sudeten Mountains form most of the northern border of the Czech Republic. The natural beauty of the region draws many hikers, mountain climbers, and other outdoor enthusiasts.

Czechoslovakia's new leaders moved quickly to create a free-enterprise economy, in which businesses could operate without extensive government control. Many new businesses were established, especially in retail trade and other service industries.

Service industries. About 45 percent of the workers of the Czech Republic hold jobs in service industries. During the Communist period, the service sector was largely undeveloped. But it is growing rapidly today. There are many new, privately owned insurance and real estate firms, medical and other professional services, repair shops, and retail stores. Hotels and travel

agencies have expanded to meet a large increase in tourism since the late 1980's.

Manufacturing and mining. Manufacturing employs about 40 percent of the labor force of the Czech Republic. Although heavy industry is still important today, light industries such as footwear, glass, and textiles are reemerging as important producers for export. The main manufacturing centers are Brno, Hradec Králové, Ostrava, Plzeň, Prague, and Ústí nad Labem.

The Czech Republic has large deposits of brown coal. The Ore Mountains contain large deposits of uranium and small amounts of antimony, mercury, and tin.

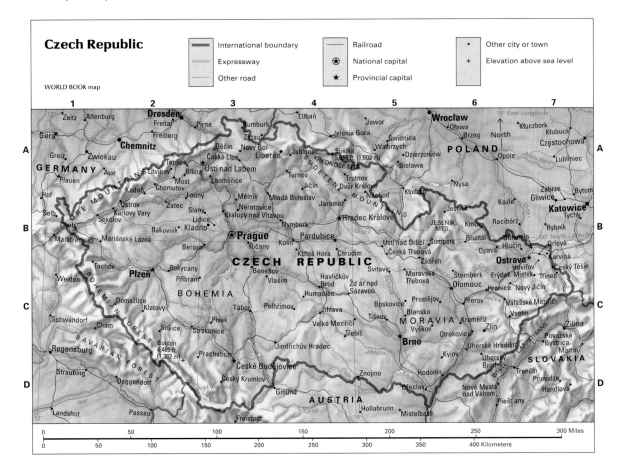

Czech Republic map index

Cities and towns

Beroun	23,790	.B 3
Blansko	19,962	.C 5
Bohumín	25,068	.B 7
Břeclav	25,495	.D 5
Brno	391,979	.C 5
Česká Lípa	33,679	.A 3
České Bu-		
dějovice	99,000	.D 3
Český Těšín	24,741	.B 7
Cheb	31,345	.B 1
Chomutov	58,105	.A 2
Chrudim	21,386	.B 4
Děčín	55,284	.A 3
Frýdek-		
Místek	66,000	.B 7
Havířov	92,000	.B 7
Havlíčkův		
Brod	25,182	.C 4
Hlučín	23,056	.B 7

Hodonín	26,584	.D 6
Hradec		
Králové	101,000	.B 4
Hranice	19,087	.C 6
Jablonec	45,459	.A 4
Jihlava	53,074	.C 4
Jindřichův		
Hradec	21,713	.C 4
Kadaň	18,657	.A 2
Karlovy Vary		
(Karlsbad)	58,541	.B 2
Karviná	70,000	.B 7
Kladno	73,000	.B 3
Klatovy	22,774	.C 2
Kolín	30,879	.B 4
Krnov	26,055	.B 6
Liberec	104,000	.A 4
Lidice	530	.B 3
Litoměřice	25,176	.A 3
Litvínov	21,452	.A 2
Louny	25,142	.B 2

Mariánské		
Lázně (Ma-		
rienbad)	18,510	.B 1
Mělník	19,494	.B 3
Mladá		
Boleslav	48,325	.B 4
Most	71,000	.A 2
Náchod	20,242	.B 5
Nový Jičín	32,495	.C 7
Olomouc	107,000	.C 6
Opava	61,545	.B 6
Orlová	33,658	.B 7
Ostrava	331,448	.B 7
Ostrov	19,591	.B 2
Otrokovice	19,628	.C 6
Pardubice	96,000	.B 4
Písek	29,068	.C 3
Plzeň	175,049	.C 2
Prague		
(Praha)	1,215,656	.B 3
Přerov	50,355	.C 6

Příbram	39,165	.C 3
Prostějov	51,081	.B 6
Sokolov	28,646	.A 2
Strakonice	23,639	.C 2
Šumperk	33,301	.B 5
Tábor	33,956	.C 3
Teplice	53,928	.A 2
Třebíč	36,130	.C 4
Třinec	44,685	.C 7
Trutnov	30,440	.A 4
Uherské		
Hradiště	37,329	.D 6
Ústí nad Labem	106,000	.A 3
Valašské		
Meziříčí	26,998	.C 7
Vsetín	31,074	.C 7
Žatec	22,832	.B 2
Žďár nad		
Sázavou	26,050	.C 4
Zlín	87,000	.C 6
Znojmo	37,983	.D 5

Physical features

Berounka (river)	.B	2
Bohemian Forest	.C	1
Boubín (peak)	.D	2
Elbe (river)	.B	3
Jeseník Mountains	.B	6
Krkonoše Mountains	.A	4
Lipenská Reservoir	.D	3
Lužnice (river)	.C	3
Morava (river)	.C	6
Mže (river)	.B	2
Oder (river)	.C	6
Ohře (river)	.B	2
Ore Mountains	.B	1
Sázava (river)	.C	4
Sněžka (peak)	.A	4
Sudeten Mountains	.A	4
Svitava (river)	.C	5
Svratka (river)	.C	5
Vltava (river)	.C	3

Sources: 1990 official estimates for largest cities; 1985 official estimates.

Agriculture employs about 10 percent of the workers of the Czech Republic. About 40 percent of the country's land is suitable for farming. Major crops are barley, corn, fruits, hops, oats, potatoes and other vegetables, rapeseed, rye, sugar beets, and wheat. Farmers also raise cattle, hogs, poultry, and sheep.

When Communists ruled Czechoslovakia, almost all the farms were either state farms or *collectives.* State farmworkers earned a salary from the government, while collective farmworkers received a share of the farm's profits, some of its products, and a small wage. Legislation was passed in 1991 that began to allow farmland to be returned to private farmers. But most farmland remains under state control.

Trade. The Czech Republic's main trading partners are Austria, France, Germany, Hungary, Italy, Poland, Russia, Slovakia, and the United States. Chief exports include automobiles, coal, footwear, iron and steel, and machinery. The country depends heavily on imports of natural gas and petroleum. Other major imports include iron ore, other ores, and automobiles.

Transportation and communication. The Czech Republic has a well-developed system of roads and railroads. There are about 35,000 miles (56,000 kilometers) of highways and 5,900 miles (9,500 kilometers) of railroads. Prague has a subway system and an international airport.

There are about 30 daily newspapers and some 1,800 other journals, newspapers, and magazines in the Czech Republic. Radio and television stations operate under both private and state ownership. Foreign news broadcasts, such as Cable News Network, are also available.

History

Early days. Celtic tribes probably lived in what is now the Czech Republic in about the 400's B.C. Germanic tribes arrived about 10 B.C. Various Slavic tribes, including the ancestors of present-day Czechs, settled in the region by about A.D. 500. The Slavs were conquered by the Avars in the 500's. The Slavs drove the Avars from the region in the 600's. Several of the Slavic tribes united to create their own state in the 800's. The state formed the core of the Great Moravian Empire, which eventually included Bohemia, southern Poland, Slovakia, and parts of western Hungary. Hungarian tribes conquered the Great Moravian Empire in 907.

The rise of Bohemia began during the 900's. The Přemyslid dynasty ruled Bohemia for almost 400 years. Under its rule, Bohemia expanded its territory and came under the protection of the Holy Roman Empire, a German-based empire that also included Austria and parts of Belgium, Italy, and the Netherlands. In 1212, Holy Roman Emperor Frederick II made Bohemia a semi-independent kingdom within the empire. Many German craftworkers and merchants settled in Bohemia in the 1200's, contributing to the region's prosperity.

Bohemia's political and economic power continued to grow in the 1300's. Prague flourished under Charles IV, who became king of Bohemia in 1346 and ruled as Holy Roman emperor from 1347. In 1348, Charles founded Charles University, the first university in central Europe, in Prague. He also brought foreign artists to Prague to make the city a major European cultural center.

The death of a priest named John Hus in 1415 triggered a series of religious wars in Bohemia. Hus led a movement to reform the Roman Catholic Church and was burned at the stake as a heretic. The wars ended in 1436 with a compromise. In 1458, Hus supporters elected Jiří of Poděbrady, a Protestant, king of Bohemia. Jiří thus became the first Protestant king in Europe. In the late 1400's, most of the Czech nobility became Protestants, and the power of the nobles increased.

Habsburg rule. In 1526, the Austrian Habsburgs (or Hapsburgs), a Catholic family, began ruling Bohemia. Bohemia remained partially independent, though the nobles lost some power. In 1618, a group of Czech Protestant nobles revolted against the Habsburgs. This revolt touched off the Thirty Years' War, a series of wars that spread through Europe.

In 1620, the Habsburg armies defeated the nobles in the Battle of White Mountain. Almost all the nobles were killed or forced into exile. Bohemia then lost most of its self-governing powers. The Habsburgs made the people convert to Catholicism. They also forced most Czechs to give up their own language and culture and adopt German.

German culture dominated Bohemia until the late 1700's. At about this time, industries began to develop in Bohemia and Moravia, and many Czech peasants moved to cities. Czech writers and other intellectuals worked to create a greater sense of national identity among Czechs. By the mid-1800's, a movement for self-government had gathered strength. But Austria continued to rule Bohemia and Moravia. In 1867, Austria and Hungary formed a monarchy called Austria-Hungary.

The creation of Czechoslovakia. During World War I (1914-1918), Tomáš G. Masaryk and other Czech leaders sought support abroad for their idea of an independent state made up of Czechs and Slovaks. At the end of the war, Austria-Hungary collapsed, and Czechoslovakia was created from a part of it. The Czechoslovak Constitution established a democratic republic.

Masaryk served as president of Czechoslovakia from 1918 until 1935, when Eduard Beneš succeeded him. The 1920's and early 1930's were generally a period of political stability and prosperity in Czechoslovakia. However, the Czech-dominated government was less successful in dealing with the country's minority groups. Many Slovaks began calling for broader powers of self-government. The *Sudeten Germans*—Germans living in the Sudetenland, the border regions of western Czechoslovakia—were also dissatisfied with Czech rule.

The Munich Agreement. In 1938, German dictator Adolf Hitler used the dissatisfaction of the Sudeten Germans to pressure Czechoslovakia to give the Sudetenland to Germany. He threatened to declare war on Czechoslovakia if his demand was not met. In an attempt to avoid war, British and French leaders gave in to Hitler's demand. They signed the famous Munich Agreement forcing Czechoslovakia to turn over the Sudetenland to Germany. Later that year, Poland and Hungary claimed parts of Czechoslovakia. In March 1939, a few months before World War II broke out, Germany seized the rest of Czechoslovakia. Slovakia became a separate state under German control, and German troops occupied Bohemia and Moravia. Beneš, who had resigned as president in 1938, established a government-in-exile in London.

The people of Bohemia and Moravia suffered greatly under German occupation. Nazis killed almost all the Jewish population. By 1945, Soviet troops had freed most of Czechoslovakia from the Germans. After World War II ended in 1945, the government-in-exile returned.

Communist rule. Beneš formed a coalition government to lead postwar Czechoslovakia. Leaders of the Communist Party held many important positions in the new government. In national elections in 1946, the Communists won more votes than any other party. In 1948, they caused a crisis that led to the resignation of non-Communist government ministers. The Communists then formed a government dominated by Communists. Beneš soon resigned and was replaced by Communist Party chairman Klement Gottwald.

Czechoslovakia's Communist leaders copied the Soviet model of Communist rule. The Communist Party became the only powerful political party. The government controlled the planning and production of all important goods. It took over nearly all the country's land and forced most farmers to join state farms or collectives. Censorship became widespread. The power of the secret police grew, and Czechoslovakia became one of the Soviet Union's most loyal allies.

The 1960's. During the 1960's, economic performance in Czechoslovakia dropped. In addition, many Slovaks wanted greater recognition of Slovak rights. In 1968, Alexander Dubček became head of the Communist Party. Under Dubček, the government introduced a program of liberal reforms known as the "Prague spring" or "socialism with a human face." The press was granted greater freedom, and citizens were given a limited role in politics. But leaders of the Soviet Union and other European Communist nations feared that Dubček's programs would weaken Communist control in Czechoslovakia. They also feared that people in other Communist countries would demand similar reforms. As a result, troops from the Soviet Union, Bulgaria, East Germany, Hungary, and Poland invaded Czechoslovakia in August 1968. Gustáv Husák replaced Dubček as head of the Communist Party in April 1969 and reversed most of the reforms. A small number of *dissidents* (political protesters) continued to oppose the government.

The Velvet Revolution. During the late 1980's, the standard of living in Czechoslovakia fell. Support for the Communist system also declined. The dissident movement grew, inspired by the democratic reforms that were taking place in the Soviet Union under Mikhail S. Gorbachev. In November 1989, large numbers of Czechs and Slovaks gathered in the streets of Prague to call for an end to Communist rule. Less than a month after the protests began, the Communist government resigned. Non-Communist leaders gained control of the government. The Federal Assembly elected Václav Havel, a non-Communist playwright, to succeed Husák as president. The end of Communist rule in Czechoslovakia occurred so smoothly and peacefully that it became known as the *Velvet Revolution*.

In free elections held in June 1990, Civic Forum—the Czech party that had emerged in 1989 to lead the Velvet Revolution—and its Slovak ally, Public Against Violence, won a majority of seats in the Federal Assembly. The Assembly reelected Havel president in July 1990.

Czechoslovakia's new leaders restored such basic civil liberties as freedom of religion, speech, and the press. New laws were passed to change the legal system, restore property rights, and establish a free-enterprise economy. Czechoslovakia also reestablished friendly relations with Western nations, including the United States.

The breakup of Czechoslovakia. After the non-Communist government took office, Czechs and Slovaks began to disagree over political and economic issues. The disagreements blocked the adoption of a new constitution and slowed economic reform. In mid-1992, Czech and Slovak leaders began to discuss splitting the country into two separate nations. Havel resigned, saying that he did not want to preside over the breakup of Czechoslovakia.

On Jan. 1, 1993, the Czech Republic and Slovakia were created to replace Czechoslovakia. Later in January, the Czech legislature elected Havel president of the Czech Republic. Sharon L. Wolchik

Related articles in *World Book* include:

Biographies

Beneš, Eduard	Hus, John
Čapek, Karel	Janáček, Leoš
Comenius, John A.	Kafka, Franz
Dvořák, Antonín	Masaryk (family)
Havel, Václav	Smetana, Bedřich

Cities

Brno	Ostrava
Karlovy Vary	Prague

History

Austria (History)	Thirty Years' War
Czechoslovakia	Warsaw Pact
Habsburg, House of	World War II (The failure of
Munich Agreement	appeasement)

Other related articles

Bohemia	Ruthenia	Slovakia
Elbe River	Silesia	Sudetenland
Moravia		

Outline

I. Government
  A. National government
  B. Local government
  C. Politics
  D. Courts
  E. Armed forces

II. People
  A. Population
  B. Ancestry
  C. Language

III. Way of life
  A. City life   E. Religion
  B. Rural life   F. Education
  C. Food and drink G. The arts
  D. Recreation

IV. Land and climate
  A. The Bohemian Mountains
  B. The Sudeten Mountains
  C. The Bohemian Basin
  D. The Bohemian-Moravian Highlands
  E. The Moravian Lowlands
  F. Climate

V. Economy
  A. Service industries   D. Trade
  B. Manufacturing   E. Transportation and
     and mining   communication
  C. Agriculture

VI. History

Slovakia is a country in central Europe that became independent on Jan. 1, 1993. It is bordered by Poland to the north, Ukraine to the east, Hungary to the south, and Austria and the Czech Republic to the west. From 1918 until Dec. 31, 1992, Slovakia and the Czech Republic were partners in the larger nation of Czechoslovakia.

Bratislava is Slovakia's capital and largest city. A Slavic people called Slovaks make up most of the country's population. About 600,000 Hungarians also live in Slovakia.

For much of its history, Slovakia formed part of larger states. Hungary ruled Slovakia from the 900's until 1918. That year, the Slovaks joined with the Czechs and with other local groups to form the new nation of Czechoslovakia.

In 1948, Communists took over Czechoslovakia's government. In 1989, following protests by large numbers of Czechs and Slovaks, the Communist government resigned and non-Communists came to power. Soon afterward, the Czechs and Slovaks began to disagree about important economic and political issues. In mid-1992, Czech and Slovak leaders decided to split Czechoslovakia into two nations, one for Czechs and one for Slovaks. On Jan. 1, 1993, the Czech Republic and Slovakia were created to replace Czechoslovakia.

Government

Slovakia is a parliamentary democracy. A one-house parliament called the National Council makes the country's laws. Voters elect the 150 members to four-year terms. A president serves as head of state. The parliament elects the president to a five-year term. The president appoints a prime minister, who serves as head of government. The prime minister is usually the head of the party with the most seats in parliament. The president also appoints a cabinet on the advice of the prime minister. The cabinet helps the prime minister carry out the executive functions of the government. The prime minister has executive authority in the government.

Facts in brief

Capital: Bratislava.
Official language: Slovak.
Official name: Slovenská Republika (Slovak Republic).
Area: 18,933 sq. mi. (49,035 km²). *Greatest distances*—east-west, 260 mi. (418 km); north-south, 130 mi. (209 km).
Elevation: *Highest*—Gerlachovský Štit, 8,711 ft. (2,655 m) above sea level. *Lowest*—308 ft. (94 m) above sea level, near the Bodrog River on the Hungarian border.
Population: *Estimated 1994 population*—5,366,000; density, 283 persons per sq. mi. (109 per km²). *1980 census*—4,991,927. *Estimated 1999 population*—5,462,000.
Chief products: *Agriculture*—barley, corn, livestock, potatoes, sugar beets, wheat. *Manufacturing*—ceramics, chemical products, machinery, petroleum products, steel, weapons. *Mining*—coal.
National anthem: "Nad Tatrou sa blýská ("Lightning Flashes over the Tatra").
Money: *Basic unit*—koruna.

Numerous political parties are active in Slovakia. The Movement for a Democratic Slovakia, a left-of-center group, is the most popular political party. The second strongest party is the Party of the Democratic Left, the successor to the Slovak Communist Party.

The Supreme Court is Slovakia's highest court. Its judges are elected by parliament.

About 50,000 soldiers make up Slovakia's armed forces. Men are required to serve for 12 months in the military after reaching the age of 18. Women enlist on a voluntary basis.

People

Ethnic groups and languages. Slovaks make up the majority of Slovakia's population. People of Hungarian descent form the second largest group. Smaller numbers of Czechs, Germans, Gypsies, Poles, Russians, and Ukrainians also live in Slovakia.

Slovak is Slovakia's official language. Czech, German, Hungarian, and Polish are also spoken. The Gypsies speak Romany, which belongs to the Indo-Iranian group

Slovakia

International boundary
Expressway
Other road
Railroad
⊛ National capital
· Other city or town

of languages. Since the end of Communist rule, tensions have surfaced between Slovaks and the Hungarian minority over language and cultural issues.

Way of life. Most of Slovakia's people live in towns and cities. The largest cities are, in order of size, Bratislava, Košice, Trnava, Nitra, Prěsov, and Žilina. Slovakia has a shortage of housing. Many urban residents live in high-rise apartments constructed during the Communist period. Most rural families live in single-family houses.

The standard of living is higher in Slovakia than it is in many other formerly Communist countries in Europe. Most families own automobiles, refrigerators, televisions, and washing machines.

The lifting of political controls and the opening of borders after the end of Communist rule have caused an increase in crime and drug abuse in Slovakia. Air and water pollution are serious threats in many parts of the country, especially in the cities.

Food and drink. *Bryndzové halušky* (noodles with sheep's cheese) is a typical Slovak dish. Hungarian food, including a spicy stew called *goulash* and other paprika-flavored dishes, is also popular. Wine is the most common alcoholic beverage. A plum brandy called *slivovice* is also popular.

Recreation. Slovakia's people enjoy a variety of leisure activities. Many people attend soccer matches and other sporting events. Skiing is also popular. City residents often spend their evenings socializing with friends in wine cellars or attending ballets, concerts, operas, or plays. Many families enjoy camping, hiking, and mountain climbing.

Religion. Most people in Slovakia are Roman Catholics. The Orthodox Church and most Protestant denominations are also active. The country has a small Jewish population. Most of Slovakia's Jews were killed by the Nazis during World War II (1939-1945).

Education. Almost all adults in Slovakia can read and write. Children are required to attend eight years of elementary school and two years of secondary school. Comenius University in Bratislava is Slovakia's leading university. Košice and Trnava also have universities.

The arts. Folk art has a long tradition in Slovakia. The best-known objects made by folk artists are baskets, glass paintings, pottery, and woodcarvings. Painted wooden houses and other forms of folk architecture are found in many regions, including the Ukrainian villages of eastern Slovakia.

Land and climate

A series of mountain ranges, part of the western branch of the Carpathian Mountains, covers most of Slovakia. The Little Carpathians and the White Carpathians dominate much of western and northwestern Slovakia. A range called the High Tatras extends along part of the country's northern border. Gerlachovský Štít, Slovakia's highest peak, rises 8,711 feet (2,655 meters) in this range. The great beauty of the range has made it a favorite vacation spot. The area is also a national park. The industrial city of Košice lies at the foot of the Carpathians.

The Danubian Lowlands make up southwestern Slovakia. The Danube River forms the southern boundary of this region. The lowlands are a fertile farming region. Farmers raise corn, wheat, and hogs there. Bratislava is the area's main industrial center.

Several rivers wind through Slovakia, including the Danube, the Hornád, the Hron, and the Váh. Firs and spruces cover many of the country's mountains. Beeches, birches, lindens, and oaks grow in lower areas. Foxes, muskrats, rabbits, squirrels, and weasels are found in the forests. Wild boars, wolves, and other wild animals roam remote mountain slopes.

Slovakia's climate varies greatly by elevation. Temperatures range from a low of 14 °F (−10 °C) in January to a high of 68 °F (20 °C) in July. Slovakia receives from 24 to 40 inches (60 to 100 centimeters) of rain, snow, and other forms of moisture annually.

Economy

Slovakia, which had been an agricultural region for most of its history, became industrialized under Communist rule. Czechoslovakia's Communist government centralized the economy after it came to power in 1948, taking control of almost all the country's land and businesses. It emphasized heavy industry, such as the manufacture of machinery and steel. Slovakia became the center of Czechoslovakia's weapons industry. Other industries that developed in Slovakia were ceramics, footwear, petroleum refining, timber, and textiles.

After the Communist government left office, Czechoslovakia's new leaders began to take steps toward establishing an economy based on free enterprise. Today, about 65 percent of all businesses in Slovakia are privately owned. However, the economic changes produced hardship in Slovakia, such as high unemployment.

Service industries and manufacturing are the mainstays of Slovakia's economy. Service industries employ about 44 percent of the country's workers. The service sector has developed rapidly since the end of Communist rule.

About 33 percent of Slovakia's work force holds jobs in manufacturing. Slovakia's main manufactured products include ceramics, chemical products, machinery, petroleum products, steel, and weapons.

Agriculture employs about 12 percent of the workers of Slovakia. Barley, corn, potatoes, sugar beets, and wheat are Slovakia's primary crops. Wine grapes are grown on the southern slopes of the High and Low Tatras and in southern Slovakia. Fruit and tobacco grow in the Váh River Valley. Slovak farmers also raise a good deal of livestock, including cattle, hogs, and sheep.

Mining and energy. Slovakia's main mineral resources are copper, iron, lead, manganese, and zinc. Deposits of brown coal lie near Handlová and Velký Krtíš.

Hydroelectric plants are an important source of energy in Slovakia. There are hydroelectric plants on the Danube, Hornád, Orava, Slaná, and Váh rivers.

Trade. Slovakia's main exports include chemical products, petroleum products, steel, and weapons. Crude oil, natural gas, and electronic products are the main imports. Austria, the Czech Republic, Germany, Hungary, Poland, and Russia are Slovakia's main trading partners.

Transportation and communication. Slovakia has about 11,400 miles (18,300 kilometers) of roads. Railroads link all the major cities and many smaller towns. Bratislava has an international airport.

Slovakia has about 20 daily newspapers and about

570 magazines and journals. Television is state-owned, as it was under Communist rule.

History

Early days. Slavic tribes settled near the Danube River in what is now Slovakia in the A.D. 400's and 500's. In 623, Slovakia became part of an empire founded by Samo, a former merchant of a Germanic people known as the Franks. In the 800's, Slovakia became part of the Great Moravian Empire established by a ruler named Mojmír. The empire also included Bohemia and Moravia, two main regions in what is now the Czech Republic. Hungarian tribes conquered the empire in 907. Hungary then ruled Slovakia for nearly 1,000 years.

Hungarian rule. A period of religious wars began in Bohemia and Moravia in the 1400's. Many Czech nobles fled Bohemia and Moravia and settled in Slovakia. From 1438 to 1453, a Czech noble controlled much of southern Slovakia. The Ottomans defeated Hungary in the Battle of Mohács in 1526 and occupied central and eastern Hungary soon afterward. Slovakia became the cultural and political center of what remained of Hungary.

During Hungarian rule, the Slovaks were pressured to give up their culture and language and become Hungarian. Beginning in the late 1700's, Slovak religious leaders tried to create a sense of national identity among Slovaks. Anton Bernolák, a Roman Catholic priest, developed a Slovak literary language based on western Slovak dialects. Jan Kollár and Pavol Šafaříc, two Slovak Protestants, developed a form of the Slovak language that combined Czech and central Slovak dialects. But Hungarian control prevented the growth of a large nationalist movement among Slovaks. In 1867, Austria and Hungary formed a monarchy called Austria-Hungary.

The formation of Czechoslovakia. At the end of World War I (1914-1918), Austria-Hungary collapsed, and the Czechs and Slovaks united to form the new nation of Czechoslovakia. Slovakia's economy was much less developed than those of Bohemia and Moravia. The Slovaks also had less experience in self-government than the Czechs did. Thus, the Czechs dominated Czechoslovakia's economy and government. Efforts to industrialize Slovakia failed, due in part to the Great Depression, the worldwide economic slump of the 1930's. Many Slovaks grew dissatisfied with Czech control, and support for extreme nationalist movements grew.

World War II. In 1938, Hungary forced Czechoslovakia to give up several areas with large Hungarian populations, including the city of Košice. These areas were along the border of Slovakia and Hungary. On March 14, 1939, faced with the threat of being divided between Germany, Poland, and Hungary, Slovakia declared its independence. Jozef Tiso, a Roman Catholic priest, was elected president. German troops occupied Czechoslovakia the following day, and Slovakia came under German influence. In September, World War II broke out. In 1944, several Slovak resistance groups fought against German control in the Slovak National Uprising.

Communist rule. At the end of the war in 1945, Slovakia once again became part of Czechoslovakia. Tiso was convicted of treason and cooperating with the Germans. He was hanged, and other high-ranking officials were punished. From 1945 until 1948, Communists and members of other political parties ruled Czechoslovakia in a coalition government. In February 1948, the Communists staged a political crisis and took over the government.

The Communist government patterned the country's economy and political structure after those of the Soviet Union. The state took control of the country's factories and almost all the other businesses. Farmers were forced to join government-owned state farms or *collectives,* in which the farmworkers jointly owned the property and farm equipment. The government silenced opposition to the Communist Party and took steps to decrease the influence of churches.

The 1960's. In the late 1960's, many Slovak Communist Party leaders and intellectuals took part in a movement to reform the Communist system. The movement came to be known as the effort to create "socialism with a human face." It was led by Alexander Dubček, a Slovak who became head of the Czechoslovak Communist Party in January 1968. But leaders in the Soviet Union and other European Communist nations feared that Dubček's program would weaken Communist control in Czechoslovakia. As a result, troops led by the Soviet Union invaded Czechoslovakia on Aug. 21, 1968.

Gustáv Husák, another Slovak, replaced Dubček as head of the Czechoslovak Communist Party in April 1969. Other leaders of the reform movement also lost their positions. The Husák government eliminated most of the reforms and reestablished tight political controls and censorship of the press.

The end of Communist rule. In November 1989, Czechs and Slovaks gathered in the streets to call for changes in the government and greater political, economic, and civil freedoms. Less than a month later, Czechoslovakia's Communist government resigned, and non-Communists gained control of the government. The first free elections since 1946 were held in June 1990. In the elections, non-Communists won a majority of seats in the legislature.

The new government began working to create a free-enterprise economy and to reverse the policies of the Communist era. However, tensions between Czechs and Slovaks slowed economic reform and prevented the adoption of a new constitution. Czech and Slovak leaders disagreed about how quickly a free-enterprise economy should be created. The Slovaks wanted the state to keep a greater role in the economy than the Czechs did. Also, the moves toward a free enterprise economy caused more hardship and unemployment in Slovakia than in Czech areas. Thus, support for nationalist parties and political leaders increased among Slovaks.

The breakup of Czechoslovakia. In parliamentary elections held in June 1992, the Movement for a Democratic Slovakia, a left-of-center party led by Vladimír Mečiar, won a majority of seats in Slovakia's parliament. Václav Klaus's Civic Democratic Party, a center-right group, won a majority of seats in the parliament of the Czech Republic. Although most Czechs and Slovaks wanted to remain united, Mečiar and Klaus began to negotiate the breakup of Czechoslovakia. On Jan. 1, 1993, Slovakia and the Czech Republic were formed to replace Czechoslovakia. In February, Slovakia's parliament elected Michal Kováč president of the new nation.

Sharon L. Wolchik

© Alex Bartel, Uniphoto

The United States government has its headquarters in Washington, D.C. The United States Capitol in that city, *above,* is where Congress meets to make the nation's laws.

United States government

United States, Government of the. The government of the United States represents, serves, and protects the American people at home and abroad. Because the United States is a nation of great wealth and military strength, the actions of its government affect all parts of the world.

The Constitution of the United States establishes the basic structure of the U.S. government. The Constitution creates a *federal system,* in which political power is divided between the national government and the governments of each state. The national government is sometimes called the *federal* government. The Constitution also creates three separate branches of government—legislative, executive, and judicial—to share the work of creating, enforcing, and interpreting the laws of the nation. The branches are represented by Congress, the President, and the Supreme Court of the United States.

The national government of the United States is the country's largest government system. It employs about 3 million civilian workers and approximately $1\frac{3}{4}$ million military personnel. Each year, it collects about $1 trillion in taxes from American citizens and corporations to help finance its work.

From the United States capital in Washington, D.C., the national government conducts thousands of activities that affect the lives of Americans. It helps fund many state government services, including job training, welfare payments, roads, and health care. It manages a social security program that provides a pension plan and other benefits to the nation's retired or disabled workers. It sets standards for programs to aid poor, aged, or disabled people. It tests food and drugs for purity and safety, conducts research on such diseases as AIDS and cancer, and sets standards to control pollution. It con-

ducts and coordinates space exploration. It oversees air travel, forecasts the weather, and runs hospitals for veterans. It maintains national parks, forests, historic sites, and museums.

The national government also deals with the governments of about 160 other nations. It works in about 85 international organizations, many of which are associated with the United Nations, that promote cooperation among nations. It operates about 275 diplomatic posts and many military posts around the world.

Principles of American government

Constitutional authority. The national government gets its authority from the American people through a written document—the Constitution of the United States. The Constitution defines the goals of the national government and what it can and cannot do.

According to the Constitution, the national government's purpose is to "establish justice, insure domestic tranquility, provide for the common defense, promote the general welfare, and secure the blessings of liberty. . . ." The Constitution grants the national government strong powers to work toward these goals. The government has direct authority over all citizens. It can collect taxes and pay debts, borrow money, negotiate with other governments, regulate trade between the states and with other countries, create armed forces, and declare war. It can also create and enforce all laws that are "necessary and proper" to carry out its constitutional goals and powers.

The Constitution also limits the authority of the government. It forbids certain laws and actions. The Bill of Rights in the Constitution describes certain basic freedoms and rights of all Americans and forbids the government to violate those rights. For example, the government must respect the people's freedoms of speech, religion, press, and peaceful assembly.

American citizens can change the Constitution. An amendment may be proposed by Congress or by a na-

---

Roger H. Davidson, the contributor of this article, is Professor of Government and Politics at the University of Maryland and co-author of Congress and Its Members.

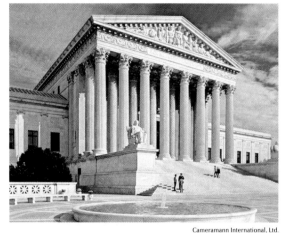

Cameramann International, Ltd.

The Supreme Court Building is where Supreme Court justices meet to interpret the laws that govern the nation.

Karen A. McCormack

The White House is the official residence of the President of the United States and also the place where the President works.

tional convention called by Congress. The amendment becomes part of the Constitution after being *ratified* (approved) by the legislatures of three-fourths of the states or by conventions in three-fourths of the states. There have been 27 amendments to the Constitution.

Separation of powers. Three separate branches share the powers of the United States government. Each branch has both *expressed powers*—those specifically listed in the Constitution—and *implied powers*—those reasonably suggested by its expressed powers. In general, the legislative branch makes the nation's laws, the executive branch enforces the laws, and the judicial branch interprets the laws if questions arise.

A system of *checks and balances* makes sure that each branch acts only within its constitutional limits. Each branch has some powers that curb, or check, those of the other two. This prevents any single government group or official from becoming too powerful.

The Constitution ensures that the branches remain separate by forbidding members of Congress from serving in another branch. In addition, executive and judicial officials may not serve in Congress. The Constitution provides that the Vice President officially preside over the Senate, one of the two bodies of Congress. However, the Senate presidency is mostly a ceremonial role, and the Vice President rarely appears in Congress.

Federalism is the division of powers between a national or central government and local authorities. The Constitution divides powers between the national and state governments. In addition, the states share and divide powers with such local political subdivisions as counties, cities, and towns.

The national, or federal, government can exercise only those powers that are listed in the Constitution or implied by the Constitution. The states, or the people, retain all powers not denied them, or not given to the national government, by the Constitution. The federal and state governments have some *concurrent* powers—that is, they both have authority to do some things. Concurrent powers include the right to tax, spend, and borrow money.

Each state has its own constitution, its own laws, and

its own legislative, executive, and judicial branches. In general, state laws and activities must not conflict with the U.S. Constitution, acts of Congress, or U.S. treaties. Through the years, the role of the federal government has increased in traditional state government activities, such as regulating businesses, providing for public schools, and protecting the people.

Representative democracy. The United States government relies on the consent of the people. The people elect a certain number of their fellow citizens to represent them in making laws and in other matters. Federal, state, and local laws regulate elections.

Political parties play an important role in elections. They select candidates to run for public office, provide opposition to the party in power, and raise funds to conduct election campaigns. They also inform voters about public affairs and about problems they believe need government action.

The United States has a *two-party system*—that is, it has two major political parties, the Democratic and the Republican. Members of these two parties hold almost

Symbols of the United States include the American flag and the Great Seal. The eagle holds an olive branch and arrows, symbolizing a desire for peace but the ability to wage war. The reverse side bears the Eye of Providence, representing God, and a pyramid dated 1776.

all the offices in the national and state governments.

Minor political parties in the United States rarely elect candidates to government offices. These parties serve chiefly to express discontent over problems that the major parties may have neglected. Often, one or both of the major parties may attempt to solve such a problem. Then the third party may disappear or be absorbed by a major party.

The legislative branch

Congress creates, abolishes, and changes federal laws, which govern the nation. Congressional lawmakers also play an important role in establishing *public policy*—what the government does or says in response to political issues.

Organization. Congress consists of two chambers—the Senate and the House of Representatives. The two chambers have about equal power. Voters in each state elect the members of each chamber, or *house.* The Senate has 100 members, 2 from each state, who serve six-year terms. About a third of the seats come up for election every two years. The House of Representatives, usually called simply the *House,* has 435 members. House members, or *representatives,* serve two-year terms. The number of representatives from each state is based on the state's population. Each state has at least one representative. The Senate and House meet in separate wings of the Capitol in Washington, D.C.

Elections are held in November of even-numbered years. The members start each two-year Congress the following January. Beginning with the First Congress (1789-1791), each Congress has been numbered.

The legislative branch includes several agencies that provide Congress with information and services. For example, the General Accounting Office *audits* (closely examines) the financial records of various departments and agencies of the federal government and reports its findings to Congress. Other support agencies of Congress include the Congressional Budget Office, the Congressional Research Service of the Library of Congress, and the Office of Technology Assessment.

In addition, each senator and representative has a personal staff to advise him or her on issues, answer mail from voters, handle publicity, and help in other ways. There are also staffs that assist committees in Congress and *aides* (assistants) for each house.

Functions. Making laws is the main job of Congress. During each two-year Congress, senators and representatives introduce about 10,000 bills. In that period, Congress passes, and the President signs into law, about 650 bills.

Congress makes laws on all kinds of matters. Some laws are major policy decisions, such as taxing and spending measures. Others deal with administrative details, such as employee benefits or the purchase of land. Still others are *commemorative* laws, which honor a group, person, or event. In 1914, for example, Congress honored mothers with a law that declared the second Sunday in May as Mother's Day. All of these laws are called *public laws* if they apply to people in general. Congress also passes a few *private laws* that apply to specific individuals, such as immigration cases.

Congress does more than make laws. It investigates the actions of the executive branch and makes sure the laws are carried out. Congress also reviews the election, qualifications, and ethical behavior of its own members. It can remove federal officials from office, including members of Congress, for serious offenses. The House brings *impeachment* (misconduct) charges against an official, and the Senate tries the official.

Each chamber of Congress has some independent duties. The Senate approves or rejects the people that the President appoints to certain high-level federal positions. It also approves or rejects treaties that the President makes. All legislation that deals with taxes or spending must start in the House.

In addition, senators and representatives spend much time serving their *constituents*—the people who elected them. They answer individuals' questions or requests, meet with visitors, and inform the public of issues. They often travel to their home states to appear at public events, study area problems, and talk with voters and local officials. In addition, legislators, usually with the help of their parties, conduct their own election campaigns, including fund-raising.

Committee system. Congress does much of its work through committees. The House has 22 *standing* (permanent) committees, each with authority over bills in a certain area, such as agriculture or banking. The Senate has 16 standing committees. Most standing committees have subcommittees to handle particular topics. In addition, each house may form temporary *special committees* or *select committees,* usually to conduct investigations. *Joint committees*—made up of members from both the House and the Senate—handle mainly research and administrative details. Most legislators serve on several committees and subcommittees.

When committees or subcommittees study bills, they may hear testimony from experts and other interested people. Committees work out amendments to the bills and other details and recommend bills to the full House or Senate for passage.

Party leadership has an important influence on Congress. Democratic and Republican members of Congress choose official party leaders for each house. Party leaders plan the legislative strategy of the party, communicate their party's position on issues to other members, and encourage members to vote along party lines. When voting on major legislation, senators and representatives weigh their party loyalty against their own judgment or the interests of their constituents. On less important bills, legislators usually vote according to their party's position.

In each house, the *majority party*—that is, the party with the most members—chooses one of its members to lead the entire chamber. The House chooses a *Speaker,* and the Senate chooses a *president pro tempore* (temporary president) to serve in the Vice President's absence. In addition, majority-party members head congressional committees.

Each party in the House and Senate also elects a *floor leader* and an assistant leader called a *whip.* The floor leaders, known as *majority leaders* or *minority leaders* depending on their party, and the whips work for passage of their party's legislative program.

In the House, the majority party has strong control over the agenda. The Speaker and the majority leader schedule the House's business and coordinate the com-

Government of the United States

The chart on this page shows the basic structure of the government of the United States. The U.S. Constitution creates three separate branches—legislative, executive, and judicial—to share government powers. In general, the legislative branch makes the nation's laws, the executive branch carries out the laws, and the judicial branch interprets the laws.

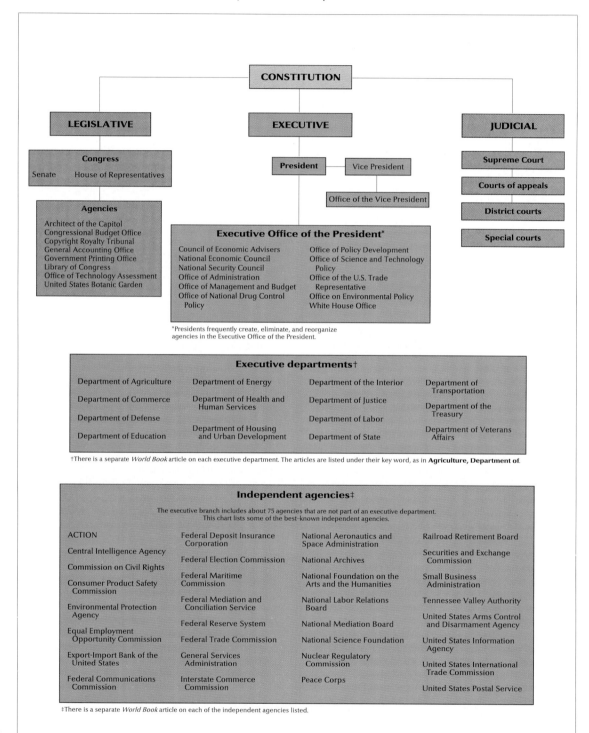

CONSTITUTION

LEGISLATIVE

EXECUTIVE

JUDICIAL

Congress

Senate   House of Representatives

President   Vice President

Office of the Vice President

Supreme Court

Courts of appeals

District courts

Special courts

Agencies

Architect of the Capitol
Congressional Budget Office
Copyright Royalty Tribunal
General Accounting Office
Government Printing Office
Library of Congress
Office of Technology Assessment
United States Botanic Garden

Executive Office of the President*

Council of Economic Advisers
National Economic Council
National Security Council
Office of Administration
Office of Management and Budget
Office of National Drug Control Policy

Office of Policy Development
Office of Science and Technology Policy
Office of the U.S. Trade Representative
Office on Environmental Policy
White House Office

*Presidents frequently create, eliminate, and reorganize agencies in the Executive Office of the President.

Executive departments†

Department of Agriculture

Department of Commerce

Department of Defense

Department of Education

Department of Energy

Department of Health and Human Services

Department of Housing and Urban Development

Department of the Interior

Department of Justice

Department of Labor

Department of State

Department of Transportation

Department of the Treasury

Department of Veterans Affairs

†There is a separate *World Book* article on each executive department. The articles are listed under their key word, as in **Agriculture, Department of**.

Independent agencies‡

The executive branch includes about 75 agencies that are not part of an executive department. This chart lists some of the best-known independent agencies.

ACTION

Central Intelligence Agency

Commission on Civil Rights

Consumer Product Safety Commission

Environmental Protection Agency

Equal Employment Opportunity Commission

Export-Import Bank of the United States

Federal Communications Commission

Federal Deposit Insurance Corporation

Federal Election Commission

Federal Maritime Commission

Federal Mediation and Conciliation Service

Federal Reserve System

Federal Trade Commission

General Services Administration

Interstate Commerce Commission

National Aeronautics and Space Administration

National Archives

National Foundation on the Arts and the Humanities

National Labor Relations Board

National Mediation Board

National Science Foundation

Nuclear Regulatory Commission

Peace Corps

Railroad Retirement Board

Securities and Exchange Commission

Small Business Administration

Tennessee Valley Authority

United States Arms Control and Disarmament Agency

United States Information Agency

United States International Trade Commission

United States Postal Service

‡There is a separate *World Book* article on each of the independent agencies listed.

mittees' work on bills. House debate rules are formal and rigid, designed to let the majority have its way.

In the Senate, a smaller and less formal body, the majority party has less control. Debate rules allow senators opposed to a bill to make *filibusters*—long speeches or other tactics designed to slow down or block the legislative process or force the bill's sponsors to compromise on its content or abandon the bill.

The lawmaking process weeds out bills that lack sufficient support. At every stage in the process, a bill's backers must bargain for the support of their fellow lawmakers. A bill is debated by one or more committees and, if approved, by the full House or Senate. Both houses must approve a bill in exactly the same form before it is sent to the President. If they adopt different versions of a bill, a *conference committee,* made up of committee leaders from both houses, may be formed to work out the differences.

For a detailed description of the lawmaking process, see the chart *How a bill becomes a law in the United States* in this article.

The executive branch

The executive branch carries out federal laws. It also creates and enforces regulations based on the laws. The President is the head of the executive branch. Fourteen executive departments and about 75 agencies handle the everyday work of administering laws and programs.

The presidency. The President is elected to serve a four-year term. The 22nd Amendment to the Constitution, approved in 1951, provides that no one can be elected to the presidency more than twice.

A nationwide presidential election is held every four years in November. The people of each state elect delegates to the Electoral College. The delegates, or *electors,* then choose the President and Vice President based on the popular votes in the states they represent. If no candidate receives a majority of Electoral College votes, the House elects the President and the Senate selects the Vice President. If the President dies, is removed from office, or becomes unable to perform the duties of office, the Vice President takes over the presidency until the next election. The President lives in the White House in Washington, D.C., and has offices there.

The President has many roles and duties. As chief executive, the President enforces federal laws, directs the preparation of the federal budget, and appoints many high-ranking officials. As commander in chief of the armed forces, the President directs foreign and national security affairs. As chief diplomat, the President negotiates treaties with other countries. As legislative leader, the President recommends laws to Congress and works to win their passage. The President may veto bills approved by Congress. The threat of a veto can influence the way Congress develops a bill.

Congress has the power to restrain most of the President's powers. Congress must approve the federal budget and the President's legislative plans. It can override a President's veto by a vote of a two-thirds majority of the members present in both houses. In addition, all treaties and high-level appointments by the President require Senate approval.

For many Americans and people around the world, the President represents the United States government.

Presidents can use their visibility in the news media to focus attention on their programs and to create public support for their policies. However, their visibility is a double-edged sword. People often blame Presidents for problems, such as an economic depression or a foreign crisis, that the President may not have caused and can do little to solve.

The Executive Office of the President consists of a number of staff agencies that provide the President with information, ideas, and advice on a wide range of issues. One agency, the Office of Management and Budget (OMB), helps plan the federal budget. The OMB also advises the President on proposed laws and regulations, shaping its recommendations to promote the President's goals. Another key unit, the White House Office, includes the President's personal aides, policy advisers, speechwriters, and lawyers.

Executive departments and agencies carry out laws and create and enforce detailed regulations based on laws. Congress creates departments and agencies to deal with particular matters. It controls the basic structure and authority of each. The Office of Management and Budget and Congress control the funding of departments and agencies. Presidents cannot create, eliminate, or reorganize departments or agencies without the approval of Congress.

Executive departments are vast organizations that conduct a wide range of government activities. Each is divided into bureaus, divisions, offices, or other units. The President, with the approval of the Senate, appoints the head of each department. The department heads form the President's Cabinet, an informal advisory group that helps the President.

Independent agencies. The executive branch includes dozens of agencies that perform government functions. These agencies are called *independent agencies* because they are not part of an executive department. Some independent agencies, such as the National Aeronautics and Space Administration and the Peace Corps, carry out programs or provide services. Others, called *regulatory agencies* or *regulatory commissions,* enforce laws dealing with aspects of American economic life. For example, the Federal Trade Commission works to protect consumers from unfair trade practices.

Government corporations are independent agencies that are organized in ways similar to businesses. They conduct commercial activities, perform services, or raise funds for the public. For example, the Tennessee Valley Authority works to develop the natural resources of the Tennessee Valley.

Control of departments and agencies. Except for high-level officials appointed by the President, executive departments and independent agencies are made up of permanent staffs of civil service workers. They establish their own ways of carrying out programs and policies. Departments and agencies may be influenced by powerful interest groups. For example, the Forest Service, a division of the Department of Agriculture, manages the national forests. It must juggle the often-conflicting needs of such groups as campers, environmentalists, ranchers, and logging companies. In addition, departments and agencies must cooperate with Congress, especially with the committees that write their laws and approve funds for their programs.

Because of these influences, Presidents may find it difficult to push departments and agencies and their programs in new directions. To have an effect, Presidents may find it necessary to create wide public support for their policies. They can also influence departments and agencies by shaping the federal budget to reflect their goals and by making sure their policies are reflected in new regulations.

The judicial branch

The judicial branch interprets the nation's laws. It is made up of a system of federal courts and judges. The Supreme Court of the United States is the highest court in the nation.

Authority of the courts. Federal courts settle disputes among citizens involving the Constitution or federal laws, and disputes between citizens and the federal government. They also hear cases involving treaties or *maritime* (sea) laws. In addition, federal courts may decide certain cases between individuals or groups from different states, and cases involving other countries or their citizens.

The courts' most important power is *judicial review*— that is, their authority to overturn laws they judge unconstitutional. Any court in the United States can declare laws or the actions of public officials illegal if they conflict with the U.S. Constitution. The Supreme Court, however, is the final authority on such matters. Judicial review provides an important check on the executive and legislative branches, as well as on state and local governments. The Supreme Court first established the power of judicial review in the famous case of *Marbury v. Madison* (1803), which struck down part of an act of Congress. Since then, the court has overturned all or parts of more than 125 federal laws and over 1,000 state laws.

Lower court system. The Constitution gives Congress the job of creating a system of lower courts. In 1789, Congress passed the Judiciary Act, which established the federal court system. Today, the system includes both *trial courts,* which conduct the first hearing of a case, and *appellate courts,* which review a trial court's decision at the request of the losing party. Most federal courts hear a wide variety of cases. Several specialized courts deal only with particular matters.

District courts are trial courts with general federal jurisdiction. There are 94 district courts in the United States and its possessions. Each state has at least one. Most federal cases begin in a district court.

Courts of appeals are appellate courts that review district court decisions on matters of law. A court of appeals can change a ruling if it decides the lower court incorrectly applied the law to the case. Courts of appeals also hear appeals of decisions made by federal agencies. The United States is divided into 12 judicial areas called *circuits,* each of which has one court of appeals. A 13th court, the United States Court of Appeals for the Federal Circuit, has nationwide jurisdiction.

Special courts. The federal court system includes several specialized courts that deal with particular matters. For example, the United States Claims Court hears cases involving claims against the federal government. The Court of International Trade settles disputes over imports. The Tax Court of the United States handles conflicts between taxpayers and the Internal Revenue Service. The Court of Military Appeals hears appeals from rulings by *courts-martial* (military courts).

The Supreme Court, the nation's highest court, is mainly an appellate court. It can review appeals from federal appellate courts and, in certain cases, appeals directly from district courts. It can also review appeals from the highest court in each state, providing the case involves an important federal question. In certain cases, the Supreme Court is a trial court. It tries disputes involving diplomats from other countries or conflicts between states. But such cases make up only a small part of its workload.

The Supreme Court has one chief justice and eight associate justices. At least six justices hear and decide each case by a majority vote. In the event of a tie, the lower court decision stands. The Supreme Court meets regularly in the Supreme Court Building in Washington, D.C.

Caseload. The Supreme Court receives thousands of appeals each year, but it can choose which ones it will hear. Each year, it hears between 100 and 150 cases. Justices select cases that raise important questions about the government system or the rights of Americans. For example, the court hears many cases based on the First Amendment guarantees of free speech and freedom of religion. In addition, justices may choose a case because it involves a question that two or more lower appellate courts have decided differently.

Effects of decisions. A Supreme Court decision has great importance. Once the court rules on a constitutional question, all other courts throughout the United States are required to follow the decision in similar cases. In this way, the Supreme Court helps guarantee legal equality to all Americans.

Supreme Court decisions are not always carried out. The court must rely on the executive and legislative branches, as well as state and local officials, to enforce its decisions. Government officials may be slow to act on rulings with which they disagree. For example, the court ruled in the 1954 case of *Brown v. Board of Education of Topeka* that public school segregation was unconstitutional. But many Southern communities moved slowly in desegregating their schools after that landmark decision. Congress or state legislatures can pass laws that bypass the Supreme Court's ruling. If a Supreme Court ruling is extremely unpopular, the Constitution itself can be amended to override the court's decision.

Judges. The President appoints all federal judges with the approval of the Senate. Most federal judges may remain in office for life. This lifetime appointment protects them from political control and helps ensure their independence from the other branches of government. However, Congress can remove judges from office through impeachment for corruption or other abuses of office.

Because of the importance of Supreme Court decisions, the political opinions of each justice are of great public interest. Presidents generally nominate individuals to the Supreme Court who share their views on important issues. Before approving each nomination, the Senate carefully examines the nominee's qualifications. Supreme Court nominees with extreme views on key issues usually face fierce opposition.

Growth of the federal government

Background. The American Colonies won their independence from Britain in the Revolutionary War in America (1775-1783). They founded the first national government of the United States in 1781 under a document called the Articles of Confederation. Under the Articles, however, the states kept much of their independence. The national government could not collect taxes, regulate trade, or force states to fulfill their obligations. Such leaders as George Washington, Benjamin Franklin, James Madison, and Alexander Hamilton feared that the weak national government would collapse. This concern about the Articles of Confederation led to the Constitutional Convention of 1787 in Philadelphia.

The state delegates at the convention wanted a strong national government but feared that it would not respect the independence of the states and the liberties of the people. In framing the Constitution, they used many ideas from the existing constitutions of New York, Massachusetts, and other states. The delegates also drew on political theories set forth by philosophers of the 1600's and 1700's. Such thinkers as England's John Locke and France's Montesquieu, for example, had urged separate governmental branches as a way to prevent tyranny.

The delegates created a bold new system of government—the Constitution of the United States. The document went into effect on June 21, 1788, when New Hampshire became the ninth state to ratify it. The first 10 amendments, called the Bill of Rights, were ratified in 1791. The Constitution is the oldest written national charter still in force. It establishes a broad framework of government, flexible enough to change as the nation changes. Through the years, government leaders have worked out the details as required by economic, political, and social conditions.

Early years. When the federal government began operating in 1789, it was a tiny establishment. That year, Congress created the first three executive departments —Foreign Affairs (later the Department of State), Treas-

---

How a bill becomes law in the United States The drawings on this page and the next three pages show how federal laws are enacted in the United States. Thousands of bills are introduced during each Congress, which lasts two years, and hundreds become law. All bills not enacted by the end of the two-year period are killed.

WORLD BOOK illustrations by David Cunningham

Ideas for new laws come from many sources. The President, members of Congress, and other government officials may propose laws. Suggestions also come from individual citizens; special-interest groups, such as farmers, industry, and labor; newspaper editorials; and public protests. Congressional committees, in addition to lawyers who represent special-interest groups, actually write most bills. Specialists called *legislative counsels* in both the Senate and House of Representatives also help prepare many bills for congressional action.

Individual citizens

Public protests

Newspaper editorials

Special-interest groups

The President

Members of Congress and other government officials

Each bill must be sponsored by a member of the House or Senate. Any number of senators or representatives may co-sponsor a bill. A bill may originate in either house of Congress unless it deals with taxes or spending. The Constitution provides that all revenue bills must be introduced in the House. By tradition, spending bills begin there also. This practice came from England.

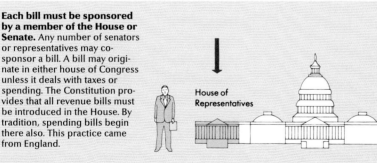

House of Representatives

Senate

Continues on the next page.

How a bill moves through Congress

The drawings on this page and the next show the normal path of a bill introduced in the House of Representatives. The process is the same for a bill introduced in the Senate, except that the House action comes after the Senate action. A bill may die at almost any stage of the process if no action is taken on it. A majority of the bills introduced in Congress fail and never become law.

Introduction in the House. A sponsor introduces a bill by giving it to the clerk of the House or placing it in a box called the *hopper.* The clerk reads the title of the bill into the *Congressional Record* in a procedure called the *first reading.* The Government Printing Office prints the bill and distributes copies.

Assignment to committee. The Speaker of the House assigns the bill to a committee for study. The House has 22 *standing* (permanent) committees, each with jurisdiction over bills in a certain area.

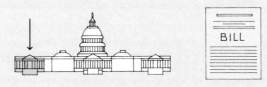

The bill goes to the Senate to await its turn. Bills normally reach the Senate floor in the order that they come from committee. But if a bill is urgent, the leaders of the majority party might push it ahead.

Committee action. The committee or one of its subcommittees studies the bill and may hold hearings. The committee may approve the bill as it stands, revise the bill, or table it.

Assignment to committee. The presiding officer of the Senate assigns the proposed law to a committee for study. The Senate has 16 standing committees.

The Senate considers the bill. Senators can debate a bill indefinitely, unless they vote or agree to limit discussion. When there is no further debate, the Senate votes. Most bills must have a simple majority to pass.

A conference committee made up of members of both houses works out any differences between the House and Senate versions of the bill. The revised bill is sent back to both houses for their final approval.

The committee studies the bill and hears testimony from experts and other interested people. In many cases, a subcommittee conducts the study. The committee may release the bill with a recommendation to pass it, revise the bill and release it, or lay it aside so that the House cannot vote on it. Releasing the bill is called *reporting it out,* and laying it aside is called *tabling.*

The bill goes on a *calendar,* a list of bills awaiting action. The Rules Committee may call for quick action on the bill, limit debate, and limit or prohibit amendments. Undisputed bills may be passed by unanimous consent, or by a two-thirds vote if members agree to suspend the rules.

Consideration by the House begins with a second reading of the bill, the only complete reading in most cases. A third reading, by title only, comes after any amendments have been added. If the bill passes by a *simple majority* (at least one more than half the votes), it goes to the Senate.

Introduction in the Senate. To introduce a bill, a senator must be recognized by the presiding officer and announce the introduction of the bill. A bill that has passed either house of Congress is sometimes called an *act,* but the term usually means legislation that has passed both houses and become law.

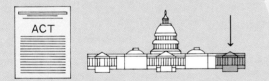

The bill is printed by the Government Printing Office in a process called *enrolling.* The clerk of the house of Congress that originated the bill certifies the final version.

The Speaker of the House signs the enrolled bill, and then the Vice President signs it. Finally, Congress sends the proposed new legislation to the White House for consideration by the President.

Action by the President

A bill passed by Congress goes to the President, who has 10 days—not including Sundays—to sign or veto it. The President may also let a bill become law by letting 10 days pass without acting.

Approval. After approving a bill, the President signs it, dates it, and often writes *approved* on it.

Veto. A vetoed bill must be returned to Congress with an explanation of the President's objections.

No action. The President might not veto the bill but may fail to sign it to show disapproval of some parts.

Reconsideration by Congress. If two-thirds of those members present approve the vetoed bill, it becomes law despite the veto.

Ten days pass. If the President holds the bill for 10 days—excluding Sundays—while Congress is in session, it becomes law without the signature of the chief executive.

If Congress adjourns within that 10-day period and the President fails to sign the bill, it dies. This procedure is called a *pocket veto.*

LAW

The bill becomes law and is given a number that indicates which Congress passed it. For example, a law enacted by the 105th Congress might be designated Public Law 105-250.

ury, and War—and the office of the attorney general. Only a few hundred clerks served the departments and Congress.

Alexander Hamilton, the nation's first secretary of the treasury, strongly influenced the early development of the U.S. government. He believed the Constitution should be interpreted loosely to give the federal government great power. Hamilton pushed bills through Congress that helped pay the nation's debt from the Revolutionary War. He also launched plans that provided for such internal improvements as roads and canals, and aided the nation's struggling new industries.

In 1803, the United States almost doubled its area in a transaction with France known as the Louisiana Purchase. The government sold much of the new land to canal and railroad companies, greatly enriching its Treasury. During the mid-1800's, the United States gained control of Texas, California, and other lands, ex-

tending its boundaries westward to the Pacific Ocean. Because of revenue from land sales, as well as taxes on imported goods, the government often collected more money than it spent during the 1800's.

The rise of big government. The size and role of the government grew as the United States expanded westward and developed into an industrial nation. Certain crises and events caused major spurts of government growth.

The American Civil War (1861-1865) led to a great increase in the size of the U.S. government. The war forced the government to build up its military forces. At the beginning of the conflict, the Regular Army of the United States consisted of about 16,000 soldiers, most of whom fought for the Union. By the last year of the war, the Army had more than 1,000,000 troops. The government also had to increase its administrative activities to arm, transport, feed, and clothe the troops. After the war, the government required record keeping and paperwork on a scale never before achieved to process pensions for war veterans.

During the late 1800's and early 1900's, federal regulations increased as the government began to actively supervise the marketplace. For example, the government passed laws curbing the power of *trusts,* large business organizations that limited competition. New laws were created to set railroad rates, improve workplace conditions, and ensure the purity of food and drugs. In addition, the government began to set aside national parks and forests, help farmers grow crops more effectively, and train students for vocational trades.

During the 1930's, the Great Depression caused the government to greatly increase its role in supervising the economy. Under the New Deal programs of President Franklin D. Roosevelt, Congress established many agencies to regulate and influence financial, business, agricultural, and industrial practices. Congress also passed laws to provide jobless benefits and old-age pensions, known as social security. In addition, the government spent billions of dollars on relief and on public works projects to create jobs. Citizens built thousands of schools, hospitals, and other public facilities.

After the Great Depression, the government continued to sponsor public works. For example, the Army Corps of Engineers and the Tennessee Valley Authority dammed rivers to provide flood control and electricity. The interstate highway program, started in 1956, was one of the largest public works projects in history.

During the 1960's, the federal government expanded again. It passed strong new civil rights laws and began to set environmental standards. It also increased its role in matters that were once handled only by state and local governments, such as education, job training, health care, and transportation.

World power. During the 1900's, the activities of the federal government spread throughout the world. Both World War I (1914-1918) and World War II (1939-1945) thrust the United States into vast multinational military campaigns in other countries.

Cold War tensions greatly influenced the federal government's foreign policy and spending for many years. The Cold War was a struggle for international power between Communist nations, led by the Soviet Union, and non-Communist nations, led by the United States. During the Cold War, which began after World War II, the United States government kept its armed forces in a state of military readiness and invested in a massive build-up of nuclear weapons. It also provided billions of dollars in aid to many non-Communist nations. The United States fought two wars, the Korean War (1950-1953) and the Vietnam War (1957-1975), in an effort to stop the spread of Communism in Asia.

In the late 1980's and early 1990's, Communist rule collapsed in most countries and the Cold War ended. In 1991, the Soviet Union broke apart. As a result, the government shifted much of its attention from foreign affairs to domestic issues, especially the economy.

Domestic challenges. In the 1990's, a long list of national problems demanded the U.S. government's attention. The nation's basic industries struggled to compete with the industries in other countries. Highways, bridges, and other essential facilities needed rebuilding.

Many measures of educational achievement were declining. In addition, Americans became increasingly concerned over signs of growing racial conflict, crime, drug abuse, and poverty, especially in the nation's cities.

Current issues in U.S. government

Current issues in United States government include debates over how much the federal government should do, how effective it is, and how democratic it is.

How much should the federal government do? People disagree on what the federal government should do about the nation's problems, and whether it has been doing too much or too little. In general, people with *liberal* political views call for the government to increase its efforts to solve economic and social problems. Those with *conservative* views believe economic and social problems are best solved when government interference is kept to a minimum. They want the government to promote traditional values.

How effective is the government? The complex system of checks and balances between the executive and legislative branches makes it difficult for government officials to take quick action. Power is constantly shifting between the President and Congress. Strong Presidents can use their position to arouse widespread public support for their plans and thus push them through Congress. The President assumes a dominant role during a crisis, especially a war or a severe economic depression, when the nation wants a strong leader. But in the absence of a crisis, the President must bargain and compromise with Congress.

In a *divided government*—when one political party wins the presidency and another controls Congress—bargaining may be especially difficult. For example, the President may want to lower taxes. But if the majority party in Congress plans to increase social programs that are funded by taxes, Congress may reject the President's proposed tax cut.

Even when one political party controls both branches, *factions* (groups) within the party can stall government action. In addition, elected officals may be influenced by many powerful special-interest groups who constantly strive for policies that benefit their members. Achieving clear-cut results or sweeping reforms under such a system is usually difficult and sometimes impossible.

How democratic is the government? Some people feel that certain features of the national government system are undemocratic and block majority rule. For example, the indirect election of the President by the Electoral College has resulted in some candidates winning with only a minority of the popular vote. Other features sometimes considered undemocratic include the appointment—rather than the election—of federal judges and the equal representation of each state in the Senate. In addition, many people believe the expense of election campaigns gives wealthy donors an unfair degree of influence on public officials.

Since the federal government began in 1789, Americans have disagreed on how their government should operate and how much it should do. Historians, political scientists, and other experts agree that no system of government can be perfect. Citizens have a right—and even a duty—to ask how their government is doing and to work to improve the system. Roger H. Davidson

West Bank is a territory in the Middle East that lies between Israel and Jordan. It covers about 2,263 square miles (5,860 square kilometers) and has about $1\frac{1}{2}$ million people. Most of them are Palestinian Arabs.

Historically part of Palestine, the West Bank was annexed by Jordan in 1950. In 1967, Israel defeated Jordan, Egypt, and Syria in a war and captured the West Bank.

East Jerusalem is the West Bank's largest city. But Israel, which includes West Jerusalem, does not consider East Jerusalem part of the West Bank. After the 1967 war, Israel made East Jerusalem a part of Israeli Jerusalem. But other countries do not recognize Israeli control.

People. Most West Bank Palestinians live in villages. About 12 percent of the Palestinians live in crowded refugee camps, where a United Nations (UN) agency provides schools and other services. Israelis make up about 15 percent of the West Bank's population. Many of the Israelis live in settlements built by the Israeli government. Many others live in East Jerusalem.

West Bank Palestinians speak Arabic. English is the most common second language. Most Palestinians are Muslims who belong to the Sunni sect of Islam. About 8 percent of the people are Christians, chiefly members of the Greek Orthodox or Greek Catholic churches.

Education is highly prized among West Bank Palestinians. It has allowed many of them to escape economic hardship for good-paying jobs elsewhere. The West Bank has five private colleges and universities.

Land and climate. The West Bank is hilly with generally thin, stony soil. Only about one-fourth of the land is suitable for farming. The Judean and Samarian Highlands, which cover most of the West Bank, have mild summers and occasional freezing temperatures and snow in winter. The Jordan River Valley, in the eastern part of the territory, has mild winters and hot summers, with temperatures reaching 120 °F (49 °C) and higher.

Much of the West Bank receives little rainfall. Only 2 to 8 inches (5 to 20 centimeters) of rain falls annually in the Jordan River Valley. Agriculture there depends on irrigation. Some areas of the highlands receive 25 inches (64 centimeters) or more of rain a year.

Economy. The West Bank has a developing economy. It has a small amount of fertile land. Its only important natural resource is stone quarried for use as building material. Agriculture, which centers on the growing of citrus fruits and olives, is the most important economic activity. But water shortages limit expansion of agricultural production. The few industries are small.

The West Bank has a fairly good road system but no railroads. An airport is in Qalandiya. Radio and television programs that are broadcast in the West Bank originate in Israel, Jordan, and Syria.

History and government. The West Bank is one of the world's most historic places. In the 1200's B.C., the Israelites settled there. The Philistines settled there at about that time. Later, the West Bank was ruled by the Assyrians, Babylonians, Persians, and Romans.

In the A.D. 600's, Arab Muslim armies conquered the West Bank. The territory was part of a series of Muslim empires almost continuously from then until the defeat of the Ottoman Turks in World War I in 1918. In 1920, as an element of a post-World War I international agreement, the West Bank became part of the British mandate of Palestine. According to the mandate, Britain was to help Palestinian Jews establish a Jewish homeland. In 1947, the UN voted to divide the mandate into an Arab state and a Jewish state. The Palestinian Arabs rejected this plan. Their Arab allies attacked Israel in May 1948, the day after that country was established as a Jewish state. Jordan occupied the West Bank when the war ended in 1949. It annexed the territory in 1950.

In 1967, Israel defeated Jordan, Egypt, and Syria in the Six-Day War. It captured the West Bank, as well as the Arab lands of the Gaza Strip, Golan Heights, and Sinai Peninsula. In 1974, King Hussein of Jordan gave up his government's responsibility for the West Bank to the Palestine Liberation Organization (PLO). In 1988, Jordan ended financial and administrative support it had continued to give the West Bank. Later that year, the PLO declared an independent Palestinian state in the West Bank and the Gaza Strip. But Israel continued to occupy and, in effect, govern both territories. In the late 1980's, violence began erupting between Israeli troops and Palestinians protesting Israel's occupation.

In 1972, Israel began allowing West Bank Palestinians to elect and operate municipal and village government councils. But the councils had little power. Real authority in the West Bank rested with the Israeli military. In September 1993, however, Israel and the PLO signed an agreement for the start of plans for self-government for, and Israel's withdrawal from, the West Bank and the Gaza Strip. The West Bank plan was to start in the city of Jericho.   Malcolm C. Peck

West Bank

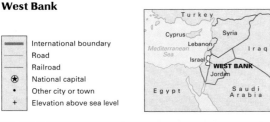

▬▬▬	International boundary
▬▬▬	Road
▬▬▬	Railroad
⊛	National capital
•	Other city or town
+	Elevation above sea level

Index

How to use the index

This index covers the contents of the 1992, 1993, and 1994 editions of *The World Book Year Book.*

Each index entry gives the edition year and the page number or numbers—for example, **Congress Party (India), 94:** 225. This means that information on this party may be found on page 225 of the 1994 *Year Book.*

When there are many references to a topic, they are grouped alphabetically by clue words under the main topic. For example, the clue words under **Constitution** group the references to that topic under numerous subtopics.

The indication (il.) means that the reference is to an illustration only, as in the **Corleone** picture on page 251 of the 1994 edition.

When a topic such as **COURTS** appears in all capital letters, this means that there is a *Year Book* Update article entitled Courts in at least one of the three volumes covered by this index. References to the topic in other articles may also appear after the topic name.

When only the first letter of a topic, such as **Craxi, Bettino,** is capitalized, this means that there is no article entitled Craxi, Bettino, but that information on this topic may be found in the edition and on the pages listed.

The "see" and "see also" cross references—for example, those under **CRIME**—refer the reader to other entries in the index.

An index entry followed by *WBE* refers to a new or revised *World Book Encyclopedia* article in the supplement section, as in **CZECH REPUBLIC, 94:** 500. This means that a *World Book Encyclopedia* article on the Czech Republic begins on page 500 of the 1994 *Year Book.*

Index

A

Aamodt, Kjetil-Andre, **94:** 378
Abacha, Sani, **94:** 318
ABC. See **American Broadcasting Companies**
Abdel Rahman, Omar, **94:** 123, 158, 191, 244, 313
Abdesselam, Belaid, **94:** 47
Abdic, Fikret, **94:** 100
Abiola, Moshood, **94:** 318
Abkhazia, **94:** 214, **93:** 251
Aborigines, **94:** 82, **92:** 77
Abortion: advertising, **93:** 38; Australia, **93:** 92; Clinton policy, **94:** 142, 337; Ireland, **94:** 244, **93:** 284; laws and court cases, **94:** 153, 389, 404, **93:** 159, 430, 432, **92:** 157-158, 161-162, 407; Protestant views, **94:** 339, **93:** 402, **92:** 376; Republican Party, **93:** 411; Roman Catholic Church, **94:** 413, **92:** 384, 385
Abruzzo, Richard, **93:** 349
Abu Musa (island), **93:** 282, 334
Academy Awards, **94:** 300, **93:** 339, **92:** 320
Accidents. See **Disasters; Safety**
ACE inhibitors, **93:** 200
Achtenberg, Roberta, **94:** 428
Acid rain, **92:** 112
Acquired immune deficiency syndrome. See **AIDS**
Adams, Gerry, **94:** 320
Adams, Michael, **94:** 117
Addiction. See **Alcoholism; Drug abuse; Smoking**
Addis Ababa, Ethiopia, **94:** 380, 381
Aden. See **Yemen**
Adenosine deaminase deficiency, **92:** 305-306
Adolescents, **94:** 133, 184, 340, **92:** 376-377
Adoption, **94:** 156, 227
ADVERTISING, **93:** 38, **92:** 40
Aegean Sea (tanker), **93:** 219
Aerospace industry. See **Aviation; Space exploration**
Afeworke, Issaias, **94:** 197
Affirmative action. See **Civil rights**
AFGHANISTAN, **93:** 39, **92:** 41; civil war, **94:** 64, **93:** 84, **92:** 71; Pakistan, **94:** 64, **93:** 39, **92:** 41; refugees, **94:** 63, **92:** 72; tables, **94:** 62, **93:** 86, **92:** 73
AFL-CIO. See **American Federation of Labor and Congress of Industrial Organizations**
AFRICA, **94:** 38-44, **93:** 40-45, **92:** 42-48; AIDS, **94:** 40, 46, **93:** 45, **92:** 331; human origins, **93:** 48, **92:** 51-52
African/African-American Summit Conference, **94:** 40
African cemetery (New York), **93:** 49-50
African Financial Community, **94:** 41-44
African National Congress, **94:** 381-382, **93:** 44, 421, **92:** 393
Afrikaner Resistance Movement, **94:** 382
Agassi, Andre, **93:** 440-441
Age of Innocence, The (film), **94:** 300
Agenda for Peace (plan), **93:** 464
Aging, **92:** 129, 130, 133, 297
Agriculture. See **Farm and farming**
Agriculture, U.S. Department of, **94:** 197, 204, 205
Ahmed, Shahabuddin, **92:** 83, 84
Aho, Esko, **92:** 319
Aideed, Mohamed Farah, **94:** 38, 53-54, 380-381, 403, 426, **93:** 421, **92:** 392
AIDS, **94:** 44-46, **93:** 46, **92:** 48; Africa, **94:** 40, **93:** 45, **92:** 331; concert, **93:** 388; drugs, **94:** 185; French scandal, **94:** 248-249; German scandal, **94:** 215; immigration ban, **94:** 224, **92:** 243; Latin America, **92:** 274; mandatory testing, **92:** 240; New York City, **92:** 324; plays, **92:** 420; prisons, **94:** 339, **92:** 372; school condom distribution, **92:** 191; stamp, **94:** 338 (il.); virus, **92:** 138
AIDS-like illness, **94:** 45
Air Force, U.S. See **Armed forces**
Air Line Pilots Association, **94:** 267
Air pollution. See **Environmental pollution**
Air traffic controllers, **94:** 269, 428
Aircraft crashes. See **Aviation disasters**
Airlines. See **Aviation**
Akalaitis, JoAnne, **94:** 415
Akashi, Yasushi, **94:** 107, **93:** 118
Akebono, **94:** 317
Akers, John F., **94:** 146
Akihito, **93:** 289
Al-Tahir (party), **94:** 263
Alabama: education, **94:** 188, 387; election, **94:** 389; energy supply, **92:** 195, 196 (il.); tables, **94:** 388, **93:** 429, **92:** 404
Alabama, University of, **92:** 246
Aladdin (film), **94:** 418, **93:** 337
Alaska: oil spill effects, **94:** 195-196; tables, **94:** 388, **93:** 429, **92:** 404

Alaska Highway, **93:** 476
ALBANIA, **94:** 46, **93:** 46-47, **92:** 48-49; Eastern Orthodox Church, **94:** 185; refugees, **92:** 48, 234, 259; Roman Catholic Church, **92:** 384; Serbia, **93:** 476; tables, **94:** 200, **93:** 236, **92:** 205. See also **Berisha, Sali**
Al-Bashir, Umar Hasan Ahmad, **93:** 408-409, 431
Albert II, **94:** 96
ALBERTA, **94:** 46, **93:** 47, **92:** 50
ALBRIGHT, MADELEINE K., **94:** 47
Alcohol, Tobacco, and Firearms, Bureau of, **94:** 158, 340, 431
Alcohol consumption, **94:** 184, **93:** 199
Alcoholism, **94:** 183, **92:** 185. See also **Drunken driving**
Alexander, Jane, **94:** 58, 413
Alexander, Lamar, **92:** 50, 148, 190
Alexei II, **94:** 185, **92:** 188
Al-Fatah, **94:** 294, **92:** 278
Algae, **93:** 376-377
ALGERIA, **94:** 47, **93:** 47, **92:** 50-51; Iran, **94:** 242; Islamic movements, **93:** 285, 408, **92:** 254; nuclear weapons, **93:** 66; tables, **94:** 42, **93:** 42, **92:** 46
Ali, Abduraham Ahmed, **92:** 392
Aliens. See **Immigration**
Aliyev, Heydar, **94:** 88
All-America City Awards, **94:** 124
Allen, George F., **94:** 192
Allen, Woody, **94:** 316, **93:** 339, 347
Allison, Davey, **94:** 85, 86, 170 (il.)
Al-Megrahi, Abdel Basset Ali, **92:** 280-281
Almsick, Franziska van, **94:** 405, 406
Al Nahyan family, **93:** 334-335
Alpha interferon, **92:** 186
ALS. See **Amyotrophic lateral sclerosis**
Al-Sabah, Jabir al-Ahmad al-Jabir, **93:** 294, **92:** 266
Al-Sulh, Rashid, **93:** 311
Altman, Robert A., **94:** 90, **93:** 99, 178, 337
Al-Turabi, Hasan, **93:** 408-409, 431
Aluminum Co. of America, **94:** 267, **93:** 296
Aluminum industry, **94:** 267
Álvarez Machain, Humberto, **93:** 329, 433
Alves dos Santos, José Carlos, **94:** 102
Alzheimer's disease, **94:** 184, **92:** 93, 236
Amalgamated Transit Union, **94:** 268
Amato, Giuliano, **94:** 247, **93:** 287
Amazon region, **92:** 98. See also **Rain forest**
Amber, **94:** 305, 310, 326
America³ (boat), **93:** 106-108
America 2000 (plan), **92:** 190
America West Airlines, **94:** 86
American Airlines, **94:** 86-87, 267, **93:** 95, 96, **92:** 83, 270
American Association for the Advancement of Science, **94:** 188
American Ballet Theatre, **94:** 162-163, **93:** 181-182, **92:** 168
American Bible Society, **92:** 382
American Broadcasting Companies, **94:** 93, 409, **93:** 439, **92:** 40, 222-224, 414-416
American Federation of Labor and Congress of Industrial Organizations, **94:** 269
American Health Security Act, **94:** 156, 218
American Hospital Association, **93:** 268-269, 274-275
American Indian. See **Indian, American**
American League. See **Baseball**
American Library Association. See **Library; Literature for children**
American Medical Association, **93:** 268-269
American Red Cross, **92:** 377
American Telephone & Telegraph Company, **94:** 408, **93:** 156, 216, 297
Americans with Disabilities Act (1990), **94:** 180, **93:** 196, **92:** 235-236, 271
America's Cup. See **Boating**
Ammaccapane, Danielle, **93:** 253, 254
Ammons, R. A., **94:** 333
Amnesty International, **94:** 139, **93:** 149, 449, **92:** 148
Ampligen, **92:** 186
Amtrak, **94:** 420
Amyotrophic lateral sclerosis, **94:** 290, **92:** 93
An Nabatiya, Lebanon, **94:** 275 (il.)
Anabolic steroids, **92:** 185
Anan Panyarachun, **94:** 417
ANAP (group), **94:** 421, **92:** 431
ANC. See **African National Congress**
Anderson, Marian, **94:** 175-177
Anderson, Terry A., **92:** 315 (il.), 316-317
Anderson, Vinton, **93:** 382
Ando, Tadao, **93:** 51, **92:** 61
Andorra, tables, **94:** 200, **93:** 236, **92:** 205
Andreotti, Giulio, **94:** 246, 249, 254 (il.), **93:** 287, **92:** 257-258

Andretti, Michael, **94:** 86, **93:** 94-95, **92:** 80
Andrew, Prince, **94:** 426
Andromeda Galaxy, **94:** 80-81
Angelou, Maya, **94:** 332
Angels in America (Kushner), **94:** 414
Angiosperms, **94:** 327
Anglicans. See **England, Church of**
Angola: civil war, **94:** 39, **93:** 41, **92:** 44; Cuba, **92:** 165; tables, **94:** 42, **93:** 42, **92:** 46
Animals: religious sacrifice, **94:** 404; *WBE*, **94:** 458. See also **Fossils; Paleontology; Zoology**
Animated film, **94:** 418, **93:** 337, **92:** 320-321
Anne, Princess, **93:** 254-255
Annenberg, Walter, **94:** 57, 189
Antall, Jozsef, **94:** 222, **93:** 276
Antarctica, **93:** 218, **92:** 199
ANTHROPOLOGY, **94:** 47-48, **93:** 48-49, **92:** 51-52
Antigua and Barbuda, tables, **94:** 273, **93:** 309, **92:** 275
Antimatter, **93:** 384
Anwar Ibrahim, **94:** 285
Aoun, Michel. See **Awn, Michel**
A.P. Indy (horse), **93:** 273-274
Apartheid. See **South Africa**
Apple Computer, Inc., **94:** 146, 147, 192, **93:** 155-156, **92:** 152
Aptidon, Hassan Gouled, **94:** 40
Aquariums. See **Zoos**
Aquifers, **92:** 457-467
Aquino, Corazon C., **93:** 382, 408, **92:** 360, 361
Arab League, **93:** 330, **92:** 193
Arabs. See **Islam; Middle East; Palestinians**
Arafat, Yasir, **94:** 245, 292-293, 406, **93:** 334, 457, **92:** 314
Arazi (horse), **93:** 273, **92:** 239
Arcangues (horse), **94:** 220-221
ARCHAEOLOGY, **94:** 49-50, **93:** 49-50, **92:** 52-53; Dead Sea Scrolls, **94:** 358-367; Persian Gulf War damage, **92:** 56-59
Archer, Dennis, **94:** 179
Archery, **94:** 386, **93:** 426, **92:** 401
ARCHITECTURE, **94:** 51-52, **93:** 50-52, **92:** 60-62; Holocaust Memorial Museum, **94:** 438-441. See also **Building and construction**
Arco Chemical Co., **92:** 387
Arctic Ocean, **93:** 359
Arctic ozone hole, **93:** 218-219
ARGENTINA, **94:** 53, **93:** 52, **92:** 62; corruption, **93:** 306; Iran terrorism, **93:** 282; military spending, **92:** 274; nuclear weapons, **93:** 64; tables, **94:** 273, **93:** 309, **92:** 275; trade pact, **93:** 273. See also **Menem, Carlos Saúl**
ARISTIDE, JEAN-BERTRAND, **94:** 54, 144, 217-218, 271-272, 427, **93:** 258, **92:** 63, 234, 235, 470
Arithmetic, **93:** 403
Arizona: elections, **93:** 215, **92:** 194; political scandal, **92:** 405; tables, **94:** 388, **93:** 429, **92:** 404
Arkansas: election, **94:** 389; tables, **94:** 388, **93:** 429, **92:** 404
ARMED FORCES, **94:** 53-56, **93:** 53-67, **92:** 63-67; aircraft crashes, **93:** 468; European army, **93:** 238; Germany, **94:** 215; manufacturing, **93:** 325, **92:** 295; married individuals, **94:** 430; military base closings, **94:** 55, 428-430; Navy scandal, **93:** 465-467; San Diego naval training center, **94:** 376. See also **Defense, U.S. Department of; Homosexuals; Persian Gulf War; Women; and specific countries**
Armed Islamic Group, **94:** 47
ARMENIA, **94:** 56, **93:** 68; independence, **92:** 438; tables, **94:** 62, **93:** 86; *WBE*, **93:** 489
Arms control. See **Nuclear weapons; Weapons**
Armstrong, Thomas N., III, **94:** 59
Army, U.S. See **Armed forces**
Arpino, Gerald, **94:** 163
ART, **94:** 57-59, **93:** 68-83, **92:** 67-69; cave, **92:** 53; freedom of expression, **93:** 177; Iraq ancient treasures, **92:** 56-59
Art Institute of Chicago, **92:** 69
Arthur Andersen and Co., **94:** 90
Arumainayagam, Raja, **92:** 244
As Nasty as They Wanna Be (recording), **93:** 388, **92:** 370
Ashbery, John, **93:** 384, **92:** 362
Ashe, Arthur, **94:** 412, **93:** 441
ASIA, **94:** 60-79, **93:** 84-88, **92:** 70-74
Asian Americans, **94:** 433, **92:** 242-243
Asimov, Isaac, **93:** 190-192
ASPIN, LES, JR., **94:** 55, 80, 106, 428, 430, **92:** 56
Aspirin, **94:** 288
Assad, Hafez al-, **94:** 406, **93:** 436, **92:** 412-413
Associated Press, **94:** 355
Association of Professional Flight Attendants, **94:** 267
Association of Southeast Asian Nations, **93:** 85-86, **92:** 71
Asteroids, **94:** 80, 384, **93:** 90, **92:** 394

Index

Index

H

Index

Index

Index

153; tables, **94:** 388, **93:** 429, **92:** 404; transportation, **93:** 449; welfare, **94:** 389. See also **Wilder, L. Douglas**
Virginia, University of, **94:** 385
Viruses, **94:** 226, 341, **92:** 137-138, 372. See also **AIDS; Public health**
Vishwa Hindu Parishad, **93:** 277
Vision, **92:** 377
Visual Artist's Rights Act (1991), **92:** 68
Vitamins, **94:** 184-185, **93:** 259
Vivas, René, **93:** 351
Vo Van Kiet, **94:** 76, **93:** 469, **92:** 453
Volcanoes: Asia, **92:** 70; Galeras, **94:** 274, 315-316; Hudson, **92:** 62, 226-228; Mt. Pinatubo, **93:** 383, **92:** 199, 226, 360, 361; Mt. Unzen, **92:** 226; undersea, **94:** 322
Volleyball, **94:** 386, **93:** 426, **92:** 401
Volvo AB (company), **94:** 405
Voting rights, **94:** 139, 403, **93:** 159, **92:** 147, 290, 408. See also **Elections**
Vouchers, Educational, **93:** 208-210
Voyage, The (Glass), **93:** 150
Vranitzky, Franz, **92:** 78

W

Wachter, Anita, **94:** 378
Wachtler, Sol, **93:** 346
Waco, Texas, **94:** 158, 340, 431
Wages, **94:** 235-240, 267, **93:** 295, 303, **92:** 268-269
Wagner, Lisa, **94:** 100
Wagner, Richard, **94:** 140
Waheed Kakar, Abdul, **94:** 325-326
Waite, Terry, **92:** 233, 317
Wajed, Hasina, **94:** 89
Walcott, Derek, **93:** 311, 316 (il.), 352, 385
Waldheim, Kurt, **93:** 92, **92:** 78
Walesa, Lech, **94:** 263, 333-334, **93:** 386, 415, **92:** 363-364
Walloons. See **Belgium**
Walsh, Lawrence E., **93:** 117, 282, 468
Walt Disney Co., **93:** 114, **92:** 320, 329
Wang Junxia, **94:** 419
Wang Xizhe, **94:** 120
Ward, Charlie, **94:** 211
Ward, Judith, **93:** 353
Wargo, Tom, **94:** 216
Warner Brothers, **93:** 387-388
Warsaw ghetto uprising, **94:** 263
Warsaw Pact, **94:** 202, **92:** 204
Washington (state): crime law, **94:** 192; elections, **92:** 405; health care, **94:** 389; tables, **94:** 388, **93:** 429, **92:** 404; taxes, **94:** 387
WASHINGTON, D.C., **94:** 433-443, **93:** 470, **92:** 453-455; city march, **93:** 136; crime, **94:** 123, 433, **93:** 470, **92:** 455; Holocaust Memorial Museum, **94:** 51, 263-264, 434-443; riots, **92:** 276; theater, **94:** 418; transportation, **92:** 424; zoo, **93:** 478. See also **Kelly, Sharon Pratt**
Washington Post, **94:** 354-355
Washington Redskins, **93:** 470, **92:** 221
Wasmosy, Juan Carlos, **94:** 327
WATER, **94:** 444, **93:** 471, **92:** 455; cancer agents, **94:** 196; farming, **93:** 240-241; ground water, **92:** 456-467; running uphill, **93:** 129-130; safety, **94:** 375; wettability, **92:** 137. See also **Drought; Environmental pollution; Ocean; Oil spills**
Water polo, **94:** 386, **93:** 426, **92:** 401
Water skiing, **94:** 386, **93:** 426, **92:** 401
Watkins, Brian, **93:** 345-346
Watkins, James D., **93:** 216
Watson, Elizabeth M., **93:** 275
Watson, Henry K., **94:** 138, 283-284
Watson, Robert, **94:** 222
Weapons: Asia, **94:** 60-62; gangs, **94:** 134; Middle East, **94:** 242-243, **93:** 284, 331-332. See also **Armed forces; Gun control; Nuclear weapons**
WEATHER, **94:** 444-448, **93:** 471-473, **92:** 468-469; cyclones, **92:** 70, 84, 469; farm production, **92:** 217; Mongolia snow, **94:** 64; storms, **94:** 376, **92:** 146; typhoons, **94:** 261, **93:** 734, **92:** 261. See also **Global warming**
Weaver, Randy, **93:** 179
Weber, Pete, **92:** 95
Weber, Vin, **94:** 368, **93:** 162
Wei Jingsheng, **94:** 120
Weicker, Lowell P., Jr., **94:** 389
Weightlifting, **93:** 426, **92:** 401
Weinberger, Caspar W., **93:** 117, 282-283, 468
Weiner, Kenneth, **92:** 181
WELFARE, **94:** 449, 934: 474, **92:** 469; census data, **92:** 130; city ills, **93:** 144, **92:** 142; New York City, **92:** 323; state programs, **94:** 389, **93:** 430. See also **Children; Homelessness; Poverty**

Wells, Clyde K., **94:** 314
Wenner, Jann S., **94:** 285
West, Togo D., Jr., **94:** 56
West Bank: Arab-Israeli conflict, **93:** 286, 332, 333, **92:** 255-257; Dead Sea Scrolls, **94:** 360, 362; peace agreement, **94:** 245, 293, 294, 406; *WBE*, **94:** 520
WEST INDIES, **92:** 470
West Virginia: steel lockout, **93:** 296-297; tables, **94:** 388, **93:** 429, **92:** 404
West Virginia, University of, **94:** 211
Western Sahara, **93:** 336, **92:** 44, 319, 448
Western Samoa: election, **92:** 339; tables, **94:** 324, **93:** 375, **92:** 338
Westinghouse Electric Corp., **93:** 217
Westray Mine (Nova Scotia), **93:** 125 (il.), 358
Wetlands, **92:** 158, 216-217
Whales, **94:** 321, **93:** 163, **92:** 477, 478
Wheat, **94:** 203, **93:** 91
Whirlpool Corp., **94:** 194
Whitaker, Pernell, **94:** 100-101, **92:** 96
White House (Moscow), **94:** 373-374
White Sox, Chicago, **94:** 92, 117
Whitman, Christine Todd, **94:** 191
Whitmire, Kathryn J., **92:** 240, 241
Whitney Museum of American Art, **94:** 59, **92:** 68
Whittle, Christopher, **94:** 189-190, **93:** 204, 210
Who's Tommy, The (musical), **94:** 376, 414
Wichita, Kans., **92:** 161-162
Wickremasinghe, Ranil, **94:** 387
Widnall, Sheila E., **94:** 56
WILDER, L. DOUGLAS, **93:** 194, **92:** 180, 470
Wildlife. See **Conservation; Endangered species; Zoology**
Wiles, Andrew, **94:** 314
Wilhelm, David C., **94:** 178
Williams, Damian M., **94:** 138, 283-284
Williams, Stanley N., **94:** 315-316
Williams, Walter Ray, Jr., **94:** 100, **92:** 95
Williams, Willie L., **93:** 321
Wilson, Allan C., **93:** 48
Wilson, Christopher, **94:** 139
Wilson, Edward O., **92:** 378
Wilson, John A., **94:** 433
Wilson, Michael Holcombe, **92:** 110, 111
Wilson, Pete, **94:** 427
Wimol Wongwanich, **94:** 413
Wind, Timothy E., **94:** 283, **93:** 148
Wind energy, **94:** 194
Windows (software), **92:** 152
Windsor Castle, **94:** 426, **93:** 257
Winger, Ron, **94:** 100
Wingti, Paias, **94:** 324, **93:** 374-375
Winston (boat), **94:** 98
Wireless networks. See **Personal communications services**
Wisconsin: Chippewa dispute, **92:** 247; education, **94:** 387-389; election, **94:** 192; flood, **94:** 203, 448; hate crimes ruling, **94:** 404; tables, **94:** 388, **93:** 429, **92:** 404; welfare, **94:** 449
Wisconsin, University of, **92:** 162, 192
Wise Use Movement, **93:** 169
Wofford, Harris L., **92:** 179, 383, 449
Wolf, Markus, **94:** 215
Wolfe, George C., **94:** 415
Wolves, **94:** 450
Women: armed forces, **94:** 56, 430, **93:** 54-55, **92:** 67; breast implants, **93:** 327; Deer appointment, **94:** 227; election gains, **93:** 214-215, **92:** 145; fashion, **94:** 158, 340, 431; gangs, **94:** 131; health studies, **92:** 297; heart disease, **92:** 236-237, 297; Islam, **94:** 245; prisons, **94:** 338-339; Protestant Church, **93:** 402; rap music, **92:** 369; Reno appointment, **94:** 368; Roman Catholic Church, **93:** 413; sex and self-esteem, **94:** 340, **92:** 376-377; smoking and child health, **94:** 344-345, 347; theater, **94:** 415. See also **Abortion; Rape; Sexual discrimination; Sexual harassment**
Wood, Bill, **94:** 222
Wood, Kimba M., **94:** 105, 142
Wool, **92:** 77
WOOLSEY, R. JAMES, JR., **94:** 449
Works Progress Administration, **93:** 78-79
World Bank, **94:** 44, 78, 79, 89, 242, **92:** 62, 190, 250
World Book supplements: *Dictionary*, **94:** 453, **93:** 479, **92:** 479; *Encyclopedia*, **94:** 456, **93:** 482, **92:** 482
World Council of Churches, **92:** 187, 382
World Cup. See **Skiing; Soccer**
World Health Organization, **94:** 45-46
World League of American Football, **93:** 245, **92:** 222
World Series. See **Baseball**
World Trade Center bombing, **94:** 123, 158, 191, 244, 313, 357

World Trade Organization, **94:** 205, 211
World War II, **94:** 212, 261, 263, 435-438
World Youth Day, **94:** 370, **92:** 384
World's Fair (1992). See **Expo '92**
Wrestling, **94:** 386, **93:** 426, **92:** 401
Wright, Frank Lloyd, **94:** 51, **93:** 52
Wrzesinski, Bryan, **92:** 327
Wuornos, Aileen Carol, **93:** 178, **92:** 164
Wyman, Donald, **94:** 315
Wyoming: conservation, **92:** 160; tables, **94:** 388, **93:** 429, **92:** 404

X

Xie Jun, **94:** 117, **92:** 138
Xu Wenli, **94:** 120

Y

Yachting. See **Boating**
Yacimientos Petroliferos Fiscales (firm), **94:** 53
YAMAGUCHI, KRISTI, **93:** 276, 363, 474, **92:** 242
Yanayev, Gennady I., **92:** 432-435
Yankee Rowe nuclear power station, **93:** 217, **92:** 197
Yanomami Indians, **94:** 102, 274
Yazdi, Mohammed, **94:** 296
Yazov, Dimitry T., **92:** 432-435
Yegorova, Lyubov, **94:** 378
Yellowstone National Park, **93:** 175
Yeltsin, Boris Nikolayevich: arms reductions, **93:** 53; Bush meeting, **93:** 117, **92:** 103; C.I.S. relations, **94:** 145; coup attempt, **92:** 434, 435, 438 (il.); India visit, **94:** 226; Japan visit, **94:** 262; political reforms and conflicts, **94:** 151, 371-374, **93:** 154, 413-416, **92:** 445; religion law, **94:** 185; Ukraine, **94:** 422, **93:** 451; U.S.S.R. collapse, **92:** 438-440
Yemen: elections, **94:** 295; Saudi Arabia, **93:** 334, 419; tables, **94:** 295, **93:** 333, **92:** 316
Yerba Buena Gardens Visual Arts Center, **94:** 57
Yermolinsky, Alex, **94:** 117
Yeutter, Clayton K., **92:** 382, 383, 451
Yoma, Amira, **92:** 62
York, Duchess of, **94:** 426, **93:** 254-255
Yoshino, Teruzo, **94:** 103
Young, Coleman A., **94:** 179, **92:** 181
Young, Kevin, **93:** 366, 372
Yu Kyong Hotel (N. Korea), **93:** 114 (il.)
YUGOSLAVIA, **94:** 449-450, **93:** 475-476, **92:** 470-475; Austria, **92:** 78; Canadian troops, **93:** 125; chess match, **93:** 131; Eastern Orthodox Churches, **92:** 187-188; German troops, **93:** 253; NATO, **94:** 202; Netherlands, **92:** 322; sports, **93:** 425, **92:** 400; tables, **94:** 201, **93:** 237, **92:** 205; U.S. relations, **93:** 117, **92:** 250. See also **Bosnia-Herzegovina; Croatia; Serbia; Slovenia; United Nations**
YUKON TERRITORY, **94:** 450, **93:** 476, **92:** 476

Z

Zah, Peterson, **94:** 226, **92:** 247
ZAIRE, **94:** 450, **93:** 476, **92:** 476; democratic reforms, **93:** 44; political changes, **94:** 40, **92:** 45; tables, **94:** 43, **93:** 43, **92:** 47
ZAMBIA, **93:** 477; democratic reforms, **93:** 44; election, **92:** 45; plane crash, **94:** 379; tables, **94:** 43, **93:** 43, **92:** 47
Zandstra, Falko, **94:** 223
Zenawi, Meles, **94:** 197, **93:** 232
Zeolites, **93:** 130
Zhelev, Zhelyu, **93:** 115, **92:** 101
Zhirinovsky, Vladimir, **94:** 371
Zhivkov, Todor, **93:** 115
Zhu Rongji, **94:** 119, **93:** 135, **92:** 141
Zia, Khaleda. See **Ziaur Rahman, Khaleda**
ZIAUR RAHMAN, KHALEDA, **94:** 89, **93:** 97, **92:** 83-84, 476
Zidovudine. See **AZT**
Ziegler, John, **93:** 272
Zimbabwe: drought, **93:** 473; tables, **94:** 43, **93:** 43, **92:** 47; United Nations, **93:** 461
Zinc mining, **92:** 317
Zionism, **93:** 458, **92:** 315, 449
Zmeskal, Kim, **93:** 373, 426, **92:** 400 (il.)
ZOOLOGY, **94:** 451, **93:** 477, **92:** 477
ZOOS, **94:** 452, **93:** 478, **92:** 477-478; architecture, **93:** 51; dinosaurs, **94:** 302-311
Zovirax (drug), **93:** 199
Zrei, Salim al-, **94:** 294
Zuckerman, Mortimer B., **94:** 318
Zulus, **92:** 393-394

Acknowledgments

The publishers acknowledge the following sources for illustrations. Credits read from top to bottom, left to right, on their respective pages. An asterisk (*) denotes illustrations and photographs that are the exclusive property of *The Year Book*. All maps, charts, and diagrams were prepared by *The Year Book* staff unless otherwise noted.

4 Robert Trippett, Sipa Press; © *Mobile Press Register* from Gamma/Liaison
5 The President Riverboat Casino; © 1993 Universal Studios/Amblin Productions from Industrial Light and Magic
8 Peter Turnley, Black Star; Reuters/Bettmann; Najlah Feanny, SABA
9 Les Stone, Sygma; Reuters/Bettmann; Greg Smith, SABA
10 AP/Wide World
12 John Paul, FSP from Gamma/Liaison; Focus on Sports
13 Reuters/Bettmann
14 Najlah Feanny, SABA
16 Reuters/Bettmann; Santosh Basak, Gamma/Liaison
18 Greg Smith, SABA
20-21 Reuters/Bettmann
22 Canapress
23 Focus on Sports; Gamma/Liaison
24 Brooks Kraft, Sygma
26 Arturo Robels, JB Pictures; Michael Amoseden, Sipa Press
27 Yoshikazu Tsuno, Agence France-Presse
28 Omar Rachidi, Sipa Press; Baldev, Sygma
29 Reuters/Bettmann
30 Peter Turnley, Black Star; Reuters/Bettmann
31 Bob Pearson, Agence France-Presse
32 Halsted, Gamma/Liaison; AP/Wide World
33 Brad Markel, Gamma/Liaison
34 Reuters/Bettmann; NASA
36 Les Stone, Sygma
38 AP/Wide World
41 Betty Press
44 AP/Wide World
48 © Javier Trueba
49 AP/Wide World
50 University of Chicago
52 Pascal Guyot, Agence France-Presse
54 Michael Hirsch, Picture Group
55 AP/Wide World
58 *The Joy of Life,* by Henri Matisse, oil on canvas, 1906, Barnes Foundation, Merion, Pennsylvania
60 Agence France-Presse
65 Noboru Hashimoto, Sygma
66 Jean Kugler, FPG; AP/Wide World
69 Bettmann
70 Sygma; UPI/Bettmann
71 AP/Wide World
72 UPI/Bettmann
73 Reuters/Bettmann
74 Mary Altier
75 Cindy Andrew
76 Andrew Holbrooke, Gamma/Liaison
77 Greg Girard, Contact Press Images
81 Dennis di Cicco
84 Chrysler Corporation
85 Joel Robine, Agence France-Presse
87 Benkt Eurenius, Pressens Bild from Gamma/Liaison
90-92 AP/Wide World
95 Richard Mackson, *Sports Illustrated* © Time Inc.

97 Esther Angert and Norman Pace, Indiana University
99 Reuters/Bettmann
101 AP/Wide World
104 Gary Wagner, Picture Group
105-108 Reuters/Bettmann
111 Canapress
112 Reuters/Bettmann
114 Brian Willer
118 © Eduardo Contreras, Chicago Tribune Company, all rights reserved, used with permission
120 Reuters/Bettmann
122 Joseph M. Sapulich*
126 © John Maso, *New York Newsday*
128 Mark Richards, DOT Pictures
129 Ray Hutchison
135 Renato Rotolo, Gamma/Liaison
139 Reuters/Bettmann
141 Jack Vartoogian
143 AP/Wide World
146 E.O. Inc.
151 © 1993 Cable News Network, Inc. All rights reserved.
153 CARLSON copyright 1993 *Milwaukee Sentinel.* Reprinted with permission of Universal Press Syndicate. All rights reserved.
154 Coalition for Habitat Conservation
157 Kristoffer Gillette, Sygma
159 KWTX-TV from Sygma
162 Sara Krulwich, NYT Pictures
164-166 Anthony Crickmay, Camera Press from Globe Photos
167 AP/Wide World
168 Archive Photos; Bettmann; UPI/Bettmann; AP/Wide World
169 LGI; UPI/Bettmann; Archive Photos; UPI/Bettmann
170 Focus on Sports; Archive Photos; AP/Wide World; UPI/Bettmann
171 AP/Wide World; Reuters/Bettmann; Archive Photos; UPI/Bettmann
172 UPI/Bettmann; Jim MacHugh, Sygma; Bettmann; UPI/Bettmann
173 UPI/Bettmann; AP/Wide World; Bettmann; Michael Jang, LGI
174-175 Van Pelt Library, University of Pennsylvania
176 Scurlock Studio
177 Van Pelt Library, University of Pennsylvania
181 Baldev, Sygma
186 AP/Wide World
189 Steve Miller, NYT Pictures
191 Bettmann
193 Agence France-Presse
195 AP/Wide World
198 CTK/Sovfoto
202 Nevers, Gamma/Liaison
204 Greg Boll
206 Dan Lecca, Anne Klein Collection
210 AP/Wide World
212 Agence France-Presse
214-216 Reuters/Bettmann
218 AP/Wide World

219 Reuters/Bettmann
220 Focus on Sports
221 Reuters/Bettmann
223 AP/Wide World
224 Craig Filipacchi, Gamma/Liaison
225 AP/Wide World
227 *Rapid City Journal*
229 REA from SABA
234 Robert Frerck, Odyssey Productions
241 Edward Carreón
243 Reuters/Bettmann
244-247 AP/Wide World
248 Massimo Sestini, Gamma/Liaison
251 Gamma/Liaison
252 Piero Guerrini, Gamma/Liaison; A. Nusca, Gamma/Liaison
253 Giuseppe Martorana, Gamma/Liaison; F. Pedone, Contrasto from SABA
254 Paolo Titolo, Contrasto from SABA
257 Livio Anticoli, Gamma/Liaison
260-266 Reuters/Bettmann
268 AP/Wide World
270 Reuters/Bettmann
274 © John Maier, Jr., *Time* Magazine
275 AP/Wide World
279 Ulf Andersen, Gamma/Liaison
282 Illustration by Emily Arnold McCully reprinted by permission of G. P. Putnam's Sons from *Mirette On The High Wire* © 1992 by Emily Arnold McCully
284 Bettmann
287 Joseph M. Sapulich*
289 © Ted Thai, *Time* Magazine
292 AP/Wide World
296 Reuters/Bettmann
299 Miramax Films
300 Warner Brothers from Shooting Star
302 © 1993 Universal Studios/Amblin, Productions from Industrial Light and Magic
305 George O. Poinar, Jr., University of California
307 © Universal City Studios, Inc. Courtesy of MCA Publishing Rights, a Division of MCA, Inc.
308 © Universal Pictures from Shooting Star. All rights reserved.
313 AP/Wide World
314 Dennis Applewhite, Sygma
316 AP/Wide World
320 Agence France-Presse
326 Paul Sereno, University of Chicago; University of Chicago Hospitals
328 AP/Wide World
333 Robert Severi, Gamma/Liaison
335 AP/Wide World
338 U.S. Postal Service
339 Ralf-Finn Hestoft, SABA
342 Tony Stone Images

345 Custom Medical
348 Carol Brozman*
350 Ralph J. Brunke*
354 Stephen Savoia, AP/Wide World
355 Reuters/Bettmann
358 © Richard Nowitz
359 Library of Congress
361 © Richard Nowitz
363 Shrine of the Book, © Israel Museum (David Harris); William L. Reed
364 M. Milner, Sygma; Israel Antiquities Authority
366 © Richard Nowitz; Library of Congress
369 AP/Wide World
370 UPI from Sipa Press
372 Robert Trippett, Sipa Press
373 Shone, Gamma/Liaison
374-378 AP/Wide World
380-381 Reuters/Bettmann
383 McDonnell Douglas
386 Reuters/Bettmann
390 Las Vegas Convention and Visitors Authority; The President Riverboat Casino
396 © Dennis Clevenger, The President Riverboat Casino; David Lee Waite; David Lee Waite
397 Grand Casinos, Minnesota
399 Duane's Photography; Rudi Von Briel
404 Reuters/Bettmann
408 Jeff Danziger in *The Christian Science Monitor* © 1993 TCSPS
410 Paul Drinkwater, NBC
412 AP/Wide World
414 Joan Marcus
417 F.A.O. Schwartz (Ralph J. Brunke*)
419 AP/Wide World
421 ABC from Sygma
423 Frank Spooner Pictures Ltd. from Gamma/Liaison
424 Reuters/Bettmann
431-432 AP/Wide World
434 Tim Hursley, Pei Cobb Freed & Partners
435 Bettmann
436 Robert C. Lautman; United States Holocaust Memorial Museum
437 Tim Hursley, Pei Cobb Freed & Partners
438 United States Holocaust Memorial Museum
439 United States Holocaust Memorial Museum; Robert C. Lautman
440 Alan Gilbert, United States Holocaust Memorial Museum
441 Robert C. Lautman; United States Holocaust Memorial Museum
443 Tim Hursley, Pei Cobb Freed & Partners
445 Laura Noel
446 Les Stone, Sygma; AP/Wide World
447-448 AP/Wide World
451 Asian Bureau for Conservation

542

Family Milestones of 1993

In the preceding pages, *The World Book Year Book* reported the major events and trends of 1993. Use these two pages to record the developments that made the year memorable for *your* family.

Family members (names) **Ages** **Family pets**

_____ _____ _____
_____ _____ _____
_____ _____ _____
_____ _____ _____
_____ _____ _____
_____ _____ _____

Births (name) **Date** **Where born** **Weight** **Height**

_____ _____ _____ _____ _____
_____ _____ _____ _____ _____
_____ _____ _____ _____ _____

Weddings (names) **Date** **Where held**

_____ _____ _____
_____ _____ _____
_____ _____ _____

Religious events _____ _____
_____ _____

Graduations _____ _____
_____ _____

Anniversaries _____ _____
_____ _____

In memoriam _____ _____
_____ _____

Awards, honors, and prizes _____ _____
_____ _____

Sports and club achievements _____ _____
_____ _____

Vacations and trips _____ _____
_____ _____

Most enjoyable books

_____

_____

_____

_____

_____

Most-played recordings and tapes

_____

_____

_____

_____

_____

Most unforgettable motion pictures

_____

_____

_____

_____

_____

Most-watched television programs

_____

_____

_____

_____

_____

Paste a favorite family photograph or snapshot here.

Date

_____

Location

_____

Occasion

_____

_____

World Book Encyclopedia, Inc., provides high quality educational and reference products for the family and school, including a FIVE-VOLUME CHILDCRAFT FAVORITES SET, colorful books on favorite topics, such as DOGS and INDIANS; and THE WORLD BOOK MEDICAL ENCYCLOPEDIA, a 1,040-page, fully illustrated family health reference. For further information, write WORLD BOOK ENCYCLOPEDIA, INC., P.O. Box 3073, Evanston, IL 60204.